Hawaii

Glenda Bendure
Ned Friary

Hawaii

4th edition

Published by
Lonely Planet Publications
Head Office: PO Box 617, Hawthorn, Vic 3122, Australia
Branches: 155 Filbert St, Suite 251, Oakland, CA 94607, USA
               10a Spring Place, London NW5 3BH, UK
               71 bis rue du Cardinal Lemoine, 75005 Paris, France

Printed by
The Bookmaker Pty Ltd
Printed in Hong Kong

Photographs by

Glenda Bendure	Ned Friary	David Russ
Michael Clark	Hawaii State Archives	Chris Salcedo

Front cover photo by Robert Holmes

First Published
August 1990

This Edition
September 1997

Although the author and publisher have tried to make the information as accurate as possible, they accept no responsibility for any loss, injury or inconvenience sustained by any person using this book.

National Library of Australia Cataloguing in Publication Data

Bendure, Glenda.
    Hawaii.

    4th ed.
    Includes index.
    ISBN 0 86442 489 2.

    1 .Hawaii – Guidebooks. I. Friary, Ned.
    II. Title. (Series: Lonely Planet travel survival kit).

919.6904041

text & maps © Lonely Planet 1997
photos © photographers as indicated 1997
climate charts compiled from information supplied by Patrick J Tyson, © Patrick J Tyson, 1997

Glenda Bendure & Ned Friary

Glenda grew up in California's Mojave Desert and first traveled overseas as a high school AFS exchange student to India.

Ned grew up near Boston, studied Social Thought & Political Economy at the University of Massachusetts in Amherst and upon graduating headed west.

They met in Santa Cruz, California, where Glenda was completing her university studies. In 1978, with Lonely Planet's first book *Across Asia on the Cheap* in hand, they took the overland trail from Europe to Nepal. The next six years were spent exploring Asia and the Pacific, with a home base in Japan, where Ned taught English and Glenda edited a monthly magazine.

The first of many extended trips to Hawaii was in 1980, when they went straight from Osaka to the green lushness of Kauai, a sight so soothing for concrete-weary eyes that a two-week vacation stretched into a four-month sojourn.

Ned and Glenda have a particular fondness for islands and tropical climates. In addition to *Hawaii*, they are also the authors of Lonely Planet's guidebooks to Honolulu, Micronesia, the Eastern Caribbean, Bermuda and Denmark, and they write the Norway and Denmark chapters of Lonely Planet's *Scandinavian & Baltic Europe on a shoestring*.

They now live on Cape Cod in Massachusetts – at least when they're not on the road.

From the Authors

Many thanks to the people who have helped us on this project: State Parks archaeologist Martha Yent; Linda Delaney from the Office of Hawaiian Affairs; Davianna McGregor of Protect Kahoolawe Ohana; Jean Greenwell of the Kona Historical Society; Andrew Perala, Communications Director for the WM Keck Observatory; Karen Reebok of the UH Astronomy program; Jon Giffin of the Division of Forestry & Wildlife; Leon Bruno of the Lyman House Memorial Museum in Hilo; Roy Damron of the Kona Reefers Dive Club; and John P Lockwood, geologist at Hawaiian Volcano Observatory.

Thanks also to those friends and travelers who have shared insights and experiences with us along the way. A special acknowledgment to Rich, Shelly and Catie Hausman and to Gareth Kernaghan, Glenn Thering and Ted Brattstrom, who have joined us in exploring many of Hawaii's more remote corners and back trails.

From the Publisher
This fourth edition of *Hawaii* is a product of Lonely Planet's US office in Oakland, California. Don Gates was the project editor, aided by Sharron S Wood. Sharron also did the proofreading with a little help from Don. Beca Lafore was responsible for the book's layout and design, and together she and Cyndy Johnsen updated the maps. The book's illustrators were Mark Butler, Hugh D'Andrade, Hayden Foell, Alex Guilbert and Rini Keagy. Hugh also produced the cover and, along with Scott Summers, contributed many hours of design advice and effort. The index was compiled by Sacha Pearson and Don.

Special thanks to Alex, Carolyn Hubbard and Caroline Liou for questions answered and problems solved.

Thanks
Thanks to the following travelers who wrote in with information: Tera & Joseph Antaree, Paul Bakker, S & R Ballmoos, Amy Bernstein, Sandra Burditt, Dr Marion Burkimsher, Jeffrey L Campbell, Kristen Caven, JM Clark, Danielle Clode, John Cofer, David & Nancy Cook, James Coulson, Kevin Davies, Mary Anne Devine, Ellen Dudley, Andrew & Larise Edwards, Terry Farrah, Effie Fletcher, Dan Fowler, Karen Gardner, Barbara J Geissler, Vivian Green, Neville & Lynne Hallam, Peter Hirsch, Caroline Hodson, Hal & Dorsey Holappa, Jackie Duffy Hook, William Hopwood, Helen Howard, Michelle House, Gay Huffman-Merriman, Nicholas Isherwood, Maxine Kamin, Sally Kane, Allan Kempe, Lisa King, Dr Karl Lang, Nancy Lecourt, Dr Howard B Levine, Barbara Lohoff, Jennie Makihara, Nancy Miceli, Wolfgang Minas, Andrew Montcrieff, Lentz Morton, Trish & Bruce Murray, Wendy & Michael Murray, Annette Oliveira, Bhavani Pathak, Kerstin Pohle, T Richard & Lucy Roaché, Su Roper, Erik Van Rossum, Michel Roussel, Lucinda F Salo, Darren Scott, Stefan H Seelen, Dee Stanley, Sharon Strait, Mike Tuggle, Anne Vaile, James Vercelline, Dr Heribert Vollmer, Gudrun Wasson, R David Weatherley, Jodie Wesley, John Z Wetmore, David Wheatley, Thomas Wiesheu, Roger Williams, Erica Wilson, Ann Wilson-Wilde.

Warning & Request
Things change – prices go up, schedules change, good places go bad and bad places go bankrupt – nothing stays the same. So, if you find things better or worse, recently opened or long since closed, please tell us and help make the next edition even more accurate and useful.

We value all of the feedback we receive from travelers. Julie Young coordinates a small team that reads and acknowledges every letter, postcard and email, ensuring that every morsel of information finds its way to the appropriate authors, editors and publishers. Everyone who writes to us will find their name in the next edition of the appropriate guide and will also receive a free subscription to our quarterly newsletter, *Planet Talk*. The very best contributions will be rewarded with a free Lonely Planet guide.

Excerpts from your correspondence may appear in updates, which are added to the end pages in reprints; in our newsletter, *Planet Talk*; or in the Postcards section of our Web site. Please let us know if you don't want excerpts from your letter published or your name acknowledged.

Contents

Map Legend

BOUNDARIES

- ·—··—··—··—··—· International Boundary
- ·—··—··—··—··—· Provincial Boundary

AREA FEATURES

Park

NATIONAL PARK   National Park

National Forest,
  Watershed Area

HYDROGRAPHIC FEATURES

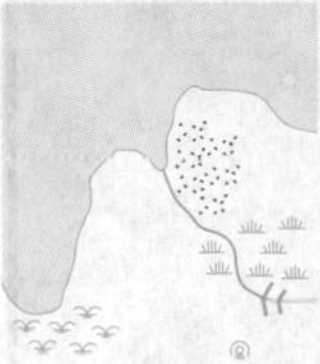

Water
Reef
Coastline
Beach
Swamp
River, Waterfall
Mangrove, Spring

ROUTES

Freeway
Primary Road
Secondary Road
Tertiary Road
Dirt Road
Trail
Ferry Route
Railway, Train Station

ROUTE SHIELDS

- (H1) Interstate Freeway
- (99) State Highway

SYMBOLS

✪	**NATIONAL CAPITAL**	✈	Airfield	⛽	Gas Station	)(	Pass
◉	**State Capital**	✈	Airport	⌐	Golf Course	⊼	Picnic Area
●	**City**	∴	Archaeological Site, Ruins	●	Hospital, Clinic	★	Police Station
●	City, Small	⊝	Bank, ATM	❶	Information	⌷	Pool
●	Town	◹	Baseball Stadium	⚚	Lighthouse	✉	Post Office
		⚐	Beach	☀	Lookout	☖	Shipwreck
		⚏	Buddhist Temple	☒	Mine	❖	Shopping Mall
■	Hotel, B&B	◐	Bus Station, Bus Stop	⚑	Monument	⚐	Skiing, Downhill
⚲	Campground	⊞	Cathedral	▲	Mountain	⚑	Skiing, Cross-country
⚐	Hostel	⌒	Cave	⏛	Museum	⌂	Stately Home
⛺	RV Park	✝	Church	✔	Music, Live	☎	Telephone
⌂	Shelter, Refugio	⚓	Dive Site	←	One-Way Street	⬛	Tomb, Mausoleum
▼	Restaurant	◔	Embassy, Consulate	⬙	Observatory	⚐	Trailhead
⛾	Bar (Place to Drink)	⋈	Foot Bridge	♣	Park	⚲	Winery
⚌	Cafe	❖	Garden	P	Parking	🐘	Zoo

Note: Not all symbols displayed above appear in this book.

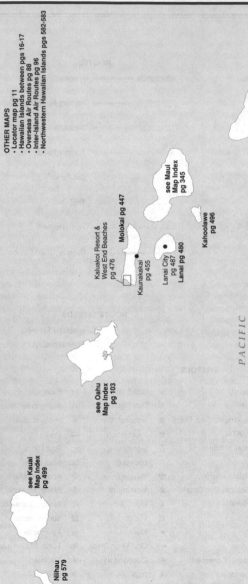

OTHER MAPS
- Locator map pg 11
- Hawaiian Islands between pgs 16-17
- Overseas Air Routes pg 88
- Inter-Island Air Routes pg 96
- Northwestern Hawaiian Islands pgs 582-583

see Hawaii
Map Index
pg 222

see Maui
Map Index pg 345

Molokai pg 447

Kaluakoi Resort &
West End Beaches
pg 476

Kaunakakai
pg 455

Lanai City
pg 487
Lanai pg 480

Kahoolawe
pg 496

see Oahu
Map Index
pg 103

PACIFIC
OCEAN

see Kauai
Map Index
pg 499

Niihau
pg 579

Map Index

0   30   60 km

0   20   40 miles

Introduction

Hawaii's natural beauty is extraordinarily grand. Mark Twain fittingly called Hawaii 'the loveliest fleet of islands that lies anchored in any ocean'. Volcanic in origin, the Hawaiian Islands are high and rugged, lushly green and cut by spectacular gorges and valleys. The beaches are beautiful, ranging from bleached white to jet black. The terrain is amazingly varied, climbing from lowland deserts to alpine mountaintops, with everything from barren lava flows to tropical rainforest found in between.

Hawaii is the world's most isolated archipelago, 2500 miles from the nearest land mass. Its isolation is so great that of the thousands of species of flora and fauna that have evolved here, over 90% exist nowhere else on earth.

Geologically, it's also unique. Hawaii has the world's most active volcano (Kilauea), its largest dormant volcano (Haleakala), its highest mountain when measured from the sea floor (Mauna Kea) and its highest sea cliffs (on Molokai).

As one of the world's leading visitor destinations, Hawaii does have the expected mass tourism, high-rise hotels and crowded beaches. But that's only one side of it.

You can also find scores of untouristed areas and secluded beaches to explore, while your accommodation options include upcountry lodges, isolated resorts and cozy B&Bs. And the best the islands have to offer is still free for hikers and backcountry campers.

The Hawaiian islands have some of the world's top surfing and windsurfing, as

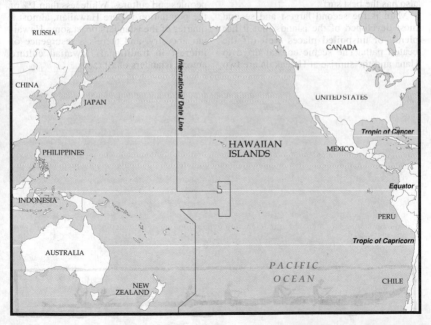

well as excellent conditions for snorkeling, swimming, diving, bodysurfing and most other water sports.

Hawaii's climate is unusually pleasant for the tropics, as near-constant trade winds prevail throughout the year. Much of the time the rain falls as short daytime showers that are accompanied by rainbows.

Hawaii's six main islands all have lovely beaches and splendid scenery. Their leeward coasts are sunny, dry and desert-like, with white sands and turquoise waters. The mountainous windward sides have tropical jungles, cascading waterfalls and pounding surf. The uplands are cool and green, with rolling pastures, small farms and ranches.

Oahu is the most crowded and developed of the islands, with Waikiki still providing half the tourist accommodations in Hawaii. Honolulu has all the pluses and minuses of urban life, from good museums and lively nightlife to congested traffic. It has wonderful restaurants, with both inexpensive ethnic foods and gourmet cuisines. Oahu also has the best surf.

Maui is the second largest and second most developed of the islands, but it has plenty of unspoiled places well off the beaten path. The scenic coastal drive to Hana and the sunrise at Haleakala are two of its highlights. Maui is also the best island for watching humpback whales.

The Big Island has two things the others don't: snow and erupting volcanoes. There's room to move, with niches for cowboys, astronomers and traditional fishing villages, as well as alternative communities settling in on the side of lava flows.

Kauai has Hawaii's greenest scenery, a deeply cut canyon resembling a mini-Grand Canyon and the famous razorback cliffs of the Na Pali Coast. The least developed of the four largest islands, it's a mecca for hikers, kayakers and other outdoor enthusiasts.

Molokai, the most Hawaiian of the islands, is charmingly rural, slow-paced and only lightly visited by tourists. Lanai, the smallest island, is undergoing a jolting transition from an economy based on pineapple growing to a new identity as a luxury resort destination.

Hawaii is ethnically diverse, with an appealing collage of East, West and Pacific peoples and cultures. While less than 1% of the population is pure Hawaiian, almost a quarter of the islanders boast some Hawaiian ancestry, and there's a resurgence of interest in traditional Hawaiian culture among islanders of all races.

Facts about Hawaii

HISTORY

Hawaii is the northern point of the huge triangle of Pacific Ocean islands known as Polynesia. The other two points of the triangle are Easter Island to the southeast and New Zealand to the southwest.

The original settlers of Polynesia, which means 'many islands', apparently followed a long migratory path through Southeast Asia, down through Indonesia and across Melanesia, before settling the Polynesian islands of Tonga and Samoa in about 1000 BC. Over the next 1500 years they migrated to the more distant islands of Polynesia, with Hawaii being one of the last areas settled.

Archaeological evidence indicates the first Polynesians arrived in Hawaii from the Marquesas between 500 and 700 AD. Among the strongest links are ancient stone statues found on Hawaii's now-uninhabited Necker Island that have striking similarities to statues found on the Marquesas.

When the first wave of Tahitians arrived in Hawaii in about 1000 AD they apparently conquered and subjugated the Marquesans, forcing them to build their temples, irrigation ditches and fishponds.

Hawaiian legends of a tribe of little people called *menehune* may well refer to the Marquesans. Indeed, the word 'menehune' is very similar to the Tahitian word for 'outcast'.

Ancient Hawaii

The earliest Hawaiians had simple animistic beliefs. Good fishing, a safe journey and a healthy child were all the result of being in tune with the spirits of nature. Their offerings to the gods consisted of prayers and a share of the harvest.

Around the 12th century, in a later wave of migration, a powerful Tahitian *kahuna* (priest), Paao, arrived on the Big Island. Convinced that the Hawaiians were too lax in their worship, Paao introduced the concept of offering human sacrifice to the gods and he built the first *luakini heiau*, a type of temple where these sacrifices took place. He also established the *kapu* system, a practice of taboos that strictly regulated all social interaction.

The kapus forbade commoners from eating the same food or even walking the same ground as the *alii*, or royalty. A commoner who crossed the shadow of a king could be put to death. Kapus prohibited all women from eating coconuts, bananas, pork and certain varieties of fish.

Paao also decided that Hawaii's blue-blood was too diluted and summoned the chief Pili from Kahiki (Tahiti) to establish a new royal lineage. With Pili as chief and Paao as high priest, a new ruling house was formed. Their dynasty was to last 700 years.

King Kamehameha the Great, like all the Big Island chiefs, traced his lineage to Pili. Likewise, Kamehameha's *kahuna nui* (high priest) descended from Paao.

Religion

In the old Hawaiian religion there were four main gods: Ku, Lono, Kane and Kanaloa.

Ku was the ancestor god for all generations of humankind, past, present and future. He presided over all male gods while his wife, *Hina*, reigned over the female gods. When the sun rose in the morning, it was said to be Ku; when it set in the evening it was Hina. Like Yin and Yang, they were responsible for heaven and earth.

Ku had many manifestations, one as the benevolent god of fishing, *Ku-ula* (Ku of the abundant seas), and others as the gods of forests and farming. People prayed to Ku when the harvest was scarce. At a time of drought or other such disaster, a temple would be built to appease Ku.

One of the most fearful of Ku's manifestations was *Kukailimoku* (Ku, the snatcher of land), the war god that Kamehameha the Great worshipped. The temples built for the worship of Kukailimoku were offered sacrifices not only of food, pigs and chickens but also of human beings.

Lono was the god in charge of the elements that brought rain and an abundant harvest. He was also the god of fertility and peace.

Kane created the first man out of the dust of the earth and breathed life into him (the Hawaiian word for man is *kane*), and it was from Kane that the Hawaiian chiefs were said to have descended.

Ku, Lono and Kane together created the earth, the moon, the stars and the ocean.

Kanaloa, the fourth major god, was often pitted in struggles against the other three gods. When heaven and earth separated it was Kanaloa who was placed in charge of the spirits on earth. Forbidden from drinking *kava*, these spirits revolted and along with Kanaloa were driven to the underworld, where Kanaloa became the ruler of the dead.

Below the four main gods, there were 40 lesser gods. The best known of them was *Pele*, goddess of volcanoes. Her sister *Laka* was goddess of the hula, and another sister, *Poliahu*, was the goddess of snow.

The Hawaiians had gods for all occupations and natural phenomena. There was a god for the tapa maker and a god for the canoe builder, shark gods and mountain gods.

NED FRIARY

Petroglyphs

The ancient Hawaiians had no written history, however they did cut petroglyphs into smooth lava rock. Many of these carved pictures are stylized stick figures depicting warriors with spears, barking dogs, birds, canoes and other decipherable images. Some are linear marks, which may have been made to record important events or represent calendars or genealogical charts.

The meanings and purposes behind Hawaiian petroglyphs are not well understood. Some may have been intentionally cryptic, while others may just be random graffiti or the carvings of a budding artist.

Most petroglyphs are found along ancient footpaths and may have been clustered at sites thought to have mana.

The Big Island has the greatest concentration of petroglyphs, with several large fields just a few minutes' walk from the road. ■

Heiaus The temples erected in ancient Hawaii, called *heiau*, were built in two basic styles, both of which were constructed of lava rock. One was a simple rectangular enclosure of stone walls built directly on the ground. The other was a more substantial structure built of rocks piled high to form raised terraced platforms. (The remains of both types can still be found throughout the islands today.)

Inside the heiaus were prayer towers, taboo houses and drum houses. These structures were made of ohia wood, thatched with pili grass and tied with cord from the native olona shrub. Tikis and god images, called *kii*, were carved of wood and placed around the prayer towers.

Heiaus were most commonly dedicated to Lono, the god of harvest, or Ku, the god of war. The heiaus built in honor of Ku were called luakini heiau and were the only ones where human sacrifices took place.

Heiaus were built in auspicious sites, often perched on cliffs above the coast or in other places thought to have *mana*, or 'spiritual power'. A heiau's significance lay not in the structure itself but focused on the mana of the site. When a heiau's mana was gone, it was abandoned.

The Makahiki

According to legend, the god Lono rode a rainbow down from the heavens to a breadfruit grove above Hiilawe Falls in Waipio Valley, where in a paradise-like setting he found Kaikilani, a beautiful princess. They fell in love, married and moved across the island to Kealakekua Bay.

When Lono discovered that a chief was lusting after Kaikilani, he became enraged and beat Kaikilani, who, as she lay dying, professed her faithful love for Lono alone. In his grief, Lono traveled restlessly around the island challenging every man he met to a wrestling match and other competitions.

After four months, a still disheartened Lono set sail on a canoe with a tall mast hung with sails made of finely woven Niihau mats. The huge canoe was laden with so much food that it took 40 men to carry it down to Kealakekua Bay. Lono promised to return one day on a floating island covered with trees and full of pigs and chickens.

Hawaiian Sports & Games

Holua racing was ancient Hawaii's most exciting spectator sport. Racers would ride prone on narrow wooden sleds, racing at high speed down steep hills along furrows that had been covered with pili grass or ti leaves to make the surface smooth. Many of the holua slide paths were a mile or two long.

Hawaiians were heavy betters and often wagered on the holua races, as well as on foot races, surfing competitions and many other sports.

Surfing is a Hawaiian creation that was as popular in old Hawaii as it is today. When the waves were up, everyone was

NED FRIARY

konane

out. There were royal surfing grounds and spots for commoners as well. Boards used by commoners were made of breadfruit or *koa* wood and were about six feet long. Only the alii were free to use the long *olo* boards, which were up to 16 feet in length and made of *wili-wili*, the lightest of native woods. The boards were highly prized possessions and were carefully wrapped in tapa cloth and suspended from the ceilings of homes.

Other popular Hawaiian games included *ulu maika*, in which rounded stone discs were rolled between two stakes, somewhat resembling bowling, and *moa pahee*, a similar game using a large wooden dart.

For the more passive, there was *konane*, a strategy game similar to checkers. Indentations were carved into a stone board to hold the pebbles of white coral and black lava that were used as playing pieces. ■

NED FRIARY

moa pahee

The Hawaiians remembered Lono each year with a harvest festival, called the *makahiki*, which lasted from October to February. Numerous inter-island competitions similar to the Olympics were held, including outrigger canoe races, fishing and surfing tournaments, foot races, wrestling matches and *holua* (sled) racing. Even during wartime, fighting would be suspended for the four months of the makahiki, so that the games and festivities dedicated to Lono could proceed.

Captain Cook

The Hawaiian Islands were the last of the Polynesian islands to be 'discovered' by the West. This is due in large part to the fact that early European explorers who entered the Pacific around the tips of either Africa or South America centered their explorations in the southern hemisphere.

Although the English were the first known Western explorers to set foot on Hawaiian shores, there is speculation that the Spanish, whose Manila galleons had been making annual runs between Mexico and the Philippines since 1565, may have

A man of the Sandwich Islands
by John Webber

stumbled upon Hawaii and kept the discovery a secret.

British explorer Captain James Cook spent the better part of a decade exploring and charting most of the South Pacific before chancing upon Hawaii as he sailed from Tahiti in search of a northwest passage to the Atlantic.

On January 18, 1778, Cook spotted the islands of Oahu, Kauai and Niihau. The winds favored approaching Kauai, and on January 19 Cook's ships, the *Discovery* and the *Resolution*, sailed into Kauai's Waimea Bay. Cook named the Hawaiian archipelago the Sandwich Islands in honor of the Earl of Sandwich.

Cook was surprised to find that the islanders had a strong Tahitian influence in their appearance, language and culture. They sailed out in canoes to welcome the ships and were eager to trade fish and sweet potatoes for nails. The islanders were not interested in the useless beads and trinkets that Cook used successfully as barter elsewhere in the Pacific. The only thing they cared to exchange for was metal, which was totally absent from their islands.

After two weeks of stocking provisions on Kauai and Niihau, Cook's expedition continued its journey north. Failing to find the fabled passages through the Arctic, Cook set sail back to Hawaii where his arrival date virtually coincided with that of his initial visit to the islands the year before.

This time he discovered the remaining Hawaiian islands. On January 17, 1779, Cook sailed into Kealakekua Bay on the Big Island, where a thousand canoes came out to greet him.

When Cook went ashore the next day he was met by the high priest and guided to a temple lined with skulls. Everywhere the English captain went people fell face down on the ground in front of him to the chant of 'Lono'.

As fate would have it, Cook had landed during the makahiki festival. The tall masts and white sails of Cook's ships and even the way he had sailed clockwise around the island all fitted the legendary descriptions

Outrigger canoe with Ala Wai Yacht Harbor and Waikiki in background

Surf shop, Haleiwa, North Shore

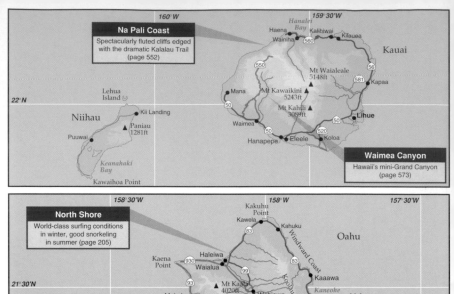

Na Pali Coast
Spectacularly fluted cliffs edged with the dramatic Kalalau Trail (page 552)

Waimea Canyon
Hawaii's mini-Grand Canyon (page 573)

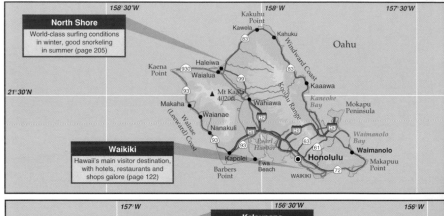

North Shore
World-class surfing conditions in winter, good snorkeling in summer (page 205)

Waikiki
Hawaii's main visitor destination, with hotels, restaurants and shops galore (page 122)

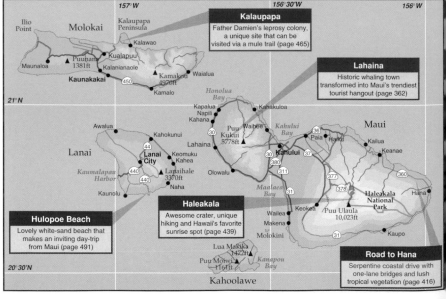

Kalaupapa
Father Damien's leprosy colony, a unique site that can be visited via a mule trail (page 465)

Lahaina
Historic whaling town transformed into Maui's trendiest tourist hangout (page 362)

Hulopoe Beach
Lovely white-sand beach that makes an inviting day-trip from Maui (page 491)

Haleakala
Awesome crater, unique hiking and Hawaii's favorite sunrise spot (page 439)

Road to Hana
Serpentine coastal drive with one-lane bridges and lush tropical vegetation (page 416)

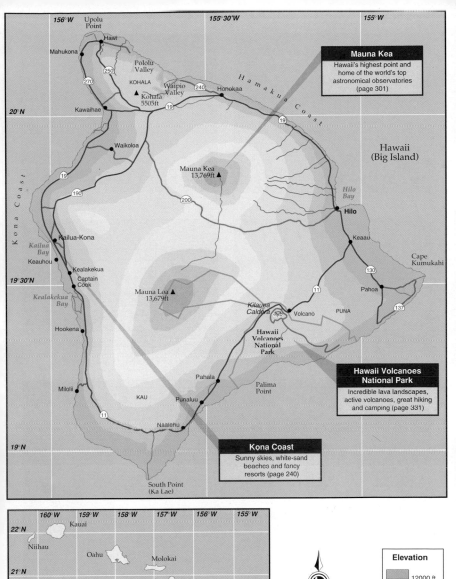

Mauna Kea

Hawaii's highest point and home of the world's top astronomical observatories (page 301)

Hawaii Volcanoes National Park

Incredible lava landscapes, active volcanoes, great hiking and camping (page 331)

Kona Coast

Sunny skies, white-sand beaches and fancy resorts (page 240)

Hawaii (Big Island)

Upolu Point

Hawi

Mahukona

Pololu Valley

KOHALA

Waipio Valley

Kohala 5505ft

Kawaihae

Honokaa

Hamakua Coast

Waikoloa

Mauna Kea 13,769ft

Kailua-Kona

Kailua Bay

Keauhou

Kealakekua

Captain Cook

Kealakekua Bay

Mauna Loa 13,679ft

Hookena

Hilo Bay

Hilo

Keaau

Cape Kumukahi

Pahoa

PUNA

Kilauea Caldera

Volcano

Hawaii Volcanoes National Park

Milolii

KAU

Pahala

Punaluu

Palima Point

Naalehu

South Point (Ka Lae)

Kona Coast

Elevation

12000 ft
10000 ft
8000 ft
6000 ft
4000 ft
2000 ft
1000 ft
Sea Level

Kauai

Niihau

Oahu

Molokai

Lanai

Maui

Kahoolawe

PACIFIC OCEAN

Hawaii

Hawaiian Islands

0 15 30 km
0 10 20 miles

Nene

Hawaiian stilt, or aeo

Black-crowned night heron, or aukuu

Red-crested cardinal

Wild peacock

of how the god Lono would reappear on the scene.

Whether the priests actually believed Cook was the reincarnated Lono or whether they just used his appearance to enhance their power and add a little flair to the festivities is unknown. What is clear is that Cook never realized that both of his arrivals to Hawaii had coincided with the makahiki festivals – he assumed this was the way things were in everyday Hawaii.

There's little wonder Cook had a favorable impression of the islands. The islanders treated his crew with open hospitality. Hawaiian men invited the sailors to boxing matches and other competitions, and the women performed dances and readily bedded down with them.

For men who had just spent months roaming inhospitable frozen tundra, this was paradise indeed.

The expedition's skilled artist, John Webber, was allowed to move freely in the villages. Today his detailed drawings of native people, costumes and village life constitute the best visual accounts of old Hawaii.

A few weeks after their arrival the crews had restocked all the supplies needed except firewood. Rather than scour the hillsides for wood, Cook directed his men to haul on board the temple railings and wooden images from the harborside temple dedicated to Lono. As Cook had been passed off as Lono himself, the priests didn't attempt to stop them.

On February 4 the English vessels and their crews headed north out of Kealakekua Bay for Maui. En route they ran into a storm off the northwest coast of the Big Island where the *Resolution* broke a foremast. Uncertain of finding a safe harbor in Maui, Cook decided to go back to Kealakekua to repair the mast – a decision that would prove to be a fatal mistake.

When they arrived at Kealakekua Bay on February 11 the islanders quickly appeared with the usual provisions to barter. The ruling alii, however, seemed upset with the ships' reappearance.

Apparently the makahiki had ended and not only was Cook's timing inauspicious, but so were the conditions of his return. This time he had arrived in a counterclockwise direction and with a broken sail.

Thievery became a big problem, and after a cutter was stolen, Cook ordered a blockade of Kealakekua Bay and then set off with a party of 11 men to the main village at the northern point of the bay. His intention was to capture the high chief Kalaniopuu and hold him until the cutter was returned. This was a tactic that Cook had used elsewhere in the Pacific and that he saw as reasonable diplomacy.

While Cook was en route to the village, a Hawaiian canoe attempting to sail out of the bay was fired upon by the English sailors. Unbeknown to Cook's crew, the canoe was transporting a lower chief, Noekema, who was killed in the musket fire.

In the meantime Cook had reached Kalaniopuu's house and the chief had agreed to go with him. But as they walked down to the shore, Kalaniopuu's wailing wife ran after him and the old chief suddenly balked and attempted to get away. In the midst of it all, word of Noekema's death reached the village, where a crowd quickly gathered.

Hoping to prevent bloodshed, Cook let the chief go, but the situation continued to escalate. As Cook was walking towards his boat, he shot at one of the armed Hawaiians who tried to block his way. The pistol misfired and the bullet bounced off the man's chest. The Hawaiians began to throw stones, and Cook ordered his men on shore to fire more shots.

Cook had always assumed, as had been the case on other Pacific islands, that if trouble developed his men could fire a few shots and the natives, upon seeing the blood, would quickly disperse. That assumption proved wrong, however, and the Hawaiians, who were now in an angry frenzy, attacked rather than retreated.

The sailors in the boats fired another round as their captain began to make his way towards them over slippery rocks. Before they could reload, the crowd of Hawaiians moved in and Cook was struck

Captain Cook's death
by John Webber

on the head. Stunned by the blow, he staggered into the shallows, where the Hawaiians beat and stabbed him, passing the daggers to share in the kill. Four other sailors also died in the battle.

In this freak melee on a shore of the Sandwich Islands, his last discovery, the life of the greatest explorer and navigator of the century came to a bloody end.

Cook's men, shocked by his death, went on a rampage. They burned a village, beheaded two of their victims and rowed across the bay with the heads on poles.

Eventually, Kalaniopuu made a truce and returned those parts of Cook's dismembered body he was able to find. The skull was returned, but it had been stripped of its skin – a common practice bestowed upon great chiefs.

Cook's remains were buried at sea in a military funeral, at which time the Hawaiians placed a kapu on the bay and also held ceremonies of their own.

A week after Cook's February 14 death, the two ships set sail, landing briefly on Oahu, Kauai and Niihau before finally leaving Hawaiian waters on March 15, 1779.

Cook and his crew left the Hawaiians a costly legacy in the iron that was turned into weapons and the introduced diseases that decimated the natives, as well as fathering the first children of mixed blood. The crews also returned home with charts and maps that would allow others to follow in their wake, and in Britain and Europe their stories and drawings were published, stirring the public's sense of adventure.

Some of Cook's crew returned to the Pacific, leading their own expeditions. Among them was Captain George Vancouver, who brought the first cattle and horses to Hawaii, and the ill-fated William Bligh, who captained the *Bounty*.

Kamehameha the Great

At the time of Cook's arrival in Hawaii in 1778, the islands were divided into separate warring chiefdoms. Kamehameha the Great, who by 1791 had become sole chief of the Big Island, was to become the first to unite all the Hawaiian Islands under one rule.

In 1795, after conquering Maui and Molokai, Kamehameha successfully invaded Oahu and established his reign there as well.

Kamehameha then made two attempts to invade Kauai, the only island not yet under his control. In 1796 his canoes were caught in a storm at sea and forced to turn back before ever reaching the island. In 1804, while Kamehameha was in Oahu again preparing for an invasion of Kauai, his warriors were struck by a deadly outbreak of a feverish disease, probably cholera, and the invasion plans were scrapped. The luck of the roll may have been Kauai's at the time, but Kamehameha's power was too obvious to ignore, so in 1810 Kauai agreed by treaty to accept Kamehameha's suzerainty.

The Sandalwood Trade

By the mid-1780s Hawaii was becoming a popular port of call for Yankee traders plying the seas between North America and China.

In the early 1790s American sea captains discovered that Hawaii had great stocks of sandalwood, which were worth a premium in China. When the captains showed interest in it, Hawaiian chiefs readily began bargaining their wood away in exchange for foreign weapons.

A lucrative three-way trade developed. From Hawaii the ships sailed to Canton and traded loads of sandalwood for Chinese silk and porcelain, which were then carried back to New England ports and sold at a high profit. In New England the ships were reloaded with goods to be traded to the Hawaiians.

Hawaii's forests of sandalwood were so vast at this time that the Chinese name for Hawaii was Tahn Heong Sahn, the 'Sandalwood Mountains'.

To try to maintain the resource Kamehameha eventually put a kapu on all sandalwood forests, giving himself total control over the trade. Even under Kamehameha's relatively shrewd management, the bulk of the profits ended up in the sea captains' pockets. Payment for the sandalwood was made in overpriced goods, originally cannons and rifles, and later exotic items such as European furniture.

While Kamehameha was careful not to use up all his forests or overburden his subjects, his successor, Liholiho, partially lifted the royal kapu, allowing island chiefs to get in on the action. The chiefs began purchasing foreign luxuries by signing promissory notes to be paid in future shipments of sandalwood.

To pay off the rising 'debts', the *makaainana* (commoners) were forced into virtual servitude. They were used like packhorses to haul the wood, the sandalwood strapped to their backs with bands of ti leaves. The men who carted the wood were called *kua leho*, literally 'calloused backs' after the thick permanent layer of calluses that they developed. It was not uncommon for them to carry heavy loads 20 miles from the interior to ships waiting on the coast. Missionaries recorded seeing caravans of as many as 3000 men carting wood during the height of the trade.

In a few short years after Kamehameha's death Hawaii's sandalwood forests were exhausted. In a futile attempt to continue the trade, Oahu's Governor Boki, who had heard of vast sandalwood reserves in New Hebrides, set sail in November 1829 with 500 men on an ill-conceived expedition to

> ## Hawaii's Alii
> Hawaii is the only US state to once have been a native-governed kingdom. Beginning with Kamehameha the Great's 1795 unification of the islands, the reign of Hawaii's *alii* (royalty) continued until the overthrow of Queen Liliuokalani by *haole* (Caucasian) businessmen in 1893. The following are the dates of the monarchs' lives.
>
> Kamehameha the Great
> c1758-1819
> Kamehameha II (Liholiho)
> 1797-1824
> Kamehameha III (Kauikeauoli)
> 1813-1854
> Kamehameha IV (Alexander Liholiho)
> 1834-1863
> Kamehameha V (Lot Kamehameha)
> 1830-1872
> Lunalilo (William C Lunalilo)
> 1832-1874
> Kalakaua (David Kalakaua)
> 1836-1891
> Liliuokalani (Lydia Liliuokalani)
> 1838-1917 ∎

harvest the trees. Boki's ship was lost at sea and the expedition's other ship, not too surprisingly, received a hostile welcome in New Hebrides.

In August 1830, 20 emaciated survivors sailed back into Honolulu Harbor. Boki had been a popular, if troubled, leader in a rapidly changing Hawaii. Hawaiians grieved in the streets of Honolulu when they heard of Boki's tragedy, and his death marked the end of the sandalwood trade.

End of the Old Religion
King Kamehameha died in 1819 at his Kamakahonu residence on the Big Island. The crown was passed to his reluctant son, Liholiho, who was proclaimed Kamehameha II. In reality the power was passed to Kaahumanu, who had been the favorite of Kamehameha's 21 wives.

Kaahumanu, who lived from 1768 to 1832, was an ambitious woman, determined to break down the ancient kapu system of taboos that restricted her powers.

Less than six months after Kamehameha's death, Kaahumanu threw a feast for women of royalty at the sacred Kamakahonu compound. Although one of the most sacred taboos strictly forbade men from eating with women, Kaahumanu forcefully persuaded Liholiho to sit beside her and join in the meal.

It was an otherwise uneventful meal; not a single angry god manifested itself. But in that one act the old religion was cast aside, along with 600 years of taboos and restrictions. Hawaiians no longer had to fear being put to death for violating the kapus, and a flurry of temple smashing and idol burning quickly followed.

Those chiefs and kahunas who resisted were easily squelched by Liholiho using the powerful army that Kamehameha had left behind. It was the end of an era.

The Missionaries

On April 19, 1820, the brig *Thaddeus* arrived from Boston with the first of the Christian missionaries to Hawaii. By a twist of fate, they landed in Kailua Bay, a stone's throw from Kamakahonu, where six months earlier Kaahumanu had feasted the overthrow of the old religion.

It was a timely arrival for the missionaries. The loss of their native religion and social structure had left the Hawaiians with a spiritual void into which the Christians zealously stepped.

The *Thaddeus* carried 23 Congregationalists, the first of 12 groups to be sent in the next three decades by the New England-based American Board of Commissioners of Foreign Missions. The leader of this initial group of missionaries was Hiram Bingham.

The missionaries befriended Hawaiian royalty and made their inroads quickly. After Queen Kaahumanu became seriously ill, Sybil Bingham nursed her back to health. Shortly after, Kaahumanu showed her gratitude by passing a law forbidding work and travel on the Sabbath.

Up until this time the Hawaiians had no written language. Using the Roman alphabet the missionaries established a written

Hawaiian language that allowed them to translate the Bible. They taught the Hawaiians to read and write and established the first 'American' high school west of the Rocky Mountains.

With encouragement from the missionaries, the Hawaiians quickly took on Western ways, Western clothing and Western laws.

Liholiho (Kamehameha II)

With Kaahumanu holding the real power, in November 1823 a floundering Liholiho set sail for England with his favorite wife to pay a royal visit to King George – although he failed to inform anyone in England of his plans.

When Liholiho arrived unannounced in London, misfitted in Western clothing and lacking in royal etiquette, the British press roasted him with racist caricatures. He never met King George. While being prepped in the social graces for their audience with the king, Liholiho and his wife came down with measles. They died in England within a few weeks of each other in July 1824.

The Whalers

Within a year of the missionaries' arrival, whalers began calling on Hawaiian ports. The first were mostly New England Yankees and a sprinkling of Gay Head Indians and former slaves. As more ships arrived, men of all nationalities roamed Hawaiian ports. Most were in their teens or twenties, ripe for adventure.

Towns sprung up with shopkeepers catering to the whalers, and saloons, brothels and hotels boomed. Honolulu and Lahaina became bustling ports of call.

From 1825 to 1870, Hawaii was the whaling center of the Pacific. It was a convenient way station for whalers hunting both the Arctic and Japanese whaling grounds. At its peak, between 500 and 600 whaling ships were pulling into Hawaiian ports each year.

Whaling brought big money to Hawaii and the dollars spread beyond the whaling towns. Many Maui farmers got their start supplying the whaling ships with potatoes;

Big Island cattle ranches grew with the demand for beef; and even the average Hawaiian could earn a little money by turning in sailors who had jumped ship.

Hawaiians themselves made good whalers, and sea captains gladly paid a $200 bond to the Hawaiian government for each *kanaka* allowed to join their crew. Kamehameha IV even set up his own fleet of whaling ships that flew under the Hawaiian flag.

Whaling in the Pacific peaked in the mid-19th century and quickly began to burn itself out. In a few short years all but the most distant whaling grounds were being depleted and whalers were forced to go farther afield to make their kills. By 1860 whale oil prices were dropping as an emerging petroleum industry was beginning to produce a less expensive fuel for lighting.

The last straw for the Pacific whaling industry came in 1871, when an early storm in the Arctic caught more than 30 ships by surprise, trapping them in ice floes above the Bering Strait. Although over 1000 seamen were rescued, half of them Hawaiian, the fleet itself was lost.

Sugar Plantations

Ko, or sugar cane, arrived in Hawaii with the early Polynesian settlers. While the Hawaiians enjoyed chewing the cane for its juices, they never refined it into sugar.

The first known attempt to produce sugar in Hawaii was in 1802, when a Chinese immigrant in Lanai boiled crushed sugar cane in iron pots. Other Chinese soon set up small sugar mills on the scale of neighborhood bakeries.

In 1835 a young Bostonian, William Hooper, saw a bigger opportunity in sugar and set out to establish Hawaii's first sugar plantation. Hooper convinced Honolulu investors Ladd & Company to put up the money for his venture and then worked out a deal with Kamehameha III to lease 980 acres of land on Kauai for $300. His next step was to negotiate with Kauai's alii for the right to use Hawaiian laborers.

In the mid-1830s Hawaii was still largely feudalistic. Commoners fished, farmed and lived on land that was under the domain of the local alii; in exchange the commoners worked when needed for the alii. Therefore, before Hooper could hire any work hands, he had to first pay the alii a stipend to free the Hawaiians from their traditional work obligations.

The new plantation system, which introduced the concept of growing crops for profit rather than subsistence, marked the advent of capitalism and the introduction of wage labor in Hawaii.

The sugar industry emerged at the same time whalers began arriving in force. Together they became the foundation for Hawaii's moneyed economy.

By the 1850s sugar plantations were established on Maui, Oahu and the Big Island, as well as on Kauai.

Sugar cane, a giant grass, only flourishes with abundant water, so plantations were limited to the rainier parts of Hawaii and even then were vulnerable to drought. In 1856 an 11-mile irrigation ditch was dug to bring mountain water to Lihue cane fields, which were suffering from a drought. While this Kauai ditch was intended as a rescue procedure, its success signaled plantation owners to the possibilities for diverting water to irrigate heretofore unsuitable lands.

In the 1870s the 17-mile Hamakua Ditch was dug on Maui, the first of several extensive aqueducts that would carry millions of gallons of water daily from upland rainforests to water-thirsty plantations. These artificial waterways turned dry central plains into drenched cane fields. Today Hawaii is still criss-crossed with hundreds of miles of working ditches and aqueducts built a century ago.

In addition to the irrigation systems, the sugar companies built flumes and railroads to carry the cane from the fields to the mills. For over 100 years, sugar formed the backbone of the Hawaiian economy.

Hawaii's Immigrants

As the sugar industry was booming, Hawaii's native population was in decline, largely as the result of diseases introduced by foreigners.

To expand their operations, the plantation owners began to look overseas for a labor supply. They needed immigrants who would be accustomed to working long days in hot weather and for whom the low wages being paid would seem like an opportunity.

In 1852 the plantation owners began recruiting laborers from China. In 1868 they went to Japan and in the 1870s they brought in Portuguese from Madeira and the Azores. After Hawaii's annexation to the USA in 1898 resulted in restrictions on Chinese immigration, plantation owners turned to Puerto Ricans and Koreans. Filipinos were the last group of immigrants brought to Hawaii to work the fields; the first wave came in 1906, the last in 1946.

Although these six ethnic groups made up the bulk of the field hands, bands of South Sea islanders, Scots, Scandinavians, Germans, Galicians, Spaniards and Russians all came in turn as well.

Each group brought its own culture, food and religion. Chinese clothing styles mixed with Japanese kimonos and European bonnets. A dozen languages filled the air and a unique pidgin English developed as a means for the various groups to communicate with one another.

Conditions varied with the ethnic group and the period. At the turn of the century Japanese contract laborers were being paid $15 a month. After annexation, the contracts were considered indentured servitude and were declared illegal under US law. Still, wages as low as a dollar a day were common up until the 1930s.

In all, approximately 350,000 immigrants came to Hawaii to work on the sugar plantations. A continuous flow of immigrant workers was required to replace those who invariably found better options elsewhere. Although some workers came for a set period to save money and return home, others worked out their contracts and then moved off the plantations to farm their own plots or start their own businesses.

Plantation towns like Koloa, Paia and Honokaa grew up around the mills, with barber shops, fish markets, beer halls and bathhouses catering to the workers.

The major immigrant populations – Japanese, Chinese, Filipino and Western European – came to outnumber the native Hawaiians. Together they created the unique blend of cultures that would continue to characterize Hawaii for generations to come.

Kamehameha III

The last son of Kamehameha the Great, Kamehameha III ruled for 30 years, from 1825 until his death in 1854. In 1840 he introduced Hawaii's first constitution, both to protect his powers and adjust to changing times. The constitution established Hawaii's first national legislature and provided for a Supreme Court.

Kamehameha III was also responsible for passing the Great Mahele land act (see below), establishing religious freedom and giving all male citizens the right to vote.

Hawaii's only 'invasion' by a foreign power occurred during Kamehameha's reign. In 1843, George Paulet, an upstart British commander upset about a petty land deal involving a British national, sailed into Honolulu commanding the British ship *Carysfort* and seized Oahu for six months. In that short period, he Anglicized street names, seized property and began to collect taxes.

To avoid bloodshed, Kamehameha III stood aside as the British flag was raised and the ship's band played 'God Save the Queen'. Queen Victoria herself wasn't flattered. After catching wind of the incident, she dispatched Admiral Richard Thomas to restore Hawaiian independence. Admiral Thomas re-raised the Hawaiian flag at the site of what is today Honolulu's Thomas Square. As the flag was raised Kamehameha III uttered the words *Ua mau ke ea o ka aina i ka pono*, meaning 'The life of the land is perpetuated in righteousness', which remains Hawaii's official motto.

The Great Mahele

The Great Mahele of 1848, which was introduced under the urging of influential missionaries, permanently altered Hawaiian concepts of land ownership. For the first time, land became a commodity that could be bought and sold.

Through the provisions of the Great Mahele, the king, who had previously owned all land, gave up title to the majority of it. Island chiefs were allowed to purchase some of the lands that they had controlled as fiefdoms for the king. Other lands, which were divided into three-acre farm plots called *kuleana*, were made available to all Hawaiians. In order to retain title, chiefs and commoners alike had to pay a tax and register the land.

The chiefs had the option of paying the tax in property and many did so. Commoners had no choice but to pay the taxes in cash. Although the act was intended to turn Hawaii into a country of small farms, in the end only a few thousand Hawaiians carried through with the paperwork and received kuleanas.

In 1850 land purchases were opened to foreigners. Unlike the Hawaiians, the Westerners jumped at the opportunity, and before the native islanders could clearly grasp the concept of private land ownership, there was little land left to own.

Within a few decades the Westerners, who were more adept at wheeling and dealing in real estate, owned 80% of all privately held lands. Even many of the Hawaiians who had gone through the process of getting their own kuleana eventually ended up selling it to the haoles for a fraction of its real value.

Contrary to the picture the missionaries had painted for Kamehameha III, the Hawaiians suddenly became a landless people, drifting into ghettos in the larger towns. With a bitter twist, many of the missionaries themselves ended up with sizable tracts of land, and more than a few of them left the church to tend their new estates.

Although Hawaiian commoners had no rights to the land prior to the Great Mahele, they were free to move around and work the property of any chief. In return for their personal use of the land they paid the chief in labor or with a percentage of their crops. In this way they lived off the land. After the Great Mahele, they were simply *off* the land.

Kamehameha IV

Kamehameha IV had a short and rather confusing reign that lasted from 1855 to 1863. He tried to give his rule an element of European regality, à la Queen Victoria, and he and his consort, Queen Emma, established a Hawaiian branch of the Anglican Church of England. He also passed a law mandating all children be given a Christian name along with their Hawaiian name, a statute that stayed on the books until 1967.

Struggles between those wanting to strengthen the monarchy and those wishing to limit it marked Kamehameha IV's reign.

Kamehameha V

The most significant accomplishment of Kamehameha V (1863-72) was the establishment of a controversial constitution that gave greater power to the king at the expense of elected officials. It also restricted the right to vote.

Kamehameha V, who suffered a severe bout of unrequited love, was the last king from a royal lineage that dated back to the 12th century. From childhood he was enraptured by Princess Bernice Pauahi, who in the end turned down his proposals, opting instead to marry American Charles Reed Bishop. Jolted by the rejection, Kamehameha V never married, yet he also never gave up on the princess. Even on his deathbed he offered Princess Bernice his kingdom, which she declined.

As the bachelor king left no heirs, his death in December 1872 brought an end to the Kamehameha dynasty. Subsequent kings would be elected by the national legislature.

Lunalilo

King Lunalilo's short reign lasted from 1873 to 1874. His cabinet, made up largely of Americans, was instrumental in paving the way for a treaty of reciprocity with the USA.

Although the USA was the biggest market for Hawaiian sugar, US sugar tariffs ate heavily into profit margins. As a means of eliminating the tariffs, most plantation owners favored the annexation of Hawaii to the USA.

The US Government was cool to the idea of annexation, but it warmed to the possibility of establishing a naval base on Oahu. In 1872 General John Schofield was sent to assess Pearl Harbor's strategic value. He was impressed with what he saw – the largest anchorage in the Pacific – and reported his enthusiasm back to Washington.

Although native Hawaiians protested in the streets and the Royal Troops even staged a little mutiny, there would eventually be a reciprocity agreement that would cede Pearl Harbor to the USA in exchange for duty-free access for Hawaiian sugar.

King Kalakaua

Although known as the 'Merrie Monarch', David Kalakaua (1874-91) ruled in troubled times.

The first challenge to the reign of Hawaii's last king came on election day. His con-

NED FRIARY
Statue of King David Kalakaua, Kalakaua Park in Hilo

tender had been the dowager Queen Emma, and when the results were announced her followers rioted in the streets, requiring Kalakaua to request aid from US and British warships that happened to be in Honolulu Harbor at the time.

Despite the initial turmoil, Kalakaua went on to become a great Hawaiian revivalist. He brought back the hula, turning around decades of missionary repression against the 'heathen dance', and composed the national anthem, *Hawaii Ponoi*, which is now the state song. He also tried to ensure some self-rule for native Hawaiians, who had become a minority in their own land.

When Kalakaua left for his first trip overseas, scores of Hawaiians came to the waterfront weeping. The last king to leave the islands, Kamehameha II, had come back in a coffin.

While in the USA, Kalakaua met with President Ulysses Grant and persuaded him to accept Lunalilo's reciprocity treaty, which the US Congress had been resisting. Kalakaua also managed to postpone the ceding of Pearl Harbor for eight years. He returned to Hawaii a hero – to the business community for the treaty, and to the Hawaiians for simply making it back alive.

The king became a world traveler, visiting India, Egypt, Europe and Southeast Asia. Kalakaua was well aware that Hawaii's days as an independent Polynesian kingdom were numbered. To counter the Western powers that were gaining hold of Hawaii, he made a futile attempt to establish a Polynesian-Pacific empire. On a visit with the emperor of Japan, he even proposed a royal marriage between his niece Princess Kaiulani and a Japanese prince, but the Japanese declined.

Visits with other foreign monarchs gave Kalakaua a taste for royal pageantry. He returned to build Iolani Palace for what the haole business community thought was an extravagant $360,000. By many influential whites, the king was perceived as a lavish spender who was fond of partying and throwing public luaus.

As Kalakaua incurred debts, he became increasingly less popular with the sugar barons, whose businesses were now the backbone of the economy. They formed the Hawaiian League in 1887 and developed their own armies, which stood ready to overthrow Kalakaua. The league presented Kalakaua with a list of demands and forced him to accept a new constitution strictly limiting his powers. It also limited suffrage to property owners, which by then excluded the vast majority of Hawaiians.

On July 30, 1889, a group of about 150 Hawaiians attempted to overthrow the new constitution by occupying Iolani Palace. Called the Wilcox Rebellion after its part-Hawaiian leader, it was a confused and futile attempt, and the rebels were forced to surrender.

Kalakaua died in San Francisco in 1891.

Queen Liliuokalani

Kalakaua was succeeded by his sister, Liliuokalani, wife of Oahu's governor John O Dominis.

Queen Liliuokalani (1891-93) was even more determined than Kalakaua in her quest to strengthen the power of the monarchy. She charged that the 1887 constitution had illegally been forced upon King Kalakaua; the Hawaii Supreme Court upheld her contention.

In January 1893, as Liliuokalani was preparing to proclaim a new constitution to restore royal powers, a group of armed haole businessmen occupied the Supreme Court and declared the monarchy overthrown. They announced a provisional government, led by Sanford Dole, son of a pioneer missionary. A contingent of US sailors came ashore, ostensibly to protect the property of US citizens, but instead of flanking the property they claimed to be protecting, the troops marched on the palace and positioned their guns at the queen's residence. Realizing it was futile to oppose US forces, the queen opted to avoid bloodshed and stepped down.

The provisional government immediately appealed to the USA for annexation, while the queen appealed to the USA to restore the monarchy. To Dole's dismay, the timing of events was to the queen's

NED FRIARY
Statue of Queen Liliuokalani, Honolulu

advantage. Democrat president Grover Cleveland had just replaced a Republican administration and his sentiments clearly favored the queen.

Cleveland sent an envoy, James Blount, to investigate the situation and determine what course of action the US Government should take.

In the meantime he received Queen Liliuokalani's niece, Princess Kaiulani, who, at the time of the coup, had been in London being prepared for the throne. The beautiful 18-year-old princess eloquently pleaded the monarchy's case. She also made a favorable impression with the American press, which largely caricatured those involved in the annexation as dour, greedy buffoons.

Cleveland ordered the US flag be taken down and the queen restored to her throne. However, the provisional government, now firmly in power, turned a deaf ear, declaring that Cleveland was meddling in 'Hawaiian' affairs.

The new government, with Dole as president, inaugurated itself as the Republic of Hawaii on July 4, 1894. Although Cleveland initially favored reversing the situation, he also knew the American public's sense of justice was thin and that ousting a government of white Americans and replacing them with native Hawaiians could backlash on his own political future. Consequently, his actions were largely limited to rhetoric.

Weary of waiting for outside intervention, in early 1895 a group of Hawaiian royalists attempted a counter-revolution that was easily squashed in a fortnight. Liliuokalani was accused of being a conspirator and placed under arrest.

To humiliate her, she was tried in her own palace and referred to only as Mrs John O Dominis. She was fined $5000 and sentenced to five years of hard labor, later reduced to nine months of house arrest at the palace.

Liliuokalani spent the rest of her life in her husband's residence, Washington Place, one block from the palace. When she died in November 1917, all of Honolulu came out for the funeral procession. To most islanders, Liliuokalani was still their queen.

Annexation

With the Spanish-American War of 1898, Americans acquired a taste for expansionism.

Not only was Hawaii gifted with Pearl Harbor, but it took on a new strategic importance being midway between the USA and its newly acquired possession, the Philippines. Annexation of Hawaii passed in the US Congress on July 7, 1898. Hawaii would enter the 20th century as a territory of the USA.

In just over a century of Western contact, the native Hawaiian population had been decimated by foreign diseases to which they had no immunities. It began with the venereal disease introduced by Captain Cook's crew in 1778. The whalers followed

with cholera and smallpox, and Chinese immigrants, who came to replace Hawaiian laborers, brought leprosy. By the end of the 19th century, the native Hawaiian population had been reduced from an estimated 300,000 to less than 50,000.

Descendants of the early missionaries had taken over first the land and now the government. Without ever having fought a single battle against a foreign power, Hawaiians had lost their islands to ambitious foreigners. All in all, as far as the native Hawaiians were concerned, the annexation wasn't anything to celebrate.

The Chinese and Japanese were also uneasy. One of the reasons for the initial reluctance of the US Congress to annex Hawaii had been the racial mix of the islands' population. There were already restrictions on Chinese immigration to the USA, and restrictions on Japanese immigration were expected to follow.

In a rush to avoid a labor shortage, the sugar plantation owners quickly brought 70,000 Japanese immigrants into Hawaii. By the time the immigration wave was over the Japanese accounted for over 40% of Hawaii's population.

In the years since the reciprocity agreement, sugar production had increased tenfold. Those who ruled the land ruled the government, and closer bonding with the USA didn't change the formula. In 1900, US president McKinley appointed Sanford Dole the first territorial governor.

World War I

Soon after annexation, the US Navy set up a huge Pacific headquarters at Pearl Harbor and built Schofield Barracks, the largest US army base anywhere. The military quickly became the leading sector of Oahu's economy.

The islands were relatively untouched by WWI, even though the first German prisoners of war 'captured' by the USA were in Hawaii. They were escorted off the German gunboat *Grier*, which had the misfortune to be docked at Honolulu Harbor when war broke out.

The war affected people in Hawaii in

other ways. Heinrich Hackfeld, a German sea captain long settled in the islands, had established Hawaii's most successful merchandise stores, BF Ehler's & Company. He had also developed a real estate empire rooted in sugar, purchasing Lahaina's Pioneer Mill, among other properties. He lost it all during WWI.

Anti-German sentiments forced Hackfeld to liquidate his holdings, and American Factors (Amfac) took over his properties, renaming the stores Liberty House.

Pineapple & Planes
In the early 20th century, pineapple emerged as Hawaii's second major export crop. James Dole, a cousin of Sanford Dole, purchased the island of Lanai in 1922 and turned it into the world's largest pineapple plantation. Although sugar remained Hawaii's top crop in export value, the more labor-intensive pineapple eventually surpassed it in terms of employment.

In 1936, Pan American flew the first passenger flights from the US mainland to Hawaii, an aviation milestone that ushered in the transpacific air age. Hawaii was now only hours away from the US West Coast.

World War II
On December 7, 1941, a wave of Japanese bombers attacked Pearl Harbor, jolting the USA into WWII. The attack caught the US fleet totally by surprise, even though there had been warnings, some of which were far from subtle.

At 6:40 am the USS *Ward* spotted a submarine conning tower approaching the entrance of Pearl Harbor. The *Ward* immediately attacked with depth charges and sank what turned out to be one of five midget Japanese submarines launched to penetrate the harbor.

At 7:02 am a radar station on the north shore of Oahu reported planes approaching. Even though they were coming from the wrong direction, they were assumed to be US planes from the mainland.

At 7:55 am Pearl Harbor was hit. Within minutes the USS *Arizona* went down in a

fiery inferno, trapping 1177 men beneath the surface. Twenty other US ships were sunk or damaged, along with 347 aircraft. More than 2500 people were killed.

It wasn't until 15 minutes after the bombing started that US anti-aircraft guns began to shell the Japanese warplanes. The Japanese lost 29 aircraft in the attack.

After the smoke cleared, Hawaii was placed under martial law and Oahu took on the face of a military camp. Already heavily militarized, vast tracts of Hawaii's land were turned over to the US armed forces for expanded military bases, training and weapons testing. Much of that land would never be returned. Throughout the war, Oahu served as the command post for the USA's Pacific operations.

Following the attack on Pearl Harbor a wave of suspicion landed on the *nisei* (people of Japanese descent) in Hawaii. While sheer numbers prevented the sort of internment practices that took place on the mainland, the Japanese in Hawaii were subject to interrogation, and their religious and civic leaders were sent to mainland internment camps.

Japanese language schools were closed, and many of the teachers arrested. Posters were hung in restaurants and other public places warning islanders to be careful about speaking carelessly in front of anyone of Japanese ancestry. Nisei were dismissed from posts in the Hawaiian National Guard and prevented from joining the armed services.

Eventually Japanese-Americans were allowed to volunteer for a segregated regiment, although they were kept on the mainland and out of action for much of the war.

During the final stages of the war, when fighting was at its heaviest, the nisei were given the chance to form a combat unit. Volunteers were called and more than 10,000 nisei signed up, forming two distinguished Japanese-American regiments. One of these, the 442nd Second Regimental Combat Team, which was sent into action on the European front, became the most decorated fighting unit in US history.

The veterans returned to Hawaii with

different expectations. Many went on to college using the GI bill, and today they account for some of Hawaii's most influential lawyers, judges and civic leaders. Among the veterans of the 442nd is Hawaii's senior US senator, Daniel Inouye, who lost an arm in the fighting.

Unionizing Hawaii
The feisty mainland-based International Longshoremen's and Warehousemen's Union (ILWU) began organizing Hawaiian labor in the 1930s.

After WWII, the ILWU organized an intensive campaign against the 'Big Five' – C Brewer, Castle & Cooke, Alexander & Baldwin, Theo Davies and Amfac – Hawaii's biggest businesses and landholders, all of which had roots in sugar.

The ILWU's six-month waterfront strike in 1949 virtually halted all shipments to and from Hawaii. The union went on to organize plantation strikes that resulted in Hawaii's sugar and pineapple workers becoming the world's highest paid.

The new union movement helped develop a political opposition to the staunchly Republican big landowners, who had maintained a stronghold on the political scene since annexation.

In the 1950s, McCarthyism, the fanatical wave of anti-Communism that had swept the mainland, spilled over to Hawaii. In the fallout, the leader of the ILWU in Hawaii, Jack Hall, was tried and convicted of being a Communist.

Post-War Hawaii
WWII brought Hawaii closer to the center stage of American culture and politics.

The prospect of statehood had long been the central topic in Hawaiian political circles. Three decades had passed since Hawaii's first delegate to the US Congress, Prince Jonah Kuhio Kalanianaole, introduced the first statehood bill in 1919. It had received a cool reception in Washington at that time, and there were mixed feelings in Hawaii as well. However, by the time the war was over, opinion polls showed that two out of three Hawaiian residents favored statehood.

Still, Hawaii was too much of a melting pot for many politicians to support statehood, particularly those from the rigidly segregated southern states. To the overwhelmingly white and largely conservative Congress, Hawaii's multiethnic community was too exotic and foreign to be thought of as 'American'.

Congress was also concerned with the success of Hawaiian labor strikes and the growth of membership in the ILWU. It all combined to keep statehood at bay until the end of the 1950s.

Statehood
In March 1959 the US Congress finally passed legislation to make Hawaii a state. On June 27 a plebiscite was held in Hawaii, with more than 90% of the islanders voting for statehood. The island of Niihau was the only precinct to vote against it.

On August 21, 1959, after 61 years of territorial status, Hawaii became the 50th state of the USA.

Hawaiian Sovereignty
Over the past decade, a Hawaiian sovereignty movement, intent on righting some of the wrongs of the past century, has come into the forefront of political issues in Hawaii. The success of the Protect Kahoolawe movement (see the Kahoolawe chapter), growing discontent over the mismanagement of Hawaiian Home Lands and the heightened consciousness created by the 1993 centennial anniversary of Queen Liliuokalani's overthrow have all served as rallying points. Things are still in a formative stage, and a consensus on what form sovereignty should take has yet to emerge.

Ka Lahui Hawaii, the largest of the many Hawaiian sovereignty groups, has adopted a constitution for a Hawaiian nation within the USA, similar to that of 300 Native American groups on the mainland who have their own tribal governments and lands. Ka Lahui Hawaii wants all Hawaiian Home Lands, as well as the title to much of the crown land taken during annexation, turned over to native Hawaiians. These lands include nearly 1¾ million acres that

Hawaiian Home Lands

In 1920, under the sponsorship of Prince Jonah Kuhio Kalanianaole, the Territory of Hawaii's congressional delegate, the US Congress passed the Hawaiian Homes Commission Act. The act set aside almost 200,000 acres of land for homesteading by native Hawaiians, who were by this time the most landless ethnic group in Hawaii. The land was but a small fraction of the crown lands that were taken from the Kingdom of Hawaii when the USA annexed the islands in 1898.

Under the legislation, people of at least 50% Hawaiian ancestry were eligible to apply for 99-year leases at $1 a year. Originally most of the leases were for 40-acre parcels of agricultural land, although more recently residential lots as small as a quarter of an acre have been allocated.

Hawaii's prime land, already in the hands of the sugar barons, was excluded from the act. Much of what was designated for homesteading was on far more barren turf.

Indeed, the first homesteading village, at Kalanianaole on Molokai, failed when the wells drew brackish waters and destroyed the newly established crops. Still, many Hawaiians were able to make a go of it, settling homesteads on Oahu, the Big Island, Kauai, Maui and Molokai. Presently there are about 5000 native Hawaiian families living on 25,000 acres of homestead lands.

Like many acts established to help native Hawaiians, administration of the Hawaiian Home Lands has been riddled with abuse. The majority of the land has not been allocated to native Hawaiians but has been leased out to big business, ostensibly as a means of creating an income for the administration of the program.

Parker Ranch on the Big Island has 32,845 acres of Hawaiian Home Lands under lease at less than $4 an acre. Kekaha Sugar, an Amfac subsidiary, leases the lion's share of Kauai's 18,569 acres of Hawaiian Home Lands, while less than 5% is made available to native Hawaiians.

In addition the federal, state and county governments have illegally, and with little or no compensation, taken large tracts of Hawaiian Home Lands for their own use. The Lualualei Naval Reservation alone constitutes one-fifth of all homestead lands on Oahu, where over 5000 native Hawaiians remain on the waiting list – some for as many as 30 years. ∎

were held by the Hawaiian Kingdom at the time of the 1893 overthrow. On Kauai alone the crown lands represent nearly half of the island, including extensive park lands, such as those along the Na Pali Coast.

Other native Hawaiian groups are also calling for self-determination. Some favor the restoration of the monarchy, others focus on monetary reparations, but the majority are looking at some form of a nation-within-a-nation model.

One sovereignty demand was addressed in November 1993, when President Clinton signed a resolution apologizing 'to Native Hawaiians for the overthrow of the Kingdom of Hawaii on January 17, 1893, with participation of agents and citizens of the United States, and the deprivation of the rights of Native Hawaiians to self-determination'. The apology went on to 'acknowledge the ramifications of the overthrow' and expressed a commitment to 'provide a proper foundation for reconciliation'.

Ka Lahui introduced state legislation to establish their group as the stewards of a new Hawaiian nation, and two other sovereignty bills were also introduced. In part to sort out the disparity between the three bills, the state legislature established the Hawaiian Sovereignty Advisory Commission to create a mechanism for native Hawaiians to determine what form sovereignty should take. The commission itself, however, became a source of conflict, as all 20 of the commission members were chosen by the governor, with 12 of those selected from nominees submitted by Hawaiian organizations. Consequently, some groups, such as Ka Lahui and Nation of Hawaii, refused to participate in the commission.

NED FRIARY

Flying the flag upside down has come to represent the sovereignty movement

In the summer of 1996, a commission-sponsored mail-in vote, open to all people of Hawaiian ancestry, was held on the ballot question 'Shall the Hawaiian People elect delegates to propose a native Hawaiian government?'. It was a first-step vote to determine if native Hawaiians wanted to establish a sovereignty process that would be based on electing delegates and holding a convention to chart out their future.

Of the 80,000 ballots mailed to native Hawaiians worldwide, some 30,000 people voted. The initiative passed 73% to 27%, but in many ways it was a far more divided vote. Some native Hawaiians, including members of Ka Lahui, felt the process was co-opted by the state, which provided funding for the ballot, and they boycotted the vote. One source of division, the commission itself, disbanded after the vote, and the state has indicated it will not provide funding for the delegate elections and con-

vention. A nonprofit group, Ha Hawaii, which includes former members of the commission, is now trying to raise $8 million for that purpose.

Although it's still an emerging process and attitudes may change as the movement takes shape, polls show that a significant majority of all Hawaii residents support the concept of Hawaiian sovereignty if it's within the framework of a nation-within-a-nation. Interestingly, the support doesn't vary greatly along ethnic lines.

Incidentally, the Hawaiian flag flown upside down as a sign of distress has come to represent the Hawaiian sovereignty movement.

GEOGRAPHY

The Hawaiian Islands stretch 1523 miles in a line from Kure Atoll in the northwest to the Big Island in the southeast. Ka Lae, on the Big Island, is the southernmost point of the USA.

The equator is 1470 miles south of Honolulu and all the main islands are in the tropic of Cancer. Hawaii shares the same latitude as Hong Kong, Bombay and Mexico's Yucatán Peninsula.

Hawaii's eight major islands are, from largest to smallest, Hawaii (the Big Island), Maui, Oahu, Kauai, Molokai, Lanai, Niihau and Kahoolawe. Together they have a total land area of 6470 sq miles, which includes 96 small nearshore islands with a combined area of less than three sq miles.

The Northwestern Hawaiian Islands lie scattered across a thousand miles of ocean west of Kauai. They consist of 33 islands in 10 clusters with a total land area of just under five sq miles.

In total, Hawaii is a bit smaller than Fiji and a bit larger than the US state of Connecticut.

Hawaii's highest mountain is Mauna Kea on the Big Island, which is 13,796 feet above sea level. According to the *Guinness Book of Records* it's the world's highest mountain (33,476 feet) when measured from the ocean floor. Mauna Loa, also on the Big Island, is Hawaii's second highest mountain, at 13,679 feet.

GEOLOGY

The Hawaiian Islands are the tips of massive mountains, created by a crack in the earth's mantle that has been spewing out molten rock for 25 million years. The hot spot is stationary, but the ocean floor is part of the Pacific Plate, which is moving northwest at the rate of about three inches a year. (The eastern edge of this plate is California's San Andreas fault.)

As weak spots in the earth's crust pass over the hot spot, molten lava bursts through as volcanoes, building underwater mountains. Some of them finally emerge above the water as islands.

Each new volcano eventually creeps northward past the hot spot that created it. The farther from the source, the lower the volcanic activity, until the volcano is eventually cut off completely and turns cold.

Once the lava stops it's a downhill battle. The forces of erosion – wind, rain and waves – slowly wash the mountains away. In addition, the settling of the ocean floor causes the land to gradually recede.

Thus the once mountainous Northwestern Hawaiian Islands, the oldest in the Hawaiian chain, are now low flat atolls that in time will be totally submerged.

The Big Island, Hawaii's southernmost island, is still in the birthing process. Its most active volcano, Kilauea, is directly over the hot spot. In its latest eruptive phase, which began in 1983 and still continues, Kilauea has pumped out more than two billion cubic yards of lava, making this the largest known volcanic eruption in Hawaii's history.

Less than 30 miles southeast of the Big Island, a new seamount named Loihi has already built up 15,000 feet on the ocean floor. The growing mounds of lava are expected to break the ocean surface within 10,000 years – however, if it were to get hyperactive, it could emerge within a century or two.

In 1987 the Woods Hole Oceanographic Institution explored Loihi with *Alvin*, the same deep-water mini-sub that had discovered the *Titanic* wreck the year before.

The Creation Myth

The early Hawaiians were astutely tuned in to geological forces and knew the order in which the islands were created. Their creation story goes something like this:

Pele, the goddess of volcanoes and fire, was born of the marriage of earth and sky. She is both Creator and Destroyer (not unlike the Hindu god Shiva). Her eruptions of molten lava both build the mountains and wreak havoc over everything in their path.

Pele was driven from her home in the northwestern shoals by a jealous older sister, Na Maka O Kahai, goddess of the seas. Pele fled to the southeast and built her home in a crater on Niihau, then on Kauai, then Oahu, and each island in turn. Each time she dug down into the fiery earth deeper than the time before, and each time she was chased away by her sister, the sea.

After being routed from her home on Haleakala on Maui, Pele crossed over to the Big Island. There she built her highest mountains yet and in their volcanic recesses made a home far from the reaches of Na Maka O Kahai.

The sea goddess, however, is still never far from Pele's doorstep. She persistently wears away at Pele's home, her waves taking on the lava, eroding it down and crushing it into sand.

In time Pele will again be forced to move on, but for now she makes her home deep in Kilauea, the most active volcano on earth. ∎

They measured Loihi's summit to be 3117 feet below the surface of the water.

Hawaii's volcanoes are shield volcanoes, which form not by explosion but by a slow build-up of layer upon layer of lava. They rise from the sea with gentle slopes and a relatively smooth surface. It's only after eons of facing the elements that their surfaces become sharply eroded. It's for this reason that the Na Pali cliffs on Kauai, the oldest of the main islands, are the most jagged in Hawaii.

Hawaii's active volcanoes are Kilauea and Mauna Loa, both on the Big Island.

The Big Island's Mauna Kea and Hualalei and Maui's Haleakala are dormant, with future eruptions possible. The volcanoes on all the other Hawaiian islands are considered extinct.

CLIMATE

Overall, Hawaii has great weather. It's balmy and warm, with northeasterly trade winds prevailing most of the year.

Average temperatures differ only about 7°F from winter to summer. Near the coast daily temperatures average a high of about 83°F and a low of around 68°F.

The rainiest time of the year is from December to March. Not only does winter have about twice the rainfall of summer, but winter storms can also hang around for days. In summer the rain is more likely to fall as passing showers. This doesn't mean winter is a bad time to go to Hawaii, it just means the weather is more of a gamble.

Rainfall varies even more with location than with season. In places like Kailua-Kona on the Big Island, you can sunbathe on the beach for all but a few days a year. At the same time you can watch typical afternoon showers pour on the hill slopes just a mile or two inland and know you're well beyond reach.

Hawaii's high volcanic mountains trap the trade winds that blow from the northeast, blocking their moisture-laden clouds and bringing abundant rainfall to the windward side of the islands. Hilo, the rainiest city in the USA with 130 inches annually, is on the windward side of the Big Island.

Conversely, the same mountains block the wind and rain from the southwesterly, or leeward, side of the islands, so it's there you'll find the driest, sunniest conditions and the calmest waters. Leeward areas generally receive only 10 to 25 inches of rain a year.

During kona weather the winds blow from the south, a shift from the typical northeast trades. The ocean swell pattern also changes at this time – snorkeling spots suddenly become surfing spots and vice versa. Kona storms usually occur in winter and are very unpredictable.

The summits of Mauna Kea and Mauna Loa on the Big Island receive snow each winter, and in some years Haleakala on Maui catches a short-lived snow cover as well. The lowest temperature ever recorded on Mauna Kea, Hawaii's coldest spot, was 11°F, while the highest temperature there was 66°F.

ECOLOGY & ENVIRONMENT

Hawaii's native ecosystems have been greatly stressed by the introduction of exotic flora and fauna species. Erosion caused by free-ranging cattle and goats and the monocrop cultures of sugar cane and pineapple have destroyed native ground-covers, resulting in washouts that sweep prime topsoil into the sea and choke out nearshore reefs. Tourism-related development has long taken its toll, particularly the proliferation of large resort hotels and golf courses, which commonly are sited on fragile coastal lands.

On the plus side, Hawaii has no polluting heavy industry, roadside billboards are not allowed and environmental awareness is more advanced than on much of the US mainland.

There are over 150 environmental groups in Hawaii, ranging from chapters of international organizations fighting to save the rainforest to neighborhood groups working to protect local beaches from impending development.

One of the broadest based is the Hawaii chapter of the Sierra Club, which has groups on all the main islands. Its activities range from political activism on local environmental issues to weekend outings for eradicating invasive plants from native forests.

The Sierra Club Legal Defense Fund (SCLDF) is in the forefront, pressing legal challenges against abuses to Hawaii's fragile environment. In conjunction with Greenpeace Hawaii, they've forced the state of Hawaii to prohibit jet skis in waters used by endangered humpback whales. On behalf of several environmental groups, SCLDF filed legal challenges halting a geothermal energy project on the Big Island that would have carved up one

Dance & Music

Ancient Hula Perhaps nothing is more uniquely Hawaiian than the hula. There are many different schools of hula, all very disciplined and graceful in their movements. Before Western contact, students spent years training in hula schools, sometimes moving to other islands to enroll with the masters.

Most ancient hula dances expressed historical events, legendary tales and the accomplishments of the great alii. Facial expressions, hand gestures, hip sway and dance steps all conveyed the story. They were performed to rhythmic chants and drum

beatings, serving to connect with the world of spirits. Eye movement was very important; if the story was about the sun the eyes would gaze upward, if about the netherworld they would gaze downward.

One school, the *hula ohelo*, was very sensual, with movements suggesting the act of procreation.

Hula dancers wore tapa cloth, not the grass skirts which were introduced from Micronesia only a hundred years ago.

The Christian missionaries thought it all too licentious for their liking and suppressed it. The hula might have been lost forever if not for King Kalakaua, the 'Merrie Monarch', who revived it in the latter half of the 19th century.

Musical Instruments The *pahu hula,* a knee drum carved from a breadfruit or coconut log, with a sharkskin drum head, was used solely at hula performances. Other hula musical instruments include *ke laau* sticks, used to keep the beat for the dancers; *iliili*, stone castanets; *puili*, rattles made from split bamboo; and *uliuli*, gourd rattles decorated with colorful feathers.

The early Hawaiians were a romantic lot. Instruments used for courting included the *ohe*, a nose flute made of bamboo, and the *ukeke*, a musical bow with a couple of strings. ■

ALL PHOTOS THIS SECTION BY NED FRIARY

Ancient Crafts

Tapa Weaving In ancient Hawaii, women spent much of their time beating *kapa* (tapa cloth) or preparing *lauhala* for weaving.

Tapa made from the *wauke* (paper mulberry tree) was the favorite. The bark was carefully stripped, then beaten with a stick. The beaters were carved with different patterns which then became the pattern of the tapa. Dyes were made from charcoal, flowers and sea urchins.

Tapa had many uses in addition to clothing, from food containers to burial shrouds. After the missionaries introduced cotton cloth and western clothing, the art of tapa making slowly faded away. These days most of the tapa for sale in Hawaii is from Samoa, with bold designs. Hawaiian tapa was different, with more delicate patterns.

NED FRIARY

Lauhala Weaving Lauhala weaving uses the *lau* (leaves) of the hala tree. Preparing the leaves for weaving is hard, messy work as there are razor-sharp spines along the leaf edges and down the center.

In old Hawaii, lauhala was woven into mats and floor coverings, but these days smaller items like hats, placemats and baskets are most common.

NED FRIARY

Wooden Bowls The Hawaiians had no pottery and made their containers using either gourds or wood. Wooden food bowls were mostly of kou or milo, two native woods which didn't leave unpleasant tastes.

Hawaiian bowls were free of designs and carvings. Their beauty lay in the natural qualities of the wood and in the shape of the bowl alone. Cracked bowls were often expertly patched with dovetailed pieces of wood. Rather than decrease the value of the bowl, patching suggested heirloom status and such bowls were amongst the most highly prized.

NED FRIARY

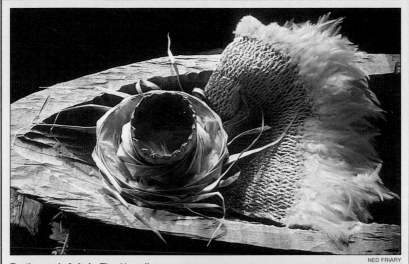

NED FRIARY

Featherwork & Leis The Hawaiians were known for their elaborate featherwork. The most impressive were the capes worn by chiefs and kings. The longer the cape, the higher the rank. Those made of the yellow feathers of the now extinct *mamo* bird were the most highly prized.

The mamo was a predominately black bird with a yellow upper tail. An estimated 80,000 mamo birds were caught to create the cape that King Kamehameha wore. It's said that bird catchers would capture the birds, pluck the desired feathers and release them unharmed. Feathers were also used to make helmets and *leis* (garlands).

The *lei palaoa*, a Hawaiian necklace traditionally worn by royalty, is made of finely braided human hair hung with a smoothly carved whale tooth pendant shaped like a curved tongue. Before foreign whalers arrived, many of these pendants were made of bone. ■

NED FRIARY

Fishponds

The early Hawaiians had a well developed aquaculture system with numerous coastal fishponds.

There were essentially two kinds of fishponds. One type was inshore and totally closed off from the sea, although generally close enough to have brackish water. These inshore ponds would be stocked with fry (young fish) and often had varying salinity levels which the Hawaiians took advantage of by cultivating different varieties of fish in different parts of the pond.

The other kind was a shorelin fishpond, created by building a long stone wall that paralleled the beach and cirved back to shore at both ends. For these walled ponds the Hawaiians built mahaka, or 'sluice gates,' that allowed young fish to swim through but kept fattened fish from swimming back out. The fish in the pond could be easily netted at any time.

Amaama (mullet) and awa (milkfish) were the two varieties of fish mist commonly raised in these dishponds. Most fishponds were strictly for the alii, and commoners were not allowed to eat the fish raised in them. ∎

Kalahuipuaa fishpond at Mauna Lani Resort, BI

Fishing shrine, South Point, BI

Kalokoeli fishpond, Kaunakakai, Molokai

'Agricultural' Golf Courses

In the late 1980s the state passed a controversial bill that allowed golf courses to be built on agriculture-zoned land. This bill led to the gobbling up of major tracts of farm land by Japanese developers and the eviction of small leasehold farmers.

Hawaii is one of the few Pacific island chains where island-grown produce has been relatively abundant, and the continued eviction of farmers who have been growing crops on the land for generations will no doubt make the islands more reliant on imported foods. One of the slogans of the resistance movement is 'No can eat golf balls'.

Currently the state has 75 golf courses, but the proposed courses on the drawing board could double that number in the not-too-distant future.

Not surprisingly, attempts to control the development of new golf courses is one of the forefront issues for island environmentalists. ■

of Hawaii's last remaining lowland rainforests.

In still another challenge, SCLDF took on both the National Rifle Association and the state to force the removal of introduced mouflon game sheep from the slopes of Mauna Kea. The sheep were found to be the primary cause for the decline of the palila, a native honeycreeper. A landmark case, it was the first time that habitat destruction was successfully defined as the 'taking' (meaning killing, harming or harassing) of an endangered species under the US Endangered Species Act.

A different approach is taken by the Nature Conservancy of Hawaii, which protects Hawaii's rarest ecosystems by buying up vast tracts of land and working out long-term stewardships with some of Hawaii's biggest landholders. One project included purchasing the Kipahulu Valley on Maui in conjunction with the state and turning the 11,000 acres over to the federal government to become part of Haleakala National Park.

On Molokai the Nature Conservancy manages the rainforest at Kamakou and Pelekunu Valley on the island's wet northeast coast and the windswept Moomomi dunes on the dry northwest coast. They also manage a crater above Hanauma Bay on

Oahu, the Waikamoi rainforest on Maui, a native dryland forest in Lanai and a Kauai nesting site for the *ao* (Newell's shearwater), a threatened species once thought extinct.

For addresses of environmental groups, see Useful Organizations in the Facts for the Visitor chapter.

FLORA & FAUNA

The Hawaiian island chain, 2500 miles from the nearest continental land mass, is the most geographically isolated place in the world.

All living things that reached Hawaii's shores were carried across the ocean on the wind or the waves – seeds clinging to a bird's feather, a floating hala plant, or insect eggs in a piece of driftwood. Probably the first to arrive on the newly emerged volcanic islands were fern and moss spores, able to drift thousands of miles in the air.

It's estimated that before human contact a new species managed to take hold in Hawaii only once every 100,000 years. New arrivals found specialized habitats ranging from desert to rainforest and elevations climbing from sea level to nearly 14,000 feet. Each species evolved to fit a specific niche in its new environment.

Climate Information

Average temperature and rainfall for various island locations by month

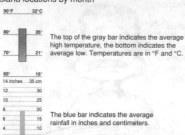

The top of the gray bar indicates the average high temperature, the bottom indicates the average low. Temperatures are in °F and °C.

The blue bar indicates the average rainfall in inches and centimeters.

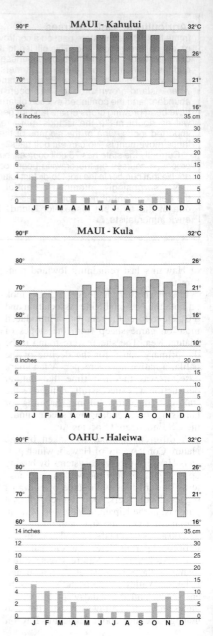

MAUI - Kahului

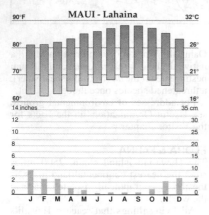

MAUI - Lahaina

MAUI - Kula

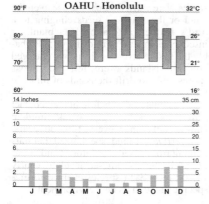

OAHU - Honolulu

OAHU - Haleiwa

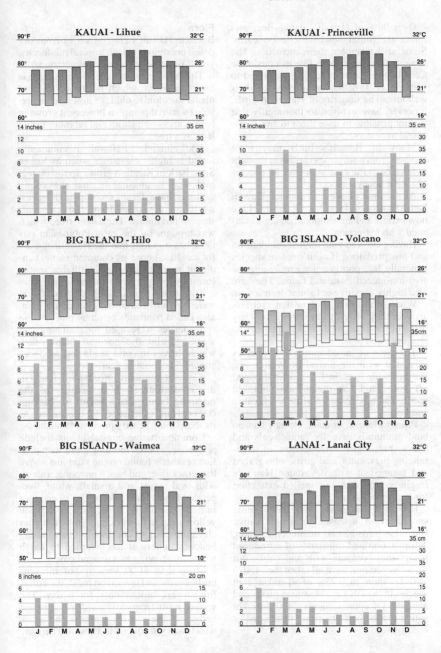

Over 90% of Hawaii's native flora and fauna are found nowhere else on earth. Some still resemble their ancestors. The *nene*, for instance, looks like its cousin the Canada goose, but its feet have adapted to walking on lava by losing most of their webbing. The majority of Hawaiian birds, however, have evolved so thoroughly that it's not possible to trace them to any continental ancestors.

Many of Hawaii's birds may have evolved from a single species, as is thought to have been the case with over 30 species of native honeycreeper.

At the time of Western contact, Hawaii had 70 native bird species. Of those, 24 are now extinct and an additional 36 are threatened with extinction.

Having evolved with limited competition and few predators, Hawaii's native species generally fare poorly among more aggressive introduced flora and fauna. They are also highly sensitive to habitat destruction.

When the first Polynesian settlers arrived, they weren't traveling light. They brought food and medicinal plants, chickens, dogs and pigs.

The pace of introducing exotic species escalated with the arrival of Westerners, starting with Captain Cook, who dropped off goats and left melon and pumpkin seeds. The next Western visitors left cattle and horses.

Prior to human contact, Hawaii had no land mammals save for monk seals and hoary bats. The introduction of free-ranging pigs, cattle and goats, who grazed and foraged at will, devastated Hawaii's fragile ecosystems and spelled extinction for many plants.

Released songbirds and game birds spread avian diseases to which native Hawaiian birds had no immunity. Erosion, deforestation and thousands of introduced plants that compete with and choke out native vegetation have all taken their toll.

Today more than 25% of all endangered species in the USA are Hawaiian plants and animals. Of approximately 2400 different native plants, half are either threatened or endangered.

Flora

Because Hawaii's climate varies from dry desert conditions to lush tropical rainforests, you'll find a wide variety of vegetation.

The most prevalent native forest tree is the *ohia lehua*, which is one of the first plants to colonize old lava flows; recognizable by its red pompom flowers, it grows in barren areas as a shrub and on more fertile land as a tree.

Koa, endemic to Hawaii, is commonly found at higher elevations, such as Kokee State Park in Kauai; it grows up to 100 feet high and is unusual in that the young saplings have fernlike compound leaves, while mature trees have flat crescent-shaped phyllodes. The *kukui* tree, which was brought by the early Polynesian settlers, has oily nuts that the Hawaiians used for candles, hence its common name, candlenut tree; it's easily identifiable in the forest by its light silver-tinged foliage.

Two trees found along the coast that were well utilized in old Hawaii are *hala*, also called pandanus or screw pine, whose spiny leaves were used for thatching and weaving; and the coconut palm *(niu)*, which thrives in coral sands and produces about 75 coconuts a year.

Kiawe, a non-native tree readily found in dry coastal areas, is a member of the mesquite family that's useful for making charcoal but is a nuisance for beachgoers, as its sharp thorns easily pierce soft sandals.

Common native coastal plants include *pohuehue*, a beach morning glory with pink flowers that's found on the sand just above the wrack line; and beach *naupaka*, a shrub with oval leaves and a small, white, five-petaled flower that looks as if it's been torn in half. The native *ilima*, with its delicate yellow-orange flowers, can grow at higher elevations but is commonly found along beaches, where it has adapted to harsh winds by growing as a ground cover.

More than 5000 varieties of hibiscus bushes grow in Hawaii; on most, the colorful flowers bloom only for a day. The variety most frequently used in landscape hedges is the red (or Chinese) hibiscus, which was introduced to Hawaii. There are also a number of native hibiscus, including the *hau* tree, whose flowers open as yellow and change to dark orange as the day goes on. The native Hawaiian white hibiscus tree *(kokio keokeo)*, which thrives in mesic forests and grows up to 60 feet high, is the only Hawaiian hibiscus with a fragrance. The pink butterfly hibiscus, another popular hedge variety, is believed to be a cross between the native white hibiscus and the introduced coral hibiscus.

Hawaii of course is abloom with scores of other tropical flowers, most introduced, including blood-red anthuriums, brilliant orange birds of paradise, colorful bougainvilleas, red ginger, torch ginger, shell ginger and various heliconias with bright orange and red bracts. There are also hundreds of varieties of orchids, all but four of which are introduced.

Fauna

Hawaiian Monk Seal The Hawaiian monk seal, so named for the cowl-like fold of skin at its neck and for its solitary habits, exists only in Hawaii. The species has remained nearly unchanged for 15 million years but is now in danger of dying out completely. Only about 1000 remain.

Hawaiian monk seals, which are sensitive to human disruption, breed and give birth primarily in the Northwestern Hawaiian Islands. In recent years, however, sightings of seals hauling themselves onto Kauai's beaches have increased.

Of the world's two other monk seal species, the Caribbean monk seal is already extinct and the Mediterranean monk seal numbers only in the hundreds.

Whales Whales are air-breathing, warm-blooded, placental mammals that lactate and nurse their young. Basically there are two types: toothed whales, which use their teeth to catch and rip apart their prey, and baleen whales, which have rows of a horny elastic material, called baleen or whalebone, that hang from the upper jaw and act as a filter to extract food from the water.

Several types of whales frequent Hawaiian waters, though it is the migrating

humpback that everyone wants to see. Luckily for whale watchers, humpback whales are coast-huggers, preferring waters with depths of less than 600 feet. Other migratory whales that pass by the islands on occasion include the fin whale, minke whale and right whale. All are baleen whales.

Hawaii's year-round resident whales, which are all toothed whales, include the sperm whale, false killer whale, pigmy killer whale, beaked whale, melon-head whale and, most common of all, the pilot whale. The latter is a small whale that often travels in large pods and, like most whales, prefers deep offshore waters.

Curiously, the early Hawaiians seem to have paid little attention to whales. They are not found in petroglyph drawings and there are virtually no legends about whales.

For information on whale watching in Hawaii, see the Outdoor Activities chapter.

Humpback Whales Humpbacks are the fifth largest of the great whales. They reach lengths of 45 feet and weigh 40 to 45 tons.

Humpbacks have distinctive long white flippers and knobby heads. They're great performers, known for their acrobatic displays, which include arching dives, lobtailing, breaching and fin splashing. In breaching, humpbacks jump almost clear out of the water and then splash down with tremendous force.

They save the best performances for breeding time. Sometimes several bull whales will do a series of crashing breaches to gain the favor of a cow, often bashing into one another, even drawing blood, before the most impressive emerges the winner.

Once one of the most abundant of the great whales, humpbacks were hunted almost to extinction and are now an endangered species. Around the turn of the century an estimated 15,000 humpbacks remained. They were still being hunted as late as 1966, when the International Whaling Commission enforced a ban on their slaughter.

The entire population of North Pacific humpbacks is now thought to be about

Whale Songs

Humpbacks are remarkable not only for their acrobatics but also for their singing. They are the only species of large whales known to do either.

Each member of the herd sings the same set of songs, in the same order. Their songs last anywhere from six to 30 minutes and evolve as the season goes on, with new phrases added and old ones dropped, so that the songs the whales sing when they arrive in Hawaii become different songs by the time they leave.

It's thought that the humpbacks don't sing in their feeding grounds in Alaska. When they return to Hawaii six months later they recall the songs from the last season and begin where they left off. The humpback's complex songs include the full range of frequencies audible to the human ear. ∎

2000. More than half of those winter in Hawaii, while most of the others migrate to Mexico.

Humpbacks feed all summer in the plankton-rich waters off Alaska, developing a layer of blubber that sustains them through the winter. One of the toothless whales, humpbacks gulp huge quantities of water and then strain it back out through the filter-like baleen in their mouths, trapping krill and small fish. They can eat close to a ton of food a day.

During their romantic winter sojourn in the warm tropical waters off Hawaii, humpbacks mate and give birth. The gestation period is 10 to 12 months.

Mothers stay in shallow waters once their calves are born, apparently as protection from shark attacks. At birth calves are about 12 feet long and weigh 3000 pounds. They are nursed for about six months and can put on 100 pounds a day in the first few weeks. Adults go without eating while in Hawaii.

Whales are highly sensitive to human activity and noise and seek out quiet coastal areas. They have abandoned areas where human activities have picked up and seem to have a particular distaste for jet skis.

Humpbacks are protected by US federal law under the Marine Mammal Protection Act and the Endangered Species Act. Approaching within 100 yards of a humpback (300 yards in cow/calf waters) is prohibited and can result in a $25,000 fine. The rules apply to everyone, including swimmers, kayakers and surfers, and are strictly enforced – whether violators are aware of the law or not.

The humpback whale has been designated Hawaii's official marine mammal.

Dolphins Dolphins, which like whales are marine cetaceans, are common to Hawaii. Spinner, bottlenose, slender-beaked, spotted, striped and rough-toothed varieties are all found in Hawaiian waters.

Dolphins are nocturnal feeders who often come into calm bays during the day to rest. Although it may seem tempting to swim out and join them, approaching the dolphins can apparently disturb their rest; in addition, it will subject swimmers to a hefty fine under the Marine Mammal Protection Act. This is a current controversy in Hawaii, as swimmers who claim that dolphins enjoy playing in the surf with humans are at odds with federal officials bent on enforcing laws against the harassment of marine mammals.

Incidentally, the *mahimahi* or 'dolphin' that you may come across on menus in Hawaii is not the mammal but a fish.

National Parks

Hawaii has two national parks: Hawaii Volcanoes National Park on the Big Island and Haleakala National Park on Maui. Among the most unique places in the US National Parks system, both Haleakala and Hawaii Volcanoes center around volcanic craters. Both have awesome scenery and include several types of terrain, from sea level to more than 10,000 feet, and from barren lava landscapes to lush tropical rainforests. They also have unique flora and fauna and are the main habitat for the nene, a number of endangered forest birds and a host of native flora. The parks offer incredible hikes, some across crater floors, and a variety of camping options. For full details on both parks, see the destination sections.

GOVERNMENT & POLITICS

Hawaii has three levels of government: federal, state and county. The seat of state government is in Honolulu.

Hawaii has a typical state government with executive power vested in the governor, who is elected to a four-year term. The present governor, Benjamin Cayetano, who took office in December 1994, is the first US state governor of Filipino ancestry.

The state's lawmaking body is a bicameral legislature. The Senate includes 25 members, elected for four-year terms from the state's 25 senatorial districts. The House of Representatives has 51 members, each elected for a two-year term.

The legislature has a typical Hawaiian casualness. The regular legislative session, which convenes on the third Wednesday of January, meets for only 60 days a year. Special sessions of up to 30 days can be convened by the governor, but otherwise that's it.

Hawaii is divided into four county governments, but unlike the mainland states, it has no municipal government. The city of Honolulu is part of Honolulu County, which governs all of Oahu; Hawaii County governs the Big Island; Kauai County governs Kauai and Niihau; and Maui County governs Maui, Molokai and Lanai.

While the leprosy colony of Kalaupapa on Molokai is called the 'county' of Kalawao, in actuality it has no county government and is under the jurisdiction of the Hawaii State Department of Health.

Each county has a mayor and county council. The counties provide services, such as police and fire protection, that on the mainland are usually assigned to cities. Development issues are usually decided at county level and are the central issue of most mayoral campaigns.

ECONOMY

Tourism is Hawaii's largest industry and accounts for about one-third of the state's income. Hawaii gets 6.6 million visitors a year. In total they spend about $10 billion in the state, but not all at the same rate. The 3.5 million visiting Americans spend an average of $135 a day, while the 1.75 million Japanese average nearly $350 a day.

The second largest sector in the economy is the US military, pumping out $3 billion annually. Agriculture is a distant third.

Sugar and pineapple, which once formed the backbone of Hawaii's economy, are rapidly losing ground. Pineapple production has ceased on Lanai, which until the early 1990s was dubbed the 'Pineapple Island', and sugar, which is still grown on Kauai and Maui, has recently disappeared from the landscape on both the Big Island and Oahu. Currently the two crops account for $175 million in sales, less than half of their value a decade ago.

Meanwhile, diversified crops, defined as all crops except sugar and pineapple, have increased two-fold over the past decade and have a combined sales value of over $250 million. Of this, Hawaii's 750 farms and nurseries sold nearly $70 million in flowers, while macadamia nuts brought in another $40 million. Other sizable crops include vegetables, fruit, coffee and seed corn.

Hawaii's former agribusiness-based economy is in the midst of change. Hawaii's 'Big Five' companies – Amfac, Castle & Cooke, C Brewer, Theo Davies and Alexander & Baldwin – all had their origins in sugar, now on the wane. The Big Five hold onto their plantations not so much for what's being produced on them, but for the potential they hold as future golf courses and condo developments – and bit by bit they're being sold off for those purposes. The biggest buyers are Japanese developers; over a third of all Japanese investment in the USA is now in Hawaii.

Hawaii's current unemployment rate of 6% is slightly higher than the US average. The cost of living is 20% higher in Honolulu than in the average US mainland city, while wages are 9% lower. For those stuck in service jobs, the most rapidly growing sector of the economy, it's tough to get by.

Native Hawaiians have the lowest median family income in Hawaii and are at the bottom of most health and welfare indicators, including high school drop-out rates, suicide rates and tragic death and major disease statistics. They also make up a disproportionately high percentage of Hawaii's homeless.

The Military Presence

Hawaii is the most militarized state in the nation.

In total, the military has a grip on 265,000 acres of Hawaiian land. The greatest holding is on Oahu, where 25% of the island is controlled by the armed forces and where there are more than 100 installations, from ridge-top radar stations to Waikiki's Fort DeRussy Beach.

Oahu is the hub of the Pacific Command, which directs military activities from the west coast of the USA to the east coast of Africa. The navy, which accounts for 40% of Hawaii's military presence, is centered at Pearl Harbor, home of the Pacific Fleet.

Despite the ending of the Cold War, the military still spends $3 billion annually in the state. It pays out $500 million in contracted services and employs 19,000 civilians directly. There are 45,000 military personnel and an additional 50,000 military dependents living on the islands.

Hawaii's politicians, while otherwise liberal-leaning, generally embrace the military presence. The Chamber of Commerce of Hawaii even has a special military affairs council that lobbies in Washington DC to draw still more military activity to Hawaii.

Nearly 3000 nuclear weapons, some 10% of the US nuclear arsenal, are stockpiled in Oahu. Pearl Harbor has the most, while other nuclear weapons are based at Schofield Barracks army base and the Kaneohe Marine Corps Air Station.

POPULATION & PEOPLE

The population of Hawaii is 1,186,600. In the island breakdown, 877,000 people live on Oahu, 137,500 on the Big Island, 106,000 on Maui, 56,100 on Kauai, 6800 on Molokai, 3000 on Lanai and 230 on Niihau.

There is no ethnic majority in Hawaii – everyone belongs to a minority. Some 32%

of the population claims 'mixed ethnicity', with a majority of those having some Hawaiian blood. As for the rest, Caucasians and Japanese each account for approximately 22% of the population, followed by Filipinos (12%), Chinese (5%), African Americans, Koreans, Samoans and Puerto Ricans. There are about 9000 full-blooded Hawaiians, less than 1% of the population.

Hawaii's people are known for their racial harmony. Race is generally not a factor in marriage. Islanders have a 50/50 chance of marrying someone of a race different than their own and the majority of children born in Hawaii are *hapa*, or mixed blood.

EDUCATION

Hawaii is the only US state to have a public education system run by the state, rather than county or town education boards. Education accounts for approximately one-third of the state budget.

Under Hawaii state law, all children between the ages of six and 18 must attend school. More than 80% of all students are enrolled in Hawaii's public school system, with the remainder in private schools.

Schools operate on a two-semester system; the first semester is from the first week of September to late December, the second from early January to the first week in June.

ARTS

Hula

Hula *halaus* (schools) have experienced an influx of new students in recent years. Some practice in public places, such as school grounds and parks, where visitors are welcome to watch. Although many of the halaus rely on tuition fees, others receive sponsorship from hotels and shopping centers and give weekly public performances in return.

There are also numerous island-wide hula competitions; two of the biggest are the Prince Lot Hula Festival held each July in Oahu and the week-long Merrie Monarch Festival, which begins on Easter Sunday in Hilo.

Music

Contemporary Hawaiian music gives center stage to the guitar, most prominently the steel guitar, an instrument designed in 1889 by Joseph Kekuku, a native Hawaiian. The steel guitar is one of only two major musical instruments invented in what is now the USA. (The other is the banjo.) The steel guitar is usually played with slack-key tunings and carries the melody throughout the song.

Some of Hawaii's more renowned slack-key guitar players include Raymond Kane, Peter Moon and Atta Isaacs Jr, and the late Gabby Pahinui and Sonny Chillingworth.

The ukulele, so strongly identified with Hawaiian music, was actually derived from the braginha, an instrument from Portugal introduced to Hawaii in the 19th century. In Hawaiian the word 'ukulele' means 'jumping flea'.

Both the ukulele and the steel guitar were essential to the lighthearted, romantic music popularized in Hawaii from the 1930s to the 1950s. *My Little Grass Shack, Lovely Hula Hands* and *Sweet Leilani* are classic examples. Due in part to the 'Hawaii Calls' radio show, which for more than 30 years was broadcast worldwide from the Moana Hotel in Waikiki, this music became instantly recognizable as Hawaiian, conjuring up images of beautiful hula dancers swaying under palm trees in a tropical paradise.

One of the more current sounds in Hawaii is Jawaiian, a blending of Hawaiian music and Jamaican reggae. Some of the better-known island musicians who incorporate Jawaiian elements include Bruddah Waltah and Hoaikane. Other popular contemporary Hawaiian musicians include soulful vocalist-composer Henry Kapono; Hapa, the duo of Kelii Kanealii and Barry Flanagan, who fuse folk, rock and traditional Hawaiian elements; and the Hawaiian Style Band, who merge Hawaiian influences with rock.

The hottest recording star of the day is Kealii Reichel, a charismatic vocalist and hula dancer, who sings Hawaiian ballads, love songs and poetic chants.

Art

Many artists draw inspiration from Hawaii's rich cultural heritage and natural beauty.

Well-known Hawaiian painter Herb Kawainui Kane creates detailed oil paintings focusing on the early Polynesian settlers and King Kamehameha's life. His works are mainly on display in museums and at gallery collections in resorts.

Another notable native Hawaiian artist is Rocky Kaiouliokahihikoloehu Jensen, who does wood sculptures and drawings of Hawaiian gods, ancient chiefs and early Hawaiians, with the aim of creating sacred art in the tradition of *makaku*, or 'creative artistic mana'.

Pegge Hopper paints traditional Hawaiian women in relaxed poses using a distinctive graphic design style and bright washes of color. Her work has been widely reproduced on posters and postcards.

Some of Hawaii's most impressive crafts are ceramics, bowls made of native woods and baskets woven of native fibers. The goddess Pele is a source of inspiration for many Big Island artists – some even use molten lava as a sculpting material.

Hawaiian quilting is another unique art form. The concept of patchwork quilting was introduced by the early missionaries, but the Hawaiians, who had only recently taken to Western cotton clothing, didn't have a surplus of cloth scraps – and the idea of cutting up new lengths of fabric simply to sew them back together again in small squares seemed absurd. Instead the Hawaiian women created their own designs using larger cloth pieces, typically with stylized tropical flora on a white background.

A more transitory art form is the creation of leis. Although the leis most widely worn by visitors are made of fragrant flowers such as plumeria and tuberose, traditional leis of mokihana berries and maile leaves were more commonly worn in old Hawaii. Both types are still made today.

SOCIETY & CONDUCT

In many ways, contemporary culture in Hawaii resembles contemporary culture in the rest of the USA.

Official Hawaii

State nickname: The Aloha State
State flower: *pua aloalo* – hibiscus
State tree: *kukui* – candlenut tree
State bird: *nene* – Hawaiian goose
State marine mammal: humpback whale
State fish: *humuhumunukunukuapuaa* – rectangular triggerfish
State motto: *Ua mau ke ea o ka aina i ka pono* – 'The life of the land is perpetuated in righteousness'.
State song: *Hawaii Ponoi* – written by King Kalakaua
State flag: Designed for King Kamehameha I prior to 1816, it has the UK's Union Jack in the upper left-hand corner. Eight stripes of red, white and blue represent the eight largest islands.
State seal: The state seal incorporates the state motto and a heraldic shield flanked by Kamehameha I on one side and the Goddess of Liberty holding the Hawaiian flag on the other. It also has taro and banana leaves, ferns, a phoenix and the statehood year of 1959. ■

Hawaiians listen to the same pop music and watch the same TV shows as Americans on the mainland. Hawaii has discos and ballroom dancing, rock bands and classical orchestras, junk food and nouvelle cuisine. The wonderful thing about Hawaii, however, is that the mainland influences largely stand beside, rather than engulf, the culture of the islands.

Not only is traditional Hawaiian culture an integral part of the social fabric, but so are the customs of the ethnically diverse immigrants who have made Hawaii their home. Hawaii is more than just a meeting place of East and West; it's also a place where the cultures merge, typically in a manner that brings out the best of both worlds.

The 1970s saw the start of a Hawaiian cultural renaissance that continues today. Hawaiian language classes are thriving, and there is a concerted effort to reintroduce Hawaiian words into modern speech. Hula classes concentrate more on the nuances of hand movements and facial expressions than on the dramatic hip-shaking that sells dance shows. Many Hawaiian artists and craftspeople are returning to traditional mediums and themes.

Certainly the tourist centers have long been overrun with packaged Hawaiiana, from plastic leis to theme-park luaus, that seems almost a parody of island culture. But fortunately for the visitor, the growing interest in traditional Hawaiiana is having an impact on the tourist industry, and authentic performances by hula students and contemporary Hawaiian musicians are increasingly easier to find.

RELIGION

Hawaii's population is religiously diverse.

Christianity has the largest following, with Catholicism being the predominant religious denomination in Hawaii. Interestingly, the United Church of Christ, which includes the Congregationalists who initially converted the islands, claim only about half as many members as the Mormons and one-tenth as many as the Catholics.

In addition, Hawaii has about 100 Buddhist temples, scores of Shinto shrines and two dozen Hindu temples. There are also Taoist, Tenrikyo, Jewish and Muslim houses of worship.

Information on Hawaii's precontact religion is in the History section.

LANGUAGE

The unifying language of Hawaii is English, although it's liberally peppered with Hawaiian phrases, loan words from the various immigrant languages and pidgin slang.

It's not uncommon to hear islanders speaking in other languages, however, as the main language spoken in one out of every four homes in Hawaii is a mother tongue other than English.

The Hawaiian language itself is still spoken among family members by about 9000 people, and Hawaiian is, along with English, an official state language.

Closely related to other Polynesian languages, Hawaiian is melodic, phonetically simple and full of vowels and repeated syllables.

Some 85% of all place names in Hawaii are in Hawaiian, and as often as not they have interesting translations and stories behind them.

The Hawaiians had no written language until the 1820s when Christian missionaries arrived and wrote down the spoken language in roman letters.

Pronunciation

The written Hawaiian language has just 12 letters. Pronunciation is easy and there are few consonant clusters.

Vowel sounds are about the same as in Spanish or Japanese, more or less like this:

a ah, as in 'father' or uh, as in 'above'
e ay, as in 'gay' or eh, as in 'pet'
i ee, as in 'see'
o oh, as in 'go'
u oo, as in 'noon'

Hawaiian has diphthongs, created when two vowels join together to form a single sound. The stress is on the first vowel, although in general if you pronounce each vowel separately, you'll be easily understood.

The consonant *w* is usually pronounced like a soft English *v* when it follows the letters *i* and *e* (the town Haleiwa is pronounced Haleiva) and like the English *w* when it follows *u* or *o*. When *w* follows *a* it can be pronounced either *v* or *w* – thus you will hear both Hawaii and Havaii.

The other consonants – h, k, l, m, n, p – are pronounced about the same as in English.

Glottal Stops & Macrons Written Hawaiian uses both glottal stops and macrons, although in modern print they are often omitted.

The glottal stop (') indicates a break between two vowels producing an effect similar to saying 'oh-oh' in English. A macron, a short straight line over a vowel, stresses the vowel.

Glottal stops and macrons not only affect pronunciation, but can give a word a completely different meaning. For example *ai* can mean 'sexual intercourse' or 'to eat', depending on the pronunciation.

All this takes on greater significance when you learn to speak Hawaiian in depth. If you're using Hawaiian words in an English-language context (this *poi* is *ono*), there shouldn't be much of a problem.

Shaka Sign

Islanders greet each other with the shaka sign, which is made by folding down the three middle fingers to the palm and extending the thumb and little finger. The hand is then usually held out and shaken in greeting. It's as common as waving. ■

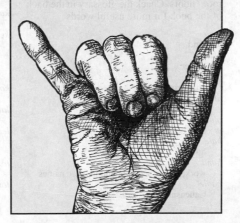

Compounds Hawaiian may seem more difficult than it is because many proper names are long and look similar. Many begin with *ka*, meaning 'the', which over time simply became attached to the beginning of the word.

When you break each word down into its composite parts, some of which are repeated, it all becomes much easier. For example: *Kamehameha* consists of the three compounds Ka-meha-meha. *Humuhumunukunukuapuaa*, which is Hawaii's state fish, is broken down into humu-humu-nuku-nuku-a-pu-a-a.

Some words are doubled to emphasize their meaning. For example: *wiki* means 'quick', while *wikiwiki* means 'very quick'.

There are some easily recognizable compounds repeatedly found in place names, and it can be fun to learn a few. For instance, *wai* means 'freshwater' – Waikiki means 'spouting water', so named for the freshwater springs that were once there. *Kai* means 'seawater' – Kailua means 'two seas'. *Lani* means 'heavenly' – Lanikai means 'heavenly sea'. *Hana* means 'bay' – Hanalei means 'crescent bay'.

Common Hawaiian Vocabulary

Learn these words first: *aloha* and *mahalo*, which are everyday pleasantries; *makai* and *mauka*, commonly used in giving directions; and *kane* and *wahine*, often on bathroom doors. Check the glossary in the back of the book for more useful words.

aina
    land
akamai
    clever
alii
    chief, royalty
aloha
    love, welcome, goodbye
aloha aina
    love of the land
hale
    house
hana
    work; or bay, a compound in place names
haole
    Caucasian

hapa
    half; or person of mixed blood
hapa haole
    half-white, used for a person, thing or idea
Hauoli Makahiki Hou
    Happy New Year
Hawaii nei
    all the Hawaiian islands, as distinguished from the Big Island
heiau
    ancient Hawaiian temple
holoholo
    to walk, drive or ramble around for pleasure
holoku
    a long dress similar to the muumuu, but more fitted and with a yoke
hui
    group, organization
hula
    traditional Hawaiian dance
imu
    underground earthen oven used in traditional luau cooking
kahuna
    wise person in any field, commonly a priest, healer or sorcerer
kalua
    traditional method of baking in an underground oven
kamaaina
    native-born Hawaiian or a long-time resident; literally 'child of the land'
kane
    man
kapu
    taboo, part of strict ancient Hawaiian social system; today often used on signs meaning 'Keep Out'
kaukau
    food
keiki
    child, children
kokua
    help, cooperation; 'Please Kokua' on a trash can is a gentle way of saying 'don't litter'
kona
    leeward, or a leeward wind
lanai
    veranda
lei
    garland, usually of flowers, but also of leaves or shells
lolo
    stupid, crazy
lomilomi
    massage

luau
    traditional Hawaiian feast
mahalo
    thank you
makai
    towards the sea
malihini
    newcomer, visitor
manini
    convict tang (a reef fish); also used to refer to
    something small or insignificant
mano
    shark
mauka
    towards the mountains, inland
mele
    song, chant
Mele Kalikimaka
    Merry Christmas
muumuu
    long, loose-fitting dress introduced by the
    missionaries
nene
    Hawaii's state bird, a native goose
ohana
    family, extended family
ono
    delicious; also the name of the wahoo fish
pakalolo
    marijuana; literally 'crazy smoke'
pali
    cliff
paniolo
    Hawaiian cowboy
pau
    finished, no more; *pau hana* means quitting
    time
puka
    any kind of hole or opening
pupu
    snack food, hors d'oeuvres; shells
puu
    hill, cinder cone
tutu
    aunt, older woman
ukulele
    stringed musical instrument
wahine
    woman
wikiwiki
    hurry, quick

Pidgin

Hawaii's early immigrants communicated
with each other in pidgin, a simplified,
broken form of English. It was a language
born of necessity, stripped of all but the
most needed words.

Modern pidgin is better defined as local
slang. It is extensive, lively and ever-
changing. Whole conversations can take
place in pidgin, or often just a word or two
is dropped into a more conventional
English sentence.

Even Shakespeare's *Twelfth Night* has
been translated (by local comedian James
Grant Benton) to *Twelf Nite O Wateva*.
Malvolio's line 'My masters, are you mad?'
becomes 'You buggahs crazy, o wat?'

Short-term visitors will rarely win
friends by trying to speak pidgin. It's more
like an insider's code that you're allowed
to use only after you've lived in Hawaii
long enough to understand the nuances.

Some characteristics of pidgin include:
a fast staccato rhythm, two-word sentences, dropping the soft 'h' sound from
words that start with 'th', use of loan
words from many languages (often Hawaiian) and double meanings that trip up the
uninitiated.

Some of the more common words and
expressions:

blalah
    big Hawaiian fellow
brah
    brother, friend; also used for 'hey you'
broke da mouth
    delicious
buggah
    guy
chicken skin
    goose bumps
coconut wireless
    word of mouth
cockaroach
    steal
da kine
    that kind of thing, whatchamacallit etc; used
    whenever you can't think of the word you
    want but you know the listener knows what
    you mean
geev em
    go for it, beat them
grinds
    food, eat; *ono grinds* is good food

haolefied
  become like a *haole*
howzit?
  hi, how's it going?
how you stay?
  how are you?
humbug
  a real hassle
like beef?
  wanna fight?
mo' bettah
  much better, the best

slippahs
  flip-flops, thongs
stick
  surfboard
stink eye
  dirty look, evil eye
talk story
  any kind of conversation, gossip, tales
tanks
  thanks; more commonly *tanks brah*
tree
  three

Facts for the Visitor

PLANNING

When to Go

Hawaii is a great place to visit any time of the year.

Although the busiest tourist season is in winter, that has more to do with weather *elsewhere*, as many visitors are snowbirds escaping cold winters back home. Essentially the weather in Hawaii is agreeable all year round. It's a bit rainier in the winter and a bit hotter in the summer, but there are no extremes and cooling trade winds modify the heat throughout the year.

In terms of cost, spring through fall can be a bargain, as hotel prices drop significantly around April 1 and most don't climb back up again until mid-December.

Naturally, for certain activities there are peak seasons. For instance, if you're a board surfer, you'll find the biggest waves in winter, whereas if you're a windsurfer you'll find the best wind conditions in summer.

Maps

If you're renting a car, the guide booklets handed out by the car rental agencies have simple maps showing the main roads. However, if you really want to explore, a more detailed road map can be invaluable.

Gousha and Rand McNally both publish good Oahu street maps, which have detailed Honolulu sections. The American Automobile Association (AAA) puts out a good Honolulu map and an all-Hawaii map, which it distributes free to its members.

The University of Hawaii (UH) Press publishes separate relief maps of Oahu, Kauai, Maui, the Big Island and Molokai/Lanai. Overall, they're the best general maps for the Neighbor Islands as they not only cover roads but also beaches, historical sites and major hiking trails. UH Press maps, which cost $3 to $4, are readily available in Hawaii bookstores and in shops frequented by tourists.

The United States Geological Survey (USGS) publishes topographical maps of Hawaii. Both full-island and detailed sectional maps are available, and there's also an individual USGS map for Hawaii Volcanoes National Park. Maps can be ordered by mail from the US Geological Survey, Box 25286, Denver Federal Center, Denver, CO 80225. Prices per map range from $2.50 to $4.

USGS maps can also be purchased at several places in Hawaii, including on Kauai at the Kauai Museum in Lihue and the Kokee State Park museum; on Oahu at the Pacific Map Center, 560 N Nimitz, Honolulu; and on the Big Island at the Middle Earth Bookshoppe in Kailua-Kona, Basically Books in Hilo and Hawaii Volcanoes National Park.

Nautical charts published by the National Oceanic and Atmospheric Administration can be ordered from the NOAA Distribution Division (☎ 301-436-6990), National Ocean Service, 6502 Lafayette Ave, Riverdale, MD 20737. Upon request NOAA will send a complete list of charts available and addresses where they can be purchased around the world. In Hawaii you can find NOAA nautical charts at the Pacific Map Center in Honolulu, Basically Books in Hilo and some larger marine supply companies.

What to Bring

Hawaii has balmy weather and a casual attitude towards dress, so for the most part packing is a breeze.

At the lower elevations it's summer all year. Shorts, sandals and a T-shirt or cotton shirt are the standard day dress. If you don't intend to spend time at higher elevations, a light jacket or sweater will be the warmest clothing you'll need.

Pack light. You can always pick up something with a floral Hawaiian print when you get there and dress island style.

An aloha shirt and lightweight slacks for men, and a cotton dress for women, is pretty much regarded as 'dressing up' on the islands. Only a few of the most exclusive restaurants require anything dressier.

Hawaii does, however, have highland areas (called 'upcountry' on the islands) as well as mountains, and most people get at least as far as the former. The upcountry can be a good 20°F cooler than the coast, and when the fog blows in and the wind picks up, it gets quite nippy. If you intend to spend any time in the upcountry, plan on another layer of clothing.

The temperature on the mountain summits on the Big Island and Maui can dip below freezing. If you're going to be camping at high elevations, you need to be prepared for cold weather; a tent, winter-rated sleeping bag, rain gear and layers of warm clothing, preferably wool, are a must.

Camping on the beach is another matter entirely. A very lightweight cotton bag is the most you'll need. Public campgrounds require tents – and because of mosquitoes they're a good idea anyway. If you don't want to pack camping gear, it can be rented on Oahu, Kauai and the Big Island.

For hiking, bring footwear with good traction. Many people just wear sneakers, although walking on lava can be tough on the ankles. Serious hikers should consider lugging along their hiking boots.

You won't regret bringing binoculars for watching whales and birds, and a flashlight is useful to explore caves. We always carry a snorkel, mask and fins, but you can also buy or rent them there. Actually, you don't need to worry too much about what to bring, as just about anything you forget to pack you can easily buy in Hawaii.

HIGHLIGHTS

Every island has its own unique highlights.

On **Oahu**, the standard attractions include Waikiki, Diamond Head, Pearl Harbor and the North Shore with its huge winter surf. Honolulu's historic downtown, with the only royal palace in the USA, and the adjacent Chinatown offer a fascinating glimpse of Hawaii's multiethnic society. Other things not to be missed include the views from Tantalus and the Nuuanu Pali Lookout.

On **Maui**, the must-do's include a trip to Haleakala summit for the sunrise, the serpentine coastal drive to Hana and a visit to historic Lahaina. Maui also has lovely beaches, top-notch windsurfing and excellent winter whale-watching opportunities.

On the **Big Island**, don't miss Hawaii Volcanoes National Park, with its fascinating landscape of steaming craters and lava flows. Rural Waipio Valley and the cascading Akaka Falls also offer splendid natural scenery. Remnants of ancient Hawaiian culture are plentiful, including heiaus at Puuhonua O Honaunau, more widely known as the Place of Refuge, and at the more-remote Mookini, where Kamehameha the Great was born.

Kauai is a favorite of naturalists and is known for its lush mountainous scenery, especially the Na Pali Coast and Kokee State Park, both of which offer excellent backcountry hiking trails. It also has the impressive Waimea Canyon, dubbed the 'Grand Canyon of the Pacific', and numerous waterways that provide excellent kayaking opportunities.

The chief attraction of **Molokai** is its rural lifestyle and slow pace. Other highlights include Papohaku, the longest beach in Hawaii; a mule trail down to the historic leprosy colony of Kalaupapa; and a shoreline of ancient fishponds.

Lanai promotes its two luxury resorts but it also offers a few off-the-beaten-path sights to explore. Its south coast has a lovely beach, Hulopoe Bay, with fine diving and snorkeling.

TOURIST OFFICES

The Hawaii Visitors Bureau (HVB) provides free tourist information on the state. On request they'll mail out a little packet containing general Hawaii-wide tourist information and booklets listing member hotels and restaurants.

Local Tourist Offices

The central HVB office (☎ 923-1811; fax 922-8991) is in the Waikiki Business Plaza,

Suite 801, 2270 Kalakaua Ave, Honolulu, HI 96815.

Tourist offices on Oahu, Maui, Kauai, the Big Island and Molokai can provide information more specific to their islands; phone numbers and addresses are in the individual island chapters.

On the US mainland, HVB maintains an office (☎ 415-248-3800, 800-353-5846; fax 415-248-3808) at 180 Montgomery St, Suite 2360, San Francisco, CA 94104.

There are also toll-free numbers that can be called from the mainland to order free glossy tourism magazines, though these can take as long as a month or two to arrive. For a magazine on all Hawaii, call ☎ 800-464-2924. For similar booklets on Maui call ☎ 800-525-6284, for Kauai ☎ 800-245-2824 (800-AH-KAUAI), for the Big Island ☎ 800-648-2441 and for Oahu ☎ 800-624-8678.

Tourist Offices Abroad
For some odd reason, the Hawaii Visitors Bureau frequently changes its overseas agents. The following are the current addresses for HVB representatives abroad.

Canada
  c/o Comprehensive Travel Industry Services, 1260 Hornby St, Suite 104, Vancouver, BC V6Z 1W2
  (☎ 604-669-6691; fax 604-683-9114)
Germany
  c/o American Venture Marketing, Siemen Strausse 9, 63263 Neu Isenburg
  (☎ 061-02-722-411; fax 061-02-722-409)
Japan
  Kokusai Building, 2nd Floor, 1-1 Marunouchi 3-chome, Chiyoda ku, Tokyo 100
  (☎ 03-3201-0430; fax 03-3201-0433)
Korea
  c/o Travel Press, 10th Floor, Samwon Building, 112-5 Sokong-Dong, Chung-ku, Seoul
  (☎ 02-773-6719; fax 02-757-6783)
Malaysia
  c/o Pacific World Travel, 2.5 & 2.6 Angkasa Raya Building, Jalan Ampang, Kuala Lumpur 50450
  (☎ 03-244-8449; fax 03-242-1129)
New Zealand
  c/o Walshes World, Dingwall Building, 87 Queen St, 2nd Floor, Auckland
  (☎ 09-379-3708; fax 09-309-0725)

Taiwan
  c/o Federal Transportation Company, 8th Floor, 61 Nanking East Rd, Section 3, Taipei
  (☎ 02-506-7043; fax 02-507-5816)
Thailand
  c/o ADAT Sales, 8th Floor, Maneeya Center Building, 518/5 Ploenchit Rd, Bangkok
  (☎ 02-255-6840; fax 02-254-1271)
UK
  Box 208, Sunbury on Thames, Middlesex TW16 5RJ
  (☎ 0181-941-4009; fax 0181-941-4011)

VISAS & DOCUMENTS
The conditions for entering Hawaii are the same as for entering any other state in the USA.

Passport & Visas
Canadians must have proper proof of Canadian citizenship, such as a citizenship card with photo ID or a passport. Visitors from other countries must have a valid passport, and most visitors also need a US visa.

However there is a reciprocal visa-waiver program in which citizens of certain countries may enter the USA for stays of 90

Hawaii Visitors Bureau warrior sign

days or less without first obtaining a US visa. Currently these countries are: Andorra, Argentina, Australia, Austria, Belgium, Brunei, Denmark, Finland, France, Germany, Iceland, Ireland, Italy, Japan, Liechtenstein, Luxembourg, Monaco, Netherlands, New Zealand, Norway, San Marino, Spain, Sweden, Switzerland and the UK. Under this program you must have a roundtrip ticket that is nonrefundable in the USA and you will not be allowed to extend your stay beyond the 90 days.

Other travelers will need to obtain a visa from a US consulate or embassy. In most countries the process can be done by mail.

Your passport should be valid for at least six months longer than your intended stay in the USA and you'll need to submit a recent photo (37 x 37 mm) with the application. Documents of financial stability and/or guarantees from a US resident are sometimes required, particularly for those from Third World countries.

Visa applicants may be required to 'demonstrate binding obligations' that will ensure their return back home. Because of this requirement, those planning to travel through other countries before arriving in the USA are generally better off applying for their US visa while they are still in their home country – rather than while on the road.

The validity period for US visitor visas depends on what country you're from. The length of time you'll be allowed to stay in the USA is ultimately determined by US immigration authorities at the port of entry.

Visa Extensions If you want, need or hope to stay in the USA longer than the date stamped on your passport, go to the Honolulu office of the Immigration & Naturalization Service (INS; ☎ 532-3721), 595 Ala Moana Blvd, *before* the stamped date to apply for an extension.

Documents

Visitors should keep in mind that US airlines, including Hawaii's inter-island carriers, now require passengers to present a photo ID as part of the airline check-in procedure. All foreign visitors (other than Canadians) must of course bring their passport. US citizens and Canadians may want to bring along a passport as well, in the event they are tempted to extend their travels beyond Hawaii. All visitors should bring their driver's license and any health insurance or travel insurance cards.

Members of Hostelling International (HI) will be able to take advantage of lower hostel rates in Oahu by bringing their membership cards. Members of the American Automobile Association (AAA) or other affiliated automobile clubs can get car rental, airfare and some sightseeing admission discounts with their membership cards. Divers should bring their certification cards.

It's a good idea to make photocopies of all your travel documents, including airline tickets and your passport or citizenship card. Keep the copies separate from the originals.

EMBASSIES
US Embassies Abroad

There are numerous US embassies around the world, including the following.

Australia
    21 Moonah Place, Canberra, ACT 2600
    (☎ 6-270-5000)
Belgium
    27 Boulevard du Régent, B-1000 Brussels
    (☎ 2-513-3830)
Canada
    PO Box 5000, 100 Wellington St, Ottawa,
    ON K1P 5T1 (☎ 613-238-5335)
Denmark
    Dag Hammarskjolds Allé 24, Copenhagen
    (☎ 31-42-31-44)
France
    2 avenue Gabriel, 75382 Paris Cedex 08
    (☎ 01-43-12-22-22)
Germany
    Deichmanns Aue 29, 53170 Bonn
    (☎ 228-3391)
Hong Kong
    26 Garden Rd, Hong Kong (☎ 523-9011)
Japan
    10-5, Akasaka 1-chome, Minato-ku, Tokyo
    (☎ 3-224-5000)
Korea
    82 Sejong-Ro, Chongro-ku, Seoul
    (☎ 397-4114)

Malaysia
376 Jalan Tun Razak, 50400 Kuala Lumpur
(☎ 248-9011)
Netherlands
Lange Voorhout 102, 2514 EJ The Hague
(☎ 70-310-9209)
New Zealand
29 Fitzherbert Terrace, PO Box 1190,
Thorndon, Wellington (☎ 4-472-2068)
Singapore
30 Hill St, Singapore 0617 (☎ 65-338-0251)
Thailand
95 Wireless Rd, Bangkok (☎ 2-252-5040)
UK
24/31 Grosvenor Square, London W1A 1AE
(☎ 0171-499-9000)

Foreign Consulates in Hawaii

There are no embassies in Honolulu, but there are numerous consulates, including those from Australia, Austria, Belgium, Brazil, Chile, the Cook Islands, Denmark, France, Germany, Hungary, India, Israel, Italy, Japan, Kiribati, Korea, Malaysia, Netherlands, Norway, Peru, Philippines, Sweden, Switzerland and Thailand.

There are also government liaison offices for Tonga, American Samoa, the Federated States of Micronesia, the Mariana Islands and the Marshall Islands.

Addresses and phone numbers are listed under 'Consulates' in the Oahu phone book yellow pages.

CUSTOMS

US customs allows each person over the age of 21 to bring one US quart of liquor and 200 cigarettes duty-free into the USA. Most fresh fruits and plants are restricted from entry into Hawaii, and there's a strict quarantine on animals.

MONEY

Costs

How much money you need for visiting Hawaii depends on your traveling style. Some people get by quite cheaply while others rack up huge balances on their credit cards.

Airfare to Hawaii is usually one of the heftier parts of the budget. Fares vary greatly, particularly from the US mainland,

so shop around. (Note that Hawaii stopovers are often thrown in free, or for a nominal charge, on trips between North America and Asian or Pacific countries.)

Flights between Hawaiian islands cost about $40 to $75 one way, depending on how you buy your tickets. Hawaii has just one inter-island ferry service, which operates between Lanai and Maui and costs $25 each way.

It can be a bit challenging to explore the islands without renting a car, except on Oahu, where there's a good inexpensive bus system. Renting a car usually costs between $150 and $200 a week.

Camping is an alternative to paying for a hotel. Every island except Lanai has at least one state park with free camping as well as inexpensive county campgrounds. In addition, Maui and the Big Island have excellent national parks with free camping.

Each of the four main islands has at least a couple of hostel-style places with dormitory beds for around $15 and either B&Bs or spartan hotels for $40 to $50. For hotels with more standard middle-class amenities expect to pay nearly double that, and if you've got your mind set on a first-class beachfront hotel, get ready to pay upwards of $125 a night. For a splurge on a luxury hotel – and Hawaii has some of the world's finest – rates generally begin around $250.

If you're staying awhile, there are ways to cut accommodation costs. Weekly and monthly condo rental rates can beat all but the cheapest hotels. Besides having more space, most condos are turn-key, with virtually everything you'll need, from towels and beach mats to a kitchen stocked with pots and pans. Being able to prepare your own meals in a condo can save a bundle on your food bill.

Another cost-cutter is to travel in the low season, generally from April to mid-December, when accommodation rates are often discounted as much as 30%.

Since much of Hawaii's food is shipped in, grocery prices average 25% higher than on the mainland. Because of the shipping costs, bulky items like cereal have the highest mark-ups, while compact items such as canned tuna have the lowest. Food in local neighborhood restaurants is a good value in Hawaii, with prices generally as cheap as you'll find on the mainland.

The good news for visitors is that lots of things in Hawaii are free. There are no parking or entrance fees at beaches or state parks, for instance, and most of Hawaii's historical sights can be explored for free.

Traveler's Checks

Foreign visitors who carry traveler's checks will find it much easier if the checks are in US dollars, but major currencies can be exchanged at Honolulu International Airport and larger banks.

Restaurants, hotels and most stores accept US dollar traveler's checks as if they're cash, so if that's what you're carrying, odds are you'll never have to use a bank or pay an exchange fee.

Credit Cards

Major credit and charge cards are widely accepted throughout Hawaii, including at car rental agencies and most hotels, restaurants, gas stations, shops and larger grocery stores. Most recreational and tourist activities in Hawaii can also be paid for by credit card. Note, however, that many B&Bs and some condominiums, particularly those handled through rental agencies, do not accept credit cards.

The most commonly accepted cards in Hawaii are Visa, MasterCard and American Express, although JCB, Discover and Diners Club cards are also accepted by a fair number of businesses.

ATMs

Automatic teller machines (ATM) are another handy plastic alternative. We long ago stopped taking traveler's checks to Hawaii, choosing instead to withdraw money from a bank account back home using ATMs. The small service charge works out cheaper than the 1% fee charged for traveler's checks and there's no need to carry a bundle of checks around.

Major banks such as Bank of Hawaii (Bankoh for short), First Hawaiian Bank

and Bank of America have extensive ATM networks throughout Hawaii that will give cash advances on major credit cards (MasterCard, Visa, American Express, Discover and JCB) and allow cash withdrawals with affiliated ATM cards. Most ATM machines in Hawaii accept bank cards from both the Plus and Cirrus systems, the two largest ATM networks in the USA.

In addition to traditional bank locations, you can also find ATMs at most large grocery stores, in mall-style shopping centers and in a growing number of convenience stores.

Currency

As is true all across the USA, US dollars are the only accepted currency in Hawaii.

The US dollar is divided into 100 cents. Coins come in denominations of one cent (penny), five cents (nickel), 10 cents (dime), 25 cents (quarter) and 50 cents (half dollar). Notes come in one-, five-, 10-, 20-, 50- and 100-dollar denominations. There is also a one-dollar coin that the government has tried unsuccessfully to bring into mass circulation and a two-dollar note that is out of favor but still occasionally seen.

Currency Exchange

Hard currency can be exchanged at larger banks, such as the ubiquitous Bank of Hawaii, or at Honolulu International Airport.

At press time, exchange rates were:

Australia	A$1	US$0.78
Canada	C$1	US$0.74
France	FF1	US$0.19
Germany	DM1	US$0.63
Hong Kong	HK$1	US$0.13
Japan	¥100	US$0.86
New Zealand	NZ$1	US$0.70
UK	UK£1	US$1.67

Tipping

Tipping practices are the same as in the rest of the USA. In restaurants, waiters expect a tip of about 15%, while 10% is generally sufficient for taxi drivers, hair stylists and the like. Hotel bellhops are typically tipped about $1 per bag.

Consumer Taxes

Hawaii has a 4.17% state sales tax that is tacked onto virtually everything, including all meals, groceries, car rentals and accommodations. An additional 6% room tax brings the total tax added to accommodation bills to 10.17%. Another tax targeted at visitors is a $2-a-day 'road use' tax imposed upon all car rentals.

POST & COMMUNICATIONS
Postal Rates

Postage rates for first-class mail within the USA are 32¢ for letters up to one ounce (23¢ for each additional ounce) and 20¢ for postcards. First-class mail between Hawaii and the mainland goes by air and usually takes three to four days.

International airmail rates are 60¢ for a half-ounce letter and 50¢ for a postcard to any foreign country with the exception of Canada (46¢ for a half-ounce letter and 40¢ for a postcard) and Mexico (40¢ for a half-ounce letter and 35¢ for a postcard).

The cost for parcels airmailed anywhere within the USA is $3 for two pounds or less, $6 for five pounds. For heavier items, rates differ according to the distance mailed.

Receiving Mail

You can have mail sent to you c/o General Delivery at any post office in Hawaii that has its own zip (post) code. An exception is on Oahu, where all general delivery mail sent to Honolulu or Waikiki is delivered to the main post office near the airport. Domestic mail is generally held for 10 days, international mail for 30 days. Most hotels will also hold mail for incoming guests.

Telephone

The telephone area code for all of Hawaii is 808. The area code is not used when making calls on the same island, but it must be added to all Hawaiian phone numbers when calling from outside the state and when calling from one Hawaiian island to another.

All phone numbers listed in this book beginning with 800 are toll-free numbers from the US mainland, unless otherwise

noted. The same numbers are sometimes toll free from Canada as well.

Pay phones can be found throughout Hawaii in public places such as shopping centers and beach parks. Local calls within Hawaii cost 25¢ at pay phones, and there's no time limit. Any call made from one point on an island to any other point on that island is a local call. Calls from one island to another are long distance.

To dial direct from one Hawaiian island to another from a pay phone, the rate from 8 am to 5 pm weekdays is $1.55 for the first minute plus 25¢ for each additional minute. From 5 to 11 pm Sunday to Friday it's $1.44 for the first minute and 16¢ for each additional minute. At all other times the rate is $1.34 for the first minute and 10¢ for each additional minute.

Most hotels add on a service charge of 50¢ to $1 for each local call made from a room phone and most also have hefty surcharges for long-distance calls. Public coin phones, which can be found in most lobbies, are always cheaper. You can pump in quarters, use a phone card or make collect calls from pay phones. In Hawaii you can make toll-free calls (those that begin with 800 or

888) from pay phones without inserting any money.

For directory assistance on the same island dial ☎ 1-411, for other islands dial ☎ 1-808-555-1212. To find out if there's an inter-island toll-free number for a business, dial ☎ 1-800-555-1212.

To make an international call direct from Hawaii, dial 011 + country code + area code + number. (An exception is to Canada, where you instead dial: 1 + area code + number.) For international operator assistance dial ☎ 0. Most international calls dialed direct from a pay phone cost about $5 for the first minute and $1 for each additional minute. The operator can give specific rate information and tell you which time periods are the cheapest for calling; these vary with the country being called.

When calling Hawaii from overseas, you must precede the number with 1, the international country code for the USA.

Fax & Email
Faxes can be sent and received through the front desk of most hotels. There are also business centers throughout Hawaii, such as Kinko's, that offer reasonably priced fax services.

If you're carrying a laptop, you may want to check in advance with your hotel to see if the room has a phone jack that can accommodate modem hook-ups; unfortunately, these are rare outside of high-end hotels.

Internet cafes (see the Online Services Appendix) where you can check your email are now popping up in Hawaii, and most have very reasonable rates. Public libraries are also online, though technically you need to have a Hawaii library card, which complicates matters for short-term visitors.

BOOKS
A wealth of books have been written about Hawaii and its people, landscapes, history, culture and unique flora and fauna. The books that follow are just a few of the recommended titles. Note that 'UH Press' in this section refers to the University of Hawaii Press in Honolulu.

People
Keneti by Bob Krauss (UH Press, 1988) is a biography of Kenneth 'Keneti' Emory, the esteemed Bishop Museum archaeologist who over the years sailed with writer Jack London, worked with anthropologist Margaret Mead and surfed with Olympian Duke Kahanamoku. Emory, who died in 1992, spent much of his life uncovering the ruins of villages and temples throughout the Pacific, recording them before they disappeared forever.

Paddling My Own Canoe by Audrey Sutherland (UH Press, 1978) details the author's adventures and ruminations while kayaking solo along the rugged, isolated north shore of Molokai. The book helped popularize wilderness kayaking in Hawaii.

Father Damien, the priest who worked in the leprosy colony on Molokai, is the subject of many books, including *Holy Man: Father Damien of Molokai* by Gavan Daws (Harper & Row, New York, 1984), *Damien the Leper* by John Farrow (Doubleday & Company, New York, 1954) and others.

Aloha Cowboy by Virginia Cowan-Smith and Bonnie Domrose Stone (UH Press, 1988) is an illustrated account of 200 years of *paniolo* life in Hawaii.

History & Politics
Hawaiian Antiquities by David Malo (Bishop Museum Press, Honolulu, 1992), written in 1838, was the first account of Hawaiian culture written by a Hawaiian. It gives an in-depth history of Hawaii before the arrival of the missionaries.

Shoal of Time by Gavan Daws (UH Press, 1974) is a comprehensive and colorful history covering the period from Captain Cook's 'discovery' of the islands to statehood.

Hawaii's Story by Hawaii's Queen by Queen Liliuokalani (Mutual Publishing, Honolulu, 1990), written in 1897, is an autobiographical account of Liliuokalani's life and the circumstances surrounding her 1893 overthrow.

The Betrayal of Liliuokalani: Last Queen of Hawaii, 1838-1917 by Helena G Allen (Mutual Publishing, Honolulu, 1990) is an insightful account not only of the queen's life but also of missionary activity and foreign encroachment in Hawaii.

Fragments of Hawaiian History by John Papa Ii (Bishop Museum Press, Honolulu, 1993), translated by Mary Kawena Pukui, is a first-hand account of old Hawaii under the *kapu* system. Ii lived in Kailua-Kona at the time of Kamehameha I.

Kauai, the Separate Kingdom by Edward Joesting (UH Press, 1984) is the authoritative history book on Kauai, the only Hawaiian island never conquered in battle.

The Hawaiian Kingdom by Ralph S Kuykendall (UH Press, Honolulu) is a three-volume set written from 1938 to 1967. It covers Hawaiian history from 1778 to 1893 and is considered the definitive work on the period.

Merchant Prince of the Sandalwood Mountains by Bob Dye (UH Press, 1997) tells the story of Chun Afong, Hawaii's first Chinese millionaire, in the context of the turbulent social and economic changes of the 18th century.

Natural History

Hawaii: The Islands of Life (Signature Publishing, 1993) has strikingly beautiful photos of the flora, fauna and landscapes being protected by the Nature Conservancy of Hawaii. The text is by respected Pacific author Gavan Daws.

The Many-Splendored Fishes of Hawaii by Gar Goodson (Stanford University Press, 1985) is one of the better of several small, inexpensive fish-identification books on the market and has good descriptions and 170 color drawings.

Hawaii's Fishes: A Guide for Snorkelers, Divers and Aquarists by John P Hoover (Mutual Publishing, Honolulu, 1993), a more expensive and comprehensive field guide, covers over 230 reef and shore fishes of Hawaii. It's fully illustrated with color photographs and gives insights on island dive sites.

Hawaii's Birds (Hawaii Audubon Society, Honolulu, 1993) is the best pocket-sized guide to the birds of Hawaii. It includes color photos and descriptions of all the native birds and many of the introduced species.

For something more comprehensive, there's *A Field Guide to the Birds of Hawaii & the Tropical Pacific* by H Douglas Pratt, Phillip L Bruner and Delwyn G Berrett (Princeton University Press, New Jersey, 1987). The 409-page book contains 45 pages of color plates.

Mammals in Hawaii by P Quentin Tomich (Bishop Museum Press, Honolulu, 1986) is the authoritative book on the mammals in Hawaii, with interesting stories on how they arrived in the islands. He includes all species of whales and dolphins found in Hawaiian waters.

Trailside Plants of Hawaii's National Parks by Charles H Lamoureux (Hawaii Natural History Association, 1976) covers common trailside plants and trees in some depth. It's a good book to have if you'll be spending time hiking in the national parks.

Plants and Flowers of Hawaii by S Sohmer and R Gustafson (UH Press, 1987) has quality color photos and descriptions of over 130 native plants of Hawaii, including information on their habitat and evolution.

Practical Folk Medicine of Hawaii by LR McBride (Petroglyph Press, Hilo, 1975) has descriptions of many native medicinal plants and their uses.

Hawaiian Culture

The Kumulipo by Martha Beckwith (UH Press, 1972) is a translation of the Hawaiian chant of creation. The chant of 2077 lines begins in the darkness of the spirit world and traces the genealogy of a royal *alii* family, said to be the ancestors of humankind.

Hawaiian Mythology by Martha Beckwith (UH Press, 1970) has comprehensive translations of Hawaii's old myths and legends.

Nana I Ke Kumu (Look to the Source) by Mary K Pukui, EW Haertig and Catherine A Lee (Hui Hanai, 1972) is a fascinating two-volume collection of information on Hawaiian cultural practices, social customs and beliefs.

The Legends and Myths of Hawaii (Charles Tuttle Company, Rutland, VT, 1985) is a collection of legends as told by King David Kalakaua. It has a short introduction to Hawaiian culture and history as well.

Niihau Shell Leis by Linda Paik Moriarty (UH Press, 1986) explains the development of the unique Hawaiian craft of shell lei making by Niihauans and illustrates the various styles.

Hawaiian Petroglyphs by J Halley Cox (Bishop Museum Press, Honolulu, 1990) lists petroglyph sites and includes extensive photos and illustrations.

Legacy of the Landscape by Patrick Vinton Kirch (UH Press, 1996) details 50 of the most important precontact Hawaiian archaeological sites, including heiaus, fishponds and petroglyphs.

Fiction

A Hawaiian Reader, edited by A Grove Day and Carl Stroven (Mutual Publishing, Honolulu, 1959), is an excellent anthology with 37 selections, both fiction and nonfiction. It starts with a log entry by Captain James Cook and includes writings from early missionaries as well as Mark Twain, Jack London, Somerset Maugham, David Malo, Isabella Bird, Martha Beckwith and others. If you only have time to read one book about Hawaii, this inexpensive paperback is a great choice.

Stories of Hawaii (Mutual Publishing, Honolulu, 1990) is a collection of 13 of Jack London's yarns about the islands.

OA Bushnell is one of Hawaii's best-known contemporary authors. UH Press in Honolulu has published his titles *The Return of Lono* (1971), a historical novel of Captain Cook's final voyage; *Kaaawa* (1972), about Hawaii in the 1850s; *Molokai* (1975), about life in the leprosy colony at Kalaupapa; *The Stone of Kannon* (1979), about the first group of Japanese contract laborers to arrive in Hawaii, and its sequel *The Water of Kane* (1980).

Talking to the Dead by Sylvia Watanabe (Doubleday & Company, New York, 1992) is an enjoyable read that portrays a sense of growing up as a second-generation Japanese-American in post-war Hawaii.

Hawaii (Fawcett, New York, 1986) is James Michener's ambitious historical novel of the islands, from their volcanic origins to their emergence as a state. This sweeping saga traces the Polynesian settlers, the arrival of the missionaries and whalers, the emergence of the sugar barons and the development of Hawaii's multiethnic society.

Outdoor Activities

Kathy Morey's *Kauai Trails* (1992), *Maui Trails* (1991), *Oahu Trails* (1993) and *Hawaii Trails* (1992), the latter to the Big Island, all by Wilderness Press, are comprehensive hiking guides with good maps and clear directions.

Hawaiian Hiking Trails by Craig Chisholm (The Fernglen Press, Lake Oswego, OR, 1994) is a good statewide hiking guide to Hawaii's best-known trails. Chisholm illustrates each hike with a USGS map of the route.

The Beaches of Oahu (1977), *The Beaches of Maui County* (1989), *Beaches of the Big Island* (1985) and *Beaches of Kauai and Niihau* (1990) are by John Clark (UH Press, Honolulu). These comprehensive books detail each island's coastline and every one of its beaches, including water conditions, shoreline geology and local history. The Maui edition includes Maui, Molokai, Lanai and Kahoolawe. If you're going to be spending a lot of time exploring beaches, these books are the ones to have.

The Divers' Guide to Hawaii by Chuck Thorne and Lou Zitnik (Hawaii Divers' Guide, Kihei, 1984) is a guide to the best shore dives on all the islands. It has comprehensive directions to sites, maps of entry points, what you'll see and hazards to expect. Although it's geared for divers it's of some value to snorkelers as well.

Diving and Snorkeling Guide to the Hawaiian Islands by Doug Wallin (Pisces Books, New York, 1991) is a good guide to both diving and snorkeling on the four main islands. It has color photos of sites and fish.

Surfer's Guide to Hawaii: Hawaii Gets All the Breaks by Greg Ambrose (Bess Press, Honolulu, 1991) describes the top surfing spots throughout the islands. Written in an entertaining style, it's packed with everything you need to know about surfing in Hawaii.

Six Islands on Two Wheels by Tom Koch (Bess Press, Honolulu, 1990) is a comprehensive guide to cycling in Hawaii. Koch encourages you to bring your own bike to Hawaii and tells you how to outfit it, where to ride and what to expect.

Reference

Although it's a bit dated, the 238-page *Atlas of Hawaii* by the Department of Geography, University of Hawaii (UH Press, 1983), is loaded with data, maps and tabulations covering everything from land ownership to seasonal ocean wave patterns.

Place Names of Hawaii by Mary Kawena Pukui, Samuel H Elbert and Esther T Mookini (UH Press, 1974) is a glossary of 4000 Hawaiian place names. The meaning and background of each name is explained.

Hawaiian Dictionary by Mary Kawena Pukui and Samuel H Elbert (UH Press, 1986) is the authoritative work on the Hawaiian language. It's in both Hawaiian-English and English-Hawaiian, with 30,000 entries. There's also a $4.95 pocket-sized version with 10,000 Hawaiian words.

There are many other Hawaiian-language books on the market, including grammar texts, conversational self-study guides and books on pidgin.

Bookstores

The four largest islands all have good bookstores with extensive Hawaiiana sections. Bookstore locations are listed under Information in each island chapter.

Ordering by Mail Island Bookshelf (☎ 503-297-4324, 800-967-5944; fax 503-297-1702; infomach@teleport.com), Box 91003, Portland, OR 97291, specializes in books on Hawaii and will mail out a comprehensive catalog on request.

The following publishers will send catalogs of their own titles that can be ordered by mail.

Bess Press
3565 Harding Ave, Honolulu, HI 96816
(☎ 734-7159, 800-910-2377; fax 732-3627; besspr@aloha.net)
Bishop Museum Press
1525 Bernice St, Honolulu, HI 96817
(☎ 848-4134; fax 841-8968)
Petroglyph Press
201 Kinoole St, Hilo, HI 96720
(☎ 935-6006; fax 935-1553)
University of Hawaii Press
2840 Kolowalu St, Honolulu, HI 96822
(☎ 956-8255, 800-956-2840; fax 988-6052)

ONLINE SERVICES

A growing number of Hawaii's hotels, B&Bs, visitor attractions and businesses are going online. Useful World Wide Web (www) sites that provide links to visitor-related topics include:

www.planet-hawaii.com
www.hawaiian-index.com
www.visit.hawaii.org

For a list of the URL addresses and individual websites of businesses mentioned throughout this book, see the Online Services Appendix.

FILMS

Dozens of feature movies have been filmed on Hawaii and scores of others have used footage of Hawaii as backdrops. One of the few that has insightfully delved into island life is *Picture Bride* (1993), starring Yuki Kudoh, with a cameo by Toshiro Mifune; filmed on Oahu, it depicts the blunt realities of 19th-century Hawaiian plantation life for a Japanese mail-order bride.

Classic movies filmed at least partially on Hawaii include: *Song of the Islands* (1942), filmed on the Big Island, starring Betty Grable and Victor Mature; *From Here to Eternity* (1953), filmed in Oahu, starring Burt Lancaster and Deborah Kerr; *Miss Sadie Thompson* (1953), filmed on Kauai, starring Rita Hayworth; *South Pacific* (1958), filmed on Kauai, with Mitzi Gaynor and Rossano Brazzi; *The Old Man and the Sea* (1958), filmed on the Big Island, starring Spencer Tracy; *Blue Hawaii* (1961), filmed on Kauai, starring Elvis Presley and Angela Lansbury; *Hawaii* (1966), filmed on Oahu and Kauai, starring Julie Andrews and Max von Sydow; *Tora! Tora! Tora!* (1970), filmed on Oahu, starring Jason Robards; *King Kong* (1976), filmed on Kauai, with Jessica Lange and Jeff Bridges; and *Raiders of the Lost Ark* (1981), filmed on Kauai, with Harrison Ford.

In the 1990s, a couple of blockbusters used Hawaii as their main base. Steven Spielberg's *Jurassic Park* (1993) was filmed in remote valleys on Kauai, while Kevin Costner's big washout *Waterworld* (1995) was filmed in the waters off the Big Island.

NEWSPAPERS & MAGAZINES

Hawaii's two main papers are the *Honolulu Advertiser*, which is published daily each morning, and the *Honolulu Star-Bulletin*, which comes out in the afternoon Monday to Saturday.

For copies of either paper, contact the Circulation Department (☎ 538-6397), Box 3350, Honolulu, HI 96801. A single Sunday paper can be sent airmail to the US mainland for $7.40 or to an overseas destination for $18.80.

The Honolulu papers are sold throughout Hawaii, but the Neighbor Islands also have their own newspapers. The *Hawaii Tribune-Herald* in Hilo, *West Hawaii Today* in Kailua-Kona, the *Maui News* in Wailuku and the *Garden Island* in Lihue are each published five to six times a week.

Several mainland newspapers are also widely available, including *USA Today, Wall Street Journal* and the *Los Angeles Times*. Look for them in the lobbies of larger hotels and in convenience stores. The best place to get international newspapers is at Borders bookstores, which carry a surprisingly wide selection.

Honolulu, Aloha and *Hawaii Magazine* are the largest general interest magazines about Hawaii. *Honolulu* is geared more towards residents and is published monthly by the Honolulu Publishing Company, 36 Merchant St, Honolulu, HI 96813. *Aloha* (Box 469035, Escondido, CA 92046) and *Hawaii Magazine* (Box 485, Mt Morris, IL 61054) have more visitor-oriented feature articles; both are published six times a year.

There are also numerous tourist magazines distributed free on the islands that are well worth perusing. They usually have simple maps, a bit of current event information, lots of ads and discount coupons for everything from hamburgers to sunset cruises.

RADIO & TV

Hawaii has about 50 AM and FM radio stations. There's a wide variety of programming, including some stations that feature Hawaiian music. More information is given under Information in the individual island chapters.

Hawaii has commercial TV stations representing the three major US networks, and cable network stations that include tourist information and Japanese language channels. Almost anything you can watch on the mainland you can watch in Hawaii.

For some local flavor, the evening news on Channel 2 ends with some fine slack-key guitar music by Keola and Kapono Beamer and clips of people waving the shaka sign.

PHOTOGRAPHY & VIDEO

Both print and slide film are readily available on all the islands. If you're going to be in Hawaii for any length of time, consider having your film developed there, as the high temperature and humidity of the tropics greatly accelerates the deterioration of exposed film. The sooner it's developed, the better the results.

Kodak and Fuji have labs in Honolulu, and island drug stores and camera shops usually send in to those labs. Longs Drugs is one of the cheapest places for both purchasing film and having it developed. All the tourist centers have one-hour print processing shops as well.

Don't leave your camera in direct sun any longer than necessary. A locked car can heat up like an oven in just a few minutes.

Sand and water are intense reflectors and in bright light they'll often leave foreground subjects shadowy. You can try compensating by adjusting your f-stop or attaching a polarizing filter, or both, but the most effective technique is to take photos in the gentler light of early morning and late afternoon.

TIME

Hawaii does not observe daylight-saving time. When it's noon in Hawaii the time in other parts of the world is: 1 pm in Anchorage, 2 pm in Los Angeles, 5 pm in New York, 10 pm in London, 11 pm in Bonn, 7 am the next day in Tokyo, 8 am the next day in Sydney and Melbourne, and 10 am the next day in Auckland.

The time difference is one hour greater during those months when other countries observe daylight saving. For example from April to October when it's noon in Hawaii it's 3 pm in Los Angeles and 6 pm in New York; and from November to March when it's noon in Hawaii it's 9 am in Melbourne and 11 am in Auckland.

Hawaii has about 11 hours of daylight in mid-winter and almost 13½ hours in mid-summer. In mid-winter the sun rises at about 7 am and sets about 6 pm. In mid-summer it rises before 6 am and sets after 7 pm.

And then there's Hawaiian Time, which is either a slow-down-the-clock pace or a euphemism for being late.

ELECTRICITY

Electricity is 110/120 V, 60 cycles, and a flat two-pronged plug is used, the same as everywhere else in the USA.

WEIGHTS & MEASURES

Hawaii, like the rest of the USA, uses the imperial system of measurement. Distances are in feet, yards and miles; weights are in ounces, pounds and tons. For those unaccustomed to the imperial system, there is a metric conversion table on the inside back cover of this book.

LAUNDRY

Many hotels, condominiums and hostels have coin-operated washers and dryers. If there's not one where you're staying, you can find commercial coin-operated laundries on all the islands. The average cost is about $1 to wash a load of clothes and another dollar to dry. Laundry locations are listed under Information in each island chapter.

HEALTH

Hawaii is a very healthy place to live and to visit. As it's 2500 miles from the nearest industrial center, there's little air pollution – other than that caused by volcanic activity. Hawaii ranks first of all the 50 US states in life expectancy, which is currently about 76 years for men and 81 years for women.

There are few serious health concerns. The islands have none of the nasties like malaria, cholera or yellow fever, and you can drink water directly out of any tap, although all stream water needs to be boiled or treated.

No immunizations are required to enter Hawaii or any other port in the USA.

Be aware that there are many poisonous plants in Hawaii, so you should never taste a plant that you cannot positively identify as edible.

If you're new to the heat and humidity, you may find yourself easily fatigued and more susceptible to minor ailments. Acclimatize yourself by slowing down your pace and setting your body clock to the more kicked-back 'Hawaiian Time'. Drink plenty of liquids.

If you're planning on a long outing or anything strenuous, take enough water and don't push yourself.

Predeparture Preparations

Health Insurance Foreign visitors should be warned that health care in the USA is expensive, and while Hawaii is the only one of the 50 states that has an extensive health insurance program, the coverage is limited to Hawaii residents.

Therefore, a travel insurance policy that covers medical expenses may be a wise idea. There are a wide variety of policies available and a good travel agent should have recommendations. While you may find a policy that pays doctors or hospitals direct, be aware that many private doctors and clinics in Hawaii will demand payment at the time of service. If you have to make a claim later, be certain to keep all documentation.

Check the small print because some policies exclude 'dangerous activities' such as scuba diving, motorcycling, anything to do with parachutes and even trekking.

Medical Kit A small first-aid kit is a sensible thing to carry, especially if you plan on camping or hiking into the backcountry.

A basic kit should have things like aspirin or Panadol for pain or fever; an antihistamine (such as Benadryl) for use as a decongestant, to relieve the itch from insect bites or to help prevent motion sickness; an antiseptic and antibiotic ointment for cuts and scratches; calamine lotion to ease the irritation from bites and stings; Band-aids and bandages; scissors; tweezers; insect repellent; and sunblock.

Bring adequate supplies of any prescription medicine or contraceptive pills you may already be taking.

Medical Care
Hawaii has 25 acute-care hospitals, 2600 physicians and 1200 dentists. While the rural islands of Molokai and Lanai have limited medical facilities, the other islands have fully staffed hospitals with modern facilities. Still, for specialized care and serious illnesses, many islanders have more confidence in Honolulu hospitals than in Neighbor Island facilities.

Medical Problems & Treatment
Leptospirosis Visitors to Hawaii should be aware of leptospirosis, a bacterial disease found in freshwater streams and ponds. The disease is transmitted from animals such as rats, mongooses and wild pigs.

Humans most often pick up the disease by swimming or wading in water contaminated by animal urine. Leptospirosis can exist in any fresh water, including idyllic-looking waterfalls and jungle streams, because the water may have washed down the slopes through animal habitats.

Leptospirosis enters the body through the nose, eyes, mouth or cuts in the skin. Wetland taro farmers, swimmers and backcountry hikers account for the majority of cases.

Symptoms can occur within two to 20 days after exposure and may include fever, chills, sweating, headaches, muscle pains, vomiting and diarrhea. More severe symptoms include blood in the urine and jaundice. Symptoms may last from a few days to several weeks.

There are a few dozen confirmed cases statewide each year. Because symptoms of leptospirosis resemble the flu and hepatitis, other cases probably go unconfirmed. Although deaths have been attributed to the disease, they are relatively rare. Leptospirosis is not specific to Hawaii and can be found on the mainland and in other countries as well.

Some precautions include wearing waterproof *tabis* (reef walkers) when hiking and avoiding unnecessary freshwater crossings, especially if you have open cuts.

Leptospirosis can be serious, yet thousands of people swim in Hawaiian streams without contracting it. The state has posted warnings at many trailheads and freshwater swimming areas. Islanders have differing opinions on leptospirosis – some never swim in fresh water because of it, while others consider it such a long shot that they take no precautions at all.

Sunburn Sunburn is always a concern in the tropics, as the closer you get to the equator the fewer of the sun's rays are blocked out by the atmosphere. Don't be fooled by what appears to be a hazy overcast day, as those rays still get through.

Sunscreen with an SPF (sun protection factor) of 10 to 15 is recommended if you're not already tanned. If you're going into the water, use one that's water-resistant. Snorkelers may want to wear a T-shirt if they plan to be out in the water a long time. You'll not only be protecting against sunburn, but potential skin cancer and premature aging of the skin.

Fair-skinned people can get both first-

and second-degree burns in the hot Hawaiian sun, and wearing a sun hat for added protection is a good idea. The most severe sun is between 10 am and 2 pm.

Prickly Heat Prickly heat is an itchy rash caused by excessive perspiration trapped under the skin. It usually strikes people who have just arrived in a hot climate and whose pores have not yet opened sufficiently to cope with greater sweating. Keeping cool by bathing often or resorting to air-con may help until you acclimatize.

Heat Exhaustion Dehydration or salt deficiency can cause heat exhaustion. Take time to acclimatize to high temperatures and make sure you get sufficient liquids. Salt deficiency is characterized by fatigue, lethargy, headaches, giddiness and muscle cramps, and in this case salt tablets may help. Vomiting or diarrhea can deplete your liquid and salt levels.

Heat Stroke This serious, sometimes fatal condition can occur if the body's heat-regulating mechanism breaks down and the body temperature rises to dangerous levels. Long, continuous periods of exposure to high temperatures can leave you vulnerable to heat stroke. Avoid strenuous activity in open sun (such as lengthy hikes or bike rides across lava fields) when you first arrive. The symptoms of heat stroke are feeling unwell, not sweating very much or at all and a high body temperature (102°F to 106°F). Where sweating has ceased the skin becomes flushed and red. Severe, throbbing headaches and lack of coordination will also occur, and the sufferer may be confused or aggressive. Eventually the victim may become delirious or convulse. Hospitalization is essential, but meanwhile get patients out of the sun, remove their clothing, cover them with a wet sheet or towel and then fan them continually.

Fungal Infections The same climate that produces lush tropical forests also promotes a prolific growth of skin fungi and bacteria. Hot weather fungal infections are most likely to occur between the toes or fingers or in the groin.

Keeping your skin dry and cool and allowing air to circulate is essential. Choose loose cotton clothing rather than synthetics and sandals rather than shoes. If you do get an infection, wash the infected area daily with a disinfectant or medicated soap. Rinse and dry well and then apply an anti-fungal powder.

Altitude Sickness On the Big Island, people planning to go to the summits of Mauna Kea or Mauna Loa need to be aware of the possibility of Acute Mountain Sickness (AMS), which occurs at high altitudes due to lack of oxygen and is potentially fatal. While AMS can generally be avoided by making gains in elevation at a slow pace, Hawaii presents an unusual situation, as most people who visit Mauna Kea summit do so by car. Many of those visitors drive straight up to nearly 14,000 feet from their hotels on the coast, a mere two-hour ride that offers no time to acclimatize. As a result AMS is a common problem for summit visitors, even though most cases are on the mild side. AMS symptoms include headaches, nausea, dizziness and shortness of breath, while confusion and lack of coordination and balance are real danger signs. With all but the mildest of symptoms, travelers experiencing signs of AMS should immediately descend to a lower elevation. For more information, see Precautions in the Saddle Road/Mauna Kea section in the Big Island chapter.

Motion Sickness Eating lightly before and during a trip will reduce the chances of motion sickness. If you are prone to motion sickness, try to find a place that minimizes disturbance – near the wing on aircraft or close to midships on boats. Fresh air usually helps; reading or cigarette smoke doesn't. Commercial antimotion-sickness preparations, which can cause drowsiness, have to be taken before the trip commences; when you're feeling sick it's too late. Ginger is a natural preventative and is available in capsule form.

HIV/AIDS HIV, the Human Immunodeficiency Virus, may develop into AIDS, Acquired Immune Deficiency Syndrome. Any exposure to blood, blood products or bodily fluids may put an individual at risk of contracting it. Apart from sexual abstinence, the most effective preventative is always to practice safe sex using condoms. It is impossible to detect the HIV-positive status of an otherwise healthy-looking person without a blood test.

HIV/AIDS can be spread through infected blood transfusions or by dirty needles – vaccinations, acupuncture, tattooing and ear-piercing are potentially as dangerous as intravenous drug use if the equipment is not clean.

If you have any questions regarding AIDS while in Hawaii, contact the AIDS/STD Hotline at ☎ 922-1313 on Oahu or ☎ 800-321-1555 from the Neighbor Islands.

Cuts & Scratches Cuts and skin punctures are easily infected in Hawaii's hot and humid climate, and infections can be persistent. Keep any cut or open wound clean and treat it with an antiseptic solution. Keep the area protected, but where possible avoid bandages, which can keep wounds wet.

Coral cuts are even more susceptible to infection because tiny pieces of coral can get embedded in the skin. These cuts are notoriously slow to heal, as the coral releases a weak venom into the wound.

Pesky Creatures Hawaii has no land snakes, but it does have its fair share of annoying mosquitoes as well as centipedes that can give an unpleasant bite. The islands also have bees and ground-nesting wasps, which, like the centipede, generally pose danger only to those who are allergic to their stings. (For information on stinging sea creatures, see Ocean Safety under Dangers & Annoyances, later.)

This being the tropics, cockroaches are plentiful; although they don't pose much of a health problem, they do little for the appetite. Condos with kitchens have the most problems. If you find that the place you're staying is infested, you can always call the manager or the front desk and have them spray poisons – which are no doubt more dangerous than the roaches!

While sightings are not terribly common, there are two dangerous arachnids on the islands: the black widow spider and the scorpion.

Black Widow Spiders Found in much of the USA, the black widow is glossy black and has a body that's a half-inch in diameter with a characteristic red hourglass mark on its abdomen. It weaves a strong, tangled web close to the ground and inhabits brush piles, sheds and outdoor privies.

Its bite, which resembles the prick of a pin, can be barely noticeable, but is followed in about 30 minutes by severe cramping in which the abdominal muscles become boardlike and breathing becomes difficult. Other reactions include vomiting, headaches, sweating, shaking and a tingling sensation in the fingers. In severe cases the bite can be fatal. If you think you've been bitten by a black widow, seek immediate medical help.

Scorpions The scorpion, confined principally to warm dry regions, is capable of inflicting a painful sting by means of its caudal fang. Like the black widow, the venom contains neurotoxins. Severity of the symptoms generally depends on the age of the victim; stings can even be fatal for very young children. Symptoms are shortness of breath, hives, swelling or vomiting. Apply diluted household ammonia and cold compresses to the area of the sting and seek immediate medical help.

While the odds of encountering a scorpion are quite low in Hawaii, campers should always check inside their hiking boots before putting them on!

Ciguatera Poisoning Ciguatera is a serious illness caused by eating fish affected by ciguatoxin, which herbivorous fish can pick up from marine algae. There is no ready way of detecting ciguatoxin, and it's not diminished by cooking. Symptoms of food poisoning usually occur three to five hours after eating.

Ciguatoxin is most common among reef fish (which are not commonly served in restaurants) and hasn't affected Hawaii's deep-sea fish, such as tuna, marlin and mahimahi. The symptoms, if you do eat the wrong fish, can include nausea; stomach cramps; diarrhea; paralysis; tingling and numbness of the face, fingers and toes; and a reversal of temperature feelings, so that hot things feel cold and vice versa. Extreme cases can result in unconsciousness and even death. Vomit until your stomach is empty and get immediate medical help.

WOMEN TRAVELERS

Women travelers are no more likely to encounter problems in Hawaii than anywhere else in the USA. We advise against hitchhiking, especially women traveling alone, but if you do, size up the situation carefully and don't hesitate to decline a ride from anyone who makes you feel uncomfortable. If you're camping, select your campground carefully, opting for popular, well-used camping areas, rather than more remote locales where you might be the only camper, as these lesser-used spots sometimes become impromptu drinking hangouts.

Women who have been abused or sexually assaulted can call the Sex Abuse Treatment Center's 24-hour hotline on Oahu at ☎ 524-7273. Similar Neighbor Island hotlines are: ☎ 245-4144 on Kauai, ☎ 935-0677 on the Big Island and ☎ 242-4357 on Maui, Molokai and Lanai.

GAY & LESBIAN TRAVELERS

Gay and lesbian travelers are taking a growing interest in Hawaii, as the state has become centerstage in the movement to legalize same-gender marriages. In December 1996 a circuit court judge ruled that state prohibitions against same-sex marriages violated the equal protection clause of Hawaii's constitution, which explicitly bans gender discrimination. While it's an important round for gay activists, the implementation of the ruling has been postponed until after the state appeals the case to the Hawaii Supreme Court.

If the supreme court rules favorably, then the state will be compelled to issue marriage licenses free of gender prejudice. Should that happen, a move to amend Hawaii's state constitution, supported largely by mainland political and religious extremists, is expected to gather momentum – the final battle in this protracted struggle may still be years away. (Incidentally, the same day that the Hawaii case went to court, the US Congress passed the 'Defense of Marriage Act', which bars federal benefits to married homosexuals and allows states to ignore gay marriages legalized in other states.)

Gay marriages aside, Hawaii is as popular a vacation spot for gays and lesbians as it is for straights. It's a liberal state, with strong minority protections and a constitutional guarantee of privacy that extends to sexual behavior between consenting adults.

Still, most of the gay scene is very low key, especially on the Neighbor Islands; public hand-holding and other outward signs of affection between gays is not commonplace.

Certainly in terms of nightlife, the main gay club scene is centered in Waikiki (see the Waikiki Entertainment section for details).

The following information sources can help gay and lesbian visitors get oriented to the islands.

The magazine *Island Lifestyle* (☎ 737-6400; ilm@tnight.com), Box 11840, Honolulu, HI 96828, is a 48-page monthly for Hawaii's gay community. It can be picked up free at clubs in Honolulu, bookstores and other locations. The latest issue can be ordered by mail; the cost is $3 within the USA, $5 overseas. Lifestyle also sells *The Pages*, a $4 directory of clubs, B&Bs, restaurants and other businesses that are supportive of the gay community.

Pacific Ocean Holidays (☎ 923-2400, 800-735-6600; fax 923-2499; poh@hi.net), 155 Paoakalani Ave, Suite 901, Honolulu, HI 96815, arranges vacation packages for gay men and women. They also produce a booklet called *Pocket Guide to Hawaii*,

Hawaiian Weddings

Many visitors come to Hawaii not only for their honeymoon, but to make their wedding vows as well.

Getting married in Hawaii is a straightforward process. The state requires that the prospective bride and groom appear in person together before a marriage license agent and pay $25 for a license, which is given out on the spot. There's no waiting period and no residence, citizenship or blood-test requirements. The legal age for marriage is 18, or 16 with parental consent.

Full information and forms are available from the Department of Health (☎ 586-4544), Marriage License Office, Box 3378, 1250 Punchbowl St, Honolulu, HI 96813. The office is open from 8 am to 4 pm Monday to Friday.

Numerous companies provide wedding services. One of these, Affordable Weddings of Hawaii (☎ 923-4876, 800-942-4554; fax 396-0959), Box 26475, Honolulu, HI 96825, will mail out a brochure with tips on planning your wedding, choosing a location, photography services etc. The amiable Reverend MC Hansen of Affordable Weddings can provide a nondenominational service, starting at $55 for a simple weekday ceremony and going up to $700 for more elaborate packages.

For something more traditional (or nontraditional, depending on your perspective), Helemano Kauihimalaihi, wearing a ti lei, performs a ceremony entirely in the Hawaiian language. He's attempted to recreate an ancient ceremony using Hawaiian chants and proverbs, draping of the bride and groom in tapa and the like. The ceremony alone costs $150, or with flowers and photos $235. For information contact Traditional Hawaiian Weddings (☎/fax 671-8420, 800-884-9505), 94-1054 Paha Place, Suite N2, Waipahu, HI 96797. ■

which is geared to the gay community and costs $5 when ordered by mail.

Christopher Travel & Tours (☎ /fax 800-969-1210; tourhi@aloha.net), in the newly renovated S Hata Building at 308 Kamehameha Ave, Suite 202, Hilo, HI 96720, is another helpful travel agency catering to the gay community. They're gay owned and operated and list more than 65 gay and gay-friendly B&B's throughout the islands.

The Gay & Lesbian Community Center (☎ 951-7000; glcc@aloha-cafe.com), 1820 University Ave, Honolulu, HI 96822 is a good source of information on local issues for both women and men.

Hawaii Equal Rights Marriage Project (HERMP), Box 11690, Honolulu, HI 96828, has spearheaded the fight to legalize gay marriages in Hawaii. You can plug into the latest by looking them up at their website (see the Online Services Appendix).

DISABLED TRAVELERS

Overall, Hawaii is an accommodating destination for travelers with disabilities, and Waikiki in particular is considered one of the more handicapped-accessible destinations in the USA. Many of the larger hotels throughout Hawaii have wheelchair-accessible rooms and as more of them renovate their facilities, accessibility improves.

The Commission on Persons with Disabilities (☎ 586-8121), 919 Ala Moana Blvd, Room 101, Honolulu, HI 96814, distributes the three-part *Aloha Guide to Accessibility,* which contains detailed travel tips for physically disabled people. Part I contains general information and covers airport access on the major islands; this section can be obtained free by mail, and with it you'll get an order form for purchasing Parts II and III, which detail accessibility to beaches, parks, shopping centers and visitor attractions and list hotels with wheelchair access or specially adapted facilities. The entire set costs $15, postage included, or $5 if you just want the section on hotels.

Wheelers of Hawaii (☎ 879-5521, 800-303-3750), 186 Mehani Circle, Kihei, HI 96753, books accessible accommodations, rents accessible vans and arranges various activities for disabled travelers.

For further general information, the Society for the Advancement of Travel for the Handicapped (SATH; ☎ 212-447-7284), 347 Fifth Ave, Suite 610, New York, NY 10016, publishes a quarterly magazine for $13 a year and has various free information sheets on travel for the disabled.

SENIOR TRAVELERS

Hawaii is a popular destination for retirees and lots of discount schemes are available, and the applicable age has been creeping lower as well.

For instance, Hawaii's biggest hotel chain, Outrigger, offers across-the-board discounts of 20% to anyone 50 years old or better, and if you're a member of the American Association of Retired Persons (AARP), they'll discount it another 5%. AARP discounts are available from other hotels as well, so whenever you book a reservation, be sure to inquire.

The nonprofit AARP itself is a good source for travel bargains. For information on joining this advocacy group for Americans 50 years and older, contact AARP (☎ 800-227-7737), 601 E St NW, Washington DC 20049.

US citizens who are 62 or older are eligible to purchase a Golden Age Passport for just $10, which allows unlimited lifetime entry into all US National Park sites, including those in Hawaii.

Information on Elderhostel study vacations is under Organized Tours in the Getting There & Away chapter.

TRAVEL WITH CHILDREN

Families with children will find lots to do in Hawaii. In addition to beaches, swimming pools and a range of water sports, Hawaii has lots of other outdoor activities and cool sightseeing attractions for kids of all ages.

If you're traveling with infants and come up short, Baby's Away rents cribs, strollers, play pens, infant seats, high chairs, gates and more on Oahu (☎ 261-2929), Maui (☎ 875-9030), Kauai (☎ 245-6259) and the Big Island (☎ 329-7475).

For more information on traveling with children, pick up a copy of Lonely Planet's

Travel with Children by Maureen Wheeler et al (1995).

USEFUL ORGANIZATIONS
State Parks

The Division of State Parks (☎ 587-0300), Box 621, Honolulu, HI 96809, provides a free brochure to Hawaii's state parks, including camping information and a brief description of each park.

Sierra Club

The Sierra Club offers guided hikes, maintains trails and is involved in conservation projects throughout Hawaii. You can get their latest newsletter, which includes a schedule of upcoming hikes, by sending $2 to the Sierra Club (☎ 538-6616), Box 2577, Honolulu, HI 96803.

In addition, the Sierra Club Legal Defense Fund plays an active role in protecting Hawaii's fragile environment. To learn more about their present struggles, write to their regional headquarters at 180 Montgomery St, Suite 1400, San Francisco, CA 94104.

Nature Conservancy

The Nature Conservancy of Hawaii protects some of Hawaii's endangered ecosystems by acquiring land and arranging long-term stewardships with landowners. They offer guided hikes into some of their preserves, most notably Kamakou on Molokai and Waikamoi in the Haleakala area on Maui. For the upcoming hike schedule or to find out more about their projects, contact the Nature Conservancy of Hawaii (☎ 537-4508) at 1116 Smith St, Honolulu, HI 96817.

American Automobile Association

The American Automobile Association (AAA), which has its only Hawaii office (☎ 528-2600) at 590 Queen St in Honolulu, can provide AAA members with information on motoring in Hawaii, including detailed Honolulu and Hawaii road maps. Members are also entitled to discounts on car rentals, Aloha Airlines tickets and some hotels and sightseeing attractions.

For information on joining AAA on the

mainland before arrival in Hawaii, call
☎ 800-564-6222. Membership dues vary
by state but average $55 the first year, $40
for subsequent years.

DANGERS & ANNOYANCES
Emergency
For police, fire and ambulance emergencies, dial ☎ 911. The inside front cover of
island phone books lists other vital service
agencies, such as poison control, coast
guard rescues and suicide and crisis lines.

If you lose your passport, contact your
consulate in Honolulu; a complete list of
consulate phone numbers can be found in
the telephone book yellow pages.

For refunds on lost or stolen American
Express traveler's checks, call ☎ 800-221-
7282; for MasterCard traveler's checks,
dial ☎ 800-223-9920.

Theft & Violence
For the most part, Hawaii is a relatively
safe place.

However the islands do have notoriety
for rip-offs from parked rental cars. The
people who break into these cars are good
at what they do; they can pop a trunk or
pull out a lock assembly in seconds to get
to loot inside. What's more, they do it not
only when you've left your car in a
secluded area to go for a long hike, but also
in crowded parking lots where you'd expect
safety in numbers.

It's certainly best not to leave anything of
value in your car any time you walk away
from it. If for some reason you feel you
must, at least pack things well out of sight
before you've pulled up to the place where
you're going to leave the car.

Other than rip-offs, most hassles encountered by visitors are from drunks. Be
tuned in to the vibes on beaches at night
and in places where young men hang out
to drink.

Overall, violent crime is lower in Hawaii
than in most mainland cities. However,
there are some pockets of resentment
against tourists as well as against off-
islanders moving in. Oahu tends to be
worse than the other islands.

Drugs
Hawaii's marijuana, called *pakalolo,* is
considered to be some of the most potent
anywhere. However, authorities have been
so successful in rooting out marijuana
crops and arresting growers that pakalolo
is, ironically, less common on Hawaii's
streets than dangerous drugs like 'ice' and
heroin. The possession of marijuana and
nonprescription narcotics is illegal on the
islands; yachties entering Hawaii should be
aware that federal authorities have been
known to seize boats after finding even
minute quantities of marijuana on board.

Tsunamis
Tsunamis, or tidal waves, are not common
in Hawaii, but when they do hit they can be
severe.

Tsunamis are generated by earthquakes
or other natural disasters. The largest to
ever hit Hawaii was in 1946, the result of
an earthquake in the Aleutian Islands.
Waves reached a height of 55.8 feet, entire
villages were washed away and 159 people
died. Since that time, Hawaii has installed a
modern tsunami warning system, which is
aired through yellow speakers mounted on
telephone poles around the islands. They're
tested on the first working day of each
month at 11:45 am for about one minute.

Although tsunamis traveling across the
Pacific can take hours to arrive, others can
be caused by earthquakes or volcanic eruptions within Hawaii. For these there may be
little warning. Any earthquake strong
enough to cause you to grab onto something to keep from falling is a natural
tsunami warning. If you're in a low-lying
coastal area when one occurs, immediately
head for higher ground.

Tsunami inundation maps in the front of
island telephone books show susceptible
areas and safety zones.

Ocean Safety
Drowning is the leading cause of accidental
death for visitors.

If you're not familiar with water conditions, ask someone. If there's no lifeguard
around, local surfers are generally helpful –

they'd rather give you the lowdown on water conditions than pull you out later. It's best not to swim alone in any unfamiliar place.

Shorebreaks Shorebreaks occur where waves break close to or directly on shore. They're formed when ocean swells pass abruptly from deep to shallow waters. If only a couple of feet high, they're generally fine for novice bodysurfers to try their hand, but otherwise they're for experienced bodysurfers only.

Large shorebreaks can hit hard with a slamming downward force. Broken bones, neck injuries, dislocated shoulders and loss of wind are the most common injuries, although anyone wiped out in the water is a potential drowning victim as well.

Rip Currents Rip currents, or rips, are fast flowing currents of water within the ocean, moving from shallow near-shore areas out to sea. They are most common in conditions of high surf, forming when water from incoming waves builds up near the shore. Essentially the waves are coming in faster than they can flow back out.

The water then runs along the shoreline until it finds an escape route out to sea, usually through a channel or out along a point. Swimmers caught up in the current can be ripped out to deeper water.

Although rips can be powerful, they usually dissipate 50 to 100 yards offshore. Anyone caught in one should either go with the flow until it loses power or swim parallel to shore to slip out of it. Trying to swim against a rip current can exhaust even the strongest of swimmers.

Undertows Undertows are common along steeply sloped beaches when large waves backwash directly into incoming surf. The outflowing water picks up speed as it flows down the slopes. When it hits an incoming wave it pulls under it, creating an undertow. Swimmers caught up in an undertow can be pulled beneath the surface. The most important thing is not to panic. Go with the current until you get beyond the wave.

STRONG CURRENT   MAN-OF-WAR   SHARP CORAL

HIGH SURF   DANGEROUS
SHOREBREAK   WAVES ON LEDGE

Warning signs on Hawaii's beaches

Rogue Waves Never turn your back on the ocean. Waves don't all come in with equal height or strength. An abnormally high 'rogue wave' can sweep over shoreline ledges such as those circling Hanauma Bay on Oahu or tear up onto beaches like Lumahai on Kauai. Over the years, numerous people have been swept into the ocean from both.

You need to be particularly cautious during high tide and in conditions of stormy weather or high surf.

Some people think rogue waves don't exist because they've never seen one. But that's the point – you don't always see them.

Coral Most coral cuts occur when swimmers are pushed onto the coral by rough waves and surges. It's a good idea to wear diving gloves when snorkeling over shallow reefs. Avoid walking on coral, which can not only cut your feet, but is very damaging to the coral.

Jellyfish Take a peek into the water before you plunge in to make sure it's not jellyfish territory. These gelatinous creatures, with saclike bodies and stinging tentacles, are fairly common around Hawaii. They're most apt to be seen eight to 10 days after the full moon, when they come into shallow near-shore waters in places such as Waikiki. They're not keen on the sun and as the day heats up they retreat from shallow waters, so encounters by beach-goers are most common in the morning. The sting of a jellyfish varies from mild to severe, depending on the variety. Unless you have an allergic reaction to their venom, the stings are not generally dangerous.

Portuguese Man-of-War The Portuguese man-of-war is a colonial hydrozoan, or a colony of coelenterates, rather than a solitary coelenterate like the jellyfish. Its body consists of a translucent, bluish, bladder-like float, which in Hawaii generally grows to four or five inches long. Known locally as 'bluebottles', they're most often found on the windward coasts, particularly after storms.

The sting of a Portuguese man-of-war is very painful, similar to a bad bee sting except that you're likely to get stung more than once from clusters of long tentacles containing hundreds of stinging cells. These tentacles can reach up to 50 feet in length. Even touching a bluebottle a few hours after it's washed up on shore can result in burning stings.

If you do get stung, quickly remove the tentacles and apply vinegar or a meat tenderizer containing papain (derived from papaya) to neutralize the toxins – in a pinch, you could use urine as well. For serious reactions, including chest pains or difficulty in breathing, seek medical attention immediately.

Fish Stings Incidences with venomous sea creatures in Hawaiian waters are rather rare. You should, however, learn to recognize scorpionfish and lionfish, two related fish that can inject venom through their dorsal spines if touched. Both are sometimes found in quite shallow water.

The Hawaiian lionfish, which grows up to 10 inches, is strikingly attractive with vertical orange and white stripes and feathery appendages that contain poisonous spines; it likes to drift along the reef, particularly at night. The scorpionfish is more drab in appearance, has shorter and less obvious spines, is about six inches in length, and tends to sit immobile on the bottom or on ledges.

The sting from either can cause a sharp burning pain, followed by numbness around the area, nausea and headaches. Immediately stick the affected area in water that is as hot as bearable (take care not to unintentionally scald the area due to numbness) and go for medical treatment.

Cone Shells Cone shells should be left alone unless you're sure they're empty. There's no safe way of picking up a live cone shell, as the animal inside has a long harpoon-like tail that can dart out and reach anywhere on its shell to deliver a painful sting. The wound should be soaked in hot water and medical attention sought.

A few species, such as the textile cone, whose shell is decorated with brown diamond or triangular shapes, have a venom so toxic that in extreme cases the sting could even be fatal.

Sea Urchins *Wana*, or spiny sea urchins, have long brittle spines that can puncture the skin and break off, causing burning and possible numbness. The spines sometimes inflict a toxin and can cause an infection. You can try to remove the spines with tweezers or by soaking the area in hot water, although more serious cases may require surgical removal.

Eels *Puhi*, or moray eels, are often spotted by snorkelers around reefs and coral heads. They're constantly opening and closing their mouths to pump water across their gills, which makes them look far more menacing than they actually are.

Eels don't attack, but will protect themselves if they feel cornered by fingers jabbing into the reef holes or crevices they occupy. Eels have sharp teeth and strong jaws and may clamp down if someone sticks a hand in their door.

Sharks

More than 35 varieties of sharks are found in Hawaiian waters, including the non-aggressive whale shark and basking sharks, which can reach lengths of 50 feet. As Hawaiian waters are abundant with fish, sharks in Hawaii are well fed and most pose little danger to humans.

Sharks are curious and will sometimes investigate divers, although they generally just check things out and continue on their way. If they start to hang around, however, it's probably time for you to go.

Outside of the rarely encountered great white shark, the most dangerous shark in Hawaiian waters is the tiger shark, which averages about 20 feet in length and is identified by vertical bars along its side. The tiger shark is not terribly particular about what it eats and has been known to chomp down on pieces of wood (including surfboards) floating on the ocean surface.

Should you come face to face with a shark the best thing to do is move casually and quietly away. Don't panic, as sharks are attracted by things that thrash around.

Some aquatic officials suggest thumping an attacking shark on the nose or sticking your fingers into its eyes, which may confuse it long enough to give you time to escape. Indeed, some divers who dive in shark waters carry a billy club or bang stick.

Avoid murky waters. After heavy rains sharks sometimes come in around river mouths.

Sharks are attracted by blood. Some attacks on humans are related to spearfishing; when a shark is going after a diver's bloody catch, the diver sometimes gets in the way. Sharks are also attracted by shiny things and by anything bright red or yellow, which might influence your choice of swimsuit color.

Unpleasant encounters with sharks are extremely unlikely, however. According to the University of Hawaii Sea Grant College, only about 30 unprovoked shark attacks were known to have occurred in Hawaii between 1900 and 1990; about a third of these were fatal. Nevertheless, in recent years, increasing numbers of both sharks and shark attacks have been reported, with attacks now occurring on average at a rate of about two or three per year.

BUSINESS HOURS

While there's a variance of half an hour in either direction, the most common office hours in Hawaii are 8:30 am to 4:30 pm Monday to Friday. Shops in central areas and malls, as well as large chain stores, are usually open into the evenings and on weekends, and some grocery stores are open 24 hours.

HOLIDAYS & SPECIAL EVENTS

With its multitude of cultures and good year-round weather, Hawaii has a seemingly endless number and variety of holidays, festivals and events. The list that follows includes the highlights.

As dates for many events change a bit from year to year, check local newspapers or inquire at one of the island tourist offices for exact schedules. Water-sport events are particularly reliant on the weather and the surf, so any schedule is tentative.

January

New Year's Day is a national holiday. Fireworks displays are held in some of the larger towns and resorts on New Year's Eve, and fireworks are shot off nonstop through the night.

Chinese New Year begins at the second new moon after winter solstice (mid-January to mid-February) with lion dances and strings of firecrackers. Honolulu's Chinatown is the center stage.

Oahu's *Narcissus Festival*, part of the Chinese New Year celebrations, runs for about five weeks and includes arts and crafts, food booths, a beauty pageant and coronation ball.

The *Hula Bowl*, the classic East/West college all-star football game, is held at Oahu's Aloha Stadium on a Saturday in January.

At the *Morey Bodyboards World Championships*, held on Oahu's North Shore in January, the world's top bodyboarders hit the Banzai Pipeline's towering waves.

Ka Molokai Makahiki, a modern-day version of the ancient makahiki festival, is held in Kaunakakai, Molokai, in mid-January. The week-long celebration features a tournament of traditional Hawaiian games and sporting events, an outrigger-canoe fishing contest and Hawaiian music and hula on the final day.

Martin Luther King Jr Day is a national holiday observed on the third Monday of the month.

The *Senior Skins Game*, a senior PGA tour golf tournament, takes place in late January at Mauna Lani Resort on the Big Island.

February

The *NFL Pro Bowl*, the annual all-star game of the National Football League, is held at Oahu's Aloha Stadium near the beginning of the month.

The *Cherry Blossom Festival*, which covers the entire month and spills over into March, features a variety of Japanese cultural events, including tea ceremonies, mochi pounding and taiko drummers. Most activities occur on Oahu.

Two PGA tour golf tournaments take place on Oahu in mid-February: the *Hawaiian Open* at Waialae Country Club and the *Hawaiian Ladies Open* at Kapolei Golf Course.

Buffalo's Big Board Surfing Classic, held at Oahu's Makaha Beach in February, is a surf contest using old-time 12-foot longboards.

Presidents' Day, a national holiday, is observed on the third Monday of the month.

The *Great Aloha Run* in Honolulu is a popular 8.2-mile fun run from Aloha Tower to Aloha Stadium on Presidents' Day.

March & April

The *East Maui Taro Festival*, held in Hana on a weekend in March, is a fun community event, featuring hula, music and food booths with taro samplings.

St Patrick's Day, March 17th, is celebrated with a parade down Waikiki's Kalakaua Ave.

The *Hawaiian Ski Cup*, a ski race down Mauna Kea, and *Pele's Cup Mauna Loa Cross Country*, the 'world's highest cross country ski race', are held on the Big Island in March – snow permitting.

Prince Kuhio Day, March 26th, is a state holiday which honors Jonah Kuhio Kalanianaole, Hawaii's first delegate to the US Congress. On his native island of Kauai there's a week-long festival, including canoe races, music and dance.

Easter falls in March or April. Many business offices are closed on *Good Friday* as well.

The *Merrie Monarch Festival*, named after King David Kalakaua, is Hawaii's biggest hula competition and Hawaiiana festival. Held in Hilo on the Big Island, it starts on Easter Sunday and lasts for a week.

The *O'Neill Invitational*, held at Maui's Hookipa Beach early in April, is the world's top international windsurfing competition.

The *Ulupalakula Thing*, a Saturday event in early April at Tedeschi Winery in Maui, is a fair-like trade show that offers the chance to sample food prepared by Maui's top chefs.

The *International Bed Race* in Oahu is an offbeat wheeled-bed race that runs along Kalakaua Ave to Kapiolani Park in late April.

May

May Day is Lei Day in Hawaii. Everybody dons a lei for this one, held on the first day of the month. There are lei-making competitions on several islands, and Oahu crowns a lei queen.

Molokai Ka Hula Piko, held on Molokai for a week in mid-May, celebrates the birth of the hula, with traditional dance performances, Hawaiian food, cultural demonstrations and visits to sacred sites.

The *Bankoh Kayak Challenge*, held in mid-May, is a 32-mile kayak race across the treacherous Kaiwi Channel, from Kaluakoi Resort on Molokai to Koko Marina, Oahu.

The *Keauhou-Kona Triathlon*, held on the last Sunday in May, is a half-Ironman with a mere 56-mile bike race, 13-mile run and 1.2-mile swim, starting at the Big Island's Keauhou Bay.

Memorial Day, on the last Monday in May, is a national holiday to honor soldiers killed in battle.

June

King Kamehameha Day is a state holiday celebrated on June 11 or the nearest weekend, with events on all islands. On Oahu the statue of Kamehameha is ceremoniously draped with leis, and there's a parade from downtown Honolulu to Kapiolani Park. On the Big Island the Kamehameha statue in the king's hometown of Kapaau is also draped with leis.

The Big Island's *Waikii Music Festival*, held at a polo grounds near Waimea on a weekend in mid-June, features top Hawaiian contemporary musicians, food booths and crafts.

The *King Kamehameha Hula & Chant Competition*, one of Hawaii's biggest hula contests, is held in Honolulu near the end of the month.

July

The Big Island's *Puuhonua O Honaunau Cultural Festival* is held at the Puuhonua O Honaunau national historical park on the weekend closest to July 1. The festival includes a 'royal court', a *hukilau* (net fishing with a seine), hula and traditional craft displays.

Independence Day, on the 4th, is a national holiday celebrated with fireworks and festivities on the main islands.

In odd-numbered years, sailboats in the *Transpacific Yacht Race* leave southern California on the July 4 weekend and arrive in Honolulu 10 to 14 days later. The race has been held since the turn of the century.

The *Makawao Rodeo* is an old-fashioned rodeo in the heart of Maui's cowboy country that lasts for a few days around the July 4th holiday.

The *TDK/Gotcha Pro* is a professional surf meet for both board surfers and bodysurfers held at Oahu's Sandy Beach, usually around mid-July.

The *Prince Lot Hula Festival*, held at Oahu's Moanalua Gardens on the third Saturday,

features hula competitors from Hawaii's major hula schools.

Kilauea Volcano Wilderness Marathon & Rim Runs at Hawaii Volcanoes National Park on the Big Island includes a 10-mile run around the rim of Kilauea, a 5.5-mile race into Kilauea Iki Crater and a 26.2-mile marathon through the Kau Desert. It's held near the end of July and draws an international crowd.

August

The *Obon* season, which is celebrated around the islands in July and August, is marked by traditional Japanese dances to honor deceased ancestors. The final event is a floating lantern ceremony at Waikiki's Ala Wai Canal on the evening of August 15.

The *Hawaiian International Billfish Tournament*, the world's number one marlin tournament, is held in Kailua-Kona on the Big Island. It lasts a week, usually beginning in early August, and includes a parade and fun events.

Admission Day is a state holiday on the third Friday that observes the anniversary of Hawaiian statehood.

The *Hawaiian Slack-Key Guitar Festival* features Hawaii's top slack key guitarists in a concert held at Honolulu's Ala Moana Beach Park.

The *Haleakala Run to the Sun* in Maui, a 36.2-mile marathon, begins at dawn at sea-level Paia and climbs 10,000 feet to the top of Haleakala. It's held in August or September.

Oahu's *Ka Himeni Ana* is a contest of old-style Hawaiian singing without amplification. All the songs are pre-WWII numbers that are sung in Hawaiian. It's held at the University of Hawaii in August or September.

September

Labor Day is a national holiday observed on the first Monday of the month.

Maui's annual *Hana Relay*, a 54-mile relay run from Kahului to Hana, is held in mid-September.

Aloha Week is a celebration of all things Hawaiian, with parades, cultural events, contests, canoe races and Hawaiian music. Festivities are staggered from mid-September to early October, depending on the island.

Na Wahine O Ke Kai, Hawaii's major annual women's outrigger canoe race, starts at sunrise at Kaluakoi, Molokai, and ends 40 miles later at Waikiki's Fort DeRussy Beach. It's held near the end of the month.

October

Columbus Day is a national holiday observed on the second Monday of the month.

Molokai Hoe is Hawaii's major men's outrigger canoe race, held near mid-month. It starts shortly after sunrise on Molokai and finishes at Waikiki's Fort DeRussy Beach about five hours later. Teams from Australia, Germany and the US mainland join Hawaiian teams in this annual competition, first held in 1952.

The Big Island's *Ironman Triathlon*, held on the Saturday in October closest to the full moon, is considered by many the ultimate endurance race. This is the triathlon that started it all and remains the world's best known. The 2.4-mile swim, 112-mile bike race and 26.2-mile marathon begins and ends at Kailua Pier.

The *Kona Coffee Cultural Festival*, a nine-day event held in Kailua-Kona in late October or early November, features a parade, a coffee-picking contest and cultural events.

November

The *Kapalua International* is a PGA tour golf tournament held in early November at Kapalua resort on Maui.

Election Day, the second Tuesday of the month, is a state holiday during election years.

Veterans Day, on the 11th, is a national holiday honoring veterans of the armed services.

The *Hawaii International Film Festival* features about 150 films from Pacific Rim and Asian nations. Films are shown throughout Oahu for a week around mid-November and on the Neighbor Islands the following week.

The *Triple Crown of Surfing* consists of three professional competitions that draw the world's top surfers to Oahu's North Shore. The events begin in November and run throughout December, with the exact dates depending on when the surf's up.

Thanksgiving is a national holiday celebrated on the fourth Thursday of the month.

December

Bodhi Day, the Buddhist Day of Enlightenment, is celebrated on the 8th with ceremonies at Buddhist temples.

The *Honolulu Marathon*, the second biggest marathon in the USA, is run mid-month along a 26-mile course from Aloha Tower to Kapiolani Park.

Christmas Day is a national holiday. Christmas festivals and craft fairs are held on all the islands throughout December.

The *Aloha Bowl* is a big collegiate football game held at Oahu's Aloha Stadium on Christmas Day and televised nationally.

First Night Honolulu, on New Year's Eve, is an alcohol-free evening of music, dance, art and family-oriented activities at 50 venues in Honolulu.

WORK

US citizens can pursue employment in Hawaii as elsewhere in the USA, while foreign visitors who are here for tourist purposes are not legally allowed to take up employment.

As Hawaii has had a relatively slow economy for the past few years, the job situation is not particularly rosy. Much of the economy is tied into the service industry, with wages hovering close to the minimum wage. For visitors, the most common work to land is waiting on tables, and if you're young and energetic there are possibilities in restaurants and clubs.

If you're hoping to find more serious 'professional' employment, note that Hawaii is considered a tight labor market, with a lack of diversified industries and a relatively immobile labor force. Those jobs that do open up are generally filled by established Hawaiian residents.

For more information on employment in Hawaii, contact the State Department of Labor & Industrial Relations (☎ 586-8700) at 830 Punchbowl St, Honolulu, HI 96813.

ACCOMMODATIONS

Hawaii has a wide variety of accommodations in all price ranges, including B&Bs, hotels and condominiums. There are also a handful of hostels and state park cabins that are quite inexpensive.

In Waikiki there are far more hotels than condos, while in Kihei and Kona the opposite is true. In most other major tourist destinations in Hawaii the number of hotels and condos are pretty evenly divided.

There are more than 75,000 hotel and condo rooms in the state. Oahu, which once boasted all of Hawaii's visitor accommodations and until 20 years ago still had 75%, has now slipped to about 50% as development continues full speed ahead on the Neighbor Islands.

Most places to stay in Hawaii have different rates for high season and low season (also called peak season and off season). High season most commonly applies to the winter period of December 15 to March 31. During this time many of the best-value places, particularly the smaller hotels and condos, are booked out well in advance. During the low season period of April to mid-December many places drop their rates by 10% to 30%, and getting the room of your choice without advance reservations is far easier.

If you are traveling with children, be aware that some B&Bs and historic inns prohibit children from staying, so it's important to inquire about their policies before making reservations.

Except where noted, the rates given in this book are the same for either singles or doubles. Rates do not include the combined room and sales tax of 10.17%, which is added to the price of all accommodations, including B&Bs.

Camping

Hawaii has numerous public campgrounds but no full-service private campgrounds of the KOA type found on the US mainland.

In general, camping in the national parks is better than in the state parks, and the state parks are better choices than the county parks.

Over the years there have been some assaults and numerous thefts targeted at off-island campers. The violence has decreased in most places, though a few campgrounds in rough areas, including the entire Waianae Coast of Oahu, are best avoided. People traveling alone, especially women, need to be particularly cautious.

In terms of theft, generally the less you look like a tourist the less likely you are to be targeted; always be careful with your valuables.

Pick your park carefully, especially the county parks. Some are well established with caretakers and attract other campers,

while others are pit stops along the road frequented mostly by drinkers.

For the most part, the farther you are from population centers, the less likely you are to run into hassles. Thieves and drunks aren't big on hiking. Backcountry camping is generally safe on all the islands – a twisted ankle, a wild boar or a cross-eyed hunter are the biggest safety concerns.

More information on all the following parks can be found in the individual island chapters.

National Parks There are two national parks in Hawaii that allow camping: Haleakala National Park on Maui and Hawaii Volcanoes National Park on the Big Island. These two parks offer some of the finest camping opportunities in Hawaii and also provide spectacular hiking. There are no camping fees at either, and the parks have both drive-up and wilderness camping areas; getting a space is seldom a problem.

State Parks The five largest islands have state park campgrounds. These range from wilderness areas that you need to backpack into to developed roadside campsites. Many also have cabins that can be rented (see the following Cabins section for details). State parks often have caretakers and better security than county parks.

Camping is allowed in the following places: on Kauai in Kokee, Na Pali Coast and Polihale state parks; on Oahu in Keaiwa Heiau, Malaekahana and Sand Island state recreation areas and Kahana Valley State Park; on Molokai in Palaau State Park; on Maui in Polipoli Spring State Recreation Area and Waianapanapa State Park; and on the Big Island in Kalopa State Park and MacKenzie State Recreation Area.

Camping in the state parks is free by permit. Developed campgrounds generally have picnic tables, barbecue grills, drinking water, toilets and showers, though the maintenance of the facilities varies greatly.

The maximum length of stay allowable at any one state park is five nights. Another camping permit for the same park will not be issued until 30 days have elapsed.

Campgrounds are open seven nights a week, except on Oahu where they are closed on Wednesday and Thursday nights. In addition, parks in forested areas may be closed during periods of drought due to extreme fire danger.

Permit applicants must be 18 and provide their address and phone number as well as an identification number (driver's license, passport or social security number) for each camper in the group. Applications should be received at least seven days in advance, but are not accepted earlier than 30 days before the intended camping date on Oahu or one year on the Neighbor Islands. Permits are issued on a first-come first-served basis, so it's best to apply as soon as possible; if you have a change of plans, be sure to cancel so other campers get a chance to use the space.

Camping permits can be obtained on weekdays from any of the following Division of State Parks offices, either in person, by mail or by phone.

Big Island
    Box 936, 75 Aupuni St, Hilo, HI 96721
    (☎ 974-6200)
Kauai
    3060 Eiwa St, Room 306, Lihue, HI 96766
    (☎ 274-3444)
Maui
    54 High St, Wailuku, HI 96793 (☎ 984-8109)
Oahu
    Box 621, 1151 Punchbowl St, Honolulu, HI
    96809 (☎ 587-0300)

County Parks All the counties have parks with camping areas, although not all are of equal standard. Some county parks have wonderful white-sand beaches and good facilities, while others are little more than unappealing roadside rest areas that have been turned into 'beach parks' simply by plopping down restrooms. Just because camping is allowed doesn't mean you'd want to camp there, or even use the beach.

Maui, which has the lion's share of Neighbor Island hotels and condos, seems more dedicated to getting your dollar than encouraging camping. Camping is allowed at only three county parks, each for only

three nights, and all have their drawbacks. The fee is $3 per person per night.

Molokai has two county parks with camping areas, one of which is delightfully set on Hawaii's largest white-sand beach. The fee is $3 per person per night.

The Big Island has 13 county campgrounds, a fee of only $1 per person per night and a maximum stay of two weeks (one week in summer) at each park.

Kauai has seven county campgrounds, including a couple of the nicest beachside camping spots in Hawaii. The fee is $3 per person per night and the maximum stay is one week at each park.

Oahu has 12 county campgrounds, a couple of which are recommendable and safe. There are no fees.

Cabins

The state has housekeeping cabins on the Big Island at Kalopa State Park and at the Kilauea and Mauna Kea state recreation areas, and on Maui at Polipoli Spring State Recreation Area and Waianapanapa State Park.

These cabins are generally simple places with a kitchen, a common area, a bathroom, one to three bedrooms, basic furnishings, bedding, hot showers and limited cooking and eating utensils. Polipoli, the most remote, has neither electricity nor refrigerators and you'll need a 4WD vehicle or good hiking boots to reach it. The cabins cost $45 per night for one to four people, $50 for five people or $55 for six people.

In addition to the housekeeping cabins, the state also has simple, enclosed A-frame shelters at Hapuna Beach State Park on the Big Island that cost $20 for one to four people.

People staying in the cabins are subject to the same five-day limit as tent campers.

Reservations can be made at any of the state park offices (listed above under Camping) and should be done as early as possible as the cabins are in high demand. Summer is the busiest time, but reservations can book up well in advance throughout the year. The state parks office does, however, get cancellations, and if someone with a reservation doesn't pay their deposit in time, the computer automatically bounces them and the site opens again.

Reservations can be made in person, by phone or by mail, with 50% of the fee due within two weeks of making the reservation. Personal checks are accepted if you're paying more than 30 days in advance, but otherwise you'll need a bank check or postal money order. The remainder is due in cash when you check in. Refunds require at least 15 days notice prior to the camping date.

In addition to the state-maintained cabins, there are concession-run cabins at Malaekahana State Recreation Area on Oahu and Kokee State Park on Kauai (see those sections for reservation information).

Hostels

Hawaii has two hostels associated with Hostelling International (HI). Both are on Oahu; one is in Waikiki and the other is a few miles away near the Honolulu campus of the University of Hawaii.

In addition, a number of private places offering inexpensive hostel-style accommodations have sprung up in the past couple of years. Private 'hostels' are located on Kauai in Kapaa; on Maui in Wailuku; on the Big Island in Kailua-Kona and Hilo; and on Oahu in Waikiki and Waimea. Some of the places are quite nice, while others are mere crash pads. Rates for a dorm bed range from about $12 to $16, and more expensive private rooms are often available as well.

B&Bs

There are hundreds of B&Bs scattered around Hawaii. Some are modest spare bedrooms in family households, others are romantic and private hideaways and a few are full-fledged inns. B&Bs generally begin around $50, although the average is closer to $70 and the most exclusive properties are $100 to $150. Many require a minimum stay of two or three days, and some give discounts for stays of a week or more. B&Bs vary greatly but for the most part they represent some of the best value accommodations to be found in Hawaii.

Because Hawaii state codes place restrictions on serving home-cooked meals, many B&Bs offer a continental breakfast or provide food for guests to cook their own. Some places do provide full home-cooked breakfasts – they just don't advertise it.

In this book, we recommend a number of B&Bs throughout Hawaii that you can book direct.

There are many other home-based B&Bs that don't handle their own reservations but sign up with B&B reservation services. Some of these agencies can book whole houses, condos and studio cottages as well. All require at least part of the payment in advance and have cancellation penalties. The following are reputable services that don't tack on needling booking fees:

Affordable Paradise Bed & Breakfast, Maria Wilson, 226 Pouli Rd, Kailua, HI 96734, books reasonably priced cottages, studios and B&Bs, with a primary focus on Oahu. Maria speaks German.
(☎ 261-1693; fax 261-7315)

All Islands Bed & Breakfast, 823 Kainui Drive, Kailua, HI 96734, books scores of host homes throughout Hawaii. There's a 3% fee if you use a credit card.
(☎ 263-2342, 800-542-0344; fax 263-0308)

Bed & Breakfast Hawaii, Box 449, Kapaa, HI 96746, is one of the larger services. For $13 they'll send you a guidebook-style directory from which you can select a B&B, or you can simply book by phone.
(☎ 822-7771, 800-733-1632; fax 822-2723; bandb@aloha.net)

Three Bears Hawaii Reservations, 72-1001 Puukala, Kailua-Kona, HI 96740, books 200 B&Bs throughout Hawaii, including many moderately priced ones. The amiable operators – Anne, Nanette and Art Stockel – speak German. (☎ /fax 325-7563, 800-765-0480; three.bears@pobox.com)

Condominiums

Condominiums are individually owned apartments that are fully furnished with everything a visitor needs, from linen and towels to dishes and cutlery. Condos have more space than hotel rooms, generally with a living room and full kitchen, and many also have washer/dryers, sofa beds and a *lanai* (veranda). Unlike hotels, most condos don't have a daily room-cleaning service.

Although some condo complexes operate similarly to hotels, with a front desk, most condos are booked through rental agents. If you're staying awhile or are traveling with several people, condos almost always work out cheaper than all but the bottom-end hotels. However, most condo units booked through rental agents have a three- to seven-day minimum stay, require deposits and have hefty cancellation fees.

Condos often offer weekly and monthly rates. The general rule is that the weekly rate is six times the daily rate and the monthly is three times the weekly.

As condo rental agencies generally deal with specific destinations, they are listed in the individual island chapters.

Hotels

In Hawaii, as elsewhere, hotels commonly undercut their standard published rates to remain as close to capacity as possible. While some hotels simply offer discounted promotional rates to pick up the slack, a few of the larger chains, such as Outrigger and Hawaiian Pacific Resorts, often throw in a free rental car. Before booking any hotel, it's worth asking if they're currently running any specials – some places actually have room/car packages for less than the 'standard' room rate!

While a good travel agent at home may know about some of these discounts, many of the best deals are advertised only in Hawaii, and to find them you'll need to pick up a Honolulu newspaper. The travel section of the Sunday *Honolulu Advertiser* (see Newspapers & Magazines, earlier) is best.

At most hotels the rooms are basically the same, with rates usually corresponding to two variables: the view and the floor. An ocean view often costs 50% to 100% more than a parking lot view, which is sometimes euphemistically called 'garden view'. Also the higher you go, the higher the tariff; the higher floors are generally quieter, especially on busy roads.

The toll-free numbers given in this book are for calls from the mainland and usually can't be dialed within Hawaii. However, some hotels will accept collect calls from the Neighbor Islands – it never hurts to try.

If you have a Hawaii driver's license, always ask about *kamaaina* rates, as many middle and top-range hotels give Hawaii residents big discounts.

The Hawaii Visitors Bureau (see Tourist Offices, earlier) will mail out on request a free annual accommodations guide listing member hotels with addresses and prices. It includes virtually all of Hawaii's resort hotels and most of those in the moderate price range.

Travel Clubs

Travel clubs can provide handsome discounts on accommodations. Essentially, hotels and condos try to fill last-minute rooms by offering cut rates to members of these clubs. In many cases you aren't allowed to book more than 30 days in advance and rooms are limited during the busiest periods. A few places even black out winter dates altogether.

Many of Hawaii's largest hotel chains participate in the two travel clubs listed below. Both allow members to book hotels directly, so they're easier to use than travel clubs that act more like reservation services.

By far the most prominent is the Entertainment program, which produces an annual book to Hawaii listing scores of hotels that offer members 50% off their standard published rates. It also has about 100 restaurants with two-for-one meals (or 50% off meals for single diners) and numerous coupons for other discounts. The books, which include a membership card, can be ordered by mail (☎ 800-374-4464) for $43 or purchased in Hawaii at Borders bookstore and other places (☎ 737-3252 for Hawaii locations).

Another popular club, Encore (☎ 800-638-0930), offers the same 50% room discounts and a similar list of hotels as Entertainment, but the dining benefits are more marginal. Annual membership costs $50.

One important difference between the two clubs is that Entertainment membership is valid for a one-year period beginning and ending December 1 – a problem for travelers who arrive in November and stay into December. Encore, on the other hand, is valid for 12 months from the time you enroll.

Keep in mind that the number of businesses participating in these programs varies significantly with the economy. When hotel occupancy is low, participation booms, and when the economy is brisk, more businesses pull out of the clubs or add restrictions. The Outrigger company, for instance, currently offers the discount at all of its Neighbor Island hotels, but it has limited participation to only half a dozen of its 20 Waikiki hotels.

Certainly these clubs will work out best for those who are in Hawaii for longer periods of time, have flexibility with hotel preferences and dates, and are traveling outside of the peak winter season.

FOOD

Eating in Hawaii can be a real treat, as the islands' ethnic diversity has given rise to hundreds of different cuisines. You can find every kind of Japanese food, an array of regional Chinese cuisines, spicy Korean specialties, native Hawaiian dishes and excellent Thai and Vietnamese food. Even McDonald's serves up saimin and Portuguese sausage, and Woolworth has sushi at the lunch counter.

Although you could spend a bundle eating out, you don't need to, as there are good, cheap neighborhood restaurants to explore on all the islands.

Hawaii also has many restaurants run by renowned chefs that feature gourmet foods of all type, including traditional continental fare. Some of the best restaurants are at the top-end hotels, although a fair number of the more successful chefs have moved on to open their own places.

Many of these 'renegade chefs' specialize in what's been dubbed 'Pacific Rim' or 'Hawaiian Regional' cuisine, which incorporates fresh island ingredients and borrows liberally from the islands' various ethnic groups. It's marked by creative com-

Fish	
Some of the most popular locally caught fish include:	
Hawaiian Name	**Common Name**
ahi	yellowfin tuna
aku	skipjack tuna
au	swordfish, marlin
kaku	barracuda
mahimahi	a fish called 'dolphin' (not the mammal)
mano	shark
onaga	red snapper
ono	wahoo
opah	moonfish
opakapaka	pink snapper
papio or *ulua*	jack fish
uhu	parrotfish
uku	gray snapper ■

binations such as kiawe-grilled freshwater shrimp with taro chips, wok-charred ahi with island greens, and Peking duck in ginger-lilikoi sauce.

Fresh fish is readily available throughout the islands. Seafood is generally expensive at places catering to tourists, but can be quite reasonable at neighborhood restaurants.

Fruit

Hawaii has an abundance of fruit including avocado, banana, breadfruit, starfruit, coconut, guava, lychee, mango, papaya, *lilikoi* (passion fruit) and pineapple. Sweet Kau oranges are grown on the Big Island.

Watermelons grown on Molokai are so famous throughout the islands that the airlines had to create special regulations for passengers carrying them out of Molokai to prevent loose melons from bombing their way down the aisles.

Wild fruits can be sometimes be found along trails; these include strawberry guava, common guava, thimbleberries, mountain apples, Methley plums and ohelo berries.

Hawaiian Food

The traditional Hawaiian feast marking special events is the *luau*. Local luaus are still commonplace in modern Hawaii for

Tropical Fruit

Pineapple Hawaii's number one fruit crop is the pineapple. Most Hawaiian pineapples are of the smooth cayenne type and weigh a good five pounds. Pineapples are fairly unique among fruits in that they don't continue to ripen after they're picked. Although they're harvested year round, the long sunny days of summer produce the sweetest pineapples.

Papaya Papayas come in several varieties. One of the best of those found in grocery stores is the Solo, a small variety with pale strawberry-colored flesh. The flavor of papayas depends largely on where they're grown. Some of the most prized are from the Kapoho area of Puna on the Big Island and the Kahuku area of Oahu. Papayas, which are a good source of calcium and vitamins A and C, are harvested all year round.

Mango Big old mango trees are abundant in Hawaii, even in remote valleys. The juicy oblong fruits are about three inches in diameter and four to six inches long. The fruits start out green but take on deeper colors as they ripen, usually reddening to an apricot color. Mangoes are a good source of vitamins A and C. Two popular varieties, Pirie and Haden, are less stringy than those usually found in the wild. Mangoes are mainly a summer fruit.

Avocado Hawaii has three main types of avocado: the West Indian, a smooth-skinned variety that matures in summer and autumn; the rough-skinned Guatemalan, which matures in winter and spring; and the Mexican variety, which has a small fruit and smooth skin. Many of the avocados now in Hawaii are a hybrid of the three. Local fruit tends to be larger and more watery than the avocados grown in California.

Starfruit The carambola, or starfruit, is a translucent yellow-green fruit with five ribs like the points of a star. It has a crisp, juicy pulp and can be eaten without being peeled.

Guava The common guava is a yellow, lime-shaped fruit, about two to three inches in diameter. It has a moist, pink, seedy flesh, all of which is edible. Guavas can be a little tart but tend to sweeten as they ripen. They're a good source of vitamin C and niacin and can be found along roadsides and trails.

Lilikoi Passion fruit is a vine with beautiful flowers that grow into small round fruits. The thick skin of the fruit is generally purple or yellow and wrinkles as it ripens. The pulp inside is juicy, seedy and slightly tart. The slimy texture can be a bit of a put-off the first time, but once you taste it you'll be hooked.

Mountain Apple The mountain apple is a small oval fruit a couple of inches long. The tree is related to the guava, though the fruit is completely different with a crispy white flesh and a pink skin. It fruits in the summer and is common along trails.

Ohelo These berries grow on low shrubs common in lava areas. It's a relative of the cranberry, similar in tartness and size. The fruit is red or yellow and is used in jellies and pies.

Breadfruit The Hawaiian breadfruit is a large, round, green fruit. It's comparable to potatoes in carbohydrates and is prepared much the same way. In old Hawaii, as in much of the Pacific, breadfruit was one of the traditional staples. ∎

events such as baby christenings. In spirit, these luaus are far more authentic than any of the commercial tourist luaus, but they're family affairs and the short-stay visitor would be lucky indeed to get an invitation to one.

The main course at a luau is *kalua* pig, which is roasted in a pit-like earthen oven known as an *imu*. The imu is readied for cooking by building a fire and heating rocks in the pit. When the rocks are glowing red, layers of moisture-laden banana trunks and green ti leaves are placed over the stones. A pig that has been slit open is filled with some of the hot rocks and laid on top of the bed. Other foods wrapped in ti and banana leaves are placed around it. It's all covered with more ti leaves and a layer of mats and topped off with dirt to seal in the heat, which then bakes and steams the food. Anything cooked in this style is called *kalua*.

The process takes about four to eight hours, depending on the amount of food. A few of the hotel luaus still bake the pig outdoors in this traditional manner and you can often go in the morning and watch them prepare and bury the pig.

Wetland taro is used to make *poi*, a paste pounded from cooked taro corms. Water is added to make it pudding-like and its consistency is measured in one-, two- or three-finger poi – which indicates how many fingers are required to bring it from bowl to mouth. Poi is highly nutritious and easily digestible, but it's an acquired taste. It is sometimes fermented to give it a zingier flavor.

Laulau is fish, pork and taro wrapped in a ti leaf bundle and steamed. *Lomi* salmon is made by marinating thin slices of raw salmon with diced tomatoes and green onions.

Other Hawaiian foods include baked *ulu* – breadfruit, *limu* – seaweed, *opihi* – tiny limpet shells that fishers pick off the reef at low tide, and *pipikaula* – beef jerky. *Haupia*, the standard dessert to a Hawaiian meal, is a custard made of coconut cream thickened with cornstarch or arrowroot.

In Hawaiian food preparation, ti leaves

are indispensable, functioning like a biodegradable version of both aluminum foil and paper plates: food is wrapped in it, cooked in it and served upon it.

Many visitors taste traditional Hawaiian food only at expensive luaus or by sampling a dollop of poi at one of the more adventurous hotel buffet meals. Although Hawaiian food is harder to find than other ethnic foods, there are a few restaurants throughout the islands that serve the real thing, and it's some of the cheapest food in Hawaii.

Local Food

The distinct style of food called 'local' usually refers to a fixed-plate lunch with 'two scoop rice', a scoop of macaroni salad and a serving of beef stew, mahimahi or teriyaki chicken, generally scarfed down with chopsticks. A breakfast plate might have Spam, eggs, kimchee and, always, two scoops of rice.

These plate meals are the standard fare in diners and lunch wagons. If it's full of starches, fats and gravies, you're probably eating local.

Snacks

Pupus is the word for all kinds of munchies or hors d'oeuvres. Boiled peanuts, soy-flavored rice crackers called *kaki mochi* and sashimi are common pupus.

Poke A local favorite is *poke*, which is raw fish marinated in soy sauce, oil, chili peppers, green onions and seaweed. It comes in many varieties – sesame ahi is a particularly delicious one – and all make a nice accompaniment with beer.

Crack Seed Crack seed is a Chinese snack food that can be sweet, sour, salty or some combination of the three. It's often made from dried fruits, such as plums and apricots, although more exotic ones include sweet and sour baby cherry seeds, pickled mangoes and *li hing mui*, one of the sour favorites. Crack seed shops often sell dried cuttlefish, roasted green peas, candied ginger, beef jerky and rock candy as well.

Shave Ice Shave ice is similar to mainland snow cones, only better. The ice is shaved as fine as powder snow, packed into a paper cone and drenched with sweet fruit-flavored syrups. Many islanders like the ones with ice cream and/or sweet azuki beans at the bottom, while kids usually opt for rainbow shave ice, which has colorful stripes of different syrups.

DRINKS
Nonalcoholic Drinks
Tap water is safe to drink, but water from freshwater streams should be boiled.

Cans of Hawaiian-made fruit juices such as guava-orange or passion fruit are stocked at most stores. If you're going for a hike and want to toss a couple of drinks in your daypack, the juices make a good alternative to sodas, as they don't explode when shaken and they taste good even when they're not kept cold.

Alcoholic Drinks
The drinking age in Hawaii is 21. It's illegal to have open containers of alcohol in motor vehicles and, although it's a common scene, drinking in public parks or on the beaches is also illegal. All grocery stores sell liquor, as do most of the smaller food marts. People in their early 20s – or those who look like they are – will need to show a driver's license, passport or similar photo ID to purchase alcohol.

Tedeschi Vineyards, a local winery on Maui, makes a good pineapple wine, grape wine and champagne.

Microbreweries have recently popped up on Oahu, Maui and the Big Island, producing a variety of British or German influenced ales and lagers. Although most sell in their own brewpubs only, the Big Island's Kona Brewing Company bottles its ales for sale in grocery stores and restaurants.

ENTERTAINMENT
Hawaii has an active and varied entertainment scene, and you won't suffer for want of nightlife. Big-name musicians from the mainland like to vacation in Hawaii, and folks like Hootie & the Blowfish, Jackson Brown, Willie Nelson and Michael Jackson include Hawaii in their tours.

There's plenty of Hawaiian entertainment as well, including contemporary Hawaiian music, slack-key guitar performances and hula shows. For detailed information, see the Entertainment sections in the island chapters.

SPECTATOR SPORTS
In part because of its isolation and relatively low population, Hawaii doesn't have major league sports teams. From October through December, however, players from Japanese, Korean and US minor-league baseball organizations come to Hawaii to hone their skills as participants in a winter baseball league. There are four teams: the Honolulu Sharks, who use the University of Hawaii's Rainbow Stadium as their home field; the West Oahu Canefires, at Hans L'Orange Field in Waipahu; the Maui Stingrays, at the War Memorial Stadium in Wailuku; and the Hilo Stars at the Wong Stadium in Hilo. Tickets cost $4 to $6; schedules are printed in the sports pages of local newspapers.

Honolulu's Aloha Stadium hosts three nationally televised football events each winter: the NFL Pro Bowl, an all-star game of the National Football League; the Hula Bowl, an all-star East/West college football game; and the Aloha Bowl, another major collegiate football game. For ticket information contact the Aloha Stadium ticket office (☎ 486-9300) as far in advance as possible.

Still, some of the most popular spectator sports in Hawaii aren't mainland imports. Surfing, boogie boarding and windsurfing contests attract some of the world's top wave riders and bring out scores of onlookers.

For information on specific sporting events, see the Holidays & Special Events section earlier in this chapter.

THINGS TO BUY
Hawaii has a lot of fine craftspeople, and quality handicrafts can be readily found on all the islands.

Woodworkers use beautifully grained native Hawaiian hardwoods, such as koa, to create calabashes and bowls. Hawaiian bowls are not decorated or ornate, but rather are shaped to bring out the natural beauty of the wood. The thinner and lighter the bowl, the finer the artistic skill and the greater the value.

There are some excellent island potters, many influenced by Japanese styles and aesthetics. Good raku work in particular can be found throughout the islands at reasonable prices.

Lauhala, the leaves of the pandanus tree that were once woven into the mats that Hawaiians slept on, are now woven into placemats, hats and baskets.

Music shops carry recorded traditional and contemporary Hawaiian music. Hula musical instruments such as nose flutes and gourd rattles are uniquely Hawaiian and make interesting gifts.

Niihau shell leis, made from the tiny shells that wash up on the island of Niihau, are one of the most prized Hawaiiana souvenirs. Elaborate pieces can cost thousands of dollars.

Hawaii's island-style clothing is colorful and light, often with prints of tropical flowers. The classiest aloha shirts are of lightweight cotton with subdued colors (like those of reverse fabric prints). Women might want to buy a *muumuu*, a loose, comfortable, full-length Hawaiian-style dress.

Foods are popular purchases. The standard souvenir is macadamia nuts, either canned or covered in chocolate. Kona coffee, macadamia nut butters, lilikoi or *poha* berry preserves and mango chutney all make convenient, compact gift items.

Pineapples are not a great choice in the souvenir department. Not only are they heavy and bulky, but they're likely to be just as cheap at home.

For those who enjoy Japanese food, Hawaii is a good place to pick up ingredients that might be difficult to find back home. Most grocery stores have a wide selection of things like dried seaweed, mochi and ume plums.

Flowers such as orchids, anthuriums and proteas make good gifts if you're flying straight home. Proteas stay fresh for about 10 days and then can be dried. Foreign visitors should check with their airline in advance, however, as there are commonly restrictions against bringing agricultural products across international borders.

Outdoor Activities

Hawaii has an exhaustive variety of sports and recreational activities available to visitors. In addition to top conditions for practically all water sports, there are also fine opportunities for hiking, biking, jogging, tennis, golf, horseback riding, you name it. There's even snow skiing on the Big Island in winter.

Hawaii is a great place to learn to dive, surf or windsurf. Equipment rental is available on the main islands, and most places that rent the equipment also give lessons to beginners. Hawaii has 750 miles of coastline, and all of its 283 beaches are public up to the high water mark.

Except for sports competitions or specialized tours, few activities require advance planning before you get to Hawaii.

More detailed information on all activities – including shops, prices and phone numbers – is given in each island chapter.

SURFING

Hawaii lies smack in the path of all the major swells that race unimpeded across the Pacific, so it comes as no surprise that the sport of surfing got its start in these islands hundreds of years ago with the early Hawaiians.

Hawaii has good surfing throughout the year, with the biggest waves hitting from November to February along the north shores of the islands. Summer swells, which break along the south shores, are usually not as frequent and nowhere near as large as the northside winter swells.

Oahu's north shore has Hawaii's top surf action. The winter swells at Waimea, Sunset Beach and the Banzai Pipeline can bring in 30-foot waves, creating the conditions that legends are made of. Waikiki has Oahu's top south shore surfing.

Maui and Kauai also have some excellent surfing spots. The Big Island and Molokai are not as notable, but it is possible to surf on both islands.

H30, a monthly magazine that interviews surfers and reports on surfing events and surf conditions, can be picked up free at surf shops around Oahu. By mail, annual subscriptions cost $36 in the USA, $72 in other countries, from H30 (☎ 488-7873), 99-1405 Koaha Place, Suite A1, Aiea, HI 96701.

WINDSURFING

Maui has some of the world's best windsurfing action, with Hookipa Beach near Paia hosting top international windsurfing competitions. Hookipa's death-defying conditions, which include dangerous shore breaks and razor-sharp coral, are for expert windsurfers only, but tamer spots that are well suited for beginners can be found on other parts of Maui, such as Kihei.

Oahu also has lots of windsurfing activity, with some spots ideal for beginners and other locales boasting advanced wave-riding conditions. Oahu's Kailua Beach attracts the biggest crowd with its excellent year-round wind.

Although Maui and Oahu are by far the top two islands for windsurfing, Kauai also has some fairly good windsurfing spots, most notably Anini Beach on its north shore, which has conditions good for both beginners and more advanced windsurfers. The Big Island doesn't rate as a windsurfing destination, although if you're there and want to windsurf, there are a couple of beaches with reasonable conditions. It's possible to rent gear and take lessons on all four islands.

Although there are good windsurfing conditions in Hawaii year round, winter can have flat periods. In general, the best winds are from June to September.

Most of the major windsurfing shops in Kailua on Oahu and in Kahului on Maui can arrange tours that package together windsurfing gear rental, accommodations and, in some cases, car rental and air fare.

DIVING

There's good year-round diving in Hawaii. Under normal conditions, the leeward shores of the islands have the best diving most months of the year. The north shores are usually best in the summer.

Hawaiian waters have excellent visibility, with water temperatures ranging from 72°F to 80°F.

The marine life around the islands is superb. Almost 700 fish species live in Hawaiian waters, with nearly one-third of those found nowhere else in the world. Divers often see spinner dolphins, green sea turtles, manta rays and moray eels. Although it's rare for divers to see humpback whales underwater, they do sometimes hear them singing.

Hawaii has underwater caves, canyons, lava tubes, vertical walls and sunken ships. There are all sorts of colorful sponges and corals, including the gem-like black coral.

The four largest islands all have some excellent diving opportunities and numerous dive shops. Complete gear can be rented, and prices are quite competitive.

If you want to experience diving for the first time, some of the dive operations offer a short beginner's 'try scuba' course for nondivers that includes a brief instruction, followed by a shallow beach or boat dive. The cost generally ranges from $60 to $90, depending upon the operation and whether a boat is used.

For those who want to jump into the sport wholeheartedly, a number of shops also offer full open-water certification courses in either PADI or NAUI. The cost generally ranges from $300 to $400, equipment included, and the entire course usually takes the better part of a week.

Snuba

If you want to get beneath the surface but aren't ready for a dive course, snuba offers an experience in between snorkeling and diving. Snuba utilizes a long air hose attached to an air tank on an inflatable raft that floats on the water's surface. The diver simply wears a mask and weight belt and can dive down as far as the air hose allows.

All snuba programs include elementary dive instruction that essentially explains how to clear your face mask and equalize ear pressure. An instructor is in the water with you during the entire dive. It makes for a quick and easy introduction to the underwater world and can certainly whet one's appetite for more serious diving. Generally, the best snuba experiences are those from boats, as you can get to better dive sites, but snuba from the beach is also available. Snuba is currently offered on Oahu, Kauai and the Big Island.

SNORKELING

Donning a mask and snorkel allows one to turn the beach into an underwater aquarium. There are numerous sites throughout Hawaii that offer splendid coral gardens and varied and abundant reef fish. Hawaii's near-shore waters harbor some 20 different kinds of butterfly fish, large rainbow-colored parrotfish, numerous varieties of wrasses, bright yellow tangs, odd-shaped filefish and ballooning pufferfish, just to list a few.

Some travelers cart along their own mask, snorkel and fins, but these can be rented on the islands from dive shops for around $15 a week or from water sports huts on some of the busier beaches, though rates tend to be higher.

KAKAYING

Kayaking is becoming increasingly popular in Hawaii, spurred in part by the newer types of stable kayaks that are suitable for beginners.

By far the most popular kayaking destination is Kauai, which offers both navigable rivers leading to scenic natural sights and ocean kayaking along the spectacular Na Pali Coast. In winter, when the north shore surf gets rough, ocean kayaking moves to the less spectacular but still pleasant south shore.

Ocean kayaking is also picking up in Maui, with the primary destination along the southwest coast – which can be a splendid whale-watching area in winter. On both Kauai and Maui you can rent kayaks to head off on your own or join guided tours.

Molokai, whose undeveloped north shore boasts the world's highest sea cliffs, is an overlooked but unsurpassed kayaking destination for those seeking solitude. Suitable for kayaking only in the calm summer months, it takes about five days to explore and is certainly not for the faint of heart. Fun Hogs, the Molokai outfitter, can set you up for the self-guided tour and also offers tamer half-day guided tours along Molokai's west and south shores.

Kayaking is more low-key on Oahu and the Big Island, but there are possibilities for rentals.

FISHING

Hawaii has some of the world's best deep-sea fishing, with Kona holding most of the world records for Pacific blue marlin. Not surprisingly, Kona has the biggest charter fishing boat industry, although charters can be arranged on other islands as well.

In addition to ocean fishing, the state maintains four public freshwater fishing areas: in Kokee on Kauai, in Wahiawa and Nuuanu on Oahu and at Waiakea on the Big Island. Stocked fish include rainbow trout, largemouth and smallmouth bass, bluegill sunfish, channel catfish, tilapia and carp.

Licenses are required for freshwater fishing. A 30-day license for nonresidents costs $3.75 (free for those ages 65 and older).

No licenses are required for saltwater fishing when the catch is for private consumption. There are, however, seasons, size limits and/or other restrictions on taking *ula* (spiny lobster), crab, octopus *(hee* in Hawaiian, and also called tako or squid), *opihi* (a kind of limpet), *limu* (seaweed) and certain species of fish. Clams and oysters cannot be taken.

Also, seek local advice before eating your catch, as ciguatera poisoning (see Health in the Facts for the Visitor chapter) has become more common in recent years.

The booklets *Hawaii Fishing Regulations* and *Freshwater Fishing in Hawaii* may be obtained free from the Division of Aquatic Resources (☎ 587-0100), Department of Land & Natural Resources, 1151 Punchbowl St, Room 330, Honolulu, HI 96813.

WHALE WATCHING

Approximately 1200 of the North Pacific's estimated 2000 humpback whales winter in Hawaiian waters, providing visitors with some fantastic whale-watching opportunities. Humpbacks begin filtering in to Hawaii around November and some stay as late as May, with most in residence from January to March.

Humpback whales prefer waters with depths of less than 600 feet, which means in Hawaii they're found relatively close to the shore. At times they can be spotted off any of the Hawaiian islands, but the largest numbers are found in the shallow waters between Maui, Lanai, Molokai and Kahoolawe. The Kona coast of the Big Island is another favored spot, as is the Penguin Bank west of Molokai.

Whales can often be seen right from shore, with the best possibilities along the

Na Ala Hele
Of special interest to hikers and naturalists is the work of Na Ala Hele, a group affiliated with Hawaii's Division of Forestry & Wildlife.

Na Ala Hele was established in 1988 with the task of documenting public access to trails as part of a movement to preserve Hawaii's natural environment and cultural heritage. Throughout the state, they've negotiated with private landowners and the military to gain access to previously restricted areas and re-establish abandoned trails.

The Na Ala Hele logo signpost is marking an increasing number of trailheads as their work continues. For more information, contact Na Ala Hele (☎ 587-0058), Division of Forestry & Wildlife, 567 S King St, Suite 132, Honolulu, HI 96813. ■

west coast of Maui. To get even closer, take one of the seasonal whale-watch cruises, which depart from all the main islands. Other possibilities for whale watching include kayaking along the shoreline or hopping on the Maui-Lanai ferry, which cruises past prime humpback territory.

See also Whales under Flora & Fauna in the Facts about Hawaii chapter.

HIKING

Hawaii has many first-rate hiking opportunities. Like the islands themselves, the hiking options are incredibly varied, from desert treks to lush rainforest walks, and from beach strolls to snowy ridgeline trails. Hikes range from short family-style nature strolls that can be walked in an hour to backcountry treks that can last several days and require backpacking in your own food, water and gear.

Despite all the development on Hawaii, it's amazing how much of the islands are still in a natural state. There are places where you could walk for days without seeing another soul.

The hiking trails of Hawaii's two national parks have no parallels anywhere. Both have barren lunar-like landscapes as well as lush, tropical forests.

Hawaii Volcanoes National Park on the Big Island has the distinction of containing both the world's most active volcano and the world's largest mountain mass. The park has breathtaking hikes down into steaming crater floors and others that climb the snowcapped summit of Mauna Loa.

At Haleakala National Park on Maui

the volcano is sleepier but equally awe-inspiring. Hikes into the caldera of the world's largest crater can take half a day, while hikes across its floor can take half a week.

Still, the premier hike in all of Hawaii is on Kauai's Na Pali Coast, where the Kalalau Trail follows an ancient Hawaiian footpath along the edges of the most spectacularly fluted coastal cliffs in Hawaii. The trail winds down into lush valleys where camping is allowed and waterfalls and ruins can be explored.

There are also hiking trails into other ancient valleys, such as Waipio on the Big Island. On Maui and the Big Island you can follow old 'king's trails' along footpaths worn through the lava by the bare feet of travelers over hundreds of years. Every island has ridgeline trails with panoramic views, as well as trails to secluded beaches and waterfalls. On some islands there are also trails in nature preserves where you can examine native plants and birds and enjoy lots of solitude.

There are organizations that offer guided hikes on the major islands, the most active of which is the Sierra Club, with branches on Oahu, Maui, Kauai and the Big Island. Send $2 to the Sierra Club, Box 2577, Honolulu, HI 96803, for a schedule of upcoming hikes, call ☎ 538-6616 for recorded information or simply look in the activity listings in local newspapers once you arrive.

Safety & Tips A number of Hawaii's hiking trails take you into steep, narrow valleys with gullies that require stream crossings. The capital rule here is that if the water begins to rise it's not safe to cross, as a flash flood may be imminent. Instead, head for higher ground and wait it out.

Flash floods are the biggest dangers on trails, followed by falling rocks. Be wary of swimming under high waterfalls, as rocks can dislodge from the top, and be careful on the edge of steep cliffs, as cliffside rock in Hawaii tends to be crumbly.

Darkness sets in soon after sunset in Hawaii, and ridgetop trails are not the place to be caught unprepared for it. It's a good idea to carry a flashlight when you're hiking, just in case.

Jeans will protect your legs from the overgrown parts of the trail, and sturdy footwear with good traction is advisable on most hikes. Hawaiian trails tend to be quite slippery when wet, so a walking stick always makes a good companion.

Hawaii has no snakes, no poison ivy, no poison oak and few dangers from wild animals. There's a slim possibility of meeting up with a large boar in the backwoods, but they're unlikely to be a problem unless cornered.

RUNNING
More than 100 road races, ranging from fun runs to triathlons, are held in the islands each year.

Hawaii's best known races are the Honolulu Marathon, held in December, which has mushroomed into a huge event in recent years, and the world-renowned Ironman Triathlon, held in Kona on the Big Island in October.

Other well-attended races include the Great Aloha Run, an 8.2-mile jaunt held in Honolulu every February; the Oahu Perimeter Relay, a 133-mile relay race around

---

Ironman Triathlon
The Ironman, the first and foremost of all triathlons, takes place each October on the sunny Kona coast, starting and ending in Kailua-Kona. It's a grueling, nonstop combination of a 2.4-mile swim, 112-mile bike race and 26.2-mile run that draws the world's top triathletes. Competitors have 17 hours to finish the race, though the top athletes cross the finish line in about half that time. The current men's record, set by Luc Van Lierde of Belgium in 1996, is eight hours and four minutes, while the women's record, set by Paula Newby-Fraser of Zimbabwe in 1992, is eight hours and 55 minutes.

The total prize purse is $250,000, with both the top male and female finishers receiving $35,000 each. The top 10 men and women across the finish line share the remainder of the purse, with the second-place finisher receiving $25,000, third-place $20,000 and fourth-place $15,000.

The world's first-ever triathlon, the Ironman began in 1978 with just 15 participants. The following year, the event was covered by Sports Illustrated, which labeled it 'lunatic'. By 1980, the Ironman was drawing enough participants to receive TV coverage on ABC's Wide World of Sports, and since that time its popularity has continued to grow by leaps and bounds.

These days, some 20,000 triathletes compete in 20 worldwide qualifiers in hopes of earning one of the 1500 entry berths in the Ironman event. The athletes who participate in the Ironman represent each US state and Canadian province and approximately 48 other countries.

Harsh Kona conditions make the event the ultimate endurance test, even by triathlon standards. Heat reflected off the lava landscape crossed by the race commonly exceeds 100°F, making dehydration and heat exhaustion major challenges. Many contenders arrive weeks before the race just to acclimate themselves. On the day of the race, nearly 5000 volunteers line up along the 140-mile course to offer water to passing racers; in all, they hand out some 12,500 gallons of water – more than eight gallons for each triathlete!

To learn more about the race, including qualifying requirements, contact Ironman Triathlon World Championship (☎ 329-0063), 75-127 Lunapule Rd, Suite 11, Kailua-Kona, HI 96740. ■

Oahu in late February; the Maui Marathon, a marathon from Kahului to Kaanapali in late March; and the Kilauea Volcano Wilderness Marathon & Rim Runs, which includes a marathon and shorter races at Hawaii Volcanoes National Park on the Big Island in late July.

The Department of Parks & Recreation of the City & County of Honolulu (650 S King St, Honolulu, HI 96813) has a schedule of annual running events that it will mail out upon request.

The bimonthly magazine *Hawaii Race* (☎ 922-4222), 3442 Waialae Ave, No 1, Honolulu, HI 96816, includes upcoming statewide race schedules, qualification details and actual entry forms for the major races. Subscriptions are $18 a year; a sample copy will be sent free on request.

MOUNTAIN BIKING

Mountain biking is gaining popularity in Hawaii, and mountain bikes can now be rented on all the main islands. While cycling along roads isn't a problem – other than the shortage of bike lanes – getting off the beaten path is a bit more complicated, since access to public forests and trails is limited.

On Maui, which just a few years ago had no legally accessible offroad trails, the Maui Mountain Bike Club has worked out an agreement with the state for bike access to some of the hiking trails in Polipoli Spring State Recreation Area; in return for access, the club helps maintain the trails.

On the Big Island, which is big on space, the county has designated a number of areas that bikers can use and has funded the publication of a new mountain biking trail map. The routes include the 45-mile Mana Rd loop that circles around Mauna Kea and the beach trail to Pine Trees on the Kona Coast.

On Kauai, the state forestry department has opened 18 of its trails to mountain bikers, including the 13-mile Powerline Trail and the Waimea Canyon Trail.

On densely populated Oahu, where mountain bikers are often pitted against hikers, there are fewer options. Bikes have been banned from the Tantalus trails because tire tracks were causing trail erosion. The state is now considering opening the trails in the dry summer months but keeping them closed to cyclists in the rainier winter season. In the meantime, the paved Tantalus Drive, which is also open to vehicle travel, remains a popular biking route.

Getting There & Away

AIR

Hawaii is a major Pacific hub and an intermediate stop on many flights between the US mainland and Asia, Australia, New Zealand and the South Pacific. Passengers on any of these routes can usually make a free stopover in Honolulu.

There are numerous airlines flying to Hawaii and a variety of fares are available. Rather than just walking into the nearest travel agent or airline office, it pays to do a bit of research and shop around first.

You might want to start by perusing the travel sections of magazines and large newspapers, like the *New York Times*, the *San Francisco Examiner* and the *Los Angeles Times* in the USA; the *Sydney Morning Herald* or Saturday's *Age* in Australia; and *Time Out* or *TNT* in the UK.

Keeping in mind that airfares are constantly changing, the fares listed throughout this chapter should at least give you an idea of relative costs. In addition to a straightforward roundtrip ticket, Hawaii can also be part of a Round-the-World or Circle Pacific ticket.

Round-the-World Tickets

Round-the-World (RTW) tickets, which allow you to fly on the combined routes of two or more airlines, can be an economical way to circle the globe.

RTW tickets are valid for one year and you must travel in one general direction without backtracking. Although most airlines restrict the number of sectors that can be flown within the USA and Canada to four, and a few heavily traveled routes (such as Honolulu to

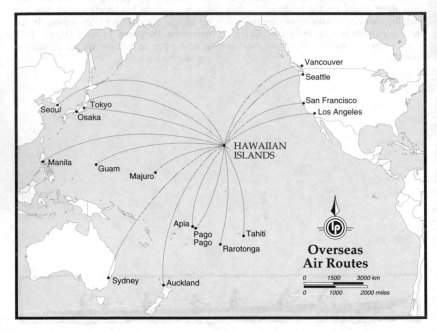

Overseas
Air Routes

Tokyo) are blacked out by some airlines, stopovers are otherwise generally unlimited.

In most cases a 14-day advance purchase is required. After the ticket is purchased, dates can usually be changed without penalty and tickets can be rewritten to add or delete stops for $25 to $50 each – depending upon the carrier.

There's an almost endless variety of airline and destination combinations possible. Because of Honolulu's central Pacific location, Hawaii can be included on most RTW tickets. As a general rule, travel solely in the Northern Hemisphere will be notably cheaper than travel that includes destinations in the Southern Hemisphere.

British Airways and Qantas Airways offer a RTW ticket that allows you to combine routes covering the South and Central Pacific regions, Asia and Europe. Because Qantas has a code-sharing partnership with American Airlines (which means you can book a flight through Qantas, such as New York-Los Angeles, using a Qantas ticket coupon though you'll actually fly with American), this RTW ticket also allows some travel within the USA. From Australia the ticket costs A$3399; from the USA it's US$3249; from London it's £1930. These fares allow unlimited stopovers. Qantas and British Airways also offer a cheaper 'Global Explorer' RTW fare to those willing to restrict their stops to six; the fare is US$2995 from the USA, £1198 from the UK and between A$2669 and A$3279 (depending upon the season) from Australia.

Qantas also offers RTWs in partnership with American Airlines, Delta Air Lines, Scandinavian Airlines, Canadian Airlines, Lufthansa, Air France and KLM.

As another example, Continental Airlines links up with either Malaysia Airlines, Singapore Airlines or Thai Airways for US$2570. With these airlines an itinerary could take you from the US mainland to Honolulu, Guam and Bali or Manila. From there, one possible routing would be to continue through Hong Kong, Saigon, Calcutta, Delhi, Istanbul, Rome and Paris before returning back to North America.

Circle Pacific Tickets

For Circle Pacific tickets, two airlines link up to allow stopovers along their combined Pacific Rim routes. Rather than simply flying from Point A to Point B, these tickets allow you to swing through much of the Pacific and eastern Asia taking in a variety of destinations – as long as you keep traveling in the same circular direction.

Circle Pacific routes essentially have the same fares: US$2579 when purchased in the USA, C$2979 when purchased in Canada, A$3299 when purchased in Australia and NZ$4049 when purchased in New Zealand.

Circle Pacific fares include four stopovers with the option of adding additional stops at US$50 each. There's a seven- to 14-day advance purchase requirement, a 25% cancellation penalty and a maximum stay of six months.

Canadian Airlines has Circle Pacific fares from Vancouver in partnership with Qantas Airways, Air New Zealand, Singapore Air, Garuda, Cathay Pacific or Malaysia airlines.

Qantas offers Circle Pacific routes in partnership with, among others, United Airlines, Delta Air Lines, Japan Air Lines, Northwest Airlines or Continental Airlines.

Air New Zealand offers the ticket in conjunction with, among others, Japan Airlines, Thai Airlines, Cathay Pacific and Singapore Airlines. United Airlines offers the ticket in combination with more than a dozen Pacific Rim carriers.

Your itinerary can be selected from scores of potential destinations. For example, a Qantas-United ticket could take you from Los Angeles to Honolulu, on to Tokyo, south to Manila, followed by Sydney and then back to Los Angeles.

Keep in mind that Circle Pacific fares are high and you may find much better deals. Air New Zealand, for instance, has recently debuted a 'Pacific Explorer' fare roundtrip from Los Angeles for US$1099 that allows stopovers at three destinations, including New Zealand, Australia, Tahiti, Hawaii, Fiji, the Cook Islands, Western Samoa and Tonga, within a two-month period.

Discount Fares from Hawaii
Hawaii is a good place to get discounted fares to virtually any place around the Pacific. Fares vary according to the month, airline and demand, but often you can find a roundtrip fare to Los Angeles or San Francisco for around $250; to Tokyo for $500; to Hong Kong or Manila for $575; to Singapore or Fiji for $650; and to Auckland, Sydney or Saigon for $800.

If you don't have a set destination in mind, you can sometimes find some great on-the-spot deals. The travel pages of the Sunday *Honolulu Advertiser* have scores of ads by travel agencies advertising discounted overseas fares.

The following agencies specialize in discount travel.

Cheap Tickets Inc, Kapiolani Blvd at Atkinson Drive, Honolulu
   (☎ 947-3717, 800-377-1000)
King's Travel, 725 Kapiolani Blvd, Honolulu
   (☎ 593-4481)
Pali Travel, 1304 Pali Hwy, Honolulu
   (☎ 533-3608; fax 524-2483)
Panda Travel, 1017 Kapahulu Ave, Honolulu
   (☎ 734-1961; fax 732-4136)

Honolulu International Airport
Honolulu International is a modern airport that's just completed a decade-long expansion. Although it's a busy place, it's not particularly difficult to get around.

The airport has all the expected services, including fast-food restaurants, lounges, newsstands, sundry shops, lei stands, gift shops, duty-free shops, a 24-hour medical clinic and a mini-hotel for naps and showers.

There's a visitor information booth, car rental counters and hotel/condo courtesy phones in the baggage claim area.

If you arrive early for a flight and are looking for something to do, the Pacific Aerospace Museum ($3) in the main departure lobby has multimedia displays on aviation.

Money Thomas Cook has foreign exchange booths spread around the airport, including in the international arrival area and in the central departure lobby next to the barber shop. On the opposite side of the same barber shop is a Bankoh ATM that gives cash advances on major credit cards and withdrawals using Cirrus and Plus systems ATM cards. As Thomas Cook adds on some hefty transaction fees, using the ATM may be a better option.

If you're in no hurry, you can avoid needling transaction fees by going to the Bank of Hawaii on the ground level across the street from baggage claim D. It's open from 8:30 am to 3 pm Monday to Thursday and to 6 pm on Fridays.

Baggage Storage There are coin-operated lockers in front of gates 13 and 24 which cost 50¢ per hour, or $3 per 24 hours, up to a maximum of 48 hours; coin changing machines are located next to the lockers.

On the ground floor of the parking structure, opposite the main overseas terminal, there are additional coin-operated lockers as well as a baggage storage service that will hold items for $3 to $10 a day, depending on the size. It's open 24 hours a day; for information call ☎ 836-6547.

Airport Shuttle The free Wiki Wiki Shuttle (☎ 836-2505) connects the more distant parts of the airport and links the main terminals with the inter-island terminals. It can be picked up streetside in front of the main lobby (on the second level) and in front of the inter-island gates.

Airlines Serving Honolulu
The following airlines have scheduled flights to Honolulu International Airport on Oahu. The numbers listed for each airline are the local Oahu numbers; those that begin with 800 can also be called toll free from anywhere within the state.

Air Canada	☎ 800-776-3000
Air Marshall Islands	☎ 949-5522
Air Micronesia	☎ 800-231-0856
Air New Zealand	☎ 800-262-1234
All Nippon Airlines	☎ 695-8008
Aloha Airlines	☎ 484-1111
America West Airlines	☎ 800-235-9292
American Airlines	☎ 833-7600
Asiana	☎ 943-0200
Canadian Airlines	☎ 800-426-7000

China Airlines	☎ 955-0088
Continental Airlines	☎ 800-523-3273
Delta Air Lines	☎ 800-221-1212
Garuda Indonesia	☎ 947-9500
Hawaiian Airlines	☎ 838-1555
Island Air	☎ 484-2222
Japan Air Lines	☎ 521-1441
Korean Air	☎ 800-438-5000
Mahalo	☎ 833-5555
Northwest Airlines	☎ 955-2255
Philippine Airlines	☎ 800-435-9725
Qantas Airways	☎ 800-227-4500
Singapore Airlines	☎ 800-742-3333
Trans Air	☎ 836-8080
TWA	☎ 800-221-2000
United Airlines	☎ 800-241-6522

US Mainland

Domestic airfares are constantly in flux. Fares vary with the season you travel, the day of the week you fly, your length of stay and the flexibility the ticket provides for flight changes and refunds. Still, nothing determines fares more than business, and when things are slow, regardless of the season, airlines will drop fares to fill the empty seats. There's a lot of competition to Honolulu from the major mainland cities, and at any given time any one of the airlines could have the cheapest fare.

The airlines each have their own requirements and restrictions, which also seem to be constantly changing. For the latest deals, either find a knowledgeable travel agent or start calling the different airlines and compare.

When you call it's important to ask for the lowest fare, as that's not always the first one they'll quote. Each flight has only a limited number of seats available at the cheapest fares. When you make reservations the agents will generally tell you the best fare that's still available on the date you give them, which may or may not be the cheapest fare that the airline is currently offering. If you make reservations far enough in advance and are a little flexible with dates, you'll usually do better.

Typically the lowest roundtrip fares from the US mainland to Honolulu are about $550 to $800 from the east coast and $300 to $450 from the west coast. Although conditions vary, the cheapest fares are generally for midweek flights and have advance purchase requirements and other restrictions. They are usually nonrefundable and nonchangeable, at least on the outbound flight (although most airlines make allowances for medical emergencies).

The following airlines fly to Honolulu from both the US east and west coasts.

American	☎ 800-433-7300
Continental	☎ 800-525-0280
Delta	☎ 800-221-1212
Northwest	☎ 800-225-2525
TWA	☎ 800-221-2000
United	☎ 800-241-6522

In addition, Hawaiian Airlines (☎ 800-367-5320) flies nonstop to Honolulu from Seattle, San Francisco and Los Angeles. Depending on the season and current promotional fares, a roundtrip ticket from Seattle is usually around $425. The standard fares from LA and San Francisco are $388 roundtrip, though Hawaiian often offers discounted fares from those cities for around $300.

Flight time to Honolulu is about 5½ hours from the west coast, 11 hours from the east coast.

Canada

The cheapest standard fares to Honolulu with Canadian Airlines are around C$450 (US$333) from Vancouver, C$650 (US$481) from Calgary or Edmonton and C$900 (US$666) from Toronto. These fares are for midweek travel, allow a maximum stay of 22 days and generally have a seven-day advance purchase requirement.

Tickets that allow longer maximum stays generally add about C$100 more on to the fares. The toll-free number for Canadian Airlines in Canada is ☎ 800-665-1177.

Central & South America

Most flights to Hawaii from Central and South America go via Houston or Los Angeles, though a few of those from the eastern cities go via New York.

Continental has flights from about 20 cities in Mexico and Central America, including San Jose, Guatemala City, Cancún and Mérida. Their lowest roundtrip fare from Mexico City to Honolulu is US$900 and allows a maximum stay of 60 days. It sometimes works out cheaper to buy two separate tickets, one to Los Angeles and then a second ticket from Los Angeles to Honolulu.

Australia
Qantas flies to Honolulu from Sydney or Melbourne (via Sydney but with no change of plane), with roundtrip fares ranging from A$1210 (US$944) to A$1479 (US-$1154), depending on the season. These tickets have a 14-day advance purchase requirement, a minimum stay of seven days and a maximum stay of 60 days. There are currently no US carriers providing service between Australia and Honolulu, though United and Continental have both done so in the past.

New Zealand
Air New Zealand has Auckland-Honolulu roundtrip fares ranging from NZ$1369 (US$958) to NZ$1519 (US$1063), depending on the season. These tickets, which have to be purchased at least seven days in advance, allow stays of up to six months. Stopovers are permitted for an additional NZ$100 per stop. The one-way fare, which allows a free stopover in Fiji, is NZ$1049 (US$734).

Fiji
Air New Zealand has a one-way fare from Nadi to Honolulu for F$916 (US$660) and a six-month excursion ticket for F$1306 (US$940).

Other South Pacific Islands
Hawaiian Airlines flies to Honolulu from Tahiti and American Samoa. From American Samoa the fare is US$403 one way, with no advance purchase required, and from US$799 roundtrip. From Tahiti to Honolulu the standard one-way fare is a steep US$1056, but there's a seven-day

'Shoppers Special' excursion ticket with no advance purchase requirement that costs US$744.

Air New Zealand flies to Honolulu from Tonga, the Cook Islands and Western Samoa. The lowest roundtrip fare from Tonga to Honolulu costs T$1125 (US$947), requires a seven-day advance purchase and allows a stay of up to 45 days. A one-way ticket costs T$647 (US$532).

From Rarotonga on the Cook Islands, Air New Zealand's cheapest roundtrip fare to Honolulu is NZ$1269 (US$888), while the one-way fare costs NZ$999 (US$699) year round.

From Apia in Western Samoa, Air New Zealand's roundtrip fare to Honolulu is WS$1355 (US$540) with no advance purchase requirement and a 90-day maximum stay. The one-way fare is WS$940 (US$375).

Micronesia
Continental, Northwest and United fly from Guam to Honolulu with roundtrip fares of around US$950. The Northwest and United flights are via Japan, while Continental offers direct flights. The tickets generally allow a stay of up to one year.

A more exciting way to get from Guam, however, would be Continental Air Micronesia's island hopper, which stops en route at the Micronesian islands of Chuuk, Pohnpei, Kosrae and Majuro before reaching Honolulu. It costs US$632 one way with no advance purchase requirement and has free unlimited stopovers. If you're coming from Asia, this is a good alternative to a nonstop transpacific flight and a great way to see some of the Pacific's most remote islands without having to spend a lot of money.

Japan
Fares in this section are in yen; there are approximately 115 yen to one US dollar.

Japan Air Lines flies to Honolulu from Tokyo, Osaka, Nagoya, Fukuoka and Sapporo. Excursion fares vary a bit with the departing city and the season, but, except at busier holiday periods, they're generally about ¥135,000 for a ticket valid for three months, with a three-day advance purchase requirement. The one-way fare from Tokyo is ¥144,600.

Two American carriers, United Airlines and Northwest Airlines, also have daily flights to Honolulu from Tokyo and Osaka. Their fares are competitive with JAL's.

An interesting alternative if you're only going one way would be to fly from Japan to Guam (¥69,400) and then pick up a Continental Air Micronesia ticket that would allow you to island hop through much of Micronesia on your way to Honolulu – for less than the cost of a direct one-way Japan-Honolulu ticket.

Southeast Asia

There are numerous airlines flying directly to Hawaii from Southeast Asia. The fares given below are standard published fares, though bucket shops in places like Bangkok and Singapore should be able to come up with much better deals. Also, if you're traveling to the USA from Southeast Asia, tickets to the US west coast are not that much more than tickets to Hawaii, and many allow a free stopover in Honolulu.

Northwest Airlines flies to Honolulu from Hong Kong, Bangkok, Manila, Seoul and Singapore. Thai Airlines, Korean Air and Philippine Airlines also have numerous flights between Southeast Asian cities and Honolulu. While there are some seasonal variations, the standard roundtrip fares average about US$1100 from Manila, US$1200 from Seoul and Bangkok, US$1500 from Hong Kong and US$1800 from Singapore.

Europe

The most common route to Hawaii from Europe is west via New York or Los Angeles. If you're interested in heading east with stops in Asia, it may be cheaper to get a Round-the-World ticket instead of returning the same way.

American Airlines has a roundtrip fare from London to Honolulu for US$1025 that allows a stay of up to 30 days. American's cheapest roundtrip fare from Paris to Honolulu is US$1075 and allows a

stay of up to three months. From Frankfurt to Honolulu the lowest fare is US $1157 for a stay of up to 30 days. All of these fares are for travel between Monday and Thursday.

United, Delta and Continental airlines have similarly priced service to Honolulu from a number of European cities.

You can usually beat the published airline fares at bucket shops and other travel agencies specializing in discount tickets. London is arguably the world's headquarters for bucket shops and they are well advertised. Two good, reliable agents for cheap tickets in the UK are Trailfinders (☎ 0171-937-5400), 194 Kensington High St, London W8 6EJ, and STA (☎ 0171-937-9962), 74 Old Brompton Rd, London SW7.

SEA

Travel agents, or shops that sell discount cruise tickets, are the best sources of information for transpacific cruises, though Hawaii-bound cruises are rare.

Once a year, usually in January, Cunard (☎ 800-221-4770) books the *Queen Elizabeth II* on a world cruise that stops in Hawaii. The boat can be picked up in Ensenada (Mexico) for a five-day cruise to Hawaii; the cost for just that segment starts at $2300, including airfare from Honolulu back to the US mainland.

ORGANIZED TOURS

There are a slew of package tours available to Hawaii. The basic ones just include airfare and accommodations, while others can include car rentals, sightseeing tours and all sorts of recreational activities. If you're interested, travel agents can help you sort through the various packages.

For those with limited time, package tours can be the cheapest way to go. Costs vary, but one-week tours with airfare and no-frills hotel accommodations usually start around $500 from the US west coast, $700 from the US east coast, based on double occupancy. If you want to stay somewhere fancy or island hop, the price can easily be double that.

Specialized Tours

In addition to traditional package tours, there are some study and environmental tours to Hawaii.

The University Research Expeditions Program (☎ 510-642-6586), University of California, Berkeley, CA 94720-7050, runs one or two work-study tours a year, assisting scholars in the field with such projects as surveying ancient petroglyphs or studying the ecology of plants that grow in lava. Most tours last two to three weeks. Rates range from $1300 to $1500, including food and simple accommodations but excluding airfare.

Elderhostel (☎ 617-426-8056), 75 Federal St, Boston, MA 02110, is a nonprofit organization offering educational programs for those aged 55 or older. The organization has its origins in the youth hostels of Europe and the folk schools of Scandinavia. There's a full range of ongoing programs, some on the Big Island in conjunction with the Lyman House Memorial Museum in Hilo and the Volcano Art Center, others at the University of Hawaii. Many programs focus on Hawaii's people and culture, while some explore the natural environment. The fee is $440 for six nights, $880 for 13 nights, including accommodations, meals and classes but excluding airfare.

Volunteer Programs

The National Park Service has a program allowing volunteers to work at Haleakala National Park on Maui and Hawaii Volcanoes National Park on the Big Island. Duties may be as varied as staffing information desks, leading hikes, trapping predatory animals, controlling invasive plants or cleaning pit toilets.

Competition is stiff; out of hundreds of applications, only a few people are selected each year. There's a preference for volunteers with a background in natural sciences and a knowledge of practicalities like first aid. A three-month (40 hours a week) commitment is required. There's no salary or help with airfare, though barracks-style housing and a small daily stipend to help pay for food are usually provided. For information write to Volunteers in Parks at Haleakala National Park, Box 369, Makawao, HI 96768 or at Hawaii Volcanoes National Park, HI 96718-0052.

Another group, the Student Conservation Association (☎ 603-543-1700), Box 550, Charlestown, NH 03603, sends a handful of people each year to work for three months as volunteers at Haleakala National Park. There are usually a few different positions that can be applied for, ranging from answering phones and issuing camping permits to assisting with the park's endangered species research. Roundtrip airfare to Hawaii, a weekly stipend of about $75 and accommodations are provided. Anyone over 18 with a high school degree may apply.

LEAVING HAWAII
Departure Taxes

There are no departure taxes to pay when leaving Hawaii.

Agricultural Inspection

All luggage and carry-on bags leaving Hawaii for the US mainland are checked by an agricultural inspector using an X-ray machine. You cannot take out gardenia, jade vine or roses, even in leis, although most other fresh flowers and foliage are permitted. You can take out pineapples and coconuts, but most other fresh fruits and vegetables are banned. Other things not allowed to enter mainland states include plants in soil, fresh coffee berries, cactus and sugar cane. Seeds, fruits and plants that have been certified and labeled for export aren't a problem.

WARNING

The information in this chapter is particularly vulnerable to change: Prices for international travel are volatile, routes are introduced and canceled, schedules change, special deals come and go, and rules and visa requirements are amended.

Airlines and governments seem to take a perverse pleasure in making price structures and regulations as complicated as possible. You should check directly with the airline or a travel agent to make sure you understand how a fare (and any ticket you may buy) works. In addition, the travel industry is highly competitive and there are many lurks and perks.

The upshot of this is that you should get opinions, quotes and advice from as many airlines and travel agents as possible before you part with your hard-earned cash. The details given in this chapter should be regarded as pointers and are not a substitute for your own careful, up-to-date research.

Getting Around

AIR

The major airports handling inter-island traffic are at Honolulu (on Oahu), Lihue (on Kauai), Kahului (on Maui), Kona and Hilo (both on the Big Island).

Smaller airports with scheduled commercial flights are: Lanai; Molokai Airport and Kalaupapa, both on Molokai; Kapalua West Maui and Hana, both on Maui; and Waimea-Kohala, on the Big Island.

Aloha Airlines and Hawaiian Airlines, the two major inter-island carriers, both have frequent flights in full-bodied jet aircraft between the five major airports.

The smaller airports are served by two commuter airlines, Island Air and Trans Air, both of which use prop planes. Hawaiian Airlines also flies to Molokai and Lanai.

Airfares

Inter-island air travel is highly competitive and the fares commonly adjust up and down to reflect the competition. The two largest carriers, Hawaiian Airlines and Aloha Airlines, both have a standard one-way fare for all flights between any two airports that they serve. That fare is currently $69, but in the recent past it's been as high as $90.

Island Air, the largest of the commuter airlines, has also dropped its inter-island fares to $69 one way.

On upstart Mahalo Air, the most recent competitor to jump into the market, all fares are $55.

Roundtrip fares on all these airlines are double the one-way fares.

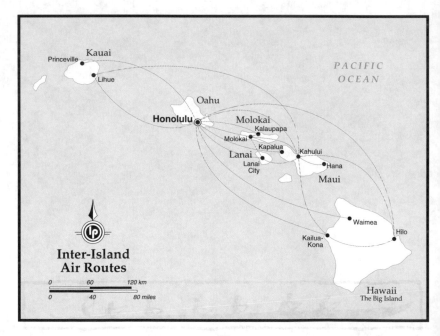

Inter-Island Air Routes

Coupons You can save a bundle by using discount coupons instead of purchasing full-fare tickets.

Hawaiian Airlines sells coupon booklets containing six tickets good for inter-island flights between any two destinations they serve. The booklets cost $318 when purchased directly from the airline. These tickets can be used by any number of people and on any flight without restrictions. You can also buy the coupons individually from discount travel agents around the islands for $40 to $45.

Aloha Airlines is more fickle with coupon books and sometimes, but not always, restricts them to use by local residents only. Still, as we go to press they're offering the best deal at the counter: a $270 book of six unrestricted coupons that are good for flights on both Aloha Airlines and its affiliate Island Air.

Mahalo generally sells its coupons only through travel agents – local discount places like Cut Rate Tickets sell them for around $30. If you find something that's cheaper, look carefully, as Mahalo issues two versions of its coupons, and the cheapest ones are restricted to residents only.

Air Passes Hawaiian Airlines offers a good-value air pass allowing unlimited air travel for a specified number of consecutive days. The cheapest pass, which is good for five days, is just a bit more than the cost of a roundtrip air ticket. You can go anywhere you please as often as you want. Reservations can be made in advance and you're free to revise your itinerary at will. Passes are nonrefundable and will not be replaced if lost or stolen.

The fare is: $189 for five days, $209 for one week, $244 for 10 days and $284 for two weeks. Of note is the fact that the one-week pass is written to allow travel between one day of the week and the same day of the next week (ie Saturday to Saturday) so it actually allows eight days of travel. Passes are $10 cheaper for children and senior citizens.

Other Discounts Aloha Airlines offers American Automobile Association (AAA) members a 25% discount off the standard ticket fare on all its inter-island flights, and its sister airline, Island Air, offers the same discount on all point-to-point flights (ie, those that don't require a connecting flight). The fare is applicable to AAA cardholders and those traveling with them. Trans Air, a small commuter airline, also offers AAA members discounted rates with one-way fares of $59.

There are also other schemes that come up from time to time, so always ask what promotional fares are currently being offered when you call to make a reservation.

Inter-Island Airlines

Hawaiian Airlines Hawaiian, which flies DC-9s, has about 175 flights a day connecting Honolulu, Lihue, Kahului, Kona, Hilo, Molokai and Lanai.

Reservation numbers for Hawaiian Airlines are:

Big Island	☎ 326-5615
Kauai	☎ 245-1813
Lanai	☎ 565-7281
Maui	☎ 871-6132
Molokai	☎ 553-3644
Oahu	☎ 838-1555
American Samoa	☎ 699-1875
Japan	☎ 03-3214-4774
Tahiti	☎ 4215-00
US mainland & Canada	☎ 800-367-5320
UK	☎ 1753-664406

Aloha Airlines Aloha Airlines, which flies 737s between Honolulu, Lihue, Kahului, Kona and Hilo, has over 200 inter-island flights a day.

Reservation numbers for Aloha Airlines are:

Big Island	☎ 935-5771
Kauai	☎ 245-3691
Maui	☎ 244-9071
Oahu	☎ 484-1111
Canada	☎ 800-235-0936
Hong Kong	☎ 2826-9111
Osaka	☎ 06-341-7241
Tokyo	☎ 03-3216-5877
US mainland	☎ 800-367-5250

Island Air Island Air serves Hawaii's smaller airports using 18-passenger deHavilland Dash 6 aircraft. As these prop planes fly lower than jet aircraft, you often get better views en route. Island Air is part of the Aloha Airgroup, so bookings can be made through Aloha Airlines as well.

Island Air has flights to Honolulu, Molokai, Kalaupapa, Kahului, Hana, Kapalua West Maui and Lanai. On some of the more remote sectors, flights are only twice daily, while the more popular routes have over a dozen flights a day.

Reservation numbers for Island Air are:

Oahu	☎ 484-2222
Neighbor Islands	☎ 800-652-6541
US mainland	☎ 800-323-3345

Mahalo Air Mahalo Air uses 46-seat ATR-42s to fly from Honolulu to Kahului, Kapalua West Maui, Kona, Lihue and Molokai. Scheduled service ranges from six flights a day between Honolulu and Molokai to 14 times a day between Honolulu and Kahului.

Reservation numbers for Mahalo are:

Oahu	☎ 833-5555
Neighbor Islands	☎ 800-277-8333
Japan	☎ 03-3597-9474
US mainland	☎ 800-462-4256

Trans Air Trans Air has twice-daily service between Honolulu and Waimea-Kohala and between Molokai and Kapalua, and flies four times a day from Honolulu to Kapalua West Maui and Molokai. Fares are $74, except the Molokai routes, which cost around $60.

Reservation numbers for Trans Air are:

Oahu	☎ 836-8080
Neighbor Islands	☎ 800-634-2090
US mainland	☎ 800-634-2090

Other Airlines Smaller commuter airlines, sometimes consisting of just a single plane, come and go with some frequency in Hawaii.

The latest entry is Molokai Air Shuttle

(☎ 545-4988), which flies a five-passenger Piper between Honolulu and Molokai; for details see Getting There & Away in the Molokai chapter.

BUS

For detailed information on each of the following bus services, see the Getting Around section in the appropriate destination chapter.

Oahu's excellent island-wide public bus system, called TheBus, makes that island the easiest one to get around without a car. You can get almost anywhere on Oahu via TheBus, and the fare is just $1 regardless of your destination.

The Big Island has a limited public bus service between Kona and Hilo and between Hilo and Hawaii Volcanoes National Park. There are a couple of other routes serving the Hilo area, but they're geared primarily for commuters and the service is infrequent. While these buses can get you between major towns, they're not practical for short sightseeing hops.

Kauai has a limited public bus service that can take visitors between island towns but doesn't cover the main tourist destinations, such as Waimea Canyon or the Kilauea lighthouse.

Maui has no county-operated buses. However, there's a limited, and rather expensive, private bus service that operates between the Kihei and Kaanapali areas. There are also inexpensive shuttles connecting Kaanapali with Lahaina.

Molokai has no buses, but there's a mule train!

TAXI

All the main islands have taxis, with the fares based on mileage regardless of the number of passengers. Rates vary, as they're set by each county, but average about $10 per five miles.

CAR

The minimum age for driving in Hawaii is 18 years, though car rental companies usually have higher age restrictions. If you're under age 25, you should call the car rental agencies in advance to check their policies regarding restrictions and surcharges.

You can legally drive in the state as long as you have a valid driver's license issued by a country that is party to the United Nations Conference on Road & Motor Transport – which covers virtually everyone.

However, car rental companies will generally accept valid foreign driver's licenses only if they're in English. Otherwise, most will require renters to show an international driver's license along with their home license.

Gasoline is about 25% more expensive in Hawaii than on the US mainland, with the price for regular unleaded gasoline averaging about $1.70 a gallon.

Road Rules

As with the rest of the USA, driving is on the right-hand side of the road.

Drivers at a red light can turn right after coming to a full stop and yielding to oncoming traffic, unless there's a sign at the intersection prohibiting the turn.

Hawaii requires the use of seat belts for drivers and front-seat passengers. State law also strictly requires the use of child safety seats for children ages three and under, while four-year-olds must either be in a safety seat or secured by a seat belt. Most of the car rental companies rent child safety seats, usually from $3 to $5 a day, but they don't always have them on hand so it's advisable to reserve one in advance.

Speed limits are posted and enforced. If you're stopped for speeding, expect to get a ticket, as the police rarely just give warnings. Cruising unmarked police cars come in the most unlikely models and colors!

Note that the word 'highway' is used very liberally in Hawaii. Just about every road of any distance gets to be called a highway, including some insignificant secondary roads and even a dirt road or two.

In this book we've given priority to using highway numbers because that's what you'll see on road signs. However, if you're

asking directions keep in mind that islanders generally refer to roads by name and few pay attention to the route numbers – many wouldn't even be able to tell you the route number of the road on which they live.

Horn honking is considered rude in Hawaii unless required for safety.

Rental

Rental cars are available on all the islands.

With most companies the weekly rate works out far cheaper per day than the straight daily rate. The daily rate for a small car with unlimited mileage ranges from around $25 to $45, while typical weekly rates are $150 to $200.

Rates vary a bit from company to company and within each company depending on season, time of booking and current promotions. If you belong to an automobile club, a frequent-flyer program or a travel club, you'll often be eligible for some sort of discount with at least one of the rental agencies.

One thing to note when renting a car is that rates for mid-size and full-size cars are often only a few dollars more per week; because some promotional discounts exclude economy-size cars, at times the lowest rate available may actually be on a larger car.

At any given time any one of the rental companies could be offering the best rates, so you can save money by shopping around. Be sure to ask the agent for the cheapest rate, as the first quote given is not always the lowest.

It's a good idea to make reservations in advance for each destination you plan on visiting. Walking up to the counter without a reservation will not only subject you to higher rates, but during busy periods, which can include weekends year round, it's not uncommon for cars to be sold out altogether.

Another advantage of advance reservations is that if you have a bottom-line car reserved and there are none in the yard when you show up, the upgrade is free.

On daily rentals, most cars are rented on a 24-hour basis, so you could get two days' use by renting at midday and driving around all afternoon, then heading out to explore somewhere else the next morning before the car is due back. Most companies even have an hour's grace period.

In Hawaii, rental rates generally include free unlimited mileage, though if you drop off the car at a different location from where you picked it up, there's usually a fee added on and sometimes a mileage charge.

Having a major credit card greatly simplifies the rental process. Without one some agents simply will not rent vehicles, while others will require prepayment by cash or traveler's checks as well as a deposit, often around $300. Some do an employment verification and credit check, while others don't do background checks but reserve the right for the station manager to decide whether to rent to you or not. If you intend to rent a car without plastic, it's wise to make your plans well in advance, as you may need to submit a written application, a process that can take up to six weeks.

Be aware that many car rental companies are loathe to rent to people who list a campground as their address on the island, and a few specifically add 'No Camping Permitted' to their rental contracts.

Most car rental companies officially prohibit use of their cars on dirt roads.

In addition to the rates, the state of Hawaii adds a $2-a-day tax on all car rentals.

Insurance Rental vehicles in Hawaii have liability insurance, which covers people and property that you might hit. Damage to the rental vehicle itself is not covered. A collision damage waiver (CDW) is available from car rental agencies for an additional $12 to $16 a day.

The CDW is not really even insurance but rather a guarantee that the rental company won't hold you liable for any damages to their car (though even here there are exclusions). If you decline the CDW, you are usually held liable for any damages up to the full value of the car. If damages do occur and you find yourself in a dispute with the rental company, you can call the state Department of Commerce & Consumer Affairs at ☎ 587-1234 and then

key in 7222 for recorded information on your legal rights.

If you have collision coverage on your vehicle at home, it might cover damages to car rentals in Hawaii. Check with your insurance company before your trip.

Some credit cards, including most 'gold cards' issued by Visa and MasterCard, offer reimbursement coverage for collision damages if you rent the car with that credit card and decline the CDW. If yours doesn't, it may be worth changing to one that does. Be aware that most credit card coverage isn't valid for rentals of more than 15 days or for exotic models, jeeps, 4WD vehicles, vans and motorbikes.

Rental Agencies The following are international companies whose cars can be booked from offices around the world. The toll-free numbers given are valid from the US mainland.

Alamo (☎ 800-327-9633) has locations at the Kona, Hilo, Kahului and Lihue airports and near the Honolulu and Kapalua West Maui airports.

Avis (☎ 800-831-8000) is at the main airports on Oahu, Maui, Kauai and the Big Island as well as a half-dozen locations around Waikiki. If you're visiting at least two islands, Avis has a handy multi-island deal that allows you to rent a car at the rate of $28 a day as long as you rent for a minimum of five days on the combined islands.

Budget (☎ 800-527-7000) is at the main airports on Oahu, Kauai, Molokai, Maui and the Big Island as well as about 35 other locations around Hawaii. All other things being equal, Budget is probably the best choice for bargain-hunters, as renters are given coupons on each island that allow free admission for one person to participating tourist attractions – it's a particularly good deal on Oahu.

Dollar (☎ 800-367-7006) is at the airports on Oahu, Kauai, Molokai, Maui and the Big Island as well as numerous locations in Waikiki.

Hertz (☎ 800-654-3131) is at the main airports on Oahu, Maui, Kauai and the Big Island as well as the Kapalua West Maui airport.

National (☎ 800-227-7368) is at the main airports on Oahu, Kauai, Maui and the Big Island and at a couple of locations in Waikiki.

There are a handful of smaller rental agencies in Hawaii as well, but this is one area in which smaller is not necessarily better. For the most part, the big companies offer newer, more reliable cars and fewer hassles.

BICYCLE

It's possible to cycle around all the Hawaiian islands. However, when you get away from coastal routes, there are some pretty hefty uphill climbs. Exploring thoroughly by bicycle is an option that's best suited for well-conditioned cyclists.

Hawaii has been slow to adopt cycle-friendly traits. Some new road projects now include cycle lanes, but such lanes are still relatively rare on the islands. Hawaii's roads also tend to be narrow and many of the main coastal routes are heavily trafficked.

There are places to rent bicycles on the four largest islands. If you bring your own bike to Hawaii, you can transport it on inter-island flights for $20.

For island-specific cycling information, see the Activities and Getting Around sections in the destination chapters.

HITCHING

Hitchhiking is not common in Hawaii. In Maui County it's outright illegal, while on the other islands it's more of a gray area and tolerance varies. All in all, hitchhiking results are mixed at best. Hitchhikers should size up each situation carefully before getting in cars, and women should be especially wary of hitching alone.

Hitchhiking is never entirely safe anywhere in the world, and Lonely Planet does not recommend it. Travelers who decide to hitch should understand that they are taking a potentially serious risk. People who do choose to hitch will be safer if they travel in pairs and let someone know where they are planning to go.

BOAT

The only inter-island ferry in Hawaii is a small 24-passenger boat that operates five times a day between Lahaina on Maui and Manele Boat Harbor on Lanai. The crossing, which takes an hour, costs $25.

TOURS

There are a number of companies doing half-day and full-day sightseeing bus tours on each island. There are also lots of specialized tours, such as whale-watch cruises, bicycle tours down Haleakala, snorkel trips to Lanai and Zodiac cruises along the Na Pali Coast, just to mention a few. All these tours can be booked after arrival in Hawaii.

Overnight Tours

If you want to visit another island but only have a day or two to spare, it might be worth looking into 'overnighters', which are mini-packaged tours to the Neighbor Islands that include roundtrip airfare, car rental and hotel accommodations. Rates depend on the accommodations you select, with a one-night package typically starting around $125 per person, based on double occupancy. You can add on additional days for an additional fee, usually about $60 per person.

If you have an air pass, the same tour companies also sell room/car packages minus the airfare – though the room/car packages offered directly by some hotels may work out cheaper.

The largest companies specializing in overnighters are: Roberts Hawaii (☎ 523-9323 on Oahu, 800-899-9323 from the Neighbor Islands and the mainland) and Pleasant Island Holidays (☎ 922-1515 on Oahu, 800-654-4386 from the Neighbor Islands).

Cruises

American Hawaii Cruises (☎ 800-765-7000), 2 N Riverside Plaza, Chicago, IL 60606, operates the cruise ship *Independence*, which makes a seven-day tour around Hawaii. The ship leaves Honolulu each Saturday all year round and visits Kauai (Nawiliwili Harbor), Maui (Kahului Harbor) and the Big Island (Hilo and Kona) before returning to Honolulu.

Rates start at $1145 for the cheapest inside cabin and go up to $3195, with the cheapest outside cabin priced at $1345. Fares are per person, based on double occupancy, and there's an additional $85 for port charges.

Although more modest than the ultra-modern mammoths that cruise the Caribbean, the *Independence* is a full-fledged cruise ship, 682 feet long, with lavish buffet meals, swimming pools and the like. Each carries a crew of 325 along with 960 passengers.

Helicopter Tours

Helicopter tours are readily available from a number of companies on the main islands. They go to some amazing places, such as over active volcanoes, along towering coastal cliffs and above inaccessible waterfalls. Prices vary depending on the destination and the length of the flight, with a 30-minute tour averaging about $125 per passenger.

Before you book one, be ready to make some inquiries. Be aware, for instance, that not every seat in all copters is a window seat. A common configuration is two passengers up front with the pilot, and four people sitting across the back. The two back middle seats simply don't give the photo opportunities proclaimed in the brochures. It's like being a mid-seat rear passenger on a scenic drive – only there's no getting out at viewpoints! People are usually seated according to weight, so if you're dishing out a lot of money, make sure you know in advance where you'll be sitting.

Oahu

The images most commonly conjured up of Hawaii are those of Oahu – places like Waikiki, Pearl Harbor and Sunset Beach.

Oahu is by far the most developed of the Hawaiian islands and, quite appropriately, has long been nicknamed 'The Gathering Place'. The island is home to 877,000 people – nearly 75% of the state's population. It's an urban scene, with highways, high-rises and crowds. If you're looking for a getaway vacation, you'd best continue on to one of the Neighbor Islands.

Still, despite all its development, in terms of scenic beauty Oahu holds its own. It has fluted mountains, aqua-blue bays and valleys carpeted with pineapple fields.

Oahu has excellent beaches. Hanauma Bay, east of Waikiki, is the most visited snorkeling spot in the islands. The North Shore has Hawaii's top surfing action, and windward Kailua is Hawaii's most popular windsurfing beach.

Honolulu is a modern city with an intriguing blend of Eastern and Western influences. Cultural offerings range from Chinese lantern parades and traditional hula performances to ballet and good museums. Honolulu has the only royal palace in the USA, fine city beaches and parks and some great hilltop views. The city is also a diner's delight, with a wonderful array of good ethnic restaurants.

Oahu can be the cheapest Hawaiian island to visit. It's the only one you can get around easily without your own transport, thanks to the inexpensive, islandwide bus system. Oahu also has some of Hawaii's cheapest accommodations, including a handful of hostels and Ys.

Almost all of Oahu's hotels and tourist facilities are centered in Waikiki. Waikiki resembles a hybrid mix of Miami Beach and Tokyo, with a population density rivaling the latter. There's a lot happening in Waikiki, but to get a better feel for what Hawaii's all about, you need to step out of

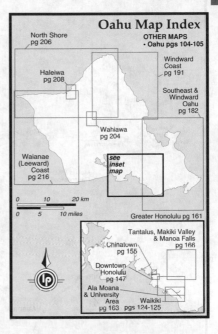

it. There are plenty of places on Oahu worth exploring.

HISTORY

Oahu was the final island conquered by Kamehameha the Great in his campaign to unite all Hawaii under his sole rule.

Prior to that, however, it was not Kamehameha but Kahekili, the aging king of Maui, who seemed the most likely candidate to grasp control of the entire island chain. Kahekili already ruled neighboring Molokai and Lanai when in the 1780s he killed his own stepson to take Oahu.

After Kahekili died at Waikiki in 1794 a power struggle ensued and his lands were divided between two quarreling relatives. His son, Kalanikupule, got Oahu and his half-brother, King Kaeokulani of Kauai,

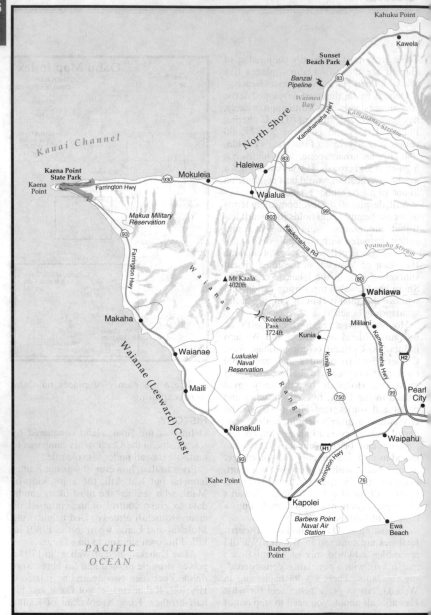

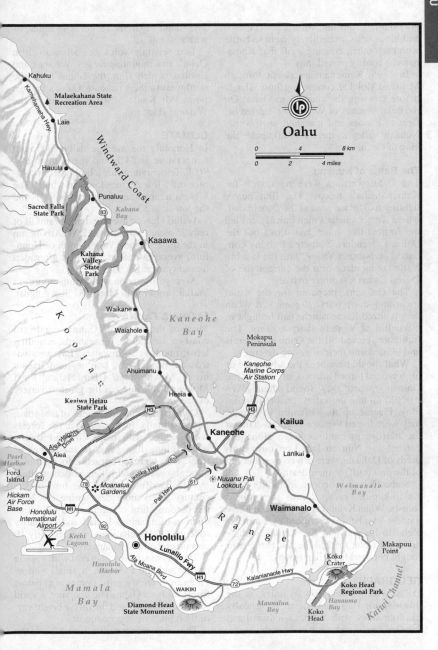

Oahu

0   4   8 km

0   2   4 miles

Kahuku

Malaekahana State
Recreation Area

Laie

Hauula

Kamehameha Hwy

Windward Coast

Punaluu

Sacred Falls
State Park

Kahana
Bay

83

Kaaawa

Kahana
Valley
State Park

K o o l a u

Waikane

Waiahole

Kaneohe
Bay

Mokapu
Peninsula

Ahuimanu

Kaneohe
Marine Corps
Air Station

Heeia

Keaiwa Heiau
State Park

H3

H3

Kaneohe

Kailua

Lanikai

63

Aiea Heights
Drive

Aiea

61

Nuuanu Pali
Lookout

Waimanalo

Waimanalo
Bay

Pearl
Harbor

Ford
Island

99

78

Moanalua
Gardens

Likelike Hwy

Pali Hwy

R a n g e

Hickam
Air Force
Base

H1

Honolulu
International
Airport

Keehi
Lagoon

92

Honolulu

Lunalilo Hwy

Ala Moana Blvd

H1

72

Kalanianaole Hwy

Makapuu
Point

Koko
Crater

Koko Head
Regional Park

Honolulu
Harbor

Mamala
Bay

WAIKIKI

Diamond Head
State Monument

Maunalua
Bay

Koko
Head

Hanauma
Bay

Kaiwi Channel

got Maui, Lanai and Molokai. The two ambitious heirs immediately went to battle with each other, creating a rift that Kamehameha readily moved into.

In 1795, Kamehameha swept through Maui and Molokai, conquering those islands before crossing the channel to Oahu. On the quiet beaches of Waikiki he landed his fleet of canoes and marched up towards Nuuanu Valley to meet Kalanikupule, the king of Oahu.

The Battle of Nuuanu

The Oahu warriors were no match for Kamehameha's troops. The first heavy fighting took place around the Punchbowl, where Kamehameha's men quickly circled the fortress-like crater and drove out the Oahuan defenders. Scattered fighting continued up Nuuanu Valley, with the last big battle taking place near the current site of Queen Emma's summer palace.

The Oahuans, prepared for the usual spear-and-stone warfare, panicked when they realized Kamehameha had brought in a handful of Western sharpshooters. The foreigners picked off the Oahuan generals and blasted into their ridge-top defenses.

What should have been the advantage of high ground turned into a death trap for the Oahuans when they found themselves wedged up into the valley, unable to redeploy. Fleeing up the cliffsides in retreat, they were forced to make their last stand at the narrow, precipitous ledge along the current-day Nuuanu Pali Lookout. Hundreds of Oahuans were driven over the top of the *pali* (cliff) to their deaths.

Some Oahuan warriors, including King Kalanikupule, escaped into the upland forests. When Kalanikupule surfaced a few months later he was sacrificed by Kamehameha to his war god Ku. Kamehameha's taking of Oahu marked the last battle ever fought between Hawaiian troops.

GEOGRAPHY

Oahu, which covers 594 sq miles, is the third-largest Hawaiian island. It basically has four sides, with distinct windward and leeward coasts and north and south shores.

The island's extreme length is 44 miles, its width 30 miles.

Two separate volcanoes arose to form Oahu's two mountain ranges, Waianae and Koolau, which slice the island from the northwest to the southeast. Oahu's highest point, Mt Kaala at 4020 feet, is in the Waianae Range.

CLIMATE

In Honolulu the average daily maximum temperature is 84°F and the minimum is 70°F. Temperatures are a bit higher in summer and a few degrees lower in winter. The highest temperature on record is 94°F and the lowest is 53°F.

Waikiki has an average annual rainfall of only 25 inches, whereas the Lyon Arboretum in the upper Manoa Valley, north of Honolulu, averages 158 inches. Mid-afternoon humidity averages 56%.

Average afternoon water temperatures in Waikiki are 77°F in March, 82°F in August.

FLORA & FAUNA

Most of the islets off Oahu's windward coast are sanctuaries for seabirds, including terns, noddies, shearwaters, Laysan albatrosses, tropicbirds, boobies and frigate birds. Moku Manu ('Bird Island') off Mokapu Peninsula has the greatest variety of species.

Oahu has an endemic genus of tree snail, the achatinella. In former days the forests were loaded with these colorful snails, which clung like gems to the leaves of trees. They were too attractive for their own good, however, and hikers collected them by the handfuls around the turn of the century. Even more devastating has been the deforestation of habitat and the introduction of a cannibal snail and predatory rodents. Of 41 achatinella species, only 19 remain and all are endangered.

The *elepaio*, a brownish bird with a white rump, and the *amakihi*, a small yellow green bird, are the most common endemic forest birds on Oahu. The *apapane*, a vivid red honeycreeper, and the *iiwi*, a bright vermillion bird, are less common.

The only other native forest bird, the

Oahu creeper, may already be extinct. This small yellowish bird looks somewhat like the amakihi, which makes positive identification difficult. The last Oahu creeper sighting was of a single bird in 1985 on the Poamoho Trail.

The most prominent urban birds are pigeons, doves, red-crested cardinals and common mynas. The myna, introduced from India, is a brown, spectacled bird that congregates in noisy flocks. Introduced game birds include pheasants, quails and francolins.

Oahu has wild pigs and goats in its mountain valleys. Brush-tailed rock-wallabies, accidentally released in 1916, reside in the Kalihi Valley. Although rarely seen, the wallabies are of interest to zoologists because they may be an extinct subspecies in their native Australia.

Oahu has some excellent botanical gardens. Foster Garden and the Lyon Arboretum both have unique native and exotic species, some of which have disappeared in the wild.

GOVERNMENT

The City & County of Honolulu is the unwieldy name attached to the single political entity governing all of Oahu.

While technically the City & County of Honolulu also includes the Northwestern Hawaiian Islands, which stretch 1300 miles beyond Kauai to Kure Atoll, for practical purposes the City & County of Honolulu refers to the island of Oahu.

Like Hawaii's other counties, there are no municipal governments. Oahu is administered by a mayor and a nine-member council, elected for four-year terms.

ECONOMY

Oahu has a 5% unemployment rate. Tourism is the largest sector of the economy, accounting for about 30% of Oahu's jobs. It's followed by defense and other government employment, which together account for 22% of all jobs.

Nearly one-fifth of Oahu is still used for agricultural purposes, mostly for growing pineapples. Sugar production, no longer profitable on Oahu, was phased out entirely in 1996. On the North Shore, around Haleiwa and Waialua, coffee trees are being introduced into former cane fields.

POPULATION & PEOPLE

Oahu's population is 877,000, with Honolulu accounting for nearly half of the total. Other sizable population centers are Pearl City, Kailua, Kaneohe, Aiea, Waipahu and Mililani.

The population is 24% Caucasian, 21% Japanese, 17% mixed ancestry other than part-Hawaiian, 16% part-Hawaiian (less than 1% pure Hawaiian), 7% Filipino and 6% Chinese, with numerous other Pacific and Asian minorities.

Approximately 14% of Oahu's residents are members of the armed forces or their dependents.

ORIENTATION

Almost all visitors to Oahu land at Honolulu International Airport, the only civilian airport on the island. It's at the western outskirts of the Honolulu district, nine miles west of Waikiki.

H-1, the main south-shore freeway, is the key to getting around the island. H-1 connects with Hwy 72, which runs around the southeast coast; with the Pali (61) and Likelike (63) highways, which go to the windward coast; with Hwy 93, which leads up the leeward Waianae Coast; and with H-2, Hwys 99 and 750, which run through the center of the island on the way to the North Shore.

By the way, H-1 is a US *interstate* freeway – an amusing term to describe a road on an island state in the middle of the Pacific.

Rush-hour traffic is heavy heading towards Honolulu in the mornings and away from it in the evenings.

Directions on Oahu are often given by using landmarks, in addition to the Hawaii-wide *mauka* (inland side) and *makai* (ocean side). If someone tells you to go 'Ewa' (a land area west of Honolulu) or 'Diamond Head' (east of Honolulu), it simply means to head in that direction.

Maps

There are simple island maps in the free tourist magazines, but if you're going to be renting a car and doing any exploring at all, it's worth picking up a good road map, especially for navigating around Honolulu. Detailed Gousha road maps (which are recommended, as they show numbered highway exits) and Rand McNally road maps are sold in stores throughout Oahu for a couple of dollars. Members of AAA or an affiliated automobile club can get a free Gousha road map from the AAA office, 590 Queen St, Honolulu. Most comprehensive – but more detailed than most visitors will need – is the 150-page *Bryan's Sectional Maps Oahu* atlas, which shows, names and indexes virtually every street on the island.

INFORMATION
Tourist Offices

The administrative office of the Hawaii Visitors Bureau (☎ 923-1811; fax 922-8991), in Waikiki at 2270 Kalakaua Ave, Suite 801, Honolulu, HI 96815, can mail out general tourist information on Oahu and the rest of the state.

To pick up tourist brochures in person, go to the Hawaii Visitors Bureau's visitor information office (☎ 924-0266) in the Royal Hawaiian Shopping Center (Hibiscus Court, 4th floor) in Waikiki, at the Lewers St end of the center.

Official Oahu
Oahu's nickname is 'The Gathering Place'. Its flower is the delicate native ilima, whose yellow-orange blossoms are the inspiration behind the island's official color. ∎

Money

There are nine banks with nearly 150 branches on Oahu, and they can easily be found in major towns. The Bank of Hawaii, Hawaii's largest bank, has a branch at the airport and at 2220 Kalakaua Ave in central Waikiki.

Banks are generally open from 8:30 am to 3 pm Monday to Thursday and from 8:30 am to 6 pm on Fridays.

Automatic teller machines (ATMs) that accept major credit cards and Cirrus and Plus system debit cards can be found at the airport, larger shopping centers, most supermarkets and numerous other locations.

Post & Communications

There are 35 post offices on Oahu. The main Honolulu post office is not in central Honolulu but at the side of the airport at 3600 Aolele St, opposite the inter-island terminal. It's open from 7:30 am to 8:30 pm Monday to Friday and 8 am to 2:30 pm on Saturdays.

All general delivery mail sent to you in Honolulu must be picked up at the main Honolulu post office. Note that any mail sent general delivery to the Waikiki post office or other Honolulu branches will either go to the main post office or be returned to the sender. If you're receiving mail in Honolulu, have it addressed to you c/o General Delivery, Main Post Office, 3600 Aolele St, Honolulu, HI 96820-3600.

A number of cybercafes, where travelers can check their email or go online, have sprung up in the Honolulu area. Near Waikiki, there's the Internet Cafe on Kapahulu Ave (see Waikiki Information). Near the UH campus, there's the Net Cafe (☎ 955-2345), at 1009 University Ave just south of Ba Le. About 10 minutes' walk north of the Ala Moana Center is the Cyber Cafe (☎ 593-1664; smooth@hawaii-cybercafe.com), across the street from El Burrito at 1311 Kapiolani Blvd.

At any of these places you can spend 15 to 30 minutes online for just a couple of dollars. In addition, Borders bookstore at the Ward Centre has a couple of computers where you can check your email for free, but there may be a long wait.

Newspapers & Magazines

The main newspapers are the morning *Honolulu Advertiser*, published daily, and the afternoon *Honolulu Star-Bulletin*, published Monday to Saturday. Subscription information is under Media in the introductory Facts for the Visitor chapter.

In addition, Oahu has numerous weekly or monthly newspapers, many of which can be picked up free around the island. These include the *Honolulu Weekly*, a progressive paper with an extensive entertainment section; the *Downtown Planet*, aimed at those who work in downtown Honolulu; and regional rags such as the *Windward Oahu News* and the *North Shore News*.

Numerous free tourist magazines are available at the airport and all around Waikiki. They can be a good source of visitor information, although most of it is paid advertising. *This Week Oahu* and *Spotlight's Oahu Gold* usually have the best discount coupons.

Radio & TV

Honolulu has 17 commercial AM radio stations, 12 FM stations and three noncommercial stations. Radio station KCCN features slack-key Hawaiian guitar on 1420 AM and 'island music', with a blend of more contemporary Hawaiian songs and reggae, on 100.3 FM. Da KINE (105.1 FM) plays classic Hawaiian music. Hawaii Public Radio is on KHPR (88.1 FM), KKUA (90.7 FM) and KIPO (89.3 FM).

There are 10 TV stations and numerous cable stations, including one featuring continuous visitor information and ads geared to tourists.

Bookstores

All of the following bookstores have good collections of books about Hawaii, travel guides and general fiction.

Borders has a new Honolulu branch in the Ward Centre on Ala Moana Blvd and another in the Waikele Center in Waipahu. There's a Barnes & Noble bookstore in Honolulu at 4211 Waialae Ave.

Another national chain, Waldenbooks, has shops in the Kahala Mall, Koko Marina Shopping Center, Windward Mall, Pearlridge Center and in Waikiki at the Waikiki Shopping Plaza and Waikiki Trade Center.

Honolulu Book Shops, a large local operation, has shops on the corner of Bishop and S Hotel Sts in downtown Honolulu and in the Ala Moana, Pearlridge and Kailua shopping centers.

Rainbow Books & Records, 1010 University Ave at S Beretania St, near the University of Hawaii, is a good place to look for used books, as well as current travel guides.

Libraries

Hawaii's statewide library system has its main library in downtown Honolulu, next to Iolani Palace. There are 21 other public libraries around Oahu, including ones in Waikiki, Kailua and Kaneohe.

Weather

The National Weather Service provides recorded weather forecasts for Honolulu (☎ 973-4380) and all Oahu (☎ 973-4381). They also have recorded tide and surf conditions (☎ 973-4383) and a marine forecast (☎ 973-4382).

Emergency

Dial ☎ 911 for all police, fire and ambulance emergencies.

Oahu has several hospitals with 24-hour emergency services. Two in the Honolulu area are Queen's Medical Center (☎ 538-9011), 1301 Punchbowl St, and Straub Clinic & Hospital (☎ 522-4000), 888 S King St at Ward. In Kailua, Castle Medical Center (☎ 263-5500), 640 Ulukahiki, is open 24 hours.

Divers with the bends are brought to the UH Hyperbaric Treatment Center (☎ 587-3425), 347 N Kuakini St, Honolulu.

A suicide and crisis line (☎ 521-4555) operates 24 hours a day.

ACTIVITIES

Beaches & Swimming

Oahu boasts more than 50 beach parks, most of which have restrooms and showers. Twenty-three are patrolled by lifeguards. The island's four distinct coastal areas each have their own peculiar seasonal water conditions. When it's rough on one side, it's generally calm on another, so you can find places to swim and surf year round.

Oahu's south shore extends from Barbers Point to Makapuu Point and encompasses the most popular beaches on the island, including the extensive white sands of Waikiki and Ala Moana.

The windward coast extends from Makapuu Point to Kahuku Point. Lovely Kailua Beach Park, Oahu's busiest windsurfing spot, also has good swimming conditions and is the best all-around beach on the windward side. Other nice beaches are at Waimanalo, Kualoa and Malaekahana.

The North Shore extends from Kahuku Point to Kaena Point. Though it has spectacular waves in winter, it can be as calm as a lake during the summer months. There are attractive sandy strands at Haleiwa, Waimea and Sunset Beach.

The leeward Waianae Coast extends from Kaena Point to Barbers Point. It's the driest, sunniest side of the island, with long stretches of white sands. The most popular beach on this side is Makaha, which sees big surf in the winter but has suitable swimming conditions in summer.

Swimming Pools The county maintains 18 community swimming pools, including ones in Kailua, Kaneohe, Pearl City, Wahiawa and Waipahu. Pools in the greater Honolulu area are at Palolo Valley District Park (☎ 733-7362), 2007 Palolo Ave; Manoa Valley District Park (☎ 988-6868), 2721 Kaaipu Ave; Booth District Park (☎ 522-7037), 2331 Kanealii Ave; and McCully District Park (☎ 973-7268), 831 Pumehana.

Surfing
Oahu has 594 defined surfing sites, nearly twice as many as any of the other Hawaiian islands. In winter, the North Shore gets some of Hawaii's most spectacular surf, with swells reaching 20 to 30 feet. This is the home of the Banzai Pipeline, Sunset Beach and some of the world's top surfing competitions.

Makaha is the top winter surf spot on the Waianae Coast. The south shore is gifted with its finest surfing waves in summer, with Waikiki and Diamond Head having some of the best breaks.

Surf News Network (☎ 596-SURF) has a recorded surf line reporting winds, wave heights and tides, updated three times a day. The National Weather Service (☎ 973-4383) also provides surf reports.

The county's Haleiwa Surf Center (☎ 637-5051), at Haleiwa Alii Beach Park, holds free surfing lessons from 9 to 11 am on Saturdays and Sundays between early September and late May. Surfboards are provided.

Surf-N-Sea (☎ 637-9887) in Haleiwa rents surfboards for $5 the first hour, $3.50 each additional hour, or $18 a day. Surf-N-Sea gives two-hour surfing lessons for $65. This and a few other shops in Haleiwa also sell new and used boards.

In Waikiki, surfing lessons can be arranged from beach concession stands like Aloha Beach Services near Duke's Canoe Club or Star Beach Boys behind the police station. The going rate is $25 for a one-hour lesson. The Waikiki concession stands also rent surfboards for around $7 an hour or $25 a day.

Planet Surf (☎ 926-2060), 421 Nahua St in Waikiki, rents surfboards/longboard tankers for $17/20 per 24 hours and also sells used surfboards. Local Motion (☎ 955-7873), 1714 Kapiolani Blvd, rents surfboards for $20 the first 24 hours, $15 for additional days or $75 a week.

H30, a monthly magazine that interviews surfers and reports on surfing events and surf conditions, is free at surf shops around the island.

Bodysurfing, Snorkeling & Boogie Boarding
On the windward coast, Waimanalo Beach Park and nearby Bellows Field Beach Park have gentle shorebreaks good for beginning bodysurfers.

The two hottest (and most dangerous) spots for expert bodysurfers are Sandy and Makapuu beach parks in southeast Oahu.

Other top shorebreaks are at Makaha on the Waianae Coast, Waimea Bay on the North Shore, Kalama Beach in Kailua and Pounders in Laie on the windward coast.

For snorkeling, Hanauma Bay on the south shore is the best year-round spot. In summer, Pupukea Beach Park on the North Shore provides excellent snorkeling.

The most popular boogie boarding place in Waikiki is at Kapahulu Groin.

Rentals If you're going to be doing much snorkeling or boogie boarding, you may be better off buying your own equipment. However, there are plenty of places to rent them.

The concession stands on Waikiki Beach generally charge about $5 an hour or $8 for two hours for boogie boards. Prime Time Sports, a concession stand at Fort DeRussy Beach, rents snorkel sets for $3 an hour, $10 for 24 hours.

A cheaper option, Planet Surf (☎ 926-2060), 421 Nahua St in Waikiki, rents snorkel sets for $5.50 a day, $15 a week, and boogie boards for $7.50 a day, $20 a week. They also sell used boards.

Snorkel Bob's (☎ 735-7944), 700 Kapahulu Ave, about a mile out of Waikiki, rents elementary snorkel sets from $2.50 a day, $14 a week, and better sets with silicone masks for $8.50 a day, $36 a week. You can also arrange to return them on one of the Neighbor Islands.

Surf-N-Sea (☎ 637-9887) in Haleiwa rents boogie boards for $3 for the first hour, $2 for each additional hour, and snorkel sets for $6.50 for half a day, $9.50 for 24 hours.

In Kailua, Naish Hawaii (☎ 262-6068), 155A Hamakua Drive, rents boogie boards for $7 a day, snorkel sets for $5.

Windsurfing

Kailua Bay is Oahu's number one windsurfing spot. It has good year-round trade winds and both flat-water and wave conditions in different sections of the bay. Windsurfing shops set up vans at Kailua Beach Park on weekdays and Saturday mornings, renting boards and giving lessons. It's a great place for beginners to try the sport.

Other good spots include Diamond Head for speed and jumps and Backyards for North Shore challenges. Fort DeRussy Beach is Waikiki's main windsurfing spot.

Naish Hawaii (☎ 262-6068, 800-767-6068) – as in windsurfing champion Robbie Naish – sells and rents equipment. The shop is at 155A Hamakua Drive, Kailua, HI 96734, but they can deliver equipment to Kailua Beach. Rental rates vary with the board and rig: beginner equipment costs $15 an hour or $30 a full day; intermediate and advanced equipment is $35 a half day, $40 to $45 a full day. Naish gives introductory group lessons for $35 for three hours. For $55 you can get a 1½-hour private lesson that includes an additional 2½ hours of board use.

Kailua Sailboard Company (☎ 262-2555), 130 Kailua Rd, Kailua, HI 96734, rents beginner equipment for $25 a half day, $30 a day or $123 a week; intermediate or advanced equipment costs $29 a half day, $38 a full day. Three-hour beginner's lessons are $39.

Waikiki Pacific Windsurfing (☎ 949-8952), in the concession stand at Fort DeRussy Beach, rents windsurfing equipment for $18 an hour, $30 for two hours; add $10 more for a lesson.

In Haleiwa, Surf-N-Sea (☎ 637-9887) rents windsurfing equipment for $12 for the first hour and $8 for each additional hour. Two-hour windsurfing lessons cost $65.

Diving

Top summer dive spots include the caves and ledges at Three Tables and Shark's Cove on the North Shore and the Makaha Caverns on the Waianae Coast. On the south shore, Hanauma Bay has calm diving conditions most of the year. There are a number of other popular dive spots between Hanauma and Honolulu that provide good winter diving.

Aloha Dive Shop (☎ 395-5922), Koko Marina Shopping Center, Honolulu, HI 96825, has two-tank boat dives off Koko Head for $75. Two-tank introductory dives also cost $75; PADI certification courses cost $375. They offer free transport from Waikiki hotels.

OAHU

Ocean Concepts (☎ 677-7975, 800-808-3483; oceanc@aloha.com), 94-547 Ukee St, Suite 303, Waipahu, HI 96797, dives the Waianae Coast, including the WWII minesweeper *Mahi*. Two-tank boat dives cost around $75 day or night, as do introductory dives.

Surf-N-Sea (☎ 637-9887), 62-595 Kamehameha Hwy, Haleiwa, HI 96712, has one-tank shore dives for $65, two-tank dives for $90. Three-day PADI certification courses cost $400 for one person, $275 each for two people, $225 each for three or more.

There are numerous other dive shops on Oahu. The following are all five-star PADI operations.

Aaron's Dive Shop, 602 Kailua Rd, Kailua, HI 96734 (☎ 262-2333; aarons@aloha.com)

Bojac Aquatic Center, 94-801 Farrington Hwy, Waipahu, HI 96797 (☎ 671-0311)

Breeze Hawaii Diving Adventure, 3014 Kaimuki Ave, Honolulu, HI 96816 (☎ 735-1857)

Dan's Dive Shop, 660 Ala Moana Blvd, Honolulu, HI 96813 (☎ 536-6181)

Hawaii Dive College, 24 Sand Island Access Rd, Honolulu, HI 96819 (☎ 843-2882)

Hawaii Pro-Dive, Waikiki Trade Center, 2255 Kuhio Ave, M7, Honolulu, HI 96815 (☎ 922-0895)

Hawaiian Island Aquatics, 834 Kilani Ave, Suite 101, Wahiawa, HI 96786 (☎ 622-3483)

Island Quest, Building 1511, Scott Pool, Pearl Harbor, HI 96860 (☎ 422-5551)

South Sea Aquatics, 2155 Kalakaua Ave, Honolulu, HI 96815 (☎ 922-0852)

Sunshine Scuba, 642 Cooke St, Honolulu, HI 96813 (☎ 593-8865)

Waikiki Diving Center, 1734 Kalakaua Ave, Honolulu, HI 96826 (☎ 955-5151)

Windward Dive Center, 789 Kailua Rd, Kailua, HI 96734 (☎ 263-2311; wdc@divehawaii.com)

Snuba Snuba Tours of Oahu (☎ 396-6163) offers snuba, a sort of scuba diving for snorkelers, at Hanauma Bay for $85 (a 3½-hour outing, including transport from Waikiki) or at Maunalua Bay in the Hawaii Kai area in conjunction with a boat cruise, kayaking, snorkeling and lunch for $105. There's also a shorter snuba experience available for $50 at Waikiki, swimming directly

out from the Outrigger Reef Hotel beach hut, where the snuba outings are booked. This is a nice opportunity to get introduced to the underwater world. All programs include elementary dive instruction, and an instructor is in the water with you during the dive.

Kayaking

Kailua Beach, which has a near-shore island that you can paddle to, is one of the most popular places for kayaking on Oahu. Waikiki, while not as interesting, also gets a fair amount of activity simply because of its high tourist density.

Twogood Kayaks Hawaii (☎ 262-5656), at 171 Hamakua Drive in Kailua, has kayak sales, rentals and lessons. One-person kayaks rent for $22 a half day or $28 a full day; two-person kayaks cost $29/39. Kailua Sailboard Company (☎ 262-2555), at 130 Kailua Rd in Kailua, has one- and two-person kayaks at the same rates.

Kayak Oahu Adventures rents kayaks at Waimea Falls Park (☎ 638-8189; waimea@lava.net) and Waikiki's Sans Souci Beach (☎ 923-0539). In Waikiki, rates for one/two-person kayaks are $10/15 an hour, $30/40 a half day. The rate is about 50% higher in Waimea. In summer they offer guided kayak/snorkel tours on the North Shore, including a 90-minute outing to Three Tables for $50.

Also in Waikiki are Prime Time Sports (☎ 949-8952) at Fort DeRussy Beach and Leahi Beach Services (☎ 922-5665) at the Outrigger Reef hotel, which rent one-person kayaks for $10 an hour, two-person kayaks for around $20.

Hiking

The trail that leads three-quarters of a mile from inside the crater of Diamond Head up to its summit is the most popular hike on Oahu. It's easy to reach from Waikiki and ends with a panoramic view of greater Honolulu.

Another nice, short hike is the Manoa Falls Trail, just a few miles above Waikiki, where a quiet walk through an abandoned arboretum of huge trees leads to a waterfall.

The Tantalus and Makiki Valley area has the most extensive trail network around Honolulu, with fine views of the city and surrounding valleys. Amazingly, although it's just two miles above the city hustle and bustle, this lush forest reserve is unspoiled and offers quiet solitude.

On the western edge of Honolulu, the Moanalua Trail goes deep into the Moanalua Valley. You can hike it on your own or join a guided Sunday walk.

At Keaiwa Heiau State Park, northwest of Honolulu, the Aiea Loop Trail leads 4½ miles along a ridge that offers views of Pearl Harbor, Diamond Head and the Koolau Range.

The Kaena Point Trail is a coastal hike through a natural area reserve on the westernmost point of Oahu. There are also longer forestry trails in the same area.

On the windward side there's a pleasant hour-long hike out to Makapuu lighthouse and a longer trail at Sacred Falls State Park that follows a narrow mountain valley to a waterfall.

There are short walks from the Nuuanu Pali Lookout, along Nuuanu Pali Drive, at Hoomaluhia Botanic Garden and along many beaches.

For more details on hikes, see the respective sections of this chapter.

Guided Hikes Notices of hiking club outings are found in the *Honolulu Star-Bulletin* 'Bulletin Board' column on weekdays and in the *Honolulu Advertiser* 'Calabash' column on Sundays.

By joining one of these outings you get to meet and hike with ecology-minded islanders. It may also be a good way to get to the backwoods if you don't have a car, as they often share rides. Wear sturdy shoes and, for the longer hikes, bring lunch and water.

The Sierra Club (☎ 538-6616) leads hikes and other outings on Saturdays and Sundays. These range from an easy 1½-mile hike to Jackass Ginger to strenuous 10-mile treks. Most outings meet at 8 am at the Church of the Crossroads at 2510

> ### Hitchhiking Weeds
> Anyone who has hiked on Oahu should scrub their shoes and wash their socks and long pants before hiking on other islands to avoid transferring clinging *Clidemia hirta* seeds, which are practically invisible. This weed has infested much of Oahu, overrunning trails and choking out native plants, but it's not yet widely established on the Neighbor Islands. It's presumed that the patches of this invasive plant found along trails on Molokai and Maui hitchhiked there on an Oahuan hiker's boot. ∎

Bingham St in Honolulu. The hike fee is $3. For a copy of the latest newsletter, which includes the hike schedule, send $2 to Sierra Club, Box 2577, Honolulu, HI 96803.

The Hawaii Audubon Society (☎ 528-1432) leads bird-watching hikes once or twice a month, usually on weekends. The suggested donation is $2. Binoculars and a copy of *Hawaii's Birds* are recommended.

The Hawaii Nature Center (☎ 955-0100), at the forestry baseyard camp in Makiki, leads hikes on most Saturday mornings for $5. Trails range from the easy 2½-mile Makiki Loop Trail to a strenuous six-mile hike up Mt Kaala, Oahu's highest point. Reservations are required.

The Hawaiian Trail & Mountain Club has guided hikes most weekends, although some are for members only. The hike fee is $2. Hikes generally range from three to 12 miles in length and from novice to advanced in difficulty. For a copy of the hiking schedule, send $1 and a self-addressed, stamped envelope to the club at Box 2238, Honolulu, HI 96804.

Horseback Riding

Kualoa Ranch (☎ 237-8515), opposite Kualoa Regional Park on the windward coast, has 40-minute trail rides in Kaaawa Valley for $25 and 1½-hour rides for $40.

The Turtle Bay Hilton (☎ 293-8811) in Kahuku has 45-minute trail rides for $35 and 1½-hour sunset rides for $65.

Hoku Ranch (☎ 622-2100) at Dole Plantation in Wahiawa has 1¼-hour trail rides past pineapple fields for $25, as well as longer rides.

Tennis

Oahu has 175 county tennis courts. If you're staying in Waikiki, the most convenient locations are the 10 lighted courts at Ala Moana Beach Park, the nine unlit courts at the Diamond Head Tennis Center at the Diamond Head end of Kapiolani Park and the four lighted Kapiolani Park courts opposite the Waikiki Aquarium. Court time is free on a first-come first-served basis.

With ground space at a premium, few Waikiki hotels have room for tennis courts. The largest facilities are at the Ilikai Hotel (☎ 944-6300), 1777 Ala Moana Blvd, which has five courts, rentals, lessons and a pro shop. Rates are $5 per hour per person for hotel guests, $7.50 for nonguests, plus a $2 charge for night play. Rackets rent for $3. It's open daily from 7 am to 10 pm.

The Pacific Beach Hotel (☎ 922-1233) on Kalakaua Ave has two courts open daily from 8 am to 6 pm and charges $5 per hour per person for guests, $8 for nonguests. Rackets can be rented for $4.

Planet Surf, at 419 Nahua St in Waikiki, rents tennis rackets for $5 a day, $20 a week.

Outside Waikiki, the Turtle Bay Hilton in Kahuku (☎ 293-6024) charges $12 per person per day, with 1½-hour playing time guaranteed; rackets rent for $7 a day. The resort also gives lessons, has a pro shop and rents shoes, baskets of balls and ball machines.

Golf

Oahu has five 18-hole municipal golf courses: Ala Wai Golf Course (☎ 733-7387) on Kapahulu Ave, mauka of the Ala Wai Canal, near Waikiki; Pali Golf Course (☎ 266-7612), 45-050 Kamehameha Hwy, Kaneohe; Ted Makalena Golf Course (☎ 675-6052), Waipio Point Access Rd, Waipahu; Ewa Villages Golf Course (☎ 681-0220) in Ewa; and West Loch Golf Course (☎ 675-6076), 91-1126 Okupe St, Ewa Beach.

Greens fees for 18 holes are $40 per person, plus an optional $14 for a gas-powered cart. The county also maintains the nine-hole Kahuku Golf Course (☎ 293-5842) in Kahuku.

The reservation system is the same at all municipal courses: call ☎ 296-2000 and key information into the recorded system as prompted. The earliest bookings are taken just three days in advance for visitors, but one week in advance for resident golfers.

The only municipal course near Waikiki is the Ala Wai Golf Course, which lays claim to being the 'busiest in the world'. Local golfers who may book earlier in the week usually take all the starting times, leaving none for visitors. However, visiting golfers who don't mind a wait may show up at the Ala Wai window and get on the waiting list; as long as the entire golfing party waits at the course, they'll usually get you on before the day is over. If you come without clubs, you can rent them for $20.

At last count, Oahu also had 18 private (and nine military) golf courses, but the number is rising, fueling many a conflict between environmentalists and overseas developers.

Running

Oahu is big on jogging. In fact, it's estimated that Honolulu has more joggers per capita than any other city in the world. Kapiolani Park and Ala Moana Park are two favorite jogging spots. There's also a well-beaten 4.8-mile run around Diamond Head crater.

Oahu has more than 75 road races each year, from one-mile fun runs and five-mile jogs to competitive marathons, biathlons and triathlons. For an annual schedule of running events with times, dates and contact addresses, write to the Department of Parks & Recreation, City & County of Honolulu, 650 S King St, Honolulu, HI 96813.

Oahu's best-known race is the Honolulu Marathon, held in December. For information send a self-addressed, stamped envelope to Honolulu Marathon Association, 3435 Waialae Ave, No 208, Honolulu, HI

96816. Those writing from overseas are asked to include two international response postage coupons.

The Department of Parks & Recreation holds a Honolulu Marathon Clinic at 7:30 am most Sundays at the Kapiolani Park Bandstand. It's free and open to everyone from beginners to seasoned marathon runners. Runners join groups of their own speed.

Skydiving
For $225, Skydive Hawaii (☎ 945-0222) will attach you to the hips and shoulders of a skydiver so you can jump together from a plane at 13,000 feet, freefall for a minute and finish off with 10 to 15 minutes of canopy ride. The whole process, including some basic instruction, takes about 1½ hours. Participants must be over 18 years of age and weigh less than 200 pounds. Arrangements can also be made to take up experienced skydivers for solo jumps. They take off daily (weather permitting) from Dillingham Airfield in Mokuleia. Pick-up service is available from Waikiki.

Organized Tours
For conventional sightseeing tours by van or bus, try E Noa Tours (☎ 591-2561), Polynesian Adventure Tours (☎ 833-3000) or Roberts Hawaii (☎ 539-9400).

Full-day, circle-island tours average $55 and generally encompass southeast Oahu, the windward coast, the North Shore and Waimea Falls Park. There are a wide variety of other tour packages, including a few that concentrate more on Hawaiian culture.

For those who actually want to get into the water and relax along the way, a good alternative island tour is offered by Alala EcoAdventures. It costs just $22 and is booked through Hostelling International Honolulu (☎ 946-0591).

Waikiki Trolley
The Waikiki Trolley is a tourist trolley bus that runs along a fixed route between Waikiki and Honolulu. There are 19 stops, including the Ala Moana Center, Honolulu Academy of Arts, Iolani Palace, Hawaii Maritime Center,

Bishop Museum, Chinatown and the Ward Centre. Sightseeing narration is provided en route and passengers can get off at any stop and then pick up the next trolley. Trolleys depart from the Royal Hawaiian Shopping Center in Waikiki every 15 minutes between 8 am and 4:30 pm. One-day passes cost $17 for adults, $5 for children ages 11 and under – a pricey alternative to the public bus.

Gliding
Glider Rides (☎ 677-3404) offers 20-minute flights on engineless piloted glider craft, towed by an airplane and then released to slowly glide back to earth. Flights leave daily, weather permitting, from the west end of Dillingham Airfield in Mokuleia between 10:30 am and 5 pm. The cost is $100 for one person or $120 for two.

At the same location, Soar Hawaii (☎ 637-3147) offers 20-minute glider rides for $120 for either one or two people. For thrill seekers, they also offer acrobatic rides with barrel rolls, spirals and stalls.

Cruises
There are numerous sunset sails, dinner cruises and party boats leaving daily from Kewalo Basin, just west of Ala Moana Park. Rates range from $20 to $100, with dinner cruises averaging about $50. Many provide transport to and from Waikiki and advertise various come-ons and specials; check the free tourist magazines for the latest offers. As some of the vessels, including a few of the 'catamarans', are large impersonal operations, you may prefer to go down to the harbor where the boats are docked and check them out for yourself before buying a ticket.

A handful of catamarans depart from Waikiki Beach, including the *Manu Kai* (☎ 946-7490), which docks behind the Duke Kahanamoku statue and charges $10 for one-hour sails, $20 for 1½-hour sunset sails. The green-sailed *Leahi* catamaran (☎ 922-5665), which departs from the beach in front of the Sheraton Waikiki, has one-hour sails for $16 and 1½-hour sunset sails for $24.

Royal Hawaiian Cruises (☎ 848-6360) runs 2½-hour whale-watching cruises from

January to April aboard the *Navatek I*, a sleek, high-tech catamaran designed to minimize rolling. It leaves daily except Mondays at 8:30 am from Pier 6, near the Aloha Tower, and costs $39 for adults and $24 for children ages three to 11.

Atlantis Submarines (☎ 973-9811) has a 65-foot, 48-passenger sightseeing submarine that descends to a depth of 100 feet about a mile off Diamond Head. The tour lasts 1¾ hours, including boat transport to and from the sub. About 45 minutes are spent cruising beneath the surface around a ship and two planes deliberately sunk to create a dive site. Tours leave from Hilton Hawaiian Village on the hour from 7 am to 4 pm daily and cost from $85 for adults, $39 for children 12 and under.

ACCOMMODATIONS

Some 90% of Oahu's 40,000 visitor rooms are in Waikiki. Unlike on the Neighbor Islands, where there are multiple destinations, all but two of Oahu's resort hotels are found in Honolulu.

The Waikiki/Honolulu area has a wide range of accommodations. The least expensive places to stay are the two HI-affiliated youth hostels and the handful of private hostel-type crash pads – all of them have dorm beds for about $15. After that, there are rooms at Ys for $30 and a few budget Waikiki hotels that start around $45. Waikiki has lots of middle-range hotels in the $65 to $100 range as well as high-priced luxury hotels.

Unless otherwise noted, rates given throughout this chapter are the same for either singles or doubles and don't include the 10.17% room tax. Most hotels have different rates for the high and low seasons. The high season is generally from December 15 to April 15, but it can vary by hotel a few weeks in either direction. The rest of the year is the low season, though a few hotels switch to high-season rates in midsummer.

To lure customers, some large chains like Outrigger and Hawaiian Pacific Resorts offer a free rental car if you request it at the time of booking. A few independent hotels occasionally throw in a car as well – it never hurts to ask whenever you book any hotel. If you had planned on renting a car, it can be a tidy savings.

Camping

Camping is allowed at 12 county beach parks, one county botanic garden and four state parks.

All county and state campgrounds on Oahu are closed on Wednesday and Thursday nights, ostensibly for maintenance, but also to prevent permanent encampments.

Although thousands of visitors use these campsites each year without incident, Oahu has more of a reputation for problems than other islands. Rip-offs, especially at roadside and beachfront campgrounds, are not uncommon.

Camping along the Waianae Coast is not recommended.

State Parks Camping is free by permit at Sand Island and Keaiwa Heiau, both in the greater Honolulu area, and at Malaekahana State Recreation Area and Kahana Valley State Park, both on the windward coast.

Keaiwa Heiau is a good choice for an inland park. A good choice for a coastal park is Malaekahana, which is also the only public park on Oahu with cabins (see the Windward Oahu section).

Camping is limited to five nights per month in each park. Permit applications must be submitted at least seven days and no more than 30 days before the first camping date. Applications may be made to the Division of State Parks by mail (Box 621, Honolulu, HI 96809), by phone (☎ 587-0300) or in person (1151 Punchbowl St, Room 131) between 8 am and 3:30 pm Monday to Friday.

County Beach Parks Camping is free at county beach parks, but permits are required. Permits are not available by mail but can be picked up between 7:45 am and 4 pm Monday to Friday at the Department of Parks & Recreation (☎ 523-4525) on the ground floor of the Municipal Office building (650 S King St, Honolulu, HI 96813), the tall gray building on the corner of King and Alapai Sts.

Camping permits are also available from any satellite city hall, including the one at the Ala Moana Center (☎ 973-2600), where they are issued from 9 am to 4:30 pm Monday to Thursday, 9 am to 5 pm on Fridays, 8 am to 4 pm on Saturdays. Other satellite city halls are in Kailua, Kaneohe and Wahiawa.

Camping is allowed at Mokuleia and Kaiaka beach parks on the North Shore; Hauula, Swanzy, Kualoa, Bellows Field, Waimanalo and Waimanalo Bay beach parks on the windward coast; and Kahe Point, Nanakuli, Lualualei and Keaau beach parks on the Waianae Coast.

Camping is allowed from 8 am Friday to 8 am Wednesday, except at Swanzy and Bellows Field beach parks, which are open only on weekends.

Kualoa, in one of Oahu's nicest beach settings, has an on-site caretaker and gates that are locked at night. Kaiaka, Bellows Field and Waimanalo Bay also have caretakers, but other beach parks don't.

County Botanic Garden Hoomaluhia Park (☎ 233-7323), an inland park in Kaneohe at the base of the Koolau Range, is unique among the county campgrounds in that it's operated by the botanic gardens division. With a resident caretaker and gates that close to noncampers at 4 pm, the park is one of the safest places to camp on Oahu.

The five grassy camping areas, each of which has restrooms, cold showers and drinking water, can accommodate up to 650 people, but often only a couple of the areas need to be opened.

Camping is allowed on Friday, Saturday and Sunday nights only. The park seldom fills and for individuals it's not necessary to make advance reservations – simply come by the park between 9 am and 4 pm Monday to Saturday to get your permit. If you prefer to get an application in advance, however, send a legal-size, self-addressed, stamped envelope to Hoomaluhia, 45-680 Luluku Rd, Kaneohe, HI 96744. There is no fee to camp at Hoomaluhia.

Backcountry Camping The state forestry allows backcountry camping along several valley and ridge trails, including three in Hauula on the windward coast and along the Waimano Trail north of Pearl City.

All backcountry camping requires a permit from the Division of Forestry & Wildlife (☎ 587-0166), 1151 Punchbowl St, Room 131, Honolulu, HI 96813. Permits are issued between 8 am and 3:30 pm Monday to Friday.

Fellow hikers on backcountry trails are likely to be pig hunters.

Camping Supplies The Bike Shop (☎ 596-0588), 1149 S King St, rents North Face internal-frame backpacks and two-person lightweight tents. The rate for each is $15/35/70 per day/weekend/week.

Omar The Tent Man (☎ 677-8785), 94-158 Leoole St, Waipahu, HI 96797, has weekly rates of $30 for lightweight two-person dome tents, $20 for sleeping bags, $22 for external-frame backpacks and $18 for stoves or lanterns. Three-day rates for those items are $25, $17, $18 and $14 respectively.

ENTERTAINMENT

The vast majority of Oahu's entertainment takes place in Honolulu, which includes but is certainly not limited to Waikiki.

The best place to look for up-to-date entertainment information is in the free *Honolulu Weekly* newspaper. Other sources are the free tourist magazines and the daily newspapers, in particular the 'Night Life' column in the Thursday edition of the *Honolulu Star-Bulletin*.

Oahu has a lively gay scene, which is centered around the Kuhio District in Waikiki.

The island has more than 40 movie theaters, including a few drive-in theaters, and a dozen theater companies that perform everything from 'South Pacific' and Broadway musicals to Mamet satires and pidgin fairy tales. Check the newspapers for current movies and plays.

More detailed information is located in the Entertainment sections under specific destinations. For festivals, fairs and sporting events, see the Special Events section in the Facts about Hawaii chapter.

Luaus

Oahu's two main luaus, *Paradise Cove* (☎ 973-5828) and *Germaine's Luau* (☎ 949-6626), are both huge, impersonal affairs held nightly out near the Barbers Point area. Both cost around $45, which includes the bus ride from Waikiki hotels (about one hour each way), a buffet dinner, drinks, a Polynesian show and related hoopla. Children pay about half price.

THINGS TO BUY

Honolulu is a large, cosmopolitan city with plenty of sophisticated shops selling designer clothing, jewelry and the like. For general crafts, the best deals are usually found at one of the craft shows that are periodically held in city parks (check the newspapers).

For kitsch souvenirs there are scores of shops selling fake Polynesian stuff, from Filipino shell hangings and carved coconuts to cheap seashell jewelry and wooden tiki statues – the largest single collection of such shops is at the International Market Place in Waikiki.

If you just want to buy a carton of macadamia nuts, Longs Drugs has better prices than most places in Waikiki. There's a Longs, as well as 200 other stores, at the Ala Moana Center, the 'largest open-air shopping center in the world' (see the Ala Moana section).

For local flavor, the Aloha Flea Market (☎ 486-1529), at Aloha Stadium out near Pearl Harbor, has some 1500 vendors from 7 am to 3 pm on Wednesdays, Saturdays and Sundays. A private shuttle bus (☎ 955-4050) to the flea market leaves from Waikiki at 7:30, 9 and 10:30 am at a cost of $6 roundtrip.

Hawaiiana Souvenirs

The Hula Supply Center (☎ 941-5379), 2346 S King St in Honolulu, sells feather leis, calabash gourds, lava-rock castanets, bamboo sticks, hula skirts and the like. Although they're intended for Hawaiian musicians and dancers, some of the items would certainly make interesting souvenirs and prices are reasonable.

Quilts Hawaii (☎ 942-3195), 2338 S King St, just a minute's walk from the Hula Supply Center, has high-quality Hawaiian quilting, including bedcovers, pillows and wall hangings. It also carries other Hawaiian crafts such as hats, koa chests and dolls. Prices are high but reasonable for the quality.

Kamaka Hawaii (☎ 531-3165), at 550 South St in Honolulu, specializes in hand-crafted ukuleles, priced from $235.

For antique and used aloha shirts, Bailey's Antique Shop (☎ 734-7628), 517 Kapahulu Ave, near Waikiki, has the island's widest selection, with prices from $10 to $1000. Bargain-hunters can sometimes find used aloha shirts and muumuus at thrift shops around the island, including the Goodwill store at 780 S Beretania St in Honolulu and the small shop (open 10 am to 2 pm weekdays) at the Waikiki Community Center, 310 Paoakalani Ave.

CDs and cassettes of Hawaiian music also make good souvenirs. You'll find an excellent collection of both classic and contemporary Hawaiian music at Borders, which has branches at the Ward Centre in Honolulu and the Waikele Center in Waipahu, and at Tower Records, which has shops behind the Ala Moana Center and at Waikiki's International Market Place. Both companies allow you to listen to various CDs before you buy.

GETTING THERE & AWAY
Air

The vast majority of flights into Hawaii land at Honolulu International Airport, the only commercial airport on Oahu. See the Getting There & Away chapter in the front of the book for information on flights to Oahu and airport facilities.

All inter-island airlines that serve the Neighbor Islands also use Honolulu International Airport. For details on flying to the Neighbor Islands, see the Getting Around chapter in the front of the book and the

Getting There & Away sections of individual Neighbor Island chapters.

GETTING AROUND

Oahu is an easy island to get around, whether you travel by public bus or private car.

Traffic in Honolulu can get quite jammed during rush hour – weekdays from 7 to 9 am and 4 to 6 pm. Expect heavy traffic in both directions on H-1 during this time, as well as when heading toward Honolulu in the morning and away in the late afternoon on the Pali and Likelike hwys. If you're heading to the airport during rush hour, give yourself plenty of extra time.

To/From the Airport

From the airport you can get to Waikiki by local bus (if your baggage is limited), by airport shuttle services, by taxi or by rental car. A taxi to Waikiki from the airport will cost about $20. The main car rental agencies have booths or courtesy phones in the airport baggage claim area.

The easiest way to drive to Waikiki from the airport is to take Hwy 92, which starts out as Nimitz Hwy and turns into Ala Moana Blvd, leading directly into Waikiki. Although this route hits more local traffic, it's hard to get lost on it.

If you're into life in the fast lane, connect instead with the H-1 Fwy heading east.

On the return to the airport from Waikiki, take note not to miss the poorly marked interchange where H-1 and Hwy 78 split; if you're not in the right-hand lane at that point, you could easily end up on Hwy 78. It takes about 20 minutes to get from Waikiki to the airport via H-1 if you don't hit traffic.

Bus Travel time is about an hour between the airport and the far end of Waikiki on city buses No 19 and 20; the fare is $1. The bus stops at the roadside median on the 2nd level, in front of the airline counters. There are two stops; it's best to wait for the bus at the first one, which is in front of Lobby 4. Luggage is limited to what you can hold on your lap or store under your seat, the latter space comparable to the space under an airline seat.

Shuttle Bus The ride between Waikiki and the airport takes about 45 minutes by shuttle bus. These buses are picked up at the roadside median on the ground level between baggage claim areas E and F. Most charge $6 for adults, $3 for children, with rates including two suitcases and one carry-on bag. Generally, you don't need reservations from the airport to Waikiki, but you do need to call at least a few hours in advance for the return van to the airport. Two of the larger companies are Airport Express (☎ 949-5249) and Rabi Transportation (☎ 922-4900).

Bus

Oahu's public bus system, called TheBus, is extensive and easy to use.

TheBus has some 80 routes, which collectively cover most of Oahu. You can take the bus to watch windsurfers at Kailua or surfers at Sunset Beach or Makaha, visit Chinatown or the Bishop Museum, snorkel at Hanauma Bay or hike Diamond Head. However, some of the island's prime viewpoints are beyond reach: TheBus doesn't stop at the Nuuanu Pali Lookout, go up to Tantalus or out to Kaena Point.

Buses stop only at marked bus stops. Each bus route can have a few different destinations. The destination is written on the front of the bus next to the number.

Buses generally keep the same number when inbound and outbound. For instance, bus No 8 can take you either into the heart of Waikiki or out away from it towards Ala Moana – so take note of both the number and the written destination before you jump on.

If you're in doubt, ask the bus driver. They're used to disoriented visitors, and most drivers are patient and helpful.

Overall, the buses are in excellent condition – if anything they're too modern. Newer buses are air-conditioned, with sealed windows and climate-control that sometimes seems so out of 'control' that drivers wear jackets to keep from freezing!

Currently, about half of the buses are equipped with wheelchair lifts and a third have bike racks that cyclists can use for free.

Although TheBus is convenient enough, this isn't Tokyo – if you set your watch by the bus here, you'll come up with Hawaiian Time. In addition to not getting hung up on schedules, buses can sometimes bottleneck, with one packed bus after another cruising right by crowded bus stops. Saturday nights between Ala Moana and Waikiki can be a particularly memorable experience.

Still, TheBus usually gets you where you want to go and as long as you don't try to cut anything close or schedule too much in one day it's a great deal.

Fares The one-way fare for all rides is $1 for adults, 50¢ for children ages six to 18. Children under the age of six ride free. You can use either coins or $1 bills; bus drivers don't make change.

Transfers, which have a time limit stamped on them, are given free when more than one bus is required to get to a destination. If needed, ask for one when you board.

Visitor passes valid for unlimited rides over four consecutive days cost $10 and can be purchased at any of the ubiquitous ABC Discount Stores.

Monthly bus passes valid for unlimited rides in a calendar month cost $25 and can be purchased at satellite city halls, 7-Eleven convenience stores and Foodland and Star supermarkets.

Seniors 65 years and older can buy a $20 bus pass valid for unlimited rides during a two-year period. Senior citizen passes are issued only at TheBus office (☎ 848-4444), 811 Middle St, Honolulu, from 7:30 am to 4 pm Monday to Friday. Bus No 1 (Kahili) or No 2 (School-Middle) goes directly to TheBus office.

Schedules & Information TheBus has a great telephone service. As long as you know where you are and where you want to go, you can call ☎ 848-5555 anytime between 5:30 am and 10 pm and they'll tell you not only which bus to catch, but also when the next one will be there. This same number also has a TDD service for the hearing impaired.

For 24-hour recorded information on getting to major destinations from Waikiki, call ☎ 296-1818 and then enter 8287.

You can get printed timetables for some routes and a handy schematic route map free from any satellite city hall (including the one at the Ala Moana Center), the Waikiki Beach police station and most libraries.

If you're going to be using TheBus extensively, it's well worth buying one of the bus guides that are sold in bookstores and convenience stores for around $3. Take time to look a few over. For instance, *Honolulu's Famous TheBus* has actual schedules, but if you're not familiar with the streets, a better choice is *Honolulu & Oahu by TheBus*, a fold-out brochure that doesn't have schedules but has maps showing major visitor destinations with bus stops and numbers. Be sure to get the most up-to-date version.

Common Routes Buses No 8, 19, 20 and 58 run between Waikiki and Ala Moana Center, Honolulu's central transfer point. There's usually a bus every 10 minutes or less. From Ala Moana you can connect with a broad network of buses to points mauka and Ewa.

Buses No 2, 19 and 20 will take you between Waikiki and downtown Honolulu.

Bus No 4 runs between Waikiki and the University of Hawaii.

Circle-Island Route It's possible to circle the island by bus, beginning at the Ala Moana Center. The No 52 Wahiawa-Circle Island bus goes clockwise up Hwy 99 to Haleiwa and along the North Shore. At the Turtle Bay Hilton, on the northern tip of Oahu, it switches signs to No 55 and comes down the windward coast to Kaneohe and down the Pali Hwy back to Ala Moana. The No 55 Kaneohe-Circle Island bus does the same route in reverse. If you do it nonstop, it takes about four hours.

To make the loop around southeast Oahu from Waikiki, it's bus No 58 to Sea Life

Park and then No 57 up to Kailua and back into Honolulu.

Because you'll need to change buses, ask for a transfer when you first board. Transfers have time limits and aren't meant to be used as stopovers, but you can usually grab a quick break at Ala Moana. Anytime you get off to explore along the route you'll need to pay a new $1 fare when you reboard.

Car

Budget (☎ 537-3600), National (☎ 831-3800), Hertz (☎ 831-3500), Avis (☎ 834-5536) and Dollar (☎ 831-2330) all have desks at Honolulu International Airport and car lots on the airport grounds. Alamo (☎ 833-4585) has its operations about a mile outside the airport, on the corner of Nimitz Hwy and Ohohia St.

All things being equal, try to rent from a company with its lot inside the airport – not only is it more convenient to do so, but, more importantly, on the way back all the highway signs lead to the in-airport car returns.

The international companies also have numerous branch locations in Waikiki, many in the lobbies of larger hotels. General rental information and toll-free numbers are in the Getting Around chapter in the front of the book.

Budget gives renters a coupon booklet that allows one free admission to many of Oahu's more expensive tourist attractions, including Sea Life Park, Waimea Falls Park, Polynesian Cultural Center and Bishop Museum. You don't even have to buy a second admission to use the coupon, so for a single traveler it's all free. This is a particularly good deal if you're renting a car for only a day or two and want to catch some of the sights.

Moped

State law requires mopeds to be ridden by one person only and prohibits their use on sidewalks and on freeways. Renters must be 18 years or older.

Blue Sky Rentals (☎ 947-0101), on the ground floor of Inn on the Park Hotel, 1920 Ala Moana Blvd, is a good Waikiki spot to rent a moped. The rates of $20 from 8 am to 6 pm, $25 for 24 hours or $105 a week include taxes and insurance.

Mopeds can also be rented at similar rates from Diamond Head Mopeds (☎ 921-2899), which has a location at the corner of Lewers St and Kuhio Ave and another on Kuhio Ave just east of the Royal Garden Hotel.

Taxi

Metered taxis charge a flag-down fee of $2 to start with, and then fares click up in 25¢ increments at a rate of $2 per mile. There's an extra charge of 35¢ for each suitcase or backpack.

Taxis are readily available at the airport and larger hotels but generally are otherwise hard to find. To phone for one, try Sida (☎ 836-0011), Charley's (☎ 955-2211), Americabs (☎ 591-8830) or City Taxi (☎ 524-2121). The latter offers a 10% discount to senior citizens over the age of 60.

Bicycle

There's a lot more traffic on Oahu than on the other islands, which makes cycling seem a lot less appealing. The State Department of Transportation has published a new 'Bike Oahu' map with possible routes divided into those for novice cyclists, those for experienced cyclists and routes that are not bicycle-friendly. The map can usually be found at the HVB visitor information center in Waikiki, or you can call ☎ 527-5044.

Planet Surf (☎ 926-2060), 419 Nahua St in Waikiki, rents mountain bikes for $15/65 a day/week and beach cruisers for $13/50.

There are also other bicycle rental places in Waikiki, including one next to InterClub Hostel Waikiki, 2413 Kuhio Ave, and Blue Sky Rentals (☎ 947-0101), 1920 Ala Moana Blvd. Both have bikes for around $20 a day.

The Hawaii Bicycling League (☎ 735-5756), Box 4403, Honolulu, HI 96812, holds bike rides around Oahu nearly every Saturday and Sunday, ranging from 10-mile jaunts to 60-mile treks. Rides are free and open to the public.

Waikiki

Once Hawaii's only tourist destination, Waikiki still accounts for nearly half of the visitor accommodations in the state with its amazing density of high-rise hotels along an attractive stretch of white-sand beach.

Waikiki is crowded with package tourists from both Japan and the US mainland. It has 25,000 permanent residents and some 65,000 visitors on any given day, all in an area roughly 1½ miles long and half a mile wide. Waikiki has 450 restaurants, 350 bars and clubs, and more shops than you'd want to count. Its 33,000 hotel and condo rooms have a year-round occupancy rate of 80%.

While the beaches are packed during the day, at night most of the action is along the streets, where window shoppers, timeshare touts and prostitutes all go about their business. A variety of live music, from mellow Hawaiian to rock, wafts from streetside clubs and hotel lounges.

Visitors who are into city lights or singles scenes often find what they're looking for here, while many seasoned travelers and a fair number of Oahu residents avoid Waikiki like the plague.

Waikiki Beach has wonderful orange sunsets, with the sun dropping down between cruising sailboats. It's the one time of day that the area approaches the romantic image that the travel brochures like to portray.

Just beyond Waikiki is Diamond Head, a landmark so dominant that it's used as a directional marker – local people say 'go Diamond Head' instead of 'head east'.

Orientation

Waikiki is bounded on two sides by the Ala Wai Canal and on another by the ocean. The eastern boundary varies according to who's drawing the line, but it's usually considered to be Kapahulu Ave.

There are two main roads: the beach road is Kalakaua Ave, named after King David Kalakaua; the main drag for Waikiki's buses is Kuhio Ave, named after Prince Jonah Kuhio Kalanianaole, a distinguished Hawaiian statesman.

City buses are not allowed on Kalakaua Ave, and trucks are prohibited at midday. Traffic on this four-lane road is one way so it's relatively smooth for driving, but pedestrians need to be cautious as cars tend to zoom by fast.

Walking along the beach is an alternative to using the crowded sidewalks. It's possible to walk the full length of Waikiki along the sand and the sea walls. Although it's rather hot and crowded at midday, it's pleasant at other times. The beach is quite romantic to stroll along at night, enhanced by both the city skyline and the surf lapping at the shore, and it's dark enough to see the stars.

Information

Tourist Offices The Hawaii Visitors Bureau has its visitor information office (☎ 924-0266) in the Royal Hawaiian Shopping Center (Hibiscus Court, 4th floor), at the Lewers St end of the center. It has racks of brochures and tourist magazines, including those for the Neighbor Islands, and is open from 8 am to 4:30 pm Monday to Friday.

Free tourist magazines, such as *This Week Oahu*, *Spotlight's Oahu Gold* and *Guide to Oahu*, can readily be found on street corners and in hotel lobbies throughout Waikiki.

Money There's a Bank of Hawaii at 2220 Kalakaua Ave, a Bank of America at 321 Seaside Ave and a First Hawaiian Bank at 2181 Kalakaua Ave. The latter has some interesting Hawaiiana murals by the renowned artist Jean Charlot.

There are numerous ATMs around Waikiki that accept major bank and credit cards. Those at Food Pantry on Kuhio Ave and the nearby 7-Eleven convenience store are both accessible 24 hours.

Post & Communications The main Waikiki post office, 330 Saratoga Rd, is open from 8 am to 4:30 pm on weekdays, except on Wednesdays, when it's open

From Swamp to Resort

At the turn of the century, Waikiki was almost entirely wetlands. It had more than 50 acres of fishponds as well as extensive taro patches and rice paddies. Fed by mountain streams from the upland Manoa and Makiki valleys, Waikiki was one of Oahu's most fertile and productive areas.

By the late 19th century, Waikiki's narrow beachfront was lined with gingerbread-trimmed cottages, built by Honolulu's more well-to-do.

Robert Louis Stevenson, who frequented Waikiki in those days, wrote:

HAWAII STATE ARCHIVES

If anyone desires such old-fashioned things as lovely scenery, quiet, pure air, clear sea water, heavenly sunsets hung out before his eyes over the Pacific and the distant hills of Waianae, I recommend him to Waikiki Beach.

Tourism took root in 1901, when the Moana opened its doors as Waikiki's first real hotel. A tram line was constructed to connect Waikiki to downtown Honolulu and city folk crowded aboard for the beach. Tiring quickly of the pesky mosquitoes that thrived in the wetlands, these early beachgoers petitioned to have Waikiki's 'swamps' brought under control.

In 1922 the Ala Wai Canal was dug to divert the streams that flowed into Waikiki. Old Hawaii lost out, as farmers had the water drained out from under them. Coral rubble was used to fill the ponds, creating what was to become Hawaii's most valuable piece of real estate. Water buffaloes soon were replaced by tourists.

Waikiki's second hotel, the Royal Hawaiian, was built in 1927 and became the crown jewel of the Matson Navigation Company.

The Royal was the land component for cruises on the *Malolo*, one of the premier luxury ships of the day. The $7.5-million ship, built while the $2-million hotel was under construction, carried 650 passengers from San Francisco to Honolulu each fortnight. The Pink Palace, as the Royal Hawaiian was nicknamed, opened with an extravagant $10-a-plate dinner.

Hotel guests ranged from the Rockefellers to Charlie Chaplin, Babe Ruth to royalty. Some of the guests brought dozens of trunks, their servants and even their Rolls Royces.

The Depression put a damper on things, and WWII saw the Royal Hawaiian turned into an R&R center for servicemen.

Waikiki had 1400 hotel rooms in 1950. In those days, surfers could drive their cars to the beach and park on the sand. In the 1960s tourism took over in earnest and by 1968

NED FRIARY

Waikiki had 13,000 hotel rooms. By 1988 that number had more than doubled.

The lack of available land has finally halted the boom. In a desperate attempt to squeeze in one more high-rise, St Augustine's Catholic Church, standing on the last speck of uncommercialized property along busy Kalakaua Ave, was nearly sold in 1989 to a Tokyo developer for $45 million. It took a community uproar and a petition to the Vatican to nullify the deal. ∎

OAHU

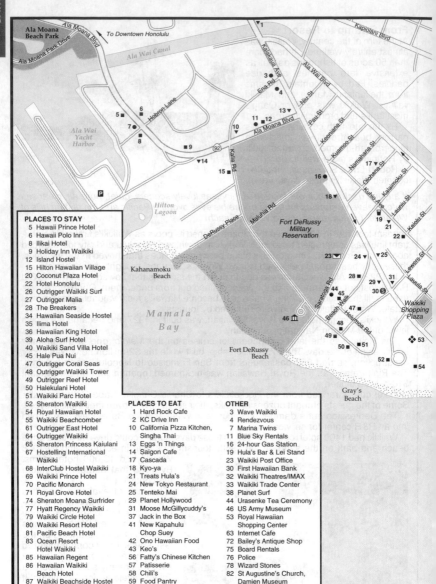

PLACES TO STAY
5   Hawaii Prince Hotel
6   Hawaii Polo Inn
8   Ilikai Hotel
9   Holiday Inn Waikiki
12 Island Hostel
15 Hilton Hawaiian Village
20 Coconut Plaza Hotel
22 Hotel Honolulu
26 Outrigger Waikiki Surf
27 Outrigger Malia
28 The Breakers
34 Hawaiian Seaside Hostel
35 Ilima Hotel
36 Hawaiian King Hotel
39 Aloha Surf Hotel
40 Waikiki Sand Villa Hotel
45 Hale Pua Nui
47 Outrigger Coral Seas
48 Outrigger Waikiki Tower
49 Outrigger Reef Hotel
50 Halekulani Hotel
51 Waikiki Parc Hotel
52 Sheraton Waikiki
54 Royal Hawaiian Hotel
55 Waikiki Beachcomber
61 Outrigger East Hotel
64 Outrigger Waikiki
65 Sheraton Princess Kaiulani
67 Hostelling International
     Waikiki
68 InterClub Hostel Waikiki
69 Waikiki Prince Hotel
70 Pacific Monarch
71 Royal Grove Hotel
74 Sheraton Moana Surfrider
77 Hyatt Regency Waikiki
79 Waikiki Circle Hotel
80 Waikiki Resort Hotel
81 Pacific Beach Hotel
83 Ocean Resort
     Hotel Waikiki
85 Hawaiian Regent
86 Hawaiian Waikiki
     Beach Hotel
87 Waikiki Beachside Hostel
88 Polynesian Hostel
     Beachclub
89 Waikiki Grand Hotel
90 Queen Kapiolani Hotel

PLACES TO EAT
1   Hard Rock Cafe
2   KC Drive Inn
10 California Pizza Kitchen,
     Singha Thai
13 Eggs 'n Things
14 Saigon Cafe
17 Cascada
18 Kyo-ya
21 Treats Hula's
24 New Tokyo Restaurant
25 Tenteko Mai
29 Planet Hollywood
31 Moose McGillycuddy's
37 Jack in the Box
41 New Kapahulu
     Chop Suey
42 Ono Hawaiian Food
43 Keo's
56 Fatty's Chinese Kitchen
57 Patisserie
58 Chili's
59 Food Pantry
60 Perry's Smorgy
62 Irifune's
66 Tanaka of Tokyo
73 Rainbow Drive-In

OTHER
3   Wave Waikiki
4   Rendezvous
7   Marina Twins
11 Blue Sky Rentals
16 24-hour Gas Station
19 Hula's Bar & Lei Stand
23 Waikiki Post Office
30 First Hawaiian Bank
32 Waikiki Theatres/IMAX
33 Waikiki Trade Center
38 Planet Surf
44 Urasenke Tea Ceremony
46 US Army Museum
53 Royal Hawaiian
     Shopping Center
63 Internet Cafe
72 Bailey's Antique Shop
75 Board Rentals
76 Police
78 Wizard Stones
82 St Augustine's Church,
     Damien Museum
84 Waikiki-Kapahulu Library
91 Kapiolani Bandstand
92 Kodak Hula Show
93 Waikiki Shell

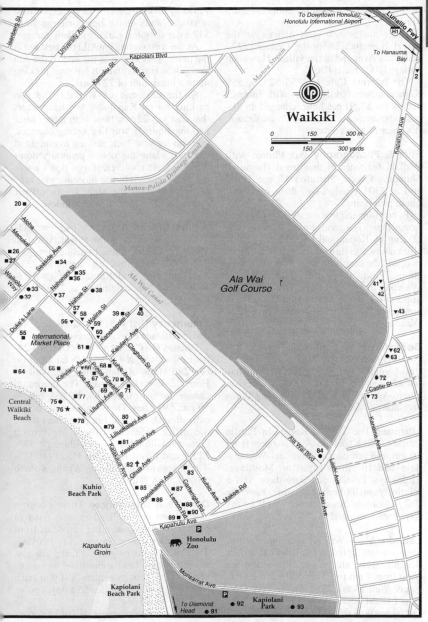

Waikiki

0   150   300 m
0   150   300 yards

*To Downtown Honolulu,
Honolulu International Airport*

*To Hanauma
Bay*

Lunalilo Fwy

H1

Kapiolani Blvd

Isenberg St

University Ave

Kamoku St

Date St

Manoa Stream

Kapahulu Ave

Manoa-Palolo Drainage Canal

Ala Wai Canal

*Ala Wai
Golf Course*

20

Aloha

Mamuku

26
27

Seaside Ave

34

Nohonani St

35
36

Nahua St

38

Waikiki Way

33
32

37

57
58

56

Walina St

59
60

39

Kanekapolei St

40

Duke's Lane

55

*International
Market Place*

61

Cleghorn St

Kalaimoku St

Kuhio Ave

41
42

43

62
63

72

Castle St

73

64

65

Kalakaua Ave

66

Koa Ave

67

68

Prince Edward St

70

71

69

Kaiulani Ave

74

75

77

76

Uluniu Ave

78

79

80

81

Liliuokalani Ave

Kealohilani Ave

*Central
Waikiki
Beach*

Kealohilani Ave

82

Ohua Ave

83

85

Paoakalani Ave

87

Cartwright Rd

86

88

Lemon Rd

89

90

Kapahulu Ave

84

Ala Wai Blvd

Kanaina Ave

Paki Ave

Lash Ave

*Kuhio
Beach Park*

Kalakaua Ave

Kuhio Ave

Makee Rd

*Kapahulu
Groin*

P

**Honolulu
Zoo**

*Kapiolani
Beach Park*

P

*To Diamond
Head*

91

92

*Kapiolani
Park*

93

Monsarrat Ave

OAHU

from 8 am to 6 pm. Saturday hours are 9 am to noon.

There are branch post offices at the Royal Hawaiian Shopping Center, 2233 Kalakaua Ave, and at the Hilton Hawaiian Village, 2005 Kalia Rd.

The Internet Cafe (☎ 735-5282), 559 Kapahulu Ave, has 10 Macs with Internet access for $7.50 per hour, charged in 10-minute increments, with a $1.25 minimum. It's open 24 hours a day.

Film & Photography Fox Photo, with Waikiki branches in the Royal Hawaiian Shopping Center, Sheraton Moana Hotel and at 2301 Kuhio Ave, does one-hour photo processing.

To buy film and to have slides processed, Longs Drugs is a good choice. It offers processing by Kodak and Fuji. Slides generally take two to three days, prints a day or two, and the cost is cheaper than at camera shops. While there are no branches in Waikiki, there's a Longs Drugs on the upper level of the Ala Moana Center and another next to Times Supermarket at 3221 Waialae Ave.

Bookstores Waldenbooks, which has good collections of Hawaiiana books, travel guides and paperback fiction, has branches at the Waikiki Trade Center on Kuhio Ave and at Waikiki Shopping Plaza on Kalakaua Ave.

Libraries The Waikiki-Kapahulu Public Library, 400 Kapahulu Ave, is open from 10 am to 8 pm on Tuesdays and Wednesdays and 10 am to 5 pm on Mondays, Thursdays, Fridays and Saturdays. It's a relatively small library, but it does have the daily Honolulu newspapers as well as the *New York Times* and *Wall Street Journal*.

Laundry Many Waikiki accommodations have on-site laundry facilities. If yours doesn't, there are public coin laundries open from 7 am to 10 pm daily at the Outrigger West Hotel, 2330 Kuhio Ave; Outrigger Coral Seas, 250 Lewers St; and the Outrigger Waikiki, 2335 Kalakaua Ave.

Parking Parking cheaply in Waikiki can be a hassle. Many of the hotels charge $8 to $12 a day for guest parking in their garages.

At the west end of Waikiki the best bet is the public parking lot at the end of the Ala Wai Yacht Harbor, which has free parking up to a maximum of 72 hours.

At the east end of Waikiki, the zoo parking lot on Kapahulu Ave has meters that cost just 25¢ an hour with a four-hour parking limit. If you like taking chances, you can try your luck parking overnight at the zoo, where the police generally don't write tickets; however, if you don't move out early enough in the morning you may be greeted with the sight of an officer placing a $25 ticket on your window.

Airline Offices Aloha Airlines (☎ 484-1111) has an office at the Royal Hawaiian Shopping Center, United Airlines (☎ 800-241-6522) is across the street at 2316 Kalakaua Ave, and Korean Air (☎ 923-1896) is on the same block at 2350 Kalakaua Ave.

Emergency Dial ☎ 911 for all police, fire and ambulance emergency services.

Doctors On Call (☎ 971-6000) has a 24-hour clinic with X-ray and lab facilities on the 2nd floor of the Outrigger Waikiki Hotel, 2335 Kalakaua Ave. The minimum charge for an office visit is $68 before 10 pm, $92 after. They'll also make house calls, though this will run more than twice the office visit cost. There are branch clinics at Hilton Hawaiian Village (☎ 973-5252) and Royal Hawaiian Hotel (☎ 923-4499), both of which are open from 8 am to around 5 pm daily.

Dangers & Annoyances There's been a clampdown on the hustlers who used to push time-shares and other con deals from every other street corner in Waikiki. They're not totally gone – there are just fewer of them (and some have metamorphosed into 'activity centers'). If you see a sign touting car rentals for $5 a day, you've probably found one.

Time-share salespeople will offer you all

sorts of deals, from free luaus to sunset cruises, if you'll just come to hear their 'no obligation' pitch. *Caveat emptor*.

Waikiki Beaches

The two-mile stretch of white sand that runs from the Hilton Hawaiian Village to Kapiolani Park is commonly called Waikiki Beach, although different sections along the way have their own names and characteristics.

In the early morning the beach belongs to walkers and joggers – and it's surprisingly quiet. Strolling down the beach towards Diamond Head at sunrise can actually be a meditative experience.

By mid-morning it looks like a normal resort beach, with boogie board and surfboard concessionaires setting up shop and catamarans pulling up on the beach offering $15 sails. By noon it is packed, and the challenge is to walk down the beach without stepping on anyone.

Most of Waikiki's beautiful white sands are not its own. Tons of sand have been barged in over the years, much of it from Papohaku Beach on Molokai.

As the beachfront developed, landowners haphazardly constructed sea walls and offshore barriers to protect their property. In the process they blocked the natural forces of sand accretion, and erosion has long been a serious problem at Waikiki.

Sections of the beach are still being replenished with imported sand, although much of it ends up washing into the ocean, where it fills channels and depressions and alters the surf breaks.

Waikiki is good for swimming, boogie boarding, surfing, sailing and other beach activities most of the year. Between May and September, summer swells can make the water a little rough for swimming, but they also make it the best season for surfing.

As a consequence of all the activity and alterations, Waikiki beaches simply aren't that good for snorkeling; the best of them is Sans Souci.

There are lifeguards and showers at many places along the beach.

Kahanamoku Beach Kahanamoku Beach, fronting the Hilton Hawaiian Village, is the westernmost section of Waikiki. It was named for Duke Kahanamoku, a surfer and swimmer who won Olympic gold in the 100-meter freestyle in 1912 and went on to become a Hawaiian celebrity.

Kahanamoku Beach is protected by a breakwater at one end and a pier at the other, with a coral reef running between the two. It's a calm swimming area with a sandy bottom that slopes gradually.

Fort DeRussy Beach Fort DeRussy Beach, one of the least crowded Waikiki beaches, borders 1800 feet of the Fort DeRussy Military Reservation. Like all beaches in Hawaii, it's public; the federal government provides lifeguards. This beach offers an alternative to frying on the sand, as it has a grassy lawn partially shaded by trees, as well as arbored picnic shelters.

The water is usually calm and good for swimming. When conditions are right, the beach is used by windsurfers, boogie boarders and board surfers. There are two beach huts, open daily, that rent windsurfing equipment, boogie boards, kayaks and snorkel sets.

Gray's Beach Gray's Beach, the local name for the beach near the Halekulani Hotel, was named for a boarding house called Gray's-by-the-Sea that stood on the site in the 1920s. On the same stretch of beach was the original Halekulani, a lovely low-rise mansion that was converted into a hotel in the 1930s. About a decade ago, the mansion gave way to the present high-rise hotel.

Because the sea wall in front of the Halekulani was built so close to the waterline, the part of the beach fronting the hotel is often totally submerged.

The section of beach between the Halekulani and the Royal Hawaiian Hotel varies in width from season to season. The waters off the beach are shallow and calm.

Central Waikiki Beach The area between the Royal Hawaiian Hotel and the Waikiki Beach Center is the busiest section of the whole beach.

Most of the beach has a shallow bottom with a gradual slope. While the swimming's pretty good here, there are also a lot of catamarans, surfers and plenty of other swimmers in the water. Keep your eyes open.

Queen's Surf and Canoe's Surf, Waikiki's best-known surf breaks, are offshore.

Waikiki Beach Center The area opposite the Hyatt Regency Waikiki is the site of the Waikiki Beach Center. It has restrooms, showers, a police station, surfboard lockers and rental concessions.

The **Wizard Stones of Kapaemahu** – four boulders on the Diamond Head side of the police station – are said to contain the secrets and healing powers of four sorcerers, named Kapaemahu, Kinohi, Kapuni and Kahaloa, who visited from Tahiti in ancient

times. Before returning back to Tahiti, they transferred their powers to these stones.

Just east of the stones is a bronze **statue of Duke Kahanamoku** (1890-1968), Hawaii's most decorated athlete, standing with one of his longboards. Considered the 'father of modern surfing', Duke, who made his home in Waikiki, gave surfing demonstrations on beaches around the world, from Sydney, Australia, to Rockaway Beach, New York. Many local surfers took issue with the placement of the statue as Duke is standing with his back to the sea, a position they say he never would have taken in real life. In response the city moved the statue as close to the sidewalk as possible.

Kuhio Beach Park Kuhio Beach Park is marked on its east end by Kapahulu Groin, a walled storm drain with a walkway on top that juts out into the ocean from the end of Kapahulu Ave.

A low breakwater sea wall runs about 1300 feet out from Kapahulu Groin, paralleling the beach. It was built to control sand erosion, and in the process two nearly enclosed swimming pools were formed. Local kids walk out on the breakwater, which is called The Wall, but it can be dangerous to the uninitiated due to a slippery surface and breaking surf.

The pool closest to Kapahulu Groin is best for swimming, with the water near the breakwater reaching overhead depths. However, because circulation is limited the water gets murky with a noticeable film of suntan oil. The 'Watch Out Deep Holes' sign refers to holes in the pool's sandy bottom that can be created by swirling currents. Those who can't swim should be cautious in the deeper areas of the pool, as the holes can take waders by surprise.

The park, incidentally, is named after Prince Kuhio, who maintained his residence on this beach. His house was torn down in 1936, 14 years after his death, in order to expand the beach.

Between the old-timers who gather each afternoon to play chess and cribbage at Kuhio's sidewalk pavilions and the kids boogie boarding off the Groin, this section

NED FRIARY
Statue of Duke Kahanamoku

Hibiscus NED FRIARY

Anthurium DAVID RUSS

Heliconia MICHAEL CLARK

Protea NED FRIARY

Plumeria NED FRIARY

Orchid

Ilima

Ohelo Berries

Fern

Ohia Lehua

of the beach has as much local color as tourist influence.

Kapahulu Groin Kapahulu Groin is one of Waikiki's hottest boogie boarding spots. If the surf's right, you can find a few dozen boogie boarders, mostly teenage boys, riding the waves.

The kids ride straight for the wall and then veer away at the last moment, drawing 'oohs' and 'ahs' from the tourists who gather to watch them. Kapahulu Groin is also a great place to catch sunsets.

Kapiolani Beach Park Kapiolani Beach Park starts at Kapahulu Groin and extends down to the Natatorium, beyond Waikiki Aquarium.

Queen's Surf is the name given to the wide midsection of Kapiolani Beach. The stretch in front of the pavilion is a popular beach with the gay community. It's a pretty good area for swimming, with a sandy bottom. The beach between Queen's Surf and Kapahulu Groin is shallow and has a lot of broken coral.

Kapiolani Beach Park is a relaxed place with little of the frenzy of activity found in front of the central strip of Waikiki hotels. It's a popular weekend picnicking spot for local families who unload the kids to splash in the water as they line up the barbecue grills.

There's a big grassy field, good for spreading out a beach towel and unpacking a picnic basket. Free parking is available near the beach along Kalakaua Ave. There are restrooms and showers at the Queen's Surf pavilion.

The surfing area offshore is called Public's.

Natatorium The Natatorium, at the Diamond Head end of Kapiolani Beach, is a 100-meter-long saltwater swimming pool built after WWI as a memorial for soldiers who died in that war. There were once hopes of hosting an Olympics on Oahu, with this pool as the focal point.

The Natatorium, which is listed on the National Register of Historic Places, is now closed and in disrepair, but there's ongoing debate about restoring the facility.

Sans Souci Beach Down by the New Otani Kaimana Beach Hotel, Sans Souci is a nice little sandy beach away from the main tourist scene. It has outdoor showers and a lifeguard station.

Many residents come to Sans Souci for daily swims. A shallow coral reef close to shore makes for calm, protected waters and provides reasonably good snorkeling. More coral can be found by following the Kapua Channel as it cuts through the reef, although beware of currents that can pick up in the channel. Check conditions with the lifeguard before venturing out.

Royal Hawaiian Hotel
The Royal Hawaiian, Hawaii's first luxury hotel, is worth a look even if you're not staying there. With its pink turrets and Moorish architecture, it's a throwback to the era when Rudolph Valentino was *the* romantic idol and travel to Hawaii was by luxury liner.

The hotel was originally on a 20-acre coconut grove, but over the years the grounds have been chipped away by a huge shopping center on one side and a high-rise mega-hotel on the other. The Royal Hawaiian is a survivor.

Inside, the hotel is lovely and airy, with high ceilings and chandeliers and everything in rose colors. The small garden at the rear is filled with birdsong, a rare sound in most of Waikiki.

Fort DeRussy
Fort DeRussy Military Reservation is a US Army post used mainly as a recreation center for the armed forces. This large chunk of Waikiki real estate was acquired by the US Army a few years after Hawaii was annexed to the USA. Prior to that it was swampy marshland and a favorite duck hunting spot for Hawaiian royalty.

The Hale Koa Hotel on the property is open only to military personnel, but there's public access to the beach and the adjacent military museum. The section of Fort DeRussy between Kalia Rd and Kalakaua Ave has public footpaths that provide a shortcut between the two roads.

US Army Museum of Hawaii

Battery Randolph, a reinforced concrete building erected in 1911 as a coastal artillery battery, houses the army museum at Fort DeRussy. It once held two formidable 14-inch disappearing guns with an 11-mile range that were designed to recoil down into the concrete walls for reloading after each firing. A 55-ton lead counterweight would then return the carriage to position.

The battery now houses a wide collection of weapons, from Hawaiian sharktooth clubs to WWII tanks, as well as exhibits on military history as it relates to Hawaii told through dioramas, scale models and period photos. There are historic displays on King Kamehameha and Hawaii's role in WWII. It's open from 10 am to 4:30 pm daily, except Mondays, Christmas and New Year's Day. Admission is free.

Oceanarium

The Pacific Beach Hotel, at 2490 Kalakaua Ave, houses an impressive three-story 280,000-gallon aquarium that forms the backdrop for two of the hotel restaurants. Even if you're not dining there, you can view the aquarium quite easily from the lobby. Divers enter the Oceanarium to feed the tropical fish daily at 11:30 am and 12:30, 6:30 and 8:15 pm.

Damien Museum

St Augustine's Church, off Kalakaua Ave and Ohua Ave, is a quiet little sanctuary in the midst of the hotel district. In the rear of the church a second building houses the modest Damien Museum, honoring Father Damien, famed for his work at the leprosy colony on Molokai. It has a video presentation on the colony, some interesting historical photos and a few of Damien's personal possessions.

As a befitting tribute to Father Damien's life, the building also houses a lunchtime soup kitchen. Museum hours are 9 am to 3 pm Monday to Friday, until noon on Saturdays; entry is free.

Ala Wai Canal

Every dawn, people jog and power walk along the Ala Wai Canal, which forms the northern boundary of Waikiki. Late in the afternoon outrigger canoe teams can be seen paddling up and down the canal and out to the Ala Wai Yacht Harbor.

Kapiolani Park

The nearly 200-acre Kapiolani Park, at the Diamond Head end of Waikiki, was a gift from King Kalakaua to the people of Honolulu in 1877. Hawaii's first public park, it was dedicated to Kalakaua's wife, Queen Kapiolani.

In its early days, horse racing and band concerts were the park's biggest attractions. Although the race track has gone, the concerts continue and Kapiolani Park is still the venue for a wide range of community activities.

The park contains the Waikiki Aquarium, the Honolulu Zoo, Kapiolani Beach Park, the Kodak Hula Show grounds, the Kapiolani Bandstand and the Waikiki Shell, an outdoor amphitheater with symphony, jazz and rock concerts. It has sports fields, tennis courts, huge lawns and tall banyan trees.

The Royal Hawaiian Band presents free afternoon concerts nearly every Sunday at the Kapiolani Bandstand. Dance competitions, Hawaiian music concerts and other activities occur at the bandstand throughout the year.

A pleasant park, it's large enough to have a lot of quiet space despite all the activity.

Waikiki Aquarium This interesting aquarium (☎ 923-9741), 2777 Kalakaua Ave, dates to 1904 and has recently completed a $3-million makeover.

The aquarium has added interactive displays, a mini-theater and an auditorium where visitors can look through a 14-foot glass window at circling sharks.

Tanks re-create various Hawaiian reef habitats, making this a great place to identify fish you've seen while snorkeling or diving. There are black-tip sharks, moray eels, flash-back cuttlefish wavering with pulses of light, and rare Hawaiian fish with names like the bearded armorhead and the sling-jawed wrasse.

There's an interesting variety of exotic marine life as well. In 1985 the aquarium was the first to breed the Palauan chambered nautilus in captivity. A couple of these sea creatures, with their unique spiral chambered shell, are on display. There are also some giant clams from Palau that were less than an inch long when acquired in 1982 and now measure over two feet, the largest in the USA.

There's also a touch tank for children, a mahimahi hatchery, green sea turtles and Hawaiian monk seals. Visitors can watch the monk seals being fed at 2:30 pm Friday to Tuesday, 1:30 pm on Wednesdays and 10 am on Thursdays.

The aquarium is open from 9 am to 5 pm daily, although entry is not allowed after 4:30 pm. Admission is $6 for adults, $4 for senior citizens over 60 and students with ID, $2.50 for children ages 13 to 17, and free for children 12 and under.

Honolulu Zoo The Honolulu Zoo (☎ 971-7171) has undergone extensive renovations that have upgraded it into a respectable city zoo, with some 300 species. The highlight is the nicely naturalized African Savanna section, which has lions, cheetahs, white rhinos, giraffes, zebras, hippos and monkeys. The zoo also has an interesting reptile section, a good selection of tropical birds and a small petting zoo.

It's open from 9 am to 4:30 pm daily except Christmas and New Year's Day. Admission is $6 for adults, $1 for children ages six to 12.

In front of the zoo there's a large banyan tree that is home to hundreds of white pigeons – escapees from a small group brought to the zoo in the 1940s.

Art in the Park Local artists have been hanging their paintings on the fence around the zoo on weekends for more than 25 years. If you're looking for a painting, this is a good opportunity to buy directly from the artist. The artwork is on display from 9 am to 4 pm on Saturdays and Sundays and from 9 am to noon on Tuesdays.

Kodak Hula Show The Kodak Hula Show, off Monsarrat Ave near the Waikiki Shell, is a staged photo opportunity of hula dancers, ti-leaf skirts and ukuleles. The musicians are a group of older ladies who performed at the Royal Hawaiian Hotel in days gone by.

This is the scene in postcards where dancers hold up letters forming the words 'Hawaii' and 'Aloha'. The whole thing is quite touristy, although entertaining if you're in the mood, and it's free.

Kodak has been hosting this show since 1939. The benches are set up stadium-style around a grassy stage area with the sun at your back. The idea is for everyone to shoot a lot of film. It works. Even though Kodak no longer monopolizes the film market, the tradition continues.

Shows are held from 10 to 11:15 am on Tuesdays, Wednesdays and Thursdays. Make an effort to be on time, because once the show starts they will only admit people in between acts.

Dolphins

The Kahala Mandarin Oriental, in the Kahala area beyond Diamond Head, has two Atlantic bottlenose dolphins in a lagoon as well as green sea turtles and tropical reef fish on display. Coached by trainers from Sea Life Park, the dolphins put on a short show for smelt and herring at 11 am and 2 and 4 pm daily. They jump and dive, stand on their tails, hula dance, play volleyball and the like. The show is free and open to the public, but parking in the hotel garage costs $6 an hour.

Places to Stay

Waikiki's main beachfront strip, Kalakaua Ave, is largely lined with high-rise hotels and $150-plus rooms. As is the norm in resort areas, most of these hotels cater to package tourists, driving the prices up for individual travelers.

Better values are generally found at the smaller hostelries on the back streets. There are hotels in the Kuhio Ave area and up near the Ala Wai Canal that are as nice as some of the beachfront hotels but half the price. If you don't mind walking 10 minutes to the beach, you can save yourself a bundle.

In many hotels the rooms themselves are the same, with only the views varying; generally the higher the floor, the higher the price. If you're paying extra for a view, you might want to ask to see the room first, as Waikiki certainly doesn't have any truth-in-labeling laws governing when a hotel can call a room 'oceanview'. While some 'ocean views' are the real thing, others are merely glimpses of the water as seen through a series of high-rises.

Waikiki has many more hotel rooms than condos. Most of Waikiki's condos are filled with long-term residents and there isn't the proliferation of vacation rental agents as on the Neighbor Islands. The best way to find a condo in Waikiki is to look in the 'Vacation Rentals' section of the daily paper, although the listings can be meager, particularly in the winter.

Places to Stay – budget

Hostels In addition to the one Hostelling International (HI) hostel, there are a number of small businesses providing hostel-like dormitory accommodations around Waikiki. They all cater to backpackers and draw a fairly international crowd. There are no curfews or other restrictions, except that some 'hostels', trying to avoid taking on local boarders, require travelers to show a passport or an onward ticket.

Hostelling International Waikiki (☎ 926-8313; fax 946-5904), 2417 Prince Edward St, Honolulu, HI 96815, is a 50-bed hostel on a back street a few short blocks from Waikiki Beach. Dorm beds cost $16. There are also four rooms for couples at $40, with small refrigerators and private bathrooms. For the private rooms, which can be booked for a maximum of five nights, paid reservations or a credit card hold are required.

Office hours are 7 am to 3 am. There's no dormitory lockout and a shared kitchen is available throughout the day. Four parking spaces are available at $5 a day. Occasionally you can be lucky as a walk-in, but at busy times reservations are often necessary a couple of weeks in advance. If you're not an HI member, there's a maximum stay of two nights and a $3 surcharge. HI membership can be purchased on site; the cost is $25 for Americans, $18 for foreigners. MasterCard and Visa are accepted.

InterClub Hostel Waikiki (☎ 924-2636; fax 922-3993), 2413 Kuhio Ave, Honolulu, HI 96815, is a well-established private hostel. It has about 75 bunk beds, arranged five to seven to a room. There's a lounge and TV room, a pool table, a washer/dryer and lockers. Try to get a bed in one of the rear units, as the rooms closest to the heavy traffic on Kuhio Ave can be very noisy. Dorm beds cost $15. The hostel also has some simple private rooms for $45 with linoleum floors, refrigerators, shared balconies and private baths.

Hawaiian Seaside Hostel (☎ 924-3306; fax 923-2110; seaside@powertalk.com), 419 Seaside Ave, Honolulu, HI 96815, occupies a two-story apartment building set back from the street in an alley off Seaside Ave. It's about a 10-minute walk from Waikiki Beach. Small dorm rooms with four bunk beds cost $13 per bed; there are curtains that can be drawn around the bunks for a bit of privacy. There's usually a separate women's dorm, though occasionally they'll put couples in it as well. You can also get semi-private rooms that have only two people in them for $15 per person. Guests have use of a kitchen after 6:30 pm. There's a courtyard with cable TV and a pool table; limited water sports equipment can be borrowed for free. About once a week there's a keg party, with all-you-can-drink beer for $6.

A clean, recommendable hostel close to the beach is *Polynesian Hostel Beachclub* (☎ 922-1340; fax 955-4470), 2584 Lemon Rd, Honolulu, HI 96815. This friendly place occupies a small three-story apartment complex with a variety of rooms. You can get a bunk bed in a small dorm (four to six people) for $15.50, one of the bedrooms in a two-bedroom apartment for $29/35 for singles/doubles or a fully private studio with a kitchen for $47 a double. Each apartment has its own toilet and shower, but only the studios have private kitchens. There's a common room with a full kitchen, a laundry area and occasional activities such as barbecues and keg parties. If you're a light sleeper, bring earplugs to ward off noise from the 6 am garbage-truck runs. Boogie boards and snorkel sets can be borrowed for free. Parking is available for $5.

Not on par but nearby is *Waikiki Beachside Hostel* (☎ 923-9566; fax 923-7525), 2556 Lemon Rd, Suite B101, Honolulu, HI 96815, another small condo complex that's been converted into hostel-style accommodations. Rates range from $16.50 a day or $99 a week for a bunk in a shared room to $65/350 a day/week for a private room.

On the west side of Waikiki is *Island Hostel* (☎ /fax 942-8748), 1946 Ala Moana Blvd, Honolulu, HI 96815, which has more than a dozen spartan studio rooms in Hawaiian Colony, an unkempt apartment building. The dorm rooms have up to six bunk beds squeezed in, a table, a TV, a small refrigerator and a bathroom; the cost is $15 a night. Some units are set up as private rooms with a double bed and can be used by couples for $45.

Hotels *Hale Pua Nui* (☎ 923-9693; fax 923-9678), 228 Beach Walk, Honolulu, HI 96815, is an older four-story building with 22 studio apartments. The rooms are not fancy and it's strictly a budget place, but each has the basics: two twin beds, a kitchenette, fan, air-con, TV and phone. The beach is but a five-minute walk away. Rates are $45/57 in the low/high season and there are discounts for stays of a week or more. There's limited on-site parking for $5 a day.

So many retirees return each winter to the 85-room *Royal Grove Hotel* (☎ 923-7691; fax 922-7508), 151 Uluniu Ave, Honzlulu, HI 96815, that it's difficult to get a room in high season without advance reservations. In the oldest wing there are

small $43 streetside units that have no air-con and are exposed to traffic noise. The main wing has $57 units that are newer but still a bit wearworn, with air-con and a lanai. Both types of rooms have a double and a twin bed, TV, kitchenette and private bath. This is an older, no-frills hotel, but unlike other places in this category it has a small pool.

A bit spiffier is the *Waikiki Prince Hotel* (☎ 922-1544), 2431 Prince Edward St, Honolulu, HI 96815, which has 30 units next door to Hostelling International Waikiki. The rooms are straightforward, but the new owner has given them a fresh coat of paint and they all have air-con, TV and private baths. There are small double rooms for $50 and larger rooms with kitchenettes for $65. Prices are a couple of dollars cheaper in the low season and the seventh night is free year round. The office is open from 9 am to 6 pm.

Places to Stay – middle

Hawaii Polo Inn (☎ 949-0061, 800-669-7719; fax 949-4906), 1696 Ala Moana Blvd, Honolulu, HI 96815, a member of the Colony chain, is at the west end of Waikiki. The 66 motel-style rooms have cinder-block walls and are lined up in rows with their entrances off a long outdoor corridor. The rooms have been renovated, and all have small refrigerators, coffeemakers, phones and TVs; some have lanais, although generally it's at the expense of room space. Rates, which have recently dropped, start at a reasonable $49/65 in the low/high season.

Waikiki Sand Villa Hotel (☎ 922-4744, 800-247-1903; fax 923-2541) is at 2375 Ala Wai Blvd, Honolulu, HI 96815, on the Ala Wai Canal. The 223 rather standard tourist-class rooms come with cable TV, refrigerators, air-con, room safes, bathtubs and small lanais. Many rooms have both a double and a twin bed, and some have views across the golf course towards Manoa Valley; the corner units have the best views. Standard rooms, which are on the lower floors, cost $66/77 in the low/high season, while upper floors are about

$10 more. There are also poolside studios with kitchenettes that can sleep up to four people for $125/140. A simple continental breakfast is included, and children under 12 stay free. Overall the hotel is a good value for this price range.

The nearby 202-room *Aloha Surf Hotel* (☎ 923-0222, 800-423-4514; fax 924-7160), 444 Kanekapolei St, Honolulu, HI 96815, is another good-value mid-range hotel. It has clean, compact rooms with air-con, TV, phone, room safe and complimentary coffee for $70/79 in the low/high season. Higher-floor rooms, which have lanais, are $10 more. There's a swimming pool and laundry room.

Waikiki Circle Hotel (☎ 923-1571, 800-922-7866; fax 926-8024), 2464 Kalakaua Ave, Honolulu, HI 96815, part of the Aston chain, is a small hotel with a great location, though it's bumped up its prices in recent years. It has 104 rooms on 13 floors, all with lanais, two double beds, room safes, phones, TVs and air-con. The hotel is older but has recently been renovated and the rooms are comfortable. This circular building has a back room on each floor that's called 'city view' and costs $120; while you can't see the ocean, these are farther from the road and quieter. Each floor also has two rooms with partial ocean views for $135 and five rooms with unobstructed ocean views from $145. Rates are $10 less in the low season. Request one of the upper-floor rooms, which have the same rates but better views.

Waikiki Grand Hotel (☎ 923-1511, 800-535-0085; fax 923-4708), 134 Kapahulu Ave, Honolulu, HI 96815, affiliated with Marc Resorts, is a 173-room hotel opposite the zoo. Although the rooms have been renovated, they are quite small and ordinary. Still, they have the standard amenities: TV, phone, air-con, mini-refrigerator, coffeemaker and a pool. Rack rates are a pricey $109 for a standard room or $129 for a room with a kitchenette, but the hotel often advertises hefty discounts in the classified section of the Honolulu papers. If you contact the front desk directly and ask for the cheapest 'special' rate, you can

commonly get a standard room for around $55 – a good deal.

Hotel Honolulu (☎ 926-2766, 800-426-2766; fax 922-3326; hotelhnl@lava.net), 376 Kaiolu St, Honolulu, HI 96815, is Waikiki's only gay hotel. It's a quiet oasis on a side street a block from busy Kuhio Ave and the heart of the gay district. The three-story hotel has the character of an unhurried inn, with helpful management, lots of hanging ferns and a peach-colored cockatoo at the front desk. The 19 main units are decorated with flair, each with its own theme ('Samurai', 'Deco Deco', 'Norma Jean' etc), and these are large and comfortable, with lanais, kitchens, ceiling fans and air-con. Studios cost $89 to $99, one-bedroom units $109 to $119. There are also five smaller, non-theme studios in an adjacent building for $75. Coffee is free, and there's a sundeck but no pool. While the guests are predominantly gay, straights are also welcome.

Ocean Resort Hotel Waikiki (☎ 922-3861, 800-367-2317; fax 924-1982), 175 Paoakalani Ave, Honolulu, HI 96815, has 451 rooms. A former Quality Inn, it's a rather ordinary place that hosts a fair number of people on low-end package tours. Still, rooms are air-conditioned and have standard amenities such as TVs, phones and room safes. Nonsmoking rooms are available, and there's a pool. Rooms begin at $98, those with kitchenettes from $135. All are $10 cheaper in the low season.

A member of Hawaiian Pacific Resorts, *Queen Kapiolani Hotel* (☎ 922-1941, 800-367-5004; fax 922-2694), 150 Kapahulu Ave, Honolulu, HI 96815, is a 313-room 19-story hotel at the quieter Diamond Head end of Waikiki. This older hotel has an aging regal theme: chandeliers, high ceilings and fading paintings of Hawaiian royalty. Standard rooms cost $104/116 in the low/high season. However, rooms are anything but standard and vary greatly in size, with some very pleasant and others so small they can barely squeeze a bed in. The simplest way to avoid a closet-size space is to request a room with two twin beds instead of a single queen. Also, be sure to get a room without interconnecting doors – they act like a sound tunnel to the next room. Some of the oceanview rooms, which cost $25 more, have lanais with fine unobstructed views of Diamond Head.

Ilima Hotel (☎ 923-1877, 800-367-5172; fax 924-8371; ilima@aloha.com), 445 Nohonani St, Honolulu, HI 96815, is a smaller hotel in a less hurried section of Waikiki, about a 10-minute walk from the beach. All 99 units are roomy and light with large lanais, two double beds, tasteful rattan furnishings, cable TV with HBO and kitchens with an oven, microwave and full-size refrigerator. The staff is friendly, the lobby has interesting Hawaiiana murals and there's a small heated pool and fitness room. Popular with business travelers and other return visitors, the Ilima offers free local phone calls and free parking, a rarity in Waikiki. Rates vary according to the floor, although the rooms themselves are the same. High-season rates start at $98/103 for singles/doubles in studios on the 4th floor and rise to $121/127 for studios on the 10th to 16th floors. There are also some one- and two-bedroom suites for $144 and $187 respectively. All rates are $12 less from April to mid-December.

Patrick Winston owns 11 pleasant units in the *Hawaiian King Hotel* (☎ 924-3332, 800-545-1948), 417 Nohonani St, Suite 409, Honolulu, HI 96815. Each has one bedroom with either a queen or two twin beds, a living room, TV, phone, air-con, ceiling fans, a lanai and a kitchen with a microwave, refrigerator and hot plate. Many also have ovens, some have a washer/dryer and all have thoughtful touches. Although it's an older complex, Patrick's units have a spiffy decor that's on par with top-end condo hotels. There's a courtyard pool. Rates are $89 to $99 in the low season and $20 more in the high season; ask about discounts. There's a four-day minimum stay.

The 200-room *Holiday Inn Waikiki* (☎ 955-1111, 800-465-4329; fax 947-1799), 1830 Ala Moana Blvd, Honolulu, HI 96815, is a recommendable mid-range

hotel at the western end of Waikiki. Rooms are modern and comfortable with either two doubles or one king bed, a desk, room safe, TV, refrigerator, coffeemaker and bathrooms with tubs and hair dryers. Some also have lanais. Rates depend on the floor, ranging from $100 to $120. There's a pool and sundeck, and the beach is about a 10-minute walk away. Unlike most hotels on busy Ala Moana Blvd, the Holiday Inn is set back from the road, so it tends to be notably quieter.

An interesting, little-known option is the *Imperial of Waikiki* (☎ 923-1827, 800-347-2582; fax 923-7848), 205 Lewers St, Honolulu, HI 96815, a pleasant all-suite time-share that rents out unfilled rooms on a space-available basis. It's a good value, especially considering it's directly opposite the Halekulani, Waikiki's most exclusive hotel, and just a two-minute walk from the beach. A studio with a double pulldown bed, queen sofa bed, toaster, coffeemaker and refrigerator costs $79 for up to two people. A small one-bedroom suite with a queen bed in the bedroom and a pull-down bed and queen sofa bed in the living room costs $99 for up to four people. There are also two-bedroom units for $169. There's a pool and a 24-hour front desk.

The Breakers (☎ 923-3181, 800-426-0494; fax 923-7174), 250 Beach Walk, Honolulu, HI 96815, is a comfortable low-rise hotel with 64 units surrounding a courtyard pool. Regular rooms, which have a double bed, a single bed and a kitchenette, cost $91 without a lanai or $97 for a 2nd-floor unit with a lanai. Large suites that have a separate bedroom with a queen bed, a living room that resembles a studio with two twin beds, a full kitchen and a table for four cost $130 for two people, $146 for four people. Both categories have air-con, TV, desks and phones. Avoid the rooms closest to Saratoga Rd, which has lots of traffic.

The 20-story *Waikiki Resort Hotel* (☎ 922-4911, 800-367-5116; fax 922-9468) is at 2460 Koa Ave, Honolulu, HI 96815. This Korean-owned hotel has a Korean restaurant, a Korean Air office and

Korean-language newspapers in the lobby. Not surprisingly, it books heavily with Korean travelers. Its clean, modern rooms have mini-refrigerators, TVs, phones, air-con, room safes and lanais. The regular rates begin at $98/108 in the low/high season; a room and car deal is available for an additional $10. Low-season rates become effective on March 1, a month before other hotels.

Coconut Plaza Hotel (☎ 923-8828, 800-882-9696; fax 923-3473), 450 Lewers St, Honolulu, HI 96815, is a quiet 80-room hotel near Ala Wai Blvd. Rooms have contemporary decor and are comfortable enough but are on the small side. Most have refrigerators, microwaves, two-burner stoves, TV, air-con and private lanais and cost $110 to $120. There are also a few rooms without cooking facilities for $97 and some larger suites for $155. Ask about promotions, as there are sometimes steeply discounted specials. Rates include continental breakfast. There's a coin laundry and some exercise machines on site.

Pacific Monarch (☎ 923-9805, 800-922-7866; fax 924-3220), 142 Uluniu Ave, Honolulu, HI 96815, is a high-rise condominium hotel with 216 units in 34 stories. The studios are good size, each with a table, desk, double bed, sofa bed, small refrigerator and two-burner hot plate. The one-bedroom units have a small bedroom and a roomy living space with a full kitchen, a dining table for four, a sofa bed and a large lanai. Aston handles more than half of the units, with low/high season rates at $120/140 for studios, $150/170 for one-bedroom units. Up to four people can stay in either a studio or a one-bedroom unit at these rates.

The *New Otani Kaimana Beach Hotel* (☎ 923-1555, 800-356-8264; fax 922-9404; webmaster@kaimana.com), 2863 Kalakaua Ave, Honolulu, HI 96815, is on Sans Souci Beach on the quieter Diamond Head side of Waikiki. It's a pleasantly low-key place with 125 units. Room rates start at $99, studios with kitchenettes at $150. All have air-con, TV, refrigerators and lanais.

Outrigger Hotels The *Outrigger* (reservations@outrigger.com), Box 88559, Honolulu, HI 96830, has bought and renovated many of Waikiki's mid-range hotels; at last count it had 20. Overall, it's a fairly good-value chain, although there's a wide range in price and quality. At any rate, with one phone call you can check on the availability of 25% of the hotel rooms in Waikiki!

Ask about promotional deals when making reservations – currently, their 'Free Ride' program provides a free Budget rental car when booking at the regular room rate and a 20% senior citizen discount.

To book rooms at any Outrigger in advance you can call ☎ 303-369-7777 or fax 303-369-9403. Outrigger also has the following toll-free numbers: ☎ 800-688-7444 from the USA and Canada; ☎ 800-124-171 from Australia; ☎ 0800-44-0852 from New Zealand; ☎ 0130-81-8598 from Germany; ☎ 0800-89-4015 from the UK; and ☎ 0031-11-3479 from Japan.

The 303-room *Outrigger Waikiki Surf* (☎ 923-7671), 2200 Kuhio Ave, is one of Outrigger's better deals in the Kuhio area. Standard hotel rooms, which cost $65 in the spring and fall, $75 in summer and $85 in winter, are small but sufficient, each with a tiny refrigerator, coffeemaker, lanai and either one queen or two twin beds. A good value are the kitchenette units, which cost $5 to $10 more but are roomier and have two double beds, a larger refrigerator and either a two-burner hot plate or a microwave. There are also one-bedroom units for up to four people for $115 year round.

If preparing your own meals is a consideration, the renovated *Outrigger Waikiki Surf East* (☎ 923-7671), 422 Royal Hawaiian Ave, right around the corner from the Outrigger Waikiki Surf, has kitchenettes in all the rooms. Rates for rooms range from $75 in the spring and fall to $95 in winter, one-bedroom units from $115 to $125.

Outrigger Malia (☎ 923-7621), 2211 Kuhio Ave, is a 328-room high-rise hotel opposite the Outrigger Waikiki Surf. Rooms are comfortable, each with a room safe, mini-refrigerator, coffeemaker, phone, TV, a tiny one-chair lanai and in most cases two double beds. Some of the rooms are wheelchair accessible. Nonsmoking rooms are available. Ask for an upper-floor room on the back side, as they're the quietest. All rooms cost the same: $85 in the spring and fall, $95 in summer and $105 in winter, while one-bedroom suites range from $120 to $135. The hotel has a rooftop tennis court and a 24-hour coffee shop.

Closer to the beach, the 109-room *Outrigger Coral Seas* (☎ 923-3881), 250 Lewers St, is a small budget hotel popular with return guests. The rooms are adequately furnished with either one queen or two double beds and a lanai. Regular rooms cost $75 in the spring and fall, $80 in summer and $85 in winter, while kitchenette units are $10 more.

The 439-room *Outrigger Waikiki Tower* (☎ 922-6424), 200 Lewers St, is a high-rise hotel a few minutes' walk from the beach. The rooms are comfortable, with a lanai, TV, room safe, small refrigerator, phone and either two doubles or a king bed. The cheapest rates are for rooms from the 12th floor down, which cost $90 in the spring and fall, $100 in summer and $110 in winter. Room on floors 14 and above are essentially the same but cost $10 more. There are also kitchenette rooms with a microwave and coffeemaker going for an additional $5.

Right on the beach, the 885-room *Outrigger Reef Hotel* (☎ 923-3111), 2169 Kalia Rd, has recently undergone a $50 million renovation. As might be expected, the rooms are spiffy, albeit without much character, and have all the usual amenities. Rates, which are the same year round, range from $155 for a nonview room to $320 for an oceanfront room.

Places to Stay – top end

The following hotels all have standard first-class amenities and in-house restaurants. All are on or across the street from the beach, and all have swimming pools.

The 298-room *Waikiki Parc Hotel* (☎ 921-7272, 800-422-0450; fax 923-1336), 2233 Helumoa Rd, Honolulu, HI 96815, is across the street from its more upmarket sister, the Halekulani. Rooms are average in size but have nice touches like ceramic tile floors, shuttered lanai doors, remote-control TV, a room safe and two phones. The hotel has a pleasantly understated elegance. Standard rooms cost $165, while the upper-level oceanview rooms top out at $250. If you book in the mid-range request the 8th floor, which has larger lanais. The hotel occasionally runs cheaper promotional rates, including a 'Park and Sunrise' deal that includes breakfast and free parking for $130 and a senior citizen's rate of $100 for those over 55 years of age.

Hawaiian Regent (☎ 922-6611, 800-367-5370; fax 921-5255; hwnrgnt@aloha.net), 2552 Kalakaua Ave, Honolulu, HI 96815, has 1346 rooms in a huge, maze-like complex. Rooms are quite ordinary for the money, with rates ranging from $170 to $260.

The 715-room *Hawaiian Waikiki Beach Hotel* (☎ 922-2511, 800-877-7666; fax 923-3656), 2570 Kalakaua Ave, Honolulu, HI 96815, looks almost like a reflection of the bigger Hawaiian Regent across the street, and the rooms are comparable though cheaper. Prices start at $110/130 in the low/high season. The best value is the Mauka Tower, an annex off to the side of the main building, where the rates are at the low end and the rooms are larger, newer and quieter than in the main hotel.

The *Sheraton* pretty much owns a little stretch of the beach, boasting 4400 rooms in its four Waikiki hotels. The toll-free numbers for all of Sheraton's Hawaii hotels are ☎ 800-325-3535 from the USA and Canada and ☎ 008-07-3535 from Australia.

The 1150-room *Sheraton Princess Kaiulani* (☎ 922-5811; fax 923-9912), 120 Kaiulani Ave, Honolulu, HI 96815, is the Sheraton's cheapest Waikiki property. It was built in the 1950s by Matson Navigation to help develop Waikiki into a middle-class destination and from the outside looks a bit like an inner-city housing project. However, the interior is more appealing and the rooms are modern. Rates begin at $145. It's in the busy heart of Waikiki, across the street from the beach.

The 793-room *Sheraton Moana Surfrider* (☎ 922-3111; fax 923-0308), 2365

Kalakaua Ave, Honolulu, HI 96815, is a special place for those fond of colonial hotels. Built in 1901, the Moana was Hawaii's first beachfront hotel. It's recently undergone a $50 million historic restoration, authentic right down to the carved columns on the porte-cochère. Despite the fact that modern wings (the 'Surfrider' section) have been attached to the main hotel's flanks, the Moana has survived with much of its original character. The lobby is open and airy, with high plantation-like ceilings, reading chairs and Hawaiian artwork. The rooms in the original building have been restored to their turn-of-the-century appearance. The furnishings are made from a different wood on each floor (koa on the 5th, cherry on the 6th), with TVs and refrigerators hidden behind armoire doors. Rates in the historic wing range from $230 for city views to $350 for ocean views.

The pink Moorish-style *Royal Hawaiian Hotel* (☎ 923-7311; fax 923-8999), 2259 Kalakaua Ave, Honolulu, HI 96815, now a Sheraton property, was Waikiki's first luxury hotel. It's a beautiful building, cool and airy and loaded with charm. The historic section maintains a classic appeal, with some of the rooms having quiet garden views. This section is easier to book too, since most guests prefer the modern high-rise wing with its ocean views. Rates are from $275 in the historic wing, $450 in the high-rise tower.

Sheraton Waikiki (☎ 922-4422; fax 922-9567), 2255 Kalakaua Ave, Honolulu, HI 96815, is an impersonal 1850-room megahotel that looms over the Royal Hawaiian Hotel. The bustling lobby resembles an exclusive Tokyo shopping center, lined with lots of expensive jewelry stores and boutiques with French names and designer labels. The hotel has central elevators that leave guests at some of the longest corridors in Hawaii. Rates range from $210 for a city view to $380 for a luxury ocean-view unit.

Hyatt Regency Waikiki (☎ 923-1234, 800-233-1234; fax 923-7839), 2424 Kalakaua Ave, Honolulu, HI 96815, has twin 40-story towers with 1230 rooms. There's a maximum of 18 rooms per floor, so it's quieter and feels more exclusive than other hotels its size. Rooms are nicely decorated in pastels with rattan furnishings and cost from $200 to $345, depending on the view. Between the towers there's a large atrium with cascading waterfalls and orchids, red torch ginger and other tropical vegetation.

Hilton Hawaiian Village (☎ 949-4321, 800-445-8667; fax 947-7898), 2005 Kalia Rd, Honolulu, HI 96815, is Hawaii's largest hotel, with 2522 rooms. The ultimate in mass tourism, it's practically a package-tour city unto itself – all self-contained for people who never want to leave the hotel grounds. It's quite a busy place, right down to the roped-off lines at the front desk, which resembles an airline check-in counter. The Hilton is on a nice beach, has some good restaurants and offers free entertainment, including Friday-night fireworks. Rates start at $175 for a garden view, $270 for an ocean view.

Halekulani Hotel (☎ 923-2311, 800-367-2343; fax 926-8004), 2199 Kalia Rd, Honolulu, HI 96815, is considered by many to be Waikiki's premier hotel. The 412 rooms, which are pleasantly subdued rather than posh, have large balconies, marble vanities, deep soaking tubs and little touches like bathrobes and fresh flowers. Rooms with garden views cost $295, while those fronting the ocean are $400. Suites start at $650.

Kahala Mandarin Oriental (☎ 739-8888, 800-367-2525; fax 739-8800; mohnl@ aol.com), 5000 Kahala Ave, Honolulu, HI 96816, is in the exclusive Kahala area, east of Diamond Head. This is where the rich and famous go when they want to avoid the Waikiki scene, a 10-minute drive away. The guest list is Hawaii's most regal: Charles and Di, King Juan Carlos and Queen Sofia and the last six US presidents. Formerly the Kahala Hilton, the 370-room hotel recently reopened after a year-long closure and a $75 million facelift. Rates start at $260 for garden-view rooms, $360 for rooms on the hotel's enclosed lagoon where dolphins swim just beyond the lanais. The presidential suite tops off at $2970.

Places to Eat

Waikiki has no shortage of places to eat, although the vast majority of the cheaper ones are easy to pass up. Generally, the best inexpensive food is found outside Waikiki, where most Honolulu residents live and eat. Waikiki's top-end restaurants, on the other hand, are some of the island's best, though they can quickly burn a hole in your wallet.

Places to Eat – budget

For inexpensive bakery items try the *Patisserie*, 2330 Kuhio Ave, at the side of the Outrigger West Hotel. It's open from 6:30 am to 9 pm daily and has reasonably good pastries, croissants, bread and coffee. If you want to eat in, there's a small sit-down area where you can get standard breakfast items, sandwiches and salads. A second *Patisserie* is located at the Edgewater Hotel at the south end of Beach Walk.

Saigon Cafe, on the 2nd floor of 1831 Ala Moana Blvd, has cheap Vietnamese food. The combination rice noodle plate, with chopped spring rolls, barbecued pork and lettuce over a bed of noodles, is a filling main dish; it costs $5 at lunch, $6 at

dinner. There's also a breakfast special of pancakes and two eggs for $1.95. It's open from 6:30 am to 10 pm daily.

New Tokyo Restaurant, 286 Beach Walk, is a popular local lunch spot with good-value Japanese food and a pleasant setting. Grilled salmon, chicken teriyaki or pork ginger, served with miso soup and rice, cost just $6 from 11:30 am to 2 pm weekdays. Dinner, served nightly from 5:30 to 9:30 pm, is a far more expensive affair, with prices from $19 to $38.

Tenteko Mai, 2126 Kalakaua Ave, is an unpretentious little place with good authentic Japanese ramen for $5.50 to $7.50. It also has tasty gyoza, a grilled garlic-and-pork-filled dumpling, for $3.75 a half dozen. The scene feels like a neighborhood eatery in Tokyo, with seating at stools around a U-shaped bar and fellow diners chatting away in Japanese. It's open from 7 am to midnight daily.

Treats Hula's, 2109 Kuhio Ave, is an open-air deli and bar in the middle of the gay district. The food is basic sandwich-and-salad fare, but it's a popular spot for gays to meet and linger over an espresso or beer. It's open from 10 am to 2 am daily.

Breakfast Ideas

Signs draped from buildings advertising breakfast specials for $2 to $4 are commonplace. *Eggs 'n' Things, Moose McGillycuddy's* and *Saigon Cafe* all have cheap breakfast specials.

Food Pantry at 2370 Kuhio Ave has a doughnut counter, while the nearby *Patisserie*, 2330 Kuhio Ave, has a full bakery that serves various pastries and a few inexpensive egg dishes.

Fast-food chains like *McDonald's* and *Burger King* offer their quick, cheap breakfasts from just about every other corner. The free tourist magazines almost always have a *Jack in the Box* coupon good for a breakfast sandwich and coffee for $1.99. If you're really hungry and not too demanding of quality, the $5 all-you-can-eat breakfast buffet at *Perry's Smorgy* is a good deal.

For between $10 and $20 you can try one of the all-you-can-eat breakfast buffets that many of the larger hotels offer, but few are worth the money. A couple of noteworthy exceptions, both with oceanview dining, are the simple breakfast buffet at the *Shore Bird Broiler* ($7) in the Outrigger Reef Hotel and the more elaborate spread at *Duke's Canoe Club* ($10) in the Outrigger Waikiki Hotel. If you don't need a water view, then the *Parc Cafe* ($11.50) in the Waikiki Parc Hotel is also a good value.

For a romantic beachfront setting right on Sans Souci Beach at the Diamond Head end of Waikiki, there's *Hau Tree Lanai* at the New Otani Kaimana Beach Hotel. It has pleasant courtyard dining shaded by a sprawling hau tree and a variety of breakfast combinations priced around $10 served from 7 to 11 am. ∎

Moose McGillycuddy's, 310 Lewers St, has 20 types of omelets for $6.50 each, but a better deal is the early-bird special, from 7:30 to 8:30 am, of two eggs, bacon and toast for $1.99. The restaurant's extensive menu of burgers, sandwiches, Mexican food and salads at moderate prices makes it popular with the college crowd. It's open for meals from 7:30 am to 10 pm daily, with breakfast served to 11 am. Drinks are half price from 4 to 8 pm, and there's music and dancing nightly.

Fatty's Chinese Kitchen, 2345 Kuhio Ave, is a hole-in-the-wall eatery in an alley at the west side of the Miramar hotel. It serves up some of the cheapest food to be found in these parts, with 'two scoop rice' or chow mein plus one hot entree for only $3. Add on $1 for each additional entree. The atmosphere is purely local, with a dozen stools lining a long bar and the cook on the other side chopping away. Fatty's is open from 10:30 am to 10:30 pm daily.

The two *Perry's Smorgy* restaurants, one at the Outrigger Coral Seas Hotel at 250 Lewers St and the other at 2380 Kuhio Ave on the corner of Kanekapolei St, offer cheap all-you-can-eat buffets. Breakfast, from 7 to 11 am, includes pancakes, eggs, ham and fresh pineapple, papaya and melon. It's a tourist crowd and the food is cafeteria quality, but you can't beat the $5 price. Lunch, which includes a reasonable fruit-and-salad bar as well as simple hot dishes like fried chicken, is from 11:30 am to 2:30 pm and costs $6. Dinner, from 5 to 9 pm nightly, costs $8.95. If it's convenient, opt for the Kuhio Ave location, as it has a surprisingly agreeable setting.

Eggs 'n' Things, at 1911 Kalakaua Ave, is an all-nighter, open daily from 11 pm to 2 pm. It specializes in breakfast fare, with prices starting at $3 for pancakes with eggs.

Wailana Coffee House at the Outrigger Malia, 2211 Kuhio Ave, is a classic diner that's open 24 hours a day. It serves inexpensive fare from an extensive menu with food that's a tad better than other similar low-end restaurants.

At the northwest side of the *International Market Place* there's a food court with about two dozen stalls selling cinnamon buns, shave ice, frozen yogurt, hot dogs and various plate lunches – nothing distinguished, but it is cheap.

Fast-food chains are well represented in Waikiki: there are three *Burger King*, four *McDonald's* and six *Jack in the Box* restaurants, the latter open 24 hours. In addition to the usual menus, they add some island touches, such as passion fruit juice, saimin and Portuguese sausage. All three chains usually have discount coupons in the free tourist magazines.

Kapahulu Ave There's a run of cheap neighborhood ethnic restaurants along Kapahulu Ave, the road that starts in Waikiki near the zoo and runs up to the H-1 Fwy. The following restaurants are grouped together about a mile up from Kalakaua Ave.

Irifune's, 563 Kapahulu Ave, is a funky little joint decorated with Japanese country kitsch. While no alcohol is served, you can bring in beer from the nearby liquor store. The gyoza plate is good at $3.50, as is the garlic tofu with vegetables at $8. There are $9 combination dinners with tempura and options such as tataki ahi, a delicious fresh tuna that's seared lightly on the outside, sashimi-like inside, and served with a tangy sauce. Lunch specials begin at $7.50. Although few tourists come up this way, the restaurant is locally popular, so you might have to wait 30 minutes to be seated at dinner, but it's well worth it. Irifune's is open from 11:30 am to 1:30 pm Tuesday to Friday and from 5 to 9 pm Tuesday to Sunday.

Ono Hawaiian Food, 726 Kapahulu Ave, is *the* place in the greater Waikiki area to get Hawaiian food served Hawaiian-style. It's a simple diner, but people line up outside waiting to get in. A kalua pig plate costs $7.10 and a laulau plate $7.35. Both come with pipikaula, lomi salmon and haupia with rice or poi. It's open from 11 am to 7:30 pm Monday to Saturday.

New Kapahulu Chop Suey, 730 Kapahulu Ave, serves big plates of Chinese food. The combination special lunch plate costs $4.15, the special dinner $5, while a score of other dishes are priced under $6. While it's certainly not gourmet, it's a lot of food for the money. It's open from 11 am to 9 pm daily.

KC Drive Inn at 1029 Kapahulu Ave, farther up the road near the freeway, features Ono Ono malts (a combination of chocolate and peanut butter that tastes like a liquid Reese's Cup) for $3 and waffle dogs (a hot dog wrapped in a waffle) for $1.80, as well as plate lunches, burgers and saimin for either eat-in or takeout. It's been a local favorite since the 1930s, complete with carhop service until just a few years back. It's open daily from 6 am to at least midnight.

If you're on foot, *Rainbow Drive-In*, at the intersection of Kapahulu and Kanaina Aves, is much closer to central Waikiki, has similar food and just as much of a local following.

See also the listing for Keo's, in the same Kapahulu neighborhood but with mid-range prices.

Grocery Stores The best place to get groceries in Waikiki is the *Food Pantry*, 2370 Kuhio Ave, which is open 24 hours a day. Its prices are higher than those of the chain supermarkets, which are all outside Waikiki, but lower than those of the smaller convenience stores. Food Pantry, like most grocery stores, accepts credit cards.

Beyond Waikiki, the easiest supermarket to get to without a car is the *Foodland* at the Ala Moana Center. There's a *Times Supermarket* at 3221 Waialae Ave, between 5th and 6th Aves, and a *Foodland* a few blocks away near the eastern intersection of King and Kapiolani Sts. There are grocery stores along Beretania St as well.

Places to Eat – middle
A good place for beachfront dining without breaking the budget is *Shore Bird Broiler* (☎ 922-2887) at the Outrigger Reef Hotel, 2169 Kalia Rd. At one end of the open-air dining room there's a big common grill where you cook your own order; mahimahi, teriyaki chicken or sirloin steak costs $13. Meals come with all-you-can-eat chili, rice

and a salad bar that includes fresh fruit. The salad bar alone costs $8. Dinner is from 4:30 to 10 pm nightly. It's a busy place, and unless you get there early expect to wait for a table – although this is scarcely a hardship, as you can hang out on the beach and watch the sun set while you wait.

Shore Bird also has a breakfast buffet from 7:30 to 11 am daily, with simple pastries, fruit, eggs and ham for $7. Look for coupons in the free tourist magazines that knock a dollar off all meal prices.

Pieces of Eight (☎ 923-6646), in the basement of the Outrigger Coral Seas hotel, 250 Lewers St, has a good-value $7.95 early-bird special from 4:30 to 6:30 pm that consists of grilled chicken or beef stir-fry, accompanied by a small salad bar. After 6:30 pm these dishes cost $12 and the salad bar is an additional $3.50, although you can usually find coupons in the free tourist magazines that can be used to add on the salad bar for free. It's open from 5 to 11 pm daily.

Chili's (☎ 922-9697), 2350 Kuhio Ave, is a popular Tex-Mex chain restaurant from the mainland that serves soft tacos with rice and beans or burgers with fries for around $8, fajitas for $13 and baby back ribs for a few dollars more. It's open from 11 am to 11 pm daily.

California Pizza Kitchen (955-5161), 1910 Ala Moana Blvd, serves up good thin-crust pizzas cooked in a wood-fired brick oven. One-person pizzas range from $7 for a traditional tomato and cheese to $10 for more intriguing creations, such as the tandoori chicken pizza with mango chutney. The restaurant also has a variety of pasta dishes, both traditional and exotic, for $8 to $12 and good green salads with generous half-order portions for $5. It's open from 11:30 am to 10 pm (to 11 pm on Fridays and Saturdays, from noon to 10 pm on Sundays).

In the same building, *Singha Thai* (☎ 941-2893), 1910 Ala Moana Blvd, is the place to go on the Ewa side of Waikiki for authentic Thai food in a somewhat upmarket setting. For starters, the grilled beef salad and the hot and sour tom yum soup are tasty house specialties. Entrees, such as spicy shrimp and shiitake mushroom stir-fry and various curry and noodle dishes, average $9 at lunch, $13 at dinner. Lunch is served from 11 am to 4 pm weekdays, dinner from 4 to 11 pm nightly. Thai dancers perform at dinner.

Duke's Canoe Club (☎ 922-2268), at the Outrigger Waikiki on Kalakaua Ave, has a nice waterfront view. The restaurant takes its name from the late Duke Kahanamoku and the outrigger canoe club that was on the beach here in earlier days. The food is a bit mass production but quite reasonable for the money. From 7 to 10:30 am there's a good breakfast buffet with granola, omelets to order and a fresh fruit selection for $10. At dinner, from 5 to 10 pm, various fresh fish preparations cost $20, or you can get a smaller portion of the fish of the day for $17. There are also chicken and steak meals from $15. All dinners include a full salad bar with cold pastas, muffins, fresh greens and fruit. A children's menu offers burgers or spaghetti and the salad bar for $5. Afternoon and evening music is presented daily (see Entertainment, below).

A fun place to dine is at *Tanaka of Tokyo*, which has branches in the Waikiki Shopping Plaza at 2250 Kalakaua Ave (☎ 922-4702) and King's Village at 131 Kaiulani Ave (☎ 922-4233). Each restaurant has 18 U-shaped teppanyaki tables that diners sit around as chefs with 'flying knives' prepare the meal. It's a set course that includes salad, miso soup, rice, shrimp appetizer and dessert; the price, which is determined by the entree you select, ranges at dinner from under $20 for chicken or salmon to $36 for lobster tail. Lunch costs $10 to $15. Look for coupons in the free tourist magazines good for 50% off one meal when two people dine together. Both restaurants are open from 11:30 am to 2 pm on weekdays and from 5:30 to 10 pm nightly.

The Honolulu branch of the *Hard Rock Cafe* (☎ 955-7383), 1837 Kapiolani Blvd, is just over the Ala Wai Canal beyond Waikiki. It's enlivened with loud rock music and decorated with old surfboards and a 1959 Cadillac 'woody' wagon hanging precariously over the bar. They serve good burgers with fries and a salad for around $8

and other all-American food, including barbecued ribs and milkshakes, but it's the hip ambiance as much as the food that draws the crowd. It's open daily from 11:30 am to 11 pm (to 11:30 pm on weekends).

Still, the trendiest spot in Waikiki is the new *Planet Hollywood* (☎ 924-7877) at 2155 Kalakaua Ave. This 2nd-floor restaurant has a flashy celluloid motif, with Hollywood memorabilia lining the walls and flicks playing on big-screen videos. Sandwiches, burgers and thin-crust pizzas cost around $10, while pastas and fajitas average $13. It's open daily from 11 am to 11:30 pm.

The *Oceanarium Restaurant* (☎ 922-1233) in the Pacific Beach Hotel, 2490 Kalakaua Ave, has standard fare with anything but standard views. The dining room wraps around an enormous three-story aquarium filled with colorful tropical fish. At breakfast, you can get oatmeal with papaya for $4, waffles or French toast for $7 or a full buffet for $13. At lunch, sandwiches average $8, while dinners begin around $15. The more expensive *Neptune's Garden*, a seafood restaurant in the same hotel, also has views of the aquarium.

Keo's (☎ 737-8240), 625 Kapahulu Ave, is widely regarded as Hawaii's top Thai restaurant. It's decorated with Thai art, sprays of orchids and a wall of photos of owner Keo Sananikone posing with celebrity diners, including the likes of Jimmy Carter, Stevie Wonder and Keanu Reeves. Prices are surprisingly moderate considering the chic reputation. House specialties include the Evil Jungle Prince entree ($11) and spring roll appetizers and green papaya salad, the latter two each $7. The most expensive items on the menu are seafood dishes for $15, so it won't break the bank to dine with the stars here. It's open from 5 pm nightly and is about a mile up Kapahulu Ave from Waikiki.

The *Parc Cafe* (☎ 921-7272) in the Waikiki Parc Hotel has continental-style dining in a pleasant setting. There are buffets for each meal, all attractively prepared with quality food on par with Waikiki's most expensive hotels. The daily breakfast buffet, from 6:30 to 10 am, includes breakfast meats, eggs, French toast, fresh fruit and pastries for $11.50. The lunch buffet, from 11:30 am to 2 pm, costs $16.50 on Wednesdays, when it features Hawaiian food; $19.50 on Sundays, when it begins at 11 am and is called brunch; and $13.50 on other days, when it's centered around a sandwich bar and taco station. All the lunch buffets include hot main dishes, salads and desserts. Dinner buffets, from 5:30 to 9:30 pm nightly, include catch of the day, prime rib, exotic salads and sumptuous desserts for $16.50 on weekdays, $24.50 on weekends, when sashimi and shellfish are included.

Places to Eat – top end

For fine Chinese dining, the *Golden Dragon* (☎ 946-5336) in the Hilton Hawaiian Village has both excellent food and a good ocean view. While the varied menu has some expensive specialties, there are many dishes, including oyster beef, roast duck and a deliciously crispy lemon chicken, that are priced around $15. It's open for dinner only, from 6 to 9:30 pm Tuesday to Sunday.

The *Surf Room* (☎ 931-7194) at the Royal Hawaiian Hotel has outdoor beachside dining, although the food tends to be pricey and not particularly distinguished. There's a $20 breakfast buffet from 6:30 to 11:30 am and a $21.50 lunch buffet from 11:30 am to 2 pm. The dinner menu changes nightly, with meat and seafood entrees averaging $25 to $30.

Michel's at the Colony Surf Hotel (☎ 923-6552), 2895 Kalakaua Ave, has for years been riding on its reputation as Oahu's most romantic restaurant. While the accolades may be a bit overstated, it's certainly pleasant – fine dining with crystal, china and chandeliers, all fronting Sans Souci Beach. The food is traditional French and prices are steep, with chateaubriand, rack of lamb and fish priced à la carte from $35 to $45. It's open daily from 5:30 to 10 pm. When you make reservations be sure to ask for a window table.

La Mer (☎ 923-2311) in the Halekulani hotel is highly regarded for both its creative French menu with Hawaiian influences and for its fine 2nd-floor ocean view. The dining is formal and men are required to wear jackets (loaners are available). Full fixed-price meals start at $85. Otherwise, à la carte entrees range from $36 to $43, including dishes such as squab with foie gras, bouillabaisse and rack of lamb. It's open nightly from 6 to 10 pm.

Waikiki's most renowned Sunday brunch buffet is at the Halekulani's *Orchid's* restaurant (☎ 923-2311). The grand spread includes sashimi, sushi, baron of beef or smoked salmon, roast suckling pig, roast turkey, salads, fruits and a rich dessert bar. There's a fine ocean view, orchid sprays on the tables and a soothing flute and harp duo. The buffet costs $32.50 (more on holidays) and lasts from 9:30 am to 2:30 pm. It's best to make advance reservations or you may encounter a long wait.

Other top-end Waikiki restaurants include *Bali* (☎ 941-2254) at the Hilton Hawaiian Village, for Hawaiian-influenced continental cuisine; *Cascada* (☎ 943-0202) at the Royal Garden at Waikiki, 440 Olohana St, for Euro-Asian specialties; and *Kyo-ya* (☎ 947-3911), 2057 Kalakaua Ave, for traditional Japanese food served by kimono-clad waitresses.

Entertainment

Waikiki has a varied entertainment scene. For updated schedule information, check the free tourist magazines and the daily newspapers.

Concerts The *Waikiki Shell* in Kapiolani Park hosts both classical and contemporary music concerts. For current schedule information, call the Blaisdell Center box office (☎ 591-2211).

Hawaiiana Waikiki has lots of Hawaiian-style entertainment, from Polynesian shows with beating drums and hula dancers to mellow duos playing ukulele or slack-key guitar.

The beachside courtyard at *Duke's Canoe Club* (☎ 922-2268) at the Outrigger Waikiki on Kalakaua Ave has become Waikiki's most popular venue for contemporary Hawaiian music. There's entertainment from 4 to 6 pm and 10 pm to midnight daily, with the biggest names – including Brother Noland, Henry Kapono and Kapena – appearing on weekend afternoons.

At the Sheraton Moana Surfrider's *Banyan Veranda*, you can listen to music beneath the same old banyan tree where 'Hawaii Calls' broadcast its nationwide radio show for four decades beginning in 1935. Typically there's harp music from 7 to 11 am, Hawaiian guitar soloists from 2 to 4:30 pm and steel-guitar music with hula dancing from 5 to 8 pm.

An older, genteel crowd gathers daily at the Halekulani Hotel's open-air *House Without a Key* restaurant for sunset cocktails, Hawaiian music and hula dancing by a former Miss Hawaii.

Coconuts (☎ 949-3811) at the Ilikai hotel often has Hawaiian contemporary music on weekends, with a $6 cover.

The *Royal Hawaiian Hotel* (☎ 923-7311) has a $74 beachside luau from 6 to 8:30 pm on Mondays, with an open bar, buffet-style dinner and Polynesian show; the price for children ages 5 to 12 is $48.

Movie Theaters *Waikiki Theatres* (☎ 971-5133), on Seaside Ave near Kalakaua, and *Marina Twins* (☎ 973-5733), 1765 Ala Moana Blvd, show first-run movies.

IMAX Theatre Waikiki (☎ 923-4629), 325 Seaside Ave, shows a 40-minute movie of Hawaii vistas throughout the day on a 70-foot-wide screen. It costs $7.50 for adults and $5 for children ages three to 11.

Dance clubs In addition to the following listings, a number of the larger Waikiki hotels have nightclubs, some with dancing, some without.

Wave Waikiki (☎ 941-0424), 1877 Kalakaua Ave, has an emphasis on alternative music and is one of Oahu's hottest dance clubs. Hours are 9 pm to 4 am nightly, the minimum age is 21 and there's no dress code. There's no cover charge before 10 pm, a $5 cover after.

Rendezvous (☎ 942-5282), a second

dance club just around the corner at 478 Ena Rd, plays techno, tribal and alternative music from 9 pm to 7 am most nights. The cover charge is usually $5 for ages 21 and older, $7 for ages 18 to 20.

At *Moose McGillycuddy's* (☎ 923-0751), 310 Lewers St, live bands play rock 'n roll from 9 pm to 1:30 am nightly. There's a $3 cover charge on weekends (free on most weekdays) and you have to be 21 to get in.

Gay Venues The gay scene is centered around the Kuhio district, along Kuhio Ave from Kalaimoku to Kaiolu St.

Hula's Bar & Lei Stand (☎ 923-0669), 2103 Kuhio Ave, an open-air video dance club with tables under a big banyan tree, is a favorite place to meet, dance and have a few drinks. It's open from 10 am to 2 am daily.

Nearby, *Treats Hula's* is also a popular gay gathering spot. Other gay hangouts seem to come and go. To find out about the most happening spots, pick up the magazine *Island Lifestyle*, free at Hula's and other gay-oriented businesses.

Comedy The *Comedy Cow* (☎ 926-2269), at Coconuts at the Ilikai hotel, has stand-up comedians at 8 pm Tuesday to Sunday

---

Tea Ceremony

The *Urasenke Foundation of Hawaii*, 245 Saratoga Rd, has tea-ceremony demonstrations on Wednesdays and Fridays, bringing a rare bit of serenity to busy Saratoga Rd. Students dressed in kimonos perform the ceremony on tatami mats in a formal tea room; for those participating it can be a meditative experience.

It costs $2 to be served green tea and sweets, or you can watch the ceremony for free. Each demonstration lasts about 30 minutes. The first sitting is at 10 am, the last at 11:30 am. Although they're not always essential, reservations can be made by calling ☎ 923-3059. Because guests leave their shoes at the door, they are asked to wear socks. The building is across the street and makai from Waikiki's post office. ∎

evenings, plus 10 pm on Fridays and Saturdays. The cost is $12 plus a two-drink minimum.

Free Entertainment A pleasant way to pass the evening is to stroll along Waikiki Beach at sunset and sample the outdoor Hawaiian shows that take place at the beachfront hotels. You can wander past the musicians playing at the Sheraton Moana Surfrider's Banyan Veranda, watch bands performing beachside at Duke's Canoe Club, see the poolside performers at the Sheraton Waikiki and so on down the line.

Hilton Hawaiian Village shoots off fireworks from the beach at 7:30 pm on Fridays, preceded at 6:15 pm by a torch-lighting ceremony and a hula show at the hotel pool. The show, minus the fireworks, also takes place from 5:45 to 6:45 pm on Saturdays. From Sunday to Thursday at 6 pm there's a brief torchlighting ceremony with Hawaiian music. All are free.

There's a worthwhile outdoor hula show at Kuhio Beach Park near the Duke Kahanamoku statue late in the afternoon on Saturdays.

The *Royal Hawaiian Shopping Center* offers a variety of free events. A Polynesian 'mini-show' is held at the center's Fountain Courtyard from 6:30 to 9 pm on Mondays, Wednesdays and Fridays and 10 to 11:30 am on Tuesdays, Thursdays and Saturdays. Hour-long hula lessons are at 10 am on Mondays, Wednesdays and Fridays, while lei-making lessons are at 11 am on Mondays and Wednesdays. On Tuesdays and Thursdays, Hawaiian quilting lessons are given at 9:30 am, ukulele lessons at 10 am and coconut-frond weaving at noon. The shopping center's brochure shows the location of each activity.

The Royal Hawaiian Band performs from 2 to 3:15 pm most Sundays, with the exception of August, at the Kapiolani Park Bandstand. It's a quintessential Hawaiian scene that caps off with the audience joining hands and singing Queen Lili-uokalani's *Aloha Oe* in Hawaiian.

At 11 am and 5:15 pm daily the *Sheraton Moana Surfrider* offers free hour-long historical tours of the old Moana Hotel, which is on the National Register of Historic Places. Tours leave from the concierge desk and are open to the public; reservations are not necessary. You can also stroll through on your own. The 2nd floor has a display of memorabilia from the early hotel days, with scripts from 'Hawaii Calls', woolen bathing suits, period photographs and a short video.

Other free things, including the Kodak Hula Show, the Damien Museum, the Oceanarium and the US Army Museum, are detailed under Waikiki sights.

Things to Buy

Waikiki has no shortage of souvenir stalls, swimsuit and T-shirt shops, quick-stop convenience marts or fancy boutiques.

The prolific ABC discount marts (33 in Waikiki at last count) are often the cheapest places to buy more mundane items, such as macadamia nuts, beach mats, sunblock and other vacation necessities.

International Market Place, in the center of Waikiki, is a collection of ticky-tacky shops and stalls set beneath a sprawling banyan tree. Although few of the stalls carry high-quality goods, if you're looking for inexpensive jewelry or T-shirts, it's worth a stroll. The market place also has a Tower Records shop with an extensive Hawaiian music section and a set-up that allows you to listen to the CDs before you buy.

The Royal Hawaiian Shopping Center, Waikiki's biggest shopping center, spans three blocks along Kalakaua Ave. It has a few dozen clothing and jewelry shops as well as numerous gift shops, the most interesting of which is The Little Hawaiian Craft Shop with a range of Hawaii-made crafts.

Liberty House, a somewhat upmarket department store with good quality clothing, is at the Waikiki Beachcomber Hotel on Kalakaua Ave.

Still, for the best deals on most items, you'll need to leave Waikiki. Try the Ala Moana Center, the Aloha Flea Market or one of the frequent craft shows that pop up around the city.

Honolulu

In 1793 the English frigate *Butterworth* became the first foreign ship to sail into what is now called Honolulu Harbor. Its captain, William Brown, named the harbor Fair Haven. Ships that followed called it Brown's Harbor. But over time the name Honolulu, which means 'Sheltered Bay', came to be used for both the harbor and the adjacent seaside district that the Hawaiians had called Kou.

As more and more foreign ships found their way to Honolulu, a harborside village of thatched houses sprouted up and the town became Hawaii's center of trade.

In 1809 Kamehameha I moved his royal court to Honolulu from Waikiki. On what today is the southern end of Bethel St, Kamehameha set up residence to keep an eye on all the trade that moved in and out of the harbor. From there Hawaiian sandalwood was shipped to Canton in exchange for weapons and luxury goods, which Kamehameha loaded into his harborside warehouses.

In the 1820s whaling ships began pulling into Honolulu for supplies, liquor and women. At the same time, Christian missionaries began coming ashore to save souls. The Protestant mission and Episcopal and Catholic churches all established their Hawaiian headquarters in downtown Honolulu.

Both groups have left their mark. Downtown are the offices of the 'Big Five' corporations that were in control of most of Hawaii's commerce by the turn of the century. It's no coincidence that their lists of corporate board members – Alexander, Baldwin, Cooke and Dole – read like a roster from the first mission ships.

The whalers left a different legacy. Hotel St, a line of bars and strip joints a few blocks from the harbor, remains the city's red-light district.

By the early 20th century Honolulu had expanded into a sprawling cosmopolitan city, but the downtown area up from the harbor remains the heart of Honolulu.

Honolulu Today

Honolulu is the only major city in Hawaii. It has a population of nearly 400,000 and is the state's center of business, culture and politics. It's been the capital of Hawaii since 1845. Honolulu International Airport and Honolulu Harbor are Hawaii's busiest ports.

Honolulu is home to people from throughout the Pacific. It's a city of minorities, with no ethnic majority.

Honolulu's ethnic diversity can be seen on almost every corner – the sushi shop next door to the Vietnamese bakery, the Catholic church around the block from the Chinese Buddhist temple, and the rainbow of school children waiting for the bus.

The main federal, state and county offices and the state's highest concentration of historic buildings are found in downtown Honolulu.

DOWNTOWN HONOLULU

Downtown Honolulu is a hodgepodge of past and present, with both sleek high-rises and stately Victorian-era buildings. There's a royal palace, a modernistic state capitol, a coral-block New England missionary church and a Spanish-style city hall all within sight of one another.

The downtown area is intriguing to explore. You can take in a Friday noon band concert on the palace lawn, lounge in the open-air courtyard of Hawaii's central library, or catch a sweeping view of the city from the top of the Aloha Tower.

Information

On weekdays downtown Honolulu has a lot of traffic congestion, which, combined with its many one-way streets and confusing intersections, can make driving a bit overwhelming for visitors.

During the week the best idea is simply to take the bus. Buses No 2, 19 and 20 run between downtown and Waikiki. On weekends the traffic is light and parking isn't difficult.

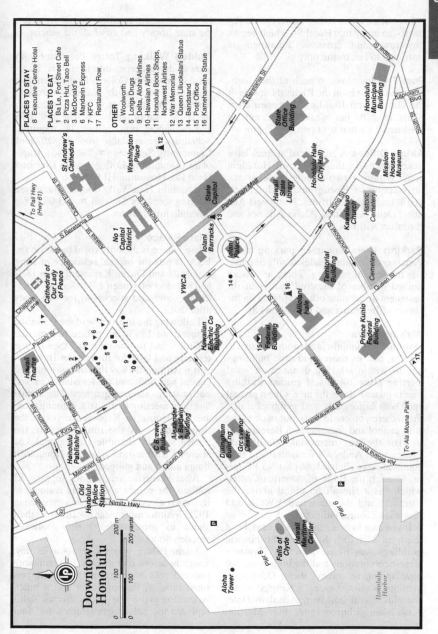

Downtown Honolulu

PLACES TO STAY
8 Executive Centre Hotel

PLACES TO EAT
1 Ba Le, Fort Street Cafe
2 Pizza Hut, Taco Bell
3 McDonald's
6 Mandarin Express
7 KFC
17 Restaurant Row

OTHER
4 Woolworth
5 Longs Drugs
9 Delta, Aloha Airlines
10 Hawaiian Airlines
11 Honolulu Book Shops,
   Northwest Airlines
12 War Memorial
13 Queen Liliuokalani Statue
14 Bandstand
15 Post Office
16 Kamehameha Statue

Lots of city bus routes converge downtown – so many that Hotel St, which begins downtown and crosses Chinatown, is restricted to bus traffic only.

Post The downtown branch of the Honolulu post office is on the Richards St side of the Old Federal Building. It's open from 8 am to 4:30 pm weekdays except on Wednesdays when it's open until 6 pm.

Airline Offices A number of airlines have ticket offices in the downtown Honolulu area. Within a two-minute walk of the intersection of Bishop and S Hotel Sts, you'll find United Airlines, Northwest Airlines, Delta Air Lines, Aloha Airlines and Hawaiian Airlines.

Parking There's metered parking along Punchbowl St and on Halekauwila St opposite the federal building. There are also a limited number of metered spaces in the basement of the state office building on the corner of Beretania and Punchbowl Sts.

Walking Tours

Downtown Honolulu is a wonderful area to wander, and its most handsome buildings are all within walking distance. A good starting place for a self-guided walking tour is Iolani Palace, the area's most pivotal spot both historically and geographically. From there you could walk out back to the state capitol and continue to S Beretania St to visit the war memorial, Washington Place and St Andrew's Cathedral and then continue down Richards St past No 1 Capitol District; the Bank of America Center, which has a Hawaiiana mural above the entrance; and the attractive YWCA and Hawaiian Electric buildings.

If you care to make the walk longer, head north on Merchant St to see the historic buildings that house some of Hawaii's largest corporations and the high-rises that have sprung up around them. Otherwise, continue southeast along S King St where the old federal building, Aliiolani Hale, Kawaiahao Church and the Mission

Houses Museum line one side of the street, the state library and city hall the other.

Guided Walking Tours For those who want to delve deeper into local lore, Kapiolani Community College leads downtown walking tours with varied historical themes – from ghosts of old Honolulu to the crime beat of the 1920s. The cost is $5 and advance registration is required. Schedules are available from the Office of Community Services (☎ 734-9245), Kapiolani Community College, 4403 Diamond Head Rd, Honolulu, HI 96816.

Honolulu TimeWalks does similar theme walking tours for $8; call ☎ 943-0371 for schedule information.

Iolani Palace

Iolani Palace is the only royal palace in the USA. It was the official residence of King Kalakaua and Queen Kapiolani from 1882 to 1891 and of Queen Liliuokalani, Kalakaua's sister and successor, for two years after that.

Following the overthrow of the Hawaiian kingdom in 1893, the palace became the capitol – first for the republic, then for the territory and later for the state of Hawaii.

It wasn't until 1969 that the current state capitol was built and the legislators moved out of their cramped quarters. The Senate had been meeting in the palace dining room and the House of Representatives in the throne room. By the time they left, the palace was in shambles, the grand koa staircase termite-ridden and the Douglas fir floors pitted and gouged.

After extensive renovations topping $7 million, the palace was largely restored to its former glory and opened as a museum in 1978. Visitors must wear booties over their shoes to protect the highly polished wooden floors.

Iolani Palace was modern for its day. Every bedroom had its own full bath with hot and cold water running into copper-lined tubs, a flushing toilet and a bidet. According to the tour guides, electric lights replaced the palace gas lamps a full four years before the White House in Washington got electricity.

The throne room, decorated in red and gold, features the original thrones of the king and queen and a kapu stick made of the long, spiral ivory tusk of a narwhal. In addition to celebrations full of pomp and pageantry, it was in the throne room that King Kalakaua danced his favorite Western dances – the polka, the waltz and the Virginia reel – into the wee hours of the morning.

Not all the events that took place there were joyous. Two years after she was dethroned, Queen Liliuokalani was brought back to the palace and tried for treason in the throne room. In a move calculated to humiliate the Hawaiian people, she spent nine months as a prisoner in Iolani Palace, her former home.

Guided tours of the palace leave every 15 minutes from 9 am to 2:15 pm Wednesday to Saturday and cost $8 for adults, $2 for children ages five to 12. Children under five are not admitted. The tours last 45 minutes. Sometimes you can join up on the spot, but it's advisable to make advance reservations by phoning ☎ 522-0832. The palace is wheelchair accessible.

Palace Grounds Before Iolani Palace was built, there was a simpler house on these grounds that King Kamehameha III used when he moved the capital from Lahaina to Honolulu in 1845. Prior to that, it was the site of a heiau.

The palace ticket window and a gift shop are in the former **barracks** of the Royal Household Guards, a building that looks oddly like the uppermost layer of a medieval fort that's been sliced off and plopped on the ground.

The **domed pavilion** on the grounds was originally built for the coronation of King Kalakaua in 1883 and is still used for the inauguration of governors and for concerts by the Royal Hawaiian Band.

The **grassy mound** surrounded by a wrought iron fence was the site of a royal tomb until 1865, when the remains of King

Kamehameha II and Queen Kamamalu (who both died of measles in England in 1824) were moved to the Royal Mausoleum in Nuuanu.

The huge **banyan tree** between the palace and the state capitol is thought to have been planted by Queen Kapiolani.

Hawaii State Library

The central branch of the state-wide library system is on the corner of King and Punchbowl Sts. Located in a beautifully restored historic building, its collection of over half a million titles is the state's best and includes comprehensive Hawaii and Pacific sections.

It's open from 9 am to 5 pm on Mondays, Fridays and Saturdays; 9 am to 8 pm on Tuesdays and Thursdays; and 10 am to 5 pm on Wednesdays.

The **Hawaii State Archives** next door holds official government documents and an extensive photo collection. It's open to the public for research.

Queen Liliuokalani Statue

The statue of Hawaii's last queen stands between the capitol and Iolani Palace. It faces Washington Place, Liliuokalani's home and place of exile for more than 20 years. The bronze statue is holding the Hawaii constitution that Liliuokalani wrote in 1893, in fear of which US businessmen overthrew her; *Aloha Oe*, a popular hymn that she composed; and *Kumulipo*, the Hawaiian chant of creation.

State Capitol

Hawaii's state capitol is not your standard gold dome. Constructed in the late 1960s, it was a grandiose attempt at a 'theme' design.

Its two legislative chambers are cone-shaped to represent volcanoes; the rotunda is open-air to let gentle trade winds blow through; the supporting columns represent palm trees; and the whole structure is encircled by a large pool symbolizing the ocean surrounding Hawaii.

Unfortunately, the building not only

symbolizes the elements but has been quite effective in drawing them in. The pool tends to collect brackish water; rain pouring into the rotunda has necessitated the sealing of skylights; and Tadashi Sato's 'Aquarius' floor mosaic, meant to show the changing colors and patterns of Hawaii's seas, got so weathered it had to be reconstructed.

After two decades of trying unsuccessfully to deal with all the problems on a piecemeal basis, the state put the facility through a thorough renovation, just completed in 1997. Visitors are free to walk through the rotunda, from where you can peer through viewing windows into the two flanking legislative chambers.

In front of the capitol is a **statue of Father Damien**, the Belgian priest who volunteered to work among the lepers of Molokai and died of their disease 16 years later, at age 49. The stylized sculpture was created by Venezuelan artist Marisol Escubar.

War Memorial

The war memorial is a sculptured eternal torch dedicated to soldiers who died in WWII. It sits between two underground garage entrances on S Beretania St, directly opposite the state capitol.

Washington Place

Washington Place, the governor's official residence, is a large colonial-style building with stately trees, built in 1846 by US sea captain John Dominis. The captain's son John married the Hawaiian princess who later became Queen Liliuokalani. After the queen was dethroned she lived at Washington Place in exile until her death in 1917.

A plaque near the sidewalk on the left side of Washington Place is inscribed with the words to *Aloha Oe*.

The large tree in front of the house on the right side of the walkway is a pili nut tree, recognizable by the buttress-like roots extending from the base of its trunk. In Southeast Asia the nuts of these trees are used to produce oil.

St Andrew's Cathedral

King Kamehameha IV, who was attracted by the royal trappings of the Church of England, decided to build his own cathedral in the capital. He and his consort Queen Emma founded the Anglican Church of Hawaii in 1858.

The cathedral's cornerstone was finally laid in 1867 by King Kamehameha V. Kamehameha IV had passed away four years earlier on St Andrew's Day – hence the church's name.

St Andrew's is on the corner of Alakea and S Beretania Sts. The building is of French Gothic architecture, shipped in pieces from England. Its most striking feature is the impressive window of hand-blown stained glass that forms the western facade and reaches from the floor to the eaves. In the right section of the glass you can see the Reverend Thomas Staley, the first bishop sent to Hawaii by Queen Victoria, alongside King Kamehameha IV and Queen Emma.

No 1 Capitol District

The elegant five-story building on Richards St opposite the state capitol houses some of the offices of the state legislature.

The building has something of the appearance of a Spanish mission, with courtyards and ceramic tile walls. Built in 1928, it served as the YMCA Armed Services building for more than five decades.

The building is owned by the Hemmeter Corporation, which put the site through a multimillion-dollar renovation and then used it briefly as its corporate headquarters. Chris Hemmeter, incidentally, was the developer behind many of the extravagant 'fantasy hotels' constructed on the Neighbor Islands in the 1980s.

Fort Street Mall

Fort Street is a pedestrian shopping mall lined with benches and an ever-growing number of high-rise buildings. While the mall is not interesting in itself, if you're downtown it's a reasonable place to eat – not as good as Chinatown, but a few blocks closer. Hawaii Pacific University, a small but growing private institution, has much of its campus at the north end of the mall.

Cathedral of Our Lady of Peace
The oldest Catholic cathedral in the USA is the Cathedral of Our Lady of Peace, at the S Beretania St end of Fort St Mall. Built of coral blocks in 1843, it's older and more ornate than St Andrew's Cathedral.

Father Damien, who later ministered to Molokai's leprosy colony, was ordained at the cathedral in 1864.

Aliiolani Hale
Aliiolani Hale ('House of Heavenly Kings') was the first major government building built by the Hawaiian monarchy. It has housed the Supreme Court since its construction in 1874 and was once also home to the legislature. The building has a distinctive clock tower and was originally designed by Australian architect Thomas Rowe to be a royal palace, although it never was used as such.

It was on the steps of Aliiolani Hale, in January 1893, that Sanford Dole proclaimed the establishment of a provisional government and the overthrow of the monarchy.

Kamehameha Statue
The statue of Kamehameha the Great stands in front of Aliiolani Hale, opposite Iolani Palace. It was cast by Thomas Gould in 1880. This one is actually a recast, as the first statue was lost at sea near the Falkland Islands. The original statue, recovered after this second version was dedicated, now stands in Kohala, the Big Island birthplace of Kamehameha.

On June 11, a state holiday honoring Kamehameha, the statue is ceremoniously draped with layer upon layer of 12-foot leis.

Honolulu Hale
City Hall, also known as Honolulu Hale, is largely of Spanish mission design with a tiled roof, decorative balconies, arches and pillars. Built in 1927, it bears the initials of

Kawaiahao Church

CW Dickey, Honolulu's most famous architect of the day. The open-air courtyard in the center of the building is sometimes used for concerts and art exhibits.

Kawaiahao Church
Oahu's oldest church, on the corner of Punchbowl and S King Sts, was built on the site where the first missionaries constructed a grass thatch church shortly after their arrival in 1820. The original was an impressive structure that measured 54 by 22 feet and seated 300 people on lauhala mats.

Still, thatch wasn't quite what the missionaries had in mind, so they designed a more typically New England-style Congregational church with simple Gothic influences.

Built between 1838 and 1842, the church is made of 14,000 coral slabs, many weighing more than 1000 pounds. Hawaiian

OAHU

NED FRIARY
Lunalilo's Tomb

divers chiseled the huge blocks of coral out of Honolulu's underwater reef.

The clock tower was donated by Kamehameha III and the clock, built in Boston and installed in 1850, still keeps accurate time.

Inside the church is breezy and cool. The rear seats, marked by *kahili* (feather) staffs and velvet padding, were for royalty and are still reserved for descendants of royalty today. The church is usually open to visitors from 8 am to 4 pm daily.

The **tomb of King Lunalilo**, the successor to Kamehameha V, is in the church grounds at the main entrance. Lunalilo ruled for only one year before his death in 1874 at the age of 39.

Around the back is a **cemetery** where many of the early missionaries are buried, including members of the Baldwin and Bingham families.

Mission Houses Museum
Three of the original buildings of the Sandwich Islands Mission headquarters still stand: the Frame House (built in 1821), the Chamberlain House (1831) and the Printing Office (1841).

Together they're open to the public as the Mission Houses Museum (☎ 531-0481), 553 S King St. The houses are authentically furnished with handmade quilts on the beds, settees in the parlor and iron pots in the big stone fireplaces.

The coral-block Chamberlain House was the early mission storeroom – a necessity, as Honolulu had few shops in those days. Upstairs are hoop barrels, wooden crates packed with dishes and a big desk with pigeon-hole dividers and the quill pen Levi Chamberlain used to work on accounts. Levi was the person appointed by the mission to buy, store and dole out supplies to the missionary families who each had an allowance. His account books show that in the late 19th century, 25¢ would buy either one gallon of oil, one pen knife or two slates.

The first missionaries packed more than their bags when they left Boston – they actually brought a prefabricated wooden house around the Horn with them! Designed to withstand cold New England winter winds, the small windows instead block out Honolulu's cooling trade winds, keeping the two-story house hot and stuffy. The Frame House, as it's now called, is the oldest wooden structure in Hawaii.

The Printing Office housed the lead-type press that was used to print the Bible in the Hawaiian language.

The Mission Houses Museum is open from 9 am to 4 pm Tuesday to Saturday. Admission is $5 for adults and $1 for children (under age six free). While you can explore the visitor center and the Chamberlain House on your own, the Printing Office and Frame House can only be seen with a guide. Guided tours are given at 9:30, 10:30 and 11:30 am and at 1, 2 and 3 pm.

Other Historic Buildings
The **Hawaiian Electric Company's** four-story administration building on the corner of Richards and S King Sts is of Spanish colonial architecture. It has an arched entranceway and ornate period lamps

hanging from hand-painted ceilings. The entrance leads into the customer service department so it's not a problem to walk in and take a look.

Diagonally opposite on Merchant St is the **Old Federal Building**, another interesting edifice with Spanish colonial features. Completed in 1922, it holds a post office and customs house.

Also noteworthy, the three-story **YWCA** at 1040 Richards St was built in 1927 by Julia Morgan, the renowned architect who designed William Randolph Hearst's San Simeon estate in California.

The **Old Honolulu Police Station** (1931) on the corner of Bethel and Merchant Sts has beautiful interior ceramic tile work in earthen tones on its counters and walls. It now houses the state departments of Housing and Finance. Also worth a look is the old **Honolulu Publishing building** across the street.

The four-story **Alexander & Baldwin building** on the corner of Bishop and Queen Sts was built in 1929. The columns at the Bishop St entrance are carved with tropical fruit and the Chinese characters for prosperity and long life. Inside the portico are ceramic tile murals of Hawaiian fish.

Samuel Alexander and Henry Baldwin, both sons of missionaries, vaulted to prominence in the sugar industry and created one of Hawaii's 'Big Five' controlling corporations. The other four – Theo Davies, Castle & Cooke, Amfac and C Brewer – all have their headquarters within a few blocks of here.

The four-story, 60-year-old **Dillingham Building** on the corner of Bishop and Queen Sts is of Italian Renaissance-style architecture, with arches, marble walls, elaborate elevator doors and an arty brick floor. It's a study in contrasts, mirrored in the reflective glass of the adjacent 30-story Grosvenor Center.

Hawaii Theatre

The neo-classical Hawaii Theatre, 1130 Bethel St, first opened in 1922 with silent films playing to the tune of a pipe organ. It ran continuous shows during the war, but the development of mall cinemas in the 1970s was its undoing.

After closing in 1984, the theater's future looked dim, even though it was on the Register of Historic Buildings. Theater buffs came to the rescue, however, forming a nonprofit group and purchasing the property from the Bishop Estate. They raised enough money to undertake a $10 million restoration.

The 1400-seat theater, which has a lovely interior with Shakespearean bas-reliefs and trompe l'oeil mosaics, has now reopened for dance, drama and music performances.

Honolulu Academy of Arts

The Honolulu Academy of Arts (☎ 532-8701), 900 S Beretania St, is an exceptional museum, with permanent Asian, European, American and Pacific art collections from ancient times to the present.

Just inside the door and to the right is a room with works by Matisse, Cézanne, Gauguin, van Gogh and Picasso. There is a welcoming place to sit in the middle of the room to take it all in.

The museum is open and airy and has numerous small galleries around six garden courtyards. The Spanish Court has a small fountain surrounded by Greek and Roman sculpture and Egyptian reliefs dating back to 2500 BC.

There are sculptures and miniatures from India, jades and bronzes from ancient China, Madonna and Child oils from 14th-century Italy and quality changing exhibits.

The Hawaiian section is small but choice, with feather leis, tapa beaters, poi pounders and koa calabashes. The adjacent collection from Papua New Guinea, Micronesia and the South Pacific includes ancestor figures, war clubs and masks.

The museum is open from 10 am to 4:30 pm Tuesday to Saturday and 1 to 5 pm on Sundays. Admission is $5 for adults, $3 for senior citizens and students, free for children under 12. There's a gift shop, library and lunch cafe.

The museum is off the tourist track and seldom crowded. Bus No 2 from Waikiki stops out front; there's metered parking behind the museum.

Aloha Tower

Built in 1926, the 10-story Aloha Tower is a Honolulu landmark that for years was the city's tallest building. In the days when all tourists arrived by ship, this icon of pre-wartime Hawaii – with its clock tower inscribed with the word 'Aloha' – greeted every visitor. Inter-island cruise ships still disembark at the terminal beneath the tower. Take a peek through the terminal windows to see colorful murals depicting the Honolulu of those bygone days.

Aloha Tower is at Pier 9, off Ala Moana Blvd at the harbor end of Fort St. The tower's top-floor observation deck offers a sweeping 360° view of Honolulu's big commercial harbor and downtown area. It's not the most scenic view of the city, but it's interesting nonetheless. The observation deck, which is reached via an elevator, is open daily from 9 am to 9 pm (to 10 pm on Fridays and Saturdays). Admission is free.

Beneath the tower is the Aloha Tower Marketplace, a new shopping center with numerous kiosks, stores and eateries.

Hawaii Maritime Center

The Hawaii Maritime Center (☎ 536-6373) is at Honolulu Harbor's Pier 7 on the Diamond Head side of the Aloha Tower. The center has a maritime museum; the *Falls of Clyde*, said to be the world's last four-masted four-rigged ship; and the berth for the double-hulled sailing canoe *Hokulea*.

The 60-foot *Hokulea* was built to resemble the type of ship used by Polynesians in their migrations. It has made a number of voyages from Hawaii to the South Pacific, retracing the routes of the early Polynesian seafarers and using age-old means of navigation, most notably wave patterns and the position of the stars. Its most recent trip took it to Rarotonga. When in port, the canoe is docked beside the museum.

Permanently on display is the 266-foot iron-hulled *Falls of Clyde*, built in Glasgow, Scotland, in 1878. In 1899 Matson Navigation bought the ship and added a deck house,

and the *Falls* began carrying sugar and passengers between Hilo and San Francisco. It was later converted into an oil tanker and eventually stripped down to a barge.

After being abandoned in Ketchikan, Alaska, where it had been relegated to the function of a floating oil storage tank, the *Falls* was towed to Seattle. A group of Hawaiians raised funds to rescue the ship in 1963, just before it was scheduled to be sunk to create a breakwater off Vancouver. With the aid of the Bishop Museum, the *Falls* was eventually brought to Honolulu and restored. Visitors can stroll the deck and walk down into the cargo holds.

The main museum has an interesting mishmash of maritime displays and artifacts, including a good whaling-era section and model replicas of ships. There's a reproduction of a Matson liner stateroom and interesting old photos of Waikiki in the days when just the Royal Hawaiian and the Moana hotels shared the horizon with Diamond Head. Both hotels belonged to Matson, who spearheaded tourism in Hawaii and ironically sold out to the Sheraton in 1959 just before the jet age and statehood launched sleepy tourism into a booming industry.

The museum is open from 8:30 am to 5 pm daily. Admission is $7.50 for adults, $4.50 for children ages six to 17 and free for kids under six.

To get there, take bus No 19 or 20 from Waikiki. By car, it's off Ala Moana Blvd, about a mile west of Ward Warehouse. There's free parking for museum visitors on Pier 6, just east of the museum.

Sand Island State Park

Sand Island is a 500-acre island on the western side of Honolulu Harbor. About a third of the island has been set aside as a state park.

The park is heavily used by locals who camp, fish and picnic there on weekends, but it has little appeal to the casual visitor and you won't find many tourists there.

Sand Island is not reached from the downtown area, but by an access road a few miles west, off the Nimitz Hwy. Sand Island Access Rd leads 2½ miles down to the park through an industrial area with a waste-water treatment plant, oil tanks, scrap metal yards and the like. The airport is directly across the lagoon and Sand Island is on the flight path.

The park has showers, restrooms and a white-sand beach, which, while cleaner than it's been in past years, still has sections posted as closed due to 'sharp metal objects' on the beach.

CHINATOWN

A walk through Chinatown is like a trip to Asia. Although it's predominantly Chinese,

it has Vietnamese, Thai and Filipino influences as well.

Chinatown is busy and colorful. It has a market that could be right off a back street in Hong Kong: fire-breathing dragons curl up the red pillars outside the Bank of Hawaii and good, cheap Asian restaurants abound. You can get tattooed, consult with an herbalist, munch on moon cakes or slurp a steaming bowl of Vietnamese soup. There are temples, shrines, noodle factories, antique shops and art galleries to explore.

Chinatown has seen some urban renewal, particularly on its downtown edge. The

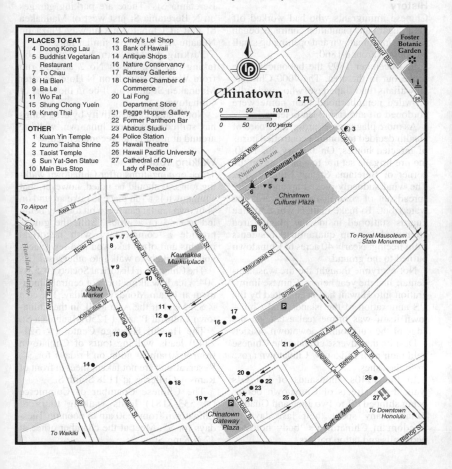

PLACES TO EAT
4 Doong Kong Lau
5 Buddhist Vegetarian
   Restaurant
7 To Chau
8 Ha Bien
9 Ba Le
11 Wo Fat
15 Shung Chong Yuein
19 Krung Thai

OTHER
1 Kuan Yin Temple
2 Izumo Taisha Shrine
3 Taoist Temple
6 Sun Yat-Sen Statue
10 Main Bus Stop

12 Cindy's Lei Shop
13 Bank of Hawaii
14 Antique Shops
16 Nature Conservancy
17 Ramsay Galleries
18 Chinese Chamber of
   Commerce
20 Lai Fong
   Department Store
21 Pegge Hopper Gallery
22 Former Pantheon Bar
23 Abacus Studio
24 Police Station
25 Hawaii Theatre
26 Hawaii Pacific University
27 Cathedral of Our
   Lady of Peace

spiffed-up image includes a new 'entranceway' at the intersection of S Hotel and Bethel Sts, marked by a small park, two marble lions and a new high-rise complex. However, despite creeping gentrification, Chinatown still has its seamy side. Just a block away on S Hotel St you'll find darkened doorways advertising 'video peeps' for 25¢ and topless nightspots with names like Risque Theatre and Club Hubba Hubba.

Places to eat in Chinatown are listed near the end of the Honolulu section.

History

Chinese immigrants who had worked off their sugar cane plantation contracts began settling in Chinatown and opening up small businesses around 1860.

In December 1899 the bubonic plague broke out in the area. The 7000 Chinese, Hawaiians and Japanese who made the crowded neighborhood their home were cordoned off and forbidden to leave.

As more plague cases arose, the Board of Health decided to conduct controlled burns of infected homes. On January 20, 1900, the fire brigade set fire to a building on the corner of Beretania St and Nuuanu Ave. The wind suddenly picked up and the fire spread out of control, racing towards the waterfront. To make matters worse, police guards stationed inside the plague area attempted to stop quarantined residents from fleeing. Nearly 40 acres of Chinatown burned to the ground.

Not everyone thought the fire was accidental. Just the year before, Chinese immigration into Hawaii had been halted by the US annexation of the islands, and Chinatown itself was prime real estate on the edge of the burgeoning downtown district.

Despite the adverse climate, the Chinese held their own and a new Chinatown arose from the ashes.

In the 1940s, thousands of US GIs walked the streets of Chinatown before being shipped off to Iwo Jima and Guadalcanal. Many spent their last days of freedom in Chinatown's 'body houses', pool halls and tattoo parlors.

Orientation & Information

Chinatown proper is immediately north of downtown Honolulu, roughly bounded by Honolulu Harbor, Bethel St, Vineyard Ave and River St. To get there by car from Waikiki, take Ala Moana Blvd and turn at Bethel St or Smith St. Or take Beretania St and head makai down Nuuanu Ave or Maunakea St. Hotel St is open to bus traffic only.

Chinatown is full of one-way streets, traffic is tight and it can be difficult to find a parking space. Your best bet for metered parking ($1 an hour, three-hour limit) is the lot off Smith St between Pauahi and N Beretania Sts. There are parking garages on N Beretania St just west of Maunakea St and at Chinatown Gateway Plaza on Nuuanu Ave that have similar rates.

Parking hassles can be avoided by taking the bus. Buses No 2 and 20 run from Waikiki; get off on N Hotel St after Maunakea St and you'll be in the heart of Chinatown.

Note that because activity by drug gangs has spilled over into Chinatown, walking around at night is not recommended.

Walking Tours

Three organizations offer Chinatown walking tours. It should be noted, however, that Chinatown is a fun place to poke around on your own, and it can feel a bit touristy being led around in a group. Still, the guides provide a commentary with historical insights and often take you to a few places you're unlikely to walk into otherwise.

The Chinatown Historical Society (☎ 521-3045) leads walking tours of central Chinatown at 10 am Monday to Friday. The cost is $5. Meet at the Asia Mall, in the Chinatown Cultural Plaza at 1250 Maunakea St.

The Hawaii Heritage Center (☎ 521-2749) leads walking tours of Chinatown from 9:30 am to noon on Fridays for $4. Reservations are not taken; meet in front of Ramsay Galleries at 1128 Smith St.

The Chinese Chamber of Commerce (☎ 533-3181) leads walking tours of Chinatown from 9:30 am to noon on Tuesdays for $5. Meet at the chamber office at 42 N King St.

Oahu Market

The heart of Chinatown is Oahu Market, the corner of Kekaulike and N King Sts.

Everything the Chinese cook needs is on display: pig heads, jasmine rice, ginger root, fresh octopus, quail eggs, slabs of tuna, long beans and salted jellyfish.

Oahu Market has been an institution since 1904. In 1984, the tenants organized and purchased the market themselves to save it from falling into the hands of developers.

Maunakea Street

Wo Fat, the distinctive pink restaurant on the corner of Hotel and Maunakea Sts, is a Chinatown landmark with a facade that resembles a Chinese temple. The oldest restaurant in Honolulu, it's been on this site since just after the Chinatown fire of 1900. However, recent renovations have stripped the interior of its once colorful Chinese decor, and now it's only the exterior that's worth a glimpse.

Shung Chong Yuein, 1027 Maunakea St, sells delicious moon cakes, almond cookies and other pastries at bargain prices. This is the place to buy dried and sugared foods – everything from candied ginger and pineapple to candied squash and lotus root. They also sell boiled peanuts, which are actually quite good if you can resist comparing them to roasted peanuts.

Across the street is **Cindy's Lei Shop**, a friendly place with leis made of maile, lantern ilima and Micronesian ginger in addition to the more common orchids and plumeria. Prices are very reasonable, starting at $3.50 for a lei of tuberose flowers. The colors and fragrances are heady.

Nuuanu Avenue

The **Chinatown Police Station**, on the corner of Hotel St and Nuuanu Ave in the Perry Block building (circa 1888), has enough 1920s atmosphere to resemble a set from *The Untouchables*.

Just down the street is the **Pantheon Bar**, now abandoned but noteworthy as the oldest watering hole in Honolulu and a favorite of sailors in days past.

Wo Fat Restaurant

Across the street, **Lai Fong Department Store** sells antiques, knickknacks and old postcards of Hawaii dating back to the first half of the century. Even walking into the store itself is a bit like stepping back into the 1940s. Lai Fong's, which has been in the same family for 70 years, also sells Chinese silks and brocades by the yard and makes silk dresses to order.

Incidentally, the **granite-block sidewalks** along Nuuanu Ave were made from the discarded ballast of ships that brought tea from China in the 19th century.

Antiques & Arts

Chinatown has a number of antique shops and art galleries. Pegge Hopper, whose prints of Hawaiian women adorn many a wall in the islands, has her gallery at 1164 Nuuanu Ave. Down the street at 1121 Nuuanu Ave is Abacus Studio, which features the colorful impressionist works of Maui artist Jan Kasprzycki. Also notable is Ramsay Galleries, 1128 Smith St, featuring finely detailed pen-and-ink drawings by the artist Ramsey and quality changing collections of works by other local artists.

A good place to browse for antiques is at Aloha Antiques and the adjacent Mahalo Antique Mall, at 926 and 930 Maunakea St. At this site about 20 vendors have set out their eclectic collections, which include everything from jewelry and Art Deco items to Asian statues and ceramics.

Chinatown Cultural Plaza

This plaza covers the better part of a block along N Beretania St from Maunakea St to River St.

The modern complex doesn't have the character of Chinatown's older shops, but inside it's still quintessential Chinatown, with tailors, acupuncturists and calligraphers alongside travel agents, restaurants and a Chinese news press. One of the kiosks inside the Asia Mall section sells nuts, dried fruit and local honey at good prices. There's a post office and restrooms.

At a small courtyard statue of Kuan Yin, elderly Chinese light incense and leave mangoes.

River St Pedestrian Mall

The River St pedestrian mall has covered tables beside Nuuanu Stream, where old men play mahjong and checkers. A statue of Chinese revolutionary leader Sun Yat-Sen stands at the end of the pedestrian mall near N Beretania St.

There are eat-in and takeout restaurants along the mall, including Japanese food, Chinese food and the peculiarly named Kent's Drive In, a hole-in-the-wall eatery serving plate lunches on the *pedestrian* walkway!

Taoist Temple

Organized in 1889, the Lum Sai Ho Tong Society was one of more than 100 societies started by Chinese immigrants in Hawaii to help preserve their cultural identity. This one was for the Lum clan, who hail from west of the Yellow River. At one time the society had more than 4000 members, and even now there are nearly a thousand Lums in the Honolulu phone book.

The society's Taoist temple on the corner of River and Kukui Sts honors the goddess Tin Hau, a Lum child who rescued her father from drowning and was later deified. Many Chinese claim to see her apparition when they travel by boat. The elaborate altar inside the temple is open for viewing when the street-level door is unlocked, which is usually from 8:30 am to 2 pm daily.

Izumo Taisha Shrine

The Izumo Taisha Shrine, across the river on Kukui St, is a small wooden Shinto shrine built in 1923. During WWII the property was confiscated by the city of Honolulu and wasn't returned to its congregation until 1962.

Incidentally, the 100-pound sacks of rice that sit near the altar symbolize good health, while the ringing of the bell placed at the shrine entrance is considered an act of purification for those who come to pray.

Foster Botanic Garden

Foster Botanic Garden covers 20 acres at the northern end of Chinatown. The entrance is on Vineyard Blvd, opposite the end of River St. The garden took root in 1850 when German botanist William Hillebrand purchased five acres of land from Queen Kalama and planted the trees that now tower in the center of the property.

Captain Foster bought the property in 1867 and continued planting the grounds. In the 1930s the tropical garden was bequeathed to the city of Honolulu and is now a city park.

The garden is laid out in groupings, including sections of palms, orchids, plumerias and poisonous plants.

If you've ever wondered how nutmeg, allspice or cinnamon grow, stroll through the Economic Garden. In this section there's also a black pepper vine that climbs 40 feet up a gold tree, a vanilla vine and other herbs and spices.

The herb garden was the site of the first Japanese language school in Oahu. Many Japanese immigrants sent their children there to learn to read Japanese, hoping to maintain their cultural identity and the option of someday returning to Japan. During the bombing of Pearl Harbor a stray artillery shell exploded into a room full of students. A memorial marks the site.

Herbs & Noodles

Chinatown herbalists are both physician and pharmacist, with a wall full of small wooden drawers each filled with a different herb. They'll size you up, feel your pulse and listen to you describe your ailments before deciding which drawers to open, mixing herbs and flowers and wrapping them for you to take home and boil up together. The object is to balance yin and yang forces. You can find herbalists at the Chinatown Cultural Plaza and along North King and Maunakea Sts.

NED FRIARY

There are also half a dozen noodle factories in Chinatown. If you look inside, you'll see clouds of white flour hanging in the air and thin sheets of dough running around rollers and coming out as noodles. One easy-to-find shop, Yat Tung Chow Noodle Factory, next to Ba Le at 150 N King St, makes nine sizes of noodles, from skinny golden thread to fat udon. ∎

At the other end of the park the wild orchid garden can be a good place for close-up photography. Unfortunately, this side of the garden is skirted by the H-1 Fwy, which detracts from what otherwise would be a peaceful stroll.

The garden's East African *Gigasiphon macrosiphon*, a tree with white flowers that open in the evening, is thought to be extinct in the wild. The tree is so rare that it doesn't have a common name.

The native Hawaiian loulu palm, taken long ago from the upper Nuuanu Valley, may also be extinct in the wild. The garden's chicle tree, New Zealand kauri tree and Egyptian doum palm are all reputed to be the largest of their kind in the USA. Oddities include the cannonball tree, the sausage tree and the double coconut palm that's capable of producing a 50-pound nut.

Foster Garden is open from 9 am to 4 pm daily. Admission costs $5 for those ages 13 and over, $1 for children. Trees are marked,

and a corresponding self-guided tour booklet is available at the entrance.

The Friends of Foster Garden provides volunteer guides who lead hour-long walking tours at 1 pm Monday to Friday. Call ☎ 522-7066 for reservations.

Kuan Yin Temple

The Kuan Yin Temple, on Vineyard Blvd near the entrance of Foster Garden, is a bright red Buddhist temple with a green ceramic-tile roof. The ornate interior is richly carved and filled with the sweet pervasive smell of burning incense.

The temple is dedicated to Kuan Yin Bodhisattva, goddess of mercy, whose statue is the largest in the prayer hall. Devotees burn paper 'money' for prosperity and good luck. Offerings of oranges, fresh flowers and vegetarian food are placed at the altar. The large citrus fruit that is sometimes stacked pyramid-style is the pomelo, considered a symbol of fertility because of its many seeds.

Hawaii's multiethnic Buddhist community worships at the temple, and respectful visitors are welcome.

GREATER HONOLULU
Bishop Museum
The Bishop Museum (☎ 847-3511), 1525 Bernice St, is considered by many to be the best Polynesian anthropological museum in the world. It also has Hawaii's only planetarium.

One side of the main gallery, the Hawaiian Hall, has three floors covering the cultural history of Hawaii. The first floor, dedicated largely to pre-Western contact Hawaii, has a full-size pili-grass thatched house and numerous other displays from carved temple images to calabashes and weapons.

One of the museum's most impressive holdings is a feather cloak made for Kamehameha I and passed down to subsequent kings. It was created entirely of the yellow feathers of the now-extinct mamo, a predominantly black bird with a yellow upper tail. Around 80,000 birds were caught, plucked and released to create this cloak.

The 2nd floor is dedicated to 19th-century Hawaii and the top floor to the various ethnic groups that comprise present-day Hawaii. Like Hawaii itself, the top floor has a bit of everything, including samurai armor, Portuguese festival costumes, Taoist fortune-telling sticks and Queen Liliuokalani's royal coach.

The Polynesian Hall contains masks from Melanesia, stick charts from Micronesia and weapons and musical instruments from across Polynesia.

The Cooke Rotunda features an exhibit detailing how ancient Pacific navigators were able to journey vast distances, tuning into the seas and the skies for direction.

The museum also has a natural history section; large seashell, flora and fauna collections; and the Kahili Room, where children can crawl under large turtle shells, try on a hula skirt or play with Hawaiian rhythm instruments.

In the Hawaiian Hall lobby, craftspeople demonstrate Hawaiian quilting, lauhala weaving, lei making and other traditional crafts from 9 am to 2 pm Monday to Friday. A hula show is presented at 1 pm on weekdays.

The Bishop Museum is open from 9 am to 5 pm daily. Admission, which has recently doubled, is now $14.95 for adults, $11.95 for children ages six to 17 (under age six free); it includes the exhibits and the planetarium.

Planetarium shows are held at 11 am and 2 pm daily. On Fridays and Saturdays there's also a show at 7 pm, which on clear nights is followed by viewing from the observatory telescope. Reservations are necessary for the evening programs. Admission to the planetarium alone costs $4.50.

The museum shop sells many books on the Pacific not easily found elsewhere as well as quality Hawaiiana gift items. There's also a snack shop that's open to 4 pm.

Getting There & Away From Waikiki or downtown Honolulu take the No 2 School St bus to Kapalama St, walk towards the ocean and turn right on Bernice St. By car, take Exit 20B off H-1, go mauka on Houghtailing St and turn left on Bernice St.

Royal Mausoleum State Monument
The Royal Mausoleum contains the remains of kings Kamehameha II, III, IV and V as well as King David Kalakaua and Queen Liliuokalani, the last reigning monarchs.

The only one missing is Kamehameha I, the last king to be buried in secret in accordance with Hawaii's old religion.

The original mausoleum building, which is usually locked, is now a chapel; the caskets are in nearby crypts. Other gravestones honor Kamehameha I's British confidante John Young and American Charles Reed Bishop, husband of Princess Bernice Pauahi Bishop.

The royal mausoleum, at 2261 Nuuanu Ave (just before the avenue meets the Pali Hwy), is open from 8 am to 4:30 pm Monday to Friday.

The **Hsu Yin Temple**, just across Nuuanu Ave from the mausoleum on Kawananakoa

NED FRIARY

Portrait of Kamehameha the Great

NED FRIARY

Lei maker, Chinatown

NED FRIARY

Can we interest you in a nice cold coconut?

Windsurfers at Kailua Beach, Oahu

Beach at Haleiwa, Oahu

Surfer, Oahu

Surfboards, Waikiki

View of Hanauma Bay, Oahu

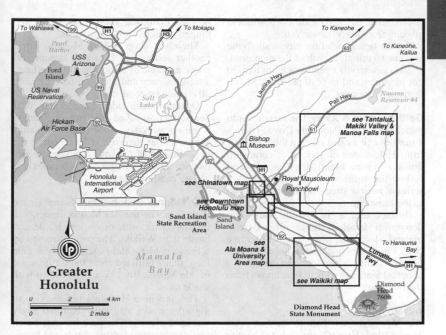

Greater Honolulu

Place, is a Buddhist temple that's worth a quick look if you're visiting the mausoleum. At the altar are the standard offerings of oranges and burning incense, while prints on the walls depict the Buddha's life story.

Punchbowl

Punchbowl is the bowl-shaped remains of a long-extinct volcanic crater. At an elevation of 500 feet it sits a mile above the downtown district and offers a fine view of the city out to Diamond Head and the Pacific beyond.

Early Hawaiians called the crater Puowaina, the 'hill of human sacrifices'. It's believed there was a heiau at the crater and that the bodies of slain kapu breakers were brought to Punchbowl to be cremated upon the heiau altar.

Today it is the site of the 115-acre National Memorial Cemetery of the Pacific. The remains of Hawaiians sacrificed to

appease the gods now share the crater floor with the bodies of more than 25,000 soldiers, more than half of whom were killed in the Pacific during WWII.

The remains of Ernie Pyle, the distinguished war correspondent who covered both world wars and was hit by machine gun fire on Ie Shima during the final days of WWII, lies in section D, grave 109. Five stones to the left, at grave D-1, lies astronaut Ellison Onizuka, the Big Island native who perished in the 1986 Challenger disaster. Their resting places are marked with the same style of flat granite stone that marks each of the cemetery's graves.

A huge memorial at the head of the cemetery has eight marble courts representing different Pacific regions and is inscribed with the names of the 26,289 Americans missing in action from WWII and the Korean War. Two additional half courts have the names of 2489 soldiers missing from the Vietnam War.

For the best view of the city, walk to the lookout 10 minutes south of the memorial.

The cemetery is open from 8 am to 5:30 pm in winter and to 6:30 pm from March through September.

Getting There & Away The entrance into Punchbowl is off Puowaina Drive. There's a marked exit as you start up the Pali Hwy from H-1; watch closely, as it comes up quickly! From there, drive slowly and follow the signs as you wind through a series of narrow streets on the short way up to the cemetery.

By bus, take a No 2 from Waikiki to downtown Honolulu and get off at Beretania and Alapai Sts, where you transfer to a No 15 bus (which runs hourly on the half hour). Ask the driver where to get off. It's about a 15-minute walk to Punchbowl from the bus stop.

Ala Moana

Ala Moana means 'Path to the Sea'. Ala Moana Blvd (Hwy 92) connects the Nimitz Hwy and the airport with downtown Honolulu and Waikiki. Ala Moana is also the name of a land area just west of Waikiki, which includes Honolulu's largest beach park and a huge shopping center.

Ala Moana Center Ala Moana Center is Hawaii's biggest shopping center, with nearly 200 shops. When outer islanders fly to Honolulu to shop they go to Ala Moana. Tourists wanting to spend the day at a mall usually head there too. Ala Moana Center is Honolulu's major bus transfer point and tens of thousands of passengers transit through daily, so even if you weren't planning to go to the center you're likely to end up there!

Ala Moana has a Sears, Liberty House, JC Penney, Longs Drugs, Foodland supermarket and Shirokiya, a department store with a Japanese food market. You'll also find local color at the Crack Seed Center, where you can scoop from jars full of pickled mangoes, rock candy, salty red ginger, cuttlefish and banzai mix.

There's a shop selling Molokai kites, another selling old Hawaiian stamps and coins, a couple of banks and airline offices, a travel agency and a good food court with 20 ethnic fast-food stalls.

On the mauka side of the center, near Sears, is a post office open from 8:30 am to 5 pm on weekdays, to 4:15 pm on Saturdays. Also at the ground level, but at the opposite end of the row, is a satellite city hall where you can get bus schedules and county camping permits.

Ala Moana Beach Ala Moana Beach Park, opposite the Ala Moana Center, is a fine city park with much less hustle and bustle than Waikiki. The park is fronted by a broad golden-sand beach, nearly a mile long, that's buffered from the traffic noise of Ala Moana Blvd by a grassy lawn with shade trees.

This is where Honolulu residents go to jog after work, play volleyball and enjoy weekend picnics. The park has full beach facilities, several softball fields and tennis courts, and free parking. It's a very popular park yet big enough to feel uncrowded.

Ala Moana is generally a safe place to swim and is a good spot for distance swimmers. However, the deep channel that runs the length of the beach can be a hazard at low tide to poor swimmers who don't realize it's there. A former boat channel, it drops off suddenly to overhead depths.

The 43-acre peninsula jutting from the Diamond Head side of the park is the **Aina Moana Recreation Area**, otherwise known as Magic Island. During the school year you can find high school outrigger teams practicing here in late afternoon. There's a nice walk around the perimeter of Magic Island and sunsets can be picturesque, with sailboats pulling in and out of the adjoining Ala Wai Yacht Harbor. This is also a hot summer surf spot.

University of Hawaii

The University of Hawaii (UH) at Manoa, the central campus of the statewide college

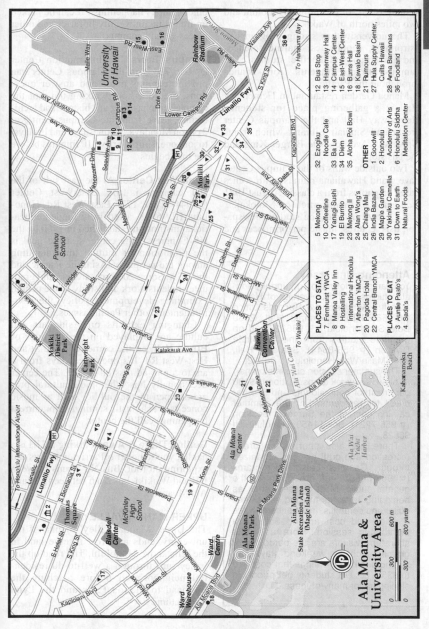

Ala Moana & University Area

system, is east of downtown Honolulu and two miles north of Waikiki.

The university has strong programs in astronomy, geophysics, marine sciences and Hawaiian and Pacific studies. The campus attracts students from islands throughout the Pacific.

Manoa Garden restaurant in Hemenway Hall is a gathering place for students. Hemenway Hall and the Campus Center are behind Sinclair Library, which fronts University Ave opposite Burger King and the bus stop.

Two outside walls of the Campus Center have grand Hawaiiana murals, with scenes based on photos from a classic August 1981 *National Geographic* article on Molokai.

Ka Leo O Hawaii, the student newspaper, lists lectures, music performances and other campus happenings. It can be picked up free at the university libraries and other places around campus.

Campus Tours The Information Center (☎ 956-7235) in the Campus Center can provide campus maps and answer questions. Free one-hour walking tours of the campus, emphasizing art, history and architecture, leave from the Campus Center at 2 pm on Mondays, Wednesdays and Fridays; to join one, simply arrive 10 minutes before the tour begins.

East-West Center At the east side of the UH campus is the East-West Center (☎ 944-7111), 1777 East-West Rd, Honolulu, HI 96848, a federally funded educational institution established in 1960 by the US Congress. The center's stated goal is the promotion of mutual understanding among the people of Asia, the Pacific and the USA. Some 2000 researchers and graduate students work and study at the center, examining development policy, the environment and other Pacific issues.

Changing exhibits on Asian art and culture are displayed on the 1st floor of **Burns Hall**, on the corner of Dole St and East-West Rd. It's open weekdays from 8 am to 5 pm; admission is free. The center occasionally has other multicultural programs open to the public, such as music concerts or scholastic seminars. For current happenings call the center.

Getting There & Away Parking at UH is a hassle; you're better off arriving by bus and exploring on foot. Bus No 4 runs between UH and Waikiki, bus No 6 between UH and Ala Moana.

UPPER MANOA VALLEY

The Upper Manoa Valley, mauka of the university, ends at forest reserve land in the hills above Honolulu. The road up the valley runs through a well-to-do residential neighborhood before reaching the trailhead to Manoa Falls and the Lyon Arboretum.

Attending University

You can get information on undergraduate studies at the University of Hawaii from the Admissions & Records Office (☎ 956-8975), Sakamaki Hall, 2530 Dole St, Honolulu, HI 96822, and on graduate studies at the Graduate Division (☎ 956-8544), Spalding Hall, 2540 Maile Way, Honolulu, HI 96822.

The summer session consists primarily of two six-week terms. Tuition is $130 per credit for nonresidents and $75 per credit for residents. For the summer catalog contact the Summer Session (☎ 956-7221), Box 11450, Honolulu, HI 96828.

There are also shorter, noncredit recreation and craft classes organized through Campus Leisure Programs (☎ 956-6468) that are open to the general public. Most classes, such as beginning hula, lei-making, slack-key guitar and ceramics, meet once or twice a week and cost around $50 for a month-long session. More useful to short-term visitors are the outdoor programs, such as weekend kayaking, surfing and hiking outings that cost $10 to $35 – but UH students get priority in signing up for many of these. ■

Manoa Falls Trail

The trail to Manoa Falls is a beautiful hike, especially for one so close to the city. The trail runs for three-quarters of a mile above a rocky streambed before ending at the falls. It takes about 30 minutes one way.

Surrounded by lush damp vegetation and moss-covered stones and tree trunks, you get the feeling you're walking through a thick rainforest a long way from anywhere. The only sounds are from the chirping birds and the rush of the stream and waterfall.

There are all sorts of trees along the path, including tall *Eucalyptus robusta*, with their soft, spongy, reddish bark; flowering orange African tulip trees; and other lofty varieties that creak like wooden doors in old houses. Many of them were planted by the Lyon Arboretum, which at one time held a lease on the property.

Wild purple orchids and red ginger grow up near the falls, adding an element to the tranquility found there. The falls are steep and drop about 100 feet vertically into a small shallow pool. The pool is not deep enough for swimming, and occasional falling rocks make it inadvisable anyway.

The trail is usually a bit muddy but not too bad if it hasn't been raining lately. Be careful not to catch your foot in exposed tree roots – they're potential ankle breakers, particularly if you're moving with any speed. The packed clay can be slippery in some steep places, so take your time and enjoy the walk.

Aihualama Trail About 75 feet before Manoa Falls, an inconspicuous trail starts to the left of the chain-link fence. This is the Aihualama Trail, well worth a little 15-minute side trip. Just a short way up you'll get a broad view of Manoa Valley.

After about five minutes you'll enter a bamboo forest with some massive old banyan trees. When the wind blows the forest releases eerie crackling sounds. It's an engaging forest, enchanted or spooky depending on your mood.

You can return to the Manoa Falls Trail or go on another mile to Pauoa Flats where the trail connects with the Puu Ohia Trail in the Tantalus area.

Lyon Arboretum

The Lyon Arboretum, 3860 Manoa Rd, is a great place to go after hiking to Manoa Falls if you want to identify trees and plants you've seen along that trail.

Dr Harold Lyon, after whom the arboretum is named, is credited with introducing 10,000 exotic trees and plants to Hawaii. Approximately half of these are represented in this 193-acre arboretum, which is part of the University of Hawaii.

This is not a landscaped tropical flower garden, but a mature and largely wooded arboretum, where related species are clustered in a semi-natural state.

The Hawaiian ethnobotanical garden has mountain apple, breadfruit and taro; ko, the sugar cane brought by early Polynesian settlers; kukui, which produced lantern oil; and ti, used medicinally since ancient times and for moonshine after Westerners arrived.

The arboretum also has herbs, spices and cashew, cacao, papaya, betel nut, macadamia nut, jackfruit and calabash trees, as well as greenhouses and classrooms.

A good choice among the arboretum's many short trails is the 20 minute walk up to **Inspiration Point**, which offers a view of the hills that enclose the valley. En route you'll encounter wonderful scents, inviting stone benches and lots of birdsong. The path loops through ferns, bromeliads and magnolias and passes by tall trees, including a bo tree, a descendant of the tree under which Gautama Buddha sat when he received enlightenment.

The arboretum is open from 9 am to 3 pm Monday to Saturday. A $1 donation is appreciated. Free guided tours (☎ 988-7378 for reservations) are given at 1 pm on the first Friday and third Wednesday of each month and at 10 am on the third Saturday of the month.

The reception center has a book and gift shop as well as helpful staff members who can give you a map of the garden and information on the arboretum's organized hikes, children's programs and one-day workshops.

Getting There & Away

From Ala Moana Center take the No 5 Manoa Valley bus to the end of the line at the junction of Manoa Rd and Kumuone St. From there it's a 10-minute walk to the road's end, where the Manoa Falls Trail begins. Lyon Arboretum is at the end of the short drive off to the left just before the trailhead.

To get there by car, simply drive to the end of Manoa Rd. There's room to park at

the trailhead, but it's not a very secure place so don't leave anything valuable in the car. Lyon Arboretum has a parking area adjacent to its gardens that's reserved for arboretum visitors only.

TANTALUS & MAKIKI HEIGHTS

Just two miles from downtown Honolulu a narrow switchback road cuts its way up the lush green forest reserve land of Tantalus and the Makiki Valley. The road climbs up almost to the top of 2013-foot Mt Tantalus, with swank mountainside homes tucked in along the way.

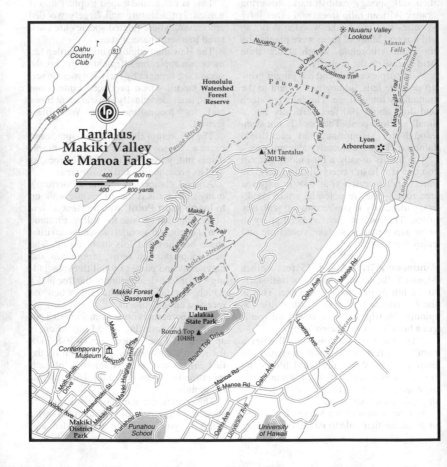

Tantalus, Makiki Valley & Manoa Falls

Although the road is one continuous loop, the western side is called Tantalus Drive and the eastern side Round Top Drive. The 8½-mile circuit is Honolulu's finest scenic drive, offering great views of the city below.

The route is winding, narrow and steep, but it's a good paved road. Among the profusion of dense tropical growth, bamboo, ginger, elephant-ear taro and fragrant eucalyptus trees are easily identified. Vines climb to the top of telephone poles and twist their way across the wires.

A network of hiking trails runs between Tantalus and Round Top drives and throughout the forest reserve, with numerous trailheads off both roads. The trails are seldom crowded, which seems amazing considering how accessible they are. Perhaps because the drive itself is so nice, the only walking most people do is between their car and the scenic lookouts.

The Makiki Heights area below the forest reserve is one of the most exclusive residential areas in Honolulu and the site of a museum of contemporary art (see below). There's bus service as far as Makiki Heights, but none around the Tantalus-Round Top loop drive.

Puu Ualakaa State Park

From Puu Ualakaa State Park you can see an incredible panorama of all Honolulu. The park entrance is 2½ miles up Round Top Drive from Makiki St. It's half a mile in to the lookout; bear to the left when the road forks.

The sweeping view from the lookout extends from Kahala and Diamond Head on the far left, across Waikiki and downtown Honolulu, to the Waianae Range on the far right. To the southeast is the University of Hawaii at Manoa, easily recognized by its sports stadium; to the southwest you can see clearly into the green mound of Punchbowl Crater; the airport is visible on the edge of the coast and Pearl Harbor beyond that.

Although for taking photos the best time to be here is during the day, this is also a fine place to watch evening settle over the

---

Rolling Sweet Potatoes

In olden times, the slopes of Puu Ualakaa ('Rolling Sweet Potato Hill') were planted with sweet potatoes, which were said to have been dug up and then rolled down the hill for easy gathering at harvest time. The hill's other name, Round Top, dates to more recent times. ■

---

city. Arrive at least 30 minutes before sunset to see the hills before they're in shadow.

The park gates are locked from 6:45 pm (7:45 pm in summer) to 7 am. For scenic views, there are a couple of pull-offs before the park.

The Contemporary Museum

The Contemporary Museum (☎ 526-0232), 2411 Makiki Heights Drive, is a delightful modern art museum occupying an estate with 3½ acres of wooded gardens.

The estate house was built in 1925 for Mrs Charles Montague Cooke, whose other former home is the present site of the Honolulu Academy of Arts.

You enter the museum through a covered courtyard with bronze gates and an arrangement of parabolic mirrors that reflect the view hundreds of times over.

Inside are galleries featuring quality changing exhibits of paintings, sculpture and other contemporary artwork by both national and international artists. A newer building on the lawn holds the museum's most prized piece, a vivid environmental installation by David Hockney based on his sets for *L'Enfant et les Sortilèges*, Ravel's 1925 opera. There's also a cafe serving lunch and afternoon desserts.

It's open from 10 am to 4 pm Tuesday to Saturday, and from noon to 4 pm on Sunday. Admission is $5 for adults and $3 for students and senior citizens; it's free for children 12 and under. Docent-led tours are conducted at 1:30 pm.

The museum, near the intersection of Mott-Smith Drive and Makiki Heights Drive, can be reached on the No 15 bus from downtown Honolulu.

Meditation Center

The Honolulu Siddha Meditation Center, 1925 Makiki St, Honolulu, HI 96822, operated by followers of Gurumayi Chidvilasananda, has early morning chanting sessions open to interested visitors.

On Wednesday and Saturday evenings, programs include an orientation to the center, a video of Gurumayi, chanting and meditation. Sometimes group meals, hatha yoga sessions and other programs are open to the public as well; for information call ☎ 942-8887.

Makiki Valley Loop Trail

Three of the Tantalus area hiking trails – Maunalaha Trail, Kanealole Trail and Makiki Valley Trail – can be combined to make the Makiki Valley Loop Trail, a popular 2½-mile hike.

The loop is through a lush and varied tropical forest that starts and ends in Hawaii's first state nursery and arboretum. In this nursery, hundreds of thousands of trees were grown to replace the sandalwood forests that had been leveled in Makiki Valley and elsewhere in Hawaii in the 19th century.

The **Maunalaha Trail** begins at the restrooms below the parking lot of the Makiki Forest baseyard. It first crosses a bridge, passes taro patches and proceeds to climb the east ridge of Makiki Valley, passing Norfolk pine, bamboo and fragrant allspice and eucalyptus trees. There are some good views along the way.

After three-quarters of a mile you'll come to a four-way junction, where you'll take the left fork and continue on the **Makiki Valley Trail**. The trail goes through small gulches and across gentle streams with patches of ginger. Near the Moleka Stream crossing are mountain apple trees (related to allspice and guava), which flower in the spring and fruit in the summer. Edible yellow and strawberry guavas also grow along the trail. There are some fine views of the city below.

The **Kanealole Trail** begins as you cross Kanealole Stream and then follows the stream back to the baseyard, three-quarters

of a mile away. The trail leads down through a field of Job's tears; the bead-like bracts of the female flowers of this tall grass are often picked to be strung in leis.

Kanealole Trail is usually muddy, so wear shoes with good traction and pick up a walking stick. Halfway down there's a grove of introduced mahogany.

Getting There & Away To get to the Makiki Forest baseyard, turn left off Makiki St and go half a mile up Makiki Heights Drive. Where the road makes a sharp bend, proceed straight ahead through a green gate into the Makiki Forest Recreation Area and continue until you reach the baseyard. There's a parking lot on the right just before the office.

You can also take the No 15 bus, which runs between downtown and Pacific Heights. Get off near the intersection of Mott-Smith Drive and Makiki Heights Drive and walk down Makiki Heights Drive to the baseyard. It's a mile-long walk between the bus stop and the trailhead.

An alternative is to hike just the Makiki Valley Trail, which you can reach by going up Tantalus Drive two miles from its intersection with Makiki Heights Drive. As you come around a sharp curve, look for the wooden post marking the trailhead on the right. You can take this route in as far as you want and backtrack out or link up with other trails along the way.

Puu Ohia Trail

The Puu Ohia Trail, in conjunction with the Pauoa Flats Trail, leads up to a lookout with a view of Nuuanu reservoir and valley. It's nearly two miles one way and makes a hardy hike.

The trailhead is at the very top of Tantalus Drive, 3.6 miles up on the left from its intersection with Makiki Heights Drive. There's a large turn-off opposite the trailhead where you can park.

The Puu Ohia Trail starts up reinforced log steps and leads past ginger, bamboo groves and lots of eucalyptus, a fast-growing tree that was planted to protect the watershed. About half a mile up, the trail reaches the top of 2013-foot Mt Tantalus (Puu Ohia).

From Mt Tantalus, the trail leads into a service road. Continue on the road to its end, where there's a Hawaiian Telephone building. The trail picks up again behind the left side of the building.

Continue down the trail until it leads into the **Manoa Cliff Trail**, which you'll go left on for a short distance until you come to another intersection, where you'll turn right onto the **Pauoa Flats Trail**. The trail leads down into Pauoa Flats and on to the lookout. The flats area can be muddy; be careful not to trip on exposed tree roots.

You'll pass two trailheads before reaching the lookout. The first is **Nuuanu Trail**, on the left, which runs three-quarters of a mile along the western side of Upper Pauoa Valley and offers broad views of Honolulu and the Waianae Mountains.

The second is **Aihualama Trail**, a bit farther along on the right, which takes you 1¼ miles to Manoa Falls through bamboo groves and huge old banyan trees. If you were to follow this route, you could then hike down the Manoa Falls Trail, a distance of about a mile, to the end of Manoa Rd and from there catch a bus back to town (see the Upper Manoa Valley section).

MOANALUA

In olden times Moanalua was a stopover for people traveling between Honolulu and Ewa as well as a vacation spot for Hawaiian royalty. In 1884 Princess Pauahi Bishop willed the valley to Samuel M Damon, and it's now privately owned by his estate.

Moanalua Gardens

Moanalua Gardens, maintained by the Damon Estate, is a large grassy park with grand shade trees. The park is the site of Kamehameha V's gingerbread-trimmed summer cottage, which overlooks a taro pond. Beyond it a Chinese-style hall is fronted by carp ponds and stands of golden-stemmed bamboo. The center of the park has a grassy stage where the Prince Lot Hula Festival is held on the third Saturday in July.

This is not a must-see spot, except during the festival, but it is a pleasant place to stroll if you happen to be passing by. To get there, take the Puuloa Rd/Tripler Hospital exit off Hwy 78 and then make an immediate right-hand turn into the gardens.

Moanalua Trail

The trail up Moanalua Valley, once cobblestoned, is now a gravel and dirt road. It's a dry area, and there is only partial shade along the trail. There are both native and introduced plants, and lots of birds. Seven stone bridges remain along the path in various stages of disrepair.

The nonprofit Moanalua Gardens Foundation (☎ 839-5334) works to preserve Moanalua Valley in its natural state. Their efforts to raise public awareness of the valley's history and environmental uniqueness helped defeat plans that would have routed the new H-3 Fwy through Moanalua Valley.

The foundation gives interpretive walks into Moanalua Valley at least one Sunday each month. The easy five-mile walks begin at 9 am, finish around 1 pm and cost $3. Reservations can be made in advance.

If you want to hike the trail on your own, the Damon Estate requests that you first call the Moanalua Gardens Foundation for permission to enter.

If you follow the road all the way in, it's about four miles. Numbered posts along the first half of the trail correspond to a self-guided brochure available for $4.95 from the foundation's office at 1352 Pineapple Place, Honolulu, HI 96819; add $4 for shipping to get it by mail.

To get to the trailhead, take the Moanalua Valley/Red Hill exit off Hwy 78 (one exit past Moanalua Gardens). Stay to the right and then follow the Moanalua Valley sign uphill 1½ miles on Ala Aolani St to where the road ends at a parking lot. There are restrooms and drinking water in the little park at the trailhead.

PLACES TO STAY
Places to Stay – budget

Hostelling International Honolulu (☎ 946-0591; fax 946-5904), 2323A Seaview Ave, Honolulu, HI 96822, is a friendly, well-run hostel in a quiet residential neighborhood near the University of Hawaii. There are seven dorms with bunk beds that can accommodate 42 travelers, with men and women in separate dorms. Rates are $12.50 for HI members, $15.50 for nonmembers. There are also two rooms for couples that cost an extra $10. If you're not a member, there's a three-night maximum stay. HI membership is sold on site for $25 for Americans, $18 for foreigners. Credit cards are accepted.

Office hours are from 8 am to noon and 4 pm to midnight. Guests must be out of the dorms from noon to 4 pm, although the TV lounge and common-use kitchen are open during the day. There's a laundry room, lockers and bulletin boards with useful information for new arrivals. From Ala Moana, catch bus No 6 or 18 (University or Woodlawn), get off on the corner of University Ave and Metcalf St and walk one block uphill to Seaview Ave. By car, take Exit 24B off the H-1 Fwy, go mauka on University Ave and turn left at Seaview Ave.

Fernhurst YWCA (☎ 941-2231; fax 949-0266), 1566 Wilder Ave, Honolulu, HI 96822, has rooms for women only in a three-story building about a mile from the university. There are 60 rooms, each intended for two guests, with two single beds, two lockable closets, two dressers and a desk. Two rooms share one bathroom. The cost is $25 per person. If you get a room to yourself, which is easier during the low season, it costs $5 more. Rates include breakfast and dinner except on Sundays and holidays; there's a small kitchen facility on each floor.

Payment is required weekly in advance; guests staying more than three days must become Y members ($30 a year). It costs an additional $20 to rent linen or you can bring your own. Although they accept tourists, most guests are local, as Fernhurst provides transitional housing for women in need. There's a laundry room, TV room and a garden courtyard with a small pool. Fernhurst is at the intersection of Wilder Ave and Punahou St on the No 4 and 5 bus lines.

The *Central Branch YMCA* (☎ 941-3344; fax 941-8821), 401 Atkinson Drive, Honolulu, HI 96814, east of the Ala Moana Center, is the most conveniently located of the YMCAs. There are 114 rooms in all. The rooms with shared bath, which are available to men only, are small and simple and resemble those in a student dorm, with an old desk, a single bed, a lamp, a chair and linoleum floors. The cost is $29 for a single, or for $40 they'll put in a rollaway bed and two people can share the room. Rooms with private bath, which are a bit nicer but still small and basic, are open to both men and women and cost $36.50/51.50 for singles/doubles. Guests receive YMCA privileges, including free use of the sauna, pool, gym and handball courts. There's also a coin laundry, a TV lounge and a snack bar. Credit cards are accepted.

The *Nuuanu Branch YMCA* (☎ 536-3556; fax 533-1286), 1441 Pali Hwy, Honolulu, HI 96813, at the intersection of Pali Hwy (Hwy 61) and Vineyard Ave, has mostly long-term tenants, but rents some rooms for $29 a day, $138 a week. Accommodations are for men only. Rooms are small and spartan, with louvered windows, a single bed and a small metal desk and chair. Bathrooms are shared. There's a microwave in the hall and guests have access to a TV lounge, the weight room and pool.

During the school year the *Atherton YMCA* (☎ 946-0253), 1810 University Ave, Honolulu, HI 96822, operates as a dorm for full-time University of Hawaii students only. During summer holidays (mid-May to mid-August) it's usually open on a space-available basis to nonstudents, although some years it's full with students year round. Rates are $20 per day for a room with a bed, dresser, desk and chair. Reservations are made by application (available by mail) with a $150 security deposit. The Y is directly opposite the university.

Places to Stay – middle

The *Pagoda Hotel* (☎ 941-6611, 800-367-6060; fax 955-5067), 1525 Rycroft St, Honolulu, HI 96814, north of Ala Moana Center, has two sections. There are studios with kitchenettes in the older apartment section, but they can feel a bit too removed from the main hotel – especially if you're checking in at night. The rooms in the hotel itself are nicer and have the usual amenities, including air-con, TV, phone, refrigerator and a central lobby. Both cost $85. There's no extra charge for children under 18 in the same room as their parents. There's nothing distinguished about this hotel, other than a restaurant with a carp pond, but it is one way to avoid jumping into the Waikiki scene.

Places to Stay – top end
The *Executive Centre Hotel* (☎ 539-3000, 800-949-3932; fax 523-1088), on the upper floors of a high-rise at 1088 Bishop St, Honolulu, HI 96813, is Honolulu's only downtown hotel. Geared for businesspeople, it's comprised of 114 large and comfortable modern suites, each with two TVs, phones with voice mail, a refrigerator, room safe and whirlpool bath. There's a heated lap pool, fitness equipment and a business center. Rates, which include continental breakfast, range from $125 for a mountain view to $180 for an executive oceanview suite with kitchen facilities.

Manoa Valley Inn (☎ 947-6019, 800-535-0085; fax 946-6168; marc@aloha.net), 2001 Vancouver Drive, Honolulu, HI 96822, on a quiet side street near the University of Hawaii, is an authentically restored Victorian inn on the National Register of Historic Places. All eight rooms are filled with antiques, one with a four-poster bed, another with furnishings that belonged to silent-film star Frances Beaumont. There's complimentary evening wine, a common parlor and a billiards room. Rates, which include continental breakfast, are $100 for rooms with a shared bathroom and $140 to $190 for rooms with a private bathroom. The inn is a Marc Resorts property.

Places to Stay – near the airport
If you need to be near Honolulu International, there are three hotels outside the airport along a busy highway and beneath

flight paths. All provide free 24-hour transport to and from the airport, about 10 minutes away.

In addition, for long layovers or midnight flights there are two cheaper places where you can catnap or just take a shower.

The more attractive option is *Sleep & Shower* (☎ 836-3044; fax 834-8985), Terminal Box 42, Honolulu, HI 96819, right in the airport's main terminal between lobbies five and six. It has 17 small, private rooms, each with a single bed and its own bathroom and shower. The place is clean and relatively quiet, although there is some vibration from the shuttle bus that runs overhead. Overnight (eight-hour) stays are $30, a two-hour daytime nap and shower cost $17.50, with additional hours for $5. Only one person is allowed to stay in each room. Showers only cost $7.50, with towels, shampoo and razors provided. It's open 24 hours. Reservations are taken for the overnight stays and MasterCard and Visa are accepted.

Nimitz Shower Tree (☎ 833-1411), 3085 N Nimitz Hwy, occupies a converted warehouse in an industrial area not far from the airport hotels. The facilities are basic; the private 'roomettes' are rows of simple cubicles with platform beds that cost $22 to $30 for an overnight sleep. You can also go there just to take a shower for $7.50. It's open 24 hours and free transport is available – look for the courtesy phone in the baggage claim area.

The renovated *Best Western Plaza Hotel-Honolulu Airport* (☎ 836-3636, 800-528-1234; fax 834-7406), 3253 N Nimitz Hwy, Honolulu, HI 96819, is a comfortable midrise hotel with 268 rooms, each with one king or two double beds, a TV and a refrigerator. The only drawback is the heavy traffic noise from the nearby highway – ask for a rear room. Rates start at $89, and nonsmoking rooms are available. There's a pool, lounge and restaurant.

Holiday Inn-Honolulu Airport (☎ 836-0661, 800-800-3477; fax 833-1738), 3401 N Nimitz Hwy, Honolulu, HI 96819, on the corner of Rodgers Blvd and Nimitz Hwy, has 308 rooms at $112, but when occupancy's not high there's a 'manager's special' at $89. The rooms are a bit tired, but this four-story hotel has typical Holiday Inn amenities, including a lounge, pool and restaurant. Guests have a choice of a king or two double beds; nonsmoking rooms are available.

Pacific Marina Inn (☎ 836-1131; fax 833-0851), 2628 Waiwai Loop, Honolulu, HI 96819, is a mile farther east in an industrial area, but on the plus side it has the least traffic noise. This three-decker motel has small, straightforward rooms for $79, but there's usually an 'airport special' for $60; they can be reached on the courtesy phone in the baggage claim area. The rooms have air-con, TVs and phones, and there's a pool on the grounds.

PLACES TO EAT

Honolulu has an incredible variety of good ethnic food, and if you know where to look it can also be quite cheap. The key is to get out of the tourist areas and eat where the locals do.

Around the University

There are some excellent restaurants in the area around the University of Hawaii at Manoa. The following listings are all within a 10-minute walk of the three-way intersection of S King St, S Beretania St and University Ave.

Coffeeline, a student hangout at the corner of University and Seaview Aves, serves coffees and vegetarian meals. Vegan soup costs $2.50, omelets, sandwiches and salads are around $4 and a few hot dishes such as spinach lasagna cost $5. It's open from 7:30 am to 4 pm Monday to Friday.

Ezogiku Noodle Cafe, at the corner of University Ave and S Beretania St, dishes up miso ramen for $5.25, gyoza for $3.50, curries, fried rice and cold noodles. While it's not gourmet quality, it is on par with similar fast-food noodle shops in Japan. It's open daily from 11 am to 11 pm.

Across the street at 1091 University Ave, a branch of the Vietnamese restaurant *Ba Le* sells good, inexpensive French rolls, croissants and sandwiches. A tasty vegetar-

ian sandwich costs $2, while a roast beef version goes for $4.

India Bazaar (☎ 949-4840), in a little shopping center at 2320 S King St, is a small cafe selling inexpensive Indian food. The vegetarian thali includes jasmine rice and three vegetable curries for $5.75, while chicken and shrimp thalis go for $7. Side orders of papadams, chapatis, samosas and raita are each under $1. It's open from 11 am to 9 pm Monday to Saturday. In the same complex a branch of *Kozo Sushi*, a decent chain operation, specializes in inexpensive sushi.

Maple Garden (☎ 941-6641), 909 Isenberg St, around the corner from S King St, is a popular local Sichuan restaurant with good food at reasonable prices. Vegetarian entrees, including a delicious eggplant in hot garlic sauce, average $6.50, while most meat dishes are about a dollar more. At lunch there are various full-plate specials for $5 to $6. It's open from 11 am to 2 pm and 5:30 to 10 pm daily.

Aloha Poi Bowl (☎ 944-0798), a little local eatery at 2671 S King St, dishes up Hawaiian fare. A meal of lomi salmon, pipikaula, poi and haupia with your choice of kalua pork, laulau or fried fish costs $7. It's open from 11 am to 2 pm and 4 to 8 pm on weekdays (closed for lunch on Tuesdays), 11 am to 9 pm on Saturdays and noon to 7 pm on Sundays.

Diem (☎ 941-8657), at 2633 S King St, is a small family-run restaurant serving some of Honolulu's best Vietnamese food. The shrimp rolls ($5.35) make excellent appetizers, while the spicy lemongrass chicken ($6.50) is a recommendable main dish. Good-value lunch specials ($7.50), including an entree, salad, rice and appetizer, are served until 4 pm daily. Diem is open daily from 10 am to 10 pm.

Chiang Mai (☎ 941-1151), 2239 S King St, serves northern Thai food. Their wonderful sticky rice, reminiscent of Japanese omochi, is served in its own little bamboo steamer. There are numerous vegetarian dishes from $6 and chicken and beef dishes from $7. It's open from 11 am to 2 pm Monday to Friday and 5:30 to 10 pm nightly.

Yakiniku Camellia (☎ 946-7595), 2494 S Beretania St, has a tasty all-you-can-cook Korean lunch buffet for $12.95 from 11 am to 3 pm. It's quality food and if you've got an appetite worked up, it's a fine deal. The mainstay is pieces of chicken, pork and beef that you select and grill at your table. Accompanying this are 18 kimchees and marinated side dishes, miso and seaweed soups, simple fresh vegetable salads and a few fresh fruits. Dinner, from 3 to 10 pm, costs $15.75 and adds on sashimi. Everything is authentic, right down to the vending machine selling the Korean-language daily.

Down to Earth Natural Foods, 2525 S King St, is a large natural foods supermarket. The store has everything from Indian chapatis to local organic produce and a dozen varieties of granola sold in bulk. It's a great place to shop, and the healthier yogurts and whole-grain breads that some of Honolulu's more with-it supermarkets sell are substantially cheaper at Down to Earth. It's open from 8 am to 10 pm daily. The store also has a vegetarian deli, for either eat-in or takeout, with a salad bar ($4 a pound), sandwiches, soups and plate lunches.

Ala Moana Center

Ala Moana Center's food court is a circus, with neon signs, 800 tiny tables crowded together and 25 fast-food stands circling it all. There's something for everyone, from salads to daiquiris, ice cream to pizza, and Chinese, Japanese, Korean, Hawaiian, Filipino, Thai and Mexican specialties.

If you've got the munchies, this is a good place to stop when you're between buses. It's like window shopping – you can walk through, preview the food and select what you want. It's open from 9 am to 9 pm Monday to Saturday and 10 am to 6 pm on Sundays.

Panda Express has good Mandarin and Sichuan food, with dishes like spicy chicken, broccoli beef and eggplant with garlic sauce. Combination plates with fried rice or chow mein and two entrees are $4.89, with three entrees $5.89. The food is fresh and you can pick what looks best from the steamer trays.

Yummy Korean BBQ is a similar concept with Korean selections that include rice and a number of tasty pickled vegies and kimchees, with plates from $5.50 to $7.

Patti's Chinese Kitchen is a big-volume restaurant with a few dozen dishes to choose from. It costs $4.75 for two selections, $5.75 for three selections, both of which include rice or noodles. If you really want to indulge, you can get a whole roast duck for $11. There's also a limited selection of dim sum and desserts, including almond cookies.

Kitchen Garden specializes in salads such as curried chicken, Thai peanut pasta, fruit, marinated vegetable and just plain green. The salads are fresh and healthy, and most are priced under $5.

Cactus Jack's offers tacos, tostadas or fajitas with rice and beans from $5 to $6, while two tasty skewers of chicken satay at nearby *Little Cafe Siam* are $2.

Also in the Ala Moana Center there's a *Foodland* supermarket open from 7 am to 11 pm daily and branches of *McDonald's*, *Häagen Dazs* and *Dunkin' Donuts*.

Ward Centre

Ward Centre, a shopping complex at 1200 Ala Moana Blvd, has a couple of coffee shops and delis, a branch of *Keo's* Thai restaurant and about a dozen other dining spots.

At the top end is the new *A Pacific Cafe Oahu* (☎ 593-0035), a branch of the renowned restaurant on Kauai. The menu features wood-fired goat-cheese pizzas, fresh fish carpaccio and similar appetizers for around $10. Entrees such as blackened ahi with hearts of palm or a rich seafood bouillabaisse average $22. The lunch menu has similar but lighter servings and prices that are about 40% less. It's open from 11:30 am to 2 pm Monday to Friday and 5:30 to 9 pm daily.

The food is a bit too Americanized at *Compadres* (☎ 591-8307), but this busy Mexican restaurant still draws a crowd and wins plenty of local awards. Combination plates with rice and beans average $10 to $15. It's open from 11:30 am to 11 pm on weekdays, until 10 on Sundays and midnight on Fridays and Saturdays.

Mocha Java/Crepe Fever, on the ground level, is a popular hangout serving good coffees, crepes, croissants, sandwiches, desserts and other light eats. It's open from 7 am to 9 pm on weekdays, 8 am to 11 pm on Saturdays and 8 am to 4 pm on Sundays. A slightly more expensive espresso bar can be found inside *Borders* bookstore at the opposite end of the complex – it closes 30 minutes before the bookstore, which is open daily from 9 am to at least 11 pm, except on Sundays when it closes at 9 pm.

Ward Warehouse

All of the following restaurants are on the upper level of Ward Warehouse, the shopping complex on the corner of Ala Moana Blvd and Ward Ave. There's free garage parking, and bus Nos 8, 19 and 20 stop there. Each restaurant has a view of the harbor, so when making reservations be sure to ask for a window table.

For cheap eats, the *Old Spaghetti Factory* (☎ 591-2513) is the best deal here. This family-style restaurant has an elaborate decor, filled with antiques, stained glass – even an old streetcar. At lunch, from 11:30 am to 2 pm on weekdays, you can get spaghetti with tomato sauce for $3.50, with clam sauce for $4.50 or with meatballs for $5.75. All meals come with warm bread and a simple green salad. Meals are about a dollar more at dinner, served from 5 to 10 pm on weekdays, 11:30 am to 10:30 pm on Saturdays and 4 to 9:30 pm on Sundays. It's certainly not gourmet, but the price is right.

Dynasty II (☎ 596-0208) is a Chinese restaurant with fine dining and good food. The à la carte menu tends to be expensive, with most entrees priced from $10 to $18. However, they commonly offer a good-value $12.95 dinner special that includes an appetizer, soup, entree with jasmine rice and dessert, each selected from a limited-choice menu. Lunch is from 11 am to 2 pm, dinner from 5:30 to 10 pm.

Stuart Anderson's (☎ 591-9292), a chain steakhouse, has lunches in the $7 to $9 range and dinners about double that. Lunch is from 11 am to 4 pm Monday to Saturday, dinner from 4 to 10 pm Monday to Saturday and noon to 9:30 pm on Sundays.

Down on the ground floor is *Coffee Works*, open daily from 7 am to 9 pm (8 am to 6 pm on Sundays), with coffees, espressos, scones, bagels and muffins.

Restaurant Row

Restaurant Row, a rather sterile complex on the corner of Ala Moana Blvd and Punchbowl St, caters largely to the downtown business crowd. There's a *Burger King*, a bakery with pastries and sandwiches, a pizzeria, an ice cream shop and about a dozen restaurants, including some recommendable ethnic ones.

Island Salsa (☎ 536-4777) has Mexican fare that's made without lard or preservatives but is otherwise near-authentic. Huge burritos, either tofu or the traditional meat variety, cost $7 to $8, while combo plates with black beans and rice cost $11. It's open daily from 11 am to 11 pm.

Payao (☎ 521-3511), a new Thai restaurant by the owners of Chiang Mai, has an extensive menu of vegetarian offerings for around $6; curries, beef, chicken and noodle dishes for around $8; and seafood dishes for a bit more. It's open from 11 am to 2:30 pm Monday to Saturday and 5 to 10 pm nightly.

Jamaican Bar & Grill (☎ 521-5855) offers up genuine Caribbean cuisine. Spicy jerk chicken or curry shrimp, served with rice and beans, mixed vegetables and corn dumpling, cost around $7 at lunch, $12 at dinner. It's open daily from 11 am to 11 pm (3 to 10 pm on Sundays).

Among the top-end places are *Ruth's Chris Steak House* (☎ 599-3860), an upmarket mainland chain restaurant offering à la carte steaks for around $25, and the relaxed and popular *Sunset Grill* (☎ 521-4409), which features grilled fresh fish and meats from around $20 at dinner and salads, calamari and sandwiches for half that price at lunch.

Fort St Mall

The Fort St Mall, a pedestrian street on the outskirts of the downtown district, has a number of cheap restaurants within walking distance of Iolani Palace. It's convenient for downtown workers and sightseers but certainly not a draw if you're elsewhere around town.

Pizza Hut, Taco Bell, McDonald's, Burger King, KFC and *Subway Sandwiches* are all near the intersection of S Hotel St and Fort St Mall.

A good local option is *Ba Le*, a branch of the Chinatown restaurant, for inexpensive sandwiches, shrimp rolls, green papaya salads and French coffees. It's open from 7 am to 7 pm on weekdays and 8:30 am to 4 pm on Saturdays.

Adjacent to Ba Le is *Fort Street Cafe*, a popular student hangout with plate lunches, pho and saimin for around $5. It's open weekdays from 7 am to 7 pm and Saturdays from 8:30 am to 4 pm.

For Chinese fast food, try *Mandarin Express*, 50 yards east of Fort St Mall at 116 S Hotel St. It features Chinese dishes served from steamer trays, but it's usually quite fresh at meal times and you can eat heartily for around $5. It's open from 9 am to 6 pm on weekdays, 10:30 am to 3 pm on Saturdays.

Chinatown

Krung Thai, 1028 Nuuanu Ave, is a good-value, family-run Thai eatery on the edge of Chinatown between the business and red-light districts. Lunch, the only meal served, is geared to the business community's 30-minute lunch breaks, with dishes ready in steamer trays. There are a dozen hot dishes to choose from, including chicken Panang, beef eggplant and vegetarian curry. One item costs $3.79, two items $4.59, and all are served with jasmine rice or noodles. It's open from 10:30 am to 2:30 pm Monday to Friday. There are tables in a quiet rear courtyard where you can enjoy your meal.

Ba Le, 150 N King St, bakes crispy French bread and is a good place for a quick inexpensive eat in Chinatown. Baguettes can be purchased for 40¢ or as sandwiches for $2 vegetarian style, $3 with meat. The vegetarian sandwich is a tangy

combo of crunchy carrots, daikon and cilantro. Sweet, strong Vietnamese coffee costs $1.50 hot or cold. There are also good croissants, shrimp rolls and tapioca puddings. It's open from 5 am to 5 pm daily.

Our favorite Chinatown eatery is the Vietnamese restaurant *To Chau*, 1007 River St, where the specialty is pho, a delicious soup of beef broth with rice noodles and thin slices of beef, garnished with cilantro and green onion. It comes with a second plate of fresh basil, mung bean sprouts and slices of hot chili pepper to add at will. The cost is $3.70, or $5 for an extra-large bowl. The shrimp rolls with a spicy peanut sauce ($2.85) are recommendable, and the restaurant also serves rice and noodle dishes, but just about everybody comes for the soup. To Chau is open from 8 am to 2:30 pm daily. It's so popular that even at 10:30 am you may have to line up outside for one of the 16 tables. It's well worth the wait.

Ha Bien, 198 N King St, next door to To Chau, is another popular Vietnamese restaurant with good, inexpensive food. Although Ha Bien specializes in noodle and long rice dishes, the menu also includes spring rolls, soups and crepes. Most dishes cost from $5 to $6. It's open from 8 am to 4 pm on weekdays, to 3:30 pm on weekends.

Doong Kong Lau, on the River St pedestrian mall, has an extensive menu that includes the expected Chinese standards as well as more exotic preparations of Hakka cuisine. There's an extensive menu with vegetable, chicken and pork dishes for $6 to $7, while seafood plates are a few dollars higher. Generous lunch specials are available for $5 to $6. If you order noodles, be sure to request the cake noodles, pressed and cooked to a crisp on the edges. It's open from 9:30 am to 8:30 pm daily.

Just west of Doong Kong Lau on the River St mall is the *Buddhist Vegetarian Restaurant*, a relatively upmarket Chinese dining spot that uses tofu and gluten in place of meats. The menu is both creative and extensive, and most dishes are priced from $7 to $10. There's also a dim sum service available at lunch. It's open from

10:30 am to 2 pm and 5:30 to 9 pm daily except on Wednesdays.

Other Places to Eat

Helena's Hawaiian Foods (☎ 845-8044), 1364 N King St, is a friendly family-run operation that's been serving excellent, inexpensive Hawaiian food since 1946. It's a totally local eatery, with 10 simple Formica-top tables and a mix of vinyl chairs and stools. The restaurant makes a delicious kalua pig, and the pipikaula and fried ahi are also notable. There's not a better place anywhere to sample various Hawaiian dishes. Nearly everything on the à la carte menu is under $2, and complete meals with poi (fresh, day-old or sour) or rice are $5 to $7. It's open from 11 am to 7:30 pm Tuesday to Friday only.

Auntie Pasto's (☎ 523-8855), 1099 S Beretania St, has very good Italian food, including a recommendable eggplant parmigiana, at moderate prices. Pasta costs $5.50 with tomato sauce, $8 with pesto or $7 heaped with fresh vegetables in butter and garlic. The parmesan cheese is freshly grated and the Italian bread is served warm. Dishes and prices are the same at lunch and dinner. Although it's off the tourist track, this popular spot attracts a crowd and you may have to wait for a table – particularly on weekends. It's open from 11 am to 10:30 pm Monday to Friday and 4 to 10:30 pm Saturdays and Sundays.

El Burrito (☎ 596-8225), 550 Piikoi St, could be a neighborhood restaurant on a back street in Mexico City. This hole-in-the-wall squeezes in about a dozen tables and serves Honolulu's most authentic Mexican food. Two tamales, enchiladas or chile rellenos with rice and beans average $9. It's open from 11 am to 8 pm Monday to Thursday, to 9 pm on Fridays and Saturdays. Expect lines at dinnertime.

Mekong (☎ 521-2025), 1295 S Beretania St, home of the original Keo's, has a similar menu to that more upmarket spinoff, but in this tiny eatery posters replace the artwork, you bring your own booze and prices are about a third less. For $6, the tasty spring rolls come with lettuce, mint leaves and peanut sauce, while most beef, chicken and vegetarian dishes are a dollar more. Nothing on the menu is over $10. It's open from 11 am to 2 pm on weekdays and 5 to 9:30 pm nightly. If you're driving, you may prefer *Mekong II* (☎ 941-6184), 1726 S King St, which has the same Thai menu and free parking in the rear.

The *Garden Cafe* (☎ 532-8734), a courtyard restaurant in the Honolulu Academy of Arts, 900 S Beretania St, offers a cultured lunch setting and a chance to support the museum. There are seatings at 11:30 am and 1 pm Tuesday to Saturday; the menu, which varies daily, includes sandwiches, soups and hot dishes such as quesadillas or fresh fish for $7 to $10. Reservations are suggested.

Pagoda Floating Restaurant at the Pagoda Hotel (☎ 941-6611), 1525 Rycroft St, has a serene garden setting and a carp pond. The breakfast menu (from 6:30 to 10:30 am) is extensive, with many choices for around $5. On weekdays, from 11 am to 2 pm, there's a lunch buffet of Japanese and American dishes for $10, or you can order off the lunch menu for less. There's also a nightly dinner buffet, from 4:30 to 9:30 pm, which costs $19 and features an array of dishes, including prime rib, Alaskan snow crab, sashimi, tempura and salad and dessert bars.

Gordon Biersch Brewery Restaurant (☎ 599-4877) is the most popular spot at the Aloha Tower Marketplace on Ala Moana Blvd. Hawaii's first microbrewery restaurant, it features its own German-style lagers accompanied by Hawaiian pupus. Salads and sandwiches are available for under $10, while hot dishes average $15. It's open from 11 am to 10 pm daily.

The hottest new restaurant in town, *Alan Wong's* (☎ 949-2526), 1857 S King St, features upmarket Hawaiian Regional cuisine. Appetizers such as sashimi, tempura ahi or duck salad cost $7 to $12, while entrees such as spicy seafood paella, beef tenderloin with Kona lobster or a delicious ginger-crusted onaga average $30. Each night they also feature a five-course 'chef's tasting menu' for $65. This is a high-energy place with a modern minimalist decor and an exhibition kitchen. It's open from 5 to 10 pm nightly.

Two good places for sushi are *Yanagi Sushi* (☎ 537-1525), 762 Kapiolani Blvd, open daily from 11 am to 2 pm and from 5:30 pm to 2 am (to 10 pm on Sundays); and *Sada's* (☎ 949-0646), 1240 S King St, open from 11 am to midnight Monday to Saturday, 5 to 11 pm on Sundays.

At the county-run People's Open Market program, farmers sell local produce for one hour a week at 22 locations around Oahu. Mondays and Wednesdays are set aside for the greater Honolulu area. Call ☎ 522-7088 for current times and locations or pick up a schedule at any satellite city hall.

ENTERTAINMENT

Honolulu has a lively entertainment scene. The best updated listings are in the free *Honolulu Weekly*, which is readily found around the downtown and university areas.

Theater & Concerts

Honolulu has a symphony orchestra, an opera company, ballet troupes, chamber orchestras and numerous community theater groups.

The newly reopened *Hawaii Theatre* (☎ 528-0506), 1130 Bethel St, is a major venue for dance, music and theater. Performances range from Russian ballet to contemporary Hawaiian music, modern dance and film festivals.

The *Blaisdell Center* (☎ 591-2211), 777 Ward Ave, presents musical concerts, Broadway shows and family events, with performers such as Stone Temple Pilots, the Honolulu Symphony, the Ice Capades and the Brothers Cazimero.

The *Academy Theatre* (☎ 532-8768) of the Honolulu Academy of Arts, 900 S Beretania St, and to a lesser degree the *East-West Center* (☎ 944-7111), adjacent to the University of Hawaii, both present multicultural theater and concerts.

Music & Dancing

Anna Bannanas (☎ 946-5190), not far from the university at 2440 S Beretania St,

features blues, Cajun, rock or reggae bands from 9:30 pm to 1:30 am Thursday to Sunday. There's usually a cover charge of $4.

The *Pier Bar* (☎ 536-2166) at the Aloha Tower Marketplace has live music nightly, including top-name contemporary Hawaiian musicians such as Willie K and Henry Kapono. Performance times vary with the night. There's usually no cover.

Rumours (☎ 955-4811) at the Ala Moana Hotel, 410 Atkinson Drive, has dancing to pre-'70s music on Fridays and '70s to '90s music on Saturdays, with country music, karaoke or ballroom dancing other nights. It's open from 5 pm (9 pm on Saturdays) to 3 am except on Mondays. The cover is $5 and the age limit is 21.

Movie Theaters

Honolulu has several movie theaters showing first-run feature films, including a nine-screen multiplex cinema at Restaurant Row (☎ 526-4171).

The *Academy Theatre* (☎ 532-8768) at the Honolulu Academy of Arts showcases American independent cinema, foreign films and avant-garde shorts. Tickets cost $4.

The *Hemenway Theatre* (☎ 956-6468) at the University of Hawaii's Hemenway Hall shows foreign flicks, select feature films and local surf films. General admission is $3.50.

Free Entertainment

In the *Ala Moana Center*, a courtyard area called Centerstage is the venue for free performances by high school choirs, gospel groups, ballet troupes, local bands and the like. There's something happening almost daily; look for the schedule in Ala Moana's free shopping magazine.

The Royal Hawaiian Band performs from 12:15 to 1:15 pm on Fridays (except August) on the lawn of the Iolani Palace.

The Mayor's Office of Culture & Arts sponsors numerous free performances, exhibits and events, ranging from street musicians in city parks to band concerts in various locales around Honolulu. Call ☎ 523-4674 for current events.

Pearl Harbor Area

On December 7, 1941, a wave of more than 350 Japanese planes attacked Pearl Harbor, home of the US Pacific Fleet.

Some 2335 US soldiers were killed during the two-hour attack. Of those, 1177 died in the battleship USS *Arizona*, which took a direct hit and sank in less than nine minutes. Twenty other ships were sunk or seriously damaged and 188 airplanes were destroyed.

USS ARIZONA MEMORIAL

Over 1.5 million people 'remember Pearl Harbor' each year with a visit to the USS Arizona Memorial. Operated by the National Park Service, the memorial is Hawaii's most visited attraction.

The visitor center includes a museum and theater as well as the offshore memorial at the sunken USS *Arizona*. The park service provides a 75-minute program that includes a 23-minute documentary film on the attack followed by a boat ride out to the memorial and back. Everything is free. The memorial and all facilities are accessible to the disabled.

The 184-foot memorial, built in 1962, sits directly over the *Arizona* without touching it. It contains the ship's bell and a wall inscribed with the names of those who perished onboard. The average age of the ship's enlisted men was 19.

From the memorial the battleship can be viewed eight feet below the surface. The ship rests in about 40 feet of water and even now oozes a gallon or two of oil each day. In the rush to recoup from the attack and prepare for war, the navy exercised its option to leave the men in the sunken ship buried at sea. They remain entombed in its hull.

The visitor center (☎ 422-2771; 24-hour recorded information 422-0561) is open from 7:30 am to 5 pm daily except Thanksgiving, Christmas and New Year's Day. There's a snack bar and a souvenir/book shop.

Programs run every 15 or 20 minutes from 8 am to 3 pm (from 7:45 am in summer) on a first-come first-served basis. As soon as you arrive, pick up a ticket at the information booth; the number on the ticket corresponds to the time the tour begins. Generally the shortest waits are in the morning; if you arrive before the first crowds, you might get in within half an hour, but waits of a couple of hours are not unknown. Summer months are busiest, with an average of 4500 people taking the tour daily, and the allotment of tickets is sometimes gone by 11 am.

Pearl Harbor survivors, who act as volunteer historians, are sometimes available to give talks about the day of the attack.

There's a little open-air museum to keep you occupied while you're waiting. It has interesting photos from both Japanese and US military archives showing Pearl Harbor before, during and after the attack. One photo is of Harvard-educated Admiral Yamamoto, the brilliant military strategist who planned the attack on Pearl Harbor even though he personally opposed going to war with the USA. Rather than relish the victory, Yamamoto stated after the attack that he feared Japan had 'awakened a sleeping giant and filled him with a terrible resolve'.

Bowfin Park

If you have to wait an hour or two for your USS Arizona Memorial tour to begin, you might want to stroll over to the adjacent Bowfin Park.

The park contains a moored WWII submarine, the USS *Bowfin*, and the Pacific Submarine Museum, which traces the development of submarines from the turn of the century to the nuclear age.

Commissioned in May 1943, the *Bowfin* sank 44 ships in the Pacific before the end of the war. There's a self-guided tour with a hand-held radio receiver that picks up recorded messages as you walk through. Admission of $8 for adults, $3 for children ages four to 12, includes entry to both the submarine and the museum.

There's no charge to enter the park and view the missiles and torpedoes spread around the grounds, look through the periscopes or inspect the Japanese *kaiten*, a suicide torpedo.

The kaiten is just what it looks like: a torpedo with a single seat. As the war was closing in on the Japanese homeland, the kaiten was developed in a last-ditch effort to ward off an invasion. It was the marine equivalent of the kamikaze pilot and his plane. A volunteer was placed in the torpedo before it was fired. He then piloted it to its target. At least one US ship, the USS *Mississinewa*, was sunk by a kaiten. It went down off Ulithi Atoll in November 1944.

The park and museum is open from 8 am to 5 pm daily.

Getting There & Away

The USS Arizona Memorial visitor center and Bowfin Park are off Kamehameha Hwy (Hwy 99) on the Pearl Harbor Naval Base just south of Aloha Stadium. If coming from Honolulu, take H-1 west to exit 15A (Stadium/Arizona Memorial). Make sure you follow highway signs for the Arizona Memorial, not Pearl Harbor.

The private Arizona Memorial Shuttle Bus (☎ 839-0911) picks up people from Waikiki hotels every 90 minutes between 7 am and 1 pm; the last bus returns at 3:30 pm. The ride takes around 40 minutes and costs $3 each way. Call to make arrangements.

To get there by public transport, take the No 20 airport bus from Waikiki, which takes about 1¼ hours.

There are also private boat cruises to Pearl Harbor leaving from Kewalo Basin for about $25, but they should be avoided as passengers are not allowed to board the memorial.

PEARL CITY

Pearl City is the largest urban area in Hawaii outside of Honolulu. It's home to about 45,000, including a lot of military personnel and civilians who work on the bases, but there's little of interest for visitors.

Honolulu Star-Bulletin 1st EXTRA

EVENING BULLETIN, EST. 1882, No. 11287   HONOLULU, TERRITORY OF HAWAII, U. S. A., SUNDAY, DECEMBER 7, 1941   ★ PRICE FIVE CENTS
Hawaiian Star, Vol. XLVIII No. 13208

WAR!

(Associated Press by Transpacific Telephone)

SAN FRANCISCO, Dec. 7.—President Roosevelt announced this morning that Japanese planes had attacked Manila and Pearl Harbor.

OAHU BOMBED BY JAPANESE PLANES

SIX KNOWN DEAD, 21 INJURED, AT EMERGENCY HOSPITAL

If you're just passing through and not going into Pearl City itself, stay on H-1 and avoid the parallel Kamehameha Hwy, as it's all stop-and-go traffic through blocks of fast-food restaurants and shopping malls.

Pearlridge Shopping Center is a massive mall that runs between H-1 and Kamehameha Hwy. A swap meet is held a block west of the shopping center on weekends at the drive-in theater.

HAWAII'S PLANTATION VILLAGE

A visit to Hawaii's Plantation Village (☎ 677-0110) in Waipahu will reward you with a glimpse of plantation life and insights into Hawaii's multiethnic heritage.

The site encompasses 30 homes and buildings set up to recreate a plantation village of the early 20th century. The cookhouse was originally on this site and the shrine was moved here; the other structures have been newly built but authentically replicate the architecture of the time.

The houses are set up with period furnishings that portray the lifestyles of the eight different ethnic groups – Hawaiian, Japanese, Okinawan, Chinese, Korean, Portuguese, Puerto Rican and Filipino – that worked Hawaii's sugar plantations. One-hour guided tours of the village are given on the hour between 9 am and 3 pm.

The setting is particularly evocative, as Waipahu was one of Oahu's last plantation towns, and its sugar mill, which operated until 1995, still looms on a knoll directly above this site. There's also a small museum detailing the lives and cultural backgrounds of plantation workers. Artifacts on display, including an ofuro bath, Korean flute, straw slippers and various tools, are accompanied by insightful interpretive write-ups. All in all, it's a quality community-based production.

It's open from 9 am to 4 pm Monday to Saturday. Admission costs $5 for adults, $3 for seniors and children five to 17.

To get there, head west on H-1, take Exit 7, turn left at the end of the offramp onto Paiwa St, then turn right onto Waipahu St, drive past the mill and turn left into the complex. The distance from H-1 is about 1½ miles.

KEAIWA HEIAU STATE PARK

This park in Aiea, north of Pearl Harbor, covers 334 acres and contains an ancient medicinal temple, campgrounds, picnic facilities and a scenic loop trail. The park is open from 7 am to sunset for day visitors. As with all state parks there are no fees.

At the park entrance is **Keaiwa Heiau**, a 100-by-160-foot single-terraced stone structure built in the 1600s and used by *kahuna lapaau* (herbalist healers). The kahunas used hundreds of medicinal plants and grew many on the grounds surrounding the heiau. Among those still found here are noni, whose pungent yellow fruits were used to treat heart disease; kukui, whose nuts were an effective laxative; ulu, whose sap soothed chapped skin; and ti leaves, which were wrapped around a person to break a fever. Not only did the herbs have medicinal value, but the heiau itself was considered to possess life-giving energy. The kahuna was able to draw from the powers of both.

People wishing to be healed still place offerings within the heiau. The offerings reflect the multiplicity of Hawaii's cultures: rosary beads, New Age crystals and sake cups sit beside flower leis and rocks wrapped in ti leaves.

Aiea Loop Trail

The 4½-mile Aiea Loop Trail begins at the top of the park's paved loop road next to the restrooms and comes back out at the campground, about a third of a mile below the start of the trail.

The trail starts off in a forest of eucalyptus trees and runs along the ridge. Other trees along the way include ironwood, Norfolk Island pines, edible guava and native ohia lehua, with its fluffy red flowers.

There are vistas of Pearl Harbor, Diamond Head and the Koolau Range. About two-thirds of the way along, the wreckage of a C-47 cargo plane that crashed in 1943 can be spotted through the foliage on the east ridge. The hike takes 2½ to three hours and is a fairly easy walk.

Camping

The camping area can accommodate 100 campers. Most sites have their own picnic table and barbecue grill. Sites are not crowded together, but because many of them are largely open there's not a lot of privacy either. There's a distant view of Honolulu's airport a couple of miles to the south.

If you're camping in winter, make sure your gear is waterproof, as it rains a lot at this 880-foot elevation, although the temperature is usually pleasant. There are restrooms, showers, a phone and drinking water.

For Oahu, it's a good choice for a campground. There's a caretaker by the front gate, and the gate is locked at night for security.

As with all Oahu public campgrounds, no camping is permitted on Wednesdays and Thursdays. Camping permits must be obtained in advance; see Camping in the Accommodations section at the start of this chapter.

Getting There & Away

From Honolulu, head west on Hwy 78 and take the Stadium/Aiea turn-off onto Moanalua Rd. Turn right onto Aiea Heights Drive at the second traffic light. The road winds up through a residential area 2½ miles to the park.

Southeast Oahu

Some of Oahu's finest scenery is along the southeast coast, which curves around the tip of the Koolau Mountains. Diamond Head, Hanauma Bay and the island's most famous bodysurfing beaches are all just a 20-minute ride from Waikiki.

East of Diamond Head, H-1 turns into the Kalanianaole Hwy (Hwy 72), passing the exclusive Kahala residential area, a run of shopping centers and some housing developments that creep up into the mountain valleys.

The highway rises and falls as it winds its way around the Koko Head area and Makapuu Point, with beautiful coastal views along the way. The area is geologically fascinating, with boldly stratified rock formations, volcanic craters and lava sea cliffs.

DIAMOND HEAD

Diamond Head is a tuff cone and crater that was formed by a violent steam explosion deep beneath the surface long after most of Oahu's volcanic activity had stopped. As the backdrop to Waikiki, it's one of the best-known landmarks in the Pacific. The summit is 760 feet high.

The Hawaiians called it Leahi and built a luakini heiau on the top where human sacrifices took place. But ever since 1825, when British sailors found calcite crystals sparkling in the sun and mistakenly thought they'd struck it rich, it's been called Diamond Head.

In 1909 the US Army began building Fort Ruger at the edge of the crater. They built a network of tunnels and topped the rim with cannon emplacements, bunkers and observation posts. Reinforced during WWII, it's been a silent sentinel whose guns have never fired.

Today there's a Hawaii National Guard base inside the crater as well as Federal Aviation Administration and civil defense facilities. Diamond Head is a state monument with picnic tables, restrooms, a phone and drinking water. The best reason to visit is to hike the trail to the crater rim for the panoramic view. The gates are open daily from 6 am to 6 pm.

Hiking

The trail to the summit was built in 1910 to service the military observation stations along the crater rim.

It's a fairly steep hike, with a gain in elevation of 560 feet, but it's only three-quarters of a mile to the top and plenty of people of all ages hike up. It takes about 30 minutes one way. The trail is open and hot,

OAHU

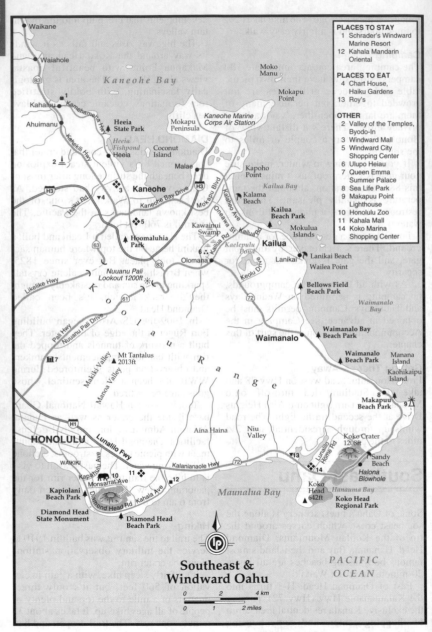

PLACES TO STAY
1 Schrader's Windward
   Marine Resort
12 Kahala Mandarin
   Oriental

PLACES TO EAT
4 Chart House,
   Haiku Gardens
13 Roy's

OTHER
2 Valley of the Temples,
   Byodo-In
3 Windward Mall
5 Windward City
   Shopping Center
6 Ulupo Heiau
7 Queen Emma
   Summer Palace
8 Sea Life Park
9 Makapuu Point
   Lighthouse
10 Honolulu Zoo
11 Kahala Mall
14 Koko Marina
   Shopping Center

**Southeast &
Windward Oahu**

0   2   4 km

0   1   2 miles

*PACIFIC
OCEAN*

so you might want to take along something to drink.

As you start up the trail, you can see the summit ahead a bit to the left, at roughly eleven o'clock.

The crater is dry and scrubby with kiawe, koa haole, grasses and wildflowers. The little yellow-orange flowers along the way are native ilima, Oahu's official flower.

About 20 minutes up the trail you enter a long, dark tunnel. Because the tunnel curves you don't see light until you get close to the end. It's a little spooky, but the roof is high enough for you to walk through without bumping your head, there is a hand rail and your eyes should adjust enough to make out shadows in the dark. Nevertheless, to prevent accidents, the park advises hikers to tote along a flashlight.

The tunnel itself seems like it should be the climax of this long climb, but upon coming out into the light you're immediately faced with a steep 99-step staircase. Persevere! After this there's a shorter tunnel, a narrow spiral staircase inside an unlit bunker and the last of the trail's 271 steps. Be careful when you reach the top – there are some steep drops.

From the top there's a fantastic 360° view taking in the southeast coast to Koko Head and Koko Crater and the leeward coast to Barbers Point and the Waianae Mountains. Below is Kapiolani Park and the orange seats of the Waikiki Shell. You can also see the lighthouse, coral reefs, sailboats and sometimes even surfers waiting for waves at Diamond Head Beach.

To reach Diamond Head from Kuhio Ave in Waikiki, take bus No 22 or 58, both of which run about twice an hour. It's a 20-minute walk from the bus stop to the trailhead above the parking lot. Once you get through the tunnel, you're in the crater.

By car from Waikiki, take Monsarrat Ave (which begins by the zoo) to Diamond Head Rd and then take the right turn after Kapiolani Community College into the crater.

Diamond Head Beach

Conditions at Diamond Head Beach are suitable for intermediate to advanced wind-surfers, and when the swells are up it's a great place for wave riding. Even as a spectator sport it's exhilarating.

The beach has showers but no other facilities.

To get there from Waikiki, follow Kalakaua Ave to Diamond Head Rd. There's a parking lot just beyond the lighthouse. Walk east past the end of the lot and you'll find a paved trail down to the beach. By bus, take No 14, which runs about once an hour.

HANAUMA BAY BEACH PARK

Hanauma, which means 'Curved Bay', is a wide, sheltered bay of sapphire and turquoise waters set in a rugged volcanic ring.

Once a popular fishing spot, it had nearly been fished out when it was designated a marine life conservation district in 1967. Now that the fish are fed instead of eaten, they swarm in by the thousands.

From the overlook you can peer into crystal waters and view the entire coral reef that stretches across the width of the bay. You can see schools of silver fish glittering, the bright blue flash of parrotfish and perhaps a sea turtle. To see an even more colorful scene, put on a mask, jump in and view it from beneath the surface.

Hanauma seems to get as many people as fish. With over a million visitors a year, it's often busy and crowded.

While it's for good reason that everyone's there, the heavy use of the bay has taken its toll. The coral on the shallow reef has been damaged by all the action, and the food that snorkelers feed the fish has increased fish populations in Hanauma well beyond what it can naturally support. In fact, many of the fish in the bay are not common to Hanauma but are more aggressive types that have been drawn in by the feeding.

A master plan is under way that aims to normalize the fish distribution and reduce the number of beachgoers from 10,000 a day to 2000. The numbers have already been nearly halved by one new restriction that prohibits tour buses from dropping off passengers to use the beach. Fish feeding will be phased out in the next few years – in the meantime, snorkelers shouldn't feed the fish anything but fish food, which can be bought at the beach concession stand.

Hanauma is both a county beach park and a state underwater park. It has a grassy picnic area, lifeguards, showers, restrooms, changing rooms and access for the disabled. The bay is closed on Wednesdays until noon but is otherwise open daily from 7 am until 6 pm in winter, until 7 pm in summer. There's a $5 admission fee for non-Hawaii residents, and there are plans to add a $1 parking fee for everyone.

The snack bar sells hot dogs, ice cream and soda. Snorkel sets can be rented at the beach concession stand from 8 am to 4:30 pm for $6.

Paths lead along low ledges on both sides of the bay. Be cautious when the sea is rough or the tide is high, as waves can wash over the ledges.

More people drown at Hanauma than at any other beach on Oahu. Although the figure is high largely because there are so many visitors at this beach, people drowning in the Toilet Bowl or being swept off the ledges have accounted for a fair number of deaths over the years.

Toilet Bowl

A 15-minute walk out to the point on the left (east) side of the bay brings you to the Toilet Bowl, a small natural pool in the lava rock. The Toilet Bowl is connected to the sea by an underwater channel, which enables water to surge into the bowl and then flush out from beneath.

People going into the pool for the thrill of it can get quite a ride as it flushes down four to five feet almost instantly. However the rock around the bowl is slippery and hard to grip, and getting in is far easier than getting out. Definitely do not try it alone.

Witches Brew

A 10-minute walk along the right (west) side of the bay will take you to a rocky point. The cove at the southern side of the point is the treacherous Witches Brew, so named for its swirling, turbulent waters.

There's a nice view of Koko Crater from there, and green sand made of olivine can be found along the way.

Snorkeling & Diving

Snorkeling is good at Hanauma Bay year round. Mornings are better than afternoons, as swimmers haven't yet stirred up the sand.

The large, sandy opening in the middle of the coral, known as the **Keyhole**, is an excellent place for novice snorkelers. The deepest water is 10 feet, although it's very shallow over the coral, so if you have diving gloves, bring them. It's well protected and usually swimming-pool calm.

Hanauma's biggest attraction is the sheer number and variety of fish. It's got big rainbow parrotfish crunching off chunks of coral, moray eels, bright yellow butterfly fish, goatfish, Moorish idols and numerous other tropicals.

For confident snorkelers, it's better on the outside of the reef, where there are larger coral heads, bigger fish and fewer people; to get there follow the directions on the signboard near the snack bar or ask the lifeguard at the southwest end of the beach. Keep in mind that because of the channel current it's generally easier getting out than it is getting back in. Don't attempt to swim outside the reef when the water is rough or choppy. Not only will the channel current be strong, but the sand will be stirred up and visibility poor anyway.

Divers have the whole bay to play in, with clear water, coral gardens, sea turtles and lots of fish. Beware of currents when the surf is up; surges near the Witches Brew, on the right-hand side; and the Molokai Express, a treacherous current that runs just outside the mouth of the bay.

Getting There & Away

Hanauma Bay is about 10 miles from Waikiki along Hwy 72. There's a large parking lot, although it sometimes fills in the middle of the day and on weekends. Parking outside a marked space will result in a parking ticket.

Bus No 22 goes to Hanauma (and on to Sea Life Park). On weekdays the first buses leave Waikiki from the corner of Kuhio Ave and Namahana St at 8:15 and 9:15 am, with subsequent buses leaving at 50 minutes past the hour until 3:50 pm. Buses leave Hanauma for Waikiki at least once every hour from 11:10 am to 5:10 pm. On weekends the buses are a little more frequent, although the times are more sporadic.

KOKO HEAD REGIONAL PARK

The entire Koko Head area is a county regional park. It includes Hanauma Bay, Koko Head, Halona Blowhole, Sandy Beach and Koko Crater.

Koko Head is backed by Hawaii Kai, an expansive development of condos, houses, shopping centers, a marina and a golf course – all meticulously planned and quite sterile in appearance.

Koko Crater and Koko Head are both tuff cones created about 10,000 years ago in Oahu's last gasp of volcanic activity.

Koko Head

Koko Head, not to be confused with Koko Crater, overlooks and forms the southwest side of Hanauma Bay.

When it's open to the public, the one-mile walk up the road to the summit offers fine coastal views that light up nicely at sunset. The road starts near the highway at the Hanauma Bay entrance.

There are two craters atop Koko Head, as well as telecommunications facilities on the 642-foot summit. The Nature Conservancy maintains a preserve in the shallow Ihihilauakea Crater, the larger of the two. The crater has a unique vernal pool and a rare fern, the *Marsilea villosa*. For information on work parties or weekend excursions to the preserve, call the Nature Conservancy (☎ 537-4508).

Halona Blowhole

About half a mile past Hanauma is a **lookout** with a view of striking coastal rock formations and crashing surf.

Nearly a mile farther is the parking lot for Halona Blowhole, where water surges through a submerged tunnel in the rock and spouts up through a hole in the ledge. It's usually preceded by a gushing sound, created by the air that's being forced out by the rushing water.

Down to the right of the parking lot is **Halona Cove**, the beach where the risque love scene with Burt Lancaster and Deborah Kerr in *From Here to Eternity* was filmed in the 1950s.

Immediately before the blowhole a small **stone monument** sits atop Halona Point. It was erected by Japanese fishers to honor those lost at sea.

Sandy Beach

Sandy Beach is one of the most dangerous beaches on the island, if measured in terms of lifeguard rescues and broken necks. It has a punishing shorebreak, a powerful backwash and strong rip currents.

Nevertheless, the shorebreak is extremely popular with bodysurfers who know their stuff. It's equally popular with spectators, who gather to watch the bodysurfers being tossed around in the transparent waves.

Sandy Beach is wide, very long and, yes, sandy. It's frequented by sunbathers, young surfers and admirers of both. When the swells are big, board surfers hit the left side of the beach.

Red flags flown on the beach indicate hazardous water conditions. Even if you don't notice the flags, always check with the lifeguards before entering the water.

Not all the action is in the water. The grassy strip on the inland side of the parking lot is used by people looking skyward for their thrills – it's both a hang glider landing site and a popular locale for kite flying.

The park has restrooms, showers, a pay phone and lifeguards.

Koko Crater

According to Hawaiian legend, Koko Crater (Kohelepelepe) is the imprint left by the vagina of Pele's sister Kapo, which was sent here from the Big Island to lure the pig-god Kamapuaa away from Pele.

Inside the crater there's a simple dryland botanic garden of plumeria trees, oleander and cacti that the county is in the process of reviving. To get there, take Kealahou St off Hwy 72 opposite the northern end of Sandy Beach. Just over half a mile in, turn left onto the one-lane road to Koko Crater Stables and continue a third of a mile to the garden, which is open daily from 9 am to 4 pm; admission is free.

On the outside of the crater on the Hanauma side there's an unmaintained hiking trail. It follows an abandoned railroad track that once served a former army missile base on the 1208-foot summit.

Places to Eat

Koko Marina Shopping Center, on the corner of Lunalilo Home Rd and Hwy 72, has a *Foodland* supermarket, standard fast-food places, a few sit-down restaurants and both shave ice and frozen yogurt shops. Best choice for local flavor is *Yummy Korean BBQ*, which offers $6 barbecued meat dishes (the chicken is a good, lean choice) with 'two-scoop rice' and four tasty marinated vegetable dishes or kimchees, including a terrific watercress and sesame variety. There are waterfront tables adjacent to the marina where you can eat.

The best upmarket option in Southeast Oahu is *Roy's* (☎ 396-9875), at Hawaii Kai Corporate Plaza on Hwy 72. Owner Roy Yamaguchi is a creative force behind the popularity of Pacific Rim cuisine, which emphasizes fresh local ingredients and blends the lighter aspects of European cooking with Japanese, Thai and Chinese influences. An exhibition kitchen sits in the center of the dining room, where Roy orchestrates an impressive troupe of sous chefs.

Starters include spring rolls, imu-oven pizzas and a variety of salads for around $7.50. The crispy lemongrass chicken, topped with a delightful cabernet curry sauce, costs $16 and makes a fine main dish. Most other meat dishes cost around $20, while fresh fish specials average $24. There are more romantic settings in Oahu, but in all other ways Roy's is a top choice for a night out – the food is attractively presented, the service attentive and the servings

good sized. It's open from 5:30 pm (5 pm on weekends) to 10 pm, and reservations are advised.

MAKAPUU POINT

About a mile north of Sandy Beach, the 647-foot Makapuu Point and its coastal **lighthouse** mark the easternmost point of Oahu. The mile-long service road to the lighthouse has recently been deeded by the federal government to Hawaii, thus opening this site to the public. The gate into the service road is locked to keep out private vehicles, but you can park off the highway just beyond the gate and walk in from there. There are fine coastal views along the way and at the lighthouse lookout.

Back on the highway, about a third of a mile farther along, there's a scenic **roadside lookout** with a view down onto Makapuu Beach, with its aqua-blue waters outlined by white sand and black lava. It's an even more spectacular sight when hang gliders are taking off from the cliffs, which serve as Oahu's top hang-gliding spot.

From the lookout you can see two offshore islands, the larger of which is **Manana Island**, also known as Rabbit Island. This aging volcanic crater is populated by feral rabbits and burrowing wedge-tailed shearwaters. They coexist so closely that the birds and rabbits sometimes even share the same burrows.

The island looks vaguely like the head of a rabbit, and if you try hard you may see it, ears folded back. If that doesn't work, you could also try to imagine it as a whale.

In front of it is the smaller **Kaohikaipu Island**, which won't tax the imagination – all it looks is flat.

There's a coral reef between the two islands that divers sometimes explore, but to do so requires a boat.

Makapuu Beach

Makapuu Beach is one of the island's top winter bodysurfing spots, with waves reaching 12 feet and higher. It also has the island's best shorebreak. As with Sandy Beach, Makapuu is strictly the domain of experienced bodysurfers who can handle rough water conditions and dangerous currents. Surfboards are prohibited.

In summer, when the wave action disappears, the waters can be calm and good for swimming.

The beach is opposite Sea Life Park in a pretty setting, with cliffs in the background and a glimpse of the lighthouse. Two native Hawaiian plants are plentiful – naupaka by the beach and yellow-orange ilima by the parking lot.

Sea Life Park

Sea Life Park (☎ 259-7933) is Hawaii's only marine park. Its 300,000-gallon aquarium has sea turtles, eels, eagle rays, hammerhead sharks and thousands of reef fish. A spiral ramp circles the 18-foot-deep aquarium, allowing you to view the fish from different depths.

In one of two outdoor amphitheaters, jumping dolphins and waddling penguins perform the standard park tricks.

In the other, the Whaler's Cove, a false killer whale and a group of Atlantic bottlenose dolphins give a choreographed performance. The dolphins tail walk, do the hula and give rides to a 'beautiful island maiden' – all bordering on kitsch.

There's a large pool of California sea lions and a smaller pool with harbor seals. There's also a section with rare Hawaiian monk seals, comprised largely of abandoned or injured pups that have been rescued from the wild; once they reach maturity, they're released back into their natural habitat. The turtle lagoon holds green sea turtles, while another section of the park has red-footed boobies, albatrosses and great frigate birds, all seabirds indigenous to Hawaii.

Hanging from the ceiling of the park's little **Whaling Museum** is the skeleton of a 38-foot sperm whale that was washed up off Barbers Point in 1980. After the Coast Guard damaged a ship propeller unsuccessfully trying to tow the 20-ton mammal out to sea, they turned the carcass over to Sea Life Park. The park removed almost 38,000 pounds of flesh from the skeleton, using many of the antique whaling tools on display in the museum. The whole process took the better part of two years.

In addition to harpoons, a try-pot used to boil down whale blubber and other whaling paraphernalia, the museum has a fine collection of whaling-era scrimshaw, from toys and bird cages to suggestive 'porno' pieces.

Sea Life Park is open daily from 9:30 am to 5 pm, with the last series of shows beginning at 3:15 pm. Admission is $19.95 for adults, $9.95 for children ages four to 12 and free for children under four.

You can visit the whaling museum and the park restaurant (sandwiches, salads and other cafeteria-style food) without paying admission. You also get a free look at the seal and sea lion pools along the walk to the museum.

Public buses No 22, 57 Kailua/Sea Life Park and 58 Hawaii Kai/Sea Life Park stop at Sea Life Park. Also, a free shuttle bus (☎ 955-3474 for a recorded schedule) leaves from major hotels in Waikiki six times a day.

WAIMANALO

Waimanalo Bay has the longest continuous stretch of beach in Oahu: 5½ miles of white sand running north from Makapuu Point to Wailea Point. A long coral reef about a mile out breaks up the biggest waves, protecting much of the shore.

Waimanalo has three beach parks with camping. The setting is scenic, although the area isn't highly regarded for safety.

Waimanalo Beach Park

Waimanalo Beach Park has an attractive beach of soft white sand and the water is excellent for swimming.

It's an in-town county park with a grassy picnic area, restrooms, changing rooms, showers, ball fields, basketball and volleyball courts and a playground. Camping is allowed in an open area near the road, but many of the campers are homeless families and it's not a scene that invites visitors.

The park has ironwood trees, but overall it's more open than the other two parks to the north. The scalloped hills of the lower Koolau Range rise up mauka of the park, and Manana Island and Makapuu Point are visible to the south.

Waimanalo Bay Beach Park

This county park, about a mile north of Waimanalo Beach Park, has Waimanalo Bay's biggest waves and thus is popular with board surfers and bodysurfers.

Locals call the park Sherwood Forest because hoods and car thieves used to hang out there in days past – it hasn't totally shaken its reputation, so keep an eye on your belongings.

The park itself is quite appealing, with beachside campsites shaded with ironwood trees. There's a lifeguard station, barbecue grills, drinking water, showers and restrooms.

Bus No 57 stops in front of the park, and it's a third of a mile walk in from the road to the beach and campground. The gate is open from 7 am to sunset.

Bellows Field Beach Park

The beach fronting Bellows Air Force Base is open to civilian beachgoers and campers on weekends only, from noon on Friday until 8 am on Monday. This long beach has fine sand and a natural setting backed by ironwood trees. The small shorebreak waves are good for beginning bodysurfers and board surfers.

There's a lifeguard, showers, restrooms and water; the 50 campsites are set out among the trees. Although it's military property, permits are issued through the county Department of Parks & Recreation.

The marked entrance is a quarter of a mile north of Waimanalo Bay Beach Park. Bus No 57 stops in front of the entrance road and from there it's 1½ miles to the beach.

Places to Eat

Bueno Nalo (☎ 259-7186) is between the two county beach parks, just north of Waimanalo's post office. Homestyle Mexican combination plates are priced around $10. It's open from 11:30 am to 9 pm daily.

There's a food mart and a bakery next door to Bueno Nalo and a *McDonald's* just south of Waimanalo Bay Beach Park.

Pali Highway

The Pali Highway (Hwy 61) runs between Honolulu and Kailua, cutting through the spectacular Koolau Range. It's a scenic little highway, and if it's been raining heavily every fold and crevice in the mountains will have a lacy waterfall streaming down it.

Many Kailua residents commute to work over the Pali, so Honolulu-bound traffic can be heavy in the morning and outbound traffic heavy in the evening. It's less of a problem for visitors, however, as most daytrippers will be traveling against the traffic. Public buses travel the Pali Hwy, but none stop at the Nuuanu Pali Lookout.

Past the four-mile marker, look up and to the right to see two notches cut about 15 feet deep into the crest of the *pali* (cliff). These notches are thought to have been dug as cannon emplacements by Kamehameha I.

The original route between Honolulu and windward Oahu was via an ancient footpath that wound its way perilously over these cliffs. In 1845 the path was widened into a horse trail and later into a cobblestone carriage road.

In 1898 the Old Pali Hwy (as it's now called) was built following the same route. It was abandoned in the 1950s after tunnels were blasted through the Koolau Range and the present multilane Pali Hwy opened.

You can still drive a loop of the Old Pali Hwy (called Nuuanu Pali Drive) and hike another mile of it from the Nuuanu Pali Lookout.

Queen Emma Summer Palace

At the Pali Hwy two-mile marker is the Queen Emma Summer Palace, which belonged to Queen Emma, the consort of Kamehameha IV.

Emma was three-quarters royal Hawaiian and a quarter English, a granddaughter of the captured sailor John Young, who became a friend and adviser of Kamehameha I. The house is also known as

Hanaiakamalama, the name of John Young's home in Kawaihae on the Big Island, where he served as governor.

The Youngs left the home to Queen Emma, who often slipped away from her formal downtown home to this cooler retreat. It's a bit like an old Southern plantation house, with a columned porch, high ceilings and louvered windows to catch the breeze.

The home was forgotten after Emma's death in 1885 and it was scheduled to be razed in 1915, as the estate was being turned into a public park. The Daughters of Hawaii rescued it and they now run it as a museum.

The house has period furniture collected from five of Emma's homes. Some of the more interesting pieces are a cathedral-shaped koa cabinet made in Berlin and filled with a set of china from Queen Victoria; feather cloaks and capes; and Emma's necklace of tiger claws, a gift from the Maharaja of India.

It's open from 9 am to 4 pm daily except holidays. Admission is $4 for adults, $1 for children under age 16.

Nuuanu Pali Drive

For a scenic side trip through a shady green forest, turn off the Pali Hwy onto Nuuanu Pali Drive, half a mile past the Queen Emma Summer Palace. The 2½-mile road runs parallel to the Pali Hwy and then comes back out to it before the Nuuanu Pali Lookout, so you don't miss anything by taking this side loop – in fact, quite the opposite.

The drive is through mature trees that form a canopy overhead, all draped with hanging vines and wound with philodendrons. The lush vegetation includes banyan trees with hanging aerial roots, tropical almond trees, bamboo groves, impatiens, angel trumpets and golden cup – a tall climbing vine with large golden flowers.

Judd Trail If you want to get off the road and into the woods, you might try Judd Trail. The full trail is a 1½-mile loop, but most people just take it as far as Jackass

Ginger, a little freshwater pool about 10 minutes in.

One mile up Nuuanu Pali Drive, there's a dirt parking lot on the right, just before a small bridge. It's best to take all valuables out of your car and leave it unlocked, as thieves are fond of smashing car windows in this area.

The trail starts below the parking lot and soon crosses a stream. It then runs parallel to the stream but goes uphill a bit, so you'll need to keep an eye out for the pool. Sometimes it's a good place for a dip, other times it's muddy; the mosquitoes are hungry!

Trees along the way include large banyans, ironwood, *Eucalyptus robusta* and Norfolk pine.

Nuuanu Pali Lookout

Whatever you do, don't miss the Nuuanu Pali Lookout (Nuuanu Pali State Park) with its broad view of the windward coast from a height of 1200 feet. From the lookout you can see Kaneohe straight ahead, Kailua to the right and Mokolii Island and the coastal fishpond at Kualoa Park to the far left.

This is *windward* Oahu – and the winds that funnel through the pali are so strong that you can sometimes lean against them. It gets cool enough to appreciate having a jacket.

In 1795, Kamehameha I routed Oahu's warriors up the Nuuanu Trail during his invasion of the island. On these steep cliffs Oahu's warriors made their last stand. Hundreds were thrown to their death over the pali by Kamehameha's troops. A hundred years later, during the construction of the Old Pali Hwy, more than 500 skulls were found at the base of the cliffs.

The abandoned Old Pali Hwy winds down from the right of the lookout, ending abruptly at a barrier near the current highway about a mile away. Few people realize the road is here, let alone venture down it. It makes a nice walk and takes about 20 minutes one way. There are good views looking back up at the jagged Koolau Mountains and out across the valley.

As you get back on the highway, it's easy to miss the sign leading you out of the parking lot, and instinct could send you in the wrong direction. Go to the left if you're heading towards Kailua, to the right if heading towards Honolulu.

Windward Coast

Windward Oahu, the island's eastern side, follows the Koolau Range along its entire length. The mountains looming inland are lovely, with scalloped folds and deep valleys. In places they come so near to the shore that they almost seem to crowd the highway into the ocean.

The windward coast runs from Kahuku Point in the north to Makapuu Point in the south. (For the Waimanalo to Makapuu area, see the Southeast Oahu section.)

The two main towns are Kaneohe and Kailua, both largely nondescript bedroom communities for workers who commute to Honolulu, about 10 miles away.

North of Kaneohe, the windward coast is rural Hawaii, where many Hawaiians struggle along close to the earth, making a living with small papaya, banana and vegetable farms. It's generally wetter on the windward side and the vegetation is lush and green.

The windward coast is exposed to the northeast trade winds. This is a popular area for anything that requires a sail – from windsurfing to yachting.

There are some nice swimming beaches on the windward coast – notably Kailua, Kualoa and Malaekahana – although many other sections of the coast are too silted for swimming. Swimmers should keep an eye out for stinging Portuguese men-of-war that are often washed in during storms.

Most of the offshore islets that you'll see along this coast have been set aside as bird sanctuaries. These tiny islands are vital habitat for ground-nesting seabirds, which have largely been driven off the populated islands by the introduction of mongooses, cats and other predators.

Two highways cut through the Koolau Range from central Honolulu to the windward coast. The Pali Hwy (Hwy 61) goes straight into Kailua. The Likelike Hwy (Hwy 63) runs directly into Kaneohe, and, although it doesn't have the scenic stops the Pali Hwy has, it is in some ways more dramatic. Driving away from Kaneohe it feels as if you're heading straight into tall fairy-tale mountains – then you suddenly shoot through a tunnel and emerge on the Honolulu side, the drama gone.

If you're heading both to and from windward Oahu through the Koolau Range, take the Pali Hwy up from Honolulu and the Likelike Hwy back for the best of both. (See the Pali Highway section for details on that drive.)

KAILUA
In ancient times Kailua was a place of legends. It was home to a giant turned into a mountain ridge, the island's first menehunes and numerous Oahuan chiefs.

But that's all history. Kailua today is an ordinary middle-class community that has one of Oahu's finest beaches. It's the third largest city in Oahu, with a population of 38,000.

Ulupo Heiau
Ulupo Heiau is a large open-platform temple, made of stones piled 30 feet high and 140 feet long. Its construction is attributed to menehunes, the little people that legends say created much of Hawaii's stonework, finishing each project in one night. Fittingly, Ulupo means 'night inspiration'.

In front of the heiau, which is thought to have been a luakini type, is an artist's rendition of how the site probably looked in the 18th century, before Westerners arrived.

If you walk out across the top of the heiau, you get a view of Kawainui Swamp, one of Hawaii's largest habitats for endangered waterbirds. Legends say the swamp's ancient fishpond had edible mud at the bottom and was home to a *moo*, or lizard spirit.

Ulupo Heiau is one mile south of Kailua Rd. Coming up the Pali Hwy from Honolulu, take Uluoa St, the first left after passing the Hwy 72 junction. Then turn right on Manu Aloha St and right again onto Manuoo St. The heiau is behind the YMCA.

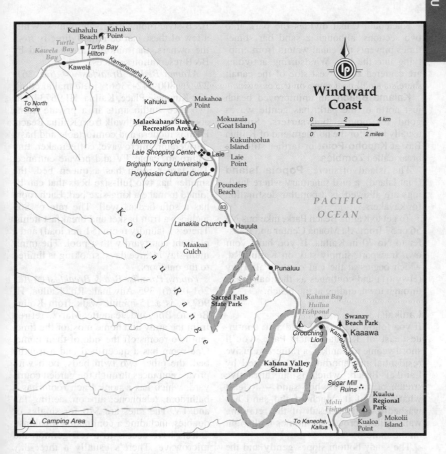

Windward Coast

Kailua Beach Park

Kailua Beach Park is at the southeastern end of Kailua Bay. This glistening white-sand beach is long and broad with lovely turquoise waters. The park is popular for long walks, family outings and a range of water activities.

Kailua Bay is the top windsurfing spot in Oahu. Onshore trade winds are predominant and windsurfers can sail at Kailua every month of the year. In different spots around the bay there are different water conditions, some good for jumps and wave surfing, others for flatwater sails. Some windsurfing companies, including Naish Hawaii and Kailua Sailboards, give lessons and rent boards at the beach park on weekdays and Saturday mornings.

Kailua Beach has a gently sloping sandy bottom with waters that are generally calm. Swimming is good year round, but sun bathers should keep in mind that the breezes favored by windsurfers also give rise to blowing sand.

The park has restrooms, showers, lifeguards, a snack shop, a volleyball court and large grassy expanses partly shaded with ironwood trees.

Kaelepulu Canal divides the park into two sections, although a sand bar sometimes prevents the canal waters from emptying into the bay. Windsurfing activities are centered at the west side of the canal; there's a small boat ramp on the east side.

Kalama Beach, an unimproved beach just north of the park, has gentle waves good for novice bodysurfers. Surfers usually head for the northern end of Kailua Bay at **Kapoho Point** or farther still to a break called **Zombies**.

The island offshore, **Popoia Island** (Flat Island), a bird sanctuary where landings are allowed, is a popular destination for kayakers.

To get to Kailua Beach Park, take bus No 56 or 57 from Ala Moana Center and transfer to No 70 in Kailua. If you have your own transport, simply stay on Kailua Rd, which begins at the end of the Pali Hwy (Hwy 61) and continues as the main road through town, ending at the beach.

Lanikai

If you follow the coastal road as it continues east of Kailua Beach Park, you'll shortly come to Lanikai, a rather exclusive residential neighborhood. It's fronted by Lanikai Beach, which is an attractive stretch of powdery white sand – at least what's left of it. Much of the sand has washed away as a result of the retaining walls built to protect the homes built right on the shore.

The sandy bottom slopes gently and the waters are calm, offering safe swimming conditions similar to those at Kailua. The twin **Mokulua islands** sit directly offshore.

From Kailua Beach Park, the road turns into the one-way Aalapapa Drive, which comes back around as Mokulua Drive to make a 2½-mile loop. There are 11 narrow beach access walkways off Mokulua Drive. For the best stretches of beach, try the one opposite Kualima Drive or any of the next three.

Places to Stay

Kailua has no hotels, but there are many furnished beachfront cottages, studios and B&B-style rooms in private homes. While a few of these can be rented directly from the owners, the majority are handled by B&B reservation services.

Akamai Bed & Breakfast (☎ /fax 261-2227, 800-642-5366; joe@makai.com), 172 Kuumele Place, Kailua, HI 96734, has two nice studio units in a private home about 10 minutes' walk from Kailua Beach. Each is modern and comfortable and has a refrigerator, microwave, coffeemaker, tiny bathroom, cable TV and private entrance. The larger room has a queen bed, the smaller has two full-size beds that can be joined to make a king-size bed. Each room has a sofa bed as well. The rate of $65 includes a fruit basket and breakfast items. There's a laundry room ($1 per load) and a pleasant courtyard with a pool. The minimum stay is three days; smoking is limited to the outdoors.

Papaya Paradise Bed & Breakfast (☎ /fax 261-0316), 395 Auwinala Rd, Kailua, HI 96734, is a 15-minute walk from Kailua Beach. Bob and Jeanette Martz, retired from the army and home most of the time, rent two rooms off the side of their home. One room has a queen bed and a trundle bed, the other two twin beds, both with private entrances through the garden courtyard, which has a pool. Each room has a bathroom, telephone, air-con, ceiling fan and TV. The rates are $70 for singles or doubles, including a continental breakfast. Guests have access to a refrigerator and microwave. There's usually a three-day minimum.

Sheffield House (☎ 262-0721; sheffield house@poi.net), 131 Kuulei Rd, Kailua, HI 96734, is a short walk from Kailua Beach and consists of two cozy rental units in the home of Paul and Rachel Sheffield. There's a guest room with a wheelchair-accessible bathroom for $50 or a one-bedroom suite with a queen bed and a separate sitting area with a queen futon sofa for $75. Each unit has a private entrance, TV, microwave, toaster oven, coffeemaker, small refrigerator and ceiling fan. There's a three-day minimum stay; breakfast is not included in the rates.

Most of the statewide B&B agencies have listings in Kailua. The two that follow are based in Kailua and book more than 50 different Kailua-area accommodations.

Affordable Paradise Bed & Breakfast (☎ 261-1693; fax 261-7315), Maria Wilson, 226 Pouli Rd, Kailua, HI 96734, books cottages from $65 and studios and B&Bs from $45 a double. Maria, who speaks German, can also arrange rooms in private homes starting at $35 for a single.

All Islands Bed & Breakfast (☎ 263-2342, 800-542-0344; fax 263-0308), 823 Kainui Drive, Kailua, HI 96734, has B&B rooms from $55 to $65 and studio apartments from $65 to $90.

In addition, *Naish Hawaii* (☎ 262-6068, 800-767-6068; fax 263-9723), 155A Hamakua Drive, Kailua, HI 96734, books windsurfing vacations with accommodations in Kailua.

Places to Eat

Kailua has several fast-food chains, such as *Burger King, Pizza Hut* and *McDonald's*, all near the intersection of Kailua and Kuulei Rds.

Kalapawai Market, on the corner of Kailua Rd and Kalaheo Ave, is a popular place to stop for coffee on the way to the beach. You have a choice of fresh brews, with a large cup for $1. They also have a few cheap eats, such as scones or chili and rice, and a good selection of wine and beer. It's open daily from 6 am to 9 pm.

The nearby *Kailua Beach Cafe*, in the Kailua Center at 130 Kailua Rd, has good breads, lunchtime sandwiches with fries for $6 and various salads for $6 to $9. Dinner dishes include Caribbean jerk chicken or fish fajitas for around $12, seafood and steak dishes for a few dollars more. It's open on weekdays from 11 am to 2:30 pm and from 5 to 9 pm and on weekends straight through from 10 am to 10 pm.

Assaggio (☎ 261-2772), 354 Uluniu St, serves good, moderately priced Italian food in a somewhat upmarket setting. At lunch, sandwiches cost around $6 and hot dishes are just a few dollars more. A good dinner choice ($13) is the spicy chicken Assaggio,

with chunks of white chicken meat, pepperoncini, mushrooms and roasted bell peppers over a bed of pasta. Other dishes include a nice eggplant parmigiana and shrimp vegetable linguine. It's open weekdays from 11:30 am to 2:30 pm and nightly from 5 to 10 pm.

Jaron's (☎ 261-4600), 201A Hamakua Drive, has a jazzy decor and a varied menu. At lunch there are salads and sandwiches or a create-your-own pasta for under $10. At dinner the menu concentrates on pastas, seafood and steaks priced from $14 to $20, green salad included. It's open for lunch from 11 am to 4 pm and for dinner from 4 to 10 pm. Jaron's is also an entertainment venue, with contemporary Hawaiian music on Thursday nights and rock or reggae bands on Fridays and Saturdays; there's a dance floor and no cover charge.

Buzz's (☎ 261-4661), a little restaurant opposite Kailua Beach Park, has lunchtime fresh fish burgers, sandwiches and salads for under $10. However, it's most popular as an evening steak house, with cuts of beef from $14 to $23. Trivia buffs can find a plaque on one of the lanai tables marking the spot where Bill and Hillary Clinton ate dinner in 1994.

The Source, 32 Kainehe St, is a small natural food store with bulk herbs and spices, vitamins, general food items and a small produce section. At lunch there's a juice bar with smoothies, tofu burgers, sandwiches, salads and soups – with the exception of smoked salmon, everything on the menu is under $5. The store is open from 9 am to 9 pm on weekdays, 10 am to 5 pm on weekends.

Across the street from the Source is *Agnes Bake Shop*, a good little bakery that makes whole-grain breads, inexpensive pastries, and Portuguese malasadas to order. The malasadas, which are intended to be eaten hot, take about 10 minutes to make and cost 50¢ each. They also serve coffee, tea and Portuguese bean soup, and there are a couple of small tables were you can sit and eat. Hours are 6 am to 6 pm daily except Mondays.

KANEOHE

Kaneohe, with a population of 36,000, is Oahu's fourth largest city.

Kaneohe Bay, which stretches from Mokapu Peninsula all the way up to Kualoa Point, seven miles north, is the state's largest bay and reef-sheltered lagoon. Although inshore it's largely silted and not good for swimming, the near-constant trade winds that sweep across the bay are ideal for sailing.

Two highways run north to south through Kaneohe. Kamehameha Hwy is closer to the coast and goes by Heeia State Park. Kahekili Hwy runs inland from the outskirts of Kaneohe, where it intersects the Likelike Hwy and continues north past Byodo-In. The highways merge into a single route, Kamehameha Hwy (Hwy 83), a few miles north of Kaneohe.

Kaneohe Marine Corps Air Station occupies the whole of Mokapu Peninsula. H-3, the controversial cross-island freeway completed in 1997, terminates at its gate.

Hoomaluhia Park

The county's youngest and largest botanic garden is Hoomaluhia, a 400-acre park in the uplands of Kaneohe. The park is planted with groups of trees and shrubs from tropical regions around the world.

It's a peaceful, lush green setting, with a stunning pali backdrop. Hoomaluhia is not a landscaped flower garden, but more of a natural preserve. A network of trails wind through the park and up to a 32-acre lake (no swimming allowed).

The little visitor center (☎ 233-7323) has displays on flora and fauna, Hawaiian ethnobotany and on the history of the park, which was originally built by the US Army Corps of Engineers as flood protection for the valley below.

The park is at the end of Luluku Rd, which starts 2¼ miles down Kamehameha Hwy from the Pali Hwy. Buses No 55 and 56 go to Windward City Shopping Center opposite the start of Luluku Rd. It's 1½ miles up Luluku Rd from the highway to the visitor center and another 1½ miles from the visitor center to the far end of the park so, if you use the bus, expect to do some walking.

The park is open from 9 am to 4 pm daily and admission is free. Guided two-hour nature hikes are held at 10 am on Saturdays

---

H-3

Environmentalists opposed the H-3 Fwy project from the beginning, concerned not only with the degradation of the pristine valleys that the new road slices across, but also with the probability that the freeway will open the rural areas of the windward coast to further development. Ironically, if the latter holds true, the H-3 is expected to *increase* traffic for Kailua-Honolulu commuters, who already contend with some of the worst traffic congestion on the island.

The H-3 Fwy, which got its impetus during the Reagan era, owes its existence in no small way to the heated Cold War mania of the day. The highway connects military bases on both sides of the island, with the Kaneohe Marine Corps Air Station at one end and the Pearl Harbor Naval Base at the other. As the post-Cold War military presence in Hawaii downsizes, the freeway's cost of $1.25 billion is being hailed as the biggest pork-barrel project in Hawaii's history. ■

and 1 pm on Sundays; call the visitor center for registration.

Weekend camping is allowed in Hoomaluhia Park. For information, see Camping in the Accommodations section at the front of this chapter.

Valley of the Temples & Byodo-In

The Valley of the Temples is an interdenominational cemetery in a beautiful setting just off the Kahekili Hwy, 1½ miles north of Haiku Rd. The main attraction is Byodo-In, the 'Temple of Equality', which is a replica of the 900-year-old temple of the same name in Uji, Japan. This one was dedicated in 1968 to commemorate the 100th anniversary of Japanese immigration to Hawaii.

Byodo-In sits against the Koolau Range. The rich red of the temple against the verdant fluted cliffs is strikingly picturesque, especially when mist settles in on the pali.

The temple is meant to symbolize the mythical phoenix. Inside the main hall is a nine-foot gold-lacquered buddha sitting on a lotus. Wild peacocks roam the grounds and hang their tail feathers over the upper temple railings.

A carp pond fronts the temple, with cruising bullfrogs and cooing doves. The three-ton brass bell beside the pond is said to bring tranquility and good fortune to those who ring it.

It's all very Japanese, right down to the gift shop selling sake cups, daruma dolls and happy buddhas. This scene is as close as you'll get to Japan without having to land at Narita.

Admission to the temple is $2 for adults, $1 for children under 12. It's open from 8:30 am to 4:30 pm daily.

On the way out, you might want to head up to the hilltop mausoleum with the cross on top and check out the view.

Heeia State Park

Heeia State Park is on Kealohi Point, just off Kamehameha Hwy. It has a good view of Heeia Fishpond on the right and Heeia-Kea Harbor on the left.

Before Western contact, stone-walled fishponds used to raise mullet and other fish for royalty were common along the coast throughout Hawaii. The **Heeia Fishpond** is an impressive survivor that remains largely intact despite the invasive mangrove that grows along its walls and takes root between the rocks.

Coconut Island, just offshore to the southeast of the fishpond, was a royal playground in times past. It was named for the coconut trees planted there by Princess Bernice Pauahi Bishop. In the 1930s it was the estate of Christian Holmes, heir to the Fleischmann Yeast fortune, who dredged the island, doubling its size to 25 acres. During the war the estate served as an R&R facility and had a brief stint as a hotel. In more recent times, air-brushed shots of Coconut Island were used in opening scenes for the *Gilligan's Island* TV series. The Hawaii Institute of Marine Biology of the University of Hawaii occupies a niche on the island, while the rest is privately owned.

You can walk around the grounds of Heeia State Park and take in the view, but otherwise there's not much to do here.

Places to Stay

Alu Bluffs Windward Bed & Breakfast (☎ /fax 235-1124, 800-235-1151), 46-251 Ikiiki St, Kaneohe, HI 96744, has two bedrooms in a cozy home filled with Old World furnishings, oil paintings, antique toys and collectibles. The Victorian Room has one double bed and costs $65, while the Circus Room has two twin beds and costs $55. Each room has a private bathroom. Originally from the Scottish Highlands, where his mother ran a B&B, host Don Munro gives guests the run of the house and provides beach towels and coolers. Breakfast and afternoon tea are included in the rates. There's a small pool and a view of Kaneohe Bay.

The 57-unit *Schrader's Windward Marine Resort* (☎ 239-5711, 800-735-5711; fax 239-6658), 47-039 Lihikai Drive, Kaneohe, HI 96744, is a spread of simple low-rise wooden buildings in a residential neighborhood. Despite the name, the ambiance is more that of a local motel than a resort. So many of the guests are military families that they offer free transport to the Kaneohe Marine Corps base. One-bedroom units range from $70 to $146, two-bedroom units from $110 to $190. All have refrigerators, microwaves, TVs and phones.

Places to Eat

The *Chart House* (☎ 247-6671) at Haiku Gardens has a lush, open-air setting with a picturesque view of a lily pond tucked beneath the Koolau Mountains. It's open from 5:30 pm nightly. The restaurant features standard steak and seafood dishes ($16 to $26) accompanied by a nice salad bar, though the real attraction is the setting. The gardens are flood-lit at night.

You can also drop by Haiku Gardens in the daytime and take a 10-minute stroll around the pond. To get there from Kamehameha Hwy, turn west on Haiku Rd just past Windward Mall; after crossing Kahekili Hwy, continue on Haiku Rd a quarter of a mile farther.

Chao Phya Thai Restaurant in the Windward City Shopping Center, 45-480 Kaneohe Bay Drive, is a family-run restaurant serving good Thai food. Most dishes on the extensive menu are priced between $6 and $8. It's open for lunch from 11 am to 2 pm Monday to Saturday and for dinner from 5 to 9 pm nightly.

The Windward City Shopping Center also has a *Foodland* supermarket, fast-food restaurants and *Kozo Sushi*, part of a local chain of fast-food shops that specialize in good, inexpensive sushi. *Burger King* and *Pizza Hut* are on the opposite side of the Kamehameha Hwy.

The Windward Mall, on Kamehameha Hwy at its intersection with Haiku Rd, is a large, two-level mall with a bank, chain department stores and numerous other shops. The mall's Food Court is sort of a mini Ala Moana, with a line of food stalls selling hot cinnamon rolls, deli items, pizza by the slice and Japanese, Chinese, Mexican and Korean meals.

WAIAHOLE & WAIKANE

Waiahole and Waikane mark the beginning of rural Oahu. The area is home to family-run nurseries and small coconut, banana, papaya and lemon farms.

Large tracts of Waikane Valley were taken over for military training and target practice during WWII, a use that continued until the 1960s. The government now claims the land has so much live ordinance that it can't be returned to the families it was leased from. This is a source of ongoing contention with local residents, who are angry that much of the inner valley remains off-limits.

KUALOA
Kualoa Regional Park

Kualoa Regional Park, a 153-acre county park on Kualoa Point, is bounded on its southwestern side by Molii Fishpond. From the road southwest of the park the fishpond is visible through the trees as a distinct green line in the bay.

Kualoa is a nice beach park in a scenic setting. The mountains looming precipitously across the road are, appropriately enough, called Pali-ku, meaning 'vertical cliff'. When the mist settles it looks like a scene from a Chinese watercolor.

The main offshore island is **Mokolii**. In Hawaiian legend, Mokolii is said to be the tail of a nasty lizard or a dog – depending on who's telling the story – that was slain by a god and thrown into the ocean. Following the immigration of Chinese laborers to Hawaii, this conical-shaped island also came to be called Papale Pake, Hawaiian for 'Chinese hat'.

Apua Pond, a three-acre brackish salt marsh on the point, is a nesting area for the endangered aeo (Hawaiian stilt). If you walk down the beach beyond the park, you'll see a bit of **Molii Fishpond**, but it's hard to get a good perspective on it from there. The rock walls are covered with mangrove, milo and pickleweed.

The park is largely open lawn with a few palm trees. It has a long, thin strip of beach with shallow waters and safe swimming.

There are picnic tables, restrooms, showers, a phone and a lifeguard. Camping is free from Friday to Tuesday nights with a permit from the county; a caretaker locks the gates at night.

Kualoa Ranch

The horses grazing on the green slopes across the road from Kualoa Regional Park belong to Kualoa Ranch. The ranch offers all sorts of activities, including horseback riding, kayaking and target shooting, with much of it packaged for Japanese honeymooners who are shuttled in from Waikiki.

Back in 1850, Kamehameha III leased about 625 acres of this land for $1300 to Dr Judd, a missionary doctor who became one of the king's advisers. Judd planted the land with sugar cane, built flumes to transport it and imported Chinese laborers to work the fields. His sugar mill trudged along for a few decades but went under just before the reciprocity agreement with the USA opened up mainland sugar markets.

You can still see the remains of the mill's stone stack and a bit of the crumbling walls half a mile north of the beach park, right alongside the road.

KAAAWA

In the Kaaawa area, the road hugs the coast and the pali moves right on in, with barely enough space to squeeze a few houses between the base of the cliffs and the road.

Swanzy, a neighborhood beach park used mainly by fishers, is fronted by a shore wall. Across the road is a 7-Eleven store, a gas station and *Kaaawa Country Kitchen*, a takeout restaurant with a couple of tables in front.

Crouching Lion

The crouching lion is a rock formation at the back of the restaurant of the same name, which comes up shortly after the 27-mile marker.

In Hawaiian legend, the rock is said to be a demigod from Tahiti who was cemented to the mountain during a jealous struggle between Pele, the volcano goddess, and her

---

Sacred Ground

Kualoa used to be one of the most sacred places on Oahu. When a chief stood on the point, passing canoes lowered their sails in respect. The children of chiefs were brought here to be raised, and it may also have been a place of refuge where kapu breakers and escaped warriors could seek reprieve from the law. It was at Kualoa that the double-hulled canoe *Hokulea* landed in 1987, following a two-year rediscovery voyage through Polynesia that retraced the ancient migration routes.

Because of its rich significance to Hawaiians, Kualoa Regional Park is listed in the National Register of Historic Places. ∎

---

sister Hiiaka. When he tried to free himself by pulling into a crouching position, he was turned to stone.

To find him, stand at the Crouching Lion Inn sign with your back to the ocean and look straight up to the left of the coconut tree. The figure, which resembles a lion, is on a cliff in the background.

The inn itself has a tour-bus ambiance. Sandwiches, salads and a few hot plates cost $7 to $12 at lunch. Dinners are about double that, although there's often a cheaper early-bird special.

Continuing north, just past the inn on the right, you get a glimpse of **Huilua Fishpond** on the coast.

KAHANA VALLEY

In old Hawaii the islands were divided into *ahupuaa* – pie-shaped land divisions reaching from the mountains to the sea that provided everything the Hawaiians needed for subsistence. Kahana Valley, four miles long and two miles wide, is the only publicly owned ahupuaa in Hawaii.

Kahana is a wet valley. Annual rainfall ranges from about 75 inches along the coast to 300 inches in the mountains. In precontact times, Kahana Valley was planted with wetland taro. The overgrown remnants of more than 130 terraces and irrigation canals have been uncovered in the valley.

In the early 20th century the area was planted with sugar cane, which was hauled north to the Kahuku Mill via a small railroad. During WWII, the upper part of Kahana Valley was taken over by the military and used for training in jungle warfare.

In 1965 the state bought Kahana Valley from the Robinson family of Kauai (owners of Niihau) in order to preserve it from development.

Kahana Valley State Park

The entrance to Kahana Valley State Park is located one mile north of the Crouching Lion Inn.

When the state purchased Kahana it also acquired tenants, many of whom had been living in the valley for a long time. Rather than evict a struggling rural population, the state created a plan allowing the 140 residents to stay on the land. The concept is to eventually incorporate the families into a 'living park', with the residents acting as interpretive guides. The development of the park has been a slow process, but after two decades of planning and negotiating, the 'living park' concept has inched forward. A simple orientation center inside the park entrance has been opened and tours are being provided to school children and local organizations.

While there are no tours for individual travelers, you can walk through the valley on your own. The orientation center has the latest information on trail conditions – keep in mind that they can be slippery when wet, and this is the wettest side of Oahu.

The most accessible of the park trails is a 1¼-mile loop trail, maintained by the Boy Scouts, that begins at the orientation center. It starts along the old railroad route, passes a fishing shrine called Kapaeleele Koa, and leads to Keaniani Kilo, a lookout that was used in ancient times for spotting schools of fish in the bay. The trail then goes down to the bay and along the highway back to the park entrance. You can find a trail map at the orientation center.

The park also takes in Kahana Bay and its tree-lined beach. The bay is set deep and narrow, and the protected beach provides safe swimming, with a gently sloping sandy bottom. The 10 beachside campsites are used primarily by island families, and there may be some turf issues for tourists. To camp here you must obtain a permit in person from the park orientation center (☎ 237-8858) or from the main state parks office in Honolulu.

PUNALUU

Punaluu is a scattered little seaside community. At Punaluu Beach Park, a narrow beach provides fairly good swimming, as the offshore reef protects the shallow inshore waters in all but stormy weather. Be cautious near the mouth of the Waiono Stream and in the channel leading out from it, as currents are strong when the stream is flowing quickly or the surf is high.

The *Paniolo Cafe*, 53-146 Kamehameha Hwy, north of the 25-mile marker, has standard salads, sandwiches and plate lunches for around $7 from 11 am to 3 pm.

SACRED FALLS STATE PARK

Sacred Falls is a 1374-acre state park with a two-mile trail leading up the narrow Kaliuwaa Valley, which folds deeply into magical-looking mountains. The park is north of the 23-mile marker.

The trail begins across an old cane field and follows Kaluanui Stream through a narrow canyon. The upper end of the trail leads to an 80-foot waterfall beneath high, rocky cliffs. The falls are nice though not spectacular and there are lots of mosquitoes.

The moderately difficult hike takes about 1½ hours. The falls may be sacred, but the hike isn't blessed. Although it's generally safe to hike, and thousands do, caution is definitely warranted. There are a couple of stream crossings on the way that have slippery rocks and, more importantly, are subject to flash flooding. Even when it's sunny on the valley floor, a quick rain storm in the mountains can wash down suddenly.

In the past decade a number of hikers have been swept to their deaths in flash floods, at least one other killed by falling rocks and another by a slip over a ledge. Other hikers have been stranded during flash flooding, a few requiring rescue by helicopter.

Flash floods give little warning. Hikers caught in them here have reported hearing a sudden loud crack and then seeing a wall of water pour down the stream bed; they've had just five seconds to reach higher ground. If the water starts to rise or you hear a rumbling, get up on a bank and wait it out. Don't try to cross the stream if the water reaches above your knees.

The trail is closed when the weather is sufficiently bad or the water level is high. Decisions are made daily and posted at the park or you can call the state parks office at ☎ 587-0300 and find out the status for that day.

Thefts from rental cars left in the parking lot are notorious and you shouldn't leave anything valuable in your vehicle here (or anywhere else, for that matter).

HAUULA

Hauula is a rather tired-looking town with a fine backdrop of hills and Norfolk pines. There's a 7-Eleven store and a few small eateries.

The in-town beach is none too appealing for swimming, but it occasionally gets waves big enough for local kids to ride. The beach is actually a county park that allows camping, although it's mostly local families that camp there.

The stone ruins of **Lanakila Church** (circa 1853) sit perched on a hill opposite Hauula Beach, next to the newer Hauula Congregational Church.

Trails

The Division of Forestry & Wildlife (☎ 587-0166) maintains three trails in the forest reserve behind Hauula: **Hauula Loop Trail** (2½ miles), **Maakua Gulch Trail** (three miles) and **Maakua Ridge Trail** (2½ miles). All three trails are through a hunting area and head into some beautiful hills. Hauula Loop and Maakua Ridge trails have good views, while the Maakua Gulch Trail crosses a stream and leads to a waterfall and pool. As flash flooding is a potential problem, the Maakua Gulch Trail should not be hiked in rainy weather or when the stream is high.

The trailhead to all three is at a bend in Hauula Homestead Rd, about a quarter of a mile up from Kamehameha Hwy. Camping is allowed along the trails. Call the Division of Forestry for information, trail maps and the required camping permits.

LAIE

Laie is thought to be the site of an ancient *puuhonua* – a place where kapu breakers and fallen warriors could seek refuge. Today Laie is the center of the Mormon community in Hawaii.

The first Mormon missionaries to Hawaii arrived in 1850. After an attempt to establish a Hawaiian 'City of Joseph' on Lanai failed amidst a land scandal, the Mormons moved to Laie. In 1865 they purchased 6000 acres of land in the area and slowly expanded their influence.

In 1919 the Mormons constructed a **temple**, a smaller version of the one in Salt Lake City, at the foot of the Koolau Range. This stately temple, which is at the end of a wide promenade, appears like nothing else on the windward coast. Although there's a visitor center where eager guides will tell you all about Mormonism, tourists are not allowed to enter the temple itself.

Nearby is the Hawaii branch of **Brigham Young University**, with scholarship programs bringing in students from islands throughout the Pacific.

Information

Laie Shopping Center, about half a mile north of the Polynesian Cultural Center, has restaurants, a supermarket, a coin laundry and a Bank of Hawaii.

Polynesian Cultural Center

The Polynesian Cultural Center (☎ 293-3333), called PCC by locals, is a 'non-profit' organization belonging to the Mormon Church. The center draws about 900,000 tourists a year, more than any other attraction on Oahu with the exception of the USS Arizona Memorial.

The park's seven theme villages represent Samoa, New Zealand, Fiji, Tahiti, Tonga, the Marquesas and Hawaii. They have authentic-looking huts and ceremonial houses, many elaborately built with twisted sennit ropes and hand-carved posts. The huts hold weavings, tapa cloth, feather work and other handicrafts.

People of Polynesian descent in native garb demonstrate poi pounding, coconut frond weaving, dances, games and the like. There's also a re-creation of an old mission house and a missionary chapel representative of those found throughout Polynesia in the mid-19th century.

Most of the people working here are Pacific Island students from the nearby Brigham Young University, who pay their college expenses by providing PCC with a source of inexpensive labor. Not all students end up at the 'village' of their home islands. Apparently there are more Samoans than Hawaiians, for instance, so you may well find a Samoan student demonstrating Hawaiian weavings. People are amiable and you could easily spend a few hours wandering around chatting or trying to become familiar with a craft or two.

The admission price includes boat rides along the waterway that winds through the park; the Pageant of the Long Canoes, a sort of trumped-up floating talent show at 2:30 pm; and 35-minute van tours of the Mormon temple grounds and BYU campus. The theme park is open daily except Sundays from 12:30 to 9:45 pm, though most activities cease by 6 pm.

Although PCC can be interesting, it is also very touristy and hard to recommend at an admission price of $27 for adults and $16 for children ages five to 11.

The 'Admission-Buffet-Show' ticket, which costs $44 for adults and $27 for children, adds on a buffet dinner and evening Polynesian show. The buffet is a mass production with uninspired food. The Polynesian song and dance show, which runs from 8 to 9:30 pm, is partly authentic, partly Hollywood-style and much like an enthusi-

astic college production, with elaborate sets and costumes.

Laie Beaches

The 1½ miles of beach fronting the town of Laie between Malaekahana State Recreation Area and Laie Point are used by surfers, bodysurfers and windsurfers.

Pounders, half a mile south of the main entrance to PCC, is an excellent bodysurfing beach, but the shorebreak, as the name of the beach implies, can be brutal. There's a strong winter current. The area around the old landing is usually the calmest. Summer swimming is generally good and the beach is sandy.

From **Laie Point** there's a good view of the mountains to the south and of tiny offshore islands. The island to the left with the hole in it is Kukuihoolua, otherwise known as Puka Rock.

To get to Laie Point, head makai on Anemoku St, opposite the Laie Shopping Center, then turn right on Naupaka St and go straight to the end.

Places to Stay

Rodeway Inn Hukilau Resort (☎ 293-9282, 800-526-4562; fax 293-8115; rodeway@ aloha.net), 55-109 Laniloa St, Laie, HI 96762, right outside the Polynesian Cultural Center, is a two-story motel with 48 rooms surrounding a courtyard pool. While not special, it's comfortable enough and the management is friendly. Each room has a lanai, cable TV, air-con and mini-refrigerator. Rates start at $79, including a continental breakfast.

Places to Eat

Laie Chop Suey in the Laie Shopping Center is a local-style eatery with standard Chinese fare. Most main dishes cost $5 to $6, while set lunch plates cost $4.75, dinner plates $5.75. It's open from 10 am to 9 pm Monday to Saturday.

The shopping center also has a grocery store, *Subway Sandwiches* and *Domino's Pizza*.

Laie's *McDonald's*, on the highway at the north end of PCC, has a little more character than the usual McDonald's. Originally built as a restaurant for the hotel next door, the building resembles a Polynesian longhouse with a peaked roof, and there's even a small waterfall inside.

MALAEKAHANA STATE RECREATION AREA

Malaekahana Beach stretches between Makahoa Point to the north and Kalanai Point to the south. The long, narrow, sandy beach is backed by ironwoods. Swimming is generally good year round, although there are occasionally strong currents in winter. This popular family beach is also good for many other water activities, including bodysurfing, board surfing and windsurfing.

Kalanai Point, the main section of the state park, is less than a mile north of Laie and has picnic tables, barbecue grills, camping, restrooms and showers.

Mokuauia (Goat Island), a state bird sanctuary just offshore, has a nice sandy cove with good swimming and snorkeling. It's possible to wade over to the island – best when the tide is low and the water's calm, but be sure to ask the lifeguard about water conditions and the advisability of crossing. Be careful of the shallow coral and sea urchins.

You can also snorkel across to Goat Island and off its beaches. Beware of a rip current that's sometimes present off the windward end of the island, where the water is deeper.

Camping

Malaekahana has the best campgrounds at this end of the windward coast. You can camp in the park's main Kalanai Point section for free if you have a state park permit. Tent sites on this side are seldom crowded, although weekends and summer are busier.

You can also rent a cabin or camp for a fee in the Makahoa Point section of the park, which has a separate entrance off the highway three-quarters of a mile north of the main park entrance. A local nonprofit group working on cultural preservation projects maintains this end and provides on-site security. Check-in is from 3 to 5 pm and the gates are locked to vehicles between 7 pm and 7 am.

There are rustic one-bedroom cabins for $50 and simpler tent cabins with slab floors for $35; both types can sleep up to six. Tent camping in this section costs $5 per person. While reservations (☎ 293-1736 weekdays from 10 am to 3 pm) are recommended, walk-in campers can usually get a tent site except during busy holiday weekends.

KAHUKU

Kahuku is a former sugar town with little wooden cane houses lining the road. The mill in the center of town belonged to the Kahuku Plantation, which produced sugar here from 1890 until it closed in 1971. The mill was a relatively small concern, unable to keep up with the increasingly mechanized competition of Hawaii's bigger mills.

Kahuku Sugar Mill

A fledgling shopping center has been set up inside Kahuku's old sugar mill, with small shops ringing the old machinery. The mill's enormous gears, flywheels and pipes have been painted in bright colors to help visitors visualize how a sugar mill works. The steam systems are red, the cane-juice systems light green, hydraulic systems dark blue and so forth. It looks like something out of *Modern Times* — you can almost imagine Charlie Chaplin caught up in the giant gears.

The center has not been wildly successful, but there's a bar, a local plate-lunch eatery, a food mart, gas station, post office, bank and a few other shops in the complex.

Kuilima Cove

The shallow Kuilima Cove, which is one of the area's best swimming spots, is fronted by the Turtle Bay Hilton, the sole hotel in Kahuku. You can park at one of the 18 free spaces for beachgoers, which are on the right just before the guard booth, and walk 10 minutes to the beach. Alternatively, there's parking inside the hotel lot for $1 for the first half hour and 50¢ for each additional half hour.

Kaihalulu Beach

Kaihalulu is a beautiful, curved, white-sand beach fronted by ironwoods. Although a shoreline lava shelf and rocky bottom make the beach poor for swimming, it's good for beachcombing – you can walk east about a mile to Kahuku Point. Local fishers cast thrownets from the shore and pole fish from the point. The dirt road just inland of the beach is also used as a horse trail.

To get there, turn into the Turtle Bay Hilton and just before the guard booth turn right into an unmarked parking lot, where there are free spaces for beachgoers. It's a five-minute walk out to the beach. There are no facilities.

Places to Stay

Turtle Bay Hilton & Country Club (☎ 293-8811, 800-445-8667; fax 293-9147), Kahuku, HI 96731, is a self-contained resort and the only major hotel on the windward and north shores. The Hilton is perched on Kuilima Point, between Turtle Bay and Kuilima Cove. All 486 rooms have ocean views. Room rates range from $180 to $330, suites from $400 to $1500. There are two golf courses, two pools, horse stables and 10 tennis courts.

You can find a better deal with *Turtle Bay Condos* (☎ 293-2800; fax 293-2169), Box 248, Kahuku, HI 96731, which handles units at Kuilima Estates, the modern condominium complex on the grounds fronting the Hilton. Rates are $95 for a regular studio, $110 for a studio with a loft and from $115/165 for a unit with one/two bedrooms. Each unit has a complete kitchen, washer/dryer, TV, phone and lanai.

Places to Eat

If you like shrimp, you can't beat *Giovanni's Aloha Shrimp*, the white truck that parks along the highway just south of the Kahuku Sugar Mill. Mozambican owners John and Connie Aragona buy fresh shrimp from local aquafarmers every morning and cook them to order using old family recipes. You have your choice of tasty shrimp scampi, conventional grilled shrimp or an ultra-fiery spicy shrimp. A plate with 12 jumbo shrimp and two scoops of rice costs a reasonable $10. There's a covered picnic area where you can sit and eat. It's open from 10:30 am to 5 pm on weekdays, to 6 pm on weekends.

There are also a few restaurants at the Turtle Bay Hilton. The *Palm Terrace* has uninspired buffets for $14 at breakfast and lunch, a few dollars more at dinner. The *Sea Tide Room* has a Sunday brunch for $27, while *The Cove* is the hotel's fine-dining restaurant.

Central Oahu

Central Oahu forms a saddle between the Waianae Mountains on the west and the Koolau Mountains on the east.

Three routes lead north from Honolulu to Wahiawa, the town smack in the middle of Oahu. The freeway, H-2, is the fastest route, and Hwy 750, the farthest west, is the most scenic. The least interesting option, Hwy 99, catches local traffic as it runs through Mililani, a modern, nondescript residential community.

Most people just zoom up through central Oahu on their way to the North Shore. If your time is limited this isn't a bad idea. There are a few sights along the way, but Wahiawa, the region's commercial center, doesn't really warrant much more than a zip through anyway.

From Wahiawa two routes, Hwy 803 (Kaukonahua Rd) and Hwy 99 (Kamehameha Hwy), lead down through pineapple country to the North Shore. Hwy 803 is a slightly shorter way to reach Mokuleia than Hwy 99 and about the same distance to Haleiwa. Both are fine scenic roads, and if you're not circling the island, you might as well go up one and down the other.

HWY 750

Highway 750 (Kunia Rd) adds a few miles to the drive through central Oahu but if you have the time it's worth it. Follow H-1 to the Kunia/Hwy 750 exit, three miles west of where H-1 and H-2 divide.

After you turn up Hwy 750 you enter plantation lands. The route runs along the foothills of the Waianae Range and the countryside remains solidly agricultural all the way to Schofield Barracks.

Up the road 2½ miles you'll come to a strip of corn fields planted by the Garst Seed Company. Three generations of corn are grown here each year, which makes it possible to develop hybrids of corn seed at triple the rate it would take on the mainland. The little bags placed over each ear of corn prevent them from being cross-pollinated.

Farther north is one of the most scenic pineapple fields in Hawaii. There are no buildings and no development – just red earth carpeted with long green strips of pineapples stretching to the edge of the mountains.

From the Hawaii Country Club, just up the road on the right, there's a distant view of Honolulu all the way to Diamond Head.

Kunia

Kunia, a little town in the midst of the pineapple fields, is home to the field workers employed by Del Monte. If you want to see what a current-day plantation village looks like, turn west off Hwy 750 onto Kunia Drive, which makes a 1¼-mile loop through the town.

Rows of grey-green wooden houses with corrugated tin roofs stand on low stilts. People take pride in their little yards, with bougainvillea and other flowers adding a splash of brightness despite the red wash of dust that blows in from the surrounding pineapple fields.

Kunia Drive intersects the highway at about 5½ miles north of the intersection of Hwy 750 and H-1 (there's a store and post office near the turn-off) and again at the six-mile marker.

Kolekole Pass

Kolekole is the gap in the Waianae Mountains that Japanese fighter planes flew through on their way to bomb Pearl Harbor. The landscape may look familiar, as the flight scene was recreated here 30 years later for the shooting of the popular war film *Tora! Tora! Tora!*

Kolekole Pass, at an elevation of 1724 feet, sits above Schofield Barracks on military property. It can be visited as long as the base isn't on some sort of military alert.

Access is through Foote Gate, on Hwy 750, a third of a mile south of its intersection with Hwy 99. After passing through the gate, take the first left onto Road A, then the first right onto Lyman Rd. The drive is 5¼ miles up past the barracks, golf course and bayonet assault course. The parking lot is opposite the hilltop with the big white cross that's visible from miles away.

The five-minute walk to the top of the pass ends at a clearing with a view straight down to the Waianae Coast. The large, ribbed stone that sits atop the ridge here is said to be the embodiment of a woman named Kolekole who took the form of this stone in order to become the perpetual guardian of the pass.

Along the side of the stone are a series of ridges, one of them draining down from a bowl-like depression on the top. Shaped perfectly for a guillotine, the depression has given rise to a more recent 'legend' that Kolekole served as a sacrificial stone for the beheading of defeated chiefs and warriors. The fact that military bases flank both sides of the pass has no doubt had a little influence on this one.

Just west of the pass the road continues through a Navy base down to the Waianae Coast, but you can't take it. The Navy base is a stockyard for nuclear weapons, and there's no public access through that side.

WAHIAWA

Wahiawa is a GI town. Just about every fast-food chain you can think of is there. Tattoo parlors and pawn shops are the town's main refinements, and if you're looking for a little excitement, there are some rough-and-tumble bars.

To go through town and visit the botanic garden, healing stones and royal birthstones, take Kamehameha Hwy (which is Hwy 80 as it goes through town, although it's Hwy 99 before and after Wahiawa). To

OAHU

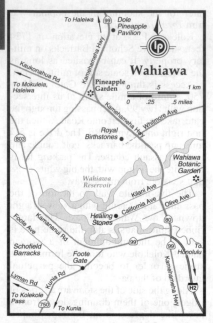

To Haleiwa 99 Dole Pineapple Pavilion

Kaukonahua Rd

To Mokuleia, Haleiwa

Kamehameha Hwy

Wahiawa

Pineapple Garden

0 .5 1 km

0 .25 .5 miles

Kamehameha Hwy Whitmore Ave

803

Royal Birthstones

Wahiawa Reservoir

Wahiawa Botanic Garden

Kilani Ave

California Ave Olive Ave

Kamananui Rd

Foote Ave

Healing Stones

80

Schofield Barracks

Foote Gate

99

99 To Honolulu

Lyman Rd

Kunia Rd

Kamehameha Hwy

H2

To Kolekole Pass

750 To Kunia

make the bypass around Wahiawa, stick with Hwy 99.

Wahiawa Botanic Garden

The Wahiawa Botanic Garden, 1396 California Ave, is a mile east of the Kamehameha Hwy. What started out in the 1920s as a site for forestry experiments by the Hawaii Sugar Planters' Association is now a 27-acre city park with grand old trees around a wooded ravine.

The park is a nice shady place to take a stroll. Interesting 60-year-old exotics such as cinnamon, chicle and allspice are grouped in one area. Tree ferns, loulu palms and other Hawaiian natives are in another. The trees are identified by markers, and the air is thick with birdsong.

The garden is open from 9 am to 4 pm daily. Admission to the park is free, as is a brochure describing some of the trees.

Healing Stones

One of the odder sights to be labeled with an HVB marker, the 'Healing Stones' are caged inside a small concrete-block 'temple' next to the Methodist church on California Ave, half a mile west of its intersection with Kamehameha Hwy.

The main stone is thought to have been the gravestone of a powerful Hawaiian chief. Although the chief's original burial place is in a field a mile away, the stone was moved long ago to a graveyard at this site. In the 1920s, people thought the stone had healing powers and thousands made pilgrimages to it before interest waned. The housing development and church came later, taking over the graveyard and leaving the stones sitting on the sidewalk.

A local group with roots in India who sees a spiritual connection between Hawaiian and Indian beliefs now visits the temple, so you may see rice, flowers or little elephant statues placed around the stones. The story is actually more interesting than the sight.

Royal Birthstones

Kukaniloko, a group of royal birthstones where queens gave birth, is just north of Wahiawa. The stones are thought to date back to the 12th century. It was said that if a woman lay properly against the stones while giving birth, her child would be blessed by the gods, and indeed, many of Oahu's great chiefs were born at this site.

These stones are one of only two documented birthstone sites in Hawaii (the other's in Kauai). Many of the petroglyphs on the stones are of recent origin, but the eroded circular patterns are original.

To get to them from town, go three-quarters of a mile north on Kamehameha Hwy from its intersection with California Ave. Turn left onto the red dirt road directly opposite Whitmore Ave. The stones, marked with a state monument sign, are a quarter of a mile down through a pineapple field, among a stand of eucalyptus and coconut trees. If it's been raining, be aware that the red clay can cake onto your car tires, and once back on the paved road the car may slide as if it's driving on ice.

Pineapple Garden

Del Monte maintains a little pineapple demonstration garden in a triangle at the intersection of Hwys 99 and 80.

Smooth cayenne, the commercial variety of pineapple grown in Hawaii, is shown in various growth stages. Each plant produces just two pineapples. The first takes nearly two years to reach maturity, the second about one year more. Other commercial varieties of pineapples grown in Australia, the Philippines and Brazil are on display, as are some varieties of purely decorative bromeliads.

You can pull off to the side of the road and walk through on your own at any time.

Dole Pineapple Pavilion

The Dole Pineapple Pavilion is on Hwy 99 less than a mile north of its intersection with Hwy 80. This touristy complex, in the heart of Oahu's pineapple country, consists of a bustling gift shop and some simple bromeliad gardens out back. Dole's processing plant sits across the street and miles of pineapple fields surround the area.

At the gift shop you can purchase pineapple juice, pineapple freezes, pineapple pastries and pineapples boxed to take home. Expect things to be a bit pricey, but the gardens are free and it makes a nice opportunity to get out and stretch. Hours are from 9 am to 6 pm daily.

the action from the beach. You can beat much of the traffic simply by coming up on a weekday.

It's believed that the earliest Polynesians to arrive on Oahu were drawn to the North Shore by the region's rich fishing grounds, cooling trade winds and moderate rain. The areas around Mokuleia, Haleiwa and Waimea all once had sizable Hawaiian settlements. Abandoned taro patches still remain in their upland valleys.

By the turn of the present century the Oahu Railroad & Land Company had extended the railroad around Kaena Point and along the entire North Shore, linking the area with Honolulu and bringing in the first beachgoers from the city. Hotels and private beach houses sprang up, but when the railroad stopped running in the 1940s the hotels shut down for good. Sections of track are still found along many of the beaches.

Waikiki surfers started taking on North Shore waves in the late 1950s and big-time surf competitions followed a few years later. Each December there are three major surf competitions, collectively known as the Triple Crown, with prize purses reaching six figures.

Surf mania prevails even in the restaurants, which serve up omelets with names like 'Pumping Surf' and 'Wipe Out'. Half the North Shore population can be found on the beach when the surf's up.

North Shore

Oahu's North Shore is synonymous with surfing and prime winter waves. Sunset Beach, the Banzai Pipeline and Waimea Bay are among the world's top surf spots and draw some of the best international surfers.

Other North Shore surf breaks may be less well known, but with names like Himalayas and Avalanche, they're not exactly for neophytes.

On winter weekends, convoys of cars make the trip up from Honolulu to watch

---

North Shore Water Conditions

With the exception of Haleiwa Beach Park, North Shore beaches are notorious for treacherous winter swimming conditions. There are powerful currents along the entire shore. If it doesn't look calm as a lake, it's probably not safe for swimming or snorkeling.

During the summer, surf conditions along the whole North Shore can mellow right out. Shark's Cove then becomes a prime snorkeling and diving spot, and Waimea Bay, internationally famous for its winter surf, turns into a popular swimming and snorkeling beach. ∎

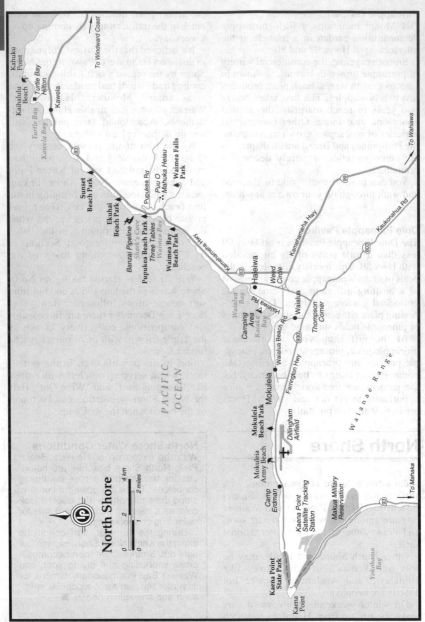

North Shore

0   1   2 miles
0   2   4 km

WAIALUA
Waialua, a quiet little town about a mile west of Haleiwa, is centered around the dusty Waialua Sugar Mill, which closed down in 1996 bringing an end to the last commercial sugar operation on Oahu.

While the Waialua area remains economically depressed, with much of the surrounding fields taken over by feral cane, other sections are newly planted in coffee and seed corn – two crops that are labor intensive and hold out some promise for new jobs.

The town has a handful of period buildings, the most interesting being the local watering hole, the Sugar Bar, which occupies the old Bank of Hawaii building down by the mill.

The most scenic route between Haleiwa and Waialua is along Haleiwa Rd.

MOKULEIA
The Farrington Highway (Hwy 930) runs west from Thompson Corner to Dillingham Airfield and Mokuleia Beach. (Both this road and the road along the Waianae Coast are called Farrington Hwy, but they don't connect, as each side reaches a dead end about 2½ miles short of Kaena Point.)

Mokuleia Beach is a six-mile stretch of white sand running from Kaiaka Bay towards Kaena Point. Although some GIs and locals come this way, the beaches don't draw much of a crowd and the area has sort of a 'boonies' feel to it. The only beach facilities are at Mokuleia Beach Park, and the nearest store is back in Waialua.

Dillingham Airfield is the take-off site for glider rides and sky diving. For details, see Activities in the front of this chapter.

Mokuleia Beach Park
Mokuleia Beach Park, opposite Dillingham Airfield, has a large open grassy area with picnic tables, restrooms, showers and a phone. Camping is allowed with a county camping permit.

Mokuleia is sandy but has a lava rock shelf along much of its shoreline. It has fairly consistent winds, making it a popular spot with windsurfers, particularly in spring and autumn. In winter there are dangerous currents.

Mokuleia Army Beach
Mokuleia Army Beach, opposite the western end of Dillingham Airfield, has the widest stretch of sand on the Mokuleia shore. Once reserved exclusively for military personnel, the beach is now open to the public, although it is no longer maintained and there are no facilities.

The beach is unprotected and has very strong rip currents, especially during winter high surf. Surfing is sometimes good.

Army Beach to Kaena Point
From Army Beach, you can drive another 1½ miles down the road, passing still more white-sand beaches with aqua waters. You'll usually find someone shorecasting and occasionally a few local people camping.

The paved road goes past YMCA Camp Erdman and then ends at a locked gate. The terrain is scrubland reaching up to the base of the Waianae Range, while the shoreline is wild and windswept. It's also a bit trashed, with the occasional torched car along the beach; this is certainly not a must-do drive.

From road's end, it's possible to walk 2½ miles to Kaena Point along state park lands, but it's more attractive from the other side (for details, see Kaena Point State Park in the Waianae Coast section).

HALEIWA
Haleiwa is the gateway to the North Shore and the main town catering to the multitude of day-trippers who make the circle island ride.

The 2500 townspeople are a multiethnic mix of families who have lived in Haleiwa for generations and more recently arrived surfers, artists and New Age folks.

Most of Haleiwa's shops are lined up along Kamehameha Ave, the main drag through town. Haleiwa has a picturesque boat harbor, bounded on both sides by beach parks. One side is known for its winter surfing, the other for the North Shore's safest year-round swimming.

OAHU

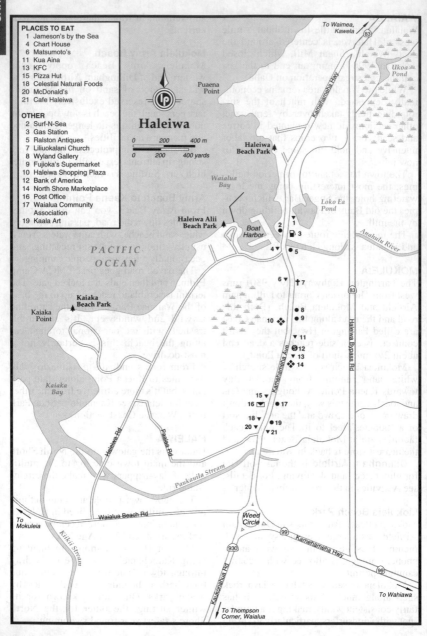

PLACES TO EAT
1 Jameson's by the Sea
4 Chart House
6 Matsumoto's
11 Kua Aina
13 KFC
15 Pizza Hut
18 Celestial Natural Foods
20 McDonald's
21 Cafe Haleiwa

OTHER
2 Surf-N-Sea
3 Gas Station
5 Ralston Antiques
7 Liliuokalani Church
8 Wyland Gallery
9 Fujioka's Supermarket
10 Haleiwa Shopping Plaza
12 Bank of America
14 North Shore Marketplace
16 Post Office
17 Waialua Community
   Association
19 Kaala Art

Haleiwa

0   200   400 m
0   200   400 yards

Puaena
Point

Haleiwa
Beach Park

Waialua
Bay

Loko Ea
Pond

Anahulu River

Haleiwa Alii
Beach Park

Boat
Harbor

PACIFIC
OCEAN

Kaiaka
Beach Park

Kaiaka
Point

Kaiaka
Bay

Haleiwa Rd

Paalaa Rd

Kamehameha Ave

Kamehameha Hwy

Haleiwa Bypass Rd

To Waimea,
Kawela

Ukoa
Pond

Paukauila Stream

Waialua Beach Rd

Kiikii Stream

To
Mokuleia

Weed
Circle

Kaukonahua Rd

Kamehameha Hwy

To Wahiawa

To Thompson
Corner, Waialua

930

99

99

83

83

The Anahulu River, which flows out along the boat harbor, is spanned by the Rainbow Bridge, so nicknamed for its distinctive arches. Take a glimpse up the river from the bridge. It's still a lushly green scene, and it's easy to imagine how it must have looked in ancient Hawaii, when the riverbanks were lined with taro patches.

In the summer of 1832, John and Ursula Emerson, the first missionaries to the North Shore, built a grass house and missionary school beside the Anahulu River. They called the school Haleiwa, meaning house *(hale)* of the great frigate bird *(iwa)*. Over time, the name came to refer to the entire village.

Information

The post office is open from 8 am to 4:15 pm on weekdays, from 9 am to noon on Saturdays. There's a Bank of Hawaii and a pharmacy in the Haleiwa Shopping Plaza and a Bank of America near KFC.

Matsumoto's

For many people the circle-island drive isn't complete without lining up at Matsumoto's tin-roofed general store for shave ice.

Hawaiian shave ice is a bit like a snow cone, although better because the ice is finer. The cloyingly sweet syrups are no different, however. Shave ice at Matsumoto's costs from $1 for the small plain version to $1.80 for a large with ice cream and sweetened azuki beans.

Liliuokalani Protestant Church

The church opposite Matsumoto's takes its name from Queen Liliuokalani, who spent summer on the shores of Anahulu River and attended services here. Although the church dates from 1832, the current building was built in 1961. As late as the 1940s, services were held entirely in Hawaiian.

Of most interest is the unusual **seven-dial clock** that Queen Liliuokalani gave the church in 1892. The clock shows the hour, day, month and year, as well as the phases of the moon. The queen's 12-letter name replaces the numerals on the clock face. A century later it still keeps accurate time. The church is open whenever the minister is in, which is usually in the mornings.

Kaiaka Beach Park

The 53-acre Kaiaka Beach Park is on Kaiaka Bay, about a mile west of town. This is a good place for a picnic, as there are shady ironwood trees, but the in-town beaches are better choices for swimming. Two streams empty out into Kaiaka Bay, muddying up the beach after heavy rainstorms. The park has an interesting view of the defunct Waialua sugar mill, and it's all quite peaceful. Kaiaka has restrooms, picnic tables, showers and seven campsites. Camping is free with a permit from the county.

Haleiwa Alii Beach Park

Surfing is king at Haleiwa Alii Beach Park. This is the site of several tournaments in the winter, when north swells can bring waves as high as 20 feet.

When waves are five feet and under, lots of younger kids bring their boards out. Any time they're six feet or better there are also strong currents and it's more suited to experienced surfers. The county (☎ 637-5051) gives free surfing lessons here on weekend mornings in winter.

The 20-acre beach park has restrooms, showers, picnic tables and a lifeguard tower. The shallow areas on the southern side of the beach are generally the calmest for swimming.

Haleiwa Beach Park

Haleiwa Beach Park is on the north side of Waialua Bay. As the beach is protected by a shallow shoal and a breakwater, the waters are usually very calm and see little wave action, although north swells occasionally ripple into the bay.

While the beach isn't Haleiwa's most appealing, this 13-acre county park has full beach facilities as well as basketball and volleyball courts, an exercise area and a softball field. It also has a good view of Kaena Point.

Places to Stay

There are no 'established' accommodations in Haleiwa proper, although people occasionally rent out rooms in their homes. You can usually find room-for-rent notices on the bulletin boards at the Coffee Gallery, Celestial Natural Foods and Haleiwa Super Market.

The other option is camping, which is allowed Friday to Tuesday nights at Kaiaka Beach Park. For details on permits, see Camping in the Accommodations section at the start of this chapter.

Places to Eat

Cafe Haleiwa, on the right as you come into town from the south, is an unpretentious eatery serving good food at honest prices. An institution of sorts on the North Shore, it has long been a haunt for local surfers. A large burrito served with terrific home fries costs $6, while two large pancakes loaded with blueberries cost $3.50. Lunch is predominantly sandwiches and Mexican fare, averaging $7. It's open from 7 am to 2 pm daily.

Celestial Natural Foods, opposite Cafe Haleiwa, has bulk foods, granolas, fresh produce, yogurts and just about everything else you'd expect to find in a good health food store. In the back of the store is *Paradise Cafe*, which is open from 10 am to 5:30 pm and has vegetable chili over brown rice for $3, sandwiches and salads for around $5 and a few Middle Eastern dishes for a tad more.

The popular *Kua Aina* in the center of town makes the North Shore's best burgers and fish sandwiches, each about $5. It's open from 11 am to 8 pm daily.

The *Coffee Gallery* in the North Shore Marketplace is a fine alternative to the burger and plate-lunch scene. It has steamed coffees, scones and tempting pastries at reasonable prices. Breakfast includes granola with soy milk for $3 and Belgian waffles topped with fruit for $6.50. Most other dishes, including soups, sandwiches, burritos and salads, fall into the same price range. There's open-air

seating at the side of the cafe, and food can be ordered for takeout. It's open daily from 8 am to 8:30 pm daily.

Cholo's in the North Shore Marketplace has reasonably priced Mexican fare. You can get a variety of combination plates for $5.50 to $9. Worth trying when they're available, fresh ahi tacos cost $3.50. It's open from 8 am to 9 pm daily.

There's a more expensive Mexican restaurant, *Rosie's Cantina*, as well as a pizza place, *Pizza Bob's*, in the Haleiwa Shopping Plaza.

Chart House (☎ 637-8005) at the boat harbor has meat and seafood dinners from $16 to $26 from 5 pm nightly. The price includes the salad bar, which has hearts of palm, artichoke hearts, fresh fruit and breads in addition to the usual greens. The salad bar alone goes for $14. Lunch, available from 11 am to 5 pm, includes sandwiches, salads and hot dishes in the $6 to $12 range.

Jameson's by the Sea (☎ 637-4336), north of the bridge, serves dinner from Wednesday to Sunday in a 2nd-floor dining room with views of the boat harbor. Seafood is the specialty, with dishes starting at $19. You can also eat in a more casual pub setting downstairs from 11 am to about 9 pm daily, with sandwiches and salads in the $8 to $10 range.

Haleiwa has two main grocery stores: *Haleiwa Super Market*, in the Haleiwa Shopping Plaza, and *Fujioka's Supermarket*, across the street.

Things to Buy

Kaala Art, next to Cafe Haleiwa, has handscreened T-shirts, batik pareos (wrapped skirts), wood sculptures, paintings and some nice tapa cloths, handmade by a Tongan woman who lives in Hawaii.

Wyland Gallery, 66-150 Kamehameha Ave, features paintings and sculptures of whales. Marine artist Wyland is best known for his many 'Whaling Wall' murals splashed on shopping-center walls around the islands.

Ralston Antiques, 66-030 Kamehameha

Ave, an operation of Crazy Shirts' owner Rick Ralston, has a collection of period toys, dolls, train sets, silver, ship models, scrimshaw, prints and Hawaiiana.

Boards Surf-N-Sea (☎ 637-9887), 62-595 Kamehameha Ave, just north of the Rainbow Bridge, rents surfboards, boogie boards, windsurfing equipment, dive gear and snorkel sets. They also offer surfing and windsurfing lessons, dive trips and sport fishing and sell new and used surfboards and sailboards.

Hawaiian Surf and Strong Current, both in the North Shore Marketplace, also sell new and used surfboards. In addition, Strong Current has a little free 'surf museum' that's essentially a collection of old surfing photos and vintage surfboards.

WAIMEA

Waimea Valley was once heavily settled. The lowlands were terraced in taro, the valley walls dotted with house sites and the ridges topped with heiaus. Just about every crop grown in Hawaii thrived in the valley, including a rare pink taro favored by the alii.

Waimea River, now blocked at the beach, originally opened into the bay and was a passage for canoes traveling to villages upstream. The sport of surfing was immensely popular here centuries ago, with the early Hawaiians taking to Waimea's huge waves on their long boards.

When Captain Cook's ships sailed into Waimea to collect water in 1779, shortly after Cook's death on the Big Island, an entry in the ship's log noted that the valley was uncommonly beautiful and picturesque.

However, Western contact wasn't kind to the area. Deforestation above the valley, from logging and the introduction of plantations, contributed to a devastating flood in Waimea in 1894. In addition to water damage, an enormous volume of mud washed through the valley, so much so that it permanently altered the shape of Waimea's shore. After the flood, most residents abandoned the valley and resettled elsewhere.

Human Sacrifices
In 1792, Captain Vancouver, who had been an officer on one of Captain Cook's vessels a decade earlier, anchored in Waimea Bay. While three of his men were collecting water on shore they were attacked and killed. It's thought that their bodies were taken up to Puu O Mahuka Heiau on the ridge above the beach and sacrificed.

When Vancouver returned a year later demanding justice, the high chief turned over three islanders. Although Vancouver doubted that these men had anything to do with the murders, he had come to set an example so he ordered their execution. ■

Waimea Bay Beach Park
Waimea Bay is a very beautiful, deeply inset bay with turquoise waters and a wide white-sand beach almost 1500 feet long. Ancient Hawaiians believed its waters were sacred.

Waimea Bay's mood changes with the seasons: It can be tranquil and as flat as a lake in summer, then savage with incredible surf and the island's meanest rip currents in winter.

Waimea has Hawaii's biggest surf and holds the record for the highest waves ever ridden in international competition. As at Sunset Beach, the huge north swells bring out crowds of spectators who throng to watch Waimea surfers perform their near-suicidal feats on waves of up to 35 feet.

On winter's calmer days the boogie boarders are out in force, but even then sets come in hard and people get pounded. Winter water activities here are not for novices.

Usually the only time the water is calm enough for swimming and snorkeling is from June to September. The best snorkeling is around the rocks on the left of the bay.

Waimea Bay Beach Park is the most popular North Shore beach. There are showers, restrooms, picnic tables and a phone, and a lifeguard is on duty daily. Parking is often tight.

Waimea Falls Park

Waimea Falls Park (☎ 638-8511), across the highway from Waimea Bay Beach Park, is a botanical garden, cultural preserve and tourist park all in one.

The main park road leads three-quarters of a mile up the Waimea Valley to a waterfall, passing extensive naturalized gardens that include sections of ginger, hibiscus, heleconia and medicinal plants. Many of the plants are labeled for identification and there are several rare species under propagation.

The park has ancient stone platforms and terraces and some replicas of thatched buildings similar to those used by early Hawaiians. Traditional hula dances, Hawaiian games and other demonstrations are given during the day. A cliff diver plunges 60 feet into the waterfall pool five times a day to thrill spectators.

The valley's natural beauty is nicely preserved, and the park is pleasant to wander through, but the cost of admission is a bit steep at $19.95 for adults, $9.95 for children ages six to 12. Those five and under are admitted free.

The best deal is to come at 4:15 pm, when the rate drops to $6.50 for adults and $4 for children. Although the demonstrations stop around this time, the grounds are less crowded and more pleasant for strolling. The park is open from 10 am to 6:30 pm daily, and there's an in-park restaurant called the *Proud Peacock*.

A free shuttle runs from Waikiki hotels at 8 and 11:30 am daily; call ☎ 955-8276 for pick-up locations. Public bus No 52 stops at the highway half a mile from the park entrance.

Kayaking Waimea River It's possible to kayak up the historic Waimea River. Kayak Oahu Adventures (☎ 638-8189), at the side of the road going into Waimea Falls Park, rents single/double kayaks for $15/30 an hour.

St Peter & Paul Church

The church of St Peter & Paul stands beneath the tall unassuming tower on the northern side of Waimea Bay. The structure was originally a rock-crushing plant, built to supply gravel for the construction of the highway in the 1930s. After it was abandoned, the Catholic church converted it into Oahu's most unlikely chapel.

Puu O Mahuka Heiau State Monument

Puu O Mahuka is a long low-walled platform heiau perched on a bluff above Waimea. The largest heiau on Oahu, its construction is attributed to the legendary menehunes.

The terraced stone walls are a couple of feet high, although most of the heiau is now overgrown. This was an excellent site for a temple, and it's well worth the drive up for the view. It can also be a fine place to watch the sunset.

Walk up above the left side of the heiau from the parking lot for a view of Waimea Valley and Waimea Bay. To the west, you can see all the way out along the coast to Kaena Point.

To get to the heiau, turn up Pupukea Rd at the Foodland supermarket. The marked turn-off to the heiau is about half a mile up the road, and from there it's three-quarters of a mile in. On the drive up there's a good view of Pupukea Beach Park.

Pupukea Beach Park

Pupukea Beach Park is a long beach along the highway that includes Three Tables on the left and Shark's Cove on the right. In the middle is Old Quarry, where a wonderful array of jagged rock formations and tide pools are exposed at low tide. This is a very scenic beach, with deep blue waters, a varied coast and a mix of lava and white sand. The rocks and tide pools are tempting to explore, but be careful – they're razor sharp, and if you slip it's easy to get a deep cut.

The waters off Pupukea Beach are a marine-life conservation district.

There are showers and restrooms in front of Old Quarry. The beach entrance is opposite an old gas station; bus No 52 stops out front. Snorkel sets and other water sports equipment can be rented from Planet Surf, at the side of the Foodland supermarket.

NED FRIARY

Mural of ancient Hawaiian life at the University of Hawaii

Three Tables Three Tables, at the western end of the beach, gets its name from the ledges rising above the water. In summer when the waters are calm Three Tables has good snorkeling and diving. It's possible to see some action by snorkeling around the tables, but the best coral and fish as well as some small caves, lava tubes and arches are in deeper water farther out. This is a summer-only spot, however. In winter, dangerous rip currents flow between the beach and the tables. Beware of sharp rocks and coral.

Shark's Cove Shark's Cove is beautiful both above and below the water's surface. The naming of the cove was done in jest – sharks aren't a particular problem.

In the summer, when the seas are calm, Shark's Cove has good snorkeling and swimming conditions as well as Oahu's most popular cavern dive. A fair number of beginning divers take lessons here,

while the underwater caves will thrill advanced divers.

To get to the caves, swim out of the cove and around to the right. Some of the caves are very deep and labyrinthine, so caution should be used exploring them. There have been a number of drownings in these caves.

The large boulders out on the end of the point to the far right of the cove are said to be followers of Pele, the volcano goddess. As an honor, she gave them immortality by turning them to stone.

Ekuhai Beach Park
The main reason people come to Ekuhai Beach Park is to watch the pros surf the world-famous **Banzai Pipeline**, a few hundred feet to the left of the park. The Pipeline breaks over a shallow coral reef and can be a death-defying wave to ride.

At Ekuhai Beach itself, many board riders and bodysurfers brave a hazardous current to ride the waves. Water conditions mellow out in summer, when it's good for swimming.

Ekuhai Beach Park is opposite the Sunset Beach Elementary School, where there's an entrance to the beach and limited parking. Parking on the highway isn't permitted, and they do tow cars away. There's a lifeguard, restrooms, showers and a phone.

Sunset Beach Park

Sunset Beach Park is just south of the nine-mile marker. This beach is Oahu's classic winter surf spot, with incredible waves and challenging breaks. For such a big name, it's surprising how easy it is to miss, as it's essentially a little roadside attraction without even a sign.

Sunset Beach is a pretty beach that invites sunbathing, but the main action is in the water.

Winter swells create powerful rips. Even when the waves have mellowed in the summer, there's still an along-shore current for swimmers to deal with. Portable toilets and a lifeguard tower are the only facilities.

Backyards, the surf break off Sunset Point at the northern end of the beach, draws a lot of top windsurfers. There's a shallow reef and strong currents to contend with, but Backyards has the island's biggest waves for sailing.

Places to Stay

The best budget place to stay on the North Shore is *Breck's On the Beach Hostel* (☎ 638-7873; brecks@netsrvind.com), 59-043 Huelo St, Haleiwa, HI 96712. Breck Trask, a single mom with a teenage daughter, treats guests like family. She has a handful of modern apartment buildings fronting a lovely stretch of Sunset Beach, just north of the beach park. There are about 21 units in all, ranging from a pleasant little $45 studio that can sleep two to three people and has its own refrigerator and bathroom to a larger two-bedroom apartment with a kitchen for $70. There are also beds for $12.50 in clean and uncrowded dorms with four to six beds. There's a group kitchen, and cheap dinners

are available. A few bicycle rentals are available at $2.50 a day. The hostel attracts an international mix of surfers and is a great place to meet youthful travelers. Breck goes to the airport to meet most flights from Australia and New Zealand. If you catch her on one of her regular runs, it's free; if you call for a ride and she sends someone to get you it's $5. Return transport to the airport is $5.

Backpackers (☎ 638-7838; fax 638-7515), 59-788 Kamehameha Hwy, Haleiwa, HI 96712, opposite Three Tables, is pretty much a surfers' hangout. It has a few different set-ups, most of it beach-house casual. The main house has four bunks to a room for $15 a bed, while a three-story house behind it has very simple double rooms for $50. Both houses have shared bathrooms and kitchens. Expect spartan decor and aging furniture, but if you're just looking for a place to crash between waves then it's an option.

A small beachfront motel across the road has eight studios with TVs, kitchens and great views. Units on the bottom floor have dorm beds for $17, while those on the top are rented out like hotel rooms for $80 to $95.

The third property, a few hundred yards away on the mauka side of the road, consists of nine cottages with either two or three bedrooms. Dorm beds are $15 while the entire cottage, which sleeps six to eight people, costs $85 to $150. Backpackers makes airport runs; rides are free to the hostel, $5 on the return.

Debbie Rezent (☎ 638-9402), 58-335 Mamao Place, Haleiwa, HI 96712, rents a pleasant studio unit above the garage at her home in a residential area near Sunset Beach. It has a deck with a peek of the ocean, two twin beds, TV, bathroom with tub and limited kitchen facilities that include a refrigerator, microwave and hot plate. The cost is a reasonable $50.

Thomsen's Bed & Breakfast (☎ 638-7947; fax 638-7694), 59-420 Kamehameha Hwy, Haleiwa, HI 96712, is one large studio unit above the garage of Norman and Dianne Thomsen's home, near Ekuhai Beach Park. It has a king bed, queen sofa bed, bathroom, kitchen area, private entrance, phone, TV and a lanai facing the mountains. It's a good value at $65, but despite the name, breakfast is not included.

At *Ke Iki Hale* (☎ 638-8229, 800-377-4030), 59-579 Ke Iki Rd, Haleiwa, HI 96712, a dozen apartments front a beautiful white-sand beach just north of Pupukea Beach Park. The rates are $132/810 by the day/week for a one-bedroom duplex and $158/995 for small two-bedroom units. There are also a couple of separate streetside units for $85.

The bulletin board at Pupukea Foodland has notices of roommates wanted and the occasional vacation rental listing.

Places to Eat

You can get fast food and plate lunches at *Sunset Diner*, opposite Sunset Beach Park, from 9:30 am to 8 pm.

D'Amicos, on the mauka side of the highway just north of Sunset Beach, has sandwiches, good New York-style pizza and breakfasts, all at moderate prices. It's open from 7 am to 9 pm daily.

Food supplies can be picked up at *Sunset Beach Store*, next to D'Amicos, or at *Kammie's Market*, next to Sunset Diner. However, the best grocery prices on the North Shore are at the *Foodland* supermarket opposite Pupukea Beach Park.

Waianae Coast

The Waianae Coast is the arid, leeward side of Oahu.

In 1793, English captain George Vancouver, the first Westerner to drop anchor here, found a barren wasteland with only a few scattered fishing huts. Just two years later, in 1795, Kamehameha invaded Oahu and the population density along the Waianae Coast swelled with Oahuans who were forced to flee from their homes elsewhere on the island. This isolated western extreme of Oahu became their permanent refuge.

Today, leeward Oahu still stands separate from the rest of the island. There are no gift shops or sightseeing buses on the Waianae Coast. When you get right down to it, other than watching surfers at Makaha, there aren't a whole lot of sights to see.

Although developers are beginning to grab leeward Waianae farmland for golf courses, leeward Oahu remains the island's least touristed side. The area has a history of resisting development and a reputation for not being receptive to outsiders. In the past, visitors have been the targets of assaults and muggings. There's still a major problem with thefts from cars and campsites, and although things aren't as hostile as they used to be, many locals aren't keen on sharing their space with tourists.

Overall, you need to be attuned to the mood of the people. This is the only place in Hawaii where the park brochures say camping opportunities are for *local* residents.

Farrington Hwy (Hwy 93) runs the length of the leeward coast. There are long stretches of white-sand beaches, some quite attractive, others a bit trashed. In winter most have treacherous swimming conditions, but at that time they also have some of the island's more challenging surfing. Although the towns themselves are ordinary, the cliffs and valleys cutting into the Waianae Range form a lovely backdrop.

At road's end, there's an undeveloped mile-long beach and a fine nature hike out to scenic Kaena Point.

KAHE POINT
Kahe Point Beach Park

Despite the name, there's no beach at this park, just the rocky cliffs of Kahe Point. The park has running water, picnic tables and restrooms, and camping is allowed, but there's little else to recommend it.

Discarded household garbage occasionally makes it over the cliffs, and the backdrop is punctuated by the smokestacks of the electric power plant across the way. Along the road in front of the park a sign welcomes visitors to the Waianae Coast.

Hawaiian Electric Beach

This sandy beach north of Kahe Point is more commonly known as Tracks, the

OAHU

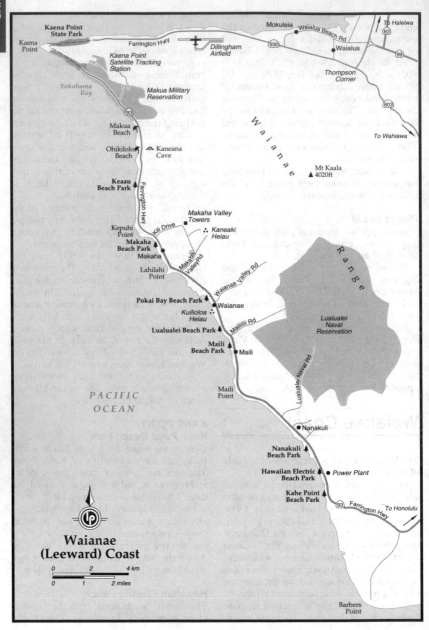

**Waianae
(Leeward) Coast**

name given to it by beachgoers who used to go there by train before the war. In summer this is a fairly calm place to swim, while in winter it's frequented by surfers.

To get there take the first turn-off after the power plant and drive over the abandoned railroad tracks. There are restrooms and a lifeguard station.

NANAKULI

Nanakuli, with a population of 9500, is the biggest town on the Waianae Coast. The site of a Hawaiian Homesteads settlement, Nanakuli has one of the largest native Hawaiian populations on Oahu. The town has supermarkets, the Waianae District Court, a bank and a few fast-food eateries.

Nanakuli is lined by a broad sandy beach park. There's swimming, snorkeling and scuba diving during the calmer summer season. In winter, high surf creates rip currents and dangerous shorebreaks.

To get to the beach park, turn left at the traffic lights on Nanakuli Ave. This is a community park, with a playground, sports fields, full beach facilities and campsites.

MAILI

Maili has a long, grassy roadside park with an endless stretch of white-sand beach. Like other places on this coast, the water conditions are often treacherous in winter but are usually calm enough for swimming in summer. There's a lifeguard station, a playground, beach facilities and a few castrated coconut palms to provide limited but safe shade.

WAIANAE

Waianae, with a population of 8800, is the second largest town on the leeward coast. It has a beach park, protected boat harbor, satellite city hall, police station, supermarkets and lots of fast-food places.

Pokai Bay Beach Park

Protected by Kaneilio Point and a long breakwater, Pokai Bay Beach Park has the calmest year-round swimming on the Waianae Coast. Waves seldom break inside

the bay, and the sandy sea floor slopes gently, making the beach a popular spot for families with children.

Snorkeling is fair by the breakwater, where fish gather around the rocks. The bay is also used by local canoe clubs, and you can watch them rowing if you happen by in the late afternoon. There are showers, restrooms and picnic tables, and a lifeguard is on duty daily.

Kaneilio Point, which runs along the south side of the bay, is the site of **Kuilioloa Heiau**. Partly destroyed by the army during WWII, the heiau has been reconstructed by a Waianae group. Because part of the point had been lost, some sections of the reconstruction had to be modified from the heiau's original design to fit the smaller space.

To get to the beach park and heiau, turn makai onto Lualualei Homestead Rd at the traffic light just after the Waianae post office.

MAKAHA

Makaha means 'ferocious', and in days past the valley was notorious for the bandits who waited along the cliffs for travelers to pass. Today, Makaha has world-class surfing as well as Oahu's best-restored heiau, a golf course and a few condos.

Makaha Beach Park

Makaha Beach is broad, sandy and crescent-shaped, with some of the most daunting winter surf in the islands. Experienced surfers and bodysurfers both hit the waves here.

The beach is home to some major surf competitions. The most colorful is Buffalo's Big Board Surfing Classic held in February using old-style surfboards called 'tankers', which are sometimes 15 feet long and weigh more than 80 pounds. As surfers today favor small, light boards, most competitors are of an older generation of surfers.

When the surf's not up, Makaha is a popular swimming beach. When the surf is up, rip currents and a strong shorebreak make swimming hazardous.

NED FRIARY
Temple offering

In summer the slope of the beach is relatively flat, while in winter the wave action results in a steeper drop. The beach sand is slightly coarse and of calcareous origin, with lots of mollusk shell fragments. As much as half of it temporarily washes away during winter erosion, but even then Makaha is still an impressive beach.

Snorkeling is good offshore during the calmer summer months. Makaha Caves, out where the waves break farthest offshore, feature underwater caverns, arches and tunnels at depths of 30 to 50 feet. It's a popular leeward diving spot.

Makaha Beach has showers and restrooms, and lifeguards are on duty daily.

Makaha Valley

For a little loop drive, turn mauka onto Kili Drive, opposite Makaha Beach Park, where the road skirts up along scalloped green cliffs into Makaha Valley. If you're there at midday, you can visit one of Hawaii's most authentically restored heiaus, which sits high in Makaha Valley at the back of a private residential estate.

An estimated 3000 wild peacocks live in the valley, including about two dozen white ones. They can be spotted, or at least heard, throughout the upper valley, and if you visit the heiau, it's not unusual to see them performing their courting rituals in the field adjacent to the parking lot.

To get to the heiau, take Kili Drive to the Makaha Valley Towers condominium complex and turn right onto Huipu Drive. Half a mile down on the left is Mauna Olu St, which leads a mile into Mauna Olu Estates and up to Kaneaki Heiau. To get to the Makaha Valley Country Club golf course, stay on Huipu Drive. Makaha Valley Rd, which intersects with Huipu Drive near the golf course, completes the loop, connecting back with the Farrington Hwy.

Kaneaki Heiau Kaneaki Heiau was originally a Lono temple, dedicated to the god of agriculture. It was later transformed into a luakini temple, and it's thought that Kamehameha used it as a place of worship after he conquered Oahu. Kaneaki Heiau remained in use until the time of Kamehameha's death in 1819.

Restoration, undertaken by the Bishop Museum and completed in 1970, added two prayer towers, a taboo house, drum house, altar and god images. The heiau was authentically reconstructed in the traditional manner using ohia logs and pili grass shipped over from the Big Island. For those interested in precontact Hawaiian culture it's a special place; the immediate setting surrounding the heiau remains undisturbed, even though the site is in the midst of a residential estate.

The guard at the Mauna Olu Estates gatehouse usually lets visitors go through to the heiau, a three-minute signposted drive past the gatehouse, between the hours of 10 am and 2 pm from Tuesday to Sunday. However, you might want to call the gatehouse (☎ 695-8174) in advance to inquire, as they can be a bit inconsistent in providing access. Admission is free.

Places to Stay

Makaha doesn't have many accommodations for short-term visitors. There are a handful of condos geared primarily to permanent residents, but none are terribly appealing and they generally require you to stay for at least a week.

Makaha Surfside (☎ 695-9574 or 524-3455), 85-175 Farrington Hwy, Makaha, HI 96792, is a four-story cinder-block apartment complex a mile south of Makaha Beach. Although it's predominantly residential, some of the 450 units are rented out on a weekly basis at $275 for studios, $400 for one-bedroom units, both with full kitchens. It's an ordinary complex, although there are pools and barbecue grills.

Makaha Shores (☎ 696-8415; fax 696-1805), Hawaii Hatfield Realty, 85-833 Farrington Hwy, Suite 201, Waianae, HI 96792, is a condo right on the northern end of Makaha Beach, with lanais overlooking the water. Studios cost $550 for one week, $800 for two weeks or $1050 a month, with a $50 cleaning fee tacked on. There are

one-bedroom units as well. It's tough to book in the high season, as a lot of retired people winter here.

Hawaii Hatfield Realty also handles units for about the same price in *Makaha Valley Towers*, the highrise complex that's tucked into the valley.

Places to Eat

Makaha Valley Country Club, overlooking the golf course at the east end of Makaha Valley Rd, is a popular lunch spot with a varied menu that includes fried chicken, teriyaki beef and yakisoba noodles.

For something on the run, a *7-Eleven* store on the corner of Farrington Hwy and Makaha Valley Rd sells inexpensive doughnuts, turnovers and simple fast-food items.

NORTH OF MAKAHA
Keaau Beach Park

Keaau Beach Park is another long, open, grassy strip, this time bordering a rocky shore, with campsites, showers, drinking water, picnic tables and restrooms. A

HAWAII STATE ARCHIVES

Making poi

sandy beach begins at the very northern end of the park, although a rough reef, sharp drop and high seasonal surf make swimming uninviting.

Driving north along the coast you'll see low lava sea cliffs, white-sand beaches and patches of kiawe. On the mauka side you'll get a glimpse into a run of little valleys.

Kaneana Cave

Kaneana Cave, a massive cave on the right-hand side of the road about two miles north of Keaau Beach Park, was once underwater. Its impressive size is the result of wave action that wore away loose rock around an earthquake crack and expanded the cavern over the millennia as the ocean slowly receded.

It's a somewhat uncanny place – often a strong wind gusts near the cave while it's windless just down the road.

Hawaiian kahunas once performed rituals inside the cave's inner chamber. Older Hawaiians consider it a sacred place and won't enter for fear it's haunted by the spirits of deceased chiefs. From the collection of broken beer bottles and graffiti inside, it's obvious not everyone shares their sentiments.

From Ohikilolo Beach, below the cave, you can see Kaena Point to the north. Ohikilolo Beach is sometimes called Barking Sands, as the sand is said to make a 'woofing' sound if it's walked on when very dry.

Nanaue the Shark Man

Hawaiian legend tells of a child named Nanaue who was born with a open space between his shoulders. Unknown to his mother, the child's father was the king of sharks who had taken on the guise of a man. Nanaue was born half human, half shark. He was human on land, but when he entered the ocean the opening on his back became a shark's mouth. After a nasty spell in which many villagers were ripped to shreds by a mysterious shark, Nanaue was discovered and forced to swim from island to island as he was hunted down. For a while he lived near Makua and took his victims into Kaneana Cave via an underwater tunnel. ■

Kaena Point Legends

Early Hawaiians believed that when people went into a deep sleep or lost consciousness, their souls would wander. Souls that wandered too far were drawn west to Kaena Point. If they were lucky, they were met here by their *aumakua* (ancestral spirit helper), who led their soul back to their body. If unattended, their soul would be forced to leap from Kaena Point into the endless night, never to return.

On clear days, Kauai can be seen from the point. According to legend, it was at Kaena Point that the demigod Maui attempted to cast a huge hook into Kauai and pull it next to Oahu to join the two islands. But the line broke and Kauai slipped away, with just a small piece of it remaining near Oahu. This is Pohaku O Kauai, a rock off the end of Kaena Point. ■

Makua

Scenic Makua Valley opens up wide and grassy, backed by a fan of sharply fluted mountains. It serves as the ammunition field of the Makua Military Reservation.

The makai road opposite the south end of the reservation leads to a little graveyard shaded by yellow-flowered be-still trees. This is all that remains of the Makua Valley community, forced to evacuate during WWII when the US military took over the entire valley for bombing practice. War games still take place in the valley, which is fenced off with barbed wire and signs that warn of stray explosives.

Makua Beach, the white-sand beach opposite the reservation, was a canoe landing in days past. A movie set of Lahaina as it appeared during the 19th century was built on Makua Beach for the 1966 movie *Hawaii*, starring Julie Andrews and Max von Sydow. No trace of the set remains.

Satellite Tracking Station

Immediately before the gate to Kaena Point State Park a road leads up to Kaena Point Satellite Tracking Station, operated by the US Air Force. The tracking station's antennas and domes sit atop the mountains above the point, a couple of them appearing like giant white golf balls perched on the ridge.

There are hiking trails above the tracking station, including a 2½-mile ridge trail that leads to Mokuleia Forest Reserve. You'll need to obtain a hiking permit in advance from the Division of Forestry & Wildlife (☎ 587-0166) to get past the air force's guard station.

KAENA POINT STATE PARK

Kaena Point State Park is an undeveloped 853-acre coastal strip that runs along both sides of Kaena Point, the westernmost point of Oahu.

Until the mid-1940s the Oahu Railroad ran up from Honolulu and around the point, carrying passengers on to Haleiwa on the North Shore.

The attractive mile-long sandy beach on this side of the point is Yokohama Bay, named for the large numbers of Japanese fishers who came through here during the railroad days.

Winter commonly brings huge pounding waves, making Yokohama a popular seasonal surfing and bodysurfing spot. It is, however, best left to the experts because of the submerged rocks, strong rip currents and dangerous shorebreak.

Swimming is pretty much limited to the summer, and then only during calm conditions. When the water's flat, it's possible to snorkel; the best spot and easiest access is at the south side of the park. There are restrooms, showers and a lifeguard station.

In addition to being a state park, Kaena Point has been designated a natural area reserve because of its unique ecosystem. The extensive dry, windswept coastal dunes that rise above the point are the

habitat of many rare native plants. The endangered Kaena akoko that grows on the talus slopes is found nowhere else.

More common plants are the beach naupaka, with white flowers that look like they've been torn in half; pau-o-Hiiaka, a vine with blue flowers; and beach morning glory, sometimes found wrapped in the parasite plant kaunaoa, which looks like orange plastic fishing line.

Seabirds common to the point include shearwaters, boobies and the common noddy, a dark-brown bird with a grayish crown. You can often see schools of spinner dolphins off the beach, and in winter humpback whale sightings are not uncommon.

Dirt bikes and 4WD vehicles once created a great deal of disturbance in the dunes, but after Kaena Point became a natural area reserve in 1983, vehicles were restricted and the situation improved. The reserve has once again become a nesting site for the Laysan albatross, and Hawaiian monk seals occasionally bask in the sun here.

Kaena Point Trail

A 2½-mile (one way) coastal hike runs from the end of the paved road at Yokohama Bay to Kaena Point, following the old railroad bed. Along the trail are tide pools, sea arches, fine coastal views and the lofty sea cliffs of the Waianae mountain range. The hike is unshaded (Kaena means 'the heat'), so take plenty of water.

Don't leave anything valuable in your car. Telltale mounds of shattered windshield glass can be found at the road's-end parking area used by most hikers; parking closer to the beach restrooms or leaving your doors unlocked can decrease the odds of having your car windows smashed.

Hawaii – The Big Island

The island of Hawaii, commonly called the Big Island, is nearly twice the size of all the other Hawaiian islands combined. Geographically, it's so incredibly varied that it resembles a mini-continent. Climates range from tropical to subarctic. Landscapes include one of just about everything: desolate lava flows, lush coastal valleys, high sea cliffs, rolling pastures, deserts and rainforests.

Geologically, it's the youngest Hawaiian island and the only one still growing. Kilauea, the most active volcano on earth, has added 500 acres of coastal land to the island since its latest series of eruptions began in 1983.

The Big Island has Hawaii's highest mountains, which rise almost 14,000 feet above sea level. Some people liken them to icebergs, not only for their seasonal snow-caps but because their summits are merely the tips of mountain masses that rise 32,000 feet from the ocean floor.

The mountains create a huge barrier that blocks the moist northeasterly trade winds and makes the leeward side of the Big Island the driest region in Hawaii. The Kona and Kohala coasts, on this sunny western side, have the island's best beaches and water conditions.

The windward east coast catches the rain and has a predominantly rugged coastline with pounding surf, lush tropical rainforests, deep ravines and majestic waterfalls.

Still, the island's most impressive scenery is at Hawaii Volcanoes National Park, which encompasses incredible volcanic sites. The park has excellent hiking and camping in locales that range from tropical beaches to the icy 13,679-foot summit of Mauna Loa. You can drive or cycle around the rim of Kilauea's huge caldera and walk across still-steaming crater floors.

The Big Island has many noteworthy historical sites, including Hawaii's best petro-

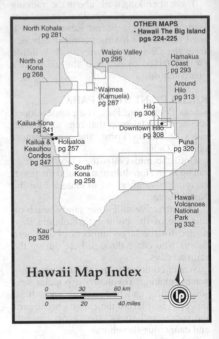

glyphs and some of its most important heiaus. It also boasts the largest privately owned cattle ranch in the USA and the world's top collection of astronomical observatories. The latter dot the summit of Mauna Kea, Hawaii's highest point at 13,796 feet.

There are two distinct centers on the Big Island. Hilo, on the lush, rainy east coast, is the island's only real city. It's the oldest city in Hawaii and it shows its age with character. But it's Kona, on the dry, sunny west coast, that attracts the visitors. Kona has the lion's share of the island's accommodations and is the center of most recreational activities, including excellent diving and deep-sea fishing.

The Big Island is big on space and few

places feel crowded. It attracts a lot of adventurous people. It's got cowboy country, traditional fishing villages, valleys with taro farmers and wild horses, and a fair number of alternative folks living off the land.

HISTORY

By and large the history of the Big Island is the history of Hawaii. It's widely believed that the first Polynesian settlers to Hawaii landed on this island. It was on the Big Island that the first *luakini heiau* (temple of human sacrifice) and the *kapu* system of strict taboos regulating all aspects of daily life came into being. It was also here, six centuries later, that the old gods were overthrown and replaced by those of the Christians.

English explorer Captain Cook died on the Big Island in 1779, a year after 'discovering' Hawaii, and this was where Kamehameha the Great rose to power.

Kamehameha the Great

Kamehameha the Great was born on the Big Island in 1758. As a young boy he was brought to Kealakekua Bay to live at the royal court of his uncle, Kalaniopuu, high chief of the island.

Kamehameha went on to become Kalaniopuu's fiercest general. To help him amass even more strength, Kalaniopuu appointed Kamehameha guardian of the war god, Kukailimoku, the 'snatcher of land'.

This war god was embodied in a coarsely carved wooden image with a bloody red mouth and a helmet of yellow feathers. Kamehameha carried it into battle with him, and it was said that during the fiercest fighting the image would screech out terrifying battle cries.

Immediately after Kalaniopuu's death in 1782, Kamehameha led his warriors against Kalaniopuu's son, Kiwalao, who had taken the throne. Kiwalao was killed and Kamehameha emerged as ruler of the Kohala region and one of the three ruling chiefs of the Big Island. The other two chiefs were Kahekili of Maui and Kamehameha's cousin, Keoua.

Kamehameha's ambitions extended well beyond sharing control of the island. In 1790, with the aid of a captured foreign schooner and two shipwrecked sailors, Isaac Davis and John Young, whom he used as gunners, Kamehameha attacked and conquered the island of Maui.

Shortly after that, Kamehameha was in Molokai preparing for an invasion of Oahu when word reached him that Keoua, chief of the Kau region, was attacking the Hamakua Coast. During those assaults Keoua had boldly pillaged Waipio Valley, which was the most sacred area on the Big Island and the site where Kamehameha had ceremoniously received his war god a decade earlier.

As an angry Kamehameha set sail for home, Keoua's soldiers beat a quick retreat back to Kau. When the withdrawing troops passed beneath the slopes of Kilauea Crater, the volcano suddenly erupted and many of the warriors were instantly killed as toxic fumes and ashes swept over them. It is the only known volcanic explosion in

HAWAII STATE ARCHIVES
Kamehameha the Great

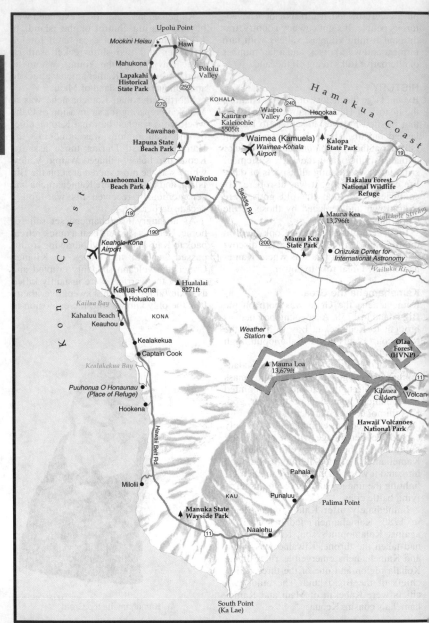

Upolu Point

Mookini Heiau
Hawi

Mahukona
Pololu
Valley
**Lapakahi
Historical
State Park**

(250)

KOHALA

(270)

▲ Kauna o
Kaleioohie
5505ft

Waipio
Valley

(240)

Honokaa

H a m a k u a   C o a s t

(19)

Kawaihae

Waimea (Kamuela)
*Waimea-Kohala
Airport*

**Kalopa
State Park**

(19)

**Hapuna State
Beach Park**

Saddle Rd

**Anaehoomalu
Beach Park** ▲

Waikoloa

**Hakalau Forest
National Wildlife
Refuge**

(19)

K o n a   C o a s t

▲ Mauna Kea
13,796ft

Kolekole Stream

(190)

(200)

**Mauna Kea
State Park** ▲

● Onizuka Center for
International Astronomy

*Keahole-Kona
Airport*

Wailuku River

▲ Hualalai
8271ft

Kailua-Kona
Holualoa

Kailua Bay

KONA

Kahaluu Beach
Keauhou

Kealakekua

Captain Cook

Olaa
Forest
(HVNP)

*Weather
Station*

▲ Mauna Loa
13,679ft

(11)

Kilauea
Caldera

Volcan

Kealakekua Bay

Puuhonua O Honaunau
(Place of Refuge)

**Hawaii Volcanoes
National Park**

Hookena

Hawaii Belt Rd

Milolii

KAU

Pahala

Punaluu

Palima Point

**Manuka State
Wayside Park** ▲

(11)

Naalehu

South Point
(Ka Lae)

**Hawaii
The Big Island**

```
0          10          20 km
0     5        10 miles
```

Hawaiian history to have resulted in mass fatalities. Casts of the soldiers' footprints, imprinted in volcanic mud and ash, remain on the trail to this day.

In the midst of these power struggles, Kamehameha was told by a prophet from Kauai that if he built a new heiau to honor his war god, Kukailimoku, he would become ruler of all the islands.

Kamehameha did so, completing Puukohola Heiau in Kawaihae in 1791. He then sent word to Keoua that his appearance was requested at the heiau for reconciliation. Keoua, well aware that this was a luakini temple, probably knew his fate was sealed, but he sailed to Kawaihae anyway.

Upon landing, Keoua and his party became the heiau's first sacrifices. With Keoua's death, Kamehameha became sole ruler of the Big Island.

Over the next few years Kamehameha conquered all the islands (except for Kauai, over which he established suzerainty) and named the entire kingdom after his home island, Hawaii.

End of an Era

Kamehameha the Great established his kingdom's royal court in Lahaina on Maui, but later returned to his Kamakahonu residence, on the north side of Kailua Bay, where he died in May 1819.

The crown was passed to his hesitant son, Liholiho, and Kamehameha's favorite wife, Kaahumanu, a spirited woman who wasn't content to be kept in her place by the old traditions.

In Kamakahonu, six months after Kamehameha's death, Kaahumanu sat down with Liholiho to eat a meal, something strictly forbidden under the kapu system. This breaking of the kapus by royalty marked the demise of the old religion. Almost immediately, temples throughout the islands were abandoned and their idols burned.

On April 4, 1820, the ship *Thaddeus* sailed into Kailua Bay with Hawaii's first Christian missionaries aboard. They landed beside Kamehameha's recently desecrated heiau at Kamakahonu. Their timing was perfect, as the recent abandonment of the

BIG ISLAND

old religion had left a vacuum into which the missionaries readily moved.

GEOGRAPHY

The Big Island has an area of 4035 sq miles and is growing as new lava spews into the sea. It's 93 miles long and 76 miles wide. The Big Island is the youngest Hawaiian island and the farthest east. Its southern tip, called South Point or Ka Lae, is the southernmost point in the USA.

The island was formed by five large shield volcanoes: Kohala, Hualalai, Mauna Kea, Mauna Loa and Kilauea. The last two are still active, with Kilauea having the distinction of being the most active volcano on earth.

Mauna Kea ('White Mountain') at 13,796 feet is the highest point in the Hawaiian Islands. It extends an additional 19,680 feet below sea level to the ocean floor and when measured from its base is the highest mountain in the world.

Mauna Loa ('Long Mountain'), just slightly lower at 13,679 feet above sea level, makes up more than half of the land mass of the Big Island and is the largest mountain mass in the world when measured from the ocean floor.

CLIMATE

Rainfall and temperatures vary more with location than with the seasons. The leeward northwest coast between Lapakahi and Waikoloa is the driest region in the state. Kawaihae, in the center of this strip, averages less than 10 inches of rain a year.

On the windward side of Mauna Kea, near the 2500-foot elevation, 300 inches of rain falls annually. So much rain is squeezed out of the clouds as they rise up Mauna Kea and Mauna Loa that only about 15 inches of precipitation reaches the summits, much of it as snow. Heavy subtropical winter rainstorms in Hilo occasionally bring blizzards to the mountains as low as the 9000-foot level.

Elevation makes enough of a difference that even within the city of Hilo, annual rainfall ranges from 130 inches on the shore to 200 inches on the higher slopes. Trivia buffs may be interested to know that Hilo has the world's largest raindrops, measuring up to 8 mm in diameter!

Annual rainfall in Volcano is 101 inches. At Kailua-Kona it's 25 inches. Although winter is wetter than summer, location again is the key. In Kona seasonal rainfall

Vog

'Vog' is a word coined on the Big Island to define the volcanic haze that has been hanging over the island since Kilauea's latest eruptive phase began in 1983. It usually blows towards Kona, and conditions can resemble city smog when the trade winds falter. Vog consists of water vapor, carbon dioxide and significant amounts of sulfur dioxide.

In the early 1990s an average of 275 tons of sulfur dioxide was being emitted from Kilauea daily, causing air quality problems on the Big Island and haze throughout Hawaii. The sulfur dioxide level exceeds standards set by the US Environmental Protection Agency an average of 22 days a year. While this shouldn't present health problems for short-term visitors, scientists are currently studying the link between vog and respiratory problems for residents. ∎

variations are marginal, while at Volcano they are about twofold.

The average daily high temperatures in January are 65°F at Hawaii Volcanoes National Park, 79°F in Hilo and 81°F in Kailua-Kona. In August, they are 71°F, 83°F and 85°F respectively. Nighttime lows are about 15° less.

FLORA & FAUNA

The *nene*, the endangered goose that is Hawaii's state bird, lives on the upland slopes of Mauna Kea, Mauna Loa and Hualalai. As recently as a hundred years ago there were an estimated 25,000 nene on the Big Island. They now number just a few hundred. Still, they're a friendly species and you might come across them, particularly at Hawaii Volcanoes National Park.

Other native birds include the endangered *palila*, a small yellow bird that survives solely on Mauna Kea's slopes, and the *io* (Hawaiian hawk), which also occupies the mountain slopes and lives only on the Big Island. Another endangered bird endemic to the Big Island is the *alala* (Hawaiian crow), which hangs on precariously with a single flock of fewer than a dozen birds.

There are wild horses in Waipio Valley and feral cattle on the slopes of Mauna Kea. The Big Island also has wild pigs, goats and sheep.

Two rare varieties of silversword grow on the Big Island, one on Mauna Kea and the other on Mauna Loa. Related to their better-known Maui cousin, they grow in remote areas well off the beaten path.

GOVERNMENT

The Big Island is one county unto itself with an elected mayor and a nine-member council.

Hilo is the county seat and political center. Rivalry is ongoing between old established Hilo and boomtown Kona; there's even a simmering separatist movement, based in Kona, aimed at dividing the island into two counties. The biggest political issue on the

Hawaii's state bird – the nene

island, as elsewhere in Hawaii, is rampant development.

ECONOMY

The Big Island's unemployment rate is 8%. Employment is fairly diversified, with retail trade, government, hotels and construction industries employing about half of the workforce.

Although the last Big Island sugar company ceased operations in 1996, agriculture still accounts for a significant sector of the economy. The island continues to produce the vast majority of Hawaii's macadamia nuts, coffee and tropical flowers, as well as four-fifths of its fruit, including papayas, bananas and oranges.

There's also an illicit underground agriculture in *pakalolo* (marijuana). Although it has declined greatly as the result of strict police surveillance, the vast majority of all marijuana confiscated in Hawaii still comes from the Big Island's Puna and Kau districts.

The Big Island has several sizable cattle ranches, which collectively produce the majority of the beef marketed in the state.

POPULATION & PEOPLE
The population of the Big Island is 137,500. Hilo has about a third of the island's population, but the Big Island's demographics are changing rapidly.

Between 1970 and 1980, North Kona (which includes Kailua-Kona) was the fastest-growing district in the state, with a growth rate of 185%. Between 1980 and 1990, neighboring South Kohala took the honors as the state's most rapidly growing district, with its population doubling.

The Big Island's ethnic breakdown is 26% part-Hawaiian, 25% Caucasian, 21% Japanese, 15% mixed non-Hawaiian and 9% Filipino. Full-blooded Hawaiians make up just 1% of the population.

ORIENTATION
The Big Island has fully serviced airports in Hilo and Kona. The Hilo Airport is in town. However, most visitors land in Kona at the Keahole-Kona Airport, which is between the island's main resort areas of Kailua-Kona and Waikoloa.

From the Keahole-Kona Airport you take Hwy 19, which runs along the Kona Coast, seven miles south to get to Kailua-Kona or 12 miles north to get to Waikoloa.

Official Hawaii
The island of Hawaii is nicknamed the Big Island. Its official flower is the ohia lehua, from a native tree that flourishes around lava flows; ceremonial leis are made from its fluffy red pompom blossoms. The island's official color is red. ∎

The Hawaii Belt Rd circles the island, taking in the main towns and many of the sights. Different segments of the road have different highway numbers and names, but it's easy to follow.

From Kona to Hilo, the northern half of the belt road is 93 miles, and the journey takes about two hours nonstop. The southern Kona-Hilo route is 125 miles and takes approximately three hours.

Maps
The best general map of the Big Island is the one published by the University of Hawaii Press; it's sold in numerous shops around the island.

INFORMATION
Tourist Offices
The Big Island has two Hawaii Visitors Bureau offices: 250 Keawe St, Hilo, HI 96720 (☎ 961-5797; fax 961-2126) and 75-5719 W Alii Drive, Kailua-Kona, HI 96740 (☎ 329-7787; fax 326-7563).

You can also receive a tourist information packet by calling ☎ 800-648-2441 and leaving your mailing address on their answering machine.

Newspapers & Magazines
West Hawaii Today (☎ 329-9311), which is the Kona Coast newspaper, and Hilo's *Hawaii Tribune-Herald* (☎ 935-6621) are both published daily except Saturday. A single copy of *West Hawaii Today* may be obtained by sending $4 to West Hawaii Today, Box 789, Kailua-Kona, HI 96745.

Free tourist magazines such as *This Week Big Island* and *Spotlight's Big Island Gold* are readily available at the airport, in hotel lobbies and around town. They're good sources of general information and include discount coupons for activities and eateries around the island.

Radio & TV
The island has six AM and 11 FM radio stations and three cable TV stations. Commercial and public TV stations are relayed from Honolulu. Channel 8 on cable TV features visitor information programs.

Libraries

There are public libraries in Kailua-Kona, Kealakekua, Holualoa, Hilo, Waimea, Pahoa, Pahala, Naalehu, Mountain View, Laupahoehoe, Kapaau, Honokaa and Keaau.

Weather

The National Weather Service has recorded forecasts for the Big Island (☎ 961-5582); for Hilo and vicinity (☎ 935-8555); and for water conditions (☎ 935-9883).

Hawaii Volcanoes National Park (☎ 985-6000) has recorded information on current volcano eruptions and viewing points.

Emergency

For police, ambulance or fire emergencies, dial ☎ 911. The crisis and help line is ☎ 329-9111 in Kona, ☎ 969-9111 in Hilo.

The main hospitals are in Hilo (☎ 969-4111) and Kealakekua (☎ 322-9311).

ACTIVITIES

The vast majority of the Big Island's recreational activities take place on the west coast. In addition to those listed here, most of the Waikoloa-area resorts have a variety of activities, including water sports, cruises and dive trips. They generally charge higher-than-average rates and advertise mainly to their guests, but they are usually open to the public as well.

Beaches & Swimming

The Big Island has 313 miles of shoreline. What it doesn't have are the expansive sandy beaches you'll find on Maui or Oahu. Most of the Big Island's beaches are sandy pockets bordering bays and coves.

The best spots are on the west coast. Kailua-Kona has a few good beaches, although the better ones are farther up the Kona Coast around Waikoloa and Kohala. Of these, Anaehoomalu and Hapuna are both beautiful, easily accessible public beaches. There are also a number of isolated gems dotting the coast that require a hike but are well worth the effort to reach.

Hilo is not as well endowed with beaches, but there are a few places to swim and snorkel on the east side of Hilo Bay.

The Puna and Kau districts have interesting black-sand beaches although generally unfavorable swimming conditions.

Swimming Pools The county has public pools at Honokaa High School in Honokaa, Kamehameha Park in Kapaau, Konawaena High School in Kealakekua, Kau High School in Pahala, Laupahoehoe High School in Laupahoehoe and at the Hoolulu Complex in Hilo. All county pools are open to the public for both lap swims and open pool use. For schedule information, call ☎ 935-2725.

In addition there's a coastal saltwater pool with public access behind the Kona by the Sea condos in Kailua.

Surfing

The Big Island is not one of the better islands for surfing, although local surfers do manage to catch waves in a number of places. Many of the island's surf spots are rocky, so surfers new to the area should check out conditions thoroughly before hitting the waves.

On the eastern side of the island, Honolii Cove, two miles north of Hilo, is popular. In Kona, favorite surfing locales include Kahaluu Beach in Keauhou and Banyans near the banyan tree north of White Sands Beach.

White Sands Beach is also one of the best places on the Kona Coast for boogie boarding and bodysurfing.

Windsurfing

The Big Island is not a real hot spot for windsurfing. Most windsurfers head to Anaehoomalu Bay in Waikoloa, which has some of the island's better wind and water conditions. You can rent boards from Ocean Sports (☎ 885-5555), the beach hut in front of the Royal Waikoloan, for $20 an hour and get a one-hour lesson for $45. The best winds are usually between 10 am and 2 pm.

Kawaihae Harbor and Hilo Bay are other spots that occasionally see some windsurfing activity.

Diving

The Big Island has excellent diving on the leeward Kona and Kohala coasts. Overall, the best conditions are in spring and summer, although there are good, calm dive spots year round.

The Kona Coast has many good shore-diving areas, including steep nearshore drop-offs with lava tubes, caves and diverse marine life. Diving is far more limited on the Hilo side, where the season is basically from April to September.

Kona has lots of dive operations. The cost of one-tank dives averages about $60, two-tank dives about $80. Several places offer introductory dives, night dives and certification courses.

One popular dive spot is Red Hill, an underwater cinder cone about 10 miles south of Kona. It has beautiful lava formations, including ledges and lots of honey-combed lava tubes nicely lit by streaks of sunlight. There are also coral pinnacles and many brightly colored nudibranchs.

Another good spot is off Kaiwi Point, south of Honokohau Harbor, where there are some respectable drop-offs and huge eagle rays, sea turtles and large fish. Nearby is Suck-em-up, a couple of lava tubes that you can swim into and let the swell pull you through, like an amusement park ride.

Kealakekua Bay has good coral and marine life in a protected cove that's calm all year round. All in all, there are about 40 boat dives along the Kona Coast, including an airplane wreck off Keahole Point.

Dive Operations The more established dive operations include the following.

Jack's Diving Locker (☎ 329-7585, 800-345-4807), 75-5819 Alii Drive, Kailua-Kona, HI 96740, at the Coconut Grove Marketplace, is a small, friendly operation and one of the best for introductory dives.

Dive Makai (☎ 329-2025), Box 2955, Kailua-Kona, HI 96745, is a personable little operation run by husband-and-wife team Tom Shockley and Lisa Choquette. They are conservation oriented and have a good word-of-mouth reputation.

Sea Paradise Scuba (☎ 322-2500, 800-322-5662), Box 580, Kailua-Kona, HI 96745, is also environmentally oriented. They're based at Keauhou Bay and tend to head south, often to Red Hill or Kealakekua Bay.

Hawaiian Divers (☎ 329-5662, 800-356-2243), Box 3060, Kailua-Kona, HI 96740, at King Kamehameha's Kona Beach Hotel, offers technical (mixed-gas) diving in addition to standard dives.

Eco-Adventures of Kona (☎ 329-7116, 800-949-3483; ecodive@ilhawaii.net), 75-5744 Alii Drive, Kailua-Kona, HI 96740, has an interesting night dive with the manta rays off the Kona Surf Hotel.

Kona Coast Divers (☎ 329-8802), 75-5614 Palani Rd, Kailua-Kona, HI 96740, is professionally run and one of the largest operations.

Kohala Divers (☎ 882-7774), Box 44940, Kawaihae, HI 96743, at the shopping center in Kawaihae, is a good operation in the Kohala area. They organize trips up the Kohala Coast.

Nautilus Dive Center (☎ 935-6939), 382 Kamehameha Ave, Hilo, HI 96720, organizes dives in the Hilo area.

Live-Aboard Boat The *Kona Aggressor* (☎ 329-8182, 800-344-5662), Live-Dive Pacific, 74-5588 Pawai Place, Building F, Kailua-Kona, HI 96740, is a 110-foot live-aboard dive boat that accommodates up to 10 guests. All-inclusive one-week trips cost $1795, starting and ending each Saturday.

Dive Club The Kona Reefers Dive Club meets on the third Friday of the month and holds shore dives (and sometimes boat dives) open to the public at 10 am on the third Sunday of the month. For more information, call the club's founder, Roy Damron (☎ 325-5422).

Snorkeling

Snorkelers will find some good spots south of Kailua-Kona. The area's most popular easy-access snorkeling haunt is Kahaluu Beach in Keauhou, which is teeming with colorful fish and makes a good place for beginners to try out the sport. The north side of the Place of Refuge is another fine drive-up snorkeling spot, although it's best suited for those with experience. While it takes a hike, horseback ride or boat to reach, there's terrific snorkeling in the calm, clear, 30-foot-deep waters near

Captain Cook's monument at the north end of Kealakekua Bay.

Snorkeling Cruises The most popular snorkeling cruise is to Kealakekua Bay. Prices include snorkeling gear, beverages and food.

Fairwind (☎ 322-2788, 800-677-9461) makes trips to Kealakekua Bay aboard a 50-foot trimaran. They leave from Keauhou Bay, which allows for more snorkeling time (about 2½ hours) than other boats. The 4½-hour tours depart at 9 am daily and cost $69 for adults and $38 for children under 17.

Captain Zodiac (☎ 329-3199, 800-422-7824) does four-hour tours aboard bouncy Zodiac rubber rafts. Departure is from Honokohau Harbor at 8 am and 1 pm daily, with pick-up possible at Kailua and Keauhou piers. The cost of $62 for adults, $52 for children ages four to 12, includes about 40 minutes of snorkeling time at Kealakekua Bay followed by visits to sea caves.

Kamanu Charters (☎ 329-2021) takes a 36-foot catamaran out of Honokohau Harbor to snorkel at Pawai Bay, just north of the Old Kona Airport. They take a maximum of 24 people, motoring down and using the sail on the way back. The 3¼-hour trips start at 9 am and cost $39 for adults, $21 for children 12 and under. They also offer a two-hour afternoon sail during the whale-watching season for $25 for adults, $15 for children.

Snorkelers can sometimes tag along with divers on dive tours if space is available. The cost is usually around $30.

Snorkeling Gear Rentals Snorkel Bob's (☎ 329-0770), off Alii Drive by the Royal Kona Resort in Kailua, has snorkel set rentals starting at $15 a week. They also rent boogie boards and corrective-lens masks.

Kona Water Sports (☎ 329-1593) at Banyan Court in Kailua rents snorkel sets and boogie boards from $8 per day, $18 per week.

The beach hut at King Kamehameha's Kona Beach Hotel in Kailua rents snorkel

sets and boogie boards for $7 per day, $15 per week.

Many of the dive shops also rent snorkel gear, though prices tend to be higher.

Snuba If you haven't tried it before, Kealakekua Bay is a great place to experience snuba, which is a sort of scuba diving for snorkelers. It's a tankless operation, with an air hose attached to an air-filled raft that floats on the surface above you. Generally you get about 30 minutes underwater before you run out of air. It's currently available only on the Fairwind snorkeling cruise and costs $45 plus the price of the cruise.

Fishing

Kona is a world-renowned deep-sea fishing spot for Pacific blue marlin, a spectacular fighting fish with a long sword. Most of the world records are held in Kona, with at least one marlin topping 1000 pounds reeled in each year. Kona is also known for its record catches of ahi (yellowfin tuna) and spearfish.

Near the Chart House restaurant at Kailua's Waterfront Row, there's an interesting 'Granders Wall' lined with photos of anglers next to their 1000-pound marlin catches.

You can watch the boats come in and see the fish weighed at Kailua Pier and Honokohau Harbor from around 11:30 am for the morning charters and from around 3:30 pm for the afternoon and full-day charters.

Kona has more than 100 charter fishing boats. The standard cost is $80 to $100 per person to go out for half a day, sharing a boat with three to five other fishers. You can also charter a whole boat and take up to six people at a cost of $225 to $400 for half a day, $300 to $800 for a full day, depending upon the boat. You might want to first take a look at the tourist magazines, which often advertise a few renegade boats at discount rates – though they'll need to be booked directly with the skippers. Prices include all fishing equipment but not food or drink.

The following centers each book numerous boats.

Kona Charter Skippers Association, 75-5663 Palani Rd, Kailua-Kona, HI 96740 (☎ 329-3600, 800-762-7546)

Kona Activities Center, Box 70, Kailua-Kona, HI 96745 (☎ 329-3171, 800-367-5288)

Kona Coast Activities, Box 5397, Kailua-Kona, HI 96745 (☎ 329-7529, 800-367-5105)

There are a number of fishing tournaments held in Kona; the granddaddy of them all is the Hawaiian International Billfish Tournament, held in early August and accompanied by a week of festive activities.

Hiking

There is excellent hiking all around the Big Island. Some of the best and most varied hikes are in Hawaii Volcanoes National Park, where trails lead across steaming crater floors, through dense native forests and up to the peak of Mauna Loa.

On the northern tip of the island there are steep coastal cliffs and deep valleys reaching down from the Kohala Mountains. From the road's end on the northwest side of the range, it's a 30-minute hike down to the beach at the bottom of Pololu Valley. On the southeast side you can take a 30-minute walk down into verdant Waipio Valley or backpack deep into remote Waimanu Valley.

North of Kona, you can hike in from the highway to secluded beaches, or explore portions of ancient footpaths and petroglyph fields. Efforts are under way by Na Ala Hele, a state-sponsored group composed mostly of volunteers, to eventually re-establish the entire 50-mile historic trail system that once ran between Kailua and Kawaihae. Mauna Lani Resort and Lapakahi State Park have easy trails, marked with interpretive plaques, around ancient fishponds and through abandoned villages.

South of Kona, a trail leads to the spot where Captain Cook died at Kealakekua Bay. In the center of the island, a strenuous hike leads to the summit of Mauna Kea,

while on the slopes below, Kalopa State Park has short, easy forest trails.

All hikes are detailed in their respective sections.

Guided Hikes The Kona Hiking Club has hikes open to all trekkers on the first Saturday and third Thursday of each month. They vary in both location and difficulty. Some hikes go into the mountains, but most take in a beach for picnics and swimming; the majority are on the west side of the island. Hikers meet at the Palani parking lot in Kailua, opposite Kona Ranch House restaurant, and usually carpool to the site. Announcements are published in the Sunday edition of *West Hawaii Today*.

Cycling

The Big Island Mountain Bike Association (☎ 961-4452) sponsors fun rides and trail-maintenance outings. In conjunction with the county, the group has published a free brochure detailing off-road trails that are open to the public. These range from easy jaunts along beaches to a hardy 45-mile circle road around Mauna Kea. The brochure can be picked up at island tourist offices and bike shops.

For bike-rental information, see Bicycle & Motor Scooter in the Getting Around section of this chapter.

Horseback Riding

Kings' Trail Rides O'Kona (☎ 323-2388) in Kealakekua takes horseback riders down the Captain Cook Trail to Kealakekua Bay for lunch and snorkeling. As the trail is a bit rough, riders must be experienced. There's a maximum of four riders per outing. The cost is $95 per person.

Kohala Naalapa (☎ 889-0022), at the intersection of Hwy 250 and Kohala Ranch Rd, has 2½-hour trail rides that cross the pastures of Kahua Ranch in Kohala and offer fine views of the coast; they depart at 9 am and cost $75. A 1½-hour afternoon ride is available in the same area; it leaves at 1 pm and costs $55.

Paniolo Riding Adventures (☎ 889-5354), on Hwy 250 in Kohala, has 2½-hour horseback rides for $85 and four-hour rides for $125. They'll select the horse according to the rider's experience, but they use real riding horses, not trail horses, and you can canter with the lead wrangler.

Dahana Ranch Roughriders (☎ 885-0057), off the Old Mamalahoa Hwy between Waimea and Honokaa, is owned and operated by native Hawaiians. Horses cross the open range of a working cattle ranch rather than following trails. Rides are by appointment only at 9 and 11 am and 1 and 3 pm daily; they last 1½ hours, cost $55 and are open to both novice and experienced riders ages four and up. Also, with a minimum of four people, a 'city slicker adventure' can be arranged at 3 pm in which riders help drive about 100 head of cattle; it takes around 2½ hours and costs $125.

Indian Summer Trail Rides (☎ 322-1818) has one-hour, 1½-hour and two-hour rides on gentle horses in the Kona area for $39 an hour.

For horseback rides in Waipio Valley, see the Waipio section.

Tennis

Many county parks on the Big Island have tennis courts. The Old Kona Airport Beach Park in Kailua-Kona has four lighted outdoor tennis courts, and if you show up with racket in hand, there's a fair chance you'll find a partner.

Hilo's Hoolulu Complex has four lighted outdoor courts and three indoor courts. The indoor courts are open daily from 8 am to 10 pm (to 6 pm on Saturdays) and cost $2 an hour per court before 4 pm, $4 an hour after; reservations are required. There's no fee or reservation system for the outdoor courts.

Other county courts that are lighted for night play are at Kailua Playground in Kailua, Greenwell Park in Captain Cook, Waimea Park in Waimea, Lincoln Park in Hilo, Papaaloa Park in the North Hilo district, Honokaa Park in Honokaa, Kamehameha Park in Kapaau, and Naalehu Park and Pahala School in the Kau district. All are free to the public.

Many of the larger hotels and resorts have tennis courts for their guests; some are also available to nonguests. The Royal Kona Resort (☎ 329-3111) in Kailua-Kona opens its four courts to the public for $4 per person per hour ($5 at night when it's lit) and rents rackets for $3.

Kings Sport & Racquet Club (☎ 329-2911) at King Kamehameha's Kona Beach Hotel in Kailua-Kona has four courts (two lighted) open to the public, charges $5 per person per day and rents rackets for $5.

In the Waikoloa area, the Mauna Kea Beach Hotel (☎ 882-7222) has 13 courts open to the public; the cost is $10 per person per day and rackets rent for $5. The Orchid at Mauna Lani (☎ 885-2000) has 10 courts open to the public; the cost is $12 per person per day and rackets rent for $5.

The Mauna Lani Racquet Club (☎ 885-7765) has 10 courts, holds various clinics and round-robin tournaments and has even hosted a Davis Cup match. Court fees are $8 per person per hour, but the courts are only open to club members or guests of the Mauna Lani Resort.

Golf

The Big Island has more than a dozen golf courses, including some world-class courses in the Waikoloa area that are laid out on top of lava flows.

All of the Big Island golf courses are 18-hole courses, except for the nine-hole Naniloa Country Club.

The island's top courses are: Mauna Kea Golf Course (☎ 882-7222) near Mauna Kea Beach; Francis Ii Brown South Course and North Course at the Mauna Lani Resort (☎ 885-6655); Waikoloa Golf Club (☎ 885-6060) and Waikoloa Kings' Golf Course (☎ 885-4647) at Waikoloa Beach Resort; Hapuna Golf Course (☎ 882-1035) at Hapuna Beach Prince Hotel; and the new Four Seasons Hulalai Golf Club (☎ 325-8000), which is open to hotel guests only with greens fees of $105.

Nonresort guests are charged $150 to $170 at each of the Mauna Lani courses, $135 at Mauna Kea, $135 at Hapuna and $95 at the two Waikoloa Resort courses. However, you can beat these fees substantially by waiting until 3 pm to tee off – fees at the Mauna Lani courses drop to $55, for example, while those at Mauna Kea drop to $85. All of the greens fees at these resorts include mandatory carts. Resort guests get discounts ranging from 20% to 50% off the standard rates.

For the island's most reasonably priced turf, the 18-hole Hilo Municipal Golf Course (☎ 959-7711), at 340 Haihai St in Hilo, charges $20 on weekdays, $25 on weekends and holidays, plus $2 for a pull cart.

Other courses around the Big Island include the following.

Kona Country Club and Alii Country Club – Keauhou; the standard cost is $100, including cart, but discounts are available during off hours (☎ 322-2595)
Makalei Hawaii Country Club – off Hwy 190 northeast of Kailua; the standard cost is $110, including cart, but it drops to $50 after 1:30 pm and all day on Wednesday and Thursday (☎ 325-6625)
Naniloa Country Club – Hilo; the cost is $30 on weekdays, $40 on weekends and holidays, plus a cart fee of $7 (☎ 935-3000)
SeaMountain Golf Course – Punaluu; the cost of $40 includes cart (☎ 928-6222)
Volcano Golf and Country Club – Hawaii Volcanoes National Park; the cost of $60 includes cart (☎ 967-7331)
Waikoloa Village Golf Club – Waikoloa village; the cost is $55 before 1 pm and $40 after, including cart (☎ 883-9621)

Skiing & Snowboarding
Skiing in Hawaii is primarily a curiosity event. Snow does fall each winter on the upper slopes of Mauna Kea, though the timing is unpredictable. The ski season usually starts anywhere from early January to late February and can run for several months. There are bad years when there's virtually no skiing and good years when the season can extend through June.

Skiing Mauna Kea is not your standard sort of skiing. The altitude can be tough and the slopes can have exposed rocks. There are no ski lodges, lifts or other facilities.

When there's snow, Ski Guides Hawaii (☎ 885-4188), Box 1954, Kamuela, HI 96743, based in Waimea, can provide a full day of skiing for $180 per person. The cost

includes use of ski equipment, transportation to Mauna Kea from Waimea, lunch and a 4WD shuttle service up the mountain after each run. If you prefer snowboarding, the cost is $190.

Sporting Competitions
The renowned Ironman Triathlon, held in Kailua-Kona each October, combines a 2.4-mile ocean swim, 112-mile bike race and 26.2-mile marathon into one exhaustive endurance event. Fifteen hundred men and women from 50 countries compete in the Ironman each year, with worldwide media coverage. The Ironman usually takes place on the Saturday nearest the full moon, so that late-finishing racers won't have to run along the highway in the dark. The event begins and ends near Kailua Pier, starting at 7 am. The first triathletes cross the finish line shortly after 3 pm and the other contenders follow throughout the afternoon and evening, with the finish line remaining open until midnight. For information on the race, contact Ironman Triathlon World Championship (☎ 329-0063), 75-127 Lunapule Rd, Suite 11, Kailua-Kona, HI 96740.

The Kilauea Volcano Wilderness Marathon and Rim Runs are held at Hawaii Volcanoes National Park in July. There are three separate races: a 10-mile run around the rim of Kilauea's caldera, a 5.5-mile race that goes down into Kilauea Iki Crater and a 26.2-mile marathon through the Kau Desert. For information, contact the Volcano Art Center (☎ 967-8222), Box 104, Hawaii Volcanoes National Park, HI 96718.

Organized Tours
Roberts Hawaii (☎ 329-1688) and Polynesian Adventure Tours (☎ 329-8008) have day-long circle-island bus tours that include Hawaii Volcanoes National Park for $50 to $60.

If you're in Hilo, Arnott's Lodge (☎ 969-7097), the local hostel, offers recommendable $35 day tours on a rotating schedule to Mauna Kea, Puna, South Point (and Green Sands Beach) and Hawaii Volcanoes National Park. These are geared for active people who prefer hiking and swimming in their outings to sitting on a bus.

Information on tours into Waipio Valley or up to Mauna Kea summit is detailed in those sections.

Helicopter & Biplane The most popular Big Island helicopter tour is a flight over Kilauea Volcano – especially when the volcano is acting up.

The cost largely depends on your departure point. Flights from the Volcano Golf Course or Hilo are about $125, from Kona about $200 and from Waikoloa about $275. However, as it's a competitive market, it's worth checking the free tourist magazines for discount coupons and calling around to compare prices.

Companies include Volcano Heli-Tours (☎ 967-7578), Hawaii Helicopters (☎ 329-4700, 800-346-2403), Mauna Kea Helicopters (☎ 885-6400, 800-400-4354), Io Aviation (☎ 935-3031, 800-942-3031), Blue Hawaiian Helicopters (☎ 961-5600, 800-247-5444), Safari Helicopters (☎ 969-1259, 800-326-3356) and Kenai Helicopters (☎ 885-5833, 800-622-3144).

Classic Aviation Corporation (☎ 329-8687, 800-695-8100) has 40-minute biplane tours over the volcano for $150 for one passenger, $99 per person for two.

Keep in mind that the volcano area is often rainy even when it's sunny in Kona. If it's raining, it's not worth going up, so call first if you're coming from the Kona side to see what the weather's like.

Dinner Cruise Capt Beans' Cruises (☎ 329-2955), the high-profile boat with the yellow lights and orange sails, has a touristy dinner cruise in the evening for ages 21 and over. It leaves at 5:15 pm from Kailua Pier, takes two hours and costs $49, including meal, drink and a Polynesian show.

Whale Watching While the best whale watching is off Maui, you can spot whales from the Big Island as well. The season for humpback whales, which are the biggest attraction, usually starts around January and runs through March or April. However,

pilot, sperm, beaked and false killer whales and five dolphin species can be found in Kona waters all year round.

Marine mammal biologist Dan McSweeney of Whale Watch (☎ 322-0028) leads three-hour whale-watching cruises aboard a 38-foot boat leaving Honokohau Harbor at 9 am daily; when business is brisk there's also a 1 pm tour. Hydrophones allow passengers to hear whale songs. The cost is $40 for adults, $30 for children ages 11 and under. The tours have a 24-hour nonrefundable cancellation policy.

A couple of the snorkeling tour boats also do whale watches during humpback season, so it's worth taking a look at listings in the tourist magazines.

Submarine & Glassbottom Boats Atlantis Submarines (☎ 329-6626, 800-548-6262) gives 45-minute submarine rides that dive down about 100 feet in a coral crevice in front of the Royal Kona Resort. The sub has 26 portholes, carries 46 passengers and departs on the hour between 10 am and 2 pm. The outing lasts two hours, including the boat ride to and from the sub, and costs $79 for adults, $39 for children.

A cheaper option is *Nautilus II* (☎ 326-2003), a 34-passenger semi-submersible. Passengers sit in a glass-windowed room beneath the surface of the water and look out at the fish as the boat edges along the reef. It leaves from Kailua Pier daily at 9:30, 10:30 and 11:30 am and 1:30 and 2:30 pm; the tour takes about 50 minutes and costs $40 for adults, $25 for children.

Cheaper still is Kona Reef Tour's (☎ 322-3102) straightforward 16-passenger glassbottom boat, which leaves from Kailua Pier and circles around the bay for about an hour. There are four trips a day and the cost is $20 for adults, $10 for children.

ACCOMMODATIONS

The Big Island has a wide range of accommodation options. As the island is so big, it's worth considering moving around and exploring from a couple of different bases.

Most of the island's accommodations are centered around Kailua-Kona, with the majority of the rooms in condos – though some of these are run like hotels with a front desk and daily rates. If you're staying a week or more, condos are usually a better deal than hotels.

At the bottom end, Kailua has a hostel-style place with dormitory beds. Otherwise, the cheapest places in the Kona area are mauka of Kailua in small local hotels in the towns of Holualoa and Captain Cook.

The Waikoloa area, north of Kailua, has the island's most expensive beach resorts. The Mauna Kea and Mauna Lani resorts attract wealthy tourists who want an elegant hideaway and not much excitement. Kona Village is even more low-key, playing out the getaway fantasy in comfortable Polynesian-style thatched huts, while the Hilton Waikoloa Village stands in sharp contrast with splashy high-tech toys and constant titillation.

Rainy Hilo doesn't see a great many visitors. While choices aren't as numerous as you might expect for a city, there are some good bottom-end to mid-range options, including a friendly hostel-like lodge.

In the uplands, Volcano and Waimea have pleasant B&Bs as well as a couple of larger hostelries. There's a scattering of other B&Bs and guesthouses around the island, including some in fine country settings. These types of accommodations have become increasingly popular throughout the Big Island and represent some of the best mid-range values.

Unless otherwise noted, the rates given in this chapter are the same for either singles or doubles and don't include the 10.17% tax.

Camping

At first glance, the list of Big Island campgrounds seems to read like some sort of 'Camping Guide to Hell': Laupahoehoe Beach, where a village was washed away in a tidal wave; Halape Beach, where an earthquake sank the shoreline 30 feet; and Kamoamoa Beach, which is now buried under a lava flow.

Despite all that, there's really little to worry about. Hawaii's lava isn't the rushing type that sweeps through campgrounds overnight, and tsunami speakers have been set up to warn of approaching tidal waves.

Some of the best and safest camping is found in Hawaii Volcanoes National Park. More detailed descriptions of specific sites can be found throughout the chapter.

State Parks Tent camping is allowed at Kalopa State Park, which has good facilities and a caretaker, as well as at MacKenzie and Manuka state parks, both of which have little to recommend them. There are no fees but permits are required.

In addition, there are A-frame shelters at Hapuna Beach and self-contained housekeeping cabins at Mauna Kea, Kalopa and Kilauea.

The booking system is computerized, and reservations can be made at state park offices on any island. The Big Island office (☎ 974-6200) is at 75 Aupuni St (Box 936), Hilo, HI 96721. The maximum length of stay at any state park is five nights a month.

The A-frame shelters at Hapuna Beach are one-room set-ups with screened windows, a picnic table and wooden sleeping platforms for up to four people. Shared facilities include restrooms, cold showers and a pavilion with refrigerator, electric range and sink. Although the shelters are elementary and offer little privacy, the cost is just $20 per night.

Cabin prices at Kilauea and Mauna Kea are $45 for up to four people, while prices at Kalopa are $55 for up to eight people. These cabins have kitchens with limited cookware and bathrooms with hot showers.

The cabins and shelters are popular with island families and commonly require booking well in advance. Cancellations do occur, however, and if you're flexible with dates, you might be able to get one without advance reservations.

County Beach Parks The county allows camping at 13 of its beach parks: James Kealoha, Kolekole, Laupahoehoe and Onekahakaha, all near Hilo; Isaac Hale in Puna; Spencer, Keokea, Kapaa, Mahukona, Hookena and Miloli'i, all on the western side of the island; and Whittington and Punaluu, both in Kau.

With the exception of Spencer, which is patrolled by a security guard, all of the county parks can be rough and noisy areas, as they're popular among late-night drinkers.

Permits are required and can be obtained by mail or in person from the Department of Parks & Recreation (☎ 961-8311), 25 Aupuni St, Hilo, HI 96720. Office hours are 7:45 am to 4:30 pm Monday to Friday, but don't cut it too close to closing time.

You can also make reservations by phone through the Hilo office and then pick up the permit at Park & Recreation branch offices around the island. In Kailua-Kona, the office is at Hale Halawai Park (☎ 329-5277), which is open weekdays from 7:45 am to 4:30 pm. At Captain Cook, the office is at the Yano Center (☎ 323-3060), opposite the Manago Hotel; it's generally staffed from noon to 2 pm, but it's best to call first. In Waimea, the office is at the community center (☎ 885-5454) at Waimea Park; it's officially staffed from 8:30 to 10:30 am but sometimes is open longer.

Daily fees are $1 for adults and 50¢ for children ages 13 to 17 (free for children 12 and under). Camping is allowed for up to two weeks in each park, except in June, July and August, when it's limited to one week in each park.

Only about half of the county parks, generally those near towns, have drinking water. Some of the others have catchment water that can be treated for drinking, while others have only brackish water that can be used for showers but is unsuitable for drinking.

Campers should also be aware that beach parks in the Puna and Kau areas are sometimes closed during winter storms.

Hawaii Volcanoes National Park The Hawaii Volcanoes National Park section of this chapter has details on the park's two drive-up campgrounds and on trail shelters and tenting sites for backcountry hikers. They're all free and rarely filled.

Camping Supplies Pacific Rent-All (☎ 935-2974), 1080 Kilauea Ave, Hilo, HI 96720, rents out simple pup tents for $8/30/60 a day/week/month, larger tents for $26/52/156 and medium-weight sleeping bags for $7/20/39. The shop also rents Coleman stoves, lanterns, water jugs and other supplies. It's open from 7 am to 5 pm on weekdays, 8 am to 5 pm on Saturdays and 9 to 11 am on Sundays. If you need gear for any length of time, you might be better off buying it at one of the discount department stores, such as Kmart or Wal-Mart in Kailua-Kona or Sears in Hilo.

ENTERTAINMENT

The Big Island entertainment scene is largely centered around the hotels in the Kona and Waikoloa areas. Most offer Hawaiian music of some type, often duos strumming guitars in the early evening, and a few hotels have dance bands, jazz groups and nightclubs as well.

Although it's a more local scene, Hilo also has a few places with music and dancing. In addition, each spring Hilo hosts the week-long Merrie Monarch Festival, the state's largest hula festival, which starts on Easter Sunday and features hula troupes from all the islands.

First-run feature films are shown at Kress Cinemas, Prince Kuhio Plaza and Waiakea Shopping Plaza in Hilo and at Hualalai Theatres and Kona Marketplace Cinemas in Kailua.

For the latest entertainment listings, check *West Hawaii Today*.

Luaus

The Kona Village Resort has one of Hawaii's more authentic luaus and offers a chance to rub shoulders with the rich and famous. It's held on Friday nights and costs $63. As the luau is complimentary to all of the resort's guests, seating for the general public is limited and sometimes books out weeks in advance.

In Kona, King Kamehameha's Kona Beach Hotel holds a popular luau on Sundays, Tuesdays, Wednesdays and Thursdays; the cost is $49. In Waikoloa, the Royal Waikoloan has a luau on Sundays and Wednesdays for $49.

All Big Island luaus include a dinner buffet, cocktails and a Polynesian show.

THINGS TO BUY

Kona coffee and macadamia nuts are the Big Island's most common souvenir items. If you're buying coffee, note that 'Kona blend' is only 10% Kona coffee, so if you want the real thing, make sure what you pick up is labeled 100%. Prices change with the market, but Kona coffee is one of the more expensive gourmet beans, priced from around $10 a pound.

Supermarkets and discount stores, such as Longs Drugs, usually have the best deals on coffee and macadamia nuts.

Shops selling local arts and crafts are plentiful. More notable ones include the Volcano Art Center in Hawaii Volcanoes National Park and the handful of galleries in the hillside village of Holualoa.

GETTING THERE & AWAY
Air

The Big Island has two main airports, in Kona and Hilo. While there are frequent flights into both airports, Kona is the busier of the two and even has a few direct flights from California with United Airlines and a twice-weekly flight from Japan.

Hawaiian Airlines (☎ 326-5615) and Aloha Airlines (☎ 935-5771) connect both airports with the other main islands. Fares on both Aloha and Hawaiian are currently $69 for flights between the Big Island and any other Hawaiian island.

Mahalo Air (☎ 800-462-4256 from the mainland, 800-277-8333 in Hawaii) flies between Honolulu and Kona an average of eight times a day and has a once-daily flight between Kona and Maui; one-way fares are $55.

There's also a small airport in Waimea that has limited service by Trans Air (☎ 800-634-2094), a little commuter airline that flies twice a day between Waimea and Honolulu. The fare is $74 one way.

More information on inter-island air travel, including discounted tickets and air passes, is in the Getting Around chapter in the front of the book.

Lava Wasteland?

Flying into Keahole-Kona Airport can be a shock if you're expecting to see tropical greenery and waving palm trees. Instead, the view from the airplane looks more like a black lava wasteland, as if the island had been paved over in asphalt. Don't panic! This is but one face of the Big Island – and even here, if you look closer, you can catch a glimpse of some fine secluded white-sand beaches squeezed between the lava and the turquoise waters. And of course once you get on the ground there's a great deal more to the island than lava landscapes . . . . ■

Hilo Airport The Hilo Airport is off Hwy 11, just under a mile south of its intersection with Hwy 19. It has a visitor information booth, newsstand, lei stand, restaurant, gift shops, taxi stand and car rental booths.

Kona Airport The Keahole-Kona Airport is on Hwy 19, about seven miles north of Kailua-Kona. It has a simple restaurant, car rental booths, visitor information booth, newsstands and a couple of gift shops. For a relatively busy airport, it's surprisingly casual and all open-air (there's not enough rain to justify sealing it up!).

GETTING AROUND
To/From the Airport

At both the Hilo and Kona airports, taxis can be picked up curbside and you'll find car rental booths lined up together on the road just outside the arrival areas.

Shuttle bus services from the Kona airport pop up from time to time, so you might want to inquire at the information booth – don't expect much, however, as the last (now defunct) shuttle service charged nearly as much as a taxi.

Bus

Hele-On is the county public bus. Service between Kona and Hilo is along the northern route of the Hawaii Belt Rd once in each direction Monday to Saturday. The bus leaves the South Kona town of Kealia at 5:45 am. Stops along the way include the Kona Surf Resort in Keauhou at 6:25 am, Waldenbooks in Kailua at 6:45 am, Parker Ranch Shopping Center in Waimea at 8:05 am and the Dairy Queen in Honokaa at 8:30 am. It arrives in Hilo at the Mooheau bus terminal at 9:45 am.

The return trip leaves Hilo at 1:30 pm and arrives in Kailua at 4:30 pm. One-way fares are $5.25 between Kailua and Hilo, $3 between Kailua and Waimea and $4.50 between Waimea and Hilo.

Drivers accept only the exact fare. Bus tickets, which are valid for $7.50 worth of travel, can be purchased in sheets of 10 for $6.75. Luggage and backpacks cost $1 extra per piece.

There are four other routes: Pahoa to Hilo, Honokaa to Hilo, Waiohinu to Hilo via Volcano, and Hilo to the Waikoloa hotels. Each route runs at least once a day in each direction Monday to Friday. The Waikoloa bus, which leaves Hilo early in the morning for the Waikoloa area hotels and returns in late afternoon, is mostly used by commuting hotel workers. However, if you're staying in Hilo and feel up for a 5:30 am departure, then it's good for a day's outing at the beach.

There's limited service around the city of Hilo for 75¢ per ride, but it mainly connects the downtown area with the outlying malls and has little practical value for most visitors.

You can get detailed schedule information by calling ☎ 935-8241 on weekdays between 7:45 am and 4:30 pm.

For information on shuttle service between Kailua and Keauhou, see Getting Around in the Kailua section.

For information on commercial bus tours, see Organized Tours under Activities earlier in this chapter.

Taxi
The taxi flag-down fee is $2 and it costs $1.70 a mile after that. The approximate fare from the Keahole-Kona Airport is $16 to Kailua, $35 to Waikoloa.

Car
The following companies have car rental booths at both the Kona and Hilo airports.

	Kona Airport	Hilo Airport
Alamo	☎ 329-8896	☎ 961-3343
Avis	☎ 327-3000	☎ 935-1290
Budget	☎ 329-8511	☎ 935-6878
Dollar	☎ 329-2744	☎ 961-6059
Hertz	☎ 329-3566	☎ 935-2896
National	☎ 329-1674	☎ 935-0891

More information on car rentals, including toll-free numbers, is in the Getting Around chapter in the front of the book.

Harper Car & Truck Rentals, at 1690 Kamehameha Ave in Hilo (☎ 969-1478) and on Kuakini Hwy in Kailua-Kona (☎ 329-6688), has 4WD vehicles adjusted for use at Mauna Kea's high altitude. Unlike other rental agencies, Harper puts no restrictions on going to the summit, although Waipio Valley remains off-limits. Isuzu Troopers and Isuzu Rodeos cost $88 a day, $527 a week; even if you purchase the optional CDW ($19), there's still a $5000 deductible.

Hilo is a good place to gas up, as gas is cheaper there than in Kona.

Bicycle & Motor Scooter
Dave's Triathlon Shop (☎ 329-4522), in the rear of Kona Square on Alii Drive in Kailua, rents quality mountain, cross-training and road bikes for $15 to $25 a day and from $60 a week. Dave also rents bike racks that can hold up to three bikes for $5 a day.

Hawaiian Pedals (☎ 329-2294), in the Kona Inn Shopping Village in Kailua, has mountain bikes for $20/70 a day/week, performance bikes for $25 a day, tandem bikes for $35 a day and car bike racks for $5 a day.

DJ's Rentals (☎ 329-1700), in a kiosk opposite King Kamehameha's Kona Beach Hotel in Kailua, rents mopeds for $8/30 an hour/day and two-person scooters for $15/50.

As Kona is the center of activity for the Ironman Triathlon, there are a few bike shops that sell and repair high-caliber equipment. Two such places are Dave's Triathlon Shop, mentioned above, and B&L Bike & Sports (☎ 329-3309) in Kailua's industrial area.

BIG ISLAND

Kona

Kona literally means 'leeward'. The Kona Coast refers to the dry, sunny west coast of the Big Island. However, to make matters a little more confusing, the name Kona is also used to refer to Kailua, the largest town on the Kona Coast. The town's name is compounded Kailua-Kona by the post office and other officialdom to avoid confusion with Kailua on Oahu.

The weather is so consistent on this side of the island that the local paper usually just alternates two forecasts: 'Sunny morning. Afternoon clouds with upslope showers' or 'Sunny morning. Cloudy afternoon with showers over the slopes'.

The afternoon showers that hit the higher slopes rarely touch the coastline just a couple of miles below. Because it sees so little rain, Kona is also dubbed the Gold Coast. It's a good bet for a sunny vacation any time of the year.

KAILUA

In the 19th century Kailua-Kona was a favorite vacation retreat for Hawaiian royalty. These days, it's the largest vacation destination on the Big Island.

It's got a lot to make it a drawing card. The weather is good, the setting on the leeward side of Mt Hualalai is pretty, and it has both ancient Hawaiian and missionary-era historic sites. Even though the town's period character is a bit stifled by trinket shops and mini-malls, it's still a fun place to poke around.

There are lots of places to stay and eat, as well as activities ranging from world-class deep-sea fishing to snorkeling cruises. Kailua is centrally located and makes a good base for exploring the entire Kona coast.

Most of Kona's condos are lined up along Alii Drive, the five-mile coastal road that runs from the town center at Kailua Bay south to Keauhou. This strip sees a lot of power walkers and joggers, particularly in the early morning hours, but the hottest activity occurs here in October when it serves as the finish line of the world-famous Ironman Triathlon.

Kailua has a few swimming, snorkeling and surfing spots, although the island's best beaches are up the coast to the north.

Information

Tourist Office The Hawaii Visitors Bureau (☎ 329-7787) is in the Kona Plaza. It's open from 8 am to noon and 1 to 4:30 pm Monday to Friday.

Money Both the Bank of Hawaii at the Hualalai Rd and Kuakini Hwy intersection and the First Hawaiian Bank at the Lanihau Center have full-service branches with ATMs.

Post & Communications The main post office is in the Lanihau Center; it's open weekdays from 8 am to 4:30 pm and Saturdays from 8 am to noon. There's also a small contract post office at the Kona Inn Shopping Village that's open weekdays from 9 am to 4:30 pm and Saturdays from 10 am to 3 pm.

Zac's Business Center (☎ 329-0006; fax 329-1021) at the North Kona Shopping Center has computers with Internet access from $6 an hour. You can check your email for a flat $3 rate, receive faxes for 50¢ a page and send faxes at varying rates.

Books & Newspapers Middle Earth Bookshoppe in the Kona Plaza and Waldenbooks in the Lanihau Center are both well-stocked bookstores with Hawaiiana and general travel sections.

KTA Supermarket and Resort Sundries at King Kamehameha's Kona Beach Hotel both sell a good selection of newspapers from the mainland. The local daily, *West Hawaii Today*, and the Hilo and Honolulu papers are available at numerous places around town.

Travel Agents Cut Rate Tickets, in the Kona Coast Shopping Center, sells discounted tickets for inter-island travel.

Laundry There are coin laundries in the North Kona Shopping Center and on Kuakini

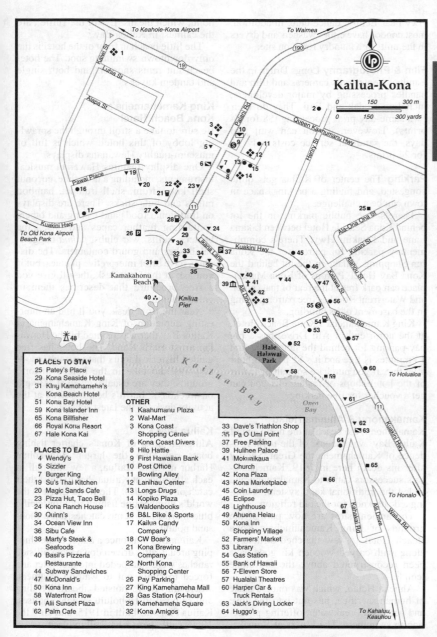

Kailua-Kona

0   150   300 m

0   150   300 yards

BIG ISLAND

To Keahole-Kona Airport

To Waimea

Kaiwi St

Luhia St

Alapa St

Pawai Place

Kuakini Hwy

To Old Kona Airport Beach Park

Palani Rd

Queen Kaahumanu Hwy

Henry St

Kuakini Hwy

Ala-Ona Ona St

Kalani St

Alahou St

Kalawa St

Hualalai Rd

Kuakini Hwy

Alii Drive

Kailua Pier

Kamakahonu Beach

Kailua Bay

Hale Halawai Park

Oneo Bay

Likana Lane

To Holualoa

To Holalo

To Honalo

To Kahaluu, Keauhou

Walua Rd

Kahakai Rd

PLACES TO STAY

25 Patey's Place
29 Kona Seaside Hotel
31 King Kamehameha's
     Kona Beach Hotel
51 Kona Bay Hotel
59 Kona Islander Inn
65 Kona Billfisher
66 Royal Kona Resort
67 Hale Kona Kai

PLACES TO EAT

4   Wendy's
5   Sizzler
7   Burger King
     Su's Thai Kitchen
20 Magic Sands Cafe
     Pizza Hut, Taco Bell
24 Kona Ranch House
30 Quinn's
34 Ocean View Inn
36 Sibu Cafe
38 Marty's Steak &
     Seafoods
40 Basil's Pizzeria
     Restaurante
44 Subway Sandwiches
47 McDonald's
50 Kona Inn
58 Waterfront Row
61 Alii Sunset Plaza
62 Palm Cafe

OTHER

1   Kaahumanu Plaza
2   Wal-Mart
3   Kona Coast
     Shopping Center
6   Kona Coast Divers
8   Hilo Hattie
9   First Hawaiian Bank
10 Post Office
11 Bowling Alley
12 Lanihau Center
13 Longs Drugs
14 Kopiko Plaza
15 Waldenbooks
16 B&L Bike & Sports
17 Kailua Candy
     Company
18 CW Boar's
21 Kona Brewing
     Company
22 North Kona
     Shopping Center
26 Pay Parking
27 King Kamehameha Mall
28 Gas Station (24-hour)
29 Kamehameha Square
32 Kona Amigos

33 Dave's Triathlon Shop
35 Pa O Umi Point
37 Free Parking
39 Hulihee Palace
41 Mokuaikaua
     Church
42 Kona Plaza
43 Kona Marketplace
45 Coin Laundry
48 Lighthouse
49 Ahuena Heiau
50 Kona Inn
     Shopping Village
52 Farmers' Market
53 Library
54 Gas Station
55 Bank of Hawaii
56 7-Eleven Store
57 Hualalai Theatres
60 Harper Car &
     Truck Rentals
63 Jack's Diving Locker
64 Huggo's

Hwy near Eclipse dance club. In addition, most condos have either washers and dryers in the units or a laundry room on site.

Film & Photography Longs Drugs in the Lanihau Center sells cameras and film and handles processing by major developers, including Kodak and Fuji. They do their own same-day print processing ($8 for 24 prints). However, if you can wait two days, the send-out service costs only $5 for 24 prints.

Parking The center of Kailua gets quite congested, and finding a parking space in town can be a challenge.

There's free public parking in the lot behind Kona Seaside Hotel between Likana Lane and Kuakini Hwy. There's complimentary parking for patrons of the Kona Inn Shopping Village in the lot behind the Kona Bay Hotel. Patrons of Kona Marketplace can park free at the rear of that center, and Waterfront Row has free patron parking in the basement of its building.

King Kamehameha's Kona Beach Hotel, at the north end of Alii Drive, has a big pay-parking lot behind the hotel. The first 15 minutes is free and it's $1 per half hour after that. If you purchase something in one of the hotel shops or restaurants you can get a voucher for free parking.

Kamakahonu & Ahuena Heiau

Kamakahonu, the beach at the north end of Kailua Bay, was the site of the royal residence of Kamehameha the Great. Shortly after his death here in 1819, Kamehameha's successors came to Kamakahonu and ended the traditional kapu system, sounding a death knell for the old religion.

The ancient sites are now part of the grounds of King Kamehameha's Kona Beach Hotel. A few thatched structures along with carved wooden kii gods have been reconstructed above the old stone temple.

Ahuena Heiau, which was once a place of human sacrifice, juts out into the cove and acts as a breakwater, offering protection to swimmers. The waters at Kamaka-

honu, which means 'Eye of the Turtle', are the calmest in Kailua Bay.

The little beach in front of the hotel is the only downtown swimming spot. The hotel beach hut rents snorkels and both single and tandem kayaks.

King Kamehameha's Kona Beach Hotel

Be sure to take a stroll through the sprawling lobby of this hotel, which is full of museum-quality Hawaiiana displays.

One display features Hawaiian musical instruments, including a nose flute, coconut shell knee drum, shell trumpet, bamboo rattles and hula sticks. There are displays on traditional foods and fishing and others containing feather capes and leis, kapa beaters, quilts, war clubs, *pahoa* daggers, calabashes and gourd containers. The displays have brief interpretive plaques, but if you ask at the front desk, they'll give you a free brochure that describes them in greater depth.

Near the front desk, you'll find an interesting depiction of King Kamehameha at Kailua Bay that was painted by the Hawaiian artist Herb Kane. The hotel has free guided historical tours that visit the indoor displays and take in the hotel's historic grounds; they are usually given at 1:30 pm on weekdays, but it's best to check at the activity desk for the latest schedule.

Kailua Pier

Although most of Kona's charter fishing boats now use the larger Honokohau Harbor north of Kailua, a few still pull in each afternoon at Kailua Pier to hoist their catch on the scales. The Kona Coast is the world's number one fishing spot for Pacific blue marlin and some catches top a thousand pounds.

Kailua Bay was once a major cattle shipping area. Cattle driven down from hillside ranches were stampeded into the water and forced to swim out to waiting steamers, where they were hoisted aboard by sling and shipped to Honolulu slaughterhouses. Kailua Pier was built in 1915, and until the 1960s cattle pens were still in place.

Cattle drive at Kailua Pier

HAWAII STATE ARCHIVES

There's a tiny patch of sandy beach on the east side of Kailua Pier that's known as **Kaiakeakua**, 'Sea of the Gods'. It once served as Kamehameha's canoe landing.

Pa O Umi Point
In the 16th century the powerful King Umi moved his royal court from Waipio to Kona. The rocky lava outcropping on the northeast side of Kailua Bay where he is thought to have landed is called Pa O Umi, 'Umi's Enclosure'.

A sea wall has been built over much of it, but when the tide is low you can see the tip of the lava point by looking over the wall in the area diagonally across the street from the Ocean View Inn.

Mokuaikaua Church
On April 4, 1820, Hawaii's first Christian missionaries landed at Kailua Bay, stepping out onto a rock that is now one of the footings for the Kailua Pier. When the missionaries landed they were unaware that Hawaii's old religion had been abolished on this same spot just a few months before. Their timing couldn't have been more auspicious. Given a favorable reception from Kamehameha's successors, the missionaries were allowed to established Hawaii's first Christian church on Kailua Bay, a few minutes' walk from Kamehameha's ancient heiau and house site.

The temporary church the missionaries erected was replaced in 1836 by the current Mokuaikaua Church, a handsome building with walls of lava rock held together with a mortar of sand and coral lime. The posts and beams are made from ohia wood, a strong termite-resistant wood hewn with stone adzes and smoothed down with chunks of coral. The pews and the pulpit are made of koa. The church steeple remains the highest structure in Kailua, at 112 feet.

There's often an interpreter around to talk about the church's history from 9 am to 4 pm Monday to Saturday. An eight-foot model of the brig *Thaddeus*, the ship that brought those first Congregational missionaries to Hawaii, is on also display.

Hulihee Palace

Hulihee Palace, a modest two-story house, was built in 1838 by Governor 'John Adams' Kuakini as his private residence.

Kuakini was also the Mokuaikaua Church contractor, and both buildings were of the same lava-rock construction. The palace got its current look in 1885, when it was plastered over inside and out by King Kalakaua, who had taken to a more polished style after his travels abroad.

The palace belonged to a succession of royal owners until the early 1900s, when it was abandoned and fell into disrepair. The Daughters of Hawaii, a group founded in 1903 by daughters of missionaries, took it over and now operate the property as a museum.

Hawaiian royalty were huge people, and everything inside the palace takes on those proportions, including a bed that is seven feet long.

Princess Ruth Keelikolani, who owned the palace in the mid-19th century, was indeed a lady of some presence and is said to have weighed more than 400 pounds. She was an earthy woman, preferring to live in a big grass hut on the palace grounds rather than being confined within the palace. After her death the wooden posts that had supported her grass hut were carved with designs of taro, leis and pineapples and used as posts in one of the beds upstairs.

The palace is furnished with antiques, many picked up on royal jaunts to Europe. Of the more Hawaiian pieces, there's a table inlaid with 25 kinds of native Hawaiian woods, some of which are now extinct, and an armoire that was made in China of Hawaiian sandalwood and inlaid with ivory. Some of Kamehameha the Great's personal war spears are also on display.

The palace is open from 9 am to 4 pm on weekdays, 10 am to 3 pm on Saturdays and 10 am to 4 pm on Sundays. Admission, which costs $4 for adults and 50¢ for children under 12, includes a 40-minute tour.

There's no charge to visit the gift shop or take a look into the stocked **fishpond** behind the palace; it once served as a queen's bath and before that was a canoe landing. The lava coastline adjacent to the fishpond is also interesting, with lots of sea urchins and scurrying black crabs camouflaged among the black rocks.

Hale Halawai Park

Hale Halawai is a quiet oceanfront park with a few shady trees. As the coast is rocky and the sand full of coral chunks, it's not a sunbathing spot, but it is a fine place to sit and read the morning paper.

A prison and courthouse once stood at the site. Now there's a pavilion used by community groups for flea markets and pancake breakfasts; a country recreation office, which issues camping permits; and free parking for park users.

Kona Brewing Company

The Kona Brewing Company (☎ 334-1133), in a warehouse adjacent to the North Kona Shopping Center, is the Big Island's first microbrewery. Started by a father and son from Oregon, this little family-run operation brews just 25 barrels at a time. Their mainstay, Pacific Golden Ale, blends pale and honey malts to produce a traditional ale. If you prefer a little island flavor, a second ale called Lilikoi Wheat has a light passion fruit bouquet. You can sample both during brewery tours from 9 am to 5 pm Monday to Saturday. There are plans to eventually add an on-site pub, local red tape notwithstanding. In the meantime, you can find these handcrafted ales in restaurants, grocery stores and convenience shops around the island.

Old Kona Airport Beach Park

The old Kona Airport, which was replaced by the current Keahole-Kona Airport in 1970, has been turned into a state recreation area and beach park. It's about a mile north of downtown Kailua, at the end of the Kuakini Hwy.

The old runway skirts a long sandy beach, but lava rocks run the length of the beach between the sand and the ocean. Although this makes for poor swimming conditions, it's ideal for fishing and exploring tide pools. At low tide the rocks reveal an intriguing system of little aquarium-like pockets holding tiny sea urchins, crabs and bits of coral.

There are a couple of breaks in the lava that allow entry into the water, including one in front of the first picnic area.

A little cove, which can be reached by a short walk from the north end of the beach, is a good area for scuba divers and confident snorkelers. The reef fish are large and plentiful, and in deeper waters there's a steep coral wall that harbors big moray eels and a wide variety of other sea creatures such as lionfish and cowries.

When the surf's up there is an offshore break that's favored by local surfers. In high surf, though, it's too rough for other water activities.

While this local park is popular with families and picnickers, it's much too big to ever feel crowded. There are restrooms, showers and covered picnic tables on a lawn dotted with beach heliotrope and short coconut palms.

In addition to the sanctioned recreational activities, the old runway also made a perfect drag strip, and because of its rowdy nighttime reputation a gate now closes off that section of the park at 8 pm.

The Kailua end of the park contains a new gym, soccer and softball fields and four outdoor lighted tennis courts.

Directly behind the tennis courts there's a break in the wall marked 'Shoreline Public Access'. This short path leads into an exclusive subdivision, but the beach fronting the subdivision, like all Hawaiian beaches, remains public. If you walk along the beach a few minutes towards downtown Kailua, you'll come to a sandy area with a big wading pool that's a few feet deep – a great spot for children.

Saltwater Pool

One of Kona's best-kept secrets is a saltwater swimming pool in a little lava outcrop so close to the ocean that waves lap in over the side carrying small tropical fish with them. It's as large as most condo pools and it's open to the public.

The pool was originally part of a retired admiral's private estate. By the time it was sold to developers (Kona by the Sea condos are here now), all coastline had become public domain.

Kona by the Sea has put in four public beach access spaces at the side of its parking lot. A gravel path on the north side of the complex leads from the parking lot down to the pool.

The admiral had good taste. You float above the ocean and can glance over the edge and watch surfers riding into shore. Still, how tempting the water will be for swimming depends on whether big waves have washed through recently, as algae tends to flourish when the water stands too long. Be careful getting into the pool, as the steps are slippery.

White Sands Beach Park

It's called White Sands, Magic Sands and Disappearing Sands, but it's all the same beach, midway between Kailua and Keauhou. In the winter when the surf is high, the sand can disappear literally overnight, leaving only rocks on the shore. And then just as magically it returns and again becomes a fine white-sand beach.

This is a very popular bodysurfing beach when the rocks aren't exposed. There's also a volleyball court, restrooms and picnic tables.

Places to Stay

In Kona, condos outnumber hotels many times over. Condos tend to be cheaper than hotels if you're staying awhile, although for advance reservations, which are recommended in the high season, there are often deposits and stiff cancellation penalties to deal with. Unlike hotels, most condos have a three-day minimum stay, and during the high season some have a seven-day minimum stay.

Places to Stay – budget

The cheapest place to stay in town is *Patey's Place* (☎ 326-7018, 800-972-7408 in Hawaii; fax 326-7640), 75-195 Ala-Ona

Ona, Kailua-Kona, HI 96740. This hostel-style accommodation is in a rather congested residential neighborhood a 10-minute walk from the town center. Dormitory beds cost $14, while simple private rooms are $25/35 for singles/doubles. There's free pick-up from the airport if you stay a minimum of two nights and a $5 fee to get back to the airport. The operation has a reputation for being a bit loose, and someone expecting the standards of an HI hostel (or Arnott's Lodge in Hilo) might not feel comfortable here. It certainly would be a good idea to look around and get your own impression before checking in.

One of the area's best deals is the *Kona Tiki Hotel* (☎ 329-1425; fax 327-9402), 75-5968 Alii Drive, Kailua-Kona, HI 96740. This older three-story complex has 15 pleasant rooms, most with a queen and a twin bed and all with refrigerators and breezy oceanfront lanais. There's friendly management, a small seaside pool and complimentary coffee, juice and breakfast pastries. Although it's right on the road, the surf usually drowns out the sound of traffic. Rates are $56 for standard rooms, $62 for rooms with kitchenettes, plus $8 more for a third person. The hotel is very popular with return visitors and generally books up well in advance during the high season. Credit cards are not accepted.

Kona Seaside Hotel (☎ 329-2455, 800-367-7000; fax 922-0052), 75-5646 Palani Rd, Kailua-Kona, HI 96740, has two sections. One's a modern six-story building with private lanais and the standard amenities, priced from $85. The older rear poolside wing is simpler and has walls that carry sound, making the $70 rate for those rooms a lesser value. You can often get a cheaper local rate on both sections if you book within Hawaii; a package that includes a free Budget rental car at $109 for two nights is perpetually advertised in the Sunday Honolulu paper. To get the best deal skip the toll-free number and call the local booking desk (☎ 922-1228). You don't have to be a Hawaii resident to qualify for the cheaper rates, but the clerk may be loath to make the reservation if you call before you arrive in the islands and give them a non-Hawaii mailing address.

For those who want to be right in the center of town, there's Uncle Billy's *Kona Bay Hotel* (☎ 329-1393, 800-367-5102; fax 935-7903), 75-5739 Alii Drive, Kailua-Kona, HI 96740. The older cinder-block buildings lack charm, but at $69 it's relatively cheap; there's a pool, and rooms have TV, air-con and phones.

Three Bears Bed & Breakfast (☎ /fax 325-7563, 800-765-0480; three.bears@ pobox.com), 72-1001 Puukala St, Kailua-Kona, HI 96740, is a delightful cedar home seven miles north of Kailua, off Hwy 190. The home has a hillside location, sweeping views of the Kona Coast and good conditions for stargazing from the lanai, where there's also a hot tub. The two comfortable guest rooms have private baths, microwaves, refrigerators, coffeemakers and cable TV. Owners Anne and Art Stockel are active in environmental issues, speak fluent German and know the island inside out. For travelers with their own transportation, Three Bears would make a good base for exploring Kona, Waimea and the Waikoloa areas. Rates, which include a hearty home-cooked breakfast and all the macadamia nuts you can crack, are $65 a night for one room, $75 for the other, with a two-night minimum stay. Anne also books other B&B accommodations in Hawaii.

Kiwi Gardens (☎ 326-1559; fax 329-6618), 74-4920 Kiwi St, Kailua-Kona, HI 96740, is a B&B about three miles north of Kailua center. Ron and Shirlee Freitas, former San Franciscans, rent three rooms in their contemporary home. One room has a queen bed with a lanai and a sunset view, another is a smaller room with a twin bed and a double bed. Both these rooms share a bath and cost $60 as a double; the smaller room can also be used as a single for $50. The third room is a master suite with a king-size brass bed, private bathroom and a lanai for $75. The house has a stylish Art Deco theme. Breakfast includes fresh bread, Kona coffee and fruits from the yard. If you're interested in deep-sea fishing, Ron has his own charter boat.

Hale Maluhia (☎ 329-5773, 800-559-6627; fax 326-5487; hi-inns@aloha.net), 76-770 Hualalai Rd, Kailua-Kona, HI 96740, is a B&B on the road to Holualoa, a couple of miles southeast of downtown Kailua. The half-dozen guest rooms center around a large rambling house that's home to the family of Ken and Ann Smith. Rates, which include breakfast, range from $55 for a small room with a double bed and shared bath to $115 for a large cottage with a king bed, private bath and deck. Add 10% for stays of less than three days. Common space includes a game room with TV and VCR.

Places to Stay – top-end

The 460-room *King Kamehameha's Kona Beach Hotel* (☎ 329-2911, 800-367-2111; fax 329-4602), 75-5660 Palani Rd, Kailua-Kona, HI 96740, is on Kailua Bay and the only beach in town. Located at the site of King Kamehameha's former residence, it has a sprawling koa-wood lobby full of interesting Hawaiiana displays. Rooms are comfortable with two double beds, a lanai, thermostatic air-con, room safe, TV and phone. There's a pool, lighted tennis courts and free guest parking. Rates range from $110 to $195, depending upon the view.

The *Royal Kona Resort* (☎ 329-3111, 800-774-5662; fax 329 9532; rkr5433@isis.interpac.net), 75-5852 Alii Drive, Kailua-Kona, HI 96740, a former Hilton, has an oceanfront location on the edge of town. There's no sandy beach, but there is a conventional swimming pool as well as a natural saltwater pool that's deep enough for swimming. The hotel also has tennis courts and a waterfront restaurant. The 452 rooms have the standard amenities including TVs, coffeemakers, refrigerators and room safes. The regular rack rate begins at $155, but there are discounted promotions, including a room and car package for $109.

Places to Stay – condominiums

Many of Kona's condominiums can be booked through more than one rental agency. For condos with an address listed, you can write directly to the condo, as they

To Kailua-Kona center

- Kona Islander Inn
- Kona Alii
- Kona Billfisher

Royal Kona Resort ■
Hale Kona Kai ■
Kona Reef ■

■ Malia Kai Apts
■ Kona Pacific
■ Kona Mansions

Alii Drive
Walua Rd

Kona Tiki Hotel ■

Sea Village ■
Kona Shores ■
Alii Villas ■
Kona Makai ■
Royal Sea-Cliff Resort ■

Casa de Emdeko ■
Kona Isle ■
Kona by the Sea ■
Kona Riviera Villa ■

Ala Kala Condo ■

Hale Kai O Kona ■
Kona Nalu ■

Kona Bali Kai ■
Banyan Tree ■

■ Holualoa Bay Villas

■ Banyan Surf Apts
■ Royal Kahili

■ Kona Palms

Kona Magic Sands ■

■ Kona White Sands

White Sands Beach

■ White Sands Village

St Peter's Church †

Kahaluu Beach

Keauhou Beach Hotel ■

Kona Lagoon Hotel ■

Keauhou-Kona Surf & Racquet Club ■

Keauhou Shopping Village

Kamehameha III Rd

Kona Coast Resort ■

Keauhou Palena ■
Kanaloa at Kona ■

Country Club Villas
Keauhou Resort Condo
Kona Country Club

Kona Surf Resort ■

Keauhou Akahi

Keauhou Punahele ■

Kailua & Keauhou Condos
not to scale

either handle their own bookings or will pass correspondence on to the agents that do. For the rest, units are handled by at least one of the following agencies; each will send their latest listings and rates upon request. It's worth comparing the listings before booking.

Hawaii Resort Management, 75-5776 Kuakini Hwy, Suite 105C, Kailua-Kona, HI 96740 (☎ 329-9393, 800-553-5035)

Kona Vacation Resorts, 77-6435 Kuakini Hwy, Kailua-Kona, HI 96740 (☎ 329-6488, 800-367-5168 from the USA, 800-800-5662 from Canada; fax 329-5480)

Triad Management, North Kona Shopping Center, Box 4466, 75-5629-M Kuakini Hwy, Kailua-Kona, HI 96745 (☎ 329-6402, 800-345-2823; fax 326-2401)

Most of Kona's condos are quite nice, have complete kitchens and are fully furnished with everything from linen to cooking utensils. The general rule is that the weekly rate is six times the daily rate and the monthly rate is three times the weekly. However, in the high season, if business is brisk, many places will offer only the daily rate, while in the off-season months of April, May and September you might be able to negotiate an even better deal.

If you wait until you arrive in Kona to look for a place, you can sometimes find a good deal under 'Vacation Rentals' in the classified ads of *West Hawaii Today*. However, this is risky during the high season, when many of the better-value places book up well in advance.

All Kona condos listed here have swimming pools unless otherwise noted.

The *Kona Islander Inn* (☎ 329-3181, 800-922-7866), 75-5776 Kuakini Hwy, Kailua-Kona, HI 96740, is an older development in the town center. Some of the units can get musty, particularly those on the bottom floor. The Aston chain handles about 30 of the 144 units and maintains a front desk. Winter rates for rooms with refrigerators range from $93 to $108, depending upon the view; the rest of the year they're $10 less.

There are also Kona Islander Inn units rented by Hawaii Resort Management, which work out to be a better deal; their office is conveniently located in the lobby. These cost from $50/245 a day/week in the low season, from $70/345 in the high season. The furnishings vary, but most rooms have TV, air-con and phones, while some also have a VCR.

Kona White Sands (konajim@ilhawaii .net), 77-6467 Alii Drive, is a two-story building with 10 bargain units, all with kitchens and lanais. One-bedroom units cost $70/420 a day/week booked through Hawaii Resort Management. The minimum stay is three days. There's no pool, but it's opposite White Sands Beach.

Kona Billfisher, at 75-5841 Alii Drive, has 65 units that are well furnished with full kitchens, lanais, queen sofa beds in the living rooms, king beds in the bedrooms and both ceiling fans and air-con. They tend to have more consistent decor and better upkeep than other moderately priced complexes. All units are closed for maintenance on the 13th and 14th of each month. When booked through Triad Management, one-bedroom units cost $65/80 for the low/high season, two-bedroom units cost $85/100. There's a three-day minimum. It's good value for this price range and within walking distance of town.

Malia Kai Apartments, mauka of the Royal Kona Resort on Walua Rd, has 21 units, each with three levels. The bottom level has a carport and washer/dryer. The 2nd floor has a lanai, a kitchen and a living room with a sofa bed. The 3rd floor has one main bedroom with sliding shoji doors separating it from another room with a sofa bed. The complex has a garden courtyard with a small pool. The layout isn't perfect for everyone, but if you're with a few people it could be economical. Rates are $510 a week in the high season, $420 in the low season, through Triad Management.

Hale Kona Kai (☎ 329-2155, 800-421-3696), 75-5870 Kahakai Rd, Kailua-Kona, HI 96740, is a real find, right on the ocean in a quiet corner just beyond the Royal

Kona Resort. The 39 one-bedroom units aren't brand new, but they're comfortable and have the usual amenities like full kitchens and cable TV. All units have waterfront lanais with great ocean views and the sound of the surf. Rates are $85 for up to two people. It's $10 more for a corner unit with a wrap-around lanai and $10 more per person for additional guests. There's a three-day minimum on most units, a $150 security deposit and no Sunday or holiday check-in.

Alii Villas (☎ 329-1288), 75-6016 Alii Drive, Kailua-Kona, HI 96740, has 126 units and is a comfortable, quiet place that attracts a fair number of seniors. The units are large and each has a private lanai, cable TV and washer/dryer. Most have a phone and sofa bed. You can either contact Alii Villas directly or book through Kona Vacation Resorts, which has one-bedroom units from $75 with a three-night minimum.

Kona Makai, on the ocean side of Alii Drive next to Alii Villas, has air-con one-bedroom units that are fully equipped with everything down to a washer/dryer and cost from $90 a day through Kona Vacation Resorts. There's an exercise room and tennis courts.

Casa de Emdeko (☎ 329-2160), 75-6082 Alii Drive, Kailua-Kona, HI 96740, is a modern complex. The one-bedroom units are pleasant and have all the standard amenities, although there's not much of an ocean view as the lanais line up at an angle facing other lanais. There are both freshwater and saltwater pools. When booked through Kona Vacation Resorts, the rates for one-bedroom units are $80/480 a day/week.

Kona Bali Kai (☎ 329-9381), 76-6246 Alii Drive, Kailua-Kona, HI 96740, is a 155-unit oceanfront complex midway between Kailua and Keauhou. Colony Hotels & Resorts (☎ 800-777-1700) maintains a front desk here and handles many of the units, which range from mountain-facing studios for $100 and one-bedroom units for $120 to two-bedroom oceanfront units for $190. If you book in advance and ask for the 'Super Saver' rate, there's often a discount on these prices. All units have full kitchens, TVs and lanais. Units are privately owned and are decorated according to the whim of the owner – some are quite nice, while others are a bit lackluster.

Royal Sea Cliff Resort (☎ 329-8021, 800-922-7866; fax 922-8785), 75-6040 Alii Drive, Kailua-Kona, HI 96740, has some of the nicest units in Kona, with large balconies, stylish furnishings and full kitchens, including washers and dryers. There are tennis courts, a couple of pools and a sauna. Aston runs it like a hotel with a front desk and there's no minimum stay. Studios cost $145/160 in the low/high season, while roomy one-bedroom units start at $165/185, two-bedroom units at $195/215. Overall, the accommodations here are ritzier than at Aston's more expensive nearby property, Kona by the Sea.

Kona Reef (☎ 329-2959, 800-367-5004; fax 329-2762), 75-5888 Alii Drive, Kailua-Kona, HI 96740, is a 130-unit condo complex run like a hotel by Hawaiian Pacific Resorts. The units have the usual amenities, including full kitchens, washer/dryers and private lanais. Rates begin at $130 for up to four people in a one-bedroom unit, which also has a sofa bed in the living room. Two-bedroom oceanfront units cost $200; rates are slightly lower in the off season.

Places to Eat – budget

Big Island Bagel Co, in Kopiko Plaza, has a range of good freshly made bagels for 75¢, as well as more expensive specialty items like pizza bagels. They also serve bagel sandwiches with fruit or potato salad for $5 and have Kona coffee, espresso and hot chocolate. You can eat in or take out. It's open from 6 am to 7 pm on weekdays and 7 am to 4 pm on weekends.

For a good cheap meal on the run try the *French Bakery* at Kaahumanu Plaza in the industrial area. Kona's best bakery, it has good French bread, huge sticky buns and hearty muffins. The Tongan bread, which costs $4.25 and is filled with cheese and spinach or ham, makes a good lunch for two and can be microwaved on request.

There are also similarly priced sandwiches. It's open from 5:30 am to 3 pm Monday to Friday, to 2 pm on Saturday.

The unassuming *Ocean View Inn*, on Alii Drive in the town center, is the best place for cheap local food. Complete breakfasts with coffee cost $2.50 to $6, while sandwiches are $2 to $3. You can get inexpensive Chinese, American and Hawaiian foods, and it's a good place to try lomi salmon or a side dish of poi. Breakfast is served from 6:30 to 11 am, lunch from 11 am to 2:45 pm and dinner from 5:15 to 9 pm. It's closed on Mondays.

Magic Sands Cafe (☎ 334-1811) is in a warehouse at the old industrial center off Pawai Place. It is a real find, with good healthy food at honest prices. Run by a caterer, who once operated a lunch wagon at Magic Sands Beach, and her husband, a former resort chef, the cafe offers fresh organic salads, hearty sandwiches and a few hot dishes. There are several vegetarian items, including a tasty grilled eggplant sandwich that's served with salad for just $4. The most expensive thing on the menu is a nice fresh fish plate for $7.50. This hole-in-the-wall cafe, which is open from 11 am to 4 pm on weekdays and until 2 pm on Saturdays, does a brisk takeout service but also has a handful of tables where you can eat in.

Kona Mix Plate in Kopiko Plaza is a popular eatery with counter service and good-value local fare. Cheeseburgers and mahimahi sandwiches are $4, while most plate lunches, including a recommendable teriyaki chicken dish, cost $5.80. It's open from 10 am to 8 pm Monday to Saturday.

Kona Healthways, a health food store in the Kona Coast Shopping Center, has fresh green salads and vegetarian sandwiches for around $4. The store sells bulk cereals, packaged goods, juices, yogurts and locally grown organic produce. It's open daily from 9 am to 8 pm (to 7 pm on Sundays).

Island Java Java, at Alii Sunset Plaza on Alii Drive, is a popular coffee shop with espresso, muffins and pies at reasonable prices. It has outdoor tables where you can linger over coffee and listen to live guitar music nightly. Also in Alii Sunset Plaza is *A Piece of The Apple*, which has a variety of tempting New York-style sandwiches, fruit smoothies and salads, and *Rico's Mexican Restaurant*, with Kona's cheapest and best-tasting Mexican food.

The 24-hour *Safeway* supermarket, above Wal-Mart at the Crossroads Shopping Center, is Kona's biggest supermarket and has a good bakery, deli and reasonably priced wines.

The Lanihau Center has a large *Sack N Save* supermarket that's open daily from 5 am to midnight, a simple deli and bakery, a pizzeria, a *Baskin-Robbins* ice cream shop and a *KFC*.

Kona also has a *McDonald's, Pizza Hut, Taco Bell, Burger King, Wendy's* and *Subway Sandwiches*.

Fresh island fruits, vegetables and flowers are available direct from the growers at bargain prices at the farmers' market that sets up opposite Waterfront Row from 7 am to 4 pm on Wednesdays, Fridays, Saturdays and Sundays.

Places to Eat – middle

Basil's Pizzeria Restaurante (☎ 326-7836), run by two Italian brothers, is one of the busiest dining spots in the center of Kailua. It has generous servings, good authentic Italian food and reasonable prices. Most dishes come with a nice Caesar salad and garlic bread. Pizzas, pastas and eggplant parmigiana are priced around $9, seafood dishes a few dollars more, sandwiches a bit less. It's open from 11 am to 10 pm daily.

Bangkok Houses (☎ 329-7746), in King Kamehameha Mall, has tasty Thai food at moderate prices. At lunch there are numerous dishes, including pad Thai, fresh ginger chicken or a flavorful Thai curry, for just $5, while at dinner the same dishes cost $8. Lunch is served from 11 am to 3 pm on weekdays, dinner from 5 to 9 pm nightly. Takeout service is also available.

Su's Thai Kitchen (☎ 326-7808), nearby on Pawai Place in the industrial area, also has good Thai food. At dinner, from 5 to 9 pm daily, most standard dishes such as beef, pork or chicken curry cost $8, while the house specialty, volcano chicken with a sweet and sour sauce, is $13. At lunch, from 11 am to 2:30 pm, you can get pad Thai or the curry of the day with rice for $6. The mood, like the food, is authentically Thai – the dining area is an informal outdoor lanai, which is lit by candles at night.

Sibu Cafe (☎ 329-1112) at Banyan Court serves Indonesian food in a casual cafe setting. Combination plates that offer three dishes (with choices like Balinese chicken, spicy Indian curry and shrimp satay) and brown rice cost around $12 at dinner. At lunch you can get combo plates for $9 or choose from a couple of good-value weekday lunch specials for just $5. It's open daily from 11:30 am to 3 pm for lunch and 5 to 9 pm for dinner. Credit cards are not accepted.

The *Sizzler* in the Kona Coast Shopping Center has a good salad bar with a selection of vegies and fresh fruit plus pasta, soup and tortillas for $9 as a meal in itself or $4 with a main course. This family-style chain restaurant, open for lunch and dinner daily, specializes in standard steak and seafood dishes with prices beginning around $10.

Michaelangelo's (☎ 329-4436), on the upper floor of Waterfront Row, has reasonable Italian food, large portions and a pleasant waterfront setting. The usual pastas are priced from $11 at dinner and $9 at lunch, a green salad included. It also has thick-crust pizzas for around $10 and a kids' menu for $5. Look for discount coupons for 25% off that you can pick up right at the door.

Kona Ranch House (☎ 329-7061), off Kuakini Hwy just south of Palani Rd, is a popular place with a varied menu and straightforward food. Breakfast plates, served from 6:30 am to 2 pm, cost $5 to $8. Lunch, available from 6:30 am to 4:30 pm, features burgers, sandwiches and a few hot dishes, mostly in the $7 to $9 range. At dinner, from 4:30 to 9 pm, there are light meals for $10 and heartier plates for a few dollars more. The menu includes ribs, teriyaki chicken and a few Mexican dishes. For a glimpse of paniolo Hawaii, check out the old photos of island ranches decorating the dining room walls.

Quinn's (☎ 329-3822), a bar on Palani Rd opposite King Kamehameha's Kona Beach Hotel, serves meals in its rear courtyard from 11 am to midnight. The crowd is mostly long-time residents who come for the consistently good fish and steak dinners. For the setting, prices aren't cheap – $8 for fish & chips or a fresh fish sandwich, $19 for an ahi dinner – but the portions are large. There are also burgers, soups and salads.

King Kamehameha's Kona Beach Hotel (☎ 329-2911) does a nice breakfast buffet from 6:30 to 10:30 am daily that costs $9.50 with hot dishes, $6 if you just want the cold dishes, which include fruit, pastries and cereal. On Sundays from 9 am to 1 pm, there is an elaborate champagne brunch for $20. On Friday and Saturday evenings, King Kamehameha's has a very good $19 seafood and prime rib buffet with everything from sashimi and crab legs to extensive salad and dessert bars. On other nights there's a more ordinary dinner menu but cheaper prices.

Places to Eat – top end

Palm Cafe (☎ 329-7765), on Alii Drive at the south end of town, is an upmarket open-air restaurant with Hawaiian regional dishes and oceanview dining. Starters such as Vietnamese spring rolls, chicken satay or sushi rolls are priced around $6, while main courses range from vegetarian yakisoba for $17 to Hunan-style lamb chops or Hawaiian mahimahi for $25. It's open for dinner nightly from 5:30 to 10 pm.

Kona Inn (☎ 329-4455), in the center of town, opened in 1929 as the Big Island's first hotel. It's now a shopping center with a large and popular restaurant of the same name. Steak and seafood dinners are in the $15 to $25 range. Light meals, which are available from 11:30 am to 10 pm, include calamari ($7) and steak sandwiches ($12).

For authentic Greek food, there's *Cassandra's Greek Taverna* (☎ 334-1066) in the Kona Marketplace, which has both indoor and streetside patio dining. For under $15 you can get souvlaki, moussaka or a gyros plate, all served with rice. Appetizers include Greek salad, hummus, stuffed calamari and pickled octopus. At lunch, served until 4 pm, there are gyro sandwiches, pita pizzas and souvlaki for around $8. It's open from 11 am to 10 pm Monday to Saturday, 4:30 to 9 pm on Sundays.

Chart House (☎ 329-2451), a popular chain restaurant at Waterfront Row, sometimes has early-bird specials, but otherwise main dishes range from $17 for grilled chicken to around $25 for filet mignon or fresh fish. All dinners include a salad bar.

Jameson's by the Sea (☎ 329-3195) at Kona Magic Sands condos, 77-6452 Alii Drive, on White Sands Beach, is a spin-off of the popular restaurant on Oahu's North Shore. The oceanside tables are about as close as you can get to the surf without getting your feet wet, but the food is not as inspired as the setting. Dinner entrees typically range from $18 to $24 for fresh fish or steak, although there's sometimes a dinner special for $14. At lunch there are sandwiches and salads for $7 to $10. It's open for lunch from 11 am to 2:30 pm Monday to Friday and for dinner from 5 to 10 pm daily.

Entertainment

With numerous restaurants and bars lined up along Alii Drive, Kona has no shortage of sunset views and happy hours. One popular watering hole is *Kona Amigos*, a 2nd-floor open-air bar and Mexican restaurant opposite the Kailua Pier. Between 3 and 6 pm there's a happy hour with cheap margaritas and draft beers, and if you get a window seat you can watch the boats pull into the harbor and hoist up the day's catch of marlin and tuna.

CW Boar's (☎ 326-7427), on Pawai Place in the industrial center, bills itself as a 'smokin sports' bar and is thick with tobacco smoke, beer drinkers and sports fans who come to watch the games on eight-foot screens. It has live music on Fridays and Saturdays and a happy hour with cheap draft beer from 3 to 6 pm daily.

The *Eclipse* (☎ 329-4686), a dance club on Kuakini Hwy, has a DJ on Fridays and Saturdays and live music on Wednesdays, Thursdays and Sundays, all from 10 pm to 1:30 am. The music varies, but is often rock or reggae, and there's a $3 cover charge.

Huggo's (☎ 329-1493), near the Royal Kona Resort, has dancing to live contemporary, pop or Hawaiian music from 9 pm to 1 am nightly. *Michaelangelo's* (☎ 329-4436) at Waterfront Row occasionally has live music on weekends.

The Mask (☎ 329-8558) in the Kopiko Plaza is a popular gay venue, with karaoke and dancing on the weekends.

Kailua has two movie theater complexes: three screens at *Hualalai Theatres* on Kuakini Hwy and two at *Kona Marketplace Cinema* in the center of town.

Luaus *King Kamehameha's Kona Beach Hotel* (☎ 326-4969) has a popular luau every Sunday, Tuesday, Wednesday and Thursday on its beach in front of Ahuena Heiau. It begins with a lei greeting at 5:30 pm, followed by torch lighting, an imu ceremony, a buffet dinner and a Polynesian show. The cost is $49 for adults, $18 for children ages six to 12. There's also limited seating at 6:45 pm, minus the dinner, which costs $25 for adults, $12 for children. If you just want to watch them bury the pig in the imu, they do that with a little commentary around 10 am on luau days.

Things to Buy

The center of Kailua is thick with small shops selling trinkets, clothing and other tourist-related goods. King Kamehameha's Kona Beach Hotel has a Liberty House department store and about 20 other shops. Kona also has a couple of new megastores, including a Wal-Mart on the north side of the Queen Kaahumanu Hwy.

You'll find good selections of Hawaiian music CDs and cassettes at Tempo Music in Kopiko Plaza and at Mele Kai Music in Kaahumanu Plaza. Beachkomers in the King Kamehameha Mall is a good place to pick up new and used aloha shirts at reasonable prices.

The Kailua Candy Company on Kaiwi St makes wonderful homemade chocolates using island fruits and nuts. You can get a peek at their operations through picture windows and free samples at their gift shop, which is open daily until 6 pm. The candies make a nice souvenir.

Getting Around

The Alii Shuttle (☎ 775-7121) makes 45-minute runs between Kailua and Keauhou nine times daily in each direction. The bus leaves the Kona Surf Resort in Keauhou at 8:30 am and every 1½ hours thereafter, with the last run at 8:30 pm. Stops are made at Keauhou Shopping Village, Keauhou Beach Hotel, Royal Kona Resort, Kona Inn Shopping Village, King Kamehameha's Kona Beach Hotel and the Lanihau Center. Return buses leave the Lanihau Center every 1½ hours from 9:20 am to 9:20 pm. This makes a good option for getting to Kahaluu Beach Park (next to the Keauhou Beach Hotel) if you're in Kailua without a car. The fare anywhere along the route is $2 each way, or you can get a day/week/month pass for $5/20/40.

KEAUHOU

Keauhou is the coastal area immediately south of Kailua-Kona. It starts at Kahaluu Bay and runs south beyond Keauhou Bay and the Kona Surf Resort.

Keauhou contains a planned community of three hotels, nine condo complexes, a shopping center and a 27-hole golf course, all neatly spaced out with a country club atmosphere. Bishop Estate, Hawaii's biggest private landholder, owns the land.

The area was once the site of a major Hawaiian settlement, which was supported by an abundance of fresh spring water. Several of these historical sites can still be explored, although they now share their grounds with the hotels and condos.

Information

Post & Communication There's a contract post office at the Keauhou Shopping Village, on the corner of Alii Drive and Kamehameha III Rd. It's open weekdays from 10 am to 4:30 pm and Saturdays from 10 am to 3 pm.

Money Inside the KTA Supermarket is a branch of the Bank of Hawaii that's open from 10 am to 7 pm on weekdays and 10 am to 3 pm on weekends. KTA also has a Bankoh ATM.

Pharmacy There's a Longs Drugs inside the Keauhou Shopping Village, as well as a small pharmacy inside the KTA Supermarket.

Other Information Keauhou has a free on-call shuttle service (☎ 322-3500) that runs around the resort between 8 am and 4:30 pm every day.

Keauhou Village Book Shop in the Keauhou Shopping Village stocks travel guides, Hawaiiana books and a few mainland dailies.

St Peter's Church

The little blue and white church on the north side of Kahaluu Bay is St Peter's Catholic Church. It dates back to 1880, although it was moved from White Sands Beach to this site in 1912. Tidal waves and hurricanes have since attempted to relocate it on a couple of occasions.

St Peter's is Hawaii's most photographed 'quaint church', and it is still used for weekend services and weddings.

Christians were not the first to deem the site a suitable place to worship the gods. At the north side of the church you'll find the remains of **Kuemanu Heiau**, a surfing temple. Hawaiian royalty, who surfed the waters at the north end of Kahaluu Bay, paid their respects at this temple before hitting the waves.

Locals keep up the surfing tradition, although high surf usually generates dangerous northward rip currents, and it's not a good spot for beginners.

Kahaluu Beach

Kahaluu, which means the 'Diving Place' in Hawaiian, is the island's best easy-access snorkeling spot. The bay is like a big natural aquarium that's loaded with colorful marine life. If you haven't tried snorkeling, this is a great place to learn. It's not even necessary to go out over your head to enjoy it!

Large rainbow parrotfish, schools of silver needlefish, brilliant yellow tangs, butterfly fish and colorful wrasses are among the numerous tropicals easily seen here.

The fish are tame enough to eat out of your hand, and if you bring along fish food, you'll be surrounded by frenzied swarms. There are lots of fish in the shallows, but generally the deeper the water the better the coral and the larger the fish. Spotted moray eels are not that hard to find either, and at high tide green sea turtles occasionally swim into the bay to feed.

An ancient breakwater, said to have been menehune-built, is on the reef and protects the bay. Still, when the surf is high Kahaluu can have strong currents that pull in the direction of the rocks near St Peter's Church, and it's easy to drift away without realizing it. Check your bearings occasionally to make sure you're not being pulled by the current.

Before jumping in, take a look at the display board by the picnic pavilion, as it has information on water conditions as well as sketches of some of the fish you'll find in the bay.

A lifeguard is on duty daily. There's a snack van selling burgers, sodas and shave ice. Another van rents snorkel sets at $4 for the first hour and $1 each subsequent hour as well as disposable Fuji underwater cameras for $18. Fish food can be purchased for $2.50.

The park has a salt-and-pepper beach composed of black lava and white coral sand. Facilities include showers, restrooms, changing rooms, picnic tables and grills. It's a popular place and often draws a crowd, particularly on weekends, so it's best to get there early.

Keauhou Beach Hotel

The grounds of Keauhou Beach Hotel, immediately south of Kahaluu Beach, contain a number of easily explored historical sites. A one-page brochure and map of the sites is available at the front desk.

The ruins of Kapuanoni, a **fishing temple**, is on the north side of the hotel. The reconstructed **summer beach house**

of King Kalakaua is inland, beside a spring-fed pond once used as a royal bath. You can peek into the simple three-room cottage and see a portrait of the king in his European-style royal dress, a Hawaiian quilt on the bed and lauhala mats on the floor.

Other heiau sites are on the south side of the hotel. The remains of the seaside **Keeku Heiau**, just beyond the footbridge that leads to the Kona Lagoon Hotel, is thought to have been a luakini heiau.

There are some interesting **tide pools** in the shelf of smooth pahoehoe lava at the south side of the hotel, best explored when the tide is low. The pools contain numerous sea urchins, including spiny and slate pencil types, and small tropical fish.

When the tide is at its very lowest you can walk out onto a flat lava tongue that is carved with numerous **petroglyphs**. The site is directly in front of the northern end of the Kona Lagoon Hotel, with most of the petroglyphs about 25 feet from the shore. Other than at low tide the petroglyphs are submerged and cannot be seen.

The Keauhou Beach Hotel grounds also has a **fertility pit**, carved wooden god images, historic *kuula* stones sacred to fishers and an ancient house site or two.

Keauhou Bay

Keauhou Bay, which has a launch ramp and space for two dozen small boats, is one of the most protected bays on the west coast.

While snorkeling can be reasonably good in the bay, it's not advised because of the boat traffic. If you come by on weekdays in the late afternoon you can watch the local outrigger canoe club practicing in the bay. There are restrooms and showers.

A stone marking the site where Kamehameha III was born in 1814 is in a small clearing just south of the harborside dive shacks. The young prince was said to have been stillborn and brought back to life by a visiting kahuna.

To get to the bay turn makai off Alii Drive onto Kamehameha III Rd. Or, alternatively, drive down Kaleopapa Rd towards Kona Surf Resort but continue to the end of the road instead of turning into the resort.

Manta Rays

If you're looking for something to do in the evening, you could go down to Kona Surf Resort and watch the manta rays that often gather in the late evening at the rocky outcrop below the resort's saltwater pool. They're attracted by the spotlights that shine down onto the ocean and thus make their best showings when there's no moon.

The wing tips of these impressive creatures measure up to 12 feet across. The manta rays cruise around in the surf, with their white underbellies flashing against the dark waters – it's hypnotic to watch.

Places to Stay

The 318-room *Keauhou Beach Hotel* (☎ 322-3441, 800-367-6025; fax 322-6586), 78-6740 Alii Drive, Kailua-Kona, HI 96740, adjoins Kahaluu Beach Park and has interesting grounds that include historical sites and tide pools. The rooms are a good size, with mini-refrigerators, TV, air-con and balconies, but the decor varies – those in the unrenovated sections are quite lackluster. Rates range from $98 to $170, depending largely upon the view. Ask for the 'Mahalo Special' when you book and you'll get a free rental car for the same rates.

Kona Surf Resort (☎ 322-3411, 800-367-8011; fax 322-3245; konasurf@ilhawaii .net), 78-128 Ehukai St, Kailua-Kona, HI 96740, is a modern, sprawling, 553-room hotel oriented to Japanese package tourists. It has some interesting Polynesian carvings and decor, a little wedding chapel, tennis courts and both saltwater and freshwater pools. The hotel is rather isolated on a rugged and rocky lava point on the south side of Keauhou Bay. Rates range from $109 to $185.

Keauhou Resort Condominiums (☎ 322-9122, 800-367-5286; fax 322-9410), 78-7039 Kamehameha III Rd, Kailua-Kona, HI 96740, has 48 units with full kitchens and washer/dryers. Although the units are about 20 years old, they are well maintained and are the cheapest in Keauhou. One-bedroom units cost from $65/90 in the low/high season with a garden view, $75/100 with an ocean view. Add about $20 more for a two-bedroom unit for up to four people. The

minimum stay is five days. It's near the golf course and there's a pool.

At the other end of the spectrum is *Kanaloa at Kona* (☎ 322-9625, 800-688-7444; reservations@outrigger.com), 78-261 Manukai St, Kailua-Kona, HI 96740, with 100 condo units ranging from $165 for a one-bedroom apartment with a golf course view to $265 for a three-bedroom unit with an ocean view. All units have lanais with wet bars as well as the standard amenities. The oceanfront units also have spas. There are three pools and two lighted tennis courts. The condo is a member of the Outrigger chain.

Other Keauhou condos are priced between the two and are largely booked through vacation rental agents. Kona Vacation Resorts (☎ 329-6488, 800-367-5168), 77-6435 Kuakini Hwy, Kailua-Kona, HI 96740, handles units in most of them.

Places to Eat

The *Kuakini Terrace* at the Keauhou Beach Hotel (☎ 322-3441) has an open-air setting and nightly buffets that include a salad bar, desserts and numerous hot dishes. The weekday buffets are good for the price ($14), with Chinese food on Mondays and Tuesdays and Hawaiian dishes on Wednesdays and Thursdays. On weekends, seafood dishes are featured but the price jumps to $22. They also do a reasonable champagne brunch on Sundays for $19. The nightly buffets are from 5 to 9 pm; Sunday brunch is from 10 am to 1:30 pm.

Rocky's Pizza (☎ 322-3223) in the Keauhou Shopping Village has average pizza, pastas and sandwiches. Eggplant parmesan served with a salad and garlic bread or a small one-item pizza costs $9. It's open from 11 am to 9 pm daily.

Drysdale's Two in the Keauhou Shopping Village specializes in sandwiches and burgers, most priced from $6 to $8, and is a hot spot for watching sports on TV. Food is served from 11 am to midnight daily.

Keauhou Shopping Village also has a *KTA Supermarket*, open from 7 am to 10 pm daily, a coffee shop, a doughnut shop, an ice cream stand and a *Wendy's*.

Entertainment

Kona Surf Resort has a free Polynesian dance show in its *Nalu Terrace* lounge from 5:30 to 7 pm on Tuesdays and Fridays.

The open-air *Makai Bar* at the Keauhou Beach Hotel often has live Hawaiian music in the early evening, which makes it a nice spot to stop for a sunset drink.

HOLUALOA

Holualoa is a sleepy village perched in the hills, 1400 feet above Kailua-Kona. The slopes catch afternoon showers, so it's lusher and cooler than on the coast below.

Holualoa is an artist's community with craft shops, galleries and a community art center, all of which makes it a fun place to poke around.

This is pretty much a one-road village, with everything lined up along Hwy 180. There's a general store, a Japanese cemetery, an elementary school, a couple of churches and a library that opens a few days a week.

From Kailua-Kona, it's a scenic four miles up Hualalai Rd to Holualoa. The landscape is bright with poinsettia flowers, coffee bushes and fruit trees of all kinds.

While Holualoa remains off the beaten path, Kona's relentless development is creeping up this way. Older homes half-hidden by jungly gardens are being joined by a jumble of new houses. It's an enviable location, with a fine view of Kailua Bay's sparkling turquoise waters below.

Kimura's Lauhala Shop

Kimura's Lauhala Shop (☎ 324-0053), at the intersection of Hualalai Rd and Hwy 180, sells items woven from lauhala, the *lau* (leaf) of the hala tree.

This was once an old plantation store selling salt and codfish. During the Depression of the 1930s, Mrs Kimura started weaving lauhala hats and coffee baskets and taking them down to the plantations to sell.

Three generations of Kimuras still weave lauhala here. Their work is supplemented by the wives of local coffee farmers, who do piecework at home when it's not coffee season.

The hardest part, the Kimuras say, is preparing the lauhala, which is messy work, complicated by the sharp spines along the leaf edges. The easy part is the weaving. Once the lauhala is ready to weave, it takes a couple of hours to make a placemat, which sells for around $10.

The most common items are placemats, open baskets, and hats of a finer weave. The shop is open from 9 am to 5 pm Monday to Saturday.

Kona Arts Center

The soul of Holualoa is the Kona Arts Center, set in a ramshackle former coffee mill with a tin roof and hot-pink doors. Carol Rogers, who's been here since 1965, directs this nonprofit organization and teaches crafts, nurturing the spirit as much as the art.

This is a community scene and everyone's welcome to join; for a monthly fee of $25, you can partake in the workshops, which include pottery, batik, tie-dye, basketry, weaving and painting.

Visitors are free to drop in to look around; the center is open from 10 am to 4 pm Tuesday to Saturday. There's also a small display area with items for sale including paintings, pottery and baskets made of natural fibers.

Galleries

Visiting galleries is the main thing to do in Holualoa.

A highlight is **Studio 7 Gallery**, which opened in 1980 to showcase the artwork of owner Hiroki Morinoue, who works in watercolors, oils, wood block and sculpture. His wife, Setsuko, is a potter and the gallery's director.

The gallery is like a little museum, and the Zen-like setting blends both Hawaiian and Japanese influences, with wooden walkways over lava stones.

In the same building as Studio 7 is the **Koa T Gallery**, which has bowls, hand mirrors, boxes and a few specialty items such as ukuleles, all made of koa.

NED FRIARY

Kii are found around prayer towers.

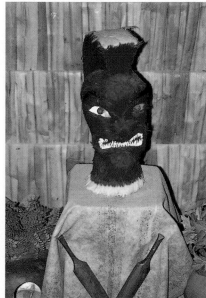

NED FRIARY

Replica of Kukailimoku, Kamehameha's war god

NED FRIARY

Preparing kalua pig for a luau, Kailua-Kona, Big Island

Steam plume from lava entering the ocean

Akaka Falls State Park, Big Island

Dropping a line at South Point, Big Island

The **Holualoa Gallery** has paintings with a Hawaiiana theme, including works by noted Big Island artist Herb Kawainui Kane, and some creative raku pottery by gallery owner Matt Lovein.

The **Country Frame Shop** is a good place to look for more affordable souvenirs, including jewelry, wood items and other crafts. **White Garden Gallery** displays watercolors with flora and fauna themes by gallery owner Shelly Maudsley White.

The old Holualoa post office building, opposite the library, houses **Hale O Kula**, the workshop of goldsmith Sam Rosen, and **Chestnut & Co**, which features weavings by Peggy Chestnut and one-of-a-kind crafts.

Holualoa's galleries are open from 10 am to 4 pm Tuesday to Saturday.

Places to Stay

Kona Hotel (☎ 324-1155), Hwy 180, Holualoa, HI 96725, in Holualoa's town center, retains the small town character (and room rates!) of a bygone era. This old local hostelry has high ceilings and some nice views. Rooms are basic with just a bed and dresser but are clean and priced at only $20/26 for singles/doubles. Bathrooms are shared and down the hall. Rumor has it that the mattresses in the street-side rooms are the most comfortable as the burly construction workers who sometimes stay during the work week favor the ocean side. With only 11 rooms, getting a room here is pretty much hit and miss, although it's generally easier on weekends.

Holualoa Inn (☎ 324-1121, 800-392-1812; fax 322-2472; holualoa@ilhawaii.net), run by Michael Twigg-Smith, Box 222, Holualoa, HI 96725, is a beautiful upmarket B&B perched atop 40 acres of sloping meadows with grand views of the Kona Coast. This contemporary house was built as a getaway by Michael's uncle, chairman of the *Honolulu Advertiser*, who at the time of construction owned a sawmill. The exterior is all western red cedar, and the interior floors are red eucalyptus from Maui. The 6000-sq-foot house has six guest rooms, each with private bath. They vary in size and decor, but all the rooms are spacious and have their own charm. If you're traveling with more than two people, the Bali suite has a separate sitting room with a queen sofa bed as well as a bedroom with a king bed – it also has unbeatable views. Guest amenities include a tile swimming pool, jacuzzi, billiard table, rooftop gazebo, living room with fireplace, TV lounge and facilities for preparing light meals. Rates, which include a continental breakfast with homegrown coffee and fruit, are $125 to $165 for up to two people and $15 more for a third person.

Places to Eat

The *Holuakoa Cafe* has pastries, bagels, coffee, espresso and herbal teas. It's open from 6:30 am to 5 pm Monday to Saturday.

You can pick up groceries at *Paul's Place*, the village's general store.

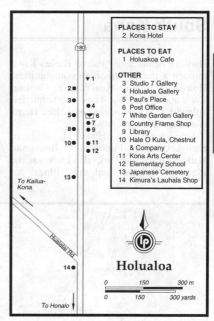

PLACES TO STAY
2 Kona Hotel

PLACES TO EAT
1 Holuakoa Cafe

OTHER
3 Studio 7 Gallery
4 Holualoa Gallery
5 Paul's Place
6 Post Office
7 White Garden Gallery
8 Country Frame Shop
9 Library
10 Hale O Kula, Chestnut & Company
11 Kona Arts Center
12 Elementary School
13 Japanese Cemetery
14 Kimura's Lauhala Shop

To Kailua-Kona

Hualalai Rd

To Honalo

Holualoa

0   150   300 m
0   150   300 yards

South Kona

Hwy 11 heads south out of Kailua-Kona through a number of small communities: Honalo, Kainaliu, Kealakekua, Captain Cook and Honaunau. These are unhurried upland towns surrounded by coffee farms and macadamia nut groves.

Side roads off Hwy 11 lead to Kealakekua Bay, Puuhonua O Honaunau National Historical Park (also known as the Place of Refuge) and the villages of Hookena and Milolii. South Kona is short on beaches, but there are a couple of excellent spots for snorkeling and diving.

HONALO

Honalo is the small village at the intersection of Hwys 11 and 180.

Daifukuji Soto Mission, in the village center on the mauka side of Hwy 11, is a big Buddhist temple with two altars, gold brocade, large drums and incense burners. Visitors are welcome to view the inside. As at all Buddhist temples, leave your shoes at the door.

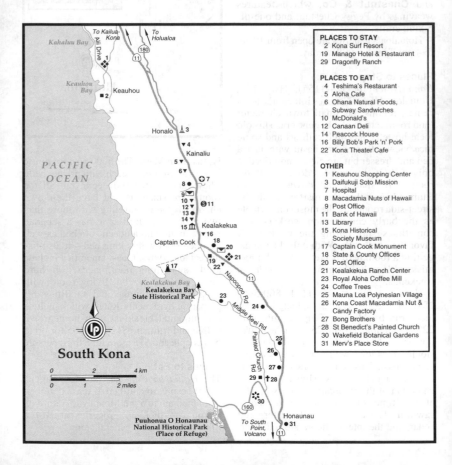

PLACES TO STAY
2 Kona Surf Resort
19 Manago Hotel & Restaurant
29 Dragonfly Ranch

PLACES TO EAT
4 Teshima's Restaurant
5 Aloha Cafe
6 Ohana Natural Foods,
   Subway Sandwiches
10 McDonald's
12 Canaan Deli
14 Peacock House
16 Billy Bob's Park 'n' Pork
22 Kona Theater Cafe

OTHER
1 Keauhou Shopping Center
3 Daifukuji Soto Mission
7 Hospital
8 Macadamia Nuts of Hawaii
9 Post Office
11 Bank of Hawaii
13 Library
15 Kona Historical
   Society Museum
17 Captain Cook Monument
18 State & County Offices
20 Post Office
21 Kealakekua Ranch Center
23 Royal Aloha Coffee Mill
24 Coffee Trees
25 Mauna Loa Polynesian Village
26 Kona Coast Macadamia Nut &
   Candy Factory
27 Bong Brothers
28 St Benedict's Painted Church
30 Wakefield Botanical Gardens
31 Merv's Place Store

South Kona

BIG ISLAND

Places to Stay & Eat

Teshima's Restaurant (☎ 322-9140) on Hwy 11 is an unpretentious place serving authentic Japanese food. The best deal is the lunch teishoku of miso soup, sashimi, sukiyaki, tsukemono (pickled cabbage) and rice, which costs $6.75 and is available only from 11 am to 1:30 pm. The same teishoku with the addition of fried fish costs $8.25 at dinner, which is served from 5 to 9 pm. There's a bar at the side of the restaurant.

In a building out back, Teshima's has 10 rooms for rent, although most are booked on a monthly basis. These small rooms are very basic, each with a double bed, a private bathroom and a cabin-like ambiance. The rate is $20/30 for singles/doubles.

KAINALIU

Kainaliu is a little town with positive energy. The focal point is the Aloha Cafe and the adjoining Alola Theatre, home of the Aloha Community Players. Check the bulletin board next to the theater for the current performance schedule; you can often find long-term room rentals posted here as well.

The town is an interesting mix of old and new influences. Shops such as the Kimura Store, which has been selling traditional fabrics and dry goods here for generations, mingle with the likes of the Blue Ginger Gallery, which sells quality crafts and New Age clothing, and Island Books, which has an up-to-date collection of used books.

Places to Eat

The *Aloha Cafe*, on Hwy 11, is the best place to eat in town and even has a distant ocean view from its outside terrace. The menu includes vegetarian dishes, good salads and fresh fish specials. A burrito or quesadilla with a side salad costs $7.50, while the most expensive dish, filet mignon, costs $18. There are also fruit smoothies, fresh-squeezed juices, espresso and desserts. It's open from 8 am to 9 pm Monday to Saturday and 9 am to 2 pm on Sundays. Bring a sweater if you come for dinner in the winter, as it can get cool in the evenings.

A little farther south on the makai side of Hwy 11 is *Subway Sandwiches*. Next to that is *Ohana Natural Foods*, a cooperative selling organic produce, fruit juices, dairy products and wrapped burritos, salads and sandwiches at reasonable prices.

KEALAKEKUA

Kealakekua means 'Path of the Gods', and there was once a series of 40 heiaus running from Kealakekua Bay north to Kailua-Kona.

These days, the town of Kealakekua is the commercial center for Kona's hill towns. The Kona Coast's hospital is on the north side of town, a quarter of a mile mauka of Hwy 11. The post office is on the corner of Hwy 11 and Halekii Rd.

Kealakekua has a good library, which is open from noon to 8 pm on Mondays, 10 am to 5 pm Tuesday to Friday and 10 am to 1 pm on Saturdays. Next door to the library is the coral mortar and lava-rock Kona Union Church, which dates back to 1854.

There's a little macadamia nut factory, Macadamia Nuts of Hawaii, on Halekii Rd, just down the hill from the post office, which offers guided tours of its operation during the August to January harvest season. At the shop out front, open from 8:30 am to 5 pm daily, you can sample and buy macadamia nut products.

Kona Historical Society Museum

Kona Historical Society (☎ 323-3222) is just south of Kona Meat Company and north of the Kealakekua Grass Shack gift shop. The stone and mortar building, built in the mid-19th century, was once a general merchandise store and post office.

These days, it houses the society's office, archives and little museum. There are some interesting displays of the area's local history, including period photos, old bottles and other memorabilia. It's open from 9 am to 3 pm Monday to Friday and admission is $1. The museum sells some nice historical postcards.

Places to Stay

Reggie's Tropical Hideaway (☎ 322-8888, 800-988-2246; fax 323-2348; banana@ ilhawaii.net), Box 1107, Kealakekua, HI

Kona Coffee

Missionaries introduced the first coffee trees to Hawaii in 1827, and by the turn of the century it was an important cash crop throughout the state. However, the erratic rise and fall of coffee prices eventually drove coffee farmers out of business on the other Hawaiian islands. Only the Big Island's Kona coffee was of high enough quality to sell at a profit during gluts in world markets.

Coffee production in Hawaii had dropped dramatically by 1980, when a rising interest in gourmet coffee sparked sales of the highly aromatic Kona beans. Today, Kona coffee is the most commercially successful coffee grown in the USA. Almost the entire harvest comes from the upland towns of South Kona, from Holualoa in the north to Honaunau in the south. The coffee trees thrive in the rich volcanic soil and the cloud cover that moves in nearly every afternoon.

Coffee, a relative of the gardenia, has fragrant white blossoms in the spring. In the summer the trees have green berries, which turn red as they ripen.

Coffee trees must be hand-picked several times a year as not all the berries ripen at once. The harvesting season begins in August. Coffee farmers at the lowest elevations may finish harvesting by December, while those at the 2000-foot level might harvest into March.

During the coffee season, buyers hang out signs announcing how much they'll pay for 'cherries', the name given to the red coffee berries. In a good year they may offer as much as a dollar a pound. ■

96750, is near central Kealakekua. There's a casual island-style room in the owner's house that has a private bath and a screened deck with a picnic table, TV, refrigerator and microwave. The cost is $55. There's also a separate two-bedroom cottage with high wooden ceilings, a full kitchen, a king bed in one bedroom, a queen waterbed in the other and a double futon in the living room. The cottage has a sunning deck with a small hot tub and is surrounded by coffee trees and privacy screens – which makes it a popular rental for naturists. The cost is $100 per night (for up to six people), with discounts for longer stays. There's also a simpler cottage available for $75.

Merryman's Bed & Breakfast (☎ 323-2276, 800-545-4390; fax 323-3749; merryman@ilhawaii.net), Box 474, Kealakekua, HI 96750, the home of former Alaskans Penny and Don Merryman, is in a quiet residential area in Kealakekua, a quarter of a mile above Hwy 11. The house is big and airy with ample windows, a large deck and lots of natural wood and exposed-beam ceilings. There are two bedrooms with a shared bath for $75 and two rooms with private bath from $95, breakfast included. Rooms are pleasantly furnished, and there's a spacious common living area and a jacuzzi for guest use.

Places to Eat

Peacock House on Hwy 11 has inexpensive Chinese food but it's rather standard fare. You can get plate lunches from steamer trays for around $5 and a wide range of entrees for not much more.

Canaan Deli, on Hwy 11, serves reasonably priced eggs, pancakes and other breakfasts from 7 am and has sandwiches and burgers for around $6. *McDonald's* is also nearby on Hwy 11.

KEALAKEKUA BAY

Kealakekua Bay is a large bay, a mile wide at its mouth. At the south end of the bay is Kealakekua Bay State Historical Park, which encompasses Napoopoo Beach and Hikiau Heiau. The north end has a protected cove with one of the best snorkeling spots on the Big Island.

Steep sea cliffs separate the two ends of the bay and there's no land passage between them. The northern end can be approached only by sea or by a hike along a dirt trail.

Kealakekua Bay is a state underwater park and marine life conservation district. Among the protected species are spinner dolphins that frequently swim into the bay. Fishing is restricted and the removal of coral and rocks prohibited.

An obelisk monument on the north side of the bay marks the spot where Captain Cook died at the water's edge.

Royal Aloha Coffee Mill

On your way down to Kealakekua Bay, stop by the Royal Aloha Coffee Mill to get a free sample of freshly brewed Kona coffee. You can also get a few insights into the coffee biz from the interpretive displays in the gift shop, where coffee, T-shirts and souvenirs are sold. It's open from 9 am to 6 pm daily.

Kealakekua Bay State Historical Park

The four-acre Kealakekua Bay State Historical Park is at the end of Napoopoo Rd, 4½ miles from Hwy 11, and encompasses Napoopoo Beach.

The park's most predominant feature is **Hikiau Heiau**, the large platform heiau above the beach. This busy park also has a boat landing, restrooms, showers and a shack near the heiau selling soft drinks and souvenirs.

Napoopoo Beach is rocky, and because it's small it often gets crowded. This is the less protected end of the bay and it can have dangerous water conditions when the surf is high and during kona storms.

There's good snorkeling at Napoopoo, but the real prize is the cove at the northern end of the bay. Some people snorkel over to the cove from Napoopoo Beach when it's calm, but it's a long haul and only strong swimmers should consider it.

Captain James Cook

Captain James Cook, the first Westerner to visit Hawaii, sailed into Kealakekua Bay at dawn on January 17, 1779. The beaches were lined with some 10,000 curious onlookers and 1000 canoes sailed out to greet him.

Cook's tall ships with high sails appeared to fulfill a prophecy of the return of the god Lono, who was to arrive on a floating island covered with tall trees.

On his first evening ashore, Cook was brought to Hikiau Heiau, where the high priest performed a series of ceremonies recognizing Cook as the incarnation of Lono.

Eleven days later at the heiau, Cook performed a burial service for sailor William Whatman, who had died of a stroke. The inauspicious death of his mate raised a few questions about Cook's own mortality as well.

On February 14, Cook was killed in a scuffle at the north end of the bay. Ironically, the world's greatest navigator was such a poor swimmer that he apparently stumbled into an angry crowd rather than swim a few yards out to a waiting boat. ■

From the park you can continue four miles south along a narrow road through scrub brush and lava to Puuhonua O Honaunau, the Place of Refuge. The road is little more than one lane, but paved and passable. Be careful if you pull over, as there are roadside trenches that are partly concealed by grasses.

Captain Cook Monument Trail

If you're up for a hardy hike, the trail to the Captain Cook Monument and the cove at the north end of Kealakekua Bay makes a good day outing. Although you'll no doubt work up a sweat, you'll be rewarded with excellent snorkeling, a natural bath once reserved for royalty and some historic sites to explore.

The trail is not consistently maintained, so it's best suited for hikers who enjoy challenging conditions. At times this can be a jungly path through tall elephant grasses, while at other times the trail is kept clear by people who use it for horseback rides to the monument.

To get to the trailhead, turn off Hwy 11 onto Napoopoo Rd and go down about 250 yards where you'll find a dirt road immediately after the second telephone pole on the right.

Start walking down the dirt road and after 200 yards it will fork – stay to the left, which is essentially a continuation of the road you've been walking on. The route is fairly simple and in most places runs between two rock fences on an old jeep road. When in doubt, stay to the left.

Eventually the coast becomes visible and the trail veers to the left along a broad ledge, goes down the hill and then swings left to the beach. Once you're at the water, the monument marking Cook's place of death is just a few minutes' walk to the left.

The hike takes about an hour down and 1½ hours up. It's hot and largely unshaded, and it's an uphill climb all the way back, so expect a good workout. There are no facilities at the bottom of the trail. Be sure to bring your own drinking water and snorkeling gear.

Snorkeling There's entry from the rocks on the left side of the cement dock in front of the Captain Cook Monument. The water starts out about five feet deep and slopes gradually to about 30 feet. The cove is protected and usually very calm. Visibility is good and both coral and fish are abundant.

Snorkeling tour boats (see the Activities section earlier in this chapter) pull into the bay in the morning, but they don't come ashore and they generally leave before lunchtime. Anyway, the cove is big enough so it doesn't feel crowded.

Exploring This area was once the Hawaiian village of Kaawaloa. Old lava stone walls still go all the way out to **Cook's Point** at the north end of the bay. There's a small light beacon on the point.

Queen's Bath, a little lava pool with brackish spring-fed water, is at the edge of the cove, a few minutes' walk from the Captain Cook Monument in the direction of the cliffs. The water is cool and refreshing, and this age-old equivalent of a beach shower is a great way to wash off the salt before hiking back – although the mosquitoes can get a bit testy here.

A few minutes beyond the Queen's Bath, the path ends at the cliffs called **Pali-kapu-o-Keoua,** the 'cliffs sacred to the chief Keoua'. The cliffs' numerous caves were the burial places of Hawaiian royalty, and it's speculated that some of Captain Cook's bones were placed here as well.

A few lower caves are accessible, but they don't contain anything other than beer cans. The ones higher up are fortunately not as easy to get to and probably still contain bones. All are sacred and should be left undisturbed.

CAPTAIN COOK

The town named for the Pacific navigator is on Hwy 11 above the bay where he met his end. Captain Cook is a small, unpretentious town with a few county and state offices, a shopping center, a hotel and a couple of restaurants. The Chevron gas station at the north side of town is open 24 hours a day.

As you continue south from town there

are a handful of roadside coffee tasting rooms that sell locally grown coffee and provide free freshly brewed samples.

If you just want to examine coffee trees, there's an unmarked pull-off for that purpose midway between the 107- and 108-mile markers, on the makai side of the road. Coffee trees are planted in the front and macadamia trees beyond.

About a mile farther south is Mauna Loa Polynesian Village, the newest incarnation of a complex that has undergone several transformations in recent years. At last look there was a gift shop, a walk-through lava tube and free coffee samples.

Places to Stay

Manago Hotel (☎ 323-2642), Hwy 11, Box 145, Captain Cook, HI 96704, is a family-run hotel that started in 1917 as a restaurant serving bowls of udon to salespeople on the then-long journey between Hilo and Kona. Those wanting to stay overnight were charged $1 for a futon on tatami mats. These days, the basic rooms in the original roadside building show their age without much grace – the furniture is rickety, the walls are thin and there are shared baths down the hall – but rates are just $22/25 for singles/doubles.

If you want comfort over character, go for one of Manago's 42 rooms in the newer wing at the rear. These motel-style rooms are ordinary but sufficient, with private baths and radios. The highlight is the unobstructed lanai view of Kealakekua Bay a mile below. Rates are $35 to $38 for singles, $38 to $41 for doubles; the higher rates are for better views. The hotel also has an atmospheric Japanese room with tatami mats for $55. There's a common TV room near the restaurant. Although its flavor is purely local, Manago draws a fair number of international travelers.

Pomaikai Farm Bed & Breakfast (☎ /fax 328-2112, 800-325-6427; nitab+b@ilhawaii .net), 85-5465 Mamalahoa Hwy, Captain Cook, HI 96704, is on Hwy 11 about three miles south of the town center. Run by Nita Isherwood, this casual place provides affordable down-home accommodations on a four-acre coffee and macadamia nut farm. Guests have use of a common kitchen and barbecue and rates include a breakfast of breads, granola, homegrown coffee and fruit. You can opt for a simple room in the roadside farmhouse for $40, have your own little converted coffee barn for $50 or stay in a new partly open-air duplex unit behind the house for $55. One of the rooms in the house has a shared bath, but the other units have private baths. There's a $10 charge for each guest beyond two and a $5 surcharge for stays of only one night. Discounts are negotiable for stays of a week or longer. Nita, who speaks fluent French, is a good resource for environmentally friendly things to do and see in the region.

Samurai House (☎ 328-9210), RR1, Box 359, Captain Cook, HI 96704, is a B&B in a traditional Japanese house that was brought over piece by piece from Japan and re-erected in Captain Cook in the 1960s. It has shoji doors, tatami mats, exposed cypress beams, a little carp pond and distant ocean views. There's a tatami room with a king bed and kitchenette for $85; a westernized studio with a full kitchen for $75; and a 'kimono room' with a refrigerator for $65. All three have private lanais. A hot tub and TV/VCR are available. Samurai House, which is on Hwy 11 a mile south of the town center, is popular with the gay community, but also welcomes straight clientele.

Places to Eat

The *Manago Restaurant* in the Manago Hotel is a Japanese version of a meat and potatoes eatery, particularly known for its pork chops. It's not health food, but the portions are large. Two big chops, rice, potato salad and side dishes such as tofu curd cost $8 while sandwiches are around $3. Breakfast is available from 7 to 9 am, lunch from 11 am to 2 pm and dinner from 5 to 7 pm. It's closed on Mondays.

If you like tasty barbecue ribs and chicken, then *Billy Bob's Park 'n' Pork*, just south of the 111-mile marker, is hard to beat. You can get a heaping plate of meat served with chili and rice for $8 or a barbecued chicken sandwich with cole slaw for $5. It's open weekdays from 11 am to 2:30 pm and nightly from 5 to 9 pm.

The Kealakekua Ranch Center on Hwy 11, about half a mile south of the Manago Hotel, has a *Sure Save* supermarket, Mexican fast food and a Chinese restaurant.

The *Kona Theater Cafe*, in the newly renovated Kona Theater accross from the Kealakekua Ranch Center, has an espresso bar and inexpensive pastries, bagels, salads and sandwiches. It's open from 6:30 am to 5 pm Tuesday to Sunday.

HONAUNAU
Honaunau's main attraction is Puuhonua O Honaunau National Historical Park, commonly called the Place of Refuge, but there are other things to see in this area as well.

On Hwy 11, just south of Middle Keei Rd, Bong Brothers has a little shop where they sell their own coffee as well as organic produce, smoothies and a few deli items.

At Merv's Place store, Hwy 160 connects with Hwy 11 and leads down to the Place of Refuge, passing Painted Church Rd, Wakefield Botanical Gardens and some rural scenery with grazing horses, stone walls and brilliant bougainvilleas.

Macadamia Nut Factory
The Kona Coast Macadamia Nut & Candy Factory, on Middle Keei Rd near Hwy 11, has a little display with a husking machine and a macadamia nut cracker. You can try it out, one nut at a time, and eat the final product.

The showroom overlooks the real operation out back, where bags of nuts are husked and sorted. The shop sells both raw and roasted macadamia nuts as well as macadamia nut honey.

St Benedict's Painted Church
This church is noted for its painted interior done by John Berchmans Velghe, a Catholic priest who came from Belgium in 1899.

Father John painted the walls with a series of biblical scenes as an aid in teaching the Bible to natives who couldn't read and designed the wall behind the altar to resemble the Gothic cathedral in Burgos, Spain.

When Father John arrived, the church was on the coast near the Place of Refuge. One of his first moves was to bring the church two miles up the slopes to its present location. It's not clear whether he did this as protection from tsunamis or just to be on the rise – both actual and symbolic – from the old gods of 'pagan Hawaii'.

The tin-roofed church still holds Sunday services, with hymns sung in Hawaiian. The church is on Painted Church Rd; turn north at the one-mile marker on Hwy 160 and go a quarter of a mile – there's usually an HVB sign pointing the way.

Wakefield Botanical Gardens
Wakefield Botanical Gardens on Hwy 160 has free self-guided walks in a largely overgrown backyard. There are some interesting plants with names like snow on the mountain and Moses in the basket, as well as cactus, bonsai and more typical tropical flowers. The gardens are owned by island artist Arlene Wakefield, who also operates an informal restaurant here.

Places to Stay
The *Dragonfly Ranch* (☎ 328-2159, 800-487-2159; fax 328-9570; dfly@aloha.net), Box 675, Honaunau, HI 96726, is a cosmic New Age retreat with a garden-like setting on Hwy 160 near Painted Church Rd. Accommodation options range from standard rooms in the main house for $70 to an open-air 'honeymoon suite' for $160 that has a king-size waterbed on a platform deck without walls; the suite does have netting to keep out the large but harmless spiders that share the gardens. For something a bit more conventional, there's a studio below the main house for $120. Rates include a breakfast of organic coffee, fruit and baked items.

Places to Eat
Wakefield Botanical Gardens has a relaxing open-air dining patio that makes for a pleasant lunch spot. A bowl of vegetable soup with chips and homemade salsa costs $4,

while sandwiches, salads and vegetarian or meat burgers are priced between $6 and $7. The restaurant is open from 11 am to 3 pm.

PUUHONUA O HONAUNAU NATIONAL HISTORICAL PARK (PLACE OF REFUGE)

Puuhonua O Honaunau National Historical Park (☎ 328-2288) encompasses ancient temples, royal grounds and a *puuhonua*, a place of refuge or sanctuary. The park fronts Honaunau Bay.

Puuhonua O Honaunau is a tongue-twister of a name that simply means 'place of refuge at Honaunau'.

In old Hawaii, breaking any of the many kapus that strictly regulated all daily inter-actions was thought to anger the gods, who might retaliate with a natural disaster or two. To appease the gods the offender was hunted down and killed.

Commoners who broke a kapu, as well as defeated warriors and ordinary criminals, could all have their lives spared by reaching the sacred ground of the puuhonua.

This was more of a challenge than it might appear. Since royalty and their war-riors lived on the grounds immediately sur-rounding the refuge, kapu breakers were forced to swim through open ocean, braving currents and sharks to get to the puuhonua.

Once inside the sanctuary, priests per-formed ceremonies of absolution that apparently placated the gods. Kapu breakers could then return home with a clean slate.

Hale O Keawe Heiau, the temple on the point of the cove, was built around 1650. The bones of 23 chiefs were buried there. It's thought that the mana of the chiefs remained in their bones and added a spiri-tual power to those who came into the grounds. The heiau has been authentically reconstructed. The carved wooden kii that stand erect beside it are said to embody the ancient gods.

The heiau is at the end of a large stone wall built around 1550. It's called the **Great Wall** and is more than 1000 feet long and 10 feet high. The west side of the wall contained the puuhonua and the east side held the royal grounds.

A self-guided walk, detailed in the park brochure, passes by Hale O Keawe Heiau, two older heiaus, a petroglyph, legendary stones, a fishpond, lava tree molds and a few thatched huts and shelters. The canoe on display is hand carved from koa wood.

There's also a stone board for konane, a Hawaiian game similar to checkers, which uses small stones of black lava and white coral. Get a copy of the game rules at the park entrance and try your hand.

Medicinal plants around the grounds include the noni tree, with its pear-sized, warty-looking fruit. The fruit, which was eaten in times of famine, tastes as bad as it smells. Its more common usage was to make dyes or as a treatment for diabetes and high blood pressure.

Check out the **tide pools** in the pahoe-hoe lava at the south end of the park. The tiny black speckles dotting the shallow pools behind the heiau are pipipi, a kind of periwinkle. Even better are the tide pools near the picnic area farther south, which harbor coral, black-shelled crabs, small fish and eels, sea hares, and sea urchins with rose-colored spines.

Twenty-minute orientation talks, some-what geared to people on tour buses who don't have time to see the whole park, are given at 10, 10:30 and 11 am and at 2:30, 3 and 3:30 pm daily.

Some of the rangers are native Hawai-ians. You'll occasionally find one dressed in a malo or tapa, demonstrating tradi-tional pili-grass thatching or canoe or kii carving.

A program in Hawaiian studies is held monthly in the park's amphitheater, usually at 7:30 pm on the first Wednesday of the month. A festival with traditional displays and food, *hukilau* (net fishing) and a 'royal court' is held on the weekend closest to July 1.

Admission is $2 per person, or $4 per family, and is good for repeated visits over one week. Fees are generally collected between about 7:30 am and 5 pm but visi-tors are free to enter and stroll the grounds between 6 am and 8 pm (to 11 pm on Fri-days and Saturdays).

Honaunau Beaches
Place of Refuge Swimming is allowed at Keoneele Cove inside the Place of Refuge. Shallow with a gradual decline, the cove was once the royal canoe landing. Snorkeling is best when the tide is rising, as the water is a bit deeper and the tide brings in fish. Sunbathing is discouraged.

South End of the Park Near the Place of Refuge visitors center, a road leads a quarter of a mile south to a beach park with picnic tables and some quiet sandy patches.

Winter surf can be rough in this area. Unless the sea is flat, it's best to stick to the Keoneele Cove area for swimming and snorkeling.

North End of the Park There's a terrific place to snorkel and dive just north of the Place of Refuge. From the park's parking lot, take the narrow road (marked with a 15 mph sign) to the left.

Go down about 500 feet and park just past the boat ramp. If you come by in the late afternoon, you'll see the Keoua Canoe Club practicing in the waters here. Incidentally, the little park mauka of the road was the original site of St Benedict's Painted Church.

Snorkelers step off a lava ledge immediately north of the boat ramp into about 10 feet of water. It then drops off fairly quickly to about 25 feet. There are some naturally formed lava steps that make it fairly easy to get in and out of the water, but there's no beach here, so it's best suited for those who are comfortable jumping into deep waters.

Visibility is excellent, with good-sized reef fish and a fine variety of corals close to shore. The predatory crown of thorns starfish can be seen here feasting on live coral polyps.

For divers, there's a ledge a little way out that drops off about 100 feet. In winter the water can get rough when the surf is high.

HOOKENA
Hookena was once a bustling village with two churches, a school, courthouse and post office. King Kalakaua sent his friend Robert Louis Stevenson here in 1889 to show him a typical Hawaiian village. Stevenson stayed a week with the town's judge and wrote about Hookena in *Travels in Hawaii*.

In the 1890s Chinese immigrants began to move into Hookena, setting up shops and restaurants. A tavern and a hotel opened and the town got rougher and rowdier.

In those days, Big Island cattle were shipped from Hookena's landing to market in Honolulu. When the circle-island road was built, the steamers stopped coming and the townspeople moved away. By the 1920s the town was all but deserted.

These days, Hookena is a tiny fishing community with a small county beach park. The storm-beaten remains of the landing are in front of the park restrooms.

Hookena is 2¼ miles down a narrow road from Hwy 11. The marked turn-off is between the 101- and 102-mile markers.

The beach has very soft black sand. The bay is backed by lava sea cliffs and there are trees for shade. When the winter surf is up, local kids with boogie boards hit the waves here.

When it's calm you can snorkel straight out from the landing. It drops off pretty quickly, from 10 feet to about 30 feet, and there's lots of coral. Don't go too far out or you may encounter strong currents. Pygmy dolphins occasionally come into the bay, sometimes as many as a hundred at a time.

Hookena is a popular weekend picnic spot for Hawaiian families, and camping is allowed with a permit from the county. It has toilets but no drinking water.

MILOLII
Milolii means 'fine twist'. Historically, the village was known for its skilled sennit twisters who used bark from the olona shrub to make fine cord and highly valued fishing nets.

Milolii villagers still live close to the sea, many making their living from fishing. Some use an age-old method resembling aqua farming in which they sail out to feed papaya and taro to opelu, a type of mackerel. After months of the fattening and taming process, they return to net the fish.

While Milolii is one of the most traditional fishing villages in Hawaii, this is more in spirit than in appearance. Old fishing shacks have been replaced with modern homes and fishers now zip out in motorized boats to do their fishing. The small village consequently holds little of direct interest to most visitors. Furthermore, Milolii residents generally prefer their isolation and are not enthusiastic about tourists poking around.

At Milolii Beach Park, past the village's little boat ramp, camping is officially allowed with a permit from the county. However, the beach park is right in the village, without a lot of space or privacy, and this is also the community's playground and volleyball court. All in all, it's not a recommendable place to camp for people who don't have ties with the village.

Milolii sits at the edge of an expansive 1926 lava flow that covered the nearby fishing village of Hoopuloa. The turn-off to Milolii is just south of the 89-mile marker on Hwy 11, from where it's five miles down a paved but steep and winding single-lane road that cuts across the lava flow. If you decide to make the drive, use a low gear, or your brakes will smoke on this one.

MacFarms of Hawaii

Just before entering the Kau district, Hwy 11 passes through the largest macadamia nut orchard in Hawaii, 3800 acres belonging to MacFarms of Hawaii. The orchards were started by a partnership that included Jimmy Stewart, Julie Andrews and other Hollywood stars.

MacFarms has introduced biological insect controls, composting and the use of grazing sheep for weed control in an effort to go organic. The orchards annually produce about 10 million pounds of nuts that are husked, processed and packaged on site.

North of Kona

Hwy 19 (Queen Kaahumanu Hwy) runs north 33 miles from Kailua-Kona up the Kona Coast to Kawaihae in the South Kohala district.

This is hot, arid country with a lava landscape. Along the road, clumps of brilliant red bougainvillea look striking against the jet-black rock, but otherwise the vegetation is mainly sparse tufts of grass that survive the dry winds. On this stretch you'll also notice the Big Island's unique version of graffiti – messages spelled out in white coral against a black lava background.

Honokohau Harbor and a new historical park are just a couple miles north of Kailua-Kona. Tiny fishing villages once dotted this sparsely populated coast but most were wiped out by the tsunami of 1946.

There are beautiful secluded beaches and coves on the north Kona Coast that are hidden from the road and accessible only by foot. Once you hike in, you'll find white-sand beaches tucked between a sea of hardened lava and a turquoise ocean. If you're not up for a hike, the new Kona Coast State Park now provides vehicle access to a nice undeveloped section of the Kona Coast.

Most of the Big Island's fanciest resorts are farther north, in the Waikoloa area of the South Kohala district. South Kohala was an important area in Hawaiian history, and there are heiaus, fishponds, petroglyphs and ancient trails that can all be explored. There are wonderful drive-up beaches at the resorts and at the nearby Anaehoomalu and Hapuna beach parks.

From much of the coast you can look inland and see Mauna Kea, and to the south of it Mauna Loa, both of which often have snowcaps in winter.

Hwy 19 is flat and straight and it's easy to zoom along, but it's also a hot spot for radar speed traps, particularly on the stretch between the airport and Kailua. Be aware that most police cruise in their own

BIG ISLAND

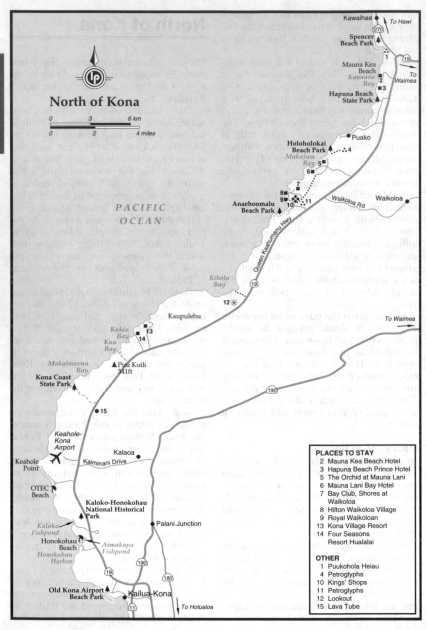

North of Kona

0   3   6 km

0   2   4 miles

PACIFIC
OCEAN

Kawaihae
To Hawi

Spencer
Beach Park

Mauna Kea
Beach
Kaunaoa
Bay

Hapuna Beach
State Park

Puako

Holoholokai
Beach Park

Makaiwa
Bay

Waikoloa Rd

Waikoloa

Anaehoomalu
Beach Park

Kiholo
Bay

To Waimea

Kaupulehu

To Waimea

Kukio
Bay

Kua
Bay

Makalawena
Bay

Puu Kuili
341ft

Kona Coast
State Park

Keahole-
Kona
Airport

Keahole
Point

Kalaoa

Kaiminani Drive

OTEC
Beach

Kaloko-Honokohau
National Historical
Park

Kaloko
Fishpond

Honokohau
Beach

Honokohau
Harbor

Aimakapa
Fishpond

Palani Junction

Old Kona Airport
Beach Park

Kailua-Kona

To Holualoa

PLACES TO STAY
2   Mauna Kea Beach Hotel
3   Hapuna Beach Prince Hotel
5   The Orchid at Mauna Lani
6   Mauna Lani Bay Hotel
7   Bay Club, Shores at
    Waikoloa
8   Hilton Waikoloa Village
9   Royal Waikoloan
13 Kona Village Resort
14 Four Seasons
    Resort Hualalai

OTHER
1   Puukohola Heiau
4   Petroglyphs
10 Kings' Shops
11 Petroglyphs
12 Lookout
15 Lava Tube

unmarked cars, anything from Trans-Ams to Broncos, and they're tough to spot.

The highway is part of the Ironman Triathlon route and wide, smooth bike lanes border both sides of the road. Cyclists should note that when the air temperature is above 85°F, reflected heat from asphalt and lava can edge the actual temperature above 100°F. There's no drinking water or services between OTEC Beach and the Waikoloa hotels.

Honokohau Harbor

Honokohau Harbor was built in 1970 to take some of the burden off Kailua Pier. The majority of the 155 slips are occupied by charter fishing boats, and these days most of Kona's catch comes in here.

The harbor is about two miles north of Kailua on Hwy 19. In case you're wondering about the plaques in front of the coconut trees that line the road down to the harbor – they name the donor for each of these trees, all planted during a beautification project.

If you want to see the charter fishing boats pull in and weigh their catches of marlin and yellowfin tuna, park near the gas station and walk to the dock at the rear of the adjacent building. The best times to see the weigh-ins are generally around 11:30 am and 3:30 pm.

The harbor complex has a couple of places where you could grab a meal and a fish market that sells delicious smoked marlin by the piece.

Honokohau Beach

Honokohau Beach, just north of the harbor, has long been Kona's nudist beach, although its days may be numbered for naturists as the beach is now part of the new Kaloko-Honokohau National Historical Park.

The beach is composed of large-grained sand, a mix of black lava, white coral and rounded shell fragments. Walking along the sand gives a good foot massage. It's not a bad beach for swimming and snorkeling, although the bottom is a bit rocky.

To get there, turn onto the Honokohau

Harbor road from Hwy 19, then turn right in front of the marina complex and follow the road a quarter of a mile. Pull off to the right after the dry dock boat yard. The trail begins at a break in the lava wall on the right about 50 feet beyond the dead end sign. It's a five-minute walk along a well-beaten path to the beach, although as development proceeds on the new park, access may change.

There are no facilities at the beach, except for pit toilets at the end of the trail. You might want to take along some insect repellent in case the gnats are feasting.

Kaloko-Honokohau National Historical Park

Kaloko-Honokohau National Historical Park (☎ 329-6881) is still in the developmental stages. It encompasses about 1200 acres and includes Aimakapa and Kaloko fishponds, ancient heiau and house sites, burial caves, petroglyphs, a holua slide, a queen's bath and the oceanfront from Kaloko to Honokohau Harbor. There's also a one-mile segment of the ancient stone footpath known as the **King's Trail**.

There's speculation that the bones of Kamehameha the Great were buried in secret near Kaloko. This, combined with the fact that Aimakapa Fishpond is a habitat for endangered water birds, was enough to help squeeze the national park designation through Congress in 1978.

The park entrance leads to **Kaloko Fishpond**, acquired in 1986 from Huehue Ranch in exchange for 300 acres of federal land on the mainland. Over the past two decades, mangrove invaded and spread rapidly throughout Kaloko Fishpond and native birds abandoned the habitat. The park service has recently finished eradicating the mangrove, a labor-intensive process that involved cutting and torching the trees, then tearing the new shoots up one by one and burning the roots. Native birds have now returned to Kaloko.

Aimakapa Fishpond, just inland from the beach, is the largest pond on the Kona Coast and an important bird habitat. Like Kaloko Fishpond, it also had to have a mangrove invasion stemmed. If you visit this brackish pond, you're likely to see *aeo* (black-necked stilts) and *alae-keokeo* (Hawaiian coots), both endangered native water birds that have made a significant return since the pond was cleared.

The **Queen's Bath** is a spring-fed pool with brackish water in the middle of a lava flow. Even though it's inland, the water level changes with the tide; at high tide, saltwater seeps in and the water in the pool rises. You can get there by walking south for about 15 minutes from Kaloko Fishpond or inland from the north end of Honokokau Beach. The queen's bath is marked by stone cairns as well as Christmas berries, always a dead giveaway that fresh water is nearby.

While most of the work within the park is still concentrating on natural restoration, trails are slowly being developed and plans call for the eventual opening of a visitor center that will feature displays on Hawaiian culture and natural history.

The unmarked park entrance is off Hwy 19, about half a mile north of the 97-mile marker. The park gates are open from 8 am to 3:30 pm daily, but there's also access from the harbor (see Honokohau Beach). A ranger is usually on site to answer questions.

Keahole Point/OTEC Beach

The turn-off leading to OTEC Beach and the Natural Energy Laboratory of Hawaii (NELH), a state hydroenergy research facility, is one mile south of the Keahole-Kona Airport.

At Keahole Point the sea floor drops steeply just offshore, providing a continuous supply of both cold water from 600-meter depths as well as warm surface waters. These are ideal conditions for ocean thermal energy conversion (OTEC).

The OTEC system operates like a steam turbine, with the difference in temperature between the cold and warm waters providing the energy source. Electricity has been successfully generated at the site, and research continues on ways to make this an economically viable energy source.

The nutrient-rich cold waters that are pumped up are also used in spin-off aquaculture projects, such as the production of salmon, Maine lobster, abalone, oysters, seaweed and spirulina.

From the highway it's about a mile in to OTEC (Wawaloli) Beach, where there are toilets, showers and drinking water. This windswept lava coastline is rocky and not very good for swimming, although there's a large naturally enclosed pool 200 yards south of the restrooms that's deep enough to wade in.

The rough dirt road that continues south from the beach leads half a mile to **Pine Trees**, one of the best surfing breaks in the Kona area.

Onizuka Space Center

The Astronaut Ellison S Onizuka Space Center (☎ 329-3441), at the Keahole-Kona Airport, pays tribute to the Big Island native who perished in the Challenger space shuttle disaster.

The little museum has exhibits about space and the role of astronauts, shows educational films and displays a moon rock, space suit and scale models of space craft. Admission is $2 for adults, 50¢ for children. It's open from 8:30 am to 4:30 pm daily.

Lava Tube

There's a big open lava tube on the mauka side of Hwy 19, north of the 91-mile marker and just before a speed limit sign. It might seem rather tame if you've been to Hawaii Volcanoes National Park but interesting if you haven't.

The tube and the expansive lava flow that surrounds the airport are both from the last eruption of Mt Hualalai, in 1801.

Kona Coast State Park

The attractive sandy beach at Mahaiula Bay has been opened to the public as part of Kona Coast State Park. The island's newest park, it has shaded picnic tables, barbecue grills and portable toilets, but is otherwise completely undeveloped. The facilities are at the south side of the beach, but the park's loveliest section is at the north end, about a five-minute walk away.

The inshore waters are shallow and gently sloping. Most of the time there's good snorkeling and swimming but during periods of high surf, which are not infrequent in winter, there's good surfing instead, particularly at the north side of the bay.

The road into the park, which begins 2½ miles north of the airport off Hwy 19, is nearly as interesting as the beach. It runs for 1¾ miles, across a seemingly endless lava flow that's totally devoid of trees and greenery, before depositing you at this little oasis. The road is quite bumpy and only partly paved, but is passable in a regular car.

If you want to explore further, a trail leads north from Kona Coast State Park about 1¼ miles to **Makalawena**, another beautiful stretch of beach. Makalawena is backed by sand dunes and contains some fine coves with good swimming and snorkeling.

On Wednesdays, Kona Coast State Park is closed and the gate at the start of the road is locked.

Kua Bay

Kua Bay, also known as Maniniowali, has a beautiful secluded beach with turquoise waters and gleaming white sands. It's picture-postcard material.

It has a gentle slope and inviting waters for swimmers most of the year and for boogie boarders and body-surfers in winter. Although it's generally calm, winter storms can generate currents in the bay.

The turn-off to the beach is just north of both the 88-mile marker and the grassy 341-foot Puu Kuili, the highest cinder cone on the makai side of the highway. Look for the stop sign and gate at the head of the road.

The road down is rough and over loose lava stones. Some people do drive in about half a mile and park near the roadside, but if you park near the highway it only takes about 20 minutes to walk in.

At the end of the road there's a path over the rocks to the south end of the beach. There are no facilities.

Kaupulehu

In ancient times, Kaupulehu was the site of a large fishing village, and a few Big Island fishers still lived along this shoreline until the tsunami of 1946 swept their homes away. The area, accessible only by boat, was then abandoned until the early 1960s, when a wealthy yachter who had anchored off Kaupulehu concluded this would be the perfect place for a hideaway hotel. The Kona Village Resort opened in 1965. It was so isolated it had to build its own airstrip to shuttle in guests – the highway that now parallels the Kona Coast wasn't built for another decade.

The Kona Village Resort remains unique among Hawaii's getaway hotels in that its accommodations are thatched Polynesian-style *hales* on stilts, which are spaced around a spring-fed lagoon and along the

---

Donkey Crossing

In the evenings, donkeys come down from the hills to drink at spring-fed watering holes and to eat seed pods from the kiawe trees along the coast between Kua and Kiholo bays. The donkeys are descendants of the pack animals that were used on coffee farms until the 1950s, when they were replaced by jeeps.

Growers, who had become fond of these 'Kona nightingales', as the donkeys were nicknamed because of their braying, released many of the creatures into the wild rather than turning them into glue. The donkeys were largely forgotten until Hwy 19 went through in 1974.

The donkeys now need to cross the road for their evening feedings, and it's worth keeping an eye out for them at night as they don't always pay attention to the 'Donkey Crossing' signs on the highway! They can sometimes be spotted in the area immediately south of the two Kaupulehu resorts. ■

white sands of Kahuwai Bay. The resort limits nonguest access, but guided tours are given daily at 11 am.

In 1996 a second upmarket hotel, the Four Seasons Resort, opened at Kaupulehu Beach, about a 10-minute walk south of Kona Village Resort. Originally begun as a multi-story resort, the developers got so much resistance from island environmentalists that they dismantled the buildings halfway through the project, replaced them with low-rise bungalows and incorporated the natural environment into their landscaping. They also opened up the shoreline, making the lovely white-sand beach at **Kukio Bay** and a string of pristine little coves to the south of it easily accessible to the public for the first time. An inviting mile-long footpath through the lava connects Four Seasons with Kukio Bay, where there's beach parking for visitors.

Places to Stay The 125 free-standing cottages at *Kona Village Resort* (☎ 325-5555, 800-367-5290; fax 325-5124; kvr@ilhawaii .net), Box 1299, Kailua-Kona, HI 96745, look like rustic thatched huts on the outside but are modern and comfortable inside with high ceilings, rattan furnishings, ceiling fans and louvered windows. In keeping with the getaway concept, the units do not have phones or TVs. Daily rates range from $300 to $585 for singles, $395 to $680 for doubles, including meals and recreational activities. Despite the obvious irony of paying this kind of money to 'go native', there seem to be few unhappy campers here.

The *Four Seasons Resort Hualalai* (☎ 325-8000, 800-332-3442; fax 325-8100), Box 1269, Kailua-Kona, HI 96745, is the island's newest luxury hotel. The 243 rooms, which are spread around three dozen low-rise buildings, are spacious with large lanais, concealed TVs, fax lines and similar amenities. Rates begin at $450 for a hotel room and top out at $5500 for the three-bedroom presidential suite. The resort has an 18-hole golf course, eight tennis courts, three oceanfront pools, a fitness club and spa, and interesting displays on Hawaiian art and culture.

Places to Eat *Pahuia*, at the Four Seasons Resort Hualalai, is an elegant oceanfront restaurant with a menu that features Hawaiian Regional cuisine, emphasizing local fish in a variety of preparations. The resort's more affordable *Beach Tree Bar & Grill* serves three meals a day, with salads and sandwiches at lunch and grilled steaks and fish at dinner.

Kona Village Resort is open for meals to nonguests, with advance reservations, except when the resort is at 100% occupancy. The daily outdoor lunch buffet, held from 12:30 to 2 pm, costs $24. There's fine dining in the *Hale Samoa*, a New Hebrides-style thatched building, where dinners average $60.

Kiholo Bay

Halfway up the coast, just south of the 82-mile marker, there's a lookout that commands a great view of Kiholo Bay. It appears like a little oasis in the midst of the lava, with intense blue waters and a line of coconut trees.

An inconspicuous trail down to the bay starts about 100 yards south of the 81-mile marker. It follows a 4WD road, the beginning of which has been blocked off by boulders to keep vehicles out. The hike down takes about half an hour.

Kiholo Bay is almost two miles wide, and the south end of the bay has a lovely, large spring-fed pond called **Luahinewai**. It's refreshingly cold and fronted by a black-sand beach. There's also good ocean swimming when it's calm.

In ancient times, Kiholo provided a respite along the King's Trail, a stone footpath that ran along the coast. It was a fishing village famous for a large fishpond built by Kamehameha. The fishpond was filled in by an 1859 lava flow.

Cattle were shipped from here in the 1890s, and there was once a small hotel. Now there are a few private homes on the bay, including one owned by country and western singer Loretta Lynn.

WAIKOLOA BEACH RESORT

Just after crossing into the South Kohala district, a single turn-off leads to the Royal Waikoloan and Hilton Waikoloa Village hotels and to Anaehoomalu Beach Park. The road is just south of the 76-mile marker.

Petroglyphs

A two-acre lava field etched with an impressive number of petroglyphs is off to the right, immediately before the Kings' Shops complex. If you park at the complex, it's about a five-minute walk along a signposted path to the etchings.

Many of the petroglyphs date back to the 16th century. Some are graphic (humans, birds, canoes), others cryptic (dots and lines). Western influences show up in the form of horses and English initials.

Although the footpath that leads through the petroglyphs is called the King's Trail, this section was actually a horse and cattle trail built in the late 19th century. The trail once connected Kailua with Kawaihae. It's possible to continue on the trail to a historical preserve at the Mauna Lani Resort, about two miles away, but it's a hot unshaded walk over lava.

Anaehoomalu Beach

Anaehoomalu Beach is a long, sandy beach that curves along an attractive bay. The waters are popular for swimming and windsurfing and have a gently sloping sandy bottom. Winter weather can produce rip currents, but most of the time the water is quite calm.

This is a fine beach for an outing if you're staying in Kona. The south end of the beach has public facilities, with showers, toilets, changing areas and parking. The north end of the beach, which fronts the Royal Waikoloan hotel, has a little fitness area with swing ropes, chin-up bars and a volleyball net.

Both ends of the bay are composed of prehistoric lava flows from Mauna Kea, with rough aa lava to the north and smooth pahoehoe to the south.

Anaehoomalu was once the site of royal fishponds, and archaeologists from the Bishop Museum have found evidence here of human habitation dating back more than a thousand years.

There are two large fishponds just beyond the line of coconut trees on the beach. A short footpath starts near the showers and winds by the fishponds, caves, ancient house platforms and a shrine. Interpretive plaques along the way explain the area's history.

The beach hut in front of the hotel can give you the latest on water conditions. They rent windsurfing equipment and snorkel sets and offer windsurfing lessons, beginning scuba lessons, boat dives, catamaran cruises and glassbottom boat rides.

A good spot for snorkeling at the north end of the beach is directly in front of the sluice gate. Here you'll find coral formations, a fair variety of tropical fish and, with a little luck, sea turtles. If you're not a snorkeler, the turtles can sometimes be seen by simply walking out onto the rock wall that encloses the sluice gate and looking down into the surrounding waters.

Hilton Waikoloa Village

The 62-acre Hilton Waikoloa Village is the most extravagant resort development on the Big Island. It so has the air of a sophisticated theme park that islanders nicknamed it 'Disneyland'.

The hotel had no beach, so it built its own. There's a four-acre saltwater lagoon stocked with tropical fish, a dolphin pool, a 'river' with a current for rafting and sprawling swimming pools with cascading waterfalls.

Canopied boats cart guests between buildings along artificial canals and there's a modernistic tram that looks like it was intended for downtown Tokyo. Because the complex is so large, both actually do function as public transport and the novelty of using and waiting for them wears off quickly.

When it opened in 1988 at a cost of $360 million, the hotel billed itself as the world's most expensive resort. But for all the extravagance it's surprisingly casual, and anyone can cruise around in the free boats and tram.

You can stroll by a multimillion-dollar **art collection** along a mile-long walkway that runs in both directions from the front lobby. The museum-quality pieces include extensive collections from Melanesia, Polynesia and Asia. It's particularly big on Papua New Guinea, with war clubs and spears, spirit boards, carved fighting shields and a partial replica of a ceremonial house. There's a collection of Han pottery that dates back 2000 years, antique dolls and Noh masks from Japan, 18th-century Burmese puppets and huge cloisonné vases. They've even managed to slip in a little Hawaiiana display with poi pounders and a few adze heads and koa bowls.

There's free parking at the hotel, but you can also walk over from the Royal Waikoloan, a quiet 15-minute stroll along the lava coast.

Places to Stay

The 545-room *Royal Waikoloan* (☎ 885-6789, 800-688-7444; fax 800-622-4852; reservations@outrigger.com), Box 5300, Waikoloa, HI 96743, is a former Sheraton hotel that's now part of the Outrigger chain. While this is the 'budget' hotel on the Waikoloa coast, the rooms are comfortable and the beachside location is far superior to that of the Hilton's. The rooms have a pleasant decor, either two double beds or one king bed, cable TV, phone, air-con and private lanai. The grounds include trails, a pool and a water sports hut, and the hotel is within walking distance of the Kings' Shops so you're not captive to resort prices for all your meals. Rates begin at $120/135 in the low/high season for a garden view; if you request it at the time of booking they'll usually add on a free rental car at no additional cost.

Hilton Waikoloa Village (☎ 885-1234, 800-445-8667; fax 885-2900), 1 Waikoloa Beach Resort, Waikoloa, HI 96743, is a megahotel with 1241 rooms and all the usual Hilton amenities. Rates start at $250/300 for garden/ocean views and go up to $3000 for the presidential suite.

There are two upscale, fully equipped condominium complexes in the area, each with a pool but about a 15-minute walk from the beach. *The Bay Club* (☎ 885-7979, 800-305-7979; fax 885-7780), 5525 Waikoloa Beach Drive, Waikoloa, HI 96743, has one-bedroom units from $180/235 in the low/high season and two-bedroom units from $225/265. Shuttle service to the beach and shopping center is provided.

The Shores at Waikoloa (☎ 885-5001, 800-922-7866), 5460 Waikoloa Beach Drive, Waikoloa, HI 96743, is an Aston-managed property. Rates start at $215/235 in the low/high season for a one-bedroom apartment, $255/275 for a two-bedroom apartment.

Places to Eat

The Kings' Shops has a little food pavilion, a couple of sit-down restaurants and a small grocery store. In the food pavilion, which is open until 9:30 pm, there's a *Subway Sandwiches* with its standard menu of submarine sandwiches and *Hawaiian Chili by Max* with chili and rice, hot dogs and chili dogs. For dinner the best option in Kings' Shops – if not in all of Waikoloa – is the new *Roy's Waikoloa Bar & Grill*, which has creative Pacific Rim cuisine at moderate prices.

The *Royal Terrace* in the Royal Waikoloan has an average breakfast buffet, served from 6 to 11 am daily, for $13 for the full spread or $9 for just the cold dishes. At dinner, the best buy is usually the daily special for around $15.

Palm Terrace, in the Hilton, is open for breakfast from 6 to 11 am and for dinner from 5 to 9:30 pm. There are good buffets at both meals. Breakfast, which has a few Japanese touches as well as the standard American dishes and pastries, costs $17.50. Dinner, which features a different ethnic buffet each night, is $23. You can also order à la carte at either meal, with breakfast main courses, dinner salads and sandwiches priced around $9. It has a pleasant and somewhat casual setting overlooking a pond with exotic water birds. Ask for a swan-view table.

The Hilton also has fine-dining Japanese, Italian and continental restaurants with prices to match the setting.

Entertainment
The *Royal Waikoloan* has a poolside luau at 6 pm on Sundays and Wednesdays. The cost of $49 for adults ($22 for children ages six to 12) includes dinner, an open bar and a Polynesian show.

The *Hilton Waikoloa Village* has a couple of bars, including the Kamuela Provision Company lounge, where guitar music is played from 6 to 10 pm.

WAIKOLOA
Waikoloa village, about six miles inland from the beach, is a modern residential development and bedroom community for workers in the nearby resorts. Although there's not much of interest for visitors passing through, the village does have condo complexes, a golf course, horse stables, a shopping center, a gas station and a bank. The 12-mile Waikoloa Rd connecting Hwys 190 and 19 runs through the village.

Places to Stay
Elima Lani (☎ 883-8288, 800-551-5264; fax 883-8170), 68-3883 Lua Kula St, Kamuela, HI 96743, is a modern 216-unit condo complex that's also on the golf course. While it's not upscale, it's comfortable enough and the grounds have a couple of swimming pools. The units have two baths and the usual amenities, including kitchens with microwaves and washers and dryers. The rate is $100 for a one-bedroom unit, $120 for a two-bedroom unit. Up to four people (six in the two-bedroom units) are allowed at these rates, although there's just a regular sofa, not a sofa bed, in the living room.

Places to Eat
The Waikoloa Highlands Shopping Center on Waikoloa Rd has a small food court with a deli, a pizzeria, a grocery store and a little sandwich and ice cream shop.

MAUNA LANI RESORT
After a brief encounter with coconut palms and bright bougainvilleas at the highway entrance, Mauna Lani Drive heads through a long stretch of lava with virtually no vegetation. Halfway along there's a strikingly green golf course sculptured into the black lava. Mauna Lani Bay Hotel is at the end of the road. The Orchid at Mauna Lani hotel and Holoholokai Beach Park are to the north.

Mauna Lani Bay Hotel
This hotel is ritzy but still low-key, a modern open-air structure centered around a breezy atrium that holds waterways, orchid sprays and full-grown coconut trees. A saltwater stream that runs through the hotel and outdoors into the sun holds small black-tipped sharks and a variety of colorful reef fish.

The hotel has good beaches and interesting historical sights; there's public access to both. A free, self-guided trail map is available at the concierge desk.

Beaches The beach in front of the Mauna Lani Bay Hotel is protected but the water is rather shallow. There's a coral reef beyond the inlet that snorkelers might want to explore. You can check at the hotel beach hut for current water conditions.

There's also a less-frequented cove down by the Beach Club restaurant, a 15-minute walk to the south.

An old **coastal foot trail** leads about a mile farther south to **Honokaope Bay**. It passes by a few historical sites, including a fishers' house site and other village remains. The southern end of Honokaope Bay is protected and good for swimming and snorkeling when the seas are calm.

Fishponds The ancient Kalahuipuaa fishponds are along the beach just south of the hotel in a shady grove of coconut palms and milo trees.

The ponds are stocked, as they were in ancient times, with awa, a Hawaiian milkfish. Water circulates from the ocean through traditional makaha sluice gates, which allow small fish to enter but keep the older fattened ones from leaving. The fish sporadically jump into the air and slap down on the water, an exercise that knocks off parasites.

The Kalahuipuaa ponds are among the few continuously working fishponds in Hawaii; the awa raised here have been used to provide stock for commercial fisheries.

Historic Trail The Kalahuipuaa Trail begins mauka of the Mauna Lani Bay Hotel, at a marked parking lot opposite the resort's little grocery store.

The trail, which is particularly pleasant in early morning or late afternoon light, offers a nice combination of historic sites and scenic views. It's also a good walk for spotting quail, northern and red-crested cardinals, saffron finches and Japanese white-eyes.

The first part of the trail meanders through a former Hawaiian settlement that dates from the 16th century, passing lava tubes once used as cave shelters and a few other archaeological and geological sites marked by interpretive plaques.

The trail then skirts fishponds lined with coconut palms and continues out to the beach, where there's a thatched shelter with an outrigger canoe and a historic cottage with a few Hawaiiana items on display. If you continue southwest past the cottage you can loop around the fishpond and make a round trip of about 1½ miles back to your starting point. If you feel like taking a break en route, there's an attractive cove at the southern tip of the fishpond that has good swimming and a lunchtime restaurant with simple fare.

Holoholokai Beach Park

Holoholokai Beach Park, north of The Orchid at Mauna Lani, has a rocky shoreline composed of a mix of coral chunks and lava. It's not a great bathing beach, although when the waters are calm there's reasonable snorkeling in the area and there can be good surf breaks in winter.

The park has showers, drinking water, restrooms, picnic tables and grills and is open from 6:30 am to 7 pm.

For those not picnicking, the main reason for visiting the park is to walk the trail to the Puako petroglyphs. To get there, take Mauna Lani Drive and turn right at the rotary, then right again on the beach road immediately before the grounds of The Orchid.

Puako Petroglyphs With more than 3000 petroglyphs, the Puako petroglyph preserve has one of the largest collections of ancient lava carvings in Hawaii.

From the north end of the beach parking lot, a well-marked trail leads to the petroglyphs three-quarters of a mile away.

The human figures drawn in simple linear forms are some of Hawaii's oldest such drawings. Those with triangular shapes and curved forms are from more recent times.

The aging petroglyphs are fragile, as the ancient lava flow into which they're carved is brittle and cracking. Stepping on the petroglyphs can damage them, so be careful not to. The only safe way to record them is with a camera. If you want to make rubbings, there are some authentically reproduced petroglyphs just a minute's walk down the trail from the parking lot that have been created for that purpose. Bring rice paper and charcoal or cotton cloth and crayons and you can make your own souvenirs of 'old Hawaii'.

Because of the sharp kiawe thorns along the trail, flip-flops (thongs) are not appropriate footwear for the walk – the thorns can easily pierce their soft soles and your feet.

Places to Stay

The *Mauna Lani Bay Hotel* (☎ 885-6622, 800-367-2323), Box 4000, Kohala, HI 96743, is widely regarded as one of the finest resort hotels in the islands. All 350 rooms have TVs, phones, room safes, minibars, private lanais and bathrobes. Rates begin at $260 for a mountain view room, $395 for an ocean view; from June through September there's a $225 run-of-the-house summer rate. In addition to the rooms, the resort also has villas with full kitchens for $395 to $630, depending upon the number of bedrooms. The Mauna Lani can be booked internationally through the Pan Pacific Hotel chain.

The luxury *Mauna Lani Point* condos at the south side of the Mauna Lani Resort are booked through Classic Resorts (☎ 667-1400, 800-642-6284), 50 Nohea Kai Drive, Lahaina, HI 96761. One-bedroom units start at $240/270 in the low/high season; two-bedroom units at $305/355.

The Orchid at Mauna Lani (☎ 885-2000, 800-325-3535), 1 N Kaniku Drive, Kohala, HI 96743, on Pauoa Bay just north of the Mauna Lani Bay Hotel, is the Waikoloa area's newest hotel. It's a rather subdued place that originally opened as a member of the Ritz but has recently affiliated with the Sheraton hotel chain. Rates for the 542 rooms start at $265 for a garden view, $395 for an ocean view.

Places to Eat
The Cafe (☎ 885-2000) at The Orchid at Mauna Lani is an upscale cafe-style restaurant with an open-air setting and good food. Appetizers and salads are priced under $10, pizzas cost $14 and Asian-Hawaiian entrees average about $23. The cafe also serves the area's best Sunday brunch (11 am to 2 pm) with everything from seafood appetizers to scrumptious desserts; the cost is $30.

There's also a tempting Sunday brunch at the Mauna Lani Bay Hotel's (☎ 885-6622) open-air *Bay Terrace*. It has a sushi and sashimi table, waffles and omelets to order, prime rib, seafood dishes and a good variety of fruits, salads and desserts. The buffet is served from 9 am to 2 pm and costs $27.50. There's a simpler breakfast buffet from 6:30 to 11 am on other days for $20 (or $12.50 continental).

The *Canoe House*, which fronts the beach beside the Mauna Lani Bay Hotel, is a romantic, open-air dinner restaurant. Run by chef David Abella (formerly of Roy's), the menu blends Mediterranean, Far East and Hawaiian influences, with an emphasis on seafood. Dishes such as lemon grass

swordfish with hearts of palm or Thai seafood curry cost $30 to $35 à la carte, while salads and appetizers will add another $8 to $20 to the tab.

The *Gallery*, adjacent to the resort's racquet club, has a pleasant alfresco setting and well-prepared continental and Pacific Rim dishes. The fresh fish is a specialty, including a mouth-watering ahi that is seared on the outside and sashimi-like inside and a recommendable onaga with a macnut crust. Most entrees cost $20 to $25, but as everything is strictly à la carte, expect dinner for two to edge up to $100.

For someplace a bit easier on the wallet, there's the *Beach Club*, a casual restaurant at the south end of Kaniku Drive overlooking a swimming cove. They serve a good burger with fries for $8 and a fish sandwich for $10. It's open from 11 am to 4 pm daily.

PUAKO
Puako is a quiet one-road coastal village where everyone either lives on the beach or across the street from it.

Puako is lined with giant **tide pools**, set in the swirls and dips of the pahoehoe lava that forms the coastline. Some of the pools are deep enough to shelter live coral and other marine life. Snorkeling can be excellent off Puako, although the surf is usually too rough in winter. A narrow beach of pulverized coral and lava lines much of the shore.

The turn-off to Puako is marked on Hwy 19 and you can also reach Puako from Hapuna Beach State Park along a passable route that's more patchwork than road.

Hoku Loa Church, which dates back to 1858, is about half a mile beyond the Puako Bay boat ramp. A plain plastered building with a few simple wooden pews, it's still used for Sunday services, but at other times it's usually locked up tight.

There are several shoreline access signs, but the easiest beach access is at the end of the village where the old road meets a section of new pavement, about three miles from Hwy 19. Here a short dirt drive leads to the water. A couple of minutes' walk north along the beach will bring you to a few petroglyphs, a konane game board chinked into the lava and tide pools deep enough to cool off in.

HAPUNA BEACH

The long beautiful stretch of white sand along Hapuna Bay is the Big Island's most popular beach.

When it's calm, Hapuna Beach State Park has good swimming, snorkeling and diving. In the winter it's a hot bodysurfing and boogie boarding beach. The high winter surf can produce strong currents close to the shore and a pounding shore-break. Waves over three feet should be left for the experts. Hapuna has had numerous drownings and many of the victims have been tourists unfamiliar with the water conditions.

There's a tiny cove with a small sandy beach about five minutes' walk to the north of the park. The water is a bit calmer there and in winter there's less sand kicked up by the waves.

The 61-acre state park includes the beach, A-frame cabins for overnight stays (see Camping in the front of this chapter) and a landscaped park with picnic facilities, showers, restrooms, drinking water and telephones. There are lifeguards on duty daily.

There's a snack bar, open from 10 am to 5 pm daily, which sells burgers, beverages and ice cream. A window at the side rents boogie boards for $5 and snorkel sets for $7.50 per half day.

Places to Stay & Eat

The 350-room *Hapuna Beach Prince Hotel* (☎ 882-1111, 800-882-6060; fax 882-1174), 1 Mauna Kea Beach Drive, Waikoloa, HI 96743, is a new resort hotel at the northern end of Hapuna Beach. It largely gears its services to Japanese tourists who aren't taken aback by the sky-high room rates. A room with a garden view is $325; add another $100 for an ocean view. The hotel has manicured lawns, a golf course, restaurants and a cocktail lounge.

MAUNA KEA BEACH

In the early 1960s, Laurance Rockefeller obtained a 99-year lease on the land around Kaunaoa Bay from his friend Richard Smart, owner of Parker Ranch. Five years later he opened Mauna Kea Beach Hotel, the first luxury hotel on the outer islands, at the north side of this bay.

Kaunaoa Bay is a gorgeous crescent bay with a white-sand beach that has since come to be known as Mauna Kea Beach. It has a gradual slope and fine swimming conditions most of the year. There's good snorkeling on the north side when it's calm. The beach is open to the public and there are parking spaces set aside for beach visitors.

The hotel lobby and grounds have displays of Asian and Pacific artwork, including bronze statues, temple toys and Hawaiian quilts. The north garden holds the most prized possession, a 7th-century pink granite Buddha taken from a temple in South India.

Places to Stay & Eat

The *Mauna Kea Beach Hotel* (☎ 882-7222, 800-882-6060; fax 880-3112), 62-100 Kaunaoa Drive, Kohala, HI 96743, is a member of the Westin hotel chain. The hotel, which recently underwent a major renovation, has all of the expected resort amenities, including a fitness center, tennis courts and an 18-hole golf course. The regular room rates start at $280 for a mountain view and rise to $500 for an upper-level ocean view, although special promotions occasionally cut these rates by about a third. The hotel's fine-dining restaurant, *Batik*, is an expensive formal affair featuring Chateaubriand and soufflés; men are required to wear jackets.

SPENCER BEACH PARK

Spencer Beach Park, off Hwy 270, just south of Kawaihae, is a popular place for families with children, as the shallow sandy beach is protected by a reef and by the jetty to the north. If anything, it's a bit too protected and the water tends to get silty.

The rocky south end of the beach past the pavilion is better for snorkeling, although entry is not as easy.

Spencer is a well-used beach park with a lifeguard station, picnic tables, toilets, showers, drinking water, changing rooms and both basketball and volleyball courts. Camping is allowed with a permit from the county. During the week, Hilo people who work on this side of the island often camp here instead of commuting.

PUUKOHOLA HEIAU

The Puukohola Heiau National Historic Site, which is off the side of the road that leads down to Spencer Beach, contains the last major temple built in Hawaii.

In 1790, after his attempt at a sweeping conquest of the islands was thwarted, King Kamehameha sought the advice of Kapoukahi, a soothsayer from Kauai. Kamehameha was told that if he built a temple to his war god here above Kawaihae Bay, then all of Hawaii would fall to him in battle. Kamehameha immediately began construction of Puukohola Heiau, completing it in 1791.

Kamehameha then held a dedication ceremony and invited his last rival on the Big Island, Keoua, the chief of Kau. When Keoua came ashore he was killed and brought up to the temple as the first offering to the gods. With Keoua's death, Kamehameha took sole control of the Big Island and then went on to fulfill the soothsayer's prophecy by conquering the other Hawaiian islands.

Puukohola Heiau, terraced in three steps, was covered with wooden idols and thatched structures, including an oracle tower, altar, drum house and a shelter for the high priest.

After Kamehameha's death in 1819, his son Liholiho and powerful widow Kaahumanu destroyed the heiau's wooden images and the temple was abandoned. These days, only the basic rock foundation remains, but it's still an impressive site.

Puukohola means 'Hill of the Whales'. Migrating humpbacks can often be seen offshore during winter.

The visitor center (☎ 882-7218), which is open from 7:30 am to 4 pm daily, has a few simple displays and someone on duty to provide a brief introduction to the park. A free brochure describes the historic sites that are spread over the park's 77 acres. There are no entrance fees.

A trail to the heiau starts at the visitor center and takes only five minutes to walk. If you arrive after hours, you can park at Spencer Beach Park and walk up to the heiau via an old entrance road that's now closed to vehicle traffic.

Just beyond Puukohola Heiau are the ruins of Mailekini Heiau, which predates Puukohola and was later turned into a fort by Kamehameha. Nearby, a heiau dedicated to shark gods lies submerged just offshore, and you can still see the stone leaning post where the high chief watched sharks bolt down the offerings he made.

The path continues down by the creek to Kamehameha's former house site. Warbling silverbills, doves and mosquitoes frequent the kiawe woods, but there's not much else to see.

The trail then leads across the highway to the site of John Young's homestead. Young, a shipwrecked British sailor, served Kamehameha as a military advisor and governor of the island. These days, all that remain are the partial foundations of two of Young's buildings; there are plans to put up an interpretive board with drawings of what the site originally looked like.

KAWAIHAE

Kawaihae has the Big Island's second largest deep-water commercial harbor. The harbor has fuel tanks and cattle pens and a little local beach park. There's not really much to attract visitors, so most stop in Kawaihae just long enough to eat and fuel up on their way to North Kohala.

Kawaihae Shopping Center on Hwy 270 has two restaurants, an ice cream and shave ice shop, a 7-Eleven convenience store, a couple of quality galleries and Kohala Divers.

BIG ISLAND

Places to Eat

Cafe Pesto (☎ 882-1071) serves up good gourmet pizza, calzones, pastas and salads. Pizzas include a tasty Greek version topped with feta cheese, fresh spinach and olive pesto and an Oriental pizza with sun-dried tomatoes, Japanese eggplant and roasted garlic. Both cost $10 for a nine-inch pizza, $16 for a 12-inch. At lunch, served until 4:30 pm, there are also hot sandwiches, including one with a generous slab of fresh fish on French bread for $9. The cafe, which is on the lower level of the Kawaihae Shopping Center, is open from 11 am to 9 pm on weekdays, to 10 pm on weekends. It can get busy at lunchtime, as it's a favorite spot for people working in the Waikoloa area.

There's more standard fare at *Tres Hombres Beach Grill* (☎ 882-1031), also in the Kawaihae Shopping Center. An enchilada, taco or tostada with rice and beans costs $8.25; two-item combination plates are a few dollars more. It's open from 11:30 am to 9 pm.

North Kohala

The northwest tip of the Big Island is dominated by a central ridge, the Kohala Mountains.

The leeward side of the ridge is dry and desert-like. The windward side is wet and lush with steep coastal cliffs and spectacular hanging valleys.

North Kohala is often bypassed by travelers, as it's off the main track, but it has a couple of impressive historical sites, a few sleepy towns to poke around in and a lovely valley lookout at the end of the road.

There are two ways to get to North Kohala, an inland road and a coastal road. You can make a nice tour by going up one and down the other.

WAIMEA TO HAWI (HWY 250)

Hwy 250 (Kohala Mountain Rd) runs north for 20 miles from Waimea to Hawi. This is a very scenic drive along the upland slopes of the Kohala Mountains. The road goes past neat rows of ironwood trees and up through rolling green hills dotted with grazing cattle.

As you head north, Maui rises out of the mist, with the red crater of Haleakala capping the skyline. Mauna Kea and Mauna Loa are visible behind you. Expansive views of the coast and Kawaihae Harbor unfold below and there's a roadside scenic lookout where you can take it all in.

There are also a couple of new subdivisions up this way, the largest being Kohala Ranch. Kohala Ranch Rd runs through the subdivision for six miles, connecting Hwys 250 and 270.

Hwy 250 peaks at 3564 feet before dropping down into Hawi.

KAWAIHAE TO POLOLU VALLEY (HWY 270)

Hwy 270 (Akoni Pule Hwy), which starts in Kawaihae, takes in the coastal sights of Lapakahi State Historical Park and Mookini Heiau and ends at a lookout above Pololu Valley.

There's a trail down to the valley floor, but even if you're not up for a hike, the view from the lookout is worth the drive.

Lapakahi State Historical Park

Lapakahi State Historical Park has the overall feel of an abandoned ghost town – which it is. Even the visitors in this desolate spot tend to be few.

This remote fishing village was settled about 600 years ago; as the terrain was rocky and dry, the villagers turned to the sea for their food. The cove fronting the village provided a safe year-round canoe landing and fish were plentiful.

Eventually some of the villagers moved to the wetter uplands and began to farm, trading their crops for fish with those who had stayed on the coast. In the process, Lapakahi grew into an ahupuaa, a wedge-shaped division of land radiating from the mountainous interior out to the sea.

In the 19th century, Lapakahi's freshwater table began to drop. This, coupled with the enticement of jobs in developing towns, led to the desertion of the village.

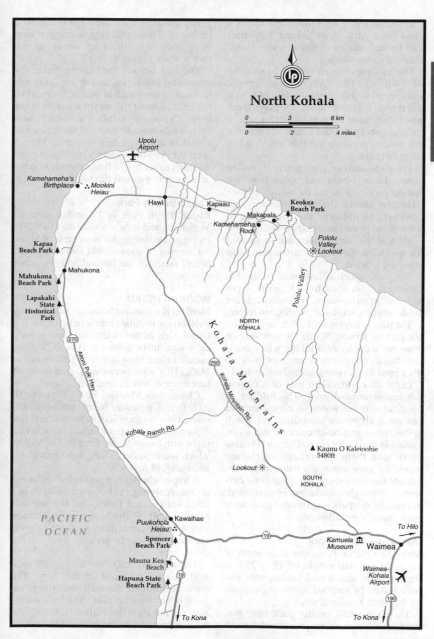

Lapakahi was a big village and this is a good-sized park. A mile-long loop trail lead to the remains of stone walls, house sites and canoe sheds.

The park encourages visitors to imagine what life was like centuries ago. People worshipped at fish shrines, a few of which still remain on the grounds. Displays show how fishers used lift nets to catch opelu, a technique still practiced today, and how the salt used to preserve the fish was dried in stone salt pans.

There's a hands-on approach to Hawaiian games. Game pieces and instructions are laid out for *oo ihe* (spear throwing), *konane* (Hawaiian checkers) and *ulu maika* (stone bowling, the object of the latter being to roll a round stone between two stakes.

Most of the trees in the park were used for medicine, food or construction, and many are labeled.

The park, which is just south of the 14-mile marker, is open from 8 am to 4 pm daily except on holidays. Trail brochures are available at the trailhead. Admission is free.

The park is largely unshaded, so it can be hot walking around. While the park service often has a cooler of drinking water available, there's no running water in the park, so it's a good idea to bring something to drink.

Lapakahi's waters are part of a marine life conservation district. The fish are so plentiful and the water so clear that you can stand above the shoreline and watch yellow tangs and other colorful fish swim around in the cove below. The coral is also good, and there's excellent snorkeling inside the cove when it's calm. However, outside the cove there are dangerous currents. Although swimming is permitted, because of the park's cultural significance sunbathing is not allowed.

Mahukona Beach Park

Mahukona Beach Park, one mile north of Lapakahi and half a mile off Hwy 270, is the site of an abandoned landing that was once linked by railroad to the sugar mills on the north Kohala coast.

There's a small county park here that has restrooms, showers, picnic tables and a grassy camping area, although it can get a bit buggy. Those planning to camp should bring their own drinking water, as the park's water is unfit to drink.

The area beyond the landing makes for interesting snorkeling and diving, although it's usually too rough in winter. Entry, via a ladder, is in about five feet of water. Heading north, it's possible to follow an anchor chain out to a submerged boiler and the remains of a ship in about 25 feet of water. There's coral on the bottom and visibility is good when it's calm. You'll find a shower near the ladder where you can rinse off.

Kapaa Beach Park

Kapaa Beach Park is 1¼ miles north of Mahukona and nearly a mile off Hwy 270. Its biggest selling point is its view of Maui.

Camping is allowed, but there's no sand beach, facilities are limited and it's rather dumpy.

MOOKINI HEIAU

Mookini is a massive heiau set atop a grassy knoll on the desolate northern tip of the Big Island. One of the oldest and most historically significant heiaus in Hawaii, it commands a clear view out across the ocean to Maui. This windswept site has a sense of timelessness and a certain eerie aura.

Chants date Mookini Heiau back to 480 AD. This is a luakini heiau, where the alii offered human sacrifices to the war god Ku.

According to legend, it was built in one night with basalt stones from Pololu Valley, which were passed along a human chain stretching 14 miles.

A kapu, which once prevented commoners from entering the heiau grounds, wasn't lifted until recent times, and the site still remains well off the beaten path. Because so few people come this way, there's a good chance it will just be you, the wind and the spirits here.

The heiau is 250 feet long, with rock walls reaching a good 25 feet high. The entrance through the wall into the heiau itself is on the west side. The long enclosure on the right immediately before the heiau entrance was the home of the *mu*, or body catcher, who secured sacrificial victims for the heiau altar. The large scallop-shaped altar on the north end of the heiau is thought to have been added by Paao, a Tahitian priest who arrived around the 12th century and introduced human sacrifice to Hawaiian worship.

The current kahuna nui priestess, Leimomi Mookini Lum, is the most recent in a long line of Mookinis tracing their lineage back to the temple's first high priest.

To get there, turn left off Hwy 270 at the 20-mile marker and go two miles down to Upolu Airport. At the airport turn left onto the road that runs parallel to the coast. Although it's usually passable, this red dirt road is rutted and bumpy and can get very muddy after heavy rains. After 1½ miles you'll come to a fork. The left road leads up to the heiau, a quarter of a mile farther.

Kamehameha's Birthplace
Kamehameha the Great was said to have been born on a stormy winter night in 1758 on this ruggedly desolate coast. If you continue straight ahead at the fork below the heiau for a third of a mile, you'll reach the stone enclosure that marks his birth site.

According to legend, Kamehameha's mother was told by a kahuna that her son would become a destroyer of chiefs and a powerful ruler. The high chief of the island didn't take well to the prophecy, and in a King Herod-like scenario he ordered the newborn killed.

Immediately after birth, the baby was taken to Mookini Heiau for his birth rituals and then into hiding in the nearby mountains.

HAWI
Hawi (pronounced Hah-vee), with a population of less than 1000, is the largest town in North Kohala. It has a post office, grocery store, gas station, coin laundry and a few galleries and restaurants.

North Kohala used to be sugar country, and Hawi was the biggest of half a dozen sugar towns. Kohala Sugar Company, which had incorporated all of the mills, closed

down its operations in 1975. Hawi now has more storefronts than stores, and although some people are beginning to be drawn this way by the area's lower property values it's still a very low-key place.

The park on Hwy 250 in front of the post office is cool and shady with giant banyan trees. Behind the park is the old sugar mill tower, a remnant of the town's former mainstay. You can still see the occasional strip of feral cane among the pastures outside town.

Places to Stay
Kohala Village Inn (☎ 889-0419), 55-514 Hawi Rd, Hawi, HI 96719, at the intersection of Hwys 270 and 250 in Hawi center, is an old-style hotel with 18 simple, clean rooms. Over the years, the place has bounced between trying to attract tourists and being given over to long-term boarders; its most recent owner has renovated it as a hotel again and given it an agreeable small-town character. A room with a double bed but no TV costs $47, while rooms with TV begin at $55. All rooms have private baths. If no one's at the front desk, walk around to the restaurant, which is managed by the same couple.

Cardinals' Haven Bed & Breakfast (☎ 884-5550), Box 53, Hawi, HI 96719, is a homey place with a lovely rural setting three miles south of Hawi center. A single guest unit in the winter home of Peter and Sonja Kamber, it consists of a bedroom with a comfortable queen bed and a living room with a small sofa bed that could accommodate one child. It's all quite straightforward but there's a TV, microwave, hot plate, coffeemaker and mini-refrigerator. From the yard you can look across cattle pastures clear out to Maui. The B&B is open only from November 20 to May 10; you can make advance reservations when it's closed by calling 206-822-3120. The rate is a reasonable $50 for two people, $60 for three, or $250 per week, breakfast of homemade breads and lilikoi jam included. Smoking is not allowed. Originally from Switzerland, the Kambers speak fluent German and French.

Places to Eat

Kohala Coffee Mill on Hwy 270 in the town center is a popular meeting place that serves fresh brewed coffees, muffins and pastries.

Kohala Health Food, on Hwy 270 opposite Kohala Coffee Mill, sells bulk and packaged health foods as well as a few dairy items.

Bamboo, immediately north of the health food store, has lunch items such as chicken satay with rice, a vegetarian black bean tostada or burgers and fries, each for $6.50. At dinner, chicken or teriyaki beef costs around $10. It's closed on Mondays.

Kohala Village Restaurant (☎ 889-0105), at the intersection of Hwys 270 and 250, is run by Carter Chu, a graduate of the Culinary Institute of America. Lunchtime favorites, which average $7, include chicken stir-fry, Honolulu fried noodles and a tasty grilled-chicken Caesar salad. At dinner, barbecued ribs, pastas and fresh fish average $15. It's open for breakfast and lunch Wednesday to Sunday until 2 pm and for dinner on Monday, Friday and Saturday evenings.

KAPAAU

The statue of Kamehameha the Great on the front lawn of the North Kohala Civic Center may look familiar. Its lei-draped and much-photographed twin stands opposite the Iolani Palace in Honolulu.

The statue was made in 1880 in Florence, Italy, by American sculptor Thomas Gould. The ship delivering it sank off the Falkland Islands, so another statue was cast from the original mold. The duplicate statue arrived in the islands in 1883 and took its place in downtown Honolulu.

Later the sunken statue was recovered from the ocean floor and completed its trip to Hawaii. This original statue was then sent here, to Kamehameha's childhood home, where it stands watching the traffic trickle along in quiet Kapaau.

Kapaau has a courthouse and police station and Kamehameha Park, which includes a large, modern gymnasium and everything from a ballpark to a swimming pool. The town also has a little library, a Bank of Hawaii and a few interesting shops.

Still, it's an aging town. The only crowd is at the senior center, which is part of the civic center. The senior citizens usually staff a table on the porch with visitor information.

Kalahikiola Church

Protestant missionaries Elias and Ellen Bond, who arrived in Kohala in 1841, built Kalahikiola Church in 1855. An earthquake damaged it in 1973, but it's since been restored and the church is still in use today.

If you want to take a look, turn mauka off Hwy 270 onto a narrow road half a mile east of the Kamehameha statue, near the 24-mile marker. The church is half a mile up from the highway.

The land and buildings on the drive in to the church are part of the Bond estate, proof enough that missionary life wasn't one of total deprivation.

If the doors of the church seem to be locked it's because they don't push or pull, but rather slide open.

Kamehameha Rock

Kamehameha Rock is on the right-hand side of the road, about two miles east of Kapaau, on a curve just over a small bridge. It's said that Kamehameha carried this rock uphill from the beach below to demonstrate his strength.

A road crew once attempted to move the rock to a different location, but although they managed to get it up onto a wagon the rock fell off – an obvious sign that it wanted to stay put. Not wanting to upset Kamehameha's mana, the workers left the rock in place.

Tong Wo Society

Immediately around the corner from Kamehameha Rock is the colorful home of the Kohala Tong Wo Society, founded in 1886. Hawaii once had many Chinese societies, providing immigrants with a place to preserve their cultural identity, speak their native language and socialize. This is the last one remaining on the Big Island. The building is not open to the public.

The two-story green building next door, once the Wo On Store, now houses the Wo On Gallery, which has a nice collection of arts and crafts made by North Kohala residents.

Places to Stay

An interesting budget possibility is at the old girls school (circa 1874) at the Bond Estate, a quarter-mile up the dirt road beyond the Kalahikiola Church. Although the school has long been closed, the estate still owns the property and leases its aging buildings out to a local family. Joleen Perez (☎ 889-5028), who lives in the cottage at the west side of the property, rents out a big room with three beds to budget travelers on a daily basis. It's a very simple place; the shower and toilet are shared with long-term residents, and there's limited use of a kitchen if you have your own pots and pans. The price is a bit negotiable but can be as cheap as $12/15 for singles/doubles.

Places to Eat

Don's Family Deli, in the town center on Hwy 270, is the best place to eat in Kapaau. Mahimahi sandwiches or tofu burgers cost $5. They also have meat and cheese sandwiches, Portuguese bean soup, espresso and good fruit smoothies. It's open from 8 am to 6 pm on weekdays, to 5 pm on weekends.

For dessert you could walk down the street to *Tropical Dreams* for a scoop of gourmet ice cream or sorbet. Tropical Dreams also makes delicious macadamia nut butters, including a nice ambrosia variety with chunks of pineapple, currants and almonds.

KEOKEA BEACH PARK

Keokea Beach Park is on a somewhat scenic rocky coast but isn't a real draw for visitors, as there's no sandy beach and it's not great for water activities.

The park is most active on weekends and camping is allowed, with a county permit, on the grassy section below the pavilion. There are covered picnic tables, restrooms, showers, drinking water, barbecue grills and electricity.

The marked turn-off is about 1½ miles before Pololu Valley Lookout. The park is about a mile in from the highway.

If you head this way, you'll pass an old Japanese cemetery on the way down to the park. Most of the gravestones are in kanji (Japanese script), and a few have filled sake cups in front of them.

POLOLU VALLEY

Hwy 270 ends at a viewpoint that overlooks secluded Pololu Valley with its scenic backdrop of steeply scalloped coastal cliffs spreading out to the east. The lookout has the kind of strikingly beautiful angle that's rarely experienced without a helicopter tour.

Pololu was once thickly planted with wetland taro. Pololu Stream fed the valley, carrying water from the remote, rainy

NED FRIARY
Kamehameha the Great

interior to the valley floor. When the Kohala Ditch was built, it siphoned off much of the water and put an end to the taro production. The last islanders left the valley in the 1940s, and the valley slopes are now forest reserve land.

Pololu Valley Trail

The trail from the lookout down to Pololu Valley only takes about 20 minutes to walk. It's steep and can be hot walking, but it's not overly strenuous. You will need to be cautious with your footing since much of the trail is packed clay that can be slippery when wet.

Cattle and horses roam in the valley; a gate at the bottom of the trail keeps them in.

The black-sand beach fronting the valley stretches for about half a mile and can make an enjoyable stroll. Driftwood collects in great quantities and on rare occasions glass fishing floats get washed up as well.

Kohala Ditch

Kohala Ditch is an intricate series of ditches, tunnels and flumes that were built to carry water from the rugged wet interior of the Kohala Forest Reserve out to the Hawi area. The source of the water is the Waikoloa Stream, midway between the Pololu and Waipio valleys.

The ditch was built in 1906 to irrigate Kohala sugar cane fields. The last Kohala cane was cut in the 1970s, but the ditch continues to be a source of water for Kohala ranches and farms.

It was engineered by a sugar man, John Hind, with the financial backing of Samuel Parker of Parker Ranch. Kohala Ditch runs 22½ miles and was built by Japanese immigrant laborers who were paid about $1 a day for the hazardous work. More than a dozen of those laborers died during the construction.

There were once miles of mule trails along the ditch that were used for maintenance, but the trails are now overgrown.

Much of the ditch runs through 19,000 acres of Kohala land, which the agricultural giant Castle & Cooke sold a few years back to a Japanese developer. ■

Surf is usually high in winter, and although it's a bit tamer in summer, there can be rip currents year round.

Waimea

Waimea has a pretty setting in the foothills of the Kohala Mountains at an elevation of 2670 feet. It's cooler than the coast, with more clouds and fog. The area has gentle rolling hills and frequent afternoon rainbows.

This is the headquarters of Parker Ranch, Hawaii's largest cattle ranch, which spreads across nearly one-ninth of the Big Island. Almost everything in Waimea is owned, run or leased by Parker Ranch.

Waimea has its cowboy influences, but it's rapidly growing and becoming more sophisticated. It's the main town serving the new subdivisions being developed on former ranches in the Kohala Mountains. While many of the newcomers are wealthy mainlanders, Waimea is also home to a growing number of international astronomers who work on Mauna Kea.

The Keck office in the town center has a short video and a model of its telescope that visitors can stop by and see during business hours (8 am to 4:45 pm weekdays).

Waimea has a couple of good dining spots and galleries, but it's not a big tourist town with a lot of action or sightseeing attractions. The museums are good for a short visit and the green pastures are scenic, but for most visitors Waimea is just a stopover on the drive between Kona and Hilo.

Information

Waimea is also referred to as **Kamuela**, which is the Hawaiian spelling of Samuel. Although some say the name comes from an early postmaster named Samuel Spencer, most claim it's for Samuel Parker of Parker Ranch fame. The result is the same: confusion. Address all Waimea mail to Kamuela.

The post office, southwest of the Parker Ranch Center, is open weekdays from 8 am to 4:30 pm, Saturdays from 10 am to 1 pm.

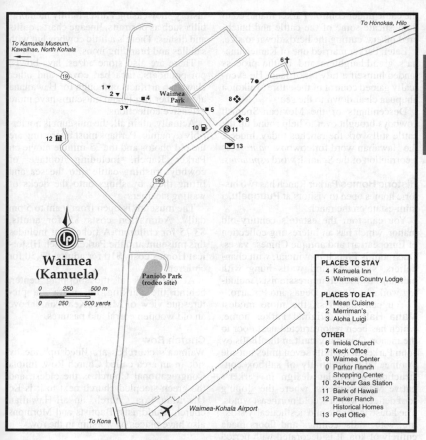

To Kamuela Museum,
Kawaihae, North Kohala

To Honokaa, Hilo

Waimea (Kamuela)

0   250   500 m
0   250   500 yards

Waimea Park

Paniolo Park
(rodeo site)

Waimea-Kohala Airport

To Kona

PLACES TO STAY
4 Kamuela Inn
5 Waimea Country Lodge

PLACES TO EAT
1 Mean Cuisine
2 Merriman's
3 Aloha Luigi

OTHER
6 Imiola Church
7 Keck Office
8 Waimea Center
9 Parker Ranch
   Shopping Center
10 24-hour Gas Station
11 Bank of Hawaii
12 Parker Ranch
   Historical Homes
13 Post Office

The Waimea-Kohala Airport, off Hwy 190, 1¾ miles south of the intersection of Hwy 19, is mainly used by private planes.

Parker Ranch

Parker Ranch claims to be the nation's largest privately owned ranch. It has 225,000 acres, 55,000 head of cattle and about 50 ranch hands. The ranch accounts for 80% of the livestock sold in Hawaii.

The first cattle arrived in Hawaii in 1793, a gift to King Kamehameha from British captain George Vancouver. To ensure the preservation of the herd, Vancouver con-

vinced the king to place a 10-year kapu on the killing of cattle.

The kapu worked, but the cattle ran wild and multiplied so quickly that they became an uncontrollable and destructive nuisance to both crops and native forests. Feral cattle still roam Mauna Kea's slopes today.

Parker Ranch owes its beginnings to John Palmer Parker, a 19-year-old from New England who arrived on the Big Island in 1809 aboard a whaler. He took one look at Hawaii and jumped ship.

Parker soon gained the favor of Kamehameha, who commissioned him to bring the cattle under control. Parker managed to domesticate some of the cattle and butchered others, cutting the herds down to size.

Later, Parker married one of Kamehameha's granddaughters and in the process landed himself a tidy bit of land. He eventually gained control of the entire Waikoloa ahupuaa clear down to the sea.

Descendants of the Mexican-Spanish cowboys brought over to help round up the cattle still work the ranches today. Indeed, the Hawaiian word for cowboy, *paniolo*, is a corruption of the Spanish word *españoles*.

Historic Homes

Parker Ranch has two historic homes open to visitors at **Puuopelu**, a mini-estate on the ranch.

You can tour the estate's century-old manor, which has an interesting collection of European art and antique Chinese vases. One room is French provincial, with chandeliers, skylights and walls hung with paintings by French impressionists, including works by Renoir, Degas and Pissarro.

You can also visit the more modest **Mana Hale**, the original Parker home, which has been reconstructed next door to the manor. Originally built in the 1840s by John Parker in the hills seven miles outside Waimea, it's essentially of saltbox construction, a popular design in Parker's native Massachusetts, where the sloping roof deflects winter's cold northeast winds. The house is simple and aesthetically striking, with walls, ceilings and floors made entirely of koa. It is decorated with period furnishings and interesting old photos of the hardy-looking Parker clan. The interior of Mana Hale was dismantled board by board and rebuilt here at Puuopelu, but the exterior is a replica.

The turn-off to the homes is on Hwy 190, about three-quarters of a mile south of its intersection with Hwy 19. Hours are 10 am to 5 pm daily (last ticket sold at 4 pm) and admission costs $7.50 for adults, $5 for children.

Visitor Center

Parker Ranch Visitor Center, in the Parker Ranch Shopping Center, is a little museum of the ranch's history showcasing Parker family memorabilia such as portraits, lineage charts, quilts and dishes. There's a little cowboy hut with saddles and branding irons.

There are also stone adzes, lava bowls, poi pounders, tapa bed covers and other Hawaiian artifacts, although for Hawaiiana alone other Big Island museums have more extensive collections.

Actually, all in all, the museum is not terribly dynamic. Perhaps most interesting are the old photos and the 25-minute movie on Parker Ranch, including footage of cowboys rushing cattle into the sea and lifting them by slings onto the decks of waiting steamers.

The museum is open from 9 am to 5 pm daily. Admission costs $5 for adults, $3.75 for children. A ticket that includes this museum and the Parker Ranch Historical Homes costs $10 for adults, $7.50 for children.

At the back of the shopping center, behind the parking lot, there's a picturesque view of Mauna Kea rising above an old wooden corral and pastures.

Church Row

Waimea's churches are lined up side by side in an area called Church Row. Imiola Congregational Church is the oldest, and the green-steepled church next to it is Ke Ola Mau Loa Church, an all-Hawaiian church. Buddhists, Baptists and Mormons also have places of worship in the row.

Imiola Congregational Church

Waimea's first Christian church was a grass hut built in 1830. It was replaced in 1838 by a wood and coral structure, built with coral stones carved out of the reef and carried inland on the backs of Hawaiian Christians. They named it Imiola, which means 'seeking salvation'.

The current building was constructed in 1857 and restored in 1976. The interior is simple and beautiful; it's built entirely of koa, most of it dating back to the original construction.

In the churchyard is the grave of missionary Lorenzo Lyons, who arrived in 1832 and spent 54 years in Waimea. Lyons

Holy Ghost Church, Waiakoa, Upcountry Maui

NED FRIARY

Blowhole, Northwest Maui

NED FRIARY

Riding into the Hana underbrush

NED FRIARY

Surfer in Paia, Maui

Haleakala Crater, Maui

Sliding Sands Trail, Haleakala National Park, Maui

wrote many of the hymns, including the popular 'Hawaii Aloha', that are still sung in Hawaiian here each Sunday. Also in the garden is the church bell, too heavy for the church roof to support.

Kamuela Museum

There's a lot of history crammed into the Kamuela Museum (☎ 885-4724) at the junction of Hwys 19 and 250. The museum contains all sorts of Hawaiiana, including tapa beaters, 18th-century feather leis braided with human hair, fish hooks made of human bones, a stone knuckle duster and a dog-toothed death cup. Some items are very rare and many once belonged to royalty. The museum has Kamehameha the Great's sacred chair and tables of teak and marble from Iolani Palace.

This museum is like one of those cluttered Chinese grocery stores that has one of everything – you just have to find it. The non-Hawaiian part of the collection ranges from a Tibetan prayer horn and stuffed moose heads from Canada to a piece of rope used on the Apollo II mission.

The future of the museum is a bit uncertain, as it's been up for sale. It's open from 8 am to 5 pm daily. Admission costs $5 for adults, $2 for children under 12.

Places to Stay

Waimea is upcountry, and if you equate Hawaii with beach life and constant sun, you may be disappointed making a base here. But if country settings and open spaces are what you're looking for, the Waimea area can be an appealing choice.

Kamuela Inn (☎ 885-4243; fax 885-8857), Box 1994, Kamuela, HI 96743, is something in between an inn and a small hotel in both layout and atmosphere. The cheaper of its 30 rooms are rather small but comfortable. Standard rooms cost $54 to $67. Suites that have refrigerators and stoves and can sleep three cost $83. Free pastries and coffee are provided in the morning.

Waimea Country Lodge (☎ 885-4100, 800-367-5004; fax 885-6711), Box 2559, Kamuela, HI 96743, is a small motel with

21 rooms. All have full baths, phones, cable TV and views of the Kohala hills out back; many also have pleasant open-beam ceilings. Be aware that there can be early-morning noise from trucks unloading at the nearby shopping center. Rooms cost $90 with kitchenette, $78 without.

Waimea Gardens Cottages (☎ 885-4550, 800-262-9912; fax 885-0559; bestbnbs@ interpac.net), Box 563, Kamuela, HI 96743, are a pair of charming cottages on the property of Barbara and Charlie Campbell, two miles west of town. Both have hardwood floors, French doors and a deck. The older unit has a full kitchen. While the newer one has more limited cooking facilities, it has many other pleasant touches, including a working fireplace. The units come stocked with a fruit basket, banana bread and Kona coffee. The rate is $115 single or double, $15 more for a third person; there's a three-day minimum stay. Barbara also runs an upmarket B&B service called Hawaii's Best Bed & Breakfasts and can book other accommodations on the island in this price range.

If you don't mind being a few miles east of Waimea, then *Mountain Meadow Ranch* (☎ 775-9376), Gay and Bill George, Box 1697, Honokaa, HI 96727, offers a pleasant country setting. Located in a quiet eucalyptus grove off the Old Mamalahoa Hwy, this seven-acre farm has gardens of citrus and macadamia trees. It would make a convenient base for exploring Waipio and the Hamakua Coast and is only about an hour's drive from Hilo. There are two rooms, one with a king bed and the other with a twin bed and a double bed. Guests share a large tiled bathroom, a dry-heat sauna and a lounge with a TV/VCR. There's no minimum stay. The cost is $55 single, $65 double; credit cards are accepted.

Places to Eat

Aloha Luigi has four little tables in the back of the convenience store at Waimea Express gas. For $8 you can get decent pastas, eggplant parmigiana or a 12-inch cheese pizza to eat in or takeout. It's open Monday to Saturday from 11 am to 8 pm.

The *Mean Cuisine* in Opelo Plaza bakes its own breads and pastries. A popular little spot with eggplant and pasta dishes for around $7 and sandwiches and good salads at reasonable prices, it's open from 6 am to 8 pm (Sundays from 9 am to 2 pm).

Merriman's (☎ 885-6822) in Opelo Plaza features Hawaiian Regional cuisine, focusing on fresh products from Big Island farmers and fishers. A specialty is the delicious wok-charred ahi, blackened on the outside and sashimi-like inside. At dinner there are a few vegetarian meals, including eggplant Sichuan or gado gado salad for $14, while most seafood and meat dishes cost $20 to $25. At lunch, there are salads, soups and sandwiches as well as a few hot grilled dishes, including a tasty coconut chicken with peanut sauce. Everything on the lunch menu is $10 or less. It's open from 11:30 am to 1:30 pm weekdays, 5:30 to 9 pm nightly.

There's a branch of *Su's Thai Kitchen* in the Parker Ranch Shopping Center, featuring moderately priced Thai food. It's open from 10 am to 9 pm daily.

The Waimea Center has *KTA Supermarket, Subway Sandwiches* and *McDonald's*, as well as a health food store, a bakery, a deli and Chinese and Korean restaurants.

Entertainment

Waimea's entertainment scene is limited, perhaps because cowboys rise at dawn and astronomers work all night!

Kahilu Theatre (☎ 885-6017), at the Parker Ranch Shopping Center, presents plays, classical music concerts, dance troupes and other productions.

Getting There & Away

Waimea is 40 miles from Kailua-Kona along Hwy 190. From Kona the road climbs out of residential areas into a mix of lava flows and dry, grassy rangeland studded with prickly pear cactus. There's a little one-room church, broad distant coastal views, wide-open spaces and tall roadside grasses that have an incredible golden hue in the morning light.

If you come back on this road at night, the highway reflectors light up like an airport runway to guide you along.

AROUND WAIMEA
Waimea to Honokaa

Hwy 19 heads east from Waimea to Honokaa through rolling hills and cattle pastures, with views of Mauna Kea to the south.

For a peaceful, scented backroad turn right off Hwy 19 onto the Old Mamalahoa Hwy just west of the 52-mile marker. (If you're coming from Hilo, turn left at the 43-mile marker opposite Tex Drive Inn and then take the next immediate right.)

The 10-mile detour winds through hill country, with small roadside ranches, old wooden fences and grazing horses. This is untouristed Hawaii. Nobody's in a hurry on this road, if they're on it at all. It can make a great alternative route for cyclists, although you'll need to be cautious as the road is narrow and winding.

Mana/Keanakolu Rd

To get closer to Mauna Kea for photography or views, you could drive part way down Mana Rd, the start of a road that curves around the eastern flank of Mauna Kea. It begins off Hwy 19 at the 55-mile marker on the eastern side of Waimea. After 15 miles the road becomes Keanakolu Rd and continues about 25 miles before reaching Summit Rd (the road leading up Mauna Kea) near the Humuula Sheep Station.

Only the first part of the Waimea section is paved. The entire road is passable on horseback or by 4WD vehicle but there are a couple of dozen cattle gates that must be opened and closed along the way. Be aware that it's mostly ranchers and hunters that come this way and it's a long way from anywhere should you get stuck en route.

Keanakolu Rd passes along the new Hakalau Forest National Wildlife Refuge, which protects a portion of the state's largest koa-ohia forest. The forest provides habitat for the hoary bat and seven endangered bird species. Only very limited access is allowed into the refuge itself; call ☎ 933-6915 for information.

David Douglas Memorial A memorial to David Douglas, the Scottish botanist for whom the Douglas fir tree is named, is on Keanakolu Rd about halfway between Waimea and the Saddle Rd. Douglas died in 1834 at this spot.

Hamakua Coast

The Hamakua Coast, the northeastern coast of the Big Island, stretches 50 miles from Waipio Valley down to the city of Hilo.

From Waimea, it's 15 miles east on Hwy 19 to the town of Honokaa. From Honokaa, you can continue nine miles northwest on Hwy 240 to reach Waipio Valley Lookout and one of the most spectacular valley views in Hawaii.

Much of the north end of the Hamakua Coast is idle agricultural land, with feral sugar cane growing in many roadside fields. The rest of the coast is rugged with luxuriant rainforests laced with streams and waterfalls.

The Hawaii Belt Rd (Hwy 19), which runs along the wet windward slopes of Mauna Kea, is an impressive engineering feat that spans deep green ravines with a series of sweeping cantilevered bridges.

Hwy 19 also passes small towns and unmarked roads leading down to unfrequented beach parks. If you're just whizzing through on your way between Kona and Hilo, at the very least make time for Waipio Valley Lookout, majestic Akaka Falls and the Pepeekeo four-mile scenic drive.

HONOKAA

Honokaa's sugar mill opened in 1873, and sugar continued to be the mainstay of this town until the Hamakua Sugar Company closed down the mill in late 1994. As a result of the closing many Honokaa residents have taken up employment in new Waikoloa resorts.

The Death of David Douglas
The circumstances surrounding the death of botanist David Douglas are somewhat mysterious, as his gored body was found trapped with an angry bull at the bottom of a pit on the slopes of Mauna Kea. Hunters commonly dug such pits and camouflaged them with underbrush as a means of trapping feral cattle, but the probability of both Douglas and a bull falling into the same hole seemed highly suspicious. Fingers were pointed at Australian Ned Gurney, an escaped convict from Botany Bay who had been hiding out in the area and who had been the last person to see Douglas alive.

Hilo authorities, unable to solve the case, packed both Douglas' body and the bull's head in brine and shipped them to Honolulu for further investigation. By the time the body arrived in Oahu, it was so badly decomposed that they hastily buried Douglas' remains at the missionary church and the case was closed. ■

Since Honokaa has its roots in sugar, most of its residents are descendants of immigrants brought here to work the plantations. The Scots and English were the first to arrive. Then came the Chinese, Portuguese, Japanese, Puerto Ricans and Filipinos in turn.

With a population of 2200, this quiet town is the biggest on the Hamakua Coast. Mamame St (Hwy 240) is the main street through town. Most of the shops lined up along it date to the 1920s and haven't changed a whole lot over the years. Honokaa has a couple of antique shops, a post office, library, swimming pool, grocery stores and a few restaurants.

Macadamia Nut Factory
Hawaiian Holiday has its macadamia nut factory on Lehua St, three-quarters of a mile down the hill from the post office. For visitors, this is basically a store where nuts and cookies are sold and the 'self-guided

A Hard Nut to Crack

Hawaii's first macadamia trees were planted in Honokaa in 1881 by William Purvis, a sugar plantation manager who brought seedlings from Australia. For 40 years the trees were grown in Hawaii, as in Australia, mainly for ornamental purposes, as the nut shells were considered too hard to crack.

Hawaii's first large-scale commercial macadamia orchard was planted in Honokaa in 1924 and it's still producing today. Macadamia nuts have proven to be one of the most commercially viable agricultural crops in Hawaii. The nuts are high in fat, protein and carbohydrates and provide a good source of calcium, phosphorous, iron, thiamine, riboflavin and niacin. ∎

tour' consists of watching factory workers through windows in the gift shop. It's open daily from 9 am to 5 pm.

Kamaaina Woods

Kamaaina Woods, on the road to the macadamia nut factory, makes quality bowls of koa, milo and mango woods, and everything sold in the shop is made there. Prices start at around $25 with many bowls going for well over $100. The thinnest and lightest bowls require the greatest skill to craft and command the highest prices.

Places to Stay

Hotel Honokaa Club (☎ 775-0678, 800-808-0678), Box 247, Honokaa, HI 96727, on Mamane St, is an older hotel with 14 basic rooms. In an effort to attract budget travelers, it has cut the rates on a few of its rooms, and visitors can now share a dorm-style room for $15 or have a small room with a sink and bed for $20/30 single/double. The shower and toilet are in the hall, and the double room has only one double bed, but these cheaper rooms are at the quieter end of the hotel. There are also rooms with private baths for $40 to $55, with the more expensive room having a queen bed, TV and 2nd-floor view.

Waipio Wayside B&B (☎ 775-0275, 800-833-8849; wayside@ilhawaii.net), Box 840, Honokaa, HI 96727, in between Honokaa and Waipio, is a gracious older home in a setting of macadamia nut trees. This smoke-free B&B is pleasant and relaxed, with hammocks on the deck and a garden gazebo. There are five nicely decorated theme rooms that vary in size and price, ranging from $60/70 single/double for a room with shared bath up to $90/100 for the attractive master bedroom suite with natural wood and a private bath. Add another $10 for stays of just one night. If you book at the lower end, ask for the Plantation Room, which is spacious and sunny. Owner Jackie Horne prepares a hearty breakfast that includes homegrown fruit and Hamakua coffee.

Paauhau Plantation House (☎ 775-7222; fax 775-7223), Box 1375, Honokaa, HI 96727, off Hwy 19 just east of the Hwy 240 turn-off into Honokaa, is a classic 70-year-old plantation manager's house with plush period furniture, a billiard room, a fireplace, and so much historic character that you might expect ghosts to come out of the walls. The bedrooms in the house are furnished with antiques. Two of them rent for $105 a night, while a large master suite with king and double beds rents for $140. There are also three pleasant cottages with cooking facilities, separate bedrooms, and sofa beds in the living rooms. The smallest costs $75, the larger ones sleep four to six people and cost $105 for two, plus $15 for each additional person. There's a tennis court on the grounds.

Places to Eat

Most people staying in the area pick up groceries at the supermarket opposite the post office, but there are a couple of reasonable places to get a bite on Mamame St at the east side of the post office intersection. *Simply Natural* serves Hilo Homemade ice cream and has sandwiches for around $4 – including a good 'awesome burger'. There's a bakery next door.

The *Honokaa Club* on Mamame St is one of the more popular local places for

Hamakua Coast

dinner although the food's quite simple, with meals such as ground beef or steak priced from $7 to $14.

Tex Drive Inn is up on Hwy 19, and if you're driving by in the morning, on your way from Waimea to Hilo, you might want to stop by for a couple of malasadas and a cup of coffee. Malasadas are Portuguese pastries of sweet fried dough, rolled in sugar and served warm – like a doughnut without the hole. The diner also serves moderately priced breakfast fare, sandwiches, burgers and plate lunches. There's a convenience store next door and a coin laundry across the road.

KUKUIHAELE

About seven miles beyond Honokaa heading towards Waipio Valley, a loop road off Hwy 240 leads to the right and down to the tiny village of Kukuihaele.

Kukuihaele means 'Traveling Light' in Hawaiian and refers to the ghostly night marchers who are said to pass through this area carrying torches on their way to Waipio. The village is less than a mile from the Waipio Lookout.

There's not much to Kukuihaele – its 'commercial center' consists mainly of the Last Chance Store and the Waipio Valley

Artworks. The latter sells quality Hawaiian-made crafts, including dyed fabrics and an extensive selection of carved wooden bowls.

Places to Stay

Waipio Valley Artworks (☎ 775-0958, 800-492-4746; fax 775-0551), Box 5070, Kukuihaele, HI 96727, rents out a contemporary two-story house on the ridge about 200 yards before the Waipio Lookout. The house has a one-bedroom apartment on the 1st floor that costs a reasonable $65 and a two-bedroom apartment on the 2nd floor that costs $90. Both units have queen-size beds, full kitchens, washer/dryers, phones, TVs and lanais with valley views. There's also a brand new two-bedroom house, with pleasant furnishings and full amenities, that's right on the cliff; the cost is $125. All rates are for double occupancy; add $15 for each additional guest. Smoking is permitted on the lanais only. Visa and Master-Card are accepted.

Another option is *Waipio Ridge Vacation Rental* (☎ 775-0603), Roger Lasko, Box 5039, Kukuihaele, HI 96727, a modern one-bedroom cottage perched above Waipio Valley, just below the lookout. The kitchen has a refrigerator, microwave, toaster oven and coffeepot, and a spectacular view of Waipio Valley from the dining table. There's a TV, a queen-size bed in the bedroom and a queen sofa bed in the living room. The cost is $75 for two people, $15 more for additional guests.

Places to Eat

Most people go into Honokaa to eat and get provisions, although there are a couple of simple options in Kukuihaele.

The village's *Last Chance Store* is just that, as there's no food or supplies in Waipio Valley. At this small grocery store you can get yogurt, crackers, canned food, beer and wine. It's open from 9 am to 6 pm daily.

The shop at the side of Waipio Valley Artworks sells Tropical Dreams ice cream, muffins, sandwiches and coffee from 8:30 am to 5 pm daily.

WAIPIO VALLEY

Hwy 240 ends abruptly at the edge of cliffs overlooking Waipio Valley. If you catch it on a day when it's not hazy, the view is glorious.

The largest and southernmost of the seven spectacular amphitheater valleys on the windward side of the Kohala Mountains, Waipio Valley is a mile wide at the coast and nearly six miles deep. Some of the near-vertical pali wrapping around the valley reach heights of 2000 feet.

Everything in Waipio Valley is lushly green, a mix of tangled jungle, flowering plants, taro patches and waterfalls. The mouth of the valley is fronted by a black-sand beach, which is divided in two by the Waipio Stream.

From the lookout you can see the switch-back trail on the opposite cliff face that leads to Waimanu Valley and get glimpses of the rugged coastal cliffs that stretch out to the northwest.

The narrow, paved, mile-long road that leads down into Waipio Valley is so steep (25% grade) that it's restricted to all but hikers and 4WD vehicles. A couple of tour companies make the run daily, but the walk down is easier than it looks. The lookout has restrooms and drinking water; it's a good idea to fill up a water bottle before going down into the valley as there are no public facilities there.

History

Waipio means 'Curving Water' and is often referred to as the 'Valley of the Kings'. In ancient times it was the political and religious center of Hawaii and home to the highest chiefs. Waipio was a very sacred place and the site of a number of important heiaus. The most sacred, Pakaalana, was also the site of one of the island's two major puuhonua.

Umi, the Big Island's ruling chief in the early 16th century, is credited with laying out Waipio's taro fields, many of which are still in production today. Waipio is also the site where Kamehameha the Great received his fearsome war god, Kukailimoku.

According to oral histories at least

10,000 people – and possibly many times more – lived in Waipio during pre-contact times. It was the most fertile and productive valley on the Big Island.

In 1823, William Ellis, the first missionary to visit the valley, guessed the population to be about 1300. Later in that century immigrants, mainly Chinese, began to settle in Waipio. At one time the valley had schools, restaurants and churches as well as a hotel, post office and jail.

In 1946 the most devastating tsunami in Hawaii's history swept great waves far back into Waipio Valley. Afterwards, most people resettled 'topside' and Waipio has been sparsely populated ever since.

Waipio Valley Today

Taro remains important in Waipio. Many of the valley's 50 or so residents have taro patches, and you may see farmers knee-deep in the muddy ponds.

Other Waipio crops include lotus (for its roots), avocados, breadfruit, oranges and limes. There are kukui and mahogany trees, huge elephant ears, Turk's cap hibiscus, air plants, ferns and vines. Pink and white impatiens climb the cliff walls along the road.

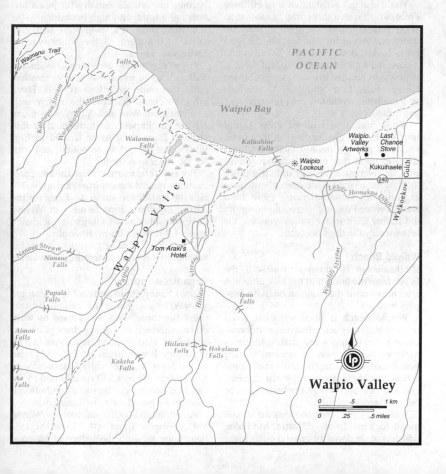

The walk from the lookout to the valley floor and back is not terribly difficult, although if you're not in good shape you may notice some forgotten muscles the next day. It takes about 30 minutes to walk down and about 45 minutes to hike back up. The road is carved into the cliffs at an angle that provides hikers with shade much of the way.

From the bottom of the hill, if you walk to the left for about five minutes there's a fair chance you'll see wild horses grazing along the stream. It's a picturesque scene set against the steep valley cliffs.

You'll also get a distant view of **Hiilawe Falls**, which with a sheer drop of more than 1000 feet is Hawaii's highest free-fall waterfall. According to legend the god Lono looked down from the heavens and discovered Kaikilani, the beautiful woman who was to become his wife, sitting beside Hiilawe Falls. Lono slid down to the falls on a rainbow – definitely the preferred way to get there.

While hiking to Hiilawe Falls is not impossible, it is challenging, as there's no real trail and it's mainly bushwhacking. Keep in mind that many valley residents who are tolerant of visitors trekking down to visit the beach aren't keen about them exploring the valley interior – there are a lot of 'Private Property' signs and generally the farther back in the valley you go, the less friendly the dogs become.

Waipio Beach

It takes about 10 minutes to walk to the beach from the bottom of the hill, although after heavy rains the road can be like a slippery mud pie.

Waipio Beach is lined with ironwood trees that act as an effective windbreak against the strong wind that sometimes picks up here. It was an ancient surfing beach that occasionally still sees some action, but there are usually rip currents and when the surf is high the waters can be outright treacherous.

Walk along the beach towards the stream mouth for a good view of **Kaluahine Falls**, which cascade down the coastal cliffs to the east. They're easier to look at than to get to, however, as the coast between Waipio Beach and Kaluahine Falls is loose lava rock and rather rough walking. The surf sometimes breaks up over the uppermost rocks, so it can also be dangerous.

Local lore has it that ghost marchers periodically come down from the upper valley to the beach and march to Lua O Milu, a hidden entrance to the netherworld.

Precautions

During heavy rains, streams in Waipio Valley can swell to the point where they become impassable, usually for just a few hours at a time, although occasionally for longer periods. It's dangerous to try to cross such streams if the water reaches above your knees.

If you're planning on hiking to Waimanu Valley, keep in mind that heavy rains can make that route hazardous as well. There are a few creeks that cross the trail, as well as a stream in Waimanu Valley, which can all become impassable torrents after rain storms. These need to be treated as life-threatening obstacles; be patient and wait for the water to subside.

Because feral animals roam the area, precautions against leptospirosis are advisable (see the Health section in the Facts for the Visitor chapter). Taro farmers in Waipio have one of Hawaii's highest incidence rates of this water-borne ailment.

Don't drink from any creeks or streams without first boiling or treating the water.

Organized Tours

Waipio Valley Shuttle offers 1½-hour tours via 4WD vans. These are essentially taxi tours for those who don't care to walk down, although the driver does point out waterfalls, identify plants and throw in a bit of history. Reservations (☎ 775-7121) can be made at Waipio Valley Artworks in Kukuihaele. It costs $30 for adults, $15 for children under 11. The tours run between 8 am and 4 pm Monday to Saturday.

An alternative to the van tours is Waipio Valley Wagon Tours' (☎ 775-9518) 1½-hour jaunt through the valley in an open mule-drawn wagon. The tour guide gives commentary on the valley's history as he wheels visitors along Waipio's rutted dirt roads and fords rocky streams. Tours leave from the Last Chance Store in Kukuihaele at 9:30 and 11:30 am and 1:30 and 3:30 pm daily, except on Sundays. Passengers are taken to the valley floor by a 4WD vehicle where they transfer to the wagon. It costs $40 for adults, $20 for children.

A more adventurous possibility for touring the valley is on horseback. Waipio on Horseback (☎ 775-7291) offers a 2½-hour ride in the valley at 9:30 am and 1:30 pm for $65. Waipio Naalapa Trail Rides (☎ 775-0419) has a 2½-hour trail ride in the valley for $75. There are no trail rides on Sundays or during bad weather.

Switchback Trail to Waimanu Valley

The switchback trail leading up the northwest cliff face of Waipio Valley is an ancient Hawaiian footpath. Although it looks arduous, and is rated moderate-to-difficult, it really isn't all that bad if you're not carrying a heavy load. It's a well-beaten path, a few feet deep in places, almost like walking in a little trough. For those who are carrying a weighty backpack, once you reach the ridge the trail gets much easier.

Doing just part of the trail makes a nice day hike from Waipio. It takes about 1½ hours from the floor of Waipio Valley to the third gulch where there are little pools and a small waterfall. The trail is used by hunters as well as hikers, and you might come across old-timers on donkeys heading for the backwoods to hunt wild boar.

The trail continues up and down a series of ravines to Waimanu Valley. From Waipio Valley to Waimanu it's about eight miles in all, and because of the numerous climbs you should allot about seven hours.

Waimanu is a smaller valley than Waipio although it's similar in appearance. It too is a beautiful deep valley with steep walls, waterfalls, a lush green valley floor and a black-sand beach.

Waimanu Valley once had a sizable Hawaiian settlement and there are many ruins from pre-contact times including house and heiau terraces, stone enclosures and old taro ponds. In the early 19th century, Waimanu was inhabited by an estimated 200 people, but by the turn of the 20th century only three families remained. Since the 1946 tsunami the valley has been completely abandoned.

Because it represents an unaltered Hawaiian freshwater ecosystem, Waimanu Valley has been set aside as a national estuarine sanctuary, and the removal of any plant or aquatic life (except for freshwater prawns and ocean fish) is forbidden.

Water is available on this route from numerous gulches, but it must be boiled or otherwise treated before drinking.

Places to Stay

Bishop Estate, which owns most of Waipio Valley, allows *camping* inland from the beach. There are only four campsites, the maximum stay is four days and you must fill out a permit application in advance. The crux of the application is a liability waiver and each camper must sign one. The permits are free and can be obtained in advance by calling ☎ 776-1104 or by writing to Bishop Estate, Box 495, Paauilo, HI 96776. The office is in Paauilo, next to the post office.

In Waimanu Valley, which is managed by the state, camping for up to six nights is allowed free by permit. There are firepits and a couple of composting outhouses. Camping reservations are taken no more than 30 days in advance by the Division of Forestry & Wildlife (☎ 933-4221), Box 4849, 1643 Kilauea Ave, Hilo, HI 96720. The actual permit can be picked up during office hours either at the forestry office in Hilo or at the state tree nursery (☎ 885-4250) in Waimea.

Tom Araki's Hotel (☎ 775-0368), c/o Sueno Araki, 25 Malama Place, Hilo, HI 96720, is back to basics on the floor of Waipio Valley. It's about a 15-minute walk inland from the bottom of the hill, just on the other side of the stream. This unpretentious place once served Peace Corps instructors who trained new recruits in the valley before they went off on assignment to other Pacific and Asian jungles.

All quite in keeping with its surroundings, the hotel's five rooms look out onto Tom's taro patch. The rooms are rustic and simple, but comfortable enough, and blankets and linen are provided. There's a communal kitchen with a gas stove, sink, dishes and cooking utensils. Kerosene lanterns provide lighting. You'll have to carry in all your own food, and it's a custom to bring along a bottle of sake to pass the evening.

Tom gets heavily booked out and suggests making reservations well in advance, although you can also take your chances and call once you arrive on the Big Island. Rates are $15 per person.

KALOPA STATE PARK

Kalopa State Park is a few miles southeast of Honokaa and about three miles inland from the marked turn-off on Hwy 19.

This unfrequented park contains 100 acres of native rainforest as well as picnic sites and some pleasant cabins that hold up to eight people. At an elevation of 2000 feet it's cooler than the coast and a bit wetter as well, averaging about 90 inches of rain a year.

The park has a pleasant hike leading to Kalopa Gulch in the adjoining forest reserve. Begin the hike along Robusta Lane, which starts on the left between the caretaker's house and the campgrounds. It's about a third of a mile to the edge of the gulch through a thick forest of tall eucalyptus trees with mossy bark. The deep gulch was formed eons ago by the erosive movement of melting glaciers that originated at Mauna Kea. A trail continues along the rim of the gulch for another mile, and a number of side trails branch west off it back into the park.

Kalopa Park also has a nature trail, beginning at the information board near the cabins, which loops for three-quarters of a mile through an ancient ohia forest where some of the trees are more than three feet in diameter. Kalopa's woods are habitat for the elepaio, an easily spotted native forest bird. It's brown with a white rump, about the size of a sparrow, and it makes a loud whistle that mimics its name.

After nearly a decade-long hiatus, the park has recently reintroduced tenting in a pleasant, grassy camping area that's surrounded by tall trees. There are new restrooms and covered pavilions with electricity, running water, barbecue grills and picnic tables. If you enjoy cool nights and don't mind being off the beaten path, this rates as one of the Big Island's more recommendable camping options. For information on booking the campground or cabins, see the Camping section near the front of this chapter.

LAUPAHOEHOE POINT

Laupahoehoe Point is midway between Honokaa and Hilo. A highway sign marks the steep winding road that leads 1⅓ miles down to the point. There are views of the coastal cliffs on the way down, and after heavy rains waterfalls come to life in all directions.

Laupahoehoe means 'leaf of pahoehoe lava'. This flat peninsula-like point jutting out from the coastal cliffs was formed by a late eruption of Mauna Kea, which poured lava down a ravine and out into the sea.

Tragedy hit Laupahoehoe on April 1, 1946, when tsunami waves up to 30 feet high wiped out the schoolhouse on the point, killing 20 children and four adults. After the tsunami the whole town moved uphill, although a few families have since settled back in. A monument on a hillock above the water lists those who died.

Laupahoehoe is a rugged coastal area and is not suitable for swimming. The surf is usually rough and pounding and can sometimes crash up over the rocks and onto the lower parking lot.

Inter-island boats once landed here. Indeed, many of the immigrants who came to work the sugar cane fields along the Hamakua Coast first set foot on the Big Island at Laupahoehoe.

The county beach park on the point has restrooms, campsites, showers, drinking water, picnic pavilions and electricity, and as it's off the highway it's relatively secluded. All this makes it convenient for camping, but makes it ideal for late-night partying too. Campers should be aware that locals sometimes use the park as a drinking hangout and it can get fairly rowdy.

KOLEKOLE PARK

This grassy park, beneath a big highway bridge, is at the side of Kolekole Stream, which flows down from Akaka Falls. There are small waterfalls, picnic tables, barbecue pits, restrooms and showers, all of which make the park a popular weekend picnic spot for families. Locals sometimes surf here, but ocean swimming is dangerous. Camping is allowed with a permit from the county, although it can be busy on weekends and in summer.

To get to the park, turn mauka off Hwy 19 at the south end of the Kolekole Bridge, about three-quarters of a mile south of the 15-mile marker.

AKAKA FALLS

To get to Akaka Falls, turn mauka off Hwy 19 onto Akaka Falls Rd (Hwy 220), midway between the 13- and 14-mile markers. The paved road passes through the town of Honomu and then climbs up through former cane fields, ending at the falls 3¾ miles away.

Honomu

Honomu is an old sugar town that might have been forgotten, if not for being on the route to Akaka Falls. As it is, things are pretty slow here, but among the village's handful of old wooden buildings you'll find two topnotch galleries, a tacky gift shop, a place to get shave ice and Ishigo's store and bakery, which has been a local landmark since 1910.

Hideo Ishigo, a spry octogenarian who still helps with the baking at Ishigo's, often sits in front of the store during the afternoon. If you happen to stop by, he loves to talk story and can tell you about little-known sights in the area. Ask to see his intriguing photo collection of old-time Honomu.

The two galleries, Hawaii's Artist Ohana and the Akaka Falls Inn & Gift Gallery, are adjacent to Ishigo's. Both galleries showcase an extensive collec-

tion of Big Island art and craft items, including fiber baskets, wooden bowls, pottery, jewelry, local fashions and paintings. They're fun to browse through even if you don't intend to buy.

Places to Stay & Eat *Ishigo's* sells inexpensive sandwiches and a few simple pastries, and both of the gift shops have small cafes selling coffee, fruit smoothies and light lunches.

Sonia Martinez, the owner of *Akaka Falls Inn & Gift Gallery* (☎ 963-5468), Box 190, Honomu, HI 96728, has two pleasant guest bedrooms in her home above the shop, which she rents for $55 and $65.

For travelers with a spiritual bent, there's *Akiko's Buddhist Bed & Breakfast* (☎ /fax 963-6422), Box 272, Hakalau, HI 96710, a mile north of Honomu. This rustic 85-year-old home has very simple rooms, with futons on the floor and shared bath. Zazen meditation, held daily at 4:30 am, is optional. Singles/doubles cost $25/40, including a modest breakfast.

HAWAII STATE ARCHIVES

Lauhala mat weaver

Akaka Falls State Park

Akaka Falls State Park has the Big Island's most impressive easy-to-view waterfall. It shouldn't be missed.

The waterfall lookout is along a delightful half-mile rainforest loop trail that takes about 20 minutes to walk. The paved trail passes through dense and varied vegetation, including massive philodendron vines, fragrant ginger, hanging heliconia, hillsides of bright impaties and cool bamboo groves. Look up and you might even find orchids growing wild in the trees.

If you start the loop trail by going to the right you'll first come to the 100-foot **Kahuna Falls**. It's a nice waterfall, but the real treat is still to come. Up ahead is **Akaka Falls**, dropping a sheer 442 feet down a fern-draped cliff. Its mood depends on the weather – sometimes it rushes with a mighty roar and other times it cascades gently. Either way it's always beautiful. With a little luck you might even catch a rainbow in the spray.

One legend says that whenever a branch of the lehua tree lands on a particular stone at the top of the falls, it will begin to rain. If so, there are apparently a lot of loose lehua branches upstream! You might want to bring an umbrella.

PEPEEKEO FOUR-MILE SCENIC DRIVE

Between Honomu and Hilo there's a delightful four-mile loop off Hwy 19. It's a drive through lush tropical jungle. The road crosses a string of one-lane bridges over little streams. In places it's almost canopied with African tulip trees, which drop their orange flowers on the road, and with passion fruit, guava and tall mango trees. The fruit can be picked up along the roadside in season.

The road is well marked on the highway at both ends, with the south end about seven miles north of Hilo.

Hawaii Tropical Botanical Garden

If somehow the four-mile scenic drive isn't enough, along the way there's also the Hawaii Tropical Botanical Garden (☎ 964-5233), a rainforest nature preserve with a lily pond, 1000 species of tropical plants and a couple of streams and waterfalls.

Visitors buy tickets at the little yellow building mauka of the road and are shuttled by van down to the valley garden at nearby Onomea Bay.

This nonprofit foundation charges $12 for adults and is free for children ages 16 and under. You're given a self-guided trail map and are free to wander as long as you like. It's open daily from 8:30 am to 5:30 pm, but the last shuttle bus goes down to the valley at 4:30 pm.

Saddle Rd/Mauna Kea

The Saddle Rd, true to its name, runs between the two highest points on the island, with Mauna Kea to the north and Mauna Loa to the south.

The road passes over large lava flows and climbs through a variety of terrains and climates. At sunrise and sunset there's a gentle glow on the mountains and a light show on the clouds. In the early morning it's crisp enough to see your breath, and if you take the spur road up to Mauna Kea you'll reach permafrost.

Although most car rental contracts prohibit travel on the Saddle Rd, it's a paved road straight across. It's narrow and there are sections where the road's surface is a bit crumbly and potholed, but it's no big deal – particularly by island standards.

Locals looking for the rationale behind the car rental ban come up with things like military convoys or evening fog. The crux of the matter seems to be that the rental agencies just don't want to be responsible for the tow charge if your car breaks down on Hawaii's most remote road.

The Saddle Rd is 50 miles long and has no gas stations or other facilities along the way. (Neither are there any gas stations on the 33-mile stretch of Hwy 190 between the Saddle Rd and Kona.)

Crossing the island on the Saddle Rd is a bit shorter than on the northern route of the

Hawaii Belt Rd, but it's also a slower road and timewise there isn't much difference either way.

To the west, the Saddle Rd starts out in cattle ranchland with rolling grassy hills and planted stands of eucalyptus trees. It's beautiful, but like the rest of the western side of the island it's changing. A new subdivision called Waikii Ranch has divided 3000 acres of the area's ranchland into million-dollar house lots and is marketing them to wealthy urban cowboys.

After about 10 miles the land starts getting rougher and the pastures and fences fewer. The military takes over where the cows leave off. Bradshaw Army Airfield comes up first, then the quonset huts of the Pohakuloa Military Camp. Most of the vehicles on the road are military jeeps and trucks, although in hunting season you'll come across a fair number of pick-up trucks as well.

MAUNA KEA

Mauna Kea is Hawaii's highest mountain, and its 13,796-foot summit has a cluster of important astronomical observatory domes.

The unmarked Summit Rd, which climbs up Mauna Kea, begins off Saddle Rd at the 28-mile marker, opposite a hunter's check station. It's a well-paved 6¼ miles to the Onizuka visitor center. The road winds up a few thousand feet in elevation. If you've got a small car, it's probably going to labor a bit, but it shouldn't be a problem making it up as far as the visitor center. A standard transmission is preferable.

Surprisingly, you don't really get closer views of Mauna Kea's peaks by driving up to the visitor center. The peaks actually look higher and the views are broader from Saddle Rd. But you'll find nice vistas from Summit Rd and you can often drive up above the clouds. Mauna Kea doesn't appear as a single main peak but rather a jumble of peaks, some black, some red-brown, some seasonally snowcapped.

Summit Rd passes through open range with grazing cattle. It's easy to spot Eurasian skylarks in the grass, and if you're lucky you might see the io, an endemic Hawaiian

hawk, hovering overhead. Both birds make their home on the grassy mountain slopes. Mauna Kea is also home to the nene goose, as well as the palila, a small yellow honeycreeper that lives nowhere else in the world.

One of the more predominant plants here is mullen, which has soft woolly leaves and shoots up a tall stalk. In spring the stalks get so loaded down with flowers that they bend over from the weight of what look like big yellow helmets. Mullen was brought in by ranchers as a free-loading weed in grass seed.

For information on skiing on Mauna Kea, see the Activities section at the beginning of this chapter.

Onizuka Visitor Center

The Onizuka visitor center (☎ 961-2180; mkvis@ifa.hawaii.edu), officially the Onizuka Center for International Astronomy, was named for Ellison Onizuka, a Big Island native and one one of the astronauts who died in the 1986 Challenger disaster.

The center shows an interesting short video on Mauna Kea's observatories. It also has photo displays of the observatories, information on discoveries made from the summit and exhibits of the mountain's history, ecology and geology.

The visitor center is currently open on Thursdays from 5:30 to 10 pm; Fridays from 9 am to 4:30 pm and 6:30 to 10 pm; and Saturdays and Sundays from 9 am to 2 pm and 6:30 to 10 pm. Note that the visitor center is commonly closed for lunch from noon to 1 pm. Because of inconsistent staffing, the hours are subject to change (and often do), so it's a good idea to call before making the trip.

Programs & Tours On Thursday to Sunday evenings, from 6:30 to 10 pm, the visitor center has a free astronomy program that includes a presentation about Mauna Kea and stargazing (weather permitting) from an 11-inch Celestron telescope. Children are welcome. Wear warm clothing.

The center also offers summit tours on Saturdays and Sundays. The tours take in the University of Hawaii's 88-inch telescope and the visitor gallery at the WM Keck Observatory.

The tour is free, but you need to provide your own 4WD transportation to the summit. If you're lucky, you might be able to catch a ride up with someone from the visitor center, but you can't count on it. Children under 16 are not allowed because of altitude health hazards. Check in at the visitor center at 1 pm; the tours usually last until 4 pm and are subject to cancellation when there's inclement weather at the summit.

Summit Observatories

The summit of Mauna Kea has the greatest collection of state-of-the-art telescopes on earth and superior conditions for viewing the heavens. Nearing 14,000 feet, the summit is above 40% of the earth's atmosphere and 90% of its water vapor. The air is typically clear, dry and stable.

Not only are the Hawaiian Islands isolated, but Mauna Kea is one of the most secluded places in Hawaii. The air is relatively free from dust and smog. Nights are dark and free from city light interference. To further the cause, streetlights on the island have been converted to low-impact sodium. Rather than using the full iridescent spectrum, these orange lights use only a few wavelengths, which the telescopes can be adjusted to remove.

Eight out of 10 nights are good for viewing. Only the Andes match Mauna Kea for cloudless nights, although air turbulence in the Andes makes viewing more difficult there.

The University of Hawaii (UH) holds the lease on Mauna Kea from the 12,000-foot level to the summit, and UH receives observing time at each telescope as one of the lease provisions. Currently nine telescopes are in operation and three more are in the making.

UH built the first telescope in 1968 with a 24-inch mirror. In comparison, the Maxwell submillimeter telescope built in 1987 by the UK, Netherlands and Canada has a 590-inch mirror.

The UK Infrared Telescope (UKIRT),

with its 150-inch mirror, was until recently the world's largest infrared telescope. It can be operated via computers and satellite relays from the Royal Observatory in England.

NASA's Infrared Telescope has measured the heat of volcanoes on Io, one of Jupiter's moons. The most active of Io's volcanoes is now named after the Hawaiian volcano goddess Pele.

Opened in 1992, the WM Keck Observatory, a project of the California Institute of Technology (Caltech) and the University of California, began operations with Keck I, the world's largest and most powerful optical/infrared telescope. In January 1996, the 390-inch Keck telescope discovered the most distant galaxy ever observed, at 14 billion light-years away. The discovery of this 'new galaxy', in the constellation Virgo, has brought into question the very age of the universe itself, because the stars making up the galaxy seemingly predate the 'big bang' that is thought to have created the universe.

Keck featured a breakthrough in telescope design. Previously the sheer weight of the glass mirrors was a limiting factor in telescope construction. The Keck telescope has an unique honeycomb design with 36 hexagonal mirror segments, each six feet across, that function as a single piece of glass.

A second Keck telescope (Keck II), a replica of the first, became operational in October 1996. The two telescopes are interchangeable and can function as one – 'like a pair of binoculars searching the sky' – allowing them to study the very cores of elliptical galaxies.

The Keck Observatory visitor gallery is open to the public from 10 am to 4 pm Monday to Friday. It has an informative display, a 12-minute video and a viewing area inside the Keck I dome that allows you to see the telescope.

Just 150 yards west of Keck is the new Japanese Subaru observatory, which is expected to open in 1999 at a cost of $170 million, the most expensive observatory yet undertaken.

Driving to the Summit

Visitors may go up to the summit in daytime, but vehicle headlights are not allowed between sunset and sunrise because they interfere with observation. What you'll see is mainly the outside of the observatory buildings, where the scientists are at work; only the WM Keck Observatory allows casual visitors.

The road to the summit is paved only as far as Hale Pohaku, the buildings just above the Onizuka center where the scientists reside. The road from the Onizuka center to the summit is recommended for 4WD vehicles only; although people occasionally go up in standard cars, this is not recommended due to problems that can occur with poor traction on the slopes. Harper Car & Truck Rentals is the only car rental company that allows its vehicles (4WD jeeps) to be driven to the summit.

The drive takes about half an hour. You should drive in the low range and loosen the gas cap to prevent vapor lock. The upper road can get iced over during winter. Be particularly careful on the way down and watch out for loose cinder.

About 4½ miles up is an area called **Moon Valley**, where the Apollo astronauts rehearsed with their lunar rover before their journey to the real moonscape.

At 5½ miles up, look to the left for a narrow ridge with two caves and black stones. That's **Keanakakoi**, 'Cave of the Adze', an ancient adze quarry. From this spot, high-quality basalt was quarried to make adzes and other tools and weapons, which were traded throughout the islands. For people interested in archaeology it's an impressive site. This is a protected area and nothing should be removed.

Precautions The summit air has only about 60% of the oxygen available at sea level and altitude sickness is not uncommon. Not only is the height a problem, but also the fact that visitors often don't take the time to properly acclimatize.

Unlike Nepal, for instance, where great heights are generally reached only after days of trekking, here you can zip up from sea level to nearly 14,000 feet by car in just two hours.

Scuba divers who have been diving within the past 24 hours risk getting the bends by going to the summit. It's recommended that children under 16, obese people, pregnant women and those with a respiratory condition, or even a cold for that matter, do not go beyond the Onizuka visitor center. Because of the demand that the altitude puts on the heart, people with a heart condition should avoid the summit as well.

Even the astronomers who work up here never fully acclimatize and are always working oxygen-deprived in the summit's thin air. Anyone who gets a headache or feels faint or nauseous should head back down the mountain. For more information, see Altitude Sickness under Health in the Facts for the Visitor chapter.

Bring warm clothing and be prepared for severe weather conditions, as temperatures can drop below freezing. Mauna Kea can have snow flurries any time of the year and winter storms can dump a couple of feet of snow overnight.

Lake Waiau

Lake Waiau is a unique alpine lake which, at 13,020 feet, is the third highest lake in the USA. It sits inside the Puu Waiau cinder cone in a barren and treeless setting.

Puu Poliahu

Just below Mauna Kea summit is the hill Puu Poliahu, home of Poliahu, the goddess of snow.

Poliahu is said to be more beautiful than her sister Pele. According to legend, during conflicts over men, Pele would get miffed and erupt Mauna Kea, Poliahu would cover it over with ice and snow, then Pele would erupt again. Back and forth they would go. The legend is metaphorically correct. As recently as 10,000 years ago there were volcanic eruptions through glacial ice caps here.

Because of its spiritual significance, astronomical domes have not been built on Puu Poliahu. ∎

Lake Waiau is rather mysterious. It's a small lake, no more than 10 feet deep and set on porous cinder in desert conditions of less than 15 inches of rainfall per year. It's fed by melting winter snows and permafrost, which elsewhere on Mauna Kea quickly evaporates. Lake Waiau has no freshwater springs and yet it's never dry.

Hawaiians used to bring the umbilical cords of their babies here and place them in the lake to give their children the strength of the mountain.

Mauna Kea Summit Trail

A six-mile hiking trail to the top of Mauna Kea starts near the end of the paved road above the Onizuka visitor center. Instead of continuing on the main 4WD road, take the road to the left. The trail begins up through wooden posts and more or less parallels the summit road. It's marked with posts and stone cairns.

The trail starts at 9200 feet and climbs almost 4600 feet. Because of the altitude it's quite strenuous and it's also easy to get sunburned. Dress in layers of warm clothing and take sunscreen and plenty of water. Give yourself a full day for this hike – most people take four to five hours to get to the summit.

It's a difficult hike, as you're walking on cinders, but there are incredible vistas and strange moonlike landscapes. The trail passes through the **Mauna Kea Ice Age Natural Area Reserve**. There was once a Pleistocene glacier here, and scratchings on rocks from the glacial moraine can still be seen.

The ancient adze quarry Keanakakoi, at 12,400 feet, is two-thirds of the way up. Lake Waiau (see above) is a mile farther.

You might be tempted to hitch a ride from someone at the Onizuka visitor center who's going to the summit and then walk down. But if you haven't spent the previous night in the mountains, there's a danger in doing this, as you won't have as much time to acclimatize.

Organized Tours

Paradise Safaris (☎ 322-2366), Box A-D, Kailua-Kona, HI 96745, conducts sunset tours of Mauna Kea summit. The tour, which costs $110, includes stargazing from their own little telescope and pick-up in Kailua-Kona, Waikoloa or Waimea.

Waipio Valley Shuttle (☎ 775-7121), Box 5128, Kukuihaele, HI 96727, operates daytime tours that go to the summit of Mauna Kea and include an observatory visit. The tour, which costs $80, including lunch, leaves from Waimea and takes about six hours. There's a four-person minimum.

Arnott's Lodge (☎ 969-7097) in Hilo also offers a daytime outing to Mauna Kea, this one including a hike to Lake Waiau; the cost is a reasonable $35.

See also Programs & Tours under the Onizuka Visitor Center heading.

Places to Stay

Mauna Kea State Park is seven miles west of Summit Rd, near the 35-mile marker. It has picnic tables, restrooms, a pay phone and 20 acres of shrubland. At an elevation of 6500 feet, the days are commonly cool and the nights cold.

The park has seven housekeeping cabins that are mostly used by hunters who hunt pigs, goats and game birds on the slopes of Mauna Kea. The cabins have basic kitchens, electric heating, bathrooms, hot showers and beds with the standard saggy mattresses.

As most hunting is restricted to weekends, that's the most difficult time to book the cabins. Nearby military maneuvers can be noisy, but otherwise it's a good base for those planning to hike Mauna Kea or Mauna Loa.

For reservations, contact the Division of State Parks (☎ 933-4200), Box 936, 75 Aupuni St, Hilo, HI 96721. Mauna Kea's rates are the same as those of other park cabins: $45 for one to four people, $5 more for each additional person.

MAUNA LOA'S NORTHERN FLANK

The road to Mauna Loa starts just east of the Summit Rd and climbs 18 miles up the northern flank of Mauna Loa to a weather station at 11,150 feet. There are no visitor facilities at the weather station.

The narrow road is gently sloping and passable in a standard car. As it's a winding, nearly single-lane drive with some blind spots, give yourself about 45 minutes to drive up. It might be wise to loosen your gas cap before you start in order to avoid vapor lock problems. Park in the lot below the weather station; the equipment used to measure atmospheric conditions is highly sensitive to exhaust.

The summit and domes of Mauna Kea are visible from here, and when conditions are just right you can see the 'Mauna Kea shadow' at sunset. It's a curious phenomenon in which Mauna Kea sometimes casts a blue-purple shadow behind itself in the sky.

Observatory Trail

The weather station is the trailhead for the Observatory Trail, which connects up with the Mauna Loa Trail after three miles. From there it's 2½ miles around the western side of Mauna Loa's caldera, Mokuaweoweo, to the summit at 13,679 feet, or two miles along the eastern side of Mokuaweoweo Caldera to Mauna Loa cabin at 13,250 feet. The cabin marks the end of the 18-mile Mauna Loa Trail, which starts down in the main section of Hawaii Volcanoes National Park.

The Observatory Trail is very steep and difficult. If you haven't been staying in the mountains, altitude sickness is very likely. The hike to the cabin takes four to six hours for strong hikers. Anyone who is not in top shape shouldn't even consider it.

Overnight hikers need to register in advance with the Kilauea Visitor Center in Hawaii Volcanoes National Park. See Back-country Hiking in the Hawaii Volcanoes National Park section for details.

Continuing on to Hilo

Heading eastward from the hunter's check station below Mauna Kea's visitor center, the terrain along Saddle Rd gradually becomes ohia-fern forest, shrubby at first, but getting thicker and taller as Hilo gets closer.

Red ohelo berries are fairly common in this area. These low shrubs are from the heath family, related to blueberries and cranberries. Like their relatives, ohelo berries are tart but edible.

Although most of the road is fine, there's one winding stretch worthy of note, as oncoming drivers often take to the center of the road to cut curves. The last part of the highway is newly paved. As the road re-enters civilization you can see Hilo Bay in the distance.

About four miles outside Hilo, Akolea Rd leads off to the left and connects in two miles to Waianuenue Ave, which passes Boiling Pots and Rainbow Falls. Alternatively, if you stay on Saddle Rd you'll soon come to Kaumana Caves on the left. For information on all three of these sites, see the Hilo section that follows.

Hilo

Hilo, the county capital and commercial center, is situated along a large crescent-shaped bay and has Hawaii's second largest port. With some 44,000 residents, Hilo accounts for nearly one-third of the Big Island's total population.

In terms of lush, natural beauty, Hilo beats Kona hands down any day – the only catch is in finding a sunny one. During an average year in Hilo, measurable rain falls on 278 days!

Although the rain dampens some spirits, it also feeds the area's waterfalls, jungle-like valleys and lush gardens. Indeed, Hilo is the center of activity for Big Island nurseries growing orchids, anthuriums and other tropical flowers that are sent to florists around the world.

Hilo is ethnically diverse, with many residents of Japanese or Filipino descent. There's also an alternative community that's been filtering in since the '70s, attracted by Hilo's affordability and the windward coast's scenic appeal.

Hilo's numerous period buildings give it a turn-of-the-century facade, but the town has had a precarious history. Hilo is a survivor that has beaten the odds. Natural forces have long threatened it from both sides, tidal waves from one and lava from the other. Two devastating

BIG ISLAND

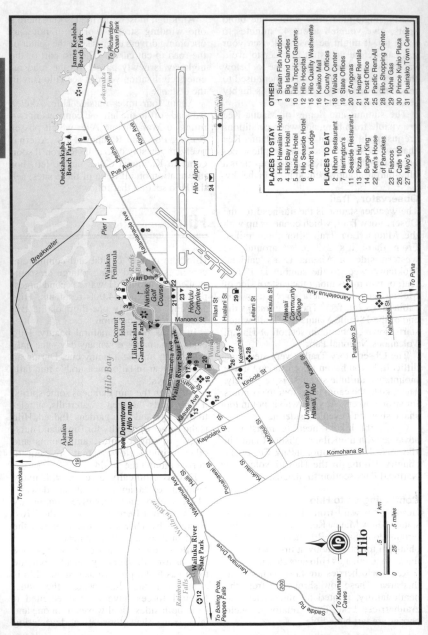

OTHER

1 Suisan Fish Auction
8 Big Island Candies
10 Hilo Tropical Gardens
12 Hilo Hospital
15 Hilo Quality Washerette
16 Kaikoo Mall
17 County Offices
18 Wailoa Center
19 State Offices
20 d'Angoras
21 Harper Rentals
24 Post Office
25 Pacific Rent-All
28 Hilo Shopping Center
29 Aloha Gas
30 Prince Kuhio Plaza
31 Puainako Town Center

PLACES TO STAY

3 Hilo Hawaiian Hotel
4 Hilo Bay Hotel
5 Naniloa Hotel
6 Hilo Seaside Hotel
9 Arnott's Lodge

PLACES TO EAT

2 Nihon Restaurant
7 Harrington's
11 Seaside Restaurant
13 Pizza Hut
14 Burger King
22 Ken's House of Pancakes
23 Flascos
26 Cafe 100
27 Miyo's

tsunamis have hit Hilo in the post-WWII era and as recently as 1984 a lava flow from Mauna Loa stopped short just eight miles above town.

Hilo's reputation for wet weather has protected it from the invasive development that has spread elsewhere on the island. In many ways Hilo is the last remaining Hawaiian city unaffected by tourism. Not that attempts haven't been made. In the 1970s Hilo built a new airport and a few deluxe hotels and started a media blitz. The airlines began direct flights from the mainland, but the tourists never showed.

'America's rainiest city' just couldn't compete with the sunny Kona Coast. The mainland flights have all been dropped and some of the hotels have been turned into condos or cheap local housing. These days, the main growth in Hilo is not related to tourism but to the rediscovery of the city – and its reasonably priced real estate – by Honolulu businesses.

Information

Tourist Offices The Hawaii Visitors Bureau (☎ 961-5797), on the corner of Haili and Keawe Sts, is open from 8 am to noon and 1 to 4:30 pm Monday to Friday.

For camping permits, the County Department of Parks & Recreation (☎ 961-8311) is at 25 Aupuni St, while the Division of State Parks (☎ 933-4200) is at 75 Aupuni St. Both are near Wailoa River State Park.

Money The Bank of Hawaii has branches at 117 Keawe St, 120 Pauahi and 417 E Kawili. There are numerous other banks around town.

Post & Communications Hilo has two post offices. The main one, which is where general delivery mail is held, is on the road into the airport. It's open Monday to Friday from 8:15 am to 4:45 pm and Saturdays from 8:30 am to 12:30 pm.

The more convenient downtown post office is in the federal building on Waianuenue Ave. It's open Monday to Friday from 8 am to 4 pm and Saturdays from 12:30 to 4 pm.

You can check your email at PostNet (☎ 959-0066), at the Price Kuhio Plaza on Hwy 11, which has an online PC. The cost is $2.50 per 15 minutes, plus 85¢ per page to print. It's open Monday to Saturday from 9 am to 7 pm, Sundays from 10 am to 4 pm.

Bookstores Basically Books (☎ 961-0144; reedbook@interpac.net), 46 Waianuenue Ave, is a book and map store specializing in Hawaiiana, including travel guides, diving guides, out-of-print books and Hawaiian literature. They also have a good general travel section and USGS topographic maps of Hawaii and the Pacific.

For quality used books, there's Still Life Books at 106 Haili St.

There are two bookstores, Waldenbooks and Book Gallery, in the Prince Kuhio Plaza on Hwy 11.

Coin Laundry Hilo Quality Washerette, 210 Hoku St, directly behind the 7-Eleven, is open from 6 am to 10 pm daily.

Emergency For police, fire and ambulance, dial ☎ 911. The hospital, Hilo Medical Center, is at 1190 Waianuenue Ave, near Rainbow Falls; for information, dial ☎ 969-4111; for the emergency room, dial ☎ 969-4100.

Airlines The ticket office of Aloha Airlines (☎ 935-9385) is in the Hilo Shopping Center, and the office of Hawaiian Airlines (☎ 935-0858) is at 120 Kamehameha Ave.

Cut Rate Tickets (☎ 969-1944), at the Puainako Town Center on Hwy 11, sells discounted air tickets.

Downtown Hilo

Downtown Hilo is an interesting mishmash of classic old buildings from the early 1900s, many on the National Register of Historic Places, and aging wooden storefronts, some newly renovated, others falling apart.

This is a good area to explore on foot. One short walk that takes in historical sites and some interesting shops starts at the intersection of Kalakaua and Keawe Sts,

BIG ISLAND

BIG ISLAND

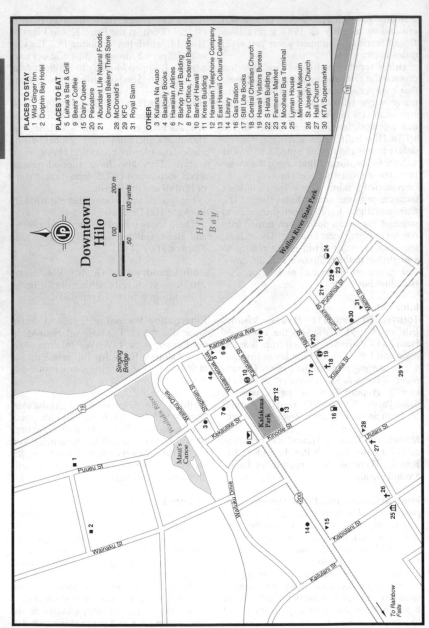

Downtown Hilo

PLACES TO STAY
1 Wild Ginger Inn
2 Dolphin Bay Hotel

PLACES TO EAT
5 Lehua's Bar & Grill
9 Bears' Coffee
15 Dairy Queen
20 Pescatore
21 Abundant Life Natural Foods,
   Oroweat Bakery Thrift Store
28 McDonald's
29 KFC
31 Royal Siam

OTHER
3 Kulana Na Auao
4 Basically Books
6 Hawaiian Airlines
7 Bishop Trust Building
8 Post Office, Federal Building
10 Bank of Hawaii
11 Kress Building
12 Hawaiian Telephone Company
13 East Hawaii Cultural Center
14 Library
16 Gas Station
17 Still Life Books
18 Central Christian Church
19 Hawaii Visitors Bureau
22 S Hata Building
23 Farmers' Market
24 Mooheau Bus Terminal
25 Lyman House
   Memorial Museum
26 St Joseph's Church
27 Haili Church
30 KTA Supermarket

0   100   200 m
0   50   100 yards

Hilo Bay

Wailoa River State Park

Singing Bridge

Wailoa River

Wailuku Drive

Maui's Canoe

Puueu St

Wainaku St

Kamehameha Ave

Shipman St

Waianuenue Ave

Kekaulike St

Kinoole St

Kalakaua Park

Kalakaua St

Haili St

Keawe St

Punahoa St

Kilauea St

Mamo St

Ululani St

Kapiolani St

Kilauai St

To Rainbow Falls

goes northwest along Keawe, up Wailuku Drive, along Kinoole St past Kalakaua Park and back down Kalakaua St.

If you wander a little further afield, you can explore the back streets, where there are little Japanese restaurants with faded kanji signs, barber shops with hand-pumped chairs and old pool halls.

The informative brochure *Walking Tour of Historic Downtown* is available free at the HVB office and some hotels.

Maui's Canoe The walk along the north end of Keawe St will lead you past a couple of period buildings that have been painstakingly renovated. The Bishop Trust Building, once a welfare office, is now a business complex, while the nearby Renaissance revival-style Kulana Na Auao building houses government offices.

If you continue walking along Keawe St just beyond Wailuku Drive, you'll be on the Puueo St Bridge, which crosses over the Wailuku River. The large rock in the river upstream on the left is known as Maui's Canoe.

Legend has it that the demigod Maui paddled his canoe with such speed across the ocean that he crash-landed here and the canoe turned to stone. Ever the devoted son, Maui was rushing to save his mother, Hina, from a water monster who was trying to drown her by damming the river and flooding her cave beneath Rainbow Falls.

Kalakaua Park In the late 1800s King David Kalakaua established Hilo as the county seat. Kalakaua Park is a quiet downtown park with a **statue** of the king sitting beneath the shade of a banyan tree, holding a taro leaf and a hula drum. The park also has a **sundial** erected by the king in 1877, a **war memorial** and a **reflecting pool** filled with carp and water lilies.

The most recent addition to Kalakaua Park is a capsule containing a collection of modern-day mementos buried during the total solar eclipse on July 11, 1991. It's intended to be opened on May 3, 2106 at the time of the next total eclipse.

The site of the king's former summer

HAWAII STATE ARCHIVES

King David Kalakaua

home, Niolopa, is opposite the park at the side of the now-closed Hilo Hotel.

Around Kalakaua Park The **federal building**, opposite the park on Waianuenue Ave, was built in 1919 of neo-classical design with high columns and a Spanish-tile roof. It still houses the federal court and downtown post office.

On the other side of the park, on Kalakaua St, the **East Hawaii Cultural Center** has taken over the old police station (circa 1932). The center hosts quality art exhibits that change monthly. Admission is free and it's open 9 am to 4 pm Monday to Saturday. A performing arts center is upstairs.

Next to the cultural center is the **Hawaiian Telephone Company building**, designed by renowned Honolulu architect CW Dickey in the 1920s. It's of Spanish-mission influence with handsome tile work and a high-hipped roof.

Lyman House Memorial Museum The Lyman House Memorial Museum (☎ 935-5021), 276 Haili St, is a first-class museum and a great place to spend a rainy afternoon.

The **Island Heritage Gallery** shows how adzes made of volcanic clink stone were used, how kukui nuts were skewered on coconut frond spines to burn as candles and other aspects of life in ancient Hawaii. Exhibits include feather leis, tapa cloth and a house made of pili grass. Mana, kahunas and *awa* (kava) drinking are all succinctly explained.

The different lifestyles of those who came as indentured immigrants and stayed on to form Hawaii's multiethnic society are all given their due. Displays include costumes, cultural artifacts and insightful interpretive plaques. From Portugal there's a braginha, the forerunner of the ukulele.

The museum has a world-class **mineral exhibit** with thousands of rocks, crystals and gemstones, including the rare 'Orlymanite' and some interesting fluorescent minerals that glow in the dark.

The **Earth Heritage Gallery** explains volcanic eruptions and lava formations with samples of spatter, olivine, Pele's tears and fine strands of Pele's hair. Other exhibits include native insects, birds, seashells and an extensive collection of land shells that represent many of the 1000 native land shell species found solely in Hawaii.

In the new **Astronomy Center** you'll not only find celestial displays, but also get an introduction to the wonders of modern astronomy via two computers linked to Mauna Kea summit observatories.

Adjacent to the museum is the **Mission House**, built by the Reverend David Lyman and his wife Sarah in 1839. The two missionaries had seven children of their own and in the attic boarded a number of island boys who attended their church school.

The mission house tour, led by an enthusiastic guide, will give you a good sense of the people who lived here. The house has many of the original furnishings, including Sarah Lyman's melodeon, rocking chair, china dishes and old patchwork quilts.

Tours of Mission House are given at 9:30, 10:30 and 11:30 am and 1, 2, 3 and 4 pm and are included in the museum admission price.

The museum is open from 9 am to 4:30 pm Monday to Saturday. Admission costs $4.50 for adults, $2.50 for children.

Churches Haili St was once called Church Row for the churches that lined up along it. The three that remain, one Catholic and two Congregational, are worth a look if you happen to be in the neighborhood.

St Joseph's Church, on the corner of Haili and Kapiolani Sts, is an attractive pink church of Spanish-mission design that looks as if it came right out of Southern California. It was built in 1919 and has stained-glass windows that open to the crosswinds and a columned entrance topped with angels.

Haili Church, at 211 Haili St, was built in 1859 with straight lines and a boxy square tower, somewhat resembling a New England barn. Services are still conducted in both Hawaiian and English.

The **Central Christian Church**, on the corner of Kilauea Ave and Haili St, was built in the Victorian style in the early 1900s by Portuguese immigrants.

Hilo Library Hilo has a good public library, at 300 Waianuenue Ave, that's open daily except Sundays until 5 pm (to 8 pm on Wednesdays and Thursdays).

The two large stones on the library's front lawn are the Naha and Pinao stones. The **Pinao Stone** was an entrance pillar to an old Hawaiian heiau.

The **Naha Stone**, from the same temple grounds, is said to weigh 2½ tons. According to Hawaiian legend it was thought that if any person had the strength to budge the stone they would also have the strength to conquer and unite all the islands. Kamehameha I reputedly met the challenge, overturning the stone in his youth.

Wailoa River State Park

Wailoa River State Park, located on the grassy expanses where Shinmachi once stood, is reached from Pauahi St. The park has two **memorials**, one dedicated to the tsunami victims and the other, an eternal flame, dedicated to the area's Vietnam War dead.

Wailoa River flows through the park, and most of **Waiakea Pond** is within the park boundaries. This spring-fed estuarine pond has both saltwater and brackish water fish species, mostly mullet. There's a boat launch ramp near the mouth of the river; only motorless boats are allowed, and fishing licenses are required.

The park's **Wailoa Center**, near the memorials, is a state-run art gallery with multimedia exhibits that change monthly. An interesting photo presentation of the tsunami damage is on display downstairs. It's open from 8 am to 4:30 pm on Mondays, Tuesdays, Thursdays and Fridays and from noon to 8:30 pm on Wednesdays. Admission is free.

Banyan Drive

Banyan Drive goes around the edge of the Waiakea Peninsula, which juts into Hilo Bay. The road skirts the Liliuokalani Gardens, the nine-hole Naniloa Golf Course and Hilo's bayfront hotels.

Banyan Drive is lined with large, sprawling **banyan trees** that were planted in the 1930s by royalty and celebrities. If you look closely you'll find plaques beneath the trees identifying the planters – they include Babe Ruth, Amelia Earhart and Cecil B De Mille.

Suisan Fish Auction Local fishers sell their catch every morning except Sundays at Suisan Fish Auction, near the intersection of Lihiwai and Banyan Drive, on the western side of the Waiakea Peninsula.

The auction is a lively local scene with the auctioneer running up the bids in Hilo's unique form of pidgin. It's open to the public with a roped-off sidewalk viewing area. Get there by 7:30 am before the auction bell rings, as the whole thing wraps up in a matter of minutes.

Next door there's a fish market with the freshest fish on the island and an outdoor

Little Tokyo & Big Tsunamis

On April 1, 1946, Hilo Bay was inundated by a tsunami that had raced its way across the Pacific from an earthquake in the Aleutian Islands. It struck at 6:54 am without warning.

Fifty-foot waves jumped the sea wall and swept into the city. They tore the first line of buildings off their foundations, carrying them inland and smashing them into the rows behind. As the waves pulled back, they sucked much of the splintered debris and a number of people out to sea.

By 7 am the town was littered with shattered buildings as far as the eye could see. The ground was not visible through the pile of rubble. Throughout Hawaii the tsunami killed 159 people and racked up $25 million in property damage. The hardest hit was Hilo, with 96 fatalities.

Hilo's bayfront 'Little Tokyo' bore the brunt of the storm. Shinmachi, which means 'New Town' in Japanese, was rebuilt on the same spot.

Fourteen years later, on May 23, 1960, an earthquake off the coast of Chile triggered a tsunami that made a beeline for Hilo at a speed of 440 miles per hour. A series of three tidal waves washed up in succession, each one sweeping farther up into the city.

Although the tsunami warning speakers roared this time, many people didn't take them seriously. The tiny tsunamis of the 1950s had been relatively harmless and some people actually went down to the beach to watch the waves.

Those along the shore were swept inland, while others farther up were dragged out into the bay. A few lucky ones who managed to grab hold of floating debris were rescued at sea. In the end there were 61 deaths and property damage of over $20 million.

Once more the Shinmachi area was leveled, but this time instead of rebuilding, the low-lying bayfront property was turned into parks and the survivors were relocated to higher ground.

All along Kamehameha Ave you can still see the curbstone cuts that once led to streets or to the driveways of businesses that made up Shinmachi. ∎

snack shop where the fishers talk story over coffee following the auction.

Liliuokalani Gardens

Hilo's 30-acre Japanese garden is named for Queen Liliuokalani, Hawaii's last queen. This picturesque waterfront park is filled with ponds complete with mullet that jump clear out of the water, little Japanese pagodas, stone lanterns, arched bridges and patches of bamboo.

The gardens are a monument of sorts to the Japanese presence in Hawaii. Many of the lanterns and pagodas that dot the park were donated by Japanese regional governments and sister cities in honor of the 100th anniversary of Japanese immigration to Hawaii.

It's a pleasant place to walk around, although after heavy rain you'll need to stick to high ground.

Coconut Island

Connected to land by a footbridge, Coconut Island sticks out into the bay opposite the Liliuokalani Gardens. The island is a county park with picnic tables and swimming but it's most popular as a recreational fishing spot. Hilo's Fourth of July fireworks display is shot off from the island and the Eastertime Merrie Monarch Festival has its opening ceremonies here.

In ancient times Coconut Island was called Moku Ola, 'Island of Life', in part due to the powers of a healing stone located on the island. Medical kahunas used the stone and invocations to cure the sick by ridding them of demonic spirits. Moku Ola also had pure spring water, which was said to bring good health, and a birthing stone that instilled mana to the children born on the island.

Beaches

Hilo is not a city for beach bums. Still, there are some decent beaches along Kalanianaole Ave, a four-mile-long coastal road on the eastern side of Hilo. The road, which is basically a continuation of Kamehameha Ave, starts in front of the Hilo Seaside Hotel.

Onekahakaha Beach Park This park is a quarter of a mile off Kalanianaole Ave; the turn-off is just before Hilo Tropical Gardens.

The park has a broad sandy-bottomed pool formed by a large boulder enclosure. As the water's just a foot or two deep in most places, it's popular with families with young children.

On the Hilo side of the park there's an unprotected cove that is sometimes used by snorkelers on calm days, but be careful as it has a seaward current. The park department cautions swimmers and snorkelers not to venture beyond the breakwater at any time.

There are campsites, restrooms, showers and a picnic area. Campers usually set up their tents around the edge of the lawn near the tree line at the Hilo end of the beach. Avoid low ground – when it rains in Hilo, it pours.

James Kealoha Beach Park Kealoha is a roadside county park known locally as Four-Mile Beach because of the distance between the park and the downtown post office. The park, which is just before the Mauna Loa Shores apartments, has camping, showers and restrooms.

For swimming and snorkeling most people go to the eastern side, which is sheltered by an island and a naturally occurring rocky breakwater. It's generally calm there, with clean, clear water and pockets of white sand.

The Hilo side of the park is open ocean and much rougher. You can sometimes find people net fishing there. It's also a popular winter surfing spot, although there are strong rip currents running out to sea.

Richardson Ocean Park This park, just before the end of the road, has a small black-sand beach fronting Hilo's most favored snorkeling site. It's also popular with boogie boarders when the waves are accommodating. The left (west) side of the bay tends to be colder due to freshwater springs in the water. On the right (east) side the springs are less common and the snorkeling is better.

The park has a lava shoreline at its east side that can be fun to explore, as it's pocketed with tiny inlets harboring black crabs and bright tropical fish. There are restrooms, showers and picnic tables, and a lifeguard is on duty daily.

Hilo Tropical Gardens

This little two-acre naturalized garden is conveniently located on the beach road at the east side of Hilo. Short walking paths wind around lily ponds and plantings of orchids, azaleas, hibiscus, ginger and other tropical flowers. There's a flower and gift shop in front, as well as a shop selling great homemade ice cream.

The garden is at 1477 Kalanianaole Ave, just past Onekahakaha Beach. It's open from 8:30 am to 5 pm daily. Admission costs $3 for adults, $1.50 for ages 13 to 18, free for children 12 and under.

Rainbow Falls

Rainbow Falls is on the western side of Hilo, off Waianuenue Ave just below the hospital.

Waianuenue, literally 'rainbow seen in water', is the Hawaiian name for this pretty 80-foot waterfall. The huge cave beneath the falls is said to have been the home of Hina, mother of Maui. The falls are usually seen as a double drop, with the two streams flowing together before hitting the large pool at the bottom.

The best time to see rainbows is in the morning, although they're by no means guaranteed, as both the sun and mist need to be accommodating. You can get a straight-on view of the falls from the lookout in front of the parking lot.

For a little diversion, take the short loop trail that begins along the steps at the left side of the falls and continues for about five minutes past a giant banyan tree and through a lush jungle-like area before leading back to the parking lot.

The site has toilets and drinking water.

Peepee Falls & Boiling Pots

Peepee Falls and Boiling Pots are up Waianuenue Ave, about 1½ miles past Rainbow Falls.

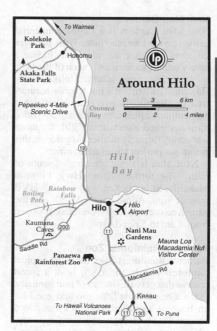

Around Hilo

Peepee Falls drop from a sheer rock face. As the water runs downstream over a series of basalt depressions in the river, it swirls and churns into bubbling pools – hence the name Boiling Pots. The bubbling effect is most pronounced after periods of heavy rain, when the water runs strongest.

Kaumana Caves

The Kaumana Caves were formed by an 1881 lava flow from Mauna Loa. As the flow subsided, the outer edges of the deep lava stream cooled and crusted over in a tunnel-like effect. The hot molten lava inside then drained out, creating these caves.

The caves are wet and mossy, thickly covered with ferns and impatiens. If you have a flashlight, you might want to explore them, although they tend to be quite drippy.

The caves, which are signposted, are three miles up Kaumana Drive (Hwy 200) on the right. There's a parking area on the opposite side of the street.

Nani Mau Gardens

Nani Mau Gardens is a large commercial garden on the tour bus route. There are over 20 acres of flowering plants, including a lovely orchid section, and much of the flora is identified with labels. Unlike many Hawaiian gardens, it's not terribly naturalized or charmingly overgrown, but rather has sculptured plantings, wide asphalt paths, tram rides and a restaurant. Still, for those who enjoy formally manicured gardens, this ambitious project has much to offer.

Nani Mau is about three miles south of Hilo. The turn-off from Hwy 11 onto Makalika St is marked with a small HVB warrior sign. Admission is $6.50, and the garden has access for the disabled. It's open from 8 am to 5 pm daily.

Panaewa Rainforest Zoo

Panaewa Rainforest Zoo, the only tropical rainforest zoo in the USA, is in a forest reserve that gets 125 inches of rain annually.

It's a respectable little zoo and good for an hour of strolling. There's a tiger in a natural pit-style cage and monkeys, reptiles, giant anteaters, a pygmy hippo and feral pigs and sheep. You can also see some of Hawaii's endangered birds, such as the nene and the Hawaiian duck, coot, hawk and owl. In addition to the 50 or so animal species that are caged here, free-roaming peacocks and guinea fowl have the run of the place.

To get there, turn off Hwy 11 onto Mamaki St (also called Kulani Hwy), a few miles south of town. The zoo is one mile west of Hwy 11. It's open from 9 am to 4:15 pm daily and admission is free.

Mauna Loa Macadamia Nut Visitor Center

Mauna Loa Macadamia Nut Visitor Center is on Macadamia Rd off Hwy 11, about five miles south of Hilo. The nearly three-mile road to the center cuts across row after row of macadamia trees, as far as the eye can see.

C Brewer Co, which owns Mauna Loa, produces most of the world's macadamia nuts. The large visitor center here caters to tour bus crowds and is essentially just a gift shop and snack bar.

To the side is a working factory, which has an outside walkway with windows that allow visitors to view the large, fast-paced assembly line inside.

The little planted area behind the visitor center, with its labeled fruit trees and flowering bushes, is worth walking through if you've come this far. The center is open from 8:30 am to 5 pm daily.

Places to Stay

Partially due to the weather, Hilo has no self-contained resorts. People don't come to Hilo to hang around a pool, but to visit the sights and then head on. Consequently, the 'vacation rental' condo market that's so common on the Kona Coast is virtually nonexistent here.

Places to Stay – budget

Arnott's Lodge (☎ 969-7097, 800-953-7773 from the Neighbor Islands; fax 961-9638), 98 Apapane Rd, Hilo, HI 96720, is a great place to connect with other travelers, if you don't mind being on the outskirts of town. This friendly, accommodating, hostel-style lodge has 36 dorm beds and 12 private rooms in a converted apartment building. It costs $17 for a bunk bed in a room with two to four people, $30 for a single room and $40 for doubles, all with shared baths and kitchen facilities. Linen and towels are provided. There's a common TV room, a coin laundry, free airport pick-up and a scheduled daily shuttle service ($1) into town.

The lodge offers a rotating schedule of well-run daily outings, including visits to Puna and Pahoa, South Point and Green Sands Beach, Hawaii Volcanoes National Park, and Mauna Kea. There's also a good barbecue ($6) a few times a week; rental bikes are available for $10 a day. Master-Card and Visa are accepted. To get to Arnott's Lodge, go east 1½ miles on Kalanianaole Ave from Hwy 11 and turn left onto Keokea Loop Rd. The lodge is about 100 yards down the road.

The popular *Dolphin Bay Hotel* (☎ 935-1466; fax 935-1523), 333 Iliahi St, Hilo, HI

96720, on a hill just above downtown, is a very friendly, family-run place. Not only is the hotel a good value but, unlike many other small inns, it welcomes travelers with children. All 18 apartment-like units have full kitchens, TVs and bathrooms, and all except the standard rooms have sunken bathtubs. Fresh-picked fruit from the backyard is available in the lobby, along with free morning coffee. Standard rooms cost $55/59 for singles/doubles, while superior rooms cost $65/69. They also have four large one-bedroom units for $79 and a two-bedroom unit for $89 for either singles or doubles. It's $10 more for each additional person. Weekly rates are available. This is one of the few hotels in Hilo with a continuously high occupancy rate and reservations are suggested.

The people at *Wild Ginger Inn* (☎ 935-5556, 800-882-1887), 100 Puueo St, Hilo, HI 96720, have taken a formerly rundown motel and given it a bright face-lift in hot pink and green Caribbean colors. Rooms in this nonsmoking inn are simple but quite adequate, and breakfast is included in the price. The rooms have private baths and either a double or two twin beds; most also have small refrigerators. Despite the central location, there's a wooded gulch behind the main wing that provides many of the rooms with nice views of bamboo and a little stream. The cost is $39/44; for stays of three or more nights it drops to $35 for either singles or doubles.

Lihi Kai (☎ 935-7865), Amy Gamble Lannan, 30 Kahoa Rd, Hilo, HI 96720, is a B&B in Amy's home perched on a cliff directly above Hilo Bay, two miles north of town. There's a small heated swimming pool and a large living room with a wonderful ocean view. There are two guest rooms – one with two twin beds, the other a king bed – that share a bath and a half and cost $50 for either a single or double with breakfast. There's a three-night minimum stay or an extra $5 charge.

Places to Stay – middle

Hilo Seaside Hotel (☎ 935-0821, 800-367-7000), 126 Banyan Drive, Hilo, HI 96720, is a 145-unit complex of two-story motel-style buildings. The rooms are simple with turquoise carpets, louvered windows, ceiling fans, air-con, TV and a small refrigerator. Avoid the rooms around the swimming pool and the streetside Hukilau wing, both of which can get a bit noisy. The nicest rooms are in the deluxe ocean wing and have balconies overlooking the hotel's carp pond and Reeds Bay. The usual room rates range from $60 to $80, but there are discounts if you book from within Hawaii (rather than toll-free from the mainland) and ask for the special – it's commonly $49.

Uncle Billy's *Hilo Bay Hotel* (☎ 935-0861, 800-367-5102; fax 935-7903), 87 Banyan Drive, Hilo, HI 96720, is a locally owned 130-room hotel with a touristy Polynesian theme. Rates range from a pricey $77 for a quite basic standard room to $92 for a much nicer oceanfront room in the main building. Rooms cost about $10 less in the low season.

Three miles north of Hilo off Hwy 19 is *Hale Kai Bjornen* (☎ 935-6330; fax 935-8439), 111 Honolii Pali, Hilo, HI 96720, a B&B in an immaculately kept contemporary home with fine views across Hilo Bay. The five ocean-facing rooms, each of which has a private bath, cable TV and either a queen or king bed, range in price from $85 to $105, with breakfast included. Guests have use of a small swimming pool, a refrigerator and the living room.

Places to Stay – top end

Hilo Hawaiian Hotel (☎ 935-9361, 800-367-5004; fax 961-9642), 71 Banyan Drive, Hilo, HI 96720, is a 285-unit high-rise hotel near Coconut Island. It's Hilo's finest hotel; the common areas are attractive, the guest rooms comfortable. Rooms have a pleasant though not distinguished decor, either a king or two smaller beds, air-con, remote-control TV and phone; most also have private lanais. Garden-view rooms, which look across the parking lot to the golf course, cost $99, while larger oceanview rooms overlooking Hilo Bay cost $130. If you request it at the time of booking, you can usually add a rental car at no extra cost.

Naniloa Hotel (☎ 969-3333, 800-367-5360; fax 969-6622), 93 Banyan Drive, Hilo, HI 96720, is a 325-room high-rise hotel – Hilo's largest. The rooms have TV, air-con and phones but are rather straightforward for the rates, which range from $100 to $160 depending on the view, and only the top-end rooms have balconies. It's popular with Japanese tour groups.

The *Shipman House Bed & Breakfast* (☎ 934-8002, 800-627-8447; bighouse@bigisland.com), 131 Kaiulani St, Hilo, HI 96720, in the town center, is an elegant Victorian mansion that has been in the Shipman family since 1901; past visitors to the home have included Queen Liliuokalani and author Jack London. The owners, Barbara-Ann and Gary Andersen, who recently returned to Hilo after 20 years in the San Francisco area, have thoroughly renovated the house. There are three B&B rooms. One is a guest room in the main house, with two antique koa twin beds, while the other two rooms, each with queen beds, are in the 1910 guest cottage. All have private baths, ceiling fans and small refrigerators. The cost is $130 for singles or doubles, breakfast included. There is no minimum stay. Smoking is not allowed indoors.

Places to Eat – budget

Miyo's (☎ 935-2273), in the back of the Waiakea Villas complex, is a charming homestyle Japanese restaurant overlooking Waiakea Pond. The atmosphere is relaxed, the food good and the prices unbeatable. Many dishes can be ordered either with fish or meat, or vegetarian style. At lunch, tempura, tonkatsu or sesame chicken – all served with rice, miso soup and salad – cost around $6. A tempura and sashimi combination is just $7. The same meals at dinner cost a dollar or two more. It's open Tuesday to Saturday from 11 am to 2 pm and 5:30 to 8:30 pm.

For a thoroughly local experience, head to *Cafe 100*, a drive-in-style eatery at 969 Kilauea Ave. It's a fun place for cheap food and perhaps the last spot in Hawaii where you can get a 35-cent cup of coffee. You can order loco moco or sandwiches for $2,

full breakfast for $3 and plate lunches from $4. There are picnic tables at the side of the building where you can chow down. It's open daily from 6:45 am to 8:30 pm (to 9:30 pm on weekends).

Bears' Coffee, 106 Keawe St, is a nice place for a light lunch or breakfast. You'll find pastries, good Belgian waffles and egg dishes (until 11:30 am), and from 10 am there are deli sandwiches, burritos and 'designer' bagels with a choice of more than a dozen fillings. Everything, except the bagel with lox, costs less than $6. It's open from 7 am to 4 pm daily except Sundays. There are both indoor and sidewalk tables, but as it's a popular gathering place, finding an empty spot at mealtimes can be challenging.

You'll find authentic Hawaiian food at *Kuhio Grille*, a casual new eatery at the north side of the Prince Kuhio Plaza that's owned by a couple of taro growers from Waipio Valley. For $8 you can get a laulau plate made with local taro leaves, poi, lomi, taro slices and haupia. In the morning, there's a breakfast special of two eggs, Spam, rice and toast for $3 and various options without the Spam for not much more. Other menu items include taro corned beef hash, burgers, saimin and the usual plate meals. It's open Monday through Friday from 5 am to 9 pm and on a 24-hour basis on weekends.

Abundant Life Natural Foods, 292 Kamehameha Ave, is a health food store with a variety of products including cheeses, yogurt, juices and bulk foods. It also has a simple deli and smoothie bar. It's open from 8:30 am to 6 pm weekdays, 8 am to 5 pm on Saturdays and 11 am to 3 pm on Sundays. Next door, *Oroweat Bakery Thrift Store* has slightly dated breads at discounted prices.

Hilo has an abundance of fast-food restaurants spread around town. The biggest concentration is at the Puainako Town Center on Hwy 11, which has *McDonald's*, *Pizza Hut*, *Jack in the Box*, *Taco Bell*, *Little Caesar's* and *Subway Sandwiches*. *Ken's House of Pancakes*, 1730 Kamehameha Ave, is open 24 hours daily.

KTA Supermarket, 323 Keawe St, a convenient downtown grocery store, is open from 7 am to 9 pm Monday to Saturday, to 6 pm on Sundays. There's a *Safeway* supermarket at the Prince Kuhio Plaza on Hwy 11 and a *Sack N Save* supermarket in the nearby Puainako Town Center. If you're heading for Volcano early in the morning, Sack N Save has coffee and doughnuts from 5 am.

Hilo has a great *farmers' market* on Wednesday and Saturday mornings on the corner of Mamo St and Kamehameha Ave. You can usually pick up three or four Kapoho papayas for $1, as well as Kau oranges and other island fruits, vegies and flowers direct from the growers at bargain prices.

Hilo's best ice cream can be found at *Hilo Homemade Ice Cream*, next to Hilo Tropical Gardens. Owner Fred Stoeber cheerfully scoops up his Hawaiian creations, including tasty poha berry, zesty ginger and other island flavors like lilikoi, coconut cream and macadamia nut. It costs $1.25 for a single scoop, $2 for a double. Hours are 10 am to 5 pm daily. From 11 am to 2 pm you can get a nice curry and rice plate for $4.

Places to Eat – middle

Royal Siam (☎ 961-6100), 68 Mamo St, has good authentic Thai food at reasonable prices. There are salads, soups and noodle dishes, as well as a selection of tasty red, green and yellow curries that can be ordered mild to hot. Beef or chicken dishes cost $7, while most seafood dishes cost around $9. The menu is extensive, with two pages of vegetarian dishes priced from $5 to $6. It's open Monday to Saturday from 11 am to 2:30 pm and 5 to 8:30 pm (to 9 pm on weekends).

Cafe Pesto (☎ 969-6640), a branch of the popular Kawaihae restaurant, is on Kamehameha Ave in the newly renovated S Hata Building, a classic 1912 building that once held the city's main department store. The restaurant serves creative pasta dishes, gourmet wood-fired pizzas and superb seafood calzones. Most items cost between $9 and $15. From 11 am to 4:30 pm there are also a few hot sandwiches available,

such as a Japanese eggplant and marinated artichoke creation, for $6.50. It's open until 9 pm Sunday to Thursday, to 10 pm on weekends.

Lehua's Bar & Grill (☎ 935-8055), 90 Kamehameha Ave, has a varied menu. At lunch there are salads, pasta dishes and sandwiches with fries for $7 to $9. Dinners, which come with salad and fries, range from $11 for chicken to $18 for steak. It's open daily from 11 am to 9 pm.

Restaurant Miwa (☎ 961-4454), 1261 Kilauea Ave, is an authentic Japanese restaurant despite its mall location in the Hilo Shopping Center. It has a sushi bar, good sashimi and a full range of Japanese dishes at moderate prices. At lunch a full-meal teishoku costs around $8, at dinner around $10, while more extensive dinner combinations cost $15. Although it's not gourmet, the food is good, with quality, price and decor comparable to a neighborhood restaurant in Japan. It's open from 11 am to 10 pm Monday to Saturday and from 5 to 9 pm on Sunday.

Ting-Hao Mandarin Restaurant (☎ 959-6288), in Puainako Town Center on Hwy 11, is Hilo's best Chinese restaurant. Vegetarian dishes such as broccoli with garlic or mapo tofu average $7, while standard Sichuan and Mandarin meat-based dishes cost $7 to $11. There's also a daily lunch special that includes two main dish selections from a steamer tray and fried rice for $4.49. No MSG is used. It's open from 10 am to 2:30 pm Monday to Friday and 4:30 to 9 pm nightly.

Fiascos (☎ 935-7666), 200 Kanoelehua Ave (Hwy 11), is a bustling place serving sandwiches, salads, pastas, fajitas and an array of meat dishes at moderate prices. There's also a reasonably good soup-and-salad bar for $6.25 alone, $4.50 with a meal. It's open from 11 am to 10 pm daily, to 11 pm on Fridays and Saturdays.

Nihon Restaurant (☎ 969-1133) at 121 Lihiwai St, next to Liliuokalani Gardens, has a fine view of Hilo Bay and a good sushi bar. At lunch the $10 'business special' includes two entrees, such as sashimi, tonkatsu or tempura, served with rice, kappamaki, miso soup and tossed salad. Dinner teishokus are a few dollars more. It's open from 11 am to 1:30 pm and 5 to 8 pm Monday to Saturday.

Places to Eat – top end
Pescatore (☎ 969-9090), 235 Keawe St, has fine dining, attentive service and Hilo's best Italian food. Lunch is a particularly good deal, with fresh fish for $10 and an array of pasta dishes ranging from $7 for bolognese to $10 for scampi alfredo. At dinner, pasta dishes are about double the lunch prices, while meat and seafood main courses average $20. One recommendable item is the *fra diavolo*, a lightly spiced dinner dish combining fresh ahi, calamari and clams over pasta. Lunch is from 11 am to 2 daily. Dinner is from 5:30 to 9 pm weekdays, to 10 pm weekends.

Harrington's (☎ 961-4966), perched on Reeds Bay, is a small waterfront restaurant with a fine view. Locally, it's a perennial favorite for special occasions, serving good seafood, steak and chicken dishes in the $15 to $20 range, salad included. Add another $8 for an appetizer such as shrimp cocktail or escargot. It's open for dinner only, from 5:30 pm nightly. Especially on weekends, dinner reservations are advisable.

Seaside Restaurant (☎ 935-8825), a family-run operation at 1790 Kalanianaole Ave, has the island's freshest fish and serves it in a delightful setting. The unpretentious dining room is a simple open-air affair that sits pondside above the family's aquafarm. You can have your pick of fresh mullet, rainbow trout, perch or catfish, all of which are raised in the pond. The local favorite is steamed mullet wrapped in ti leaves, but there are other preparations to choose from. The meals, which include rice, salad, apple pie and coffee, cost a reasonable $17 and are served from 5 to 8:30 pm Tuesday to Sunday. It's best to call ahead for reservations so meals can be planned in advance.

Entertainment
Nighttime musical entertainment is not one of Hilo's strong points. *Fiascos*, on Hwy 11

near Banyan Drive, has country line dancing on Thursday evenings, live rock or contemporary Hawaiian music on Friday and Saturday; there's no cover charge. *Lehua's Bar & Grill*, 90 Kamehameha Ave, occasionally has a band on weekends, with varying cover charges.

d'Angoras, a bar and nightclub at 101 Aupuni St, has a DJ with dancing to rock and Top 40 music Thursday to Sunday from 9:30 pm and a jazz band on Sunday from 3 to 6 pm; there's usually a cover charge of $3 to $5.

Harrington's, on Reeds Bay, has Hawaiian or contemporary music, usually acoustic guitar or keyboards, in its lounge from 7 pm on weekends.

Uncle Billy presents a hula show during dinnertime, from 6 pm nightly, at the *Hilo Bay Hotel* restaurant.

Periodically there are community plays, dances and concerts at the *East Hawaii Cultural Center* on Kalakaua St; check the Hilo paper for the current schedule.

Movie Theaters *Kress Cinemas*, in the meticulously renovated Art Deco-style Kress Building at 174 Kamehameha Ave, is the most atmospheric place to take in a little celluloid. It shows standard first-run Hollywood films, as do the movie theaters at *Prince Kuhio Plaza* on Hwy 11 and *Waiakea Shopping Plaza* at 88 Kanoelehua Ave, just south of Ken's House of Pancakes.

Things to Buy
Hilo has several shopping centers. The largest is the Prince Kuhio Plaza, at the south side of town on Hwy 11, which has 65 stores, including Liberty House, Penthouse, Hilo Hattie, Sears, Longs Drugs, Safeway, Woolworth, a camera shop and a one-hour photo place.

Big Island Candies, 500 Kalanianaole Ave, sells chocolate-covered macadamia nuts, cookies and other sweet treats made on site. From the gift shop, you can sample the products and sip on a free cup of coffee while watching candy being hand-dipped on the other side of plate-glass windows. It's open from 8:30 am to 5 pm daily.

Puna

Puna is the diamond-shaped easternmost point of the Big Island. Its main attractions are in lava: vast fields of it covering former villages, an ancient forest of lava tree molds, lava tide pools and black-sand beaches.

Kilauea Volcano's active east rift zone slices clear across Puna. The most recent series of eruptions has been spewing lava since 1983. These days, the highway into Puna ends abruptly at the 1990 lava flow that buried the former village of Kalapana.

Not surprisingly, Puna has Hawaii's cheapest real estate. The closer to the rift, the greater the volcanic activity and the cheaper the land gets.

While a growing number of people are drawn to Puna by the idea of homesteading, many have found it tough making a living off a lava flow. For years, growing pakalolo has been a potentially lucrative alternative, although changing public attitudes and mounting police pressures have made it an increasingly less appealing one. Paramilitary raids, intense herbicide sprayings and helicopters with infrared sensors that allow authorities to see into people's homes have sharply curtailed the growing. Nonetheless, the majority of all pot confiscated by Hawaii police is still taken in Puna.

Deserved or not, Puna has the reputation of being less than friendly. If you're traveling the main roads you probably won't pick up on those vibes at all, but if you're cruising around off the beaten path you may raise a suspicious eye.

Some crops take well to lava and Puna is a major producer of anthuriums, grows the best papayas in Hawaii, and grows many of the orchids that get credited to Hilo.

Puna is not known for its beaches, and for the most part waters along the coast are subject to strong currents and rip tides.

Orientation

Keaau is the entrance to Puna, where Hwys 11 and 130 intersect. From there, Hwy 130 goes south 11 miles to Pahoa and then continues on to the coast.

Maps that show Hwy 130 winding down through Puna and up the Chain of Craters Road to Hawaii Volcanoes National Park were made obsolete in 1988 when a lava flow buried a large section of the road; active lava tunnels have continued flowing over that stretch of road to this day. Consequently, the national park can be entered only via the Hawaii Belt Rd (Hwy 11), which makes Puna more time-consuming to visit, as you need to backtrack out the same way you go in.

KEAAU

Keaau is the small town at the northern end of Puna. If you need to pick up supplies or get something to eat, the Keaau Shopping Center, at the intersection of Hwys 11 and 130, has a supermarket, post office, Dairy Queen, natural foods store and a couple of small local eateries.

PAHOA

The heart of Puna is Pahoa, a funky little town with raised wooden sidewalks, cowboy architecture and an untamed edge. There are influences from the '60s and '70s, but there are other more timeless ones as well. The Akebono Theater, which was built in 1917 and is one of the oldest theaters in Hawaii, has recently been reopened for both movies and live concerts.

If you'd like to take a look at life on a lava flow as you're driving around, stop by Pahoa Realty on Main St and pick up their free subdivision map and listings. Prices start as low as $4500 for a small lot (no electricity, water by catchment, gravel roads) on Kilauea's active east rift zone.

Wild orchids grow like weeds along the roadsides around Pahoa and throughout Puna. There are fields of cultivated orchids and lots of anthurium nurseries as well.

Places to Stay

The *Village Inn* (☎ 965-6444), Box 1987, Pahoa, HI 96778, has five 2nd-story rooms in a historic wooden building on Main St, adjacent to the theater. It's partly funky,

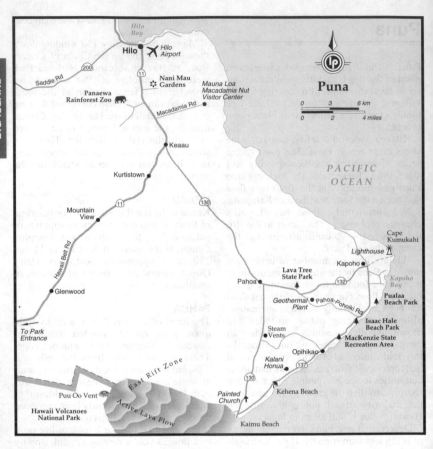

Puna

0   3   6 km
0   2   4 miles

Hilo Bay
Hilo
Hilo Airport

Saddle Rd
(200)

(11)
Nani Mau Gardens
Mauna Loa Macadamia Nut Visitor Center

Panaewa Rainforest Zoo

Macadamia Rd

Keaau

PACIFIC OCEAN

Kurtistown

(11)
(130)

Mountain View

Hawaii Belt Rd

Cape Kumukahi

Lighthouse

Kapoho

Glenwood

Lava Tree State Park

Pahoa
(132)

Kapoho Bay

Geothermal Plant
Pahoa-Pohoiki Rd

Pualaa Beach Park

To Park Entrance

Steam Vents

Isaac Hale Beach Park

MacKenzie State Recreation Area

Opihikao

East Rift Zone

Kalani Honua
(137)

(130)

Kehena Beach

Puu Oo Vent
Active Lava Flow

Painted Church

Hawaii Volcanoes National Park

Kaimu Beach

slanted hardwood floors and all, and partly classy, with rooms furnished with authentic Victorian-era antiques. All rooms have cable TVs and mini-refrigerators. Rates are $30 for singles or doubles in rooms with shared bath, $40 for rooms with private baths. Credit cards are accepted.

Bamboo House (☎ 965-8322), Box 1546, Pahoa, HI 96778, a cottage rented by the owner of the natural foods store, is on a side street in the center of town. One side of a duplex cottage, it's clean, comfortable and pleasantly airy. It even has a bit of tropical decor with Japanese and Hawaiian

floral touches. The unit has one bedroom as well as a small living room with a queen sofa bed, mini-refrigerator and cable TV. Another nearby building is also being converted into a vacation rental. Rates are a reasonable $45 per night, or $35 a night for three nights or more. Smoking is not allowed; credit cards are accepted.

The cheapest place to crash is *Pahoa Station Rooms* (☎ 936-4676), a small, simple boarding house above the shops at the east end of Main St in the town center. The rooms are very basic – a bed, TV and window fan – and share toilets and showers.

Rates are $25 a night, $100 a week and $200 a month.

Places to Eat

Luquin's, on Main St in Pahoa's town center, has good, authentic Mexican food. A single taco or enchilada costs $2.50, while combination plates are priced from $6. Huevos rancheros with tortillas, rice and beans cost $5 and are served all day; it's open from 11 am to 9 pm daily.

Huna Ohana, on Main St near Luquin's, is an incense-scented metaphysical bookstore and espresso cafe. Eggs with potatoes and toast, a Belgian waffle with fresh fruit and whipped cream, and various vegetarian lunches average $4 to $5. They also serve organic Kona coffee and make good fruit smoothies. It's open from 8 to 11 am for breakfast and 11 am to 5 pm for lunch Monday to Saturday.

Paolo's Bistro (☎ 965-7033), also on Main St in the town center, has genuine Northern Italian fare. Most pasta dishes, which are served with a cup of minestrone, cost $8 to $10, while the most expensive item on the menu, cioppino (seafood stew), costs $15. Add another $4 for a salad or tiramisu. Paolo's is currently open for dinner only, from 5:30 to 9 pm Tuesday through Sunday.

Pahoa Natural Groceries, across from the Bank of Hawaii in the center of town, is a well-stocked natural foods store with a dairy section, bakery items, inexpensive salads and healthy sandwiches such as cheese and avocado on whole-wheat bread. It's open from 9 am to 9 pm daily (to 6 pm on Sundays).

Pahoa also has a ribhouse restaurant, Chinese and Thai restaurants, a *Dairy Queen* and an old grocery store where you'll find the local bulletin board.

Onward from Pahoa

The usual route after Pahoa is a triangle that goes down Hwy 132 past Lava Tree State Park to Kapoho, then continues on Hwy 137 along the shore to the lava flow at Kaimu Beach and comes back to Pahoa via Hwy 130. Conveniently, Hwys 137 and 130

still connect, though they do so at the very edge of a lava flow.

From Pahoa, Hwy 132 passes through a tropical forest reserve. The area is very lush and jungle-like, with ferns growing on the bark of trees and a thick ground cover of impatiens. If you're short on time, a good alternative is Pahoa-Pohoiki Rd, which is also a nice rainforest drive along a narrow road lined by old mango trees and papaya groves.

LAVA TREE STATE PARK

The lava molds at Lava Tree State Park were created in 1790 when this former ohia rainforest was engulfed in pahoehoe from Kilauea's east rift zone. The lava was free-flowing and moved quickly, like a river flooding its banks.

As the molten lava ran through the forest, some of it began to congeal around the moisture-laden ohia trunks while the rest of the flow moved on through and quickly receded.

Although the trees themselves burned away, the molds of lava that had formed around them remained. Now, 200 years later, there's a ghost forest of lava shells.

Puna & Pele

In the Hawaiian language there are several proverbial expressions that link Puna with the volcano goddess Pele. As an example, to express anger, someone might say *Ke lauahi malla o Pele ia Puna*, 'Pele is pouring lava out on Puna'.

Equally common are both historic and modern stories of a mysterious woman traveling alone through Puna. Sometimes she's young and attractive, other times she's old and wizened, and often she's seen just before a volcanic eruption. Those who stop and pick her up hitchhiking or show some other kindness are often protected from the lava flow.

After the 1960 lava flow destroyed the village of Kapoho, stories circulated about how the lightkeeper in the spared Kapoho lighthouse had offered a meal to an elderly woman who had showed up at his door on the eve of the eruption. ■

A 20-minute loop walk winds around the 'lava trees'. Some are a good 10 feet high, while others are short enough to look down into and shelter ferns within their hollows.

Be careful if you walk off the path, as in places the ground is crossed by deep cracks, some hidden by new vegetation. It's speculated that one deep fracture, which was caused by an earthquake at the same time as the flow, may have drained much of the lava back into the earth.

The park is on Hwy 132, 2½ miles east from its intersection with Hwy 130. The mosquitoes can be wicked.

KAPOHO

Hwy 132 heads east through orchards of papaya and long rows of vanda orchids to what was once Kapoho, a farming town of about 300 people.

On January 13, 1960, a fountain of fire half a mile long shot up in the midst of a sugar cane field just above Kapoho. The main flow of liquid pahoehoe lava ran towards the ocean but a slower moving off-shoot of aa lava crept towards the town, burying orchid farms in its path.

Earthen barricades were built and fire hoses frantically pumped water onto the lava, but none of the attempts to harden or divert the flow worked.

On January 28 the lava entered Kapoho and buried the town. A hot springs resort and nearly 100 homes and businesses disappeared beneath the flow.

One bizarre phenomenon occurred when the river of lava approached the sea at **Cape Kumukahi**. Within a few feet of the cape's lighthouse the lava parted into two flows and circled around it, sparing the lighthouse from destruction. If you want to take a look, the site is 1¾ miles down the dirt road that continues beyond the intersection of Hwys 132 and 137. However, while the parted lava flows are still visible, the old lighthouse has been replaced by a modern light. Cape Kumukahi, which means 'first beginning' in Hawaiian, is the easternmost point in the state.

The most dominant landscape feature in the Kapoho area is the **Kapoho Crater**, an ancient 420-foot cinder cone. The hill is lush green with thick vegetation and has a small crater lake on top of it.

One of the earliest legends of volcanic activity in Kapoho goes back to the 14th century. It seems that Kahavari, a young Puna chief, was holding a holua (sledding) contest on the slopes of Kapoho Crater. One of the spectators was an attractive woman who stepped forward and challenged the chief to a race.

Kahavari tossed the woman an inferior sled and charged down the hill, daring her to overcome him. Halfway down he glanced over his shoulder and found her close behind, racing down atop a wave of molten lava. It was of course the volcano goddess Pele, who chased Kahavari clear out to sea, where he narrowly escaped in a canoe. Everyone and everything in Pele's path was buried in the flood of lava.

Hwy 137

Hwy 137 (Kalapana-Kapoho Beach Rd) is barely above water level, bordered by invasive milo and hala trees that look as if they plan to reclaim the road. In a few places it's so overgrown there's almost a tunnel effect, with just a lacy bit of light filtering in through the trees. The road sometimes floods during winter storms and high surf.

Kapoho Tidepools

Kapoho Tidepools are in the Kapoho Vacationland subdivision, a mile south of the lighthouse. This network of tide pools is formed in lava basins, some of which are deep enough for swimming and snorkeling.

To get there, turn makai off Hwy 137 onto Kapoho Kai Drive and then turn left on Waiopai. There's a sign for public access, but parking can be a hassle.

PUALAA BEACH PARK

One of the few safe swimming spots on the Puna coast is Pualaa Beach Park, off Hwy 137 one mile north of Isaac Hale Beach Park. Recently turned into a park by the county, the star attraction is a lovely thermal spring-fed pool set in lava rock, roughly 60 feet in diameter and deep enough for swimming.

The water temperature averages about 90°F, but the pool has an inlet to the ocean (which pounds upon the seawall rocks at the makai side of the pool) so the water is kept clean. On weekdays it's generally a quiet spot, while on weekends it's popular with families. The park has picnic tables, pit toilets and usually a lifeguard on duty. The pool is directly behind a long yellow house; parking is on the opposite side of the road.

ISAAC HALE BEACH PARK
Isaac Hale Beach Park, which is on Pohoiki Bay on Hwy 137, has a shoreline of chunky lava rocks. This county park is small, but on weekends there's usually a frenzy of local activity, including picnics and fishing.

The park has Puna's only boat ramp. Local kids like to swim near the ramp, which is somewhat protected by a breakwater, and there are sometimes surfers at the south side of the bay.

Camping is allowed, but it's not a very attractive option, as the camping area is virtually in the parking lot.

The park has toilets but no drinking water or showers.

MACKENZIE STATE RECREATION AREA
There's no beach at MacKenzie State Recreation Area but rather 40-foot sea cliffs with a surging surf that sometimes breaks three-quarters of the way up. There's good fishing from the cliffs for ulua, a jack fish that favors turbulent waters.

This 13-acre park on Hwy 137 is quiet and secluded in a grove of ironwood trees. There's a soft carpet of needles underfoot. Both tent and trailer camping are allowed with a permit from the state, but the facilities, which include picnic tables and pit toilets, are run down and there's no drinking water.

An old Hawaiian coastal trail, called the

King's Trail, passes through the park. It runs parallel to the ocean about 75 yards in from the cliffs. If you take it northeast from the parking lot for about three minutes, you'll come across the opening of a long **lava tube**, which is marked by a low thicket of ferns.

OPIHIKAO
The village of Opihikao is marked by a little Congregational church and a couple of houses.

Kalani Honua, a New Age conference and retreat center, is 2½ miles southwest of Opihikao village, midway between the 17- and 18-mile markers. A wide diversity of workshops take place at the center, including tai chi retreats, alternative health and fitness courses, heritage programs focusing on Hawaiian culture and weekend workshops geared to the gay and lesbian community. Visitors are welcome to stop by and take a look around. There's a simple cafe and gift shop at the office.

Places to Stay & Eat
Kalani Honua (☎ 965-7828, 800-800-6886), RR2 Box 4500, Pahoa, HI 96778, caters mostly to groups but also welcomes individual travelers on a space-available basis.

There are 31 rooms, most in two-story cedar lodges with exposed-beam ceilings, lots of natural wood and a screened common area with shared kitchen. Singles/doubles cost $75/85 with a private bath, $60/70 with a shared bath. There are also private cottages with one bedroom, bath and living room for $85/95.

Tents can be pitched on the grounds for $15/25 singles/doubles. There's a sauna, pool and tennis court for guests.

The center has a work scholar program that provides room and board in exchange for 30 hours of work per week; a three-month commitment is required. This could be an interesting budget option for a lengthy stay in Hawaii.

The dining room, which serves buffet-style vegetarian meals, is open to the public. Breakfast costs $7, lunch $9 and dinner $13. Dining room hours are short: from 7:30 to 8:30 am for breakfast, noon to 1 pm for lunch and 6 to 7 pm for dinner. From 10 am to 6 pm you can also get soda, snack items and a few simple microwaveable foods at the small cafe adjacent to the office.

KEHENA BEACH
Kehena Beach, at the base of a cliff, is a black-sand beach created by a 1955 lava flow. Shaded by coconut and ironwood trees, the beach is a pleasant and free-spirited nude sunbathing spot.

When the water is calm, swimming is usually safe, but during periods of heavy surf there can be powerful currents and dangerous undertows. In winter it's not unusual for dolphins to come close to the shore and swim with bathers.

Kehena is off Hwy 137, immediately south of the 19-mile marker. Look for cars parked at the side of the road and you'll find the start of the path down to the beach, a five-minute walk away. Don't leave valuables in your car.

End of the Road
For years, the village of Kalapana sat precariously beneath Kilauea's restless east rift. When the current series of eruptions began in 1983 the main lava flow moved down the slope to the west of Kalapana. Much of the early flow passed through a series of lava tubes, which carried the molten lava down to the coast and into the sea. During pauses in the eruption in 1990, the tubes feeding lava to the ocean cooled long enough to harden and block up. When the eruption started again, the lava flow, no longer able to take its previous course, was redirected towards Kalapana. By the end of 1990 the entire village, including 100 homes, was buried.

Today the road (Hwy 137) ends abruptly at Kaimu Beach on the eastern edge of Kalapana. Kaimu, formerly the most famous black-sand beach in Hawaii, is now encased under a sea of hardened lava that flowed over the sandy beach and clear into the bay. Opposite the beach, the drive-in

restaurant where the tour buses used to park was ironically spared – a boarded-up reminder of the attraction that Kaimu once was. The rest of the coastal village is gone.

HWY 130
From the edge of the lava flow at Kaimu Beach, a side road leads up to Hwy 130, which goes back to Pahoa. There are a couple of sights along the way.

You can also take a short detour on the eastern stub of the old national park road, which is now cut off by a lava flow a mile west of the Painted Church. Where the road meets the lava you can usually see billowing steam clouds created by molten lava pouring into the sea a few miles away.

Painted Church
The Star of the Sea is a little white Catholic church noted for its interior murals painted in trompe l'oeil style to create the effect of being in a large cathedral. The painting style is primitive, but the illusion of depth is amazingly effective. The church also has a nice stained-glass window of Father Damien, who was with the parish before he moved to the leprosy colony on Molokai.

The church, which was in the town of Kalapana, was moved just before lava flows swept over the site. It currently sits along Hwy 130, at the 20-mile marker, waiting for a more permanent home.

Steam Vents
At the 15-mile marker, 3½ miles south of Pahoa, for some less than obvious reason a big blue highway sign marks a scenic view. While the scenery is not particularly special, if you look closely you'll notice steam rising from steam vents on the makai side of the road.

Only a few minutes' walk away are some low spatter cones with hollowed out natural steam baths inside, perfect for a sauna. To get there, take the path leading down from the scenic lookout; when the path forks, bear right and walk to the cinder cone, which has a couple of pieces of wood inside that serve as seats.

Kau

The Kau district stretches from South Kona along the southern flanks of Mauna Loa, taking in the entire southern tip of the island all the way up to Hawaii Volcanoes National Park.

Kau is sparsely populated, with only about 5000 people and three real towns. Much of it is dry and desert-like. Indeed, the highest temperature ever recorded in the state was in Kau in the town of Pahala: 100°F in April 1931. However, Kau also has some lush areas in the foothills, where macadamia nuts and most of Hawaii's oranges are grown.

MANUKA STATE WAYSIDE PARK
Manuka State Wayside Park is an eight-acre arboretum off Hwy 11 near the 81-mile marker. The trees and bushes, planted here between the mid-1930s and the 1950s, include 48 native Hawaiian species and 130 introduced species. Many are labeled, some with both Latin and common names.

Camping is allowed by permit in the three-sided covered shelter, which has space for about five sleeping bags. In a pinch it might be OK for an overnight break between Hilo and Kona, but it's quite close to the road. While camping under the trees looks tempting, it's prohibited. There are restrooms and picnic tables.

The park is in the midst of the 25,500-acre Manuka Natural Area Reserve, which reaches from the slopes of Mauna Loa clear down to the sea where it takes in a couple of heiaus and other ruins.

The **Manuka Nature Trail**, a two-mile interpretive loop, begins above the parking lot. The trail crosses ancient lava flows and goes through a varied mesic forest that contains both rainforest and dry lowland plants. A detailed brochure explaining the flora along the trail can be picked up from the state parks office in Hilo.

HAWAIIAN OCEAN VIEW ESTATES
A few miles east of Manuka there's a grocery store, a plate lunch eatery, a pretty good pizzeria, a Texaco gas station, a post office and a hardware shop. This is the commercial center, such as it is, for Hawaiian Ocean View Estates and a couple of other isolated southside subdivisions.

This area remains one of the last sunny expanses of land in Hawaii to be totally free of resorts. A large, controversial development that had been proposed for the barren Kahuku Coast just west of South Point has, to the relief of island environmentalists, gone belly up.

Places To Stay
South Point Bed & Breakfast (☎ 929-7466), Box 6589, Ocean View, HI 96704, is in Hawaiian Ocean View Estates, just mauka of Hwy 11. There are three comfortable units, each with a private entrance and bath. Rates, which include a breakfast of fresh fruit, granola and muffins, are $55

Devastation Day
Kau was the center of devastation in the massive 1868 earthquake, the worst Hawaii has ever recorded. For five full days from March 27 the earth was rattled almost continuously by a series of tremors and quakes. Then in the afternoon of April 2 the earth shook violently in every direction and an inferno broke loose from beneath the surface.

Those fortunate enough to be uphill watched as a rapidly moving river of lava poured down the hillsides and swallowed up everything in its path, including people, homes and cattle. Within minutes the coast was inundated by tidal waves and villages near the shore were swept away.

This deadly triple combination of earthquakes, lava flows and tidal waves permanently changed Kau's landscape. Huge cinder cones came crashing down the slopes and there was one landslide that buried an entire village. You can see the 1868 lava flow along the highway two miles west of the South Point turn-off. The old village of Kahuku lies beneath it. ■

BIG ISLAND

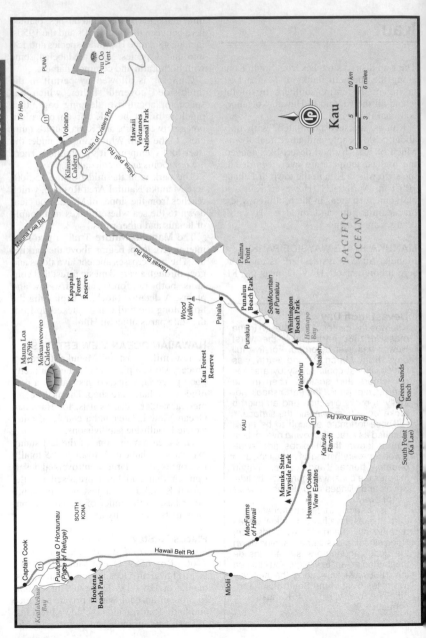

Kau

a double for the two smaller rooms and $10 more for the larger unit, which has a kitchenette. The rate is discounted for stays of three or more nights.

Bougainvillea Bed & Breakfast (☎ /fax 929-7089; peaceful@interpac.net), Box 6045, Ocean View, HI 96704, in the home of Martie and Don Nitsche, is also in Hawaiian Ocean View Estates but on the makai side of Hwy 11. This casual B&B has comfortable rooms, each with private bath, private entrance and VCR (no TV reception, but there's a video library). Singles/doubles cost $49/59, breakfast included. There's a swimming pool and hot tub set back behind the house that makes a nice spot for stargazing. If you come by without a reservation, you can usually find Martie at the Texaco station, which she manages.

SOUTH POINT

South Point is the southernmost spot in the USA. In Hawaiian it's known as Ka Lae, which means simply 'the point'.

South Point has rocky coastal cliffs and a turbulent ocean. It was the site of one of the earliest Hawaiian settlements and may have been where the first Polynesians landed. Much of the area is now under the jurisdiction of Hawaiian Home Lands.

The turn-off to South Point is midway between the 69- and 70-mile markers. South Point is 11 miles south of Hwy 11, at the end of a well-paved one-lane road. There are packed shoulders most of the way allowing cross-traffic to pass without having to stop.

South Point Rd starts out in house sites and macadamia nut farms, which soon give way to grassy pastures. The winds are strong here, as evidenced by the trees, some bent almost horizontal with their branches trailing along the ground.

Kamaoa Wind Farms

As you go over a hill along this country drive you suddenly come upon rows of huge high-tech windmills lined up in a pasture beside the road. With cattle grazing beneath it's a surreal scene; the unearthly whirring

sound is what you might expect an alien invasion to sound like.

Each of these wind turbine generators can produce enough electricity for 100 families. It's thought, theoretically at least, that by using wind energy conversion the state could produce more than enough electricity to meet its needs.

Four miles south of the windmills, you'll pass a few abandoned buildings wasting away. Until 1965 this was a Pacific Missile Range Station that tracked missiles shot from California to the Marshall Islands.

Ka Lae

Ten miles down from the highway, South Point Rd forks and the road to the left goes to Kaulana boat ramp and a small cove.

The road to the right leads to the rugged coastal cliffs of South Point. The confluence of ocean currents just offshore makes this one of Hawaii's most bountiful fishing grounds. Locals fish from the cliffs, many precariously hanging out over the edge of steep lava ledges. Red snapper and ulua, a jack fish, are particularly plentiful.

Ruins at Ka Lae include those of a heiau and a well-preserved fishing shrine. The outcrop on the west side of the fishing shrine is a good place to find some of the numerous canoe mooring holes that were long ago drilled into the rock ledges. Ancient Hawaiians used to anchor one end of a rope through the holes and tie the other end to their canoes. The strong currents would pull the canoes straight out to deep turbulent waters where they could fish without getting swept out to sea.

The wooden platforms built on the edge of the cliffs have hoists and ladders that are used to get things to and from the small boats that anchor below.

There's a large unmarked and unprotected hole in the lava directly behind the platforms where you can watch water rise and fall as the waves rush in. Keep an eye out for it, particularly if you have children with you, as it's not obvious until you're almost on top of it.

Walk down past the beacon and continue along the wall to get to the southernmost point in the USA. There are no markers here, no souvenir stands, just crashing surf and lots of wind.

Green Sands Beach

If you want to explore the area further, go back to the fork and take the road to Kaulana boat ramp. Beside the ramp you'll find pockets of green sand sparkling in the sun. These are olivine crystals worn from the lava cliffs by a relentless and pounding surf.

The highest concentration of green sand in Hawaii is at Green Sands Beach, a 2½-mile hike along the 4WD road heading northeast from the boat ramp. The walk is not difficult, though once you reach Green Sands you'll need to scramble down the cliffside to get to the beach. If you have a high-riding 4WD vehicle you could consider driving in, but the road is rough and the drive takes about 25 minutes.

Pick a calm day to visit, as during periods of high surf the entire beach can be inundated. A couple of minutes beyond Kaulana boat ramp the trail passes the site of Kapalaoa, an ancient fishing village.

WAIOHINU

After South Point, Hwy 11 winds down into a pretty valley and the sleepy village of Waiohinu, which sits nestled beneath green hills. On the right as you enter the town is the quaint little wooden Kauahaao Church, white with green trim, dating from 1841.

Shirakawa Motel is 500 feet ahead on the left, and about 150 yards beyond it on the same side of the road is a monkeypod tree planted by Mark Twain in 1866. The original tree fell in a typhoon in 1957, but hardy new trunks have sprung up and it's once again full grown.

In the village center is Wong Yuen's Chevron gas station, which is open from 8 am to 7 pm daily and has a small convenience store at the side.

Places to Stay

Margo's Corner (☎ /fax 929-9614), Box 447, Naalehu, HI 96772, at the home of Margo Hobbs and Philip Shaw, offers bicyclists and backpackers a place to pitch a tent and store gear while exploring the Kau area. Margo, who runs a little food co-op on site, enjoys meeting travelers from around the world. Guests are welcome to have breakfast and dinner with the family, which includes three teenagers. Meals are vegetarian and incorporate vegetables and fruit from the family's organic garden. Guests have use of the family bathroom and Margo has set up a couple of tent areas with pebbly mounds to allow drainage, though you can also pitch your tent on the grass if you prefer. No specific fee is charged, but a donation or work exchange should be given; those who eat meals with the family typically offer about $20 a day. The house is on Wakea St, a couple of miles southwest of Waiohinu center, off Kamaoa Rd. Call ahead for reservations.

Shirakawa Motel (☎ 929-7462), Box 467, Naalehu, HI 96772, is a green, weather-beaten motel with 13 basic units. The motel is plain but adequate, and the setting is beneath the green hills is lovely. Rooms, which have private baths and twin beds, cost $30/35 for singles/doubles, $42 for a kitchenette unit, tax included. There are no phones or TVs, but at dusk myna birds commonly provide a little show as they flock through the area squawking.

Kiari Resorts (☎ 929-8148, 800-333-4175), Box 624, Naalehu, HI 96772, is a B&B on a 10-acre macadamia nut farm half a mile south of Waiohinu center. Centered around an expansive contemporary home with open-beam ceilings, it has four guest rooms, all large with private baths and lanais. Most interesting is the Honeymoon Suite, which has a separate bedroom, a good-sized sitting area and lots of windows looking out onto the lush grounds. There's a tennis court, a pool and a common TV lounge. Singles/doubles go for $85/100, breakfast included. This upmarket B&B would not only make a nice option for honeymooners (weddings on the lawn can be arranged), but also for anyone seeking a B&B that offers plenty of private space.

Places to Eat

Mark Twain Square is a reasonably priced village restaurant that sits under the shade of Twain's monkeypod tree. The menu is simple; you can get sandwiches for around $4 or a plate lunch for $5.50. It's open from 8:30 am to 6 pm weekdays, 8:30 am to 5 pm on Saturdays.

NAALEHU

Naalehu's claim to fame is being the southernmost town in the USA. It's two miles east of Waiohinu and a few inches to the south.

Modest as it is, Naalehu is the region's shopping center. It has a couple of grocery stores and eateries, a gas station, public library, post office, elementary school and the Kau police station.

Naalehu closes up early, so don't count on getting food or gas here if you're driving back to Kona from Hawaii Volcanoes National Park at night.

Places to Eat

The best place to eat in town is the *Naalehu Fruit Stand* on Hwy 11, a reasonably priced produce stand, health food store, pizzeria and sandwich shop all in one. The ovens out back bake bread in the morning and pizzas to order ($8) from 11 am. The shop sells prepared sandwiches such as teri-tofu on homemade whole-wheat bread for $2.75, or you can get a sub with the works for a bit more. Macadamia nut bars and other pastries cost about a dollar. It's open from 9 am to 6:30 pm daily (to 5 pm on Sundays), and there are a few picnic tables near the front steps where you can eat.

WHITTINGTON BEACH PARK

Two miles beyond Naalehu there's a pull-off with a scenic lookout above Honuapo Bay. From the lookout you can see the cement pilings of the old Honuapo Pier, which was used for shipping sugar and hemp until the 1930s.

Honuapo Bay is the site of Whittington Beach Park; the turn-off is one mile from the lookout. Although there are tide pools to explore, there's really no beach at Whittington and the ocean is usually too rough and dangerous for swimming. Endangered green sea turtles, which can sometimes be seen offshore, apparently have been frequenting these waters for a long time, as Honuapo means 'caught turtle' in Hawaiian.

Camping is allowed with a permit, and it's far enough from the highway to offer a little privacy. Overall, the park makes a pretty good choice for a county campground, but avoid setting up near the street light by the parking lot, as the light stays on all night and illuminates much of the lawn where tenting is allowed. Whittington has toilets and sheltered picnic tables, but there's no potable water.

PUNALUU

Punaluu is a small bay with a black-sand beach that was once the site of a major Hawaiian settlement and in later days an important sugar port. The most visited section of the beach, the area fronting the now-closed Punaluu Black Sands Restaurant, is lined with coconut trees and backed by a duck pond. The ruins of the Pahala Sugar Company's old warehouse and pier are a short walk away at the north end of the beach. Sitting on a rise above it is the site of Kaneeleele Heiau.

Punaluu Beach Park, a county park just to the south, has restrooms, showers, drinking water, picnic pavilions and camping. It's a flat, grassy area right on the beach and a nice place to camp, although it's very open with no privacy and there can be a fair amount of activity here during the day. At night you can drift off to sleep to the sounds of crashing surf.

Be careful walking about, as the area's black sands are used as nesting sites by hawksbill turtles. Swimmers should be aware that the waters along the beach can have a strong undertow, and there's a particularly dangerous rip current pulling out from the boat channel near the pier.

If heading east on Hwy 11, the first turn-off you'll reach in Punaluu is the entrance to SeaMountain, Kau's only condo complex. To get to the beach park take the turn-off marked Punaluu Park, which is less than a mile farther along Hwy 11.

Places to Stay & Eat

SeaMountain at Punaluu (☎ 928-6211, 800-344-7675), Box 340, Pahala, HI 96777, is a small condo complex with all the amenities you'd expect to find in Kona, albeit there's certainly much less to do in this area. The complex has a pool, tennis courts and a golf course.

The studios are big – almost as large as one-bedroom units elsewhere – some one-bedroom units are two-level with cathedral ceilings. All have TVs and phones. Rates start at $90 for studios, $110 for one-bedroom units and $135 for two-bedroom units. Ocean views cost about $15 more and all rates are $10 lower in the off season. There's a two-day minimum stay.

Currently, the only place to eat at sleepy Punaluu is at the golf course pro shop at SeaMountain, which serves lunchtime sandwiches from 10:30 am to 2 pm.

PAHALA

Pahala, on the north side of Hwy 11, is really two little towns side by side. Down by the old mill is the original sugar town, with old dusty shacks, cars rusting in the yards and 'Beware of Dog' signs. In contrast, the north side of town has tract homes, gas stations, a hospital, a bank, a community center and a modern grocery mart. If you're looking for a quick meal, there's also Alii Bakery, which has cinnamon sweet bread, inexpensive sandwiches and plate lunches.

Kau Agribusiness, which once had 15,000 acres of sugar cane planted for 15 miles in either direction from Pahala, closed its sugar mill in 1996. The company has now introduced groves of macadamia nut trees on much of the former cane land.

WOOD VALLEY

About four miles up the slopes from Pahala is remote Wood Valley and the **Buddhist temple and retreat center** of Nechung Dorje Drayang Ling. The temple, which has a quiet 25-acre setting, was built in the early 20th century by Japanese sugar cane laborers who lived in the valley.

In 1975 a Tibetan lama, Nechung Rinpoche, took up residence here, and in 1980 the Dalai Lama visited to dedicate the temple. Since that time many Tibetan lamas

have conducted programs here and the Dalai Lama himself returned to visit in 1994. In addition to its teachings of Buddhism, the center is also used by groups conducting Zen meditation, yoga classes and other New Age and spiritual programs. If you're interested, the center can send you a list of upcoming workshops.

Places to Stay

Nechung Dorje Drayang Ling (☎ 928-8539; fax 928-6271), Box 250, Pahala, HI 96777, has a two-story building with a meditation hall and two pleasant guest rooms on the upper floor. One guest room has a queen platform bed and Japanese decor, the other has a king bed and Hawaiian decor; singles/doubles cost $35/45. The ground floor also has a couple of simpler rooms with twin beds for $5 less and a dormitory for $18 a night. There's a two-day minimum stay and all rooms share a bath. Guests must bring their own food; a kitchen is available. There's a library of books on Buddhist culture, and guests are welcome to join in morning services. For those seeking a peaceful retreat the temple is a special place.

Wood Valley Bed & Breakfast (☎ 928-8212, 800-854-6754), Box 37, Pahala, HI 96777, tucked back a mile beyond the temple, is an earthy little alternative B&B in the home of Jessie Hillinger. An interesting old house that sits on 12 acres, the B&B has three simple rooms that share a bath. It's a cozy place, not ideal for those who want privacy but suited for those who enjoy a homey, shared setting. There's a wood-fired steam bath ($5) and an open-air bathtub overlooking the woods; if you want to loosen tense muscles, Jessie can provide lomi massage ($40). Rates, which include breakfast of fresh eggs and fruit from the yard, are $35/55 for singles/doubles. Guests are allowed to use the kitchen to fix other meals. There's a two-night minimum stay. Campers can pitch a tent on the grounds for $10 per person, including use of the bathhouse but not the kitchen. This B&B is gay-friendly and straight-friendly too.

TO HAWAII VOLCANOES NATIONAL PARK

Hawaii Volcanoes National Park begins 12 miles from Pahala. Hwy 11 cuts across an 11-mile stretch of the park. There are no fees to drive through on the highway nor to explore the Mauna Loa side of the park.

Kilauea's southwest rift zone runs through this part of the Kau Desert, makai of the road. The rift runs for 20 miles, all the way from the summit of Kilauea down to the coast.

You'll know you're getting closer to the center of Hawaii Volcanoes National Park when the signs start reading 'Caution, Fault Zones. Watch for Cracks in Road'.

Before you reach the entrance to the park you'll pass Mauna Loa Rd. There are tree molds near the turn-off, a hiking trail through a native forest a mile farther up, and the trailhead to the Mauna Loa summit at the end of the road. All are detailed in the following Hawaii Volcanoes National Park section.

Hawaii Volcanoes National Park

Hawaii Volcanoes National Park is hands down the most unique park in the US National Parks system. It's a huge area that not only contains two active volcanoes, but also terrain ranging from tropical beaches to the subarctic summit of Mauna Loa.

The centerpiece of the park is Kilauea Caldera, the sunken center of Kilauea Volcano. This still-steaming crater, where molten lava boils just beneath the surface, is said to be the home of Madame Pele, goddess of volcanoes. Both a foot trail and a paved road circle the caldera's rim.

The park's landscape is geologically awesome, with dozens of craters and cinder cones, hills piled high with pumice, and hardened rivers of lava that have frozen rock-solid on the hillsides complete with ripples and waves. There are also native bird reserves, rainforests and fern groves that

Volcanic Formations

Hawaii's volcanoes are shield volcanoes, formed by repeated gentle eruptions, building up over time as thin layers of lava are deposited one on top of another. As the mountains get higher and wider, long cracks break open down their gently stretched slopes. These are called fault zones, or rift zones, and lava eruptions may come from these cracks (as is currently the case with Kilauea) as well as from the summit crater.

Craters are formed when volcanic hills release their lava and collapse back into themselves.

'Pahoehoe' and 'aa' are Hawaiian words that are now used worldwide to describe the earth's two major types of lava. Pahoehoe refers to the rivers of lava that flow smooth and unbroken. When pahoehoe begins to harden it twists into rope-like coils and swirls, as the outer skin cools and stiffens, while the hotter lava underneath continues to move a little.

Aa is rough and jumbled lava that moves so slowly that the tip of the flow hardens. It's only the molten lava pushing from behind that keeps the flow moving, with the hard lava at the front piling up and falling over itself, slowing rolling and clunking its way along. ∎

either have been spared by lava flows or have since grown over them.

The park is one of Hawaii's best places for camping and hiking. It has 140 miles of amazingly varied hiking trails and two free drive-up campgrounds in addition to back-country camping.

The park encompasses about a quarter of a million acres of land – more than the entire island of Molokai – and it's still growing.

Kilauea's southeast rift has been actively flowing since 1983, taking everything in its path with it. The coastal road to Puna was blocked by lava in 1988. The Wahaula Visitor Center on the south coast went under the next year, and the entire village of Kalapana, with more than a hundred homes, was buried in lava in 1990. Since that time the flows have crept farther west, engulfing

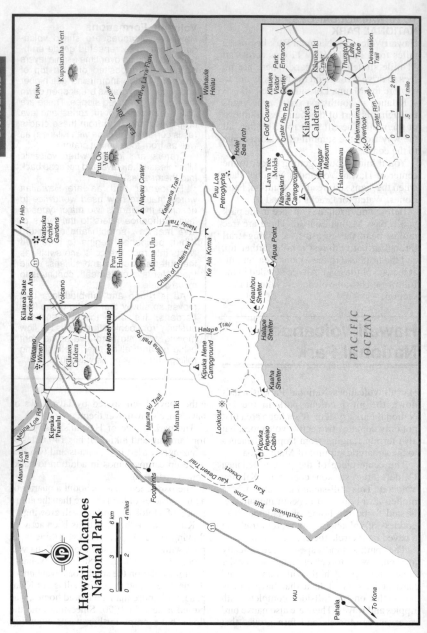

Hawaii Volcanoes National Park

Kamoamoa Beach in 1994 and later claiming an additional mile of the road. The situation is so tentative that the ranger station at the south end of the park operates out of a trailer that can be hauled back each time a new flow comes its way.

The current series of eruptions, which is the longest in recorded history, has spewed out more than two billion cubic yards of new lava.

What you'll be able to see will depend on the current volcanic activity. During the day distant steam clouds from the vents can usually be seen clearly from the end of Chain of Craters Rd. After dark, the lava tubes on the mountainside glow red in the night sky and lava lakes at the top of vents reflect light onto passing clouds.

Although many visitors expect to see lava fountains spurting up into the air, this is certainly the exception rather than the rule. But whenever Pele does put on one of her spectacular fireworks displays, cars stream in from all directions. In Hawaii, people generally run *to* volcanoes, not away from them.

Orientation

The park's main road is Crater Rim Rd, which circles the moonscape sights of Kilauea Caldera. It's possible to take in the drive-up sites in an hour – and if that's all the time you have it's unquestionably worth it. Still, it's far better to give yourself a good three hours to allow time for a few short walks and stops at the visitor center and museum.

The park's other scenic drive is the Chain of Craters Rd, which leads south 20 miles to the coast, ending at the site of the most recent lava activity. Allow about three hours down and back to stop at all the scenic points along the way.

While you can get a good sense of the place in one full day, it would be easy to spend days, if not weeks, exploring this vast and varied park.

Information

The park's 24-hour hotline (☎ 985-6000) has recorded information on current volcanic activity and directions to the best viewing sites.

Fees The park entrance fee of $10 per vehicle is good for multiple entries in a seven-day period. Visitors entering on foot or bicycle through the check station are charged $5 each. The check station is staffed from about 8:30 am to 4:30 pm daily, although the park is open 24 hours.

National park passes are sold here, including an annual pass for $50 that covers Haleakala on Maui and all other US National Park sites. US citizens with disabilities can get a pass allowing free entry, and those age 62 or older can buy a $10 pass good for all US National Parks.

Access for the Disabled Many of the park sites are accessible to the disabled, including the Kilauea Visitor Center, Jaggar Museum, Volcano Art Center and Volcano House hotel. Many of the pull-ups along Crater Rim Drive and the Chain of Craters Rd are free of curbstones. A few of the park's shorter trails, including Devastation Trail and an eastern section of the Crater Rim Trail near Waldron Ledge, have been converted to make them wheelchair accessible.

Climate The park has a wide range of climatic conditions that vary with elevation and the weather can be moody as well. Rain and fog move in quickly, and on any given day it can change from hot and dry to cool and damp. Near Kilauea Crater, temperatures average about 15°F cooler than in Kona. It's a good idea to wear clothing in layers.

Road Closures During periods of prolonged drought, both Mauna Loa Rd and Hilina Pali Rd are subject to closure due to fire-hazard conditions.

Precautions Hawaiian volcanoes are seldom violent and most of the lava that flows from cracks in the rift zones is slow moving. The eruptions don't spew out a lot of ash or poisonous gases either, which is what accounts for most volcano-related deaths in other parts of the world.

There have been only two known violent explosions of Hawaiian volcanoes – both from Kilauea, in 1790 and in 1924. The only direct fatality from a volcanic eruption in this century was during the 1924 explosion, when a boulder was tossed onto the leg of a photographer who then bled to death.

People with respiratory and heart conditions, pregnant women, infants and young children are advised to avoid the areas where sulfur fumes are most highly concentrated, including Sulphur Banks and the Halemaumau Overlook.

Other potential hazards include deep cracks in the earth and thin lava crust, which may mask hollows and lava tubes. If you stay on marked trails, you shouldn't have any problems. All park warning signs should be taken seriously.

Crater Rim Rd

Crater Rim Rd is a field trip in vulcanology. This amazing 11-mile loop road skirts the rim of Kilauea Caldera with marked stops at steam vents and crater lookouts. From roadside parking areas, short trails lead through a lava tube, a native rainforest and a forest devastated by pumice. There are also trailheads for longer hikes into and around the caldera.

Natural forces have rerouted Crater Rim Rd on a few occasions. Earthquakes in both 1975 and 1983 rattled it hard enough to knock sections of the road down into the caldera.

The most interesting stops are at Jaggar Museum, Halemaumau Overlook, Devastation Trail and Thurston Lava Tube. If you take Crater Rim Rd in a counter-clockwise direction, you'll start off at the visitor center.

Unlike the Chain of Craters Rd, Crater Rim Rd is relatively level, making it a good road for cyclists.

Kilauea Visitor Center The visitor center is a good place to get oriented to the park. Rangers here have the latest information on volcanic activity, interpretive programs,

guided walks, backcountry trail conditions and the like. They have free pamphlets for a few of the park trails and sell an excellent selection of books on volcanoes, hiking and park flora.

The center contains a small **theater** where a 25-minute film on the geology of Kilauea volcano is played on the hour from 9 am to 4 pm. Although the films change periodically, footage usually includes flowing rivers of lava and some of the most spectacular lava fountains ever to be caught on film.

In addition, commercial videos of the most recent eruptions run continuously in the center's tiny museum, where you'll also find a few volcano-related exhibits. The center is open daily from 7:45 am to 5 pm.

Volcano Art Center The Volcano Art Center (☎ 967-7511), next door to the visitor center, sells island pottery, paintings, weavings, woodwork, sculpture and other arts and crafts. The pieces are of high quality, with many one-of-a-kind items, and it's worth a visit just to admire the workmanship even if you're not up for shopping.

The center is in a former Volcano House lodge, built in 1877. The nonprofit organization that runs it offers workshops on crafts and hula dancing and sponsors concerts, plays and other activities. It's open from 9 am to 5 pm daily.

Sulphur Banks The first stop beyond the art center is the Sulphur Banks, where the day-glo colors and piles of steaming rocks look like a landscape from another planet.

This is one of many areas where Kilauea lets off steam, releasing hundreds of tons of sulfuric gases daily. As the steam reaches the surface, it deposits sulfur around the mouths of the vents, giving them a froth of fluorescent yellow crystals. The pervasive smell of rotten eggs is from the hydrogen sulfide wafting from the vents.

Steam Vents There are a few open, non-sulfurous steam vents at the next pull-off, although they're not particularly remarkable. Rainwater that sinks into the earth is heated by the hot rocks below and rises back up as steam.

More interesting is the two-minute walk beyond the vents out to a part of the crater rim aptly called **Steaming Bluff**. The cooler it is, the more steam there'll be. A plaque on the rim tells a legend about the struggles between Pele and the pig-god Kamapuaa.

Jaggar Museum This museum is worth a visit both for its displays and for the fine view of Halemaumau Crater. Halemaumau sits within Kilauea Crater and is sometimes referred to as the 'crater within the crater'. Detailed interpretive plaques at the lookout explain the geological workings of volcanoes. When the weather is clear, there's also a good view of Mauna Loa to the west, 20 miles away.

The museum is named after Thomas A Jaggar, former head geologist at the Massachusetts Institute of Technology (MIT) and the first scientist to undertake in-depth studies of Kilauea. Jaggar led the group of geologists who lowered the first thermometer into Halemaumau's lava lake in the summer of 1911. It registered 1832°F before melting. Today an observatory at this site has Kilauea completely wired, making it the most studied volcano anywhere in the world.

Jaggar Museum is open from 8:30 am to 5 pm daily. It has photo displays, a section on Pele, seismographs, tiltmeters and printed updates showing the current status of volcanic activity. The museum also sells videos and books.

The museum is at **Uwekahuna Bluff**, the site of an infamous hut that once sat right on the edge of the crater. Local kahunas are said to have tricked people into entering the building, where they slipped through a false-bottomed floor to the crater pit below.

Drivers should be careful of the nene that congregate in the museum parking lot and at other tourist stops on the south side of the caldera. The nene move slowly and have a suicidal tendency of walking up to moving cars, looking for handouts. Feeding the nene contributes to the road-deaths of these endangered birds and is strictly prohibited.

After leaving the museum you'll pass the **Southwest Rift**, where you can stop and take a look at the wide fissure slicing across the earth.

Halemaumau Overlook The next attraction is Halemaumau Overlook, which is perched on the crater rim, just a five-minute walk from the parking area. For at least a hundred years (from 1823, when missionary William Ellis first recorded the sight in writing), Halemaumau was a boiling lake of lava that alternately rose and fell, overflowing its banks and then receding.

This fiery lake attracted people from all over the world. Some observers compared it to the fires of hell, while others saw primeval creation. Mark Twain wrote of staring down at:

... circles and serpents and streaks of lightning all twined and wreathed and tied together .... I have seen Vesuvius since, but it was a mere toy, a child's volcano, a soup kettle, compared to this.

In 1924 seeping water touched off a massive steam explosion that blew up the lava lake, causing huge boulders and mud to rain down and setting off a lightning storm. When it was over, the crater had doubled in size and the lava activity had ceased. The crust has since cooled, although the crater still steams and the area is pungent with the smell of sulfur.

All of the Big Island is Pele's territory, but Halemaumau is her home. During special ceremonies the hula is performed in her honor here, and throughout the year those wishing to appease Pele leave flowers, coins and other offerings at the crater rim.

Ohelo, a bush about two feet high with clusters of bright red berries, is one of the early takers to lava and grows near the site. Before eating any of the tart berries, which are said to personify Pele's sister Hiiaka, some should first be offered to Pele.

The Halemaumau Overlook is at the start of the **Halemaumau Trail**, which runs three miles across Kilauea Caldera to the visitor center. Although few people who aren't hiking the full trail venture past the overlook, it's an easy half-mile walk to the site of a 1982 lava flow and is well worth the 30 minutes it takes to walk there and back. The spewed lava along the trail has interesting textures and colors, and there's an eerie sense of the earth's raw power.

Devastation Trail After the Halemaumau Overlook, Crater Rim Rd continues across the barren Kau Desert and then through the fallout area of the 1959 eruption of Kilauea Iki Crater. At that time, ash and pumice blown southwest of the crater buried a mile of Crater Rim Rd eight feet deep and the road had to be plowed by tractors, much like clearing snow after a blizzard.

Devastation Trail is a half-mile walk across a former rainforest devastated by cinder and pumice from that eruption. Everything green was wiped out. What remains today are dead ohia trees, stripped bare and sun-bleached white, standing stark against the black landscape. Indeed, it's so barren and desolate it could be the movie set for a post-nuclear scene.

The trail is paved and there are parking lots on each end. The prominent cinder cone along the way is **Puu Puai**, 'Gushing Hill', formed during the 1959 eruption. The northeast end of the trail looks down into Kilauea Iki Crater.

Chain of Craters Rd intersects Crater Rim Rd opposite the west side parking area for Devastation Trail.

Thurston Lava Tube On the east side of the Chain of Craters Rd intersection, Crater Rim Rd passes through the rainforest of native tree ferns and ohia that covers Kilauea's windward slope.

The Thurston Lava Tube Trail is an enjoyable 15-minute loop walk that starts out in ohia forest, goes through an impressive lava tube and then through a fern grove. The cibotium tree ferns here grow to a height of 20 feet.

Lava tubes are formed when the outer crust of a river of lava starts to harden but the liquid lava beneath the surface continues to flow on through. After the flow has drained out, the hard shell remains. Thurston Lava Tube is a grand example – it's tunnel-like and almost big enough to run a train through.

You'll likely hear a lot of birdsong along this walk. The apapane, a native honeycreeper, is easy to spot at the upper end of the trail. It has a red body and silvery-white underside and flies from flower to flower drinking from the yellow blossoms of the mamane tree and the red pompom-like flowers of the ohia tree.

Kilauea Iki Crater When Kilauea Iki burst open in a fiery inferno in November 1959 the whole crater floor turned into a bubbling pool of molten lava. Its fountains reached record heights of 1900 feet, lighting the evening sky with a bright orange glow for miles around. At its peak it gushed out two million tons of lava an hour.

From Kilauea Iki Overlook there's a good view of the mile-wide crater below. Today a trail runs across the crater floor. The hike is not unlike walking on ice – here, too, there's a lake below the hardened surface, although in this case it's molten lava, not water. For more information, see Hiking Trails in this section.

Chain of Craters Rd
Chain of Craters Rd winds 20 miles down the southern slopes of Kilauea Volcano, ending abruptly at a lava flow on the Puna Coast. It's a good, paved, two-lane road, although there's no gas, food, water or other services along the way.

From the road you'll have striking vistas of the coastline far below, and for miles the predominant view is of long fingers of lava reaching down to the sea.

In some places the road slices through lava and in other places it's paved over it. You'll see both aa lava, which is crusty and rough, and pahoehoe lava, which is as shiny and black as fresh tar. You can sometimes also find thin filaments of volcanic glass known as Pele's hair in the lava cracks and crevices.

In addition to endless lava expanses, the road takes in an impressive collection of sights, including a handful of craters that you can literally pull up to the rims of and peer into. Some are so new there's no sign of life, while others are thickly forested with ohia lehua, wild orchids and ferns.

Chain of Craters Rd once connected through to Hwys 130 and 137, allowing traffic between the volcano and Hilo via Puna. Lava flows closed the road in 1969 but by 1979 it was back in service, rerouted slightly. Flows from Kilauea's active east rift cut the link again in 1988 and have since buried a nine-mile stretch of the road.

Hilina Pali Rd Hilina Pali Rd starts 2¼ miles down Chain of Craters Rd and leads five miles in to Kipuka Nene campground. It's another four miles to Hilina Pali, a lookout at 2283 feet with a view of the southeast coast. The end of the road is the trailhead for the Kau Desert Trail and for the Kaaha and Hilina Pali trails, which lead down to the coast. They are all hot, dry, backcountry trails.

Mauna Ulu In 1969, eruptions from Kilauea's east rift began building a new lava shield, which eventually rose 400 feet above its surroundings. It was named Mauna Ulu, 'Growing Mountain'.

By the time the flow stopped in 1974 it had covered 10,000 acres of parkland and added 200 acres of new land to the coast.

It also buried a 12-mile section of Chain of Craters Rd in lava as deep as 100 yards. There's still a surviving half-mile portion of the old road, which you can follow to the lava flow by taking the turn-off on the left 3½ miles down Chain of Craters Rd. Just beyond this is Mauna Ulu itself.

A moderately easy three-mile roundtrip hike, the **Puu Huluhulu Overlook Trail** begins at the parking area, crosses lava flows from 1974 and goes to the top of a 150-foot cinder cone, where there's a panoramic view that includes Mauna Loa, Mauna Kea, Kilauea and the east rift zone.

As you continue down Chain of Craters Rd you'll be passing over Mauna Ulu's extensive flows.

Ke Ala Koma About halfway along the road, at an elevation of 2000 feet, is Ke Ala Koma, a covered shelter with picnic tables and a superb ocean view. This would be a great place to unpack a lunch, at least on days when the wind's not whipping.

After Ke Ala Koma the road begins to descend along a series of winding switchbacks, some deeply cut through lava flows.

Puu Loa Petroglyphs The Puu Loa Trail leads to a field of petroglyphs carved into the lava by early Hawaiians. The site, about a mile in, is along an ancient trail between Kau and Puna and has one of the largest concentrations of petroglyphs in Hawaii. A boardwalk runs around a large group of them and offers some fine photo opportunities. Puu Loa ('Long Hill') was also a place where Hawaiians brought the umbilical cords of their babies in the hope that burying them there would bring their children long lives.

The marked trailhead begins on the Chain of Craters Rd midway between the 16- and 17-mile markers and makes for an interesting hour-long walk that's suitable for all ages.

Holei Sea Arch About 2½ miles after the petroglyphs and just before the 19-mile marker, look for the sign marking the Holei Sea Arch. This rugged section of the coast has sharply eroded lava cliffs, called Holei Pali, which are constantly being pounded by crashing surf.

The high rock arch carved out of one of the cliffs is impressive, although the wave action has numbered its days. The ocean, which is a strikingly deep blue, provides a picturesque backdrop to the scene.

End of the Road Chain of Craters Rd ends at the coast near Laeapuki, where hardened lava flows seal off the road. Rangers staff a trailer here that acts as a sort of visitor information center, but there are no other facilities.

In recent times most of the lava flowing from Kilauea's east rift has been coming from the Puu Oo Vent. When the molten lava, which is carried down the hillsides in lava tubes, hits the ocean, it heats the water to a boil and produces an immense acidic steam plume.

Park rangers have marked a trail over the hardened lava that puts you close enough to the action to get a good view but keeps you safe from harm. The trail is often rerouted as a consequence of the lava flows; however, it always makes for an intriguing walk, generally taking about 30 minutes. The walk is over crisp, shiny lava, and you

need to watch your footing, as there are sharp jags of lava as well as cracks and holes in the brittle surface. It's recommended that you wear sturdy shoes with good traction.

The steam plumes are impressive to see from a distance but extremely dangerous to attempt to view up close. Not only can the explosive clash between molten lava and seawater shoot scalding water and debris hundreds of feet into the air, but the lava crust itself forms in unstable ledges, called lava benches, that eventually collapse into the ocean without warning. Many curiosity seekers have been hurt by attempting to get too close. In 1993 one of these lava benches collapsed, sending an islander to his fiery death and burning more than a dozen people in the ensuing steam explosion.

The rangers know which areas are safe and which aren't; listen to them, heed all signs and don't stray from the marked trails. If you plan to stay in the area after dark to observe the red glow, be sure to take a flashlight, as there are no artificial lights in the area.

Incidentally, the ancient Wahaula Heiau (see the sidebar) is separated from the end of the road by an active lava tube, so there's currently no access to it.

Mauna Loa Rd

Mauna Loa Rd leads off Hwy 11 about 2¼ miles west of the visitor center. The road provides access to the eastern approach of Mauna Loa, the world's highest active volcano. Mauna Loa has erupted more than 18 times in the past century; the last eruption began in March 1984 and lasted 21 days.

The **Mauna Loa Trail**, which climbs the slopes of Mauna Loa, begins at the end of the road, 13½ miles from Hwy 11. For further details, see Hiking Trails, below.

Lava Tree Molds Near the start of Mauna Loa Rd there's a turn-off to some lava tree molds. These tube-like holes were formed when a lava flow engulfed the rainforest that stood here. Because the trees were so waterlogged the lava hardened around them instead of burning them on contact. As the

---

Wahaula Heiau

Wahaula Heiau was the first luakini heiau built in Hawaii. Its construction is credited to Paao, a Tahitian high priest who migrated here in the 12th century. Paao not only introduced human sacrifice into temple ceremonies, but also the concept of *mana*, a divine power that could be held by the royal chiefs as well as embodied in the temple grounds themselves.

A strict social system of *kapus* (taboos) were enacted to protect that mana. Commoners were forbidden to eat the same foods or walk the same grounds as chiefs for fear they would absorb the chiefs' mana. Those who broke the kapus were put to death.

Mana was an elusive element that could be lost. When a temple no longer had its mana it was abandoned and a new one built elsewhere. Wahaula Heiau never lost it – it was the last luakini temple where royalty worshipped before the Hawaiian gods were abandoned.

In 1989 a lava flow buried the entire Wahaula area, including the nearby visitor center, which stood just 150 feet away from the heiau. The heiau was mysteriously spared, however, when the molten lava literally parted at its walls and skirted around the main temple and the high priest's house on its way to the sea. Subsequent lava flows have continued to spare the site. Apparently it still has some mana left! ■

trees disintegrated, deep holes where the trunks once stood were left in the ground.

Some of the molds are very close to the parking lot, making it easy to get a quick glimpse.

Kipuka Puaulu Kipuka Puaulu, a unique sanctuary for native flora and fauna, is about 1½ miles up Mauna Loa Rd. The mile-long **Kipuka Puaulu Loop Trail** runs through this 100-acre oasis of Hawaiian forest.

About 400 years ago a major lava flow from Mauna Loa's northeast rift covered most of the surrounding area. Pele spared this bit of land when the flow parted, creating an island forest in a sea of lava. In Hawaiian, it's known as a *kipuka*.

Kipuka Puaulu is a tiny ecopreserve of rare endemic plants, insects and birds. The lava that surrounds the kipuka has served as a protective barrier against intruding foreign species.

Koa is the largest of the trees here. The younger trees have fern-like leaves that are replaced with flat, crescent-shaped leaf stalks as the koa matures and rises above the forest floor. The tree provides a habitat for ferns and climbing peperomia that take root in its moist bark.

Kipuka Puaulu is delightfully quiet, except for the chirping of birds. The natives include the inquisitive elepaio and three honeycreepers – the amakihi, apapane and iiwi. All of these birds are sparrow size and brightly colored. The honeycreepers have slender curved beaks that enable them to drink nectar from the flowers of native trees.

Also along the trail is a **lava tube** in the dark depths of which a unique species of big-eyed spider was discovered in 1973.

Hiking Trails

The park has an extensive network of hiking trails, spanning from sea level to over 13,000 feet. The hikes range from short, easy walks to serious backcountry treks. Trails strike out in a number of directions – across crater floors, down to secluded beaches, across the Kau Desert,

through native forests and up to snow-capped Mauna Loa.

Crater Rim Trail The Crater Rim Trail is an 11-mile hiking trail that runs roughly parallel to Crater Rim Rd. On the north side the trail is along the crater rim, while on the south side it runs outside the paved road.

Because the vehicle road is designed to take in the main sights, you'll actually miss a few of them by hiking. If you have wheels of some sort, you might want to consider riding around the crater rim and saving your hiking legs for trails into areas inaccessible by car or bike.

Halemaumau Trail Diagonally across the road from the visitor center there are signs marking the way to a number of trailheads, including the Halemaumau Trail.

The first section of the Halemaumau Trail passes briefly through a moist ohia forest, with tall ferns and flowering ginger. It then descends about 500 feet to the floor of **Kilauea Caldera** and continues for three miles across the surface of this still-active volcano.

In ancient times the caldera was much deeper, but in the past century overflows from Halemaumau Crater as well as eruptions from the caldera floor have built it up.

The process is easy to visualize, as the trail crosses flow after flow, beginning with one from 1974 and continuing over flows from 1885, 1894, 1954, 1971 and 1982, each distinguished by a different shade of black. The trail is marked with *ahu*, stone cairns created with piled lava rocks.

Shortly after breakfast on April 30, 1982, geologists at the Hawaiian Volcano Observatory watched as their seismographs and tiltmeters unexpectedly warned of an imminent eruption. The park service quickly closed off Halemaumau Trail and cleared hikers from the crater floor. Before noon a half-mile fissure broke open in the crater and began spewing out a million cubic meters of lava!

This 1982 flow created a landscape that is both very barren and hauntingly beautiful. The lava has incredible textures, unusual shapes and deep black tones accented with orange, rust and ocher.

Although there hasn't been another major eruption here since 1982, on March 24, 1996, the tiltmeters again indicated that the caldera was inflating rapidly. However, that crisis ended the same day when the magma suddenly shifted downrift to the Puu Oo vent, allowing Kilauea Caldera to subside without erupting.

Halemaumau Trail ends about 3½ miles from the visitor center at **Halemaumau Overlook**. Needless to say there's no shade on the trail and it can be very hot. Take water with you, as there's none at the lookout.

Kilauea Iki Trail When Kilauea Iki Crater exploded in 1959, its lava fountains set a new height record of 1900 feet. When the ash finally settled, it covered the entire area southwest of the crater.

Kilauea Iki Trail begins near the parking lot of the Thurston Lava Tube and descends 400 feet to the crater floor. From there it goes clear across the mile-long crater, passing the main vent on the way. The crater floor is still steaming and there's molten lava beneath the hardened surface.

After you ascend the crater wall on the far side, you'll be on **Byron Ledge**, the ledge that separates Kilauea Iki from Kilauea Caldera. By looping around to the right, you can get back to the parking lot via the Crater Rim Trail, which skirts the north rim of Kilauea Iki. Altogether this popular loop hike is about 3½ miles long.

If you want to check it out before hiking, there's a drive-up lookout half a mile north of the Thurston Lava Tube.

Footprints Trail The Footprints Trail is the beginning of the **Mauna Iki Trail**, which leads to a network of trails through the Kau Desert. The trailhead is between the 37- and 38-mile markers on Hwy 11, nine miles southwest of Kilauea Visitor Center. The footprints are an easy three-quarter-mile hike in from the highway.

In 1790, a violent and massive explosion at Kilauea wiped out a regiment of warriors who were retreating to Kau after attacking Kamehameha's sacred Waipio Valley. The men were literally stopped in their tracks, suffocated by a rare cloud of poisonous gases. A shower of hot mud and ashes hardened around them, leaving a permanent cast of their footprints.

Two hundred years later, you can still count the toes in a few of the prints – although it takes some imagination these days, as most of the trailside footprints have been seriously damaged by vandals. Still, it's a pleasant walk.

Halape Trail The 7¼-mile trail to Halape starts from Kipuka Nene campground off Hilina Pali Rd. Halape was an idyllic beachfront campground bordered by coconut trees until November 29, 1975, when the strongest earthquake in 100 years shook the Big Island. Just before dawn, rock slides from the upper slopes sent most of the 36 campers running towards the sea, where the coastline suddenly sank. As the beach submerged beneath their feet a series of tsunamis swept the campers up, carrying them first out to sea and then tossing them back up on shore. Miraculously, only two people died.

The earthquake left a fine **sandy cove** inland of the former beach, and despite its turbulent past Halape is still a lovely spot. Swimming is good in the protected cove, but there are strong currents in the open ocean beyond the cove. Halape has catchment water, a pit toilet and a three-walled shelter.

Halape is one of only a half-dozen Hawaiian nesting sites for the endangered hawksbill sea turtle. The park service, which is trying to balance the need for protecting the turtles' habitat with visitor accessibility issues, has relocated the campsites east of the cove in an area that's unsuitable for nesting. Campers should be careful not to set up tents in areas that are marked as turtle nesting sites; keep sites clean of food scraps, which attract cats and mongooses that prey upon turtle eggs and hatchlings; and minimize the use of night lighting, which can disorient the turtles.

Mauna Loa Trail The Mauna Loa Trail begins at the end of Mauna Loa Rd, 13½ miles north of Hwy 11 and about an hour's drive from the visitor center. Overnight hikers are required to register at the visitor center, which also has the latest information on trail and cabin conditions.

This is a rugged 18-mile trail that ascends 6600 feet. The ascent is gradual, but the elevation makes it a serious hike and it takes a minimum of three days.

Two simple cabins are available to hikers on a first-come first-served basis: Red Hill cabin has eight bunks with mattresses and Mauna Loa summit cabin has 12.

The trail rises out of an ohia forest and above the tree line, climbing seven miles to Red Hill at 10,035 feet. This leg of the hike takes four to five hours. From Red Hill there are fine views of Mauna Kea to the north and Haleakala on Maui to the northwest.

It's 11 miles and a full day's hike from Red Hill to the summit cabin at 13,250 feet. The summit has a subarctic climate, and temperatures normally drop to freezing at night all year round. Winter snowstorms can last a few days, bringing snow packs as deep as nine feet. Occasionally, snow falls as low as Red Hill and covers the upper end of the trail.

It is important to acclimatize, as altitude sickness is not uncommon. Common symptoms are headache, nausea and shortness of breath. For minor symptoms, deep breathing brings some relief, as does lying down with your head lower than your feet. If the symptoms are more serious, get to a lower elevation immediately.

Hypothermia from the cold and wind is another hazard. A good windproof jacket, wool sweater, winter-rated sleeping bag and rain gear are all essential.

Backcountry Camping Hiking shelters and simple cabins are available along some of the park's longer backcountry trails. There's no fee to use them.

In addition to the two cabins along the Mauna Loa Trail, there's a small cabin at Kipuka Pepeiao along the Kau Desert Trail and coastal area shelters at Keauhou,

Halape and Kaaha. All have limited water catchment, which should be treated before drinking.

The visitor center keeps track of current water supplies and trail conditions.

In addition to the sites with shelters, there are two primitive camping areas that have pit toilets but no shelter or water. The seaside Apua Point campsite is along the Puna Coast Trail, about 6½ miles west of the Puuloa parking area off Chain of Craters Rd. The Napau Crater campsite, just three miles west of the erupting Puu Oo vent, is reached via a 5¼-mile hike on the Naulu and Kalapana trails.

All overnight hikers are required to register and obtain a free permit at the visitor center before heading out. Permits are issued on a first-come basis, but no earlier than noon on the day before your hike. There's a three-day limit at each backcountry camping site.

Essential backpacking equipment that the park service recommends for any of the backcountry trails includes a first aid kit, a flashlight with extra batteries, a minimum of two quarts of water, emergency food, a compass, a mirror (for signaling), broken-in boots, complete rain gear, cooking stove with fuel (open fires are prohibited), sunscreen and a hat.

More information on backcountry hiking, including a basic trail map, can be obtained at the visitor center or by writing to Hawaii Volcanoes National Park, HI 96718.

Volcano

The village of Volcano, about a mile east of the park, has a couple of general stores, a place to gas up, a post office, a few eateries and a growing number of B&B-type places to stay.

There's also the little **Volcano Winery** at the end of the golf course road, a mile from Hwy 11, which offers samples of Volcano's first wines. Although the winery is still in its infancy, the curious may want to stop by the tasting room to try its ambitious vintages, which come in flavors such as guava and passion chablis. It's open daily from 10 am to 5 pm.

BIG ISLAND

Akatsuka Orchid Gardens, between the 22- and 23-mile markers on Hwy 11, about four miles east of Volcano village, is a nursery with beautiful orchids that's worth a stop. Women get a free orchid blossom to pin in their hair.

Places to Stay – in Volcano

At *My Island B&B* (☎ 967-7216; fax 967-7719), Box 100, Volcano, HI 96785, Gordon and Joann Morse rent out three bedrooms with shared bathrooms in their home from $40/60 singles/doubles, including breakfast. There are also a couple of $75 studio units adjacent to the house that have kitchens, TVs, phones and bathrooms. The B&B is a quarter-mile east of Kilauea Lodge, on the left after Wright Rd. Gordon enjoys piling guests high with information on the Big Island – which he proclaims to be 'the *only* Hawaiian Island worth visiting' – and the living room is stacked with books on volcanoes, a few written by former guests.

Volcano Inn (☎ 967-7773; fax 967-8067; volcinn@aloha.net), Box 963, Volcano, HI 96785, consists of half a dozen pleasant units built by the owner, Ron Ober. The most economical ($55) are two cozy units in a modern duplex cabin with electric heaters, queen beds, bathrooms with tubs, refrigerators, coffeemakers and picture windows looking out on a fern and ohia forest. The other units vary from a studio with kitchenette for $65 to a two-bedroom house for $95. There's a discount of 10% for a two-night stay and 20% for a three-night stay. The rates cover up to two people in the smaller units and four in the larger; the duplex cabins can also be rented out as singles for $45. All units have phones with free local calls; breakfast is not included.

Lokahi Lodge (☎ 985-8647, 800-457-6924), Box 7, Volcano, HI 96785, is a newer B&B in a contemporary house built specifically for the purpose. There's a spacious common area with a wood-burning stove, an upright piano and a pleasant dining area, where an ample continental breakfast is provided. Each room has its own private entrance. All four rooms are

good-sized, have a pleasant decor that includes wallpaper and frilled curtains, and are furnished with two extra-long double beds and bathrooms with tubs. Rates are $75 for singles or doubles. MasterCard and Visa are accepted.

Hale Ohia (☎ 967-7986, 800-455-3803; fax 967-8610), Box 758, Volcano, HI 96785, a B&B on an old estate, has pleasant grounds that include a hot tub in the backyard. Three of the four units are in a two-story building (formerly the gardener's cottage) at the side of the main house. On the top floor there's a contemporary three-bedroom unit with a full kitchen while the first floor has two suites with refrigerators and coffeemakers but no cooking facilities. There's also a guest bedroom in the main estate house and a separate one-bedroom cottage with a fireplace and kitchenette behind the house. Rates, which include continental breakfast, are from $75 to $95 for doubles, $15 more for each additional person.

Kilauea Lodge (☎ 967-7366; fax 967-7367), Box 116, Volcano, HI 96785, on the main road in Volcano village, has a variety of accommodations, including four pleasantly renovated rooms in what was formerly a YMCA dormitory. These rooms cost $105 and have the sort of country comfort you'd find in a fine inn, with working fireplaces, quilts, high ceilings and bathrooms with tubs. A newer adjacent building has a common area with a large fireplace and seven cheery rooms at $90. Avoid room Nos 7 and 8, which are right off the common room and can get a bit noisy. The lodge also has a couple of cottages from $120. All rooms are nonsmoking, and prices include a full breakfast for two in the lodge's restaurant.

The state maintains *Niaulani Cabin*, a housekeeping cabin half a mile east of the national park. The cabin sits all by itself in the seven-acre ohia forest of Kilauea State Recreation Area, on Kalanikoa Rd near Volcano village. The cabin has two bedrooms, a living room, hot showers, a stove and refrigerator. Rates are $45 for up to four people and $5 more for each additional person, but it's a long shot getting in. For reservations contact the Division of State Parks (☎ 933-4200), Box 936, 75 Aupuni St, Hilo, HI 96721, where you also pick up the key.

Places to Stay – in the park

Namakani Paio Cabins are 10 dreary, windowless plywood cabins at the national park's Namakani Paio Campground. Each has one double bed, two single bunk beds and electric lights, but there are no power outlets or heating. There are communal showers and restrooms. It can get cold at night, so bring a sleeping bag if you have one. (Or bring a tent as well and you can stay in the adjacent campground for free.)

Booking is done through Volcano House, where you pay and pick up your bag of linen. The rate is $32 for up to four people, and there's a $10 deposit for keys and linen.

Volcano House (☎ 967-7321; fax 967-8429), Box 53, Hawaii Volcanoes National Park, HI 96713, is opposite the national park visitor center. Although it has an enviable location, perched right on the rim of Kilauea Caldera, most of the room views are disappointing. By and large, the lower-level rooms look out onto a walkway and even some of those on the upper floor have only a partial view of the crater. The rooms are rather small and straightforward, but they do have some koa furnishings and a bit of character. The best (and most expensive) are the 2nd-story rooms in the main building. Rates are $79 to $131.

Camping The park has two drive-up campgrounds. Camping is free and the campgrounds are not usually crowded, although things can pick up in summer. There's no registration or reservation system – it's simply on a first-come first-served basis. Camping is officially limited to seven days per campground per year. Because of the elevation, nights are crisp and cool at both Namakani Paio (4000 feet) and Kipuka Nene (3000 feet) campgrounds.

Namakani Paio Campground, the park's busiest campground, is just off Hwy 11, about three miles west of the visitor center.

If you're on your way between Hilo and Kona, it's a convenient place to stop for the night. The open tent sites are in a small meadow with little privacy, although it's surrounded by fragrant eucalyptus trees. There are restrooms, water, fireplaces and picnic tables. From the campground it's about a one-mile hike to the Jaggar Museum and Crater Rim Trail.

Kipuka Nene Campground is about five miles down Hilina Pali Rd, off Chain of Craters Rd. It's the less developed of the two campgrounds, but there's a water catchment system, toilets and a shelter with picnic tables. True to the campground's name, a few friendly nene reside nearby. Consequently, the campground is usually closed between November and March during the breeding season. Because of problems with people feeding the endangered nene, and the fact that campers' food attracts cats and other nene predators, there is some uncertainty about the future use of this site for camping; check at the visitor center to be sure it's open before driving out.

For information on backcountry camping in the national park, see Backcountry Camping at the end of the earlier Hiking Trails section.

Places to Eat

If you're trying to see the park in a day, you can save time by bringing lunch and having a picnic wherever you are at noon. If you don't happen to be near the park entrance, it's a long haul from most points in the park out to a restaurant.

The only in-park public restaurant is at *Volcano House* (☎ 967-7321), which serves up a cafeteria-quality breakfast buffet from 7 to 10:30 am for $9.50 and a lunch buffet from 11 am to 2 pm for $12.50. The quality of the food is better at dinner (5:30 to 8:30 pm), with main courses ranging from $15 for pork medallions to $22 for shrimp scampi. While the dining-room view overlooking Kilauea Caldera is magnificent, it can be matched in the adjacent snack shop, which has chili, simple sandwiches, yogurt, juice and coffee. The snack shop is open from 10:30 am to 4:30 pm.

The *Volcano Country Club Restaurant* at Volcano Golf Course has a simple menu with light salads, Hawaiian stew and burgers with fries, all priced around $8. It's open daily for breakfast from 7 to 10 am and for lunch from 10:30 am to 3 pm.

Alii Bakery & Drive-In, a small local diner adjacent to Volcano Store in Volcano village, has good 65¢ cinnamon rolls as well as breakfasts, sandwiches and plate lunches for around $5. It's open from 8 am to 4:30 pm daily. There are a couple of booths where you can eat or you can order takeout for a picnic in the park.

The best food in Volcano is at *Kilauea Lodge* (☎ 967-7366), which is only open for dinner, from 5:30 to 9 pm daily. Reservations are recommended. Dinners of beef, seafood and chicken begin at around $18, and there's always at least one pasta dish on the menu priced around $15. The atmospheric dining room has high wooden ceilings, island artwork and window tables looking out onto a fern forest. It also has a big stone fireplace, built in 1938 when this was a YMCA camp, embedded with an international collection of stones and coins.

Getting There & Away

The park is 29 miles from Hilo and 97 miles from Kona.

The public bus running between Hilo and Waiohinu stops at the visitor center (and at Volcano village) once in each direction Monday to Friday. It leaves the visitor center for Hilo at 8 am and returns from Hilo at 2:40 pm. The ride takes about one hour and costs $2.25.

Maui

Maui has much to lure visitors, including superb scenery, diverse landscapes, world-class windsurfing and excellent conditions for most other water sports. The sunny west coast is lined with beautiful white-sand beaches. Maui's warm coastal waters are the main wintering grounds for North Pacific humpback whales, making it prime whale-watching country.

In the 1960s, Hawaii's first major resort development outside Waikiki was built on Maui. Since that time, Maui has become the most visited and the most developed of the Neighbor Islands. As might be expected, the resort action all centers around the beaches of West Maui.

The main tourist destinations – Lahaina, the Kaanapali area and the Kihei strip – are urbanized experiences, complete with traffic and crowds. But Maui does have another side. It's quite easy to escape the touristed West Maui scene by heading to the east coast or the uplands. Making a base in the small towns of Haiku, Kula or Hana is a totally different experience. Those towns sit beneath Haleakala, the massive mountain that provides the scenic backdrop to all of East Maui. Its slopes hold native rainforests, eucalyptus groves and open pastures with large cattle ranches.

Haleakala Crater, with a summit of 10,023 feet, is the centerpiece of Haleakala National Park. The crater is an extraordinary landscape of spewed red cinders and gray lava hills. Haleakala is the world's largest dormant volcano, its crater so big that an entire city could fit inside. There are some incredible hiking trails across the crater floor, and sunrise at the summit is awe-inspiring.

Kula, at a cool 3000-foot elevation on Haleakala's western slopes, is Maui's garden land. Flowers and vegetables that ordinarily don't have a chance in the tropics thrive up here. Upcountry also has the island's only winery.

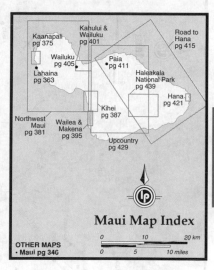

Maui Map Index

OTHER MAPS
• Maui pg 346

The windward side of Haleakala is lush, wet and rugged. The famed Hana Hwy runs down the full length of it, winding its way above the coast through tropical jungle and past roadside waterfalls. It's the most beautiful coastal road in Hawaii.

HISTORY

Before Western contact, Maui had three major population centers: the southeast coast around Hana, the Wailuku area and the district of Lele (present-day Lahaina).

In the 14th century, Piilani, the chief of the Hana district, conquered the entire island. During his reign Piilani accomplished some impressive engineering feats. He built Maui's largest temple, Piilanihale Heiau, which still stands today, as well as an extensive island-wide road system. Almost half of Maui's highways still bear his name.

The last of Maui's ruling chiefs was Kahekili. During the 1780s he was the most

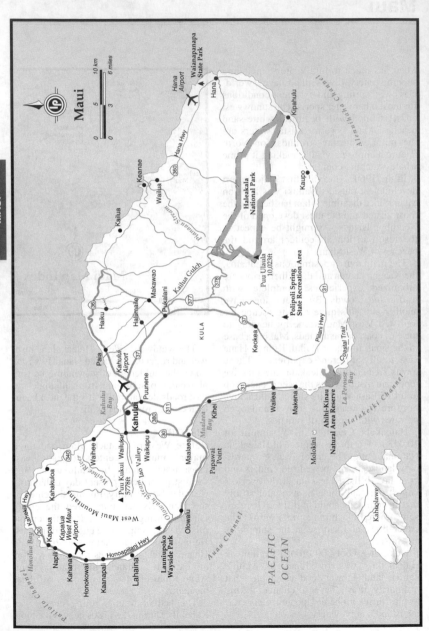

powerful chief in Hawaii, bringing both Oahu and Molokai under Maui's rule.

In 1790, while Kahekili was in Oahu, Kamehameha the Great launched a bold naval attack on Maui. Using foreign-acquired cannons and the aid of two captured foreign seamen, Isaac Davis and John Young, Kamehameha defeated Maui's warriors in a fierce battle at Iao Valley.

An attack on his own homeland by a Big Island rival forced Kamehameha to withdraw from Maui, but the battles continued over the years. When Kahekili died on Oahu in 1794, his kingdom was divided. In 1795, Kamehameha invaded Maui again, and this time he conquered the entire island and brought it under his rule.

In 1800, Kamehameha established Lahaina as his main home and royal court. It remained the capital of Hawaii until 1845.

Whaling Days

Both the whalers and the missionaries arrived in Lahaina in the early 1820s. They were soon at odds.

Shortly after his arrival in 1823, William Richards, Lahaina's first Protestant missionary, converted Maui's Governor Hoapili to Christianity. Under Richards' influence, Hoapili began passing laws against drunkenness and debauchery.

After months at sea, the whalers weren't looking for a prayer service when they pulled into port. Ready for grog and women, they didn't take kindly to the puritanical influences of New England missionaries. To most sailors, there was 'no God west of the Horn'.

In 1826, when English captain William Buckle of the whaler *Daniel* pulled into port, he was outraged to discover Lahaina had a new 'missionary taboo' against womanizing. Buckle's crew came to shore seeking revenge against Richards, but a group of Hawaiian Christians came to Richards' aid and chased the whalers back to their boat.

Following Captain Buckle's purchase of a Hawaiian woman, Richards wrote to Buckle's hometown newspaper reporting the details. A libel suit followed. Richards

Maui's Home

According to legend, the Polynesian demigod Maui was wandering the Pacific on a fishing expedition when his fishhook snagged the sea floor. He tugged with such a powerful force that the islands of Hawaii were yanked to the surface. He then claimed the island of Maui and made it his home. ■

was summoned to Honolulu to be tried, but he was acquitted.

In 1827, after Governor Hoapili arrested the captain of the *John Palmer* for allowing women to board his ship, Palmer's crew shot a round of cannonballs at Richards' house. The captain was released, but laws restricting liaisons between seamen and native women stayed.

After Governor Hoapili's death, laws against liquor and prostitution were no longer strictly enforced, and whalers began to flock to Lahaina. By the mid-19th century, two-thirds of the whalers coming into Hawaii landed in Lahaina, which had replaced Honolulu as the favored harbor. In 1846 almost 400 ships pulled into port.

By the 1860s the whaling industry started to fizzle. The depletion of the last hunting grounds in the Arctic and the emergence of the petroleum industry spelled the end of the US whaling era.

Whaling had been the base of Maui's economy. After the whalers left, Lahaina became all but a ghost town.

Sugar

As whaling was declining, sugar was on the rise. Two of the first planters were Samuel Alexander and Henry Baldwin, sons of prominent missionaries.

In 1870 they began growing sugar cane on 12 acres in Haiku, and the next year they added another 500 acres. It was the beginning of Hawaii's biggest sugar company.

In 1876, Alexander & Baldwin began construction of the Hamakua Ditch, which carried water from the mountainous interior to the Haiku plantations 17 miles away. This system turned Wailuku's dry central plains into green sugar land. Sugar remained the backbone of the economy until tourism took over in the 1960s.

GEOGRAPHY

Maui, the second largest Hawaiian island, arose from the ocean floor as two separate volcanoes. Lava flows and soil erosion eventually built up a valley-like isthmus between the two, linking them in their present form. The flat isthmus provides a fertile setting for fields of sugar cane and has given Maui the nickname 'The Valley Island'.

The eastern side of Maui, the larger and younger of the two, is dominated by Haleakala, which has a summit elevation of 10,023 feet. This dormant volcano has a massive crater-like valley containing numerous cinder cones and vents. Haleakala last erupted in 1790, which on the geological clock means it could just be snoozing.

The West Maui Mountains dominate West Maui, with Puu Kukui, at 5778 feet, the highest point.

The rainy northeast sides of both mountain masses are cut with deep ravines and valleys that lead down to the coast. White-sand beaches run along much of the island's western shoreline.

Maui's total land area is 728 sq miles.

Molokini

The largely submerged volcanic crater of Molokini lies midway between Maui and Kahoolawe. Half of the crater rim has eroded away, leaving a crescent moon shape that rises 160 feet above the ocean surface. Its land area is about 18 acres.

Molokini has clear waters with abundant fish and coral, making it a popular snorkel and dive spot.

The US Navy used to shell Molokini for target practice, and live bombs are still found on the crater floor. A few years ago demolition experts removed three that were in just 20 feet of water.

CLIMATE

Maui's west coast is largely dry and sunny. The southeast coast and the Kula uplands receive more rain and commonly have intermittent clouds.

Temperatures vary more with elevation than season. The variance between winter and summer is only about 7°F in most places. The average August temperatures (over a 24-hour period) are 77°F in Hana, 78°F in Lahaina and Kihei, 79°F in Kahului and 50°F at Haleakala summit.

The lowest temperature ever recorded at the summit of Haleakala was 14°F, and temperatures hovering around freezing are common on winter nights. The mountain even gets an occasional winter snowcap.

Average annual rainfall is 69 inches in Hana, 13 in Kihei, 15 in Lahaina, 19 in Kahului and 44 at Haleakala summit.

Puu Kukui, the highest peak of the West Maui Mountains, gets 400 inches of rain a year. The peak is Maui's wettest spot, although it sits just five miles from the dry Wailuku plains.

FLORA & FAUNA

It's on Maui that you are most likely to see the endangered nene goose and the rare silversword plant. Haleakala is the habitat for both. Maui is also the best island for viewing humpback whales.

At least six birds native to Maui are found nowhere else in the world. These are the Maui parrotbill, the Maui nuku-puu, the Maui creeper, the Maui akepa, the crested honeycreeper and the poouli, all of which are endangered. The poouli, quite amazingly, wasn't discovered until 1973, when it was sighted by a group of University of Hawaii students working in a secluded area of the Hana rainforest.

Maui also has feral pigs, goats and game birds, all of which are hunted both for recreational purposes and to control the damage that these introduced species cause to the habitat.

Humpback Whales

After spending their summers in Alaska, more than half of all humpback whales in the North Pacific come to Hawaii for the winter. The largest numbers are found in the shallow waters between Maui, Lanai and Kahoolawe.

Humpbacks have tail flukes with distinctive individual markings, making them easy to identify. The Pacific Whale Foundation has counted over a thousand humpback whales off Maui in recent seasons.

NED FRIARY

Humpback whale flukes

The peak season for humpbacks in Hawaii is the same as for tourists from cold-weather climates. Some whales arrive as early as November and a few stay as late as May, with most in residence from January to March.

The western coastline of Maui from Olowalu to Makena (and the eastern shore of Lanai) are the chief birthing and nursing grounds for wintering humpbacks. Federal law protects these 'cow/calf waters' and prohibits boats and swimmers from approaching within 300 yards of the whales.

Humpbacks like to stay in shallow water when they have newborn calves, apparently as a safeguard against shark attacks. Maalaea Bay is a favorite nursing ground.

Humpbacks are highly sensitive to human disturbance and noise. Around Lahaina where the waters are buzzing with activity, they generally stay well offshore.

The best bet for whale spotting if you're in the Lahaina area is to go south at least as far as Launiupoko Wayside Park. Maui's finest shoreline whale-watching spots are the stretches from Olowalu to Maalaea Bay and from Keawakapu Beach to Makena Beach.

GOVERNMENT

Maui County consists of the islands of Maui, Molokai, Lanai and uninhabited Kahoolawe. The county seat is in Wailuku.

The county is governed by an elected mayor with a four-year term and nine council members with two-year terms.

ECONOMY

Maui's unemployment rate is 7%. The major industries are tourism, sugar cane and pineapple production, cattle grazing and diversified agriculture.

Surprisingly, more land on Maui is used for grazing dairy and beef cattle than for any other purpose. For every acre of sugar, there are three acres of ranch land.

Kula is one of the state's major flower- and vegetable-producing regions, accounting for more than half of the cabbage, lettuce, onions and potatoes grown in Hawaii and for almost all of the commercially grown proteas and carnations.

After Oahu, Maui captures the lion's share of Hawaii's tourist industry, accounting for roughly half the visitor accommodations on all the outer islands combined. Numbers, however, don't equate to bargains here. Maui has the highest room rates in Hawaii, averaging $150 a night, about 25% higher than the state average.

POPULATION & PEOPLE

Maui has a population of 106,000. The Wailuku district, which includes the sister towns of Wailuku and Kahului, is home to half of the island's residents.

Ethnically, 26% of the population is Caucasian, 16% Japanese, 15% Filipino and 2% Hawaiian. About one-third of Maui's residents consider themselves to be of 'mixed blood', with two-thirds of these having some Hawaiian ancestry.

ORIENTATION

Most visitors to Maui land at the main airport in Kahului.

From Kahului, it's five miles to Paia down Hwy 36 and another 45 miles to Hana.

Upcountry (Kula) is 15 miles from Kahului on Hwy 37. From there it's another 20 miles up to the summit of Haleakala.

It's about 10 miles to Kihei from Kahului along Hwy 311.

It's 25 miles from Kahului to Lahaina via Hwys 380 and 30, and four miles more from Lahaina to Kaanapali.

Be aware that most main roads are called 'highways' whether they're a busy four lanes or just a country road. Islanders refer to highways by name, rarely by number. If you ask someone how to find Hwy 36, chances are they won't know – ask for the Hana Hwy instead.

Maps

The best map for getting around the island is the University of Hawaii Press map of Maui, which not only covers the roads well, but shows beaches and major sights. It can be purchased at convenience shops and bookstores around the island.

INFORMATION
Tourist Offices

The Maui Visitors Bureau (☎ 244-3530; fax 244-1337), Box 580, Wailuku, HI 96793, has its office at 1727 Wili Pa Loop, opposite the Wailuku post office. It's open from 8 am to 4:30 pm Monday to Friday. If you call ☎ 800-525-6284 before you go, the bureau will send its 'travel planner', a packet containing brochures and other promotional information.

Other Tourist Information For details on Kaanapali, contact the Kaanapali Beach Resort Association (☎ 661-3271, 800-245-9229), 2530 Kekaa Drive, Suite B1, Lahaina, HI 96761. For information on Wailea, contact the Wailea Destination Association (☎ 879-4258, 800-782-5642), 3750 Wailea Alanui Drive, Wailea, HI 96753. Both organizations will mail out brochures on accommodations at their resorts.

Newspapers & Magazines

Maui's main newspaper, the *Maui News* (☎ 244-3981, 800-827-0347), Box 550, Wailuku, HI 96793, has good coverage of local and off-island news and comes out daily except Saturday. The Sunday edition can be mailed to the US mainland for $5.50, postage included. It can be ordered by phone using a credit card.

There are several small community newspapers that focus on local issues, including the *Lahaina News*, *South Maui Times*, *Haleakala Times* and *Maui Bulletin*.

Free tourist magazines such as *This Week On Maui* and *Spotlight's Maui Gold* are full of ads, discount coupons, simple maps and general sightseeing information. They're worth picking up at the airport and island hotels and restaurants.

Radio & TV

Maui has numerous radio stations, including KPOA (93.5 FM and 107.3 FM), which plays Hawaiian music from 1 am to 8 pm daily, followed by tropical jazz until 1 am.

All the major US mainland TV networks are available on cable. Cable TV Channel 7

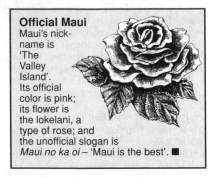

Official Maui

Maui's nickname is 'The Valley Island'. Its official color is pink; its flower is the lokelani, a type of rose; and the unofficial slogan is *Maui no ka oi* – 'Maui is the best'. ∎

has ongoing programs on Hawaii geared for visitors.

Bookstores
The island's largest bookstore, the new Borders Books & Music on Dairy Rd in Kahului, has an impressive collection of novels, travel guides, Hawaiiana books, magazines and international newspapers. Waldenbooks, with branches in Kahului, Kihei and Lahaina, also has good selections of Hawaiiana and travel books.

Libraries
There are public libraries in Kahului, Wailuku, Lahaina, Hana, Makawao and Kihei.

Weather
For the National Weather Service's recorded forecast of weather conditions on Maui, Molokai and Lanai, call ☎ 877-5111.

For a recreational forecast, including conditions at Haleakala and along the road to Hana, sunrise and sunset times and general marine conditions, call ☎ 871-5054. For a more extensive marine forecast, including surf conditions, winds and tides, call ☎ 877-3477.

Emergency
Dial ☎ 911 for police, ambulance or fire emergencies. The county crisis and help line is ☎ 244-7407.

The island's largest hospital, Maui Memorial Hospital (☎ 244-9056), 221 Mahalani St, Wailuku, and the smaller Hana Medical Center (☎ 248-8294) in Hana both have 24-hour emergency service.

ACTIVITIES
Beaches & Swimming
Maui has lots of fine beaches, some of Hawaii's best windsurfing and board surfing and plenty of good swimming, snorkeling and bodysurfing spots.

The northwest coast from Kaanapali up to Honolua Bay and the southwest coast from Maalaea down to Makena are largely fringed with white-sand beaches. This western side is dry and sunny, and water conditions are generally calmer than on the windward northern and eastern coasts.

Most of the west coast beaches are backed by hotel and condo developments – good if you're looking to stay right at the beach, not so good if you prefer seclusion. Some of the best undeveloped beaches are Slaughterhouse Beach and Honolua Bay in the north and Makena's Big and Little beaches in the south.

Swimming Pools The county maintains heated swimming pools free to the public in Wailuku, Lahaina and Pukalani. For current schedule information, call ☎ 243-7411 for the Wailuku pool on the corner of Wells and Market Sts, ☎ 243-7394 for the pool at Baldwin High School in Wailuku, ☎ 661-7611 for the Lahaina Aquatic Center and ☎ 572-1479 for the spiffy new pool at the Upcountry Swimming Complex in Pukalani.

Surfing
Maui has some unbeatable surfing spots, with peak surfing conditions from November to March. Hookipa Beach near Paia has surfing almost year-round, with incredible winter waves. When conditions are right, Honolua Bay on the northwest coast has the island's top action.

The Maalaea Pipeline, at the south side of Maalaea Bay, has a very fast break, best during south swells. However, this break, which *Surfer* magazine has described as one of the world's 10 best, could be seriously altered if a proposed expansion of Maalaea Harbor is allowed to go through.

A number of places give surfing lessons for beginners, including Andrea Thomas' Maui Surfing School (☎ 875-0625), Nancy Emerson's School of Surfing (☎ 244-7873), Lahaina Surfing School (☎ 667-5999), Second Wind (☎ 877-7467), Kaanapali Windsurfing School (☎ 667-1964), Hawaiian Sailboarding Techniques (☎ 871-5423) and Maui Mistral (☎ 871-7753).

Lessons typically take 1½ to two hours and cost $50 to $60. Most places guarantee that students of all ages will be surfing at the end of the lesson.

The most popular beaches for bodysurfing are Baldwin Beach Park, Fleming Beach Park and those in the Kihei area.

Both surfboards and boogie boards can be rented at numerous locations around Maui, including many of the windsurfing shops.

Hi-Tech Surf Sports (☎ 877-2111) rents surfboards for $18/90 a day/week at its Kahului (425 Koloa) shop and boogie boards for $8/45 at its Paia (Baldwin Ave) shop.

Maui Mistral, 261 Dairy Rd, Kahului, rents boogie boards for $7.50/15 a day/week, surfboards for $20/100.

Reef Watchers (☎ 874-3467) at Suda's Store, 61 S Kihei Rd in Kihei, rents boogie boards for $5 a day.

Reef Divers (☎ 667-7647), 578 Front St, Lahaina, rents boogie boards for $4/15 a day/week.

Windsurfing

Maui is a mecca for windsurfers. Some of the world's best windsurfing is at Hookipa Beach in Paia, though it's suitable for experts only. Spreckelsville Beach in Paia is for intermediate and advanced windsurfers. Kanaha Beach in Kahului is good for beginners, as are parts of the Kihei coast.

In Maalaea Bay, winds are usually strong and blow offshore towards Kahoolawe, good for advanced speed sailing. During the winter, on those occasions when kona winds blow, the Maalaea-Kihei area is often the only place windy enough to sail and becomes the main scene for all windsurfers.

Overall, Maui is known for its consistent winds, and windsurfers can find action in any month. Although trade winds can blow at any time of the year and flat spells could also hit anytime, generally the windiest time is June to September and the flattest from December to February.

The Maui Boardsailing Association has developed a 'sail safe' program with windsurfing guidelines; brochures with the guidelines are available at the windsurf shops.

Most windsurfing shops are based in Kahului; the following shops sell and rent windsurfing gear and either give lessons themselves or do it through an affiliate that works out of the same shop.

Hawaiian Island Surf & Sport, 415A Dairy Rd, Kahului, HI 96732
  (☎ 871-4981, 800-231-6958)
Hi-Tech Surf Sports, 425 Koloa, Kahului, HI 96732 (☎ 871-5423, 800-736-6284)
Maui Windsurf, 520 Keolani Place, Kahului, HI 96732 (☎ 877-4816, 800-872-0999)
Sailboards Maui, 397 Dairy Rd, Kahului, HI 96732 (☎ 871-7954, 800-328-8877)
Second Wind, 111 Hana Hwy, Kahului, HI 96732 (☎ 877-7467)
Windrigger Maui/Maui Mistral, 261 Dairy Rd, Kahului, HI 96732
  (☎ 871-7753, 800-345-6284)

Shops generally rent boards and rigs for about $50/275 a day/week, which usually includes swapping privileges that let you try different equipment.

Windsurfing lessons, either one-day classes or multiday packages, can be arranged for any level. Introductory classes for beginners are usually held at Kanaha Beach or at the north side of Kihei, last two to three hours and cost around $60, equipment included.

Most of the Kahului shops also sell windsurfing gear and can book package tours that include accommodations and gear rental.

In northwest Maui, a smaller operation, the Kaanapali Windsurfing School (☎ 667-1964), rents windsurfing equipment and gives beginner lessons in front of Whalers Village on Kaanapali Beach. The cost is $45 for a 90-minute lesson. Rentals without lessons cost $20 for one hour, $45 for three hours.

Diving & Snorkeling

Some dive and snorkel boat tours go along the Maui shoreline, but the main destinations are the sunken volcanic crater of Molokini and the island of Lanai. Although a few dive boats take snorkelers, and some snorkeling tours take divers, as a rule you'll be better off going out on a tour that's geared for the activity you're doing.

For snorkeling from the beach, the best spots are Black Rock at the Sheraton in

Kaanapali; Olowalu, south of Lahaina; around the rocky points of Wailea and Makena beaches; and in summer at Honolua Bay and Slaughterhouse Beach on the northwest shore. Kapalua Bay is generally one of the calmest places for snorkeling all year round. Maui Dive Shops has a good free map that details the island's best diving and snorkeling spots.

Kaanapali	Whalers Village (☎ 661-5117)
Kahana	Kahana Gateway (☎ 669-3800)
Kahului	Kaahumanu Center (☎ 871-2111)
Kihei	Azeka Place II (☎ 879-3388)
	Kamaole Center (☎ 879-1533)
	Kihei Town Center (☎ 879-1919)
Lahaina	Lahaina Cannery Mall (☎ 661-5388)
	626 Front St (☎ 667-0722)
Wailea	Wailea Shopping Village
	(☎ 879-3166)

Molokini Molokini is Maui's most popular snorkeling tour site. The fish are tame and numerous and the water is clear.

Morning is the best time to snorkel Molokini, as winds pick up in the afternoon. The fish are given their breakfast call by boat captains who drop in loaves of bread to start the action.

For divers, Molokini has walls, ledges, white-tipped reef sharks, manta rays, turtles and a wide variety of other marine life.

Although the snorkeling and diving is good, a score of tour boats crowd the islet every day and all of the activity has taken a toll on the reef. Some sections have been permanently damaged, largely from dropped and dragged anchors that have carved swaths in the coral.

Black coral was once prolific in Molokini's deeper waters. However, most of it made its way into Lahaina jewelry stores before Molokini was declared a conservation district in 1977.

Lanai Lanai also has clear waters, but without the crowds. The most common destination is Hulopoe Bay.

Hulopoe is a big, beautiful beach that was once secluded but now has a luxury hotel at its northern end. The reef at the southern end harbors large schools of fish and is good for snorkeling.

For divers, the nearby Cathedrals offers intriguing geological formations, including caves, arches and connecting passageways.

Dive Shops & Boat Dives Maui has a number of dive operations. The most prolific is Maui Dive Shops, which has the following branches around the island.

Maui Dive Shops offers introductory dives for beginners for $59; two-tank dives for $75 off West Maui or $100 at Molokini; and four-day certification courses go for around $300.

Lahaina Divers (☎ 667-7496, 800-998-3483), 143 Dickenson St, Lahaina, HI 96761, has two-tank dives to either Lanai or Molokini, one-tank introductory dives for $79 and shore night dives for $55. A five-star PADI operation, they also offer three-day certification courses for $265 and lead advanced drift and deep-water dives.

Reef Divers (☎ 667-7647), 578 Front St, Lahaina, HI 96761, has two-tank dives to Molokini for $95, introductory dives for $89. It's a competitive operation, and prices for certification courses have recently been as low as $200.

Ed Robinson's Diving Adventures (☎ 879-3584), Box 616, Kihei, HI 96753, is operated by underwater photographer Ed Robinson, who offers two-tank dives for $105.

Snorkeling Tours & Rentals Numerous snorkeling cruises leave for Molokini daily from Maalaea Harbor. Boats are usually out from about 7 am to noon and average $40 to $60, including snacks and snorkeling gear. Competition is heavy, so deals and discount coupons are easy to come by. Tickets are sold at activity booths around the island.

Snorkeling gear can be rented at reasonable prices from most dive shops and at inflated prices from hotel beach huts.

Reef Divers (☎ 667-7647) in Lahaina has some of the best rates, with snorkel sets from $3 a day. Maui Dive Shops (see Dive Shops for locations) rents snorkel sets with silicone masks for $7.50/15 a day/week.

MAUI

High-profile Snorkel Bob's has come-on rates of $15 a week for its cheaper snorkel gear, but you'll probably want better quality and prices will rise accordingly. There are three Maui locations: 161 Lahainaluna Rd in Lahaina (☎ 661-4421), 34 Keala Place in Kihei (☎ 879-7449) and Napili Village Hotel in Napili (☎ 669-9603).

Reef Watchers (☎ 874-3467) at Suda's Store, 61 S Kihei Rd in Kihei, rents snorkel sets for just $2.50 a day.

Kayaking

South Pacific Kayaks (☎ 875-4848, 800-776-2326; kayak@maui.net), at the Rainbow Mall in Kihei, rents single kayaks from $20 a day and doubles from $40, including car racks, paddles and life vests. Three-hour guided kayak tours (some dubbed 'whale watch') are offered for $55. Five-hour outings around the La Perouse area cost $85, including snorkeling and lunch.

Kelii's Kayak Tours (☎ 874-7652; kelii@maui.net) offers guided ocean kayak tours, with stops for snorkeling. There's a daily 2½-hour trip from Makena to the La Perouse area for $55, a Papawai Point area sunset tour on Saturdays for $55 and a 4½-hour tour along Maui's north shore with lunch for $85.

Other Maui kayak operations are Makena Kayak Tours (☎ 879-8426), Maui Sea Kayaking (☎ 572-6299) and Tradewind Kayak Maui (☎ 879-2247).

Hiking

Haleakala National Park has some extraordinary trails across the moonscape-like Haleakala Crater, varying from half-day walks to overnight treks. In the Oheo section of the park, which is south of Hana, there's a trail to two impressive waterfalls.

Polipoli Spring State Recreation Area in Maui's Upcountry has an extensive trail system in cloudforest. One of these, the Skyline Trail, leads up to Haleakala summit.

Several pull-offs along the Hana Hwy lead to short nature walks. There's also a pleasant coastal trail between Waianapanapa State Park and Hana Bay.

A nice choice north of Wailuku is the scenic Waihee Ridge Trail, which branches off the Kahekili Hwy. From La Perouse Bay, on the other side of the island, there's a hardy coastline hike over a lava footpath. And, of course, Maui has many white-sand beaches perfect for strolls. Hikes are detailed in their respective sections.

Sierra Club The Maui branch of the Sierra Club leads hikes or service trips once or twice a month on weekends. The schedule is posted in the Datebook section of the *Maui News*. There's no fee, but a small donation is appreciated.

The service trips sometimes involve helping to rid the island of invasive exotic plants, such as myconia and banana poka. The latter, a not-so-benign relative of the edible passion fruit vine, has run rampant over native forests on the Big Island and Kauai, but is kept relatively controlled on Maui thanks in large part to the Sierra Club. Their eradication tactics include bagging fruit and seedlings, pulling up vines and spraying herbicide on the roots.

Cycling

Each morning before dawn, groups of cyclists gather at the top of Haleakala for the thrill of coasting 38 miles down the mountain, with a 10,000-foot drop in elevation.

Companies offering this activity include Maui Downhill (☎ 871-2155, 800-535-2453), Maui Mountain Cruisers (☎ 871-6014, 800-232-6284) and Mountain Riders (☎ 242-9739, 800-706-7000).

Generally it's an all-day affair (eight to 10 hours), starting with hotel pick-up at around 3 am, a van ride up the mountain for the sunrise and about 3½ hours of biking back down. It's not a nonstop cruise, as cyclists must periodically pull over for cars following behind, and the primary exercise is squeezing the brakes – it's estimated there's only 400 yards of pedaling on the entire trip! The going rate is a steep $115, which includes bike, helmet, transportation and meals.

Bikes are generally modified with special safety brakes, and each group is followed by an escort van. Pregnant women, children under 12 and those less than five feet tall are usually not allowed to ride.

Aloha Bicycle Tours (☎ 249-0911, 800-749-1564) offers a non-sunrise tour geared for hardier cyclists that begins with a glide down the Haleakala Crater Rd, but instead of continuing downhill to the coast, takes in various Upcountry sights before ending at the winery. The cost of $79 doesn't include hotel pick-up.

If you don't feel the need for a group outing or a guide to bring you back down the mountain, Upcountry Cycles (☎ 573-2888) will rent you a 21-speed mountain bike with helmet, backpack, map and weather gear and give you a van ride up to Haleakala summit from their shop in Pukalani, at 81 Makawao Ave in Pukalani Square. The cost is $29 in the daytime, $50 in time for the sunrise.

Bicycle rentals are detailed in the Getting Around section later in this chapter.

Horseback Riding

Maui has lots of ranch land and some of Hawaii's best opportunities for trail rides. The most unusual ride meanders down into Haleakala Crater via Sliding Sands Trail.

Pony Express (☎ 667-2200) is in a eucalyptus grove on Haleakala Crater Rd, 2½ miles up from Hwy 377. Their half-day Haleakala Crater ride leaves at 9:30 am, takes four hours and covers 7½ miles; it's open to novice riders and costs $120, including a picnic lunch on the crater floor. A full-day version covers 12 miles, goes to Kapalaoa Cabin and costs $150. On weekdays there are rides across the rolling meadows of Haleakala Ranch that cost $35 for one hour, $60 for two hours.

Charles Aki Jr (☎ 248-8209), c/o Kaupo Store, Kaupo, HI 96713, arranges weekend overnight pack trips into Haleakala Crater from his home in Kaupo. The cost is $300 per person, with two to three people, and includes camping equipment or cabin fees and meals. As Charles is a working cowboy, trips require advance notice of at least a couple of weeks and a deposit.

Thompson Ranch (☎ 878-1910) in Keokea has 1½-hour trail rides for $45, as well as longer and more expensive rides, including outings into Haleakala Crater.

Rainbow Ranch (☎ 669-4991) in Napili, open Monday to Saturday, offers 90-minute rides for $75, two-hour sunset rides for $100, 3½-hour picnic rides for $135 and various other options. They can pick up and drop off in the Kaanapali-Kapalua area.

Hana Ranch Riding Stables (☎ 248-8211) has one-hour guided trail rides along the Hana coast at 8 and 9:30 am and 2 pm Monday to Saturday for $30 and two-hour rides at 4 pm Tuesday and Thursday for $59.

Oheo Stables (☎ 667-2222), one mile southwest of Oheo Gulch, offers three-hour horseback rides within the Kipahulu District of Haleakala National Park. The rides depart at 11:30 am and 2:30 pm, move at a casual pace, visit waterfalls and cost $95.

Makena Stables (☎ 879-0244), on the old Makena Rd in Makena, has a variety of trail rides from Makena up the slopes to Ulupalakua Ranch; three-hour rides cost $105.

Hang Gliding

Under the name Hang Gliding Maui (☎ / fax 572-6557), German-born Armin Engert offers instructional tandem hang-gliding flights off the slopes of Haleakala, providing a scenic descent of nearly 10,000 feet down to the coast. The outing lasts about four hours and costs $250, including transportation from Pukalani, basic instruction and about 35 minutes of flight time in a tandem harness with Armin.

Armin also provides 45-minute motorized hang-gliding instructional flights in an open-cockpit ultralight for $150.

Tennis

The county maintains tennis courts at these places: Lahaina Civic Center, Lahaina; Maluuluolele Park, Lahaina; Wells Park, Wailuku; War Memorial Complex, Wailuku; Kahului Community Center, Kahului; Kalama Park, Kihei; Hana Ball Park, Hana; Eddie Tam Memorial Center, Makawao; and Pukalani Community Center, Pukalani. All county courts are free to the public on a first-come first-served basis and are lit for night play.

Numerous hotels and condos have tennis courts for their guests. There are tennis courts open to the public on a fee basis at the Wailea Tennis Club (☎ 879-1958) in Wailea; Makena Tennis Club (☎ 879-8777) in Makena; Kapalua Tennis Garden (☎ 669-5677) and Village Tennis Center (☎ 665-0112) in Kapalua; and the Maui Marriott (☎ 667-1200) and Royal Lahaina Tennis Ranch (☎ 661-3611) in Kaanapali.

Rates at the Makena Tennis Club are $18 per court per hour. At the Royal Lahaina the cost is $5 per person per hour or $7.50 per day. At the other resort clubs, rates are quoted at $10 to $12 per person 'per day', although only the first hour of playing time is guaranteed and the courts are subject to space availability after that. Rackets can be rented at all tennis clubs for $4 to $6 a day ($2.50 at Royal Lahaina); some clubs also rent tennis shoes.

Golf

Maui has 16 golf courses open to the public. They include, in order by listing, one municipal, five private and 10 resort courses. All are 18-hole, par-71, -72 or -73 courses except Maui Country Club, which is nine-hole, par-37.

Grand Waikapu Country Club in Waikapu charges $200 for greens fees, cart and use of the spa (☎ 244-7888).

Kaanapali Beach Resort has two courses (North and South) in Kaanapali; greens fees and cart cost $100 for resort guests, $120 for nonresort guests at either course; twilight rates are $62 (☎ 661-3691).

Kapalua Golf Club has three courses in Kapalua; greens fees and cart cost $75 for resort guests and $115 for nonguests at the Bay and Village courses, $80 for guests and $125 for nonguests at the Plantation course; all have $62 twilight fees after 2 pm (☎ 669-8044). The Bay Course has plantings of native flora and uses only minimal chemicals, a combination that has made it Hawaii's only course to be recognized as a 'Certified Audubon Cooperative Sanctuary'.

Makena Golf Course has two courses (North and South) in Makena; greens fees and cart cost $120, but there's a $70 twilight rate after 2 pm (☎ 879-3344).

Maui Country Club in Spreckelsville is open to the public on Mondays only and charges $45, including a cart (☎ 877-0616).

Pukalani Country Club in Pukalani charges $63 for greens fees and cart if you tee off in the morning, $42 if you tee off after noon (☎ 572-1314).

Sandalwood Golf Course in Waikapu, next to the Waikapu Country Club, charges $75 for greens fees and cart (☎ 242-4653).

Silversword Golf Course in Kihei charges $69 for greens fees with shared cart and has a $44 twilight rate (☎ 874-0777).

Waiehu Municipal Golf Course, north of Wailuku, charges greens fees of $25 on weekdays, $30 on weekends and holidays, plus $7.50 per person for a shared cart. Clubs rent for $13.50 a day. This is a busy little course, and reservations for starting times are taken up to two days in advance (☎ 243-7400).

Wailea Golf Club has three courses in Wailea; greens fees with cart cost $85 for Wailea resort guests and $125 for the general public at the Blue & Emerald courses, $5 more at the Gold Course (☎ 875-5111).

Organized Tours

Maui has a handful of sightseeing tour companies. Tours to Hana and Haleakala are the most popular.

Polynesian Adventure Tours (☎ 877-4242) has tours of Hana for $68 and of Haleakala, central Maui and Iao Valley for $54. There's also a Haleakala sunrise tour for $50. Children under 12 are charged about 75% of the adult fare.

TransHawaiian (☎ 877-7308) has Hana tours for $65 and Haleakala sunrise tours for $49. Children under 12 are charged 65% of the adult fare.

Helicopter & Biplane Numerous helicopter companies take off from the heliport at Kahului Airport for trips around the island. Some cross the channel and tour Molokai's spectacular north shore as well.

Most companies advertise in the free tourist magazines. Prices are competitive, with many running perennial specials, offering free use of video cameras and the like.

Typical are 30-minute tours of the West Maui Mountains for around $100,

45-minute tours of Haleakala and Hana for $130 and one-hour circle-island tours for $180.

Helicopter companies operating on Maui include Sunshine Helicopters (☎ 871-0722, 800-544-2520), Blue Hawaiian (☎ 871-8844, 800-247-5444), Hawaii Helicopters (☎ 877-3900, 800-367-7095), Air Maui (☎ 877-7005) and Alex Air (☎ 871-0792).

Biplane Barnstormers (☎ 878-2860) offers open-cockpit biplane rides, ranging from $99 for a 20-minute sightseeing flight to $450 for a 100-minute circumnavigation of the island. Unlike the helicopters, which charge a per-person rate, the cost for the biplane is the same for either one or two passengers.

Cruises Maui has enough dinner cruises, sunset sails, deep-sea fishing and charter sailboats to fill a book. Most leave from Lahaina or Maalaea, a few from Kihei and Kaanapali.

You can get current rates and information from activity booths all around Maui or from the tourist magazines – or just go down to Lahaina Harbor where the booths and the boats are lined up and check out the scene for yourself.

Atlantis Submarines (☎ 667-7816) has a 65-foot sub that carries 48 passengers down to a depth of about 100 feet in the waters off Lahaina to see coral and fish. Tours leave from Lahaina Harbor via a catamaran every hour on the hour from 8 am to 3 pm daily. The cost is $79 for adults, $39 for children.

If you want a similar effect at half the price, the semi-submersible Nautilus (☎ 667-2133) is a glassbottom boat with a submerged lower deck that has underwater viewing windows similar to those on the sub. It leaves Lahaina Harbor five times a day and costs $30 for adults, $16 for children ages six to 12 (free for children under six).

Whale Watching The peak humpback whale-watching season is from January to the end of March, though there are usually

whales around Maui for a month or so on either side.

In season, whale-watching cruises are heavily advertised, and you'll have no trouble finding one. Whale-watch boats range from double-hulled sailboats to large cruise vessels. Most leave from Maalaea or Lahaina harbors, a few from Kihei and Kaanapali. A two- to three-hour tour usually costs $25 to $40 for adults, half price for children. Some companies have hydrophones to hear whale songs, some claim to donate a portion of the ticket price to whale conservation groups and some guarantee whale sightings or give another boat tour free.

Many of the boats that take snorkelers to Molokini in the morning go out whale watching in the afternoon. During the season there's a good chance of spotting whales on the snorkeling trip to Molokini itself.

The nonprofit Pacific Whale Foundation (☎ 879-8811, 800-942-5311) has numerous daily cruises from both Maalaea and Lahaina for $31 for adults and $17 for children. They often cut the rate for the first and last boats out of both harbors to just $20 for adults, $12.50 for children. The foundation uses a 50-foot sailboat from Lahaina and a 53-foot motorboat from Maalaea. Whale sightings are guaranteed, or you'll get a coupon good for another free trip. A portion of the profits go to the foundation's marine conservation projects.

To Lanai Club Lanai (☎ 871-1144, 800-531-5262) sails a 70-passenger catamaran to secluded Kahalepalaoa Beach on Lanai's east coast. The cost of $89 includes all you can eat and drink and a few water activities. The boat leaves Lahaina's Pier 4 at 7:30 am and returns at 3:30 pm.

Trilogy Excursions (☎ 661-4743, 800-874-2666) operates a day tour by catamaran from Lahaina to Lanai's Hulopoe Beach. The cost of $149 includes breakfast, a barbecue lunch, snorkeling and a brief land tour of Lanai.

MAUI

In addition, some of Maui's dive shops offer dive or snorkel outings to Lanai. See also the Getting There & Away section of this chapter for information on the Lanai-Lahaina ferry, which deposits passengers at Manele Bay, a stone's throw from lovely Hulopoe Beach.

ACCOMMODATIONS

Other than camping, the cheapest places to stay on Maui are the Banana Bungalow and Northshore Inn in Wailuku, both of which have dorm beds for around $15.

Maui also has some studio-style cottages and apartments that rent from about $50, with the bulk of these found in the Haiku-Paia area. There are a number of B&Bs spread throughout the island, offering some very pleasant places to stay for around $75.

Kihei has the highest concentration of Maui's mid-range accommodations, most of it in condos. Other mid-range accommodations can be found in Kahului, Lahaina and Honokowai. The lower end of the mid-range is about $60 to $80, but it's easy to spend well over $100 a night and not be in anything exclusive.

Maui's two biggest resort developments are Kaanapali Beach Resort and Wailea Resort, both of which have luxury hotels and condos. Prices for the cheapest condos start around $140. The beachfront hotels start around $150 in Kaanapali and $200 in Wailea, though the more exclusive hotels have room rates that are easily double that.

Overall, rates can be substantially lower during the low season (mid-April to mid-December), when you get to pick and choose. During the high season, the better condo deals usually require reservations far in advance.

Condominiums

Maui has many more condo units than hotel rooms. Some condo complexes are booked only through rental agents. Others operate more like a hotel with a front desk, though even in those places some of their units are usually handled by rental agents.

Overall, the best rates are through the agents, but you'll have to deal with advance

payments, and in some cases there may be security deposits and cleaing fees as well.

Most agents require deposits within one to two weeks of booking, with full payment due within the 30 days prior to arrival. Cancellation policies vary, but there will be a hefty charge (or no refund at all) for canceling within the last month. The minimum stay is usually four to 14 days, depending on the place and season.

Each of the agents listed here handles a number of condo complexes and will send listings with rates, making it possible for you to compare values. The 800 numbers that follow can be called toll free from the continental USA, and most can also be called from Canada.

AA Oceanfront Condominium Rentals, 2439 S Kihei Rd No 206A, Kihei, HI 96753 (☎ 879-7288, 800-488-6004; fax 879-7500)

Bello Realty, Box 1776, 2395 S Kihei Rd, Kihei, HI 96753 (☎ 879-2598, 800-541-3060; fax 879-3329)

Condominium Rentals Hawaii, 362 Huku Lii Place No 204, Kihei, HI 96753 (☎ 879-2778, 800-367-5242 in the USA, 800-663-2101 in Canada, 0014-800-123-212 in Australia; fax 879-7825; crh@maui.net)

Hawaiian Apartment Leasing Enterprises, 479 Ocean Ave Suite B, Laguna Beach, CA 92651 (☎ 714-497-4253, 800-854-8843; fax 714-497-4183)

Kihei Maui Vacations, Box 1055, 2395 S Kihei Rd, Kihei, HI 96753 (☎ 879-7581, 800-541-6284; fax 879-2000)

Klahani Resorts, Box 11108, 505 Front St, Lahaina, HI 96761 (☎ 667-2712, 800-669-0795; fax 661-5875)

Kumulani Rentals, Box 1190, 1993 S Kihei Rd, Kihei, HI 96753 (☎ 879-9272, 800-367-2954; fax 874-0094)

Maui Condo & Home Realty, Box 1840, 2511 S Kihei Rd, Kihei, HI 96753 (☎ 879-5445, 800-822-4409; fax 874-6144)

Maui Network, Box 1077, Makawao, HI 96768 (☎ 572-9555, 800-367-5221; fax 572-8553)

Camping

Maui has fewer camping options than the other islands. Waianapanapa State Park and Haleakala National Park are good choices for places to camp.

In addition to the federal, state and county campgrounds listed here, there's also a church-sponsored campground at Olowalu, which is described in that section.

State Parks Polipoli Spring State Recreation Area and Waianapanapa State Park, the only state parks on Maui with camping areas, both have tent sites and cabins. Permits are required. The maximum length of stay is five consecutive nights at each site, and tent camping is free.

Polipoli, in Upcountry, has one primitive cabin and a primitive road into it, which usually requires a 4WD vehicle. Waianapanapa, near Hana, has 12 housekeeping cabins that are very popular and must be reserved well in advance. The cost is $45 for up to four people, $55 for six people.

For camping permits or cabin reservations, contact the Division of State Parks (☎ 984-8109), State Office Building, 54 High St, Wailuku, HI 96793. Office hours are from 8 to noon and 1 to 4 pm weekdays.

County Parks Maui has three county parks that allow camping: Baldwin and Rainbow, both in the Paia area, and Kanaha, on the beach north of the airport.

Permits cost $3 per day (50¢ for children under 18), and camping is limited to three consecutive nights at each campground.

Permits are available by mail or in person from the Department of Parks & Recreation (☎ 243-7389), Camping Permit Office, 1580 Kaahumanu Ave, Wailuku, HI 96793. The office is in the War Memorial Complex at Baldwin High School in Wailuku.

Haleakala National Park Tent camping is allowed at Hosmer Grove, which is at the crater section of the park, and at Oheo Gulch on the coast south of Hana. They are both fine sites, though Oheo has no drinking water. There are no fees or permits required.

Tent camping is also allowed by permit inside the crater, and there are cabins as well. Full details are in the Haleakala section.

Each national park campground has a limit of three days a month.

ENTERTAINMENT
Maui's entertainment scene is second only to Oahu's, with a wide variety of music from rock and jazz to mellow Hawaiian guitar.

Casanova in Makawao sometimes has top-name musicians. Otherwise, most of the action is in Lahaina and at the resort hotels, especially in Kaanapali and Wailea. See the relevant destination sections for more information.

The new *Maui Arts & Cultural Center* in Kahului, which has both 300- and 1200-seat indoor theaters and a large outdoor amphitheater, is the venue for performances by the Maui Symphony Orchestra, Maui Academy of Performing Arts and other community theater and cultural organizations. It's also one of the hottest places in Hawaii for big-name concerts – recent performers have included Hootie & the Blowfish, Jackson Browne and Blues Traveler. For a current schedule of events, call the box office at ☎ 242-7469.

For Maui's gay community, Little Beach in Makena is a daytime meeting spot; *Hamburger Mary's* in Wailuku and Casanova's in Makawao (especially on Thursdays) are evening spots. There's also an Upcountry social club that meets regularly for movies, dinner or other activities and welcomes visitors; for information, call *Club Kula* (☎ 876-0000), a gay B&B in Kula.

The *Maui News* is the best source of current entertainment information, particularly the 20-page 'Maui Scene' insert in the Thursday paper and in the Sunday paper's more concise 'Calendar' page.

Hawaiiana
Luaus are held regularly in Lahaina, Kaanapali and Wailea. All include a buffet dinner with Hawaiian foods and a Polynesian show and cost around $55. The Old Lahaina Luau in Lahaina puts on one of the more authentic productions.

The Napili Kai Beach Club in Napili has Friday dinner shows that feature hula dancing by local children. There are free hula shows in Lahaina, Kaanapali and Wailea shopping centers. Details on specific luaus and hula shows are given throughout the chapter.

THINGS TO BUY

For local arts and crafts, some of the best deals are at the Lahaina Arts Society's gallery in Lahaina and at the Maui Crafts Guild in Paia. See the Lahaina and Paia sections for details.

Maui Blanc, Maui's own pineapple wine, is a decent-quality wine that makes a good gift. It sells for about $8 a bottle at liquor and grocery stores around the island.

Proteas are a Maui specialty. The best deal is to buy direct from the Upcountry farms where they are grown.

Several businesses sell food and flowers, including leis, proteas, papayas, pineapples, Maui onions and husked coconuts, which are agriculturally preinspected and delivered to the airport for you to pick up on your way out. Two such places are Take Home Maui (☎ 661-8067), 121 Dickenson St, Lahaina, and Airport Flower & Fruit (☎ 243-9367), 532 Keolani Place, Kahului.

GETTING THERE & AWAY

Air

The island's main airport is in Kahului. Maui also has two smaller commuter airports with scheduled air service: Kapalua West Maui Airport and Hana Airport.

For information on discounted tickets and air passes, see the Getting Around chapter in the front of the book.

Kahului Airport Hawaiian Airlines (☎ 871-6132) and Aloha Airlines (☎ 244-9071) fly directly to Kahului from Oahu, Kauai and the Big Island. Both airlines fly an average of twice hourly from Honolulu, with the last flight leaving Honolulu at 8 pm with Aloha and 10 pm with Hawaiian. From the Big Island, both airlines have three direct flights a day from Kona and Hawaiian Airlines also has two direct flights a day from Hilo. From Kauai, Aloha Airlines has four daily nonstop flights; all other Kauai-Maui flights go via Honolulu. One-way fares on either airline are $69, roundtrip fares are double that.

Mahalo Air (☎ 800-277-8333) flies between Honolulu and Kahului about a dozen times a day and from Kahului to both Molokai and Kona once a day; one-way fares are $55.

Island Air (☎ 800-652-6541) flies to Kahului from Honolulu a dozen times a day, and from Molokai, Lanai and Hana two to four times a day. One-way fares are $69.

From the US mainland, Kahului Airport is served by United, American and Delta airlines.

Kahului Airport has car rental booths, a lei stand, restaurant, cocktail lounge, snack bar, visitor information booth, gift shops and newsstand.

Kapalua West Maui Airport This is a small airfield with a 3000-foot runway that's incapable of handling jet aircraft. The airport is between Kapalua and Kaanapali, about two miles from each.

Island Air (☎ 800-652-6541), the main carrier flying into Kapalua West Maui, has a dozen flights a day from Honolulu; the first leaves Honolulu at 6:45 am, the last at 4:25 pm. The current fare is $69.

Trans Air (☎ 800-634-2094) flies between Honolulu and Kapalua West Maui four times a day and between Molokai and Kapalua twice a day. The one-way fares are $74.

Hana Airport Island Air flies to Hana twice daily from Honolulu, Kahului and Molokai. The fares are $91 one way.

Ferry

Expeditions (☎ 661-3756, 800-695-2624) runs a small ferry five times daily between Maui and Lanai. Not only is it much cheaper than flying, but if you take the boat in winter, there's a fair chance of seeing whales along the way. The boat leaves Lahaina Harbor from the public pier in front of the Pioneer Inn at 6:45 and 9:15 am and 12:45, 3:15 and 5:45 pm, arriving at Manele Boat Harbor in Lanai about an hour later. The boat leaves Lanai at 8 and 10:30 am and 2, 4:30 and 6:45 pm. The one-way fare is $25 for adults and $20 for children ages two to 11. Reservations can be made by phone in advance; tickets are purchased on the boat.

GETTING AROUND
To/From the Airport

TransHawaiian (☎ 877-0380) has an airport shuttle bus that leaves from the Kahului Airport on the hour between 9 am and 4 pm daily. The bus goes to Kaahumanu Center in Kahului ($1), where it's possible to connect onward to either the Kihei-Wailea or Lahaina-Kaanapali areas. The fare from the airport to either destination is $13.

In addition, Speedi Shuttle (☎ 875-8070) has airport transfers on demand, with advance reservations. The price depends on the destination and the size of the group. For example, the cost for two people is $20 to Wailea, $28 to Lahaina, while a single person pays $18 and $24 respectively. There's a courtesy phone at the baggage claim area.

The TransHawaiian bus, as well as taxi dispatchers, are found outside the baggage claim area.

Bus

Maui has no public bus service, but Trans-Hawaiian operates the following tourist-oriented shuttle routes. Schedules are subject to change, so it's wise to call (☎ 877-0380) before planning your day.

The 'Whalers Village Shopping Express' runs three times a day from major hotels in Wailea and Kihei directly to the Whalers Village shopping center in Kaanapali. The fare is $15 one way, but the return trip is free if you show a receipt for any purchase (even a pack of gum will do) from one of the Whalers Village shops.

The 'Maui Shopping Express' stops at many of the island's largest shopping centers. It operates half a dozen times a day between Kaanapali, Lahaina, the airport, Kihei, Wailea and the Maui Prince Hotel in Makena. Most of the buses transfer in Kahului at the Kaahumanu Center. Fares are on the high side, with a one-day pass costing $30. The one-way fare from the Lahaina or Wailea areas to Kahului (including the airport) is $10 to $13 and from Wailea to Lahaina or Kaanapali is $15; roundtrip fares are double.

The 'West Maui Shopping Express' shuttle operates throughout the day between the Ritz-Carlton in Kapalua and the Wharf Cinema Center in Lahaina. The first bus heads southbound from the Ritz at 8 am and northbound from Lahaina at 9:15 am. En route stops include the Whalers Village shopping center in Kaanapali, Embassy Suites in Honokowai, Kahana Gateway Shopping Center in Kahana and Napili Plaza in Napili. The cost is $1.

In addition, a double-decker 'Lahaina Express' shuttle makes numerous runs daily between Kaanapali and Lahaina for $1, and Wailea and Kaanapali both have free resort-wide shuttle services; see the respective destination sections for details.

Taxi

Taxi fares are regulated by the county. The minimum flag-down fare is $1.75; the first mile totals around $3.50, and each additional mile is about $1.75.

Approximate one-way fares from the Kahului airport are $5 to $10 to places around Kahului, $12 to Paia, $16 to $30 to Kihei, $45 to Lahaina, $50 to Kaanapali and $60 to Kapalua.

Car

Alamo (☎ 871-6235), Avis (☎ 871-7575), Budget (☎ 871-8811), Dollar (☎ 877-6526), Hertz (☎ 877-5167) and National (☎ 871-8851) all have booths at Kahului Airport.

Budget has a car rental booth at the Kapalua West Maui Airport, while Alamo, Avis, Dollar and National have offices on Hwy 30 in nearby Kaanapali and will pick up at that airport. Dollar is the only rental agency for Hana Airport.

For more information on the national chains, including toll-free numbers, look in the Getting Around chapter in the front of the book.

In Lahaina, Wheels R Us (☎ 667-7751), at 150 Lahainaluna Rd, rents older compact cars for $25/130 a day/week, jeeps for $40/215. Drivers under age 25 are charged $6 extra a day. If you don't have a credit card, a $300 cash deposit is accepted and you must purchase the otherwise optional $9 per-day CDW insurance.

MAUI

In Kahului, Word of Mouth (☎ 877-2436, 800-533-5929), 150 Hana Hwy, rents older cars for around $115 a week, and if they're not busy, they'll rent by the day for $20. Credit cards are required, and the minimum age is 25.

Bicycle & Moped

South Maui Bicycles (☎ 874-0068), 1993 S Kihei Rd, Kihei, rents quality mountain bikes for $17 for a 24-hour period, $79 for a week.

Kukui Activity Center (☎ 875-1151), at the back of the Kukui Mall in Kihei, rents mopeds for $28/125 a day/week and mountain bikes from $12 a day. They provide free pick-up in the Kihei-Wailea area.

Wheels R Us (☎ 667-7751), 150 Lahainaluna Rd, Lahaina, rents mopeds for $30/140 a day/week and mountain bikes for $9 a day (until 4 pm) or $15 for 24 hours.

A&B Moped Rental (☎ 669-0027), 3481 Lower Honoapiilani Rd, Honokowai, rents mopeds for $24 a day, mountain bikes from $15.

Other places that rent bicycles are West Maui Cycles, with shops in Lahaina (☎ 661-9005) and Kahana (☎ 669-1169), and Island Biker (☎ 877-7744) in Kahului.

Information on cycle tours is under Cycling in the earlier Activities section of this chapter.

Lahaina

In ancient times Lahaina was a royal court for Maui chiefs and the bread basket, or, more accurately, the breadfruit basket, of West Maui. After Kamehameha I unified the islands, he set up his base in Lahaina, and the capital remained there until 1845. Hawaii's first stone church, first missionary school and first printing press were all in place in Lahaina by the early 1830s.

The whaling years reached their height in Lahaina in the 1840s, with hundreds of ships pulling into port each year. The town took on the whalers' boisterous nature, opening dance halls, bars and brothels.

Hundreds of sick or derelict sailors, who had either been abandoned or jumped ship, roamed the streets. Herman Melville, who later penned *Moby Dick*, was among the multitudes that landed in Lahaina.

These days, Lahaina's streets are jammed with tourists. The old wooden shops that once housed saloons and provision stores are now crammed with boutiques and galleries.

While there are plenty of interesting historical sites to see, Lahaina is abuzz with commercial activity; if you're expecting something quaint and romantic, you may well be disappointed. The coastal setting and mountain backdrop *is* pretty, however, and it's easy to see why people have been drawn here. There are soft breezes off the water and fine sunset views of Lanai.

Orientation

Lahaina's chief attractions are 18th-century historical sites. Sightseeing spots include homes of missionaries, prisons for sailors and graveyards for both.

The focal point of Lahaina is its bustling small-boat harbor, which is backed by the old Pioneer Inn and Banyan Tree Square. Half of Lahaina's sights are clustered in this area, while the other half are scattered around town.

The main drag and tourist strip is Front St, which runs along the shoreline. If Front St seems too hectic, you can stroll inland a block or two to the residential streets, where you'll find Lahaina's quieter, more Hawaiian side.

Information

Tourist Offices The Lahaina Visitors Center, on the 1st floor of the Old Courthouse, has racks of tourist brochures and sells the University of Hawaii's Maui map and a few souvenir items. It's open from 9 am to 5 pm daily.

Money Bank of Hawaii in the Lahaina Shopping Center is open from 8:30 am to 3 pm Monday to Thursday, until 6 pm on Fridays. The First Hawaiian Bank has branches on the corner of Wainee and Papalaua Sts, and up on the Honoapiilani Hwy.

MAUI

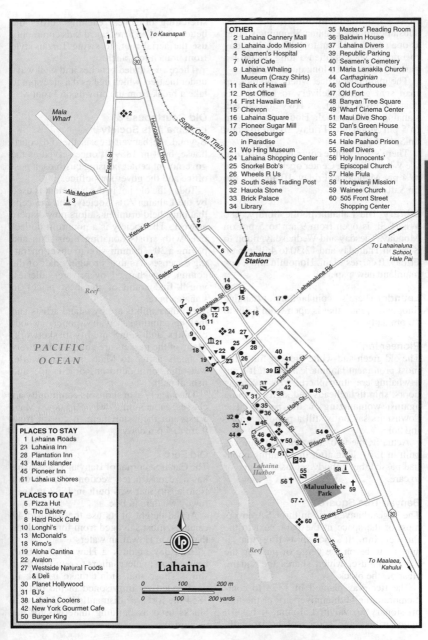

OTHER
2 Lahaina Cannery Mall
3 Lahaina Jodo Mission
4 Seamen's Hospital
7 World Cafe
9 Lahaina Whaling
   Museum (Crazy Shirts)
11 Bank of Hawaii
12 Post Office
14 First Hawaiian Bank
15 Chevron
16 Lahaina Square
17 Pioneer Sugar Mill
20 Cheeseburger
   in Paradise
21 Wo Hing Museum
24 Lahaina Shopping Center
25 Snorkel Bob's
26 Wheels R Us
29 South Seas Trading Post
32 Hauola Stone
33 Brick Palace
34 Library

35 Masters' Reading Room
36 Baldwin House
37 Lahaina Divers
39 Republic Parking
40 Seamen's Cemetery
41 Maria Lanakila Church
44 Carthaginian
46 Old Courthouse
47 Old Fort
48 Banyan Tree Square
49 Wharf Cinema Center
51 Maui Dive Shop
52 Dan's Green House
53 Free Parking
54 Hale Paahao Prison
55 Reef Divers
56 Holy Innocents'
   Episcopal Church
57 Hale Piula
58 Hongwanji Mission
59 Wainee Church
60 505 Front Street
   Shopping Center

PLACES TO STAY
1 Lahaina Roads
23 Lahaina Inn
28 Plantation Inn
43 Maui Islander
45 Pioneer Inn
61 Lahaina Shores

PLACES TO EAT
5 Pizza Hut
6 The Bakery
8 Hard Rock Cafe
13 McDonald's
18 Kimo's
19 Aloha Cantina
22 Avalon
27 Westside Natural Foods
   & Deli
30 Planet Hollywood
31 BJ's
38 Lahaina Coolers
42 New York Gourmet Cafe
50 Burger King

To Kaanapali

Mala
Wharf

Ala Moana

Reef

PACIFIC
OCEAN

Front St

Honoapiilani Hwy

Sugar Cane Train

Kenui St

Baker St

Papalaua St

Lahaina
Station

To Lahainaluna
School,
Hale Pai

Lahainaluna Rd

Dickenson St

Hale St

Luakini St

Prison St

Canal St

Wainee St

Lahaina
Harbor

Maluuluolele
Park

Shaw St

Reef

To Maalaea,
Kahului

Lahaina

0   100   200 m
0   100   200 yards

Post & Communications The post office substation in the Lahaina Shopping Center is open from 8:15 am to 4:15 pm Monday to Friday. There's often a long wait for a parking space and a long queue inside.

The main post office, where you pick up mail sent general delivery to Lahaina, is near the civic center, on Hwy 30 between Lahaina and Kaanapali. Hours are 8:30 am to 5 pm Monday to Friday, 10 am to noon on Saturdays.

There's also a little contract post office at the Wharf Cinema Center open from 10 am to 4 pm Monday to Friday, 10 am to 1 pm on Saturdays.

Library The Lahaina public library, 680 Wharf St, is open from 9 am to 5 pm on Monday, Tuesday and Wednesday, noon to 8 pm on Thursday and 12:30 to 4:30 pm on Friday. It carries Maui, Honolulu and a few mainland newspapers.

Laundry There's a coin laundry at Lahaina Shopping Center that is open from 6 am to 10 pm daily.

Pioneer Inn

The old green-and-white Pioneer Inn is the most prominent landmark in town. It's got a whaling-era atmosphere, with swinging doors, ship figureheads and signs warning against womanizing in the rooms. The downstairs saloon is still a popular watering hole.

Actually, the two-story Pioneer Inn was built in 1901, long after the whaling boom had passed, but nobody seems to notice or to care.

Banyan Tree Square

The largest banyan tree in the USA covers most of the space in the park next to the Pioneer Inn. It's so sprawling that it appears to be on the verge of pushing the old courthouse, which shares the square, clear off the block.

The tree was planted in 1873 to commemorate the 50th anniversary of the first missionary arrival in Lahaina. It has 16 major trunks and scores of horizontally stretching branches reaching across the better part of an acre. Local kids commonly use the aerial roots to swing Tarzan-style from branch to branch.

There are shaded benches and walkways under the tree, which makes it a nice spot to take a break from the crowds on Front St.

Old Courthouse & Lahaina Arts Society

Beyond the banyan tree is the old courthouse, built in 1859. It once served as the government center housing customs, a post office and the governor's office.

Today the old jail in the basement is used by the Lahaina Arts Society, and the cells that once held drunken sailors now display artwork. The society is a nonprofit collective, with artists donating their time and paying a 30% commission to cover operating expenses. As that's roughly half of the commission charged by private galleries, you'll find some of the best prices in Lahaina here.

All the exhibits are by island artists and include paintings, jewelry, pottery, woodcarvings and some quality basketwork. Many of the baskets are composed entirely of fibers native to Maui, such as wattle, watsonia, philodendron, draco, ape and fishtail palm.

The society also sponsors community art classes, and a number of well-known Maui artists got their start here. It's open from 9 am to 5 pm daily.

Old Fort

The Canal St corner of Banyan Tree Square has a reconstructed section of coral wall from a fort that was built in 1832 to keep rowdy whalers in line.

At the height of its use the fort had 47 cannons, most salvaged from foreign ships that sank in Hawaiian waters.

Each day at dusk a Hawaiian sentinel beat a drum to alert sailors to return to their ships. Those that didn't make it back in time ended up imprisoned in the fort. In 1854 the fort was dismantled and its coral blocks used as building materials for the new prison.

Canal St

Canal St, bordering Banyan Tree Square, used to be part of a canal system that ran through Lahaina. An enterprising US consul officer built this section of the canal in the 1840s to allow whalers easier access to fresh water supplies – for a fee, of course.

Because of problems with mosquitoes, most of the canal system was filled in long ago. Incidentally, Hawaii had no mosquitoes at all until the whalers brought them in from North America in their water barrels.

Lahaina Harbor

The four cannons on the waterfront opposite the old courthouse were raised from the wreck of a Russian ship that went down in Honolulu Harbor in 1816.

They now point directly at Lahaina's crowded small-boat harbor, which is filled with glassbottom boats, windjammers, sport fishing boats, whale-watchers and sunset sailboats. Booths lining the edge of the harbor sell tickets for most of the cruises, as do the ubiquitous activity booths around town.

The Carthaginian

In 1972, the 960-ton *Carthaginian*, one of the last square-riggers in Hawaii, was on its way from Maui to Honolulu for repairs when it hit a reef outside Lahaina Harbor and sank. The wooden-hulled *Carthaginian* belonged to a class of swift brigantines that made freight runs between New England, Hawaii and China in the 19th century.

The *Carthaginian* that now sits in Lahaina Harbor is a steel-hulled vessel that was converted into a replica of the original. After being brought to Lahaina in 1973, the 97-foot brig had to be completely restored and all the masts and yards handcrafted – a process that took a full seven years.

Although the most attractive view of the ship is from the outside, you can also board the boat for $3 for adults (no charge for accompanying children). Below deck there's a tiny theater where films on whales are shown continuously. It's open from 10 am to 4 pm daily.

Masters' Reading Room

The Masters' Reading Room, on the corner of Front and Dickenson Sts, is the office of the Lahaina Restoration Foundation (☎ 661-3262), the group most instrumental in preserving Lahaina's historical sites, including the Baldwin House, Wo Hing Temple and Hale Pai.

During the whaling years the building was a reading room for sea captains. From here they could keep an eye on happenings in the harbor across the road. The original construction of coral and stone blocks has been preserved.

Baldwin House

The Baldwin House, next door to the Masters' Reading Room, is the oldest building in Lahaina, built in 1834. It was home to the Reverend Dwight Baldwin, a missionary doctor. The exterior of the coral and rock building once resembled the Reading Room, but it has since been plastered over. The walls beneath the plaster are a full 24 inches thick, which keeps the house cool all year round.

It took the Baldwins 161 days to get to Hawaii from their native Connecticut. These early missionaries traveled neither fast nor light, and the house still holds the collection of china and furniture they brought with them around the Horn.

The entrance fee of $3 ($5 per family) includes a brief tour. It's open from 10 am to 4:30 pm daily, with the last tour beginning at 4:15 pm.

Library Area

The entire area surrounding the Lahaina public library was once the site of a royal taro field. It was also the location of the first Western-style building in Hawaii, the **Brick Palace**, erected by King Kamehameha I so he could keep watch on arriving ships. Despite the grand name, this 'palace' was a modest two-story structure built around 1800 by two Botany Bay convicts. All that remains today is the excavated foundation, which can be found on the ocean side of the library.

The nearby **Hauola Stone** is a water-worn lava stone on the shoreline. To spot it, look to the right as you face the ocean – it's the middle stone. The Hawaiians believed this flat, seat-shaped stone emitted healing powers to those who sat on it.

If you walk north down Front St past the library, there's a row of interesting **turn-of-the-century buildings** along the street, best appreciated from the sea wall sidewalk.

Wo Hing Temple

The Wo Hing Temple, on Front St, was built in 1912 by the Chinese community in Lahaina. This two-story building functioned largely as a meeting hall, though for a period after WWII it was also used as a home for elderly Chinese men.

As Lahaina's ethnic Chinese population declined, so too did the building. It was restored and turned into a museum by the Lahaina Restoration Foundation in 1983. There are cultural artifacts and period photos downstairs and a Taoist shrine upstairs.

The tin-roofed cookhouse next door (built detached because of the danger of fire) has been set up as a little theater that shows fascinating films taken in Hawaii by Thomas Edison during his visits to the islands in 1898 and 1905.

NED FRIARY
Whaling ship figurehead

Against the wall there's a collection of little opium bottles found during the clean-up of the grounds. The museum is open from 10 am to 4:30 pm Monday to Friday. Admission is free, though donations are appreciated.

Lahaina Whaling Museum

Lahaina Whaling Museum is a display of whaling-era artifacts along one wall of the Crazy Shirts store at 865 Front St. It's authentic, free and open from 9 am to 10 pm daily.

The collection includes antique harpoons, harpoon guns, scrimshaw and photos of the *Carthaginian* sinking outside Lahaina Harbor in 1972. The figurehead hanging from the ceiling in the front of the store was salvaged from the ship. It had been carved in 1965 to prepare the *Carthaginian* for its feature role in the movie *Hawaii*, the adaptation of James Michener's epic novel.

Outside on the back porch there's a rusty old cannon and anchor and a whaler's try-pot once used for boiling down blubber.

Holy Innocents' Episcopal Church

The interior of Holy Innocents' Episcopal Church, 561 Front St, is decorated with a Hawaiiana motif.

Paintings on the front of the koa altar depict a fisher in an outrigger canoe and Hawaiian farmers harvesting taro and breadfruit. Above the altar is a Hawaiian Madonna and Child; a Lahaina mother and infant were the models for the painting.

Until the turn of the century the church property was the site of a vacation home belonging to Queen Liliuokalani, Hawaii's last reigning monarch.

Hale Piula

A couple of steps and a grassy building foundation between the Episcopal Church and the 505 Front St shopping center is all that remains of Hale Piula, Lahaina's half-hearted attempt at a royal palace.

Construction on the palace was started in the late 1830s but never completed – Kamehameha III preferred to sleep in a

Hawaiian-style thatched house, and at any rate decided to move the capital to Honolulu halfway through the project. The building was used for a short time as a government office, but most of the stones were later carted away and used to build the harborside courthouse.

Maluuluolele Park

Maluuluolele Park, opposite Hale Piula, was once the site of a large pond containing a legendary *moo* (water dragon). An island in the center of the pond was home to Maui chiefs and at times to kings Kamehameha I, II and III. Called Mokuula, which means 'sacred island', it held an ornate burial chamber for royalty.

The park's present name is literally 'the breadfruit shade of Lele' ('Lele' was the ancient name for Lahaina).

In 1918 the island was leveled and the pond filled in. Today the park has basketball courts, tennis courts, a baseball field and not a hint of its fascinating past.

Wainee Church

Wainee Church, 535 Wainee St, was built in 1832 as the first stone church in Hawaii. It's gone through a barrage of changes since.

The steeple and bell collapsed in 1858. In 1894 the church was torched by royalists because its minister supported the annexation of Hawaii. A second church, built to replace the original, burned to the ground in 1947 and the third was blown away in a storm a couple of years later. One could get the impression that the old Hawaiian gods didn't take kindly to the house of this foreign deity!

The fourth version has been standing since 1953. It's now called Waiola Congregational Church and holds regular services.

The **cemetery** next door is more interesting than the church. Here lies Governor Hoapili, who ordered the original church built; Queen Keopuolani, once the highest ranking woman in Hawaii and wife of Kamehameha I; and the Reverend William Richards, Lahaina's first missionary. Some of the old tombstones have interesting inscriptions and photo cameos.

Hongwanji Mission

The Lahaina Hongwanji Mission, 551 Wainee St, was built in 1927. It's usually locked, but the front doors are glass so you can glance in. Unlike Buddhist temples in Japan, this one has rows of wooden pews. Services are held each Sunday in English and once a month in Japanese.

Hale Paahao Prison

Hale Paahao ('stuck-in-irons house'), Lahaina's old prison, was built in 1852 by convicts who dismantled the old harborside fort and carried the stone blocks here to construct these eight-foot-high prison walls.

Inside, one of the whitewashed cells has an authentic-looking 'old seadog' mannequin with a recorded story about 'life in this here calaboose'.

In another cell you'll find a list of offenses and arrests for the year 1855. The top three offenses were drunkenness (330 arrests), adultery and fornication (111) and 'furious riding' (89). Others include profanity, aiding deserting sailors, drinking awa and giving birth to bastard children. Hawaiians could collect bounties by turning in sailors that jumped ship or fooled around with local women. There's also a copy of a 16-year-old seaman's diary vividly describing his time spent in the prison. Admission is free.

Seamen's Cemetery

The Seamen's Cemetery on Wainee St is next to Maria Lanakila Church, the first Catholic church on Maui.

It's basically a local cemetery, with only one seaman's tombstone that can be identified. However, historical records indicate that numerous sailors from the whaling era were buried here, including a shipmate of Herman Melville's from the *Acushnet*.

Pioneer Sugar Mill

It's hard to think of tourist-jammed Lahaina as a sugar town, but it is. The Pioneer Sugar Mill has been a prominent part of Lahaina for 130 years, and its cane fields still stretch for 17 miles along the coast.

MAUI

The dusty mill, which sits on both sides of Lahainaluna Rd on the slopes above the town center, stands in sharp contrast to all the tourist activity below.

Lahainaluna Seminary

Lahainaluna Seminary, established by Christian missionaries in 1831, was the first US educational institution west of the Rockies.

One of the school's early graduates was David Malo, a respected Hawaiian philosopher. He became Hawaii's first native rights spokesperson, warning in his early writings in 1837 that Hawaii was about to be swallowed up by the masses of foreigners arriving on its shores. His book *Hawaiian Antiquities* is regarded as the best account of ancient Hawaiian history and culture.

Lahainaluna is now Lahaina's public high school, considered one of the finest in the state. Malo is buried on the hillside above the school.

The school is at the end of Lahainaluna Rd, 1⅓ miles above the mill. There's a nice view of Lahaina with Lanai in the background from the school's lower parking lot.

Hale Pai Hale Pai, a printing house on Lahainaluna's grounds, was the site of the first printing press in Hawaii. Although the main purpose of the press was to make the Bible available to Hawaiians, it also was used to produce other works, including the first Hawaiian botany book and, in 1834, Hawaii's first newspaper.

Examples of early books are on display at Hale Pai. You can use a replica of the original Ramage press to hand print your own copy of a page from the first Hawaiian primer.

Volunteers staff the building, and it's usually open from 9 am to 2 pm Monday to Friday. Admission is free but donations are appreciated.

Seamen's Hospital

In 1844 the building at 1024 Front St was leased by the US government and turned into a hospital for sick and abandoned seamen.

Officials at the hospital were notorious for embezzlement. Sailors who weren't sick and others long since dead were commonly signed onto the hospital books. A US warship with a board of inquiry was sent by the American government to investigate the corruption, but the ship and its findings mysteriously disappeared at sea on the return home!

The seamen's hospital has been completely restored and is now used as an office by Paradise Network, a local television station. A huge anchor on the lawn marks the site.

Lahaina Jodo Mission

A large bronze statue of Buddha overlooks the compound of Lahaina Jodo Mission, off the north end of Front St, just before the bridge. The statue was put up in 1968 in celebration of the centennial of Japanese immigration to Hawaii. With its back to the mountains, the Buddha looks out over the Pacific towards Japan.

Opposite the mission, in the sandy cemetery along the beach, the county has moved a number of graves that have been disinterred by high surf in the past few years.

Just to the north is the long **Mala Wharf**, constructed in the 1920s to allow inter-island ferries to land passengers directly ashore. It never made the grade. Rough seas prevented the ferries from pulling up alongside the pier, forcing them to continue shuttling passengers across the shallows of Lahaina Harbor in small boats.

The wharf is now crumbling and closed, though Mala does have a new launch ramp for small boats nearby.

Lahaina Beaches

Lahaina is not known for its beaches, which are largely shallow and rocky. The section near the Lahaina Shores is swimmable, but your best bet is to go north to Hanakaoo Beach Park or to Kaanapali. If you don't have a car, use the free trolley bus (see Lahaina's Getting Around section, later).

Places to Stay

Hotels & Condos *Maui Islander* (☎ 667-9766, 800-367-5226; fax 661-3733), 660 Wainee St, Lahaina, HI 96761, is a 372-unit sprawling hotel set back a few blocks from Front St. The hotel is standard fare without a great deal of character. Rooms have cable TV, air-con, ceiling fans and safes. There's a pool, a tennis court and a barbecue area. Rates are $84 for a room with a refrigerator, $96 for a studio with kitchen and $114 (for up to three people) for a one-bedroom suite. You can add on a rental car for $20 more a day, or $10 a day if you stay six nights or more.

You couldn't be more in the middle of the action than at the *Pioneer Inn* (☎ 661-3636, 800-457-5457; fax 667-5708), 658 Wharf St, Lahaina, HI 96761. It can be noisy from the traffic, the throngs of tourists and the raucous bar, but this two-story, turn-of-the-century hotel has plenty of character. However, the funky old harborfront rooms for which the inn was best known are no longer available. Instead, there are a few dozen renovated rooms in the newer wing facing Front St and Banyan Square. These rooms are reasonably comfortable, with queen beds, lanais, air-con and private baths, but pricey at $90 to $120.

The best-value condo in the Lahaina area is *Lahaina Roads* (☎ 661-3166, 800-624-8203), 1403 Front St, Lahaina, HI 96761, north of the town center, near the Lahaina Cannery Mall. All of its 42 units are oceanfront with full kitchens, lanais, TVs and phones with free local calls. There's a beachside swimming pool. Roomy one-bedroom units have a sofa bed in the living room and cost $100 for up to four people. There's a 10% discount for seven nights or more. The minimum stay is three days.

Lahaina Shores (☎ 661-4835, 800-628-6699; fax 661-1025), 475 Front St, Lahaina, HI 96761, is a 155-room condo run like a hotel. It's on the beach next to the 505 Front St shopping center, at the south side of town. Mountain-view studios cost $110/120 in the low/high season, one-bedroom units cost $135/160. Add on another $20/30 low/high for an ocean view. There's a small pool.

The *Lahaina Inn* (☎ 661-0577, 800-669-3444; fax 667-9480), 127 Lahainaluna Rd, Lahaina, HI 96761, is a restored turn-of-

the-century hotel, a project of Crazy Shirts owner Rick Ralston, who spent over $3 million restoring this 13-room hostelry. The rooms are small but delightfully atmospheric – each has hardwood floors, floral wallpaper, antique furnishings and a lanai. Modern conveniences include air-con, private bath, telephone and piped-in classical music, but no TV. Room rates are $89 and $99, while suites are $129. Prices, which include continental breakfast, are the same for singles and doubles. Children under the age of 15 are not allowed.

The *Plantation Inn* (☎ 667-9225, 800-433-6815; fax 667-9293), 174 Lahainaluna Rd, Lahaina, HI 96761, is an elegant two-story Victorian-style inn with hardwood floors, antique furnishings, stained glass and a tiled pool. The 18 rooms and suites range from $119 to $219 in the high season, about 15% less in the low season. Classy and comfortable, it's arguably the nicest place to stay in Lahaina. Prices include a continental breakfast at Gerard's, the restaurant at the front of the inn.

B&Bs *Aloha Lani Inn* (☎ 661-8040; fax 661-8045; tony@maui.net), 13 Kauaula Rd, Box 11475, Lahaina, HI 96761, about a two-minute walk south of Lahaina Shores, is a modest home with a couple of guest rooms that cost $55/65 for singles/doubles. There's a two-night minimum. Breakfast is not included, but guests are allowed kitchen privileges.

More comfortable is the *Old Lahaina House* (☎ 667-4663, 800-847-0761; fax 667-5615), Box 10355, Lahaina, HI 96761, also just a few minutes south of Lahaina Shores. Sherry and John Barbier have four guest rooms in their home. Two rooms have king beds, private baths and refrigerators and rent for $85/95 for singles/doubles. The other three rooms, which cost $60/69, each have two twin beds and share a bath. All five rooms have TV and air-con, and there's a pool out back. Except on Sundays, a breakfast of pastries and fruit is included in the rates.

The following B&Bs are in a pleasant residential area about four miles north of

MAUI

Lahaina just inland from Hwy 30, a 10-minute walk from Wahikuli beach park.

House of Fountains (☎ 667-2121, 800-789-6865; fax 667-2120), 1579 Lokia St, Lahaina, HI 96761, is an attractive 7000-sq-foot contemporary residence with six pleasant rooms. All have TV/VCRs, air-con, ceiling fans, queen beds, private baths and mini-refrigerators. The smallest is $85 a day while the largest, a commodious suite, costs $115. Guests share a large, well-equipped kitchen, laundry facilities, a pool and jacuzzi. A full breakfast, which includes cold cuts and other European-style fixings, is served on the ocean-view deck. German is spoken. All in all, it's a real find for travelers looking for a touch of luxury in a personal setting.

The GuestHouse (☎ 661-8085, 800-621-8942; fax 661-1896), 1620 Ainakea Rd, Lahaina, HI 96761, is another upmarket contemporary home set up as a B&B. It has four roomy suites, each with a private lanai, air-con, TV, ceiling fan, refrigerator, phone, queen bed and either a hot tub or a jacuzzi. Three of the rooms also have a twin bed. Singles/doubles cost $85/89. There's also a simpler room for $55/59 with TV, refrigerator, air-con and shared bath. Guests have access to laundry facilities and the use of beach gear, ranging from suntan lotion to snorkel sets. Breakfast is included in the rates.

More casual is *Garden Gate Bed & Breakfast* (☎ 661-8800; fax 667-7999; ggbb@maui.net), Box 12321, Lahaina, HI 96761, in the home of Welmoet and Ron Glover. A private studio in the back of the house has a queen bed, sofa bed, TV/VCR, fan, air-con, cooking facilities and phone for $95. For those who enjoy being part of the family scene, there's also a small room in the main house that has a double bed, fan, air-con and shared bath for $55. Breakfast is included in both rates. There's a hot tub and shared use of a washer and dryer.

Camping The nearest campground is in Olowalu, five miles south of Lahaina. Details are in the Olowalu section.

Places to Eat – budget

The Bakery, on Limahana Place on the north side of town, is Lahaina's best bakery. In addition to freshly baked bread, they have huge sticky buns and muffins for under $2 and sandwiches made to order for $5. It opens at 5:30 am daily, closing at 3 pm on weekdays, 2 pm on Saturdays and noon on Sundays. To get there, turn mauka off Hwy 30 onto Hinau St at Pizza Hut.

New York Gourmet Cafe, a reasonably priced deli at 180 Dickenson St, serves a variety of salads and sandwiches for $5 to $7. It also has breakfast items, including French toast and eggs, and deli specials such as chicken cutlets. Hours are from 7 am to 10 pm daily.

Westside Natural Foods & Deli, 193 Lahainaluna Rd, sells organic produce, yogurt, fresh juice and a variety of bulk trail mixes and granolas. There's a salad bar and a few hot vegetarian dishes for $5 a pound and good vegetarian sandwiches for $3.50. It's open from 7:30 am to 9 pm, except on Sundays when it's open from 8:30 am to 8 pm.

Lahaina has numerous fast-food restaurants, including *Burger King* at 632 Front St; *McDonald's*, on the corner of Wainee and Papalaua Sts; and *Pizza Hut* on Hwy 30.

The Wharf Cinema Center on Front St has a *Subway Sandwiches* shop, an *Orange Julius*, a *TCBY* frozen yogurt shop, a pancake place and an inexpensive Korean restaurant.

Lahaina Square, off Wainee St, has a *Foodland* supermarket, a 24-hour *Denny's* restaurant, *Jack in the Box* and *Maui Tacos*.

Lahaina Cannery Mall, in a former pineapple cannery on the northern side of town between Front St and Hwy 30, has a 24-hour *Safeway* supermarket with takeout salads and good deli, produce and wine sections. The mall also has an inexpensive Greek eatery, a moderately priced Mexican restaurant and a cafe with fresh ground coffee and deli fare.

Places to Eat – middle

Lahaina Coolers, 180 Dickenson St, has good food at reasonable prices with a varied menu that includes salads for $3 to $8 and creative pizza, pasta and Thai dishes, most priced from $10 to $12. You can also get burgers and fries for a few dollars less. From 7 to 11:15 am daily there's an extensive breakfast menu, with egg dishes, pancakes and lox and bagels. It's open until midnight daily.

Kimo's, 845 Front St, is a popular oceanfront restaurant with a sunset view. Lunch is mainly sandwiches in the $6 to $10 range, while dinner features chicken, seafood and steaks for $15 to $20, including Caesar salad and warm muffins. Lunch is from 11 am to 3 pm and dinner from 5 to 10:30 pm.

The *Hard Rock Cafe*, 900 Front St, has good burgers and sandwiches, including a vegie burger, club sandwich or bacon-guacamole cheeseburger for around $7. All come with fries and a green salad. There are also a few hot dishes such as steak, barbecued chicken and fajitas for $11 to $15. Food is served daily from 11:30 am to 10 pm. Expect a bit of a wait at mealtimes, when a line often forms outside the door.

The trendiest place to be seen is *Planet Hollywood* at 744 Front St. The restaurant has a celluloid decor and Hollywood stockholders who make cameo appearances when they're on the island. Among those who occasionally show their face are Arnold Schwarzenegger, Sylvester Stallone and Melanie Griffith. A Cajun chicken sandwich, barbecue pizza or Asian salad costs $10; fajitas, ribs and pastas are a few dollars more. You can also just go in and linger over a beer. It's open from 11 am to midnight, but meal service ends at 10:30 pm.

BJ's (☎ 661-0700), 730 Front St, is a southern California chain restaurant serving Chicago-style pizza. You can get a large cheese pizza for $12.50 (add $1.50 for each topping) and sandwiches and pastas from $7. Until 4 pm there's a lunch special of a mini-pizza and salad for $6.25. It's open daily from 11 am to late at night and has a 2nd-floor ocean view.

Aloha Cantina, 839 Front St, has oceanfront dining and Tex-Mex food at moderate prices. There are numerous plates, such as two tacos or enchiladas with rice and beans, for around $12. It's open for lunch and dinner from 11 am to 10 pm.

Places to Eat – top end

Longhi's (☎ 667-2288), 888 Front St, is one of Lahaina's busiest upper-end restaurants. At lunch, sandwiches and pastas begin at around $8, while seafood dishes such as fresh ahi and prawns amaretto average $12. The same seafood dishes cost $20 to $24 at dinner, and the pastas start around $13. Longhi's has an extensive wine list and is open from 7:30 am to 10 pm.

Avalon (☎ 667-5559), 844 Front St, features Hawaiian Regional cuisine. Although not always consistent, the food is usually good for the price. For starters, the summer rolls in Thai peanut sauce and the Indonesian satay are a treat at $6. There are vegetarian dishes such as salads or gado-gado over brown rice for around $10, chicken dishes for under $20 and seafood and steaks for a bit more. If you dine from 5 to 6 pm there's sometimes an early-bird special featuring half off the second dinner. Avalon is open from 11:30 am to 10:30 pm daily.

David Paul's Lahaina Grill (☎ 667-5117), at 127 Lahainaluna Rd in the historic Lahaina Inn, is a popular fine dining spot with excellent Pacific Rim cuisine and an intimate setting. A specialty here is the spicy tequila shrimp with firecracker rice for $27. Other main courses range from butternut ravioli ($19) to lobster risotto ($38). Appetizers such as seared ahi salad or Thai-style oysters cost $13. There's also a prix fixe meal that includes appetizer, entree, dessert and coffee for $45. It's open for dinner only, from 6 to 10 pm nightly.

Pacific'O (☎ 667-4341), 505 Front St, has an ocean view and imaginative food. Appetizers include sashimi or a salad of Kula-grown greens with grilled tofu and warm shiitake dressing for under $10. Main dinner dishes range from kiawe-grilled chicken in a garlic black bean sauce for $15 to imu-style fish for $23. At lunch there are simpler offerings such as fish & chips, sandwiches and fries, or Oriental chicken salad for under $10. It's open from

MAUI

11 am to 4 pm for lunch, 5:30 to 10 pm for dinner.

Gerard's (☎ 661-8939) serves traditional French country cooking in a pleasant setting at the Plantation Inn, 174 Lahainaluna Rd. The menu changes regularly, but rack of lamb and comfit duck are house standards; à la carte entrees range from $23 to $30. It's open for dinner only, from 6 to 9:30 pm daily.

Entertainment

Lahaina has lots of action, most of it on Front St.

World Cafe (☎ 661-1515) at the Lahaina Center, 900 Front St, is a happening place for live music, with the island's top reggae, rock and contemporary Hawaiian bands. It occasionally gets some big names – Hootie & the Blowfish did an impromptu jam here in 1996. There's usually a $5 cover charge.

Longhi's (☎ 667-2288), 888 Front St, has a good dance floor but doesn't have entertainment every week. When something is happening, it's usually live rock bands from 10:30 pm on Friday and Saturday, with a cover charge of $5 to $10, depending on the band.

Cheeseburger in Paradise (☎ 661-4855), 811 Front St, usually has two groups nightly, one from 4:30 to 7:30 pm and the other from 8 to 11 pm. Expect mellow rock and easy-listening sounds, Jimmy Buffett style. There's no cover charge.

Pacific' O (☎ 667-4341), overlooking the beach at 505 Front St, has live jazz from 9 pm to midnight on Thursdays, Fridays and Saturdays, with no cover charge.

Aloha Cantina (☎ 661-8788), 839 Front St, has live music on Friday and Sunday nights, usually folk and soft rock, and there's no cover.

There's a free Hawaiian/Tahitian dance show at 2 pm on Wednesdays and Fridays at the Lahaina Center at 900 Front St and a free keiki hula show at 1 pm on Sundays at the Lahaina Cannery Mall.

Luaus The Old Lahaina Luau (☎ 667-1998), on the beach behind the Lahaina Cannery Mall, has a buffet dinner with open bar, Hawaiian music and a show from 5:30 to 8:30 pm nightly. The cost is $57 for adults, half-price for children ages 12 and under.

Cinemas Lahaina Cinemas at the Wharf Cinema Center and Front Street Theatres at the Lahaina Center (both ☎ 661-3347) are multiscreen theaters showing first-run movies.

The Hawaii Experience Domed Theater (☎ 661-8314), 824 Front St, shows a 40-minute film about Hawaii on a giant 180° screen on the hour from 10 am to 10 pm daily. It costs $7 for adults, $4 for children ages four to 12.

Things to Buy

Lahaina has numerous arts and crafts galleries, some with high-quality collections and others more mediocre. A good place to start is the Lahaina Arts Society, a Maui collective with an extensive gallery in the old harborside courthouse.

'Art Night', held from 6:30 to around 9 pm on Fridays, is the time when Lahaina galleries schedule their openings, occasionally with entertainment and hors d'oeuvres.

South Seas Trading Post, 780 Front St, stands apart from all the gaudy tourist shops on Front St. It sells Tongan tapa, Papua New Guinean face masks and items from Southeast Asia. The collection depends on the owner's last jaunt abroad, but is always intriguing.

Dan's Green House, at 133 Prison St, sells *fuku-bonsai*, created when the roots of the common house plant schefflera (octopus tree) grow around a lava rock becoming quasi-bonsai. They are treated for export and cost from $25.

Getting Around

Shuttle Bus The Lahaina Express shuttles between the Wharf Cinema Center in Lahaina and the Kaanapali resort, a ride of about 20 minutes. The fare is $1, and the bus runs in each direction about once every 45 minutes. The first southbound bus leaves the Whalers Village shopping center in Kaanapali at 9:30 am, and the last leaves at 9:15 pm.

Parking Finding a space for your car in Lahaina can be a challenge. Front St has on-street parking, but there's always a line of cruising cars. Your best bet is the corner of Front and Prison Sts, where there's free public parking with a three-hour limit. There are also a few private parking lots, the biggest being Republic Parking on Dickenson St, which charges $1.50 for up to two hours, $6 all day and $1 for overnight parking.

LAHAINA TO MAALAEA

The stretch between Lahaina and Maalaea has pretty mountain scenery, but during winter most people are craning their necks to look seaward as they drive along. This is a prime whale-watching road.

Launiupoko Wayside Park

Launiupoko Wayside Park, 2½ miles south of Lahaina, is most popular as a picnic spot and as a place to watch the sun set behind Lanai. There are showers, toilets, picnic tables, changing rooms and a pay phone.

Olowalu

There's little to mark Olowalu other than Olowalu General Store and a seemingly misplaced expensive French restaurant named *Chez Paul*.

When the water is calm, there's good snorkeling around the 14-mile marker, south of the general store. The coral reef here is large and shallow, and there's a narrow sandy beach to lie on, though be careful of kiawe thorns.

Olowalu, which means 'many hills', has a lovely setting with cane fields backed by the West Maui Mountains.

Camping *Camp Pecusa* (☎ 661-4303), 800 Olowalu Village, Lahaina, HI 96761, run by the Episcopal Church, has a low-profile 'tentground' available to individuals on a first-come first-served basis. It's at the side of a cane field, half a mile south of the Olowalu General Store, on the makai side of the road. Camping is on dirt but in shade and along a beach.

The campground is very basic, but it does have a solar-heated shower, a couple

> **The Olowalu Massacre**
> Olowalu Beach was the site of an infamous massacre in 1790. After a skiff was stolen from the US ship *Eleanora* and burned for its iron nails and fittings, Captain Simon Metcalfe retaliated by tricking the Hawaiians into sailing out in their canoes to trade. He then gunned them down with his cannons, killing an estimated 100 people. ∎

of outhouses, drinking water and picnic tables. A caretaker lives on the grounds, making this the most secure place in Maui to camp. No alcohol is allowed, and there's a maximum stay of seven nights in any 30-day period. They don't take advance reservations, but there's usually space available. The cost is $5 per person per night.

Papawai Point

The whole area between Olowalu and Makena is humpback cow/calf waters, and in the winter whale watching can be fantastic from the shore.

There are a couple of inconspicuous roadside lookouts just south of the 10-mile marker, but they are unmarked and difficult to negotiate when there's heavy traffic. Your best bet is to drive a little farther to Papawai Point, a clearly marked scenic lookout with a big parking lot.

Because the point juts into the waters at the western edge of Maalaea Bay, a favored humpback nursing ground, it's a good whale-sighting spot. Papawai Point is also good for sunsets, with Lanai, Kahoolawe and Molokini visible.

The popular bumper sticker 'I Brake For Whales' has particular significance along this stretch of road. Although they are usually spotted farther offshore, humpbacks occasionally breach as close as 100 yards from the coast. Forty tons of whale suddenly exploding straight up through the water can be a real showstopper! Unfortunately, some of the drivers whose heads are jerked oceanward by the sight slam on their brakes and others don't, with rear-ender potential.

MAUI

MAUI

LAHAINA TO KAANAPALI

On the stretch from Lahaina to Kaanapali the driving can be aggressive and traffic often jams up, particularly during morning and late-afternoon rush hours.

Sugar Cane Train

The old train that once carried sugar cane from the fields to the mill has been restored and now takes tourists on a joy ride through the cane fields between Kaanapali and Lahaina.

At the Kaanapali end, the train can be boarded on the mauka side of Hwy 30 off Puukolii Rd. To get to the Lahaina station, turn up Hinau St off Hwy 30 at Pizza Hut.

From the Wharf Cinema Center, a free bus connects with Lahaina station departures, while the free Kaanapali resort shuttle services the Kaanapali station.

The train (☎ 661-0089), which makes the six-mile journey six times a day, takes about half an hour each way and costs $13.50 roundtrip or $9.50 one way. Children ages three to 12 are half price.

Wahikuli Wayside Beach Park

There's a wayside park on a narrow strip of beach between the highway and the ocean, two miles north of Lahaina. With a gift for prophecy, the Hawaiians aptly named this coastal stretch Wahikuli or 'noisy place'.

The beach is mostly backed by a black-rock retaining wall, though there's a small sandy area. If you don't mind the traffic noise, the swimming conditions are usually fine. There are showers, restrooms, picnic tables and a pay phone.

Across the street from the beach is Lahaina's civic center, police station and main post office.

Hanakaoo Beach Park

Hanakaoo Beach Park is a long sandy beach just south of Kaanapali Beach Resort. As with all public beach parks, the parking here is free.

The park has full facilities and a lifeguard on duty daily. The beach has a sandy bottom, and water conditions are usually quite safe for swimming. However, southerly swells, which sometimes develop in the summer, can create powerful waves and shorebreaks, while the occasional kona storm can kick up rough water conditions in winter.

You can snorkel down by the second clump of rocks on the south side of the beach park or walk a few minutes north to the Hyatt and snorkel out by the green buoy.

Hanakaoo Beach is also called Canoe Beach, as the Lahaina, Kahana and Napili canoe clubs all store their canoes here. You can see them paddling up and down the coast in the early mornings and late afternoons. It's a pretty scene.

Kaanapali

Kaanapali is a high-rise resort community. Despite the opulence of some of its hotels, the overall development is rather generic – the influence is as much southern Californian as Hawaiian.

In the late 1950s, Amfac, owner of the Pioneer Sugar Mill, earmarked 600 acres of relatively barren sugar cane land for development as the first resort outside Waikiki. The first hotels, the Royal Lahaina and the Sheraton Maui, opened in 1962.

Now Kaanapali Beach is lined with six oceanfront hotels, each with its own shops and restaurants. The resort also includes six condominiums, two 18-hole golf courses, 40 tennis courts and the Whalers Village shopping center.

Kaanapali has three miles of sandy beach and offers pleasant views across the Auau Channel to Lanai and Molokai.

While Kaanapali is not a 'getaway' in the sense of avoiding the crowds, it has its quieter niches. The north side of Black Rock and the condos up around the golf course are less bustling than the central beach area.

Beach Walk

A mile-long beach walk runs between the Hyatt and the Sheraton. In addition to the coastal scenery, both the Hyatt and the

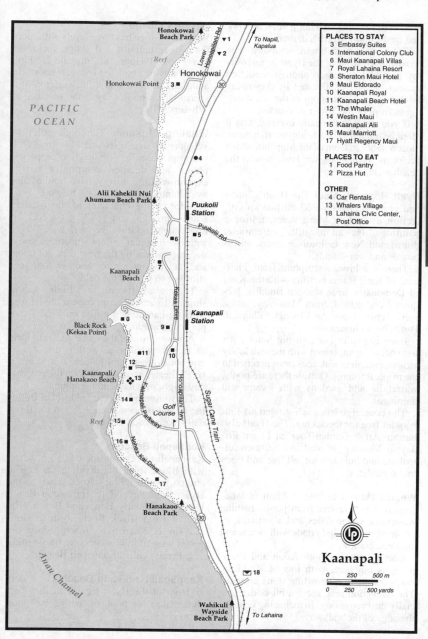

Kaanapali

Westin have some striking garden artwork and landscaping worth a detour.

The 17-foot-high bronze sculpture 'The Acrobats' in front of the Hyatt is noteworthy and makes a nice photo silhouetted against the sunset. Created by Australian John Robinson, it's a copy of the one standing in front of the Tower of London.

If you stroll in the early evening, you'll often be treated to beachside entertainment, most notably in front of the Marriott, which performs its luau on the lawn beside the beach walk.

Hyatt Regency Maui The Hyatt's lobby and grounds contain a $2 million art collection, including Ming vases, Balinese paintings, Hawaiian quilts, ceremonial drums and New Guinean artifacts, storyboards and war shields.

There's a bronze sculpture from Thailand of King Rama battling with the King of Demons; a large wooden Buddha, lacquered and gilded, from Mandalay; and a spirit figure from the Misingi village in Papua New Guinea.

Even if you're not into big hotels, it's hard not to be impressed with the lush lobby atrium, complete with cockatoos perched in the tropical foliage. Outside there are pools, waterfalls and gardens with swans and flamingos.

The concierge has a self-guided art tour booklet free for the asking. The Hyatt also has an 'Art & Garden Tour' at 11 am Friday to Monday, as well as afternoon lei-making and hula lessons, all free and open to the public.

Westin Maui The Westin Maui is landscaped with five free-form pools, rushing waterfalls, water slides and a network of artificial streams and ponds with swans and crowned cranes.

Garden statuary, both Asian and European, is big here, with lots of Buddhas, vases and pairs of growling stone animals. The collection may seem a bit odd, especially the bronze dogs in menacing poses at the edge of the walkways.

Whalers Village

Whalers Village has three levels with more than 50 restaurants and shops, including Fox Photo 1-Hour Lab, upscale clothing stores, a wine shop and souvenir shops. In addition, you can find a full skeleton of a sperm whale on display at the entrance to Whalers Village.

Whaling Museum The high point of Whalers Village is its small but top-notch whaling museum. A collection of period photos and detailed interpretive boards explain whaling history, from how whales were hunted to the uses of whale oil.

A lot of the character of the whalers comes through, and you'll get a feel for how rough and dirty the work was. Wages were so low that sailors sometimes owed the ship money by the time they got home and had to sign up for another four-year stint just to pay off the debt.

There are harpoons, logs from whaling ships, all sorts of scrimshaw, a model of a whaling barque and a film on whales that plays continuously.

A newer wing of the museum has models of various whales, as well as displays of jaw bones, teeth and baleen. It also has a small theater showing films on the present-day plight of whales and dolphins.

The museum is on the 3rd level of Building G and is open from 9:30 am to 10 pm daily. Admission is free.

Kaanapali Beaches

Kaanapali can be considered two beaches, with Black Rock the dividing mark. The stretch south of Black Rock down to the Hyatt (and beyond to Hanakaoo Beach Park) is officially Hanakaoo Beach. The stretch from Black Rock north to Honokowai is Kaanapali Beach. Since the resort was built, however, the whole thing is generally called Kaanapali Beach.

Kaanapali/Hanakaoo Beach The waters in front of the Hyatt have a shallow reef that makes for poor swimming but good snorkeling.

Much of the stretch between the Sheraton and the Hyatt can be dangerous, particularly on the point in front of the Marriott, where strong currents sometimes develop. As a general rule, waters are rougher in winter, though actually the worst conditions can occur in early summer if there's a southerly swell. Be careful in rough surf, as the waves can pick you up and bounce you onto the coral reef that runs from the southern end of the Westin down to the Hyatt. Check with the hotel beach huts for the day's water conditions.

Black Rock Black Rock, also known as Kekaa Point, is the rocky lava promontory that protects the beach in front of the Sheraton. This is Kaanapali's safest and best spot for swimming and snorkeling.

You can snorkel along the southern side of Black Rock, where there's some nice coral and schools of fish that are used to being fed. The real prize, however, is the horseshoe cove cut into the tip of the rock, where there's more pristine coral, abundant tropical fish and a family of eagle rays.

There's often a current to contend with off the point, which can make getting to the cove a little risky, but when it's calm you can swim right around into the horseshoe. Check with the Sheraton beach hut or snorkelers in the water regarding current conditions. Black Rock is also a popular shore dive spot. If you want to see what the horseshoe cove looks like, you can peer down into it by taking the short footpath from the Sheraton beach to the top of Black Rock.

Alii Kahekili Nui Ahumanu This new beach park at the north side of Kaanapali Beach is dedicated to Kahekili Nui Ahumanu, the last king of Maui. The park, which is on a nice section of the beach, has free parking, showers, changing rooms, toilets, a covered picnic pavilion and barbecue grills.

To get there from Honoapiilani Hwy, turn left onto Kai Ala Drive (opposite Puukolii Rd) and then bear right. The

---

Souls Leap

According to traditional Hawaiian beliefs, Kekaa Point, the westernmost point of Maui, is a place where the spirits of the dead leap into the unknown and are carried to their ancestral homeland.

The rock itself is said to have been created during a scuffle between the demigod Maui and a commoner who questioned Maui's superiority. Maui chased the man to this point, killed him, turned his body into rock and cast his soul out to sea. ■

---

waters here are open ocean, but inshore it's usually calm and good for swimming.

This is a good walking beach. If you walk north for about 20 minutes, there's a reef around Honokowai Point with clear waters that are good for snorkeling when it's calm.

Places to Stay

All Kaanapali accommodations are either on the beach or within walking distance of it, and all have the expected amenities, including swimming pools.

International Colony Club (☎ 661-4070; fax 661 5856), 2750 Kalapu Drive, Lahaina, HI 96761, has 44 freestanding cottages spread over 10 acres. They are nice and spacious with big lanais and have phones (free local calls) and cable TV. The complex is about 30 years old and was one of the first in Kaanapali, back when tastes were simpler and the island wasn't as crowded. There are two large heated swimming pools. One-bedroom units cost $105 and two-bedroom units are $125; there's no extra per-person cost, and some of the units can hold up to six people.

Maui Kaanapali Villas (☎ 667-7791, 800-922-7866), 45 Kai Ala Drive, Lahaina, HI 96761, is an Aston property on the edge of Kaanapali, 200 yards south of Alii Kahekili Nui Ahumanu Beach Park. As is common with Aston properties, rooms are individually owned, and overall it's of a less meticulous standard than other Kaanapali properties. Hotel rooms with refrigerators cost $125/145 in the low/high season, and studios with kitchens start at $155/180.

Kaanapali Beach Hotel (☎ 661-0011, 800-262-8450; fax 667-5978; mauikbh@ aloha.net), 2525 Kaanapali Pkwy, Lahaina, HI 96761, has an enviable beachside location near Black Rock. The hotel's 430 rooms are spread across a number of three- to six-story wings. While it's an older complex, it's well maintained and is pleasantly low-key. The rooms have lanais, refrigerators, safes and TVs. Prices start at $145 for a garden view, $190 for an ocean view. If you ask for the 'Free Ride' special, the rate includes a free rental car.

Maui Eldorado (☎ 661-0021, 800-688-7444; reservations@outrigger.com), 2661 Kekaa Drive, Lahaina, HI 96761, is a low-rise condo complex up the hill from the beach. It has a slower pace and a friendlier atmosphere than the big resort hotels. The units are individually owned, so they vary, but some are quite nicely furnished, with wallpapered bathrooms, wicker furniture and the like. The studios are big, with kitchens completely set apart from the bedrooms, and start at $145/160 in the low/ high season, while one-bedroom units for four people start at $170/200.

Kaanapali Royal (☎ 661-4804, 800-688-7444; reservations@outrigger.com), 2560 Kekaa Drive, Lahaina, HI 96761, is a low-rise condo complex with large, comfortable units. It has an unhurried hillside location near the golf course, a few minutes' walk from the beach. The condos are smartly furnished, each with a full kitchen and a sunken living room with a sofa bed. The one-bedroom units start at $150/165 in the low/high season for up to four people, the two-bedroom units from $175/190 for up to six people.

Royal Lahaina Resort (☎ 661-3611, 800-447-6925; fax 661-3538), 2780 Kekaa Drive, Lahaina, HI 96761, has 540 rooms on a broad stretch of beach on the north side of Black Rock. Standard rooms in the high-rise section cost from $195. Cottages, which are nicely clustered and spread out

down to the beach, cost from $255. The resort has 11 tennis courts and three pools.

The Whaler (☎ 661-4861, 800-367-7052), 2481 Kaanapali Pkwy, Lahaina, HI 96791, is a 360-unit high-rise condo complex that looks rather boxy from the outside but is quite pleasant inside, with marble baths, private lanais and modern amenities. Studios with garden views cost $195 in the high season. There are also one-bedroom units from $245 and two-bedroom units from $325.

The *Maui Marriott* (☎ 667-1200, 800-228-9290; fax 667-0692), 100 Nohea Kai Drive, Lahaina, HI 96761, has 720 guest rooms in two long high-rises. Regular rack rates start at $270, but there are often cheaper package deals that include breakfast and a car. It's pleasant enough, but not exceptional for the price.

The *Sheraton Maui Hotel* (☎ 661-0031, 800-325-3535; fax 661-0458), 2605 Kaanapali Pkwy, Lahaina, HI 96761, has the prime beach spot, behind Black Rock. Completely rebuilt to the tune of $150 million, this 510-room hotel reopened in 1997 as a luxury hotel with rates beginning at $270 for a garden-view room and climbing to $3000 for a top-end suite.

The *Westin Maui* (☎ 667-2525, 800-228-3000; fax 523-3958), 2365 Kaanapali Pkwy, Lahaina, HI 96761, is a 762-room high-rise hotel. It has waterfalls flowing into free-form pools and a garden full of statuary. The hotel itself is not as distinguished as the grounds, but then the Westin wasn't built from scratch – it's a remake of the old Maui Surf. Rates start at $245 for rooms in the old wing.

The 815-room *Hyatt Regency Maui* (☎ 661-1234, 800-233-1234; fax 667-4498), 200 Nohea Kai Drive, Lahaina, HI 96761, is the premier hotel on Kaanapali Beach. Not only does it have interesting artwork, but there's a massive meandering swimming pool with a swim-through grotto and a 130-foot water slide. The rooms, which have standard Hyatt decor and amenities, begin at $245, or $335 with an ocean view.

Places to Eat

Hotels All of the Kaanapali hotels have restaurants, some formal and expensive, others more casual.

The cheapest spot to eat is at the *Pizza Hut* at the Maui Marriott's poolside kiosk, open from 11 am to 7 pm daily, where one-person pizzas cost $4.

The Marriott's *Moana Terrace* (☎ 667-1200) has a good-value soup, pasta and salad buffet Monday to Thursday nights from 5 to 9 pm. The cost is $10.95 as a meal in itself, plus $3.75 if you also order an entree. On Friday nights the salad buffet includes prime rib and fish and costs $13.75; on Saturday nights it includes seafood dishes and jumps to $21.95; on Sundays it's with pasta and costs $11.25. Prices are reduced for children. Dining is either indoors or on the adjacent open-air terrace.

Nikko (☎ 667-1200) is a Japanese teppanyaki restaurant at the Marriott, open daily for dinner only. It has a pleasant atmosphere with authentic Japanese food cooked at your table and a good ocean view from the window. Complete dinners include miso soup, salad, rice and teppanyaki vegetables, all accompanying main dishes like sesame chicken ($22) and lobster tail ($37).

Lahaina Provision Company at the Hyatt has a Chocoholic Bar, an all-you-can-indulge sugar rush of chocolate goodies served from 6:30 to 11 pm nightly. It's $6 with a meal, $8 alone. The restaurant features moderately expensive grilled meats and seafood.

Whalers Village Whalers Village has three beachfront restaurants. The most interesting food is at the *Hula Grill*, which has outdoor dining, a kiawe grill, a wood-fired pizza oven and evening hula dancing. Hawaiian Regional cuisine is featured. Sandwiches and fries or pizzas are priced under $10, pastas from around $15 and fresh fish around $22. The drawback is the service, which can be slow and indifferent.

The other two beachfront restaurants offer more standard fare. The *Rusty Harpoon* has

burgers with fries for around $8, chicken dinners for $17 and pricier fresh fish meals. *Leilani's*, next door, is a bit cheaper, with $6 burgers from 11:30 am to 11 pm at the ground-level dining area and chicken and steak dishes, served upstairs, for around $15 at dinner.

The *Maui Yogurt* takeout shop has sandwiches and salads for under $5, as well as frozen yogurt, juices and fruit. Whalers Village also has a *Häagen Däzs* ice cream shop and a small food court with a *McDonald's*, a Korean eatery with plate lunches, a Japanese soba shop and a stall selling pizza by the slice.

Breakfast Buffets Kaanapali has a number of breakfast buffets where you could easily while away the better part of a morning.

The *Hyatt Regency Maui* has a good breakfast buffet in a superb setting at Swan Court. One side of the restaurant is in the open air and overlooks a large swan pond, artificial waterfalls and a Japanese garden. The buffet is served from 7 to 11:30 am, costs $16.25 and includes fresh fruit, Danish pastries, an omelet station, blintzes and more.

The *Maui Marriott* has a decent breakfast buffet from 6:30 to 11 am daily at its Moana Terrace, with fresh fruit, yogurt, cereals, pastries, eggs Benedict and Belgian waffles. It costs $15.75 for a full breakfast or $12.75 for a continental breakfast, which consists of everything except the hot dishes. There's a pleasant garden patio but no ocean view.

The Westin's *Cooks on the Beach* also does a reasonably good breakfast buffet, but there's nothing special about the setting, and at $17.50 it's the most expensive option. The buffet is from 6:30 to 11 am daily.

The bargain of the breakfast buffets is at *Kaanapali Mixed Place*, off the lobby of the Kaanapali Beach Hotel. Here you can get fresh pineapple, eggs, sausage, steamer trays of French toast, cereals and coffee. While not a notable culinary experience, you can eat your fill for $7.95. Breakfast is

MAUI

from 6 to 10:45 am daily. There's also a reasonable lunch buffet for the same price from 11 am to 2 pm.

Entertainment

The Kaanapali hotels feature a variety of entertainment, including dance bands, pianists, Hawaiian music and Polynesian revues.

Solo guitarists play mellow contemporary music in the Hyatt's *Weeping Banyan* from 6 to 9 pm nightly.

In the courtyard of the Kaanapali Beach Hotel there's a free hula show from 6:30 to 7:30 pm nightly, and Hawaiian music from 6 to 9:30 pm nightly.

The Maui Marriott's *Makai Bar* has contemporary music nightly. The Marriott also has a comedy club in its *Lobby Bar* at 8:30 pm on Mondays and Fridays, with a $12 cover charge.

Whalers Village has a free Hawaiian hula show on its center stage at 1 pm on Sundays and Wednesdays. There's often contemporary or Hawaiian music outdoors in the evening at one of the Whalers Village restaurants.

Luaus The Kaanapali luaus include an imu ceremony, open bar, buffet dinner and Polynesian show with music and dance. Reservations are required. Most of the shows are held outdoors, so you can get a preview of them by walking along the beach.

The Hyatt Regency Maui (☎ 667-4420) has its 'Drums of the Pacific' luau from 5 to 8 pm most nights. The cost is $55 for adults, $25 for children.

The Royal Lahaina Resort (☎ 661-3611) has a luau from 5:30 pm nightly for $55 for adults, $28 for children, though sometimes one accompanying child is allowed for free.

The Maui Marriott (☎ 661-5828) has a luau from 5 to 8 pm nightly. The cost is $57 for adults, $25 for children.

Astronomy You can look at the night sky through giant binoculars and a 16-inch telescope from the rooftop of the Hyatt Regency Maui. Its one-hour star-gazing programs (☎ 661-1234) are at 8, 9 and 10 pm

nightly and cost $12 for adults, $6 for children.

Getting Around

Shuttle Buses A free shuttle runs between the Kaanapali hotels, Whalers Village shopping center, the golf course and the sugar cane train's Kaanapali station about 20 times a day between 7:15 am and 10:15 pm.

For information on the shuttle between Kaanapali and Lahaina, see Getting Around in the Lahaina section. Three other shuttle buses connect Kaanapali with Kapalua, south Maui and Kahului; for details, see the Getting Around section near the front of this chapter.

Parking There's free beach access parking at many of the Kaanapali hotels, but the number of spaces is limited and they're earmarked strictly for beachgoers. The Hyatt also has free 'self parking' for hotel visitors at its south side. Otherwise, the cheapest pay parking is at the Whalers Village shopping center, which charges $1 for the first two hours and 50¢ for each additional half hour.

Northwest Maui

North of Kaanapali the road forks. The main road is Honoapiilani Hwy (Hwy 30), and the parallel shoreline road is Lower Honoapiilani Rd.

If you just want to zip up to the beaches, bypassing the condos and resorts, stick to Hwy 30. Cyclists may want to come this way as well, as the highway has a wide shoulder lane marked as a bike route.

Napili Bay, Kapalua Beach, Slaughterhouse Beach and Honolua Bay are all fine beaches on Maui's curving northwest coast.

HONOKOWAI

To the degree that Kaanapali is a planned community, Honokowai is an unplanned one, consisting mainly of a stretch of condos squeezed between the shoreline and Lower Honoapiilani Rd.

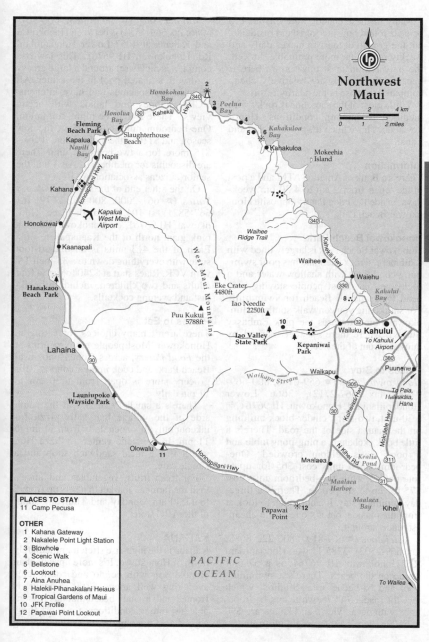

Northwest Maui

0   2   4 km
0   1   2 miles

PLACES TO STAY
11 Camp Pecusa

OTHER
1   Kahana Gateway
2   Nakalele Point Light Station
3   Blowhole
4   Scenic Walk
5   Bellstone
6   Lookout
7   Aina Anuhea
8   Halekii-Pihanakalani Heiaus
9   Tropical Gardens of Maui
10 JFK Profile
12 Papawai Point Lookout

PACIFIC
OCEAN

Many of these condos were intended to be year-round housing for island residents, but the growth in tourism makes daily and weekly rentals far more profitable. Indeed, the only reason most tourists are here is because the condos are relatively cheap compared to those at the nearby resorts.

While most of the shoreline is rocky with mediocre swimming conditions, Honokowai does have fine views of Molokai and Lanai.

Information

There's a Bank of America ATM and a post office, open from 9 am to 4:30 pm weekdays, inside the Food Pantry opposite Honokowai Beach Park.

Honokowai Beach Park

Honokowai Beach Park is largely lined with a submerged rock shelf and has poor swimming conditions with shallow water and a rocky bottom. Most people staying here head to Kaanapali Beach for swimming. For snorkeling you can walk south to Honokowai Point (towards the pink Embassy Suites), where there's a reef marked by buoys in front of the hotel.

Places to Stay

Honokowai Palms (☎ 669-6130, 800-669-0795; fax 667-2712), 3666 Lower Honoapiilani Rd, Honokowai, HI 96761, is a 30-unit, two-story, cinder-block building on the mauka side of the road. There's a little book exchange, a ping-pong table and a pool that's seldom crowded. One-bedroom condo units cost $65 for up to four people, while two-bedroom units cost $75 for up to six people. There's a three-day minimum stay. It's not much to look at from the outside, but it's one of the cheapest places around.

Kaleialoha (☎ 669-8197, 800-222-8688; fax 669-2502), 3785 Lower Honoapiilani Rd, Honokowai, HI 96761, is a 67-unit condo on the beach. There's a swimming pool and barbecue area. Studios, which face the road, cost $75, while one-bedroom units with ocean views and lanais are $90 to $100. There's a three-night minimum.

Mahina Surf (☎ 669-6068, 800-367-6086; fax 669-4534) is between Honokowai and Kahana at 4057 Lower Honoapiilani Rd, Honokowai, HI 96761. This low-rise complex is nicely set around a large grassy yard with a heated pool in the center. All 56 units are spacious and have kitchens, VCRs, phones and lanais with ocean views. There's a three-night minimum. One-bedroom units cost $95 in the low season and $110 in the high season. It costs $15 more for a two-bedroom unit. There are discounts for members of AAA and the senior-citizens association AARP.

On the other end of the scale is *Embassy Suites* (☎ 661-2000, 800-362-2779; fax 667-5821), at 104 Kaanapali Place, Honokowai, HI 96761, on Honokowai Point, a pink giant north of the Kaanapali resorts. Each of the 413 units is an 820-sq-foot suite with everything down to a 35-inch TV with VCR. Rates start at $240 for up to four adults and two children, including breakfast and evening cocktails.

Places to Eat

There aren't many choices for eating in Honokowai. Most people buy groceries at the *Food Pantry*, across from Honokowai Beach Park, and cook in their condos. This grocery store is open from 6:30 am to 11 pm daily.

There's a small *Pizza Hut* at the south side of the village that sells pizza for takeout only; it's open daily from 11 am to 11 pm. In the same center as Pizza Hut, you'll find a local sandwich shop and a simple cafe.

For fresh fruits, vegetables and juices, visit the farmers' market that sets up from 7 to 11:30 am Monday and Thursday south of the ABC store.

KAHANA

Kahana is the high-rise stretch immediately north of Honokowai. It's more upscale than Honokowai, with condo and room rates averaging well above $100. Kahana is fronted with a sandy beach that has reasonable swimming conditions; for snorkeling, a good area is along the rocky outcropping at the north side of the Kahana Sunset condominium complex.

Information

The Kahana Gateway shopping center, off Hwy 30 half a mile north of the Kapalua West Maui Airport, has a gas station, a Bank of Hawaii with a 24-hour ATM and a coin laundry that's open from 6 am to 10 pm daily.

Places to Stay

Noelani (☎ 669-8374, 800-367-6030; fax 669-7904), 4095 Lower Honoapiilani Rd, Kahana, HI 96761, has a friendly atmosphere and 50 nicely furnished units right on the beach. All have ocean-facing lanais, phones with free local calls, full kitchens, sofa beds and VCRs; all but the studios have a washer/dryer. There are two pools. Studios cost $87, one-bedroom units $110. Two-bedroom, two-bath units cost $140 for up to four people, and three-bedroom units cost $170 for up to six people. There's a three-day minimum. It's a good deal for this area.

Kahana Reef (☎ 669-6491, 800-253-3773; fax 669-2192), 4471 Lower Honoapiilani Rd, Kahana, HI 96761, is a four-story, 88-unit condo. All units are oceanfront and most are nicely furnished. There's a small pool on the ocean with a great view of Molokai. The studios, which cost $105, are almost as large as one-bedroom units elsewhere and have single and double day beds, as well as a tiny second room with a single bed. For another $10 you can get a very large one-bedroom unit. A third person costs $8 extra.

Royal Kahana (☎ 669-5911, 800-447-7783), 4365 Lower Honoapiilani Rd, Kahana, HI 96761, is a Marc Resorts property. The units are spacious, modern and comfortable, with full kitchens, bathtubs, TVs, VCRs and phones. All but the studios have a washer/dryer, and most have private ocean-facing lanais. There's a heated pool, two tennis courts, a small fitness room and a sauna. The location is convenient, just a few minutes' walk from the Kahana Gateway. Rates begin at $149 for a studio, $179 for a one-bedroom unit and $219 for a two-bedroom unit. If you're a member of one of the travel clubs in which Marc participates, such as Entertainment, the rate drops 50%, making it a particularly appealing deal.

Places to Eat

The best bet for places to eat is the Kahana Gateway shopping center, which has a *McDonald's*; a frozen yogurt and ice cream shop; the *Kafe Kahana*, with average pastries and sandwiches; and the *Whalers General Store*, a small grocery store with a few fast-food items that's open from 6:30 am to 11 pm daily.

The Kahana Gateway also has *Roy's Kahana Bar & Grill* (☎ 669-6999), a branch of the renowned Roy's in Honolulu. Centered around a large exhibition kitchen, the restaurant features contemporary regional dishes such as lemongrass chicken in a Thai curry sauce for $18 and a delicious blackened yellowfin ahi for $26. Roy's also serves superb appetizers, interesting imu-style pizzas and some of the island's most scrumptious desserts.

The adjacent *Roy's Nicolina* (☎ 669-5000), a sister restaurant under the same management, also serves Pacific Rim dishes. It doesn't have the exhibition kitchen, but otherwise the food, atmosphere and prices are essentially the same as at Roy's Kahana Bar & Grill. Each evening one of the two restaurants offers a special three-course meal for $35 that includes an appetizer, salad and entree – each course from a selection of two items. Both Roy's are open for dinner only from 5:30 to 9:30 pm nightly.

NAPILI

Napili Beach is a beautiful, curving, golden-sand beach, with excellent swimming and snorkeling when it's calm. Big waves occasionally make it into the bay in the winter, attracting bodysurfers but also creating strong rip currents. To get to the beach from Lower Honoapiilani Rd, turn down Hui Drive.

Napili Kai Beach Club, built in 1962, was the first hotel north of Kaanapali. To protect the bay, as well as their investment, Napili Kai residents organized area land-owners and petitioned the county to create a zoning bylaw restricting all Napili Bay buildings to the height of a coconut tree.

The law was passed in 1964, long before the condo explosion took over the rest of West Maui, and consequently Napili is one of the more relaxed niches on the coast. It attracts a fair number of return visitors, the majority of them retirees escaping main-land winters.

Most of Napili's condos are on the beach and for the most part away from the road and the sound of traffic.

Places to Stay

Hale Napili (☎ 669-6184, 800-245-2266; fax 665-0066), 65 Hui Drive, Napili, HI 96761, is an 18-unit condo on Napili Beach, with friendly Hawaiian management. The rooms have phones with free local calls, TVs, ceiling fans and lanais. Garden studios cost $90, oceanfront studios $115 and one-bedroom units $135. It has a three-day minimum stay, and there's no pool.

Napili Sunset (☎ 669-8083, 800-447-9229; fax 669-2730), 46 Hui Drive, Napili, HI 96761, has studios with garden views for $95 and one-bedroom beachfront units for $175. All have full kitchens, although the furnishings in some of the units can be a bit worn. There's a three-day minimum, and rates are about $20 cheaper in summer.

Napili Surf (☎ 669-8002, 800-541-0638; fax 669-8004), 50 Napili Place, Napili, HI 96761, is a motel-style, painted cinder-block place at the south end of Napili Bay. The 53 units are pleasant, the grounds well kept, and there's a pool. High season rates range from $99 for studios with a garden view to $190 for one-bedroom units with ocean views; during the low season rates are about 10% cheaper. There's a five-day minimum, and credit cards are not accepted.

Napili Kai Beach Club (☎ 669-6271, 800-367-5030; fax 669-5740), 5900 Honoapi-ilani Rd, Napili, HI 96761, is a sprawling 180-unit hotel at the northern end of Napili Bay. The staff is friendly – almost pamper-ing. The units are tasteful, with Polynesian

decor and nice touches like shoji doors. The catch here is the price: studios start at $160 without a kitchen, $180 with one.

Places to Eat

The Napili Plaza, at the junction of Napili-hau St and Hwy 30, has a grocery store open from 6:30 am to 11 pm daily; a *Subway Sandwiches* shop; the *Coffee Store*, which has good pastries and coffees; and *Maui Tacos*, which has healthy, inexpen-sive Mexican food. The plaza also has *Koho Grill & Bar*, a local sit-down restau-rant with an extensive menu of hot dishes, sandwiches and burgers.

For a more appealing setting, the *Sea House Restaurant* at Napili Kai Beach Club has open-air dining with a sunset view. The usual breakfast offerings and lunchtime burgers, fish & chips and papaya salad are all priced from $6 to $10. Dinners, which include fish and steaks, are in the $15 to $25 range. There's live Hawaiian dinner music from Saturday to Thursday. The restaurant also has a worthwhile dinner show at 6:30 pm on Fridays for $35, which features hula dancing by area children; reservations are required (☎ 669-6271) for the show. Res-taurant hours are 8 to 11 am, noon to 2 pm and 6 to 9 pm.

The *Napili General Store* in the Napili Village complex sells groceries, liquor, wrapped sandwiches and a few mediocre fast-food items. It's open from 7:30 am to 10 pm daily.

KAPALUA

The Kapalua resort development has the upmarket Kapalua Bay and Ritz-Carlton hotels, some luxury condos, a few restau-rants and three golf courses. It's a small, uncrowded development – the most exclu-sive in northwest Maui – but truth to tell, if you're not a well-to-do golfer, there's not a lot to do here.

Kapalua Beach

Kapalua Beach, at Kapalua Bay, is a pretty white-sand crescent beach with a fine view of Molokai across the channel. The long rocky outcroppings at both ends of the bay make Kapalua Beach the safest year-round swimming spot on this coast.

There's good snorkeling on the right side of the beach, where you'll find lots of large tangs, butterfly fish, wrasses and orange slate-pencil sea urchins.

Take the unmarked paved drive immediately north of Napili Kai Beach Club to get to a parking area with about 25 beach access spaces, restrooms and showers. A tunnel from the parking lot leads under the Bay Club restaurant to the beach.

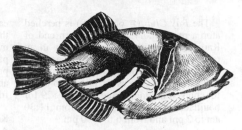

Hawaii's state fish, the
humuhumunukunukuapua̒a

Fleming Beach Park

DT Fleming Beach Park on Honokahua Bay, at the north side of Kapalua, is a county beach park with restrooms, picnic facilities, showers and a pay phone.

The long sandy beach is backed by iron-wood trees. There's good surfing and body-surfing, with winter providing the biggest waves. The shorebreaks can be tough, however, and this beach is second only to Hookipa for injuries.

Take notice of the sign warning of dangerous currents – the beach has seen a number of drownings over the years. The reef out on the right is good for snorkeling, but only when it's very calm. There's a lifeguard on duty daily.

The Honokahua sand dunes just south of Fleming Beach were excavated in 1988 during the construction of the Ritz-Carlton hotel. After skeletal remains were found, construction was halted, the bodies were reinterred and the hotel was resituated mauka of the seaside graves. The Honokahua burial ground is thought to contain the remains of over 1000 Hawaiians who were buried between 950 AD and the 18th century.

Places to Stay

Kapalua Bay Hotel & Villas (☎ 669 5656, 800-367-8000; fax 669-4690) at 1 Bay Drive, Kapalua, HI 96761, is a luxury complex with hotel rooms from $260. There are also one-bedroom condos with modern conveniences and large lanais; prices start at $200 on the hillside near the golf course and $340 along the bay.

One-bedroom condos in the same resort development can be rented from Ridge Rentals (☎ 669-9696, 800-326-6284; fax 669-4411), 10 Hoohui Rd, Suite 301, Kahana, HI 96761, for $115/745 a day/week in the low season, $165/1110 in the high season. There are also two-bedroom, three-bath units for $175/1175 in the low season, $240/1500 in the high. Ridge Rentals has a five-day minimum stay.

The *Ritz-Carlton* (☎ 669-6200, 800-241-3333; fax 669-3908), 1 Ritz-Carlton Drive, Kapalua, HI 96761, has 550 rooms and suites with the usual Ritz standards and decor. Rates range from $285 to $2800.

Places to Eat

Honolua Store is an old general store with a cafeteria-style deli serving local food such as stew and fried chicken. Plate lunches are available from about 10 am to 2:30 pm, either 'hobo' style (a hot dish and rice) for $3.50 or a full plate for $5.50. There are also sandwiches and salads for around $4. Everything's takeout only. To get there, turn up Office Rd half a mile north of Kapalua Bay Hotel.

While the setting looks somewhat exclusive, the *Plantation House Restaurant* (☎ 669-6299), at the Plantation Course golf course, is the best place in these parts for a reasonably priced sit-down brunch. From 8 am to 3 pm, eggs Benedict, salads and sandwiches cost about $8. Dinner is a pricier affair with seafood, duck and meat dishes averaging $20 to $25. There's a fine view across the fairway clear down to the ocean.

MAUI

The *Bay Club* (☎ 669-8008) is perched atop a promontory at the southern end of Kapalua Bay with a beautiful view in an open-air setting. At lunch, there are creative salads and sandwiches for around $10. At dinner, entrees are priced from $24 for chicken in ginger-lime sauce to $29 for bouillabaisse. It's open daily from 11:30 am to 2 pm and from 6 to 9:30 pm.

HONOLUA & MOKULEIA BAYS

Kapalua marks the end of development on the West Maui coast. From here on it's rural Hawaii, with golf carts giving way to pickup trucks and old cars with surfboards tied on top. The coast gets lusher, greener and more scenically rugged as you go along.

About a mile north of Fleming Beach are Mokuleia Bay (Slaughterhouse Beach) and Honolua Bay. The two bays are separated by the narrow Kalaepiha Point and together form the Honolua-Mokuleia Bay Marine Life Conservation District. Fishing is prohibited, as is collecting shells, coral, rock or sand. In the winter both bays see heavy surf and sand erosion.

In winter, Honolua Bay has such perfect waves that it's made the cover of numerous surfing magazines. The bay faces northwest, and when it catches the winter swells it has some of the best surfing to be found anywhere in the world.

Slaughterhouse Beach

Named for the slaughterhouse that once sat on the cliffs above, this is a hot bodysurfing spot during the summer when the rocks aren't exposed. It's also a popular nude beach.

In summer there's excellent snorkeling in both bays. Both sides of Honolua Bay have good reefs with lots of different coral formations, while the midsection of the bay has a sandy bottom. Honolua Stream empties into the bay and it can get quite murky after heavy rains.

When it's calm you can snorkel around Kalaepiha Point from one bay to the other. In addition to seeing coral and reef fish, you might get lucky and spot a sea turtle.

There's no designated parking area or easy access. There are a few pull-offs along the road (including one north of the 32-mile marker) where beachgoers commonly park their cars and scramble along rough paths down to the beach. Don't leave valuables in your car, as this area is notorious for vehicle break-ins.

Kahekili Hwy

As you continue north beyond Honolua and Mokuleia bays the road climbs, offering some nice coastal views. The beaches along this section are open ocean with rough water conditions.

It's possible to continue around on this coastal road to Wailuku (see Kahekili Hwy at the end of the Kahului-Wailuku section). The last stop for gas and provisions on this side of Wailuku is at the Honolua Store in Kapalua.

Kihei

Kihei extends six miles along Maui's southwest coast, on the leeward side of Haleakala. Maalaea Bay is to the north, the more exclusive Wailea resort to the south.

Kihei is fringed with sandy beaches its entire length and has near-constant sunshine. It has long attracted sunbathers, boogie boarders, windsurfers and Kahului families on weekend picnics.

The beaches have views of Lanai and Kahoolawe as well as West Maui, which because of the deep cut of Maalaea Bay looks like a separate island from here.

Twenty years ago Kihei was a long stretch of undeveloped beach with kiawe trees, a scattering of homes and a church or two. Over the past decade it's had the dubious distinction of being Maui's fastest growing community, with development continuing nonstop.

South Kihei Rd, which runs the full length of Kihei, is lined with condos, gas stations, shopping centers and fast-food places in such congested and haphazard disarray that it's the example most often cited by antidevelopment forces on other

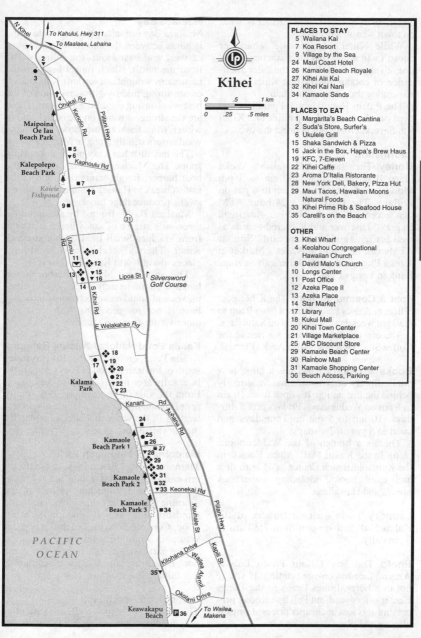

Kihei

0   .5   1 km
0   .25   .5 miles

PLACES TO STAY
5 Wailana Kai
7 Koa Resort
9 Village by the Sea
24 Maui Coast Hotel
26 Kamaole Beach Royale
27 Kihei Alii Kai
32 Kihei Kai Nani
34 Kamaole Sands

PLACES TO EAT
1 Margarita's Beach Cantina
2 Suda's Store, Surfer's
6 Ukulele Grill
15 Shaka Sandwich & Pizza
19 Jack in the Box, Hapa's Brew Haus
19 KFC, 7-Eleven
22 Kihei Caffe
23 Aroma D'Italia Ristorante
28 New York Deli, Bakery, Pizza Hut
29 Maui Tacos, Hawaiian Moons
     Natural Foods
33 Kihei Prime Rib & Seafood House
35 Carelli's on the Beach

OTHER
3 Kihei Wharf
4 Keolahou Congregational
     Hawaiian Church
8 David Malo's Church
10 Longs Center
11 Post Office
12 Azeka Place II
13 Azeka Place
14 Star Market
17 Library
18 Kukui Mall
20 Kihei Town Center
21 Village Marketplace
25 ABC Discount Store
29 Kamaole Beach Center
30 Rainbow Mall
31 Kamaole Shopping Center
36 Beach Access, Parking

Neighbor Islands. To them, Kihei is what no town wants to become.

While Kihei's 'condoville' character doesn't win any prizes for aesthetics, it has one advantage for visitors – the sheer abundance of condos means that Kihei's rates are among the cheapest in Maui.

The Piilani Hwy (Hwy 31) parallels and bypasses the start-and-stop traffic of S Kihei Rd. Several crossroads connect the two.

Information

Money The Bank of Hawaii at Azeka Place II is open from 8:30 am to 3 pm Monday to Thursday, 8:30 am to 6 pm on Fridays. The bank has a 24-hour ATM that accepts MasterCard, Visa, American Express, Discover and JCB credit cards as well as Cirrus and Plus debit cards. Similar ATMs can be found at Azeka's Market at Azeka Place and at the American Savings Bank in Longs Center.

Post & Communications The Kihei post office, at Azeka Place, is open from 9 am to 4:30 pm weekdays, 9 to 11 am on Saturdays.

You can check your email for free at the Coffee Store (☎ 875-4244) at Azeka Place II.

Books & Library Kihei has a large new public library on Waimahaihai St, directly behind the fire station. It's open from 10 am to 6 pm on Wednesdays, Fridays and Saturdays, 10 am to 5 pm on Thursdays and noon to 8 pm on Tuesdays.

There's a branch of the Waldenbooks chain in the Kukui Mall. Aloha Books, in the Kamaole Beach Center, sells both new and used books, including paperback novels and Hawaiiana.

Laundry There's a coin laundry at the Kukui Mall that is open from 7:30 am to 8 pm daily.

Photo The Fox 1-Hour Photo Lab at Azeka Place has on-site printing. If you're not in a hurry, Longs Drugs in the Longs Center offers send-out Fuji and Kodak processing services at cheaper prices; Longs is also a good place to pick up film.

Maalaea Bay

Maalaea Bay runs along the south side of the isthmus between the two mountain masses of west and east Maui. Prevailing winds from the north, which funnel between the mountains straight out towards Kahoolawe, create strong midday gusts and some of the best windsurfing conditions on Maui. These are the strongest winds on the island, and in winter, when the wind dies down elsewhere, windsurfers still fly along in Maalaea Bay.

The bay also has a couple of hot surfing spots. The Maalaea Pipeline, south of the boat harbor, freight-trains right and is the fastest break in Hawaii. Summer's southerly swells produce huge tubes.

Maalaea Bay is fronted by a continuous three-mile stretch of sandy beach that runs from Maalaea Small Boat Harbor south to Kihei. There's beach access at several places along North Kihei Rd (Hwy 31).

The area near Maalaea harbor has a handful of moderately priced condo complexes and could make a convenient central base if not for problems with theft and other visitor-targeted crimes.

Kealia Pond National Wildlife Refuge

Kealia Pond, on North Kihei Rd two miles south of the intersection of Hwys 31 and 30, is a saltwater marsh and bird sanctuary. From the side of the road you can usually spot Hawaiian stilts, an endangered species, wading in the water. It's also a habitat for the Hawaiian coot, egrets and herons.

Maipoina Oe Iau Beach Park

Maipoina Oe Iau Beach Park, at the northern end of Kihei, has a long sandy beach. Swimming and sunbathing is best in the morning before the wind picks up, while windsurfing is generally good in the afternoon. Consequently, the beach is a popular venue for windsurfing lessons.

The park, whose name means 'forget me not', is dedicated to Maui's war veterans. It has full facilities.

Kalepolepo Beach Park

The waters off Kalepolepo Beach Park offer only mediocre swimming, but this is one of the few places in Maui where you can see the stone wall remains of a fishpond.

Koieie Fishpond was built in the 16th century by King Umi of the Big Island. It was used to raise mullet for the alii.

David Malo's Church

Another historic site at the northern end of Kihei is the church built in 1853 by David Malo, a noted philosopher and the first Hawaiian ordained to the Christian ministry. While most of the church was dismantled long ago, a three-foot-high section of the church walls still stands. Eighteen pews are lined up inside the stone walls, where open-air services are held on Sunday mornings. David Malo's Church is at 100 Kulanihakoi St, at the side of the Trinity Episcopal Church.

Another notable church in the area is the little green-and-white **Keolahou Congregational Hawaiian Church** at 131 S Kihei Rd, which was established in 1920. Many of the 1000 Tongans living on Maui belong to the congregation, and services are held in Tongan at 5:30 pm on Sundays.

Kalama Park

Kalama Park, opposite Kihei Town Center, is a local park with ball fields, tennis and volleyball courts, playground, picnic pavilions, restrooms and showers. The park is long and grassy, but the beach is shallow and unappealing for swimming.

Kamaole Beach Park

Kamaole Beach is one long beach divided into three sections by rocky points. All three are pretty golden-sand beaches, though sometimes powerful kona storms temporarily wipe out much of the sand.

Each section is along the roadside opposite condos and shopping centers. All three sections have full beach facilities and a lifeguard.

Water conditions vary greatly with the weather, but there's usually good swimming. For the most part these beaches have sandy bottoms with a fairly steep drop, which tends to create good conditions for bodysurfing as well.

Koieie Fishpond

In a story with an unusual menehune twist, the Koieie Fishpond at Kalepolepo Beach Park was said to have been built by regular-sized Hawaiians. After the workers protested that the work couldn't be done properly without the help of the menehune, the chief in charge angrily ordered that when the job was finished the workers were to be cooked in an imu. The night before the last rock was to be placed, the menehune came down from the mountains and carried away every stone. Only after the threats against the Hawaiian laborers were withdrawn did the menehune return with the stones and rebuild the fishpond. ∎

For snorkeling, the southern end of Kamaole Beach Park 3 has some rocks near shore harboring a bit of coral and a few tropical fish, though the Wailea beaches to the south are far better.

Keawakapu Beach

Keawakapu Beach is bordered on its north end by the southernmost Kihei hotels and on its south end by Mokapu Beach and the Wailea resort area. More scenic and less crowded than the roadside Kihei beaches, Keawakapu is a sandy beach with a sandy bottom. Snorkeling is fairly good at the rocky outcrop at the southern end.

As there's no reef off Keawakapu, the state has been working to develop an artificial reef here for the past 30 years. In the original drop they used piles of car bodies, but in recent years they've switched to 'fish shelters' made of old tires embedded in concrete; about 1000 of these shelters have been dropped some 500 yards offshore.

There's a fine view from the beach, and during the winter whales cavort in the surrounding waters, sometimes coming quite close to shore.

To get to Keawakapu, go south on S Kihei Rd until it ends. There you'll find 25 public parking spaces and an outdoor shower.

Places to Stay

Kihei is packed with condos, but there are few hotels. In many places along S Kihei Rd the traffic will challenge you to get a good night's sleep, so when you book be sure to avoid rooms facing the road.

In addition to the following listings, scores of Kihei condos can be booked through rental agents; for details see Condominiums under Accommodations in the front of this chapter.

Condos *Wailana Kai* (☎ 877-5796), 34 Wailana Place (mailing address: Mary Caravalho, 255-E Alamaha St, Kahului, HI 96732), is on a quiet cul-de-sac a block back from the beach at the one-mile marker. It has a small pool and 10 pleasant units, each with cable TV, full kitchen and everything you'd expect in a more expensive condo except the price. One-bedroom units cost $60 in the low season and $70 in the high season. Two-bedroom units for up to four people cost $80/90 low/high. Credit cards are not accepted.

Village by the Sea, also known as *Kauhale Makai*, is a six-story concrete-block complex at 938 S Kihei Rd. Ninety of the 160 condo units are vacation rentals booked through Maui Condo & Home Realty (☎ 879-5445, 800-822-4409; fax 874-6144), Box 1840, Kihei, HI 96753. All units have lanais and the standard amenities such as kitchens, cable TV and phones, and while the location is not special, the interiors are on par with many of Kihei's pricier condos. Studios cost $65/75 in the low/high season, one-bedroom units $75/95, two-bedroom units $90/120. It has a pool, sauna and tennis court. There is a three-day minimum stay, and weekly and monthly discounts are available.

Kihei Kai Nani (☎ 879-1430, 800-473-1393; fax 879-8965), 2495 S Kihei Rd, is a friendly place with 180 low-rise apartments, about 30 of which are in the rental pool. All are one-bedroom units with full modern kitchens, ceiling fans, good-sized balconies and phones with free local calls. The decor varies with the unit, but most are quite pleasant for this price range. The hotel is opposite Kamaole Beach Park 2; the grounds have a pool, shuffleboard and barbecue grills, and there are restaurants and shops within easy walking distance. The rate is $61/78 in the low/high season, and there's a three-day minimum stay. Between mid-April and mid-December the rate drops to $50 a day for stays of 14 days or more.

Kamaole Beach Royale (☎ 879-3131, 800-421-3661), 2385 S Kihei Rd, Kihei, HI 96753, is a seven-story condo opposite Kamaole Beach Park 1 but set back from the road. It's quiet, with open rangeland behind and ocean views from the top floors. Units are spacious and well furnished with private lanais, modern kitchens, washer/dryers, TVs and phones with free local calls; most also have VCRs and air-con. It's a particularly good value during the low season, when one-bedroom units cost $70, two-bedroom units $85. Both are $25 more in the high season. There's a cleaning charge of $50 for stays of four nights or less, and credit cards are not accepted.

Kihei Alii Kai (☎ 879-6770, 800-888-6284; fax 879-6221), Box 985, 2387 S Kihei Rd, Kihei, HI 96753, set back from the main road a two-minute walk from Kamaole Beach Park 1, is a 127-unit complex with a pool, sauna and tennis courts. The units are big and most are quite nice for the money; all have a washer/dryer and cable TV. One-bedroom units cost $65/90 in the low/high season for up to two people, and two-bedroom units cost $80/105 for up to four people. The minimum stay is three days.

Koa Resort (☎ 879-3328, 800-541-3060), 811 S Kihei Rd, Kihei, HI 96753, has 54 large, comfortable units spread over 5½ acres. All are equipped with full kitchens, a washer/dryer, lanai, cable TV, etc. There are two tennis courts, a putting green, a spa and a large swimming pool. One-bedroom units cost $85/105 in the low/high season, while two-bedroom units cost $100/130. The minimum stay is four days.

Kamaole Sands (☎ 874-8700, 800-535-0085), 2695 S Kihei Rd, Kihei, HI 96753, is its own condo city with 440 units in 10 four-story buildings. The units are very large and have modern amenities – cable TV, full kitchen, lanai, washer/dryer, two bathrooms and a living room with a sofa bed – but the complex itself is big and impersonal. Kamaole Sands is directly opposite Kamaole Beach Park 3 and has a pool, jacuzzi, tennis courts and a poolside restaurant. Marc Resorts, which handles the front desk, charges a steep $150 for one-bedroom units (for up to four people) and $190 for two-bedroom units (up to six people), but there are a number of discount schemes, such as the Entertainment program, that can cut those rates in half.

Hotels & B&Bs The *Maui Coast Hotel* (☎ 874-6284, 800-895-6284; fax 875-4731), 2259 S Kihei Rd, Kihei, HI 96753, is a modern seven-story hotel affiliated with the Canadian Coast Hotels chain. The 264 rooms are comfortable and pleasantly decorated, all with air-con, ceiling fans, mini-refrigerators, coffeemakers, safes, remote-control TVs, phones, lanais, sofa beds and either a king or two double beds. The hotel has complimentary washers and dryers, a heated pool, tennis courts and a restaurant. As it's set back from the road, the hotel is quieter than most Kihei condos. Standard room rates begin at $129, suites at $149, but there are usually discounts available during the low season.

Wonderful World B&B (☎ 879-9103; amauibnb@maui.net), 2828 Umalu Place, Kihei, HI 96753, is in the contemporary home of Eva and Jim Tantillo in a residential neighborhood about half a mile inland from Kamaole Beach Park 3. There are three nicely furnished units on the ground floor: a one-bedroom unit with a full kitchen for $95, a simpler one-bedroom unit for $85 and a studio for $75. Each is good-sized with a private entrance, private bath, cable TV, VCR, phone with free local calls and at least a microwave, refrigerator and toaster oven. In addition, there's an upstairs master bedroom that has a refrigerator and coffeemaker but no cooking facilities for $65. Guests have access to a washer and dryer. Rates include breakfast served on the ocean-view lanai.

Ann and Bob Babson (☎ 874-1166, 800-824-6409; fax 879-7906; babson@mauibnb.com), 3371 Keha Drive, Kihei, HI 96753, rent two upstairs bedrooms and a small apartment in their hillside home in the Maui Meadows area, about a mile above Wailea. From the living room there's a nice view of Kahoolawe, Molokini and Lanai. One bedroom has a queen-size bed and a mini-refrigerator and costs $70. The master bedroom has a private deck, wraparound windows, a skylight and a jacuzzi and costs $85. If you want more privacy, there's a downstairs one-bedroom apartment with cooking facilities for $85 and a separate cottage adjacent to the house for $105. All have TVs, phones and private baths; prices for the upstairs bedrooms include breakfast. There's a three-day minimum stay.

Places to Eat

These Kihei restaurants are listed in order from north to south.

Margarita's Beach Cantina in Kealia Beach Plaza, 101 N Kihei Rd, has average Mexican food but a great sunset-facing deck overlooking the water. You can get a single taco, enchilada or burrito with rice and beans for $7 and the usual combination plates for $9 to $14. There are also burgers with fries for around $8. It's open from 11:30 am to midnight daily. From 2:30 to 5 pm there's a happy hour with $1 margaritas.

The snack shop adjacent to *Suda's Store*, 61 S Kihei Rd, has cheeseburgers and saimin for about $2.50 as well as hot dogs and shave ice. On the other side of the store is *Surfer's*, a small bar and grill serving burgers and fries for $6; it's open from noon to 2 am daily. On Tuesdays and Fridays from 1:30 to 5 pm a farmers' market, with local fruits and vegetables, sets up in Suda's parking lot.

The new *Ukulele Grill* (☎ 875-1188), in the open-air longhouse at Maui Lu Resort, 575 S Kihei Rd, has an old-fashioned Hawaiian atmosphere and good food at moderate prices. Breakfast is served from 7 to 11 am daily, with fruit plates, Belgian waffles and egg dishes for $4 to $7. Dinner, from 5:30 to 9 pm nightly, features creative island dishes such as orange hoisin chicken, imu-style ribs or miso grilled prawns for $15 to $20. There's live Hawaiian music from 6 pm.

Stella Blues, a casual cafe and deli in the Longs Center, 1215 S Kihei Rd, opens at 8 am daily and has coffees, desserts, kosher meat sandwiches and numerous vegetarian options. Full breakfasts averaging $7 are served until 11 am. Most sandwiches, salads and burgers cost between $6 and $8. At dinner, which is served from 5 pm, you can also order hot dishes such as Cajun eggplant, spinach lasagna and Thai chicken for $12 to $15 with salad.

There's a *McDonald's* across from the Longs Center.

Azeka Place has a *Baskin-Robbins* ice cream shop, a *Taco Bell*, a *Pizza Hut*, an *International House of Pancakes* and a local sandwich shop. On the south side of Azeka Place is a *Star Market* supermarket with a deli and a fresh salad bar.

In Azeka Place II, opposite Azeka Place, is *Panda Express*, a fast-food chain Mandarin restaurant with about a dozen dishes, such as broccoli beef and spicy chicken with peanuts, served from steamer trays. The food is tasty, the servings generous and the price a good value at $5 for any two dishes with rice or chow mein. You can eat in or order takeout. It's open from 10:30 am to 9 pm daily.

Azeka Place II also has *A Pacific Cafe Maui* (☎ 879-0069), an offshoot of chef Jean-Marie Josselin's Kauai restaurant. Despite its shopping center locale, it's *the* place to eat Pacific Rim food in Kihei. The menu changes nightly. Starters such as sushi tempura or warm seafood salad are around $10. Main dishes range from $16 for the vegetarian entree to $25 for fresh fish. It's open nightly from 5:30 to about 10 pm. During busy periods, reservations are necessary.

Shaka Sandwich & Pizza (☎ 874-0331) at 1295 S Kihei Rd, tucked back behind Jack in the Box, has good pizza. An 18-inch pizza costs from $13, while a single slice of cheese pizza is $1.65. There's also a variety of sandwiches, including a recommendable Philly cheese steak, for around

$4. Shaka is open from 10:30 am to 9 pm and has delivery service with a $10 minimum order. It's closed on Sundays.

Adjacent to Azeka Place II is a *Jack in the Box* that has reasonably good fast food and is always offering some sort of discounted promotion.

The new *Hapa's Brew Haus* (☎ 879-9001), in the Lipoa Center at the corner of Lipoa St and S Kihei Rd, is Kihei's only brew pub. The half-dozen homemade lagers include Maui Moonset, a light beer, and Black Lava, a nearly jet-black brew. It has a full menu of pub-style meals, including salads, pizzas, baby back ribs and bratwurst with sauerkraut, all for $10 or less. It's open from 11 am to midnight, with live music nightly.

Another popular pizzeria is *Pair O' Dice Pizza* at the Kukui Mall, 1819 S Kihei Rd, which offers a choice of mozzarella or soy cheese and prices similar to Shaka's. Kukui Mall also has a bakery and a branch of the barbecued-rib chain restaurant *Tony Roma's*.

There's a 24-hour *Foodland* supermarket at Kihei Town Center and a *KFC* and a *7-Eleven* convenience store immediately to the north.

Alexander's (☎ 874-0788), 1913 S Kihei Rd, at the north side of Village Marketplace, is a popular spot for fried fish & chips, with a choice of mahimahi, ono or ahi for $6. It's open daily from 11 am to 9 pm. The food is prepared for takeout, but there are a few lanai tables outside.

Kihei Caffe, opposite Kalama Park at 1945 S Kihei Rd, is a little cafe with cappuccino, Kona coffee, homemade pastries and good karma. Fresh salads, tabouli and sandwiches, as well as a range of breakfast offerings, including tempting banana macnut pancakes, are priced from $5 to $6. It's open from 5 am (6 am on Sundays) to at least 3 pm daily.

Aroma D'Italia Ristorante (☎ 879-0133), 1993 S Kihei Rd, is a small restaurant with a dozen cafe tables and home-style Italian food at honest prices. Pasta dishes range from spaghetti marinara for $6.50 to pesto shrimp on linguine for $13. It's open from 11:30 am to 2 pm and 5 to 9 pm every day but Sunday. Alcohol is not served, but you're free to bring in your own beer or wine.

New York Deli in the Dolphin Plaza, 2395 S Kihei Rd, has hearty sandwiches for $6 and tortellini and Greek and fruit salads for about $3 a half pound. It's open from 8 am to 9 pm daily. Next door at the *Kihei Bakery* you can get a cup of coffee and a doughnut for just $1.25. The center also has a hole-in-the-wall taco shop, a sushi bar and a takeout *Pizza Hut*. There are a couple of small tables in front of the bakery where you can sit and eat.

Hawaiian Moons Natural Foods, in the Kamaole Beach Center at 2411 S Kihei Rd, has an organic produce section, yogurts, juices, trail mix, bulk grains, granolas and a few organic wines. It also has a small deli where a healthy vegetarian sandwich with dairy or soy cheddar costs $5. It's open from 8 am to 8 pm Monday to Saturday, to 6 pm on Sundays.

Also in the Kamaole Beach Center is *Maui Tacos*, a popular local eatery with tacos and burritos made with lard-free beans and fresh salsas. Everything can be made with or without meat, and most items are from $2 to $5. You can either eat in or order for takeout.

The Kamaole Shopping Center, 2653 S Kihei Rd, has a *Denny's* family-style restaurant open 24 hours; *Canton Chef*, which has a full range of moderately priced Chinese dishes; and *Cinnamon Roll Fair*, which sells warm cinnamon rolls for $2.35.

Kihei Prime Rib & Seafood House (☎ 879-1954), 2511 S Kihei Rd, is a popular old standby with a water view and good steaks and fish. Regular dinners cost $16 for chicken and $20 for fish or prime rib, including a salad bar. However, from 5 to 6 pm, you can get the same items as an early-bird special for $15. It's open nightly from 5 to 10 pm.

Kihei's fine-dining Italian restaurant, *Carelli's on the Beach* (☎ 875-0001), 2980 S Kihei Rd, has a romantic waterfront setting. Main dishes range from pastas for around $20 to zuppa di mare cioppino for $30. Appetizers are about half that. Though expensive, it's trendy among celebrities

and always packs in a crowd. It's open for dinner only, from 5:30 to 10 pm nightly.

Entertainment

Kihei is not known for its entertainment scene, but the new *Hapa's Brew Haus* (☎ 879-9001) at 41 Lipoa St has picked things up substantially. It has a dance floor and live music nightly, with the likes of musician Willie K and the popular Maui rock band The Missionaries; the cover charge varies, but is often around $5.

The Sports Page Grill & Bar (☎ 879-0602) in the Kamaole Beach Center, 2411 S Kihei Rd, has big-screen TVs with sports broadcasts, live music on Wednesdays and a comedy show on Saturdays.

Kukui Mall (☎ 875-4533) has a four-screen movie theater.

Things to Buy

Kihei is overflowing with souvenir, gift and clothing shops of all sorts. The Village Marketplace, opposite Kalama Park, has a collection of stalls selling cheap T-shirts, swimwear, jewelry and souvenir items.

Tropical Disc, in the Dolphin Plaza at 2395 S Kihei Rd, has a good selection of Hawaiian music and a headphone set-up for previewing some of the more popular releases.

A good place to look for quality aloha shirts and other Hawaiian clothing is at Liberty House department store and at Penthouse, its discount outlet, both at Azeka Place II.

On the opposite side of S Kihei Rd, Azeka Place has a couple of shops selling fashionable lightweight cotton clothing. Tropical Tantrum has Indonesian batik clothing, while Red Dirt & Teal Seas specializes in T-shirts dyed with Hawaiian red clay. Island Memories in Azeka Place has Hawaiian-made handicrafts.

Maui Dive Shop in Azeka Place II sells reef walkers, boogie boards, snorkels, fins and wet suits. Tropics, next door, also carries boogie boards as well as a few surfboards. The ABC Discount Store, opposite Kamaole Beach Park 1, has liquor, $1 beach mats, suntan lotion and other practical items for visitors.

MAUI

Wailea & Makena

WAILEA
As soon as you enter Wailea you'll be struck by the contrast to the cluttered commercialism of Kihei – everything is green, manicured and precise.

Wailea has a few swank hotels on the beach, a number of low-rise condo villas, a pair of golf courses, a shopping center and a tennis club that's been nicknamed 'Wimbledon West'.

Wailea's interesting lava rock coastline is broken by attractive golden-sand beaches. From Wailea and neighboring Makena there are good views of Lanai, Kahoolawe and Molokini, and during winter there's superb shoreline whale watching.

Orientation
If you're heading to Wailea beaches from Lahaina or Kahului, be sure to take the Piilani Hwy (Hwy 31) and not S Kihei Rd. It's less than 10 minutes' drive this way, whereas the Kihei strip can be a tedious 30 minutes through congested traffic.

Wailea's main road is Wailea Alanui Drive, which after Polo Beach changes its name to Makena Alanui as it continues south to Makena.

Information
A free shuttle bus (☎ 879-2828) runs every 30 minutes around the Wailea resort connecting the hotels, shopping center, golf courses and tennis club.

Wailea Shopping Village, in front of the Aston Wailea Resort, has a First Hawaiian Bank, a couple of uninspired eateries, a little grocery store and a few boutiques.

Wailea Beaches
Wailea's beaches begin with the southern end of Keawakapu Beach and continue south with Mokapu, Ulua, Wailea and Polo beaches. They are all lovely strands with free public access, parking, showers and restrooms. Some also have picnic tables and barbecue grills.

While Wailea's beaches generally have good swimming conditions, occasional high surf and kona storms can create dangerous shorebreaks and rip currents.

Ulua Beach Ulua Beach is a little gem between the Aston Wailea Resort and the Renaissance Wailea Beach Resort. The first road south of the Renaissance leads to the beach parking lot.

When it's calm, Ulua Beach has the area's best snorkeling. There's coral at the rocky outcrop on the right side of the beach and you can usually spot long needlefish, schools of goatfish, unicorn tangs and other tropicals. Snorkeling is best in the morning before the winds pick up. When the surf's up, forget snorkeling – in its place there's apt to be good bodysurfing.

During WWII, US Marines trained for the invasion of Tarawa off this beach, and consequently it was referred to locally as Tarawa Beach until the developers of Wailea resort came in and renamed it Ulua.

Wailea Beach Wailea is the largest and widest of Wailea's beaches. The inshore waters along the sandy beach slope gradually and are good for swimming. When the water's calm, there's good snorkeling around the rocky point on the south side of the beach. Divers entering the water at Wailea Beach can follow an offshore reef that runs down to Polo Beach. At times there's a gentle shorebreak suitable for bodysurfing.

Beach access is from the road running between the Four Seasons Resort and the Grand Wailea Resort, both of which front Wailea Beach.

Polo Beach Polo is fronted by a condo development and by the Kea Lani Hotel, but the south end is seldom crowded.

When there's wave action, boogie boarders and bodysurfers usually find a good shorebreak at Polo Beach. When the waters are calm, the rocks at the north end of the beach are good for snorkeling. At low tide the lava outcropping at the south end of the beach has some interesting little tide pools that harbor spiny sea urchins and a few small fish.

To get to Polo Beach, turn down Kaukahi St after the Kea Lani Hotel. There's a large beach parking lot on the right, near the end of the road.

Palauea Beach Palauea Beach is along Makena Rd, a quarter of a mile south of Polo Beach. The kiawe brushland between the beach and the road is marked private property, though there are breaks in the fence where beachgoers cross. A fair number of people use the beach for surfing and bodysurfing. It's more secluded and less frequented than Polo Beach, but otherwise much the same, sans the development. You can walk to Palauea Beach from Polo Beach in less than 10 minutes.

Wailea Beach Walk

For a delightful stroll, take the shoreline path that runs for 1¼ miles from the Aston Wailea Resort to the Kea Lani, connecting the Wailea beaches and the resort hotels that front them. The path winds above jagged lava points that separate the beaches and is landscaped with native Hawaiian flora, some of which is identified by plaques. In winter this is one of the best walks in all of Hawaii for spotting humpback whales – on a good day you may be able to spot more than a dozen of them frolicking in the waters offshore.

Some of the luxury hotels you'll pass along the beach walk are also worth strolling through, most notably the Grand Wailea Resort, which has $30 million of artwork and some strikingly elaborate waterways and landscaping on its grounds.

Places to Stay

The *Aston Wailea Resort* (☎ 879-1922, 800-922-7866; fax 875-4878), 3700 Wailea Alanui Drive, Wailea, HI 96753, has 516 rooms spread across a number of low-rise buildings and a mid-rise tower. For Wailea, it's an unpretentious, low-key operation. Although it's a relatively older hotel, the rooms have the usual resort-class amenities. Garden-view rooms cost $245; ocean

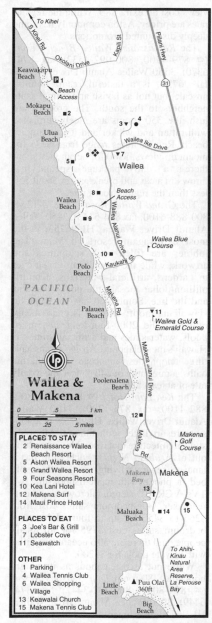

MAUI

Wailea & Makena

```
0        .5        1 km
0    .25      .5 miles
```

PLACES TO STAY
2 Renaissance Wailea
   Beach Resort
5 Aston Wailea Resort
8 Grand Wailea Resort
9 Four Seasons Resort
10 Kea Lani Hotel
12 Makena Surf
14 Maui Prince Hotel

PLACES TO EAT
3 Joe's Bar & Grill
7 Lobster Cove
11 Seawatch

OTHER
1 Parking
4 Wailea Tennis Club
6 Wailea Shopping
   Village
13 Keawalai Church
15 Makena Tennis Club

views cost an extra $80. While the regular rates are pricey, Aston commonly has some deeply discounted promotions.

The *Renaissance Wailea Beach Resort* (☎ 879-4900, 800-992-4532; fax 874-5370), 3550 Wailea Alanui Drive, Wailea, HI 96753, is a tasteful resort hotel – upscale, but not as lavish and formal as its neighbors to the south. The grounds are lush, the 350 rooms are nicely furnished with rattan and wicker and it's on a quiet beach. Regular rates range from $275 for mountain views, $380 for ocean views, but there's a 'daily package' special that throws in a car and breakfast for about $50 less than the regular room rate.

The *Grand Wailea Resort* (☎ 875-1234, 800-888-6100; fax 874-5143), 3850 Wailea Alanui Drive, Wailea, HI 96753, is the most extravagant resort on Maui. The lobbies are filled with sculptures and artwork, while the grounds are given over to gardens, artificial waterfalls, a multi-million-dollar mosaic tile pool, fountains and the like. Some of it has an upmarket Hawaiiana motif; all of it is unabashedly opulent. The 2000-foot-long system of pools, water slides and artificial grottos is Hawaii's most elaborate. All 767 rooms have three telephones, an ocean view, marble baths, a minimum of 640 sq feet and a daily rate of at least $380.

The *Kea Lani Hotel* (☎ 875-4100, 800-882-4100; fax 875-1200), 4100 Wailea Alanui Drive, Wailea, HI 96753, is a 450-suite resort hotel with fanciful Moorish-style architecture that resembles something out of *Arabian Nights*. Each suite has a lanai, a separate living room with a sofa bed, a phone with modem hook-up, two TVs, VCR, CD stereo, microwave and coffeemaker. One-bedroom suites cost from $265 to $450 for up to four adults, two-bedroom suites cost $795 for up to six people, and there are also oceanfront villas with private pools for $1200.

While not as ostentatious as its neighbors, the 380-room *Four Seasons Resort* (☎ 874-8000, 800-332-3442; fax 874-6449), 3900 Wailea Alanui Drive, Wailea, HI 96753, has open-air lobbies, lots of

marble and a series of pools and fountains. Rates begin at $295.

Destination Resorts (☎ 879-1595, 800-367-5246; fax 874-3554; drh@maui.net), 3750 Wailea Alanui Place, Wailea, HI 96753, books about 300 units in half a dozen complexes around the Wailea and Makena area. While they aren't cheap, most of the condos are quite nice and represent far better value than Wailea's luxury hotels. Studio and one-bedroom condos in Wailea begin at $140, while the high end tops off with three-bedroom oceanfront units costing $575.

Places to Eat

The Wailea resort hotels offer full buffet breakfasts for around $20, but none have a particularly outstanding spread. If you want to concentrate on fresh fruit, cereals and pastries, then the *Palm Court* at the Renaissance Wailea Beach Resort allows you to choose items from just the cold table for $10.

Cafe Ciao (☎ 875-4100) at the Kea Lani Hotel has both a deli and an outdoor cafe, with excellent food at affordable prices. Takeout deli items, available from 6:30 am to 10 pm, include tortellini, kung pao chicken or eggplant caponata for around $5, as well as muffins and tempting desserts such as tiramisu and white chocolate mousse. The courtyard cafe, open from 11 am to 10 pm, has pastas and wood-fired pizzas from around $12 at lunch, $14 at dinner. There are also good meat and fish dishes; a recommendable dinner selection is the crispy salmon with fresh spinach and wine sauce for $18.

Joe's Bar & Grill (☎ 875-7767), at 131 Wailea Ike Place, overlooking the courts at the Wailea Tennis Club, is a new restaurant run by the owners of the popular Haliimaile General Store. Open for dinner from 5:30 to 9:30 pm, it offers American standards such as grilled lamb chops with mint glaze, New York steak and lobster pie. Most entrees are priced from $16 to $26, while appetizers and salads go from $6 to $12.

Seawatch (☎ 875-8080), at the Gold & Emerald Course Clubhouse, is perched on a hillside with a great ocean view and both indoor and veranda dining. A breakfast favorite is the smoked-salmon eggs Benedict, while at lunch there are sandwiches, salads and stir-fried noodles – all averaging $8. Dinner features the likes of seafood pasta, kiawe-grilled chicken and miso-chili tiger prawns for $21 to $25. It's open daily from 8 am to 3 pm for breakfast and lunch and from 5:30 pm for dinner.

Lobster Cove/Harry's Sushi Bar (☎ 879-7677) is a busy dinner spot overlooking the Blue Golf Course, up the hill from Wailea Shopping Village. Specialties at the Cove include lobster and fresh fish; the latter can be prepared in a number of ways, including grilled Thai-style with curry. Seafood prices are quoted daily; entrees generally begin around $20. The sushi bar is popular with late-night diners, with most items priced à la carte from $6 to $10. Dinner in the main dining room is served from 5:30 to 10 pm, while the sushi bar stays open to 1 am.

Cafe Kula in the Grand Wailea Resort (☎ 875-1234) is an open-air cafe open from 6 am to 3 pm daily. It has simple fare, including cinnamon rolls or muffins for $3, muesli or granola for $4, crepes for $6; add $2 for a cup of coffee. The hotel's *Bistro Molokini* has pizza and pastas for around $15 and is open from 11:30 am to 10 pm daily. The Grand Wailea also has two expensive dinner restaurants: the *Kincha*, which has Japanese fare, and the *Humuhumu*, serving seafood and steaks in a Polynesian-style longhouse surrounded by carp ponds.

Seasons (☎ 874-8000), the fine-dining restaurant at the Four Seasons Resort, specializes in contemporary American cuisine with a Hawaiian accent. The food is good, if not always consistent; expect dinner for two to cost about $150.

Entertainment

The Wailea hotels often have some sort of music in their restaurants and lounges. The Grand Wailea Resort's high-tech *Tsunami* nightclub has dancing nightly.

The Wailea Shopping Village presents a free Polynesian dance show at 1:30 pm Tuesdays and offers hula classes for children and adults at 4:30 pm Wednesdays (☎ 572-5864 for information).

The Aston Wailea Resort has a luau at 5:30 pm on Tuesdays, Thursdays and Fridays for $52 for adults, $26 for children. It's held on the lawn near the beach, and you can see some of the show for free from the beach walk. The musicians are good, though they have a tendency to drift into pop medleys. The Renaissance Wailea and the Grand Wailea Resort have less frequent luaus.

MAKENA

Until recently, Makena was a sleepy and largely overlooked area at the end of the road. Its center was the abandoned Makena Landing, with its small and predominantly Hawaiian village.

In the 1980s the Seibu Corporation bought up 1800 acres of Makena above the landing, and a development similar to Wailea is now in the making. So far there's a golf course, a tennis center, the Maui Prince Hotel and a new bypass road to it all.

Makena's dominant shoreline feature is Puu Olai, a 360-foot cinder hill a mile south of the landing. Just beyond Puu Olai, Makena has two knockout beaches adjoining each other. They are commonly called Big and Little beaches or, together, Makena Beach.

Big Beach is a huge sweep of glistening sand and a prime sunset-viewing locale with straight-on views of Molokini and Kahoolawe. Little Beach is a secluded cove and Maui's most popular nude beach.

In the late 1960s Makena was the site of an alternative-lifestyle camp and took on the nickname 'Hippie Beach'. The tent city lasted until 1972, when police finally evicted everyone on health code violations. More than a few of Maui's now-graying residents can trace their roots on the island to the camp at Makena Beach.

Makena Beach has recently become a state park, and long-term plans call for the addition of full beach facilities, but for now it remains in a largely natural state except for a couple of pit toilets and picnic tables.

MAUI

MAUI

Makena Bay

To explore the older side of Makena, turn right down Makena Rd after Makena Surf condos and go about a mile to Makena Bay.

In the 19th century, Makena was the busiest landing on this side of Maui. Cattle from Ulupalakua Ranch and other Upcountry ranches were brought down the hillsides and shipped to market in Honolulu from **Makena Landing**. By the 1920s, inter-island boat traffic had shifted to other ports on the island, and Makena lost its economic base.

Makena Landing is now a local recreational area with boat-launching facilities, showers, toilets and picnic tables. There's good snorkeling along the rocks at the south side of the landing.

South of the landing is the **Keawalai Congregational Church**, which dates to 1832 and is one of Maui's early missionary churches. The current building was built in 1855 with three-foot-thick walls made of burnt coral rock. A small congregation still meets for Sunday services, which are held in a mix of Hawaiian and English. The church graveyard has a fine bayside view and old tombstones with interesting cameo photographs.

The sheltered cove fronting the church is protected by two rocky outcrops, and its waters are almost always calm. The showers and restrooms opposite the church are the nearest facilities to Big Beach.

Makena Rd ends shortly after the church at a cul-de-sac on the ocean side of Maui Prince Hotel.

Maluaka Beach

At the southern end of Makena Bay is Maluaka Beach, a beige-sand beach fronting the Maui Prince Hotel. The beach, which slopes down from a low sand dune, has a sandy bottom in its center and rocky formations at each end that might provide decent snorkeling.

Big Beach

Big Beach is the sort of scene that people conjure up when they dream of a Hawaiian

beach – beautiful and expansive, with virtually no development on the horizon.

The Hawaiian name for Big Beach is Oneloa, literally 'Long Sand'. This golden-sand beach is well over half a mile long and as broad as they come, with clear turquoise waters.

The turn-off to the main parking area for Big Beach is about a mile past the Maui Prince Hotel. There's a second parking area a quarter of a mile to the south. You can also park alongside the road and walk in, but thefts and broken windshields are commonplace in the area and the parking lots are a safer bet. Watch for kiawe thorns in the woods behind the beach.

Big Beach is open ocean, with powerful rip currents and dangerous shorebreaks during periods of heavy surf.

Little Beach

Little Beach is hidden by a rocky outcrop that juts out from Puu Olai, the cinder cone that marks the north end of Big Beach.

A trail over the rock links the two and takes just a few minutes to walk. From the top of the trail there's a splendid view of both beaches.

Little Beach fronts a sandy cove that usually has a gentle shorebreak ideal for bodysurfing and boogie boarding. Snorkeling along the rocky point is good when the water is calm.

A trail continues for five minutes beyond Little Beach to an area where lava outcrops reach into the clear deep water like giant fingers. When it's very calm, divers and confident snorkelers sometimes explore these formations, which have caves and abundant marine life.

Little Beach, also known as Puu Olai Beach, is a popular nudist beach, despite posted signs to the contrary.

Beyond Makena

Makena Rd continues as a narrow paved road for 2½ miles after Big Beach. The road goes through the Ahihi-Kinau Natural Area Reserve before ending at La Perouse Bay. Because of the road's narrow width, and two-way traffic, it can be a very slow drive and is not really suitable for a quick sightseeing excursion.

Ahihi-Kinau The Ahihi-Kinau Natural Area Reserve covers 2045 acres and includes sections of Ahihi Bay and Cape Kinau.

Maui's most recent lava flow created most of the cape on its way to the sea in 1790. The reserve has lava tide pools, coastal lava tubes and all the aa lava you could ever want to see.

It has been designated a natural area reserve because of its distinctive marine life habitat and its unique geological features, including anchialine pools and *kipukas* (areas of land spared when lava flows around it). The removal of any flora, fauna or lava is prohibited.

The remains of a coastal Hawaiian village sit between lava flows at Ahihi Bay, its old sites marked by walled and terraced platforms.

There's a little roadside cove with good snorkeling just one-tenth of a mile south of the first reserve sign. It's quite rocky and can be a bit challenging getting in, but the cove has lots of coral and fish.

La Perouse Bay The paved road ends just short of La Perouse Bay. Although you may be able to drive all the way in on the 4WD road, you can also park where the asphalt ends and walk down to the coast. A 10-minute foot trail leads over the lava and along the water, passing a few tiny coves with sandy patches before reaching La Perouse Bay. The bay is rather rocky and marginal for most water activities, other than advanced diving, but there are good hiking possibilities in the area.

King's Hwy Coastal Trail From La Perouse Bay it's possible to continue on foot along the old King's Hwy. This ancient trail follows the coastline across jagged barren lava flows, so hiking boots are a good idea. It's a dry area with no water and little vegetation, and it can get very hot.

The first part of the trail is along the

sandy beach at La Perouse Bay. Right after the beach it's possible to take a ¾-mile spur trail down to the lighthouse at the tip of Cape Hanamanioa.

Alternatively, you could continue on the King's Hwy as it climbs up through rough aa lava inland for the next two miles before coming back to the coast at an older lava flow. In that area there are a number of old Hawaiian house foundations and pebble and coral beaches.

Places to Stay
The *Maui Prince Hotel* (☎ 874-1111, 800-228-3000; fax 879-8763), 5400 Makena Alanui, Wailea, HI 96753, turns inward in typical Japanese fashion. From the outside it looks like a fortress, but the interior incorporates a fine sense of Japanese aesthetics. The five-story hotel surrounds a courtyard with waterfalls and streams, carp ponds, raked rock gardens and bougainvillea draped from the balconies. All 300 rooms have at least partial ocean views and rack rates from $230, although there are often special promotions that include a room, car and breakfast for a few dollars less than the regular rates.

Places to Eat
Cafe Kiowai is the least expensive restaurant in the Maui Prince Hotel. At lunch, served until 5 pm, there are moderately priced salads and sandwiches as well as a

MAUI

The Lost Explorer

In May 1786 the renowned French explorer Jean François de Galaup La Perouse became the first Westerner to land on Maui. As he sailed into the bay that now bears his name, scores of Hawaiian canoes came out to greet him and trade.

After leaving Hawaii, La Perouse mysteriously disappeared in the Pacific. While no one knows his fate, some historians speculate that he and his crew were eaten by cannibals in the New Hebrides. ■

few hot dishes for $15 to $20. At dinner the best deal is a $13 soup and salad buffet that's offered from Monday to Thursday. On weekends there are more elaborate seafood or Oriental food buffets for $30.

Hakone at the Maui Prince has kimono-clad waitresses and authentic Japanese food, including a sushi bar. There are a number of full meals with appetizer, rice and soup in the $25 to $35 range. It's open from 6 to 9:30 pm Tuesday to Saturday.

The *Prince Court* at the Maui Prince has Hawaiian Regional cuisine, with main dishes priced from $20 for coconut curry chicken to $34 for filet mignon and lobster. It's open nightly from 5:30 pm. There's also an indulgent Sunday champagne brunch from 9:30 am to 1 pm for $32.

Kahului-Wailuku Area

Kahului and Wailuku, Maui's two largest communities, flow together to form a single urban sprawl. This is where regular folks live, work and shop.

Kahului is the commercial center. The main road, Kaahumanu Ave, is a collection of stores, banks and office buildings and a mile-long strip of shopping centers. Kaahumanu Ave continues into Wailuku where it becomes W Main St. Wailuku, the county seat, is the more distinctive and less hurried end of it all. This is an older town with back streets of curio shops, mom-and-pop stores and hole-in-the-wall ethnic restaurants.

Kahului Harbor, Maui's deep-water commercial port, services barges, cargo ships and the occasional cruise liner. This one's geared for work – there are no charming wharves or sailboats.

Maui's main airport is in Kahului. After landing, most people drive right out of town and don't come back until they're ready to leave. And, with a few exceptions, unless you're up for mall shopping, there's really not much in Kahului for visitors.

Wailuku, which you'll pass through on the way to Iao Valley State Park, has a few historic places of interest and makes for a

good lunch break and stroll. Wailuku also has some of Maui's cheapest places to stay.

Information
The main county and state office buildings are next to each other on High St in downtown Wailuku. The county parks office, which issues county camping permits, is on Kaahumanu Ave at Baldwin High School.

Tourist Offices The Maui Visitors Bureau (☎ 244-3530) is in Wailuku at 1727 Wili Pa Loop, near the post office. It's open from 8 am to 4:30 pm Monday to Friday.

Money The Bank of Hawaii has branches at 2105 Main St in Wailuku and 27 Puunene Ave in Kahului. Both have ATMs that accept major credit and debit cards.

Post & Communications Wailuku's post office is at 250 Imi Kala St, on the north side of town. Kahului's post office is on Puunene Ave. Both are open weekdays from 8:30 am to 5 pm, to noon on Saturdays.

The Coffee Store (☎ 871-6860) in the Kaahumanu Center in Kahului provides free Internet access.

Kinko's (☎ 871-2000), next to Pinata's at 395 Dairy Rd in Kahului, has computer rentals, fax transmissions, photocopying and other business services.

Bookstores & Libraries The Kahului public library, 90 School St, is open from 10 am to 5 pm on Mondays, Thursdays, Fridays and Saturdays and 10 am to 8 pm on Tuesdays and Wednesdays.

The Wailuku public library, 251 High St, is open from 10 am to 8 pm on Mondays and Thursdays, 10 am to 5 pm on Tuesdays, Wednesdays and Fridays.

There are Waldenbooks bookstores at both the Kaahumanu Center and the Maui Mall.

Travel Agents There are two discount travel agencies a five-minute drive from the airport. Both sell air coupons for inter-island flights for around $40. Maui Airport Travel (☎ 871-7666) is in the shopping

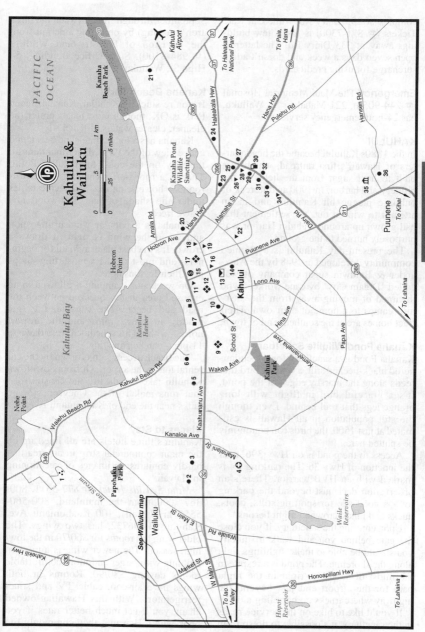

PACIFIC
OCEAN

Kanaha Beach Park

Kahului Airport

Kahului & Wailuku

0   .25   .5   .75   1 km
0   .25   .5   .75   1 miles

Kanaha Pond Wildlife Sanctuary

Kahului Bay

Hobron Point

Kahului Harbor

Nehe Point

Kahului Beach Rd

Waiehu Beach Rd

Iao Stream

Papohaku Park

See Wailuku map

Wailuku

To Iao Valley

Waile Reservoirs

Hopoi Reservoir

To Lahaina

Kahekili Hwy

Honoapiilani Hwy

Kahului Park

Kaahumanu Ave

Kamehameha Ave

School St

Lono Ave

Hina Ave

Papa Ave

Puunene Ave

Daily Rd

Alamaha St

Hana Hwy

Amala Rd

Hobron Ave

Pulehu Rd

Hansen Rd

To Paia, Hana

To Haleakala National Park

Haleakala Hwy

Puunene

To Kihei

MAUI

complex at 395 Dairy Rd, while Cut Rate Tickets (☎ 871-7300) is just a few buildings away at 333 Dairy Rd. The latter is open seven days a week and doesn't add a surcharge for using credit cards.

Emergency The Maui Memorial Hospital (☎ 244-9056), 221 Mahalani St, Wailuku, has 24-hour emergency service.

KAHULUI

In the 1880s Kahului became the headquarters of Hawaii's first railroad, which was built to haul sugar from the fields to the refinery and harbor. In 1900 an outbreak of bubonic plague hit Kahului, and in an attempt to wipe it out, the settlement that had grown up around Kahului Harbor was purposely burned to the ground.

The present-day Kahului is a planned community developed in 1948 by the Alexander & Baldwin sugar company. It was called 'Dream City' by cane workers who dreamed of moving away from the dusty mill camps to a home of their own. Their tract homes are at the southern end of town.

Kanaha Pond Wildlife Sanctuary

Kanaha Pond is a sanctuary for the endangered black-necked stilt, a wading bird that feeds along the marshy edges of the pond. It's a graceful bird in flight with long orange legs that trail behind. Even though the stilt population in all Hawaii is estimated at just 1500, the birds can commonly be spotted here.

Access to the pond is on Hwy 396, near the junction of Hwy 36. The parking lot is marked with an HVB warrior. There's an observation deck just beyond the parking lot – a good site for spotting stilts, coots, ducks and black-crowned night herons.

Upon entering the sanctuary, if you close the gate behind you and walk in quietly you should be able to make sightings right along the shoreline. The pond is a respite in the midst of suburbia, right in the flight path for the airport and just beyond the highway where trucks go barreling along.

If you'd like to hike on the service roads in the sanctuary, it's possible to do so from

September through March (when the birds aren't nesting) by obtaining a permit from the Division of Forestry and Wildlife (☎ 984-8100), State Office Building, 54 High St, Wailuku.

Kanaha Beach Park

If you're stuck in Kahului, Kanaha Beach Park is OK, though most locals prefer the cleaner, clearer waters of Kihei.

Kanaha has a long white-sand beach and a nice view of the West Maui Mountains all the way up the coast to Hakuhee Point. There's a roped-off swimming area, restrooms, showers, phones and picnic tables under the shade of hau, ironwood and kiawe trees.

Kanaha is a popular windsurfing spot, and when the wind is right, it draws a crowd. It's the best place in Maui for beginners, and most of the windsurfing shops give their lessons here.

On weekends, camping is allowed in an exposed area that's squeezed between the road and beach. The sites tend to get muddy in heavy rains and the airport noise – with flights scheduled from dawn to 11 pm – can be annoying.

The beach access sign is down by the car rental lots at the airport. Or from downtown Kahului take Amala Rd, the coastal road that runs makai of the Chevron storage tanks near the end of Kaahumanu Ave.

Places to Stay

Kahului's three hotels are all lined up on the main commercial strip in an area that hardly conjures up images of vacationing in Hawaii.

Maui Seaside Hotel (☎ 877-3311, 800-367-7000 from the mainland, 800-560-5552 in Hawaii), 100 Kaahumanu Ave, Kahului, HI 96732, has two wings. The older wing has rooms for $60/70 in the low/high season. The newer wing is a modern building with larger and more comfortable rooms costing $80/90. Rooms in both wings have air-con, cable TV and small refrigerators. With this Hawaiian-owned chain, you'll get much better rates if you book within Hawaii – they commonly run discounted specials in Sunday's *Honolulu Advertiser* that include a room and car for less than the standard room rates.

Next door, the adjacent *Maui Beach Hotel* and *Maui Palms Hotel* are Hawaiian Pacific Resorts properties (☎ 877-0071, 800-367-5004; fax 596-0158). Both are older and lackluster, and the main attraction is the rates, which have inched down in recent years. Prices at the 103-room Maui Palms Hotel start at $55, while those at the 154-room Maui Beach Hotel are from $80. Free shuttle service is provided from the airport, but if you reserve in advance, there's often a car/room package for the same price as the room alone.

Places to Eat

The second level of the Kaahumanu Center has a food court with a handful of good fast-food ethnic eateries, including *Little Cafe Siam*, *Yummy Korean BBQ*, *Panda Express*, *Edo Japan* and *Maui Tacos*, all of which have dishes for around $5. There's also a *McDonald's*, a fresh-juice bar called *Juiceland* and a *Mama Brava* with big slices of pizza for $2. The best bet is just to walk around and see what catches your eye. The food court is open from 11 am to 9 pm Monday to Saturday and from 11 am to 6 pm on Sunday.

The *Coffee Store*, a casual little place on the ground level of the Kaahumanu Center, roasts its own coffee and serves it straight or as espresso or cappuccino. Croissant sandwiches or quiche cost $4, lasagna is $6.50 and there are scrumptious pastries such as baklava and white-chocolate raspberry cheesecake. The shop, which is open daily, has only a few cafe tables and gets crowded at lunchtime.

A fun place on the upper level of the Kaahumanu Center is the *Sharktooth* microbrewery. You can observe the operation's stainless steel hopper and tanks through glass windows behind the bar – the taps lead directly from the tanks. There are five brews, ranging from a pale ale (Hula Girl) to sweet dark ale (Da Kine). Most popular of the lot is Sharktooth, a decent amber ale with a slight floral aroma. For

$2.25 you can get two-ounce samples of all five ales, or a 10-ounce glass of one. Prices are 75¢ cheaper during happy hour, from 3 to 6 pm daily. They also have pupus, sandwiches, $8 plate lunches and $20 steaks. It's open from 11 am to 11 pm, except on weekends when it closes at 1 am.

If you're in the Maui Mall, the best place to have lunch is *Stanton's*. Sandwiches such as tofu burger or hot pastrami are $6 or less. At breakfast there are bagels, croissants and egg dishes. Hours are 8 am to 6 pm weekdays (to 9 pm on Fridays), 9 am to 4:30 pm on weekends. The Maui Mall also has a few fast-food restaurants, an ice cream shop, an *International House of Pancakes* and *Maui Natural Foods*, a standard mall-style health food store.

Pinata's Mexican Food, 395 Dairy Rd, has a fast-food atmosphere but serves up Mexican fare that's good for the price. A taco, enchilada, rice and beans plate costs $6, a single burrito $3. It's open from 10:30 am to 7 pm Monday to Saturday.

Maui Coffee Roasters, 444 Hana Hwy, serves the coffee of the day at 50¢ a cup or $1 for a large mug. It also has good cappuccino, scones, muffins and sandwiches. It's open from 7:30 am to 6 pm weekdays, 8 am to 5 pm on Saturdays and 9 am to 3 pm on Sundays.

Maui Bakery & Bagelry, 201 Dairy Rd, specializes in bagels but also has pastries and sandwiches. Its hours are Monday to Saturday from 6:30 am to 5:30 pm.

There's a *Pizza Hut*, *Taco Bell*, *Jack in the Box* and *Sizzler* steak house lined up on Kamehameha Ave between Puunene Ave and Alamaha St, and *McDonald's* is nearby on Puunene Ave.

You'll find a *Safeway* supermarket on Kamehameha Ave, a *Foodland* supermarket at the Kaahumanu Center and a *Star Market* at the Maui Mall.

Entertainment

The main venue on Maui for theater, big-name music concerts, foreign film series and art exhibits is the new *Maui Arts & Cultural Center* on Kahului Beach Rd. It's a great place to catch a performance; the indoor theaters are acoustically outstanding and the seats are very comfortable. There's no permanent art museum, but rather exhibits that change on an ongoing basis; entry is free, though donations are appreciated. Call ☎ 242-2787 to find out if there's something currently on display. Tours of the center are given at 11 am on Wednesdays.

First-run movies are shown at *Kaahumanu* multiscreen theater (☎ 244-8934) in the Kaahumanu Center.

Sharktooth (☎ 871-6689) in the Kaahumanu Center presents live rock music on Tuesday nights. *Stanton's* (☎ 877-3711) in the Maui Mall occasionally has live blues and jazz on weekends.

Things to Buy

The Kaahumanu Center, on Kaahumanu Ave, is the area's largest mall, with about 50 shops, including Liberty House (and its Penthouse discount shop) and Sears. The Maui Mall on Kaahumanu Ave has Longs Drugs, Woolworth and a one-hour photo-processing shop.

For some local flavor try the Maui Swap Meet, which is held from 7 am to noon on Saturdays on Puunene Ave, just south of the Kahului post office.

PUUNENE

Puunene is a working plantation village surrounded by sugar cane fields and centered around a mill run by the Hawaiian Commercial & Sugar Company. When the mill is in operation the air hangs heavy with the sweet smell of sugar.

The power plant next to the mill burns residue sugar cane fibers called bagasse to run the mill machinery that extracts and refines the sugar. With a capacity of 37,000 kilowatts, it's one of the world's largest biomass power plants. Excess electricity is sold to Maui Electric.

Puunene's main attraction is the sugar museum opposite the mill.

Sugar Museum

The Alexander & Baldwin Sugar Museum is a worthwhile little museum that tells the history of sugar in Hawaii. Displays explain how sugar cane grows and is harvested, complete with an elaborate working scale model of a cane-crushing plant.

What's most interesting, however, are the images of people. The museum traces how Samuel Alexander and Henry Baldwin gobbled up vast chunks of Hawaiian land and fought tooth and nail with an ambitious Claus Spreckels to gain access to Upcountry water. They then dug extensive irrigation systems that made large-scale sugar cane plantations a possibility.

Representing the other end of the scale is a turn-of-the-century labor contract from the Japanese Emigration Company stating that the laborer shall be paid $15 a month for working 10 hours a day in the field, 26 days a month (minus $2.50 banked for return passage to Japan). Interesting period photos and artifacts of plantation life are also on display.

The museum (☎ 871-8058), originally the home of the mill's superintendent, is at the intersection of Puunene Ave and Hansen Rd. It's open from 9:30 am to 4:30 pm Monday to Saturday (and on Sundays in summer). Admission is $4 for adults, $2 for children ages six to 17.

WAIKAPU

The Honoapiilani Hwy (Hwy 30), which runs along the east side of the West Maui Mountains, passes through the town of Waikapu just a couple of miles south of Wailuku.

Although Waikapu has a new golf course sitting above its pineapple fields, it remains quite rural. Its only sight is **Maui Tropical Plantation**, which features a touristy narrated tram ride past fields of sugar cane, pineapple and tropical fruit trees. The ride, which takes about 40 minutes, costs $9.

There's also a shop selling fresh fruit and a free-admission section that includes a nursery, a few taro plants and a couple of very simple exhibits on agriculture.

If you're driving by, you might want to make a quick stop, but it's not worth going out of your way. Its hours are from 9 am to 5 pm daily.

WAILUKU
Wailuku sits beneath the eastern flank of
the West Maui Mountains and is an interesting juxtaposition of old and new. While
the central area serves as the county capital,
complete with a few mid-rise government
buildings, the back streets are lined with a
colorful hodgepodge of older shops and
neighborhood restaurants. Wailuku is
unabashedly local – there's nothing touristy
in the whole town.

It's a fun town for strolling. Begin walking
north from West Main St on Market St,
which has a handful of pawn shops, galleries
and antique shops, some of them intriguingly
cluttered affairs. One of the more interesting
shops is Traders of the Lost Art, which has
ancestral carvings and ritual art from Papua
New Guinea, Oceania and the Antipodes
and inexpensive used aloha shirts. Other
shops have a mishmash of goods that
include Hawaiiana, Thai and Indonesian
handicrafts and lots of odds and ends.

Kaahumanu Church
Kaahumanu Church, on the corner of West
Main and High Sts, dates from 1837,
making it the oldest Congregational church
in Maui. The present building was built in
1876 by missionary Edward Bailey.

The church was named in honor of Queen
Kaahumanu, who cast aside the old gods
and burned temple idols, allowing Christianity to flourish. She visited Wailuku in 1832
and in her ever-humble manner requested
that the first church bear her name.

The old clock in the steeple was brought
around the Horn in the 19th century, and it
still keeps accurate time. Hymns are sung
in Hawaiian at Sunday morning services.

Bailey House Museum
Bailey House, a five-minute walk up Iao
Valley Rd from Kaahumanu Church, was
home to the family of missionary Edward
Bailey, who came to Wailuku from Boston,
Massachusetts, in 1837.

MAUI

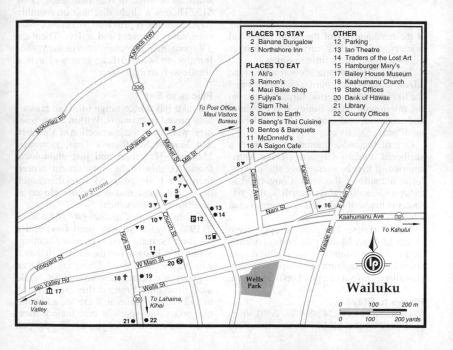

NED FRIARY

Uncle Sol Kawaihoa at the
Bailey House Museum

The building, also called Hale Hoikeike, is the headquarters of the Maui Historical Society, which has turned the former mission house into a little museum.

There's a Hawaiiana section with stone adzes, tapa, bottle gourds, calabashes and the like, as well as period furnishings from the missionary days. Bailey was a painter and engraver, and many of his works are on display.

One of the most interesting sights is a surfboard used by Olympian Duke Kahanamoku; it can be seen above the parking lot at the side of the shed. Compare it to today's sleek fiberglass boards – this six-footer is made of redwood and weighs in at a hefty 150 pounds!

Bailey House Museum is open from 10 am to 4 pm Monday to Friday. Admission is $4 for adults, $1 for children ages six to 12. The museum gift shop has quality Hawaiiana crafts and a good book selection.

Places to Stay

Northshore Inn (☎ 242-8999), 2080 Vineyard St, Wailuku, HI 96793, in a funky old building right in the center of Wailuku, is popular with European windsurfers. Its new owner has spiffed the place up a bit and turned it into a decent budget accommodation. There are a few simple rooms with shared baths at $27/37 for singles/doubles and a handful of dorm rooms, which have four to six bunks to a room and cost $14 per bunk. Add $1 (for the entire length of stay) to rent a cover sheet and another dollar if you want a blanket. There's a TV near the front desk and a small group kitchen. The inn is open only to travelers, and a passport or airline ticket may be required to book a room.

Banana Bungalow (☎ 244-5090, 800-746-7871; fax 242-9324), 310 Lower Market St, Wailuku, HI 96793, is a modest hostel-type place with cheap beds and both international travelers and long-term borders. Private rooms are simple but generally clean and cost $33/40 for singles/doubles, while space in one of the dorm rooms, which have three to four beds each, costs $15. There's a slight discount on monthly stays. Bedding is provided. All guests share community showers and toilets. There's a TV room, group kitchen, coin laundry, shed for storing windsurfing gear and a free shuttle to Kanaha Beach.

Places to Eat

Wailuku has a nice range of good, reasonably priced restaurants. Within a few minutes' walk from the intersection of Vineyard and Market Sts there's Thai, Japanese, Mexican, Hawaiian and just plain local food. As this is the government center, there are a lot of good weekday lunch deals, but most restaurants are closed at lunchtime on weekends.

Saeng's Thai Cuisine (☎ 244-1567), 2119 Vineyard St, has good food and a pleasant setting with open-air dining. While it's known for its curries, it has a wide range of dishes. There are a dozen vegetarian offerings for around $8, while most meat and shrimp dishes are in the $8 to $12 range. At lunch, there are a handful of good-value specials that include rice, salad and an entree for just $6.50. It's open from 11 am to 2:30 pm on weekdays and 5 to 9:30 pm nightly.

Two blocks away and run by a relative, *Siam Thai* (☎ 244-3817), 123 N Market St, also has good food. Although the atmosphere is more local in flavor, the food is nearly the same as at Saeng's and the hours are identical.

Bentos & Banquets (☎ 244-1124), 85 Church St, has takeout lunch specials from 10 am to 2 pm weekdays that are quite popular with local businesspeople. The menu changes daily, though a few dishes like roast pork, teriyaki steak and vegetarian tofu are standards. Most lunches cost around $6.

Maui Bake Shop & Deli, a small family-run operation at 2092 Vineyard St, has a wide variety of good breakfast pastries and desserts as well as soups, salads and sandwiches at reasonable prices. It's open from 6 am to 5:30 pm on weekdays and 7 am to 3 pm on Saturdays.

At *Ramon's* (☎ 244-7243), 2101 Vineyard St, you can get a Spanish omelet with home-fries for $5, an enchilada with rice and beans for $7 and standard Mexican combination plates for a few dollars more. It's open Monday to Saturday from 7 am to 10 pm.

Fujiya's (☎ 244 0206), 133 Market St, has a variety of Japanese dishes for around $8 and some good dinner teishoku combinations for $10. Hours are 11 am to 2 pm Monday to Friday and 5 to 9 pm Monday to Saturday.

Aki's, 309 N Market St, serves Hawaiian food. Kalua pig with cabbage and salad costs $5, a small octopus with coconut milk is $3.50 and a side of poi is $1.60. It's a local experience. Hours are 11 am to 9 pm Monday to Saturday, 5 to 9 pm on Sundays.

A Saigon Cafe (☎ 243-9560), on the corner of Main and Kaniela Sts, has excellent Vietnamese pho soup and various meat and vegetarian entrees, such as chicken in lemongrass or curry tofu with jasmine rice for around $7. A fun dish is banh hoi, which is somewhat like a Vietnamese version of fajitas, served with a plate of mint leaves, rice noodles, assorted vegetables and shrimp or tofu, which you roll up

into rice-paper wraps. The restaurant doesn't have a sign and is a bit challenging to reach, but it's worth the effort; to get there, take Central Ave to Nani St and then turn south on Kaniela St. It's open daily from 10 am to 10 pm (to 9 pm on Sundays).

Down to Earth, on the corner of Central Ave and Vineyard St, is a well-stocked natural food store with reasonable prices, fresh organic produce and good dairy and juice sections. For takeout there's a salad bar for $4.50 a pound, sandwiches and a few hot dishes. It's open from 8 am to 7 pm on weekdays, 8 am to 6 pm on Saturdays and 10 am to 5 pm on Sundays.

For the less health-oriented, there's a *McDonald's* on Main St.

Entertainment

Local theater groups present plays at the circa-1928 *Iao Theatre* on Market St, which has recently been restored after years of neglect. It's pleasantly casual, and cross-breezes keep it cool and comfortable inside. For schedule information, call ☎ 244-8680.

Hamburger Mary's (☎ 244-7776), a restaurant and bar at 2010 Main St, is a popular night spot for the gay community. Dance videos are played from 10 pm to 2 am Monday to Saturday.

IAO VALLEY RD

In 1790, Kamehameha I attacked Kahului by sea and quickly chased the defending Mauian warriors up into precipitous Iao Valley. Those unable to escape over the mountains were slaughtered along the stream. The waters of Iao Stream were so choked with bodies that the area was called Kepaniwai, meaning 'Dammed Waters'.

Today much of the upper valley along the stream is park land. Iao Valley Rd leads into the Iao Valley State Park, passing a few sights along the way.

Tropical Gardens of Maui

If you're looking for a botany lesson, Tropical Gardens of Maui has in-depth interpretive plaques explaining the background of many of the plants here. Even though it's a relatively new garden, the plantings are varied and in the past few years they've matured enough to make this a worthwhile sight. It's open from 9 am to 4:30 pm Monday to Saturday; admission is $3.

Kepaniwai County Park

Kepaniwai County Park is dedicated to Hawaii's varied ethnic heritage.

Like Hawaii itself, there's a little bit of everything mixed in, including a Hawaiian hale with a pili grass roof, a Filipino house, a little New England missionary home and a Portuguese garden with a statue of the Virgin Mary overlooking a bubbling fountain and outdoor bread oven.

Most colorful are the Asian gardens, with their pavilions, stone pagodas and miniature bridges over flowing water. Amid the gardens is a Chinese pavilion, red and white with a green ceramic tile roof, and the requisite statue of Sun Yat-sen. Nearby a bronze statue of two Japanese sugar cane workers in traditional garb commemorates the centennial of Japanese immigration to the islands.

Iao Stream, which runs through the park, is bordered by pavilions with tables and barbecue pits that are often used for picnics and parties.

JFK Profile

A half mile after Kepaniwai Park you'll come to a bend in the road where there are often a few cars pulled over and people staring off into Pali Eleele, a gorge on the right. One of the rock formations on the cliff face looks surprisingly like John F Kennedy's profile. There's a pipe set up as a scope to help you find the obvious.

If parking is difficult here, just continue on to Iao Valley State Park, as it's only a couple of minutes' walk from there back to the profile viewing site.

Iao Valley State Park

Iao Valley State Park is nestled in the mountains at the 2250-foot elevation, three miles out of central Wailuku. The valley is named for Iao, the beautiful daughter of Maui and Hina.

Iao Needle, a rock pinnacle that rises 1200 feet from the valley floor, is said to be Iao's clandestine lover, captured by Maui and turned to stone.

Clouds often rise up the valley, forming a shroud around the top of Iao Needle. A stream meanders beneath the needle, and the steep cliffs of the West Maui Mountains form a scenic backdrop.

A two-minute walk from the parking lot, you'll reach a bridge where most people stop to photograph Iao Needle. However, just before the bridge there's a walkway looping downhill by the stream and if you take it you'll find the nicest photo angle – one that captures the stream, bridge and Iao Needle together.

Over the bridge, a short walkway leads up to a sheltered lookout with another fine view of Iao Needle.

The park is open daily from 7 am to 7 pm; there's no admission fee.

HALEKII & PIHANAKALANI HEIAUS

Halekii-Pihanakalani Heiaus State Monument marks one of Maui's most important precontact historical sites.

Kahekili, the last ruling chief of Maui, lived here, and Keopuolani, wife of Kamehameha I and mother of Kamehamehas II and III, was born at this site. After the decisive battle of Iao in 1790, Kamehameha I came to these heiaus to worship his war god Ku, offering what is thought to have been the last human sacrifice on Maui.

The two adjoining heiaus are atop a knoll and have a commanding view of the entire region, clear across the plains of central Maui and up the slopes of Haleakala. The temples were built with stones carried up from Iao Stream.

Halekii (literally 'House of the Idol'), the first heiau, has stepped stone walls and a flat grassy top. (Watch out for bullhead thorns if you're wearing flip-flops.) The pyramid-like mound of Pihanakalani Heiau is directly ahead, a five-minute walk away.

Pihanakalani, which means 'gathering place of supernatural beings', is fairly overgrown with kiawe, wildflowers and weeds.

Few people come this way, and as you approach doves fly up from the bushes.

Despite the state monument status, the government has been somewhat negligent in protecting the heiaus. This is one of the fastest growing residential areas on Maui, and construction and gravel removal along both sides of the hill have been so widespread that some conservationists are fearful that the heiau site itself is being undermined.

Nevertheless, a certain spiritual essence still emanates from the site. Ignore the industrial warehouses and tract homes and concentrate instead on the heiaus and the wide vistas to imagine it all through the eyes of the Hawaiians 200 years back. It must have been an incredible scene.

To get there from Waiehu Beach Rd, turn mauka onto Kuhio Place, three-quarters of a mile south of the intersection of Hwys 340 and 330. Then take the first left off Kuhio Place onto Hea Place and drive up through the gates. The heiaus are less than half a mile from Hwy 340.

KAHEKILI HWY

Kahekili Hwy (Hwy 340) curves around the undeveloped northeastern side of the West Maui Mountains. It's ruggedly scenic, with deep ravines, eroded red hills and rock-strewn pastures. The coastline is rocky lava sea cliffs and open ocean.

The route is pastoral and quiet with a couple of waterfalls, blowholes and one-lane bridges. It's common to spot cowhands on horseback and egrets riding the backs of lazy cows.

The northern end of the road is at Honokohau, the south at Wailuku, a distance of about 22 miles.

Like its counterpart to the south (the Piilani Hwy around the southern flank of Haleakala), Hwy 340 is shown either as a black hole or an unpaved road on most tourist maps. The road, however, is paved its entire length – though much of the drive is very winding and narrow, with blind curves and the occasional sign warning of falling rocks.

The road between Honokohau and Kahakuloa is largely two lanes and easygoing, while the section between Kahakuloa and Waihee is mostly one lane (with two-way traffic) and has a few sections cliffside without shoulders. While most of the road is posted 15 mph, there are sections where it's a mere 5 mph. But taking it slowly is the whole point anyway.

Waiehu & Waihee

Waiehu Beach Rd turns into Kahekili Hwy at the northern end of Wailuku and heads through the little towns of Waiehu and Waihee.

Waiehu Municipal Golf Course is down near the shore, bordered by two county beach parks that have poor swimming conditions and limited appeal, other than for strolling and beachcombing.

Waihee Ridge Trail

A side road up to the Boy Scouts' Camp Mahulia is a pretty, winding drive through open pasture that leads to the start of the Waihee Ridge Trail. This trail is a peaceful, seldom-trodden route offering varied scenery and breathtaking views of the interior.

The drive up, which begins mauka just before the seven-mile marker, is a one-lane paved road. Be prepared to stop for cattle crossing the pavement.

The trailhead is a mile up, on the left just before the camp, marked with a Na Ala Hele sign and a squeeze-through 'turnstile' through the fence. There's a little parking area to the left of the trailhead.

The trail is three miles one way and takes about three hours roundtrip. Consider packing a lunch, as there's a picnic table with an unbeatable view at the end. It's a well-defined trail that crosses forest reserve land, and though it's a bit steep, it's a fairly steady climb and not overly strenuous.

Starting at an elevation of 1000 feet, the trail climbs a ridge, passing from pasture to cool forest, much of it through groves of rainbow eucalyptus trees. Guava trees are also prominent along the trail, and if you look closely, you can usually find thimbleberries too. From the three-quarter-mile post, panoramic views open up with a spectacular scene that sweeps clear down to the ocean along the Waihee Gorge and deep into the interior valleys. The ridge-top views are similar to those you'd see from a helicopter, though the stillness along this route can only be appreciated by those on foot. The trail ends at the 2563-foot peak of Lanilili, where there are great views in all directions.

Waterfalls & Gardens

Back on the highway, you'll pass a gentle waterfall on the left, rain permitting. For another waterfall view, stop at the pull-off a tenth of a mile north of the eight-mile marker and look down into the ravine below, where you'll see a picture-perfect waterfall framed by double pools.

Shortly before reaching the nine-mile marker, a sign marks the driveway up to Aina Anuhea tropical gardens, a private estate offering a 20-minute walk through gardens with labeled plants and a 25-foot waterfall where you can take a dip. It costs $3.

Kahakuloa

The village of Kahakuloa is at the base of a small green valley. Although there are only a few dozen simple homes, Kahakuloa ('Tall Lord') has two churches. The little tin-roofed Catholic mission sits hillside at the southern end of town just off the road, while on the valley floor is the green wooden Protestant church with a red-tile roof.

Up out of the valley at the northern edge of town there's a pull-off with a good view of the village and the rugged coastline. The rise on the south side of Kahakuloa Bay is Kahakuloa Head, 636 feet high.

Bellstone

Pohaku Kani is a large bellstone at the inland side of the road just past the 16-mile marker.

If you hit the bellstone with a rock on the Kahakuloa side where the deepest indentations are, you might be able to get a hollow sound. It's pretty resonant if you hit it right, but it takes some imagination to hear it ring like a bell.

Pastures & Cliffs

The wide turn-off about half a mile beyond the 16-mile marker looks down over a clifftop plateau with a rugged coast and crashing surf. The stretch of green turf practically invites you to walk from the road down to the cliffs and out along the coastline. Although it's unshaded, it would be a fine place to break out a bottle of wine and a picnic lunch.

This is hilly country, with rocky cattle pastures and tall sisal plants. There are a number of viewpoints and pull-offs where you can stop and explore.

Stone cairns are piled everywhere. They look like religious offerings, but most are just the creations of sightseers and are of no significance.

Blowhole

When the water is surging, there's a blowhole visible from the road just past the 20-mile marker. It comes up after a sharp bend in the road. During the winter season, you can sometimes spot humpbacks breaching offshore in this area as well.

Nakalele Point Light Station

About half a mile farther, there's a walk out to the light station at the end of Nakalele Point. The coastline has interesting pools, arches and other formations worn out of the rocks by the pounding of the surf. As elsewhere in Maui, don't leave valuables in your car at the parking area. The smashed glass from broken windshields is indicative of the break-ins that take place here.

As you continue north along the road, Molokai comes into view, and the scenery is very lush on the way to Honokohau Bay.

Paia

Paia is an old sugar town with a fresh coat of paint.

As part of the original Alexander & Baldwin sugar plantation, Paia had a population of about 8000 in the early 20th century, more than triple its present size. In

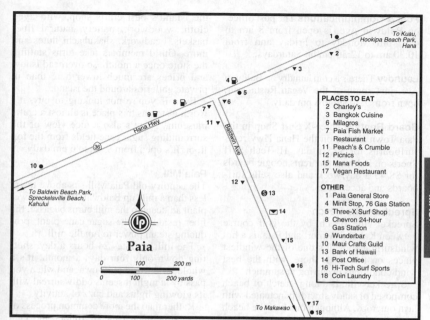

Paia

PLACES TO EAT
2 Charley's
3 Bangkok Cuisine
6 Milagros
7 Paia Fish Market Restaurant
11 Peach's & Crumble
12 Picnics
15 Mana Foods
17 Vegan Restaurant

OTHER
1 Paia General Store
4 Minit Stop, 76 Gas Station
5 Three-X Surf Shop
8 Chevron 24-hour Gas Station
9 Wunderbar
10 Maui Crafts Guild
13 Bank of Hawaii
14 Post Office
16 Hi-Tech Surf Sports
18 Coin Laundry

To Kuau, Hookipa Beach Park, Hana

To Baldwin Beach Park, Spreckelsville Beach, Kahului

To Makawao

Hana Hwy

Baldwin Ave

MAUI

those days most of Paia's residents lived in plantation camps on the slopes above the sugar mill.

The mill is still open, though its heyday is past. During the 1950s many of the town's residents moved to Kahului, shops closed down and Paia began to collect cobwebs.

In the early 1980s windsurfers began to discover nearby Hookipa Beach and Paia was dubbed the 'Windsurfing Capital of the World'.

Today, Paia has as many windsurfers as sugar cane workers. They come from all over the world, including Germany, France and Australia, giving Paia more of an international flavor than any other small town in Hawaii.

Paia has small grocery stores that have been in the same families for generations and offbeat shops selling Balinese clothing and antique aloha shirts. Many of the old wooden storefronts are painted in bright tones of rosy pink, sunshine yellow and sky blue, adding to the town's unique character.

The Hana Hwy (Hwy 36) runs straight through the center of Paia – this is the last real town before Hana and the last place to gas up your car.

Paia is also a link to the Upcountry; Baldwin Ave leads from the center of town up to Makawao.

Information
Mana Foods on Baldwin Ave has a good bulletin board, with rooms for rent tacked up amid notices of such things as windsurfing lessons, Tibetan pulsing healing and Congolese dancing.

Money Bank of Hawaii on Baldwin Ave is open from 8:30 am to 3 pm Monday to Thursday, 8:30 am to 6 pm on Fridays. If you want to make a credit card or ATM card withdrawal, there's a Bankoh money machine at the Minit Stop.

Post & Communications The post office, on Baldwin Ave, is open from 8 am to 4:30 pm Monday to Friday and from 10:30 am to 12:30 pm on Saturdays.

Laundry There's a coin laundry on Baldwin Ave, just south of the Vegan Restaurant, open from 7:30 am to 8 pm daily.

Board Rentals Three-X Surf Shop in the Paia Town Center on the Hana Hwy rents surfboards for $25 a day. Hi-Tech Surf Sports on Baldwin Ave rents boogie boards for $8/45 a day/week and also sells surfboards and accessories.

Spreckelsville Beach

Spreckelsville Beach, by the golf course between Kahului Airport and Paia, is a hot windsurfing spot. It's one of the windiest places on the north shore, with the best wind conditions occurring in summer.

Spreckelsville is a long stretch of beach composed of sandy strands punctuated with lava outcrops. Although much of the beach is rocky, there are spots with reasonably good swimming.

To get there turn makai on Nonohe Rd, which runs along the west side of the Maui Country Club. Turn right when the road ends and look for the beach access sign.

Baldwin Beach Park

Baldwin Beach Park, a big county park about a mile west of Paia, has a long sandy beach with good bodysurfing. There are showers, restrooms, picnic tables, a phone and camping. The park also has a well-used baseball and soccer field, which tends to make it a rather congested scene.

The tent spaces are on a flat grassy spot by the road, surrounded by a chain-link fence. Even with the high visibility it's not a particularly secure place to stay, and in past years there have been some serious assaults on campers at this site.

Maui Crafts Guild

Maui Crafts Guild, on the left as you come into town from Kahului, is a collective of Maui artists and craftspeople. It is the island's best crafts shop, with dyed cloth, woodwork, pottery, natural fiber baskets, beadwork, shakuhachi flutes and more. Guild members take turns staffing the store once a month, so overhead is low and prices are much lower here than in private galleries around the island.

Even if you're not looking to buy, it's worth a stop as this place is almost a crafts museum. There's also a nice view of the surrounding sugar cane fields from the top floor. It's open from 9 am to 6 pm daily.

Paia Mill

The century-old Paia Mill sits above town, less than a mile up Baldwin Ave. The power plant adjacent to the mill burns bagasse, the fiber residue of the sugar cane plant, producing steam power to run the mill.

The mill operates 24 hours a day, shutting down only four days a month. It's a whole little world of its own, and when you pass by at night it seems oddly surreal with its glowing lights and buzz of activity.

Rather than the more common process of squeezing sugar cane by rollers, the Paia Mill flushes juice out of shredded sugar cane in a process resembling that of a drip coffeemaker.

Mantokuji Buddhist Mission

Mantokuji, a circa-1921 Buddhist temple with an ocean view and a big gong in the yard, is on the Hana side of town. It's fronted with a graveyard of kanji-engraved stones, some decorated with colorful tropical flowers. During the summer, the Obon holidays are observed here with religious services and Japanese dances.

Hookipa Beach Park

Hookipa, which has long been one of Maui's prime surfing spots, has more recently established itself as Hawaii's premier windsurfing beach. It has good year-round action for both – winter has the biggest waves for board surfers and summer has the most consistent winds for windsurfers.

Hookipa Beach attracts the world's top windsurfers. It is the site of several international tournaments, including the Da Kine

Hawaiian Pro Am in April and the Aloha Classic in October or early November.

Between the strong currents, dangerous shorebreak and razor-sharp coral, this is unquestionably an area for experts. As a spectator sport, it's great – if you come by at the right time, you'll be watching some of the best action to be found anywhere.

Hookipa is just before the nine-mile marker; look for the line of cars on the lookout above the beach. This county park has restrooms, showers, pay phones and picnic pavilions.

Places to Stay

While Paia has no hotels, there are a number of smaller private places to stay. Most are rented out through B&B booking services, though you can also find rooms by checking bulletin boards around Paia and in the 'Vacation Rentals' column in the *Maui News* classifieds. If you're staying any length of time, you might be able to get a room in a shared house for as little as $300 a month.

The four places that follow can be booked direct. With the exception of Hale Aloha, which is midway between Kuau and Paia, they are all near the eight-mile marker in Kuau. Kuau is about two miles west of downtown Paia and is the closest neighborhood to Hookipa.

Mike Doherty (☎ 579 9430; fax 579-8322), 4 Kalholo Place, Paia, HI 96770, has a small apartment house with three units that he rents out as *North Shore Vacation Rentals*. There's a good-sized studio as well as a one-bedroom unit that rent for $50 a night and a two-bedroom unit that rents for $1200 a month. Each has a private bath, cooking facilities and cable TV. Most guests are windsurfers, and the location is close enough to the beach that you can keep sails rigged in the yard, walk down the street and sail away. Guests have free use of a washer and dryer. There's storage space for up to 30 boards and a work space for board repair.

Hale Aloha (☎ /fax 579-9849), 16 Kulani Place, Paia, HI 96779, is a two-story plantation-style house with large airy lanais and a nice laid-back character. It's about 500 yards mauka of the Hana Hwy in a quiet setting on the edge of cane fields. There are three studios with microwaves and small refrigerators that rent for $50 (two have ocean views); a one-bedroom unit for $75 and a roomy two-bedroom unit with a full kitchen for $100. Each unit has a fan, phone, TV and VCR, and there's surfboard storage and free use of a washer and dryer. There's usually a three-day minimum, but that can be flexible if things are slow, and discounts can be arranged for longer stays.

Terry and Margit Tolman (☎ 579-8282, 800-398-6284; fax 579-9953), Box 108, Paia, HI 96779, have two units called *Hookipa Haven*. A one-bedroom apartment on the 1st floor of their home rents for $60. It has a queen bed, kitchen, bathroom, private entrance and a futon couch in the living room. There's also a fully furnished two-bedroom cottage on the grounds that costs $85 for two people or $95 for four; note that the walls are open at the ceiling, so there's no sound barrier between the rooms. There's a $150 deposit in the studio, $200 in the cottage. Margit runs a vacation rental service and books other accommodations in the Paia and Haiku areas, as well as elsewhere on Maui, with daily rates starting at about $50 for studios. German is spoken.

Mama's Vacation Rentals (☎ 579-9764; fax 579-8594), 799 Poho Place, Paia, HI 96779, rents two garden-view one-bedroom apartments for $75 and two beachfront two-bedroom apartments for $150, all adjacent to Mama's Fish House. Each unit has a kitchen, cable TV, VCR, stereo and phone. All have queen beds; the two-bedroom units also have two twin beds and a queen sofa bed. If you don't stay a minimum of three nights, there's a $35 cleaning fee. Smoking is not allowed.

Places to Eat

Picnics, 30 Baldwin Ave, is a deli with both takeout and eat-in services. Sandwiches include a nice vegetarian spinach nut burger with cheddar cheese ($5.50) as well as more traditional fillings like roast beef or turkey. There are good breakfast pastries for around $1.50, including large cinnamon rolls and orange pecan scones. Picnics also has fruit and vegetable salads, cappuccino and espresso. There's a guide to the Hana Hwy on the back of the takeout menu, and they prepare box lunches for the road. Hours are 7 am to 7 pm daily.

Peach's & Crumble Cafe & Bakery on Baldwin Ave has muffins, croissants and peach crumble squares for $1.25 to $2.50 and sandwiches such as Mexican avocado, nutty vegie burger and smoked salmon for around $5. They also make picnic lunches ($7) to go. It's open from 6:30 am to at least 6 pm daily.

The *Vegan Restaurant* (☎ 579-9144), 115 Baldwin Ave, serves tasty vegetarian food at reasonable prices. It costs $5 for a vegan burger or a large salad. The menu includes a variety of imaginative dishes with Thai, Mexican and Japanese influences; most hot dishes cost $9. As there are only a dozen small cafe tables, it's best to arrive early for dinner to avoid a long wait. It's open from 4 to 8:30 pm daily.

Milagros (☎ 579-8755), on the corner of Baldwin Ave and the Hana Hwy, is a popular little Tex-Mex cafe with both indoor and sidewalk dining. Two tacos or enchiladas served with rice and beans cost $6.50. There are also salads, sandwiches and burritos for around the same price. It's open from 8 am to 9:30 pm.

Paia Fish Market Restaurant (☎ 579-8030), on the opposite corner of Baldwin Ave and the Hana Hwy, specializes in fresh fish, which you'll find on display in a refrigerated case at the counter. A good choice is the grilled fish sandwich on a whole-wheat bun, which costs $6 with ono or mahimahi. Fish & chips cost $7 at lunch, $10 at dinner. It's open from 11 am to 9:30 pm daily.

Charley's (☎ 579-9453) on the Hana Hwy is a popular place for a late breakfast. Both breakfast and lunch fare are served from 7 am to 2:30 pm, with omelets, sandwiches and burritos all priced around $7. Dinner, from 5 to 10 pm, includes pizza, pastas and calzones for under $10 and a few more elaborate dishes such as shrimp scampi for around $15.

For authentic Thai food, the family-run *Bangkok Cuisine* (☎ 579-8979), 120 Hana Hwy, has a menu that includes curries, pad Thai and various shrimp, fish, meat and vegetarian dishes, most priced from $8 to $10. It's open from 11 am to 3 pm and 5 to 9:30 pm daily.

Mana Foods on Baldwin Ave is a large, down-to-earth health food store with a good variety of juices, yogurts, bulk nuts, granola, cheeses and organic produce. It also has fresh baked breads, including a loaf filled with tomatoes and feta cheese ($3) that makes a meal in itself. There's a small salad bar and a few inexpensive takeout hot dishes. Mana is open from 8 am to 8 pm daily and like most grocery stores in Hawaii takes credit cards.

Although pricey, *Mama's Fish House* (☎ 579-8488), along the Hana Hwy in Kuau, just east of Paia center, has excellent fish and a nice ocean view. There are always three to five different types of fresh fish, priced at $24 for lunch and around $30 at dinner. There are half a dozen preparations, including a traditional saute in wine and garlic butter, but the local favorite is pan-fried fish with Maui onions and chili peppers. Add another $6 for a salad, double that for an appetizer. It's open daily from 11 am to 2:30 pm for lunch, 5 to 9:30 pm for dinner. Hawaiian residents get a 20% discount.

Entertainment

The *Wunderbar* (☎ 579-8808), Paia's most popular watering hole, has the island's longest monkeypod bar and a full range of European beers, including Warsteiner on tap. Rock bands play on Friday nights from 10 pm to 12:30 am; the cover charge is typically $3 to $5.

Road to Hana

The Hana Hwy runs from central Maui to the village of Hana and beyond to the pools of Oheo Gulch. While all the islands some incredible scenery, the Hana Hwy ranks as *the* most spectacular coastal drive

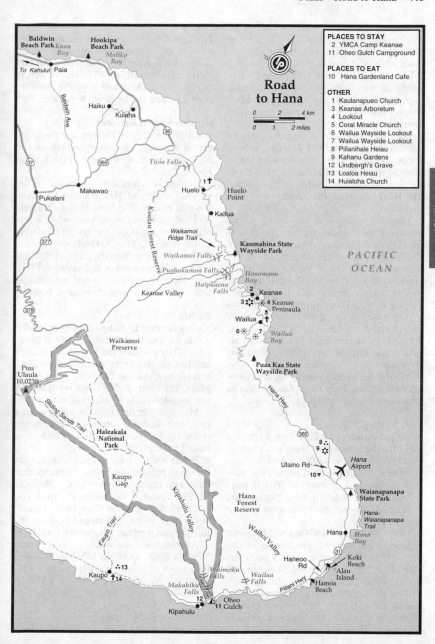

Road to Hana

0   2   4 km
0   1   2 miles

PLACES TO STAY
2   YMCA Camp Keanae
11 Oheo Gulch Campground

PLACES TO EAT
10 Hana Gardenland Cafe

OTHER
1   Kaulanapueo Church
3   Keanae Arboretum
4   Lookout
5   Coral Miracle Church
6   Wailua Wayside Lookout
7   Wailua Wayside Lookout
8   Piilanihale Heiau
9   Kahanu Gardens
12 Lindbergh's Grave
13 Loaloa Heiau
14 Huialoha Church

Baldwin Beach Park
Hookipa Beach Park
Kuau Bay
Maliko Bay
To Kahului
Paia
Haiku
Kuiaha
Baldwin Ave
Makawao
Pukalani
Twin Falls
Huelo
Huelo Point
Kailua
Koolau Forest Reserve
Waikamoi Ridge Trail
Waikamoi Falls
Puohokamoa Falls
Haipuaena Falls
Kaumahina State Wayside Park
PACIFIC OCEAN
Keanae Valley
Honomanu Bay
Keanae
Keanae Peninsula
Wailua
Wailua Bay
Waikamoi Preserve
Puaa Kaa State Wayside Park
Puu Ulaula 10,023ft
Sliding Sands Trail
Haleakala National Park
Kaupo Gap
Kaupo Trail
Kipahulu Valley
Hana Forest Reserve
Waihoi Valley
Hana Hwy
Ulaino Rd
Hana Airport
Hana Gardenland Cafe
Waianapanapa State Park
Hana
Hana Bay
Hana-Waianapanapa Trail
Kaupo
Loaloa Heiau
Huialoha Church
Waimoku Falls
Makahiku Falls
Wailua Falls
Lindbergh's Grave
Oheo Gulch
Kipahulu
Haneoo Rd
Koki Beach
Alau Island
Hamoa Beach
Pillani Hwy

in Hawaii. This road, which was built in 1927 using convict labor, is also very narrow; in many places it's essentially 1½ lanes wide, with two-lane traffic!

The Hana Hwy is a cliff-hugger as it winds its way deep into lush valleys and back out above a rugged coastline, snaking around more than 600 twists and turns along the way.

One-lane bridges mark dozens of waterfalls. Some are tiny and Zen-like, others sheer and lacy. The 54 bridges to Hana have 54 poetic Hawaiian names taken from the streams and gulches they cross – names like Heavenly Mist, Prayer Blossoms and Reawakening.

The valleys drip with vegetation. There are dense rainforests, bamboo groves and fern-covered hillsides. African tulip trees add bright splashes of orange.

It would take about two hours to drive straight through from Kahului to Hana. But this is not a drive to rush. If you're not staying over in Hana, get an early start to give yourself a full day. There are short trails to hike, mountain pools to dip in and a couple of historic sites to check out, all just a few minutes beyond the road for those with time to explore.

Remember to pull over if local drivers are behind you. They have places to get to and move at a different pace.

Paia to Hwy 360

A couple of miles past Paia the road passes Hookipa Beach, where there's a clifftop vantage point of the surfing action.

After Hookipa, fields of sugar cane give way to rows of pineapples. You'll pass through Haiku, but there's not much to see as it's a spread-out little town, most of it up the slopes.

Hwy 365, which leads up to Makawao and other Upcountry towns, comes in just after the 16-mile marker. At this point the Hana Hwy changes from No 36 to No 360 and the mile markers begin again at zero.

The road then changes dramatically, slicing through cliffs and becoming more of a mountain road than a highway. Hana is 35 scenic miles away.

Huelo

Huelo Rd, half a mile past the three-mile marker, is a passable dirt road that leads down to Kaulanapueo Church, a coral and stone church built in 1853. The church is likely to be locked, and if you're short on time, this one can be easily bypassed.

Koolau Forest Reserve

After Huelo, the road winds and the vegetation becomes increasingly lush as the highway runs along the edge of the Koolau Forest Reserve.

Koolau, which means 'windward', is the windward side of Haleakala and catches the rain clouds. The coast in this area gets 60 to 80 inches of rain a year, while a few miles up on the slopes the annual rainfall is an impressive 200 to 300 inches.

The reserve is heavily forested and cut with numerous gulches and streams. From here there seems to be a one-lane bridge and a waterfall around every other bend.

Kailua

Kailua is home to many of the people who work for the East Maui Irrigation Company. They maintain the 75 miles of ditches and tunnels that bring water from the rainforests to the cane fields of dry central Maui. The century-old system is capable of carrying 450 million gallons of water a day.

Many of the dirt roads leading mauka from the highway are the maintenance roads for the **Koolau Ditch**, which runs inland paralleling the highway.

If you want to take a closer look, stop at the small pull-off just before the bridge that comes up immediately after the eight-mile marker. Just 100 feet above the road you can see a section of the ditch, built of hand-hewn stone block, that meanders down the hillside and then tunnels into the rock face.

As you leave the village, you'll notice Norfolk pines up on the hillside, followed by a grove of painted eucalyptus trees with rainbow-colored bark, then a long stretch of bamboo and more painted eucalyptus.

Waikamoi Ridge Trail

Waikamoi Ridge Trail is a peaceful loop

trail through tall trees with wonderful fresh scents. You're welcomed by a sign: 'Quiet. Trees at Work'.

Pull off at the unmarked turn-off half a mile after the nine-mile marker. The trailhead is up on the left beyond the covered picnic table.

This is an easy trail, three-quarters of a mile long. The grand reddish trees are *Eucalyptus robusta*. Note the huge climbing philodendron vines wrapped around them – they provide an apt illustration of the etymology of philodendron, a Greek word meaning 'lover of trees'! The trail also passes lots of hala, ferns and paperbark eucalyptus trees.

Especially if you're walking with children, keep an eye out for occasional metal spikes and tree roots that protrude along the path. From the ridge at the top there's a good view of the winding Hana Hwy.

Waikamoi Falls

Waikamoi Falls is at the bridge just before the 10-mile marker. There's a waterfall and pool near the road. It's possible to walk a short way up to a higher waterfall, but the rocks can be slippery and the bottom waterfall is prettier anyway.

Past Waikamoi, bamboo grows almost horizontally out from the cliff side creating a canopy effect over the road.

Puohokamoa Falls

At the 11-mile marker, near the bridge of the same name and just a few minutes' walk from the road, is Puohokamoa Falls – yet another pretty waterfall. Because it has more parking space and a couple of picnic tables, it's more visited than the Waikamoi or Haipuaena waterfalls.

Haipuaena Falls

Haipuaena Falls, half a mile after the 11-mile marker, is a gentle little waterfall with a wonderful pool deep enough for swimming.

Most people don't know this one's here as you can't see the pool from the road. If you want to take a dip but don't have a bathing suit, this seems like a good choice.

There's space for just one car, on the Hana side of the bridge. To reach the falls walk upstream for a couple of minutes. Wild ginger grows along the path and ferns hang from the rock wall behind the waterfall, making for a quite idyllic setting.

Kaumahina State Wayside Park

Kaumahina State Wayside Park is shortly after the 12-mile marker. A two-minute walk up the hill under the park's tall eucalyptus trees provides a broad ocean vista, with Keanae Peninsula to the southeast. The park has picnic tables, restrooms and a large parking area.

Honomanu Bay

For the next several miles, the scenery is particularly magnificent, opening up to a new vista as you round each bend. If you're on this road after heavy rains you can expect to see waterfalls galore crashing down the mountains.

Just after crossing the bridge at the 14-mile marker, an inconspicuous and very rough gravel road heads down to Honomanu Bay and a rocky black-sand beach. The water's usually too turbulent for swimming and it's mostly used by surfers and fishers, though on very calm days it's possible to snorkel and dive there.

Keanae

Keanae is about halfway to Hana. The YMCA Camp Keanae is midway between the 16- and 17-mile markers. Within the next half mile the Keanae Arboretum, the road to Keanae Peninsula and the Keanae Peninsula Lookout come up in quick succession.

Keanae Valley, which extends down from the Koolau Gap in Haleakala Crater, averages 150 inches of rain a year.

Keanae Arboretum Although it's not well maintained, this arboretum, three-quarters of a mile past the 16-mile marker, has six acres of trees and numerous ornamental and food plants. Introduced tropical plants include painted eucalyptus trees and thickets of golden-stemmed bamboo with green stripes that look like the strokes of a Japanese shodo artist.

A trail leads up past heliconia, ti, banana, guava, breadfruit, ginger and other fragrant plants. The higher ground has dozens of varieties of Hawaiian taro in irrigated patches.

Keanae Peninsula The road that leads down to Keanae Peninsula is just beyond the arboretum.

Lanakila Ihiihi O Iehova Ona Kaua (Keanae Congregational Church) is an attractive old (1860) stone church about half a mile down. This is one church made of lava rocks and coral mortar whose exterior hasn't been covered over with layers of whitewash. And rather than locked doors, there's a guest book and a 'Visitors Welcome' sign.

Keanae is a quiet little village with colts and goats roaming freely. At the end of the road there's a scenic coastline of jagged rock and pounding waves. The rock island down the coast is Mokumana Island, a seabird sanctuary.

Keanae Peninsula Lookout There's a good view of Keanae village, with its squares of planted taro fed by Keanae Stream, at an unmarked pull-off just past the 17-mile marker. Look for the mailbox under the tsunami speaker.

Keanae Peninsula was formed by a later eruption of Haleakala that flowed through Koolau Gap down Keanae Valley. Outlined with a black lava coastline, the peninsula still wears its birthmark around the edges. It's very flat, like a leaf floating on the water.

Places to Stay The *YMCA Camp Keanae*, on a knoll overlooking the coast, has three guest cabins that can sometimes fill with groups on weekends but are otherwise usually available for individual travelers as hostel-style dorms for $10 per person. The cabins have bunk beds, but you have to bring your own sleeping bag, food and cookware. Cooking is done on hibachi-style barbecue grills that are available from the caretaker. If you prefer to set up a tent, you can do that instead of staying in the cabins. There's no pool, but you can take a dip in nearby Ching's Pond. Because of space limitations, advance reservations are required and there's a three-night limit. Reservations are made through the Maui YMCA office (☎ 242-9007), 250 Kanaloa Ave, Kahului, HI 96732.

Fruit Stands
There are a couple of informal places where you can buy fresh fruit along the road. Waianu Fruit Stand, just past the Keanae Peninsula Lookout, also has banana bread, coffee, ice cream, shave ice, a 24-hour soda machine and a pay phone.

Three-quarters of a mile farther is Uncle Harry's snack shop, run by the family of the late Harry Kunihi Mitchell, a native Hawaiian rights advocate who wrote the popular 'Mele O Kahoolawe' (Song of Kahoolawe) and represented the Hawaiian people in the Nuclear Free Pacific movement. This snack shop sells fruit, smoothies, chips and hot dogs.

Wailua
Take Wailua Rd makai immediately after Uncle Harry's to get to **Our Lady of Fatima Shrine**, Wailua's main attraction.

This little white and blue chapel, built in 1860, is also known as the Coral Miracle Church. The coral used in the construction came from a freak storm that deposited coral rocks onto a nearby beach. Before this, men in the congregation had been diving quite deep but were only able to bring up a few pieces of coral at a time. After the church was completed, another rogue storm hit the beach and swept all the leftover piles of coral back into the sea. Or so the story goes.

The chapel has just half a dozen little pews. The current congregation now uses St Gabriel's Mission, the larger pink-shingled church out front.

From Wailua Rd you can also get a peek of the long cascade of **Waikani Falls**, which is just to the left of Wailua Lookout up on the Hana Hwy.

Wailua Rd dead ends half a mile down, though you might not want to go that far, as driveways blocked off with logs and milk crates prevent cars from turning around.

Wailua Wayside Lookout
Back on the Hana Hwy, just before the 19-mile marker, Wailua Wayside Lookout comes up on the right. It has a broad view into Keanae Valley, which appears to be a hundred shades of green. There are a couple of waterfalls in sight, and if it's clear, you can look up at Koolau Gap, a break in the rim of Haleakala Crater.

If you climb up the steps to the right, you can get a good view of Wailua Peninsula, but there's a better view of it at a large paved turn-off a quarter of a mile down the road.

Puaa Kaa State Wayside Park
Halfway between the 22- and 23-mile markers is Puaa Kaa State Wayside Park, where a tranquil waterfall empties into a pool before flowing down into a ravine.

There are shaded picnic tables along the stream, a pool large enough for swimming, restrooms and a pay phone. The only disadvantage to the site is the many stray cats that pester picnickers.

Hana Gardenland
Just before the 31-mile marker is Hana Gardenland, a combination landscape nursery, gift shop and cafe (see Places to Eat, Hana). There's a pleasant two-minute path shaded with exotic plants, the shop features Maui-made crafts and the nursery sells bromeliads and orchids. It's open from 9 am to 5 pm daily.

Kahanu Gardens
Kahanu Gardens (☎ 248-8912), a 126-acre botanical garden on Kalahu Point, a few miles north of Hana, is under the jurisdiction of the National Tropical Botanical Garden. This nonprofit group is involved in the propagation and conservation of rare and medicinal plants, and the garden features ethnobotanical collections of numerous Polynesian trees, including kukui, hala, breadfruit and hau.

The Kahanu grounds are also the site of **Piilanihale Heiau**, the largest heiau on Maui. Built by Piilani, the 14th-century Mauian chief who is also credited with construction of many of the coastal fishponds and taro terraces in the Hana area, the garden can only be visited on a guided tour; a new schedule is still in the making, but tours will likely take place on Tuesdays and Thursdays and cost around $15.

Waianapanapa State Park
The road into Waianapanapa State Park is immediately after the 32-mile marker, half a mile south of the turn-off to Hana Airport. This 122-acre park has 12 cabins, tent camping, picnic pavilions, restrooms, showers and drinking water.

The road ends at a parking lot above Pailoa Bay, which is surrounded by a scenic coastline of low rocky cliffs. There's a natural lava arch on the right side of the bay. A short path from the parking lot leads down to the small black-sand beach, which is unprotected and usually has strong rips. When it's very calm the area around the arch is said to be good for snorkeling. Check it out carefully, though, as people have drowned here.

Caves Two impressive lava-tube caves are just a five-minute walk from the parking lot along a loop path. On the outside the caves are covered with ferns and flowering impatiens. Inside they're dripping wet and cool.

Waianapanapa means 'glistening waters' and, should you be tempted to take a dip, the clear mineral waters will leave you feeling squeaky clean.

On certain nights of the year, the waters in the cave turn red. Legend says it's the blood of a princess and her lover who were killed in a fit of rage by the princess's jealous husband after he found them hiding together here. Less romantic types account it to swarms of tiny bright red shrimp called *opaeula* that occasionally emerge from subterranean cracks in the lava.

Hana-Waianapanapa Trail A coastal trail that parallels the ancient King's Hwy leads

MAUI

south about two miles from the park to Kainalimu Bay, just north of Hana Bay. Some of the original smooth lava stepping stones are still in place along the trail.

Beyond the park cabins, the trail passes blowholes and the ruins of a heiau. There are gorgeous coastal views with cobalt blue water below craggy black lava outcrops. The most predominant vegetation is hala and beach naupaka, the latter with delicate white flowers that look as if they've been torn in half.

From the end of the trail it's about a mile farther to the center of Hana.

Camping Tent camping is free with a permit. The housekeeping cabins, which generally book up months in advance, cost $45 for up to four people, plus $5 for each additional person. Permits and reservations must be obtained in advance through one of the state park's district offices; Maui's is at 54 High St, Wailuku, HI 96793 (☎ 984-8109).

Hana

Separated from Kahului by 54 bridges and almost as many miles, Hana's isolation has thus far protected it from development, and even though a line of traffic passes through each day, not many visitors stay on.

Hana sits beneath the rainy slopes of Haleakala, surrounded by green pastures and a jagged black coastline. In ancient times it was the heart of one of Maui's largest population centers. The village itself was thought to have been reserved for the alii.

In the late 19th century, Chinese, Japanese and Portuguese laborers were brought in to work the newly planted sugar cane fields and Hana became a booming plantation town. A narrow-gauge railroad connected the fields to the Hana Mill. In the 1940s Hana could no longer compete with larger sugar operations in central Maui and the mill shut down.

In 1943, San Francisco businessman Paul Fagan, who owned Puu O Hoku Ranch on Molokai, purchased 14,000 acres in Hana. Starting with 300 Herefords, Fagan converted the cane fields to ranch land.

A few years later, Fagan opened a six-room hotel as a getaway resort for his well-to-do friends. Geographically and economically, Hana Ranch and the hotel became the hub of town.

Today, Hana Ranch still has a few thousand head of cattle worked by Hawaiian cowhands. When the cattle are ready for Oahu stockyards, they're trucked all the way up the Hana Hwy to Kahului Harbor.

Hana is not a grand finale to the magnificent Hana Hwy, and people expecting great things are often disappointed. While the setting is pretty, the town itself is simple and sedate. What makes Hana special is more apparent to those who stay on. There's an almost timeless rural character, and though 'Old Hawaii' is an oft-used cliche elsewhere, it's hard not to think of Hana in such terms.

Hana is one of the most Hawaiian communities in the state. Many of Hana's 1900 residents have Hawaiian blood and a strong sense of ohana, or extended family. If you spend time around here you'll hear the words 'auntie' and 'uncle' a lot.

People in Hana hold on to their traditional ways and have largely been successful in warding off the kind of changes that have altered much of the rest of Maui. Their latest round was beating down a plan by outside developers to build a golf course and luxury home development on pasture lands above the Hana Ranch headquarters.

A small community of celebrities, such as George Harrison and Kris Kristofferson, have long had homes in the Hana area.

Information

Hana Ranch Center is the commercial center of town. It has a post office, open from 8 am to 4:30 pm weekdays; a tiny Bank of Hawaii, open Monday to Thursday from 3 to 4:30 pm and Fridays from 3 to 6 pm; and the Hana Ranch Store, which sells groceries, liquor and general supplies and is open from 7 am to 6:30 pm daily.

MAUI

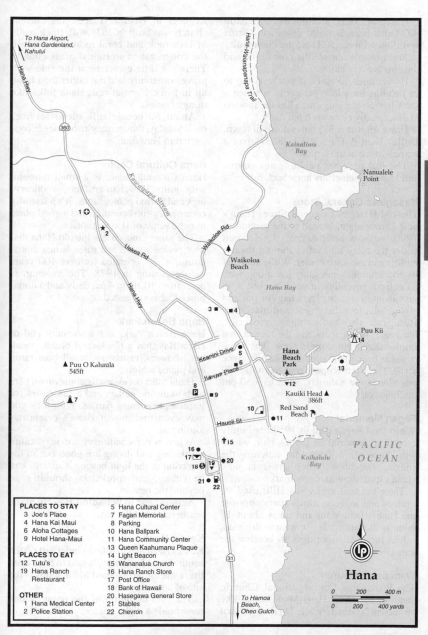

To Hana Airport,
Hana Gardenland,
Kahului

Hana Hwy

360

Hana-Waianapanapa Trail

Kainalimu
Bay

Nanualele
Point

Keaninapanapa Stream

Uakea Rd

Waikoloa Rd

Waikoloa
Beach

Hana Hwy

Hana Bay

▲ Puu O Kahaula
545ft

Keanini Drive

Keawa Place

Puu Kii
14

Hana
Beach
Park

13

▼12

Kauiki Head ▲
386ft

Red Sand Beach

8 P
9

10

Hauoli St

11

† 15

16
17
18

19
20

21
22

PACIFIC
OCEAN

Kaihalulu
Bay

31

Hana

0   200   400 m
0   200   400 yards

To Hamoa
Beach,
Oheo Gulch

PLACES TO STAY
3 Joe's Place
4 Hana Kai Maui
6 Aloha Cottages
9 Hotel Hana-Maui

PLACES TO EAT
12 Tutu's
19 Hana Ranch
     Restaurant

OTHER
1 Hana Medical Center
2 Police Station

5 Hana Cultural Center
7 Fagan Memorial
8 Parking
10 Hana Ballpark
11 Hana Community Center
13 Queen Kaahumanu Plaque
14 Light Beacon
15 Wananalua Church
16 Hana Ranch Store
17 Post Office
18 Bank of Hawaii
20 Hasegawa General Store
21 Stables
22 Chevron

Hasegawa General Store has a Bankoh ATM that accepts credit cards and Cirrus and Plus debit cards. There are community bulletin boards outside the post office and the two grocery stores.

Hana closes up early. If you're going to be heading back late, get gas in advance – the Chevron station, which has the longest hours, usually closes at 6 pm daily.

Hana Airport is 3½ miles north of town. Dollar Rent-A-Car (☎ 248-8237) has a branch office at the airport.

The ball park has public tennis courts, and Hana Ranch offers horseback riding.

Hasegawa General Store

The old Hasegawa General Store, Hana's best-known sight, burned to the ground in 1990. After a brief hiatus, it relocated under the rusty tin roof of the old theater building in the town center. While some of its character was inevitably lost along with its eclectic inventory, it's still packed with just about everything from bags of poi and aloha dolls to fishing gear and machetes. Hasegawa also has clothing, groceries, hardware, newspapers and the record that immortalized the store in song. The business has been in the Hasegawa family since 1910. The store is open from 8 am to 5:30 pm Monday to Saturday, 9 am to 3:30 pm on Sundays.

Fagan Memorial

When Paul Fagan died in 1959 his family erected a memorial on Lyon's Hill, which was Fagan's favorite spot for watching the sunset. The huge hilltop cross is now Hana's most dominant landmark.

There's a trail up Lyon's Hill, used by cyclists and joggers, which starts opposite the Hotel Hana-Maui and takes about 15 minutes to walk up. If you want to drive up, ask at the hotel front desk to borrow the gate key.

Wananalua Church

The Wananalua Congregational Church, south of the Hotel Hana-Maui, looks like an ancient Norman church. On the National

Register of Historic Places, the current church was built in 1838 with thick walls of lava rock and coral mortar to replace the congregation's original grass church. There's a little cemetery at the side with graves randomly laid out rather than lined up in rows. Even at rest, Hana folks like things casual.

About 50 people still attend services each Sunday, though they're no longer conducted in Hawaiian.

Hana Cultural Center

Hana Cultural Center is a small museum with quilts, Hawaiian artifacts, woodcarvings and period photographs. It's a friendly community-run operation and a good place to get a sense of Hana's roots.

The same grounds has the old Hana district police station and three-bench courthouse, which operated for over 100 years before closing in 1978. The museum is open from 10 am to 4 pm daily and a donation of $2 is suggested.

Hana Beach Park

Hana Beach Park, at the southern end of Hana Bay, has a black-sand beach, snack bar, showers, restrooms, small boat ramp and picnic tables.

Hana folks occasionally come down here with ukuleles, guitars and a few beers for impromptu evening parties. With luck you may even find one of Hana's celebrities joining in.

When water conditions are very calm, snorkeling and diving are good out in the direction of the light beacon. Currents can be strong, and snorkelers shouldn't go beyond the beacon.

Surfers head to **Waikoloa Beach**, at the northern end of the bay.

Kauiki Head

Kauiki Head, the 386-foot cinder hill on the south side of Hana Bay, is said to have been the home of the demigod Maui and was the site of an ancient fort.

The islet at the tip of the point, which now holds a light beacon, is Puu Kii or

'Image Hill'. The name can be traced to a huge idol that the great king Umi erected here in the 16th century to ward off invaders. In 1780 the Mauian chief Kahekili successfully fought off a challenge by Big Island chiefs at Kauiki Head.

Queen Kaahumanu, the favorite wife of Kamehameha I and one of the most powerful women in Hawaiian history, was born in a cave here in 1768. It was Kaahumanu who destroyed the ancient kapu system and freed women from restrictive taboos.

A trail to a plaque noting her birth starts along the hill at the side of the wharf at Hana Beach Park. It leads through ironwood trees towards the light beacon, passing by a tiny red-sand beach. The walk to the rock where the plaque is mounted is only mildly interesting, but then again it takes just five minutes. Watch where you step, as some of the trail is a bit crumbly.

Red Sand Beach

Red Sand Beach (Kaihalulu Beach), on the south side of Kauiki Head, is favored by nude sunbathers. It's a gorgeous little cove with sand eroded from the red cinder hill and beautiful turquoise waters.

Although the cove is partly protected by a lava outcrop, the currents can be dangerous if the surf is up. Water drains through a break on the left side, which should be avoided.

The path to the beach is at the end of Uakea Rd beyond the ballpark. It starts across the lawn at the lower side of the Hana Community Center, where a steep trail continues down to the beach, less than 10 minutes away.

The curious can also find an interesting overgrown Japanese cemetery just two minute's walk east from the community center, a remnant of the sugar cane days.

Places to Stay

Joe's Place (☎ 248-7033), Box 557, Hana, HI 96713, on Uakea Rd, has 12 rooms that cost $45 with shared bath, $55 with private bath, for either one or two people. Most rooms have two single beds, though a few have double beds. Rooms are small and basic, but clean and comfortable enough. Guests have access to a community kitchen and TV room.

Aloha Cottages (☎ 248-8420), Fusae Nakamura, Box 205, Hana, HI 96713, is on Keawa Place, opposite the Hotel Hana-Maui. There is one studio with twin beds and limited cooking facilities (a hot plate, toaster and refrigerator) for $60. There are also three two-bedroom cottages, each with full kitchens, a queen bed and two twin beds for $75 for two people, $10 for each additional person. All of the units are straightforward; none have phones, but messages are taken.

Hana Kai Maui (☎ 248-8426, 800-346-2772; fax 248-7482), Box 38, Hana, HI 96713, at the north side of town, is a modern though not fancy 19-unit condo. Units have full kitchens and lanais with fine ocean views of Hana Bay, in earshot of the breaking surf. Studios cost $110 to $125 for double occupancy; one-bedroom units are $125 to $145 for up to four people.

Hamoa Bay Bungalow (☎ 248-7884; fax 248-8642), Jody Baldwin, Box 773, Hana, HI 96713, is a pleasant new cottage within walking distance of Hamoa Beach. Set in the midst of tropical greenery, the cottage has Balinese decor and is equipped with a kitchen, king-size bed, jacuzzi tub and screened lanai. The cost is $125 to $150, depending on the season, with a breakfast of fresh fruit and muffins. Amenities include laundry facilities and a small movie library (no cable TV). There's a two-person maximum, and smoking is not allowed.

The *Hotel Hana-Maui* (☎ 248-8211, 800-321-4262; fax 248-7202), Hana, HI 96713, is one of Maui's more exclusive getaway hotels. On 23 acres in the center of town, the Hana-Maui is low profile, more like a plantation estate than a luxury hotel. Everything's very airy and open, with Hawaiian accents from local art to quilt bedspreads. The 92 rooms are mostly in one-story row cottages that have bleached hardwood floors, tiled baths, a view over a private garden and French doors to trellised patios. Pampering has its price – rates range from $395 to $795.

Vacation Rentals There are a few vacation rental agencies handling cottages and houses in the Hana area. As the properties can vary greatly in quality and maintenance, it's recommended that you get specific details, preferably with current photos, before sending a deposit.

Hana Alii Holidays (☎ 248-7742, 800-548-0478; fax 248-8595; duke@maui.net), Box 536, Hana, HI 96713, manages about two dozen places, a mix of condos, private homes and cottages that can be rented by the day, week and month. Daily rates range from a studio condo at $75 to an estate home for $275.

Blair's Original Hana Plantation Houses (☎ 923-0772, 800-228-4262; fax 922-6068), Box 249, Hana, HI 96713, rents a dozen houses. At the low end there's a little Japanese-style studio with an efficiency kitchen and a jacuzzi on the deck for $80 and at the high end a two-bedroom home on a black-sand beach for $160. The houses are about 10 minutes outside town, and all have cooking facilities. Rates are for up to two people; add $10 for each extra person.

Hana Bay Vacation Rentals (☎ 248-7727, 800-959-7727), Box 318, Hana, HI 96713, also manages a handful of properties that average $100 a day.

Camping There's tent camping and cabins at Waianapanapa State Park, just north of Hana (see the Road to Hana section), and tent camping at Oheo Gulch, 10 miles south of Hana (see the Hana to Kipahula section). If you plan to camp at Oheo, you'll need to stock up on food and water in Hana.

Places to Eat

Tutu's, a fast-food grill at the beach park at Hana Bay, is open from 8:30 am to 4 pm daily, though the grill closes 30 minutes earlier. Hamburgers and vegie sandwiches cost $2.75, mahimahi burgers $3.75. Tutu's also has $6 plate lunches, ice cream and shave ice.

A good lunch stop is the *Hana Gardenland Cafe* (☎ 248-7340), three miles north of town on the Hana Hwy, which runs with the motto: 'nothing even close to a hamburger'. Here you'll find a garden setting and a menu that emphasizes locally grown fruits and vegies. Organic green salads, pizza, quiche, pasta and sandwiches on whole-wheat bread average $7. You can also get fresh-squeezed juices, Hana fruit smoothies, espresso and desserts. It's open from 9 am to 5 pm daily.

The *Hana Ranch Restaurant* (☎ 248-8255) at the Hana Ranch Center is open for lunch from 11 am to 3 pm daily, with a buffet that includes a simple salad bar and a few lackluster hot dishes for $9. At dinner, offered from 6 to 8 pm on Fridays and Saturdays, meals range from $15 for a smoked half chicken to around $25 for steak, salad bar included.

At the side of Hana Ranch Restaurant is a takeout counter open daily from 6:30 am to 4 pm on Wednesdays, Fridays and Saturdays and until 7 pm on other days. It has standard breakfast fare for around $5, plate lunches for $6.25 and saimin, burgers and sandwiches for a bit less. They also sell ice cream, and there are picnic tables outside where you can chow down.

The *Hotel Hana-Maui* (☎ 248-8211) serves three meals a day in a cheery open-air dining room. At lunch (11:30 am to 2 pm), dishes such as tropical fruit salad, clubhouse sandwiches or fish are priced from $13 to $18. Dinner (6 to 9 pm) offers main course dishes such as pasta with vegetables for $21 and catch of the day for $29, with salads and appetizers for around $10. The food is quite straightforward considering the high price.

On Tuesday evenings the hotel offers a luau dinner on Hamoa Beach, with pleasantly low-key local entertainment. Reservations are required, as it only takes place if at least 30 people sign up; the cost is $55. Local musicians perform at the hotel bar a couple of nights a week.

Bring groceries from Kahului if you plan to stay awhile, as the Hana grocery stores have only a limited selection.

Hana to Kipahulu

From Hana, the road continues on to Kipahulu, passing Oheo, the southern end of Haleakala National Park. It's an incredibly lush stretch, perhaps the most beautiful part of the entire drive. As it continues south from Hana, the road changes its name to the Piilani Hwy.

The road from Hana to Oheo is narrow and winding. Between the hairpin turns, one-lane bridges and drivers trying to take in all the sights, it's a slow-moving 10 miles.

You'll get extra coastal views by detouring along the 1½-mile Haneoo Rd loop, which runs past Koki and Hamoa beaches and a couple of ancient shoreline fishponds. The turn-off is half a mile south of Hana Ranch headquarters.

Koki Beach is at the base of a red cinder hill less than half a mile from the start of the loop. Most of Koki's sand washes away in winter, leaving a rocky shoreline. Local surfers who know the coastline sometimes surf here, but rocks and strong currents make it hazardous for newcomers.

The offshore rock topped by a few coconut trees is Alau Island, a seabird sanctuary. The trees were planted years ago by a couple of Hana residents so they'd have coconuts to drink from while fishing off the island.

A little farther is Hamoa Beach, a nice gray-sand beach that's used by the Hotel Hana-Maui but is accessible to everyone. The beach has showers, restrooms and a lifeguard on duty. When the surf's up, there's good surfing and bodysurfing, though be aware that rip currents can sometimes be present. When seas are calm, swimming in the cove is good. Public access is down the steps below the hotel's bus-stop sign.

As you continue south, there are waterfalls down the cliffs, orchids growing out of the rocks, and lots of breadfruit and coconut trees. There's even a statue of the Virgin Mary tucked into a rock face on the side of the road.

Wailua Falls, three miles before Oheo, is particularly attractive with its 100-foot drop visible from the road. There's usually a couple of people at the waterfall pull-off selling hand-painted T-shirts and the like.

OHEO GULCH

Oheo Stream dramatically cuts its way through Oheo Gulch as a lovely series of waterfalls and wide pools, each one tumbling into the next one below. In fair weather you can swim in them. A two-mile trail runs up the stream bed.

There was once a large Hawaiian settlement spread throughout the Oheo area, and the stone remains of more than 700 structures have been identified. These early villagers cultivated taro and sweet potatoes in terraced gardens.

Kipahulu Valley

In the 1960s, 11,000 acres of Kipahulu Valley were jointly purchased by the Nature Conservancy and the state of Hawaii for preservation. The valley, which borders the main body of Haleakala National Park and stretches southeast to the coast, was turned over to the US Department of the Interior and added to the national park in 1969. The coastal Oheo Gulch area is part of the Kipahulu Valley property.

The upper Kipahulu Valley is a pristine rainforest of koa and ohia trees that is refuge to endangered native plants and birds. The Maui parrotbill, whose sole population lives in this valley, has a habitat range of just over eight miles. Fewer than 500 of the birds survive. Also in Kipahulu Valley is the entire population of the Maui *nuku-puu*, Hawaii's most endangered honeycreeper – about 30 birds in all. The parrotbill and nuku-puu are both beautiful forest birds, about five inches long, with bright yellow underbellies.

The upper part of the valley gets up to 300 inches of rain a year and is swampy with dense vegetation. In an effort to protect the habitat, no public access is allowed. ∎

One of the expressed intentions of Haleakala National Park is to manage the Oheo area 'to perpetuate traditional Hawaiian farming and *hoonanea*' – a Hawaiian word meaning to pass the time in ease, peace and pleasure.

Not so long ago Oheo Gulch was dubbed 'Seven Sacred Pools' in a tourism promotion scheme. There are actually 24 pools from the ocean all the way up to Waimoku Falls, and they were never sacred (although it was kapu for menstruating women to bathe in them).

The park's ranger station (☎ 248-7375) is staffed from 9 am to 5 pm daily to answer questions. There are occasionally Hawaiian culture demonstrations and short ranger-led walks, and there's usually a three-hour guided hike to Waimoku Falls on Saturdays at 9:30 am. You'll find restrooms near the visitors' parking lot, but there's no drinking water or food at Oheo.

Lower Pools

A 20-minute path from the Oheo Gulch parking lot heads down to the lower pools and then loops back via the road, with interpretive signs along the way. The ranger station is near the start of the trail. A few minutes down, the trail comes to a broad grassy knoll with a beautiful view of the Hana coast. On a clear day you can see the Big Island across the Alenuihaha Channel, 30 miles away. It would be a fine place to break out a picnic basket.

The large freshwater pools along the trail are almost terraced one atop the other, connected by gentle cascades. They're usually calm and great for swimming, though the water's brisk. The second big pool below the bridge is a favorite.

If it's been raining heavily and the water is flowing too high and fast, the pools are closed and signs are posted. Still, at any time, heavy rains in the upper slopes can bring a sudden torrent of rising waters. If the water starts to rise, get out immediately. People have been swept from these pools out to sea by flash floods. The ocean below is not inviting at all – it's quite rough and is populated by gray sharks!

Actually, the biggest cause of injury here is from falls on slippery rocks. Another hazard is the submerged rocks and ledges in some of the pools. Check them out carefully before diving in.

Oheo is home to a rare goby fish that spends the first stages of its life in the ocean, but returns to breed in the upper stream. It works its way up the chain of pools and waterfalls by using its front fins as suction cups on the rocks.

Waterfall Trails

Opposite the parking lot is a trail leading up to Makahiku Falls (half a mile) and Waimoku Falls (two miles). The path passes large mango trees and lots of guava, forking after about 10 minutes.

Makahiku Falls, a long bridal-veil waterfall that drops into a deep gorge, is just off to the right. Thick green ferns cover the sides of 200-foot basalt cliffs where the fall cascades. The scene is quite rewarding for such a short walk.

To the left of the overlook there's a path that goes up to the top of the waterfalls, where there's a popular skinny-dipping pool. Around midday the pool is quite enjoyable, but by late afternoon the sun stops hitting it and the mosquitoes move in.

Rocks above the waterfall protect the pool as long as the water level isn't high. A cut on one side lets the water fall over the cliff. Examine it carefully before getting in, and if the water starts to rise once you are in, get out immediately – a drop over this sheer 184-foot falls could obviously be fatal!

Waimoku Falls is a thin, lacy 400-foot waterfall dropping down a sheer rock face. The walk to the falls is made all the more special by three thick bamboo groves. When you come out of the first grove, you'll see the waterfall in the distance. By the time you emerge from the third thicket, you're there.

It takes about 45 minutes to hike the 1½ miles to Waimoku Falls from the Makahiku Falls viewpoint. The upper part of the trail is muddy, with a boardwalk over sections of it. There are ancient farm sites with abandoned taro patches along the way, although it takes a keen eye to recognize them. Mosquitoes thrive along the stream bed.

As the pool under Waimoku Falls was partially filled in by a landslide caused by an earthquake in 1976, it's not terribly deep, but at any rate swimming is not recommended due to the danger of falling rocks.

If you want to take a dip, there are better pools to swim in along the way. About 100 yards before Waimoku Falls you'll cross a little stream. If you go left for 10 minutes up the stream there's an attractive waterfall and a little pool about neck deep. There's not really a trail, but you can walk alongside the stream to get to it.

There's also a nice pool in the stream about halfway between the Makahiku and Waimoku falls.

Places to Stay

The national park has a campground about half a mile southeast of the main Oheo Gulch visitor's area. The campground is Hawaiian style: free and undeveloped – just a huge open pasture. There are some incredible places to pitch a tent on grassy cliffs right above the coast and the pounding surf. Not only is the scenery stunning, but the camping area is set amid the ruins of an old Hawaiian village, making this quite a powerful place to be.

In winter there are usually only a handful of tents here. It gets quite a few campers in summer, but even then it's large enough to handle everyone who shows up. There are pit toilets and a few picnic tables but *no* water. Permits aren't required, though camping is officially limited to three nights each month.

KIPAHULU

The village of Kipahulu is less than a mile south of Oheo. Around the turn of the century Kipahulu was one of several sugar plantation villages in the Hana area. It had a working mill from 1890 to 1922. Following the closure of the mill, there were unsuccessful attempts to grow pineapples before ranching took hold in the late 1920s.

Today Kipahulu has both exclusive estates and more modest homes. A scattering of fruit stands are set up along the roadside, some attended by elderly women who string leis and sell bananas, papayas and woven lauhala hats. This is the end of the line for most day visitors who have pushed beyond Hana.

Lindbergh's Grave

The Hana area was home to aviator hero Charles Lindbergh during the last years of his life. He began visiting in the 1960s, built a cliffside home in Kipahulu in 1968 and died of cancer in Maui in 1974.

Lindbergh is buried in the graveyard of Palapala Hoomau Congregational Church. His simple grave is surrounded by a chain and marked with little US flags.

Would-be visitors sometimes get the location mixed up with St Paul's Church, which sits on the highway three-quarters of a mile south of Oheo, but the dirt drive down to Palapala Hoomau Church is a quarter of a mile beyond that, on the makai side of the road. Turn in at the gate just past the wooden cistern at the end of the field.

Palapala Hoomau Church, with its 26-inch-thick walls and simple wooden pews, dates from 1864. The church is known for its window painting of a Polynesian Christ dressed in the red and yellow feather capes worn only by Hawaii's highest chiefs.

The churchyard is a peaceful place, with sleepy cats lounging around, waiting for a nice warm car hood to sprawl out on.

GETTING THERE & AWAY

A lot of people leave Oheo in mid-afternoon to head back up the Hana Hwy. Some of them, suddenly realizing what a long trek they have ahead, become very impatient drivers.

You might want to consider leaving a little later, which would not only give you more sightseeing time, but allow you to avoid the rush. Getting caught in the dark returning north on the Hana Hwy does have certain advantages. You can see the headlights of oncoming cars around bends that would otherwise be blind, and the traffic is almost nonexistent.

There are no shortcuts back, but sometimes there is another option.

From Kipahulu, the Piilani Hwy (don't be misled by the term 'highway' – there's barely a road in places!) heads west through Kaupo up to Keokea in Kula. It's usually passable, but not always, and it shouldn't be done in the dark.

The Oheo Gulch ranger station usually has the latest information on road conditions. Another option is to drive to the south end of Kipahulu and talk to people coming from the Kaupo direction. Most likely they've either just driven down from Kula or else have started up the road from Kipahulu, found road conditions bad and turned around.

For more details on the drive, see the Piilani Hwy section of this chapter.

Upcountry

Upcountry, the highland area of East Maui on the western slopes of Haleakala, has some of Maui's finest countryside, with rolling hills, grazing horses and green pastures. You have to drive through Upcountry to get to Haleakala National Park, but it's well worth visiting for its own sake.

Upcountry is uncrowded and dotted with small towns. A fair chunk of the area is occupied by ranches, with Haleakala Ranch covering vast spreads to the north and Ulupalakua Ranch to the south.

Kula, in the center of it all, has rich farmland where most of Maui's vegetables and flowers are grown. On the mountainside above Kula are the delightful cloudforests of Polipoli. Upcountry sightseeing spots include landscaped gardens and a winery tasting room.

From Upcountry you can look across the central plains to the West Maui Mountains and get a good view of the Maui coastline and the neighboring islands. Daytimes are cooler in Upcountry, and nights can be downright brisk.

PAIA TO MAKAWAO
Baldwin Ave (Hwy 390) runs seven miles from Paia up to Makawao. It starts amid sugar cane, passes the Paia Mill and then runs up through pineapple fields interspersed with little open patches where cattle graze.

There are two churches along Baldwin Ave. The **Holy Rosary Church**, with its memorial statue of Father Damien, comes up first on the right, and the attractive **Makawao Union Church**, a stone block building with stained-glass windows, is farther along on the left. The latter, built in 1916, is on the National Register of Historic Places.

The roadside **Rainbow Park** is at the three-mile post. It has a covered picnic table, a portable toilet and camping, but it's in a low area that can get soggy during rainy periods.

On the left just after the five-mile marker is Kaluanui, the former nine-acre plantation estate of sugar magnates Harry and Ethel Baldwin, which now houses the **Hui Noeau Visual Arts Center**. The two-story plantation home with Spanish-style tile roof was designed by famed Honolulu architect CW Dickey in 1917. Maui's first mule-powered centrifugal sugar mill was once on the site.

The nonprofit group Hui Noeau (☎ 572-6560) offers community classes in printmaking, weaving, batik and dozens of other visual arts at the center. The main house features changing exhibits and a gift shop, while the stables at the back have been turned into a ceramics studio. The gallery and gift shop are open from 10 am to 4 pm Monday to Saturday.

Haliimaile
Haliimaile is a little pineapple town on the edge of an expansive cane and pineapple plantation. The main attraction is the old general store, circa 1918, which has been converted into one of the better upscale restaurants on this side of Maui.

Places to Eat With high ceilings and plantation-era decor, *Haliimaile General Store* (☎ 572-2666) features a mix of nouvelle and Asian cooking influences. At dinner, served from 5:30 to 9:30 pm, main dishes

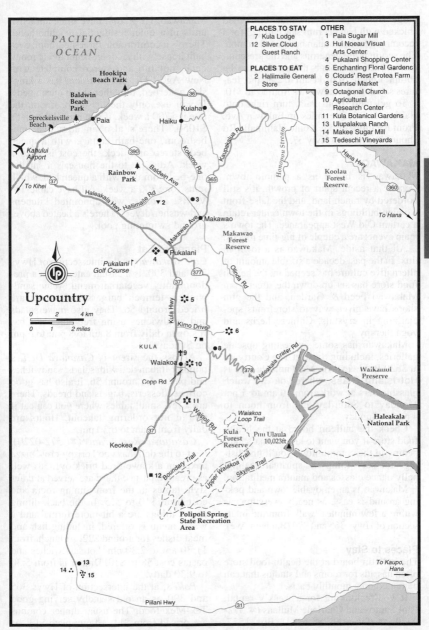

PLACES TO STAY
7 Kula Lodge
12 Silver Cloud
    Guest Ranch

PLACES TO EAT
2 Haliimaile General
   Store

OTHER
1 Paia Sugar Mill
3 Hui Noeau Visual
   Arts Center
4 Pukalani Shopping Center
5 Enchanting Floral Gardens
6 Clouds' Rest Protea Farm
8 Sunrise Market
9 Octagonal Church
10 Agricultural
    Research Center
11 Kula Botanical Gardens
13 Ulupalakua Ranch
14 Makee Sugar Mill
15 Tedeschi Vineyards

PACIFIC
OCEAN

Hookipa Beach Park
Baldwin Beach Park
Spreckelsville Beach
Kahului Airport
To Kihei
To Hana
To Kaupo, Hana

Paia
Haiku
Kuiaha
Koolau Forest Reserve
Rainbow Park
Makawao
Makawao Forest Reserve
Pukalani
Pukalani Golf Course

Upcountry

0   2   4 km
0   1   2 miles

Kula
Waiakoa
Copp Rd
Keokea

Kokomo Rd
Kaupakalua Rd
Honopou Stream
Hana Hwy
Baldwin Ave
Haleakala Hwy Haliimaile Rd
Makawao Ave
Kula Hwy
Kimo Drive
Waipoli Rd
Olinda Rd
Haleakala Crater Rd

Waiakoa Loop Trail
Kula Forest Reserve
Boundary Trail
Upper Waiakoa Trail
Skyline Trail
Puu Ulaula 10,023ft

Waikamoi Preserve
Haleakala National Park

Polipoli Spring State Recreation Area

Piilani Hwy

MAUI

range from $18 for Jawaiian blackened chicken with banana rum sauce to $23 for a recommendable Sichuan barbecued salmon. The servings are generous and the presentation attractive, though the service can be abrupt. Lunch, from 11 am to 2:30 pm, features salads and sandwiches from $7 to $10.

To get there from Paia, turn right onto Haliimaile Rd, five miles up Baldwin Ave. From Kahului, turn left onto Haliimaile Rd about 4½ miles up Hwy 37.

MAKAWAO

Makawao is billed as a paniolo town. Despite a recent spurt of growth, it's still bordered by ranch land, and the false-front wooden buildings in the town center retain a certain Old West appearance. The town's main events are a couple of big-time rodeos.

All that aside, Makawao is a town in flux. In the past decade a sizable amount of alternative culture has seeped in: the health food store has set up down the street from Makawao Feed & Garden, and the gun shops have given way to storefronts specializing in crystals, Chinese herbs and yoga therapy.

Makawao has some interesting upscale galleries, including those at The Courtyard at 3620 Baldwin Ave. Most notable here is **Hot Island Glass**, where you can watch glassblowers at work from 10 am to 5 pm Monday to Saturday and from noon to 4 pm on Sunday.

Check the bulletin board at the health food store if you want to know what's happening in the community – you'll find listings for such things as spiritual healing, belly dance classes and mantra meditation.

Makawao is an enjoyable town and poking around is easy, as nearly everything is within a few minutes' walk from the intersection of Hwys 365 and 390 (Baldwin Ave).

Places to Stay

The bulletin board at the health food store often has ads for rooms and studios that can be rented on a monthly basis.

If you're looking for a weekly rental, Paul Santos and Charlene Mullens (☎ 572-0020; ☎ /fax 800-788-6284), Box 1527, Makawao, HI 96768, have three attractive units in a quiet residential neighborhood. There's a comfortable three-bedroom, two-bath house with an open-beam living room, deck, hot tub and stereo complete with New Age CDs; one bedroom has a king-size waterbed, the others have queen beds. If you use only the master bedroom, the rate is $700 a week; if you use all three, it's $1050. There's also an attractive one-bedroom, one-bath cottage with a queen bed, stereo and deck; the cost is $525 a week. Adjacent to the house is a smaller one-bedroom unit with a queen bed, which rents for $300 a week. All have cable TV, VCRs, phones, well-appointed kitchens and washer/dryers. There's a heated above-ground swimming pool.

Places to Eat

Cafe Makawao, at the intersection of Hwys 365 and 390, is a casual eatery with a predominantly vegetarian menu. Vegie sandwiches, tempeh burgers and salads are priced around $6. They also make salads and sandwiches using free-range poultry. It's open daily from 8 am to 8 pm (to 6 pm on Sundays).

Across the street is *Casanova Deli*, a popular Italian deli with salads, sandwiches and pastas for around $6. It also has good coffees, desserts, bagels and breads. There are a few small tables where you can eat if you're not ordering takeout. Hours are daily from 8 am to 6:30 pm.

Casanova Restaurant (☎ 572-0220), next to the deli, has good crispy-crust pizza baked in a kiawe-fired brick oven, as well as creative pastas; these are served at cafe-style tables in the front dining room and cost from $10 to $15. In the back dining room, things are a bit more formal and a wider menu is offered, including fish and meat dishes for around $22. At lunch, from 11:30 am to 2:30 pm, hot sandwiches and pastas cost $8 to $10. Dinner is from 5:30 to 9:30 daily.

Polli's, at the intersection of Hwys 365 and 390, is an old standby serving good Tex-Mex food. The usual dinner combos are priced from $11, a fajita plate $13. At lunch a chili relleno or a single enchilada with rice and beans costs $6.50. Vegetarians can order dishes with tofu instead of meat. It's open from 11 am to 10 pm daily.

Makawao Steak & Fish House on Baldwin Ave is a straightforward steak and seafood restaurant with filet mignon or fresh fish of the day for $25, including a spinach or Caesar salad. It's open from 5 to 9:30 pm nightly.

Kitada's Restaurant, in a funky old building on Baldwin Ave opposite the steak house, has been making saimin here for generations; the servings are generous and the prices cheap. It's open from 6 am to 1:30 pm Monday to Saturday.

Down to Earth Natural Foods, across from Casanova at 1169 Makawao Ave, has organic produce, bulk and packaged foods, a dairy section, juices, sandwiches and a small salad bar. The store is open from 8 am to 8 pm daily.

Entertainment
Casanova (☎ 572-0220) is East Maui's hottest music spot, bringing in mainland performers as well as some of Hawaii's top musicians. There are often live bands from Thursday to Sunday, anything from rock, reggae and Jawaiian to Cajun. The cover charge is often $5 to $8 for local bands, $15 to $20 for big names.

There's sometimes acoustic music on Fridays at the *Courtyard Deli*.

HAIKU
Scenic back roads head out in all directions from Makawao, and almost any one you choose to explore will make a prime country drive.

Some of those roads lead through Haiku, a scattered community that stretches north from Makawao down the slopes to the Hana Hwy. From Makawao, take Kaupakalua Rd (Hwy 365) north. After a mile, turn left onto Kokomo Rd, which passes through pineapple fields before reaching the modest village that marks the center of Haiku.

Alexander & Baldwin grew their first 12 acres of sugar cane near Haiku, and there was once both a sugar mill and pineapple

cannery here. Today the old cannery houses a few local eateries, a grocery store and a hardware store.

Haiku is seeing a bit of a revival. Its rural character and its proximity to Makawao and Hookipa have attracted a number of new residents, including windsurfers, artists and New Age folks. The area has some good-value places to stay and makes a fairly convenient base for exploring the whole island.

Places to Stay
Bamboo Mountain Sanctuary (☎ 572-5106), 911 Kaupakalua Rd, Haiku, HI 96708, makes an interesting place to stay if you're looking for a meditative experience. Occupying a rustic plantation house on the grounds of a New Age retreat center, it has five simple rooms with futon-style beds that go for $55/75, breakfast included. Showers are in the hall. The setting is serene, with verandas overlooking the surrounding forest, and guests have access to a kitchen and a meditation room; massage and yoga can be arranged.

Lanikai Farm (☎ 572-1111; fax 572-3498), Margaret and Achim Koebke, 100 S Lanikai Place, Box 797, Haiku, HI 96708, is a contemporary home in a residential neighborhood about a 10-minute drive from Hookipa Beach. The house has three guest rooms, each with a queen bed, a small refrigerator and shared bath. There's a common room with a TV, VCR and microwave and a squash court on the premises. Well-behaved children are welcome. Both English and German are spoken. Rates, which include breakfast, are $60/65 for singles/doubles, with a slight discount for stays of five days.

Haikuleana (☎ 575-2890; fax 575-9177), 555 Haiku Rd, Haiku, HI 96708, is a pleasant B&B in an older plantation-style house that retains some graceful period touches. There's a central dining area and a sitting room with antiques and wicker furnishings. It has four guest rooms, three with queen beds, one with two twin beds, and each with a private bath. Singles/doubles cost $85/95 with a two-night minimum. Breakfast is included, children

MAUI

under six are not accepted and smoking is not allowed. It's about 1⅓ miles up Haiku Rd from Hwy 36, near the Haiku Chapel.

Pilialoha (☎ 572-1440; fax 572-4612; heyde@mauigateway.com), Machiko and Bill Heyde, 2512 Kaupakalua Rd, Haiku, HI 96708, is a delightful cottage in upcountry Haiku, about two miles from the center of Makawao. Set in a eucalyptus grove, the terraced cottage has hardwood oak floors, sliding glass doors leading to a deck, a bedroom with a queen bed and a second room with a single bed. There's a fully equipped kitchen, a washer/dryer, a phone and a living room with VCR, cable TV and a queen sofa bed. Machiko, an artist, has quilted and painted the pillows and adds other charming touches, such as roses cut fresh daily from her garden. The cost is $95 for one or two people, $10 for each additional person. There's a two-day minimum stay, and smoking is allowed outdoors only. Kona coffee, tea, fruit and homemade granola and breads are provided for breakfast; if you don't eat sugar, Machiko will bake with honey.

Halfway to Hana House (☎ 572-1176), Box 675, Haiku, HI 96708, is not actually in Haiku, but about five miles south of it, on the road to Hana. It consists of a cozy studio unit at the side of the home of Gail Pickholz, a friendly host who welcomes visitors to join her in kayaking, snorkeling and other outings. The studio has a private entrance and bath, a double bed, microwave, toaster oven, coffee pot and an unobstructed view across treetops to the ocean. The cost is $55/65 for singles/doubles with breakfast, $50/55 without. There's a two-night minimum; smoking is not allowed.

PUKALANI

Pukalani, on the way to Haleakala, is a residential community with a population of 6000, making it the biggest Upcountry town.

Pukalani is two miles from Makawao along Hwy 365. Midway between the two towns is a picture-perfect ranch scene with rolling pastures, horses, grazing cattle and a mountain backdrop. Beyond this the rows of pineapple start up again.

If you're coming from Kahului, the Haleakala Hwy (Hwy 37) climbs for six miles through cane fields before reaching Pukalani. If you just want to go to Haleakala or Kula, there's a new bypass that skirts around Pukalani; if you want to see the town, stay on Hwy 37.

Information

The Pukalani Terrace Shopping Center, south of the intersection of Hwys 365 and 37, has a coin laundry and a bank with a 24-hour ATM. There are a couple of gas stations on Hwy 37 in the center of Pukalani; the Chevron station is open from 4 am to 11 pm daily.

Places to Eat

The Pukalani Terrace Shopping Center has a carry-out *Pizza Hut* open from 11 am to at least 10 pm; a *Foodland* supermarket with a deli and bakery, open daily from 5 am to midnight; a *Subway* sandwich shop and a Chinese restaurant.

There's a *McDonald's* a little farther up the highway, next to a convenience store that sells fried chicken and giant steak fries by the piece.

Pukalani Terrace Country Clubhouse (☎ 572-1325) is where Pukalanians head when they want to go out. It's located above the golf course, three-quarters of a mile past the shopping center on Pukalani St. There's a reasonably good salad bar with soup that costs $7 at dinner, $5.25 at lunch, or $3 when ordered with a meal. Complete Hawaiian plates, which include kalua pig, lomi salmon, poi and haupia, cost about $8, while chicken and beef dishes are a few dollars more. Standard breakfast fare is around $5. The dining room has a good view down to the ocean and is open from 8 am to 2 pm and 5 to 9 pm daily. Things can be a bit hectic at lunch, as the restaurant is a popular stop for Japanese tour buses.

KULA

Kula is the agricultural heartland of Maui. The average elevation is 3000 feet. Crops such as lettuce, tomatoes, carrots, cauliflower and cabbage thrive in Kula's warm days, cool nights and rich volcanic soil. No gourmet cook in Hawaii would be without sweet Kula onions.

During the California Gold Rush in the mid-19th century, Hawaiian farmers in Kula shipped so many potatoes off to the miners that the area became known as 'Nu Kaleponi', the Hawaiian pronunciation for New California. In the late 19th century, Portuguese and Chinese immigrants moved in to farm the Kula area after they had worked off their contracts on the sugar plantations.

Kula grows most of Hawaii's proteas, large bright flowers with an unusual flair. Some, like the pincushion varieties, are very delicate, and others have spine-like petals.

Almost 90% of the carnations used in leis throughout Hawaii are grown in Kula, as are many of the chrysanthemums.

Hwy 377 (Haleakala Hwy) and Hwy 37 (Kula Hwy) are both scenic. Take your pick, or go up one and down the other.

Gardens

All of Kula is a garden, but if you want to take a closer look, you can visit several established walk-through gardens.

Clouds' Rest Protea Farm, one mile off Hwy 377 along Upper Kimo Drive, has a little garden area with plants identified by plaques. You can stroll through it for free from 8 am to 4:30 pm daily. Cut protea are on sale at rock-bottom prices at the farm and at more typical prices by mail order.

Sunrise Market, on Hwy 378 on the way to Haleakala, has a free roadside garden with a small but select group of proteas.

Kula Botanical Gardens is a mature garden of tropical plants, pleasantly overgrown and shady. It's on Hwy 377, three-quarters of a mile up from the southern intersection of Hwys 377 and 37. The garden is open from 9 am to 4 pm daily and admission is $4 for adults, $1 for children.

The more recently established **Enchanting Floral Gardens** is sunny, open and orderly, with both tropical and cool-weather flowers. It has a colorful collection, with most plants labeled in both Japanese and English. It's on Hwy 37 at the 10-mile marker and is open from 9 am to 5 pm daily. Admission is $4 for adults, $2.50 for children.

The University of Hawaii maintains a 20-acre **Agricultural Research Center** in Kula. It's there that Hawaii's first proteas, natives of Australia and South Africa, were established in 1965. You can walk through rows of their colorful descendants, as well as dozens of new hybrids under development. The protea has more than 1400 varieties and is named after the Greek god Proteus, who was noted for his ability to change form.

There are now over 50 protea farms in Hawaii supplying fresh cut flowers to florists on the US mainland, Japan and Europe. The nearest is just across the street from the research center.

Some sections of the garden are used for experiments in plant pathology and are thus closed to visitors, but the rest of the garden is open to the public on weekdays except Fridays, the day set aside for pesticide spraying.

The research center is about a half-mile above town; to get there, take Copp Rd (between the 12- and 13-mile markers on Hwy 37) and turn left on Mauna Place.

Octagonal Church

The octagonal Holy Ghost Church is a hillside landmark in Waiakoa village. This distinctive white church has a roof that glints silver in the sun and is easily visible from the highway. Built in 1897 by Portuguese immigrants, the church's beautifully ornate interior looks like it came right out of Portugal, and much of it did. Because of termite problems, the church was dismantled and completely renovated in 1992.

Places to Stay

Kula View Bed & Breakfast (☎ 878-6736), Susan Kauai, Box 322, Kula, HI 96790, is less than a mile south of Hwy 37 in Waiakoa at 140 Holopuni Rd. Occupying the 2nd floor of Susan's home, the B&B is a pleasant studio room with nice views of the garden and distant ocean. The room has a dining

MAUI

table, desk, queen bed, mini-refrigerator, toaster oven, coffee pot, shower, deck and private entrance. The rate of $75 includes a breakfast of homemade muffins, juice, local fruit and coffee. Smoking is not allowed.

Kula Lodge (☎ 878-1535, 800-233-1535), RR1 Box 475, Kula, HI 96790, on Hwy 377, has five cottages in the same complex as its restaurant. All have private decks and are pleasant but not notably special for the money. Cheapest is a studio without a view for $100. There are two cottages for $120, each with a queen bed and a small loft with two futons, and two larger $150 cottages with a similar set-up but with twin beds in the loft and the addition of gas fireplaces. It costs $30 for each occupant beyond two. There are no TVs or phones, and breakfast is not included in the rates.

Camp Kula (☎ 876-0000), Box 111, Kula, HI 96790, is a gay B&B on seven secluded Upcountry acres with views of central Maui. There are two guest rooms. The Prince Kuhio Room has a single bed and a shared bath for $42 to $50, depending on the season, while the Queen Emma Suite has a king bed, TV, VCR and private bath for $52/65 for singles/doubles in the low season, $62/78 in the high season. Rates include a breakfast of herbal teas, homegrown fruits and baked goodies. HIV-positive guests are welcome.

Places to Eat

The dining room at the *Kula Lodge* is on a knoll and has wraparound windows and a splendid view of central and northern Maui and the ocean beyond. Breakfast features multigrain pancakes, tofu scramble and eggs Benedict, priced from $5 to $8. At lunch, burgers and sandwiches cost around $9, while the dinner menu includes pastas for $15, steak for around $20 and the fresh catch of the day at market prices. It's on Hwy 377, less than a mile north of Haleakala Crater Rd. It's open daily for breakfast from 6:30 to 11:15 am, for lunch and dinner from 11:30 am to 8:30 pm.

Kula Sandalwoods Restaurant, just past Kula Lodge on the mauka side of Hwy 377, is open daily from 6:30 am to 1:30 pm (to noon on Sundays). Breakfast, which is served until 11 am, includes omelets and waffles, while lunch includes sandwiches and salads. Most items go for $5 to $10.

Sunrise Market is a quarter of a mile up from the intersection of Hwys 378 and 377 on the way to Haleakala. You can pick up your morning coffee here along with bakery items, wrapped sandwiches and fresh and dried fruits. The store is open from 7:30 am to 4 pm daily.

Kula Country Store, a quarter of a mile south of the Octagonal Church in Waiakoa, is a small grocery store with a popular deli counter. It has lasagna or sandwiches for around $4, plate lunches for about a dollar more, and a few bakery and breakfast items. The store is open from 6 am to 6 pm on weekdays and from 7:30 am to 2:30 pm on weekends.

POLIPOLI SPRING STATE RECREATION AREA

Polipoli Spring State Recreation Area is high up in the Kula Forest Reserve on the western slope of Haleakala. The park is in a coniferous forest with picnic tables, camping and a network of trails. It's not always possible to get all the way to the park without a 4WD, but it's worth driving even part way up for the view.

Waipoli Rd, the road to the park, is off Hwy 377 just under half a mile before its southern intersection with Hwy 37. There's a Na Ala Hele sign marking the beginning of Waipoli Rd.

Waipoli is a narrow, switchbacking one-lane road. The drive is often through layers of clouds that drift in and out of groves of eucalyptus and past open rangeland (watch for cattle on the road). When the clouds lift there are vast views across green rolling hills to the islands of Lanai and Kahoolawe.

Few people venture up this way, and, except for the symphony of bird calls, everything is still.

When the clouds are heaviest, visibility is measured in feet. The road has some soft shoulders, but the first six miles are well paved. The road then enters the forest reserve and turns to dirt. When it's muddy, the next four miles up to the state park are not worth trying in a standard car.

The whole area was planted during the 1930s by the Civilian Conservation Corps (CCC), a Depression-era work program. Several of the trails pass through old CCC camps. There are stands of redwood, ash, cypress, cedar and pines. It all looks somewhat like the northern California coast.

Waiakoa Loop Trail

The trailhead to the Waiakoa Loop Trail starts at the hunter check station five miles up Waipoli Rd. Walk three-quarters of a mile down the grassy spur road on the left to a gate marking the trail that starts out in pine trees.

Since a fire some years back, the trail has not been well maintained, and it may not be possible to do the whole three-mile loop. However, you can start from the left side of the loop and walk about two miles to where it connects with the Upper Waiakoa Trail.

Upper Waiakoa Trail

The Upper Waiakoa Trail is a maintained seven-mile trail that was reconstructed a few years ago by the Na Ala Hele group. The trail begins off Waiakoa Loop at an elevation of 6000 feet, climbs 1800 feet, switchbacks and then drops back down 1400 feet.

It's stony terrain, but high and open and provides good views. Bring a full canteen of water.

The trail ends on Waipoli Rd between the hunter check station and the campground. If you want to start at this end of the trail, keep an eye out for the trail marker for Waohuli Trail, as the Upper Waiakoa Trail begins across the road.

Boundary Trail

The four-mile Boundary Trail is a marked and maintained trail that begins about 200 yards beyond the end of the pavement. Park to the right of the cattle grate that marks the boundary of the Kula Forest Reserve.

This is a steep downhill walk that crosses gulches and goes down deep into the woods, where there's eucalyptus, pine and cedar as well as a bit of native forest. In the afternoon the fog generally rolls in and visibility fades.

Skyline Trail

It's possible to hike 8½ miles from the summit of Haleakala to Polipoli campground at 6200 feet. At Haleakala National Park, go past the summit and take the road to the left just before Science City.

The first 6½ miles is down Skyline Trail, a dirt road used to maintain the state park. It starts at the 9750-foot elevation in an open terrain of cinder and craters.

After three miles you'll reach the tree line, which is at 8500 feet and begins in a native mamane forest. In the winter mamane is heavy with clusters of delicate yellow flowers that look like sweet-pea blossoms.

Skyline Trail merges into the Haleakala Ridge Trail and then connects with the Polipoli Trail, which spurs half a mile to the campground.

There's solitude on this walk. If the clouds treat you kindly, there are broad views as you pass from the barren summit into the dense cloudforest.

Places to Stay

Besides tent camping, Polipoli has one housekeeping cabin at $45 for up to four people, reserved through the state park system. Unlike the other state cabins, this one has gas lanterns but no electricity or refrigerator.

Come properly prepared, as this is cold country; winter temperatures frequently drop below freezing at night. There are restrooms, but no showers. Fellow campers are likely to be pig hunters.

KEOKEA

Around the turn of the century, Keokea was home mainly to Hakka Chinese who farmed the remote Kula region.

Although there's not much to it, Keokea is the last real town before Hana if you're swinging around the southern part of the island. It has a coffee shop and two small stores, the Fong Store and the Ching Store, the latter with a gas pump.

The village's green-and-white St John's Episcopal Church was built in 1907 to serve the Chinese community. 'St John's House of Worship' is still written in Chinese above the door.

On a clear day there are good views of West Maui and Lanai from the church and elsewhere along the roadside.

Places to Stay

Halemanu Bed & Breakfast (☎ /fax 878-2729), Carol Austin, 221 Kawehi Place, Kula, HI 96790, is in a lovely contemporary home set beneath the Kula Forest Reserve off Waipoli Rd. Accommodation is in a room with a queen bed, private bath, phone and deck. A TV and VCR are available in the loft. Carol, a travel columnist for the *Maui News*, is a very outgoing person who enjoys showing her guests around and occasionally joins them for impromptu hikes and snorkel outings. The cost is $75/85 for singles/doubles. There's a two-day minimum.

Bloom Cottage (☎ /fax 878-1425), RR2 Box 229, Kula, HI 96790, is a two-bedroom free-standing cottage in Keokea. There's a fireplace in the living room to ward off evening chills. The cottage also has a kitchen, TV, VCR and front porch. The rate is $105 for doubles, $15 for each extra person, with breakfast fixings provided. There's a two-night minimum stay, and smoking is not allowed.

Silver Cloud Guest Ranch (☎ 878-6101, 800-532-1111; fax 878-2132; slvrcld@maui .net), RR2 Box 201, Kula, HI 96790, is a former ranch turned B&B on Thompson Rd, just over a mile from central Keokea. The atmospheric plantation home has six guest rooms, all with private baths. The cheapest room ($75) is small and simple, while the most expensive ($115) is large and airy with a private porch and a fine ocean view. The house has a formal living room with hardwood floors, a fireplace, a piano and lots of upholstered chairs and love seats that invite lounging.

In addition, the bunkhouse out back has been converted into five small studios with kitchenettes and French doors leading to a little porch; a couple have nice ocean views. Avoid unit No 1, as the adjacent furnace is noisy. Rates are $95 to $135 but, as might be expected, the bunkhouse is not as refined as the plantation house. There's also a separate cottage with a wood-burning stove and covered lanai for $135. Breakfast is included in all rates, trail rides are available and credit cards are accepted.

Places to Eat

Upcountry folks gravitate to *Grandma's Coffee House* (☎ 878-2140) on Hwy 37 for homemade pastries and fresh dark-roasted Maui coffee. This cheery little place also has sandwiches and a few lunch items for around $6 and dinner specials such as ginger chicken with rice for a few dollars more. It opens at 7 am, closing at 3 pm on Sundays, 5 pm on Mondays and Tuesdays and 8 pm Wednesday to Saturday, the only nights dinner is available.

The family that owns Grandma's has been growing coffee beans on the slopes of Haleakala since 1918. If you want to see what coffee trees look like, just walk out to the side porch.

ULUPALAKUA RANCH

From Keokea, Hwy 37 winds south through ranch country with good views of Kahoolawe and the little island of Molokini. Even on overcast days you can often see below the clouds to sunny Kihei on the coast.

Tedeschi Vineyards, in the middle of Ulupalakua Ranch, is 5½ miles south of Keokea.

In the mid-19th century, Ulupalakua Ranch was a sugar plantation owned by whaling ship captain James Makee. The 25,000-acre ranch has been owned by Pardee Erdman and family since 1963. It's a working ranch with about 6000 head of cattle, 600 Merino sheep and 150 head of Rocky Mountain elk.

Ulupalakua Ranch Store, opposite the ranch headquarters, is a small local store selling cowboy hats, T-shirts, souvenirs, frozen elk sausage, snack items and Haagen-Dazs ice cream bars. It's open from 9 am to 5 pm Monday to Friday, 10 am to

4:30 pm on weekends. Be sure to check out the wooden cowboys on the front porch that were carved by local artist Reems Mitchell.

Tedeschi Vineyards

Tedeschi Vineyards (☎ 878-6058) planted its first grapes in 1976. While waiting for the vines to mature, the vineyard began producing Maui Blanc, a pineapple wine that is surprisingly light and dry.

Tedeschi now makes four wines from grapes, including champagne, red, rose and blush zinfandel, which you can try out in the tasting room from 9 am to 5 pm daily. Winery tours are given once an hour on the half hour between 9:30 am and 2:30 pm.

Opposite the winery, you can see the remains of the three stacks of the Makee Sugar Mill, built in 1878.

Piilani Hwy

The Piilani Hwy (Hwy 31) curves along the southern flank of Haleakala. From Tedeschi Winery it's 25 rugged miles to the town of Kipahulu, near Oheo Gulch, the southern end of Haleakala National Park.

Someday, in an asphalt future, this may well be a real highway with cars zipping along in both directions. For now, it's an unspoiled adventure. In different sections, this isolated road is of broken pavement, gravel, dirt or stones. It takes a good two hours to drive it.

Signs such as 'Motorists Assume Risk of Damage Due to Presence of Cattle' and 'Narrow Winding Road, Safe Speed 15 mph' give clues that this is not your standard highway.

The hardest part is finding out if the road is currently open and passable. Many tourist maps mark it as impassable, and car rental agencies say that just being on it is a violation of their contract.

There are a couple of possibilities for getting the latest on road conditions. While the best is word of mouth from other drivers, you can also call the Oheo Gulch ranger station (☎ 248-7375) daily between 9 am and 5 pm or the county public works department (☎ 248-8254) weekdays between 6:30 am and 3 pm.

The trickiest section of the drive is around Kaupo, where the road goes over three rocky creek beds. These are usually dry and pose little problem. But after hard rains, streams flow over the roads making passage difficult, if not dangerous. Flash floods sometimes wash away portions of the road, making it impossible to get through until it's repaired.

The best way to approach the road is with an early morning start. Take something to munch, plenty to drink and check your oil and spare tire. Go slowly enough so you don't bottom out. It's a long haul to civilization if you break down, and the tow charge is said to be around $400. If all goes well, it's possible to be soaking in one of Oheo's pools by early afternoon.

For the first 15 miles after the winery the road is reasonably good; some sections have been upgraded, while others are patchwork asphalt sprinkled with potholes. There are five unpaved miles, the roughest section of which is around Kaupo, where, depending on when it was last graded, there can be some torturous climbs over rocky riverbeds.

A 4WD is recommended, or at least a high riser with a manual transmission. Still, when all is said and done, we have driven this road in a low-slung compact car and, somewhat to our amazement, managed to not scrape bottom at all. There were sections where we had to take it very slow, but other than being bounced and rattled, we had no problems.

Keokea is the last place on the Kula side to get gas and something to eat. In the Oheo Gulch area you might find a fruit stand, but there's no drinking water, gas stations or other services until Hana.

Tedeschi Vineyards to Kaupo

South from Tedeschi Vineyards, groves of fragrant eucalyptus trees soon give way to a drier and scrubbier terrain. It's open rangeland with cattle grazing alongside and moseying across the road.

A few miles south of the winery the road crosses an expansive lava flow dating from 1790, Haleakala's last eruption. This flow, which is part of the Kanaio Natural Area Reserve, is the same one that covers the La Perouse area of the coast south of Makena. It's still black and barren all the way down to the sea.

Just offshore is the crescent island of Molokini with Kahoolawe beyond. The large grassy hills between here and the sea are volcanic cinder cones.

Painters sometimes set up their easels along the roadside to paint scenes of the grassy rock-strewn hills and the distant ocean. There's such a wide-angle view that the ocean horizon is noticeably curved.

As the road continues it runs in and out of numerous gulches and crosses a few bridges, gradually getting closer to the coast. Around the 28-mile marker, keep an eye out for a natural lava sea arch. As you continue, there are a couple of black-sand beaches.

Kaupo

Kaupo Gap is a deep and rugged valley with the only lowlands on this section of the coast. The village of Kaupo is around the 35-mile marker. However, don't expect a developed village in any sense of the word, as Kaupo is spread out and there's really not much to see. This is home for the scattered community of paniolos who work the Kaupo Ranch, many of them third-generation ranch hands.

Kaupo General Store, on the east side of the gap, is 'the only store for 20 miles'. Officially the hours are from 9 am to 5 pm Monday to Saturday, but they can be a bit flexible, so it's best not to count on it being open. On the west side of the store, Auntie Jane commonly sets up an afternoon lunch wagon selling burgers and sandwiches.

Kaupo was once heavily settled. It has three heiaus from the 18th century and two churches from the 19th century. Loaloa Heiau, the largest, is a registered national historical monument. All three heiau sites are mauka of Huialoha Church.

Huialoha Church, which is less than a mile east of the store, is on the rocky black-sand Mokulau Beach. The attractive white-washed church, built in 1859 and restored in 1978, is surrounded by a stone wall and a few windswept trees. Mokulau, which means 'many small islands', is named for the rocks just offshore. The area was an ancient surfing site.

From here the road curves in and then out, at which point it's well worth stopping and looking back for a picturesque view of the church across the bay. There used to be a landing in the bay for shipping Kaupo Ranch cattle, and you can still see steps leading down into the water on a rock jutting out into the ocean. This area is cool and forested, with sisal plants on the hillsides.

The road winding into Kipahulu skirts the edge of rocky cliffs and the vegetation picks up, with hala and guava trees. As you return to civilization, the road is shaded with big mango trees, banyans, bougainvillea and wiliwili trees with red tiger-claw blossoms. For details on Kipahulu, see the end of the Hana to Kipahulu section.

Haleakala

Haleakala Crater is an awesome geological wonder. It resembles the surface of the moon, with a seemingly lifeless crater floor dotted with high majestic cinder cones. Haleakala is the world's largest dormant volcano, 7½ miles long and 2½ miles wide. It last erupted 200 years ago.

Haleakala National Park centers around the crater, offering impressive views from its rim and hikes across the crater floor.

Haleakala (literally 'House of the Sun') has long been considered Maui's soul. The summit is thought to be an energy vortex, a natural power point for magnetic and cosmic forces. In ancient times it was a spiritual center for Hawaiian kahunas.

Whether it's the lingering mana of the gods who once made their home here or the geological forces of the earth that still release an occasional tremor, Haleakala does emanate a sense of omnipresent power.

The requisite pilgrimage to witness the sunrise at the rim of the crater can be an experience that borders on the mystical. Mark Twain referred to it as 'the sublimest spectacle' he'd ever seen.

Morning is usually the best time for viewing the crater. Later in the day, warm air generally forces clouds higher and higher until they pour through the two gaps and into the crater.

Although sunrises get top billing, sunsets can be impressive too. Sometimes there's a high, thin layer of cirrus clouds and a lower layer of fluffier clouds, with the sunset reflecting colors on both levels. At other times, however, it's completely clouded over.

Haleakala National Park stretches from Haleakala Crater down to the pools of Oheo Gulch on the coast south of Hana. There are separate entrances to both sections of the park, but no passage between them. For information on the Oheo Gulch area, see the Hana to Kipahulu section earlier in this chapter.

Geology

In its prime, Haleakala probably reached a height of 12,000 feet before water erosion began to eke out two large river valleys. The valleys eventually eroded into one another, forming what today is known as Haleakala Crater. The valley gaps, Koolau Gap on the northwest side and Kaupo Gap on the southeast, are dominant features in the crater wall.

Later eruptions have added numerous cinder cones to the floor of Haleakala. The yellow colors are from sulfur, the reds from iron oxide.

Information

It's a good idea to check on weather conditions (☎ 871-5054) before driving up. It's not uncommon for it to be cloudy at Haleakala when it's clear on the coast. A drizzly sunrise is a particularly disappointing non-event after getting out of bed at 4 am. The *Maui News* prints a sunrise schedule.

MAUI

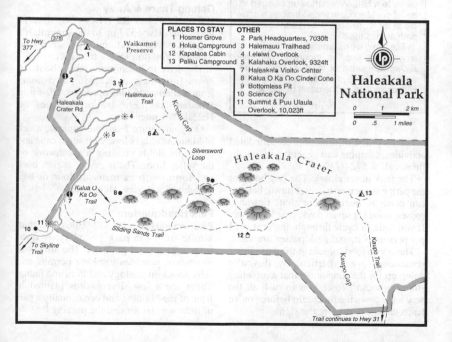

PLACES TO STAY
1 Hosmer Grove
6 Holua Campground
12 Kapalaoa Cabin
13 Paliku Campground

OTHER
2 Park Headquarters, 7030ft
3 Halemauu Trailhead
4 Leleiwi Overlook
5 Kalahaku Overlook, 9324ft
7 Haleakala Visitor Center
8 Kalua O Ka Oo Cinder Cone
9 Bottomless Pit
10 Science City
11 Summit & Puu Ulaula Overlook, 10,023ft

Haleakala National Park

0   1   2 km
0   .5   1 miles

To Hwy 377
(378)
Waikamoi Preserve
1
2
3
Haleakala Crater Rd
Halemauu Trail
Koolau Gap
4
5
6
Silversword Loop
Haleakala Crater
Kalua O Ka Oo Trail
7
8
9
13
11
10
To Skyline Trail
Sliding Sands Trail
12
Kaupo Gap
Kaupo Trail
Trail continues to Hwy 31

House of the Sun

Legend says that long ago the goddess Hina was having problems drying her tapa cloth because the days were too short. Her son Maui, the prankish demigod for whom the island is named, decided to take matters into his own hands.

One morning he went up to the mountaintop and waited for the sun. As it came up over the mountain Maui lassoed the rays one by one and held on until the sun came to a halt. When the sun begged to be let go, Maui demanded that as a condition for its release it hereafter slow its path across the sky.

The sun gave its promise, the days were lengthened and the mountain became known as House of the Sun. There are about 15 more minutes of daylight at Haleakala than on the coast below. ■

For recorded information on scheduled activities, camping and general park conditions, call ☎ 572-7749.

The park never closes. The pay booth at the park entrance opens after dawn, but you can drive through before that. Entrance passes, good for seven days, cost $4 per car. If you walk or cycle through, the cost is $2 per person. National park passes are valid.

There's no food for sale in the park. Bring something to eat, particularly if you're going up for the sunrise, so that a growling stomach doesn't force you to rush all the way back down the mountain before you've had a chance to explore the sights.

Activities

Fifteen-minute natural history talks are held at the summit building at 9:30, 10:30 and 11:30 am daily.

Park rangers lead a guided, moderately strenuous two-hour hike that goes about a mile into the crater down Sliding Sands Trail (meet at the trailhead) at 10 am on Tuesdays and Fridays.

Guided hikes into the Waikamoi Preserve leave from Hosmer Grove campground at 9 am on Mondays and Thursdays and last about three hours.

Other activities are scheduled less frequently. For example, guided hikes along the 12-mile Sliding Sands-Halemauu Trail are led once or twice a month, and there are evening stargazing programs periodically in summer.

Bicycle tours down Haleakala via the park road and horseback rides into the crater are detailed in the Activities section near the front of the Maui chapter.

Getting There & Away

Haleakala Crater Rd (Hwy 378) runs 11 miles from Hwy 377 up to the summit. It's a good paved road, but it's steep and winding. You don't want to rush it.

The drive to the summit takes about 1¼ hours from Paia or Kahului, two hours from Lahaina. If you need gas, fill up in Pukalani as there are no services on Haleakala Crater Rd.

On your return from the summit, much of Maui unfolds below, with sugar cane and pineapple fields creating a patchwork on the valley floor. The highway snakes back and forth, with as many as four or five switchbacks in view all at once.

Park Headquarters

Park headquarters (☎ 572-9306), less than a mile from the park boundary, is open from 7:30 am to 4 pm daily. The office has brochures, provides camping permits and sells books on geology and flora and fauna. There are a few silverswords planted in front of the building and occasionally a pair of nene wander around the parking lot.

Hosmer Grove

Hosmer Grove, three-quarters of a mile before park headquarters, has a pleasant half-mile loop trail that begins in the campground. The trail starts in a forest of introduced trees and then passes into native Hawaiian shrubland.

The exotics in Hosmer Grove were introduced in 1910 in an effort to develop a lumber industry in Hawaii. They include incense cedar, Japanese sugi, Douglas fir, eucalyptus and various pines. Although the trees adapted well enough to grow, they didn't grow fast enough at these elevations to make tree harvesting practical. Thanks to this failure, there's a park instead.

Native plants include ohelo, pukiawe, mamane, pilo and sandalwood. There are wonderful scents along the trail and lots of bird calls.

Walking through either Hosmer Grove or the nearby Waikamoi Preserve, you might see the native iiwi or apapane, both fairly common sparrow-size birds with bright red feathers. The iiwi has a very loud squeaking call, orange legs and a curved salmon-colored bill. The apapane is a fast-moving bird with a black bill, black legs and a white undertail. It feeds on the nectar of ohia flowers.

You might also see the melodious laughing thrush, also called the spectacle bird for the circles around its eyes that extend back like a pair of glasses, and the greenish Japanese white-eye, also with eye circles. These two are foreign species.

Waikamoi Preserve

Waikamoi Preserve is a 5230-acre reserve adjoining Hosmer Grove. In 1983, Haleakala Ranch conveyed the land's management rights to the Nature Conservancy.

The area contains native koa and ohia rainforest and is a habitat for Hawaiian forest birds, including a number of rare and endangered species. The yellow-green Maui creeper and the crested honeycreeper, while both endangered, are more common than some of the others. The crested honeycreeper is a beautiful but aggressive bird that often dive-bombs apapane and chases them off branches.

The conservancy has hikes on the second Saturday of each month. Reservations are required and can be made by calling the conservancy office (☎ 572-7849). More

---

The Sunrise Experience

Sunrise at Haleakala is an unforgettable experience. As you drive up the mountain in the dark, the only sights are lights: a sky full of stars, scattered city lights resembling a large connect-the-dots drawing, and a distant fishing boat or two on the dark horizon.

About an hour before sunrise, the night sky begins to lighten and turn purple-blue and the stars fade away. Interesting silhouettes of the mountain ridges appear.

Plan to arrive 30 or 40 minutes before the actual sunrise. The gentlest colors show up in the moments just before dawn. The undersides of the clouds lighten up first, accenting the night sky with pale silvery slivers and streaks of pink.

About 20 minutes before sunrise, the light intensifies on the horizon in bright oranges and reds, much like a sunset. Turn around for a look at Science City, whose domes turn a surreal pink.

Temperatures hovering around freezing and a cold wind are the norm at dawn. There's often a frosty ice in the top layer of cinders, which crunches underfoot.

If you don't have a winter jacket or sleeping bag to wrap yourself in, take a warm blanket from your hotel. This will give you the option of sitting outside in a peaceful spot to take it all in rather than huddling for heat inside the crowded visitor center.

Everyone comes out for the grand finale. The moment the sun appears, the earth awakens and everything glows.

Every morning is different, but once the sun is up the silvery lines and the subtleties disappear. The best photo opportunities are before the sun rises. ■

Nene

The native nene, Hawaii's state bird, is related to and resembles the Canada goose. It has been brought back from the verge of extinction (only 30 birds remained in 1951) by a captive breeding and release program.

Currently, Haleakala's nene population is holding steady at about 200. The birds generally nest in high cliffs surrounded by rugged lava flows with sparse vegetation.

Nene are rather curious. Many hang out where people do, from the crater floor cabins to park headquarters. Unfortunately, they don't do well in an asphalt habitat, and many have been run over by cars. ■

frequent are the guided hikes led by the National Park Service, which enter the preserve from Hosmer Grove campground at 9 am on Mondays and Thursdays.

Leleiwi Overlook

Leleiwi Overlook is midway between park headquarters and the visitor center. From the parking lot it's a five-minute walk out to the overlook, from where you can see the West Maui Mountains and both sides of the isthmus connecting the two sides of Maui. You also get another angle on Haleakala Crater.

In the afternoon, if weather conditions are right, you might see the Brocken specter, an optical phenomenon that occurs at high elevations. Essentially, by standing between the sun and the clouds your image is magnified and projected onto the clouds. The light reflects off tiny droplets of water in the clouds, creating a circular rainbow around your shadow.

Kalahaku Overlook

Kalahaku Overlook is about a mile above Leleiwi Overlook. The lower section has a fenced enclosure containing lots of silversword, from seedlings to mature plants.

The upper section has an observation deck looking down into Haleakala Crater. With the help of the deck's information plaque, you can clearly identify seven cinder cones on the crater floor below.

For photography, afternoon light is best. In the early morning you can get more favorable light by walking a few minutes down an unmarked path to the left of the observation deck.

Haleakala Visitor Center

The visitor center, on the rim of the crater, is the main sunrise-viewing spot. It's open from shortly before sunrise to 3 pm daily.

The center has displays on geological and volcanic evolution and a recording explaining what you see looking out of the window into the crater floor 3000 feet below. Books on geology, plants and the national park are for sale here, and there's usually a ranger on duty.

Summit

The Puu Ulaula (Red Hill) Overlook, at 10,023 feet, is Maui's highest point. The octagon summit building at the overlook has wraparound windows, and on clear days you can see the Big Island, Lanai, Molokai and even Oahu. The summit building is half a mile uphill from the visitor center.

The 37-mile drive from sea level to the summit of Haleakala is said to be the highest elevation gain in the shortest distance anywhere in the world.

Science City

On the Big Island's Mauna Kea, scientists study the moon. Here at Haleakala, appropriately enough, they study the sun.

Science City, just beyond the summit, is outside park headquarters and off-limits to visitors. It's under the jurisdiction of the University of Hawaii, which owns some of the domes and leases other land for a variety of private and government research projects.

In addition to UH's solar observatory, the university's Institute of Astronomy operates a lunar ranging facility. Purdue University and the University of Wisconsin jointly operate a gamma ray telescope.

Defense-related projects include laser technology related to the 'Star Wars' project, satellite tracking and identification and a deep-space surveillance system. The newest military telescope, built in 1996 at a cost of $123 million, is capable of identifying a grapefruit-size object flying in space hundreds of miles away.

Places to Stay

Camping Free tent camping is allowed at three campgrounds in the Upcountry section of the park and one on the coast at Oheo Gulch. Information on the Oheo Gulch area is in the Hana to Kipahulu section of this chapter.

Hosmer Grove is a drive-up campground immediately after the park entrance. It has a picnic shelter, toilets, water and grills. Permits are not required, though there's a three-day limit per month. It's busier in summer than in winter and is often full on holiday weekends. Located at the 6800-foot elevation, it tends to be cloudy and a bit wet.

There are two backcountry campgrounds inside Haleakala Crater. One is at Holua, four miles down Halemauu Trail, and the other is at Paliku at the trail's end. Both are below steep cliffs, though Holua is dry and barren while Paliku is lush and wet.

Permits are required for backcountry camping. They are issued at park headquarters on a first-come first-served basis between 8 am and 3 pm on the day of the hike. Camping is limited to three nights in the crater each month, with no more than two consecutive nights at either campground.

Each campground is limited to 25 people. Permits can go quickly if large groups show up, a situation that is more likely to occur in summer.

The campsites have pit toilets and water. Fires are prohibited, and you'll need to carry all your trash out.

Cabins There are three primitive cabins along trails in the crater, one each at Holua, Kapalaoa and Paliku, which were built by the CCC in the 1930s. Each has a wood-burning stove, some cooking utensils, 12 bunks with sleeping pads (but no bedding), pit toilets and a limited supply of water and firewood. Hiking distances from the crater rim range from four to 10 miles.

Cabin fees are $40 per night for a group of one to six people, $80 for seven to 12 people. There's a three-day limit, with no

Silversword

The strikingly beautiful silversword with its pointed silver leaves is a distant relative of the sunflower. The plant grows for four to 25 years before blooming just once.

In its final year, it shoots up a flowering stalk sometimes as high as nine feet. During the summer the stalk flowers with hundreds of maroon and yellow blossoms. When the flowers go to seed in late autumn, the plant dies.

The silversword, found only in Hawaii, was nearly wiped out in the early 20th century by grazing feral goats and by people who took them for souvenirs. It's making a comeback due to efforts by the park service, who have fenced in sections of the park to protect the plants. ∎

more than two consecutive nights in any cabin. Each cabin is rented to only one party at a time.

The problem here is the demand, which is so high the park service actually holds a lottery to award reservations! To enter, your reservation request must be received two months prior to the first day of the month of your proposed stay (for example, requests for cabins on any date in July must arrive before May 1). Your chances are increased if you have alternate dates.

Only written reservation requests are accepted (no phone or fax). To receive a request form, write to Cabin Lottery Request, Haleakala National Park, Box 369, Makawao, HI 96768.

Do not send money with your request form. If you are selected in the lottery, you will be notified, at which point the fees will have to be paid in full at least three weeks prior to the reservation date. They can be paid by Visa, MasterCard, check or money order.

HIKING THE CRATER

Hiking the crater floor offers a completely different angle on Haleakala's lunar landscape. Instead of peering down from the rim, you're looking up at the walls and towering cinder cones. It looks so much like a moonscape that US astronauts trained here before going to the moon.

The crater floor is a very still place to walk. Cinders crunching underfoot is often the only sound.

The trails inside the crater connect with each other and are marked at junctions.

The weather at Haleakala can change suddenly from dry, hot conditions to a cold, windswept rain. Although the general rule is sunny in the morning and cloudy in the afternoon, fog and clouds can blow in at any time.

No matter what the weather is like at the start of a hike, be prepared for temperatures that can drop into the 50s (°F) during the day and the 30s at night, at any time of year. Hikers without proper clothing risk hypothermia.

The climate also changes radically as you walk across the crater floor. In the four miles between Kapalaoa and Paliku cabins, rainfall varies from an annual average of 12 inches to 300 inches. December to May is the wetter season.

With the average elevation on the crater floor at 6700 feet, the relatively thin air means that hiking can be quite tiring. The higher elevation also means that sunburn is more likely. Take sunscreen, rain gear, a few layers of clothing and a full canteen of water.

Sliding Sands Trail

Sliding Sands, the summit trail into the crater, starts at the south side of the visitor center parking lot. The trail leads 9¾ miles to the Paliku campground and cabin, passing Kapalaoa cabin at 5¾ miles. The first six miles of the trail follow the south wall of the crater.

From Kapalaoa to Paliku, the descent is gentle and the vegetation gradually increases. Paliku (6380 feet) is beneath a sheer cliff at the eastern end of the crater. In contrast to the crater's barren western end, the heavy rainfall in this area makes for grassy campsites, with ohia forests climbing the slopes.

Sliding Sands-Halemauu Trail

One of the most popular day hikes for people in good shape is the 12-mile hike that starts down Sliding Sands Trail and returns via Halemauu Trail. It's a strenuous full-day outing.

Sliding Sands starts out at 9780 feet and descends steeply over loose cinders down to the crater floor. If you hike it after catching the sunrise you'll walk directly into a gentle warmish wind and the rays of the sun. There are great views on the way down but, except for a few shrubs, there's no vegetation in sight.

Four miles down, after an elevation drop of 2500 feet, a spur trail leads north about a mile to the Halemauu Trail.

Once on the Halemauu Trail it's possible to take a short loop to the **Bottomless Pit**. Legends say the pit leads down to the sea, though the park service says it's just 65 feet deep. It's basically a large hole in the ground of limited interest.

About 1½ miles up the Halemauu Trail,

the short **Silversword Loop** passes by silversword plants in various stages of growth. If you're here in summer, you should be able to see plants in bloom.

About a mile farther along Halemauu Trail is Holua cabin and campground. There's a large **lava tube** here that's worth exploring. At 6960 feet this is one of the lowest areas along this hike, and there are impressive views of the crater walls rising a few thousand feet to the west. From the cabin it's four miles to the Halemauu trailhead.

Because of its steep descent, Sliding Sands Trail makes a better entry trail into the crater than a return trail. The Halemauu trailhead, at an elevation of 8000 feet, is an easier exit.

Halemauu trailhead is on Hwy 378, six miles below the visitor center (and the trailhead to Sliding Sands) and 3½ miles above park headquarters. If you haven't arranged to be picked up or left a car at the trailhead, you could try your luck hitchhiking.

Halemauu Trail

If you're not up for a long hike, you might try doing just part of the Halemauu Trail. Even hiking in the first mile to the crater rim gives a fine view of the crater with Koolau Gap to the east. It's fairly level up to this point.

If you were to continue on the trail and hike down the switchbacks to Holua cabin and back, the eight-mile roundtrip would make a fine, hardy day hike. From the trailhead to the bottom of the pali the trail descends 1400 feet. Once on the floor of the crater the trail follows the west wall for about a mile to Holua cabin at 6960 feet. The trail continues another six miles to Paliku cabin.

Halemauu trailhead, 3½ miles above park headquarters, is marked. There's a fair chance you'll find nene in the parking lot.

Kalua O Ka Oo Trail

Two miles down the Sliding Sands Trail (a descent of 1600 feet), a spur trail leads up the Kalua O Ka Oo cinder cone, about half a mile to the north.

Midway along Kalua O Ka Oo Trail are some silversword plants. From the visitor center to Kalua O Ka Oo and back it's a hardy three-hour hike. Because of the uphill climb back, this is a good hike to do early in the morning to avoid the midday heat.

Kaupo Trail

From Paliku campground on the eastern edge of the crater floor, it's possible to continue another nine miles down to Kaupo on the southern coast. The first 3½ miles of the trail drops 2500 feet in elevation before reaching the park boundary. It's a rocky trail through rough lava and brushland. The last 5½ miles pass through Kaupo Ranch property on a rough jeep trail as it descends to the Kaupo Gap, exiting at the east side of the Kaupo General Store. There are fine coastal views along the way.

The 'village' of Kaupo is a long way from anywhere, with very little traffic. Still, what traffic there is – largely sightseers braving the circle-island road – moves slow enough along Kaupo's rough road to start conversation. If you have to walk the final stretch, it's 10 miles to Oheo Gulch and what will seem like hordes of people and traffic. If you do need to spend the night in Kaupo, hikers are allowed to camp outside the walls at the Huialoha Church.

This is a strenuous hike, and because of the remoteness and the ankle-twisting conditions it's not advisable to hike it alone. The National Park Service publishes a Kaupo Trail brochure that people considering the hike should pick up in advance.

Molokai

Molokai is the last stronghold of rural Hawaii. It manages to hold out in a sort of time warp: no packaged Hawaiiana, no high-rises, more farmers than tourists.

If you're looking for lots of action or anything slick, Molokai isn't the place. Instead, you can walk along Hawaii's largest beach with barely another soul in sight, or take the cliffside mule trail down to the old leprosy colony of Kalaupapa. Molokai offers quiet hikes, spectacular valleys, a wildlife park and a handful of historical sites.

Molokai is the most Hawaiian of the main islands, with almost 50% of its population of native Hawaiian ancestry. It's only sparsely populated, with but a handful of small towns.

According to ancient chants, Molokai is a child of Hina, goddess of the moon. This is a place to get in touch with basics.

In the morning you can sit on the edge of an 800-year-old fishpond and watch the sun rise over Haleakala on distant Maui. In the evening you can watch the sun set behind the silhouette of Molokai's royal coconut grove.

Molokai retains so much small-town character that at times it seems more like some forgotten outpost in the South Pacific than the island between the high-rises of Maui and Waikiki.

HISTORY

Molokai had powerful sorcerers whose reputations were respected throughout the islands. Through carvings of poisonwood idols and other elaborate rituals, they were able to keep potential invaders at bay. For centuries, the battling armies of Maui and Oahu were careful to bypass Molokai.

By the 18th century, magic wasn't enough to protect Molokai from outside influences. Internal dissent among the alii of Molokai, largely over access to valuable fishing grounds at Moomomi, led them to align with chiefs from other islands. Oahu,

Maui and the Big Island all got involved in the ensuing power struggle.

Eventually the king of Oahu, Peleioholani, established his rule over Molokai. When the daughter he left on Molokai was captured and killed by Molokai chiefs, Peleioholani hastily returned to the island and struck back with a vengeance. Those Molokai chiefs who were unable to flee to Maui were captured and roasted alive.

Oahu continued to rule over Molokai until 1785. Over the next decade, warring Maui and the Big Island took alternate turns ruling Molokai until Kamehameha the Great finally united all the islands in 1795.

The first detailed description of the island was recorded by Captain George Vancouver, a British navigator, who anchored off Molokai in 1792. His guesstimate placed Molokai's population at around 10,000.

When the missionaries arrived in the 1830s, they did a more detailed count, estimating Molokai's total population at 8700.

Molokai's largest settlements were on the rainy south coast of the eastern half of the island. The shallow waters and coastal indentations there were ideal for the construction of fishponds, and in the valley wetlands, taro patches flourished.

The missionaries found the densest populations between Kamalo and Waialua, and it is in this area that they established their first missions. Some of the churches still stand today.

Kalaupapa Peninsula had the island's other major settlement, with about 2500 people. The north shore valleys of Halawa, Pelekunu and Wailau were also populated. Molokai's central plains and dry western half were only lightly settled.

Ranching & Agriculture

Cattle and sheep, which were introduced in the mid-19th century, had a major impact on Molokai. Grazing resulted in widespread destruction of native vegetation,

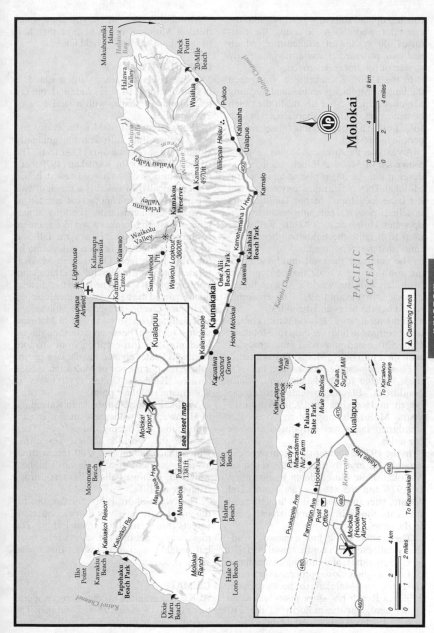

MOLOKAI

causing upland soils to wash down into the coastal fishponds. As a result, the centuries-old system of aquaculture, which had long provided Hawaiians with a ready source of food, was destroyed.

In the 1850s, Kamehameha V acquired the bulk of Molokai's arable land, forming Molokai Ranch. After his death the ranch became part of the Bishop Estate, which sold it off to a group of Honolulu businesspeople in 1897.

A year later the American Sugar Company, a division of Molokai Ranch, attempted to develop a major sugar plantation in central Molokai. They built a railroad system to haul the cane, developed harbor facilities and installed a powerful pumping system to draw up water. However, by 1900 the well water used to irrigate the fields had become so saline that the crops failed.

The company then got into honey production on such a scale that at one point Molokai was the world's largest honey exporter. In the mid-1930s an epidemic wiped out the hives and the industry.

In the meantime, Molokai Ranch continued its efforts to find 'the crop for Molokai'. Cotton, rice and numerous grain crops all took their turn biting Molokai's red dust.

Finally, pineapple took root as the crop most suitable for the island's dry, windy conditions. Plantation-scale production began in Hoolehua in 1920. Within 10 years Molokai's population tripled as immigrant labor was introduced to work the fields.

In the 1970s, competition from overseas brought an end to pineapple's reign on Molokai. Dole closed down its operation in 1976 and the other island giant, Del Monte, later followed suit. It brought hard times and the highest unemployment levels in the state.

Then cattle raising, long a mainstay, suddenly collapsed. In a controversial decision in 1985, the state, after finding an incidence of bovine tuberculosis, ordered every head of cattle on Molokai to be destroyed. Molokai Ranch has since restocked some of its herd, but the majority of the 240 smaller cattle owners called it quits.

Molokai Ranch still owns about one-third of Molokai, which is more than half of the island's privately held lands.

GEOGRAPHY

Molokai is Hawaii's fifth-largest island. It is 38 miles long, 10 miles wide and roughly rectangular in shape, with a land area of 264 sq miles.

The western half of Molokai is dry and arid, with rolling hills and the gradually sloping range of Maunaloa (1381 feet). The island's highest point, Kamakou (4970 feet), is in the middle of the rugged eastern half.

Geologically, Molokai is a union of two separate shield volcanoes that erupted to form two distinct islands. The lofty mountains of eastern Molokai acted like a screen, capturing the clouds. Heavy rainfall and stream erosion then cut deep valleys into its towering north face. Dry western Molokai formed into more modest hills and tableland. Later eruptions spilled lava into the channel that separated the two, forming the Hoolehua Plains and creating present-day Molokai.

Kalaupapa, on the north side of Molokai, seems to have been an afterthought by Madame Pele. An eruption from offshore Kauhako Crater created the flat lava peninsula long after the rest of Molokai had been formed. Kauhako Crater, at 400 feet, is Kalaupapa's highest point.

Molokai's North Shore, from Kalaupapa to Halawa, is a wilderness area of coastal mountains and deeply cut valleys. They include the world's highest sea cliffs, which reach heights of 3300 feet with an average gradient of 58°. Hawaii's highest waterfall, Kahiwa Falls (1750 feet), drops from these cliffs.

The North Shore is spectacular, but for the most part its steep slopes and rainforests are virtually impenetrable. The main way to get into the valleys is by boat, but rough winter seas restrict that to the summer season.

CLIMATE

At Kaunakakai, the average daily temperature is 70°F in winter, 78°F in summer. The average annual rainfall is 27 inches.

FLORA & FAUNA
The two most dominant forest types on Molokai are kiawe in the drier areas and ohia lehua in the wetter. Along the banks of streams, which were once heavily cultivated with taro, forests of kukui and guava now dominate.

The axis deer that run free in Molokai are descendants of eight deer sent from India in 1868 as a gift to King Kamehameha V. Feral pigs, introduced by the early Polynesian settlers, roam the upper wetland forests, and feral goats inhabit the steep canyons and valley rims. All three wreak havoc on the environment and are hunted game animals.

Native water birds include the common moorhen, Hawaiian coot and black-necked stilt, which are all endangered. Molokai also has five native forest birds, mostly in the undisturbed upland forests, and the Hawaiian owl.

GOVERNMENT
Kalaupapa Peninsula is a county unto itself, called Kalawao, which is essentially administered by the State Department of Health. The rest of Molokai, along with neighboring Lanai, is swallowed up in the mire of Maui County.

Most administrative decisions affecting Molokai are made on Maui. Since many community planning and development issues are decided at a county level, the island of Maui, with 12 times Molokai's population, has the clout.

ECONOMY
Molokai has a double-digit unemployment rate that's triple the state average.

After the huge pineapple plantations left Molokai in the late 1970s, islanders began to more intensely develop small-scale farming.

Molokai has rich soil, and some feel the island may have the potential to be Hawaii's 'breadbasket'. Significant crops include watermelons, dryland taro, macadamia nuts, sweet potatoes, string beans and onions.

The Kaunakakai area has some of the world's best growing conditions for seed corn. Hawaii's climate makes it possible to produce three generations of hybrids each year versus only one on the mainland. Corn for seed has been raised in Hawaii since the late 1960s, and much of the corn produced in the USA can trace its roots to Molokai.

In 1991, coffee trees were planted on formerly fallow pineapple fields in Kualapuu and now cover some 600 acres.

POPULATION & PEOPLE
Molokai has a population of 6800. Outside of Niihau, Molokai is the most Hawaiian of the islands, with almost 50% of its people Hawaiian or part-Hawaiian. Filipino is the

Molokai Plan
In the early 1980s a Maui County Committee was appointed to create a community plan to address development issues on Molokai. The committee conducted hearings and surveys on Molokai, and much to the surprise of Molokai residents – who were used to being bullied by Maui prodevelopment forces – the recommendations put forth in the final plan were tuned in to their own feelings on growth.

The Molokai Plan calls for the preservation of Molokai's rural lifestyle and the maintenance of agriculture as the basis of the economy. It also calls for all resort development to be limited to the West End and to be low-rise. The Molokai Plan has been widely accepted as the guiding code for land use on Molokai and is referred to whenever there are disputes over development – which is often.

Water use is a particularly hot issue on Molokai, with both farmers and West End developers vying for the island's limited supply.

You can pick up a lot of local antidevelopment sentiment simply by noticing bumper stickers on Molokai pickup trucks, which bear slogans such as 'Molokai Is Too Small To Be Big' and 'Keep Molokai Molokai'. ■

next largest ethnic group, followed by Japanese and Caucasian.

The large Hawaiian population is in part due to the Hawaiian Homes Act of 1921 that awarded 40-acre blocks of land to people with at least 50% Hawaiian ancestry. The purpose of the act was to encourage homesteading among native Hawaiians, who had become the most landless ethnic group in Hawaii. The first settlements under the act were made on Molokai.

ORIENTATION

Molokai lies midway in the Hawaiian chain, 26 miles southeast of Oahu and nine miles northwest of Maui. Lanai is nine miles directly south.

The airport is on the island's flat central plains, more or less in the center of Molokai. Take a right turn when you leave the airport to get to Hwy 460. At the highway, to the left it's seven miles to Kaunakakai, the main town; to the right it's 13 miles to Kaluakoi Resort on the west coast.

This one highway is Molokai's main road, stretching from east to west. From Kaunakakai westward it's called Hwy 460 (Maunaloa Hwy). From Kaunakakai eastward it's Hwy 450 (Kamehameha V Hwy).

Maps

The best map of Molokai, albeit not perfect, is the Molokai-Lanai map published by the University of Hawaii Press; it's sold in shops around Kaunakakai.

Exploring Molokai

Molokai is not the place to explore dirt roads just to see what's there. People on the

island spend a lot of time outdoors, and their yards are extensions of their homes. Many dirt paths that seem like they could be roads are just driveways into someone's backyard. In addition, as on all the islands, there's a bit of pakalolo growing here and there. All in all, folks aren't too keen on outsiders cruising around on their private turf.

On the other hand, if there's a fishpond you want to see and someone's house is between the road and the water, it's usually easy to stop and strike up a conversation. Molokai people are generally receptive and friendly. If you ask permission first, they'll usually let you cross their property. If you appear interested, they might even share a little local lore and history – the old-timers in particular can be fascinating to listen to.

INFORMATION
Tourist Offices

The Molokai Visitors Association (☎ 553-3876; fax 553-5288), Box 960, Kaunakakai, HI 96748, distributes tourist information about Molokai. From the US mainland and Canada, call toll free ☎ 800-800-6367; from within Hawaii, call ☎ 800-553-0404.

Money

There are half a dozen banks and credit unions on the island; the Bank of Hawaii in Kaunakakai is the largest.

Post & Communications

The main post office is in downtown Kaunakakai; there are also post offices in Hoolehua, Kualapuu, Maunaloa and Kalaupapa.

Newspapers

Molokai's two weekly newspapers, both distributed free around the island, provide a glimpse of island life. The more substantial of the two is *The Dispatch* (☎ 553-3293), Box 440, Kaunakakai, HI 96748, which has a progressive stance on local issues and is published each Thursday; subscriptions sent to the US mainland cost $50 a year. The *Molokai Advertiser-News* (☎ 558-8253; molokai@aloha.net), HC 1, Box 770,

---

Official Molokai

Molokai's official flower is the white kukui blossom, its official color is green and its nickname is 'The Friendly Island'. ∎

Kaunakakai, HI 96748, is published each Wednesday.

The *Maui News*, *Honolulu Advertiser* and *Honolulu Star-Bulletin* are sold at the airport and from vending machines in front of C Pascua Store in Kaunakakai.

Film & Photography

Molokai Sight & Sound in Kaunakakai sells film and does in-house film processing; a 24-exposure roll of prints costs $10 for overnight service, $2 more for one-hour service. It's open from 9 am to 8:30 pm daily.

Weather

For recorded weather and marine forecasts by the National Weather Service, call ☎ 552-2477.

Emergency

Dial ☎ 911 for police, ambulance and fire emergencies. Molokai General Hospital (☎ 553-5331) in Kaunakakai has 24-hour emergency service. The Molokai Helpline (☎ 553-3311) provides crisis counseling.

ACTIVITIES
Beaches & Swimming

Papohaku Beach on the west coast is the broadest and longest sandy beach in all of Hawaii. Although it's a great walking beach, it's not safe for swimming. However, just a few miles south of Papohaku is Dixie Maru Beach, a popular family beach with a small protected bay.

For something less frequented, Kawakiu Beach is a beautiful crescent beach north of Kaluakoi Golf Course with fine coastal views and good swimming when seas are calm. Moomomi Beach, on the north coast, is another secluded coastal stretch, this one backed by expansive dunes.

In terms of swimming, the Kaunakakai area is a dud, with a coastline of silty, shallow waters. Most Kaunakakai visitors drive to the southeastern end of the island, where the beach around the 20-mile marker offers some of Molokai's best swimming and snorkeling. Rock Point, not far from there, and Halawa Bay, at the end of the road, are popular surfing spots.

There are other beaches in remote places, but Molokai is about the last place you'd need to torture yourself with washed-out roads or trips through jungles simply to get away from it all. For those who have ever fantasized about having a vast secluded beach to themselves, all that's needed is to drive up to the miles of gleaming sand at Papohaku and start walking.

Molokai Fish & Dive in Kaunakakai rents snorkel sets for $9 a day and boogie boards for $7; you can buy a mask and snorkel for $20. Fun Hogs at the Kaluakoi Hotel rents snorkel sets for $7.50 a day and body boards with fins for $15 a day.

Swimming Pools The Mitchell Pauole Center in Kaunakakai has a 25-meter pool free to the public from 8:30 am to noon daily except Thursdays and Sundays, and from 1 to 4:30 pm daily. It's not uncommon to have the pool to yourself, particularly in winter, when islanders consider the pool water to be cold.

Hiking

Molokai has a handful of hiking opportunities. The Nature Conservancy's Kamakou Preserve offers unique rainforest hikes in the island's rugged interior and out to scenic valley overlooks.

The Palaau State Park area has a couple of good hiking options. One, the hike down the mule trail to Kalaupapa, not only offers fine views, but also provides a way to get to the peninsula without dishing out a lot of money. A less frequented trail from the Kalaupapa Overlook provides a pleasant hour-long hike through a forest of fragrant eucalyptus and ironwood.

On the west side of the island, there's an easy hike to secluded Kawakiu Beach from the Kaluakoi Golf Course. The expansive white sands of Papohaku Beach and Moomomi Beach offer fine walks as well.

All trails are detailed in their respective sections.

Kayaking

Fun Hogs Hawaii (☎ 552-2242), in the beach hut at the Kaluakoi Hotel, rents kayaks in summer. The cost is $25/40 for four/eight hours for a one-person kayak, and $40/55 for a two-person kayak.

From June through August, Fun Hogs conducts guided shoreline kayak tours to Kawakiu Bay or along the south coast for $40 per person, snorkeling gear included. For experienced kayakers, they can also make arrangements for a self-guided North Shore kayak/camping trip from Halawa Valley all the way back to Kepuhi Beach, a trip of about five days.

Tennis
The Mitchell Pauole Center in Kaunakakai has two lighted tennis courts just beyond the pool. Like everywhere else in Molokai, you're not likely to find a crowd waiting.

Cycling
Fun Hogs Hawaii (☎ 552-2242) at the Kaluakoi Hotel rents 21-speed mountain bikes for $6 an hour, $15 a day, including helmets and gloves. Bike racks rent for $5 a day. Fun Hogs also offers guided off-road mountain-biking tours.

Horseback Riding
Molokai Ranch (☎ 552-2791, 800-254-8871) offers 1½-hour guided horseback rides at 8:30 am daily for $60. The rides cross ranch pasture, providing views of the ocean and Lanai. For the more adventurous, they can also organize a 'paniolo roundup', complete with barrel racing, pole vending and cattle herding; the cost is $75 per person with a minimum of six people.

Molokai Horse & Wagon Ride (☎ 558-8132) offers 1½-hour guided horseback rides for $40.

Golf
The Kaluakoi Golf Course (☎ 552-2739) has an 18-hole par 72 course open from 7 am to 6:30 pm, a driving range, a putting green and a pro shop. The cost for 18 holes, including a cart, is $55 for resort guests, $75 for nonguests. Clubs can be rented for $22, shoes for $10.

Although most tourists stick to the resort golf course, the Ironwood Hills Golf Club

(☎ 567-6000) in Kalae is the course of choice by islanders and is a real test of skill. It's open from 7 am to 5 pm daily. Fees are $10 for nine holes or $14 for 18 holes, plus $7 to $14 for carts.

Organized Tours
Taxi & Van Tours Kukui Tours & Limousines (☎ 553-5133) has three-hour island tours for $24 per person; these include Kaunakakai and Maunaloa towns, Kaluakoi Resort, Purdy's Macadamia Nut Farm and the Kalaupapa Overlook. Seven-hour tours, which add on a ride through eastern Molokai, cost $42. There's a three-person minimum. Kukui also has sightseeing vans that can be chartered at an hourly rate of $54 with a two-hour minimum.

Friendly Isle Tours (☎ 553-9046) has similar tours at similar prices.

Molokai Off-Road Tours & Taxi (☎ 553-3369) offers 4WD tours, including 'a rain-forest adventure' of the interior forests for $53 with a four-person minimum.

Wagon Ride Molokai Horse & Wagon Ride (☎ 558-8132, 800-670-6965), Box 1528, Kaunakakai, HI 96748, is a small local operation that combines a horse-drawn wagon ride from the beach at Mapulehu to Iliiliopae Heiau with coconut husking and hula lessons, followed by lunch. While it's touristy, most people enjoy themselves. The ride leaves at 10:30 am Monday to Saturday and the cost is $37 for adults, $18.50 for children six to 12. To get there, look for a big mango grove, makai side, a quarter of a mile past the 15-mile marker on Hwy 450.

Sailing & Whale Watching The waters between Molokai, Lanai and Maui are a frequent winter site for cavorting humpbacks.

Molokai Charters (☎ 553-5852), Box 1207, Kaunakakai, HI 96748, has a $30 two-hour sunset sail and a $40 four-hour sail that includes whale watching in season. There's also a full-day $75 trip to Lanai that includes snorkeling and lunch. All sailings are from Kaunakakai aboard *Satan's Doll*, a 42-foot sloop. The boat goes out with a minimum of four people.

Fun Hogs (☎ 552-2242) at the Kaluakoi Hotel takes a 28-foot catamaran on snorkeling excursions up the west coast to Ilio Point during the summer when the surf is low. Sailing excursions and whale-watching outings are sometimes also available. The cost is $50.

Joe Reich (☎ 558-8377), Box 825, Kaunakakai, HI 96748, has a 31-foot boat, the *Alyce C*, that can be chartered for fishing trips, whale-watching jaunts and inter-island runs.

ACCOMMODATIONS

Molokai has a total of three hotels and five condominium complexes.

The Kaunakakai area has two hotels, Pau Hana Inn and Hotel Molokai, and one condo, Molokai Shores. All three front a beach with a good view of Lanai, but with waters unsuitable for swimming; each place does, however, have a swimming pool.

Molokai's only resort is Kaluakoi, on the west coast. It has one hotel, a golf club, three condo complexes and attractive white-sand beaches.

The only other development, the Wavecrest condos, are 13 miles east of Kaunakakai, on Molokai's wetter, lusher eastern side. Molokai also has a handful of B&Bs.

Unless otherwise specified, the rates given in this chapter are the same for both singles and doubles.

Camping

Camping is allowed at Palaau State Park, at Waikolu Lookout, at the county beach parks of Papohaku and One Alii and at the Kapuaiwa Coconut Grove.

State Parks Camping is free at Palaau State Park and at Waikolu Lookout, the latter just outside Kamakou Preserve. There's a five-day maximum stay at each site. Permits, which are required, may be obtained at the Department of Land & Natural Resources office (☎ 567-6891), the unmarked building just south of the post office on Puupeelua Ave (Hwy 480) in Hoolehua. It's open between 7:30 am and 4 pm Monday to Friday.

County Parks The Department of Parks & Recreation (☎ 553-3204) at the Mitchell Pauole Center in Kaunakakai issues camping permits for Papohaku and One Alii county parks. The office is open from 8 am to 4 pm Monday to Friday. Permits cost $3 per adult and 50¢ per child (age 17 and under) per day and can be obtained by mail (Box 1055, Kaunakakai, HI 96748) or in person. Permits are limited to three consecutive days; if you want to camp longer, you must return to the county parks office every three days for a new permit. Both parks have restrooms, drinking water, showers and picnic areas.

Hawaiian Home Lands The Department of Hawaiian Home Lands (☎ 567-6296), Box 198, Hoolehua, HI 96729, on Puukapele Ave in Hoolehua, issues permits for only one group each night for camping at Kapuaiwa Coconut Grove, on the shore just west of Kaunakakai. The cost is $5 per night for the entire site. While it's usually booked by groups for parties, reunions and the like, individual travelers can stay when it's available. The site has electricity, water, picnic tables, barbecue grills, restrooms and showers.

THINGS TO BUY

Craft fairs, which are held a couple of times a month at Kaluakoi Hotel, are a good way to meet local artists who sell their own lauhala weavings, quilts, pottery, woodwork and other handcrafts.

Just about every shop in Kaunakakai has an assortment of T-shirts proclaiming Molokai's rural pride. With slogans like 'Keep Hawaiian Lands in Hawaiian Hands' and 'Molokai Mo Bettah', they make a good souvenir. Molokai Sight & Sound in Kaunakakai sells Hawaiian music cassettes and CDs.

Molokai-grown coffee can be purchased at the Coffees of Hawaii center in Kualapuu and in grocery stores around the island. Or you could take back the same stash islanders do when they leave Molokai: an island-grown watermelon and some Molokai bread from Kanemitsu Bakery.

MOLOKAI

GETTING THERE & AWAY

Air

Island Air (☎ 567-6115, 800-652-6541 within Hawaii) flies direct to Molokai a dozen times a day from Honolulu, four times from Kahului and twice from Hana. The one-way fare is currently $69, though at times it climbs as high as $91.

Hawaiian Airlines (☎ 553-3644, 800-367-5320 from the US mainland) flies direct to Molokai at 4:45 pm daily from Honolulu. The full one-way fare is $88, but you can sometimes book it for $50 by asking for the 'last flight out' price. Note that with the exception of a 6 am flight on weekends, other Molokai flights booked by Hawaiian Airlines are code-shares that will have you flying with Mahalo, and in those cases it's cheaper to book direct with Mahalo.

Mahalo Air (☎ 800-277-8333) flies direct to Molokai five times a day from Honolulu and once a day from Kahului. One-way fares are $61, but if you buy coupons from a travel agent, it'll only cost about half that.

Molokai Air Shuttle (☎ 567-6847 in Molokai, 545-4988 in Oahu) flies a five-passenger Piper between Honolulu and Molokai on demand about eight times a day. Unlike other commuter airlines, it doesn't hit up tourists for higher prices. The cost is just $25 one way, $45 roundtrip. The catch is that you'll need to have your own car (or take a taxi) on the Honolulu side, as they're at the back side of the airport, off Lagoon Drive.

Trans Air (☎ 800-634-2094), another small commuter airline, flies a few times a day between Molokai and Honolulu, and

between Molokai and Kapalua West Maui. It charges residents $30 one way, but tourist prices are double that.

Information on flights to and from Kalaupapa is in the Kalaupapa section.

Molokai Airport Molokai Airport, sometimes called Hoolehua Airport, has car rental booths, a snack bar, a liquor lounge, a lei stand, restrooms, pay phones and a visitor information booth that is rarely staffed. The Molokai newspapers can be picked up free, and off-island papers are for sale.

The snack bar, which is open from 6:30 am to 6 pm daily, sells breakfast and lunch plates for $5 to $6, cheeseburgers for $3, and carries loaves of Molokai bread.

GETTING AROUND

Taxi

There are no metered taxis on Molokai, but a couple of companies provide taxi services for set fees. The taxis occasionally meet flights, but to be assured of a ride from the airport, you should make advance reservations.

From the airport, Kukui Tours & Limousines (☎ 553-5133) charges, with a two-person minimum, $8 per person to Kaluakoi Resort or Kaunakakai or $19 to Wavecrest condos.

Friendly Isle Tours (☎ 553-9046) also offers taxi services and airport transfers by prearrangement.

Car

Renting a car on Molokai is just about essential if you intend to explore the island. However, as there are currently only two companies operating on Molokai, it's best to book well in advance, especially if you're planning on going over on a weekend.

Budget (☎ 567-6877) and Dollar (☎ 567-6156) both base their operations at the airport. Note that rental vehicles are officially not supposed to be driven on dirt roads, and there may be restrictions against camping as well. See the Getting Around chapter in the front of the book for general rental information and toll-free numbers.

There are gas stations in Kaunakakai, Maunaloa and Kualapuu.

ALOHA SLOW DOWN THIS IS MOLOKAI

NED FRIARY

Kaunakakai

Kaunakakai, Molokai's biggest town, takes much of its character from what it doesn't have. There's not a single traffic light, no shopping centers and no fast-food chains.

Most of Molokai's businesses are lined up along Ala Malama St, the town's broad main street. The stores have aging wooden false fronts that give Kaunakakai the appearance of an old Wild West town. There

are a couple of restaurants, a bakery, a post office, a pharmacy and one of just about everything else a small town needs. The tallest point is still the church steeple.

Kaunakakai is a town that hasn't changed its face at all for tourism. It has an almost timeless quality and a nice slow pace.

Information

Since Molokai doesn't have a daily newspaper, bulletin boards around Kaunakakai are the prime source of news and announcements. The board next to the Bank of Hawaii is the most extensive.

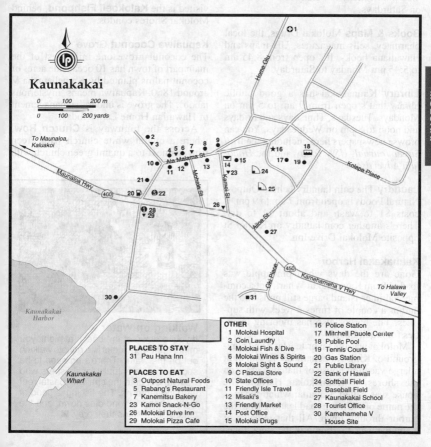

Kaunakakai

Scale: 0 – 100 – 200 m / 0 – 100 – 200 yards

To Maunaloa, Kaluakoi
Maunaloa Hwy (460)
To Halawa Valley
Kamehameha V Hwy (450)

OTHER
1 Molokai Hospital
2 Coin Laundry
4 Molokai Fish & Dive
6 Molokai Wines & Spirits
8 Molokai Sight & Sound
9 C Pascua Store
10 State Offices
11 Friendly Isle Travel
12 Misaki's
13 Friendly Market
14 Post Office
15 Molokai Drugs
16 Police Station
17 Mitchell Pauole Center
18 Public Pool
19 Tennis Courts
20 Gas Station
21 Public Library
22 Bank of Hawaii
24 Softball Field
25 Baseball Field
27 Kaunakakai School
28 Tourist Office
30 Kamehameha V House Site

PLACES TO STAY
31 Pau Hana Inn

PLACES TO EAT
3 Outpost Natural Foods
5 Rabang's Restaurant
7 Kanemitsu Bakery
23 Kamoi Snack-N-Go
26 Molokai Drive Inn
29 Molokai Pizza Cafe

MOLOKAI

Tourist Offices The Molokai Visitors Association (☎ 553-3876), at the corner of Hwys 450 and 460, can give you brochures and the lowdown on what's happening around the island. The office is open from 8 am to 4:30 pm Monday to Friday.

Money The Bank of Hawaii, on Ala Malama St, is open from 8:30 am to 3 pm Monday to Thursday, 8:30 am to 6 pm on Fridays. There's a 24-hour ATM out front.

Post & Communications The post office, on Ala Malama St, is open from 9 am to 4:30 pm Monday to Friday and 9 to 11 am on Saturdays.

Books & Maps Molokai Drugs, the local pharmacy, sells magazines, UH maps and Hawaiiana books. It's open from 8:45 am to 5:45 pm Monday to Saturday.

Library Kaunakakai has a good public library that's open from 9 am to 5 pm on Mondays, Tuesdays, Thursdays and Fridays and noon to 8 pm on Wednesdays. You can browse newspapers here, including the *Wall Street Journal, USA Today* and the *Honolulu Advertiser*.

Laundry The coin laundry behind Outpost Natural Foods is open from 7 am to 9 pm. It costs $1 to wash and about $1 to dry. There's another coin laundry on Kamoi St opposite Molokai Drive Inn.

Kaunakakai Harbor
Gone are the days when pineapple was loaded from Kaunakakai Wharf, but a commercial inter-island barge still pulls into the harbor a couple of times a week with supplies. The harbor also has mooring facilities for small boats.

Molokai was the favorite island and playground of King Kamehameha V, who built a large vacation house of thatched grass on the shores of Kaunakakai Harbor. The house was called Malama, which today is the name of the main road leading from the harbor through town. All that remains of Kamehameha V's home is the stone foundation, now overgrown with grass. It's on the right side of the road before the wharf, mauka of the canoe shed.

Fishponds
Molokai's southeast coast is dotted with the largest concentration of ancient fishponds in Hawaii. Grazing by cattle and sheep introduced in the mid-1800s resulted in widespread erosion, and the clay that washed down from the mountains choked out the ponds. Over the years efforts have been made to revive a few of the fishponds, although without much commercial success.

One of the most impressive and easily visited is the **Kalokoeli Fishpond**, behind Molokai Shores condos.

Kapuaiwa Coconut Grove
The coconut grove one mile west of the main part of town has 10 oceanside acres of coconut palms planted by Kamehameha V around 1860. Kapuaiwa means 'mysterious taboo'. The grove is under the management of Hawaiian Home Lands today.

Across the highway is **Church Row**, where a quaint white church with green trim sits next to a quaint green church with

Walking on Water
If you're down at the beach at night, you might spot what looks like ghosts walking out on the water. There's no need to be spooked – it's actually local fishers who walk far out onto the shallow coastal reef carrying lanterns. The fishing is good at night when the wind dies down, and the lantern light stuns their prey. ■

white trim and so on down the line. Any denomination that gets a handful of Hawaiian members gets its own little tract of land to put up a church. Some of the more recent arrivals include Mormons and Jehovah's Witnesses.

One Alii Beach Park

One Alii, three miles east of Kaunakakai, is the beach park nearest to town. As the water is shallow and swimming conditions are poor, the park is used mainly for picnics, parties and camping. Two memorials erected in the park commemorate the 19th-century immigration of Japanese to Hawaii.

Places to Stay

Pau Hana Inn (☎ 553-5342, 800-423-6656), Box 860, Kaunakakai, HI 96748, is the closest hotel to the town center. The cheapest of its 39 rooms are those in the long house at $45, which are small and simple but sufficient, with either two twin beds or a double bed, and a toilet and shower. Try to get one of the end rooms on the ocean side, which are lighter and airier. There are five other room categories, topping off with beachfront suites for $125. Pau Hana means 'work's over', and its bar is a popular drinking hole; it can get noisy on weekends, when a live band plays until 1 am. Between the bar and the beach is an impressive 100-year-old Bengalese banyan tree.

Hotel Molokai (☎ 553-5347, 800-423-6656; fax 553-5047), Box 546, Kaunakakai, HI 96748, about two miles east of town, has 55 units with a Polynesian design of sorts. While the hotel is a bit funky, the overall atmosphere is the most in keeping with the character of Molokai. The rooms, which are in clusters of two-story buildings, vary greatly. As noise from people walking on the creaky wooden floors travels down to the lower level, it's best to spend the extra money for one of the upper lanai units, which are also the roomiest. These cost $90, and most have a king and two twin beds as well as a large lanai. Standard rooms cost $59. Rooms have small refrigerators and fans. There's no TV, but sunsets and stargazing from the beachside hammock can be unbeatable. The future of the hotel is a bit iffy, as it's in need of renovation and up for sale.

Molokai Shores (☎ 553-5954, 800-535-0085; fax 553-5954; marc@aloha.net), Box 1037, Kaunakakai, HI 96748, about 1½ miles east of town, has 100 condo units, 26 of which are in the rental pool. Most are decorated nicely and each has a kitchen, sofa bed, cable TV, lanai and ceiling fans. Ask for a unit on the 3rd floor as they are quieter and have cathedral ceilings. One-bedroom units cost $125 for up to four people, and two-bedroom units cost $159 for up to six people, but discount schemes can cut the rates substantially. There's a pool and coin-operated laundry on the premises. It's a member of Marc Resorts.

Ka Hale Mala (☎ 553-9009; cpgroup@aloha.net), 7 Kamakana Place, Box 1582, Kaunakakai, HI 96748, is a delightful three-room apartment about four miles east of Kaunakakai. Occupying the ground level of the contemporary home of Jack and Cheryl Corbiell, an amiable Canadian couple, this stands as the best accommodation value on the island. The spotless 840-sq-ft apartment has exposed beam ceilings and a lanai that looks out on surrounding gardens. There's a living room with two twin beds, TV and stereo, a separate dining room with a fully equipped kitchen, a private bathroom with a tub and a bedroom with two twin beds. Guests are free to borrow snorkeling gear and mountain bikes. Cheryl cooks a full breakfast that includes fresh fruit from the garden and specialties such as taro pancakes or poi muffins. The rate is $70 for two people and $15 more for each additional person. If you prefer to prepare your own breakfast, the price is $5 less per person.

Bed & Breakfast Molokai (☎ 553-5048), Hannah and Will Johnstone, Box 295, 141 Kahinani St, Kaunakakai, HI 96748, is 1½ miles east of Kaunakakai, upslope from Molokai Shores. This studio unit, which is detached from the main house, has two twin beds, a small refrigerator, a hot plate, cable TV and a private bath. The owners spend half the year in Scotland, so the

MOLOKAI

rental is available from the beginning of November to the end of March only. The rate of $75 includes a hearty Scottish breakfast. Children are not allowed, and there's a two-night minimum. Will is a retired economist and Hannah, who grew up on Molokai, is the author of a book on Moomomi Beach ecology.

Camping Camping is allowed with a county permit at *One Alii Beach Park*, a roadside park on a shallow beach three miles east of Kaunakakai. While the campsites are near the water, they have little privacy, and because the park is close to town, it tends to be well used.

A second camping option that's sometimes available in the Kaunakakai area is at *Kapuaiwa Coconut Grove*, on Hawaiian Home Lands property, just west of town. However, this spot is often booked up far in advance as camping permits are issued to just one group at a time and priority is given to native Hawaiians.

For booking information for both campgrounds, see Camping under Accommodations earlier in this chapter.

Places to Eat

Kanemitsu Bakery makes *the* Molokai bread that is shipped around the islands, as well as a variety of Danish pastries and doughnuts. The cinnamon apple crisp ($1) is a favorite. The restaurant in the back of the bakery is the island's most popular breakfast spot. Eggs, toast, ham and coffee go for $4.25, sandwiches and burgers for $2.25 and plate lunches for about double that. The restaurant is open from 5:30 am to 1 pm, the bakery from 5:30 am to 6:30 pm; both are closed on Tuesdays.

Outpost Natural Foods has the standard collection of natural foods and vitamins as well as fresh produce, some of it organic. *Oasis Juice Bar* inside the store makes good burritos and sandwiches for $3.50 and salads for $5. They also have a daily special, such as vegie enchilada or lasagna and salad for around $6. The juice bar is open from 10 am to 3 pm Sunday to Friday, and there's a picnic table out back where you can eat. The store is open from 9 am to 6 pm Sunday to Thursday and 9 am to 3:30 pm on Fridays.

Kamoi Snack-N-Go, behind the post office, is a combination convenience store and ice cream shop that's open daily from 9 am to 9 pm (from noon on Sundays). It sells about 30 different flavors of the gourmet Honolulu-made Dave's Ice Cream at a reasonable $1.60 for a one-scoop cone.

Molokai Pizza Cafe (☎ 553-3288), in a small complex behind the tourist office, is open from 11 am to 10 pm Sunday to Thursday, to 11 pm on weekends. The pizza is good, with single-topping versions priced at $10 for a medium (12 inches) that's big enough for two – although if you're really hungry, the large is only $2 more. Other items include sub sandwiches, lasagna and spaghetti & meat balls, all priced around $7.50. The restaurant also has Mexican food on Wednesdays and occasionally offers other special meals, such as prime rib dinners.

Pau Hana Inn serves rather standard fare at moderate prices. Breakfast, from 6:30 to 10:30 am, includes a recommendable Molokai-bread French toast with ham and coffee for $5 and various egg dishes. At lunch, from 11 am to 2 pm, there are sandwiches for around $5 and a few hot dishes for a bit more. Dinner, from 6 to 9 pm, features meat and fish meals averaging $15. The dining room fireplace is sometimes lit on cool winter evenings, adding a cozy touch.

Molokai Drive Inn has inexpensive hamburgers, breakfasts and $5 plate lunches. The food is takeout, but there are picnic tables at the side where you can chow down. This place used to be a Dairy Queen, but Molokai wasn't quite ready for a fast-food chain so the sign came down. It's open from 6 am to 10 pm daily.

Rabang's Restaurant, a simple local eatery, has Filipino lunch plates such as turkey tail adobo, tripe or pig's feet for around $5, as well as burgers and shave ice. It's open from 7 am to 9 pm daily.

Misaki's and *Friendly Market* are the island's major grocery stores and are open from 8:30 am to 8:30 pm Monday to Saturday. Misaki's, which is also open from 9 am to noon on Sundays, has the island's cheapest wine prices, though the selection is limited.

Molokai Wines & Spirits carries a good assortment of imported beers and a wide selection of wine at reasonable prices. The shop, which is open from 9 am to 10 pm daily, also has Häagen-Däzs ice cream and a few food items.

Entertainment

The local band FIBRE (Friendly Isle Band Rhythmic Experience!) plays dance music – including oldie standards, rock & roll and Hawaiian songs – from 9:30 pm to midnight on Fridays and Saturdays at *Pau Hana Inn*. The cover charge is $5. There's a DJ ('adult disco') from 9 am to 1 pm on Thursdays for $4. The action is out on the patio, with the band playing under the big banyan tree.

Other than this, the baseball field in Kaunakakai is the most active spot on the island. For some local flavor, you could go down and cheer on the Molokai Farmers as they compete against their high school rivals, the Lanai Pinelads.

East Molokai

The 28-mile drive from Kaunakakai to Halawa Valley is along the Kamehameha V Hwy (Hwy 450) and takes about 1½ hours one way. It's a good paved road from start to finish. Check your gas gauge before starting off, as there are no gas stations after Kaunakakai.

The road edges alongside the ocean for much of the drive, with the mountains of East Molokai rising up to the north. The terrain starts out relatively dry and becomes greener and lusher as you head east. It's all quite pastoral, with small homes tucked into the valleys, horses grazing at the side of the road and silver waterfalls dropping down the mountainsides.

The beaches along this stretch are mostly shallow and silted and not so good for swimming until about the 20-mile marker. The last part of the road is narrow, with lots of hairpin bends and scenic coastal views, winding up to a clifftop view of Halawa Valley.

KAWELA

The **Kakahaia Beach Park**, a grassy roadfront park in Kawela, shortly before the six-mile marker, has a couple of picnic tables but little other reason to stop. Should you pull over, pick your spot carefully, as the loaded coconut trees are like aerial bombers. This beach park is the only part of the **Kakahaia National Wildlife Refuge** open to the public. Most of the 40-acre refuge is mauka of the road. It includes marshland with a dense growth of bulrushes and an inland freshwater fishpond that has been expanded to provide a home for the endangered Hawaiian stilt and coot.

Farther inland is the **Kawela puuhonua**, a place of refuge that was used in ancient times by those running from the law or hiding from personal enemies. The stone ruins are on a high ridge separated by deep gulches and nearly impossible to reach.

In 1795, Kamehameha the Great invaded Molokai with such a large force that his war canoes were lined up for a full four miles along this coast. He quickly brought Molokai under his command and from here went on to invade Oahu, the last battle in a campaign that united all the Hawaiian islands.

KAMALO

The biggest attraction in Kamalo, a small village about 10 miles east of Kaunakakai, is the roadside St Joseph's Church.

St Joseph's Church

Two of the four Molokai churches Father Damien built outside the Kalaupapa Peninsula are still standing, including St Joseph's in Kamalo. This simple one-room wooden church built in 1876 has a steeple and bell, five rows of pews and some of the original wavy glass panes. A statue of Damien and a little cemetery are at the side. Only the yellow tsunami-warning speaker brings the scene into the 20th century.

Across the road, a minute's stroll up a driveway leads to a self-service fruit hut that usually has limes, grapefruits, coconuts and papayas for sale.

Smith-Bronte Landing

Just over three-quarters of a mile after the 11-mile marker, a small wooden sign makai of the road notes the site where pilot Ernest Smith and navigator Emory Bronte safely crash-landed their plane at the completion of the world's first civilian flight from the US mainland to Hawaii.

They left California on July 14, 1927, coming down in Molokai 25 hours and two minutes later. Oahu was the intended destination. A little memorial plaque is set among the kiawe trees and grasses where they landed.

Places to Stay

Kamalo Plantation Bed & Breakfast (☎ /fax 558-8236), HC 1, Box 300, Kaunakakai, HI 96748, is in a fruit orchard opposite St Joseph's Church. There are two bedrooms that share a bath in the main house. The smaller bedroom has two twin waterbeds; the larger room has a TV, microwave and two twin beds that can be made up as a king. Each room has a refrigerator. Rates, which include breakfast, are $55 and $65 respectively. If you prefer to have a private bath, you can pay $10 more to keep the smaller room unbooked. There's also an adjacent studio-style cottage with two twin beds, a sofa bed and a full kitchen that costs $75 and would be quite suitable for a couple with a child. A breakfast of homemade breads and homegrown fruits is provided. The grounds, which have the stone foundation of an ancient heiau, are pleasantly quiet. The friendly owners, Glenn and Akiko Foster, are good sources of information about little-known hiking trails and other things to do.

UALAPUE

The Wavecrest condo development is at the 13-mile marker in Ualapue.

Shortly beyond Wavecrest you'll spot **Ualapue Fishpond** on the makai side of the road. Molokai once had more than 60 productive fishponds, constructed from the 13th century onward. Built of lava rock upon the reefs, their slatted sluice gates allowed small fish into the pond where they were fed and fattened, but prevented the mature fish from swimming back out. A ready supply of fish could then be easily scooped up with a net as needed. The Ualapue Fishpond was restored a few years ago and restocked with mullet and milkfish, two species that were raised there in ancient times.

Beyond this, look for the defunct Ah Ping Store and its old gas pump at the roadside. This classic building of faded green wood with a red tin roof was a Chinese-owned grocery store in the 1930s.

Places to Stay

Wavecrest Resort (☎ 558-8103, 800-367-2980; fax 558-8206), HC 1, Box 541, Kaunakakai, HI 96748, is a 126-unit condo complex that has about 40 units in the rental pool. The condos are divided into categories depending largely upon the decor and when they were last renovated. Rates range from $109 for a lackluster standard garden unit to $139 for a cheery deluxe oceanfront unit. All have separate bedrooms, a roomy living room with a sofa bed, a kitchen, TV and lanai. There are also two-bedroom units for $149 to $169. Breezes blow right through the oceanfront units, which have great views of Maui and Lanai from the lanai. Maximum occupancy is four people in the one-bedroom units and six in those with two bedrooms. Weekly discounts are available. The resort has a pool, tennis courts and a coin laundry.

KALUAAHA

The village of Kaluaaha is about two miles past Wavecrest. The ruins of Molokai's first church are here, a bit off the road on the mauka side, but (barely) visible if you keep an eye out. **Kaluaaha Church** was built in 1844 by Molokai's first missionary, Harvey R Hitchcock. There was talk of rebuilding the church a decade ago, but the rusting old steel rods in the original structure thwarted the plan.

Our Lady of Sorrows Church is a quarter of a mile past the Kaluaaha Church site. The present Our Lady of Sorrows is a 1966 reconstruction of the original wooden-frame building built in 1874 by Father Damien.

From the church parking lot, a fine view of an ancient **fishpond** and the high-rise-studded shores of West Maui provide an incongruous backdrop.

ILIILIOPAE HEIAU

Iliiliopae is the largest and best-known heiau on Molokai and is thought to be the oldest as well. Approximately 300 feet long and 100 feet wide, it is about 22 feet high on the east side and 11 feet high at the other end. It is strikingly level. It's believed the heiau may have originally been three times its current size, reaching out beyond Mapulehu Stream.

The path to the heiau is mauka of the highway, nearly half a mile past the 15-mile marker, immediately after a little bridge. It starts on a dirt drive on the east side of the creek. After a 10-minute walk a footpath leads off to the left, opposite a house. The heiau is two minutes farther.

Although once a site of human sacrifice, Iliiliopae is today silent except for the chittering of birds. African tulip trees line the trail to the site, a peaceful place whose stones still seem to emanate vibrations of a powerful past. A good place to sit and take it all in is on the north side, up the steps to the right of the heiau.

Visiting the heiau is usually straightforward, but since it is on private property, it's advised that you check with the tourist office to see if permission to visit currently needs to be obtained in advance.

PUKOO

The village of Pukoo was once the seat of local government – complete with a court-house, jail, wharf and post office – until the plantation folks built Kaunakakai and centered everything there. The population

shifted away from Pukoo, and it's been a sleepy backwater ever since. Now bit by bit islanders are beginning to move back to the Pukoo area, and while it's not exactly suburbia, you'll notice a handful of newer homes as the road continues.

In the village, just before the 16-mile marker, a road marked 'shoreline access' leads a few hundred yards to a sandy beach with shallow waters.

Places to Stay

Honomuni House (☎ 558-8383), HC 1, Box 700, Kaunakakai, HI 96748, is a pleasant guest cottage just beyond the Honomuni Bridge, about a mile east of Pukoo. The cottage is studio-style, with a kitchen, bath and outdoor deck and shower. The living room area has a sofa bed, a TV and a small dining table made of monkeypod wood from the grounds. Rates are $80 for two,

---

Iliiliopae Sacrifices

Legend says Iliiliopae Heiau was built in one night by menehunes who brought *iliili* (stones) over the mountains from Wailau Valley. In return for their efforts, each was given one *opae* (shrimp), hence the temple's name.

Lono, the god of harvest, and Ku, the god of war, were both worshipped here. Human sacrifices were made at this heiau, always on the eve of a full moon. Drums were beaten to call all males to the temple where, upon the priest's direction, all fell prone and the victims to be sacrificed were brought to the platform. Amid chanting and rituals these victims, always male, were strangled to death and their bodies later burned.

One local legend tells of a man, Umoekekaua, who lost nine of his 10 sons to sacrifice at Iliiliopae. He became so outraged that he went with his only remaining son to Pelekunu Valley to enlist the aid of Kauhuhu, the shark god. Kauhuhu sent a torrent of rain, flooding the heiau and washing the priests responsible for the sacrifices into Pukoo Harbor, where they were duly eaten by sharks. ■

plus $10 for each additional adult. There's no extra charge for children. Breakfast is not included, but bananas and other seasonal fruits are provided, as are eggs when the hens are laying. Host Patty McCartney and her family live in a large house on the same grounds.

Places to Eat
The *Neighborhood Store 'N' Counter*, near the 16-mile marker, is not only a well-stocked little grocery store but is also the only place to get a meal on the east side. The food is quite good and includes omelets, burgers and plate lunches that range from teriyaki chicken to fresh fish specials. It's open from 8 am to 6 pm daily except Wednesdays. There are picnic tables at the side.

WAIALUA
Waialua is a little roadside community around the 19-mile marker. The attractive little Waialua Congregational Church, which marks the center of the village, was built of stone in 1855. The nearby Waialua Beach is the site of Molokai's keiki surf competitions.

Sugar Mill Remains
Three-quarters of a mile after the 19-mile marker, begin looking for the remains of a stone chimney, a remnant of the Moanui Sugar Mill, which processed sugar from a nearby plantation until it burned down in the late 1800s. The ruins are about 50 feet mauka of the road, just before a stand of tall ironwood trees.

Twenty-Mile Beach
A stretch of white-sand beach pops up right along the roadside at the 20-mile marker. There are places to park just beyond that. During the winter, when other Molokai beaches are rough, this is the area everyone directs you to for swimming and snorkeling.

However, when the tide is low the water is sometimes too shallow for snorkeling inside the reef. Snorkeling is much better beyond the reef, but unless it's very calm the currents can be dangerous.

Rock Point
The point of rocks sticking out as the road swings left before the 21-mile marker is called, appropriately enough, Rock Point. This is a popular surfing spot where local competitions sometimes take place.

Onward to Halawa
After the 21-mile marker the road starts to wind upwards. Tall grasses just at the edge seem to be trying to reclaim the road, while ironwood trees and the spindly spikes of sisal plants dot the surrounding hills.

It's a good paved road – the only problem is there's not always enough of it. In places, including some cliff-hugging curves, it's really only wide enough for one car, and you'll need to do some horn tooting. The road levels out just before the 24-mile marker, where there's a view of the small island of Mokuhooniki, a seabird sanctuary.

The fenced grassland in this area is part of Puu O Hoku Ranch, Molokai's second largest cattle ranch. A grove of sacred kukui trees on the ranch property marks the grave of Lanikaula, a famous kahuna of the late 16th century. Over the years, many islanders claim to have seen the night lanterns of ghost marchers bobbing along near the grove.

After passing the 25-mile marker, the jungle begins to close in and the scent of eucalyptus fills the air. One and a quarter miles after the 25-mile marker there's a turn-off with a great panoramic view of Halawa Valley – if the viewpoint is overgrown, just park and walk down the road a little farther to reach a clearing. In the winter, this is also a good place to watch for whales breaching off the coast.

There are lots of 'beep as you go' hairpin bends on the one-lane road that leads down to the valley, but the road is in good condition and the incline is reasonably gradual.

HALAWA VALLEY
Halawa Valley once had three heiaus, two of which are thought to have been used for human sacrifice. Little remains of the sites. In the mid-19th century, the fertile valley had a population of about 500 people and

produced most of Molokai's taro as well as many of its melons, gourds and fruits. Taro production declined over the years, coming to an abrupt end in 1946, when a massive tsunami swept up Halawa Valley, wiping out the farms and much of the community. A second tsunami washed the valley clean in 1957. Only seven families now remain in Halawa. Sunday services are still occasionally held in Hawaiian at the valley's little church.

Halawa Beach Park

Halawa Beach was a favored surfing spot for Molokai chiefs and remains so today for local kids. This beach has double coves separated by a rocky outcrop, with the north side a bit more protected than the south. When the water is calm, there's good swimming, but both coves are subject to dangerous rip currents when the surf is heavy. There can also be strong currents when Halawa Stream, which empties into the north cove, is flowing heavily.

Halawa Beach Park has restrooms and running water; the water, which is piped down from the upper valley, does not meet health standards and should be treated before drinking. The old building before the park is the remains of a village church that burned down a few decades ago.

Central Molokai

Central Molokai takes in the Hoolehua Plains, which stretch from windswept Moomomi Beach in the west to the former plantation town of Kualapuu. The central part of the island also has forested interiors leading to Kamakou, a unique rainforest preserve that embraces the island's highest mountain, Kamakou peak (4961 feet). On the north side of central Molokai is Kalaupapa Peninsula, the site of the leprosy colony.

The most trodden route in central Molokai is the drive up to the Kalaupapa Overlook, where you'll find one of the prettiest views on Molokai. It takes about 15 minutes to drive the 10 miles from Kaunakakai.

Turning north off Hwy 460 onto Hwy 470 (Kalae Hwy), the road starts in dry grasslands and climbs pass a coffee plantation, the town of Kualapuu, a restored sugar mill, a community of single-rooster dwellings, a mule stable and the trail down to the Kalaupapa Peninsula. The road ends at Palaau State Park, site of the Kalaupapa Overlook.

KUALAPUU

Kualapuu is the name of both a 1017-foot hill and the village that has grown up north of it.

At the base of the hill is the world's largest rubber-lined reservoir. It can hold up to 1.4 billion gallons of water, which is piped in from the rainforests in East Molokai and is presently the source of water for both the Hoolehua Plains and the dry West End.

Del Monte set up headquarters in this area in the 1930s, and Kualapuu developed into a plantation town. The center of Del Monte's activities covered the spread between Kualapuu and the nearby Hoolehua homesteads.

In 1982, Del Monte decided to phase out its Molokai operations and the economy came tumbling down. Old harvesting equipment sat rusting in overgrown pineapple fields for a decade before Coffees of Hawaii leased out the abandoned fields and replanted them with coffee saplings. Long rows of coffee trees now extend down the slope from the town center. The first harvests, under the label Malulani Estate, have reached the market. Kualapuu is banking on this new crop to spur its revival, and indeed the operation has grown into the town's largest employer, with some 20 people working there year round and about 50 during the harvest season of September to January.

If you want to try out the final product, stop by Coffees of Hawaii, in the village center, where there's a little cafe with free coffee samples and a gift shop selling packaged coffee and a few handicraft items. There are occasionally mule-drawn wagon tours of the coffee fields for $14.

Places to Eat

The *Kualapuu Cookhouse* (☎ 567-6185) is a busy little place for such a small town. There are breakfast omelets and numerous plate lunches, including a nice chicken stir-fry with rice, for around $7. You can also order a cup of chili for $2 and burgers for around $4. Homemade pies are another specialty – for sheer indulgence try a slice of the chocolate macnut pie. The restaurant is open from 7 am to 9 pm Monday through Saturday.

KALAE
RW Meyer Sugar Mill

Four miles north of Hwy 460, in Kalae, is the sugar mill built by Rudolph W Meyer, an industrious German immigrant.

Meyer was on his way to the California gold rush when he dropped by Hawaii, married a member of Hawaiian royalty and in the process landed a tidy bit of property. He eventually found his gold in potatoes, which he grew and exported to the Californian miners. Other hats he wore were overseer of the Kalaupapa leprosy settlement and manager of King Kamehameha V's ranchlands.

In the 1850s, Meyer established his own ranch and exported cattle from Palaau village. In one infamous incident, after finding his herd declining, he had all the men of Palaau charged with cattle rustling and sent off to a jailhouse in Honolulu.

In the late 1870s, when a new reciprocity treaty gave Hawaiian sugar planters the right to export sugar duty-free to the US, Meyer turned his lands over to sugar and built this mill. The sugar mill operated for about 10 years.

A lot of time and money has gone into authentically restoring the mill, including the complete rebuilding of a 100-year-old steam engine and other rusting machinery abandoned a century ago. The mill, which is on the National Register of Historic Places, is the last of its kind. If you're into sugar mills, antique steam engines and that sort of thing, you'll certainly find it interesting.

The sugar mill (☎ 567-6436) is open from 10 am to 2 pm Monday to Saturday. Admission is $2.50 for adults, $1 for students.

A building behind the sugar mill contains a small display of Molokai's history through period photos and a few Hawaiiana items. Meyer and his descendants are buried in a little family plot out back.

Ironwood Hills Golf Course

There are no polo shirts here. Ironwood Hills is a delightfully casual golf course, with crabgrass growing in the sand pits and local golfers who actually look like they're having fun. The course is down the red dirt road at the tree-lined edge of the pasture immediately south of Meyer Sugar Mill.

Originally built by Del Monte for its employees, the course was maintained by Molokai residents after Del Monte left and is now open to all. For more information, see Activities in the front of this chapter.

PALAAU STATE PARK

Palaau State Park is at the end of Hwy 470. The park's main sight, the Kalaupapa Overlook, is just a few minutes' walk from the parking lot. In the opposite direction, a five-minute trail through a grove of ironwoods leads to a phallic-shaped rock. Both trails are marked and easy to follow. The park has campsites, picnic areas and lovely stands of paperbark eucalyptus.

Kalaupapa Overlook

The Kalaupapa Overlook provides a scenic overview of the entire Kalaupapa Peninsula from the edge of a 1600-foot cliff. It's like an aerial view without the airplane.

Interpretive plaques identify the landmarks below and explain Kalaupapa's history as a leprosy colony. The village where all Kalaupapa's residents now live is visible, but Kalawao, the original settlement and site of Father Damien's church and grave, cannot be seen from here.

The **lighthouse** at the northern end of the peninsula once had the most powerful beam in the Pacific. The 700,000-candlepower Fresnel crystal lens cast its light until 1986, when it was taken down and replaced by an electric light beacon.

Kalaupapa means 'Flat Leaf', an accurate description of the lava slab peninsula created when a low shield volcano poked up out of the sea long after the rest of Molokai had been formed. The dormant Kauhako Crater, visible from the overlook, contains a little lake over 800 feet deep.

Kalaupapa residents use the term 'topside' to refer to all of Molokai outside their peninsula. Seen from the overlook, the reason is obvious.

Whether or not you get down to Kalaupapa itself, a visit to the overlook is a must. Because of the angle of the sun, the best light for photography is usually late morning to mid-afternoon.

Hiking There's an old trail that continues directly beyond the last plaque at the overlook. For one of Molokai's nicest forest walks, simply follow this trail for about 30 minutes. Few people go this way and it's very peaceful – if you're lucky you might even spot deer crossing the trail.

The path, on a carpet of soft ironwood needles, passes through a thickly planted forest of ironwood and eucalyptus, dotted here and there with Norfolk pine. These diagonal rows of trees were planted during a 1930s Civilian Conservation Corps (CCC) reforestation project. The trees create a canopy over the trail, and, as is generally true under ironwood and eucalyptus trees, there's little undergrowth to obscure the way.

There's no destination – the joy here is the woods. Eventually the trail winds down into a gully and peters out a little after that.

Phallic Rock

Kauleonanahoa, literally 'the penis of Nanahoa', is Hawaii's premier phallic stone, poking up in a little clearing inside an ironwood grove. Nature has endowed it well, but it's obviously been touched up by human hands.

Although it's said that women who bring offerings and spend the night here will return home pregnant, there apparently is no danger in just going to have a look.

Places to Stay

Camping is free at Palaau State Park. The camping area is in a grove of eucalyptus and ironwood trees that is cool and shady in summer, but can feel a bit dark and damp when it's rainy in winter. In winter you may well have the place to yourself, and even in the summer you're unlikely to find a crowd. The camping area is usually quite peaceful, with the only sounds coming from the roosters from the 'cock farm' and the braying of mules from the nearby stables.

There are restrooms, cement picnic tables and fireplaces, but there are no showers and the tap water is not fit for drinking.

KALAUPAPA PENINSULA

Kalaupapa Peninsula appears both strikingly beautiful and strikingly lonely. Set at the base of majestic and formidable cliffs, it has been a leprosy settlement for more than a century. The trip to the peninsula – accessible only by mule, on foot or by small plane – is one of Molokai's major attractions. It's also a pilgrimage of sorts for admirers of Father Damien (Joseph de Veuster), the Belgian priest who devoted the latter part of his life to helping people with leprosy, before dying of the disease himself.

Kalaupapa Peninsula is a national historical park jointly managed by the Department of Health and the National Park Service. It is unique among historic parks in that many of the people whose lives are being interpreted are still living on the site.

Though no longer required for medical reasons, old state laws that require everyone who enters the settlement to have a 'permit' and allow entry only to those 16 years of age and older are maintained to protect the privacy of the patients. There's no actual paper permit. A reservation with either Damien Tours or Molokai Mule Ride (see Tours under Getting There & Around, below) is considered a permit.

Only guests of Kalaupapa residents are allowed to stay overnight. There are no stores or other public facilities for visitors.

History

Ancient Hawaiians used Kalaupapa as a refuge when caught in storms at sea. The peninsula held a large settlement at the time of early Western contact, and the area is rich in archaeological sites.

The first case of leprosy in Hawaii was diagnosed in 1835, one of many diseases introduced by foreigners, this one probably by Chinese laborers. Alarmed by the spread of the disease, in 1865 King Kamehameha V signed into law an act that banished people with leprosy to Kalaupapa Peninsula.

It was a one-way trip. Kalaupapa Peninsula is surrounded on three sides by some of Hawaii's roughest and most shark-infested waters and on the fourth by the world's highest sea cliffs. Once the afflicted arrived on Kalaupapa Peninsula, there was no way out, not even in a casket. Hawaiians called leprosy *mai hookaawale*, which means separating sickness, a disease all the more dreaded because it tore families apart forever.

Father Damien arrived at Kalaupapa in 1873. He wasn't the first missionary to come, but he was the first to stay.

Damien nursed the sick, wrapped bandages on oozing sores, hammered coffins and dug graves. On the average he buried one person a day. He put up more than 300 houses – each little more than four walls, a door and a roof, but still a shelter to those

NED FRIARY
Friendly advice from Kalaupapa

cast here. He was a good carpenter. Some of the solid little churches he built earlier around the Big Island and Molokai still stand today.

The original settlement was in Kalawao, at the wetter eastern end of the peninsula. Some of the afflicted arrived in boats, whose captains were so terrified of the disease that they would not land but instead dropped patients overboard into the bay. Those who could swam to shore.

Early conditions were unspeakably horrible. Before modern medicine, leprosy manifested itself in dripping, foul-smelling sores. Eventually there was loss of sensation and tissue degeneration that could lead to fingers, toes and noses becoming hideously deformed or falling off altogether.

In 1888, Damien installed a water pipeline to the sunnier western side and the settlement moved to where it is today. Over the years, some 8000 people have come to Kalaupapa Peninsula to die. During Damien's time, lifespans here were almost invariably short.

Yet even in Damien's day leprosy was one of the least contagious of all communicable diseases. All in all, more than 1100 volunteers have worked with patients at Kalaupapa, but only Damien contracted leprosy. He died in 1889 at the age of 49. In 1995, Damien was beatified by Pope John Paul II and is now a candidate for sainthood.

Damien's work inspired others. Brother Joseph Dutton arrived in 1886 and stayed 44 years. In addition to his work with the sick, he was a prolific writer who kept the outside world informed about what was happening in Molokai. Mother Marianne Cope arrived a year before Damien died. She stayed 30 years, helping to establish a girls' home and encouraging patients to live life to the fullest. She is widely considered to be the mother of the hospice movement.

In 1909, a fancy medical facility called the US Leprosy Investigation Station opened at Kalawao. However, the hospital was so out of touch – requiring patients to sign themselves in for two years, live in seclusion and give up all Hawaiian-grown food – that even in the middle of a leprosy colony it attracted only a handful of patients. It closed four years later.

Although sulfone antibiotics have been used successfully to control leprosy since the 1940s, isolation policies in Kalaupapa weren't abandoned until 1969.

Kalaupapa Today

Today, fewer than 100 patients live on Kalaupapa Peninsula. It's an old population, getting older, with only a few people younger than 50. Some of the elderly have become blind or weakened. Others fish or tend gardens, although lots of people just stay glued to their TVs.

Current residents are free to leave, but Kalaupapa is the only home most of them know. They have been given guarantees that they can stay in Kalaupapa Peninsula throughout their lifetimes. To minimize the impact on residents, the park requires all visitors to join a guided tour.

While the state of Hawaii officially uses the term 'Hansen's Disease' for leprosy, many Kalaupapa residents consider that to be a euphemism that fails to reflect the stigma they have suffered and continue to use the old term.

Things to See & Do

On typical tours the village looks nearly deserted. The sights are mainly cemeteries, churches and memorials. Places where residents go to talk story – the post office, store and hospital – are pointed out, but no stops are made. Visitors are not allowed to photograph the residents. Kalaupapa is a tourist attraction, but its people are not.

Stops are made in town at **memorials** for Father Damien and Mother Marianne and at a **mini-museum** where photographs of the original settlement are on display and books are for sale. The tours then go across the peninsula to Kalawao.

St Philomena Church (better known as 'Father Damien's Church') in Kalawao was built in 1872. You can still see where Damien cut open holes in the floor so that the sick who needed to spit could attend church and not be ashamed. The graveyard at the side contains Damien's gravestone and

Father Damien's Church

original burial site, although his body was exhumed in 1936 and returned to Belgium.

The view from Kalawao is one of the island's finest. It looks out on the pali of the northeast coast, each successive cliffside jutting out behind the one in front, each looking more like a shadow in the mist. The park boundaries include the Waihanau, Waialeia and Waikolu valleys, east of the peninsula.

The **rock island** just offshore is the legendary home of a giant shark. From some angles it looks like a shark's head coming straight up out of the water, while from other angles it looks like a dorsal fin.

Getting There & Around

The switchback mule trail down the pali is the only land route to the peninsula. No matter how you get there, you cannot wander around Kalaupapa Peninsula by yourself. You must take a guided tour.

Air Kalaupapa has a little air strip at the edge of the peninsula and air service via small prop planes. Passengers must first book a tour with Damien Tours or Molokai Mule Ride before buying air tickets.

MOLOKAI

Molokai Air Shuttle (☎ 567-6847) has a 9 am flight from Molokai Airport, returning at 2 pm, every day but Sunday. The cost is $50 roundtrip.

Island Air (☎ 567-6115) flies daily between Honolulu and Kalaupapa via Molokai Airport. The flight leaves Honolulu at 7:30 am and arrives in Kalaupapa 45 minutes later. The return flight leaves Kalaupapa at 3:30 pm. The fare is $35 each way between Molokai and Kalaupapa, $91 between Honolulu and Kalaupapa.

On Foot The two-mile hike along the mule trail takes about one hour going down, a bit longer going up. It's best to begin hiking by 8 am, before the mules start to go down, to avoid walking in fresh dung. The narrow trail is rutted in places and can be slippery and muddy if it's been raining, but otherwise it's not terribly strenuous.

The trail starts on the right (east) side of Hwy 470 just north of the mule stables. Don't be intimidated by the 'Unauthorized persons keep out' sign at the start of the path. If you have tour reservations, this is the trail in.

Mule Ride One of the best-known outings in the islands, the mule ride down the pali to Kalaupapa, is again up and operating after a two-year hiatus.

The tour begins at the mule stables at 8 am with a short riding instruction. At around 8:30 am, riders hit the trail, which begins opposite the stables. The mules arrive in Kalaupapa around 10 am, and shortly thereafter a bus tour of the peninsula begins. Lunch is included in the price of $120. Expect to return back to the stables at around 3:30 pm. Wear loose trousers, closed shoes and a windbreaker.

While the mules move none too quickly – actually, hiking can be faster – there's a certain thrill in trusting your life to these sure-footed beasts while descending 1600 feet on 26 narrow cliffside switchbacks.

Reservations are made through Molokai Mule Ride (☎ 567-6988, 800-567-7550; fax 567-6244), Box 200, Molokai, HI 95757.

Tours Damien Tours (☎ 567-6171 or 567-6675), Box 1, Kalaupapa, HI 96742, does land tours for people who come to Kalaupapa on foot or by plane. Richard Marks, who runs Damien Tours, is a wonderful storyteller, an oral historian and the third generation of his family to be banished to Kalaupapa. He leads the best tour of Kalaupapa. Reservations must be made in advance and the cost is $30. Bring your own lunch. The tours pick up visitors at both the airport and the bottom of the trail.

Molokai Mule Ride can also organize land tours ($38, lunch included) for those who fly in or hike down on their own.

KAMAKOU

The mountains that form the spine of Molokai's east side reach up to Kamakou, the island's highest peak (4970 feet). Over half of Molokai's water supply comes from the Kamakou rainforest.

Hawaiian women used to hike up to the top of Kamakou to bury the afterbirth of their babies, a process that assured their children would reach great heights in life. These days islanders come to the forest to pick foliage for leis as well as to hunt pigs, deer and goats.

The Nature Conservancy's Kamakou Preserve is a near-pristine forest that is home to more than 250 native plants and some of Hawaii's rarest birds. With its mountaintop perch, Kamakou has some splendid views of the north shore valleys that unfold below. Just before the preserve entrance, Waikolu Lookout offers a panoramic view of remote Waikolu Valley, while a hike inside the preserve leads to another lookout, this one into the spectacular Pelekunu Valley.

Kamakou is a treasure, but it doesn't come easy: It is protected in its wilderness state in part because the rutted dirt road leading to it makes it a challenge to reach.

To Kamakou Preserve

Coming from Kaunakakai on Hwy 460, turn right three-quarters of a mile after the three-mile marker, immediately before

Manawainui Bridge. The paved road ends shortly at the Kalamaula hunter check box. The 10-mile drive from the highway to Waikolu Lookout takes about 45 minutes, depending on road conditions. During the rainy season, vehicles leave tracks and the road tends to get progressively more rutted until it's regraded in the summer.

A 4WD is recommended and may be essential. In dry weather, some people do make it as far as the lookout in a car, but if it's been raining heavily, it's not advisable to try. In places where the road is narrow, if one person gets stuck the whole road is blocked.

From the Kalamaula hunter check box, the road starts out fairly smoothly, but deteriorates as it goes along. Bear left at the first fork, about five minutes' drive up the dirt road, and from there just follow the main road all the way in.

Although there's no visible evidence of it from the road, the Kalamaula area was once extensively settled. It was here that Kamehameha the Great knocked out his two front teeth in grieving the death of a female high chief that he had come to visit.

The landscape starts off shrubby, dry and dusty, later turning to woods of eucalyptus with patches of cypress and Norfolk pines. The trees were planted in the 1930s by the CCC to stem the erosion and watershed loss caused by the free-range cattle policies of earlier times.

The Molokai Forest Reserve starts about 5½ miles in. A short loop road on the left leads to a former Boy Scout camp that's now used by the Nature Conservancy. After another 1½ miles, there will be an old water tank and reservoir off to the left. Just past this a sign marked 'Kakalahale' points to the right. (This is one of several 4WD roads used by hunters that lead south to the coast or to Kaunakakai. Once the roads leave forest reserve land they run across private property, often with closed gates along the way.) It's two miles more to the Sandalwood Pit and one mile past that to Waikolu Lookout and Kamakou Preserve.

Sandalwood Pit

Lua Moku Iliahi, or Sandalwood Measuring Pit, is a hull-shaped grassy depression on the left side of the road. It takes a little imagination to get the whole picture, as over the years water erosion has rounded the sides.

The sandalwood pit was dug in the early 19th century, shortly after the lucrative sandalwood trade began. In the frenzy to make a quick buck to pay for the foreign goods they craved, the alii forced the *makaainana* (commoners) to abandon their crops and work the forest.

The pit was dug out to the exact measurements of a 75-foot-long ship's hold and filled with fragrant sandalwood logs cleared from the nearby forest. When the pit was full, the wood was hauled down to the harbor for shipment to China. The sea captains made out like bandits, while the makaainana broke their backs.

After all the mature trees were taken, the makaainana pulled up virtually every new sapling in order to spare their children the misery of another generation of forced harvesting. In the end, the sandalwood forests literally disappeared on Molokai and elsewhere in Hawaii.

Waikolu Lookout

Waikolu Lookout, at 3600 feet, provides a spectacular view into Waikolu Valley and out to the ocean beyond. Even if you're not able to spend time in Kamakou Preserve, the lookout is a fine destination in itself. If it's been raining recently, you'll be rewarded with numerous waterfalls streaming down the sheer cliffsides. Waikolu means 'Three Waters' – presumably named for the three drops in the main falls. Morning is the best time for views, as afternoon trade winds commonly carry clouds to the upper level of the canyon.

These steep mountains effectively prevent the rain clouds from entering Molokai's dry central plains. In 1960, a 5½-mile tunnel was bored into the western side of Waikolu Valley. It now carries up to 28 million gallons of water each day down to the Kualapuu Reservoir.

A grassy picnic and camping area is directly opposite the lookout. If you can bear the mist and cold winds that sometimes blow up from the canyon, this could make a good base camp for hikes into the preserve. The site has pit toilets but no water supply. For more information, see the Camping section in the front of the Molokai chapter.

Kamakou Preserve

In 1982, Molokai Ranch conveyed to the Nature Conservancy of Hawaii the rights to manage the Kamakou Preserve, which starts immediately beyond Waikolu Lookout. Its 2774 acres of native ecosystems include cloudforest, bogs, shrubland and habitat for many species of endangered plants and animals.

Much of the preserve is forest of ohia lehua, a native tree with fluffy red blossoms whose nectar is favored by native birds. The forest is home to two rare birds that live only on Molokai (Molokai creeper and Molokai thrush) and to the bright red apapane, the yellow-green amakihi and the pueo (Hawaiian owl). Other treasures are tree ferns, native orchids and silvery lilies.

The road deteriorates quickly from the preserve entrance. Don't even consider driving it without a 4WD vehicle. Even with a 4WD, if you're not used to driving in mud and on steep grades it can be challenging. There are a few spots where it would be easy to flip a vehicle.

The Nature Conservancy asks visitors to sign in and out at the preserve entrance. Check out the sign-up sheet, where visitors write short entries on everything from car breakdowns to trail conditions and bird spottings.

Occasionally, portions of the preserve are closed to the public. At such times, notices are posted at Kaunakakai's post office, Kalamaula hunter check box and the preserve entrance.

Hiking As Kamakou is a rainforest, trails in the preserve can be very muddy. Rain gear is a good idea, and you should bring along an ample supply of drinking water.

The best hiking trail is the **Pepeopae Trail**, which goes east one mile to an overlook with a stunning view of Pelekunu Valley. The trail is along a raised wooden boardwalk over Pepeopae Bog. The extensive boardwalk allows hikers access to this unique area while protecting the fragile ecosystem from being trampled. Pepeopae is a nearly undisturbed Hawaiian montane bog, a mysterious miniature forest with stunted trees and dwarfed plants. The area gets about 180 inches of rain each year.

There are two ways to get to the Pepeopae Trail. The easiest is to walk from Waikolu Lookout about 2½ miles along the main jeep road to the trailhead. It's a nice forest walk that takes just over an hour. There are some side roads along the way, but they're largely overgrown and it's obvious which is the main road. You'll eventually come to the 'Pepeopae' sign marking the start of the trail, which branches to the left.

The second and far muddier way is to take the **Hanalilolilo Trail**. It begins on the left side of the road about five minutes' walk past Waikolu Lookout, shortly after entering the preserve.

The Hanalilolilo Trail climbs 500 feet through a rainforest of moss-covered ohia trees and connects up with Pepeopae Trail after 1½ miles. If you approach via the Hanalilolilo Trail, turn left when you reach the Pepeopae Trail and you'll have about a half-mile walk up to the summit overlooking Pelekunu Valley.

From the Pelekunu Valley Overlook you get a view of majestic cliffs, and if it's not clouded over you can see down the valley out to the ocean.

Pelekunu Valley is also under the stewardship of the Nature Conservancy. The Pelekunu Valley Preserve covers nearly 6000 acres, extending from sea level up to a height of almost 5000 feet here at the valley's upper rim. This inaccessible valley has one of the few remaining perennial streams in Hawaii. It's an important habitat for gobies and river shrimp that return from the ocean each year to swim up and lay their eggs in the fresh water of Pelekunu Stream.

Give yourself a good half day to do the entire hike from the Kamakou Preserve entrance and back. If you'd like to shorten the walk, consider one of the **guided hikes** led by the Nature Conservancy, as they enter the reserve in 4WD vehicles and start hiking from the Pepeopae trailhead. These guided hikes also give visitors insights into the history and ecology of the preserve.

The conservancy's hikes are conducted monthly, usually on the first or second Saturday. The cost and reservation information is the same as for Moomomi hikes; see the end of the Moomomi Beach section, below, for more details.

In addition, Fun Hogs (☎ 552-2242) at the Kaluakoi Hotel arranges guided hikes to Kamakou that include 4WD transport into the preserve. There's a four-person minimum. The cost is $40 per person and the outing lasts about six hours, with about half of that time spent hiking.

HOOLEHUA

Hoolehua is the dry plains area that separates eastern and western Molokai. Here, in the 1790s, Kamehameha the Great trained his warriors in a year-long preparation for the invasion of Oahu. Hoolehua was settled as an agricultural community in 1924 as part of the Hawaiian Homes Act, which made public lands available to native Hawaiians. The land was divided into 40-acre plots. By 1930, more than half of Molokai's ethnic Hawaiian population was living on Hawaiian homesteads.

The first homestead was attempted closer to the coast at Kalanianaole, but it failed when the well water pumped to irrigate crops turned brackish. Many of those islanders then moved up to Hoolehua, where homesteaders were already planting pineapple, a crop that required little water. As the two giant pineapple companies established operations in Molokai, homesteaders found it increasingly difficult to market their own pineapples and were eventually compelled to lease their lands to the plantations.

These days, there is a reliable water supply and crops that are more diversified,

including coffee, sweet potato, papaya and fresh herbs.

Orientation & Information

Three paved roads run east to west, with dirt crossroads going north to south. The post office and the adjacent Department of Land & Natural Resources office are on Puupeelua Ave (Hwy 480), just south of where it intersects with Farrington Ave.

Farrington Ave is Hoolehua's main street with a fire station, Episcopal church and Molokai's high school. The Hawaiian Home Lands office is up on Puukapele Ave.

Puukapele Ave leads westward and merges into another paved road that deceptively appears to be a find, heading beachward, but the road ends at the Western Space & Missile Center, a radio receiving station for the US Air Force. Here, a bunch of odd metal towers and wire cables look for all the world as if grown-up kids have been playing with a giant Erector Set.

Purdy's Macadamia Nut Farm

Tuddie Purdy runs the best little macadamia nut farm tour in all of Hawaii. Everything is Molokai scale. You can crack open macadamia nuts on a stone with a hammer and sample macadamia blossom honey scooped up with slices of fresh coconut.

Unlike tours on the Big Island that focus on processing, Purdy takes you into his orchard and explains how the nuts grow. A single macadamia tree can simultaneously be in various stages of progression – with flowers in blossom, tiny nuts just beginning and clusters of mature nuts. His 1½ acres of mature trees are over 60 years old and grow naturally: no pesticides, herbicides, fertilizers or even pruning.

Admission is free. Macadamia nuts (roasted or raw) and honey are for sale. To get to the farm head north, turn left onto Farrington Ave from Hwy 470 and after one mile turn right onto Lihi Pali Ave, just before the high school. It's a third of a mile up, on the right.

The hours are a bit flexible, but you might find Purdy there from 9:30 am to

Mail Home Some Aloha

Postmaster Margaret Keahi-Leary of the Hoolehua post office stocks baskets of unhusked coconuts that you can address and mail off as a unique (and edible!) 'postcard'. These coconuts, which Margaret gathers on her own time, are free for this 'post-a-nut' purpose, and she keeps a few felt pens on hand so you can jot down a message on the husk. Priority mail postage to anywhere in the USA costs $3 for a average-sized coconut. The Hoolehua post office is open from 7:30 to 11:30 am and 12:30 to 4:30 pm Monday to Friday. ■

NED FRIARY

3:30 pm Monday to Friday, 10 am to 2 pm on Saturdays.

MOOMOMI BEACH

Moomomi Beach, on the western edge of the Hoolehua Plains, is ecologically unique. It stands as one of the few undisturbed coastal sand dune areas left in Hawaii. Among its native grasses and shrubs are at least five endangered plant species that exist nowhere else on earth. It is one of the few places in the populated islands where green sea turtles still find a habitat suitable for breeding.

Evidence of an adze quarry and the fossils of a number of long-extinct Hawaiian birds have been unearthed here, preserved over time by Moomomi's arid sands. In 1988, the Nature Conservancy purchased 920 acres of Moomomi from Molokai Ranch and established Moomomi Preserve. Moomomi is not lushly beautiful, but windswept, lonely and wild.

To get there, turn off Hwy 460, east of the airport, onto Hwy 480. Then turn left onto Farrington Ave and head west. The paved road ends after about three miles. From there, it's 2½ miles farther along a red dirt road that is in some areas quite smooth and in others deeply rutted. In places you may have to skirt along the edge of the road and straddle a small gully. The road condition varies, depending on when it's last been graded, and it could be difficult going if it's muddy. Still, it's usually passable in a standard car, although the higher the vehicle the better.

A little over two miles after the paved road ends the road forks. Bear to the right and follow this road half a mile down to the beach. If it gets too rough, there's a spot halfway down this last stretch where you can pull off to the right and park.

At the end of the road is Moomomi Bay and a little sandy beach used by sunbathers. The rocky eastern point that protects the bay provides a perch for fishers. There are no facilities here, just the foundations of a bathhouse that burned down years ago. This area is part of the Hawaiian Home Lands.

The lovely beach that people refer to as Moomomi is not here, but at Kawaaloa Bay, a 20-minute walk to the west. Kawaaloa is a broad white-sand beach. The wind, which picks up steadily each afternoon, blows the sand into interesting ripples and waves.

The high hills running inland are actually massive sand dunes. The coastal cliffs, which have been sculptured into jagged abstract designs by wind and water, are made of sand that has petrified due to Moomomi's dry conditions.

The narrower right side of Kawaaloa Bay is partially sheltered, however the whole beach can be rough when the surf is up and swimming is discouraged. Kawaaloa collects a lot of drifting debris, some of it driftwood and some of it less romantic. Visitors may collect human-made objects found along the coast but should not take any natural objects, including flora, rocks and coral.

There's a fair chance you'll have Kawaaloa to yourself, but if you don't you can always walk farther on to one of the other sandy coves along the shore. Most of the area west of here is open ocean with strong currents.

Because of the fragile ecology of the dunes, visitors should stay along the beach and on trails only. Foot access is allowed without a permit via the route described, although visitors with a 4WD vehicle can also get a gate key from the Nature Conservancy and drive directly in to Kawaaloa Bay. To do that a permit application and $25 key deposit are required.

The conservancy leads monthly guided hikes of Moomomi, usually on the third Saturday of the month. The cost of $10 for conservancy members and $20 for nonmembers includes transport to and from the preserve. As it's common for hikers to fly over from other islands to join in, the pickup run includes Molokai Airport. Reservations are required and must usually be made well in advance.

To get a hike schedule or make reservations, contact The Nature Conservancy of Hawaii (☎ 553-5236), Molokai Preserves, Box 220, Kualapuu, HI 96757. If you're writing, include a self-addressed, stamped envelope.

The Nature Conservancy office is the small blue building at the intersection of Hwys 460 and 470. The office hours are generally from 7:30 am to 3 pm Monday to Friday (closed for lunch).

West End

The Maunaloa Hwy (Hwy 460) heads west from Kaunakakai, passes Molokai Airport, and then climbs into the high grassy rangeland of Molokai's arid western side.

Hwy 460 is about 17 miles long and the drive takes about half an hour from its start in Kaunakakai to its end at Maunaloa. It's a good paved road all the way, as are the roads to and around Kaluakoi Resort and down to Papohaku and Dixie Maru beaches. Most other West End roads, however, are privately owned dirt roads that are locked off to the public.

Molokai Ranch owns most of the land on this side of the island. Access is at the whim of the ranch but generally requires special permission.

From Molokai's West End beaches, the twinkling lights of Oahu are just 26 miles away. The view is of Diamond Head to the left, Makapuu Point to the right.

West End Development
In the 1970s, Molokai Ranch joined with Louisiana Land & Exploration Company to form the Kaluakoi Corporation. They proposed developing western Molokai into a major suburb of Honolulu, complete with a ferry service. The plan called for 30,000 private homes on the heretofore uninhabited west coast. A vocal anti-growth movement boomed quicker than the buildings could, however, and the plan was scrapped.

In its place a somewhat more modest master plan was drawn up for the development of Kaluakoi Resort that called for 1100 hotel units, 1200 condo units, 1000 single-family homes and a 15-acre shopping center.

Only 200 of the condo units, one 18-hole golf course and one of the four planned hotels have thus far been built. The 290-room hotel never really took off and the occupancy rate has been so low that part of it has been turned into condos. The house lots have been subdivided, but as of yet fewer than 100 houses have been built, mostly exclusive homes scattered along the edge of the beach and up on the bluff.

MAUNALOA
The long mountain range that comes into view on the left past the 10-mile marker is Maunaloa, which means 'Long Mountain'. Its highest point is Puunana at 1381 feet. In

MOLOKAI

addition to being the site of Hawaii's first hula school and one of the Hawaiian Islands' most important adze quarries, Maunaloa was also once a center of sorcery.

The name Maunaloa not only refers to the mountain range, but also the town at the end of the road. Built in the 1920s by Libby, McNeill & Libby, this little plantation town was the center of the company's pineapple activities on Molokai. Dole, which acquired Libby, McNeill & Libby in 1972, closed down operations in Maunaloa in 1975.

These days about 400 people live in the area, most working for Molokai Ranch or at Kaluakoi Resort.

Maunaloa is a town in flux. Molokai Ranch, which owns the land that the town sits on, has been replacing many of the old plantation-era cottages with modern housing and adding new conveniences, including a business center and movie theater. Some of the housing is geared for local residents, but the town is also being targeted for growth, with plans for 250 new house lots in all.

Information

The Molokai Ranch office is on the right as you enter town.

The little rural post office, opposite the Molokai Ranch office, is open from 8 am to 4:30 pm Monday to Friday.

Molokai Sorcery

According to legend, fire gods who roamed the heavens as shooting stars landed on Maunaloa, where they inhabited a grove of trees. Unsuspecting men who tried to cut down the possessed trees were poisoned upon touching the wood, until at last one of the gods explained to a kahuna how to cut the trees down. The kahunas were then able to carve the poisoned wood into images that harnessed the force of the gods. During the 17th century it became a powerful sorcery that could be sent off into the night to wreak vengeance upon enemies. It was potent stuff, and none of Molokai's neighbors dared to violate Molokai's sovereignty in those days. ■

The village gas station, the only one on the West End, is open from 7:30 am to 5:30 pm Monday to Saturday.

Places to Eat

The town's main eatery is the *Village Grill*, which is currently in the process of taking over the old JoJo's Cafe. It plans to be open daily for lunch and dinner with a menu that includes salads, burgers and steaks. Also going in is a mini *KFC*, with the usual fried chicken offerings, at the side of the new movie theater. Otherwise, pick up supplies at the village grocery store.

Things to Buy

Big Wind Kite Factory sells designer kites of all shapes and styles. Owner Jonathan Socher's kites have a reputation throughout the islands for their creative flair. Many of the kites, which have tropical fish and other island-influenced designs, are made on site, and if you're there at the right time you can watch the process. An extension of the kite factory is the gift shop next door, which has sarongs and wood carvings from Bali, horn scrimshaw from Molokai deer, books and jewelry. Both are open from 8:30 am to 5 pm Monday to Saturday and 10 am to 2 pm on Sundays.

SOUTHWEST BEACHES

If you really want to get off the beaten track, there are a couple of remote beaches south of Maunaloa. However, getting to them is not easy, as access – which is via rutted dirt roads across Molokai Ranch land – is restricted to one or two weekends per month. The ranch posts the opening days in the local papers.

The most frequented spots are **Halena Beach**, a broad white-sand beach with a protective reef, and **Hale O Lono Beach**, the starting point of the Molokai-to-Oahu outrigger canoe race that's held each year during Aloha Week. Two miles to the east of Halena is the abandoned Kolo Wharf. Libby, McNeill & Libby shipped Maunaloa pineapples from Kolo until moving their operations to Kaunakakai Harbor in the 1950s.

MOLOKAI RANCH WILDLIFE PARK

In the late 1960s, Molokai Ranch began importing antelope in an effort to control the rapid spread of kiawe trees, which were encroaching onto their cattle pastureland. The antelope, which feed on kiawe in their native habitat, adapted so well to Molokai that the ranch later started importing other rare exotic animals to breed for game parks and zoos. When Kaluakoi Resort opened, Molokai Ranch began providing sightseeing tours for the resort's guests.

Animals native to Africa, India, Asia and South America roam the park's 350 acres. The more numerous are the eland, Indian blackbuck and oryx, all strikingly marked antelopes; Barbary sheep, with thick curved-back horns; and sika deer from Japan.

There are also a few zebras, giraffes, rheas and East African crowned cranes. Flocks of wild turkey, ring-necked pheasant, francolin, quail and other game birds have flown in on their own.

The park's grassy hillsides and scrubby kiawe trees look so convincingly like the Serengeti that both US and Japanese film companies have used it to fake African backdrops.

The tour along the park's dirt roads is usually by van, but if 10 or more people sign up they sometimes take an open-air wagon that provides good photo opportunities. Stops are made for animal sightings, giraffe feedings and photography.

The tours, which last about 1¾ hours, leave Kaluakoi Resort at 8 am, 10 am and 1:30 pm from Tuesday to Saturday and at 10:30 am only on Sundays – call ahead, though, as the schedule changes occasionally. It costs $35 for adults, $18 for children ages 13 to 17 and $10 for children ages three to 12. Reservations can be made by calling ☎ 552-2791 or 800-254-8871.

KALUAKOI RESORT

Off Hwy 460 at the 15-mile marker, a road leads down to Kaluakoi Resort. The 6700-acre development includes Kaluakoi Hotel & Golf Club, the condominium complexes of Kaluakoi Villas, Paniolo Hale and Ke Nani Kai, private house lots and a beautiful windswept coast. Overall, it's a low-key and unobtrusive development that's pleasantly quiet and uncrowded.

Kepuhi Beach

Kepuhi is the white-sand beach in front of Kaluakoi Hotel. During the winter the surf breaks close to shore, carrying a tremendous amount of sand to and fro. Experienced surfers take to the northern end of the beach.

Swimming conditions are often dangerous here. Not only can there be a tough shorebreak, but strong currents can be present even on calm days. Check with the folks at the hotel beach hut for the latest water conditions. The hut rents snorkel sets for $7.50 a day and boogie boards for $5 an hour.

Kaiaka Rock

A five-minute hike up to the top of this 110-foot-high promontory at the south end of Kepuhi Beach rewards strollers with a nice view of Papohaku Beach. To get there, take the golf course road (Kaiaka Rd) to its end from where the trail begins. At the top you'll find the remains of a pulley that was once used to carry cattle down to waiting barges for transport to Oahu slaughterhouses. There was also a 40-foot heiau on the hilltop until 1967 when the US Army bulldozed it under. There have been on-again off-again plans to build a luxury hotel at Kaiaka Rock.

Places to Stay

Kaluakoi Hotel & Golf Club (☎ 552-2555; fax 552-2821), Box 1977, Maunaloa, HI 96770, has rooms that are fairly standard for a resort hotel, although they're not too spiffy and are on the small side. The cost is $95 for a garden view, $115 for an ocean view. There are also condo-style units that start at $140 for a studio, $165 for a one-bedroom. The hotel has an 18-hole golf course, wearworn tennis courts, a pool, a restaurant and a couple of small stores.

About 75 units of the Kaluakoi Hotel are under separate management and booked as *Kaluakoi Villas* (☎ 552-2721, 800-525-1470; fax 525-2201), Box 200, Maunaloa,

MOLOKAI

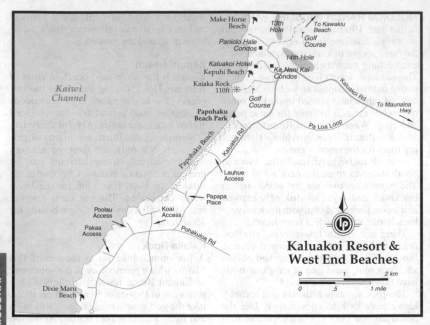

Make Horse Beach
13th Hole
To Kawakiu Beach
Golf Course
Paniolo Hale Condos
14th Hole
Kaluakoi Hotel
Ke Nani Kai Condos
Kepuhi Beach
Kaluakoi Rd
Kaiaka Rock 110ft
Kaiwi Channel
Golf Course
To Maunaloa Hwy
Papohaku Beach Park
Pa Loa Loop
Papohaku Beach
Kaluakoi Rd
Lauhue Access
Papapa Place
Poolau Access
Koai Access
Pakaa Access
Pohakuloa Rd
Dixie Maru Beach

Kaluakoi Resort & West End Beaches

0   1   2 km
0   .5   1 mile

HI 96770. The units each have a private lanai, TV and kitchenette with a refrigerator, coffeemaker and four-burner stove. While the walls are on the thin side and the decor is lightly faded, they are pleasant enough and can be a good value if you get a discounted rate. Standard rates are $120 to $145 for studio units, $145 to $195 for one-bedroom units, but they offer an array of discounts that can cut those prices by half. Ask for a 2nd-floor unit, as they have cathedral ceilings and many have a peek of the ocean.

Paniolo Hale (☎ 552-2731, 800-367-2984; fax 552-2288), Box 190, Maunaloa, HI 96770, is a 77-unit condominium. The units are airy and each has a kitchen, ceiling fans, TV, washer/dryer and screened lanai. In the low season studios cost $95, one-bedroom, two-bath units cost $115 and two-bedroom units cost $145. In the high season all rates are $20 more. Up to two people can stay in the studios and four in

the other units. The minimum stay is usually three nights, although a couple of the units sometimes allow a two-night stay. There's a 10% weekly discount. The complex has a pool and barbecue grills. The office is open only from 8 am to 4 pm Monday to Saturday.

Ke Nani Kai (☎ 552-2761, 800-888-2791; fax 552-0045), Box 126, Maunaloa, HI 96770, is a 120-unit condominium. Units are individually owned so they vary significantly in their upkeep and decor. Each has a kitchen, lanai, washer/dryer and TV; most have a sofa bed in the living room. The units on the 2nd floor have high exposed-beam ceilings and the best of them are arguably the nicest on Molokai. Rack rates are $125 for up to four people in a one-bedroom unit, $160 for up to six people in a two-bedroom, two-bath unit. Units with ocean views are $20 more, but it's a distant and partial view. There's a pool and two tennis courts. The minimum stay is two nights. Various discount schemes, such as the Entertainment card, can cut the rack rates by as much as half.

Places to Eat

The only restaurant at the resort is the *Ohia Lodge* (☎ 552-2555) at Kaluakoi Hotel. The dining room is pleasant and the food is reasonably good. Expect a standard breakfast of pancakes or eggs to run around $7, while dinner prices range from $14 for chicken stir-fry to $22 for steak and shrimp. Every Friday there's a buffet dinner, sometimes Mexican, sometimes Asian, which includes hot dishes, salad bar, desserts and coffee for under $20. The restaurant is open from 6:30 to 10:30 am and 6 to 9 pm.

Lunch is at the hotel's snack bar, which is open daily from 11 am to 4 pm, to 5 pm on weekends, and sells simple fare such as burgers for $4, teriyaki chicken plates for $5.50.

The hotel also has a sundries shop with wine, beer and a few convenience foods at inflated prices.

PAPOHAKU BEACH

Papohaku Beach lays claim to being Hawaii's largest beach. It's 2½ miles long and vast enough to hold the entire population of Molokai without getting crowded, although that would be an unlikely scenario. There's seldom more than a handful of beachgoers, even on sunny days, and at times you can walk the shore without seeing another soul.

It's a beautiful beach and easy to reach, so why are so few people there? Well, for one, it can be windy. But the main drawback is the water itself, which is usually too treacherous for swimming.

Yet for barefoot strolling it's a gorgeous stretch, with soft golden sands gleaming in the sun and wisps of rainbows tossed up in the crashing surf.

There are seven well-marked beach access points leading off Kaluakoi Rd; all have outdoor showers and paved parking lots. The first three lead to Papohaku Beach. The first access, the most developed of the seven, is Papohaku Beach Park, a grassy landscaped park with campsites, showers, changing rooms, restrooms, drinking water and thorny kiawe trees.

From the third access, off Papapa Place, there's a broad view of all Papohaku Beach stretching north with the sun at your back. The large concrete tunnel at this end of the beach was used to load sand onto barges for shipping to Honolulu. The sand was used in construction and to build up Waikiki beaches until environmental protection laws put a halt to the sand mining operation in the early 1970s. This beach is a good place to find small puka shells of the type used to make necklaces. It's also a great place to catch the sunset.

The next three beach accesses lead to rocky coastline, more suitable for fishing than other water activities.

Places to Stay

Papohaku Beach Park is a choice site for camping, beautiful and quiet, with the surf lulling you to sleep and the birds waking you up. The tent sites are grassy and level. Secure your tent carefully, as the wind sometimes picks up with hardy gusts. The camping area has two sections; they are watered by timed sprinklers on different days of the week, so pay attention to the sign that tells which days each area is scheduled for watering – there's nothing more depressing than finding your tent and belongings soaked!

For information on permits, see Camping in the Accommodations section at the front of this chapter.

DIXIE MARU BEACH

The beach at the end of the road, which the ancient Hawaiians knew as Kapukahehu, is now called Dixie Maru after a ship that went down in the area long ago.

Dixie Maru is the most protected cove on the west shore and the most popular swimming area. Consequently, there are usually a fair number of families here. The waters are generally calm, except when the surf is high enough to break over the mouth of the bay.

MAKE HORSE BEACH

Make (pronounced 'mah-kay') Horse Beach supposedly takes its name from days past when wild horses were run off the cliff north of here. *Make* means 'dead' in Hawaiian. This pretty little white-sand beach is more secluded than the one in front of Kaluakoi Hotel. It's a good place for sunbathing, but it's not safe for swimming.

To get there, turn off Kaluakoi Rd onto the road to Paniolo Hale condos and then turn left as if going to the condo complex. Either park just beyond the condos and walk a quarter of a mile down to the golf course or drive the rutted dirt road to the end, where there's a little spot to park. From there, cross a narrow stretch of fairway and you're on the beach.

KAWAKIU BEACH

Kawakiu, north of the Kaluakoi Resort complex, is a broad crescent beach of white sand and bright turquoise waters.

In 1975, Kawakiu was a focus of Molokai activists, who began demanding access to private, and heretofore forbidden, beaches. The group, Hui Alaloa, marched to Kawakiu from Moomomi in a successful protest that convinced Molokai Ranch to provide public access to this secluded West End beach.

To get there, turn off Kaluakoi Rd onto the road to Paniolo Hale, but instead of turning left down to the condos, continue straight towards the golf course. Where the paved road ends, there's space to pull over and park just before crossing the greens. There are restrooms and drinking water

here at the 14th hole. It's the last chance to get water.

The red dirt road that continues down to the beach should be OK with a 4WD and might also be passable in a standard car. However, it's quite rocky in places, and if you did bottom out or brush one of the rocks on the side, it could put a dent in things. Anyway, why bother driving when it's a pleasant half-hour hike down to the beach?

After the golf course the road passes through ranchland with kiawe trees. Trees that died during the drought of the mid-1980s now stand bleached white by the sun, making interesting silhouettes against the blue sky.

You'll come first to a rocky point at the southern end of the bay. Before descending to the beach, scramble around up here for a scenic view of the coast south to the sands of Papohaku Beach and north to Ilio Point.

When seas are calm, Kawakiu is generally safe for swimming, though that's more common in summer than winter. When the surf is rough, there are still areas where you can at least get wet. On the southern side of the bay there's a little sandy-bottomed wading pool in the rocks. The northern side has an area of flat rocks over which water slides to fill up a shallow shoreline pool.

On weekends there's usually a few families picnicking under the kiawe trees, but at other times you may well have the place to yourself.

Locals occasionally camp here as well, but there are no facilities.

Lanai

Until recently Lanai was a one-crop, one-company, one-town island. The latter two still hold true.

For over half a century Castle & Cooke, which owns 98% of Lanai, ran the island as its own private pineapple plantation. For a time nearly one-fifth of the world's pineapples came from Lanai, but competition from more cheaply produced Costa Rican and Philippine pineapples gradually eroded the profitability of the Lanai crop.

Castle & Cooke has now ceased its commercial pineapple operations completely and is turning rural Lanai into an exclusive tourist destination, under the slogan 'Hawaii's Private Island'. During the past few years they have opened two luxury resorts, both with 18-hole golf courses, and the first of the island's million-dollar vacation homes have been built.

Until 1990, Lanai had only one little hotel with just 10 rooms. The few visitors who came this way were largely hunters, hikers and independent travelers trying to avoid the tourist scene on the other islands. Now, with its two new resorts, Castle & Cooke is gambling that enough wealthy visitors in search of seclusion will show up to make it all pay off.

On the surface the hotels, with 350 rooms combined, haven't altered things all that radically. The center of Lanai remains Lanai City – not a city at all, but merely a small plantation town of tin-roofed houses. It's still home to all but a few dozen of Lanai's 2800 residents, most of whom work for the Lanai Company, the nonagricultural subsidiary of Castle & Cooke.

Lanai has bright red earth, dry and dusty gullies, forested ravines, white-sand beaches and cool, foggy uplands. The island also has some obscure archaeological sites and petroglyphs and the last native dryland forest in Hawaii.

Although Lanai can be interesting to explore, many of the sights are a good distance from town, along rutted dirt roads that require a 4WD vehicle.

Not surprisingly, Lanai can be quite expensive to visit. One of the easiest ways to get a glimpse of it is to take the ferry over from Maui in the morning, snorkel at Hulopoe Bay, which has the island's finest beach, and then take the boat back in the afternoon.

Spirits in the Night

According to legend, Lanai was a land of *akua* (spirits), and they alone roamed the island until the 15th century.

It was at this time that Kaululaau, the young prince of Maui, lived in what is today the town of Lahaina. He was a mischievous child. After he had torn out breadfruit trees that his father had just planted, it was decided to banish him to uninhabited Lanai, an almost certain death.

Not one to be easily intimidated, Kaululaau learned to trick the evil spirits of Lanai. During the day the akua would see him on the beach and ask where he spent his nights, hoping to ambush him in his sleep. He convinced them that he slept in the surf, though when darkness fell he slipped off to the shelter of a cave.

Night after night, the akua returned to the beach and rushed out to look for Kaululaau in the waves. The longer they searched, the more exhausted they got, until finally the pounding surf overcame them. Kaululaau continued his pranks until at last all 400 of Lanai's akua had either perished or fled to Kahoolawe.

Kaululaau's family had given him up for dead, when Mauians noticed a light from a fire across the Auau Channel, which separates Maui and Lanai. When they went over to investigate, they found Kaululaau alive and well and the island devoid of spirits. Kaululaau was brought back to Maui a hero. ■

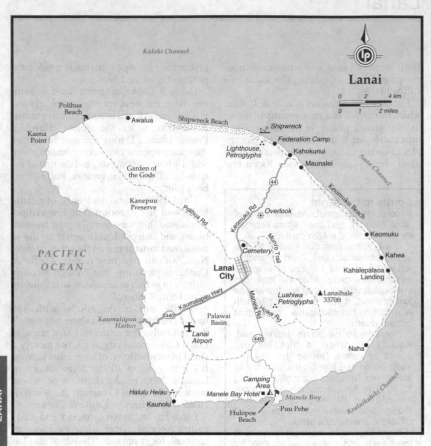

Lanai

0   2   4 km
0   1   2 miles

Kalohi Channel

Polihua
Beach

Kaena
Point

Awalua

Shipwreck Beach

Shipwreck

Federation Camp

Lighthouse,
Petroglyphs

Kahokunui

Maunalei

Auau Channel

Garden of
the Gods

Kanepuu
Preserve

Polihua Rd

Keomuku Rd

44

Overlook

Keomuku Beach

Keomuku

PACIFIC
OCEAN

Cemetery

Murro Trail

Kahea

Kahalepalaoa
Landing

Lanai City

Luahiwa
Petroglyphs

Lanaihale
3370ft

Manele Rd

Hoike Rd

Kaumalapau Hwy

Naha

Kaumalapau
Harbor

440

Palawai
Basin

Lanai
Airport

440

Halulu Heiau

Kaunolu

Camping
Area

Manele Bay Hotel

Manele Bay

Hulopoe
Beach

Puu Pehe

Kealaikahiki Channel

HISTORY

Archaeological studies indicate Lanai was
never heavily settled. Villages were relatively
small and scattered throughout the island.

Since ancient times, Lanai has been under
the rule of its more dominant neighbor,
Maui. In 1778, when the Big Island chief
Kalaniopuu was routed in a failed attempt to
invade Maui, he decided to take his revenge
on tiny Lanai and sent warriors under the
command of Kamehameha.

Kamehameha's troops were brutal. They
killed everyone they found and virtually
depopulated Lanai. When English explorer

George Vancouver sailed by Lanai in 1792,
he saw no villages and noted that the island
might at best be only sparsely populated.

Due to a treacherous ocean swell, which
by the 1820s had already claimed a couple
of foreign ships, would-be visitors were
dissuaded from landing on Lanai's shores.
In 1823, a missionary named William Ellis
became the first Westerner to step ashore.
He guessed the island's population to be
around 2000.

Although the early missionaries didn't
spend much time on Lanai, they still had an
influence. They introduced the heretofore

NED FRIARY

Molokai Church, Kaunakakai, Molokai

RICK GERHARTER

Kalaupapa Village, Molokai

RICK GERHARTER

View of the north coast from Kalaupapa Peninsula, Molokai

NED FRIARY

Halawa Valley, Molokai, from roadside lookout

NED FRIARY

Girls on beach, Kaunakakai Harbor, Molokai

NED FRIARY

Weighing in at fishing tournament, Molokai

unknown concept of adultery to Hawaii, and in the 1830s Maui women accused of that criminal offense were banished to the barren northwestern side of Lanai as punishment.

Mormons

In the 1850s the Mormons moved in and set up a community at Palawai Basin, south of present-day Lanai City. Their intention was to establish a 'City of Joseph' in Hawaii.

The community floundered until 1861, when a new charismatic elder, Walter Gibson, arrived. Mormons from around the islands poured in, as did money to buy Palawai Basin. At the height of it all, there was one Mormon for every Lanaian.

Gibson, a shrewd businessman, handled the financial matters for the community – including the acquisition of land. Things got sticky when it was discovered that he had made the land purchases in his own name, rather than in the church's. In 1864, after refusing to transfer the title of his Lanai holdings to the mother church in Salt Lake City, he was excommunicated by church leader Brigham Young.

This apparently suited Gibson just fine. Unable to gain title to the property, the Lanai congregation faded away and the 300 or so Mormons left for Laie on Oahu's north shore, where their church is still based today.

Gibson held onto the prime Lanai real estate he had cornered. Equally calculating in the political arena, in the early 1880s, Gibson became a friend and confidant of King Kalakaua and came to hold a number of positions in Kalakaua's cabinet, including that of premier.

Sugar & Cattle

Upon his death, Gibson left the land to his daughter, Talula Lucy. In 1888, she and her husband, Frederick Hayselden, established the Maunalei Sugar Company and developed a landing at Kahalepalaoa on Lanai's east coast. A water pumping station went up at nearby Keomuku, the surrounding area was planted with sugar cane and the whole shebang was connected by a little railroad. Over 400 Japanese laborers were brought in to work the fields. The sugar days were short lived, however. By 1901 the pumps were drawing saltwater, the sugar cane had died and the whole enterprise had folded.

After the dismal failure with sugar, the land was sold off to ranching interests. In 1910 the newly formed Lanai Company consolidated most of the holdings and established cattle ranching on a larger scale. The following year, New Zealander George Munro was hired to manage the ranch and a landing for shipping cattle to off-island markets was established at Manele Bay.

In 1917, the Baldwin brothers, sons of missionaries from Maui, purchased the Lanai Company. With the exception of a small haole-held ranch and about 500 acres held by Lanaians, the Baldwins owned the entire island.

Pineapples

In 1922, Jim Dole paid $1.1 million for Lanai, a mere $12 an acre. It was just enough for the Baldwins to buy the Ulupalakua Ranch that they had long coveted on Maui. With the purchase of Lanai, Dole, who had already established pineapple production on Oahu, doubled his holdings of cultivable Hawaiian land.

Sugar Roots

The short-lived Maunalei Sugar Company, which had high hopes of turning Lanai into a bustling sugar cane plantation at the end of the 19th century, was not the first try at the sugar business on Lanai.

In 1802, a Chinese man landed on Lanai with granite rollers to crush sugar cane, which had been growing freely on the islands since the arrival of the first Polynesians. Using iron pots, he boiled the crushed cane down into a sugary syrup. Although his name has been lost to history, this man is commonly credited with being the first person to attempt commercial sugar production in Hawaii. This particular enterprise was a failure, but it was such Chinese know-how that became the basis for the Maunalei Sugar Company and other sugar mills throughout Hawaii. ■

Hula dancer with dog-tooth leg ornaments and feather rattle – by John Webber

Dole's Hawaiian Pineapple Company poured $4 million into Lanai to turn it into a plantation island. It built the plantation town of Lanai City, dredged Kaumalapau to make it a deep-water harbor, put in roads and water systems, cleared the land and planted pineapples. By the end of the 1920s production was in full swing.

Dole had marketed his pineapples well and was producing bumper crops – the future looked rosy. Then the Great Depression hit the mainland and sales plummeted. The newly popular canned pineapples were suddenly seen as an exotic extra, one that most Americans could easily do without in hard times.

After an $8 million loss in 1932, a reorganization took place. Castle & Cooke purchased much of the stock and eventually gained a controlling interest in Dole. They've been the dominant force on Lanai ever since.

GEOGRAPHY

Lanai is the sixth-largest Hawaiian island. It's 18 miles long, 13 miles wide and shaped like a teardrop. It has an area of 140 sq miles.

Lanai lies nine miles south of Molokai and nine miles west of Maui. The name Lanai means 'hump'. When viewed from Maui it looks somewhat like the back of a whale rising out of the water.

The island was formed by a single volcano, Palawai, now long extinct. The large flat basin of Palawai crater contains most of Lanai's arable land.

Lanai's terrain and climate are dominated by a ridge running from the northwest to the southeast. It reaches a height of 3370 feet at Lanaihale. From there, a series of gulches radiate down to the east coast, ending at a strip of coastal flats.

The western side of the ridge is a cool central plateau, which includes Lanai City at 1620 feet.

The southwest coast has sheer sea cliffs, some higher than 1000 feet. Northwest Lanai is dry and barren and slopes gently down to the coast.

CLIMATE

Lanai City has a mild climate. The lowest temperature on record is 46°F, the highest 88°F. Average temperatures range from 73°F in the summer to 66°F in the winter. Evenings can be brisk, commonly dipping down to around 50°F in winter.

Lanai is rather dry. Molokai to the north and Maui to the east draw much of the rain out of the moisture-laden trade winds before they reach Lanai.

Annual rainfall averages 37 inches in Lanai City and 10 to 15 inches along most of the coast. The difference is great enough that when it's overcast in Lanai City, chances are that Shipwreck Beach or Manele Bay will be sunny.

As with the rest of Hawaii, October to April is the rainiest season. Even the island's drier areas can get soaked with heavy rainfall during winter storms.

FLORA & FAUNA

Lanai has suffered the greatest loss of native forests, plants and birds of any of the main Hawaiian islands, the result of drastic overgrazing.

Lanai has about 8000 axis deer, descendants of a herd of eight brought to Molokai from India in 1868. The deer were introduced to Lanai in 1920 and are more prolific than on Molokai, the only other Hawaiian island where they roam free.

Mouflon sheep were introduced to Lanai in 1954 and inhabit the island's gullies and ridges. Both the deer and sheep are hunted.

Lanai has no mongooses, which eat the eggs of ground-nesting birds, so introduced game birds thrive. Ring-necked pheasants, francolins, chukar partridges, quails, doves and wild turkeys are all common.

However, the island has only two endemic birds remaining – the Hawaiian owl and the *apapane* (native honeycreeper) – and they are scarce.

The most noticeable types of vegetation are thorny kiawe trees, common in Lanai's dry coastal areas, and stately Norfolk Island pines, which abound around Lanai City. Lanai has a unique native dryland forest, under the protection of the Nature Conservancy.

GOVERNMENT

Lanai is part of Maui County, but control of the island is largely in the hands of Castle & Cooke, which owns all but 2% of Lanai. Total county and state land accounts for just over 100 acres. Beaches on Lanai, as elsewhere in Hawaii, are public domain under state jurisdiction.

ECONOMY

About 80% of Lanai's 1200 workers are employed by the Lanai Company, mostly in its resort operations.

Although visitors will see a couple of high-profile pineapple fields, these small patches are only 'show fields' – the last commercial pineapple harvest was in 1992. Some of the former pineapple fields have been given over to forage crops and cattle and hog raising, but the importance of agriculture and ranching is secondary at best.

Lanai's transition from a plantation economy to a tourism-oriented service economy hasn't been entirely smooth. The resorts initially mounted millions of dollars in operating losses, although occupancy rates climbed with the opening of a second golf course in 1994. The Lanai Company now intends to build hundreds of luxury homes geared for wealthy, second-home owners who have bypassed Lanai up to now. If it all develops according to plan, Lanai's population could more than triple to 10,000 in the next decade.

In addition, there are new proposals to replace nearly half of Lanai City's aging homes, which are owned and maintained by the Lanai Company. Most of these new replacement homes are expected to sell for $120,000 to $250,000, prices that are well beyond the reach of many Lanaians.

POPULATION & PEOPLE

Lanai has seen some dramatic rises and declines in its population. It had dropped well below 200 when Dole arrived in 1922.

Lanai's current population has risen to 3000, but that's still about 10% less than it was during pineapple's heyday in the 1950s. All but a few dozen of Lanai's residents live in Lanai City. The largest ethnic group is Filipino (51%), followed by Japanese (18%), Caucasian (11%) and part-Hawaiian (9.2%).

Approximately a third of the people living on Lanai were born in the Philippines.

ORIENTATION

Lanai has only one town, Lanai City, which is smack in the center of the island. The town is laid out in a sensible grid pattern, which makes it easy to find your way around.

Outside Lanai City there are only three paved roads: Keomuku Rd (Hwy 44), which heads northeast towards Shipwreck Beach;

LANAI

Official Lanai

Lanai has long had the nickname 'The Pineapple Island', but the newest promotional slogan is 'Hawaii's Private Island'. Lanai's official color is yellow and its official flower is kaunaoa, a thin yellow-orange parasitic vine. ■

Kaumalapau Hwy, which heads west to Kaumalapau Harbor; and Manele Rd, which goes south to Manele and Hulopoe bays. Both Kaumalapau Hwy and Manele Rd are marked Hwy 440, even though they are two distinct roads.

The airport is on Kaumalapau Hwy, 3½ miles from town.

Maps

As Lanai has so few roads and relatively few visitors, it may come as no surprise that there's no proliferation of road maps. The University of Hawaii's joint Molokai-Lanai map shows Lanai's topography as well as geographical and archaeological sites. The Lanai Company has a simpler fold-out map that shows Lanai City, the grounds of the two resorts and the island's main roads; it can be picked up free at the hotels.

Dirt Roads

Most roads on Lanai are dirt roads, many of them built in days past to service the pineapple fields; their conditions vary from good to impassable, largely as a result of the weather.

If you rent a 4WD vehicle and plan to travel these roads, ask the rental agency for the current best routes to out-of-the-way sights – often there are a few alternatives, and they know which roads are washed out and which are passable. If you do go off the beaten path and get stuck, it can be a long walk back to town and you can expect to get hit up for the towing and repair fees.

INFORMATION

There's no local daily newspaper, but you can buy the *Maui News* from a box in front of International Food & Clothing in Lanai City. Community notices, including items for sale and houses for rent, are posted on bulletin boards outside the post office and the three grocery stores.

Money

There are two banks in Lanai City, both on Lanai Ave. The First Hawaiian Bank, near 7th Street, is open Monday to Thursday

from 8:30 am to 3 pm, on Fridays until 6 pm. First Federal Savings, on the opposite side of the post office, has the same Friday hours as First Hawaiian but is open until 4:30 pm on other days.

Post & Communications

Lanai's post office, at the east side of Dole Park in Lanai City, is open from 9 am to 4:30 pm on weekdays and 10 am to noon on Saturdays.

Library

Lanai's library is on Fraser Ave in Lanai City, adjacent to the school. It's a fairly large library with a good collection of newspapers, including *USA Today*, the *Wall Street Journal* and Neighbor Island papers. It's open from 8 am to 5 pm Tuesday to Friday and 1 to 8 pm on Mondays.

Laundry

There's a coin laundry open 24 hours a day on 7th St in Lanai City.

Weather

For recorded weather forecasts and water conditions call ☎ 565-6033.

Emergency

For all emergencies call ☎ 911. Lanai Community Hospital (☎ 565-6411) on 7th St in Lanai City has 24-hour emergency service.

ACTIVITIES

There's a public recreation center in Lanai City, next to the school, with a 75-foot-long pool, a basketball court and a couple of lighted tennis courts.

Both the Manele Bay Hotel and the Lodge at Koele have 18-hole designer golf courses complete with dress codes and $100 greens fees ($150 for nonguests), cart included.

The Cavendish Golf Course, a local nine-hole course on the north side of Lanai City, is the only free golf course in Hawaii and a popular recreation spot for islanders. Anyone can play; simply bring your clubs and begin – no dress codes, no fees.

The two resort hotels offer a variety of activities, including tennis, diving and horseback riding; however, fees are generally quite high and many of the activities are limited to hotel guests.

GETTING THERE & AWAY
Air
Island Air (☎ 565-6744, 800-652-6541) flies to Lanai from Honolulu 10 times a day and from Kahului on Maui three times a day. Hawaiian Airlines (☎ 565-7281) flies to Lanai from Honolulu once a day on weekdays, twice daily on weekends. On both airlines the one-way fare is currently $69; for the same price, you can fly between Lanai and any other island, with connections via Honolulu.

For information on discounted tickets and air passes, see the Getting Around chapter in the front of the book.

Ferry
Expeditions (☎ 661-3756 on Maui, 800-695-2624) operates a small passenger ferry between Lahaina on Maui and Manele Boat Harbor on Lanai. The boat departs Lahaina at the dock in front of the Pioneer Inn daily at 6:45 and 9:15 am and 12:45, 3:15 and 5:45 pm. The boat departs Manele daily at 8 and 10:30 am and 2, 4:30 and 6:45 pm. The trip takes 45 minutes to an hour. One-way fares are $25 for adults and $20 for children ages two to 11. Reservations can be made in advance; tickets are purchased on the boat.

This is a great way to get to Lanai. Although the ride can be jolting when the seas are rough, it's usually quite pleasant. During the winter there's a good chance of seeing whales.

Tours
For details on diving, snorkeling and sailing tours to Lanai from Maui, see the Activities section in the Maui chapter.

GETTING AROUND
To/From the Airport
The Lodge at Koele and Manele Bay Hotel have a shuttle bus that meets hotel guests at the airport; with advance notice Hotel Lanai will also provide free airport pickup. Lanai City Service provides taxi service from the airport, and if you have reservations for a rental car, they provide free transfers to their in-town office.

Shuttle Bus
The resorts run a free shuttle bus between the Manele Bay Hotel and the Lodge at Koele for their guests, although nonguests can try their luck catching a ride. It runs about once an hour on weekdays, every half an hour on weekends.

Taxi
Lanai City Service provides a limited taxi service. The cost is $5 per person between the airport and town and $10 per person between Manele Bay and town. If you're flying in, it's best to call and make arrangements in advance. Otherwise, once you arrive you'll have to call to see if someone is available to come and get you (they're not always); there's a courtesy phone in the baggage claim area.

If you're coming from Maui by ferry, Lanai City Service's shuttle van generally goes down to meet the first two morning ferries.

Car
Only one car rental company operates on Lanai, and consequently the rates are high.

Lanai City Service (☎ 565-7227, 800-342-7398 in Hawaii, 800-367-7006 from the mainland), on Lanai Ave in Lanai City, is affiliated with Dollar Rent A Car. Unlike its affiliates on other islands, Dollar requires a one-day deposit to make a booking on Lanai and there are no discounts available. Compact cars rent for $60 a day and 4WD Jeep Wranglers for $119.

While there are many dirt roads in fine condition that could easily be driven, Lanai City Service restricts all its cars to paved roads – the 4WD jeeps may be driven on most dirt roads. The jeeps are usually available on short notice, but the cars can be in short supply and sometimes need to be booked a week or more in advance.

LANAI

Around the Island

LANAI CITY

Lanai City is nestled among Norfolk pines on a cool central plateau beneath the slopes of Lanaihale Mountain. For an old plantation town, it's a tidy little place. Houses are brightly painted and many have lovely front gardens with flowering plants and trees.

The center of town is Dole Park, a large grassy park lined with Norfolk pines. The park stretches six blocks from Fraser Ave to Lanai Ave, the two main roads in town.

Lanai's restaurants are on the north side of the park and the grocery stores are on the south side. To the east of the park are the post office, hospital and Hotel Lanai. To the west are the school and recreation center, with houses spread out for half a dozen blocks on either side – and that's about it.

At sunset, walking through the town and looking at the pines silhouetted against the crimson sky can be a delight. On Sunday mornings, a stroll by the Hawaiian church on the corner of 5th and Gay Sts will treat you to fine melodies of choir music.

While the new resorts are bringing change, this is still a place where you can unwind. It's hard to imagine a town less hurried than Lanai City – most shops even close for a siesta between noon and 1:30 pm.

Walks

Strollers will find a pleasant short hike behind the Lodge at Koele. Simply take the road on the Lanai City side of the lodge to its end at the golf cart parking lot. From there take the path along the golf cart route for a 15-minute walk past stands of Norfolk pines, artificial ponds and golf course landscaping. It ends at a hilltop bench, where there's a plaque bearing the poem 'If' by Rudyard Kipling.

It's also possible to walk from the back of the golf course up to the Munro Trail on a path called the Koele Nature Hike. A brochure detailing this five-mile roundtrip hike is available from the Activities Desk at the Lodge at Koele.

Places to Stay

Dreams Come True (☎ 565-6961, 800-566-6961; fax 565-7056; gblue@aloha.net), Michael and Susan Hunter, 547 12th St, Lanai City, HI 96763, is a B&B in a period plantation house with three guest bedrooms. The home is furnished with Asian antiques; two of the bedrooms have four-poster beds and all have private baths. There's a large common room with cable TV. Rates, which include a continental breakfast of homemade breads and fresh fruit from the yard, are $55/75 for singles/doubles. The Hunters also rent out a nearby three-bedroom, two-bath house that can sleep up to six for $190 a day and have two Jeep Cherokees that guests can rent for $100 a day (no insurance).

Hotel Lanai (☎ 565-7211, 800-321-4666; fax 565-6450), Box A 119, Lanai City, HI 96763, was built by Dole in 1923 to house plantation guests. It still maintains a rustic mountain lodge ambiance that's a throwback to the island's plantation era. The 10 restored rooms are pleasantly simple with hardwood floors, pedestal sinks, bleached pine furnishings, patchwork quilts and painted wooden walls that are anything but soundproof. There are various bed combinations, ranging from two twins to one king-size bed. Each room has a private bathroom and costs $95 to $105, with the more expensive rooms having front porches overlooking Lanai City. There's also a one-bedroom cottage in the rear that has a separate sitting room with a sofa bed for $135 a night. Rates include continental breakfast.

The *Lodge at Koele* (☎ 565-7300, 800-321-4666; fax 565-4561), Box 774, Lanai City, HI 96763, is a low-rise 102-room hotel with the ambiance of an overgrown plantation estate. The hotel maintains a genteel image, complete with afternoon tea, lawn bowling and croquet. Its lobby, called the Great Hall, is stuffed with an eclectic collection of antiques, artwork and upholstered furnishings and boasts Hawaii's two largest stone fireplaces. Guest rooms, which have a plantation-era decor, are quite nicely appointed with four-poster beds, private

To Shipwreck Beach

Keomuku Rd

■ 1

44

Cavendish
Golf Course

To Garden
of the Gods

Lanai City

0   100   200 m
0   100   200 yards

To Lanai Airport,
Kaumalapau Harbor

Kaumalapau Hwy

Manele Rd

440

440

To Hulopoe Bay,
Manele Bay

3rd St

Fraser Ave

Gay St

4th St

Houston St

Ilima St

Jacaranda St

Koele St

Lanai Ave

Matana St

5th St

† 2

6th St

● 3

7th St

● 4

8th St

● 5

● 6

18 ★

19 ▼

20

21 ●

9th Ct

10th St

11th St

12th St

13th St

7 ● 8 ● 9 10 11 12
▼ ▼

13 ●

14
Ⓢ

15 ▼

● 16

17 ✚

Queens Ave

Nani St

■ 24

22 23
Ⓢ

● 25

26
■

12th St

PLACES TO STAY
1 Lodge at Koele
24 Hotel Lanai
26 Dreams Come True

PLACES TO EAT
11 Blue Ginger Cafe
12 Tanigawa's
19 Pele's Garden

OTHER
2 Hawaiian Church
3 Lanai Elementary
   & High School
4 Library
5 Recreation Center
6 Government Offices
7 Maui Community College
8 Lanai Art Program
9 Coin Laundry
10 Heart of Lanai Art Studio
13 Lanai Playhouse
14 First Hawaiian Bank
15 Post Office
16 Castle & Cooke Offices
17 Hospital
18 Police Station
20 Pine Isle Market
21 International Food
    & Clothing
22 Richard's Shopping Center
23 First Federal Savings
25 Lanai City Service

Dole Park

LANAI

lanais, marble bathrooms, VCRs and the like. The rooms cost from $315 to $475, while suites, which include butler service, start at $600.

Places to Eat

The *Blue Ginger Cafe*, a little bakery and cafe, makes muffins and cinnamon buns and serves up three meals a day. A nice breakfast choice is the Belgian waffles for $4.25. The cafe also serves inexpensive hamburgers and saimin and $6 plate lunches. At dinner, specials such as shrimp tempura or scampi go for around $10. It's open from 6 am to 9 pm daily, with breakfast served until 11 am.

Tanigawa's serves up the most popular burgers on Lanai – you can get one with the works for a mere $2. The restaurant, which has an old-style counter where you can sit over coffee and watch the bacon sizzle on the grill, has breakfast dishes and lunch plates for around $6. Hours are from 6:30 am to 1 pm; it's closed on Wednesdays.

Pele's Garden on 8th St is a combination deli and health food store. The latter, which is open Monday to Friday from 9:30 am to 6:30 pm, has dry goods, vitamins, teas and a frozen food section. The deli, open from 11 am to 7 pm on Mondays, Tuesdays and Thursdays and 11 am to 11 pm on Fridays and Saturdays, has sandwiches for around $5 and fresh-squeezed juices, most from local produce, some organic.

The Rotisserie at Hotel Lanai has a chef with New Orleans roots and a dining room with a fireplace, high ceilings and hardwood floors. Dinner, which is currently the only meal being served, includes Creole eggplant pasta or Louisiana-style pork ribs for $15 and country French duck confit for $20. There are also Caesar salads for $8 and pizzas from $11. It's open nightly from 5:30 to 9 pm, although the bar stays open to midnight as long as there are still customers.

At the Lodge at Koele, the lobbyside *Terrace Dining Room* overlooks the hotel gardens. Breakfast menu items such as hot cakes, salmon omelets or bread pudding as well as lunchtime salads and sandwiches cost $10 to $14. At dinner, main courses

such as clams on penne pasta, vegetarian 'meatloaf' or grilled fish are $16 to $20. Breakfast is served from 7 to 11 am, lunch from 11 am to 6 pm and dinner from 6 to 9:30 pm.

The Lodge's formal dining room is also open for dinner, serving entrees such as rack of lamb or venison from Lanai axis deer for $35 to $40.

The island's largest grocery stores, *Richard's Shopping Center* and *Pine Isle Market*, are near each other on 8th St. Both are open from at least 8:30 am to noon and 1:30 to 6:30 pm Monday to Saturday. *International Food & Clothing* on Ilima St stays open during the noontime siesta, has Sunday hours (from 8:30 am to noon) and carries the widest selection of wine and beer.

Entertainment

People go to bed early in Lanai and there's no real nightlife, although the *Lodge at Koele* usually has mellow Hawaiian music from 7 to 10 pm in its Great Hall lobby.

The *Lanai Playhouse*, the island's movie theater, shows current feature films for $6.

Things to Buy

Lanai Art Program on 7th St is the site of the community arts program and the place to purchase locally made arts and crafts. The items, all made by Lanai residents, include watercolors, painted T-shirts and silk scarves, jewelry and raku ceramics. It's open from 9 am to 4 pm Monday to Saturday.

Heart of Lanai Art Studio, a few doors east on 7th St, has more upmarket items from artists throughout Hawaii. It's open from 1 to 6 pm Monday to Saturday.

SHIPWRECK BEACH & KEOMUKU

Hwy 44 runs 8½ miles from town to the northeast coast. The highway is narrow but well paved. To get there, head north on Lanai Ave and bear right on Keomuku Rd (Hwy 44).

The road heads into hills and pastures with grazing cattle. The uplands here are often cool, with fog and cloud cover drifting in and out. The Lodge at Koele is on Hwy 44, a mile above town.

A mile past the lodge is a paved road on the right that leads to the Munro Trail (for trail information, see the Munro Trail heading later in this chapter). The road to the trailhead, which is lined with Norfolk pines, ends in half a mile at a cemetery with gravestones in Japanese and Filipino. Sake offerings are placed at some of the Japanese graves. Pinwheels, bunny rabbits and pink flamingoes adorn sites where Filipino children are buried.

Back on Hwy 44, three miles out of town, there's a pull-off to the right with a beautiful vista. Straight ahead is the undeveloped southeast shore of Molokai and its tiny islet of Mokuhooniki, while the view to the right is of Maui and the Kaanapali high-rises.

From the lookout, the road slopes down to the coast. The scenery is punctuated by interesting rock formations sitting atop the eroded red earth, similar to those found at Garden of the Gods. Later, a shipwreck comes into view.

The paved road ends near the coast. A dirt road to the left leads to Shipwreck Beach and a former lighthouse.

Shipwreck Beach

Shipwreck Beach is the name given to nine miles of Lanai's northeast shore. It starts at Kahokunui at the end of Hwy 44 and goes up to Polihua Beach. True to its name, there are a couple of shipwrecks as well as a coastline that's good for beachcombing.

The dirt road that heads left from the highway ends after 1¾ miles at the site of a former lighthouse on a lava point. Only the cement foundations of the lighthouse remain. When it's dry, the road is usually passable by car, but you'll miss the beach walk. An alternative is to hike (or drive) in about half a mile from the end of the paved road, cut down to the beach and walk to the lighthouse from there. You can walk back by the road, which is quicker.

Lots of driftwood washes up on this windswept beach. Some of the pieces are identifiable as sun-bleached timbers from shipwrecks – hulls, side planks, perhaps even a gangplank if your imagination is active. There are also fishing nets, ropes and the occasional glass float.

It's likely to be just you and the driftwood, although about 20 minutes up the beach there's a cluster of small wooden beach shacks called Federation Camp, which is sometimes used by Filipino fishers. The lighthouse is 10 minutes farther.

The beach sand is a bit soft and sinks underfoot, making this a good walk for your calves. The sand gradually changes colors as you walk along. In some places it's a colorful, chunky mixture of rounded shells and bits of rock that look like some sort of beach confetti.

A low rock shelf lines much of the shore and the shallow, murky waters are not good for swimming or snorkeling.

Up on the slopes some of the beach pohuehue (morning glory) is entwined with an airplant that looks something like yellow-orange fishing line. This is Lanai's official flower, a leafless parasitic vine called kaunaoa.

Petroglyphs From the lighthouse foundations, markings lead directly inland for about five minutes to some small petroglyphs. The simple figures are etched on large boulders on the right side of the path, down the slope past the 'Do Not Deface' sign.

The rocky path is through groundcover of flowering golden ilima and pink and yellow lantana. The former is native, while the latter was introduced to Hawaii just 40 years ago and has escaped from cultivation to become a major pest throughout the islands.

Keep your eyes open for animals – sightings of mouflon sheep on the inland hills are not uncommon. The males have curled-back horns and the more dominant ones travel with a harem of females.

Up the Beach It's about 15 minutes farther up the beach to a rusting WWII Liberty ship that washed up on the reef. You can see the shipwreck clearly from the lighthouse.

LANAI

This is the point where most people turn around and head back, but it's possible to walk another six miles down to **Awalua**, which long ago was the location of a north shore landing. There's another shipwreck at Awalua but not much else. The beach is generally windy and the hike is hot and dry, although the farther down the beach you go, the prettier it gets.

Keomuku Beach

Keomuku Beach is the stretch of shore that runs from Kahokunui, at the end of Hwy 44, south to Kahalepalaoa Landing.

The dirt road is likely to be either dusty or muddy, with deep ruts, though if you're lucky enough to catch it after it's been graded, it's not so bad. Still, it's a 4WD road. When the tide is low, locals do much of the drive down on the beach sand rather than bump along on the road. This uninhabited coast is not particularly attractive and there's not much to see, other than a few marginal historical sites, scattered groves of coconuts and lots and lots of kiawe.

Real diehards can go the full 12 miles down to **Naha**, at the end of the road. It may take as long as two hours one way, depending on road conditions.

Less than a mile down the road is **Maunalei**. An ancient heiau that once sat there was taken apart by Frederick Hayselden, who used its stones to build a cattle fence. He later lost his shirt in the ill-fated Maunalei Sugar Company. Islanders believed the temple desecration was what caused the wells to turn salty and kill off the sugar cane Hayselden had planted.

Keomuku, 5¾ miles south of Hwy 44, was the center of the short-lived sugar cane plantation. There's little left to see other than the reconstructed Ka Lanakila O Ka Malamalama Church, originally built in 1903 after Maunalei Sugar collapsed. The ruins of a couple of fishponds are along the coast, but not easily visible.

Another heiau at **Kahea**, 1½ miles south of Keomuku, was also dismantled by Maunalei Sugar Company, this time to build a railroad to transport the sugar to Kahalepalaoa Landing. Kahea, meaning 'red stains', was a luakini heiau where human sacrifices were made.

Kahalepalaoa Landing, just south of Kahea, has the best beach on this end of the island and is used by Club Lanai, which operates day outings from Maui. The road onward to Naha really doesn't offer much more scenery for the effort, but should you want to continue, it's about four miles farther. Naha is occasionally used by local fishers but is not a good place for swimming.

MANELE BAY & HULOPOE BAY

Lanai's best beach, Hulopoe, is reached by a 20-minute drive down Manele Rd, a paved road that starts just south of town. The beach is 7½ miles south of the intersection of Manele Rd and Kaumalapau Hwy.

About 1½ miles down Manele Rd, an unusually wide dirt road comes in diagonally to the left. This is Hoike Rd, which leads to the Munro Trail and the Luahiwa Petroglyphs.

After four miles Manele Rd veers to the left and a mile farther there's a small pull-off with a pretty coastal view of both Manele Bay to the left and Hulopoe Bay to the right. The island beyond is Kahoolawe.

Manele Boat Harbor

Manele Harbor is a scenic, crescent-shaped natural harbor backed by sheer cliffs. Lanai folks like to fish from the stone breakwater that sticks out into the mouth of the bay.

Manele is a very protected harbor and a popular sailboat anchorage. Lanai is one of the easier islands to sail to from Honolulu (although 'easy' is a relative term – the waters can be quite rough).

In the early 20th century, cattle were herded down to Manele Bay for shipment to Honolulu. The remains of a cattle chute, which was used to load them directly onto the ships, can be seen by walking around the point to the right at the end of the parking lot.

Stone ruins from a Hawaiian fishing village and concrete slabs from the days of cattle ranching are up on the hill above the parking lot. The ruins are now largely overgrown with kiawe and ilima.

Inside Manele Bay, coral is abundant near the cliffsides, where the bottom quickly slopes off to about 40 feet. Beyond the western edge of the bay, near Puu Pehe Rock, is First Cathedrals, a popular dive site. Off the parking lot are restrooms, showers, drinking water, picnic tables and a little harbormaster's office. If you arrive by boat, it's a 10-minute walk from Manele Bay to Hulopoe Beach.

Hulopoe Beach

Hulopoe Beach is a gently curving white-sand beach. It's long and broad and protected by a rocky point to the south. On the north side of the bay, the Manele Bay Hotel sits on a low seaside terrace.

Even with the hotel, this is a pretty quiet beach. Generally, the most action occurs when the boats from Maui pull in with snorkelers.

Some of Lanai's best snorkeling is found on the left side of the bay, where there are lots of colorful coral and reef fish.

Also on that side, just beyond the sandy beach, there's a low lava shelf with tide pools worth exploring. One area has been blasted out, making a protected pool for children. Cement steps lead down to the pool from the rocks. It looks as if every kid on Lanai rushed down to scrawl their name in the cement when it was poured in August 1951.

Hulopoe Beach has a landscaped park with solar-heated showers, restrooms, picnic tables, pay phones, drinking water and campsites.

Both Manele and Hulopoe bays are part of a marine life conservation district in which the removal of coral and rocks is prohibited and many fishing activities are restricted. Water activities can be dangerous during kona storms, when strong currents and swells prevail.

Puu Pehe Cove

From Hulopoe Beach, a short path leads south to a point with interesting coastal formations. The peninsula of land separating Hulopoe and Manele bays is a volcanic cone that's sharply eroded on its southerly

Puu Pehe

According to local lore, an island girl named Puupehe was so beautiful that her lover decided to make their home in a secluded coastal cave, lest any other young men in the village set eyes on her. One day the lover was up in the mountains fetching water when a kona storm suddenly blew in. He rushed down the mountain, but by the time he arrived the waves had swept into the cave, drowning Puupehe.

The islanders brought a tapa cloth and prepared to bury the girl in the village. But Puupehe's lover slipped off with her body at night and carried it out to the top of a nearshore islet, where he erected a tomb and laid her to rest within. Immersed in grief, he then jumped into the surging waters below and was dashed back onto the rock. The islanders recovered his body, wrapped it in the tapa they had prepared for Puupehe and buried him in the village. ■

seaward edge. Here on the point, the lava has rich rust-red colors with swirls of gray and black in fascinating patterns. The texture is bubbly and brittle – so brittle that huge chunks of the point have broken off and fallen onto the coastal shelf below. There's a small sea arch below the point.

Puu Pehe is the name of the cove to the left of the point as well as the sea stack just offshore. This islet, also called Sweetheart's Rock, has a tomb-like formation on top that figures into Hawaiian legend.

Places to Stay

Hotels The 250-room *Manele Bay Hotel* (☎ 565-7700, 800-321-4666; fax 565-2483), Box 774, Lanai City, HI 96763, overlooking Hulopoe Beach, has spacious lobbies that are partially open-air and adorned with artwork and antiques. There's a reading room with a dark-wood decor and leather-bound books, lots of Italian marble floors and a central lounge with sofas, elegant chairs and a grand piano. Rooms are quite pleasant, all with four-poster beds, lanais and marble baths. Rates are $250 for

LANAI

a room without a view, $525 for an ocean-front room and from $775 for suites.

Camping Surprisingly, even with the hotel up and running, camping is still allowed at six campsites just a minute's walk from Hulopoe Beach.

As long as the Lanai Company (☎ 565-3982), Box 310, Lanai City, HI 96763, continues issuing permits, here's how it goes: There's a $5 registration fee per campsite plus $5 per person per night. The maximum length of stay is seven consecutive days. Reservations can be made by mail or phone. Fees must be paid within five days of confirmation of the reservation.

Sometimes you can get permits without advance reservations if the campground's not full. Permits are issued at the Lanai Company, in the Castle & Cooke offices opposite the post office.

Places to Eat

The Manele Bay Hotel serves breakfast in its *Hulopoe Court* from 7 to 11 am. The setting has a bit of everything: high ceilings with showy chandeliers, ornate Chinese vases and a view of the ocean. There's a full breakfast buffet for $18 or a continental version with fruit, pastries and cereals for $12. You can also order à la carte, but expect to run up a similar tab. The restaurant also serves dinner from 6 to 9:30 pm, with dishes such as grilled eggplant salad and tandoori chicken priced from $15 to $25.

The *poolside grill*, open from 11 am to 5 pm, is the main lunch venue, with light eats such as mahimahi sandwiches with fries and a variety of salads for around $15.

The *Club House* at the hotel golf course has sandwiches, salads, pastas and fish & chips for $10 to $20. It's open from 11 am to 5 pm year round as well as from 6 to 9 pm in the busier winter season.

The hotel's open-air *Ihilani Dining Room*, which is elegant and quite pleasant, serves fine French food at dinner. Appetizers include oysters mignonette and escargot priced from $15 to $25, and entrees such as fresh fish, Maine lobster or local venison go for around $45.

KAUNOLU

Kaunolu was the site of an early Hawaiian fishing village that was abandoned in the mid-19th century. It has the greatest concentration of ruins on Lanai.

Kaunolu was a vacation spot for Kamehameha the Great, who went there to fish the prolific waters of Kaunolu Bay. Kamehameha also held tournaments and sporting events at Kaunolu and had a house up on the bluff on the eastern side of the bay.

Kaunolu Gulch separates the two sides of the bay. Most of the house sites sit on the eastern side. The now-overgrown Halulu Heiau, on the western side, once dominated the whole scene. The heiau included a puuhonua, where renegade kapu breakers could be absolved from their death sentences. There are a number of petroglyphs, some on the southern side of the heiau.

Beyond the heiau ruins, the Palikaholo sea cliffs rise more than 1000 feet. Northwest of the heiau there's a high natural stone wall along the perimeter of the cliff. Look for a break in the wall at the cliff's edge where there's a sheer 90-foot drop. This is Kahekili's Jump, named after a Lanaian chief. There's a ledge below it that makes diving into the ocean here a bit death-defying. Apparently, Kamehameha used to amuse himself by making upstart warriors leap from this cliff.

Dr Kenneth Emory of Oahu's Bishop Museum did an extensive survey of Kaunolu in 1921 and counted 86 house sites, 35 stone shelters and a number of grave markings, pens and gardens. These days most of the sites are simply too overgrown with kiawe even to recognize.

There are a couple of ways to get to Kaunolu. The easiest is to go south from Lanai City down Manele Rd. At three quarters of a mile past the nine-mile marker, there's a sharp bend in the road. Rather than follow Manele Rd as it bears left to Manele Bay, go straight ahead onto an access road that begins as pavement but soon turns to dirt. Just before reaching a brightly painted water pipe, a sign marks the turn-off to Kaunolu; turn left onto this dirt road, which leads south in the direction of the lighthouse. If the road hasn't been washed out by rain recently, you may be able to make it most of the way down with a 4WD vehicle, but odds are you'll have to walk the last mile or so.

KAUMALAPAU HARBOR

Kaumalapau, Lanai's commercial harbor, is 6½ miles west of town, at the end of the airport road. The harbor was built for shipping pineapples; now that the industry is gone, it's a rather sleepy place. These days, the main traffic here is the cargo boat that comes in once a week from Oahu.

You can often find people fishing from the boulder jetty for awa (milkfish), a good-tasting fish that's a common catch in the bay. Scuba divers sometimes use the bay as well, as the deep waters at Kaumalapau are extremely clear.

As along most of the southwest coast, Kaumalapau has sheer coastal cliffs.

NORTHWEST LANAI

To get to sights in the northwest part of Lanai, go north up Fraser Ave in Lanai City and, shortly after it turns to dirt, turn right onto Polihua Rd. This dirt road passes along former pineapple fields and the Nature Conservancy's Kanepuu Preserve before reaching the Garden of the Gods after about 5½ miles.

The section leading up to Garden of the Gods is a fairly good, albeit dusty, road that usually takes about 20 minutes from town. To get from Garden of the Gods to Polihua Beach is another matter, however, as the road down to the beach is very rocky and narrow and is suitable only for a 4WD. Depending on when it was last graded, it could take anywhere from 20 minutes to an hour.

Kanepuu Preserve

The Nature Conservancy manages 462 acres at Kanepuu, a diverse native dryland forest that is the last of its kind in all of Hawaii. Native plants include iliahi (Hawaiian sandalwood), olopua (an olive), lama (in the persimmon family), a morning glory, a native gardenia and fragrant vines of maile and huehue.

Native dryland forests once covered 80% of Lanai and were also common on the leeward slopes of other Hawaiian islands, but feral goats and cattle did them in. Credit for saving this one goes to naturalist and former ranch manager George Munro, who realized the need to protect this ecosystem and fenced hoofed animals out in the 1920s.

The Kanepuu Preserve is about six miles northwest of Lanai City. Castle & Cooke retains title to the land, but has given the Nature Conservancy an easement to the forest in perpetuity.

Garden of the Gods

There's no garden at Garden of the Gods, but rather a dry and barren landscape of strange wind-sculpted rocks in rich shades of ocher, pink and brown. The colors change with the light and are much nicer and gentler in the early morning and late afternoon.

How godly they appear depends on what you're looking for. Some people just see rocks, while others find the formations hauntingly beautiful.

Polihua Beach

Polihua Beach, on the northwestern tip of the island, is a broad, 1½-mile-long white-sand beach. It has a great view of the entire south coast of Molokai. Although it's a gorgeous beach, strong winds kicking up the sand often make it uncomfortable, and water conditions are treacherous all year round.

Polihua means 'eggs in the bosom' and refers to the green sea turtles that used to nest here en masse. After a long hiatus, the now-endangered turtles are beginning to return.

MUNRO TRAIL

The Munro Trail is an 8½-mile dirt road that can either be hiked or driven in a 4WD vehicle. On foot, it's a full day's hike. If you're driving and the road is in good condition, it takes about 1½ hours. However, be aware that the road can get very muddy (particularly in winter and after heavy rainstorms) and jeeps occasionally get stuck.

Drivers also need to watch out for sheer drops; the road can be quite dangerous when wet.

To start, head north on Hwy 44, the road to Shipwreck Beach. About a mile past the Lodge at Koele turn right onto the paved road that leads to a cemetery half a mile down.

The Munro Trail starts at the left of the cemetery. It goes through sections planted with eucalyptus and up along the ridge, where it's fern-draped and studded with Norfolk pines.

The trail is named after naturalist George Munro, who planted the trees along this trail and elsewhere around the island to provide a watershed. He selected species that draw moisture from the clouds and fog, both of which are fairly common in the high country (more so in the afternoon than in the morning).

Before the Munro Trail was upgraded to a dirt road, it was a footpath. It's along this trail that islanders tried to hide from Kamehameha when he went on a rampage in 1778. Hookio Battleground, where Lanaians made their last stand, is just above Hookio Gulch, about 2½ miles from the start of the trail.

The Munro Trail looks down upon a series of deep ravines that cut across the eastern flank of the mountain and it passes Lanaihale, which at 3370 feet is the highest point on Lanai. On a clear day you can see all the inhabited Hawaiian islands except Kauai and Niihau from various points along the route. The trail ends on Hoike Rd, which is a little more than 1½ miles south of the intersection of Manele Rd and Kaumalapau Hwy.

Luahiwa Petroglyphs

The Luahiwa Petroglyphs are carved onto about three dozen boulders spread over three acres. This is Lanai's highest concentration of petroglyphs and includes a wide variety of forms thought to have been carved during different eras. There are lots of dogs in various poses, linear and triangular human figures and a canoe or two. Unfortunately, many of the petroglyphs are quite weathered.

It's a little challenging to get there, but basically you turn onto Hoike Rd and then head for the water tower on the ridge. The boulders are near the head of a ravine north of the road, below the trees.

Kahoolawe

Kahoolawe, the uninhabited island seven miles off the southwest coast of Maui, was used exclusively by the US military as a bombing target from WWII until 1990. Although the bombing has stopped, the island remains off limits due to the stray ammunition that peppers Kahoolawe and its surrounding waters.

The channel between Lanai and Kahoolawe, as well as the westernmost point of Kahoolawe itself, is named Kealaikahiki, meaning 'pathway to Tahiti'. When ancient voyagers made the journey between Hawaii and Tahiti, they lined up their canoes at this departure point.

More than 500 archaeological sites have been identified on Kahoolawe. They include several heiaus and many koa shrines and kuula stones dedicated to the gods of fishermen. Puu Moiwi, in the center of the island, has one of Hawaii's largest ancient adze quarries.

In 1981, Kahoolawe was added to the National Register of Historic Places as a significant archaeological area. For nearly a decade the island had the distinction of being the only place of such merit that was being used for target practice.

Kahoolawe has become a symbol of the separation of Hawaiians from their land and a focal point in the growing Hawaiian rights movement.

HISTORY
Prisoners & Opium

Since ancient times Kahoolawe has been under the rule of Maui.

From 1830 to 1848, Kaulana Bay, on the island's northern side, was used as a place of exile for Mauian men accused of petty crimes. (Female outcasts were sent to Kaena Point on the northwestern tip of Lanai.)

Kahoolawe proved to be less of a 'prison isle' than intended. In 1841, some of the prisoners managed to swim to the Makena area of Maui, where they stole food and canoes and paddled back with their booty. Later raids included one to Lanai, where they picked up female prisoners and brought them back to Kahoolawe.

Kahoolawe's secluded southwestern side was used for decades by smugglers importing illegal Chinese opium. To avoid detection, they'd unload their caches at Hanakanaea Bay (commonly known as Smugglers Bay) on arrival from China and come back later in small fishing boats to pick them up.

In more recent times, Smugglers Bay served as the site of a US military base camp.

Overgrazing

Kahoolawe was once a green and forested island. It is now largely barren, and pili grass and kiawe trees are the main forces in keeping the dry red soil from blowing away completely.

The first attempt at ranching was in 1858 by RC Wyllie, the Scotsman who developed a sugar plantation at Princeville on Kauai. Wyllie leased the entire island of Kahoolawe from the Territory of Hawaii, but the sheep he brought over were diseased and the venture failed. Those sheep that survived were left to roam freely, causing serious damage to native plants.

Over the years, the territory granted a series of leases to other ranchers. Cattle were first brought over around 1880, and sheep were also tried again. Land mismanagement was the order of the day.

By the early 1900s, feral goats, pigs and sheep had dug up, rooted out and chewed off so much of Kahoolawe's vegetation that the island was largely a dust bowl.

Kahoolawe Ranch

The most successful ranching operation on Kahoolawe was run from 1918 to 1941 by Angus MacPhee, the former manager of Maui's Ulupalakua Ranch.

When MacPhee got his lease from the

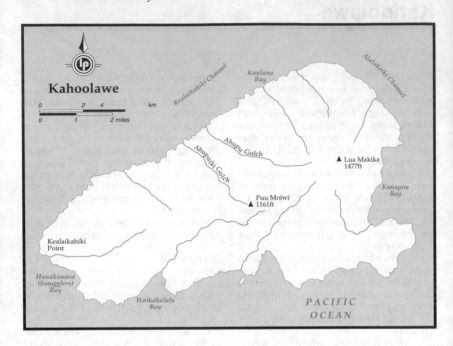

territorial government in 1918, Kahoolawe was overrun with goats and looked like a wasteland. MacPhee rounded up 13,000 goats, which he sold on Maui, and built a fence across the width of the entire island to keep the remaining goats at one end. He then brought in large redwood tanks to store water and planted grasses and groundcover.

Once the land was again green, MacPhee created Kahoolawe Ranch Company in partnership with Harry Baldwin, a sugar plantation owner. Cattle were brought over and raised for the Honolulu market. Ranching Kahoolawe was not easy, but MacPhee, unlike his predecessors, was able to make it profitable.

Inez MacPhee Ashdown, Angus' daughter, has written her story in *Kahoolawe* (Topgallant Publishing Co, Honolulu, 1979). The book includes legends of Kahoolawe, as told to her by native Hawaiians, as well as the ranch's history.

A Bombing Target

In 1939, Kahoolawe Ranch subleased part of the island to the US Army for bombing practice and moved their cattle and ranch hands over to Maui.

After the attack on Pearl Harbor in 1941, the military took all of Kahoolawe and began bombing the entire island. Ranch buildings and water cisterns were used as targets and reduced to rubble.

Of all the fighting that took place during WWII, Kahoolawe was the most bombed island in the Pacific – even though the 'enemy' never fired upon it.

After the war, civilians were forbidden to return to Kahoolawe. MacPhee, incidentally, was never compensated for his losses.

In 1953, a presidential decree gave the Navy official jurisdiction over the island. It stated that when Kahoolawe was no longer 'needed' that the live ordnance would be cleaned up and the island returned to the Territory of Hawaii.

Kahoolawe Movement

In the mid-1960s, Hawaii politicians began petitioning the federal government to return Kahoolawe to the state. In 1976, a small group of Hawaiians set out in boats and occupied the island in an attempt to attract greater attention to the bombings. There were a series of occupations, some lasting more than a month.

During one of the 1977 crossings, group members George Helm and Kimo Mitchell mysteriously disappeared in the waters off Kahoolawe. Helm had been an inspirational Hawaiian-rights activist, and with his death the Protect Kahoolawe Ohana movement sprang up. Helm's vision of turning Kahoolawe into a sanctuary of Hawaiian culture and identity became widespread among islanders.

In June 1977, two group members, Walter Ritte Jr and Richard Sawyer, were tried for trespassing on Kahoolawe and sentenced to six months in jail.

In a letter to President Jimmy Carter asking that the two men be pardoned, Daniel Inouye, US Senator from Hawaii, wrote:

... it was a form of protest against, what was to them, the unconscionable desecration of the land by the Navy's continued bombing of Kahoolawe. *Aloha aina*, love for the land, is an important part of the Native Hawaiian religion and culture . . . . Kahoolawe has become a symbol of the resurgence of the Hawaiian people, a movement formulating for many Hawaiians a renewed respect for their culture and their history.

Kahoolawe Today

In 1980, in a court-sanctioned consent decree, the Navy reached an agreement with Protect Kahoolawe Ohana that allowed the Ohana regular access to the island. It also required the Navy to preserve archaeological sites, eradicate goats and control soil erosion.

Although the bombing continued, the decree restricted the Navy from using live ordnance on part of the island and from bombing historic sites. In 1982 the Ohana began to go to Kahoolawe to celebrate makahiki, the annual observance that honors Lono, god of agriculture and peace.

Maui County, of which Kahoolawe is a part, adopted a planning document in 1982 calling for a 20-year phase-out of the military and the development of Kahoolawe as a historical and cultural site, with Protect Kahoolawe Ohana as the stewards of the land. The Navy, however, refused to recognize the document.

In what many Hawaiians saw as the ultimate insult to their heritage, the US military offered Kahoolawe as a bombing target to foreign nations during biennial Pacific Rim exercises. In an unanticipated backlash for the military, the exercises brought recognition of what was happening in Kahoolawe into a broader arena. An international movement against the bombing, led by environmentalist and union groups in New Zealand, Australia, Japan and the UK, resulted in those countries withdrawing from the Kahoolawe exercises. With only the US and Canada willing to participate, the exercises finally stopped.

In the late 1980s, Hawaii's first Hawaiian governor, John Waihee, and other state politicians became more outspoken in their demands that Kahoolawe be returned to Hawaiians. In October 1990, as Hawaii's two US senators, Daniel Inouye and Daniel Akaka, were preparing a congressional bill to stop the bombing, President Bush issued an order to halt military activities. The senators' bill, which became law the next month, requires the island to be cleared of munitions and restored to a pre-war condition. It also established a federally funded Kahoolawe Conveyance Commission to prepare recommendations on terms for the conveyance of the island to the state of Hawaii.

On May 7, 1994, in a ceremony marked by Hawaiian rituals, chants and prayers, the US Navy signed over control of Kahoolawe to Governor Waihee and the state of Hawaii. Following the signing, 100 native Hawaiians dressed in traditional malo and tapa cloaks went to Kahoolawe to perform sunrise rituals honoring the return of the island. Among the ceremonies was the placing of leis at memorial plaques for Helms and Mitchell.

One enormous obstacle that remains is the cleaning up of live ordnance from

KAHOOLAWE

Kahoolawe. The federal government has established a $400 million fund for that purpose, but the cleanup now underway will take the better part of a decade to complete. In the meantime, a new state entity, the Kahoolawe Island Reserve Commission, has taken over administration of the island and is in the process of developing a new master plan. Proposals for the island's future range from establishing a marine sanctuary to making the island the center for a new Hawaiian nation.

GEOGRAPHY

Kahoolawe is 11 miles long and six miles wide, with a land area of 45 sq miles. With the help of a vivid imagination, its shape can be seen as a crouching lion facing eastward.

A ridge runs diagonally across the island, and the terrain is gently sloping. The highest point is the 1477-foot Lua Makika, at the site of the caldera that formed the island. It's a dry, arid island with only 10 to 20 inches of rainfall annually.

Because of its windblown red dust, Kahoolawe often appears to have a pink tinge when viewed from Maui, particularly in the afternoons, when the breezes pick up. At night, it's pitch black, devoid of any light.

GETTING THERE & AWAY

There's no public access to the island unless you're a member or guest of the Ohana.

Two weekends per month, offshore waters 20 fathoms or deeper are open to local fishers, but at all other times boats are prohibited from going within two miles of Kahoolawe. As the island and its near-shore waters are still dangerous, due to the unexploded ordnance, shoreline access is expected to remain off limits to the public until the final stages of the cleanup, which is currently scheduled to be completed in 2003.

Kauai

If you're looking for lush scenery, Kauai is a great choice – the island is so richly green that it's nicknamed 'The Garden Island'.

 ' Kauai is the oldest of the main Hawaiian land masses and arose from the sea as a high, smooth island. Over time, heavy rains have eroded deep valleys, while pounding waves and falling sea levels have cut steep cliffs.

Kauai's central volcanic peak, Mt Waialeale, is the wettest place on earth and feeds seven rivers, including Hawaii's only navigable one. A deep north-south rift slices the western end of the island, creating the impressive Waimea Canyon.

The North Shore is lushly mountainous, with waterfalls, beautiful beaches and stream-fed valleys. The northwest coast is lined by the steeply fluted Na Pali sea cliffs, Hawaii's foremost hiking destination.

Movie makers looking for scenery bordering on fantasy have often found it in Kauai. *South Pacific* and *Raiders of the Lost Ark* were both filmed on Kauai's North Shore. The remote Honopu Valley on the Na Pali Coast was the jungle home of King Kong, while the Hanapepe and Limahuli valleys served as locations for Steven Spielberg's *Jurassic Park*.

Kauai is the least developed of the four major islands, and most of its interior is mountainous forest reserve. The Alakai Swamp is poised on a high, cliff-bound plateau, about 1000 feet below Mt Waialeale. There, clouds and mist that rarely lift support a unique ecosystem where trees grow knee high.

Kauai is dry and sunny on its southern and western sides, with long stretches of white sand beaches. Sugar cane fields cover large portions of the island just inland from the coast in a semicircle from the northeast to the west.

Kauai's main attraction is its stunning natural beauty. There are hiking trails into some incredible places.

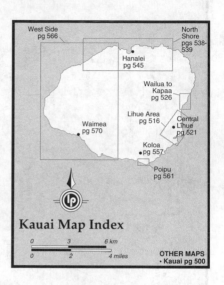

Kauai Map Index

HISTORY

Kauai was probably settled between 500 and 700 AD by Polynesians who migrated from the Marquesas Islands. Archaeological finds, including identical ring-shaped poi-pounding stones found both in Kauai and the Marquesas, support the connection.

While in Hawaiian lore there are no direct references to the Marquesan culture, Kauai is often referred to as the home of a race of little people called menehunes. Legend after legend tells of happy Disney-like elves coming down from the mountains to produce great engineering works in stone.

It seems likely that when the first wave of Tahitians arrived in about 1000 AD they conquered and subjugated the Marquesans, forcing them into slavery to build the temples, irrigation ditches and fishponds now attributed to the menehunes.

The Tahitian term for 'outcast' is *manahune*. And the diminutive social status the

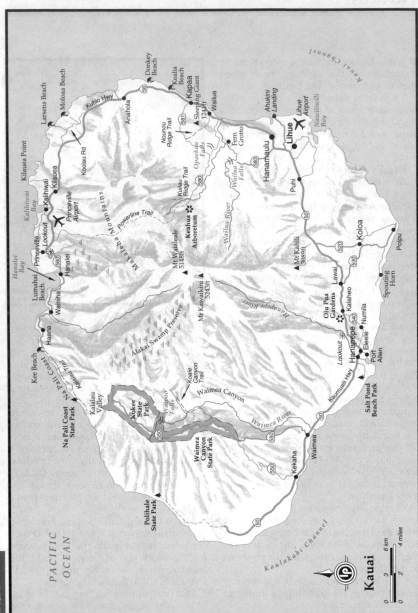

PACIFIC
OCEAN

Kauai

KAUAI

Hurricane Iniki

On September 11, 1992, Hurricane Iniki, the most powerful storm to strike Hawaii in a century, made a direct hit on Kauai. Packing gusts of 165 miles per hour, Iniki felled thousands of trees and caused serious damage to an estimated 50% of the buildings on Kauai.

While some of the structures destroyed by Iniki were aging wooden buildings, others were wings of beachfront resorts that were battered by 30-foot waves. Most homes throughout the island had windows blown out, many lost roofs and others were simply laid to waste – in all, 5000 homes were damaged and 1300 were totally destroyed. A combination of powerful gusts and abrupt changes in atmospheric pressure caused some buildings to literally shatter, as if hit by a bomb blast. Although nearly 100 people were injured by flying debris, quite amazingly only two people were killed.

Even though Kauai is small and lightly populated, the total value of the damage to the island was $1.6 billion, making Iniki the third costliest disaster in US history. Particularly hard hit were Kauai's two main resort areas – Poipu and Princeville – and many of the vacation rentals that did survive had to be turned into temporary housing for Kauai's 8000 newly homeless residents. Tourism, brought to a standstill after the storm, made a slow recovery. Most hotels took at least a year to get back on line, although a few of them, still sorting through red tape, have yet to even begin repairs.

As for the natural environment, Kauai is again lushly green, and to the casual eye there's not much to indicate that the hurricane ever occurred. However, while many stripped trees have sprouted new leaves, extensive sections of the Hawaiian koa forest failed to recover. Opportunistic exotic plants – such as guava, blackberry and banana poka, a member of the passion fruit family – have spread through large tracts of what were predominantly native woodlands prior to Iniki.

It will take many years before the storm's impact on the island's endangered flora and fauna is fully understood, but the decline of native forest habitat has had detrimental effects. Four species of endangered or threatened native birds have not been spotted on Kauai since the hurricane. ■

Marquesans had in the eyes of their conquerors may have given rise to tales of a dwarf-size race.

The menehunes may have created the temples, but the Tahitian settlers created the legends. While the stonework remains, the true identity of Kauai's 'little people' is lost.

During the second wave of Tahitian migration, around the 12th century, a high chief named Moikeha arrived at Wailua with a fleet of double-hulled canoes. There, in the royal court, Moikeha was received by Kauai's aging *alii-nui* (high chief), Puna.

Puna gave his daughter to Moikeha in marriage, and upon Puna's death Moikeha became the alii-nui of Kauai. Moikeha introduced taro and sweet potatoes to Kauai and sent his son Kila back to Tahiti to fetch the *pahu hula*, a sharkskin drum essential for use in hula temples. This type of drum is still used in hula performances today.

Early Settlements

Kauai is the most isolated of the major islands, lying 72 miles from Oahu, its nearest neighbor. It was never conquered by another Hawaiian island, and its history is one of autonomy.

Kauai was settled most intensively along river valleys near the coast, such as Wailua, Waimea and Hanalei. Even valleys that were difficult to reach, like Kalalau and Nualolo on the Na Pali Coast, had sizable settlements. When winter seas prevented canoes from landing on the northern shore, trails down precipitous ridges and sennit-rope ladders provided access.

When Captain Cook landed on Kauai in 1778, he estimated the island had 50 villages with a total population of about 30,000. Missionaries in the 1820s estimated it to be closer to 10,000. Historians tend to side with the missionaries and discredit Cook's estimates, but considering the

Sandwich Islander wearing a gourd helmet
by John Webber

deadly diseases Cook's men left behind, it's possible both were correct.

Kaumualii
Kaumualii was the last chief to reign over an independent Kauai. Though he was a shrewd leader and Kauai's warriors were fierce, it was apparently the power of Kaumualii's kahunas that protected him from the advances of Kamehameha the Great.

In 1796, Kamehameha, who had conquered all the other islands, sailed with an armada of war canoes towards Kauai. A mysterious storm suddenly kicked up at sea, forcing him to turn back to Oahu, and he never reached Kauai's shores.

During the next few years, both Kamehameha and Kaumualii continued to prepare for war by gathering foreign weaponry and trying to ally foreign ships to their cause.

In 1804, Kamehameha was once again on the shores of Oahu ready to attack Kauai. However, on the eve of the invasion, an epidemic of what was probably cholera struck the island of Oahu, decimating his warriors and forcing yet another delay.

While Kamehameha's numerically superior forces had Kaumualii unnerved, Kaumualii's uncanny luck had a similar effect on Kamehameha. They reached an agreement in 1810 that recognized Kaumualii as the alii-nui of Kauai but ceded the island of Kauai to the Kingdom of Hawaii.

It was essentially a truce, and the plotting continued, with Kaumualii never fully accepting Kamehameha's suzerainty.

Russian Presence
In January 1815, a Russian ship loaded with seal skins was wrecked off Waimea, and Kaumualii confiscated the cargo. In November, the Russian-American Company sent their agent, Georg Anton Schaeffer, to retrieve it.

When Schaeffer arrived in Hawaii, he saw opportunity in the rift between Kaumualii and Kamehameha. In Kauai he exceeded his authority by entering into an agreement with Kaumualii in which he claimed the Russians would provide a ship and military assistance for the invasion of Oahu. In return Kaumualii offered the Russians half of Oahu plus all the sandalwood on Oahu and Kauai. In September 1816, Hawaiian laborers under Schaeffer's direction began to build forts in Waimea and Hanalei.

Later that year, when Russian naval explorer Otto von Kotzebue visited Hawaii, he informed Kamehameha that the Russian government did not endorse Schaeffer's alliance. Kamehameha, tired of all the scheming, ordered Kaumualii to kick the Russians out or face the consequences. In May 1817, Schaeffer was escorted to his ship and forced to leave Kauai.

The End of a Kingdom
When Kamehameha died in 1819 he was succeeded by his son Liholiho, who didn't trust Kaumualii's loyalties any more than his father had. In 1822, Liholiho set off for

KAUAI

Kauai in an 83-foot luxury schooner he had purchased from Western traders in exchange for sandalwood.

In Kauai, Liholiho tricked Kaumualii into going out for a cruise. He then kidnapped him and took him to Oahu, where Kaumualii was forced to marry Kamehameha's widow, Kaahumanu. In the grand scheme of royal design, this served to bring Kaumualii into the fold. When Kaumualii passed away in 1824, so too did the Kingdom of Kauai.

GEOGRAPHY

Shaped like a slightly compressed ball, Kauai is 33 miles wide and 25 miles from north to south. The highest elevation is Mt Kawaikini (5243 feet).

The fourth largest of the Hawaiian Islands, Kauai has an area of 558 sq miles.

Kauai arose as a single volcano, of which Mt Waialeale is the eastern rim. Moisture-laden trade winds blow into the deep North Shore valleys, which channel the winds up to the top of Mt Waialeale. Near its 5148-foot summit, cooler temperatures cause the moisture to condense, creating the heaviest rainfall on earth.

CLIMATE

Kauai's temperature varies more with location than season. Average coastal temperatures are 70°F in February and 77°F in August. At Kalalau Beach the temperature seldom drops below 60°F, while a few thousand feet above at Kokee State Park it dips into the 30s during winter nights. Kokee averages a crisp 55°F in February and 65°F in August.

Kauai's average annual rainfall is about 40 inches, but variances are extreme. Waimea in the south averages 21 inches, while Princeville in the north averages 85 inches. And Mt Waialeale in the swampy interior averages a whopping 486 inches, the world record.

Summer trade winds keep the humidity from becoming oppressive and bring in refreshing showers.

Winter is far less predictable. It's quite possible to have fairly continuous down-pours for a week at a time in midwinter. Then again, it might be all blue skies and calm seas. We've experienced both.

FLORA & FAUNA

Kauai has the largest number of native bird species in Hawaii. It is the only major island free of mongooses, which prey upon the eggs of ground-nesting birds.

The greatest concentration of Kauai's native forest bird species is found in the remote Alakai Swamp. Many of these species are endangered, some having fewer than 100 birds remaining.

The Kauai oo, the last of four remaining species of Hawaiian honeyeaters, was thought to be extinct until a nest with two chicks was discovered in Alakai Swamp in 1971. However, the call of the oo was last heard in 1987 – that of a single male.

Alakai Swamp is unique in that it has 10 times as many native birds as introduced. (Elsewhere in Hawaii introduced birds outnumber the natives many times over.) Not only is the swamp inhospitable to exotic bird species, but due to its high elevation it is one of the few places in Hawaii where mosquitoes, which transmit avian diseases, do not flourish.

The ao, or Newell's shearwater, is a threatened seabird that once nested on all the major Hawaiian islands; today it nests almost exclusively in the mountains of Kauai. The ao digs earthen burrows and

The ao, or Newell's shearwater

lays just one egg each year. It has a call that sounds like a braying donkey.

The ao, which flies only between dusk and dawn, often fails to see utility wires strung across its path to the sea. Despite some success of a forestry program that recovers some of the birds that crash-land, as many as a thousand birds still die in this way each year.

Of Hawaii's two native mammals, the hoary bat lives in Kokee State Park and the Hawaiian monk seal occasionally hauls out on Kauai beaches. You'll never know where the monk seals will show up, but they don't necessarily avoid people – we've seen them in such heavily touristed areas as Poipu Beach Park and the Coconut Plantation beach in Wailua. It's fine to observe these endangered creatures, but give them a wide berth so as not to disturb them.

Wild pigs, goats and black-tailed deer are nonnative mammals that are hunted.

The most common tree in Kauai forests is the ohia lehua. Koa, guava, kiawe and kukui trees are also plentiful.

GOVERNMENT
Kauai County is composed of the islands of Kauai and Niihau. There's an elected mayor with a four-year term and seven county council members with two-year terms.

ECONOMY
Since Hurricane Iniki hit in 1992, Kauai has experienced high unemployment; it currently hovers around 10% – almost twice the state average. The high rates are in part attributed to the general decline of tourism-related businesses in the lean years after Iniki and to the fact that some of the larger South Shore resort hotels, tied up with insurers over storm-related claims, have yet to reopen.

Kauai's labor force is 29,500. The service industry, including hotels, accounts for 42% of all workers. It is followed by wholesale and retail trade at 21%, government at 12% and agriculture at 4%.

The sugar industry still cultivates 30,000 acres on Kauai, but mechanization has streamlined its labor force to fewer than a thousand employees. Other sizable crops grown commercially are guava, taro and papaya. Attempts to diversify as sugar production declines have resulted in the introduction of new crops including seed corn, sunflower seed and coffee.

POPULATION & PEOPLE
The population of Kauai is 56,100. People of Hawaiian and part-Hawaiian ethnicity make up 25% of Kauai's population; those of mixed ethnicity other than part-Hawaiian comprise 19%, followed by Japanese (18%), Caucasian (18%) and Filipino (17%).

ORIENTATION
Kauai is roughly circular. A belt road runs three-quarters of the way around the island, from Haena in the north to Polihale in the west.

Most travelers arrive at the main airport in Lihue, the county capital, on the east coast. From Lihue the road runs north past Wailua and Kapaa, continuing up to Princeville resort and Hanalei before ending at the eastern edge of the Na Pali cliffs.

South of Lihue a side road leads down to the resort beaches at Poipu, while the main road continues west to Waimea. In Waimea, one road goes west to the arid Barking Sands region and another heads north along the Waimea Canyon into Kokee State Park.

Maps
The University of Hawaii map of Kauai is good for general sightseeing, as it shows beaches, heiaus and other sightseeing spots as well as major hotels. However, the best road map is *Hawaii, Maui & Kauai Map of the Neighbor Islands* produced by Compass Maps. Both are sold in bookshops and other stores around the island.

For hiking, you can get a quality fold-out topographical map of Kauai that shows the island's network of trails by stopping by the Division of Forestry & Wildlife office, 3060 Eiwa St, Room 306, Lihue, HI 96766. You can also request one by mail; enclose a 10-by-13-inch manila envelope with $1.01 postage.

INFORMATION
Tourist Offices
The Hawaii Visitors Bureau (☎ 245-3971) has its Kauai office at Lihue Plaza Building, 3016 Umi St, Suite 207, Lihue, HI 96766.

A toll-free hotline that can answer visitor-related questions about Kauai can be reached at ☎ 800-262-1400 from 6 am to 4 pm Monday to Friday.

To get a 'vacation planning kit', call ☎ 800-245-2824 (AH-KAUAI) toll-free from the USA – but note that it can take well over a month to arrive.

Money
The Bank of Hawaii has branches in Lihue, Kapaa, Princeville, Hanalei, Hanapepe and Waimea. The downtown Lihue branch has a 24-hour ATM. First Hawaiian Bank has ATMs in its Lihue, Kapaa, Koloa and Waimea branches, and ATMs can be found in many island grocery stores.

There are Western Union money transfer stations at Star Market in the Kukui Grove Center in Lihue and at Foodland markets in Waipouli and Princeville.

Newspapers & Magazines
Kauai's main newspaper, *The Garden Island* (☎ 245-3681), Box 231, Lihue, HI 96766, is published Monday to Saturday.

Free tourist magazines such as *This Week Kauai*, *Spotlight's Kauai Gold* and *Kauai Beach Press* can be picked up at the airport, hotels and major shopping centers. All are loaded with ads and activity information. Also worth picking up is the free *Menu Magazine*, which prints menus of many of Kauai's restaurants.

Kauai Magazine, a full-color quarterly magazine with articles about island life and attractions, is sold in bookstores for $4.

Radio & TV
Kauai has three AM and three FM radio stations. KUAI (720 AM) has a Hawaiian music program from 6 to 11 pm on Sundays and plays Hawaiian music sporadically at other times.

Commercial and public TV stations are relayed from Honolulu, and cable TV is

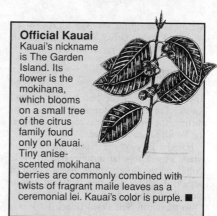

Official Kauai
Kauai's nickname is The Garden Island. Its flower is the mokihana, which blooms on a small tree of the citrus family found only on Kauai. Tiny anise-scented mokihana berries are commonly combined with twists of fragrant maile leaves as a ceremonial lei. Kauai's color is purple. ∎

available in most communities. KVIC, on TV cable channel 15 or 18, is a visitor information channel that shows continuous videos on sightseeing attractions.

Libraries
There are public libraries in Lihue, Hanapepe, Kapaa, Koloa and Waimea.

Bookstores
Borders bookstore in Lihue, behind the Kukui Grove Center, is Kauai's biggest bookstore and has comprehensive collections of novels, travel guides, Hawaiiana books, magazines and foreign newspapers.

The Waldenbooks chain, which has travel and Hawaiiana sections, has a store in Kauai Village shopping center in Waipouli. The Kauai Museum in Lihue and Tin Can Mailman in Kapaa also sell Hawaiiana books.

Weather
The National Weather Service provides recorded local weather information (☎ 245-6001) and marine forecasts (☎ 245-3564).

Emergency
Dial ☎ 911 for police, ambulance and fire emergencies.

The main hospital, Wilcox Memorial Hospital (☎ 245-1100) at 3420 Kuhio Hwy in Lihue, and the smaller Kauai Veterans

Memorial Hospital (☎ 338-9431), 4643 Waimea Canyon Drive, Waimea, both have 24-hour emergency room services.

ACTIVITIES
Beaches & Swimming
There are respectable beaches all around Kauai. For most water activities except surfing, the North Shore is tops in summer, the South Shore in winter.

Hanalei Bay on the North Shore is the island's most popular summer beach, while Poipu, on the South Shore, has a string of beautiful white-sand beaches that swimmers flock to in winter.

To the west, Salt Pond Beach Park is a popular family beach with protected swimming. Farther west, Kekaha, Barking Sands and Polihale have expansive white-sand beaches, though with open ocean and often treacherous water conditions.

The beaches around Lihue and Kapaa are generally not great for swimming. The safest one is Lydgate Beach in Wailua, a large family park with a boulder retaining wall that creates a protected year-round swimming pool.

Many of Kauai's beaches have rough water conditions at various times of the year and caution is warranted. Kauai has an average of nine drownings a year, about half of those on the North Shore between October and May.

There are year-round lifeguards at Salt Pond Beach Park, Poipu Beach Park, Lydgate Beach Park and Hanalei Bay.

Swimming Pools The county has swimming pools free to the public in Kapaa at Kapaa Beach Park (☎ 822-3842) and in Waimea (☎ 338-1271) next to the high school.

Surfing
Kauai has 330 named surfing sites. Generally, the best surfing is on the north coast in winter, the south in summer and the east during transitional swells.

Hanalei Bay is a very good spot for North Shore surfing, as well as boogie boarding and bodysurfing. Tunnels and Cannons are two other popular North Shore surf spots.

The area around the Sheraton at Poipu Beach is a top summer surf spot. Pakalas, near Makaweli, and Majors Bay at Barking Sands are two West Side favorites.

When the breaks are on the east coast, Kealia and the Coco Palms area can have good surf conditions.

For a recorded surf report, updated twice daily, call ☎ 246-4441, extension 1521.

Margo Oberg (☎ 742-8019), a former World Cup surfing champion, gives surfing lessons at Poipu Beach. The cost is $45 for a 1½-hour class.

Nukumoi Beach & Surf Company (☎ 742-8019) near Poipu Beach Park rents surfboards for $5 an hour, $20 a day or $60 a week.

Seasports Divers (☎ 742-9303) at Poipu Plaza in Poipu rents surfboards for $20 a day, $100 a week.

Kayak Kauai, in Hanalei (☎ 826-9844) and Kapaa (☎ 822-9179), rents surfboards for $20/70 a day/week and gives surfing lessons for $25 per hour.

Hanalei Surf Company (☎ 826-9000), in the Hanalei Center in Hanalei, rents soft surfboards for $12/50 a day/week, fiberglass boards for $15/65 and wet suits for $4/17.

Windsurf Kauai (☎ 828-6838) offers 1½-hour surfing lessons in winter at Hanalei Bay for $50, including all-day use of the board.

Snorkeling & Boogie Boarding
On the North Shore, Kee Beach has good snorkeling most of the year. Nearby Tunnels Beach has excellent snorkeling in summer, but be cautious of currents.

On the South Shore, the section of Poipu Beach in front of the Renaissance Waiohai Beach Hotel is one of Kauai's best snorkeling spots for beginners. Another good snorkeling spot in Poipu is at the Koloa Landing. On the West Side, you can try Salt Pond Beach Park in Hanapepe.

For boogie boarding, Brennecke's in Poipu is Kauai's hottest spot, while on the North Shore Hanalei Bay attracts the biggest crowds.

Snorkel sets and boogie boards can be rented at lots of places. Most of the beach huts at the resort hotels charge about $5 an hour, while in-town shops are much more reasonable.

Hanalei Surf Company (☎ 826-9000), in the Hanalei Center in Hanalei, rents snorkel sets (including corrective masks) or boogie boards for $5/20 a day/week, snorkel vests for $4/17.

Pedal & Paddle (☎ 826-9069) in the Ching Young Village in Hanalei rents snorkel sets or boogie boards for $5 a day, $20 a week. Corrective masks or boogie fins cost $2/5 a day/week more.

Kayak Kauai, in Hanalei (☎ 826-9844) and Kapaa (☎ 822-9179), rents snorkel sets and boogie boards for $6 to $8 the first day, $4 each additional day, or $20 a week.

Kauai Snorkel Rentals (☎ 823-8300) in the Coconut Marketplace in Wailua rents boogie boards for $5 a day and $20 a week, snorkel sets for $4/10 a day/week (with corrective masks $8/20).

Snorkel Bob's, at 4480 Ahukini Rd in Lihue (☎ 245-9433) and 3236 Poipu Rd in Koloa (☎ 742-2206), rents elementary snorkel sets from around $15 a week.

Seasports Divers (☎ 742-9303) at Poipu Plaza in Poipu rents snorkel gear and boogie boards for $4 to $8 a day, $20 to $25 a week.

Nukumoi Beach & Surf Company (☎ 742-8019), opposite Poipu Beach Park, rents snorkel sets and boogie boards for $5/15 a day/week.

Windsurfing

Beginner windsurfers usually start off at Anini Beach on the North Shore or at Nawiliwili Bay. Tunnels Beach in Haena, Mahaulepu Beach on the South Shore and Salt Pond Beach in Hanapepe attract more advanced windsurfers, although Anini is also a top-notch place for speed sailing when the wind is up.

At Anini Beach, Windsurf Kauai (☎ 828-6838), Box 323, Hanalei, HI 96714, and Anini Beach Windsurfing (☎ 826-9463), Box 1602, Hanalei, HI

96714, offer lessons for all levels year round. Both charge $65 for a three-hour lesson and rent boards for around $25 an hour, $60 a day.

True Blue (☎ 246-6333), at the Kauai Marriott on Nawiliwili Bay, Box 1722, Lihue, HI 96766, rents windsurfing equipment for $20 an hour and gives two-hour lessons for $85.

Diving

Popular summer diving spots on the North Shore include Kee Beach, Tunnels and Cannons, all shore dives in the Haena area. Cannons is particularly special; it's a wall dive, with crevices and lava tubes sheltering all sorts of marine life.

Koloa Landing and Poipu Beach Park in Poipu are easy beach dives. On those rare days when kona winds blow from the

Portuguese man-of-war

south, east-side diving is good and Ahukini Landing becomes a favored site. There are a number of offshore boat dives available as well, including dives around Niihau.

Dive shops sometimes give a free introductory scuba lesson at resort hotel pools; for information check at the hotel beach huts or call the dive shops.

Most dive shops offer two-tank dives with equipment for around $90 for shore dives, $100 for boat dives. Most also offer night dives for around $70, introductory dives for beginners for around $80 and certification courses for around $400. Dive Kauai and Fathom Five Divers are the island's five-star PADI operations.

Four recommendable dive operations are:

Dive Kauai, 976 Kuhio Hwy, Kapaa, HI 96746
    (☎ 822-0452)
Fathom Five Divers, 3450 Poipu Rd, Box 907,
    Koloa, HI 96756
    (☎ 742-6991, 800-972-3078)
Seasports Divers, at Poipu Plaza in Poipu, Box
    638, Koloa, HI 96756 (☎ 742-9303)
Sunrise Diving Adventures, near the Kauai
    Marriott at 3412 Rice St in Lihue
    (☎ 822-7333, 800-695-3483)

Snuba If you'd like to get underwater without loading down with dive equipment, you might consider snuba, in which you breathe through an air hose attached to a tank that floats on the water surface. Snuba Tours of Kauai (☎ 823-8912) offers snuba from Lawai Beach in Poipu for $55.

Kayaking
With all its waterways, Kauai has some of Hawaii's best kayaking.

One pleasant outing is up the Hanalei River, which goes through the wildlife refuge and meanders deep into Hanalei Valley. The riverfront is lushly beautiful, often canopied by overhanging trees. The journey is about nine miles roundtrip, but if it's been dry recently and the water level is low you might not be able to go up nearly that far. Another popular but quite busy route is up the Wailua River to the Fern Grotto, which is about seven miles roundtrip. Each outing takes three to four hours.

Other popular kayaking spots include the Hanapepe, Waimea and Huleia rivers.

Kayak prices include paddles, life vests and a car rack set-up. With the exception of Outfitters Kauai, which is closed on Sundays, all the following shops are open from at least 9 am to 5 pm daily.

Pedal & Paddle (☎ 826-9069) in the Ching Young Village in Hanalei rents one-person kayaks for $25 a day and two-person kayaks for $30 a half day, $45 a day.

Kayak Kauai, in Hanalei (☎ 826-9844) and Kapaa (☎ 822-9179), rents one-person kayaks for $35 a day, two-person kayaks for $60 a day. They also have three-hour guided tours of either the Hanalei River or Wailua River for $55. In the summer, full-day guided sea kayaking trips along the Na Pali Coast cost $130, and multiday Na Pali excursions that combine kayaking, hiking and camping cost $175 per day. In the winter there's a full-day ocean kayak tour on the South Shore for $105.

Kauai Water Ski & Surf Company (☎ 822-3574), opposite the Sizzler steak house on Kuhio Hwy in Wailua, delivers kayaks and sea cycles to the Wailua River, making it a practical choice for those without a rental car. The daily rate is $25/50 for single/double kayaks and $75 for sea cycles that can hold up to four people.

Outfitters Kauai (☎ 742-9667) in the Poipu Plaza in Poipu rents one-person kayaks for $30 a day, two-person kayaks for $45 a day. Guided kayak trips along the South Shore are held year round, last four hours and cost $65. They also offer full-day $130 guided tours along the Na Pali Coast in summer.

Island Adventure (☎ 245-9662) leads 2½-hour guided kayak trips up the Huleia River past the Menehune Fishpond and the Huleia National Wildlife Refuge for $42 for adults, $21 for children under 12.

Fishing
For deep-sea sport fishing, Gent-Lee Charters (☎ 245-7504), True Blue Charters (☎ 246-6333) and Sea Lure Fishing Charters (☎ 822-5963) take boats out of Nawiliwili Harbor. Anini Fishing Charters (☎ 828-1285)

and Robert McReynolds Fishing Charters (☎ 828-1379) are based at Anini Beach.

Kauai has largemouth and smallmouth bass in some of its private freshwater reservoirs. Two guide services providing freshwater charters are JJ's Big Bass Tours (☎ 332-9219) and Cast & Catch (☎ 332-9707).

There's rainbow trout in several streams, reservoirs and ditches in Kokee State Park. The season begins on the first Saturday in August and runs for 16 days, usually continuing on weekends and holidays through September. A valid state freshwater license is required (on Kauai, call ☎ 274-3344).

Hiking

Kauai has some excellent hikes. The best known is the spectacular 11-mile Kalalau Trail, which hugs the rugged Na Pali Coast.

Kokee State Park is also a hiker's paradise, with the largest concentration of trails on Kauai. Some of these trails lead to splendid views of the Na Pali Coast. Others include short nature walks, mountain stream trails and a muddy trek through the unique Alakai Swamp.

South of Kokee, backcountry trails lead down into the picturesque Waimea Canyon, forking into abandoned river valleys.

There are also some pleasant hiking opportunities in the Kapaa-Wailua area, including a trail that goes across the chest of the Sleeping Giant mountain. A couple of scenic ridgetop trails start at Keahua Arboretum in Wailua, including the Powerline Trail, which goes all the way to Princeville, and the shorter Kuilau Ridge Trail.

These hikes are all detailed in their respective sections.

Guided Hikes The Kauai division of the Sierra Club offers guided hikes, usually on weekends, ranging from strolls up the Sleeping Giant to overnighters in Waimea Canyon. Advance registration is required and a donation of $3 is suggested. For a hike schedule, send a self-addressed stamped envelope to the Sierra Club, Box 3412, Lihue, HI 96766. On Kauai, updated information can be obtained by calling Sierra Club member Micco Godinez at Kayak Kauai (☎ 826-9844).

Cycling

Mountain biking is becoming more popular on Kauai, and many of the island's forest reserve trails, including the 13-mile Powerline Trail, are accessible to mountain bikers. The Division of Forestry & Wildlife (☎ 274-3433), 3060 Eiwa St, Room 306, Lihue, HI 96766, has a new brochure that lists the trails open to mountain bikers and offers a few ecology and safety tips.

If you prefer to be with a group, the following places provide guided tours.

Kauai Coasters (☎ 639-2412) has a bike tour down the Waimea Canyon road, starting at sunrise from the Kalalau Lookout. The 12-mile ride takes about 1½ hours, mostly coasting downhill. The entire outing lasts about four hours, depending on your pick-up point, and costs $65 including a continental breakfast.

Outfitters Kauai (☎ 742-9667) at Poipu Plaza in Poipu also has bicycle tours in the Waimea/Kokee area for $65, bike/hike outings for $78.

Kayak Kauai has easy three-hour guided cycling tours leaving from their shops in Hanalei (☎ 826-9844) and Kapaa (☎ 822-9179). The cost is $45.

Kayak Kauai and Outfitters Kauai also rent bikes. Information on rentals is in the Getting Around section of this chapter.

Horseback Riding

CJM Country Stables (☎ 742-6096) has rides in the Mahaulepu Beach area. There's a three-hour breakfast ride for $71, a two-hour morning ride for $56 and a two-hour afternoon ride for $53. The stables are in Poipu, 1½ miles east of the Hyatt hotel.

Princeville Ranch Stables (☎ 826-6777), on Hwy 56 just past Princeville Airport, offers a $105 four-hour ride across ranch lands to a waterfall for a picnic and swim, a $95 three-hour ride to Anini Beach, where they break for a swim, and a $55 scenic two-hour ride on rangeland.

Both stables are closed on Sundays.

Tennis

There are county tennis courts, which are free and open to the public, at the following locations: Wailua Houselots Park and Wailua Homesteads Park, both in Wailua; Hardy St, near the convention hall in Lihue; opposite Kauai Community College in Puhi; Kapaa New Park in Kapaa; near the fire station in Koloa; Kalawai Park in Kalaheo; near Hanapepe Stadium in Hanapepe; and on the corner of Hwys 550 and 50 in Kekaha.

Some hotels have tennis courts available for their guests. The following places are open to the general public. All rent rackets for $5.

Kauai Lagoons Racquet Club (☎ 246-2414), adjacent to the Kauai Marriott in Lihue, has seven courts. The cost is $20 per court per hour, but there are also cheaper clinics and round-robins.

Kiahuna Tennis Club (☎ 742-9533) in Poipu has 10 courts and charges $10 per person per hour, although women pay just $1 on Tuesdays and there are $5 round-robins on Wednesdays.

Hyatt Regency Kauai (☎ 742-1234) in Poipu has four courts and charges $20 per court per hour.

Princeville Tennis Center (☎ 826-3620) in Princeville has six courts and charges $10 per person, which allows at least 1½ hours of play.

Hanalei Bay Resort (☎ 826-6522) in Princeville has eight courts and a full tennis program, charging $6 per person per hour.

Golf

Kauai has one municipal golf course, one local course and six resort courses. Major tournaments are hosted at Princeville's Prince course and at the Poipu Bay Resort. The Kauai Lagoons' Kiele course and Princeville's Makai course are also top rated.

Wailua Golf Course (☎ 241-6666), a county-owned 18-hole par-72 course, is a highly regarded public course and very heavily played. Reservations for two people or more are taken up to seven days in advance. Greens fees are $25 on weekdays and $35 on weekends. Cart rentals cost $14, club rentals $16.

Kukuiolono Golf Course (☎ 332-9151) in Kalaheo is a nine-hole par-36 course on an old estate with a grand hilltop view and an earthy appeal. Greens fees are just $7 and pull carts cost $2 more.

Princeville resort (☎ 800-826-1105) has two courses: the 18-hole par-72 Prince (☎ 826-5000) and the 27-hole par-72 Makai (☎ 826-3580). Greens and cart fees for the Makai course are $95 for guests staying in Princeville and $115 for nonguests. Fees for the Prince course are $120/150. In addition, there are handsome 'matinee discounts' at both courses if you wait until the afternoon to tee off. Club rentals cost $30.

The Kauai Lagoons Golf Club (☎ 241-6000, 800-634-6400), north of the Kauai Marriott in Lihue, has two 18-hole par-72 courses. The Kiele course costs $145, the Lagoons course $100. Clubs rent for $30.

The Poipu Bay Resort Golf Course (☎ 742-8711, 800-858-6300), an 18-hole par-72 course adjacent to the Hyatt Regency Kauai, charges Hyatt guests $85, nonguests $135. Prices drop to $75 after noon, $45 after 3 pm. Carts are included in the rate; club rentals start at $30.

Also in Poipu, the Kiahuna Golf Club (☎ 742-9595), an 18-hole par-70 course run by the Sports Shinko Group, charges $27 for nine holes, $53 for 18 holes ($35 after 1 pm on weekdays), including a cart. Clubs rent for $23.

Organized Tours

Minivan In Kauai, most sightseeing tour prices vary with the pick-up point.

Polynesian Adventure Tours (☎ 246-0122) has full-day minivan tours that include Wailua, Fern Grotto, Koloa, Poipu, Waimea, Waimea Canyon and the Kalalau Lookout for $58 with pick-up in Lihue or Wailua, $63 from Poipu, $70 from Princeville. Half-day North Shore tours that take in Hanalei, Haena and Kee Beach cost $33 from Lihue or Wailua, $28 from Princeville, $43 from Poipu. Half-day Waimea Canyon tours cost $39 from Lihue or Wailua, $43 from Poipu, $59 from Princeville. Full-day outings that squeeze in both the Waimea Canyon and the North Shore cost $60 from Lihue or Wailua, $65 from Princeville or Poipu.

TransHawaiian (☎ 245-5108) and Roberts Hawaii (☎ 245-9101) offer similar tours at comparable prices. In addition, Kauai Paradise Tours (☎ 246-3999; fax 245-2499) specializes in full-day sightseeing tours narrated in German for around $100.

Kauai Mountain Tours (☎ 245-7224, 800-452-1113) tours Waimea Canyon and Kokee State Park in 4WD vans that are capable of detouring from the beaten path to take in sights along forest dirt roads. Tours last six to seven hours and cost $84, lunch and hotel pick-up included.

All tour companies offer discounted prices for children.

Helicopter Many wilderness hikers resent the intrusion of helicopters into otherwise serene areas, and local environmentalists have successfully stopped their landings on Na Pali Coast beaches. However, these 'Kauai mosquitoes' that are an irritant to people on the ground no doubt offer some pretty spectacular views as they swoop into Waimea Canyon, run along the Na Pali Coast and seek out hidden waterfalls.

About a dozen helicopter companies offer flights around Kauai. The free tourist magazines advertise most of them and often have discount coupons.

The going rate is about $100 for a 45-minute 'circle-island tour' zooming by the main sights. There's usually some sort of 'ultimate splendor' tour that can add on 20 minutes and run up another $50 to $75. Most of the helicopter offices are either in Lihue near the corner of Hwy 56 and Ahukini Rd or at the side of the airport.

Cruises Like the other islands, Kauai has its fair share of catamaran picnic sails, sunset cruises and the like. It also has something the other islands don't: the spectacular Na Pali Coast.

Several boat companies have cruises down the Na Pali Coast. Most use small craft that can hug the coast and enter sea caves. The typical tour lasts four hours, goes down the coast as far as Nualolo, includes snorkeling when seas are calm and costs $75 to $85. If you just want a quick look at the coast without spending that much, a couple of companies also offer two-hour mini-tours for around $55.

The smoothest rides are generally in the summer. For most of the winter the seas are too rough for near-shore activities such as sea-cave exploration and on some days it's simply too rough for the boats to go out at all. A few companies then switch to the calmer southern shore for snorkeling cruises and whale-watching tours.

The following four companies are all within a few minutes' walk of one another near the intersection of Hwy 560 and Aku Rd in Hanalei, making it easy to shop and compare. The boats leave from the mouth of the Hanalei River, except for Captain Zodiac, which leaves from Tunnels Beach.

Captain Zodiac (☎ 826-9371, 800-422-7824) uses bouncy Zodiac rafts. Na Pali Adventures (☎ 826-6804) and Catamaran Kahanu (☎ 826-4596) use power catamarans, which, while not as adventurous as Zodiac rafts, offer a far smoother ride. Hanalei Sea Tours (☎ 826-7254, 800-733-7997) has both Zodiac rafts and power catamarans.

ACCOMMODATIONS

Three areas in Kauai – Poipu, Princeville, and the strip from Lihue to Kapaa – have almost all the island's hotels and condos.

For the most part, Kauai's beach hotels are a bit expensive. The cheapest begin around $85, although the majority are nearly double that. Condos have a similar price range but tend to be a better deal, particularly if you're traveling in a group.

The best accommodations deals on the island are found in the scattering of B&Bs that have sprung up in recent years. The Wailua area has the greatest concentration of B&Bs, with prices averaging about $50/60 for singles/doubles. Many are in fine homes that are very comfortable and scenically situated a few miles up the slope from the coast. Wailua also makes a good base for exploring, as it's midway between the North Shore and Kokee State Park.

The cheapest places to stay, other than campgrounds, are the dorm beds at the

Kauai International Hostel in Kapaa at $15 per person and the bunkhouses at the YMCA in Haena at $12 per person. From $25 to $40, there are basic cabinettes at Kahili Mountain Park near Koloa and rooms at spartan in-town hotels in Lihue.

Camping

Kauai has some fine camping spots. Some are drive-up beach parks, some are in dense forest and others are at the end of day-long hikes into remote valleys.

There are camping areas at three state parks, seven county parks and at forest reserve trailside camps in Waimea Canyon and the nearby Kokee area.

State Parks Camping is allowed at Kokee, Polihale and Na Pali Coast state parks. Permits are required and are free. They are issued from 8 am to 4 pm Monday to Friday from the Division of State Parks (☎ 274-3444), 3060 Eiwa St, Room 306, Lihue, HI 96766, and at state park offices on other islands.

Up to 10 people may be listed on each permit, but the person applying for the permit must show an ID (such as a driver's license or passport) for each person. Permits may be obtained by mail if a photocopy of each camper's ID (with the ID number and birth date clearly readable) is sent. If you don't have time to send for an official application form, this information can be written on a regular sheet of paper; be sure to specify the exact dates and which park(s) you want to stay at (in Na Pali Coast State Park, you'll have to specify which of the three campgrounds you'll be at on which nights).

Permits may be applied for as early as a year in advance. During the busy summer period of May to September, Na Pali Coast campsites are often booked out many months ahead, so apply for your permit as far in advance as possible. If you change your mind about camping once you get your permit, be sure to cancel, as otherwise you'll be tying up an empty space and preventing someone else from camping.

Camping is allowed for up to five consecutive nights at each state park within a 30-day period. For the Na Pali Coast, this means a maximum of five nights on the entire Kalalau Trail, with no two consecutive nights at either Hanakapiai or Hanakoa.

The Milolii Valley section of Na Pali Coast State Park, accessible only by small boat, is open May to September and has a three-day limit. Captain Zodiac (☎ 826-9371) and Hanalei Sea Tours (☎ 826-7254) can drop campers off at Milolii for a roundtrip fee of around $150. On rare occasions when the surf gets too high, the pick-up service may be delayed, so campers should carry extra provisions.

County Beach Parks Camping is allowed at Haena, Hanalei, Anini, Anahola, Hanamaulu, Salt Pond and Lucy Wright parks. Haena, Anini and Salt Pond are all on nice beaches and are good choices. Camping is allowed at Hanalei Beach Park on weekends and holidays only.

All county campgrounds have showers and restrooms, and most have covered picnic pavilions and barbecue grills. There's a typical Hawaiian free style to the campgrounds, so don't expect to find numbered sites or caretakers.

Permits, which are required, are $3 per night for adults, free for children under 18 (no fees for Hawaii residents). There's a limit of seven consecutive days at each campground, and a limit of 60 days of camping a year.

Permit applications can be made by mail if a completed form and payment are received at least one month in advance. Otherwise, pick up the permits in person from 8 am to 4:30 pm Monday to Friday at the Division of Parks & Recreation (☎ 241-6660), 4444 Rice St, Suite 150, Lihue, HI 96766, in the Lihue Civic Center at the corner of Hwys 50 and 56.

You can also just set up camp and wait for the ranger to come around and collect, but if you do this the fee jumps to $5 per person. Be aware that rangers sometimes wake up campers late at night or as early as

Secret Beach, North Shore, Kauai

NED FRIARY

View of Na Pali Coast from Kee Beach, Kauai

NED FRIARY

NED FRIARY

View of patchwork taro fields, Hanalei Valley, Kauai

NED FRIARY

Na Pali Coast, Kauai

GLENDA BENDURE

Swinging bridge over Hanapepe River, Kauai

5 am to collect fees, and if they determine the camping area is too full, campers without permits can be asked to move.

Waimea Canyon The Division of Forestry & Wildlife allows backcountry camping at four sites along trails in Waimea Canyon and at two sites (Sugi Grove and Kawaikoi) in the Kokee State Park area. Camping is limited to four nights in the canyon and three nights in the Kokee area within a 30-day period.

Camping permits, which are required and are free, can be picked up in person between 8 am and 4 pm Monday to Friday, from the forestry office at 3060 Eiwa St, Room 306, Lihue, HI 96766. You can also get the permits mailed to you in advance by writing (or by calling ☎ 274-3433); simply tell them the name and address of each camper, the camping area in which you want to stay (Waimea or Kokee) and the dates you plan to camp.

Cabins Cabins run by a private concessionaire are available in Kokee State Park. There are also cabins in a mountain setting at Kahili Mountain Park, north of Koloa. See the relevant sections for more information.

Camping Supplies Pedal & Paddle (☎ 826-9069), in Ching Young Village in Hanalei, rents two-person dome tents for $10/30 a day/week, backpacks for $5/20, daypacks for $4/12 and light blankets, trail stoves and sleeping pads each for $3/10. They sell the same supplies they rent and have a selection of hiking books, maps and backpacking items. The store is open daily from 9 am to 5 pm, and a bit later in summer.

Kayak Kauai (☎ 826-9844), on Hwy 560 in Hanalei, rents two-person tents or backpacks for $8/30 a day/week, camping stoves or sleeping bags for $6/20, sleeping pads for $3/10 and daypacks for $4/15. It's open from 8 am to 5:30 pm daily.

Outfitters Kauai (☎ 742-9667), in the Poipu Plaza in Poipu, rents backpacks for $4 to $8 a day and sells topographical maps of Kauai. It's open from 9 am to 5 pm Monday to Saturday.

ENTERTAINMENT

Most of Kauai's entertainment scene is at the larger hotels. The main dance clubs are Kuhio's Nightclub at the Hyatt Regency Kauai in Poipu and Gilligan's at the Outrigger Kauai Beach hotel in Lihue, both with DJs.

You can listen to live Hawaiian music at some of the resort poolside bars and on the North Shore at the Hanalei Gourmet in Hanalei and the Hanalei Bay Resort in Princeville.

The main tourist luaus are at Kauai Coconut Beach Resort and Smith's Tropical Paradise in Wailua.

Free hula shows are presented at the Coconut Marketplace in Wailua, the Kukui Grove Center in Lihue and the Hyatt Regency Kauai in Poipu.

There are movie theaters in the Kukui Grove Center in Lihue and the Coconut Marketplace in Wailua.

For more details on specific venues, see the relevant town sections in this chapter. Check the local paper or the free tourist magazines for the latest entertainment schedules.

THINGS TO BUY

Popular souvenir items include Niihau shell leis, island-made baskets and paintings of Kauai landscapes. While the early harvests of Kauai-grown coffee have not been as highly regarded as the gourmet Kona coffee, the price is a relative bargain; some of the best prices on both coffees can be found at discount stores such as Longs Drugs.

Good places to look for locally made arts and crafts include Kilohana Plantation in Puhi, Ching Young Village in Hanalei, Kauai Museum in Lihue and shopping centers around the island.

Kauai's largest shopping center, the Kukui Grove Center in Lihue, has a Kauai Products Store that sells everything from

Sunshine Markets

For island-grown fruits and vegetables that are both fresher and much cheaper than grocery store produce, try to catch one of the farmers' markets, known locally as Sunshine Markets. Not only will you find bargain prices on fruits like papayas, oranges and avocados, but you'll also find items such as passion fruit and guava that aren't sold in supermarkets at all.

The organizers keep the markets on a fixed schedule, but occasionally there are adjustments; call ☎ 241-6390 for the latest. The current schedule is: at Koloa Ballpark in Koloa at noon on Mondays; on Hwy 560 just west of Hanalei at 2 pm on Tuesdays; at Kalaheo Neighborhood Center in Kalaheo at 3:30 pm on Tuesdays; at Kapaa New Town Park in Kapaa at 3 pm on Wednesdays; near the United Church of Christ in Hanapepe at 3 pm on Thursdays; at Kilauea Neighborhood Center, opposite Kong Lung Center in Kilauea, at 4:30 pm on Thursdays; at Vidinha Stadium in Lihue at 3 pm on Fridays; and at Kekaha Neighborhood Center in Kekaha at 9 am on Saturdays.

Get there early. As a matter of fact, it's best to be there before the starting time, as once the whistle blows there's a big rush and people begin to scoop things up quickly. Depending on the location, it can all wrap up within an hour or so. ■

Niihau shell jewelry to Kauai coffee. An excellent selection of Hawaiian music, as well as a nifty headphone set-up that enables you to preview virtually all CDs, can be found at the nearby Borders bookstore.

GETTING THERE & AWAY
Air
Kauai's main airport is in Lihue.

Hawaiian Airlines (☎ 245-1831) flies nonstop from Honolulu to Lihue every hour on the hour from 6 am to 8 pm and Aloha Airlines (☎ 245-3691) operates nearly twice an hour during the same period. Aloha also has a few nonstop flights between Lihue and Kahului on Maui as well as several daily flights between Lihue and Kona on the Big Island that require a stop in Honolulu but no change of planes. One-way fares are currently $69 on either airline.

Mahalo Air (☎ 800-277-8333) flies between Honolulu and Lihue nearly a dozen times a day, with a one-way fare of $55.

Kauai also has a small commuter airport in Princeville on the North Shore. However, with the recent pull-out of its sole passenger carrier, Island Air, the airport currently has no commercial service.

For more information on air travel, including discounts and air passes, see the Getting Around chapter in the front of the book.

Lihue Airport The Lihue Airport has a modern terminal, an airstrip that can handle direct flights from the US mainland and agricultural inspection for passengers leaving the state.

There's also a restaurant, cocktail lounge, flower shop, gift shop and newsstand with island maps. You can find stands loaded with activity and accommodations brochures in the baggage claim area.

GETTING AROUND
Kauai has a limited public bus service, and while it connects most towns on the island, it's not geared for visitors and won't take you off the beaten path or out to major destinations such as Kilauea Lighthouse, Waimea Canyon or Kokee State Park. Consequently, renting a car is almost essential for exploring the island in depth.

Kauai's main roads are straightforward and easy to follow, but if you plan on doing a lot of exploring, consider picking up a good road map, such as the *Hawaii, Maui & Kauai Map of the Neighbor Islands* by Compass Maps.

Surprisingly, Kauai does have rush-hour traffic jams, especially in central Lihue and on the highway between Lihue and Kapaa. To reduce rush-hour congestion, temporary cones are sometimes set up on Hwy 56 in the Wailua area to create 'contra-flow' lanes, opening an additional lane by changing the usual direction of traffic flow.

To/From the Airport

The public bus does not stop at Lihue Airport. Taxis can be picked up curbside in front of the arrival area. Car rental booths are lined up on the other side of the street, opposite the arrival and departure gates.

Bus

The public bus has two main routes, both originating in the county capital of Lihue and operating seven or eight times a day on weekdays and four times a day on Saturdays. One route heads north to Hanalei; stops along the way include Coconut Market Place in Wailua, the library in Kapaa and the Princeville Shopping Center. The second route operates between Lihue and Kekaha, Kauai's westernmost town, making en route stops in Kalaheo, Eleele, Hanapepe and Waimea.

In addition, there's a bus four times a day on weekdays from Lihue to Koloa and Poipu and an hourly local Lihue bus, geared largely for retired residents, that runs between Lihue's shopping centers.

In Lihue the buses can be boarded on Eiwa St, near the county office building. Buses are white with a green sugar cane motif and are marked 'Kauai Bus'. Destinations are posted in the front window; the fare on all routes is $1 per ride. You can get more information on the bus by calling ☎ 241-6410 from 7 am to 5 pm Monday to Saturday.

If you plan to get around by bus, keep in mind that there's no service on Sundays. Carry-on bags have a size limit of 7-by-14-by-22 inches; boogie boards are not allowed and nothing can be stored in the aisles.

The latest bus schedule is printed in the *Hawaii Penny Saver*, a free shopping paper that can be found in grocery stores and other shops. You can also pick up a bus schedule from most bus drivers or at the county office building in Lihue.

Information on commercial sightseeing bus tours is under Organized Tours in the earlier Activities section of this chapter.

Car

Budget (☎ 245-1901), Hertz (☎ 245-3356), Avis (☎ 245-3512), Alamo (☎ 246-0645), Dollar (☎ 245-3651) and National (☎ 245-5636) have car rental booths at Lihue Airport.

More information, including toll-free numbers, is in the introductory Getting Around chapter in the front of the book.

Taxi

Taxis charge $2 at flagfall and then $2 a mile, metered in 25¢ increments. The fare from Lihue Airport is about $17 to Coconut Plantation in Wailua, $20 to Kapaa and $30 to Poipu.

Taxi companies include Akiko's Taxi (☎ 822-7588), on the east side; North Shore Cab (☎ 826-6189), based in Princeville; and Poipu Taxi (☎ 639-2044), for service on Kauai's south side.

Bicycle

Bicycle rentals generally include use of a helmet, lock, water bottle and car rack.

Kayak Kauai, in both Hanalei (☎ 826-9844) and Kapaa (☎ 822-9179), rents 21-speed mountain bikes for $20/70 a day/week, tandem bikes for the same price and beach cruisers for $15/60.

Pedal & Paddle in the Ching Young Village in Hanalei (☎ 826-9069) rents 21-speed mountain bikes for $15/80 a day/week and beach cruisers for $10/50.

Outfitters Kauai (☎ 742-9667) in the Poipu Plaza in Poipu rents mountain bikes for $20 to $33 a day, road bikes for $30 and tandem bikes for $35. There are discounts for rentals of more than three days.

See Cycling in the earlier Activities section for information on cycling outings.

East Side

LIHUE

Lihue is the county capital, the island's commercial center and the arrival point of most visitors to Kauai. Although it's the island's central town, its population is only 5500 and it's essentially a grown-up plantation town. It has inexpensive local hotels and restaurants and the island's main

Lihue Area

To Wailua, Kapaa

56

Kalepa Ridge

Kuhio Hwy

Wailua County Golf Course

Aston Kauai Beach Villas
Outrigger Kauai Beach

Kalepa Forest Reserve

Hanamaulu Beach Park

Hanamaulu

Hehi Rd

Hanamaulu Rd

Hanamaulu Restaurant

Gas Station

Kapule Hwy

To Wailua Falls

583

Maalo Rd

570

Ahukini Rd

Wilcox Memorial Hospital

See Central Lihue map

Old Lutheran Church

56

Lihue

Hoomana Rd

Rice St

51

50

Grove Farm Homestead

Nawiliwili Rd

Borders

58

Kaumualii Hwy

Kukui Grove Center

Kilohana Plantation

Kauai Community College

Puhi

Puhi Rd

Fisherman's Galley

To Poipu, Waimea

Hulemalu Rd

Menehune Fishpond Overlook

Huleia National Wildlife Refuge

Menehune Fishpond

Huleia Stream

Haupu (Hoary Head) Ridge

Ahukini Landing

PACIFIC OCEAN

Hanamaulu Bay

Ahukini Rd

Lihue Airport

Kamilo Point

Lighthouse

Ninini Point

Kauai Marriott

Pacific Ocean Plaza

Garden Island Inn

Kalapaki Beach

Nawiliwili Beach Park

Nawiliwili Bay

Nawiliwili Harbor

Waapa Rd

Carter Point

Kawai Point

0   .5   1 km
0   .3   .6 miles

KAUAI

shopping mall. There are a few sights of interest, but Lihue itself is rather ordinary, with no special charm.

Information
Tourist Offices The Hawaii Visitors Bureau (☎ 245-3971), 3016 Umi St, on the 2nd floor of the Lihue Plaza, is open from 8 am to 4 pm Monday to Friday. If you're looking for brochures and printed information, however, the racks at the airport are much better stocked.

Money The bank is open from 8:30 am to 3 pm Monday to Thursday, to 6 pm on Fridays, and has a 24-hour ATM.

Post & Communications The post office is opposite the museum on Rice St, next to the Bank of Hawaii. Post office hours are from 8 am to 4:30 pm Monday to Friday, 9 am to 1 pm on Saturdays.

Library The Lihue Public Library, 4344 Hardy St, is open from 10 am to 8 pm on Mondays and Wednesdays, 9 am to 5 pm on Tuesdays, Thursdays and Fridays and 9 am to 1 pm on Saturdays.

Laundry There's a coin laundry in the Rice Shopping Center.

Kauai Museum
A few hours at the Kauai Museum (☎ 245-6931), 4428 Rice St, will give you a good overview of the island's history.

The displays begin with Kauai's volcanic genesis from the ocean floor, then move on to describe the island's unique ecosystems. The 1st floor covers early Hawaii, with the likes of hula instruments, poi pounders and tapa-making tools.

Upstairs the sugar cane workers and missionaries arrive on the scene. A replica of a plantation worker's spartan shack sits opposite the spacious bedroom of an early missionary's house, furnished with a four-poster koa bed and Hawaiian quilts. It is to these folks that Hawaii traces its multiethnic roots and vastly unequal distribution of land and wealth. The displays are accompanied by well-written interpretive presentations of life in old Kauai.

The gift shop has a good selection of Hawaiiana books and a small collection of koa bowls and other handicrafts. If you only want to visit the gift shop, which is inside the museum lobby, you can enter without paying.

The museum is open from 9 am to 4 pm Monday to Friday and 10 am to 4 pm on Saturdays. Admission is $5 for adults, $3 for children ages 13 to 17 and $1 for children ages six to 12. If you run out of time, ask for a free re-entry pass when you leave.

Lihue Sugar Mill
The conveyer belt that crosses over Hwy 50 just south of its intersection with Hwy 56 transports crushed sugar cane to the Lihue Sugar Mill. The mill produces raw sugar crystals that are shipped to California to be refined. Molasses is also made here, and if you happen by on one of those days, you'll find the air laden with the sweet, thick smell of the syrup.

Old Lutheran Church
From the outside, the oldest Lutheran church in Hawaii is just one more quaint Hawaiian church. From the inside, it's much more interesting.

German immigrants styled their church to resemble the boat that brought them from their homeland to Hawaii in the late 19th century. The floor has been built to slant like the deck of a ship, the balcony resembles a captain's bridge and ship lanterns hang from the ceiling. The current building was actually constructed in 1983, but it's an almost exact replica of the original 1885 church that was leveled by Hurricane Iwa in 1982.

The immigrants themselves now lie at rest in the church cemetery on a knoll overlooking the cane fields in which they toiled.

The church is a quarter of a mile up Hoomana Rd, which is just west of the intersection of Hwys 56 and 50.

Wailua Falls
Wailua Falls is a scenic 80-foot waterfall just north of Lihue. From Lihue, turn left

onto Maalo Rd (Hwy 583), a narrow paved road that weaves through sugar cane fields. The road ends at the falls at precisely 3.94 miles – as the highway marker fastidiously proclaims.

Wailua, which means 'two waters', is usually seen as two falls. However, after heavy rains it becomes one wide rushing waterfall and you can watch fish being thrown out beyond the powerful waters for a flying dive into the pool below.

This is not a waterfall to explore from the top. A sign at the parking lot near a closed path reads, 'Slippery rocks at top of falls. People have been killed'. There are plenty of stories told of people sliding off the rocks, some miraculously grabbing roots and being rescued and others not so lucky.

A third of a mile before the road's end, at a large dirt pull-off, there's an eroded trail that leads to the base of the falls. The steep trail down to the river can be very slippery when wet, if not outright hazardous. As the trail along the bottom follows the riverbed to the base of the falls, that part of the path commonly floods over and may be barely discernible after heavy rains. However, all said and done, local kids do manage to scramble their way through the overgrowth to the waterfall. If you decide to give it a try, expect to work up a sweat; it can be humid enough along the riverbed to steam up eyeglasses.

Back on the road, keep an eye out for wood roses, a flower commonly used in dried floral arrangements. The vines, which bear bright yellow flowers shaped like morning glories, are especially thick around the bridge half a mile down the road from the waterfall.

Hanamaulu

Hanamaulu is a little village between Lihue and Wailua along Hwy 56 that's significant in Hawaiian folklore as the birthplace of Kauai's legendary hero Kawelo. Today, it's a sleepy town with just a few businesses, including an old-fashioned Japanese restaurant, a hole-in-the-wall post office and a doughnut shop that closes each day as soon as the doughnuts are gone.

Three-quarters of a mile from the village center, **Hanamaulu Beach Park** is at the inside of Hanamaulu Bay, a deep protected bay with a boulder breakwater part way across its mouth. The park has camping with full facilities, but it's more of a local hangout than a visitor destination. The waters are occasionally closed due to pollution.

From Hwy 56, turn makai onto Hanamaulu Rd at the 7-Eleven store and after a quarter-mile turn right onto Hehi Rd. As you enter the park, you'll first go under the highway bridge and then the arched trestle of an abandoned railroad bridge.

Ahukini Landing

If you've got some time to kill before your flight, you could drive down to the end of Hwy 570 to Ahukini Landing, 1½ miles beyond the airport. The road runs through cane fields and crosses a series of narrow-gauge railroad tracks that were once used to bring sugar cane down to the landing. Ilima and chain of love grow along the road.

Ahukini State Recreation Pier, at the end of the road, consists largely of cement pillars and the decaying framework of the old pier. A wooden walkway runs out across it, providing a prime locale for pole fishing. At the head of the bay is Hanamaulu Beach.

Ninini Point

The lighthouse on Ninini Point stands 100 feet above the shore, marking the northern entrance to Nawiliwili Bay. The road down to the lighthouse begins off Hwy 51, a little over half a mile south of its intersection with Hwy 570. Although you'll have to go through a guard gate and cross the Kauai Lagoon Golf Course property to get to the coast, access is free to visitors.

The 2½-mile drive from the gatehouse to the lighthouse skirts between the airport fence and the golf course. After two miles the pavement ends and the road continues as dirt; this section is sometimes too rough to pass in a low-slung car, and you may have to hike the last 10 minutes of it.

Not only is there a fine view from the lighthouse, but nearby is one of the few sections of accessible shore in the area where

Hawaiians can still fish, pick opihi and gather limu as they've done for generations.

Kalapaki Beach

Kalapaki Beach, a sandy beach sheltered by points and breakwaters, is off Hwy 51 at Nawiliwili Bay. Swimming is usually good, even in the winter, unless storms kick the surf up.

The beach is backed by the Kauai Marriott but is open to the public. There's free beach access parking close to the water at the north side of the hotel.

Nawiliwili Beach Park

Nawiliwili Beach Park is largely a parking lot facing an ocean retaining wall. From here you can look across to the light beacon on Kukui Point, and at the far end of the parking lot you can also see the lighthouse on the more distant Ninini Point.

There's no beach at the beach park, but if the waters in Nawiliwili Stream are not running strongly you could cross over to Kalapaki Beach.

Right at the mouth of the stream is an old shelter under ironwood trees with a wooden sign reading 'Pine Tree Inn' – it's an impromptu neighborhood open-air bar of sorts. Old-timers gather here during the day with ice chests of beer to talk story and play music.

Nawiliwili Harbor

Nawiliwili Harbor is a deep-water port with a commercial harbor and an adjacent small-boat harbor. Several deep-sea fishing boats are based at the small-boat harbor, which has a picturesque setting backed by the edge of the Haupu (Hoary Head) Ridge.

Waapa Rd runs southwest past the harbor and then connects with Hulemalu Rd, which leads up to an overview of the Menehune Fishpond.

Menehune Fishpond Overlook

Half a mile up Hulemalu Rd there's a lookout on the left with a view of the Alakoko Fishpond, more commonly called the Menehune Fishpond. In the background is the misty Haupu Ridge.

The fishpond, created by a stone wall that runs along a bend in Huleia Stream, was said to have been built in one night by menehunes. The stone wall is now covered by a thick green line of mangrove trees. Morning is a good time for viewing as in the afternoon you look into the sun.

The **Huleia National Wildlife Refuge** lies along the north side of Huleia Stream. Once planted with taro and rice, the area now provides breeding and feeding grounds for endemic waterbirds. The refuge is not accessible to the public.

If you continue about a mile past the fishpond overlook and then turn right onto Puhi Rd, you'll come out to Hwy 50 opposite the community college.

Grove Farm Homestead

The Grove Farm Homestead Plantation Museum, up Nawiliwili Rd (Hwy 58), 1¾ miles from Waapa Rd, is a preserved farmhouse built in 1864 by George Wilcox, son of missionaries Abner and Lucy Wilcox. It's somewhat like the house of an old aunt, a bit musty and filled with memories. Rocking chairs sit on a covered porch. One room is lined with bookshelves stuffed with a home library, with koa calabashes and a model ship on top. In one corner a card table is set up, waiting for a couple of people to sit down to a wild game of cribbage.

Two-hour tours are given at 10 am and 1 pm on Mondays, Wednesdays and Thursdays. Reservations are required (☎ 245-3202); space sometimes fills up a week or so in advance. The cost is $5 for adults, $2 for children 12 and under.

Kilohana Plantation

Kilohana, 1½ miles south of Lihue on Hwy 50, is the 1930s sugar plantation estate of Gaylord Parke Wilcox, once head of Grove Farm Plantation. The Tudor-style mansion built by Wilcox was the most distinguished house on Kauai in its day.

The home has been restored, with most of the rooms turned into shops that sell artwork, antiques and handicrafts. It was a nice way to preserve the old estate, and you get to look around without being charged an admission fee.

Visitors are free to wander through rooms full of antiques. The hallways hold cases of stone poi pounders and other Hawaiian artifacts, and Oriental rugs litter the hardwood floors. There's also Gaylord's, a restaurant in a U-shaped courtyard setting around the lawn.

Many island galleries rent space at Kilohana, giving it one of the widest collections of arts and crafts on Kauai. On the 1st floor, a former cloakroom is now the Hawaiian Collection Room, which sells finely strung Niihau shell leis and scrimshaw.

The upstairs bedrooms have likewise been turned into shops, with displays laid out even in the bathrooms and closets. The works include wood carvings of whales and dolphins, contemporary paintings by local artists, jewelry and dolls.

Kilohana (☎ 245-5608) is open from 9:30 am to 9:30 pm Monday to Saturday, until 5 pm on Sundays. The 35-acre grounds are still part of a working farm, and turn-of-the-century carriages pulled by Clydesdale horses give 20-minute tours at $8 for adults and $4 for children under 12.

Queen Victoria's Profile

The rock profile of Queen Victoria, part of the Haupu (Hoary Head) Ridge, can be seen from a marked 'scenic view' pull-off in front of the Kauai Community College along Hwy 50 in Puhi.

It takes some imagination, but here's how to find it: Position yourself midway in the pull-off facing the mountains to the south. Look across the highway at the phone pole, then over to the metal light pole in the background to the right. The queen's crowned head is under the arch of the lamp – the crown is the high part at the right, her chin lower and to the left.

Supposedly, she's shaking her thin pointy finger at an imaginary William, saying 'Na, Willy, Willy', hence the harbor's name.

Places to Stay – budget

Lihue has some of Kauai's cheapest hotels, though they're generally drab places and, except for Motel Lani, are filled mostly with local residents. You'll get a place to sleep, but by no means are these vacation spots.

The family-run *Motel Lani* (☎ 245-2965), 4240 Rice St, Box 1836, Lihue, HI 96766, is the best budget choice, though it's at a busy intersection. There's a long cinder-block building with six $32 rooms that are basic but clean and have private baths, air-con and mini-refrigerators. There are also three 'deluxe' rooms for $52 that are larger and have TVs. There's a two-day minimum stay or a $2 surcharge.

The *Hale Lihue Hotel* (☎ 245-2751), 2931 Kalena St, Lihue, HI 96766, has 20 rooms for $22/25/30 a single/double/triple. Rooms have two twin beds and private baths, but are quite spartan with zilch for atmosphere.

The *Tip Top Motel* (☎ 245-2333; fax 246-8988), 3173 Akahi St, Box 1231, Lihue, HI 96766, has a couple dozen rooms in two-story cinder-block buildings. Rooms

---

Princess Hina's Profile

Long before Europeans decided that the vague rock profile on the Haupu Ridge looked like Queen Victoria, the Hawaiians had their own story. They call it Hina-i-uka.

Long ago Peleula, a princess from Oahu, sailed to Kauai to check out rumors that the island had the most handsome men in Hawaii. Hina, a Kauai princess, welcomed her with a royal banquet. At the banquet was Kahili, a young chief from Kilauea, who caught the fancy of both women. To compete for his affections they danced the hula.

Peleula's dance was stunning. But Hina, who was perfumed with the scent of Kauai's endemic mokihana berries, was absolutely mesmerizing, and she became Kahili's lover. The people of Kauai carved one ridge of the Haupu mountains into the image of Hina, with her finger up to warn off women from other islands. ∎

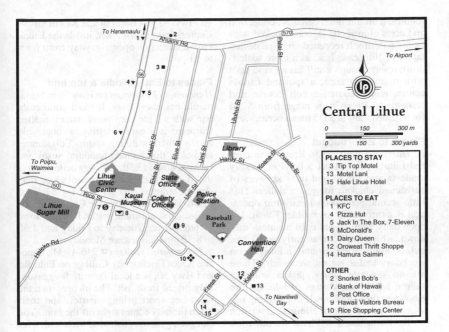

Central Lihue

0   150   300 m

0   150   300 yards

PLACES TO STAY
3   Tip Top Motel
13   Motel Lani
15   Hale Lihue Hotel

PLACES TO EAT
1   KFC
4   Pizza Hut
5   Jack In The Box, 7-Eleven
6   McDonald's
11   Dairy Queen
12   Oroweat Thrift Shoppe
14   Hamura Saimin

OTHER
2   Snorkel Bob's
7   Bank of Hawaii
8   Post Office
9   Hawaii Visitors Bureau
10   Rice Shopping Center

are basic with twin beds, air-con and louvered windows but they do have TV and private baths. The rate is $44.

Places to Stay – middle & top end

The *Garden Island Inn* (☎ 245-7227, 800-648-0154), 3445 Wilcox Rd, Lihue, HI 96766, is an older three-story hotel that was extensively renovated after Hurricane Iniki. It has 21 small but tidy rooms with TVs, ceiling fans, mini-refrigerators and coffeemakers. The rate is $55 for ground-floor rooms and $65 for rooms on the 2nd floor with small private lanais. The hotel is near an industrial area and at the side of a rather busy road, so expect to hear some traffic noise. On the plus side, it's within walking distance of Kalapaki Beach and a couple of good restaurants.

A few miles north of downtown Lihue is the *Outrigger Kauai Beach* (☎ 245-1955, 800-688-7444; fax 246-9085; reservations@outrigger.com), 4331 Kauai Beach Drive, Lihue, HI 96766, which has 341 rooms

costing from $130 with a mountain view to $180 with an ocean view. The hotel was originally built as a Hilton and has the standard design and amenities you'd expect of that chain, including large free-form swimming pools and tennis courts.

On the same beachfront property as the Outrigger, the *Aston Kauai Beach Villas* (☎ 245-7711, 800-922-7866), 4330 Kauai Beach Drive, Lihue, HI 96766, has one-bedroom condos at $170 for up to four people and two-bedroom units at $245 for up to six people. Rates are $20 cheaper in the low season.

The 618-room *Kauai Marriott* (☎ 245-5050, 800-228-9290; fax 241-6025), Kalapaki Beach, Lihue, HI 96766, is an upmarket hotel with an interesting history. Originally built as the Kauai Surf, its very construction as the island's first multistory resort led to a successful campaign to limit the height of future hotels on Kauai to that of a coconut tree. In the late 1980s, it was remade into a luxury hotel with marble

KAUAI

lobbies, a multimillion dollar art collection and acres of artificial lagoons stocked with exotic wildlife. It reopened after the devastation of Hurricane Iniki as a more scaled-down resort, though it still has a grand pool with marble jacuzzis, a spa and fitness center, tennis courts, a golf course and restaurants. Room rates range from $225 for a garden view to $375 for an ocean view.

Places to Eat – budget

At *Hamura Saimin*, 2956 Kress St in central Lihue, you can get a bowl of freshly made saimin for $3 and tasty skewers of barbecued chicken for just a dollar. This little second-generation family-run operation is a throwback to an older Kauai. It's open daily from 10 am until business dies down, which might be as early as 10 pm, but is more often around midnight on weekdays and 2 am on weekends. There are no separate tables, just a winding saimin bar where visitors and locals rub elbows as they slurp bowls of steaming hot saimin. The one rule of etiquette is written on the menu board – 'Please do not stick gum under counter'!

Kauai Chop Suey, in the Pacific Ocean Plaza at 3501 Rice St, has lots of standard Cantonese dishes for around $7, including about a dozen vegetarian dishes. Kauai is not known for its Chinese restaurants, but this one has good, reasonably priced food. The menu is the same at lunch (11 am to 2 pm Tuesday to Saturday) and dinner (4:30 to 9 pm Tuesday to Sunday).

Cafe Kauai, an espresso cafe inside the Borders bookstore, has sandwiches, pastries and a variety of newspapers that you can read while sipping your coffee. It's open from at least 8 am to 9:30 pm daily, except on Sundays when it closes at 7:30 pm.

Vim N Vigor in the Rice Shopping Center is a small health food store that carries vitamins, granola and other standard products.

The *Oroweat Thrift Shoppe* on the corner of Rice and Kalena Sts has day-old bakery products at discounted prices.

There's a *McDonald's, Jack in the Box, Pizza Hut* and *KFC* clustered together on Hwy 56 and a *Burger King* and *Taco Bell*

on Hwy 50 just north of the Kukui Grove Center. *Star Supermarket*, inside the Kukui Grove Center, is open everyday from 6 am to 11 pm.

Places to Eat – middle & top end

Hanamaulu Restaurant on Hwy 56 in Hanamaulu has many faces. It has a good sushi bar with a little carp pond, tatami-matted tearooms in a garden setting, a robatayaki and a no-frills dining room. Full dinner teishokus that include tempura, sushi and sashimi cost $13.50. An even better deal is the special plate meal of miso soup, rice, shrimp tempura and teriyaki for $7.50 at lunch, $9 at dinner. Average Chinese dishes are available at similar prices. It's open from 10 am to 1 pm Tuesday to Friday and 4:30 to 8:30 pm daily except Mondays.

Fisherman's Galley (☎ 246-4700), opposite Kauai Community College on Puhi Rd and Hwy 50, is a local favorite for reasonably priced fresh fish. The owners own the Gent-Lee sport fishing charter, and their catch literally comes right off the boat. You can get a generous fish sandwich with fries or fish & chips for $8 or a broiled fish dinner for about twice that. It's open daily from 11 am to 9 pm.

Tokyo Lobby (☎ 245-8989), in the Pacific Ocean Plaza, is a thoroughly authentic Japanese restaurant both in terms of atmosphere and food. The lunch menu includes noodle dishes, donburi and chicken teriyaki plates for around $8 and good sushi and sashimi for a bit more. At dinner, there is a wide range of meals with soup, salad and rice for $12 to $15. It's open from 11 am to 2 pm Monday to Saturday and from 5 to 9:30 pm nightly.

The best-value restaurant at the Kauai Marriott is the beachside *Duke's Canoe Club* (☎ 246-9599), which has a nice atmosphere and a selection of fresh fish with half a dozen different preparations for $20, a good salad bar included. There are also chicken, pasta and steak dishes from $15. It's open for dinner from 5 to 10 pm, with live Hawaiian music nightly.

Gaylord's (☎ 245-9593) at Kilohana Plantation has a pleasant open-air estate setting, though the food is ordinary and pricey. Lunch is from 11 am to 3 pm daily except Sundays, with sandwiches and salads for $9. Dinner, from 5 pm nightly, has entrees ranging from $17 for chicken to $24 for steak. On Sundays, there's a brunch from 9:30 am to 3 pm, with dishes from $10 to $15.

Entertainment

The main nightclub in these parts is *Gilligan's* (☎ 245-1955) at the Outrigger Kauai Beach, which has dancing and a DJ from 9:30 pm to 1 am on Fridays and Saturdays with a $5 cover. The minimum age is 21.

The cafe at Borders bookstore in Lihue has live music every Sunday from 5 to 7 pm. Most of the musicians are islanders promoting their latest CDs, ranging from contemporary tunes played on ukulele and Hawaiian slack-key guitar to environmental music. There's no cover charge.

There's a free hula show at 6 pm on Fridays at the Kukui Grove Center.

Kukui Grove Cinema in the Kukui Grove Center shows standard Hollywood movies.

Things to Buy

Kukui Grove Center, at the intersection of Hwy 50 and Hwy 58, is Kauai's main shopping mall. The major department stores are Liberty House and its discount Penthouse branch, Sears and Longs Drugs. The center also has a one-hour photo shop and several clothing and gift shops. The nearby Borders has an excellent collection of books, CDs and cassettes, including lots of Hawaiiana options.

For Hawaiian-made handicrafts, the gift shops at Kilohana and the Kauai Museum are good places to start.

WAILUA

The three-mile stretch of Kuhio Hwy (Hwy 56) from Wailua to Kapaa is largely a scattering of shopping centers, restaurants, hotels and condos. Wailua doesn't really have a town center. Most of its sights are clustered around the Wailua River.

Long ago, Wailua was the site of Kauai's royal court, with 'Seven Sacred Heiaus'

running from the mouth of the Wailua River up to the top of Mt Waialeale. Six of these heiau sites are within a mile of the river mouth. Five are visible, while the sixth is abandoned in a sugar cane field on the northern side of the Wailua River. All date back to the early period of Tahitian settlement and are considered to be typical menehune construction.

Wailua River State Park is a hodgepodge of sites that includes most of the heiaus, sections of the Wailua River bank, the Fern Grotto, the riverboat basin and a public boat ramp.

Wailua River, 11¾ miles long, is the only navigable river in Hawaii. Although most people travel this waterway on packaged riverboat tours, the more adventurous kayak or water-ski on it.

Lydgate Beach Park

Lydgate Beach Park is a popular family beach with protected swimming in a large seawater pool created with stone walls. It's fun for kids but deep enough for adults to swim in as well. The open ocean beyond often has strong currents, and there have been many drownings on both sides of the Wailua River mouth, just north of Lydgate. The park has changing rooms, restrooms, showers, large picnic pavilions and safe drinking water.

Lydgate is makai of the Kauai Resort Hotel, down Leho Drive.

Hikina A Ka La Heiau

Hikina A Ka La (Rising of the Sun) Heiau is the long, narrow heiau aligned directly north to south at the far end of the Lydgate Beach parking lot.

The heiau is thought to have been built around 1200 AD. Boulders still outline the shape, but most of the stones have long since been removed.

At the northern end of the heiau, a bronze plaque on a large stone reads 'Hauola, City of Refuge'. The mounded grassy area behind the plaque is all that remains of this former refuge for kapu breakers.

The stone with bowl-shaped depressions, 10 feet to the left of the plaque, is an adze grinding stone. While it's easy to recognize, the stone hasn't always been in this upright position since to grind a correct edge it would have to be flat. There are also a couple of flat stone saltpans on the grounds.

If you look straight out across the bay, you can see the remains of a heiau on Alakukui Point. Only the foundation stones are discernible, as the heiau site has been landscaped over in a carpet of condo grass. In ancient times, torches were lit on the point at night to help guide outrigger canoes.

If you walk straight down to the beach while looking towards Alakukui Point, you may find a few ancient stones with petroglyphs on them, though they're usually hidden under shifting sands.

Malae Heiau

Malae Heiau is in a thick clump of trees growing on the edge of a sugar cane field, a mere 40 feet mauka of the highway across from the Kauai Resort Hotel. Although this is the largest heiau on Kauai, covering two acres, it's thickly overgrown with grasses and Java plum trees and almost impossible to explore.

In the 1830s the missionaries converted Deborah Kapule, the last Kauaian queen, to Christianity, and she converted the interior of Malae Heiau into a cattle pen. Except for these alterations, it's relatively well preserved, thanks largely to its impenetrable overgrowth. The stone walls, which encompass an altar, are up to 10 feet high and eight feet wide.

The heiau is on state property, and there are plans to eventually incorporate it into the Wailua River State Park system.

Incidentally, the Java plums found at the site make a nice wine, but should you be tempted to try the fresh fruit, you'll find they're bitter enough to dry out your mouth!

Fern Grotto

Kauai's busiest tourist attraction is the riverboat tour up the Wailua River to the Fern Grotto, complete with corny jokes and packaged sentimentality to the tune of Elvis' 'Hawaiian Wedding Song'.

The riverboats are big with wide, flat bottoms – very simple, like covered barges. Some people compare them to cattle boats even before they pack the tourists on. The grotto, a large musty cave beneath a fern-covered rock face, is pretty enough but not a must-see sight.

Smith's Motor Boat Service (☎ 821-6892) and Waialeale Boat Tours (☎ 822-4908) both charge $15 for adults and $7.50 for children under 12, and one or the other leaves the Wailua Marina about once an hour between 9 am and 3 pm.

Smith's Tropical Paradise

Smith's Tropical Paradise (☎ 821-6895) at Wailua Marina has a loop trail through theme gardens, open from 8:30 am to 4 pm daily. Admission is $5 for adults, $2.50 for children under 12. Three evenings a week there's a luau and Polynesian show; see Entertainment in this section for details.

A woman of the Sandwich Islands
by John Webber

KAUAI

Hwy 580

Highway 580, also known as Kuamoo Rd, begins at the traffic light off Hwy 56 at Coco Palms. It passes heiaus, historical sites, Opaekaa Falls and Wailua Homesteads before reaching Keahua Arboretum, the starting place for a couple of backcountry trails.

Coco Palms

The Coco Palms resort was built on the site of Kauai's ancient royal court, in the midst of an historic 45-acre coconut grove.

There's a Hawaiian design to it all, with lagoons and thatched cottages, and it looks a bit like a movie set. In fact, the hotel's outdoor chapel was originally built in 1954 for the movie *Sadie Thompson* with Rita Hayworth. The highest-profile wedding that took place at Coco Palms was that of Elvis Presley and Joan Blackman in *Blue Hawaii*. Although Hurricane Iniki did extensive damage to the hotel that has yet to be repaired, the little chapel in the palms remains open for weddings.

Holoholoku Heiau

Holoholoku, a luakini heiau, is a quarter of a mile up Hwy 580 on the left. Like all the Wailua heiaus, this one was of enclosure-type construction, with stone walls built directly on the ground rather than with terraced platforms.

This whole area used to be royal property, and here on the west side of the grounds, against the flat-backed birthstone, queens gave birth to future kings. This stone is marked by a plaque reading 'Pohaku Hoohanu'. Another stone a few yards away, marked 'Pohaku Piko', was where the *piko* (umbilical cords) of the babies were left.

Above the temple where Hawaiian royalty were born, steps lead to a hilltop cemetery where later-day Japanese laborers lie at rest.

Poliahu Heiau

Poliahu Heiau, perched high on a hill overlooking the meandering Wailua River, is named after the snow goddess Poliahu, one of Pele's sisters. This relatively well preserved heiau is thought to have been of the luakini type.

Poliahu Heiau is immediately before the Opaekaa Falls lookout, on the opposite side of the road.

Bellstone

Immediately south of Poliahu Heiau, on the same side of the road, look for a 'Falling Rocks' sign that marks a short, rutted dirt drive leading to a bellstone. Because of the road angle it's easiest to approach coming downhill from Poliahu.

In old Hawaii, Wailua River was a naval entrance, and the bellstone at this lookout was thought to have been used by sentries to warn of attacks as well as to ring out announcements of royal births.

There are actually two stones at the end of the drive, one with an all-too-perfect petroglyph whose age is suspect. Archaeologists question just which stone may have been the bellstone. Although you can find depressions in the stones, they may well be the result of modern-day poundings by people trying to check out the resonance for themselves.

A short path down from these rocks leads to a vista of the river, where you can commonly see cattle grazing on the banks below and hear the amplified narration from the passing riverboats.

Opaekaa Falls

Opaekaa Falls is a high, broad waterfall which, depending upon recent rainfall, usually flows as a double cascade. The peaks of the Makaleha Mountains form a scenic backdrop, and white-tailed tropicbirds can often be seen soaring in the valley below the falls. The marked turn-off to the viewpoint is 1½ miles up Hwy 580. For the best angle, walk up the sidewalk past the parking lot towards the bridge.

From across the highway you can look down on the winding Wailua River and the thatched huts of the abandoned Kamokila Village. A former sightseeing spot that was set up to resemble an old Hawaiian village, Kamokila was used as a setting for the 1995 movie *Outbreak* with Dustin Hoffman.

KAUAI

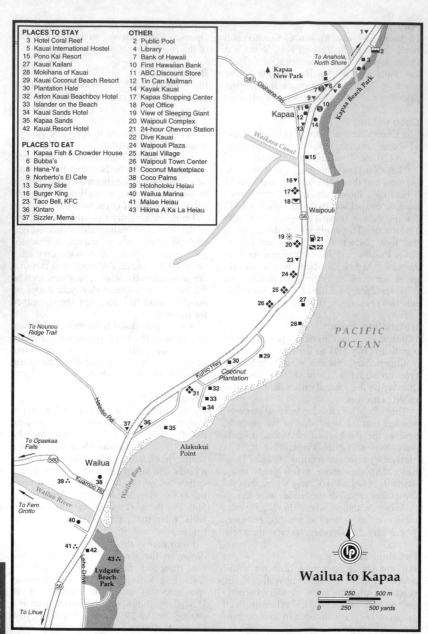

PLACES TO STAY
3 Hotel Coral Reef
5 Kauai International Hostel
15 Pono Kai Resort
27 Kauai Kailani
28 Mokihana of Kauai
29 Kauai Coconut Beach Resort
30 Plantation Hale
32 Aston Kauai Beachboy Hotel
33 Islander on the Beach
34 Kauai Sands Hotel
35 Kapaa Sands
42 Kauai Resort Hotel

PLACES TO EAT
1 Kapaa Fish & Chowder House
6 Bubba's
8 Hana-Ya
9 Norberto's El Cafe
13 Sunny Side
16 Burger King
23 Taco Bell, KFC
36 Kintaro
37 Sizzler, Mema

OTHER
2 Public Pool
4 Library
7 Bank of Hawaii
10 First Hawaiian Bank
11 ABC Discount Store
12 Tin Can Mailman
14 Kayak Kauai
17 Kapaa Shopping Center
18 Post Office
19 View of Sleeping Giant
20 Waipouli Complex
21 24-hour Chevron Station
22 Dive Kauai
24 Waipouli Plaza
25 Kauai Village
26 Waipouli Town Center
31 Coconut Marketplace
38 Coco Palms
39 Holoholoku Heiau
40 Wailua Marina
41 Malae Heiau
43 Hikina A Ka La Heiau

To Anahola,
North Shore

Kapaa
New Park

Olehena Rd

Kapaa

Kapaa Beach Park

Waikaea Canal

Waipouli

Kuhio Hwy

To Nounou
Ridge Trail

PACIFIC
OCEAN

Coconut
Plantation

Haleilio Rd

To Opaekaa
Falls

Wailua

Kuamoo Rd

Alakukui
Point

Wailua Bay

To Fern
Grotto

Wailua River

Leho Drive

Lydgate
Beach
Park

To Lihue

Wailua to Kapaa

0   250   500 m
0   250   500 yards

KAUAI

Wailua Homesteads

In the Wailua Homesteads area, on the west side of the Sleeping Giant mountain, the government once gave 160-acre parcels to people willing to work the land. Most early homesteaders used the land to graze cattle, though at one point Dole grew pineapples in the area. Today Wailua Homesteads is largely a mix of spacious residential lots and pastoral countryside reminiscent of Pennsylvania Dutch farmland.

The main through road is Hwy 581 (Kamalu Rd), which connects with Hwy 580.

Nounou Ridge (Sleeping Giant) Trail

The Nounou Ridge Trail climbs up the Sleeping Giant to a summit on the giant's upper chest, affording views of both the east coast and the highland valleys. It's a well-maintained trail that takes 1½ to two hours roundtrip. Because the trail is somewhat steep, it provides a hardy workout.

There are two trailheads, both marked. The trail on the western side is a shaded forest trail of tall trees and moss-covered stones. The trail on the eastern side, which is more open and a bit longer, begins at a parking lot a mile up Haleilio Rd in Wailua Houselots.

The trail up the western side of the mountain starts on Hwy 581 (Kamalu Rd), near house No 1068. Walk through a metal gate marked as a forestry right of way and up along a small cattle pasture to the trailhead. If you have a car, note that there's no parking at the trailhead, but there's trail access and a parking area at the end of Lokelani Rd, which is off Kamalu Rd a bit farther north. If you pick up the trail there, it will deposit you on the same pasture but closer to the woods.

This is a wonderful trail to do early in the morning, when it's relatively cool and you can watch the light slowly spread across the valley below. The packed trail can get slippery when wet, so look for a walking stick. Hikers sometimes leave them near the trailhead.

The eucalyptus at the trailhead soon gives way to a tall, thick forest of Norfolk pines that were planted in a Civilian Conservation Corps (CCC) reforestation program during the 1930s. About five minutes into the woods, right after the Norfork pines begin, there's a fork. Veer left up the path with the large rock beside it.

The trail passes through thick strawberry guava bushes that can grow up to 15 feet high; in places the guava creates a canopied tunnel-like effect. Strawberry guava has a small red fruit that's eaten whole and is considered the sweetest of any guava.

A few minutes below the summit, the eastern and western trails merge on the ridge. Continue up to the right past some hala trees. On the summit is a picnic table shelter that offers protection from the rain. Passing showers can create some incredible valley rainbows. To the west there's a 180° view of Wailua and the Makaleha Mountains.

Below to the east you can see Kapaa, sugar cane fields, Wailua Houselots, Coco Palms and the Wailua River. To the right of the riverboat docks and mauka of the Kauai Resort Hotel there's a square, dark green area in the sugar cane field. This is Malae Heiau, now overgrown with Java plums.

If you go south across the picnic area, the trail continues. About five minutes up there's a rocky area where you can sit and enjoy the view. The ridge continues up the giant's chin. Should it tempt you, size it up carefully. It's sharp, and loose rocks and slides are visible.

Kuilau Ridge Trail

For the effort, the Kuilau Ridge Trail is one of the most visually rewarding trails on the island. The marked trailhead is on the right just before Hwy 580 crosses the stream at the Keahua Arboretum, 3.9 miles up from the junction of Hwys 580 and 581. Don't leave anything of value in your car.

The maintained trail starts up a wide dirt path that is also used by horses and the occasional renegade dirt biker. There's a dense growth of native plants along the way, including koa trees, ohia lehua and thickets of ti, and there's plenty of birdsong as well. In the upper reaches, there are hillsides covered with lush ferns and broad vistas of the mountains. A few thimbleberries grow wild along the trail, and there are many trail-side guava trees.

The hike climbs up to a broad ridge that offers views into valleys on both sides and clear down to the coast. You can see Kapaa to the east and the island's uninhabited central region to the west. It takes about 35 minutes to walk the 1¼ miles up to the grassy clearing on the ridgetop, where there are a couple of picnic tables and a great view of Mt Waialeale, due west.

Beyond the clearing, the Kuilau Ridge Trail continues as a narrow footpath offering even more spectacular views, ending in about a mile at the Moalepe Trail. If you don't want to go that far, at least walk a little of it, as some of the best vistas are along the next half mile of the trail, which continues to the right past the picnic area.

If you go left at the connection with the Moalepe Trail, you'll come to a viewpoint after about 10 minutes. If you go right on Moalepe, you'll come out on Olohena Rd in Wailua Homesteads about 2¼ miles down.

Coconut Plantation

Coconut Plantation is a resort development with four hotels, a condominium and a shopping center. It fronts a half-mile-long beach partially shaded by ironwood trees.

Water activities are restricted due to the low lava shelf that runs along most of the beach and the strong currents that prevail beyond. The best section for swimming is in front of Kauai Sands Hotel, which has a break in the lava shelf. You'll also find a beachside shower there.

While water conditions are mediocre, the beach makes for good strolling. The beach sand is unique, each little piece polished to a high gloss. The large grassy field between the Kauai Coconut Beach Resort and the Aston Kauai Beachboy Hotel is popular with egrets and the occasional kite flyer.

The resort's shopping center, Coconut Marketplace, has 70 different stores, including Liberty House, a kite shop, Fox Photo one-hour processing, art galleries, boutiques and gift shops. All are open at least from 10 am to 8 pm.

Places to Stay – B&Bs & Cottages

If you don't need to be on the beach, the following Wailua B&Bs represent some of the best-value accommodations on Kauai. The listings in this section are all in the Wailua Homesteads area, about three miles from the coast in a rural setting. All are within a mile or so of the intersection of Hwys 581 and 580.

Rosewood B&B (☎ 822-5216; fax 822-5478; rosewd@aloha.net), 872 Kamalu Rd, Kapaa, HI 96746, is a beautifully restored 85-year-old plantation home belonging to Rosemary and Norbert Smith. Upstairs is a pleasant master bedroom with a king bed and a tiled bath with sunken tub as well as a roomy second bedroom with two twin beds and private bath. Each costs $65, breakfast included, and has a view of grazing cattle with a mountain backdrop.

There are also two guest cottages on the grounds, both with breakfast fixings provided. The charming Victorian ($115) is light and airy, with high ceilings, natural oak floors, a master bedroom with a queen bed, an upstairs loft with two twin beds, a full kitchen, ceiling fans, TV and phone. The second cottage ($85) is simpler and studio-style, with coconut-frond thatching on the roof and screened windows all around that open to a garden with birdsong. It has a king bed, queen-size futon, kitchenette, ceiling fans, indoor toilet, outdoor hot shower and barbecue grill.

A third building, the Bunkhouse, has three straightforward but comfortable rooms geared for budget travelers. Each has its own sink, coffeemaker, toaster and small refrigerator. All share a toilet and outdoor shower. Rates, without breakfast, are $40 each for the two smallest rooms, $50 for the largest. All accommodations are nonsmoking. Rosewood also handles other cottages and condos around Kauai.

The *House of Aleva* (☎ 822-4606), Ernest and Anita Perry, 5509 Kuamoo Rd, Kapaa, HI 96746, is a B&B right on Hwy 580, two miles up from Coco Palms. Ernest is a retired merchant seaman and Anita is a retired nurse who reads palms and makes ceramic Hawaiiana sculptures. They rent out two upstairs rooms with a shared bath in their home, at $55 a double. The rooms have queen beds with comfortable mattresses, phones, TV and mini-refrigerators. There's also a smaller downstairs room with a twin bed that rents for $40 single. Rates include continental breakfast. Photos of past guests, which line one wall, include a fair number of European travelers.

Kauai's first B&B is still called *Kay Barker's B&B* (☎ 822-3073, 800-835-2845), Box 740, Kapaa, HI 96746, though Kay has passed away and the place is now run by her son Gordon. While the house is a little more modest than some of the other Wailua B&Bs, it's still quite comfortable. The back yard looks out onto a field with grazing cattle and borders the trail to the Sleeping Giant. There are four bedrooms, each with a private bath, which cost $45 to $60 for singles, $55 to $70 for doubles, breakfast included. Guests have use of a refrigerator; smoking and social drinking are allowed. A separate two-room cottage with a microwave, sink and refrigerator costs $70/80 for singles/doubles, $10 more for each additional person.

Inn Paradise (☎ 822-2542; mcinch@ aloha.net), Major and Connie Inch, 6381 Mukana Rd, Kapaa, HI 96746, has three delightful units with nice touches like Persian carpets, rattan furnishings and quality Hawaiiana wall prints. Each has a phone, cable TV, refrigerator, microwave, toaster, coffeemaker and private entrance. The three units are in a guesthouse that stands separate from the Inchs' contemporary home. All share a lanai with an unspoiled view of pasture and mountains. The Prince Kuhio room, which has a king bed, costs $60. The Queen Kapule suite, which has a king bed and a separate living room with a Murphy bed, costs $75. The King Kaumualii unit, which is equipped like a small house, has two bedrooms, one with a king bed, the other two twins, and a full kitchen; it costs $100. Additional guests beyond two in the smaller units or four in the larger are $7 more. There's a two-night

minimum; rates include breakfast provisions and use of a washer and dryer.

Hale Kahawai (☎ 822-1031; fax 823-8220; bandbkauai@aol.com), Arthur Lucas and Thomas Hart, 185 Kahawai Place, Kapaa, HI 96746, is a B&B that's popular with gay and lesbian travelers. This pleasant contemporary home has lovely mountain views from the rear deck, where there's a hot tub. Guests have access to a kitchen and a spacious living room with a 35-inch TV. Two small rooms with queen beds and shared bath cost $60/70 for singles/ doubles, while a third upstairs room with king bed and private bath is $10 more. There's also an apartment on the ground level with a kitchenette, full bath, queen bed and sofa bed for $90. Rates include a breakfast of fruit, cereal and Thomas' homemade bread.

Royal Drive Cottages (☎ 822-2321), Bob Levine, 147 Royal Drive, Kapaa, HI 96746, consists of two studio cottages on a quiet street just off Hwy 580. The cottages have a pleasant Hawaiian simplicity that's wholly adequate, each with two twin beds, phone, refrigerator, microwave, hot plates and coffeemaker. One of the units also has a screened lanai and cable TV. The cottages do have corrugated metal roofs and this is a wet island – some people find the sound of rain on tin romantic, while it might keep others awake. The rate for either cottage is $80.

Hale Lani (☎ 822-5216; fax 822-5478), 5780 Lokelani Rd, Kapaa, HI 96746, is an immaculate two-bedroom cottage that would make an ideal home away from home. Built by a Seattle couple as a future retirement residence, it has oak floors, cathedral ceilings, a washer/dryer, ceiling fans, a fully equipped kitchen and a living room with a stereo system, TV and VCR. There's a double bed in one bedroom, a king bed in the other. The price is a reasonable $100 for up to six people, plus a cleaning charge of $50 that covers the entire stay. This is a nonsmoking property in a quiet neighborhood at the base of the Sleeping Giant Trail.

Places to Stay – Hotels & Condos

Wailua's hotels and condos all have swimming pools and the usual standard resort facilities.

Kauai Sands Hotel (☎ 822-4951, 800-367-7000; sandsea@hawaii.net), 420 Papaloa Rd, Kapaa, HI 96746, is part of the Hawaiian-owned Sand & Seaside hotel chain. The rooms, which are in a series of two-story buildings that mostly surround the lawn and pool, are a bit plainer than those in neighboring hotels, but it's a good value, especially if you book at the rates commonly advertised within Hawaii: around $55 for a room only, $128 for two nights with a car. Otherwise, the rate quoted to people who call from the mainland using the toll-free number is $85 for standard rooms, $120 for rooms with kitchenettes.

Kapaa Sands (☎ 822-4901, 800-222-4901; fax 822-1556), 380 Papaloa Rd, Kapaa, HI 96746, has 24 condo units set up in either duplexes or fourplexes. All have kitchens, lanais, louvered windows to catch the breeze, and at least a partial ocean view. While the complex is an older one, the units were thoroughly renovated after Hurricane Iniki and are a relatively good value at $80 for studios for one or two people and $104 for two-bedroom units for up to four people. Oceanfront units cost $10 more. There's a three-day minimum stay in the low season, seven days in the winter.

The *Aston Kauai Beachboy Hotel* (☎ 822-3441, 800-847-7417; fax 822-0843), 484 Kuhio Hwy, Kapaa, HI 96746, is a modern beachfront hotel with 243 rooms in blocks of three-story buildings. Although undistinguished, the rooms are pleasant enough and have either one king or two double beds, aircon, lanai, TV, mini-refrigerator and room safe. Rates range from $105 to $145, depending on the view and the season, but there are often promotional discounts.

Islander on the Beach (☎ 822-7417, 800-847-7417; fax 822-1947), 484 Kuhio Hwy, Kapaa, HI 96746, has 195 hotel rooms in half a dozen three-story buildings. Rooms have king or double beds, refrigerators, coffeemakers, air-con, TVs, room safes and lanais. Rates range from $98 for a garden-

view room to $128 for an oceanfront room. There's a poolside bar.

Kauai Resort Hotel (☎ 245-3931, 800-367-5004; fax 596-0158), 3-5920 Kuhio Hwy, Kapaa, HI 96746, run by Hawaiian Pacific Resorts, is north of Lydgate Beach Park and next to the Wailua Golf Course. Standard rooms, which are on the small side, begin at a pricey $124, but that rate usually throws in a free rental car with advance reservations. The hotel commonly participates in discount schemes that can cut the rates by as much as half.

On the highway side of Coconut Plantation is *Plantation Hale* (☎ 822-4941, 800-775-4253; fax 822-5599; reservations@outrigger.com), 484 Kuhio Hwy, Kapaa, HI 96746. Now part of the Outrigger chain, the complex has 160 spacious one-bedroom units with modern furnishings, two doubles or one king bed in the bedroom, a queen sofa bed in the living room, a separate full kitchen, a phone, air-con, ceiling fans and two TVs. The rate of $110/125 in the low/high season is the same for up to four people, which makes it a good value for small groups. Outrigger often throws in a free rental car with advance reservations and offers various discounts.

Kauai Coconut Beach Resort (☎ 822-3455, 800-222-5642; fax 822-1830), Box 830, Kapaa, HI 96746, a former Sheraton, is a 309-room hotel at the quieter north end of Coconut Plantation. The rooms are comfortable, with either two doubles or a king bed, a TV, room safe, mini-refrigerator, coffeemaker and tiny lanai that can barely fit two people. The 4th-floor rooms are the nicest, as they have high ceilings that make the rooms feel a bit larger. Rates are $125 for a standard room, $175 for an ocean view, but discounts are common. If you book in advance and request the car-room deal, you can usually get a rental car at no extra cost.

Places to Eat

Sizzler steak house, 4361 Kuhio Hwy, has a good salad bar that includes greens, fresh fruit and a taco and pasta bar. As an all-you-can-eat meal by itself, the cost is $8 at lunch, $9 at dinner; if you're ordering a separate meal, it costs $4 to add on the salad bar. Chicken and burgers begin at $6 at lunch, and steaks cost $9 to $15 at dinner.

Mema (☎ 823-0899), within the same complex as the Sizzler, has pleasant decor and some of the best Thai food in all Hawaii. The shrimp rolls served on a bed of fresh lettuce and mint leaves make a nice appetizer, while the chicken red chili with coconut milk is a recommendable entree. There's a good-value dinner for two that includes both of the aforementioned dishes plus green papaya salad, a shrimp broccoli entree and delicious warm tapioca pudding for $33. Or you can order from a range of chicken, beef and pork dishes for around $8, shrimp or fish dishes for $10. Most dishes can also be prepared vegetarian. At dinner it's best to arrive early or call ahead to make reservations. It's open from 11 am to 2 pm on weekdays and 5 to 9:30 pm daily; takeout is available.

The popular *Kintaro* (☎ 822-3341), opposite Sizzler, has Japanese dinners priced from $13 to $20. This large restaurant has a good sushi bar and a teppanyaki room where the chef prepares food at your table with 'flying knives'. It's open from 5:30 to 9:30 pm Monday to Saturday.

The restaurant at the *Aston Kauai Beachboy Hotel* in Coconut Plantation has a peek of the ocean and a basic breakfast buffet that includes fresh fruit, egg dishes and breakfast meats for $7.50; it's served from 6:30 to 10 am.

There are a handful of food kiosks in the Coconut Marketplace. Best among them are *Aloha Kauai Pizza*, with good moderately priced pizzas and calzones; the *Fish Hut*, with fresh fish sandwiches for $5 and fish & chips for $7; and *Harley's Ribs-N-Chicken*, which has Cajun chicken sandwiches for $5 and a good Caesar salad with lemon-pepper chicken for $6.25. Coconut Marketplace also has a couple of sit-down restaurants, an average cafe/bakery and a convenience store that sells snacks and liquor. All are open at least from 11 am to 8 pm.

Entertainment
Coconut Marketplace Cinemas in the Coconut Marketplace is a two-screen theater showing first-run movies.

Free hula shows take place at the Coconut Marketplace at 5 pm on Mondays, Wednesdays, Fridays and Saturdays.

Kauai Coconut Beach Resort (☎ 822-3455) has a luau at 6 pm nightly. It includes an open bar, dinner and a rather standard Polynesian revue. The cost is $49 for adults, $28 for children ages five to 11. You can catch a glimpse of it from the hotel parking lot. If you're interested in seeing the imu preparation, you can watch the pig being stuffed with hot rocks and buried at 10:45 am.

Smith's Tropical Paradise (☎ 821-6895), at Wailua Marina, has a luau with cocktails, dinner and show at 6 pm on Mondays, Wednesdays and Fridays. It costs $47 for adults, $27 for children ages seven to 13 and $18 for children ages three to six.

WAIPOULI
Waipouli is the mile-long strip between Coconut Plantation and Kapaa. Its biggest draw is its shopping centers, which are not only the area's largest, but also contain some of Kauai's best places to eat.

Information
Money A Bankoh ATM, which accepts major credit and debit cards, is inside the Foodland supermarket in the Waipouli Town Center.

Post & Communication The Kapaa post office, in the Kapaa Shopping Center, is open from 8:30 am to 5 pm Monday to Friday, from 10 am to noon on Saturdays.

Laundry There's a coin laundry in the Kapaa Shopping Center.

Sleeping Giant
There's a marked viewpoint just north of the Waipouli Complex where you can see the outline of the Sleeping Giant, who is taking his eternal rest stretched out atop Nounou Ridge with his head in Wailua and his feet in Kapaa.

KAUAI

Legend tells of a friendly giant who fell asleep on the hillside after eating too much poi at a luau. When his menehune friends needed his help, they tried to awaken him by throwing stones, but the stones bounced from his full belly into his open mouth. As the stones lodged in the giant's throat, he died in his sleep and turned into rock.

A hiking trail runs across the ridge connecting Wailua Houselots and Wailua Homesteads (see the Wailua section). The giant's forehead, the highest point on the ridge, is 1241 feet.

Places to Stay

Mokihana of Kauai (☎ 822-3971), 796 Kuhio Hwy, is a time-share complex that rents to nonmembers on a space-available basis. It has 80 studio units on the beach and while they're rather plain, each has twin beds, a hot plate, a refrigerator and a lanai with an ocean view for $65.

The front desk at Mokihana also handles the 57 two-bedroom time-share units at nearby *Kauai Kailani*. These units have full kitchens, two twin beds in one room and a double in the other, and cost $65 in the inland wing and $75 in the oceanside building; rates cover up to four people.

Don't expect anything upmarket, as the units have a strictly economy feel, but they're adequate and the price is a bargain, particularly during the high season. You can also make advance reservations through Hawaii Kailani (☎ 206-676-1434, 800-682-8945; fax 206-676-1435), 119 N Commercial St, Suite 1400, Bellingham, WA 98225.

Places to Eat

The *King & I* (☎ 822-1642) in Waipouli Plaza has good Thai food at reasonable prices. The spring rolls make a nice starter, while the green curry, which gets its color from fresh basil, lime leaves and lemongrass, is an excellent choice for an entree. The curries, like most other dishes on the menu, cost $7 for meat varieties, $9 for shrimp or fish. All can be prepared mild, medium or hot. The restaurant has both Thai and brown rice, and virtually any dish

can be ordered vegetarian. It's open daily from 4:30 to 9:30 pm, to 10 pm on Fridays and Saturdays.

The *Aloha Diner*, a local eatery in the Waipouli Complex, is the place to try authentic Hawaiian food, including good laulau and lomi salmon. You can order à la carte, or get complete lunches from about $6, dinners for about $10. It's open Tuesday through Saturday from 10:30 am to 3 pm and from 5:30 to 9 pm.

Papaya's Natural Foods in Kauai Village is a well-stocked health food store with a cafe serving wholesome salads, sandwiches and casserole-style warm dishes. Hearty vegie burgers cost $5 and plate lunches are $6 to $8. Papaya's is open from 9 am to 8 pm Monday to Saturday. There are outside tables in front of the store.

A Pacific Cafe (☎ 822-0013) in Kauai Village is a bustling, high-energy restaurant that serves excellent Pacific Rim cuisine. French chef Jean-Marie Josselin has a creative menu with dishes like fresh snapper in a delicate Thai curry sauce and Chinese roast duck with ginger-lime glaze. Starters and soups range from $6 to $10, and main dishes are $20 to $25. The main dish portions are generous, so you might want to skip (or share) a starter. For an indulgent dessert, try the caramel chocolate mousse. A Pacific Cafe is a class act, with artful presentation and attentive service – if you're saving one night for a splurge on Kauai, this is certainly a top choice. Hours are from 5:30 to 10 pm; reservations are usually essential, certainly on holidays and weekends.

At the opposite end of the gastronomic scale are the slew of fast-food eateries, including *KFC* and *Taco Bell* north of Waipouli Plaza, *Subway Sandwiches* in Kauai Village, *Burger King* at the Kapaa Shopping Center and *McDonald's* and *Pizza Hut* in the Waipouli Town Center.

A good alternative to fast food is the 24-hour *Safeway* supermarket in Kauai Village, which has a deli counter with fried chicken and salads, a bakery with doughnuts and bread and a fish counter with eight kinds of poki, including a delicious sesame-ahi variety. In addition, the store has some of the cheapest wine prices on the island.

Foodland supermarket in the Waipouli Town Center is open daily from 6 am to 11 pm. They have a good selection of doughnuts and breakfast pastries, cheap hot coffee and even a couple of cafe-style tables.

Big Save supermarket, open from 7 am to 11 pm daily, is in the Kapaa Shopping Center.

KAPAA

Kapaa is an old plantation town with a small commercial center that is half-local, half-tourist oriented. As unimposing as it appears, Kapaa is one of Kauai's largest towns. However most of the residential area is well inland of the center and you can walk the main drag in just 10 minutes.

While many of its historic buildings were leveled by Iniki, most of the reconstruction has been in keeping with the town's original character rather than adopting the shopping mall appearance that predominates to the south of Kapaa. The town has the island's only hostel, a small hotel, a few restaurants and a couple of water sports and clothing shops.

Information

Money Bank of Hawaii and First Hawaiian Bank have branches on Kuhio Hwy in the town center.

Library & Books Kapaa Public Library, 1464 Kuhio Hwy, is open from 9 am to 5 pm on Mondays, Wednesdays and Fridays and noon to 8 pm on Tuesdays and Thursdays.

Tin Can Mailman, a bookstore at 1353 Kuhio Hwy, has a good collection of new and used Hawaiiana books.

Kapaa Beach Park

Kapaa Beach Park begins along the north side of Kapaa, where there's a ball field, picnic tables and a public swimming pool. The beach continues south for about a mile; the section fronting the Pono Kai condos has one of the nicer sandy sections. Along the length of the beach, a shoreline

foot and bicycle path follows a former cane-rail line and passes over a couple of old bridges along the way. If you're staying in the area, the path makes an appealing alternative to walking along the highway to and from town.

Places to Stay

Kauai International Hostel (☎ 823-6142, 800-858-2295 within Hawaii), 4532 Lehua St, Kapaa, HI 96746, is a private hostel in the center of Kapaa. There are about 30 dorm beds, four to six to a room, and five simple private rooms with double beds. The dorm beds cost $15, the private rooms $40. All rooms, including the private rooms, have shared bathrooms. The hostel has a common dining room, kitchen, TV room and coin laundry. Bags can be stored for free while you're hiking, and day trips ($30) are usually available about twice a week, as long as a minimum of four people have signed up. The hostel is popular with European visitors, and there's usually someone around who speaks German and French. Note that there's a no-refund policy, so if you're going to be paying for several days in advance, make sure that this is where you want to be for that entire period.

The *Hotel Coral Reef* (☎ 822-4481, 800-843-4659; fax 822-7705), 1516 Kuhio Hwy, Kapaa, HI 96746, is a small family-run hotel with two sections. The newest and best-value rooms are in the main building, which was rebuilt after Iniki and has a handful of $59 rooms with private bath, TV and either one queen or a double and twin bed. Rooms in the older seaside building have oceanfront lanais and a bit more room but are not as spiffy and cost $89. Complimentary coffee and homemade breads are available at breakfast time in the lobby. There's no pool, but it's right on the beach.

Keapana Center (☎ 822-7968, 800-822-7968), 5620 Keapana Rd, Kapaa, HI 96746, is a relaxing New Age B&B with a scenic hilltop location three miles above Kapaa center. There are three rooms with shared bath at $40/55 singles/doubles and two rooms with private bath at $55/70. The rooms are small and suitably simple, and rates include continental breakfast and use of the hot tub. There's a common-use refrigerator and microwave, a large airy lounge and a platform for sunrise stretching with a splendid view of the Anahola Mountains. Metaphysical books are loaned free, and massage is available for a fee. No pre-teen children are allowed.

The beachfront *Pono Kai Resort* (☎ 822-9831), 4-1250 Kuhio Hwy, Kapaa, HI 96746, is a well-maintained 219-room condominium at the south side of Kapaa. Units are roomy and well equipped, with full kitchens including dishwashers and microwaves, living rooms with queen sofa beds, air-con, ceiling fans, cable TV, VCR and lanais. There's a pool, spa, tennis courts and beach and it's within walking distance of the town center. Although most people book through Marc Resorts (☎ 800-535-0085), which manages some of the units here, its rates begin at a steep $159 for a one-bedroom unit and $199 for a two-bedroom two-bath unit. For a better deal, contact RCIM (☎ 909-736-2112, 800-438-6493), which handles the majority of Pono Kai's units as time-share properties. RCIM commonly has a few unoccupied units that it rents out to the general public at $119/149 for one-/two-bedroom condos; for stays of a week, the seventh night is free.

Places to Eat

All of these restaurants except Kapaa Fish & Chowder House are within a few minutes walk of each other on Kuhio Hwy (Hwy 56), near its intersection with Olohena Rd.

Bubba's, opposite the hostel, has hot dogs, chili dogs, fish & chips and a range of burgers, all priced under $5. It's open from 10:30 am to 6 pm Monday to Saturday.

Hana-Ya is a little Japanese restaurant with a small sushi bar and a few tables. Soba or oyako donburi cost around $6 and there's a full menu of other dishes priced from $6 to $15. It's open from 11:30 am to 2 pm weekdays and from 5:30 to 9:30 pm Sunday to Friday.

Norberto's El Cafe (☎ 822-3362), Kauai's original Mexican restaurant, serves hearty portions of the usual Mexican fare,

with full dinner plates priced from $12 to $15. You can wash it down with margaritas or Mexican brew. It's open from 5:30 to 9 pm daily, except Sundays.

Kapaa Fish & Chowder House (☎ 822-7488) on Kuhio Hwy, half a mile north of Kapaa center, has good fresh fish. Main dishes, which are served with a house salad, include calamari ($16), shrimp scampi ($17) and fresh fish of the day or a steak and fish combo for around $20. Children's portions are half price. It's open for dinner only from 5:30 pm daily.

You can pick up fresh fruit and vegetables at *Sunny Side*, a large produce stand at the south side of Kapaa.

KAPAA TO KILAUEA

The drive north from Kapaa heads through fields of sugar cane in varying stages of growth, from newly planted seed cane to mature stalk. Beyond the fields, the jagged edges of the Anahola mountain peaks cut their way through the clouds. In the other direction, there are glimpses of bright blue ocean and distant bays.

A couple of scenic lookouts just north of Kapaa are worth pulling over for. Sunsets can be particularly nice if there's a low tide with waves breaking over the shallows and fishers out with their throw nets.

Kealia Beach

The long, pretty beach at the 10-mile marker is Kealia Beach. During transitional swells, Kealia can be a good place for surfing. There are no facilities here.

After rain storms the beach tends to be heavily littered with tree limbs that are carried down Kealia Stream, which empties at the south side of the beach.

Donkey Beach

Donkey Beach is best known as a nudist beach, frequented largely by gay visitors, though it's used by both clad and unclad sunbathers. This lovely windswept sandy beach is hidden from the road and takes some effort to reach.

The trail to Donkey Beach begins about half a mile past the 11-mile marker; look for cars parked at the side of the road. It's a 10-minute walk down a well-worn path beside a sugar cane field and through a narrow stretch of coastal ironwoods.

Because of the strong winds along the coast here, all the ironwood trees lean away from the shore and those right at the beach are so blown over they almost look like shrubs. Naupaka and ilima grow in the sand along the shadeless beach. There are no facilities. From October to May, high surf creates dangerous rip currents and a powerful shorebreak.

Anahola

Anahola is a small, scattered village, much of it spread out along Anahola Bay. This wide bay was an ancient surfing site, and its break is still popular with surfers today.

Anahola Beach Park, a county park on Hawaiian Home Lands, sits at the south side of the bay. To get there, turn off Hwy 56 onto Kukuihale Rd at the 13-mile marker, drive a mile down and then turn onto the dirt beach road.

Anahola's modest commercial center consists of the Anahola post office, Duane's burger stand and a small general store grouped together at the side of Hwy 56, just south of the 14-mile marker.

Just to the north, on the mauka side of the road, the quaint little **Anahola Baptist Church** is backed by a picturesque mountain setting.

Places to Stay On Anahola Bay, *Mahina Kai* (☎ /fax 822-9451; trudy@aloha.net), Box 699, 4933 Aliomanu Rd, Anahola, HI 96703, is a B&B that caters to the gay and lesbian community. The contemporary home has Asian-Pacific touches, such as shoji doors and a swimming pool and hot tub in a Japanese garden. It's a nice, quiet place to relax. There are three rooms with private bathrooms at $95/115 singles/doubles, breakfast included, as well as a two-bedroom apartment with kitchenette that costs $150 for two people, $175 for four.

Places to Eat The popular *Duane's Ono Charburger* sells good sandwiches and

burgers for $4 to $7. The best deal is the basic burger, as more expensive burgers basically add a dollop of sauce on top. There are outdoor picnic tables where you can chow down. It's open from 10 am to 6 pm daily (from 11 am on Sundays).

Whaler's General Store, next door to Duane's, has hard-boiled eggs for a quarter, hot dogs for a dollar and cold beer. It's open daily from 6:30 am to 9:30 pm.

Hole in the Mountain

Although the Hole in the Mountain, once an obvious sight, was largely filled in by a landslide in the 1980s, a speck of it is still visible. Slightly north of the 15-mile marker, look back at the mountain down to the right of the tallest pinnacle and you'll be able to see a shimmer of light coming through a small opening in the rock face.

Legend says the original hole was created when a giant threw his spear through the mountain, causing the water stored within to gush forth as waterfalls. Incidentally, after the landslide closed the hole, Hawaii began to experience one of the worst droughts in its history.

Koolau Rd

Koolau Rd is a peaceful drive through rich green pastures with white egrets and a smattering of bright wildflowers. Take it as a scenic loop off the highway or to get to Moloaa Beach or Larsens Beach. Both the road and the beaches are well off the tourist track. Neither beach has any facilities.

Koolau Rd connects with Hwy 56 half a mile north of the 16-mile marker and again one-tenth of a mile south of the 20-mile marker.

Moloaa Beach To get to Moloaa Beach coming from the south, turn right onto Koolau Rd and after 1¼ miles turn right onto Moloaa Rd. The road ends three-quarters of a mile down at a few beach houses. As the road near the beach is narrow, finding a place to park can be quite challenging.

Moloaa is very rural, with horses grazing on the hills above the crescent-shaped bay. The northern end of the beach before the rocky outcrop is somewhat protected for swimming, though it's not all that deep. The whole bay can have strong currents when the surf is rough.

Larsens Beach Larsens is a long golden-sand beach, good for solitary strolls and beachcombing. Although it's a bit shallow for swimming, snorkeling can be good when the waters are very calm, which is generally in the summer only. Beware of a current that runs westward along the beach and out through a channel in the reef.

Often the Holstein cattle that graze the hills above the beach are the only company you'll encounter. However, if the tide is low, you may well see a few Hawaiian families on the outer edge of the reef collecting an edible seaweed called *limu kohu*. The seaweed found at Larsens is considered to be some of the finest in all Hawaii.

The turn-off to Larsens Beach is off Koolau Rd, a little more than a mile down from the north intersection of Koolau Rd and Hwy 56, or just over a mile north of the intersection of Moloaa and Koolau Rds. Turn makai on the dirt road there and then take the immediate left. It's one mile to the parking area and then a five-minute walk downhill to the beach.

North Shore

Kauai's North Shore has an unhurried pace and incredible scenery. It has deep mountain valleys, rolling cattle pastures, ancient taro fields, white-sand beaches and the rugged Na Pali Coast.

The North Shore is lush and often wet. In winter that can mean days on end of rain, but in summer it usually means brief showers followed by rainbows. On bright full-moon nights you might even see a moonbow – a rainbow colored with moonbeams.

Rainy days are almost dream-like. The tops of the mountains become shrouded in clouds that alternately drift and lift revealing a series of waterfalls that plunge down the face of the mountains.

The North Shore takes in the seabird sanctuary at Kilauea and a couple of small coastal villages before reaching the resort community of Princeville with its condos and golf courses.

But it's the area beyond, from Hanalei Bridge to Kee Beach at road's end, that best embodies the North Shore spirit. This is a part of Hawaii that has resisted mass tourism and stalled development. Its appeal is not in creature comforts but in stunning natural beauty. It attracts people tuned in to the environment. Over the years musicians like Graham Nash and Buffy Sainte-Marie and numerous other alternative-minded folks have made Kauai's North Shore home.

KILAUEA

Kilauea is a former sugar plantation town whose main attraction is its picturesque lighthouse and seabird sanctuary at Kilauea Point. The sanctuary is the most visited site on the North Shore and shouldn't be missed.

Kolo Rd, the main turn-off into Kilauea, is a third of a mile beyond the 23-mile marker on Hwy 56. On Kolo Rd, you pass a gas station, a post office with a mini-mart and then an Episcopal church, all in quick succession. Kilauea Rd starts opposite the church and ends two miles later at Kilauea Point.

Episcopal Church

The little Christ Memorial Episcopal Church attracts attention because of its striking lava-rock architecture. It was built in 1941, but the interesting lava-rock headstones in the churchyard are much older, dating back to when the original Hawaiian Congregational Church stood on this site.

Also near the corner, diagonally opposite the church, is Aloha International, which has an exhibit of traditional Hawaiiana, including musical instruments and leis, that you can view for free.

Kilauea Bay

If you're looking for someplace new to explore, you might try Rock Quarry Beach at Kilauea Bay. Also known as Kahili Beach, it's a nice sandy beach and the site of an abandoned rock quarry and steamer landing. This remote beach is mostly used by local fishers, but when the surf is unusually high, surfers also take to these waters. Swimmers should be aware of strong near shore currents when the surf is up.

Public access is via Wailapa Rd, which begins midway between the 21- and 22-mile markers. Follow Wailapa Rd north for a half-mile beyond Hwy 56 and then turn left on the dirt road that begins at a yellow water valve. The dirt road, which continues for a half-mile before ending at the beach, is usually in fairly good shape and passable in a car.

Kilauea Point

Kilauea Point (☎ 828-1413), a national wildlife refuge, is the northernmost point of the inhabited Hawaiian Islands. Topped by a lighthouse that was built in 1913, it's picture-postcard material.

Four species of birds come to Kilauea to nest, most leaving after their young have been hatched and reared. Red-footed boobies, the most visible, are abundant on the cliffs to the east of the point, where they build nests of sticks and leaves in the trees. They nest from February to September, with their peak egg laying occurring in spring.

Wedge-tailed shearwaters arrive by April and stay until November, nesting in burrows that they dig into Kilauea Point. Another readily spotted species is the red-tailed tropicbird, which nests along the cliff edges from March to October. If you're lucky, you'll spot a pair flying in loops, performing their courtship ritual.

Laysan albatross are at Kilauea from about November to July. Some nest on Mokuaeae Rock, straight off the tip of the point. Other albatross nesting sites are on the grassy clearing to the west of Kilauea Point. If you look out beyond this clearing, you can also see Secret Beach, divided into three scalloped coves by lava fingers.

Great frigate birds nest on the Northwestern Hawaiian Islands, not Kauai, though these aerial pirates do visit Kilauea Point to steal food from other birds. Great frigate birds can be spotted circling above

Kilauea Point year-round. You won't see the distinctive red throat balloon that the male puffs out to attract females though, as they're not here for courtship. Frigate birds, which have a wing span of seven feet and a distinctive forked tail, are beautiful when they soar.

While birds are certainly the main attraction at Kilauea Point, with a little luck you might also spot sea turtles swimming in the cove at the base of the cliffs. During winter it's not unusual to see whales pass by the point.

The refuge is open from 10 am to 4 pm daily, except on federal holidays. Admission is $2 for adults, free for children under 12. Binoculars and scopes are available to use and books on flora and fauna are for sale.

Even outside opening hours it's worth driving to the end of Kilauea Rd for the picturesque view of the lighthouse and point.

Guava Kai Plantation

The Guava Kai Plantation has 480 acres of guava trees that produce juice for Ocean Spray and a handful of other juice companies. A visitor center doles out small samples of guava juice and sells guava products. There's also a path through a garden planted with tropical flowers that's good for a short stroll.

To get there, turn mauka onto Kuawa Rd from Hwy 56, just north of the 23-mile marker and a quarter of a mile south of the Kolo Rd turn-off to Kilauea. The visitor center, which is open daily from 9 am to 5 pm, is about a mile from the highway.

As you go up the road past rows of guava trees it might seem like the fruit is too big to be the same guava that grows wild elsewhere on the island – in fact these guava trees are hybrids whose fruit grows to half a pound, twice the normal size.

Places to Eat

The *Farmer's Market*, a grocery store with a good deli, is in the Kong Lung Center, half a mile up Kilauea Rd. The deli has a variety of sandwiches on whole-wheat bread, good hummus rolls and salads. The store is open from 8:30 am to 8:30 pm

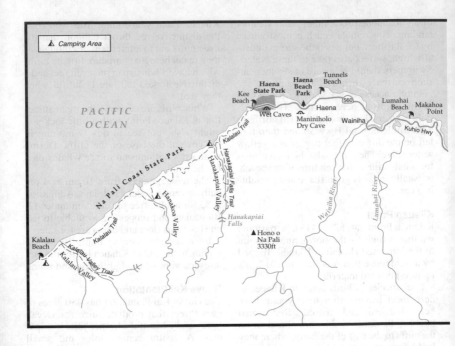

daily, the deli from 10 am to 2 pm Monday to Saturday and 9 am to 1 pm on Sundays.

Kilauea Bakery & Pau Hana Pizza, tucked in the back of the Kong Lung Center, sells breakfast pastries, pizza and breads. From 11 am to around 3 pm there's gourmet pizza by the slice for $2.75. Whole pizzas, available until closing, cost from $11.25 for a 12-inch cheese version; optional toppings range from pepperoni to soy-based 'mozzarella' and feta cheese. It's open from 6:30 am to 9 pm daily except Sundays. There are tables on the lawn where you can eat, weather permitting.

A good place for a sit-down meal in these parts is the *Roadrunner Cafe*, at 2430 Oka St, a right turn off Kilauea Rd one block prior to the Kong Lung Center. This family-run operation is a combination bakery and cafe, with hearty breads, healthy salads and Mexican fare. An ahi salad with fresh tuna and local organic greens costs $7, as do a pair of fish tacos

served with rice and beans. Most items can also be ordered in meat, tofu or vegan versions. It's open from 7 am to 8 pm Monday to Saturday and 8:30 am to 1:30 pm on Sundays.

For a down-home treat, stop at *Banana Joe's*, the bright yellow shack on the mauka side of Hwy 56, just north of the Kolo Rd turn-off to Kilauea. They dish up a nice fruit frosty, made solely of frozen fruit that is squeezed through a processor and is as smooth as ice cream. The papaya and pineapple flavors are the best. A bowl of this ($2) and a granola bar ($1.25) make a nice snack. You can also buy dried banana and jackfruit strips and a few fresh fruit items grown on the adjacent six-acre plot. The stand is open from 9 am to 6 pm daily.

KALIHIWAI
Kalihiwai Rd was a loop road going down past Kalihiwai Beach, connecting with the

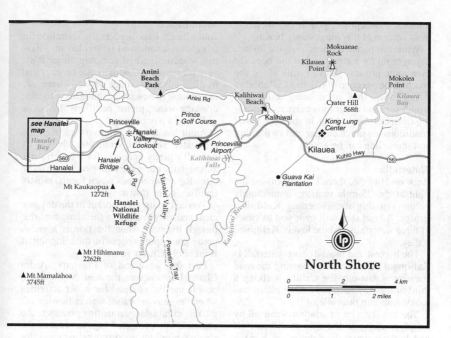

North Shore

highway at two points, until the tidal wave of 1957 washed out the bridge over Kalihiwai River. The bridge was never rebuilt and now there are two Kalihiwai roads, one on each side of the river.

The Kalihiwai Rd half a mile west of Kilauea leads down a mile to **Kalihiwai Beach**. At the very end of the road you can still see the pillars that once supported the bridge. The river empties out into a wide, deep bay. The broad, sandy beach is a popular spot for all kinds of activities, including picnicking, swimming, boogie boarding, bodysurfing and, when the northwest swells roll in, some daredevil surfing along the cliff at the east end of the bay. The river is popular with kayakers. The beach has no facilities.

As you take Kalihiwai Rd back up to the highway, look to the left as soon as you see the 'Narrow Bridge' sign; you'll spot a picturesque waterfall that's partially hidden in a little valley.

Secret Beach

Secret Beach is a gorgeous golden-sand beach backed by sea cliffs and jungle-like woods. The beach is well off the beaten path and access to it has changed frequently over the years, so very few visitors discover it. Secret Beach is frequented mostly by Kauai's alternative community and nude sunbathers, and while tourists aren't exactly welcomed, unobtrusive visitors who can blend in are unlikely to encounter any problems.

To get there, turn down the Kalihiwai Rd half mile west of Kilauea and then turn right onto the first dirt road, which is a tenth of a mile from Hwy 56. The road ends at a parking area a third of a mile down.

The well-defined trail begins from the parking lot along a barbed wire fence that separates the woods from a horse pasture. After two minutes it leads downhill through ironwood trees and mixed jungle growth. All in all, the trail only takes about five minutes and deposits you at the western-most section of this long, sandy beach.

While this part of the beach is quite idyllic, if you're up for a stroll or feel the need for even more privacy, you can walk along the beach in the direction of Kilauea Lighthouse.

The beach has open seas, with high winter surf and dangerous currents prevailing from October to May. In summer, water conditions are much calmer and swimming and snorkeling can be good.

Waterfalls

Back on Hwy 56, there's a pull-off on the right at the 25-mile marker, immediately before crossing the sweeping Kalihiwai Bridge. A brief stop will treat you to views of three waterfalls and the lovely Kalihiwai Valley.

The highest and most distant waterfall is **Kalihiwai Falls**, seen by crossing the road (beware of fast-moving traffic), walking a third of the way onto the bridge ahead and looking up into the valley.

You can see a bit of another waterfall by simply walking to the side of the pull-off and looking down over the edge. For the third you must walk back along the road a minute or two towards Lihue. The waterfall is just above the road.

ANINI

Anini has a long beach that's fronted by vast reef flats and backed by a beach park. To get there take the Kalihiwai Rd on the Hanalei side of the bridge and then bear left onto Anini Rd. It's about 1½ miles from the highway to the beach.

Over the years there's been talk of connecting Princeville and Anini by a direct coastal road, but local resistance to the plan has kept the road at bay. For now, Anini's dead-end street means little traffic, keeping this area unhurried and quiet.

Still, Anini is growing, and a number of exclusive homes have been built in recent years, including some by people with Hollywood connections. Don't expect to see Anini's best-known vacation home owner, Sylvester Stallone, however, as he's sold his property and moved on.

Anini Beach

Anini Beach Park borders the shoreline for more than a mile and is divided into day-use, windsurfing and camping areas. It's a very pleasant spot, with gentle breezes and tropical almond shade trees. There are restrooms, showers, changing rooms, drinking water, picnic pavilions, barbecue grills and a pay phone.

Anini has a good campground, right on the water, with the campsites shaded by trees. It's pretty spacious for a beach park, although the camping area gets a little more crowded on weekends when locals, mostly families, come down.

You can swim and snorkel in the day-use area, and also in front of the camping area, though it's best when the tide is high. A pretty good spot is opposite the midpoint of Kauai Polo Club's fence.

Past the west end of the park, Anini Channel cuts across the reef. While some people use the channel for water activities when the seas are calm, waters flowing off the reef create dangerous rip currents in the channel. The protected lagoon west of the channel provides good snorkeling and safer water conditions.

At the far end of Anini you can watch people walk way out onto the shallow reef of Anini Flats, picking opihi, net fishing and catching octopus.

PRINCEVILLE

Princeville, Kauai's biggest development, traces its haole roots to Robert Wyllie, a Scottish doctor who later became foreign minister to Kamehameha IV. In the mid-19th century, Wyllie bought a large coffee plantation in Hanalei and began planting sugar.

When Queen Emma and Kamehameha IV came to visit in 1860, Wyllie named his plantation and surrounding lands Princeville in honor of their young son, Prince Albert. The plantation later became a cattle ranch, and in 1968 ground was broken for the Princeville Resort.

Today, Princeville is a planned community spread over 11,000 acres on a promontory between Hanalei Bay and Anini Beach. It has a dozen condo complexes, a luxury hotel, hundreds of private homes, a couple of championship golf courses, restaurants, tennis courts, a shopping center and even its own little airport.

While it may seem out of place on the North Shore, and it certainly stands in sharp contrast to the free-spirited communities that lay beyond, Princeville's manicured grounds are spacious, the condos are low-rise and the development is uncrowded compared to its counterparts on other islands.

Information
Princeville Center has a gas station, supermarket, medical clinic, one-hour photo shop, Bank of Hawaii, ice cream shop and a few restaurants and boutiques. There's a post office inside the Foodland supermarket.

Princeville Chevron is open from 6 am to 9 pm daily. If you're heading towards Kee Beach at the end of the road, this is the last place to buy gas.

Kuhio Hwy changes from Hwy 56 to Hwy 560 at the 28-mile marker in front of Princeville Center. The 10-mile stretch from this point to Kee Beach at the end of the road is one of the most scenic drives in all of Hawaii.

Princeville Hotel
The Princeville Hotel offers a splendid view of Hanalei Bay and the Bali Hai mountains. The luxury hotel was erected amidst a great deal of controversy in 1985. Locals, who were miffed at losing one of their favorite sunset spots, nicknamed the bluffside building 'The Prison'. The hotel was indeed dark and inward-looking, and it so failed to incorporate its surroundings that the owners closed it down in 1989. Over the next two years the hotel was gutted and virtually rebuilt. The current Princeville Hotel has a lobby with floor-to-ceiling windows offering 180° views of Bali Hai. It also has marble floors, posh furniture, pools of flowing water and a smattering of antiques and artwork, but the real attraction is the view.

The site of a short-lived Russian fort, called **Fort Alexander**, and a shelter with interpretive displays can be found on a grassy knoll at the northwest side of the hotel. The display points out a couple of stones that were once part of the fort's foundation, but there's little else to see from that era.

Princeville is not known for its beaches, but there's a reasonably good-sized one, **Puu Poa Beach**, between the Princeville Hotel and the mouth of the Hanalei River. On the opposite side of the hotel, below the Puu Poa condos, **Pali Ke Kua** (also called Hideaways) is a secluded, sandy pocket of beach that has good swimming and snorkeling when it's calm. High surf, common in winter, can generate dangerous currents at both beaches.

Powerline Trail
In the 1930s, electric transmission lines were run along the mountains and a 13-mile maintenance route now known as the Powerline Trail was created. There is occasional talk of turning it into a real inland road connecting Princeville to Wailua, but environmental concerns make it unlikely to happen anytime soon.

To get to the trailhead, take the paved road going uphill from Princeville Ranch Stables, a third of a mile after the 27-mile marker on Hwy 56. The pavement ends at a water tank 1¾ miles up; even if you don't plan to hike the trail, the road makes for a pretty drive, offering fine mountain views and glimpses of Hanalei Bay.

The trail continues from the end of the pavement along a rutted 4WD dirt road used mainly by hunters and the power company. It's a full day's walk to its end at the Keahua Arboretum and is recommended only in dry weather.

Places to Stay
Sometimes you can find someone renting out a bedroom in their condo or home for about $50 a day. Most people list their rooms on the bulletin board outside the Foodland supermarket in Princeville Center, though occasionally someone will run an ad in the newspaper.

Some of Princeville's condo complexes are perched on cliffs, while others are by the golf course. While all of the complexes have some units that are vacation rentals, many units are occupied as year-round housing.

Princeville was hit hard by Hurricane Iniki and all of its condominium complexes suffered extensive damage, some of them taking a couple of years to reopen. Consequently, almost all have been thoroughly renovated and have a spiffy appearance.

Most condo complexes are represented by a number of different rental agents. While agents offer cheaper prices than direct bookings at a front desk, be aware that there may be cleaning fees, minimum stays and other restrictions. Three agents with fairly extensive Princeville rental listings, all with offices at Princeville Center, are:

Kauai Paradise Vacations, Box 1080, Hanalei, HI 96714 (☎ 826-7444, 800-826-7782; fax 826-7673; kpvl@aloha.net)
Oceanfront Realty, Box 3570, Princeville, HI 96722 (☎ 826-6585, 800-222-5541; fax 826-6478; ori@aloha.net)
Pacific Paradise Properties, Box 3195, Princeville, HI 96722 (☎ 826-7211, 800-800-3637; fax 826-9884)

Sealodge is an older complex and the quarters can be a bit cramped, but it's high on a cliff and many of the 86 units have great sunrise views across the expansive coral reef of Anini. If you leave the windows open, the surf is guaranteed to give you nautical dreams. One-bedroom units can be booked through the rental agents listed above for around $100.

Pali Ke Kua, a pleasant upmarket property near the Princeville Hotel, can be booked through Marc Resorts (☎ 922-9700, 800-535-0085; fax 922-2421; marc@aloha.net), which maintains an office at the complex. Rates range from $169 for a one-bedroom garden-view unit to $239 for a two-bedroom oceanview unit. There's a two-night minimum stay. The same Marc Resorts office also handles a couple of simpler units for $105 in the nearby *Hale Moi* complex, though most are occupied by long-term residents. Marc

offers numerous discount schemes that can cut rates by 20% to 50% – so their properties can be a bargain.

Hanalei Bay Resort (☎ 826-6522, 800-367-5004; fax 826-6680), 5380 Honoiki Rd, Princeville, HI 96722, has both hotel-style rooms and condo units. The hotel rooms range from $150 for a mountain view to $230 for an ocean view. Studios begin at $165, one-bedroom condos at $275 and two-bedroom condos at $380. The units are pleasant, there are fine views of Hanalei Bay and the grounds have a couple of swimming pools, including a large free-form one, and eight tennis courts.

The above rates apply to Castle Resorts, which manages the front desk and 230 of the 280 units here. You can usually find better deals through a couple of the condo rental agents listed in this section. A good one to start with is Kauai Paradise, which handles several Hanalei Bay Resort units, with rates starting from $100/120 for rooms/studios.

The *Cliffs at Princeville* is an older complex with one of the more ordinary settings, but its units have been refurbished and it remains relatively cheap for pricey Princeville. The units are large and have one bedroom, front and rear lanais, two bathrooms and all the usual condo amenities. It's adjacent to the golf course and there's a pool. Village Resorts (☎ 826-6219, 800-367-7052) maintains a front desk at the complex and handles 42 of the units, charging $155 to $225, but you should be able to get a better deal through an agent.

The *Princeville Hotel* (☎ 826-9644, 800-325-3535; webmaster@princeville.com), Box 3069, Princeville, HI 96722, a Sheraton property, has 252 luxury rooms with king beds, marble bathrooms and modern amenities that run the gamut from original oil paintings with dimmer-controlled spotlights to liquid-crystal windows between the bedroom and bath that can be turned from opaque to clear with the flick of a switch. Rates are $290 for a garden view, $435 for an ocean view and $3500 for the royal suite.

Places to Eat

Foodland supermarket in the Princeville Center has a bakery section with cheap doughnuts and pastries and a deli with plate lunches and other takeout items. The deli's tasty fried chicken breasts are the area's best value at $1.29 – grab a can of fruit juice and you've got yourself a cheap lunch. The store is open from 7 am to 11 pm daily.

Hale Java in the Princeville Center is open from 6:30 am to about 9:30 pm. It has good cafe food, including breakfast items, soups, sandwiches and deli salads at moderate prices. There are also pizzas from $8.50 to $20, depending on the size and toppings.

Chuck's Steak House in the Princeville Center has standard fare such as burgers and sandwiches for $5 to $8 at lunch and a dinner menu that ranges from $17 for chicken to $27 for steak and shrimp. Lunch is from 11:30 am to 2:30 pm weekdays only, dinner from 6 to 10 pm nightly.

The Princeville Restaurant & Bar at the Prince golf course, half a mile west of the Princeville Airport, has a broad view, a country club setting and average food at reasonable prices. At breakfast, from 8 to 11 am, a Belgian waffle or banana pancakes with an egg and bacon cost $6. At lunch, from 11:30 am to 3 pm, there are sandwiches, salads and good-value daily specials for $8 to $10. It's open daily for breakfast and lunch only.

The *Bali Hai Restaurant* in the Hanalei Bay Resort has open-air dining with a wonderful view of Hanalei Bay and the Bali Hai mountains. At breakfast, from 7 to 11 am, you can get a 'taro patch breakfast' of two fried eggs, Portuguese sausage, poi pancakes and taro hash browns for $8.25 or macnut waffles for $6.75. At lunch, from 11:30 am to 2 pm, sandwiches with fries average $10. Dinner, from 5:30 to 10 pm, costs from $17 for vegetable stir-fry to $26 for cioppino. The food's OK, but the view's the real attraction.

Cafe Hanalei in the Princeville Hotel has a striking view of Hanalei Bay, but expect to pay a premium for it. There's a breakfast buffet with waffle and omelet stations, pastries, fruit and a few hot dishes for $20.50, while at lunch, sandwiches are priced from $12 to $17. The breakfast buffet is from 6:30 to 11 am Monday to Saturday, to 9:30 am on Sundays. Lunch is from 11 am to 2 pm Monday to Saturday.

La Cascata, also in the Princeville Hotel, has a lovely view of Bali Hai and specializes in upscale Italian food, with à la carte seafood and meat dishes averaging $28, pasta dishes from $20. It's open from 6 to 10 pm nightly.

Entertainment

At the Hanalei Bay Resort's *Happy Talk* lounge, there's contemporary music most nights from 6:30 to 9:30 pm and a jazz jam session on Sundays from 2 to 5 pm.

The Princeville Hotel (☎ 826-2788) has a luau from 6 to 10 pm on Thursdays; the cost of $49 for adults and $30 for children includes an imu ceremony, Hawaiian food and live music and dance.

HANALEI VALLEY

Just beyond Princeville, the Hanalei Valley Lookout provides a spectacular bird's-eye view of the valley floor with its meandering river and spread of patchwork taro fields. Be sure not to miss it.

The Hanalei National Wildlife Refuge encompasses 917 acres of the valley, stretching up both sides of Hanalei River. The wetland taro farms in the refuge produce two-thirds of Hawaii's commercially grown poi taro, while at the same time serving as habitat for endangered water birds.

In precontact time the valley was planted in taro, but in the mid-1800s rice farming was introduced into Hanalei Valley to feed the Chinese laborers who worked the sugar cane fields. The rice grew so well that by the 1880s it became a major export crop. Now taro once again predominates.

From the lookout, to the lower right, you can glimpse the North Shore's first one-lane bridge, opened in 1912. Also visible are the twin peaks of Hihimanu, which in Hawaiian means 'beautiful.'

Hanalei Bridge

The seven one-lane bridges between Hanalei River and the end of the road not only link this part of the North Shore to the rest of the island, they also protect it from runaway development.

Big cement trucks and heavy construction equipment are beyond the bridges' limits. Even large package-tour buses are kept at bay.

Over the years, developers have introduced numerous proposals to build a two-lane bridge over Hanalei River, but North Shore residents have successfully beaten them all down.

While it's not a frequent occurrence, during unusually heavy rains the road between the taro fields and the river can flood and the Hanalei Bridge remains closed until it subsides.

After the Hanalei Bridge, the valley widens. Buffalo belonging to Hanalei Garden Farms graze in the pastures to the right. Having shed their thick woolly fur for a short tropical coat, these creatures are raised for their meat and are the source of the buffalo burgers and kebabs found on Kauai menus.

Ohiki Road

If you want to go into Hanalei Valley, turn left onto Ohiki Rd immediately after Hanalei Bridge. The drive parallels the Hanalei River, starting in taro fields and later passing banana trees, bamboo thickets, hau trees, ferns and wild ginger. It dead ends after two miles.

Snow-white egrets are common along the road. Night herons and endangered Hawaiian water birds reside in the valley too, including coots, stilts, the Hawaiian duck and the coot-like Hawaiian gallinule with its bright red bill.

HANALEI

After the Hanalei Bridge, Hwy 560 runs parallel to the Hanalei River. The mile before Hanalei village is a very pastoral scene of taro patches and grassland. There's no development of any kind and no buildings in sight. Take away the telephone poles and asphalt road and this is how it's looked for centuries.

Hanalei has a pleasant low-key village center. The village took a severe battering during Hurricane Iniki, losing many of its old wooden buildings, but fortunately most of the reconstruction has been done in a period style matching the original character of the town.

Hanalei is friendly, casual and slow. If you're in a hurry, you're in the wrong place.

Information

The Hanalei post office is on Hwy 560 in the village center, and there's a branch of the Bank of Hawaii in the adjacent Ching Young Village shopping center.

There are several shops in Hanalei geared to outdoor sports. Kayak Kauai specializes in kayak rentals and tours, but also rents bicycles, camping gear, surfboards and snorkel sets. Pedal & Paddle in Ching Young Village rents kayaks, bicycles, camping gear and snorkel sets. Hanalei Surf Company in the Hanalei Center rents surfboards, boogie boards and snorkel sets. A handful of Na Pali Coast boat-tour companies have their offices near the corner of Hwy 560 and Aku Rd. For more information on all of these, see the Activities section at the front of this chapter.

Ching Young Village

The old Ching Young Store, the North Shore's main general store since the turn of the century, has evolved into the larger Ching Young Village shopping center. The original Ching Young Store now houses Evolve Love, a cooperative gallery with handpainted silk clothing, jewelry, koa woodwork and other handicrafts by local artisans.

Opposite Ching Young Village is the old Hanalei elementary school, which has been renovated and turned into the Hanalei Center complex, with a restaurant and a couple of shops. The building is on the Hawaii Register of Historic Places.

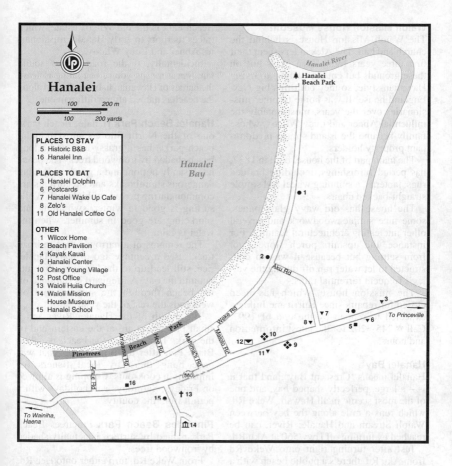

Hanalei

PLACES TO STAY
5 Historic B&B
16 Hanalei Inn

PLACES TO EAT
3 Hanalei Dolphin
6 Postcards
7 Hanalei Wake Up Cafe
8 Zelo's
11 Old Hanalei Coffee Co

OTHER
1 Wilcox Home
2 Beach Pavilion
4 Kayak Kauai
9 Hanalei Center
10 Ching Young Village
12 Post Office
13 Waioli Huiia Church
14 Waioli Mission
   House Museum
15 Hanalei School

Waioli Huiia Church

Hanalei's first missionaries, the Reverend and Mrs William Alexander, arrived in 1834 in a double-hulled canoe. Their church, hall and mission house are in the middle of town, set on a huge manicured lawn with a beautiful mountain backdrop. These folks knew how to pick property.

The picturesque Waioli Huiia Church is a favorite subject for watercolorists. The green wooden church retains an airy Pacific feel, with large windows that open outwards and high ceilings. The doors remain open during the day, and visitors are welcome to go inside. A Bible printed in Hawaiian in 1868 is on display on top of the old organ. The Waioli Church Choir, the island's best, sings hymns in Hawaiian at the 10 am Sunday service.

Waioli Mission Hall, to the right of the church, was built in 1836. The hall, which originally served as the church, was built of coral lime and plaster with a distinctive high-pitched roof to handle Hanalei's heavy rains. An old church graveyard is beside the hall.

KAUAI

Waioli Mission House Museum

The Waioli Mission House is behind the church and hall. The Alexanders spent their first three years living in a grass hut on these grounds but couldn't adjust to living Hawaiian-style, so they built this big New England house. It was home to other missionaries over the years, most notably the influential Abner and Lucy Wilcox, whose family became the island's most predominant property holders.

The main part of the house, built in 1837, has period furnishings, including braided rugs, lanterns, a spinning wheel and simple straight-backed chairs.

The house has old wavy glass panes, some nice simple woodwork and several other interesting architectural features. For instance, the upstairs porch slopes, not from settling but because it was so constructed to let water run off during the valley's frequent torrential rains.

The mission house, which has been closed for repairs since Hurricane Iniki, is expected to reopen by the end of 1997. Call ☎ 245-3202 for the latest information and hours.

Hanalei Bay

Hanalei means 'Crescent Bay', and that it is – a large, perfectly shaped bay, and one of the most scenic in all Hawaii. Weke Rd, which runs a mile along the bay between Waioli Stream and Hanalei River, can be reached by turning off Hwy 560 at Aku Rd.

Just after turning right onto Weke Rd from Aku Rd, there's a public beach with a picnic pavilion. The more appealing Hanalei Beach Park is about half a mile farther, at the end of Weke Rd. Pinetrees Beach Park is in the opposite direction.

Each of the three beaches has restrooms, showers, drinking water, picnic tables and grills. Hanalei Beach Park is the best place for catching the sunset, as you can see Bali Hai from there. It's a popular summer anchorage for sailboats.

The big brown house with the wraparound porch mauka of the road and midway between the pavilion and Hanalei

Beach Park is the old Wilcox estate, which traces its roots to early Hanalei missionaries Abner and Lucy Wilcox.

Incidentally, if the road names sound familiar, it means you're beginning to learn the names of Hawaiian fish – each road along the beach is named after a different one.

Hanalei Beach Park Hanalei Beach Park, one of the North Shore's most popular beach parks, has a grassy area and a long beach shaded by ironwood trees. The beach has a sandy bottom and a gentle slope, but dangerous shorebreaks and rip currents are common during periods of high surf. While surfing is good in winter, swimming and snorkeling are good in summer, when the water is calm.

The remains of a narrow-gauge railroad track, used a century ago to haul Hanalei rice, still lead up to the long pier that juts out into the bay. A lifeguard is stationed on the beach through the summer and on weekends the rest of the year.

The mouth of the Hanalei River and a small boat ramp are at the eastern end of the park. That part of the beach is called Black Pot, after the big iron pot that was once hung there by local fishers for impromptu cook-outs. Camping is allowed on Fridays, Saturdays and holidays with a permit from the county.

Pinetrees Beach Park Pinetrees Beach Park, named by surfers, is actually shaded by ironwood trees.

From Weke Rd, turn either onto Hee Rd, which has the bigger parking lot, or Amaama Rd, which has the restrooms and showers. This section of the beach is also known locally as Toilet Bowls. Pinetrees has some of the bay's highest winter surf and is the site of various surfing contests.

Places to Stay

The *Historic B&B* (☎ 826-4622; jbshepd@aloha.net), Jeff and Belle Shepherd, Box 1662, Hanalei, HI 96714, occupies the oldest Buddhist temple on Kauai, built in Lihue in 1901 and moved to the center of Hanalei in 1985. This is a pleasant little place, with tasteful decor that includes antique furniture and Jeff's own artwork. There are three guest rooms with shoji sliding doors; two rooms have bamboo four-poster queen beds with canopied mosquito nets, while the other has twin beds. The rate is a reasonable $55/65 for singles/doubles, with a two-night minimum; one-night stays are allowed, if space permits, for a $10 surcharge. Breakfast is included. Credit cards and small children are not accepted.

Bed & Breakfast & Beach (☎ 826-6111), Box 748, Hanalei, HI 96714, is in a large house, a two-minute walk from the beach pavilion section of Hanalei Bay. There are four rooms, each furnished with queen beds, except for the largest room, which has a king. All have their own bath, either attached or just outside the room. The contemporary house has a wraparound 2nd-floor lanai and hardwood floors. Rates range from $65 to $95, breakfast included, with a two-night minimum stay. There's also a two-bedroom house nearby, which can be rented by the week for $725, plus $50 per person beyond two.

Across the street, Mary and Dave Cunning (☎ /fax 826-4116), Box 720, Hanalei, HI 96714, rent *Ohana Hanalei*, a pleasant studio unit attached to the side of their home. The daily rate is $65; for stays of a week the seventh night is free. The unit has its own entrance and bath, a king bed, refrigerator, microwave, coffeemaker, cable TV and a phone with free local calls.

Hanalei Inn (☎ 826-9333), Box 1373, Hanalei, HI 96714, is an older local hostelry with five simple, lackluster units on Hwy 560, on the west side of the village. Rates are $55 to $75, with the more expensive units having kitchenettes.

Bali Hai Realty (☎ 826-7244, 800-404-5200; fax 826-6157), Hanalei Trader, 5-5016 Kuhio Hwy, Box 930, Hanalei, HI 96714, books vacation rental homes in the Hanalei area, as well as in Haena, Princeville and Anini. Rates begin at around $700 a week.

Places to Eat – budget

Tropical Taco, which parks its old green van in the parking lot adjacent to Kayak Kauai, dishes out decent $5 burritos and other simple Mexican fare from about 11 am to 3:30 pm daily except Mondays. There are a couple of picnic tables where you can sit and eat.

Hanalei Gourmet in the Hanalei Center has both a deli and a restaurant. Breakfast includes reasonably priced muffins and pastries, as well as a couple of egg dishes or a bagel with lox and cream cheese priced around $7. Sandwiches cost from $6 for tuna or avocado to $10 for smoked salmon. They also make fairly good deli salads and sell sandwich meats over the counter. The deli hours are from 10 am (8 am on weekends) to 9 pm; dinner is served until 9:30 pm.

Old Hanalei Coffee Co, west of the Hanalei Center, has good homemade bagels and fresh brewed coffee, each for $1.50, and hearty, relatively cheap breakfasts. It's open daily from 7 am to 3 pm, with later hours in summer.

For surfers and other early risers, the *Hanalei Wake Up Cafe* on Aku Rd is open daily by 6 am with omelets, custard French toast or half a papaya with yogurt and granola for $5 to $7.

For inexpensive hot dogs, corn dogs and hamburgers, there's *Bubba's* at the west side of the Hanalei Center, open daily from 10:30 am to 6 pm.

Pizza Hanalei (☎ 826-9494) at Ching Young Village has good pizza at reasonable prices. A 10-inch cheese pizza on either traditional white or a crisp whole-wheat crust topped with sesame seeds is $8.25, plus $1.20 per topping. The spicy calzone-style pizzarittos are loaded with cheese and vegies and make a good meal for $5. At lunchtime you can also buy slices of pepperoni or pesto pizza for $2.75. It's open from 11 am to 9 pm daily.

Next door, *Hanalei Natural Foods* sells juices, organic fruit and vegetables, wrapped sandwiches, vitamins and other health food items. It's open from 8:30 am to 7 pm daily.

Zababaz, a vegetarian deli at the back of

Evolve Love at Ching Young Village, has sandwiches, curries, $6 plate lunches and Lappert's ice cream. It's open from 10 am to 6 pm daily.

The *Big Save* supermarket at Ching Young Village is open daily from 7 am to 9 pm.

Places to Eat – middle to top end

Zelo's (☎ 826-9700), the most bustling sit-down restaurant in Hanalei, has burgers with fries for $6 at lunch and $8 at dinner, a fish Caesar salad for $13 and fresh fish of the day for around $23. It's open for meals daily from 11:30 am to 3:30 pm and from 5:30 to 9:30 pm (10 pm on Fridays and Saturdays).

Postcards (☎ 826-1191), a trendy new vegetarian (and seafood) cafe, is a bit pricey but good, and everything's organic. Breakfast, served from 8 to 11 am, includes granola with yogurt or a simple breakfast burrito for $6, egg dishes for a bit more. Dinner, from 5:30 to 9:30 pm, features the likes of fish tacos with rice and beans for $12.50, Thai coconut curry with tempeh satay for $15 and blackened fresh fish with taro fritters and papaya salsa for around $20. They don't have a liquor license, but you can bring your own wine or beer.

Hanalei Dolphin (☎ 826-6113), at the east side of the village on the Hanalei River, is a steak-and-seafood restaurant. At lunch, from 11 am to 3 pm, you can get fish burgers, sandwiches or salads from around $6 and eat on the outdoor patio. At dinner, from 5:30 to 10 pm, meals range from chicken or frozen mahimahi for $15 to king crab and tenderloin for $25.

Entertainment

Hanalei Gourmet (☎ 826-2524) has live music from 8:30 to 10:30 pm nightly, anything from jazz or rock to Hawaiian; there's no cover charge. Happy hour is from 3:30 to 5:30 pm. *Zelo's* (☎ 926-9700), which also has a bar, sometimes has live music as well.

HANALEI TO WAINIHA
Waikoko Beach

The western part of Hanalei Bay, called Waikoko Beach, has a sandy bottom, is protected by a reef and is shallower and

calmer than the middle of the bay. There are beachside places to park under ironwood trees around the four-mile marker, but no facilities.

Winter surfing is sometimes good off Makahoa Point, the western point of the bay, called Waikokos by surfers.

Lumahai Beach

Lumahai is the gorgeous mile-long stretch of beach where Mitzi Gaynor promised to wash that man right out of her hair in the 1958 musical *South Pacific*. It's a broad white-sand beach with lush jungle growth on one side and tempestuous open ocean on the other.

This is a good beach for walking and exploring. Around some of the lava outcrops you can find green sand made of olivine.

There are two ways onto Lumahai. The first and more scenic is a three-minute walk that begins at a pull-off along a stone retaining wall three-quarters of a mile past the four-mile marker. Park in the direction of the traffic flow to avoid a ticket. The trail to the beach starts at a 'No Lifeguard' sign and goes down the slope to the left.

The lava point at this eastern end of the beach offers protection from the winds that often blow from the Princeville direction. These rocks are a rather popular place for sunbathing and for being photographed, but size it up carefully, as people have been washed away by high surf and rogue waves. Lumahai has dangerous shore-breaks and is not a beach to turn your back on. It's particularly treacherous in winter, though there are strong currents all year round. Because of the numerous drownings that have occurred here, Lumahai has been nicknamed Luma*die* by locals.

Back on the road, there are a couple of lookouts with views down onto Lumahai. The first is at the five-mile marker, though the next one that pops up around the bend has a better angle.

The other access onto Lumahai Beach is along the road at sea level at the western end of the beach, just before crossing the Lumahai River Bridge. The beach at this end is lined with ironwood trees. Across the road is Lumahai Valley, open and flat with ranchland and some grazing horses and cattle.

WAINIHA

Wainiha has a tiny general store that's the last place before the end of the road where you can buy groceries and beer. It's open from 9:30 am to 6:30 pm daily.

Ancient house sites, heiau sites and old taro patches reach deep into the Wainiha Valley. The valley is said to have been the last hideout of the menehunes. In fact, as late as the mid-1800s, 65 people in the valley were officially listed as menehune on the government census!

Wainiha Powerhouse Rd

For a glimpse into an older Hawaii, take a side trip up Wainiha Powerhouse Rd, which begins off Hwy 560 shortly before the seven-mile marker. It leads up into Wainiha Valley, a narrow valley with steep green walls.

This narrow road is lined with simple tin-roofed homes, old rusting pickup trucks and sleeping dogs. At 1½ miles up, an incongruous manicured estate with a cool blue stream meandering through it suddenly comes into view. Shortly after this you arrive at the Wainiha hydroelectric plant, built in 1906 by McBryde Sugar Co and still pumping out juice today. Beyond the powerhouse the road turns to dirt and begins to feel more private.

Places to Stay

Tassa Hanalei (☎ /fax 826-7298), Box 856, Hanalei, HI 96714, at the home of Ileah Van Hubbard, occupies a remote riverside niche in Wainiha Valley. The best unit is an airy studio cottage with a queen bed, full kitchen, sofa bed, deck and glass doors that look out onto a fine mountain scene; it costs $125 per couple, $140 for a family of four. Two rooms that are attached to the main house and have private entrances but share a garden (outdoor) bathroom cost $65/85 for singles/doubles. There's a hot tub, and massage is available for $85, colonic therapy for $35.

HAENA

Haena has houses on stilts, little beachfront cottages, a few vacation homes, the YMCA camp, large caves, campsites and beautiful sandy beaches. It also has the only condo complex and restaurant beyond Hanalei.

Tunnels Beach

Tunnels is a big horseshoe-shaped reef that has great diving and snorkeling when the water is calm, which is generally limited to the summer. There's a current as you head into deeper water. When conditions are right, you can start snorkeling near the east point and let the current carry you westward. It's more adventurous than Kee Beach, and the coral is beautiful.

Tunnels was not named after the caves and other crevices in the underwater walls but by surfers for its tubular winter surf break at the outer corner of the reef. The beach is popular with both windsurfers and board surfers, though dangerous rip currents that prevail from October to May make it suitable for experts only.

To get there, look for cars parked at the side of the road near phone pole No 144, midway between the eight- and nine-mile markers opposite the beach access road. Or you can park at Haena Beach Park and walk along the beach to Tunnels.

Haena Beach Park

Haena Beach is a beautiful curve of white sand. To the right, you can see the horseshoe shape of Tunnels outlined by breaking waves. To the far left is Cannons, another good dive spot. Haena itself is not protected by reefs and has very strong rip currents and powerful shorebreaks from October to May.

The county beach park has campsites, covered picnic tables, restrooms, showers, grills and a pay phone. There are usually a few hikers from the Kalalau Trail camping here. It's a bit over a mile to the trailhead and this is a safer place to park a car than the end of the road if you're going on to Kalalau.

Maniniholo Dry Cave

Three large sea caves, which were part of the coast thousands of years back, are mauka of the road between Haena and Kee Beach. One is dry and two are wet.

According to legend, they were created when the goddess Pele dug into the mountains looking for a place on Kauai's North Shore to call home.

Maniniholo Dry Cave, across the road from Haena Beach Park, is a deep broad cave that you can walk into. Dry is a relative term, as the dripping water that constantly seeps from the cave walls keeps the interior of Maniniholo damp and humid.

Limahuli

Limahuli is the last valley before the start of the Na Pali Coast. Much of it is still virgin forest.

The National Tropical Botanical Garden, a nonprofit group that preserves and propagates rare native plants, owns 1000 acres of the valley. The Limahuli garden contains collections of Hawaiian ethnobotanical and medicinal plants and other endangered native species. A trail passes old stone terraces planted with taro and various fruiting trees. Endemic trees along the way include the endangered Kokio hauheleula, which has a red hibiscus-like blossom, and the equally beautiful but more common ohia lehua tree.

The garden starts at a concrete driveway on the mauka side of the highway just before the stream that marks the Haena State Park boundary.

It's open from 9:30 am to 4 pm Tuesday to Friday and on Sundays. It costs $10 to walk through the garden on your own, accompanied by a self-guided tour booklet, or $15 to join a two-hour guided tour (☎ 826-1053 for reservations).

Wet Caves

Haena State Park includes the two wet caves as well as Kee Beach. The caves, which are near each other, less than a quarter of a mile from the end of the road, are usually marked with HVB warrior signs. The first, Waikapalae Wet Cave, is just a few minutes' walk uphill from the road along the rutted drive with the stop

sign. The second, Waikanaloa Wet Cave, is easier to spot, as it's right at the south side of the road going to Kee Beach.

Both caves are big, deep, dark and dripping, with pools of very cold water. Divers sometimes explore them, but the caves can be dangerous and it's certainly best to go with an experienced local diver the first time.

Kee Beach

Kee Beach is commonly called 'the beach at the end of the road', which it is.

On the left side of the beach is the distinctive 1280-foot cliff that marks the start of the Na Pali Coast. Almost everyone calls it Bali Hai, its name in *South Pacific*. The Hawaiian name is Makana, which means 'gift'. A heiau and ancient hula school site are' at its base.

Snorkeling is good at Kee Beach, which has a variety of tropical fish. A reef protects the right side of the cove, and except on high surf days, it's usually calm. The left side is open and can have a powerful current, particularly in winter.

When it's really calm – generally only in summer – snorkelers cross the reef to the open ocean where there's great visibility, big fish, large coral heads and the occasional sea turtle. It makes the inside of the bay look like kid's stuff, but check it out carefully because breaking surf and strong currents can create dangerous conditions.

When the tide's at its lowest you can actually walk a great distance out on the reef without getting your feet wet and peer down into tide pools.

Showers, changing rooms, drinking water, restrooms and a pay phone are tucked back in the woods behind the parking lot.

There are several ways to get views down the Na Pali Coast from Kee Beach. One way is to walk the first 30 minutes of the Kalalau Trail. Another is to take the short walk out around the point at the left side of the beach.

Or, simply walk down the beach a few minutes to the right and look back as the cliffs unfold, one after the other.

Kaulu Paoa Heiau

To make the five-minute walk out to Kaulu Paoa Heiau, take the path on the western side of the beach. The walk is shaded by tropical almond trees, which drop their edible nuts along the trail. Follow the stone wall as it curves uphill and you'll reach the heiau almost immediately.

The overgrown section at the foot of the hill is one of the more intact parts of the heiau, but don't stop there. Instead, continue walking up the terraces towards the cliff face. Surf pounding below, vertical cliffs above – what a spectacular site to worship the gods from!

Beneath the cliff face, large stones retain a long flat grassy platform. A thatched-roofed halau, a longhouse used as a hula school, once ran the whole length of the terrace. Here, dances to Laka, the goddess of hula, were performed. In ancient Hawaii, this was Kauai's most sacred hula school and students from all the islands aspiring to learn hula came to Kaulu Paoa.

Fern wreaths, rocks wrapped in ti leaves, leis and other offerings to Laka are still placed into the crevices of the cliff face. The site is sacred to native Hawaiians and should be treated with respect. Night hula dances are still performed on special occasions.

Lohiau's House Site

Lohiau's house site is just a minute's walk above the parking lot at Kee Beach. At the Kalalau Trail sign, go left along the barely discernible dirt path to a vine-covered rock wall. This overgrown level terrace runs back 54 feet to the bluff and is said to have been the home of Lohiau, a 16th-century prince.

Legend says that the volcano goddess Pele was napping one day under a hala tree in Puna on the Big Island when her spirit was awakened by the sound of distant drums. Her spirit rode the wind in the direction of the sound, searching each island in turn until she finally arrived at Kee Beach. Here she found Lohiau above the heiau beating a hula drum, surrounded by graceful hula dancers.

Taylor Camp

If you walk down Kee Beach about 15 minutes to the northeast, you'll come to a stream and the site of the former Taylor Camp.

In the late 1960s, a little free-style village of tents and tree houses sprang up on property owned by actress Elizabeth Taylor's brother. Reports of drugs, orgies and pipe organ music in the middle of the night eventually got the authorities to crack down on the camp. When the state tried to evict everyone on public health grounds, the campers challenged them in court claiming squatters rights. The 'squatters' eventually lost and the property was condemned and incorporated into the state park system. Taylor Camp remains part of North Shore folklore, though there's nothing left to see. ■

Pele took the form of a beautiful woman and captured Lohiau's heart. They became lovers and moved into this house. In time Pele had to go back to the Big Island, leaving a lovesick Lohiau behind. His longing quickly got the better of him, and on this site he died from his grief.

Places to Stay

The *Kauai YMCA-Camp Naue* (☎ 826-6419 or 246-9090; fax 246-4411), Box 1786, Lihue, HI 96766, in Haena, just before the eight-mile marker on Hwy 560, has rustic coed bunkhouses on the beach. It costs $12 for one of the 50 bunks, which have mattresses but no linen or blankets. As there are five separate rooms (with six, eight or 14 beds), couples or groups of friends can sometimes have a room to themselves. To pitch a tent costs $10 for the first person and $7 for each extra person. There are hot showers, but the kitchen is reserved for large groups only. While there are no lockers, the camp is a safe place and theft hasn't been a problem. Guests can stay a maximum of seven nights; check-in is allowed until it gets dark. The Y doesn't accept reservations, but unless there's a large group staying they can usually take everyone who shows up. Call ahead, however, as in summer and some other holiday periods the camp is commonly booked by children's groups, at which times it's closed to travelers. It's a 10-minute walk to Tunnels Beach.

Hanalei Colony Resort (☎ 826-6235, 800-628-3004; fax 826-9893; hcr@aloha .net), Box 206, Hanalei, HI 96714, is an older but renovated low-rise condo complex on the east side of Haena. Each of the 54 units has a full kitchen, a lanai and two bedrooms, although one of the bedrooms is really a sitting area with two twin beds that's separated from the rest of the living room by sliding doors. The complex is right on the beach, and there's a swimming pool and barbecue area. This is a place to listen to the surf: there are no TVs, radios or room phones. Rates range from $115 for a garden view to $195 for oceanfront in the low season, $135 to $220 in the high season. The rates are the same for up to four people and for weekly stays the seventh night is free.

Places to Eat

Charo's is on the beach, beside Hanalei Colony Resort. At lunch, there are sandwiches with fries for under $10, while dinner dishes range from chicken for $13 to fresh fish for $19. There's also a bar, but the splashy 'Tropical Fiesta' revue of days past is gone, as Charo moved the show to Waikiki.

NA PALI COAST

In Hawaiian, *na pali* means simply 'the cliffs'. Indeed, these are Hawaii's grandest.

The Na Pali Coast is the rugged 22-mile stretch between the end of the road at Kee Beach in the north and the road's opposite end at Polihale State Park in the west. It has the most sharply fluted coastal cliffs in Hawaii.

Kalalau, Honopu, Awaawapuhi, Nualolo and Milolii are the five major valleys on the Na Pali Coast. These deep river valleys once contained sizable settlements.

In the mid-19th century missionaries established a school in Kalalau, the largest valley, and registered the valley population at about 200. Influenced by Western ways, people gradually began moving to towns, and by the end of the century the valleys were largely abandoned.

The Na Pali valleys, with limited accessibility and abundant fertility, have long served as a natural refuge for people wanting to escape one scene or another. While Koolau the Leper is the best known, there have been scores of others.

Getting There & Away

Precarious trails once led from the upland Kokee area down to the valley floors along the Na Pali Coast. In some places footholds were gouged into cliffsides and in others rope ladders were used. These trails no longer exist.

Only Hanakapiai, Hanakoa and Kalalau valleys can still be reached on foot, solely along the 11-mile Kalalau coastal trail.

The only other access is by boat. Landings are limited to the Kalalau, Nualolo and Milolii valleys and are largely restricted to summer when the seas are calm. Milolii, part of the Na Pali Coast State Park, has primitive camping. For more information on Milolii see the Camping section at the start of this chapter.

Captain Zodiac (☎ 826-9371) is permitted to drop off and pick up backpackers in Kalalau Valley during the summer months, which gives people the option of hiking the Kalalau Trail just one way. The Zodiac ride leaves from Tunnels Beach and costs $70 per passenger, including your pack. For those who prefer to hike without a backpack, Captain Zodiac will also drop off or pick up a pack in Kalalau, charging $30 each way. The boat operates daily, weather permitting, from May through September. If you're considering this option, there is one caveat: Rough surf at Kalalau has been known to prevent landings for several days in a row.

In addition to approaching the Na Pali Coast from the North Shore, you can also look down into the Na Pali valleys from Kokee State Park. The park has a drive-up lookout right on the rim of Kalalau Valley as well as hardy hikes out to clifftops that offer gorgeous views into Awaawapuhi and Nualolo valleys (for details, see Kokee State Park in the West Side section of this chapter).

Kalalau Trail

Kalalau is Hawaii's premier trail. It's common to come across hikers here who have trekked in Nepal or climbed to Machu Picchu. The Na Pali Coast is similarly spectacular, a place of singular beauty.

The Kalalau Trail is basically the same ancient route used by the Hawaiians who once lived in these remote north coast valleys. The trail runs along high sea cliffs and winds up and down across lush valleys before it finally ends below the steep fluted pali of Kalalau. The scenery is breathtaking, with sheer green cliffs dropping into brilliant turquoise waters.

While hikers in good shape can walk the 11-mile trail straight through in about seven hours, it's less strenuous to break it up and spend a night camping in one of the two valleys along the way.

In winter there are generally only a few people at any one time hiking all the way in to Kalalau Valley, but the trail is heavily trodden in summer. As it's a popular hike for islanders as well as visitors, weekends tend to see the most use.

The hike can be divided into three parts: Kee Beach to Hanakapiai Valley (two miles); Hanakapiai to Hanakoa Valley (four miles); and Hanakoa to Kalalau Valley (five miles).

The first two miles of the hike makes a popular day trip, and permits are not required for those going only as far as Hanakapiai Valley. Even if you're not planning to stay overnight, a permit is officially required to continue on the Kalalau Trail beyond Hanakapiai; day-use hiking permits are available free from the state parks office in Lihue.

The trail is part of Na Pali Coast State Park. Camping is allowed in all three valleys, but is limited to five nights total, with no two consecutive nights in Hanakapiai or Hanakoa. State camping permits are required (for details, see the Camping section at the start of this chapter).

Kee Beach to Hanakapiai The two-mile trail to Hanakapiai is a delightfully scenic hike. Morning is a good time to be going west, and the afternoon to be going east, as you have both the sun at your back and good light for photography.

The trail weaves through kukui and ohia trees and then back out to clearings with fine coastal views. There are purple orchids, wildflowers and a couple of tiny Zen-like waterfalls. The black nuts half buried in the clay are kukui, polished smooth by the scuffing of hundreds of hiking shoes.

Just a quarter of a mile up the trail you can catch a fine view of Kee Beach and the surrounding reef. After 30 minutes you get your first view of the Na Pali Coast. Even if you weren't planning on a hike, it's well worth coming this far.

Hanakapiai has a sandy beach in the summer. In the winter the sand washes out and it becomes a beach of boulders, some of them sparkling with tiny olivine crystals. The western side of the beach has a small cave with dripping water and a miniature fern grotto.

The ocean is dangerous here, with unpredictable rip currents year round. It's particularly treacherous during winter high surf conditions, but summer trades also bring powerful currents. Hanakapiai Beach is matched only by Lumahai for the number of drownings on Kauai.

If you're just doing a day hike and want to walk farther, it makes more sense to head up the valley to Hanakapiai Falls than it does to continue another couple of miles on the coastal trail.

Hanakapiai Falls The two-mile hike from Hanakapiai Beach to Hanakapiai Falls takes about 2½ hours roundtrip. Because of some tricky rock crossings, this trail is rougher than the walk from Kee Beach to

Hanakapiai Beach. Due to the possibility of flash floods in the narrow valley, the Hanakapiai Falls hike should only be done in fair weather.

The trail itself is periodically washed out by floodwaters and sections occasionally get redrawn, but the path is not that difficult to follow, as it basically goes up the side of Hanakapiai Stream. The trail is not maintained, and in places you may have to scramble over and around tree trunks and branches.

There are trails on both sides of the stream, but the main route heads up the stream's western side. About 50 yards up, there are old stone walls and guava trees. If the guavas are ripe, it's a good place to stock up. There are also some big old mango trees along the way.

Ten minutes up from the trailhead you'll find thickets of green bamboo interspersed with eucalyptus. Off to the left, a picnic table is shaded by horizontally leaning bamboo with wild ginger behind it. It's Eden-like.

Also along the trail is the site of an old coffee mill, although all that remains to be seen is a little of the stack.

The first of four or five stream crossings is about 25 minutes up at a sign that warns:

'Hazardous. Keep away from stream during heavy rainfall. Stream floods suddenly.'

Be particularly careful of your footing on the rocky upper part of the trail. Some of the rocks are covered with a barely visible film of slick algae. It's like walking on glass.

Hanakapiai Falls is spectacular, with a wide pool gentle enough to swim in. Directly under the falls the cascading water forces you back from the rock face, a warning from nature as rocks can fall from the top.

This is a very peaceful place to spend a little time meditating. It's a beautiful lush valley, though it's not terribly sunny near the falls because of the incredible steepness.

Hanakapiai to Hanakoa Just 10 minutes up the trail from Hanakapiai to Hanakoa there's a nice view of Hanakapiai Beach, but from there the trail goes into bush and the next coastal view is not for another mile. This is the least scenic part of the trail.

The camping site at Hanakoa is tucked into the valley about half a mile inland. Of the three camping areas, Hanakoa is the wettest. It also tends to have the most mosquitoes.

The valley is lovely and Hanakoa Stream has pools perfect for swimming. There's a waterfall about a third of a mile up the

---

Koolau the Leper

Koolau was a *paniolo* (cowhand) who contracted leprosy in 1893. Rather than accept separation from his family and banishment to Molokai's leprosy colony, as was the law at the time, Koolau hiked down into Kalalau Valley, taking along his wife and young son. Shortly after, a sheriff and deputy showed up to clear the valley of renegade lepers. Koolau was the only resister. That night, in the light of a full moon, the sheriff snuck up the valley hoping to take Koolau in his sleep. In self-defense, Koolau shot the sheriff.

When word reached Honolulu, a shipload of soldiers was sent to land on Kalalau Beach. As they marched up the valley they met Koolau's gunfire. After two of the soldiers were shot off the ridge and a third accidentally killed himself, they switched strategies. Just before dawn they blasted Koolau's hideaway with cannon fire, not knowing he had slipped through their lines the night before. From a nearby waterfall Koolau watched as the soldiers loaded up and set sail. They never returned, and Koolau lived the rest of his days in the valley undisturbed.

Eventually the son, and then Koolau, died of leprosy. Both are buried on a valley hillside. When Koolau's wife, Piilani, left the valley she found Koolau had largely been forgotten. A decade later a visiting reporter, John Sheldon, recorded her story. Jack London later wrote *Koolau the Leper*, a more fictionalized account. ■

valley, but it's rough getting up there as the path is overgrown. The valley was formerly settled by farmers who grew taro and coffee, both of which still grow wild.

Hanakoa to Kalalau This is the most difficult part of the trail, although without question the most beautiful. Make sure you have at least three hours of daylight left.

About a mile out of Hanakoa Valley, you'll reach the coast again and begin to get fantastic views of Na Pali's jagged edges. There are some very narrow and steep stretches along this section of the trail, so make sure your gear is properly packed and be cautious of your footing. A little past the halfway mark, you'll get your first view into Kalalau Valley.

The large valley has a beach, a little waterfall, a heiau site, some ancient house sites and some interesting caves that are sometimes dry enough to sleep in during the summer.

An easy two-mile trail leads back into the valley to a pool in Kalalau Stream with a natural water slide. If you have a quick hand, you might try your luck at catching prawns that live in the stream.

Valley terraces where Hawaiians cultivated taro until 1920 are now largely overgrown with Java plum and guava. Feral goats scurry up and down the crumbly cliffsides and drink from the stream.

Kalalau Valley has fruit trees, including mango, papaya, orange, banana, coconut, guava and mountain apple. During the 1960s and 1970s, people wanting to get away from it all tried to settle in Kalalau, but forestry rangers eventually routed them out.

Warnings & Information This is rugged wilderness and hikers should be well prepared. In places the trail runs along steep cliffs that can narrow to little more than a foot in width, which some people find unnerving. However, hikers accustomed to high-country trails generally enjoy the hike and don't consider it unduly hazardous. The Sierra Club, which occasionally leads hikes into Kalalau, classifies the trail as moderate to strenuous. Like other Hawaiian trails, the route can be muddy and slippery if it's been raining – at such time, a walking stick makes a good companion.

Accidents are not unknown. Most casualties along the Kalalau Trail are the result of people trying to ford swollen streams, walking after dark on cliffside trails or swimming in treacherous surf. Keep in mind that the rock that the cliffs are composed of is loose and crumbly; don't try to climb the cliffsides, and don't camp directly beneath them as goats commonly dislodge stones that tumble down the sides. Still, for someone who's cautious and aware, this can be a hike into paradise.

There's no shortage of water sources along the trail, but all drinking water must be boiled or treated.

Bring what you need, but travel light. You won't want to have extra shifting weight on stream crossings or along cliff edges. Shoes should have good traction; it's certainly not a trail for flip-flops. If you bring a sleeping bag, make it a light one.

The state parks office in Lihue can provide a Kalalau Trail brochure with a basic map. There is also information posted at the Kee Beach trailhead.

Break-ins to cars left overnight at Kee Beach are very common. Some people advise leaving cars empty and unlocked to prevent smashed windows. It's generally safer to park at the campground at Haena Beach Park. Or, better yet, get a lift to the end of the road. Whatever you do, don't leave valuables in a locked car.

Kayak Kauai (☎ 826-9844) in Hanalei will store vehicles for $5 a day, as well as packs for $3, and can transport hikers from their shop to the trailhead for $8 per person, with a two-person minimum.

You can usually arrange to leave extra luggage wherever you've been staying. Other possibilities include the Lihue Airport, where baggage storage can be arranged through the airport porters for $3 per bag per day, and at the general store in Wainiha, on Hwy 560 en route to Kee Beach, which stores bags for $2 per day.

South Shore

Poipu is Kauai's main beach resort area. It's typically sunny, and for the larger part of the year, including winter, it has calm waters good for swimming and snorkeling. During the summer the surf kicks up and it becomes a surfers' haunt.

The village of Koloa, three miles inland from Poipu, was the site of Hawaii's first sugar plantation. This sleepy town could have doubled for Dodge City before it got caught up in Poipu's boom. Now most of its shops are geared for tourists, and it catches the overflow from neighboring Poipu.

Poipu and Koloa are about 10 miles south of Lihue. To get there, take Hwy 520 (Maluhia Rd) from Hwy 50 (Kaumualii Hwy).

Tree Tunnel

Immediately after turning down Maluhia Rd you enter the Tree Tunnel, a mile-long stretch of road canopied by swamp mahogany trees, a type of eucalyptus. Originally, the tree tunnel was more than double this length but when Hwy 50 was re-routed south, most of the tunnel was lopped off.

In 1992, Hurricane Iniki brought down many of the branches, temporarily destroying the tunnel effect, but by and large it has filled back in nicely.

The cinder hill to the right about two miles down Maluhia Rd is Puu O Hewa. From its top the ancient Hawaiians raced wooden holua sleds down paths covered with oiled pili grass. To add even more excitement to this popular spectator sport, the Hawaiians crossed two sled paths near the middle of the hill. The paths were about five feet wide, and if you strain your eyes you might be able to see the X on the hillside where they crossed.

Hewa means 'wrong' or 'mistake'. The hill's original name was lost when a surveyor jotted 'Puu O Hewa' (wrong hill) on a map he was making and it mistakenly went off to the printer like that.

The two grassy hills to the left of the road are Mauna Kalika, or Silk Mountain.

Two American entrepreneurs introduced Chinese silkworms here in the 1830s in an attempt to develop a Hawaiian silk industry. The climate proved unsuitable for the silkworms, so the hills, like the rest of the surrounding area, were eventually given over to sugar cane.

KOLOA

Hawaii's first sugar plantation was started in Koloa in 1835. The raw materials had arrived long before: sugar cane with the original Polynesian settlers and small-scale refinery know-how with the earliest Chinese immigrants. However, large-scale production didn't begin until William Hooper, an enterprising 24-year-old Bostonian, arrived in Kauai and made inroads with the alii.

With financial backing from Honolulu businesspeople, he leased land in Koloa from the king and paid the alii a stipend to release commoners from their traditional work obligations. He was then free to hire Hawaiians as wage laborers, and Koloa became Hawaii's first plantation town.

Koloa Rd (Hwy 530), which runs between Koloa and Lawai, is the best way to leave Koloa if you're heading west – it's a pleasant drive through pastures, cane fields and tree-covered hills.

Sugar Exhibits

Any sugarologists in the crowd? The field at the intersection of Hwy 520 and Koloa Rd is for you.

In a tiny garden a dozen varieties of sugar cane are labeled with faded interpretive markers. Some are noted for their high tonnage, others for high sucrose and some for their good ratooning abilities, though the different varieties have all grown to twist and clump together. Who knows, maybe there's a great new hybrid sprouting up among the tangles!

The stone stack in another corner of the field is a relic from one of Koloa's early mills and dates back to 1841.

In the center of the field, the principal ethnic groups that worked the plantations are immortalized in a **sculpture**. The Hawaiian wears a malo and has a poi dog by

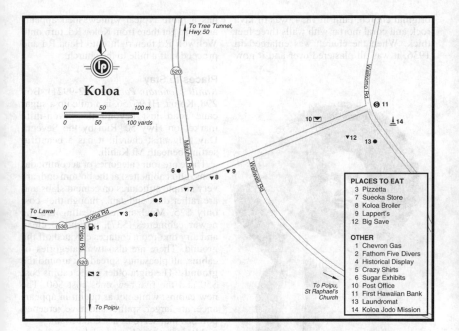

Koloa

0   50   100 m
0   50   100 yards

To Tree Tunnel,
Hwy 50

To Lawai

To Poipu

To Poipu,
St Raphael's
Church

PLACES TO EAT
3   Pizzetta
7   Sueoka Store
8   Koloa Broiler
9   Lappert's
12 Big Save

OTHER
1   Chevron Gas
2   Fathom Five Divers
4   Historical Display
5   Crazy Shirts
6   Sugar Exhibits
10 Post Office
11 First Hawaiian Bank
13 Laundromat
14 Koloa Jodo Mission

his side. The Chinese, Korean, Japanese, Portuguese, Filipino and Puerto Rican groups are likewise in native field dress. You may notice that the plaque on the wall curiously gives reference to a haole overseer – present-day islanders found the depiction of this Caucasian plantation boss seated on a high horse so unacceptable that at the last minute he was omitted from the sculpture.

If you want to learn more about the history of sugar, there are informative plaques at the sculpture display.

Old Koloa

With it's aging wooden buildings and false storefronts, Koloa has the appearance of an Old West town. It was a thriving plantation village and commercial center that largely went bust after WWII.

While its history is sugar, its present is unmistakably tourism. The former fish markets, barber shops, bathhouses and beer halls are now boutiques, galleries and restaurants.

The building that houses Crazy Shirts was until recently the Yamamoto General Store. Moviegoers would line up at Yamamoto's for crack seed and soft drinks, until the theater across the street burned down. On the sidewalk in front of the store is a sculpture by Maui artist Reems Mitchell. The courtyard behind the store looks onto the former town hotel, where you'll find a little display on Koloa's history, including a Japanese bath and some period photos.

At the east side of town is the Koloa Jodo Mission, which dates back to 1910. The Buddhist temple on the left is the original, while next to it is a newer and larger temple where services are now held. During services the smell of incense and the sound of beating drums fills the air.

St Raphael's Catholic Church

St Raphael's, the oldest Catholic church on Kauai, is the burial site of some of the first Portuguese immigrants to Hawaii. The

KAUAI

original church, built in 1854, was of lava rock and coral mortar with walls three feet thick. When the church was enlarged in 1936, it was all plastered over and it now has a more typical whitewashed appearance. To get there from Koloa Rd, turn onto Weliweli Rd then right onto Hapa Rd and proceed half a mile to the church.

Places to Stay

Kahili Mountain Park (☎ 742-9921), Box 298, Koloa, HI 96756, is a mile up a sugar cane road just beyond the seven-mile marker on Hwy 50. Run by the Seventh Day Adventist church, it has a beautiful setting beneath Mt Kahili.

There are four categories of accommodations. Old cabinettes, at the bottom end, are very simple structures on cement slabs and are rather dark and dank, though they cost only $25. Much more appealing are the newer cabinettes ($37), which are clean and airy one-room cottages elevated off the ground. There are also two categories of cabins, all pleasantly spread out around the grounds. The eight older rustic cabins cost $50 and the five new ones cost $60. The new cabins, while not as quaint in appearance, are larger, spiffier and have screened porches that serve as a second room.

All categories have bed linens, a two-burner gas stove, pots and pans, a sink and a refrigerator; cabinettes have shared showers and toilets, while cabins have private bathrooms. Cabinettes hold five people, cabins hold four. Rates given are for up to two people, with each additional person charged $10. It's an unbeatable value and only about a 20-minute drive to the beaches in Poipu. As they commonly book out during the high season, advance reservations are advised.

Places to Eat

All of the following places to eat, as well as a *Lappert's* ice-cream shop, are on Koloa Rd near its intersection with Maluhia Rd.

The snack shop at the side of Sueoka Store sells burgers, cheese sandwiches and saimin for $1.50 each and plate lunches for $4. It's open daily from 10 am to 3 pm.

Pizzetta is a small pizzeria with average fare – a slice of cheese pizza is $2.75, while a whole pizza costs $12. It's open from 11 am to 9 pm daily.

NED FRIARY
Statue detail of Filipino caneworker

KAUAI

Sugar mill at Koloa

NED FRIARY

Koloa Broiler (☎ 742-9122) is in a funky old tin-roofed wooden building that used to be a soft drink bottling plant. The 'menu' is a display case of raw meat and fish. Diners get to be cooks, preparing their own orders over a communal gas grill. Dishes range from $7 for a burger to around $12 for chicken or steak and $15 for fresh fish. The portions are generous and a simple buffet of rice, beans and salad is included. It's open from 11 am to 10 pm daily.

POIPU

Poipu is about three miles south of Koloa down Poipu Rd. Other than its lovely sandy beaches, Poipu's most popular attraction is the Spouting Horn blowhole. To get to Spouting Horn, turn right off Poipu Rd onto Lawai Rd, just past Poipu Plaza, and continue for 1¾ miles.

Prince Kuhio Park

Prince Kuhio Park is about half a mile down Lawai Rd, across from tiny Hoai Bay. Here you'll find **Hoai Heiau** and a monument honoring Jonah Kuhio Kalanianaole, the Territory of Hawaii's first delegate to the US Congress. It was Prince Kuhio who spearheaded the Hawaiian Homes Commission Act, which provided homesteads for native Hawaiians. The remains of a fishpond and an ancient Hawaiian house platform are also on the grounds.

Baby Beach

A protected swimming area just deep enough for children is off Hoona Rd, east of Prince Kuhio Park. Look for the marked beach access post marking the pathway between the road and the beach. Adults may want to walk west down the beach to reach a sandy break with fewer rocks and deeper water.

Lawai Beach

Lawai Beach is west of Prince Kuhio Park, opposite Lawai Beach Resort. It's a little rocky, but during winter the water is usually quite clear and snorkelers will find an abundance of tropical fish. When the surf's up in summer, the beach is inundated with surfers.

Opposite the beach, you'll find restrooms, a shower and public parking. At the east

KAUAI

side of the beach, adjacent to the Beach House Poipu restaurant, there's a shop that rents boogie boards for $5 a day, snorkel sets for $6.

Kukuiula Bay

Kukuiula Bay, about a half mile east of Spouting Horn, is a small boat harbor maintained by the state and mostly used by fishing and diving boats. The beach is rocky and more suitable for pole fishing than other water activities. There are nine mooring spaces, a launch ramp and a concrete wharf.

Spouting Horn Beach Park

Spouting Horn is a blowhole that has its days. Sometimes it has a pretty good spout, other times it's simply a nonevent. The waves, the tides and the overall force of the sea rushing into the lava tube decide how much water surges through the spout. Listen for the low whooshing that precedes the rushing water – it sounds like a whale breathing.

During the height of the day, tour buses pull in and out of the parking lot and there's often a small crowd with cameras clicking away. Jewelry and trinket stalls line the walkway from the parking lot down to the viewing area. You can avoid the tour bus crowd by arriving in the late afternoon, which is also the best time to see rainbows that are sometimes cast in the spray by the sun.

Allerton Gardens

The Allerton Gardens (☎ 742-2623), in the remote Lawai Valley east of the Spouting Horn area, were started in the 1870s by Queen Emma, who built a summer cottage on the site. Chicago industrialist Robert Allerton later bought the property and expanded the gardens in the 100-acre estate.

In 1971 the site became part of the National Tropical Botanical Garden, which propagates tropical and endangered plant species and does research in ethnobotanical and medicinal plants.

The gardens can only be entered on a guided tour. The tours are at 9 am, 11:30 am and 2 pm Tuesday through Sunday, last 2½

hours, depart from the Spouting Horn parking lot and cost $25. Reservations are required.

Koloa Landing

Koloa Landing, at the mouth of Waikomo Stream, was once Kauai's largest port. It not only served to ship sugar grown on Koloa Plantation, but whalers also called at Koloa Landing to resupply provisions. In the 1850s local farmers used the landing to ship Kauai-grown oranges and sweet potatoes to California gold miners. The landing lost its importance after an island-wide road system was built, and it was abandoned in the 1920s. Other than a small county boat ramp, there's nothing left to see.

Beneath the water it's another story. Koloa Landing is a popular snorkeling and diving spot. Its protected waters reach depths of about 30 feet and it's generally calm all year, although kona winds can sometimes create rough water conditions. The area has some underwater tunnels and a good variety of coral and fish. For the best sights, swim out to the right after entering the water.

Poipu Beach

The long stretch of white sand running from the Sheraton east to Poipu Beach Park is generally referred to as Poipu Beach. It's actually three attractive crescent beaches separated by narrow rocky points. The turquoise waters are good for swimming, bodysurfing, windsurfing, board surfing and snorkeling.

Cowshead, the rocky outcropping at the west end of the beach near the Sheraton, has Poipu Beach's best boogie boarding and bodysurfing breaks. Top surfing spots are Waiohai, which is off the east side of Poipu Beach, and First Break, offshore in front of the Sheraton. Slow, gentle waves more suitable for beginners can be found inshore along the beach.

Poipu Beach Park

Poipu Beach Park, at the end of Hoowili Rd, has a lifeguard station, shallow nearshore waters and safe swimming, making

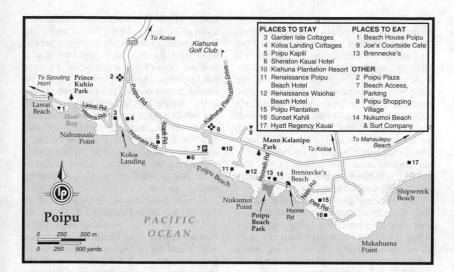

Poipu

3 Garden Isle Cottages
4 Koloa Landing Cottages
5 Poipu Kapili
6 Sheraton Kauai Hotel
10 Kiahuna Plantation Resort
11 Renaissance Poipu
    Beach Hotel
12 Renaissance Waiohai
    Beach Hotel
15 Poipu Plantation
16 Sunset Kahili
17 Hyatt Regency Kauai

PLACES TO EAT
1 Beach House Poipu
9 Joe's Courtside Cafe
13 Brennecke's

OTHER
2 Poipu Plaza
7 Beach Access,
   Parking
8 Poipu Shopping
   Village
14 Nukumoi Beach
    & Surf Company

it one of the most popular weekend destinations for families on the South Shore.

Nukumoi Point extends into the water at the western side of the park. At low tide you can walk out on the point and explore tide pools that shelter small fish and sea urchins. You'll find the best snorkeling at the west side of the point, where there are swarms of near-tame fish.

Beach facilities include restrooms, showers and picnic tables. Snorkel sets, boogie boards, beach chairs and umbrellas can be rented across the street at Nukumoi Beach & Surf Company.

Brennecke's Beach

Brennecke's has good shorebreaks that make it the South Shore's best spot for bodysurfing and boogie boarding. It breaks very close to shore and is suitable only for the experienced. While it's best when surf is highest, which is generally in the summer, there's some respectable action in winter as well. Beware of strong rips that are present with high surf. The beach is only a small pocket of sand and the waters can get crowded. For safety reasons, fins are not allowed and surfboards are prohibited.

Brennecke's is off Hoone Rd, just east of Poipu Beach Park.

Shipwreck Beach

Shipwreck Beach, the sandy beach fronting the Hyatt Regency Kauai, also sees some top bodysurfing and boogie boarding conditions. There are a couple of challenging near-shore surf breaks that attract local board surfers as well. The water conditions here are not for novices, and the pounding shorebreak and high surf make for treacherous swimming conditions along the entire beach.

Mahaulepu Beach

Secluded Mahaulepu Beach, a couple of miles beyond Shipwreck Beach, has lovely white sands, sheltered coves, tide pools, lithified sand dunes and sea cliffs.

At various times of the year Mahaulepu is good for surfing, windsurfing, boogie boarding and snorkeling. In precontact times the area was heavily settled, and many important historic sites lie buried beneath the cane fields and shifting beach sands. People still claim to see ghost marchers coming in from the sea at night along the beach.

KAUAI

The property is owned by Grove Farm, which provides visitors with beach access from 7:30 am to 6 pm in winter, until 7 pm in summer. The easiest way to get there is to drive past the Hyatt and continue on the cane road for 1½ miles, at which point the road will be blocked by a gate. Turn right, continue past the gravel plant and after a third of a mile you'll come to a gatehouse, from where it's half a mile to the beach parking area at the end of the road. A short trail to the beach begins at the right side of the parking area. This will bring you to a popular windsurfing spot and a convenient place from which to explore.

One striking geological feature in the area is a **cinder cone** with a cave that you can walk deep into. To get there, walk west along the beach for about a third of a mile. After crossing a little stream, the trail going inland leads to the cave, a couple of minutes away. In the cave's center you'll find an opening looking straight up to the heavens – it feels like you're sitting in a little volcano.

Or, instead of heading to the cave, walk east along the beach for about 10 minutes and you'll reach scenic **Kawailoa Bay**, which is surrounded by sand dunes to the west and protected by jutting sea cliffs to the east. The bay has a lovely beach, and it's not uncommon to find a few Hawaiians net-fishing in the waters along the shore.

Places to Stay – budget

Koloa Landing Cottages (☎ 742-1470, 800-779-8773; fax 332-9584; dolfin@ aloha.net), 2704B Hoonani Rd, Poipu, HI 96756, occupies five cottages across the street from Koloa Landing. All cottages have TVs, phones and full kitchens. Studio units, which have queen beds, cost $60. Full cottages, which have both a queen bed and two twins, cost from $70 for two people in a smaller unit to $110 for four people in the largest unit. A cleaning fee of $20 for studios, $40 to $60 for the cottages, is tagged onto the bill. Reserve as far in advance as possible, as the place is often booked solid.

Poipu Plantation (☎ 742-6757, 800-733-1632; bandb@aloha.net), 1792 Pee Rd, Koloa, HI 96756, consists of nine condo-style units and a 1930s home with three B&B rooms. The best deals are the condos, which are modern and comfortable with tropical rattan furniture, air-con, TVs and full kitchens. They cost from $85 to $95 for one-bedroom units, $110 for two-bedroom units. While not as spacious, the B&B accommodations are pleasant enough, have private baths, include breakfast and cost $70 for a room in the back with either a queen or a king bed, $75 for the front room with a king bed. There's a hot tub, barbecue area and a laundry room with coin-op washers and dryers.

Garden Isle Cottages (☎ 742-6717, 800-742-6711), 2666 Puuholo Rd, Poipu, HI 96756, has seven pleasant units above Koloa Landing. The studios, which have a double and single bed, refrigerator and coffeemaker, cost $75 for garden views, $95 for ocean views. One-bedroom apartments with oceanview lanais, queen beds, kitchens and roomy living rooms start at $121 for doubles; extra guests are $10 each. All the units have TVs, ceiling fans and abstract paintings and sculpture by owner/artist Robert Flynn. Garden Isle also rents a studio ($86) and a large suite ($149) in a separate house on a hill near Poipu Crater. Amenities at the latter include a lap swimming pool.

Sunset Kahili (☎ 742-1691, 800-827-6478; fax 742-6058; sunset@aloha.net), 1763 Pee Rd, Poipu, HI 96756, is an older, well-maintained five-story condo with friendly management. Each of the 36 units has an ocean view, a washer/dryer, cable TV and lanai. Rates for the lower two floors are $100 for two people in a one-bedroom unit and $130 for up to four people in the two-bedroom units. The top floors are $10 more. The minimum stay is three nights, with prices dropping gradually the longer you stay. It can be difficult to book from January through March, particularly if you're looking for a longer stay, as a lot of retirees return here each year to spend the winter.

Gloria's Spouting Horn Bed & Breakfast (☎ /fax 742-6995), 4464 Lawai Beach Rd,

Poipu, HI 96756, is a lovely oceanside B&B just a few minutes' walk from Spouting Horn. There are three comfortable bedrooms, all fronting the ocean. Each has a refrigerator, microwave, phone, TV, VCR, a bath with a deep soaking tub and a seaside balcony. Rates, which include breakfast, are $160 for singles or doubles with a three-day minimum, except around the Christmas holidays when the rate is $185 and the minimum is seven days.

Places to Stay – top end

The three large resort hotels on Poipu Beach – *Renaissance Poipu Beach Hotel, Renaissance Waiohai Beach Hotel* and *Sheraton Kauai Hotel* – were severely damaged by Hurricane Iniki and remain closed. The Sheraton (☎ 800-325-3535) is beginning to rebuild and is expected to be open by early 1998. There are still no reopening dates for the other two hotels.

Poipu Kapili (☎ 742-6449, 800-443-7714; fax 742-9162), 2221 Kapili Rd, Koloa, HI 96756, a new 60-unit seaside condominium complex, is one of Poipu's best top-end values. The units are large and nicely furnished; each is privately owned and about 45 of them are in the rental pool. They have ocean views, ceiling fans, full kitchens, and a queen-size sofa bed in the living room. One bedroom units, which have either a queen or king bed, cost from $155. The two-bedroom units typically have a king bed in the master bedroom and two twins in the second bedroom and begin at $205. There's a three-day minimum, though it's waived when things are slow; rates drop about 10% on stays of two weeks. There's a tennis court and swimming pool.

Kiahuna Plantation (☎ 742-6411, 800-688-7444; fax 742-1698; reservations@outrigger.com), 2253 Poipu Rd, Koloa, HI 96756, is a 333-unit condominium complex spread across acres of quiet garden-filled grounds between Poipu Rd and Poipu Beach. The units are pleasant, each with a full kitchen, a living room with a sofa bed and a large balcony. Prices mainly reflect the distance from the water: $175 for a one-bedroom garden-view unit for up to four

people, $400 for a one-bedroom oceanfront unit. Two-bedroom condos cost $305 to $450 for up to six people. If you book at the lower end, request a 3rd-floor unit, as some have glimpses of the ocean despite being in the garden-view category. The Outrigger chain, which manages the property, offers numerous promotions that can cut the rates by as much as half. There's a two-day minimum stay.

Poipu's most exclusive hotel is the 600-room *Hyatt Regency Kauai* (☎ 742-1234, 800-233-1234; fax 742-6229), 1571 Poipu Rd, Poipu, HI 96756. It's quite elegant with airy lobbies adorned with antiques, and its central building nicely incorporates the ocean view into its design. There are also the requisite artificial lagoons and waterways spread around the resort grounds. Garden-side rooms start at $275, while the best suites climb to $2500. There are restaurants, a health spa, tennis courts and a golf course.

Places to Stay – vacation rentals

The Poipu Beach Resort Association (☎ 742-7444; fax 742-7887; info@poipu-beach.org), Box 730, Koloa, HI 96756, has a brochure listing most of Poipu's accommodations.

The following vacation rental companies book condos and private homes in the Poipu area.

Suite Paradise, at Poipu Plaza, 2827 Poipu Rd, Poipu, HI 96756 (☎ 742-7400, 800-367-8020; fax 742-9121)

Grantham Resorts, Box 983, Poipu, HI 96756 (☎ 742-7220, 800-325-5701; fax 742-9001)

R&R Realty & Rentals, 1661 Pee Rd, Poipu, HI 96756 (☎ 742-7555, 800-367-8022; fax 742-1559)

Kauai Vacation Rentals, 3-3311 Kuhio Hwy, Lihue, HI 96766 (☎ 245-8841, 800-367-5025; fax 246-1161)

Places to Eat – budget

Taqueria Nortenos in the Poipu Plaza has cheap Mexican food. This is essentially a takeout place with some indoor picnic tables at the side. The meatless burrito is a good value at $2.80, while two enchiladas with rice and beans cost $4.50. The food is fine for the price and it's open from 11 am to 10 pm daily except Wednesdays.

Joe's Courtside Cafe at the Kiahuna Tennis Club is a good choice for reasonably priced breakfast fare. You can get a bowl of granola, a bagel or half a papaya for $2 and various breakfast standards like pancakes and omelets for around $6. It's open from 7 to 11 am for breakfast and from 11 am to 2 pm for lunch, which features salads, sandwiches and burgers for $5 to $8.

Poipu Shopping Village, at the corner of Poipu Rd and Kiahuna Plantation Drive, has *Amigo's*, a basic Mexican restaurant with $8 plates that include rice and beans; *Shipwreck Subs*, a simple sandwich stand; and *Rusty's*, which has reasonably priced gourmet pizza, salads, burgers and sandwiches.

Keoki's Paradise (☎ 742-7535) in the Poipu Shopping Village has an open-air Polynesian motif with artificial waterfalls, lit torches and hanging vines. While it's a bit contrived, it somehow all works quite nicely. The food is reasonably good, and dishes, which come with a Caesar salad, include vegetarian lasagna for $11, Balinese chicken for $15 and catch of the day for $20. It's open for dinner from 5:30 to 10 pm daily. A simpler cafe menu of burgers and sandwiches is offered near the bar from 11 am to 11:30 pm.

Brennecke's, a touristy restaurant and bar opposite Poipu Beach Park, has an ocean view and good but pricey fish dishes. A fresh fish sandwich costs $11 at lunch, while beef or vegetarian burgers are a few dollars cheaper. A salad bar can be added on for an additional $4. Dinner dishes, which include the salad bar, range from chicken stir-fry for $16 to fresh catch for $22. It's open daily, from 11:30 am to 4 pm for lunch, 4 to 10 pm for dinner.

Places to Eat – top end

In the Poipu Shopping Village is *Roy's Poipu Bar & Grill* (☎ 742-5050), a branch of the famed Roy's on Oahu. It has good Hawaiian Regional cuisine and a changing menu of creative dishes. Soups, salads and appetizers cost $5 to $8, while main courses range from $16 for chicken to $23 for fresh fish. It's open for dinner only, from 5:30 to 9:30 pm nightly.

If the setting is as important as the food, then the best place in Poipu for good Hawaiian Regional cuisine is the *Beach House Poipu* (☎ 742-1424) on Lawai Rd. Operated by chef Jean-Marie Josselin, who also owns A Pacific Cafe in Kapaa, this new restaurant has an open-air waterfront setting right on Lawai Beach. Appetizers such as wild mushroom dim sum or grilled fish nachos with lilikoi sauce are under $10, while main courses, which include the likes of pistachio-crusted salmon, seafood risotto or rack of lamb, cost $20 to $25. It's open from 5:30 to 10 pm nightly.

If you want top-notch food without burning a hole in your wallet, *Pattaya Asian Cafe* (☎ 742-8818) in the Poipu Shopping Village has wonderful Thai and Chinese dishes. Run by the same chef who operates Mema's in Wailua, it has a wide range of items for $8 to $10, including some excellent curries and flavorful dishes such as stir-fried eggplant with fresh basil. It's open for lunch from 11:30 am to 2:30 pm Monday to Saturday, for dinner from 5 to 9:30 pm nightly.

The *Ilima Terrace* (☎ 742-6260) at the Hyatt Regency Kauai offers a different buffet each night. It's not a lavish spread, but it's certainly sufficient, the quality is good and there's a pleasant waterview setting. The buffets include a small salad bar, fruits, cheeses and half a dozen tempting desserts. A couple of nights a week, prime rib is featured, while on other nights it's either a Mediterranean buffet or an island-style spread with a few Hawaiian dishes like pipikaula salad thrown in. The buffets are served from 5 to 9 pm and cost $24. The Ilima Terrace also has a breakfast buffet for $16.50 and a Sunday brunch for $20.

Entertainment

On most days the Hyatt Regency Kauai has a short but picturesque torch-lighting ceremony and hula show before sunset in its open-air *Seaview Terrace*, just off the lobby. On Tuesdays and Saturdays, a children's hula troupe performs at 6:15 pm.

The Hyatt's *Kuhio's Nightclub* has dancing to a DJ playing Top 40 music from 9 pm to 1 am on Fridays and Saturdays. The cover charge is $5 and there's a bit of a dress code (no tank tops or T-shirts).

West Side

The top destinations on Kauai's West Side are Waimea Canyon and Kokee State Park, both with ruggedly spectacular scenery.

It's 38 miles along Kaumualii Rd (Hwy 50) from Lihue to Polihale State Park, the farthest accessible point on the West Side. This is sugar country, with cane lining the roadside much of the way.

KALAHEO

Kalaheo, an old sleepy Portuguese community, is quintessentially local in flavor. Pig hunting is popular in this town, which accounts for all the hunting dogs in tiny backyard cages.

The town's main shops are clustered around the intersection of Hwy 50 and Papalina Rd. They include a couple of food marts, the post office and Kalaheo's restaurants. There's a coin laundry behind Kalaheo Steak House on Papalina Rd.

Kukuiolono Park

Kukuiolono Park (☎ 332 9151) is an unassuming little golf course with gardens and scenic views. Kukuiolono means 'light of Lono', referring to the torches that Hawaiians once placed on this hill to help guide canoes safely to shore.

From Hwy 50, turn left onto Papalina Rd in Kalaheo. Just short of a mile turn right onto Puu Rd and then make an immediate right, which takes you through an old stone archway and up into the park. A neat little Japanese garden is at the end of the parking lot.

The park gates are open from 6:30 am to 6:30 pm. The nine-hole golf course is open to the public on a first-come first-served basis. Greens fees are a mere $7. The little clubhouse has an inexpensive snack shop and a fine view clear down to the coast.

Puu Rd Scenic Drive

Puu Rd is a scenic side loop with small ranches, grand mango trees and fine coastal views. It's a winding road, only one lane with some blind curves, but nothing tricky if you drive slowly. This is such a quiet country road it's quite possible you won't even encounter another car.

After leaving Kukuiolono Park, turn right onto Puu Rd to start the drive. It's just over three miles back to Hwy 50 this way. About halfway along you'll look down on Port Allen's oil tanks and the town of Numila with its old sugar mill.

Down the slope on the west side of the road are coffee trees, part of a total of 4000 acres that have been planted between Koloa and Eleele. The coffee, on McBryde Sugar Company property, is one of the company's grander schemes for diversifying crops on land that was formerly planted solely in sugar cane.

Olu Pua Gardens

Olu Pua (☎ 332-8182) is a 12-acre plantation estate with gardens that contain a fine collection of tropical plants, including palms, hibiscus and orchids. The Olu Pua estate home, built in 1931 by noted Honolulu architect CW Dickey, served as the headquarters for Alexander & Baldwin's Kauai Pineapple Plantation.

Olu Pua is at the end of a long driveway that starts mauka of the intersection of Hwy 50 and Hwy 540. Guided tours of the gardens and the estate house are given six times a day at 30 minutes after the hour from 9:30 am to 2:30 pm. It costs $12 for adults, $6 for children ages five to 12.

Places to Stay

Classic Vacation Cottages (☎ 332-9201; fax 332-7645; clascot@hawaiian.net), Dick and

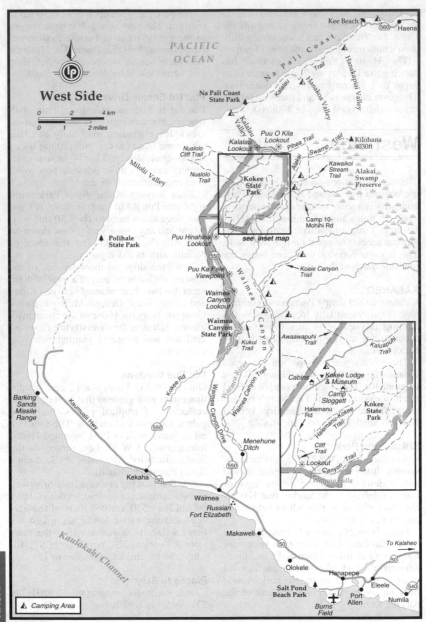

PACIFIC
OCEAN

West Side

0   2   4 km
0   1   2 miles

**Polihale
State Park**

**Barking
Sands Missile
Range**

Kaumualii Hwy

Kekaha

50

Waimea
*Russian
Fort Elizabeth*

Makaweli

50

Olokele

Kee Beach

560   Haena

N a   P a l i   C o a s t

Kalalau
Trail

Hanakapiai Valley

Hanakoa Valley

Hanakapiai
Trail

**Na Pali Coast
State Park**

Miloli Valley

Nualolo
Cliff Trail

Nualolo
Trail

Kalalau
Valley

*Puu O Kila
Lookout*

Kalalau
Lookout

Pihea Trail

Alakai   Swamp   Trail

▲ Kilohana
4030ft

Kawaikoi
Stream Trail

Alakai
Swamp
Preserve

Kokee
State
Park

Puu Hinahina
Lookout

see inset map

Camp 10-
Mohihi Rd

550

Koaie Canyon
Trail

Puu Ka Pele
Viewpoint

W a i m e a

Waimea
Canyon
Lookout

**Waimea
Canyon
State Park**

Kukui
Trail

C a n y o n

Waimea River

Kokee Rd

Waimea Canyon Drive

Waimea Canyon Trail

550

Menehune
Ditch

Kaulakahi   Channel

Awaawapuhi
Trail

Kaluapuhi
Trail

Cabins

Halemanu
Rd

▼ Kokee Lodge
& Museum

Camp
Sloggett

Halemanu-Kokee
Trail

Kokee
State
Park

Cliff
Trail

Lookout
Canyon   Trail

Waipoo Falls

Waimea

Hanapepe

Salt Pond
Beach Park

Port
Allen

Burns
Field

50

Eleele

Numila

540

To Kalaheo

50

△ *Camping Area*

KAUAI

Wynnis Grow, Box 901, Kalaheo, HI 96741, is in Kalaheo, half a mile up from Hwy 50. There's a studio for $65 with a queen-size bed, a skylight and French doors to a little porch. A one-bedroom unit above the studio has high ceilings, a lanai and a peek at the ocean for $68. A simpler third unit at the side of the main house costs $65. All have sofa beds, kitchens and cable TV. For additional guests beyond two, add $10 more.

If you prefer to be in a secluded country setting, *Strawberry Guava* (☎ /fax 332-7790; lauria@hawaiian.net), Joe and Lauria Sullivan, Box 271, Lawai, HI 96765, is perched on a hillside above Lawai Valley, just east of Kalaheo. This is a contemporary home with separate side wings containing three guest rooms, each with a private bath. One is a cozy bedroom with a splendid view for $60. The other two are suites with separate living rooms containing a TV and VCR; these cost $75. Breakfast, included in the rates, is served on an outdoor deck with bucolic views.

Places to Eat

The *Bread Box* on Papalina Rd sells good whole-grain breads, tasty macnut rolls for $1.30 and coffee for just 25¢. It's open Tuesday to Saturday from 4 am to noon, or until the bread sells out.

Kalaheo Coffee Co, on Hwy 50 at the side of the Menehune Food Mart, is a friendly cafe with good coffee, espresso and pastries – try the pumpkin muffins. For around $5, you can get lunchtime sandwiches or various breakfast offerings, including Belgian waffles or ham and eggs. It's open daily from 6 am to 4 pm (Sundays from 7 am to 2 pm).

Brick Oven Pizza (☎ 332-8561) on Hwy 50 is a popular place with small (10-inch) pizzas priced from $8.35, large ones (15-inch) from $18. The pizzas come in a choice of whole-wheat or white crust. The restaurant also has sandwiches, good salads, wine and beer. It's open from 11 am to 10:30 pm daily except Mondays.

The new *Pomodoro* (☎ 332-5945), on Hwy 50 opposite Brick Oven Pizza, operated by an Italian couple from Brooklyn,

serves up some of the finest Italian food on the island. Pastas, which are made fresh, range from $10 to $15, while chicken, scampi and calamari dishes are priced from $17 to $20. It's open for dinner only, from 5:30 to 10 pm nightly.

A good place for meat and potatoes is the *Kalaheo Steak House* (☎ 332-9780) on Papalina Rd. It's open from 6 to 9 pm nightly, with dinner offerings ranging from teriyaki chicken for $13 to filet mignon for $19.

HANAPEPE VALLEY LOOKOUT

The scenic lookout that comes up shortly after the 14-mile marker gives a view deep into Hanapepe Valley. The red clay walls of the cliffs are topped by bright green cane like a sugar frosting.

The same Robinson family that owns the island of Niihau also has substantial land holdings in these parts, including a hideaway estate deep in Hanapepe Valley.

While old king sugar may dominate the scene surrounding Hanapepe Valley, if you glance towards the opposite side of the road from the lookout you'll see Kauai's newest commercial crop – coffee trees.

ELEELE, NUMILA & PORT ALLEN

Eleele is largely a residential area of limited interest to visitors. It does have a shopping center at the 16-mile marker with a Big Save supermarket, bank, post office, coin laundry, a McDonald's and a pretty good Thai restaurant.

Hwy 540 is an alternate route that leads off Hwy 50 just after Kalaheo and connects back to Hwy 50 at Eleele. It passes through fields of coffee trees and swings by Numila, a former cane town with dusty wooden houses surrounding an old sugar mill that's been converted into a coffee processing facility. If you head down this way on weekdays, there's a little shop offering samples and sales of Kauai Coffee.

Port Allen, immediately south of Eleele on Hanapepe Bay, is both a commercial harbor and one of Kauai's busiest recreational boat harbors. The state-run small craft harbor here is protected by breakwaters and has launch ramps, berthing and mooring spaces.

KAUAI

Glass Beach

Glass Beach, just east of Port Allen, is a cove piled high with colorful bits of glass that have been worn into smooth pebble-like pieces. The glass comes from a long abandoned dump site nearby, and its weathering is the result of decades of wave action. At certain times of the year the glass is deep enough to scoop up by the handful, while at other times it's largely washed out to sea.

To get to the little cove, take the last left before entering the Port Allen commercial harbor, drive past the fuel storage tanks and then curve to the right down a dirt cane road that leads 100 yards to the beach.

HANAPEPE

Before Hurricane Iniki hit, Hanapepe was one of the best preserved historic towns in Hawaii. Parts of *The Thorn Birds* were filmed here because Hanapepe bore such a close resemblance to the dusty Australian outback of days past.

While the hurricane wreaked havoc on the town's old wooden buildings, claiming about half of them, Hanapepe still has lots of character and a nice unhurried pace that invites lingering.

The turn-off into Hanapepe is marked by a sign on Hwy 50.

Hanapepe Rd, the town's main street, retains a decidedly period face, with small local stores and a few art galleries. Most interesting is Kauai Fine Arts, which occupies the former bowling alley and has a collection of antique maps and prints, including works related to Captain Cook's explorations.

Be sure to take a stroll over the **swinging bridge**, which crosses the Hanapepe River, opposite Kauai Fine Arts. Its funky old predecessor fell victim to Iniki, but in a community-wide effort this new bridge was erected in 1996.

If you want to take a **scenic side drive** through a niche of 'old Hawaii', turn mauka onto Awawa Rd, which runs north from Hanapepe Rd at the west side of the Hanapepe River. This narrow road is bordered by cliffs on one side and by taro patches and grazing horses on the other. After a mile, Awawa Rd forks. If you take the dead-end street to the left, there's more rural scenery and lots of tall trees. After three-quarters of a mile you'll have to turn around and come back to the 'main' road, where you can turn left and loop back to town along a dirt drive. However, there's one tricky section where the road crosses a cement bridge that's really little more than a weir. Because the river flows *over* rather than under this bridge, you'll need to gauge the depth of the water on top before deciding whether or not to continue. If it's only a couple of inches deep, you shouldn't have any problem crossing, but if it's more than that, turn around and return the way you came.

Salt Pond Beach

Kauai has long been known for its alae salt, a sea salt with a red tint that comes from adding a bit of iron-rich earth. The salt is made by letting seawater into shallow basins called salt pans and allowing it to evaporate. When dry, the salt crystals are scraped off. Native Hawaiians still make salt this way down on the coast south of Hanapepe.

Salt Pond Beach Park is just beyond the salt ponds. It has a sandy beach, campsites, covered picnic tables, barbecue grills, a pay phone, showers and a lifeguard on duty daily. Water in the cove gets up to 10 feet deep and is good for swimming laps – four times across equals half a mile. Both ends of the cove are shallow and good for kids.

To get to Salt Pond Beach, turn left just past the 17-mile marker onto Lele Rd, then right onto Lokokai Rd.

Places to Eat

The *Hanapepe Bookstore* (☎ 335-5011), in the town center on Hanapepe Rd, is a good cafe-style restaurant specializing in vegetarian fare. Breakfast, served from 8 to 11 am, includes multigrain pancakes or waffles topped with macnuts and real maple syrup for around $5, as well as fresh croissants and pastries made on site. Lunch, from 11 am to 2 pm, includes garden burgers, sandwiches, a pasta special or baked frittata with a Caesar salad – all for under $8. Dinner is available from 6 to 9 pm on Thursdays, Fridays and Saturdays only (reservations suggested) and features creative pasta meals priced from $16 to $19. The restaurant is closed on Sundays and Mondays.

On the highway section of town there's also *Sinaloa*, a moderately priced Mexican restaurant; *Green Garden Restaurant*, an old standby that's popular with tour buses; and a *Lappert's* ice cream shop.

OLOKELE

Olokele exists for the Olokele Sugar Company. Of the 220 employees, mostly field laborers, 200 live in Olokele.

The road to the sugar mill, which comes up immediately after the 19-mile marker, is shaded by tall trees and lined with classic turn-of-the-century lampposts. Taking this short drive offers a glimpse into real plantation life. Everything is covered with a layer of red dust from the surrounding sugar cane fields and mill. Rather than fight it, many of the houses are painted in beige-red tones.

MAKAWELI

Makaweli is headquarters for Gay & Robinson, Niihau Ranch and Niihau Helicopters, all enterprises of the Robinson family, the owners of Niihau. Quite a few native Niihauans live in this area, many of them working for the Robinsons. Once or twice a week an old military landing craft makes the 17-mile trip between Niihau and Makaweli Landing.

RUSSIAN FORT ELIZABETH

The remains of Russian Fort Elizabeth stand above the east bank of the Waimea River. Hawaiian laborers started building the fort in 1816 under the direction of Georg Anton Schaeffer, an agent of the Russian-American Company. The alliance between the Russians and Kauai's King Kaumualii proved to be a short-lived one, and the Russians were tossed out in 1817, the same year the fort was completed.

You can take a short walk through this curious period of Kauai's history. The most intact part of the fort is the exterior lava-rock wall, which is eight to 10 feet high in places and largely overgrown with scrub and colorful wildflowers. The seaward side was designed like the points of a star, but it takes close observation to get the effect.

The fort has a good view of the western bank of the Waimea River, where Captain Cook landed. Bear right down the dirt road that continues past the parking lot and you'll find a vantage above the river mouth with a view of Waimea Pier and the island of Niihau. There are restrooms and a pay phone at the parking lot.

WAIMEA

Waimea (which means 'reddish water') was the site of an ancient Hawaiian settlement. It was at Waimea, on January 19, 1778, that Captain Cook first came ashore on the Hawaiian Islands. In 1820 the first wave of missionaries to Hawaii also selected Waimea as a landing site. In 1884, Waimea Sugar moved in and Waimea developed into a plantation town. Today, Waimea remains the biggest town on this side of the island.

If you want to explore, Waimea Library, at the 23-mile marker, has a map of historical buildings that can be photocopied and used for a self-guided walking tour. The library (☎ 338-6848) is open from noon to 8 pm Mondays and Wednesdays and from 9 am to 5 pm Tuesdays, Thursdays and Fridays.

Waimea Canyon Drive (Hwy 50) heads north from town to Kokee State Park.

Lucy Wright Park

The Cook landing site is noted with a simple plaque on a nondescript rock on the western side of Waimea River. The plaque is on the beach at Lucy Wright Park, on Ala Wai Rd, just over the Waimea Bridge. This county park also has a ball field, picnic tables, restrooms and showers. Camping is allowed on a flat grassy area, but it's at the side of the road in town and doesn't have much appeal.

KAUAI

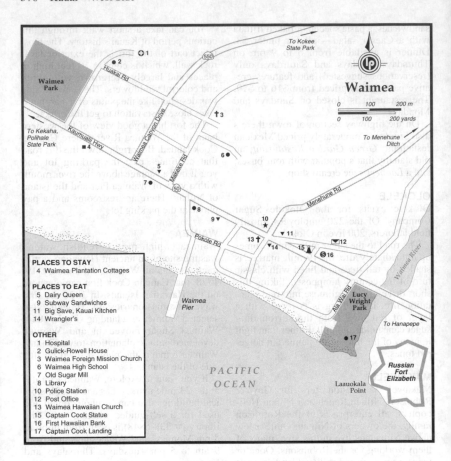

Waimea

PLACES TO STAY
4 Waimea Plantation Cottages

PLACES TO EAT
5 Dairy Queen
5 Subway Sandwiches
11 Big Save, Kauai Kitchen
14 Wrangler's

OTHER
1 Hospital
2 Gulick-Rowell House
3 Waimea Foreign Mission Church
6 Waimea High School
7 Old Sugar Mill
8 Library
10 Police Station
12 Post Office
13 Waimea Hawaiian Church
15 Captain Cook Statue
16 First Hawaiian Bank
17 Captain Cook Landing

Captain Cook Statue

The statue of Captain Cook in the center of town is a replica of the original statue by Sir John Tweed that stands in Whitby, England. The Pacific's greatest navigator, clutching his charts and decked out in his best captain finery, now watches over traffic on Hwy 50.

Waimea Pier

Until Port Allen was built, Waimea was the region's main harbor. It was a major port of call for whalers and traders during the mid-19th century, and plantations started exporting sugar from here later in the century.

Waimea Pier, off Pokole Rd, is now used primarily for pole fishing, crabbing and picnicking.

Waimea Churches

The Waimea Foreign Mission Church was originally a thatched structure built in 1826 by the Reverend Samuel Whitney, the first missionary to Waimea. Whitney and his wife are buried in the churchyard. The present church was built of sandstone blocks and coral mortar in 1858 by the Reverend George Rowell.

In 1865, Reverend Rowell had a spat

with some folks in the congregation and went off and built the **Waimea Hawaiian Church**, a wooden frame church that was downed in the 1992 hurricane but has since been rebuilt.

It was Rowell who finished building the Gulick-Rowell House, at the end of Huakai Rd. Construction began in 1829, making it the oldest house still standing in Kauai. The two-story stone-block house is now privately owned and not open to the public.

Menehune Ditch

The Menehune Ditch is a stone and earthen aqueduct built prior to Western contact. Kauai's legendary little people, the menehune, are said to have built the ditch in one night. The ditch was an engineering masterpiece with rocks carefully squared and joined to create a watertight seal.

When Captain Vancouver visited Waimea at the end of the 18th century he walked up the river valley atop the wall of this ditch, which also served as a footpath. He estimated the walls to be a full 24 feet high. These days most of the ancient waterway lies buried beneath the road, but one section about two feet high can still be seen. The ditch still diverts water from the Waimea River along and through the cliff to irrigate the taro patches below.

To get there, turn at the police station onto Menehune Rd and go about 1⅓ miles up Waimea River. The ditch is along the left side of the road after a very small parking area.

On the drive up to the ditch, notice the scattered holes in the cliffs to the left. They are Hawaiian burial caves. One group of seven caves behind the Waimea Shingon Mission was explored by Wendell Bennett of the Bishop Museum in the 1920s. At that time each of the caves held a number of skeletal remains, some in canoe-shaped coffins and others in hollowed-out logs.

Places to Stay

Waimea Plantation Cottages (☎ 338-1625, 800-992-4632; fax 338-2338), 9600 Kaumualii Hwy, Waimea, HI 96796, is a collection of nearly 50 plantation workers' homes that date to the early 1900s. The wooden cottages, which are clustered in a coconut grove, are cutesy-rustic right down to their tin-roofed porches. They've been thoroughly restored and pleasantly furnished with appropriately simple decor. Rates are pricey, ranging from $180 for a one-bedroom cottage that sleeps two to $260 for a three-bedroom cottage that can sleep eight.

Places to Eat

Wrangler's, in the center of town on Hwy 50, has a varied menu and average food. At lunch, which is available weekdays until 5 pm, you can get chicken katsu with salad, an enchilada with rice and beans or a burger with fries for $6.50. Dinner, served from 5 to 9 pm Monday to Saturday, features steaks for around $15.

Kauai Kitchen, next to Big Save supermarket, has standard plate lunches for around $5. There's a *Subway Sandwiches* and a *Dairy Queen* farther west on Hwy 50.

KEKAHA

Kekaha has great beaches, or rather it has one long glorious stretch. The road follows the beach for about two miles, with roadside parking all along the way. This is open ocean, and when the surf is high there can be dangerous currents; when there's no swell, you can usually find swimmers here. Niihau and its offshore island, Lehua, are visible from the beach.

There's a very inconspicuous shower just mauka of the highway between Alae Rd and Amakihi Rd; restrooms and picnic tables are farther in.

A few blocks inland from the beach is Kekaha Rd, the main village street, which runs parallel to the highway. It has a grocery store, a post office and the last gas station before the end of the road. The village's most dominant feature is its working sugar mill, which is visible from the highway.

On its eastern end, Kekaha Rd comes out to Hwy 50 near the Kikiaola Small Boat Harbor. This state harbor has one launch ramp and eight mooring spaces.

Kekaha is Kauai's westernmost town, and as you continue on towards Polihale it's a rural scene, with the inland cliffs getting higher and the ravines deeper. Corn and sunflowers, which are planted for seed production, grow in fields along the road. Cattle and cattle egrets feed in the pastures.

Places to Stay
Mindy's (☎ 337-9275), 8842 Kekaha Rd, Box 861, Kekaha, HI 96796, is the only accommodations alternative beyond Waimea (other than camping) and would make a good base for exploring Kokee and the southwest coast. Mindy and Dave Heri rent a pleasant 2nd-story apartment above their home, with a large deck, a full kitchen and a living room with a double sofa bed. The bedroom has a double bed and a cane field view. The place is modern and comfortable, with ceiling fans throughout, TV, phone, radio and a shower/tub combination in the bathroom. The rate is $55 for one person, $5 for each additional person up to four; add $10 more if you're staying for just one night. Complimentary fruit and coffee are provided.

Places to Eat
On Kekaha Rd at the base of Hwy 550, there's a small center with a *Menehune Food Mart*, which has groceries, wrapped sandwiches and takeout salads, and *Lappert's*, which sells ice cream, plate lunches, fried chicken and burgers.

BARKING SANDS
Barking Sands Pacific Missile Range, a US Navy base, usually has at least one stretch of its beach open to the public. For a recorded message on current access, dial ☎ 335-4229.

The road in is at the 'Pacific Missile Range Facility' sign, less than half a mile after the 32-mile marker. At the gate they ask to see your driver's license and then explain where you can go, which is usually the beach about two miles south of the gate, which locals call **Majors Bay** and the military calls RecArea No 3.

This broad curving sweep of fine golden sand is a good sunbathing and walking beach,

though it's open and hot. The scrub brush behind the beach offers no shade, but it hardly matters, as the vegetation line is the DMZ line and you're forbidden to go beyond it anyway.

In winter, Majors Bay is a popular surfing spot, although as with all West Side beaches the waters can be dangerous. There are no facilities. The purple-tinged island of Niihau can be seen on the horizon.

On very sunny days, when the wind is blowing off the water just right, the moving sands make sounds similar to barking dogs, hence the area's name.

The missile range facility at Barking Sands provides the above-ground link to a sophisticated sonar network that tracks more than 1000 sq miles of the Pacific. Established during WWII, it's been developed into the world's largest underwater listening device. The equipment is sensitive enough to pick up the songs of wintering humpback whales, and the base has gathered the most comprehensive collection of humpback whale soundtracks ever recorded.

POLIHALE
Polihale is near-desert. When it's raining everywhere else, beachgoers head this way.

Polihale has a beautiful long white-sand beach with aqua-colored water that often comes to shore in huge explosive waves. Expert surfers occasionally give Polihale a try, but strong rip currents make the waters treacherous for swimming.

Polihale State Park is about five miles from the Barking Sands military base. Turn left three-quarters of a mile north of the base entrance onto a wide dirt road that runs through sugar cane fields. The road is a bit bumpy but passable. Set your odometer at zero here.

At 3⅓ miles, at a large spreading tree in the middle of the road, a turn-off leads to the only safe swimming spot in the area. To get there, turn left at the tree and then after a quarter of a mile follow the road up the hill to the right to the base of the dunes. Walk a couple of minutes to the north along the beach and you'll come to **Queen's Pond**, where a large semicircle of reef comes almost to shore creating a protected swimming pool. When the seas are relatively calm the reef blocks the longshore currents; however, when surf breaks over the reef and into the pool a dangerous rip current runs towards an opening at the southern end of the reef. The rest of the beach is bordered by open sea.

To get to **Polihale State Park** go back to the tree at the main cane road, turn left and continue down a mile. A turn-off on the left leads to a camping area with restrooms, outdoor showers, drinking water and a picnic pavilion. Farther down, other camping areas are in the dunes just above the beach amid thorny kiawe trees.

At the very end of the beach is Polihale Cliff, marking the western end of the Na Pali Coast. Combined with the untamed ocean and vast expansive beach, it's a magnificent sight. Sunsets here can be a meditative experience.

There's a terraced **heiau** towards the base of the cliff. It was originally on the beach, but over the years shifting sands have added a 300-foot buffer between the heiau and the sea. The heiau is so overgrown that even after you tramp into the brush and find it, it's really hard to get a perspective on it. Wasps are another obstacle – if you're allergic to stings, forget about exploring this one.

WAIMEA CANYON

Waimea Canyon is nicknamed the 'Grand Canyon of the Pacific'. This may sound like promotional hype, but it's not a bad description. Although it's smaller and 200 million years younger than the famed Arizona canyon, the Waimea Canyon is certainly grand.

The canyon's colorful river-cut gorge is 2785 feet deep. The river that runs through it, the Waimea-Poomau, is 19½ miles long, Kauai's longest. All in all, it seems incredible that such an immense canyon could be tucked inside such a small island.

The view of the canyon is usually a bit hazy. The best time to be there is a sunny day after it's been raining heavily – at such times, the earth's a deeper red and waterfalls cascade throughout the canyon, providing unbeatable scenery.

Waimea Canyon Drive

Waimea Canyon Drive (Hwy 550) starts in Waimea. The road is 19 miles long, ending at lookouts with terrific views into Kalalau Valley on the Na Pali Coast.

The views start about a mile up from Waimea and get better and better as the road climbs. There are plenty of little scenic lookouts where you can stop to take it all in. The one at 1¾ miles looks down on the Waimea River and the taro patches that are irrigated by the Menehune Ditch. About 2½ miles up there are good views across cane fields to Kekaha Beach with Niihau in the background. From there on it's all canyon views.

WAIMEA CANYON STATE PARK

The southern boundary of Waimea Canyon State Park is about six miles up. Waimea Canyon Drive and Kokee Road, both labeled Hwy 550, merge nearby. Kokee Rd, which climbs up from Kekaha, also has scenic views, but not of the canyon. After the two roads merge, the single road continuing north is called Kokee Rd.

Iliau Nature Loop

The marked trailhead for the Iliau Nature Loop comes up shortly before the nine-mile marker. Just a hundred feet up the trail there's a bench with a scenic view, though for the best angle take a two-minute walk to the left where a cliffside bench provides a topnotch view into Waimea Canyon. After heavy rainfall, waterfalls explode down the sheer rock walls across the gorge.

Iliau Loop starts at the first bench and takes about 10 minutes to walk. Iliau, a plant endemic to western Kauai, grows along the trail, with stalks up to 10 feet high. Like its cousin the silversword, iliau grows to a ripe old age. Then for a grand finale it bursts open with blossoms and dies.

Scenic Lookouts

The most scenic of the lookout points along this stretch, **Waimea Canyon Lookout** is clearly signposted a third of a mile north of the 10-mile marker. The lookout offers a sweeping view of Waimea Canyon from a perch of 3100 feet. The prominent canyon running in an easterly direction off Waimea is Koaie Canyon, which is accessible to backcountry hikers.

As you continue up the road, Waipoo Falls can be seen from a couple of small unmarked lookouts before the 12-mile marker and then at the **Puu Ka Pele Viewpoint**, shortly before the 13-mile marker. When the light is right a rainbow shows up in the spray of the 800-foot falls. Across the road from the viewpoint is a picnic area with barbecue pits, restrooms and water, as well as Camp Hale Koa, a Seventh Day Adventist camp.

Puu Hinahina Lookout, at 3640 feet, is at a marked turn-off between the 13- and 14-mile markers. There are two lookouts close to the parking lot. One has a fine view down Waimea Canyon clear out to the coast, while the other has a view of Niihau.

Waimea Canyon Trails

For serious hikers, there are trails that lead deep into Waimea Canyon. The trailhead for the **Kukui Trail** is shortly before the nine-mile marker. This trail continues from the Iliau Nature Loop at a sign-in box and picnic table. From there the Kukui Trail makes a steep 2000-foot descent down the western side of Waimea Canyon, 2½ miles to the Waimea River. Wiliwili Camp is at the end of the trail.

The **Koaie Canyon Trail** begins at Kaluahaulu Camp, half a mile up the Waimea River from the end of the Kukui Trail. From there it runs east for three miles along the southern side of Koaie Canyon. There are some good swimming holes in the stream along the way and at the end of the trail. This trail should be avoided during stormy weather due to the danger of flash flooding.

The canyon's fertile soil once supported an ancient Hawaiian settlement. It's long abandoned, but the remains of a heiau and some house sites are still discernible. The Koaie Canyon Trail passes Hipalau Camp and ends at Lonomea Camp.

All four camps on these trails are part of the forest reserve system. Although they have simple open-air shelters, there are no facilities and the stream water needs to be treated before drinking. Information on permits is given in the Camping section near the beginning of this chapter.

A third trail in this area is the eight-mile **Waimea Canyon Trail**, which runs south from Wiliwili Camp to the town of Waimea, ending on Menehune Rd. Much of the trail is along a 4WD road that leads to a hydroelectric power station. While there's public access along the route, the trail passes over private property so no camping is allowed. There are a number of river crossings, making the trail best considered only during periods of dry weather.

During weekends and holidays, all of these trails are fairly heavily used by pig hunters.

KOKEE STATE PARK

The Kokee State Park boundary starts beyond the Puu Hinahina Lookout. After the 15-mile marker, you'll pass park cabins, Kokee Lodge, a museum and a campground one after the other. Kokee Lodge is not an overnight lodge but a restaurant and the concessionaire station for the nearby cabins.

The ranger station in Kokee hasn't been staffed for years, but the helpful people at the Kokee Museum can provide a little assistance, including basic information on current trail conditions. There's also an information board and trail map posted outside the museum.

Kokee Museum

A good place to learn about Kauai's ecology is the Kokee Museum (☎ 335-9975), which features displays of local trees, birds, climate and geology. There are also detailed topographical maps of the area and a glass case of poi pounders, stone adze heads and other historic artifacts. Quality koa bowls, a good selection of books and inexpensive trail maps are for sale. The museum is open from 10 am to 4 pm daily. Admission is free, though it's appreciated if visitors drop a dollar or so in the donation box.

Ask at the museum for the brochure to the short nature loop trail out back. The brochure corresponds to numbered plants and trees, many of them native Hawaiian species, beginning with a koa tree directly behind the museum.

By the way, the chickens that congregate in the museum parking lot are not the common garden variety but *moa*, or jungle fowl. Early Polynesian settlers brought moa to Hawaii, and they were once common on all the main islands. Now the moa remain solely on Kauai, the only island that's free of mongooses, an introduced mammal that preys on the eggs of ground-nesting birds.

Kalalau Lookouts

The two Kalalau Valley lookouts at the end of the road are not to be missed.

The first, the **Kalalau Lookout**, is at the 18-mile marker. From a height of 4000 feet you can see deep into the green depths of the valley straight out to the sea. When the weather is cooperative, late afternoon rainbows sweep so deeply into Kalalau Valley that the bottom part of the bows curve back inward. Bright-red apapane birds feed from the flowers of the ohia lehua trees near the lookout railings.

Kalalau Valley was once the site of a large settlement and was joined to Kokee by a very steep trail that ran down the cliffside. These days the only way into the valley is along the coastal Kalalau Trail from Haena on the North Shore.

The cone-shaped pinnacles along the valley walls look rather like a row of sentinels standing at attention. One legend says that rain has sculptured the cliffsides into the shape of the proud chiefs who are buried in the mountains.

The mushroom-shaped white dome and satellite dishes visible on the hill as you walk back to the parking lot are part of the Kokee Air Force station.

The paved road continues another mile to **Puu O Kila Lookout**. This is the last leg of the aborted Kokee-Haena Hwy, which would have linked Kokee with the North Shore, thus creating a circle-island road. One look at the cliffs at the end of the road and you'll understand why the scheme was scrapped.

Meadow Spirits

According to legend, Kanalohuluhulu Meadow, opposite Kokee Museum, was once a forested hideout for an evil *akua* (spirit) who enjoyed harassing people passing through on their way to Kalalau Valley. Distraught travelers appealed to the great god Kanaloa to protect them from the akua. Kanaloa responded by ripping out all the trees and declaring that they were never again to grow here, thus destroying the akua's hiding place. These days the meadow is full of good vibes and makes a nice place to throw a frisbee. ∎

The Pihea Trail that climbs the ridge straight ahead runs along what was to be the road.

From this lookout you get another view into Kalalau Valley and a glance inland towards the Alakai Swamp. A sign here points to Waialeale, the wettest spot on earth.

Kokee State Park Trails

Kokee State Park is the starting point for about 45 miles of trails, some maintained by the park service, others by the forestry. Pig and goat hunters use some of these trails during the hunting season, so it's a good idea for hikers to wear brightly colored clothing.

Three of the trails – Nualolo, Awaawapuhi and Pihea – offer clifftop views into valleys on the Na Pali Coast. A couple of trails go into the swampy bogs of Alakai Swamp, while others are easy nature trails.

Halemanu Rd Trails Halemanu Rd, the starting point for several scenic hikes, is just north of the 14-mile marker. Whether or not the road is passable in a non-4WD vehicle often depends on whether it's been raining recently. Keep in mind that the clay roads provide no traction when wet and even if you're able to drive a car in, should it begin to rain driving out can be another matter!

The first hike is **Cliff Trail**, where a short five-minute walk leads to an overlook into

Waimea Canyon. From there you can continue along **Canyon Trail**, a rather strenuous 1¾ miles one way that follows the canyon rim, passes Waipoo Falls and ends at Kumuwela Lookout with views down the canyon to the ocean beyond. On both trails there's a good chance of spotting feral goats scrambling along the canyon walls.

A little farther down Halemanu Rd is the start of **Halemanu-Kokee Trail**. This easy 1¼-mile (each way) nature trail passes through a native forest of koa and ohia trees that provide a habitat for native birds, including the iiwi, apapane, amakihi and elepaio. One of the common plants found on this trail is banana poka, a member of the passion fruit family and a serious invasive pest. It has pretty pink flowers, but it drapes the forest with its vines and chokes out less aggressive native plants.

Nualolo & Awaawapuhi Trails The Nualolo and Awaawapuhi trails each go out to the very edge of sheer cliffs, allowing you to peer down into valleys that are otherwise accessible only by boat. The valley views are extraordinarily beautiful.

The Nualolo and Awaawapuhi trails connect via the Nualolo Cliff Trail. You can combine the three trails to make a hardy day hike of about 10 miles. Then you'll have to either hitch a ride or walk an additional two miles back down the road to where you started.

Bring plenty of water, as there's none along the way. Edible plants along the trail include blackberries, thimbleberries, guava and passion fruit.

Wild goats, prolific in the North Shore valleys, are readily spotted along the cliff walls. Capable of breeding at five months of age, the goats have no natural predators in Hawaii, and their unchecked numbers have caused a fair amount of ecological damage.

The 3¾-mile Nualolo Trail starts between the cabins and Kokee Lodge. The trail begins in cool upland forest and descends 1500 feet, ending with a fine view from Lolo Vista Point, a lookout on the valley rim. There's a USGS survey marker at the lookout, at an elevation of 2234 feet.

The trailhead for the Awaawapuhi Trail begins at a small parking area just after the 17-mile marker. The trail descends 1600 feet, ending after 3¼ miles at a steep and spectacular pali overlooking Awaawapuhi and Nualolo valleys. The hike starts in an ohia forest. About half a mile down the trail, the forest becomes dryer and koa begins to mix in with the ohia. Some of the trees and plants along the trail are marked; a corresponding interpretive nature guide is available from the forestry office in Lihue and sometimes at the Kokee Museum. Awaawapuhi means 'valley of ginger'. Kahili, a yellow ginger, is seen at marker number nine.

The two-mile Nualolo Cliff Trail is very scenic and offers numerous viewpoints into Nualolo Valley. There's even a picnic table where you can break for lunch along the way. The Nualolo Cliff Trail connects at the Nualolo Trail near the 3¼-mile mark and at the Awaawapuhi Trail a little short of the three-mile mark.

Kawaikoi Stream Trail The Kawaikoi Stream Trail begins between the Sugi Grove and Kawaikoi campgrounds, off Camp 10-Mohihi Rd. This is a scenic mountain stream trail of about three miles roundtrip. It starts out following the southern side of Kawaikoi Stream, then heads away from the stream and makes a loop, coming down the northern side of the stream before reconnecting with the southern side. If the stream is running high, don't make the crossings.

Kawaikoi Stream is popular for rainbow trout fishing, which is allowed during an open season in August and September. Fishing licenses are required.

Camp 10-Mohihi Rd is up past the museum on the right. Like many of the dirt roads in Kokee, when it's dry, ordinary cars can usually make it at least part way in. However on those occasions when it's really wet and rutted, even 4WD vehicles can have difficulty.

Pihea Trail The Pihea Trail starts from the Puu O Kila Lookout and combines coastal views with an opportunity to see some of the Alakai wilderness. The beginning of the trail was graded in the 1950s, before plans to make this the last leg of the circle-island road were abandoned.

The first mile of the trail runs along the ridge, offering fine views into Kalalau Valley, before coming to the Pihea Lookout, a viewpoint that requires a steep scramble to reach. The Pihea Trail then turns inland through wetland forest and at about 1¾ miles crosses the Alakai Swamp Trail. If you turn left here, you can continue on for about two miles through the Alakai Swamp to Kilohana Lookout. If you go straight instead, you will reach the Kawaikoi campground in about two miles.

Alakai Swamp Trail Alakai Swamp is inaccessible enough that even invasive plants haven't been able to choke out the endemic swamp vegetation, and native bird species still have a stronghold.

There are parts of the swamp that receive so little sunlight that the moss grows thick and fat on all sides of the trees. Most people that see this swamp see it from a helicopter, but it's possible to walk through a corner of it by taking the Alakai Swamp Trail.

This rough 3½-mile trail starts off Camp 10-Mohihi Rd and goes through rainforest and bogs before reaching Kilohana Lookout perched on the rim of Wainiha Pali. If it's not overcast – and that's a big 'if', considering this is the wettest place on earth – hikers will be rewarded with a sweeping view of the Wainiha and Hanalei valleys to the north. While the trail has been upgraded since Iniki and most of it spanned with boardwalks, this can still be an extremely wet and slippery trail, and in places you can expect to have to literally slog through mud. It's certainly a trail that's best suited for doing in the relatively drier summer season.

If your car can't make it down Camp 10-Mohihi Rd, parking at the Puu O Kila Lookout and approaching the Alakai Swamp Trail via the Pihea Trail is probably your best bet.

Kaluapuhi Trail The Kaluapuhi Trail, a forest trail leading to a plum grove, is about two miles long. The trailhead starts at the highway a quarter of a mile past the 17-mile marker. This is a busy trail during midsummer, when lots of islanders come up to pick the wild plums.

Places to Stay

Lodges *Kokee Lodge* (☎ 335-6061), Box 819, Waimea, HI 96796, manages the 12 cabins in Kokee State Park. The oldest cabins are a little tired, have just one large room and cost $35. Better are the two-bedroom cedar cabins at $45. Both types of cabins have one double and four twin beds, as well as basic kitchens, linens, blankets, hot showers and wood stoves. Rates are the same for up to six people. State park rules limit stays to five days. The cabins are often booked up well in advance, although cancellations do occur and you can occasionally get a cabin at the last moment if you're flexible.

The YWCA's *Camp Sloggett* in Kokee State Park has a lodge that sleeps 10 people, a hostel-style bunkhouse that holds 40 and a cement slab platform for tent camping. A bed in the bunkhouse costs $20; guests must provide their own bedding and towels, but there's a kitchenette with pans and bathrooms with hot showers. Tent campers, who pay $10 per person, have a barbecue pit for cooking and use of the showers and toilets in the bunkhouse. For the bunkhouse and tent sites, call the caretaker (☎ 335-6060) to check availability. The lodge is rented to only one group at a time; the per-person rate is the same as the bunkhouse, with a minimum charge of five people on weekdays and eight people on weekends. Bookings for the lodge are made through the YWCA (☎ 245-5959), 3094 Elua St, Lihue, HI 96766. All rates are discounted for Hawaii residents. Camp Sloggett is about half a mile east of the park museum down a dirt road that's usually passable in an ordinary car.

Camping There's a campground right at Kokee State Park and two forest reserve campgrounds just beyond the park boundaries. For information on camping at the

YWCA's Camp Sloggett, see the Lodges section, above.

Kokee State Park's campground is immediately north of the meadow at Kokee Lodge. The sites are in an uncrowded grassy area beside the woods and have barbecue pits, picnic tables, drinking water, restrooms and showers. Camping is free and allowed for up to five nights, but state camping permits must be obtained before arriving in Kokee.

If you want to get farther off the main track, the Kawaikoi and Sugi Grove campgrounds are about four miles east of Kokee Lodge, off the 4WD Camp 10-Mohihi Rd in the forest reserve adjacent to the state park. Each campground has pit toilets, picnic shelters and fire pits. You'll need to carry in your own water or treat the stream water before drinking it.

The Kokee area campgrounds are at an elevation of almost 4000 feet and nights are crisp and cool. This is sleeping bag and warm clothing country.

For more information on camping permits, see Camping in the Accommodations section earlier in this chapter.

Places to Eat

Kokee Lodge is the only place to eat north of Waimea. Open from 9 am to 3:30 pm daily, the menu includes Portuguese bean soup, quiche, chili, salads and sandwiches for $7 or less and lilikoi pie for $4. The gift shop in front of the restaurant is open to 4 pm and sells canned soup, candy bars and soft drinks.

If you're staying in the cabins or campgrounds, be sure to bring ample provisions, as the nearest stores (and gas station) are in Waimea, 15 miles away.

Niihau

Niihau has long been closed to outsiders, earning it the nickname 'The Forbidden Island'.

No other place in Hawaii has more successfully turned its back on change than Niihau, which has no paved roads, no airport, no island-wide electricity and no telephones.

Niihau is a native Hawaiian preserve and is the only island in the state where the primary language is stilll Hawaiian. The entire island, right down to the church, belongs to the Niihau Ranch, which is privately owned by the non-Hawaiian Robinson family. They are highly protective of Niihau's isolation.

Most of Niihau's 230 residents live in **Puuwai**, a settlement on the dry western coast, and make their living working the

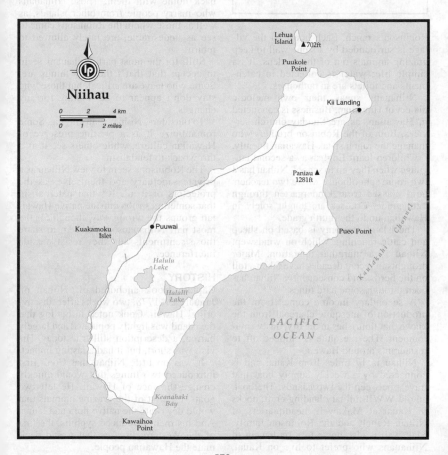

Niihau Shell Leis

Niihauans create fine handcrafted necklaces made of tiny seashells painstakingly strung in spiral strands and intricate patterns. These Niihau shell leis are Hawaii's most highly prized and priced. They are sold in fine jewelry shops and craft galleries on the other islands, some for well over $1000.

The shells used in the necklaces are found mainly on Niihau beaches, where they are collected by sifting through the sand. Smaller numbers of these shells can also be found on Kauai. ■

Robinson's ranch. Each house in the village is surrounded by a stone wall to keep grazing animals out of the gardens. It's a simple life; water is collected in catchments and toilets are in outhouses.

Niihauans speak their own melodic dialect of Hawaiian. Business is conducted in Hawaiian, as are Sunday church services. Both of the Robinson brothers who manage the ranch speak Hawaiian fluently.

Children learn English as a second language when they go to school. Niihau has a two-room schoolhouse where two teachers hold classes from kindergarten through 12th grade. Courses are taught solely in Hawaiian up to the fourth grade.

The island economy is based on sheep and cattle ranching, which on windswept Niihau is a marginal operation. Major droughts in recent decades have taken a toll on the herds, and consequently Niihau has been through some hard times.

A secondary income comes from the production of mesquite charcoal from the kiawe that flourishes in the dry, dusty environment. The mesquite is shipped off to restaurants around Hawaii.

Niihau is 17 miles from Kauai and is connected by a weekly supply boat that travels between the two islands. The boat, an old WWII military landing craft, docks in Kauai at Makaweli, headquarters of Niihau Ranch and the Robinson family. Makaweli is also home to a settlement of Niihauans who prefer to live on Kauai,

though many of them still work for the Robinsons.

Niihau is by no means a living-history museum of Hawaiians stuck in time. Although it's got a foot in the past, it takes what it wants from the present. The supply boat brings sodas as well as poi, and the island has more dirt bikes than outrigger canoes.

Niihau residents are free to go to Kauai to shop, have a few beers (Niihau itself is dry) or just hang out. What they are not free to do is bring friends from other islands back home with them. Those Niihauans who marry people from other islands, as well as those whom the Robinsons come to see as undesirable, are rarely allowed to return.

Still, for the most part, Niihauans seem to accept that that's the way things are. Some who leave are critical, but those who stay don't appear to be looking for any changes.

To outsiders, Niihau is an enigma. Some romanticize it as a pristine preserve of Hawaiian culture, while others see it as a throwback to feudalism.

The Robinsons seem to view Niihau as a private sanctuary and themselves as the protectors of it all. It's that paternalism that sometimes rubs outside native Hawaiian groups the wrong way, though for the most part Niihauans don't seem to share those sentiments and they resist outside interference.

HISTORY

Captain Cook anchored off Niihau on January 29, 1778, two weeks after 'discovering' Hawaii. Cook noted in his log that the island was lightly populated and largely barren, a description still true today. His visit was short, but it had a lasting impact.

It was on little Niihau that Cook first introduced two things that would quickly change the face of Hawaii. He left two goats, the first of the grazing animals that would devastate the native flora and fauna. And his men introduced syphilis, the first of the Western diseases that would decimate the Hawaiian people.

In 1864, Elizabeth Sinclair, a Scottish widow who was moving from New Zealand to Vancouver when she got side-tracked in Hawaii, bought Niihau from King Kamehameha V for $10,000. He originally tried to sell her the 'swampland' of Waikiki, but she passed it up for the 'desert island'. Interestingly, no two places in Hawaii today could be further apart, either culturally or in land value.

Mrs Sinclair brought the first sheep to Niihau from New Zealand and started the ranching operation that her great-grandsons continue today.

GEOGRAPHY
Niihau is the smallest of the inhabited Hawaiian Islands. It is 18 miles long and six miles wide, with a total area of 70 sq miles. It has 45 miles of coast and the highest elevation is 1281 feet. The island is semi-arid, in the lee of Kauai.

Niihau's 860-acre Halalii Lake is the largest in Hawaii, though even during the rainy winter season it's only a few feet deep. In the summer it sometimes dries up to a mud pond. About 50% of Hawaii's endangered coots breed on Niihau – when there's enough water.

GETTING THERE & AWAY
Although outsiders are not allowed to visit Niihau, the Robinsons have 'opened up' the island – at least slightly – via pricey helicopter flights.

Niihau Helicopters (☎ 335-3500), Box 370, Makaweli, HI 96769, has no set schedule; tours should be arranged well in advance. The tours, which last about three hours and take off from Burns Field in Kauai, cost $250 per person. The helicopter generally makes one of two stops, either at **Puukole Point** on the northern end of the island, or at **Keanahaki Bay**, on the southern end of the island, where Captain Cook landed. They fly over much of Niihau but avoid Puuwai village, where people live.

The helicopter was purchased for emergency medical evacuations and the tours are given in an effort to defray the cost.

Northwestern Hawaiian Islands

The Northwestern Hawaiian Islands, also called the Leeward Islands, stretch from Kauai nearly 1300 miles across the Pacific in an almost straight northwesterly line.

Volcanic in origin, the islands once jutted up high above sea level as the main Hawaiian Islands do now. However, they are slowly slipping back into the sea as a result of a sagging of the ocean floor and the ongoing forces of erosion. Where the mountains once raised their heads, coral reefs now appear like flower leis left floating on the water.

There are 10 island clusters in all, and together the clusters have 33 islands, all of which are small. They include atolls, each with a number of low sand islands formed on top of coral reefs, as well as some single-rock islands and a reef that is mostly submerged.

Listed according to their order from Kauai, the clusters are Nihoa, Necker Island, French Frigate Shoals, Gardner Pinnacles, Maro Reef, Laysan Island, Lisianski Island, Pearl and Hermes Atoll, Midway Islands and Kure Atoll.

The total land area of all the Northwestern Hawaiian Islands together is just under five sq miles, though the atoll lagoon areas are a hundred times that.

All the islands except Kure Atoll (a state seabird sanctuary) and the Midway Islands are part of the Hawaiian Islands National Wildlife Refuge. Established in 1909 by US President Theodore Roosevelt, it is the

Northwestern Hawaiian Islands

oldest and largest of the national wildlife refuges. In 1988, Midway was given a separate refuge status as Midway Atoll National Wildlife Refuge.

With the exception of Midway, visitors are not allowed on the Northwestern Hawaiian Islands unless they have permits, and these are granted only in the rarest of circumstances. Human activities are simply too disturbing to the fragile ecosystem. The only human habitation in the Hawaiian Islands National Wildlife Refuge is at Tern Island, and that is for wildlife researchers.

The Northwestern Hawaiian Islands come under the political, though not the practical, jurisdiction of the City & County of Honolulu.

FAUNA

The Northwestern Hawaiian Islands are home to around 15 million seabirds, all of which find room for at least a foothold. Endangered Hawaiian monk seals, green sea turtles and four endemic land birds also live there.

Seabirds

Eighteen seabird species nest on these islands, feeding on the abundant fish that live around the submerged reefs. They include frigate birds, boobies, albatrosses, terns, shearwaters, petrels, tropicbirds and noddies.

The sooty terns are the most abundant, numbering several million. These screeching black-and-white birds also nest on the offshore islets of Oahu's windward coast.

Shearwaters and petrels lay their eggs in burrows that they dig in the sandy soil. The roofs of the burrows can easily collapse under the feet of unobservant walkers, which is one reason why visitors are discouraged.

NW ISLANDS

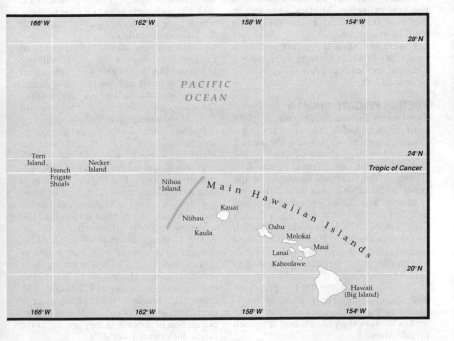

Land Birds

The Laysan duck, Laysan finch, Nihoa finch and Nihoa millerbird, endemic to Laysan and Nihoa islands respectively, are all listed as endangered or threatened species.

This is not because their numbers are declining, but because these species exist in only one place on earth and are therefore susceptible to the introduction of new diseases and predators or the disruption of their habitat. One rat from a shipwrecked boat, weed seed from a hiker's boot or an oil slick washing ashore could mean the end of the species.

Monk Seals

The endangered Hawaiian monk seal, which exists only in Hawaii, uses Kure Atoll, the French Frigate Shoals and Laysan, Lisianski, Nihoa and Necker islands for pupping grounds. The seals are easily disturbed by human contact.

In the 19th century, the seals were hunted nearly to extinction. Military operations in the area during and after WWII also resulted in a decline.

Fewer than 200 seal pups are born each year, many of which die from shark attacks. The total species population is estimated to be about 1200.

FRENCH FRIGATE SHOALS

The French Frigate Shoals consist of 13 sand islands and a 135-foot rock, La Perouse Pinnacle, named after the French explorer who was almost wrecked on the reef. One of the sand islands, 37-acre Tern Island, is the field headquarters for the Hawaiian Islands National Wildlife Refuge.

Most of Tern Island is covered by an airfield left over from the days when the US Coast Guard had a loran (radio navigation system) station there. The old Coast Guard barracks now house two US Fish & Wildlife Service refuge managers and up to a dozen volunteers.

Tern Island is home to 17 species of seabirds and many Hawaiian monk seals. Ninety percent of the green sea turtles that nest in the Hawaiian Islands nest at French Frigate Shoals.

LAYSAN ISLAND

Laysan Island is a classic example of how human interference can wreak havoc on island ecology.

Laysan is 1.45 sq miles in size; though small, it's actually the largest of the Northwestern Hawaiian Islands. From 1890 to 1904, Laysan was mined for guano, the phosphate-rich bird droppings used for fertilizer. Houses were built, mules were brought ashore as pack animals and ships docked to take the guano away.

There were once millions of birds on Laysan – mostly Laysan albatrosses, otherwise known as gooney birds. In addition to guano mining, albatross eggs were collected by the hundreds of thousands to be sold for their albumen, a substance used in photo processing.

As each albatross lays just one egg a year, an 'egging' sweep could destroy an entire year's hatch. Hunters also ravaged the island. In one six-month period alone, 300,000 birds were killed for their feathers, which were used by milliners to make hats for fashionable ladies.

There are now about 160,000 pairs of Laysan albatrosses on the island, still one of the world's largest colonies. Albatrosses sometimes court and dance for five annual mating seasons before actually mating. Once they do mate, pairs stay together for life and sometimes live for 30 years.

Rabbits, introduced to Laysan first as pets for the workers' children and later for breeding, virtually destroyed the island's vegetation, and where they left off sandstorms took over. The loss of native food plants spelled the end of the three endemic land birds: the Laysan flightless rail, Laysan honeycreeper and Laysan millerbird. The rabbits were finally exterminated in 1923.

The Laysan duck reached the brink of extinction as a result of the activities of rabbits and hunters. Their numbers were reduced to just six by 1911, but they're making a modest comeback. Laysan ducks swim in the brackish lagoon in the center of the island, their only habitat. With a current population of about 300, they are one of the rarest ducks in the world.

The Laysan finch, the population of which was once as low as 100 thanks to the rabbits, is once again common on Laysan Island and has also been introduced to Pearl and Hermes Atoll. Unlike its honeycreeper cousins on the main Hawaiian islands, which feed on nectar, the Laysan finch has become carnivorous and feeds on seabird eggs as well as the carcasses of dead seabirds.

There are also more than one million sooty terns nesting on Laysan.

NECKER & NIHOA

Necker and Nihoa, the two islands closest to the main Hawaiian Islands, were probably settled more than a thousand years ago. Archaeological remains of stone temple platforms, house sites, terraces and carved stone images suggest that the early settlers on these islands were from the Marquesas.

Necker and Nihoa are not coral atolls but rugged, rocky islands, each less than a quarter of a square mile. Nihoa is the highest of the Northwestern Hawaiian Islands, with sheer sea cliffs and a peak elevation of 910 feet.

Two land bird species live only on tiny Nihoa and nowhere else.

The Nihoa finch, which like the Laysan finch is a raider of other birds' eggs, is hanging in there with a population of a few thousand. Attempts were made in 1967 to develop a back-up colony in case something happened to the birds on Nihoa, but it failed when all 42 finches sent to the French Frigate Shoals died.

The gray Nihoa millerbird, related to the old world warbler family, is rare and secretive. It wasn't even discovered until 1923 and was so named because it eats miller moths. Approximately 400 birds remain.

MIDWAY ISLANDS

The Midway Islands, best known as the site of a pivotal WWII battle between Japanese and American naval forces, is the only place in the Northwestern Hawaiian Islands open to tourism.

Midway, which in the postwar era served as a naval air facility with some 3000 personnel, was one of several military bases targeted for closing at the end of the Cold War. In 1996, the military transferred jurisdiction of Midway to the US Fish & Wildlife Service and began an intense environmental cleanup that's scheduled to be completed by late 1997.

The US Fish & Wildlife Service, while maintaining a limited presence on Midway, has entered into an agreement with a private company to handle most of the atoll's operations. Midway Phoenix Corporation not only has a defense contract to maintain Midway's airfield, which is used for refueling and fisheries-enforcement operations by the US Coast Guard, but is also being allowed to develop the island for ecotourism purposes.

The company has spent half a million dollars renovating former officers' quarters into hotel rooms and installing a satellite cellular phone system. It's now opening the atoll to low-impact tours geared for naturalists and divers. Access to some of Midway's white-sand beaches will be limited in order to minimize disturbance to Hawaiian monk seals, and diving and other activities will be guided.

Initial tours, which have a limit of 30 visitors, are already underway, but once the US Navy completes its cleanup, tours are expected to be fully operational, and up to 100 visitors will be allowed on Midway at any one time.

More than a million seabirds nest on Midway, including the world's largest colony of Laysan albatrosses, which are so thick during the months of November through July that they virtually blanket the ground. Sand Island, where the facilities are situated, is the largest island in the three-island Midway Atoll and averages about a mile across. In addition to its dense colonies of seabirds, Sand Island has a scattering of early 20th-century relics, including the remains of a cable station that dates to 1903 and WWII-era bunkers and anti-aircraft guns. The surrounding waters harbor coral gardens, unusual tropical fish and schools of spinner dolphins.

Getting There & Away

Midway can only be visited on a guided tour. A five-day package begins around $1700, including activities, accommodations, meals and airfare from Kauai via a 19-passenger turboprop plane. Those interested in dive tours should contact Midway Dive-N-Snorkel (☎ 888-329-9559; fax 421-0444), 3901 Mokulele Loop 29, Lihue, HI 96766. For ecology tours, contact Oceanic Society Expeditions (☎ 415-441-1106, 800-326-7491), Fort Mason Center, Bldg E, San Francisco, CA 94123.

Glossary

aa rough and jagged lava type

ahi albacore (yellowfin) tuna

ahu stone cairns used to mark a trail; or an altar or shrine

ahupuaa a traditional land division, usually in a wedge shape from the mountains to the sea

aikane friend

aina land

akamai clever

aku skipjack tuna

akua god, spirit, idol

akule bigeye mackerel

alii chief; royalty

aloha the traditional greeting, meaning love, welcome, goodbye

aloha aina love of the land

amaama mullet

amakihi small yellow green bird, one of the more common of the native birds

ao Newell's shearwater (a seabird)

apapane bright-red native Hawaiian honeycreeper

au marlin

aumakua ancestral spirit helper

auwe Oh my! Alas!

awa kava, made into an intoxicating brew; milkfish

awapuhi wild ginger

bento the Japanese word for a box lunch

cilantro coriander leaves (also known as Chinese parsley)

crack seed snack foods, usually dried fruits or seeds, either sour, salty or sweet

elepaio a brownish forest bird with a white rump

hala pandanus; the leaves are used in weaving mats and baskets

hale house

hana work; or bay, when used as a compound in place names

haole Caucasian; literally 'without breath'

hapa half; person of mixed blood

hau indigenous lowland hibiscus tree, the wood of which is often used for outrigger canoes

haupia coconut pudding

Hawaii nei all the Hawaiian Islands, as distinguished from the Big Island

heiau ancient stone temple, a place of worship in Hawaii before Western contact

Hina Polynesian goddess (wife of Ku, one of the four main gods)

holoholo to walk, drive or ramble around for pleasure

holoku a long dress similar to the muumuu, but more fitted and with a yoke

holua sled or sled course

honu turtle

hoolaulea celebration, party

huhu angry

hui group, organization

hukilau net fishing with a seine, involving a group of people; the word can also refer to the feast that follows

hula traditional Hawaiian dance

hula halau hula school or troupe

humuhumunukunukuapuaa rectangular triggerfish

iiwi a bright-vermilion forest bird with a curved, salmon-colored beak

iliahi Hawaiian sandalwood

iliili stones

ilima native groundcover with a delicate yellow-orange flower

imu underground earthen oven used in traditional luau cooking

kahuna wise person in any field; commonly a priest, healer or sorcerer

kahuna nui high priest

kahili a feather standard, used as a symbol of royalty

kalo see 'taro'

kalua traditional method of baking in an underground oven (imu)

kamaaina native-born Hawaiian or a long-time resident; literally 'child of the land'
kanaka human being; usually refers to native Hawaiians
Kanaloa god of the underworld
kane man; also the name of one of four main Hawaiian gods
kapa see 'tapa'
kapu taboo, part of strict ancient Hawaiian social system
kaunaoa a thin parasitic vine
kava a mildly narcotic drink made from the roots of *Piper methysticum*, a pepper shrub
keiki child, children
ki see 'ti'
kiawe a relative of the mesquite tree introduced to Hawaii in the 1820s, now very common; its branches are covered with sharp thorns
kii image, statue
kipuka an area of land spared when lava flows around it; an oasis
ko sugar cane
koa native hardwood tree often used in woodworking of native crafts
kohola whale
kokua help, cooperation
kona leeward, or a leeward wind
konane ancient Hawaiian board game similar to checkers
koolau windward side
Ku Polynesian god of many manifestations, including god of war, farming and fishing
kukui candlenut tree; the official state tree, its oily nuts were once used in lamps
kuleana an individually held plot of land
kupuna grandparent, elder
kuula fishing shrine

lanai veranda
lauhala leaves of the *hala* plant used in weaving
laulau wrapped package; pork or beef with salted fish and taro leaves, wrapped in ti or banana leaves and steamed
lei garland, usually of flowers, but also of leaves or shells
lilikoi passion fruit
limu seaweed
lio horse

lolo stupid, crazy
lomi to rub or soften; 'lomi salmon' is raw, diced salmon marinated with tomatoes and onions
lomilomi massage
Lono Polynesian god of harvest, agriculture, fertility and peace
loulu native fan palms
luakini a type of heiau dedicated to the war god Ku and used for human sacrifices
luau Hawaiian feast

mahalo thank you
mahele to divide; usually refers to the missionary-initiated land divisions of 1848
mahimahi 'dolphin', a type of fish unrelated to the marine mammal
maile native twining plant with fragrant leaves often used in leis
makaainana commoners; literally 'people who tend the land'
makaha sluice gates, used in fishponds
makahiki ancient annual four-month winter harvest festival dedicated to Lono, when sports and celebrations replaced all warfare
makaku creative artistic mana
makai towards the sea
malasada a fried dough served warm, similar to a doughnut
malihini newcomer, visitor
malo loincloth
mana spiritual power
manini convict tang (a reef fish); also used to refer to something small or insignificant
mano shark
mauka towards the mountains; inland
mele song, chant
menehune the 'little people' who according to legend built many of Hawaii's fishponds, heiaus and other stonework
milo a native shade tree with beautiful hardwood
moo water spirit, water lizard or dragon
mu a 'body catcher', who secured sacrificial victims for the heiau altar
muumuu a long, loose-fitting dress introduced by the missionaries

naupaka a native shrub with delicate white flowers

Neighbor Islands the term used to refer to the main Hawaiian islands outside of Oahu
nene a native goose; Hawaii's state bird
nisei people of Japanese descent
noni Indian mulberry; a small tree with yellow, warty, smelly fruit that is used medicinally
nuku puu a native honeycreeper with a bright yellow underbelly

ohana family, extended family
ohelo low-growing native shrub with edible red berries, related to cranberries; said to be sacred to Pele
ohia lehua native Hawaiian tree with tufted feathery pompom-like flowers
okole buttocks
olo surfboards used by the alii
onaga red snapper
ono delicious; also the name of the wahoo fish
opae shrimp
opakapaka pink snapper
opihi edible limpet

pahoehoe quick and smooth flowing lava type
pakalolo marijuana; literally 'crazy smoke'
pali cliff
palila native honeycreeper
paniolo a Hawaiian cowboy; the word is derived from the Spanish *españoles*, as Hawaii's first cowboys were Mexican
pau finished, no more
Pele goddess of fire and volcanoes, who lives in Kilauea volcano
pho a Vietnamese soup of beef broth, noodles and fresh herbs
piko navel, umbilical cord
pili a bunch grass, commonly used for thatching houses
pilikia trouble
pipikaula a salted, dried beef served broiled
poha gooseberry

poi a gooey paste made from taro roots, a staple food of the Hawaiian diet
poke chopped raw fish marinated in soy sauce, oil and chili peppers
Poliahu goddess of snow
pua aloalo a hibiscus flower
pueo Hawaiian owl
puhi moray eels
puka any kind of hole or opening
pupu snack food, hors d'oeuvres; shells
puu hill, cinder cone
puuhonua place of refuge

saimin a Japanese noodle soup

tabi Japanese reef-walking shoes
talk story to strike up a conversation, make small talk
tapa cloth made by pounding the bark of the paper mulberry tree, used for early Hawaiian clothing. In Hawaiian: *kapa*
taro a plant, with green heart-shaped leaves, cultivated in Hawaii for its edible rootstock. The root is mashed to make poi. In Hawaiian, taro is pronounced *kalo*.
teishoku Japanese word for fixed-plate meal
teppanyaki Japanese style of cooking with an iron grill
ti common native plant; its long shiny leaves are used for a variety of things, including plates and hula skirts. In Hawaiian: *ki*
tutu older woman; used out of respect for any older woman

ukulele a stringed musical instrument derived from the 'braginha', which was introduced to Hawaii in the 19th century by Portuguese immigrants
ulu breadfruit
ulu maika ancient Hawaiian game

wahine woman
wana sea urchin
wikiwiki hurry, quick

Appendix – Online Services

FACTS FOR THE VISITOR
TOURIST OFFICES
Hawaii Visitors Bureau
www.visit.hawaii.org

BOOKS
Island Bookshelf
www.teleport.com/~infomach/

University of Hawaii Press
www2.hawaii.edu/uhpress/uhphome.html

GAY COMMUNITY
Christopher Travel & Tours
www.icchi.com/tourhi

Gay & Lesbian Community Center
www.tnight.com/glcc

Hawaii Equal Rights Marriage Project
www.xq.com/hermp

Island Lifestyle www.tnight.com/ilm

Pacific Ocean Holidays
www.tnight.com/poh

B&B RESERVATION SERVICES
Bed & Breakfast Hawaii
planet-hawaii.com/bandb

OUTDOOR ACTIVITIES
SPORTS MAGAZINES
H30 www.h3o.com

Hawaii Race
www.runningnetwork.com/hawaiirace

GETTING THERE & AWAY
AIRLINES
Air Canada www.aircanada.ca

Air New Zealand www.airnz.com

All Nippon Airlines
www.ana.co.jp/index-e.html

America West Airlines
www.americawest.com

American Airlines www.amrcorp.com

Asiana Airlines www.asiana.co.kr

Canadian Airlines www.cdnair.ca

China Airlines www.china-airlines.com

Continental Airlines
www.flycontinental.com

Delta Air Lines www.delta-air.com

Island Air www.alohaair.com/aloha-air

Japan Air Lines www.jal.co.jp

Korean Air www.koreanair.com

Northwest Airlines www.nwa.com

Qantas Airways www.qantas.com.au

Singapore Airlines
www.singaporeair.com

TWA www.twa.com

United Airlines www.ual.com

GETTING AROUND
AIRLINES
Aloha Air www.alohaair.com/aloha-air

Hawaiian Airlines www.hawaiianair.com

Mahalo Air www.islander-magazine.com/
mahaloschedule.html

CAR RENTAL AGENCIES
Alamo www.freeways.com/bookit

Avis www.avis.com

Dollar www.dollarcar.com

Hertz www.hertz.com

National www.nationalcar.com

OAHU
INTERNET CAFES
Cyber Cafe hawaii-cybercafe.com

Internet Cafe www.aloha-cafe.com

NEWSPAPERS
Honolulu Weekly
www.honoluluweekly.com

ACTIVITIES
Aaron's Dive Shop
www.aloha.com/~aarons

Ocean Concepts
www.aloha.com/~oceanc

Windward Dive Center
www.divehawaii.com

PLACES TO STAY
Breck's On the Beach Hostel
www.netsrvind.com/hostels/brecks

Hawaiian Regent hoohana.aloha.net

Ilima Hotel www.pete.com/ilima

Manoa Valley Inn
planet-hawaii.com/marcresorts/

New Otani Kaimana Beach Hotel
www.kaimana.com

Outrigger hotel chain
www.outrigger.com

Sheffield House
www.poi.net/~sheffieldhouse

SIGHTSEEING ATTRACTIONS
Polynesian Cultural Center
www.polynesia.com/

BIG ISLAND

ACTIVITIES
Big Island Mountain Bike Association
www.interpac.net/~mtbike

Eco-Adventures of Kona www.travel-base.com/activities/scuba/eco-adventures/

PLACES TO STAY
Hale Maluhia www.hawaii-bnb.com/halemal.html

Hilton Waikoloa Village
www.hilton.com/hotels/koahwhh

Holualoa Inn www.konaweb.com/hinn

Kanaloa at Kona www.outrigger.com

Kona Bali Kai
www.pope.com:80/travelex/kona4.htm

Kona Surf Resort
www.ilhawaii.net/konasurf

Merryman's Bed & Breakfast
www.ilhawaii.net/merrymans

Pomaikai Farm Bed & Breakfast
civic.net/webmarket/hawaii/pomaikai

Reggie's Tropical Hideaway
www.ilhawaii.net/~banana

Royal Waikoloan www.outrigger.com

Waimea Gardens Cottages
planet-hawaii.com/hea/bestbnb

Waipio Ridge Vacation Rental
www.pope.com:80/travelex/waipio.htm

Waipio Wayside B&B
www.stayhawaii.com/wayside.html

SIGHTSEEING ATTRACTIONS
Hawaii Volcanoes National Park
www.nps.gov/havo

Onizuka Center for International Astronomy
www.ifa.hawaii.edu

MAUI

ACTIVITIES
Aloha Bicycle Tours
www.maui.net/~bikemaui

PLACES TO STAY
Aloha Lani Inn
www.maui.net/~tony/index.html

Ann & Bob Babson www.mauibnb.com

Destination Resorts
www.maui.net/~drh

Kaanapali Royal www.outrigger.com

Old Lahaina House
www.mauiweb.com/maui/olhouse

Pilialoha www.mauigateway.com/~heyde

Silver Cloud Guest Ranch
www.maui.net/~slvrcld

INTERNET CAFES
The Coffee Store
maui.net/~jstark/mauicofe.html

BUSINESS SERVICES
Kinko's www.kinkos.com

MOLOKAI
NEWSPAPER
Molokai Advertiser-News
planet-hawaii.com/molokai

PLACES TO STAY
Ka Hale Mala
www.molokai.com/kahalemala

Molokai Shores
planet-hawaii.com/marcresorts/

LANAI
PLACES TO STAY
Dreams Come True
www.go-native.com/

KAUAI
PLACES TO STAY
Garden Island Inn, Lihue
planet-hawaii.com/g-i-inn/

Hanalei Colony Resort, Haena
www.hcr.com

Historic B&B, Hanalei
planet-hawaii.com/~bubba/B&B/for.html

Kauai Paradise Vacations, Princeville
planet-hawaii.com/paradise/

Kiahuna Plantation, Poipu
www.outrigger.com

Koloa Landing Cottages, Poipu
planet-hawaii.com/koloa

Oceanfront Realty, Princeville
www.oceanfrontrealty.com

Outrigger Kauai Beach, Lihue
www.outrigger.com

Pali Ke Kua, Princeville
planet-hawaii.com/marcresorts/

Plantation Hale, Wailua
www.outrigger.com

Poipu Beach Resort Association, Poipu www.poipu-beach.org/poipu

Poipu Plantation, Poipu
planet-hawaii.com/bandb

Princeville Hotel, Princeville
www.princeville.com

Rosewood B&B, Wailua
planet-hawaii.com/rosewood/index.html

Index

LONELY PLANET JOURNEYS

JOURNEYS is a unique collection of travel writing – published by the company that understands travel better than anyone else. It is a series for anyone who has ever experienced – or dreamed of – the magical moment when they encountered a strange culture or saw a place for the first time. They are tales to read while you're planning a trip, while you're on the road or while you're in an armchair, in front of a fire.

JOURNEYS books catch the spirit of a place, illuminate a culture, recount a crazy adventure, or introduce a fascinating way of life. They will always entertain, and always enrich the experience of travel.

'Idiosyncratic, entertainingly diverse and unexpected . . . from an international writership'
– The Australian

'Books which offer a closer look at the people and culture of a destination, and enrich travel experiences'
– American Bookseller

FULL CIRCLE
A South American Journey
Luis Sepúlveda

(translated by Chris Andrews)

Full Circle invites us to accompany Chilean writer Luis Sepúlveda on 'a journey without a fixed itinerary'. Whatever his subject - brutalities suffered under Pinochet's dictatorship, sleepy tropical towns visited in exile, or the landscapes of legendary Patagonia - Sepúlveda is an unflinchingly honest yet lyrical storyteller. Extravagant characters and extraordinary situations are memorably evoked: gauchos organizing a tournament of lies, a scheming heiress on the lookout for a husband, a pilot with a corpse on board his plane . . . Part autobiography, part travel memoir, *Full Circle* brings us the distinctive voice of one of South America's most compelling writers.

Luis Sepúlveda was born in Chile in 1949. Imprisoned by the Pinochet dictatorship for his socialist beliefs, he was for many years a political exile. He has written novels, short stories, plays and essays. His work has attracted many awards and has been translated into numerous languages.

'Detachment, humor and vibrant prose' – El País

'an absolute cracker' – The Bookseller

Australia | **Council** for the Arts

This project has been assisted by the Commonwealth Government through the Australian Council, its arts funding and advisory body.

LONELY PLANET PHRASEBOOKS

Building bridges,
Breaking barriers,
Beyond babble-on

Nepali phrasebook

Spanish phrasebook

Ethiopian Amharic phrasebook

Russian phrasebook

USA phrasebook

Greek phrasebook

Latin American Spanish phrasebook

Listen for the gems

Speak your own words

Ask your own questions

Master of your own image

- handy pocket-sized books

- easy to understand Pronunciation chapter

- clear and comprehensive Grammar chapter

- romanization alongside script to allow ease of pronunciation

- script throughout so users can point to phrases

- extensive vocabulary sections, words and phrases for every situation

- full of cultural information and tips for the traveler

'... vital for a real DIY spirit and attitude in language learning.' – Backpacker

'the phrasebooks have good cultural backgrounders and offer solid advice for challenging situations in remote locations'
– San Francisco Examiner

'... they are unbeatable for their coverage of the world's more obscure languages'
– The Geographical Magazine

Arabic (Egyptian)
Arabic (Moroccan)
Australian
  Australian English,
  Aboriginal and Torres Strait
  languages
Baltic States
  Estonian, Latvian,
  Lithuanian
Bengali
Brazilian
Burmese
Cantonese
Central Asian
Central Europe
  Czech, French, German,
  Hungarian, Italian and Slovak
Eastern Europe
Ethiopian Amharic
Fijian
French
German
Greek

Hindi/Urdu
Indonesian
Italian
Japanese
Korean
Lao
Latin American Spanish
Malay
Mandarin
Mediterranean Europe
  Albanian, Croation, Greek,
  Italian, Macedonian, Maltese,
  Serbian, Slovene
Mongolian
Nepali
Pidgin (Papua New Guinea)
Pilipino (Tagalog)
Quechua
Russian
Scandinavian Europe
  Danish, Finnish, Icelandic,
  Norweign and Swedish

South East Asia
  Burmese, Indonesian, Khmer,
  Lao, Malay, Tagalog (Pilipino),
  Thai and Vietnamese
Sri Lanka
Swahili
Thai
Thai Hill Tribes
Tibetan
Turkish
Ukrainian
USA
  US English, Vernacular Talk,
  Native American languages and
  Hawaiian
Vietnamese
Western Europe
  Basque, Catalan, Dutch,
  French, German, Irish, Italian,
  Portuguese, Scottish, Gaelic,
  Spanish (Castilian) and Welsh

LONELY PLANET TRAVEL ATLASES

Lonely Planet has long been famous for the number and quality of its guidebook maps. Now we've gone one step further and in conjunction with Steinhart Katzir Publishers produced a handy companion series: Lonely Planet travel atlases – maps of a country produced in book form.

Unlike other maps, which look good but lead travellers astray, our travel atlases have been researched on the road by Lonely Planet's experienced team of writers. All details are carefully checked to ensure the atlas corresponds with the equivalent Lonely Planet guidebook.

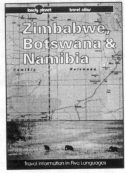

The handy atlas format means no holes, wrinkles, torn sections or constant folding and unfolding. These atlases can survive long periods on the road, unlike cumbersome fold-out maps. The comprehensive index ensures easy reference.

- full-colour throughout
- maps researched and checked by Lonely Planet authors
- place names correspond with Lonely Planet guidebooks
  – no confusing spelling differences
- legend and travelling information in English, French, German, Japanese and Spanish
- size: 230 x 160 mm

Available now:
Chile & Easter Island • Egypt • India & Bangladesh • Israel & the Palestinian Territories •Jordan, Syria & Lebanon • Kenya • Laos • Portugal • South Africa, Lesotho & Swaziland • Thailand • Turkey • Vietnam • Zimbabwe, Botswana & Namibia

---

LONELY PLANET TV SERIES & VIDEOS

Lonely Planet travel guides have been brought to life on television screens around the world. Like our guides, the programmes are based on the joy of independent travel, and look honestly at some of the most exciting, picturesque and frustrating places in the world. Each show is presented by one of three travellers from Australia, England or the USA and combines an innovative mixture of video, Super-8 film, atmospheric soundscapes and original music.

Videos of each episode – containing additional footage not shown on television – are available from good book and video shops, but the availability of individual videos varies with regional screening schedules.

Video destinations include: Alaska • American Rockies • Australia – The South-East • Baja California & the Copper Canyon • Brazil • Central Asia • Chile & Easter Island • Corsica, Sicily & Sardinia – The Mediterranean Islands • East Africa (Tanzania & Zanzibar) • Ecuador & the Galapagos Islands • Greenland & Iceland • Indonesia • Israel & the Sinai Desert • Jamaica • Japan • La Ruta Maya • Morocco • New York • North India • Pacific Islands (Fiji, Solomon Islands & Vanuatu) • South India • South West China • Turkey • Vietnam • West Africa • Zimbabwe, Botswana & Namibia

The Lonely Planet TV series is produced by:
Pilot Productions
The Old Studio
18 Middle Row
London W10 5AT UK

For video availability and ordering information contact your nearest Lonely Planet office.

Music from the TV series is available on CD & cassette.

PLANET TALK

Lonely Planet's FREE quarterly newsletter

We love hearing from you and think you'd like to hear from us.

*When...*is the right time to see reindeer in Finland?
*Where...*can you hear the best palm-wine music in Ghana?
*How...*do you get from Asunción to Areguá by steam train?
*What...*is the best way to see India?

For the answer to these and many other questions read PLANET TALK.

Every issue is packed with up-to-date travel news and advice including:

* a letter from Lonely Planet co-founders Tony and Maureen Wheeler
* go behind the scenes on the road with a Lonely Planet author
* feature article on an important and topical travel issue
* a selection of recent letters from travellers
* details on forthcoming Lonely Planet promotions
* complete list of Lonely Planet products

To join our mailing list contact any Lonely Planet office.

Also available: Lonely Planet T-shirts. 100% heavyweight cotton.

LONELY PLANET ONLINE

Get the latest travel information before you leave or while you're on the road

Whether you've just begun planning your next trip, or you're chasing down specific info on currency regulations or visa requirements, check out Lonely Planet Online for up-to-the-minute travel information.

As well as travel profiles of your favourite destinations (including maps and photos), you'll find current reports from our researchers and other travellers, updates on health and visas, travel advisories, and discussion of the ecological and political issues you need to be aware of as you travel.

There's also an online travellers' forum where you can share your experience of life on the road, meet travel companions and ask other travellers for their recommendations and advice. We also have plenty of links to other online sites useful to independent travellers.

And of course we have a complete and up-to-date list of all Lonely Planet travel products including guides, phrasebooks, atlases, Journeys and videos and a simple online ordering facility if you can't find the book you want elsewhere.

www.lonelyplanet.com
or
AOL keyword: lp

LONELY PLANET PRODUCTS

Lonely Planet is known worldwide for publishing practical, reliable and no-nonsense travel information in our guides and on our web site. The Lonely Planet list covers just about every accessible part of the world. Currently there are eight series: *travel guides, shoestring guides, walking guides, city guides, phrasebooks, audio packs, travel atlases* and *Journeys* – a unique collection of travel writing.

EUROPE

Amsterdam • Austria • Baltic States phrasebook • Britain • Central Europe on a shoestring • Central Europe phrasebook • Czech & Slovak Republics • Denmark • Dublin • Eastern Europe on a shoestring • Eastern Europe phrasebook • Estonia, Latvia & Lithuania • Finland • France • French phrasebook • Germany • German phrasebook • Greece • Greek phrasebook • Hungary • Iceland, Greenland & the Faroe Islands • Ireland • Italian phrasebook • Italy • Lisbon • Mediterranean Europe on a shoestring • Mediterranean Europe phrasebook • Paris • Poland • Portugal • Portugal travel atlas • Prague • Russia, Ukraine & Belarus • Russian phrasebook • Scandinavian & Baltic Europe on a shoestring • Scandinavian Europe phrasebook • Slovenia • Spain • Spanish phrasebook • St Petersburg • Switzerland • Trekking in Spain • Ukrainian phrasebook • Vienna • Walking in Britain • Walking in Switzerland • Western Europe on a shoestring • Western Europe phrasebook

Travel Literature: The Olive Grove: Travels in Greece

NORTH AMERICA

Alaska • Backpacking in Alaska • Baja California • California & Nevada • Canada • Florida • Hawaii • Honolulu • Los Angeles • Mexico • Miami • New England • New Orleans • New York City • New York, New Jersey & Pennsylvania • Pacific Northwest USA • Rocky Mountain States • San Francisco • Southwest USA • USA phrasebook • Washington, DC & the Capital Region

CENTRAL AMERICA & THE CARIBBEAN

Bermuda • Central America on a shoestring • Costa Rica • Cuba • Eastern Caribbean • Guatemala, Belize & Yucatán: La Ruta Maya • Jamaica

SOUTH AMERICA

Argentina, Uruguay & Paraguay • Bolivia • Brazil • Brazilian phrasebook • Buenos Aires • Chile & Easter Island • Chile & Easter Island travel atlas • Colombia • Deep South • Ecuador & the Galápagos Islands • Latin American Spanish phrasebook • Peru • Quechua phrasebook • Rio de Janeiro • South America on a shoestring • Trekking in the Patagonian Andes • Venezuela

Travel Literature: Full Circle: A South American Journey

ANTARCTICA

Antarctica

ISLANDS OF THE INDIAN OCEAN

Madagascar & Comoros • Maldives • Mauritius, Réunion & Seychelles

AFRICA

Africa - the South • Africa on a shoestring • Arabic (Moroccan) phrasebook • Cape Town • Central Africa • East Africa • Egypt • Egypt travel atlas • Ethiopian (Amharic) phrasebook • Kenya • Kenya travel atlas • Malawi, Mozambique & Zambia • Morocco • North Africa • South Africa, Lesotho & Swaziland • South Africa, Lesotho & Swaziland travel atlas • Swahili phrasebook • Trekking in East Africa • West Africa • Zimbabwe, Botswana & Namibia • Zimbabwe, Botswana & Namibia travel atlas

Travel Literature: The Rainbird: A Central African Journey • Songs to an African Sunset: A Zimbabwean Story

THE LONELY PLANET STORY

Lonely Planet published its first book in 1973 in response to the numerous 'How did you do it?' questions Maureen and Tony Wheeler were asked after driving, bussing, hitching, sailing and railing their way from England to Australia.

Written at a kitchen table and hand collated, trimmed and stapled, *Across Asia on the Cheap* became an instant local bestseller, inspiring thoughts of another book.

Eighteen months in South-East Asia resulted in their second guide, *South-East Asia on a shoestring*, which they put together in a backstreet Chinese hotel in Singapore in 1975. The yellow bible', as it quickly became known to backpackers around the world, soon became *the* guide to the region. It has sold well over half a million copies and is now in its 9th edition, still retaining its familiar yellow cover.

Today there are over 240 titles, including travel guides, walking guides, language kits & phrasebooks, travel atlases and travel literature. The company is the largest independent travel publisher in the world. Although Lonely Planet initially specialised in guides to Asia, today there are few corners of the globe that have not been covered.

The emphasis continues to be on travel for independent travellers. Tony and Maureen still travel for several months of each year and play an active part in the writing, updating and quality control of Lonely Planet's guides.

They have been joined by over 70 authors and 170 staff at our offices in Melbourne (Australia), Oakland (USA), London (UK) and Paris (France). Travellers themselves also make a valuable contribution to the guides through the feedback we receive in thousands of letters each year and on our web site.

The people at Lonely Planet strongly believe that travellers can make a positive contribution to the countries they visit, both through their appreciation of the countries' culture, wildlife and natural features, and through the money they spend. In addition, the company makes a direct contribution to the countries and regions it covers. Since 1986 a percentage of the income from each book has been donated to ventures such as famine relief in Africa; aid projects in India; agricultural projects in Central America; Greenpeace's efforts to halt French nuclear testing in the Pacific; and Amnesty International.

'I hope we send people out with the right attitude about travel. You realise when you travel that there are so many different perspectives about the world, so we hope these books will make people more interested in what they see. Guidebooks can't really guide people. All you can do is point them in the right direction.'

– Tony Wheeler

LONELY PLANET PUBLICATIONS

Australia
PO Box 617, Hawthorn 3122, Victoria
tel: (03) 9819 1877 fax: (03) 9819 6459
e-mail: talk2us@lonelyplanet.com.au

USA
Embarcadero West, 155 Filbert St, Suite 251,
Oakland, CA 94607
tel: (510) 893 8555 TOLL FREE: 800 275-8555
fax: (510) 893 8563
e-mail: info@lonelyplanet.com

UK
10a Spring Place,
London NW5 3BH
tel: (0171) 428 4800 fax: (0171) 428 4828
e-mail: go@lonelyplanet.co.uk

France:
71 bis rue du Cardinal Lemoine, 75005 Paris
tel: 1 44 32 06 20 fax: 1 46 34 72 55
e-mail: 100560.415@compuserve.com

World Wide Web: http://www.lonelyplanet.com
or AOL keyword: lp

MAIL ORDER

Lonely Planet products are distributed worldwide. They are also available by mail order from Lonely Planet, so if you have difficulty finding a title please write to us. North American and South American residents should write to Embarcadero West, 155 Filbert St, Suite 251, Oakland CA 94607, USA; European and African residents should write to 10a Spring Place, London NW5 3BH; and residents of other countries to PO Box 617, Hawthorn, Victoria 3122, Australia.

NORTH-EAST ASIA

Beijing • Cantonese phrasebook • China • Hong Kong • Hong Kong, Macau & Guangzhou • Japan • Japanese phrasebook • Japanese audio pack • Korea • Korean phrasebook • Mandarin phrasebook • Mongolia • Mongolian phrasebook • North-East Asia on a shoestring • Seoul • Taiwan • Tibet • Tibet phrasebook • Tokyo

Travel Literature: Lost Japan

MIDDLE EAST & CENTRAL ASIA

Arab Gulf States • Arabic (Egyptian) phrasebook • Central Asia • Central Asia phrasebook • Iran • Israel & the Palestinian Territories • Israel & the Palestinian Territories travel atlas • Istanbul • Jerusalem • Jordan, Syria & Lebanon travel atlas • Lebanon • Middle East • Turkey • Turkish phrasebook • Turkey travel atlas • Yemen

Travel Literature: The Gates of Damascus • Kingdom of the Film Stars: Journey into Jordan

ALSO AVAILABLE:

Travel with Children • Traveller's Tales

INDIAN SUBCONTINENT

Bangladesh • Bengali phrasebook • Delhi • Hindi/Urdu phrasebook • India • India & Bangladesh travel atlas • Indian Himalaya • Karakoram Highway • Nepal • Nepali phrasebook • Pakistan • Rajasthan • Sri Lanka • Sri Lanka phrasebook • Trekking in the Indian Himalaya • Trekking in the Karakoram & Hindukush • Trekking in the Nepal Himalaya

Travel Literature: In Rajasthan • Shopping for Buddhas

SOUTH-EAST ASIA

Bali & Lombok • Bangkok • Burmese phrasebook • Cambodia • Ho Chi Minh City • Indonesia • Indonesian phrasebook • Indonesian audio pack • Jakarta • Java • Laos • Lao phrasebook • Laos travel atlas • Malay phrasebook • Malaysia, Singapore & Brunei • Myanmar (Burma) • Philippines • Pilipino phrasebook • Singapore • South-East Asia on a shoestring • South-East Asia phrasebook • Thailand • Thailand's Islands & Beaches • Thailand travel atlas • Thai phrasebook • Thai audio pack • Thai Hill Tribes phrasebook • Vietnam • Vietnamese phrasebook • Vietnam travel atlas

AUSTRALIA & THE PACIFIC

Australia • Australian phrasebook • Bushwalking in Australia • Bushwalking in Papua New Guinea • Fiji • Fijian phrasebook • Islands of Australia's Great Barrier Reef • Melbourne • Micronesia • New Caledonia • New South Wales • New Zealand • Northern Territory • Outback Australia • Papua New Guinea • Papua New Guinea phrasebook • Queensland • Rarotonga & the Cook Islands • Samoa • Solomon Islands • South Australia • Sydney • Tahiti & French Polynesia • Tasmania • Tonga • Tramping in New Zealand • Vanuatu • Victoria • Western Australia

Travel Literature: Islands in the Clouds • Sean & David's Long Drive